Rover 75 & MG ZT

Owners Workshop Manual

R M Jex

Models covered *(4292 - 400)*

Saloon & Estate (Tourer / ZT-T), including special/limited editions

Petrol engines:	1.8 litre (1796 cc), 4-cyl, inc. turbo
	2.0 litre (1997 cc) & 2.5 litre (2497 cc) V6
Turbo-Diesel engines:	2.0 litre (1950 cc)

Does NOT cover models with 4.6 litre V8 petrol models

ABCDE
FGHIJ
KLMNO
PQ

A book in the **Haynes Service and Repair Manual Series**

ISBN-10: **1 84425 292 2**
ISBN-13: **978 1 84425 292 3**

British Library Cataloguing in Publication Data
A catalogue record for this book is available from the British Library.

Printed in the USA

Haynes Publishing
Sparkford, Yeovil, Somerset BA22 7JJ, England

Haynes North America, Inc
861 Lawrence Drive, Newbury Park, California 91320, USA

Editions Haynes
4, Rue de l'Abreuvoir
92415 COURBEVOIE CEDEX, France

Haynes Publishing Nordiska AB
Box 1504, 751 45 UPPSALA, Sverige

Contents

LIVING WITH YOUR ROVER 75 / MG ZT

Contents

Advanced driving

Many people see the words 'advanced driving' and believe that it won't interest them or that it is a style of driving beyond their own abilities. Nothing could be further from the truth. Advanced driving is straightforward safe, sensible driving - the sort of driving we should all do every time we get behind the wheel.

An average of 10 people are killed every day on UK roads and 870 more are injured, some seriously. Lives are ruined daily, usually because somebody did something stupid. Something like 95% of all accidents are due to human error, mostly driver failure. Sometimes we make genuine mistakes - everyone does. Sometimes we have lapses of concentration. Sometimes we deliberately take risks.

For many people, the process of 'learning to drive' doesn't go much further than learning how to pass the driving test because of a common belief that good drivers are made by 'experience'.

Learning to drive by 'experience' teaches three driving skills:

- ☐ Quick reactions. (Whoops, that was close!)
- ☐ Good handling skills. (Horn, swerve, brake, horn).
- ☐ Reliance on vehicle technology. (Great stuff this ABS, stop in no distance even in the wet...)

Drivers whose skills are 'experience based' generally have a lot of near misses and the odd accident. The results can be seen every day in our courts and our hospital casualty departments.

Advanced drivers have learnt to control the risks by controlling the position and speed of their vehicle. They avoid accidents and near misses, even if the drivers around them make mistakes.

The key skills of advanced driving are **concentration,** effective all-round **observation, anticipation** and **planning.** When **good vehicle handling** is added to these skills, all driving situations can be approached and negotiated in a safe, methodical way, leaving nothing to chance.

Concentration means applying your mind to safe driving, completely excluding anything that's not relevant. Driving is usually the most dangerous activity that most of us undertake in our daily routines. It deserves our full attention.

Observation means not just looking, but seeing and seeking out the information found in the driving environment.

Anticipation means asking yourself what is happening, what you can reasonably expect to happen and what could happen unexpectedly. (One of the commonest words used in compiling accident reports is 'suddenly'.)

Planning is the link between seeing something and taking the appropriate action. For many drivers, planning is the missing link.

If you want to become a safer and more skilful driver and you want to enjoy your driving more, contact the Institute of Advanced Motorists at www.iam.org.uk, phone 0208 996 9600, or write to IAM House, 510 Chiswick High Road, London W4 5RG for an information pack.

Working on your car can be dangerous. This page shows just some of the potential risks and hazards, with the aim of creating a safety-conscious attitude.

General hazards

Scalding

• Don't remove the radiator or expansion tank cap while the engine is hot.

• Engine oil, automatic transmission fluid or power steering fluid may also be dangerously hot if the engine has recently been running.

Burning

• Beware of burns from the exhaust system and from any part of the engine. Brake discs and drums can also be extremely hot immediately after use.

Crushing

• When working under or near a raised vehicle, always supplement the jack with axle stands, or use drive-on ramps. ***Never venture under a car which is only supported by a jack.***

• Take care if loosening or tightening high-torque nuts when the vehicle is on stands. Initial loosening and final tightening should be done with the wheels on the ground.

Fire

• Fuel is highly flammable; fuel vapour is explosive.

• Don't let fuel spill onto a hot engine.

• Do not smoke or allow naked lights (including pilot lights) anywhere near a vehicle being worked on. Also beware of creating sparks (electrically or by use of tools).

• Fuel vapour is heavier than air, so don't work on the fuel system with the vehicle over an inspection pit.

• Another cause of fire is an electrical overload or short-circuit. Take care when repairing or modifying the vehicle wiring.

• Keep a fire extinguisher handy, of a type suitable for use on fuel and electrical fires.

Electric shock

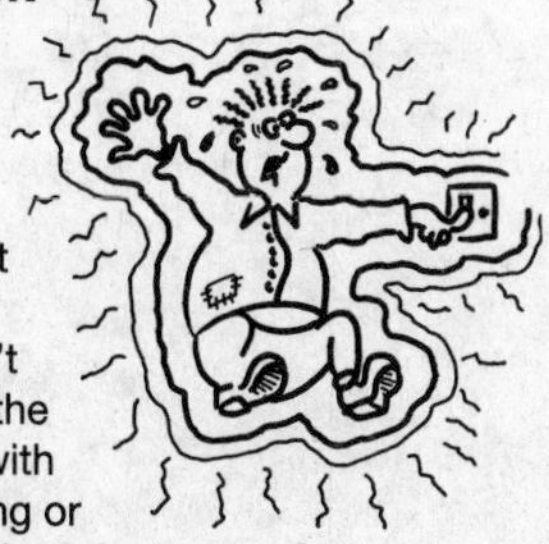

• Ignition HT voltage can be dangerous, especially to people with heart problems or a pacemaker. Don't work on or near the ignition system with the engine running or the ignition switched on.

• Mains voltage is also dangerous. Make sure that any mains-operated equipment is correctly earthed. Mains power points should be protected by a residual current device (RCD) circuit breaker.

Fume or gas intoxication

• Exhaust fumes are poisonous; they often contain carbon monoxide, which is rapidly fatal if inhaled. Never run the engine in a confined space such as a garage with the doors shut.

• Fuel vapour is also poisonous, as are the vapours from some cleaning solvents and paint thinners.

Poisonous or irritant substances

• Avoid skin contact with battery acid and with any fuel, fluid or lubricant, especially antifreeze, brake hydraulic fluid and Diesel fuel. Don't syphon them by mouth. If such a substance is swallowed or gets into the eyes, seek medical advice.

• Prolonged contact with used engine oil can cause skin cancer. Wear gloves or use a barrier cream if necessary. Change out of oil-soaked clothes and do not keep oily rags in your pocket.

• Air conditioning refrigerant forms a poisonous gas if exposed to a naked flame (including a cigarette). It can also cause skin burns on contact.

Asbestos

• Asbestos dust can cause cancer if inhaled or swallowed. Asbestos may be found in gaskets and in brake and clutch linings. When dealing with such components it is safest to assume that they contain asbestos.

Special hazards

Hydrofluoric acid

• This extremely corrosive acid is formed when certain types of synthetic rubber, found in some O-rings, oil seals, fuel hoses etc, are exposed to temperatures above $400^{\circ}C$. The rubber changes into a charred or sticky substance containing the acid. *Once formed, the acid remains dangerous for years. If it gets onto the skin, it may be necessary to amputate the limb concerned.*

• When dealing with a vehicle which has suffered a fire, or with components salvaged from such a vehicle, wear protective gloves and discard them after use.

The battery

• Batteries contain sulphuric acid, which attacks clothing, eyes and skin. Take care when topping-up or carrying the battery.

• The hydrogen gas given off by the battery is highly explosive. Never cause a spark or allow a naked light nearby. Be careful when connecting and disconnecting battery chargers or jump leads.

Air bags

• Air bags can cause injury if they go off accidentally. Take care when removing the steering wheel and/or facia. Special storage instructions may apply.

Diesel injection equipment

• Diesel injection pumps supply fuel at very high pressure. Take care when working on the fuel injectors and fuel pipes.

Warning: Never expose the hands, face or any other part of the body to injector spray; the fuel can penetrate the skin with potentially fatal results.

Remember...

DO

• Do use eye protection when using power tools, and when working under the vehicle.

• Do wear gloves or use barrier cream to protect your hands when necessary.

• Do get someone to check periodically that all is well when working alone on the vehicle.

• Do keep loose clothing and long hair well out of the way of moving mechanical parts.

• Do remove rings, wristwatch etc, before working on the vehicle – especially the electrical system.

• Do ensure that any lifting or jacking equipment has a safe working load rating adequate for the job.

DON'T

• Don't attempt to lift a heavy component which may be beyond your capability – get assistance.

• Don't rush to finish a job, or take unverified short cuts.

• Don't use ill-fitting tools which may slip and cause injury.

• Don't leave tools or parts lying around where someone can trip over them. Mop up oil and fuel spills at once.

• Don't allow children or pets to play in or near a vehicle being worked on.

The Rover 75 was introduced into the UK in June 1999, replacing the previous Rover 600 and 800 ranges. Developed during the period when Rover was owned by BMW, this thoroughly modern front-wheel-drive car was apparently based on a 5-series platform, but had retro styling cues from successful Rovers of the 1950s and 60s. Rover claim that the car is built to far higher standards than any preceding model, with an extra-stiff bodyshell boasting precise shutlines. The 75 was designed to be a luxury car, with many models featuring a traditional wood-and-leather interior, while the later MG ZT derivatives had a more sporting feel, in keeping with the famous octagonal badge.

The petrol engine range features well-proven K-series units seen in previous MG/Rover models, but with a turbo version of the 1.8 litre four-cylinder unit, and a new 2.0 litre version of the KV6. The diesel engine is a BMW-derived modern common-rail unit.

Production moved from Oxford to Longbridge in Spring 2001, at which time the range grew to include the five-door 'Tourer' estate car. In July the same year, the re-launch of the MG brand spawned the ZT Saloon, then later the ZT-T Sportswagon – 'driving enthusiast' versions of the Rover 75 underneath, with heavily-revised suspension, a sports interior, skirts, spoilers and mesh grilles. All models received a facelift in Spring 2004, which mostly amounted to revised bumpers and headlights; production finally ceased in April 2005, when Rover ceased trading.

All models have front-wheel-drive, with a five-speed manual transmission (or an optional five-speed automatic, offering three selectable modes). The front suspension is of conventional MacPherson strut type, incorporating rear-facing L-shaped lower arms attached to a subframe, and an anti-roll bar. At the rear, BMW's independent multi-link Z-axle and subframe is used, modified for a front-wheel-drive application.

The car has a high equipment level, even at the lower end of the model range. All feature electric windows and mirrors, CD player, and remote central locking. Leather trim, climate control, alloy wheels and electric heated seats are among the equipment fitted higher up the range.

Your Rover/MG manual

The aim of this manual is to help you get the best value from your car. It can do so in several ways. It can help you decide what work must be done (even should you choose to get it done by a garage). It will also provide information on routine maintenance and servicing, and give a logical course of action and diagnosis when random faults occur. However, it is hoped that you will use the manual by tackling the work yourself. On simpler jobs it may even be quicker than booking the car into a garage and going there twice, to leave and collect it. Perhaps most important, a lot of money can be saved by avoiding the costs a garage must charge to cover its labour and overheads.

The manual has drawings and descriptions to show the function of the various components so that their layout can be understood. Tasks are described and photographed in a clear step-by-step sequence.

References to the 'left' and 'right' of the car are in the sense of a person in the driver's seat, facing forwards.

Acknowledgements

Thanks are due to Draper tools Limited, who provided some of the workshop tools, and to all those people at Sparkford who helped in the production of this manual.

We take great pride in the accuracy of information given in this manual, but car manufacturers make alterations and design changes during the production run of a particular car of which they do not inform us. No liability can be accepted by the authors or publishers for loss, damage or injury caused by any errors in, or omissions from, the information given.

The following pages are intended to help in dealing with common roadside emergencies and breakdowns. You will find more detailed fault finding information at the back of the manual, and repair information in the main chapters.

If your car won't start and the starter motor doesn't turn

- ☐ Open the bonnet and make sure that the battery terminals are clean and tight.
- ☐ Switch on the headlights and try to start the engine. If the headlights go very dim when you're trying to start, the battery is probably flat. Try jump starting (see next page) using another car.

If your car won't start even though the starter motor turns as normal

- ☐ Is there fuel in the tank?
- ☐ Has the engine immobiliser been deactivated? This should happen automatically when the key is inserted and turned to the first position.
- ☐ If it's a model with automatic transmission, the selector must be in N or P.
- ☐ Is there moisture on electrical components under the bonnet? With the ignition off, wipe off any obvious dampness with a dry cloth. Spray a water-repellent aerosol product (WD-40 or equivalent) on ignition and fuel system electrical connectors like those shown in the photos. Pay special attention to the ignition coil wiring connectors.

A Check the condition and security of the battery connections (unclip the battery cover for access).

B With the ignition off, remove the engine top cover and check that the wiring connectors are securely connected to the ignition coils (petrol models).

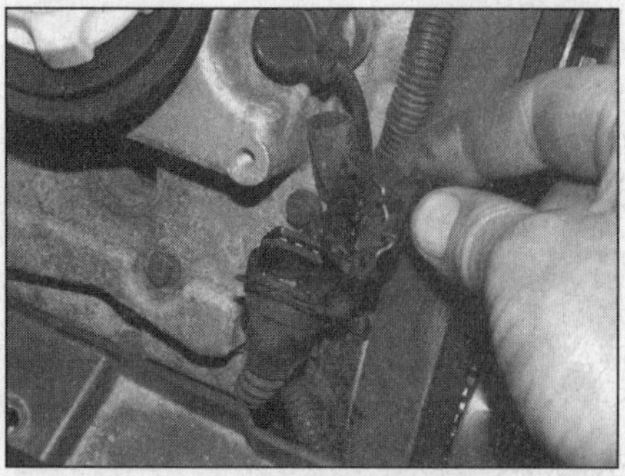

C Check that the camshaft position sensor wiring plug is securely connected.

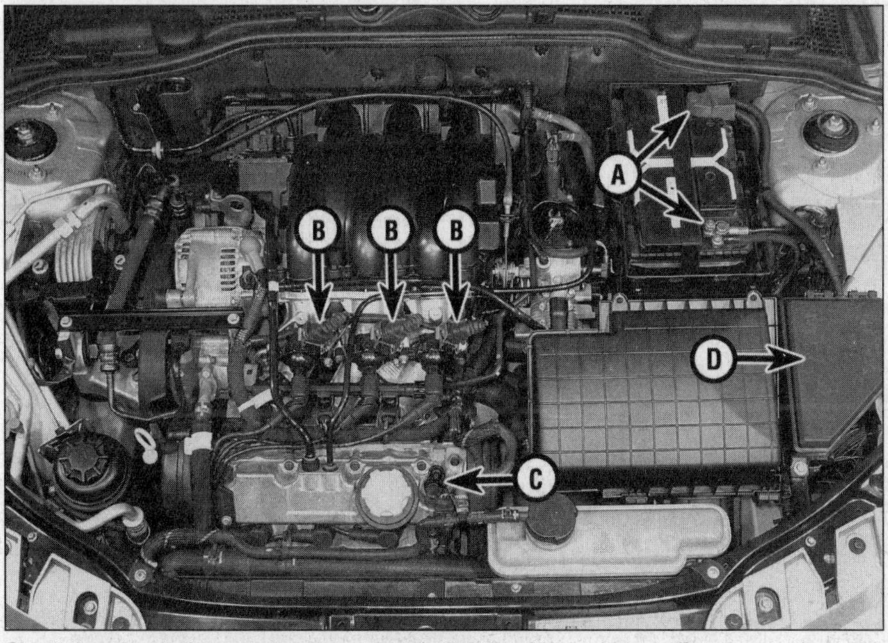

Check that electrical connections are secure (with the ignition switched off) and spray them with a water-dispersant spray like WD-40 if you suspect a problem due to damp.

D With the ignition off, check the fuses and relays in the engine compartment fusebox.

Jump starting

When jump-starting a car using a booster battery, observe the following precautions:

✔ Before connecting the booster battery, make sure that the ignition is switched off.

✔ Ensure that all electrical equipment (lights, heater, wipers, etc) is switched off.

✔ Take note of any special precautions printed on the battery case.

✔ Make sure that the booster battery is the same voltage as the discharged one in the vehicle.

✔ If the battery is being jump-started from the battery in another vehicle, the two vehicles MUST NOT TOUCH each other.

✔ Make sure that the transmission is in neutral (or PARK, in the case of automatic transmission).

HAYNES HiNT ***Jump starting will get you out of trouble, but you must correct whatever made the battery go flat in the first place. There are three possibilities:***

1 The battery has been drained by repeated attempts to start, or by leaving the lights on.

2 The charging system is not working properly (alternator drivebelt slack or broken, alternator wiring fault or alternator itself faulty).

3 The battery itself is at fault (electrolyte low, or battery worn out).

1 Connect one end of the red jump lead to the positive (+) terminal of the flat battery

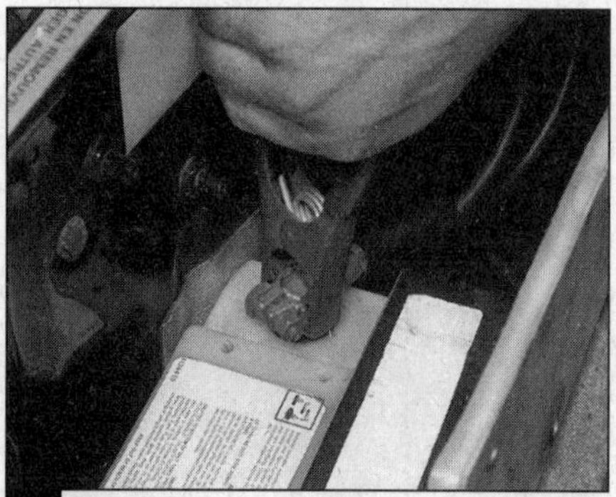

2 Connect the other end of the red lead to the positive (+) terminal of the booster battery.

3 Connect one end of the black jump lead to the negative (-) terminal of the booster battery

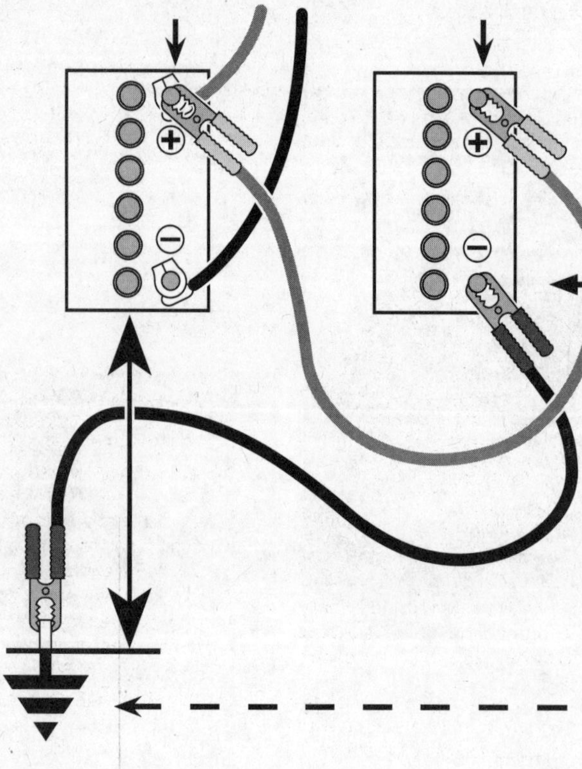

4 Connect the other end of the black jump lead to a bolt or bracket on the engine block, well away from the battery, on the vehicle to be started.

5 Make sure that the jump leads will not come into contact with the fan, drive-belts or other moving parts of the engine.

6 Start the engine using the booster battery and run it at idle speed. Switch on the lights, rear window demister and heater blower motor, then disconnect the jump leads in the reverse order of connection. Turn off the lights etc.

Wheel changing

Warning: Do not change a wheel in a situation where you risk being hit by another vehicle. On busy roads, try to stop in a lay-by or a gateway. Be wary of passing traffic while changing the wheel – it is easy to become distracted by the job in hand.

Preparation

- ☐ When a puncture occurs, stop as soon as it is safe to do so.
- ☐ Park on firm level ground, if possible, and well out of the way of other traffic.
- ☐ Use hazard warning lights if necessary.
- ☐ If you have one, use a warning triangle to alert other drivers of your presence.
- ☐ Apply the handbrake, and engage first or reverse gear (or P on automatic transmission).
- ☐ Chock the wheel diagonally opposite the one being removed – a couple of large stones will do for this.
- ☐ If the ground is soft, use a flat piece of wood to spread the load under the jack.

Changing the wheel

1 The spare wheel and tools are located in the luggage compartment, under the boot carpet. Lift the carpet, then lift out the tool/storage tray. Unscrew the spare wheel retainer anti-clockwise, and lift out the spare wheel.

2 The vehicle jack is stored in the tool tray just removed (Saloon models), which also contains the wheelbrace, towing eye, and hub cap removal tool. Rover 75 Tourer models have the jack and tools located around the spare wheel well.

3 Prise off the wheel trim or wheel centre cap from the punctured wheel, using the end of the wheelbrace or the hooked tool. Use the wheelbrace to loosen each wheel bolt by half a turn. Models with alloy wheels have one locking bolt per wheel, removed using the adaptor provided, after taking off the bolt cap.

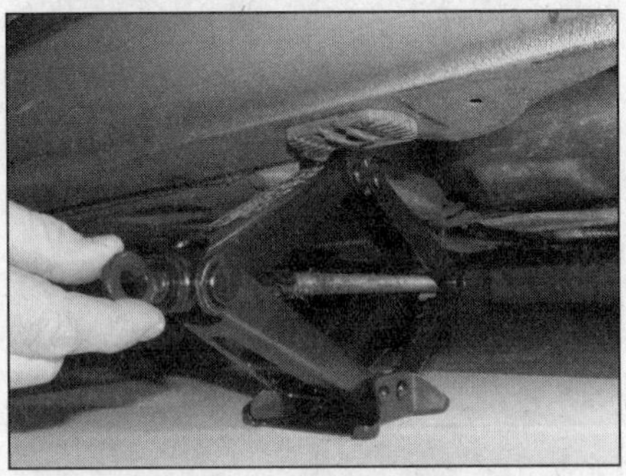

4 Locate the domed jack head into the jacking point nearest the wheel to be changed. The jacking points are small plates on the base of the door sill, with a central recess for the jack head. Only use the jack on firm, level ground.

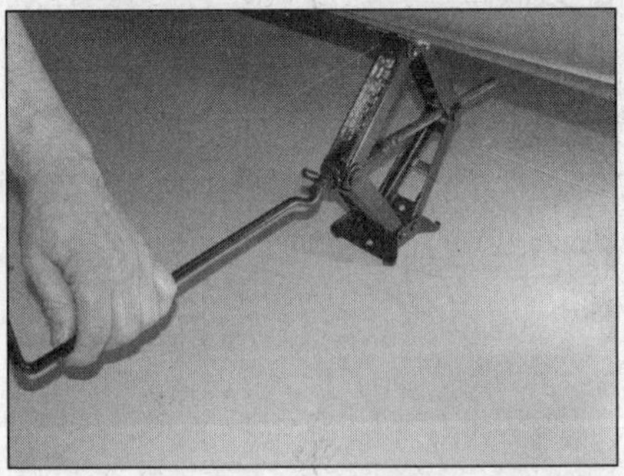

5 Turn the jack handle clockwise until the wheel is raised clear of the ground. Remove the bolts and lift the punctured wheel clear.

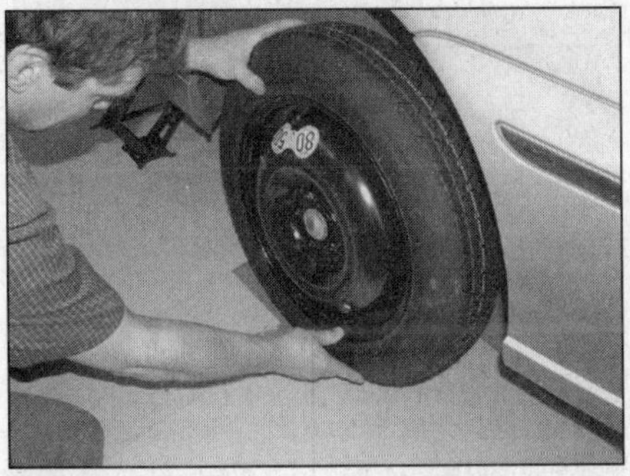

6 Fit the spare wheel, refit the wheel bolts, and tighten moderately with the wheelbrace.

7 Lower the car to the ground, then finally tighten the wheel bolts in a diagonal sequence. Refit the wheel trim or centre cap, where possible.

Note: *On MG ZT models, the narrow space saver spare wheel should* ***not*** *be fitted on the front. With a front puncture, fit the spare on the rear, then fit the good rear tyre in place of the punctured front.*

Finally...

- ☐ Remove the wheel chocks.
- ☐ Stow the jack and tools in the car.
- ☐ Check the tyre pressure on the wheel just fitted. If it is low, or if you don't have a pressure gauge, drive to the garage and inflate the tyre to the right pressure.
- ☐ Ideally, the wheel bolts should be slackened and retightened to the specified torque at the earliest opportunity.
- ☐ The space saver spare wheel is for temporary use only. Drive with extra care, especially when cornering – limit yourself to a maximum of 50 mph, and to the shortest possible journeys.
- ☐ Have the damaged tyre or wheel repaired as soon as possible.

Identifying leaks

Puddles on the garage floor or drive, or obvious wetness under the bonnet or underneath the car, suggest a leak that needs investigating. It can sometimes be difficult to decide where the leak is coming from, especially if the engine bay is very dirty already. Leaking oil or fluid can also be blown rearwards by the passage of air under the car, giving a false impression of where the problem lies.

Warning: Most automotive oils and fluids are poisonous. Wash them off skin, and change out of contaminated clothing, without delay.

HAYNES HiNT ***The smell of a fluid leaking from the car may provide a clue to what's leaking. Some fluids are distinctively coloured. It may help to clean the car carefully and to park it over some clean paper overnight as an aid to locating the source of the leak. Remember that some leaks may only occur while the engine is running.***

Sump oil

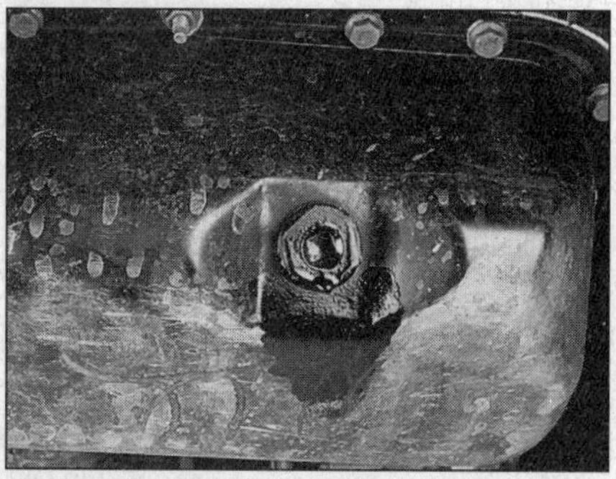

Engine oil may leak from the drain plug...

Oil from filter

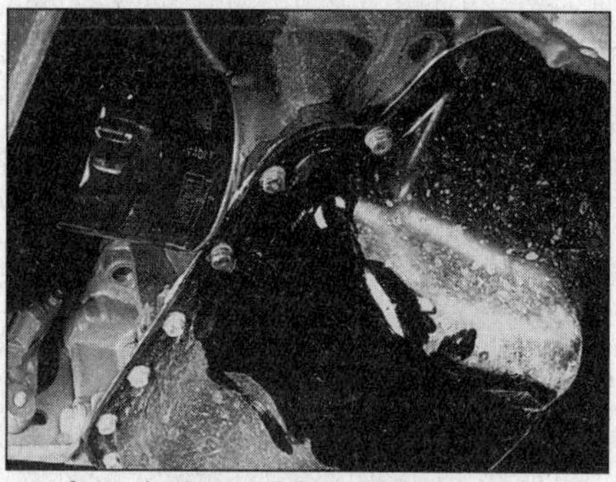

...or from the base of the oil filter.

Gearbox oil

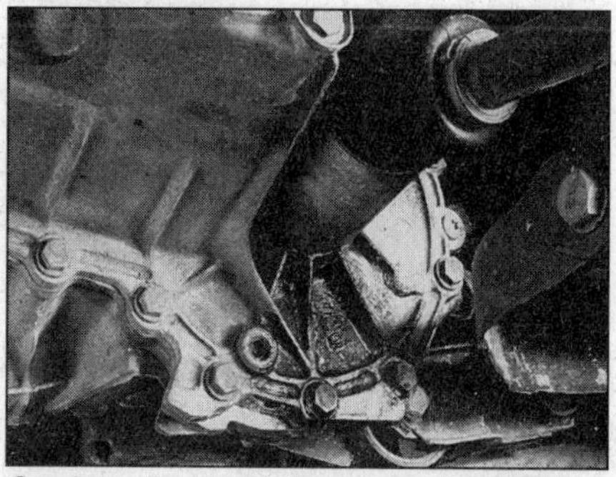

Gearbox oil can leak from the seals at the inboard ends of the driveshafts.

Antifreeze

Leaking antifreeze often leaves a crystalline deposit like this.

Brake fluid

A leak occurring at a wheel is almost certainly brake fluid.

Power steering fluid

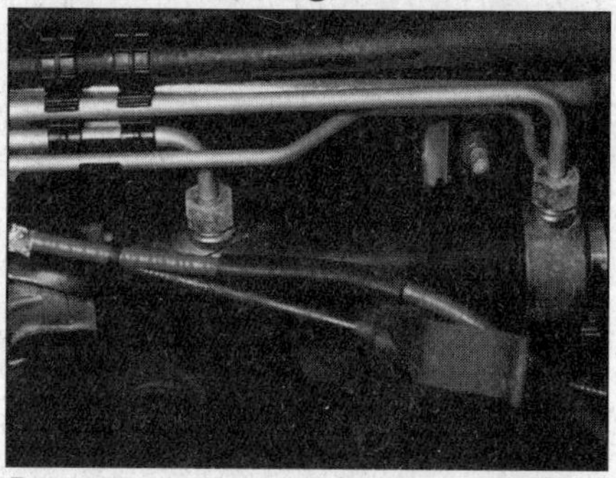

Power steering fluid may leak from the pipe connectors on the steering rack.

Towing

When all else fails, you may find yourself having to get a tow home – or of course you may be helping somebody else. Long-distance recovery should only be done by a garage or breakdown service. For shorter distances, DIY towing using another car is easy enough, but observe the following points:

☐ Use a proper tow-rope – they are not expensive. The vehicle being towed must display an ON TOW sign in its rear window.

☐ Switch on the ignition when the vehicle is being towed, so that the steering lock is released, and that the direction indicator and brake lights will work.

☐ Before being towed, release the handbrake and select neutral on the transmission.

☐ On models with automatic transmission, the car **must** be towed with its front wheels raised clear of the ground, or transmission damage may occur. Otherwise, the safe towing speed is no more than 30 mph, for no further than 30 miles.

☐ Note that greater-than-usual pedal pressure will be required to operate the brakes, since the vacuum servo unit is only operational with the engine running.

☐ Greater-than-usual steering effort will also be required.

☐ The driver of the car being towed must keep the tow-rope taut at all times to avoid snatching.

☐ Make sure that both drivers know the route before setting off.

☐ Only drive at moderate speeds and keep the distance towed to a minimum. Drive smoothly and allow plenty of time for slowing down at junctions.

☐ A front towing eye is located with the jack in the luggage compartment (see *Wheel changing*); a rear towing eye is located centrally under the rear bumper. To fit the front towing eye, prise out the cover on the side of the front bumper, and remove it. Screw the towing eye in as far as it will go. Tighten the towing eye with the wheelbrace.

Introduction

There are some very simple checks which need only take a few minutes to carry out, but which could save you a lot of inconvenience and expense.

These 'Weekly checks' require no great skill or special tools, and the small amount of time they take to perform could prove to be very well spent, for example:

☐ Keeping an eye on tyre condition and pressures, will not only help to stop them wearing out prematurely, but could also save your life.

☐ Many breakdowns are caused by electrical problems. Battery-related faults are particularly common, and a quick check on a regular basis will often prevent the majority of these.

☐ If your car develops a brake fluid leak, the first time you might know about it is when your brakes don't work properly. Checking the level regularly will give advance warning of this kind of problem.

☐ If the oil or coolant levels run low, the cost of repairing any engine damage will be far greater than fixing the leak, for example.

Underbonnet check points

◀ **1.8 litre petrol**

A *Engine oil level dipstick*
B *Engine oil filler cap*
C *Coolant reservoir (expansion tank)*
D *Brake and clutch fluid reservoir*
E *Washer fluid reservoir*
F *Power steering fluid reservoir*
G *Battery*

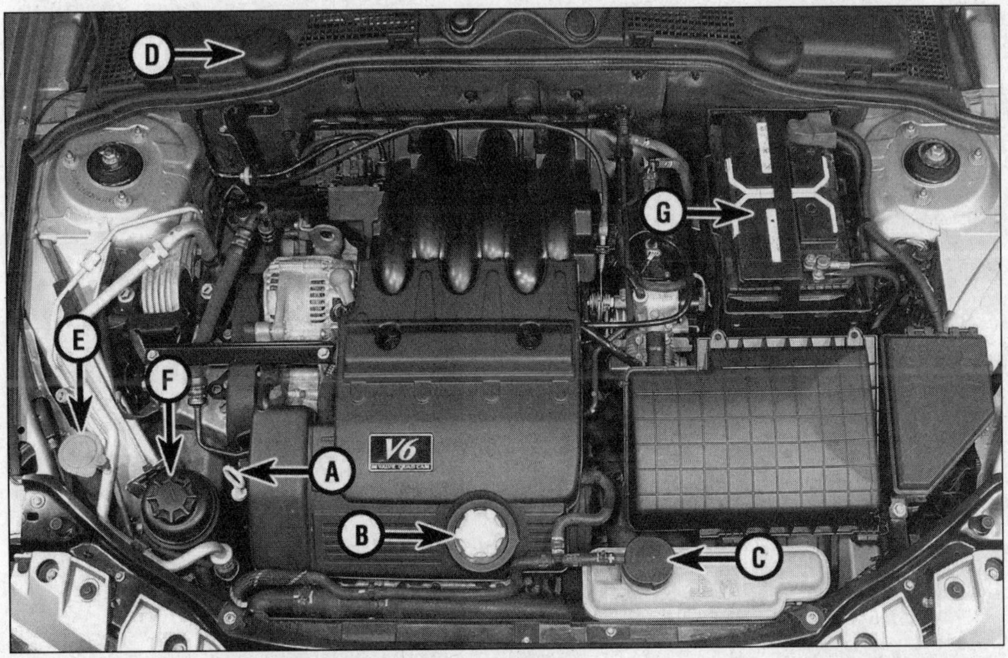

◀ **V6 petrol**

A *Engine oil level dipstick*
B *Engine oil filler cap*
C *Coolant reservoir (expansion tank)*
D *Brake and clutch fluid reservoir*
E *Washer fluid reservoir*
F *Power steering fluid reservoir*
G *Battery*

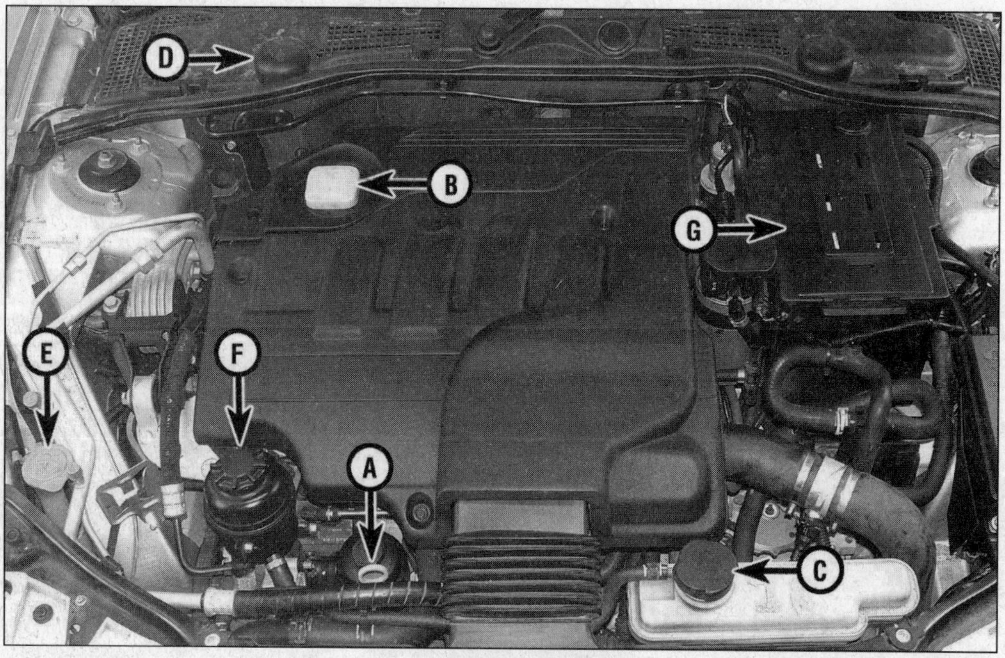

◀ Diesel

A *Engine oil level dipstick*
B *Engine oil filler cap*
C *Coolant reservoir (expansion tank)*
D *Brake and clutch fluid reservoir*
E *Washer fluid reservoir*
F *Power steering fluid reservoir*
G *Battery*

Engine oil level

Before you start

✔ Make sure that your car is on level ground.
✔ Check the oil level before the car is driven, or at least 5 minutes after the engine has been switched off.

> **HAYNES HiNT** ***If the oil is checked immediately after driving the car, some of the oil will remain in the upper engine components, resulting in an inaccurate reading on the dipstick.***

The correct oil

Modern engines place great demands on their oil. It is very important that the correct oil for your car is used (see *Lubricants and fluids*).

Car care

- If you have to add oil frequently, you should check whether you have any oil leaks. Place some clean paper under the car overnight, and check for stains in the morning. If there are no leaks, the engine may be burning oil (see *Fault finding*).
- Always maintain the level between the upper and lower dipstick marks (see photo 3). If the level is too low, severe engine damage may occur. Oil seal failure may result if the engine is overfilled by adding too much oil.

1 Pull out the dipstick. The dipstick is located at the front of the engine on all engines except the 1.8 litre petrol, which has the dipstick at the back (see *Underbonnet check points* for exact location). Wipe the dipstick clean, insert it into the tube as far as it will go, then withdraw it again.

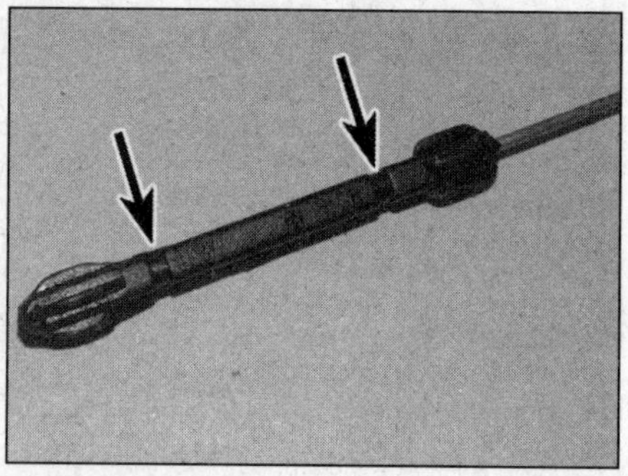

2 Note the oil level on the end of the dipstick, which should be within the 'hatched' area, or between the upper and lower notches. If the engine is very hot, the oil level may appear to be above the upper mark, owing to thermal expansion. Approximately 1.0 litre of oil will raise the level from the lower to the upper mark.

3 Oil is added through the filler cap, located on top of the engine, towards the rear on all except V6 engines. Unscrew and remove the cap.

4 Top-up the level, adding only a small amount of oil at a time. A funnel may help to reduce spillage. Add the oil slowly, checking the level on the dipstick often. Don't overfill.

Brake and clutch* fluid level

**The brake fluid reservoir also supplies fluid to the clutch master cylinder.*

Safety first!

- If the reservoir requires repeated topping-up, this is an indication of a fluid leak somewhere in the brake or clutch system, which should be investigated immediately.
- The fluid level in the reservoir will drop slightly as the brake pads wear down, but the fluid level must never be allowed to drop below the MIN mark.
- If a leak is suspected, the car should not be driven until the braking system has been checked. Never take any risks where brakes are concerned.

Warning: Brake fluid can harm your eyes and damage painted surfaces, so use extreme caution when handling and pouring it.

Do not use fluid that has been standing open for some time, as it absorbs moisture from the air, which can cause a dangerous loss of braking effectiveness.

1 The reservoir is located at the back of the engine compartment, on the driver's side. First unclip the plastic scuttle panel, by pressing back the two tabs at the front.

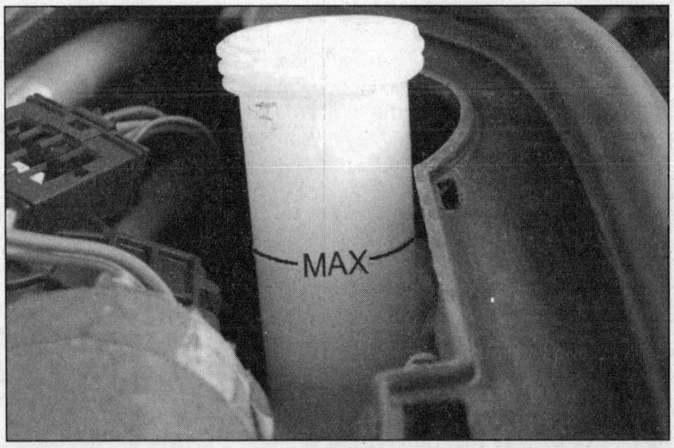

2 The fluid level should be between the MAX and MIN level marks on the filler neck, and should never fall below the MIN level.

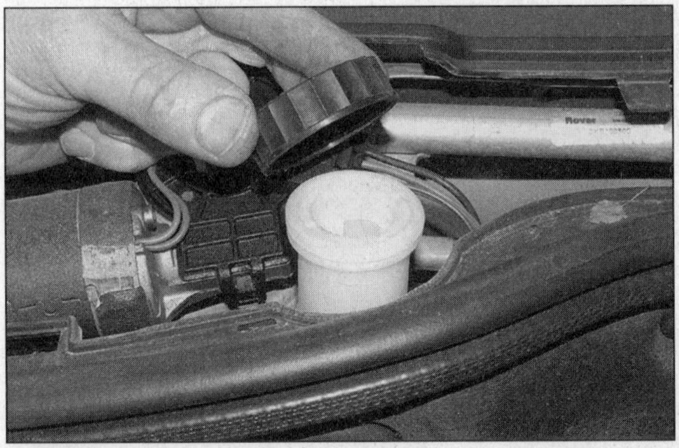

3 If topping-up is necessary, wipe the area around the filler cap with a clean rag, then unscrew the cap. When adding fluid, it's a good idea to inspect the reservoir. The fluid should be changed if it appears to be dark, or if dirt is visible.

4 Carefully add fluid, avoiding spilling it on surrounding paintwork. Use only the specified hydraulic fluid; mixing different types of fluid can cause damage to the system and/or a loss of braking effectiveness. After filling to the correct level, refit the cap securely. Wipe off any spilt fluid.

Tyre condition and pressure

It is very important that tyres are in good condition, and at the correct pressure - having a tyre failure at any speed is highly dangerous. Tyre wear is influenced by driving style - harsh braking and acceleration, or fast cornering, will all produce more rapid tyre wear. As a general rule, the front tyres wear out faster than the rears. Interchanging the tyres from front to rear ("rotating" the tyres) may result in more even wear. However, if this is completely effective, you may have the expense of replacing all four tyres at once!

Remove any nails or stones embedded in the tread before they penetrate the tyre to cause deflation. If removal of a nail does reveal that the tyre has been punctured, refit the nail so that its point of penetration is marked. Then immediately change the wheel, and have the tyre repaired by a tyre dealer.

Regularly check the tyres for damage in the form of cuts or bulges, especially in the sidewalls. Periodically remove the wheels, and clean any dirt or mud from the inside and outside surfaces. Examine the wheel rims for signs of rusting, corrosion or other damage. Light alloy wheels are easily damaged by "kerbing" whilst parking; steel wheels may also become dented or buckled. A new wheel is very often the only way to overcome severe damage.

New tyres should be balanced when they are fitted, but it may become necessary to re-balance them as they wear, or if the balance weights fitted to the wheel rim should fall off. Unbalanced tyres will wear more quickly, as will the steering and suspension components. Wheel imbalance is normally signified by vibration, particularly at a certain speed (typically around 50 mph). If this vibration is felt only through the steering, then it is likely that just the front wheels need balancing. If, however, the vibration is felt through the whole car, the rear wheels could be out of balance. Wheel balancing should be carried out by a tyre dealer or garage.

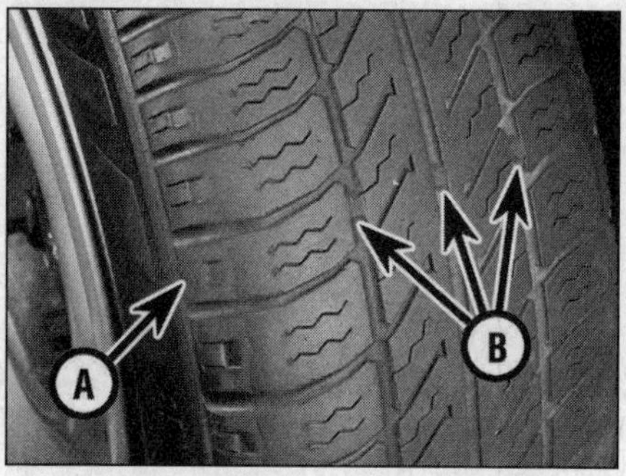

1 ***Tread Depth - visual check***

The original tyres have tread wear safety bands (B), which will appear when the tread depth reaches approximately 1.6 mm. The band positions are indicated by a triangular mark on the tyre sidewall (A).

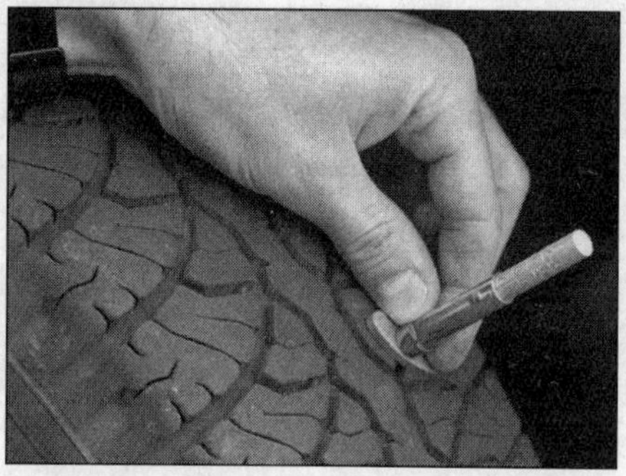

2 ***Tread Depth - manual check***

Alternatively, tread wear can be monitored with a simple, inexpensive device known as a tread depth indicator gauge.

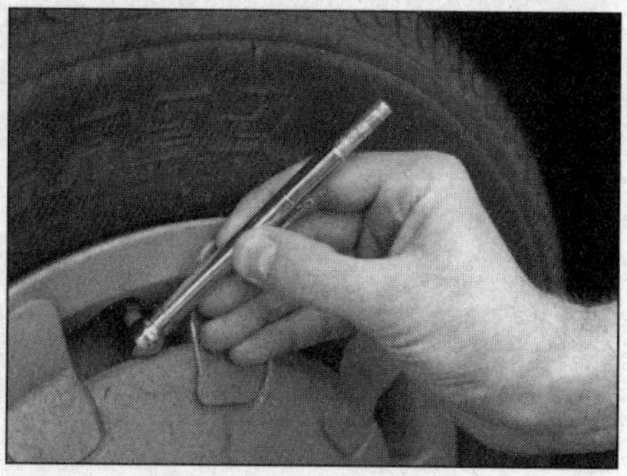

3 ***Tyre Pressure Check***

Check the tyre pressures regularly with the tyres cold. Do not adjust the tyre pressures immediately after the vehicle has been used, or an inaccurate setting will result.

Tyre tread wear patterns

Shoulder Wear

Underinflation (wear on both sides)
Under-inflation will cause overheating of the tyre, because the tyre will flex too much, and the tread will not sit correctly on the road surface. This will cause a loss of grip and excessive wear, not to mention the danger of sudden tyre failure due to heat build-up.
Check and adjust pressures
Incorrect wheel camber (wear on one side)
Repair or renew suspension parts
Hard cornering
Reduce speed!

Centre Wear

Overinflation
Over-inflation will cause rapid wear of the centre part of the tyre tread, coupled with reduced grip, harsher ride, and the danger of shock damage occurring in the tyre casing.
Check and adjust pressures

If you sometimes have to inflate your car's tyres to the higher pressures specified for maximum load or sustained high speed, don't forget to reduce the pressures to normal afterwards.

Uneven Wear

Front tyres may wear unevenly as a result of wheel misalignment. Most tyre dealers and garages can check and adjust the wheel alignment (or "tracking") for a modest charge.
Incorrect camber or castor
Repair or renew suspension parts
Malfunctioning suspension
Repair or renew suspension parts
Unbalanced wheel
Balance tyres
Incorrect toe setting
Adjust front wheel alignment
Note: *The feathered edge of the tread which typifies toe wear is best checked by feel.*

Coolant level

Warning: DO NOT attempt to remove the expansion tank pressure cap when the engine is hot, as there is a very great risk of scalding. Do not leave open containers of coolant about, as it is poisonous.

Car care

● With a sealed-type cooling system, adding coolant should not be necessary on a regular basis. If frequent topping-up is required, it is likely there is a leak. Check the radiator, all hoses and joint faces for signs of staining or wetness, and rectify as necessary.

● It is important that antifreeze is used in the cooling system all year round, not just during the winter months. Don't top-up with water alone, as the antifreeze will become too diluted.

1 The coolant level varies with the temperature of the engine. The expansion tank is located at the front of the engine compartment, in front of the air cleaner housing. Wait until the engine is cold, then remove the cap on the expansion tank.

2 The coolant MAX and MIN level markings are either visible inside the tank, or on the side (V6 engines). When cold, the level should be up to the MAX mark.

3 If necessary, add a mixture of water and antifreeze to the expansion tank, until the coolant is up to the MAX mark visible inside the filler neck. Use antifreeze of the same type (and colour) as that which is already in the system. Refit the cap securely.

Power steering fluid level

Before you start

✔ The level should be checked when the engine is cold (ie, before the car is driven), with the wheels pointing straight-ahead.

Safety first!

● The need for frequent topping-up indicates a leak, which should be investigated immediately.

1 The power steering fluid reservoir is located behind the right-hand headlight on all except 1.8 litre engine models, which have the reservoir behind the engine (see *Underbonnet check points* for exact location). The fluid level should be checked with the engine stopped.

2 The reservoir cap has a dipstick incorporated underneath. Unscrew the filler cap and wipe the dipstick clean, then screw it fully back into place. Unscrew it once more, and note the fluid level, which should be between the upper and lower notches on the dipstick.

3 Top-up the fluid level to the upper mark, using the specified type of fluid (do not overfill the reservoir), then refit and tighten the filler cap.

Battery

Caution: Before carrying out any work on the battery, read the precautions given in 'Safety first!' at the start of this manual.

✔ Make sure that the battery tray is in good condition, and that the clamp is tight. Corrosion on the tray, retaining clamp and the battery itself can be removed with a solution of water and baking soda. Thoroughly rinse all cleaned areas with water. Any metal parts damaged by corrosion should be covered with a zinc-based primer, then painted.

✔ Periodically (approximately every three months), check the charge condition of the battery as described in Chapter 5A.

✔ If the battery is flat, and you need to jump start your car, see *Roadside repairs*.

1 The battery is located at the rear of the engine compartment, on the passenger side. To access the battery, unclip and remove the top cover. The exterior of the battery should be inspected periodically for damage such as a cracked case or cover.

2 Check the tightness of the battery cable clamps to ensure good electrical connections. You should not be able to move them. Also check each cable for cracks and frayed conductors.

HAYNES HiNT

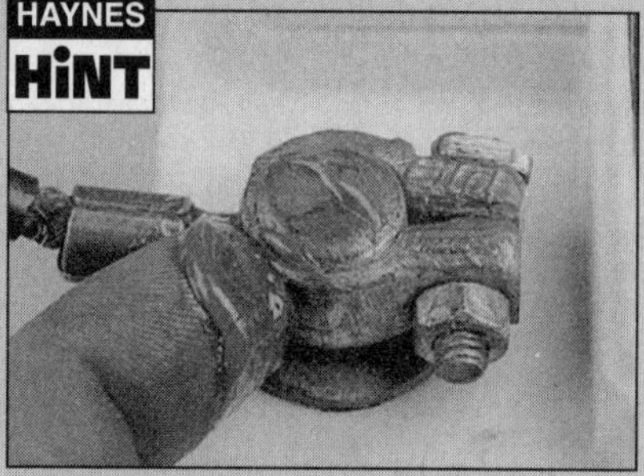

Battery corrosion can be kept to a minimum by applying a layer of petroleum jelly to the clamps and terminals after they are reconnected.

3 If corrosion (white, fluffy deposits) is evident, remove the cables from the battery terminals, clean them with a small wire brush, then refit them. Automotive stores sell a tool for cleaning the battery post . . .

4 . . . as well as the battery cable clamps.

Wiper blades

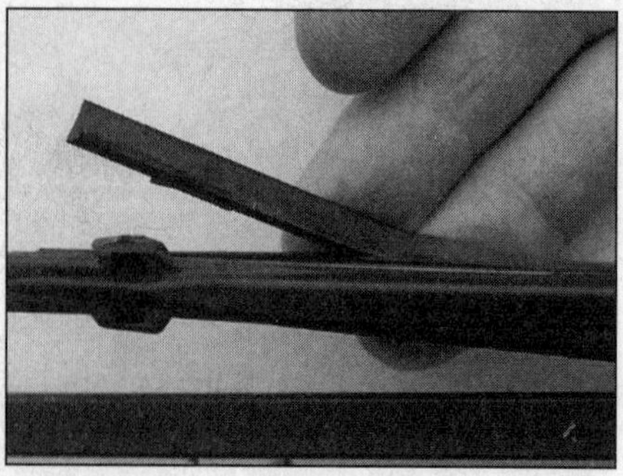

1 Check the condition of the wiper blades; if they are cracked or show any signs of deterioration, or if the glass swept area is smeared, renew them. For maximum clarity of vision, wiper blades should be renewed annually, as a matter of course.

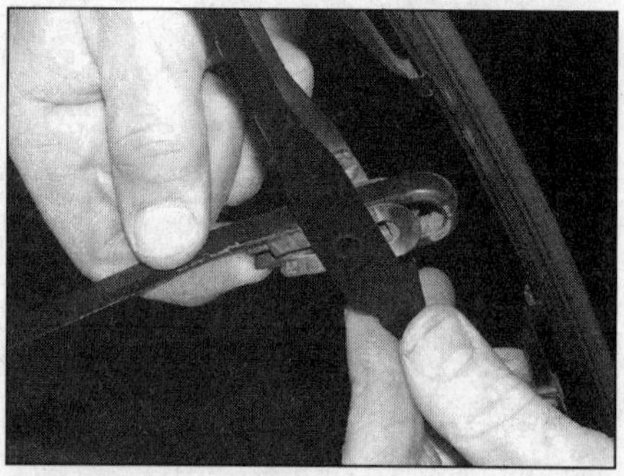

2 To remove a windscreen wiper blade, pull the arm fully away from the screen until it locks. Swivel the blade through 90°, then depress the locking clip at the base of the mounting block, and slide the blade out of the hooked end of the arm.

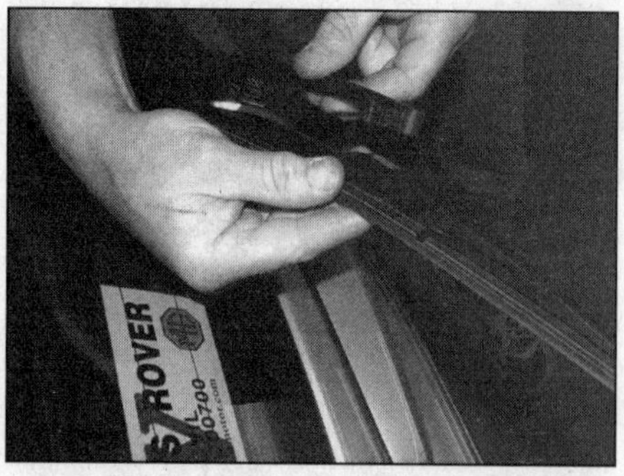

3 Don't forget to check the tailgate wiper blade as well (Tourer models), which unclips directly from the arm.

Electrical systems

✔ Check all external lights and the horn. Refer to the appropriate Sections of Chapter 12 for details if any of the circuits are found to be inoperative.

✔ Visually check all accessible wiring connectors, harnesses and retaining clips for security, and for signs of chafing or damage.

HAYNES HiNT ***If you need to check your brake lights and indicators unaided, back up to a wall or garage door and operate the lights. The reflected light should show if they are working properly.***

1 If a single indicator light, brake light or headlight has failed, it is likely that a bulb has blown and will need to be renewed. Refer to Chapter 12 for details. If both brake lights have failed, it is possible that the brake light switch operated by the brake pedal has failed. Refer to Chapter 9 for details.

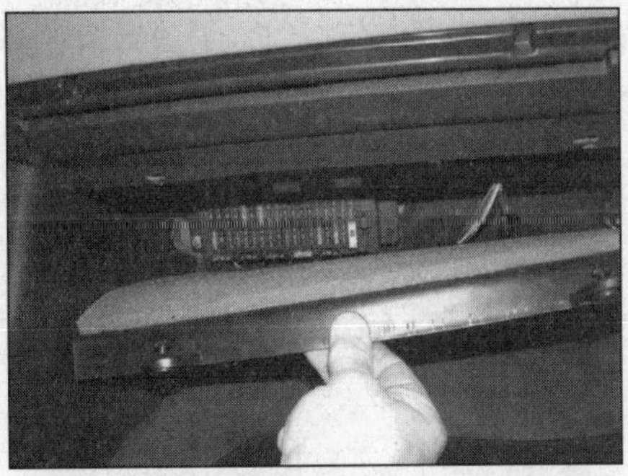

2 If more than one indicator light or headlight has failed, it is likely that either a fuse has blown, or that there is a fault in the circuit (see Chapter 12). The main fuses are mounted behind the glovebox. Remove the lower trim panel, then release the two clips to lower the fusebox cover.

3 To renew a blown fuse, remove it using the plastic tweezer tool provided. Fit a new fuse of the same rating, available from car accessory shops. It is important that you find the reason that the fuse blew (see Electrical fault finding in Chapter 12).

Screen washer fluid level

● Screenwash additives not only keep the windscreen clean during foul weather, they also prevent the washer system freezing in cold weather – which is when you are likely to need it most. Don't top-up using plain water as the screenwash will become too diluted, and will freeze during cold weather.

⚠ ***Warning: On no account use coolant antifreeze in the washer system – this could discolour or damage paintwork***

1 The windscreen/tailgate washer fluid reservoir filler neck is located at the front of the engine compartment, behind the right-hand headlight. Unclip and remove the cap.

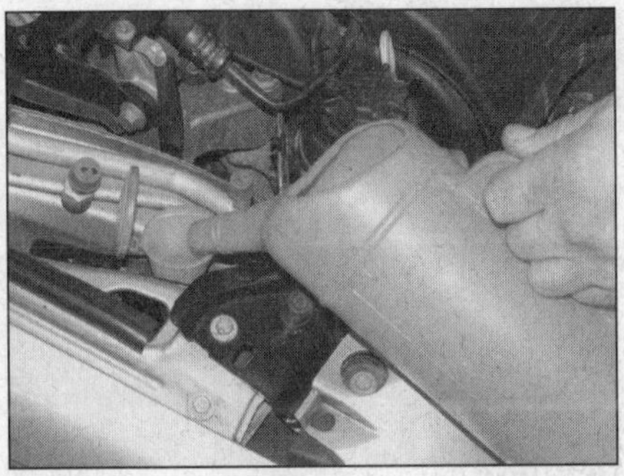

2 When topping-up the reservoir, a screenwash additive should be added in the quantities recommended on the bottle. The bottle can safely be filled until the level is visible inside.

Lubricants and fluids

Engine (petrol)	Engine oil, SAE 10W-40, to specification ACEA A2 or A3*
Engine (diesel)	Engine oil, SAE 10W-40 or 15W-40, to specification ACEA A3 **and** B3
Cooling system	Ethylene glycol antifreeze with Organic Acid Technology (OAT) corrosion inhibitors, meeting BTC coding type 4E (Havoline Extended Life Coolant (XLC) or Unipart OAT Antifreeze & Summer Coolant)
Manual transmission	Texaco MTF 94 or Burmah Oil MTF 1067
Automatic transmission	Texaco N402
Brake and clutch systems	Hydraulic fluid to DOT 4 (Shell Donax YB)
Power steering system	Dexron III type fluid

** 1.8 litre turbo engines and MG ZT 190 models should* ***only*** *use engine oils to ACEA A3 specification.*

Tyre pressures

Note: *Pressures given here are a guide only, and apply to original-equipment tyres – the recommended pressures may vary if any other make or type of tyre is fitted. Check with the car handbook for latest recommendations, and for usage other than that quoted below.*

Rover 75 models	**Front**	**Rear**
Petrol models:		
Saloon	2.1 bar (30 psi)	1.9 bar (28 psi)
Tourer:		
All except V6 automatic models	2.2 bar (32 psi)	2.2 bar (32 psi)
V6 automatic models	2.3 bar (33 psi)	2.3 bar (33 psi)
CDT Diesel models:		
Saloon	2.2 bar (32 psi)	2.1 bar (30 psi)
Tourer	2.3 bar (33 psi)	2.3 bar (33 psi)
CDTi Diesel models	2.2 bar (32 psi)	2.2 bar (32 psi)
MG ZT models	2.2 bar (32 psi)	2.2 bar (32 psi)
Space-saver spare tyre (for rear use only on MG ZT)	4.2 bar (61 psi)	4.2 bar (61 psi)

Chapter 1 Part A:
Routine maintenance & servicing – petrol models

Contents

Degrees of difficulty

Easy, suitable for novice with little experience	**Fairly easy,** suitable for beginner with some experience	**Fairly difficult,** suitable for competent DIY mechanic	**Difficult,** suitable for experienced DIY mechanic	**Very difficult,** suitable for expert DIY or professional

Lubricants and fluids

Lubricants and fluids	Refer to *Weekly checks*

Capacities

Engine oil (including oil filter)	
1.8 litre engine	4.5 litres
V6 engines	5.2 litres
Cooling system (total capacity)	
1.8 litre engine	6.2 litres
V6 engines	7.5 litres
Transmission	
Oil/fluid change:	
Manual	1.4 litres
Automatic	4.0 litres
From dry:	
Manual	1.6 litres
Automatic	8.0 litres
Washer fluid reservoir	
All models	6.0 litres
Fuel tank	
All models	65.0 litres

Cooling system

Antifreeze mixture:	
50% antifreeze	Protection down to -48°C

Note: *Refer to antifreeze manufacturer for latest recommendations.*

Ignition system

	Type	Gap*
Spark plugs (all models)	GSP 66527	1.0 mm

* *The spark plug gap quoted is that recommended by MG Rover for their plugs listed above. If spark plugs of any other type are to be fitted, refer to their manufacturer's recommendations.*

Brakes

Friction material minimum thickness (nominal)	1.5 mm

Tyre pressures

See end of *Weekly checks* on page 0•18

Torque wrench settings

	Nm	lbf ft
Automatic transmission:		
Drain plug	45	33
Level plug	14	10
Cylinder block coolant drain plug (V6 engines)	20	15
Engine oil drain plug	25	18
Front seat bolts	45	33
Ignition coil mounting bolts	8	6
Manual transmission drain and filler/level plugs	35	26
Roadwheel bolts	125	92
Seat belts:		
Front belt pretensioner-to-seat bolt	30	22
Front belt-to-adjuster bolt	33	24
Mountings to vehicle body	50	37
Spark plug cover bolts (1.8 litre engines)	8	6
Spark plugs	25	18

The maintenance intervals in this manual are provided with the assumption that you, not the dealer, will be carrying out the work. These are the minimum maintenance intervals recommended by us for cars driven daily. If you wish to keep your car in peak condition at all times, you may wish to perform some of these procedures more often. We encourage frequent maintenance, because it enhances the efficiency, performance and resale value of your car.

If the car is driven in dusty areas, used to tow a trailer, or driven frequently at slow speeds (idling in traffic) or on short journeys, more frequent maintenance intervals are recommended.

When the car is new, it should be serviced by a factory-authorised dealer service department, in order to preserve the factory warranty.

Every 250 miles or weekly

- ☐ Refer to *Weekly checks*

Every 7500 miles or 6 months, whichever comes first

- ☐ Renew the engine oil and filter (Section 3)

Note: *MG Rover recommend that the engine oil and filter are changed every 15 000 miles or 12 months. However, oil and filter changes are good for the engine, and we recommend that the oil and filter are renewed more frequently, especially if the car is used on a lot of short journeys.*

Every 15 000 miles or 12 months, whichever comes first

- ☐ Reset the service indicator (Section 4)
- ☐ Check all components, pipes and hoses for fluid leaks (Section 5)
- ☐ Check the condition and tension of the auxiliary drivebelt(s) (Section 6)
- ☐ Check the operation of all lights, wipers/washers and the horn (Section 7)
- ☐ Check the condition and operation of the seat belts (Section 8)
- ☐ Lubricate all hinges and locks (Section 9)
- ☐ Check the handbrake, and adjust if necessary (Section 10)
- ☐ Check the brake pads and discs for wear (Section 11)
- ☐ Check the steering and suspension components for condition and security (Section 12)
- ☐ Check the condition of the driveshaft gaiters (Section 13)
- ☐ Check the roadwheel bolts are tightened to the specified torque (Section 14)
- ☐ Check the braking system rubber hoses (Section 15)
- ☐ Carry out a road test (Section 16)

Every 30 000 miles or 2 years, whichever comes first

- ☐ Renew the pollen filter, where applicable (Section 17)
- ☐ Renew the air filter (Section 18)
- ☐ Check the transmission oil/fluid level (Section 19)
- ☐ Check the condition of all accessible engine/transmission mountings (Section 20)

Every 45 000 miles or 3 years, whichever comes first

- ☐ Renew the timing belt(s) (Section 21)

Note: *Although the normal interval for timing belt renewal is 90 000 miles or 6 years, it is strongly recommended that the interval suggested above is observed, especially on cars which are subjected to intensive use, ie, mainly short journeys or a lot of stop-start driving. The actual belt renewal interval is therefore very much up to the individual owner, but bear in mind that severe engine damage will result if the belt breaks.*

Every 60 000 miles or 4 years, whichever comes first

- ☐ Renew the spark plugs (Section 22)
- ☐ Renew the automatic transmission fluid (Section 23)

Every 90 000 miles or 6 years, whichever comes first

- ☐ Renew the manual transmission oil (Section 24)
- ☐ Renew the auxiliary drivebelt(s) (Section 25)

Every 2 years, regardless of mileage

- ☐ Renew the brake fluid (Section 26)

Every 4 years, regardless of mileage

- ☐ Renew the coolant (Section 27)

Underbonnet view of a 1.8 litre engine model

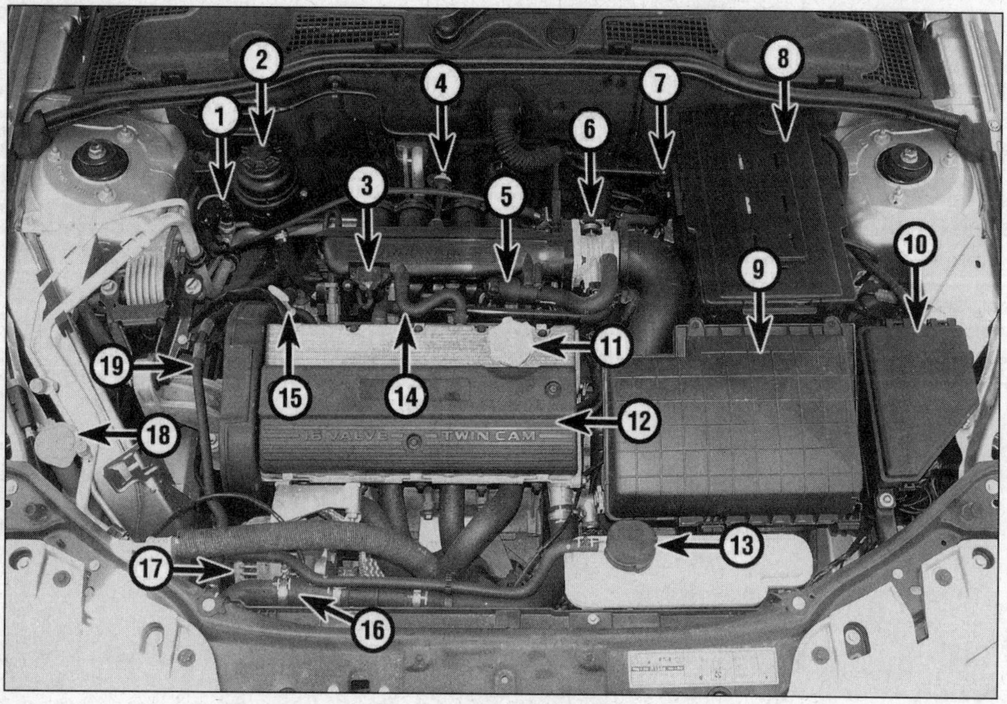

1 *Air conditioning trinary pressure switch*
2 *Power steering fluid reservoir*
3 *Manifold absolute pressure (MAP) sensor*
4 *Brake servo one-way valve*
5 *Idle air control valve*
6 *Throttle body*
7 *Canister purge valve*
8 *Battery*
9 *Air cleaner housing*
10 *Engine compartment fusebox*
11 *Engine oil filler cap*
12 *Spark plug cover*
13 *Coolant expansion tank*
14 *Breather hose*
15 *Engine oil dipstick*
16 *Radiator top hose*
17 *Alternator*
18 *Washer fluid reservoir*
19 *Heater return hose*

Underbonnet view of a V6 engine model

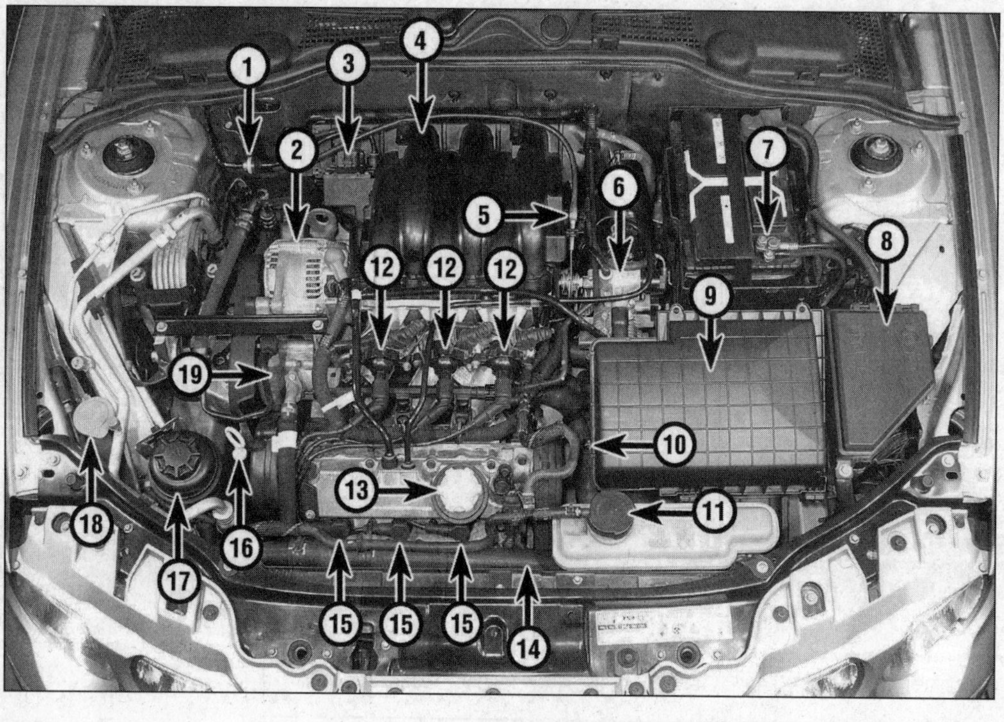

1 *Brake servo vacuum hose*
2 *Alternator*
3 *VIS motor*
4 *Inlet manifold upper chamber*
5 *Accelerator cable*
6 *Throttle body*
7 *Battery negative terminal*
8 *Engine compartment fusebox*
9 *Air cleaner housing*
10 *Cooling system bleed screw*
11 *Coolant expansion tank*
12 *Ignition coil*
13 *Engine oil filler cap*
14 *Radiator top hose*
15 *Ignition HT lead*
16 *Engine oil dipstick*
17 *Power steering fluid reservoir*
18 *Washer fluid reservoir*
19 *Power steering pump*

Front underbody view

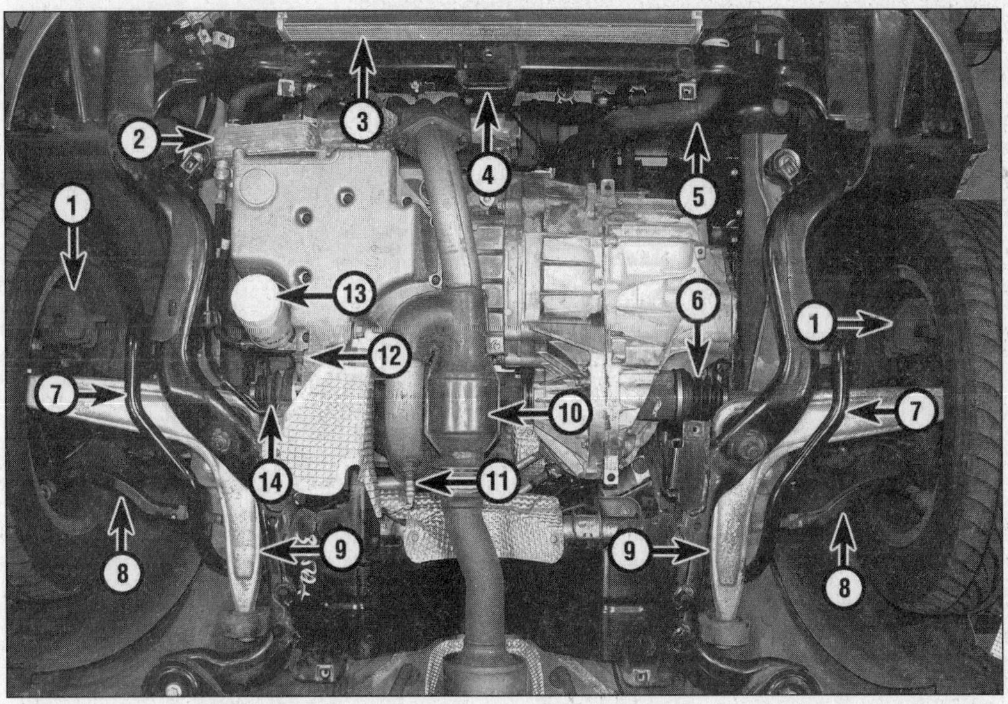

1 Front brake caliper
2 Engine oil cooler
3 Air conditioning condenser
4 Front jacking/support point
5 Radiator bottom hose
6 Left-hand driveshaft
7 Front anti-roll bar
8 Track rod
9 Front suspension lower arm
10 Catalytic converter
11 Oxygen sensor
12 Engine oil drain plug
13 Engine oil filter
14 Right-hand driveshaft

Rear underbody view

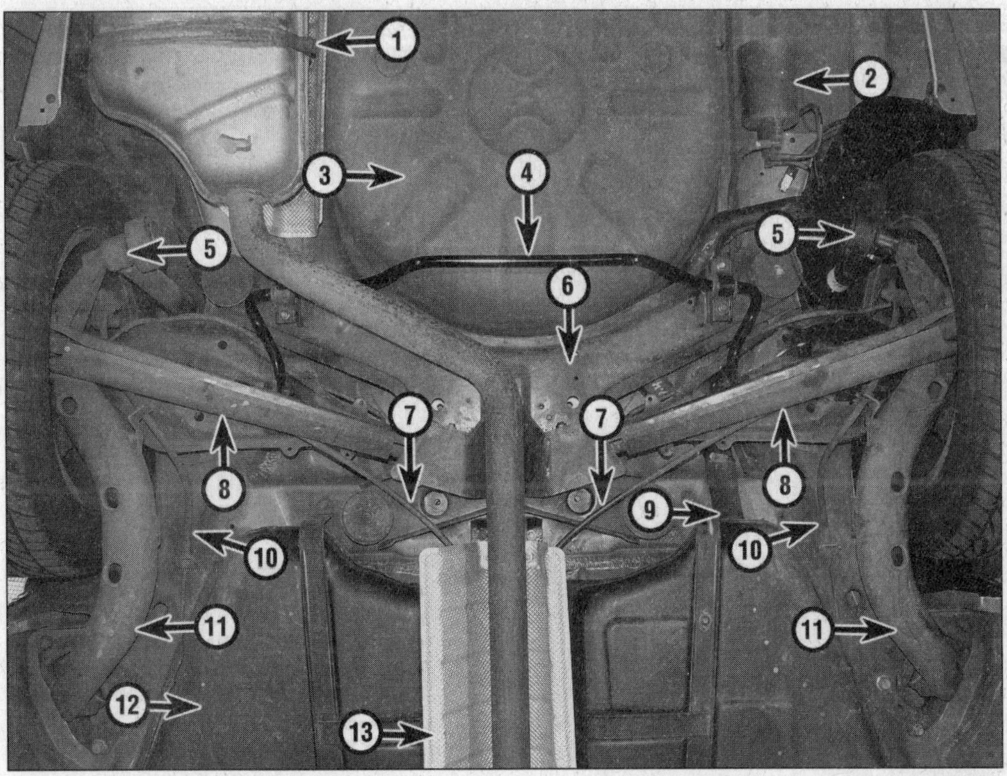

1 Exhaust rear silencer
2 Charcoal canister
3 Spare wheel well
4 Rear anti-roll bar
5 Rear shock absorber
6 Rear subframe
7 Handbrake cables
8 Rear lower arms
9 Fuel filler hose
10 Rear brake pipes/hoses
11 Rear trailing arms
12 Fuel tank
13 Heat shield

1 General information

1 This Chapter is designed to help the home mechanic maintain his/her car for safety, economy, long life and peak performance.

2 The Chapter contains a master maintenance schedule, followed by Sections dealing specifically with each task in the schedule. Visual checks, adjustments, component renewal and other helpful items are included. Refer to the accompanying illustrations of the engine compartment and the underside of the car for the locations of the various components.

3 Servicing your car in accordance with the mileage/time maintenance schedule and the following Sections will provide a planned maintenance programme, which should result in a long and reliable service life. This is a comprehensive plan, so maintaining some items but not others at the specified service intervals, will not produce the same results.

4 As you service your car, you will discover that many of the procedures can – and should – be grouped together, because of the particular procedure being performed, or because of the proximity of two otherwise-unrelated components to one another. For example, if the car is raised for any reason, the exhaust can be inspected at the same time as the suspension and steering components.

5 The first step in this maintenance programme is to prepare yourself before the actual work begins. Read through all the Sections relevant to the work to be carried out, then make a list and gather all the parts and tools required. If a problem is encountered, seek advice from a parts specialist, or a dealer service department.

2 Regular maintenance

1 If, from the time the car is new, the routine maintenance schedule is followed closely, and frequent checks are made of fluid levels and high-wear items, as suggested throughout this manual, the engine will be kept in relatively good running condition, and the need for additional work will be minimised.

2 It is possible that there will be times when the engine is running poorly due to the lack of regular maintenance. This is even more likely if a used car, which has not received regular and frequent maintenance checks, is purchased. In such cases, additional work may need to be carried out, outside of the regular maintenance intervals.

3 If engine wear is suspected, a compression test (refer to Chapter 2A or 2B, as applicable) will provide valuable information regarding the overall performance of the main internal components. Such a test can be used as a basis to decide on the extent of the work to be carried out. If, for example, a compression test indicates serious internal engine wear, conventional maintenance as described in this Chapter will not greatly improve the performance of the engine, and may prove a waste of time and money, unless extensive overhaul work is carried out first.

4 The following series of operations are those most often required to improve the performance of a generally poor-running engine:

Primary operations

a) Clean, inspect and test the battery (refer to 'Weekly checks').
b) Check all the engine-related fluids (refer to 'Weekly checks').
c) Check the condition and tension of the auxiliary drivebelt(s) (Section 6).
d) Renew the spark plugs (Section 22).
e) Check the condition of the air filter, and renew if necessary (Section 18).
f) Check the condition of all hoses, and check for fluid leaks (Section 5).

5 If the above operations do not prove fully effective, carry out the following secondary operations:

Secondary operations

All items listed under *Primary operations*, plus the following:

a) Check the charging system (Chapter 5A).
b) Check the ignition system (Chapter 5B).
c) Check the fuel system (Chapter 4A or 4B).

Every 7500 miles or 6 months

3 Engine oil and filter renewal

1 Frequent oil and filter changes are the most important preventative maintenance procedures which can be undertaken by the DIY owner. As engine oil ages, it becomes diluted and contaminated, which leads to premature engine wear.

2 Before starting this procedure, gather together all the necessary tools and materials. Also make sure that you have plenty of clean rags and newspapers handy, to mop-up any spills. Ideally, the engine oil should be warm, as it will drain more easily, and more built-up sludge will be removed with it. Take care not to touch the exhaust or any other hot parts of the engine when working under the car. To avoid any possibility of scalding, and to protect yourself from possible skin irritants and other harmful contaminants in used engine oils, it is advisable to wear gloves when carrying out this work.

3 Remove the oil filler cap.

4 Firmly apply the handbrake, then jack up the front of the car and support it on axle stands (see *Jacking and vehicle support*).

5 Remove the engine undertray, which is secured by a number of quick-release screw fasteners **(see illustration)**.

6 Using a spanner, or preferably a socket and bar, slacken the drain plug about half a turn. On 1.8 litre engines, the drain plug is at the front of the sump, while V6 engines have the drain plug at the rear, next to the oil filter **(see illustrations)**. Position the draining container under the drain plug, then remove the plug completely.

3.5 Removing the engine undertray

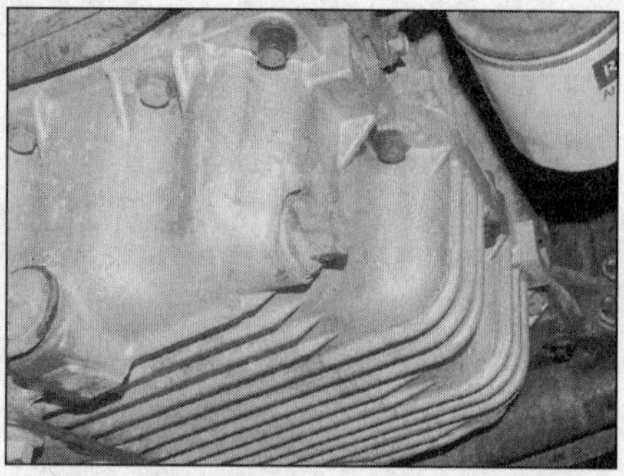

3.6a Engine oil drain plug is at the front on 1.8 litre engines . . .

3.6b . . . while V6 engines have it at the rear

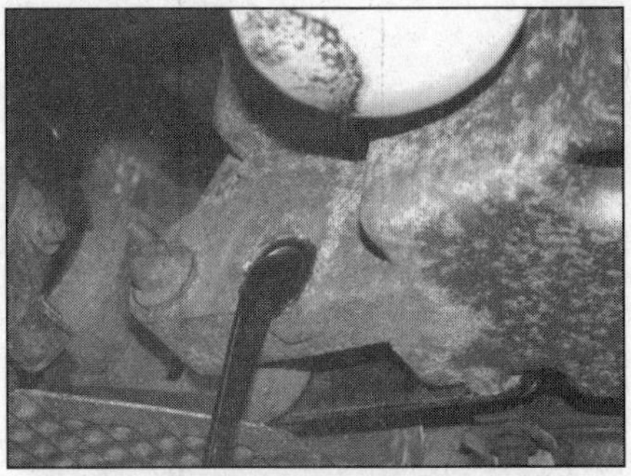

3.7 Allow time for the oil to drain

3.9a Oil filter is horizontal on 1.8 litre engines . . .

3.9b . . . and vertical on the V6

3.12a Apply clean oil to the filter sealing ring . . .

3.12b . . . then screw it into position

3.14 Use a funnel when pouring in the engine oil

HAYNES HiNT ***As the plug releases from the threads, move it away sharply, so that the stream of oil from the sump runs into the container, not up your sleeve.***

7 Allow some time for the oil to drain, noting that it may be necessary to reposition the container as the oil flow slows to a trickle **(see illustration)**.

8 After all the oil has drained, wipe the drain plug with a clean rag. Clean the area around the drain plug opening, then refit the plug, complete with a new washer, and tighten it to the specified torque.

9 Move the container into position under the oil filter. On 1.8 litre engines, the oil filter is horizontal, and located at the front; V6 engines have the filter mounted vertically, at the rear **(see illustrations)**.

10 Use an oil filter removal tool to slacken the filter initially, then unscrew it by hand the rest of the way. Empty the oil from the old filter into the container.

11 Use a clean rag to remove all oil, dirt and sludge from the filter sealing area on the engine.

12 Apply a light coating of clean engine oil to the sealing ring on the new filter, then screw the filter into position on the engine **(see illustrations)**. Tighten the filter firmly by hand only – **do not** use any tools. Once the filter has seated, it should only need tightening by a further half-turn to secure it.

13 Remove the old oil and all tools from under the car, refit the undertray, then lower the car to the ground.

14 Fill the engine through the filler hole, using the correct grade and type of oil (refer to *Weekly checks* for details of topping-up). Pour in half the specified quantity of oil first, then wait a few minutes for the oil to drain into the sump **(see illustration)**. Continue to add oil, a small quantity at a time, until the level is up to the lower mark on the dipstick. Adding approximately a further 1.0 litre will bring the level up to the upper mark on the dipstick.

15 Start the engine and run it for a few minutes, while checking for any sign of leakage from the oil filter seal or the sump drain plug. Note that there may be a delay of a few seconds before the oil pressure warning light goes out when the engine is first started, as the oil circulates through the new oil filter and the engine oil galleries before the pressure builds-up.

16 Stop the engine, and wait a few minutes for the oil to settle in the sump once more. With the new oil circulated and the filter now completely full, recheck the level on the dipstick, and add more oil as necessary.

17 Dispose of the used engine oil safely, with reference to *General repair procedures*.

Every 15 000 miles or 12 months

4 Service indicator resetting

1 The service indicator must be reset after each service, but this can only be done using the MG Rover Testbook, or equivalent resetting tool.

2 However, by temporarily bridging two of the pins in the diagnostic socket under the steering column, the display will reset.

Caution: It should be stressed that the following is NOT an official MG Rover procedure, and is undertaken at the owner's risk, but it does appear to work. If the wrong pins are used, apparently all that happens is a fuse blows, but we do not recommend testing this theory.

3 A bridging wire will be needed, to temporarily link two of the pins in the diagnostic socket. This need only be a short piece of stiff insulated wire, which should be stripped at each end as little as possible. Also, each bared end of this wire should be carefully twisted up, or ideally tinned with solder, to avoid stray strands from arcing other pins than those required. If a low-amp fuse can be incorporated into the bridging wire, this may help to avoid blowing the car's fuses if the wrong pins are used.

4 Turn the ignition switch to the second position (ignition and warning lights on).

5 Seen from under the steering column, the pin arrangement is as shown below:

16	15	14	13	12	11	10	09
08	07	06	05	**04**	03	02	01

6 Join pin number 8 to pin number 4 using the bridging wire, and hold in this position for up to 4 seconds. This should reset the oil service display. Holding the same pins for between 8 and 25 seconds will reset the inspection and time services.

7 This procedure may require more than one attempt to be successful. On completion, switch off the ignition.

5 Hose and fluid leak check

Coolant

Warning: Refer to the safety information given in 'Safety first!' and Chapter 3 before disturbing any of the cooling system components.

1 Carefully check the radiator and heater coolant hoses along their entire length. Renew any hose which is cracked, swollen or which shows signs of deterioration. Cracks will show up better if the hose is squeezed. Pay close attention to the clips that secure the hoses to the cooling system components. Hose clips that have been overtightened can pinch and puncture hoses, resulting in cooling system leaks.

HAYNES HiNT

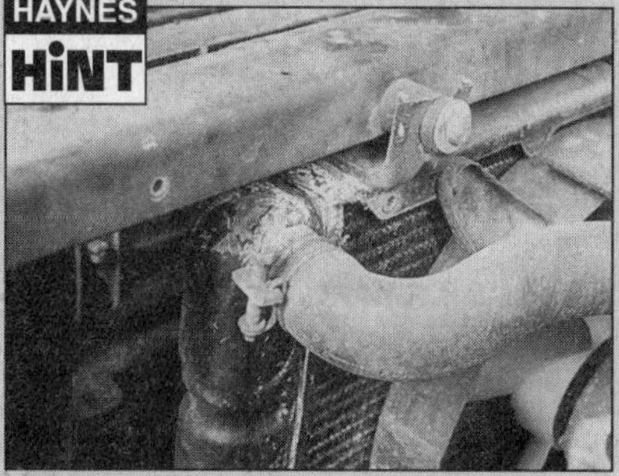

A leak in the cooling system will usually show up as white- or rust-coloured deposits on the areas adjoining the leak.

2 Inspect all the cooling system components (hoses, joint faces, etc) for leaks. Where any problems of this nature are found on system components, renew the component or gasket with reference to Chapter 3.

3 A leak from the cooling system will usually show up as white or rust-coloured deposits on the area surrounding the leak **(see Haynes Hint)**.

5.7 Check fuel lines and connections under the car

5.8 Oil leaking from the transmission bellhousing suggests crankshaft oil seal failure

5.9 Check the oil cooler hoses on V6 engines

5.10 Check the power steering pump hose connections

Fuel

Warning: Refer to the safety information given in 'Safety first!' and Chapter 4A or 4B before disturbing any of the fuel system components.

4 Check all accessible fuel lines at their underbonnet connections.

5 Examine each fuel hose/pipe along its length for splits or cracks. Check for signs of leakage, which could be anything from a damp hose to an area of bodywork adjacent to the hose which seems especially clean (from being 'washed' by leaking fuel).

6 To identify fuel leaks between the fuel tank and the engine bay, the car should raised and securely supported on axle stands. Inspect the fuel tank and filler neck for punctures, cracks and other damage. The connection between the filler neck and tank is especially critical. Sometimes a rubber filler neck or connecting hose will leak due to loose retaining clamps or deteriorated rubber.

7 Carefully check all rubber hoses and metal fuel lines leading away from the fuel tank **(see illustration)**. Check for loose connections, deteriorated hoses, kinked lines, and other damage. Pay particular attention to the vent pipes and hoses, which often loop up around the filler neck and can become blocked or kinked, making tank filling difficult. Follow the fuel supply and return lines to the front of the car, carefully inspecting them all the way for signs of damage or corrosion. Renew damaged sections as necessary.

Engine oil

8 Inspect the area around the camshaft cover, cylinder head, oil filter and sump joint faces. Bear in mind that, over a period of time, some very slight seepage from these areas is to be expected – what you are really looking for is any indication of a serious leak caused by gasket failure. Engine oil seeping from the base of the timing belt cover or the transmission bellhousing may be an indication of crankshaft or input shaft oil seal failure **(see illustration)**. Should a leak be found, renew the failed gasket or oil seal by referring to the appropriate Chapters in this manual.

9 On V6 engine models with air conditioning, check the oil cooler pipes for signs of oil leakage **(see illustration)**.

Power-assisted steering fluid

10 Examine the hose running between the fluid reservoir and the power steering pump, and the return hose running from the steering rack to the fluid reservoir. Also examine the high-pressure supply hose between the pump and the steering rack **(see illustration)**.

11 Check the hoses leading to the fluid cooler at the front of the engine bay. Look for deterioration caused by corrosion and damage from grounding, or debris thrown up from the road surface.

12 Pay particular attention to crimped unions,

5.16 Check the ABS unit for fluid leaks

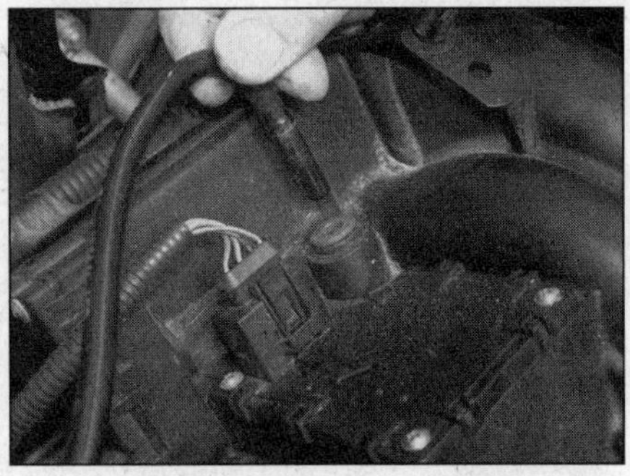

5.21 Check the security of the vacuum hoses

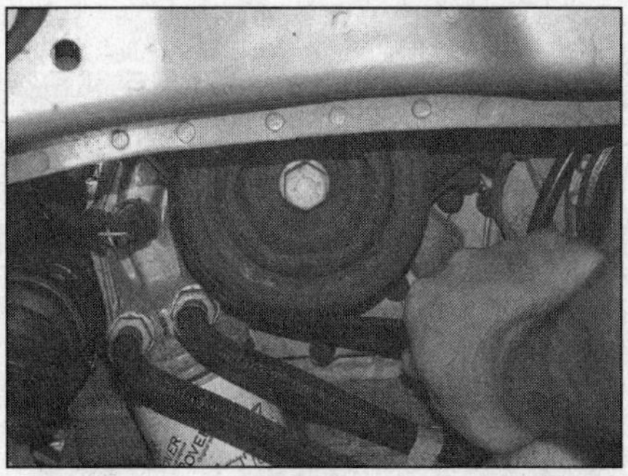

6.5 Twist the drivebelt to check it properly

and the area surrounding the hoses that are secured with adjustable worm-drive clips.

Air conditioning refrigerant

Warning: Refer to the safety information given in 'Safety first!' and Chapter 3, regarding the dangers of disturbing any of the air conditioning system components.

13 The air conditioning system is filled with a liquid refrigerant, which is retained under high pressure. If the air conditioning system is opened and depressurised without the aid of specialised equipment, the refrigerant will immediately turn into gas and escape into the atmosphere. If the liquid comes into contact with your skin, it can cause severe frostbite. In addition, the refrigerant contains substances which are environmentally damaging; for this reason, it should not be allowed to escape into the atmosphere.

14 Any suspected air conditioning system leaks should be immediately referred to a MG Rover dealer or air conditioning specialist. Leakage will be shown up as a steady drop in the level of refrigerant in the system.

15 Note that water may drip from the condenser drain pipe, underneath the car, immediately after the air conditioning system has been in use. This is normal, and should not be cause for concern.

Brake (and clutch) fluid

Warning: Refer to the safety information given in 'Safety first!' and Chapter 9, regarding the dangers of handling brake fluid.

16 With reference to Chapter 9, examine the area surrounding the brake pipe unions at the master cylinder for signs of leakage. Check the area around the base of fluid reservoir, for signs of leakage caused by seal failure. Also examine the brake pipe unions at the ABS hydraulic unit **(see illustration)**.

17 If fluid loss is evident, but the leak cannot be pinpointed in the engine bay, the brake calipers and underbody brake lines and should be carefully checked with the car raised and supported on axle stands, as described in Section 15. Leakage of fluid from the braking system is serious fault that must be rectified immediately.

18 Refer to Chapter 6 and check for leakage around the hydraulic fluid line connections to the clutch master cylinder at the bulkhead, and to the clutch slave cylinder on the transmission.

19 Brake/clutch hydraulic fluid is a toxic substance with a watery consistency. New fluid is almost colourless, but it becomes darker with age and use.

Unidentified fluid leaks

20 If there are signs that a fluid of some description is leaking from the car, but you cannot identify the type of fluid or its exact origin, park the car overnight and slide a large piece of card underneath it. Providing that the card is positioned in roughly in the right location, even the smallest leak will show up on the card. Not only will this help you to pinpoint the exact location of the leak, it should be easier to identify the fluid from its colour. Bear in mind, though, that the leak may only be occurring when the engine is running!

Vacuum hoses

21 Although the braking system is hydraulically-operated, the brake servo unit amplifies the effort you apply at the brake pedal, by making use of the vacuum available in the inlet manifold (see Chapter 9). Vacuum is ported to the servo by means of a large-bore hose **(see illustration)**. Any leaks that develop in this hose will reduce the effectiveness of the braking system, and may affect engine running.

22 In addition, many of the underbonnet components, particularly the emission control components, are driven by vacuum via narrow-bore hoses. A leak in a vacuum hose means that air is being drawn into the hose (rather than escaping from it) and this makes leakage very difficult to detect. One method is to use an old length of vacuum hose as a kind of stethoscope – hold one end close to (but not in) your ear and use the other end to probe the area around the suspected leak. When the end of the hose is directly over a vacuum leak, a hissing sound will be heard clearly through the hose. Care must be taken to avoid contacting hot or moving components, as the engine must be running when testing in this manner. Renew any vacuum hoses that are found to be defective.

6 Auxiliary drivebelt check

General

1.8 litre models

1 Two auxiliary drivebelts are fitted at the right-hand side of the engine – one for the power steering pump, with the other for the alternator and air conditioning compressor (where fitted). An automatic tensioner is fitted on the power steering drivebelt, so setting the drivebelt tension is unnecessary. For the other belt, a similar tensioner is also fitted on models with air conditioning, but those without have a manually-tensioned alternator drivebelt.

V6 models

2 All V6 models have a single drivebelt on the right-hand side of the engine, with an automatic tensioner.

Checking

3 Due to their function and material makeup, drivebelts are prone to failure after a long period of time, and should therefore be inspected regularly.

4 Since the drivebelt is located very close to the right-hand side of the engine compartment, it is possible to gain better access by raising the front of the car and removing the right-hand front wheel. On 1.8 litre models, remove the engine undertray, which is secured by a number of quick-release screw fasteners; on V6 models, remove the right-hand front wheel arch liner as described in Chapter 11, Section 22.

5 With the engine stopped, inspect the full length of the drivebelt for cracks and separation of the belt plies. It will be necessary to turn the engine (using a spanner or socket and bar on the crankshaft pulley bolt) in order to move the belt from the pulleys so that the belt can be inspected thoroughly. Twist the belt between the pulleys so that both sides can be viewed **(see illustration)**. Also check for fraying, and glazing which gives the belt a shiny appearance. Check the pulleys for nicks, cracks, distortion and corrosion.

6 Small cracks in the belt ribs are not usually

serious, but look closely to see whether the crack has extended into the belt plies. If the belt is in any way suspect, or is known to have seen long service, renew it as described in Section 25.

7 If the belt appears to be too slack (or has actually been slipping in service), this either indicates a problem with the belt tensioner (where applicable), or may indicate external contamination of the belt (eg, by oil or water). In the case of models without air conditioning, the alternator belt may just have stretched and require adjustment.

8 If the belts are satisfactory, refit the wheel arch liner or engine undertray, and the right-hand front wheel, and lower the car to the ground. Tighten the wheel bolts to the specified torque.

Renewal and adjustment

9 If the belts require renewal or adjustment, refer to Section 25.

7 Electrical equipment check

1 Check the operation of all electrical equipment, ie, lights, direction indicators, horn, etc. Refer to the appropriate Sections of Chapter 12 for details if any of the circuits are found to be inoperative.

2 Note that stop-light switch adjustment is described in Chapter 9.

3 Visually check all accessible wiring connectors, harnesses and retaining clips for security, and for signs of chafing or damage. Rectify any faults found.

8 Seat belt check

1 Check the seat belts for satisfactory operation and condition. Pull sharply on the belt to check that the locking mechanism engages correctly.

2 Pull each belt out fully, and inspect the entire length of webbing for fraying and cuts. Check that the belts retract smoothly and without binding into their reels.

3 Check that the seat belt mounting bolts are tight, and if necessary tighten them to the specified torque wrench setting.

4 Also check the front seats for signs of excessive movement, and if necessary retighten the seat mounting bolts.

9 Hinge and lock lubrication

1 Work around the car and lubricate the hinges of the bonnet, doors and tailgate with light oil.

2 Lightly lubricate the bonnet release mechanism with a smear of grease.

3 Check carefully the security and operation of all hinges, latches and locks, adjusting them where required. Check the operation of the central locking system.

4 Check the condition and operation of the boot lid or tailgate struts, renewing them if either is leaking or no longer able to support the boot lid or tailgate securely when raised.

10 Handbrake check and adjustment

Checking

1 The handbrake should be fully applied (and capable of holding the car on a slope) after approximately three clicks of the ratchet. The operating cables will stretch over time, and adjustment will be needed.

2 The handbrake is a conventional design, having separate cables for the two rear wheels, and a front cable with an equaliser plate which operates both rear cables equally. The handbrake is adjusted by means of a nut attached to the front cable.

3 With the rear of the car raised and supported (see *Jacking and vehicle support*), check that the rear wheels are free to turn with the handbrake fully released.

4 Apply the handbrake one click at a time, and check whether the rear wheels can still be turned. If the handbrake does not appear to be working equally on both wheels, this may indicate a problem with either the rear cable or the handbrake shoes on the less-operative side (see Chapter 9 for more details).

Adjustment

Note: *This simplified procedure is intended only to compensate for stretch in existing cables. If the limit of adjustment mentioned below is reached, the more elaborate procedure described in Chapter 9 should be followed to compensate for wear in the handbrake shoes.*

5 If the handbrake appears to be working evenly, but requires an excessive amount of lever movement to operate, the front cable should be adjusted as follows. First, unclip and remove the gaiter around the handbrake lever **(see illustration)**.

6 With the lever released, tighten the adjuster nut by half a turn, then recheck the operation of the handbrake and repeat if necessary **(see illustration)**. Do not over-adjust, as this may accelerate the stretching of the front cable – the length of exposed thread above the adjuster nut should **not** exceed 25 mm. When the handbrake operation is satisfactory, check that the rear wheels are free to turn when the handbrake is fully released.

7 On completion, lower the car to the ground. Refit the handbrake gaiter to the centre console.

11 Brake pad and disc wear check

1 Apply the handbrake, then jack up the front of the car and support it securely on axle stands (see *Jacking and vehicle support*). Remove the front roadwheels.

2 The brake pad thickness, and the condition of the disc, can be assessed roughly with just the wheels removed **(see Haynes Hint)**. For a comprehensive check, the brake pads should be removed and cleaned. The operation of the caliper can then also be checked, and the condition of the brake disc itself can be fully examined on both sides. Refer to Chapter 9 for further information.

3 On completion, refit the roadwheels and lower the car to the ground.

10.5 Unclip the handbrake lever gaiter from the centre console

10.6 Handbrake cable adjuster nut

HAYNES HiNT

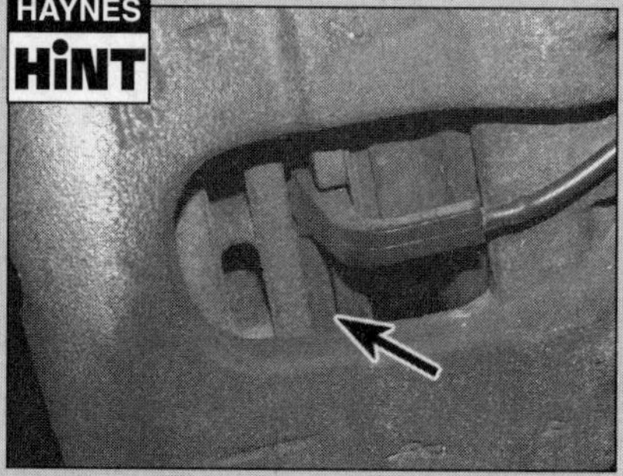

The pad thickness check can be carried out via the inspection hole at the front of the caliper.

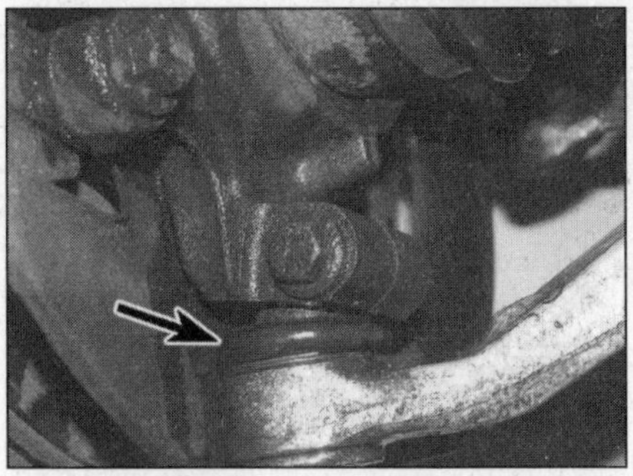

12.2a Check the lower balljoint dust covers . . .

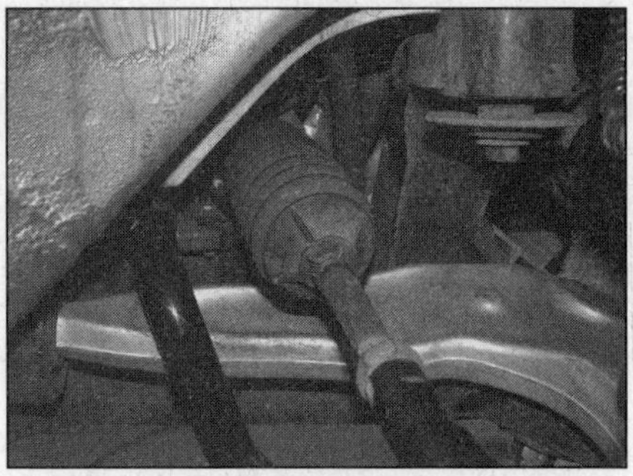

12.2b . . . and the steering rack gaiters for signs of damage

12.4 Grasp the roadwheel top and bottom, and try to rock it

4 Similarly, with the front wheels chocked, jack up the rear of the car, release the handbrake, and check the rear brake pads and discs.

12 Steering and suspension check

Front suspension and steering

1 Raise the front of the car, and securely support it on axle stands (see *Jacking and vehicle support*).

2 Visually inspect the balljoint dust covers and the steering rack-and-pinion gaiters for splits, chafing or deterioration **(see illustration)**. Any wear of these components will cause loss of lubricant, together with dirt and water entry, resulting in rapid deterioration of the balljoints or steering gear.

3 Check the power steering fluid hoses for chafing or deterioration, and the pipe and hose unions for fluid leaks. Also check for signs of fluid leakage under pressure from the steering gear rubber gaiters, which would indicate failed fluid seals within the steering gear.

4 Grasp the roadwheel at the 12 o'clock and 6 o'clock positions, and try to rock it **(see illustration)**. Very slight free play may be felt, but if the movement is appreciable, further investigation is necessary to determine the source. Continue rocking the wheel while an assistant depresses the footbrake. If the movement is now eliminated or significantly reduced, it is likely that the hub bearings are at fault. If the free play is still evident with the footbrake depressed, then there is wear in the suspension joints or mountings.

5 Now grasp the wheel at the 9 o'clock and 3 o'clock positions, and try to rock it as before. Any movement felt now may again be caused by wear in the hub bearings or the steering track rod balljoints. If the outer balljoint is worn, the visual movement will be obvious. If the inner joint is suspect, it can be felt by placing a hand over the rack-and-pinion rubber gaiter and gripping the track rod. If the wheel is now rocked, movement will be felt at the inner joint if wear has taken place.

6 Using a large screwdriver or flat bar, check for wear in the suspension mounting bushes by levering between the relevant suspension component and its attachment point. Some movement is to be expected, as the mountings are made of rubber, but excessive wear should be obvious. Also check the condition of any visible rubber bushes, looking for splits, cracks or contamination of the rubber.

7 With the car standing on its wheels, have an assistant turn the steering wheel back-and-forth, about an eighth of a turn each way. There should be very little, if any, lost movement between the steering wheel and roadwheels. If this is not the case, closely observe the joints and mountings previously described. In addition, check the steering column universal joints for wear, and also check the rack-and-pinion steering gear itself.

Rear suspension

8 Chock the front wheels, then jack up the rear of the car and support securely on axle stands (see *Jacking and vehicle support*).

9 Working as described previously for the front suspension, check the rear hub bearings, the suspension bushes and the shock absorber mountings for wear.

Shock absorbers

10 Check for any signs of fluid leakage around the shock absorber body, or from the rubber gaiter around the piston rod. Should any fluid be noticed, the shock absorber is defective internally, and should be renewed. **Note:** *Shock absorbers should always be renewed in pairs on the same axle.*

11 The efficiency of the shock absorber may be checked by bouncing the car at each corner. Generally speaking, the body will return to its normal position and stop after being depressed. If it rises and returns on a rebound, the shock absorber is probably suspect. Also examine the shock absorber upper and lower mountings for any signs of wear.

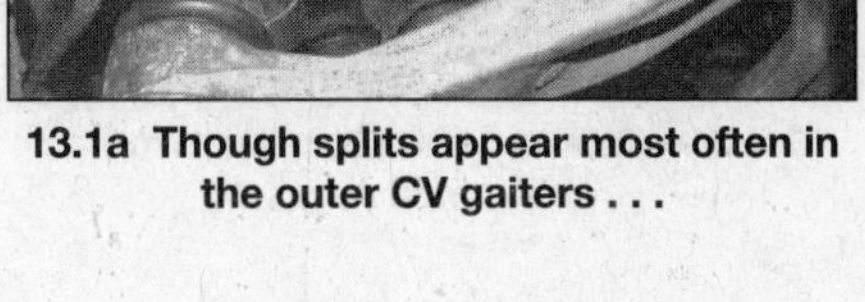

13.1a Though splits appear most often in the outer CV gaiters . . .

13 Driveshaft gaiter check

1 With the car raised and securely supported on stands, turn the steering onto full lock, then slowly rotate the roadwheel. Inspect the condition of the outer constant velocity (CV) joint rubber gaiters while squeezing the gaiters to open out the folds. Check for signs of cracking, splits or deterioration of the rubber which may allow the grease to escape and lead to water and grit entry into the joint. Also check the security and condition of the retaining clips. Repeat these checks on the inner CV joints **(see illustrations)**. If any damage or deterioration is found, the gaiters should be renewed as described in Chapter 8.

14 Roadwheel bolt tightness check

1 Remove the wheel trims or alloy wheel centre covers, and slacken the roadwheel bolts slightly.

2 Tighten the bolts to the specified torque, using a torque wrench.

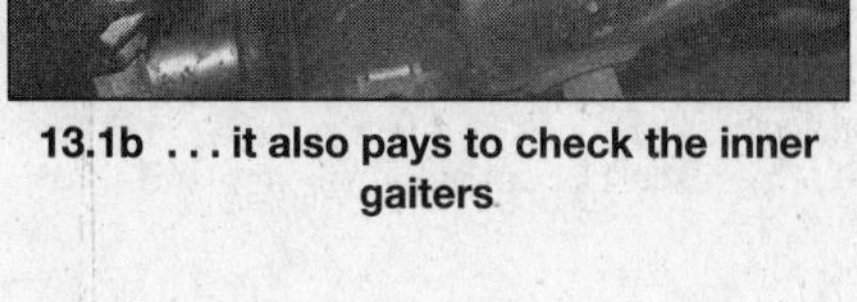

13.1b . . . it also pays to check the inner gaiters

15 Braking system rubber hose check

1 Position the car over an inspection pit, on car ramps, or jack it up one wheel at a time (see *Jacking and vehicle support*).
2 Inspect the braking system rubber hoses fitted to each brake caliper. Look for perished, swollen or hardened rubber, and any signs of cracking, especially at the metal end fittings **(see illustration)**. If there's any doubt as to the condition of any hose, renew it as described in Chapter 9.

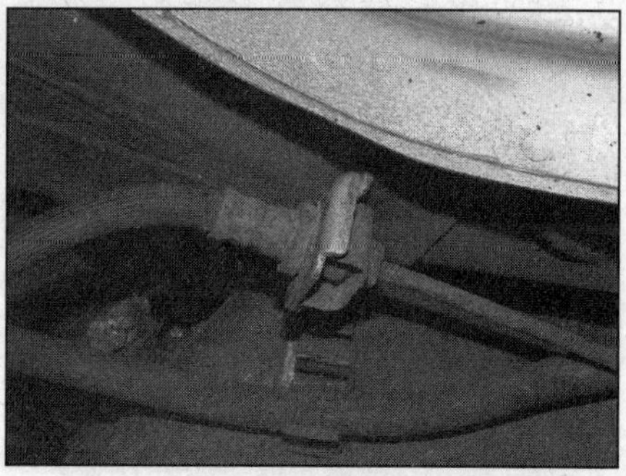
15.2 Check the condition of the brake flexible hoses

16 Road test

Instruments and facia switches

1 Check the operation of all instruments and electrical equipment.
2 Make sure that all instruments read correctly, and switch on all electrical equipment in turn, to check that it functions properly.

Steering and suspension

3 Check for any abnormalities in the steering, suspension, handling or road 'feel'.
4 Drive the car, and check that there are no unusual vibrations or noises.
5 Check that the steering feels positive, with no excessive 'sloppiness', or roughness, and check for any suspension noises when cornering and driving over bumps.

Drivetrain

6 Check the performance of the engine, clutch, transmission and driveshafts.
7 Listen for any unusual noises from the engine, clutch and transmission.
8 Make sure that the engine runs smoothly when idling, and that there is no hesitation when accelerating.
9 Check that, where applicable, the clutch action is smooth and progressive, that the drive is taken up smoothly, and that the pedal travel is not excessive. Also listen for any noises when the clutch pedal is depressed.
10 Check that all gears can be engaged smoothly without noise, and that the gear lever action is smooth and not abnormally vague or 'notchy'.
11 Listen for a metallic clicking sound from the front of the car, as the car is driven slowly in a circle with the steering on full-lock. Carry out this check in both directions. If a clicking noise is heard, this indicates wear in a driveshaft joint (see Chapter 8).

Braking system

12 Make sure that the car does not pull to one side when braking, and that the wheels do not lock when braking hard.
13 Check that there is no vibration through the steering when braking.
14 Check that the handbrake operates correctly, without excessive movement of the lever, and that it holds the car stationary on a slope.
15 Test the operation of the brake servo unit as follows. Depress the footbrake four or five times to exhaust the vacuum, then start the engine. As the engine starts, there should be a noticeable 'give' in the brake pedal as vacuum builds-up. Allow the engine to run for at least two minutes, and then switch it off. If the brake pedal is now depressed again, it should be possible to detect a hiss from the servo as the pedal is depressed. After about four or five applications, no further hissing should be heard, and the pedal should feel considerably harder.

Exhaust system

16 Listen carefully for any unusual noises from the system, which might indicate that it has started blowing, or that the mountings may be deteriorated, allowing the system to hit the underside of the car.
17 If any noises are detected, inspect the system with the car raised and supported on axle stands (see *Jacking and vehicle support*). Leaks are often accompanied by sooty stains, and are most common at the joints, and at welded sections, where pipes enter silencer boxes. Check the condition of the rubber mountings – if they are cracked or perished, fit new ones.

Every 30 000 miles or 2 years

17 Pollen filter renewal

Note: *If the pollen filter is wet when removed, this is a sign that its housing may be filling up with water, due to blocked drain channels. Since the engine control module shares this housing, any sign of this problem should be investigated without delay, to avoid possible ECM damage. Only models with air conditioning appear to be fitted with a pollen filter. Those without have a restrictor plate fitted instead, to limit the ram effect of incoming air – if wished, this plate can apparently be removed a pollen filter fitted.*
1 Open the bonnet, then release and lift off the passenger-side half of the windscreen outer grille panel, which is secured by two tabs at the front edge **(see illustration)**.
2 Pull off the rubber weatherstrip at the front of the windscreen cowl panel on the passenger side **(see illustration)**.
3 Remove the three clips at the rear, and the single screw/clip at the front, then lift up the

17.1 Unclip and remove the windscreen outer grille panel

17.2 Peel off the weatherstrip

17.3a Prise up . . .

17.3b . . . and remove the rear clips . . .

17.3c . . . and the screw/clip in front . . .

17.3d . . . then slide out the shield panel (seen with frame removed)

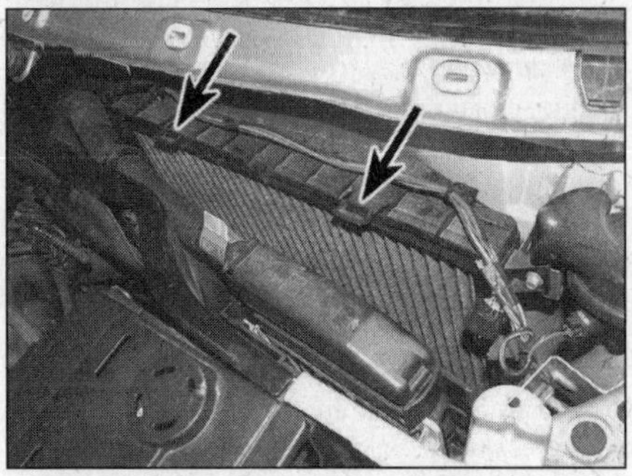

17.4a Release the two clips at the top . . .

17.4b . . . and lift out the pollen filter

passenger side of the windscreen cowl panel frame. Slide out the passenger-side water shield panel **(see illustrations)**.

4 Release the two clips, and lift the pollen filter out straight upwards **(see illustrations)**.

5 Ensure that the filter housing is clean (and dry – refer to the note at the start of this Section). While the filter is removed, check that the drain holes in its housing are clear. Fit the new filter, observing any direction-of-fitting markings.

6 Refit the removed components in the reverse order of removal.

18 Air filter element renewal

1 The air cleaner is located at the side of the engine.

2 Remove the two screws at the rear of the air cleaner housing, and lift the upper cover for access to the element below **(see illustration)**. To remove the cover completely (which is not necessary for element renewal), loosen the Jubilee clip and disconnect the inlet air duct from it.

3 Remove the filter element, noting which way round it is fitted **(see illustration)**.

4 Wipe clean the interior surfaces of the cover and base.

5 Insert the new element, making sure that it is seated correctly in the base.

6 Refit the cover and secure with the two screws.

19 Transmission oil/fluid level check

1 If possible, leave the car on the ground for this check – if the car is raised for better access underneath, it must be level to ensure accurate refilling.

Manual transmission

2 Remove the engine undertray, which is secured by a number of quick-release screw fasteners.

3 Clean the area around the filler/level plug, which is located on the end face of the transmission, directly behind the right-hand driveshaft **(see illustration)**.

4 Unscrew the filler/level plug, which will probably be very tight.

5 The level must be just below the bottom edge of the filler/level plug hole (use a cranked tool such as an Allen key to check the level). If necessary, top-up the level with the specified grade of oil (see *Lubricants and fluids*) until the oil just starts to run out. Allow any excess oil to flow out until the level stabilises.

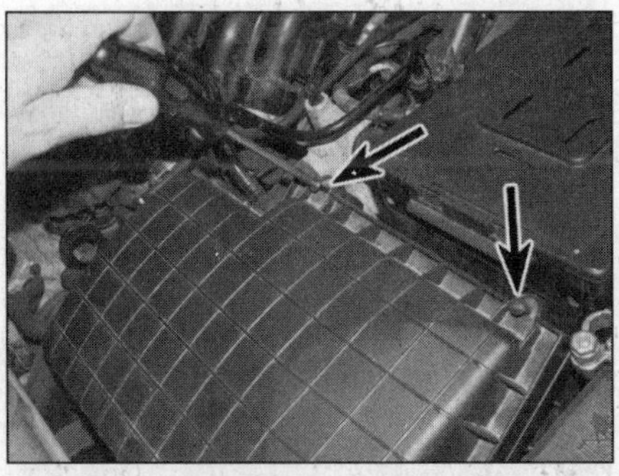

18.2 Remove the two rear screws from the air cleaner

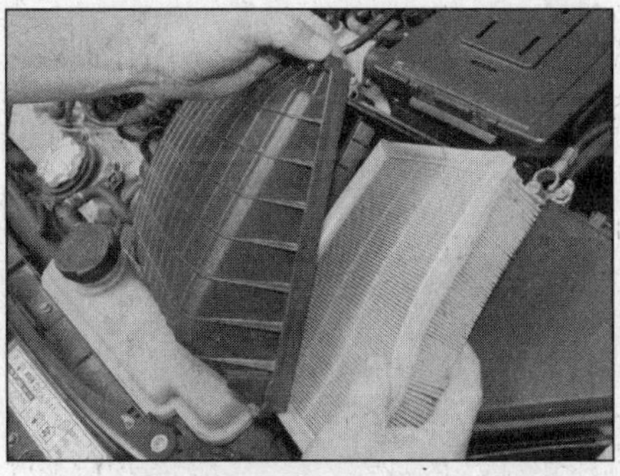

18.3 Lift the cover at the rear, and withdraw the element

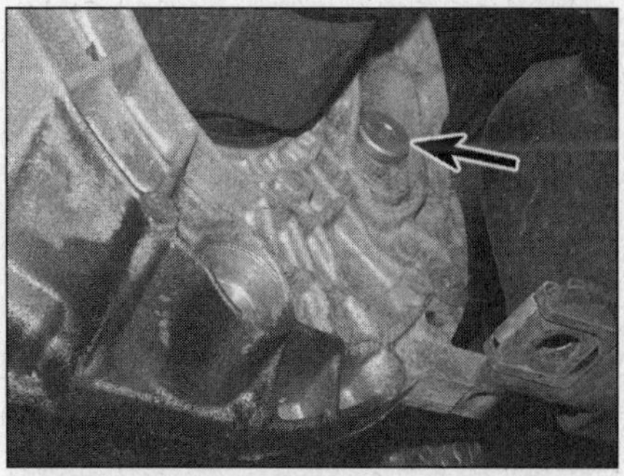

19.3 Manual transmission oil filler/level plug

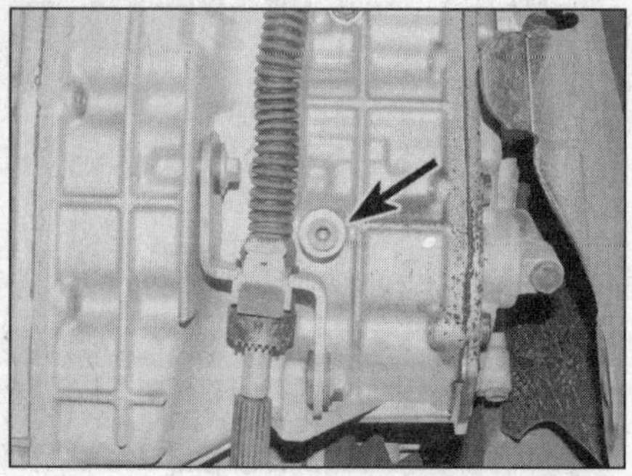

19.10 Automatic transmission fluid level plug

6 When the level is correct, clean and refit the filler/level plug, then tighten it to the specified torque.

7 Refit the engine undertray on completion.

Automatic transmission

⚠ ***Warning: The transmission fluid may be extremely hot.***

8 Remove the engine undertray, which is secured by a number of quick-release screw fasteners.

9 The fluid level is checked with the transmission at operating temperature, and with the engine running. Starting at P, and with the footbrake firmly pressed, move the selector lever through each position. Pause in each position for a few seconds, then return to position P.

10 Clean the area around the level plug, which is located directly below the selector cable – it may even be necessary to detach the cable for better access **(see illustration)**.

11 Using a 5 mm Allen key, unscrew the filler/level plug, which will probably be very tight. Recover the sealing ring – a new one will be needed when refitting.

12 The level must be just below the bottom edge of the level plug hole (use a cranked tool such as an Allen key to check the level). With the engine running, allow any excess fluid to drain.

13 If the level is correct, refit the plug using a new sealing washer, and tighten it to the specified torque. Switch off the engine.

14 If topping-up is required, switch off the engine and remove the air cleaner as described in Chapter 4A or 4B.

15 Clean around the filler pipe on top of the transmission – it is vital that no dirt enters the transmission at any stage. Pull out the filler plug.

16 Start the engine, then slowly add clean fluid of the specified type (see *Lubricants and fluids*). Add small amounts at a time, until fluid starts to flow from the level plug hole, then refit the filler plug firmly into its pipe. Refit the air cleaner as described in Chapter 4A or 4B.

17 Move the selector lever through all positions as described in paragraph 9, and allow any excess fluid to run out.

18 When the level stabilises, stop the engine. Refit and tighten the level plug (with a new sealing washer) to the specified torque.

19 Refit the engine undertray on completion.

20 Engine mounting check

1 Check the condition of the rubber sections of the engine left- and right-hand mountings, and examine the right-hand mounting (which has a hydraulic mount) for signs of fluid leakage.

2 As far as possible, check that the engine mounting bolts are fully tight, referring to Chapter 2A or 2B as applicable.

3 Jack up the front of the car, and support it on axle stands (see *Jacking and vehicle support*).

4 Check the condition and security of the engine rear mounting link.

Every 45 000 miles or 3 years

21 Timing belt renewal

Refer to Chapter 2A (1.8 litre engines) or 2B (V6 engines). V6 engines have a total of three timing belts, and all three should be renewed together.

Every 60 000 miles or 4 years

22 Spark plug renewal and ignition system check

Spark plug renewal

1 The correct functioning of the spark plugs is vital for the correct running and efficiency of the engine. It is essential that the plugs fitted are appropriate for the engine; suitable types are specified at the beginning of this Chapter, on the Vehicle Emissions Control Information (VECI) label located on the underside of the bonnet (only on models sold in some areas) or in the owner's handbook. If the correct type is used and the engine is in good condition, the spark plugs should not need attention between scheduled renewal intervals. Spark plug cleaning is rarely necessary, and should not be attempted unless specialised equipment is available, as damage can easily be caused to the firing ends.

1.8 litre engines

2 Remove the spark plug cover from the top of the engine – this is secured by three screws **(see illustration)**.

3 Unclip the HT leads from the top of the engine. Disconnect the HT lead from Nos 2 and 4 spark plugs by pulling upwards on the end fitting, not the lead **(see illustration)**.

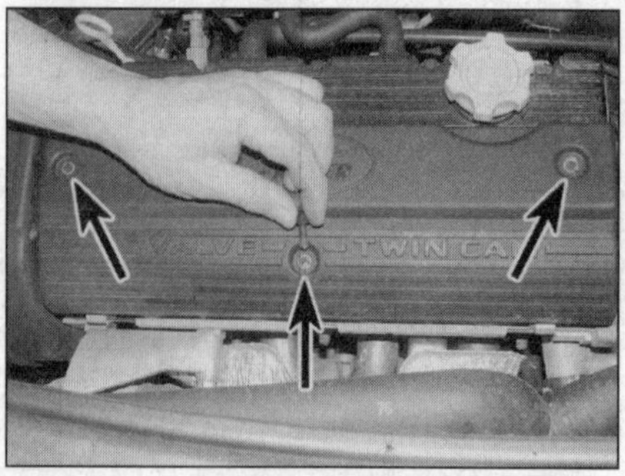

22.2 The spark plug cover is secured by three bolts

22.3 Disconnect the HT leads from plugs 2 and 4

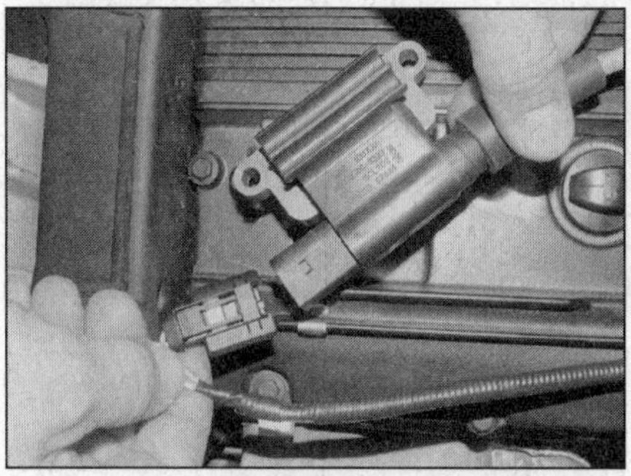

22.4 Unscrew the bolts, then disconnect the coils and pull them off

22.6 Unscrew the plugs from the cylinder head

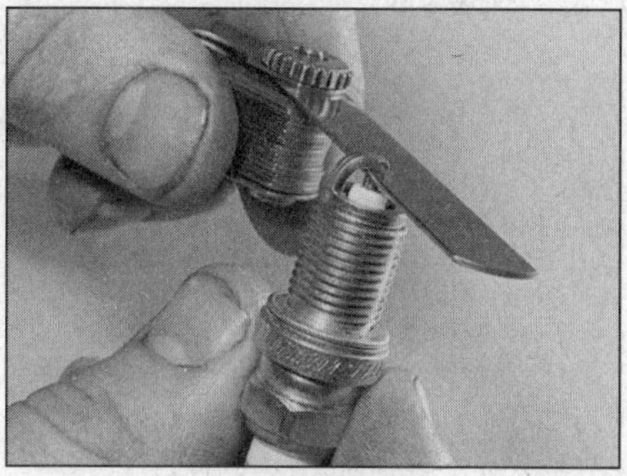

22.11a Measure the plug gap using a feeler blade . . .

4 Remove the two bolts from each of the coils. Disconnect the coil wiring plug (the HT lead can be left in place), then pull the coil upwards off the spark plug **(see illustration)**.

5 It is advisable (if possible) to remove any dirt from the spark plug recesses using a clean brush, vacuum cleaner or compressed air before removing the plugs, to prevent dirt dropping into the cylinders.

6 Unscrew the plugs from the cylinder head using a spark plug spanner, suitable box spanner or a deep socket and extension bar **(see illustration)**. Keep the socket aligned with the spark plug – if it is forcibly moved to one side, the ceramic insulator may be broken off. As each plug is removed, examine it as follows.

7 Examination of the spark plugs will give a good indication of the condition of the engine. If the insulator nose of the spark plug is clean and white, with no deposits, this is indicative of a weak mixture or too hot a plug (a hot plug transfers heat away from the electrode slowly, a cold plug transfers heat away quickly).

8 If the tip and insulator nose are covered with hard black-looking deposits, then this is indicative that the mixture is too rich. Should the plug be black and oily, then it is likely that the engine is fairly worn, as well as the mixture being too rich.

HAYNES HiNT

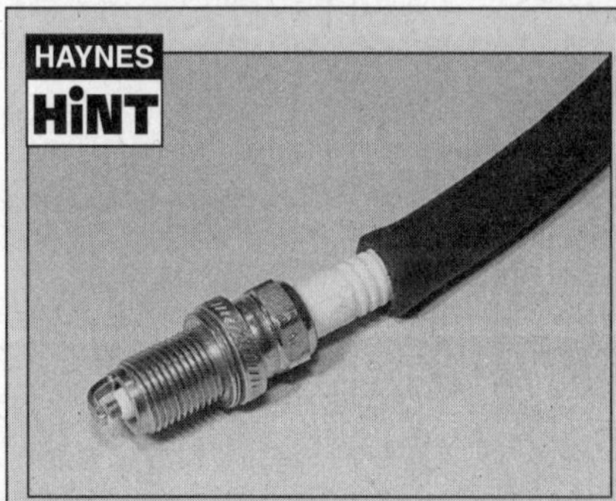

It's often difficult to insert spark plugs into their holes without cross-threading them. To avoid this possibility, fit a short length of rubber or plastic hose over the end of the spark plug. The flexible hose acts as a universal joint, to help align the plug with the plug hole. Should the plug begin to cross thread, the hose will slip on the spark plug, preventing thread damage to the aluminium cylinder head.

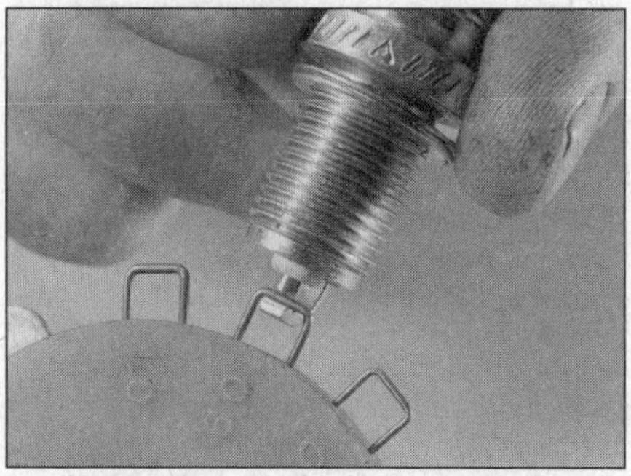

22.11b . . . or a wire gauge . . .

22.12 . . . and if necessary, bend the outer electrode to set the gap

9 If the insulator nose is covered with light tan to greyish-brown deposits, then the mixture is correct and it is likely that the engine is in good condition.

10 The spark plug electrode gap is of considerable importance as, if it is too large or too small, the size of the spark and its efficiency will be seriously impaired. The gap should be set to the value given in the Specifications at the beginning of this Chapter.

11 To set the gap, measure it with a feeler blade and then bend open, or closed, the outer plug electrode until the correct gap is achieved. The centre electrode should never be bent, as this may crack the insulator and cause plug failure, if nothing worse. If using feeler blades, the gap is correct when the appropriate-size blade is a firm sliding fit **(see illustrations)**.

12 Special spark plug electrode gap adjusting tools are available from most motor accessory shops, or from some spark plug manufacturers **(see illustration)**.

13 Before fitting the spark plugs, check that the threaded connector sleeves are tight, and that the plug exterior surfaces and threads are clean **(see Haynes Hint)**.

14 Remove the rubber/plastic hose (if used), and tighten the plug to the specified torque using the spark plug socket and a torque wrench. Refit the remaining spark plugs in the same manner.

15 Refit the HT leads to spark plugs 2 and 4, and the ignition coils to plugs 1 and 3. Reconnect the coil wiring plugs and HT leads, and tighten the coil mounting bolts to the specified torque. Finally, refit the spark plug cover, and tighten the screws securely.

V6 engines

16 Remove the two bolts and unclip the engine top cover **(see illustrations)**. Recover the washers and rubber grommets from the bolt holes, and store them for refitting.

22.16a Remove the two bolts . . .

22.16b . . . and lift off the engine top cover

22.17 Peel up the rubber seal from the rear bulkhead

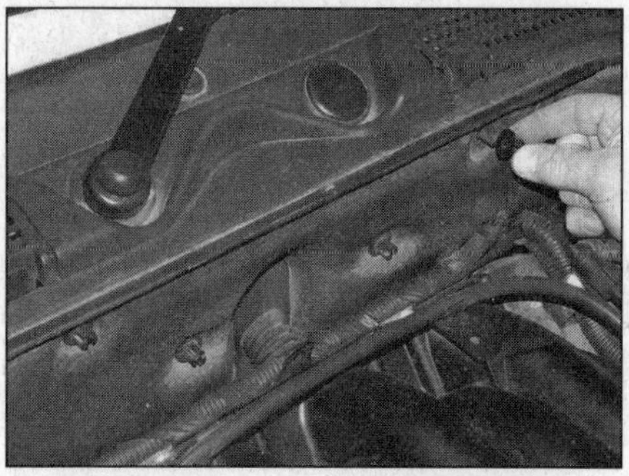
22.18a Remove the plastic nuts . . .

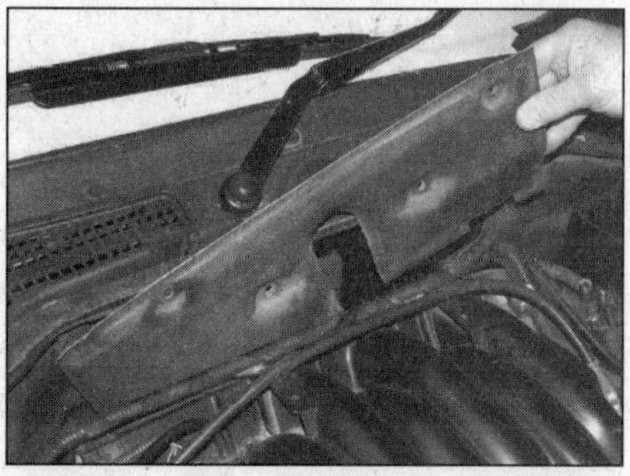
22.18b . . . and take off the soundproofing panel

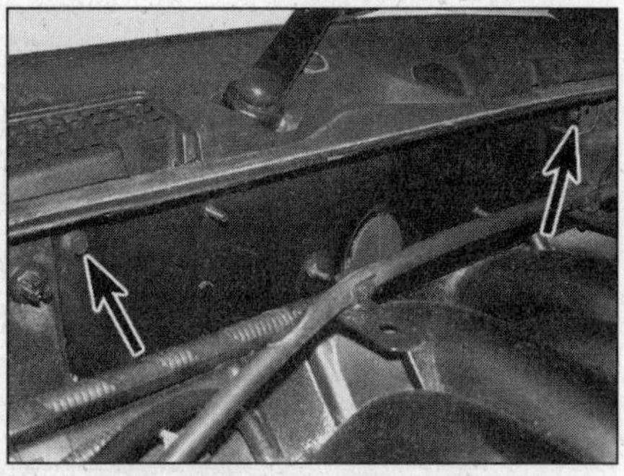
22.19a Remove the two bolts . . .

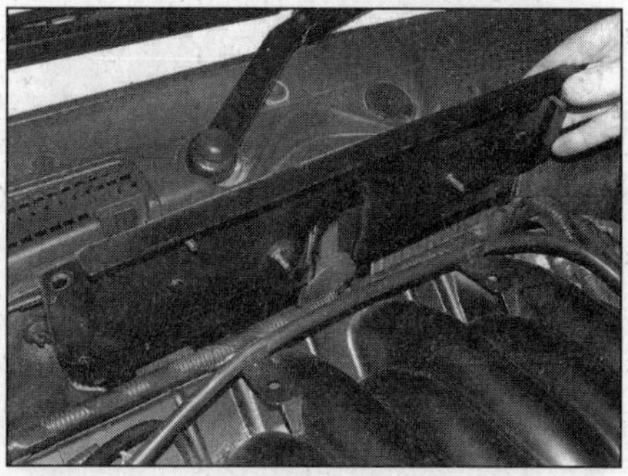
22.19b . . . and lift out the metal access panel

22.20a Lift the locking clip and disconnect the coil wiring plugs . . .

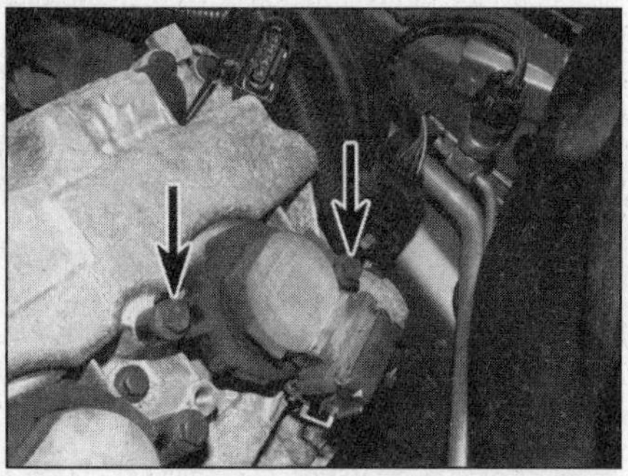
22.20b . . . then unscrew the two bolts from each coil . . .

22.20c . . . and lift them off the spark plugs

17 Peel up the rubber weatherseal at the rear of the engine compartment **(see illustration)**.

18 Remove the four nuts securing the central soundproofing panel, then lift it off the wiring harness which passes through the bulkhead **(see illustrations)**.

19 Remove the two bolts and take out the access panel behind the soundproofing **(see illustrations)**.

20 On the rear bank of the engine, lift the locking clips and disconnect the wiring plug from each of the three ignition coils. Remove the two bolts securing each coil, then lift them off the spark plugs **(see illustrations)**.

21 On the front bank of the engine,

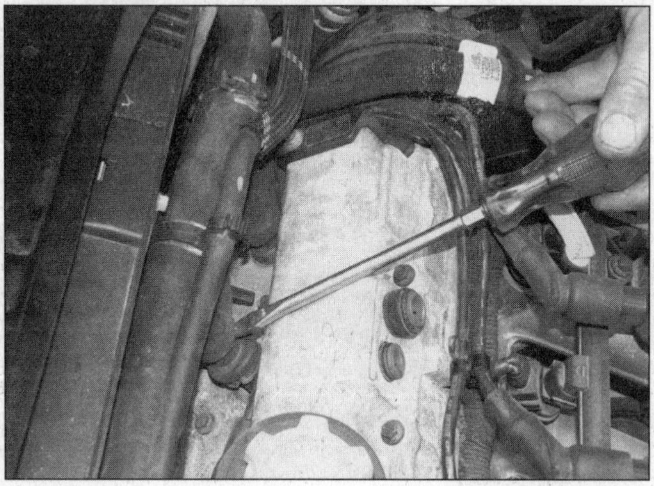
22.21a If necessary, prise the HT leads off the front plugs . . .

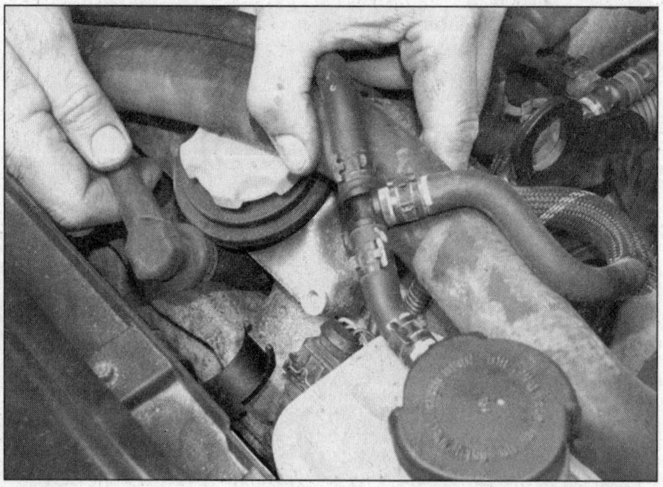
22.21b . . . and disconnect them, holding the coolant hoses clear

22.22a Clearance is limited on the front plugs . . .

disconnect the three HT leads from their spark plugs, noting their fitted positions **(see illustrations)**. The coolant hoses hinder access, but they can be lifted clear sufficiently, without disconnecting them.

22 Fit the new spark plugs as described in paragraphs 5 to 14 **(see illustrations)**.

23 Refit the HT leads to the front three spark plugs. Refit the coils to the rear three plugs, then reconnect the coil wiring plugs, and tighten the coil mounting bolts to the specified torque.

24 On completion, refit the rear access panel and soundproofing, then refit and secure the engine top cover.

Ignition system check

Warning: Voltages produced by an electronic ignition system are considerably higher than those produced by conventional ignition systems. Extreme care must be taken when working on the system with the ignition switched on. Persons with surgically-implanted cardiac pacemaker devices should keep well clear of the ignition circuits, components and test equipment.

25 The front spark plug (HT) leads should be checked whenever new spark plugs are fitted. First, mark the leads for fitted position, by wrapping tape around each one and marking it – on our car, we used F, C and R, for Front, Centre and Rear **(see illustration)**.

26 Check inside the end fitting for signs of corrosion, which will look like a white crusty powder. Push the end fitting back onto the spark plug, ensuring that it is a tight fit on the plug. If not, remove the lead again, and use

22.22b . . . but it is possible to remove them

pliers to carefully crimp the metal connector inside the end fitting until it fits securely on the end of the spark plug.

27 Using a clean rag, wipe the entire length of the lead to remove any built-up dirt and grease. Once the lead is clean, check for burns, cracks and other damage. Do not bend the lead excessively, nor pull the lead lengthwise – the conductor inside might break.

28 Disconnect the other end of the lead from the ignition coil **(see illustration)**. Check for corrosion and a tight fit in the same manner as the spark plug end. Refit the lead securely on completion.

29 Check the remaining leads one at a time, in the same way.

30 If new spark plug (HT) leads are required, purchase a set for your specific car and engine.

31 Even with the ignition system in first-class condition, some engines may still occasionally experience poor starting attributable to damp ignition components. To disperse moisture, a water-dispersant aerosol can be very effective.

23 Automatic transmission fluid renewal

Warning: The transmission fluid may be extremely hot.

1 The fluid should ideally be drained with the transmission at operating temperature. For this reason, it is advisable to wear gloves for this procedure, to protect your hands from hot fluid and surrounding components.

2 Referring to Chapter 4A or 4B as applicable, remove the air cleaner assembly. Pull out the plug from the fluid filler pipe on top of the transmission.

3 Park the car on level ground, and remove the engine undertray, which is secured by a number of quick-release screw fasteners. If possible, leave the car on the ground – if the car is raised for better access underneath, it must be level to ensure accurate refilling.

4 Position a container (of at least 4.0 litre capacity) under the transmission drain plug, which is a hex-headed bolt at the rear of the housing. Clean the area around the drain plug **(see illustration)**.

5 Remove the drain plug, and recover the sealing washer – a new one should be obtained for refitting.

6 When the fluid has finished draining, refit the drain plug with a new washer, and tighten it to the specified torque.

7 Clean around the filler pipe on top of the transmission – it is vital that no dirt enters the transmission at any stage.

8 Slowly add 3.5 to 4.0 litres of clean fluid of the specified type (see *Lubricants and fluids*) through the filler pipe, then clean and refit the filler plug.

9 Start the engine. With the footbrake firmly pressed, move the selector lever through each position. Pause in each position for a few seconds, then return to position P.

10 Clean the area around the level plug, which is located directly below the selector cable – it may even be necessary to detach the cable for better access **(see illustration 19.10)**. Position a container under the level plug.

11 Using a 5 mm Allen key, unscrew the filler/level plug, which will probably be very tight. Recover the sealing ring – a new one will be needed when refitting.

12 Allow any excess fluid to run out. If none emerges, add a little fluid through the filler pipe on top of the transmission, until it just runs from the level hole. Move the selector through all its positions, finishing at P, then wait for the excess fluid to run out.

13 When the level stabilises, stop the engine. Refit and tighten the level plug (with a new sealing washer) to the specified torque.

14 Refit the engine undertray on completion.

22.25 Mark the HT leads for position before removing them

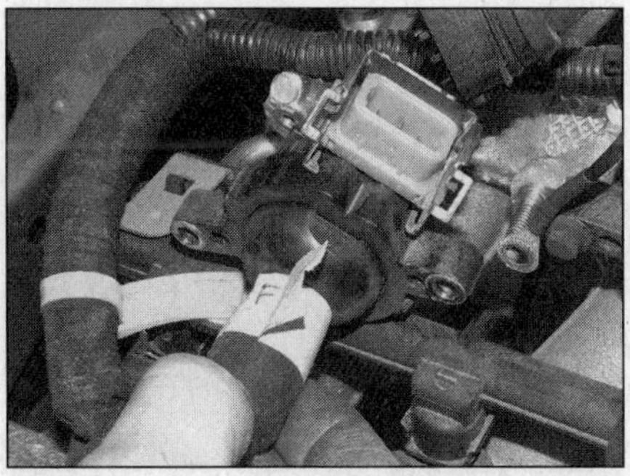

22.28 Disconnecting the HT leads from the ignition coils

23.4 Unscrew the transmission fluid drain plug

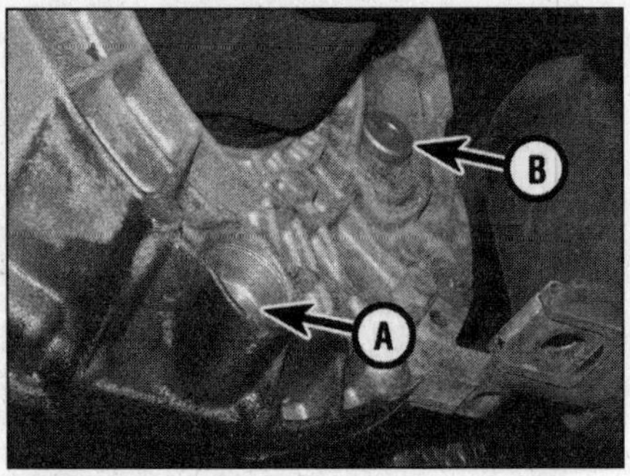

24.6 Manual transmission drain plug (A) and filler/level plug (B)

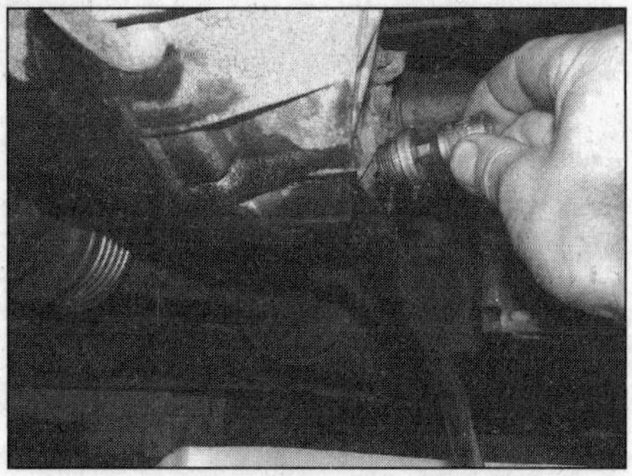

24.7 Draining the transmission oil

Every 90 000 miles or 6 years

24 Manual transmission oil renewal

1 The oil is best drained when the transmission is hot, after a run, but this is not essential. If the oil is drained hot, take precautions against scalding from hot oil, and against burning yourself on hot components.
2 Position the car over an inspection pit, on car ramps, or jack it up, but make sure that it is level.
3 Remove the engine undertray, which is secured by a number of quick-release screw fasteners.
4 Clean the area around the filler/level plug, which is located on the end face of the transmission, directly behind the right-hand driveshaft.
5 Unscrew the filler/level plug, which will probably be very tight.
6 Similarly, clean around the drain plug, which is also on the right-hand end of the housing, but below and in front of the driveshaft, and surrounded by a collar **(see illustration)**.
7 Position a suitable container below the drain plug, then unscrew the plug and allow the oil to drain **(see illustration)**.
8 When the oil has finished draining, refit the drain plug, and tighten it to the specified torque.
9 Ensuring that the car is as level as possible, fill the transmission using the specified grade of oil (see *Lubricants and fluids*) via the filler hole. This can be an awkward operation, especially if the car has been lowered to the ground to get it level **(see Haynes HInt)**.
10 The level must be just below the bottom edge of the filler/level plug hole (use a cranked tool such as an Allen key to check the level). Continue filling until the oil just starts to run out. Allow any excess oil to flow out until the level stabilises.
11 When the level is correct, clean and refit the filler/level plug, then tighten it to the specified torque.

25 Auxiliary drivebelt renewal and adjustment

1.8 litre models

1 Loosen the right-hand front wheel bolts. Raise the front of the car, and support it on axle stands (see *Jacking and vehicle support*). Remove the right-hand front wheel.
2 Remove the engine undertray, which is secured by a number of quick-release screw fasteners, and the right-hand wheel arch liner as described in Chapter 11, Section 22.

Power steering pump

3 Using a 13 mm spanner on the automatic tensioner's hex fitting, turn the tensioner clockwise to release the belt tension **(see illustration)**.
4 To hold the tensioner in the belt-released position, insert a 3 mm diameter pin (such as a small Allen key) through the hole in the tensioner's hex fitting. Turn the tensioner clockwise until the pin enters the hole in the tensioner backplate.
5 Remove the drivebelt from the pulleys, noting how it is fitted and any direction-of-rotation markings.
6 Fit the new belt onto the two pulleys, ensuring it locates correctly in the grooves.
7 Turn the tensioner slightly clockwise using the spanner on the hex fitting, and withdraw the holding pin. Release the spanner and allow the tensioner to act on the belt.

Alternator without air conditioning

8 Remove the power steering pump drivebelt as described previously in this Section.
9 Loosen the alternator upper pivot bolt and nut, in front of the timing belt upper cover **(see illustration)**.
10 Working in the wheel arch, loosen the bolt securing the alternator adjustment bracket to the engine.
11 From underneath, loosen the adjuster clamp bolt, then turn the adjuster bolt anti-clockwise to release the belt tension **(see illustration)**. **Note:** *The adjuster bolt should not require much force to turn – if it is stiff, apply a maintenance*

HAYNES HiNT

Take a piece of hosepipe (half a metre should be enough), and insert a smaller section of metal or plastic pipe which is a close fit in the filler/level hole. With a funnel on the other end, the transmission can be filled quite easily – add the oil in small amounts at a time when the transmission is almost full.

25.3 Turn the tensioner clockwise using a spanner

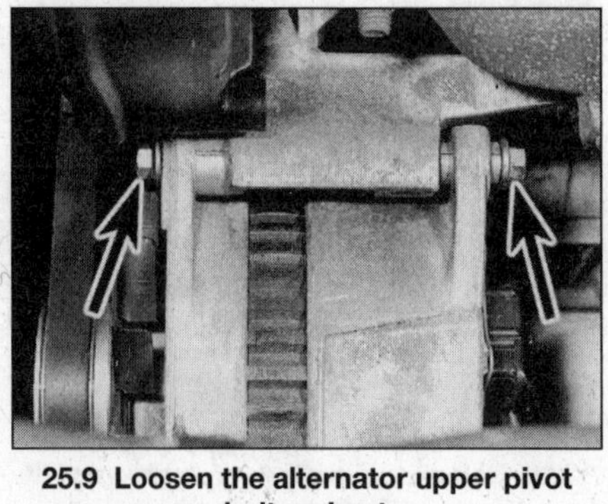

25.9 Loosen the alternator upper pivot bolt and nut

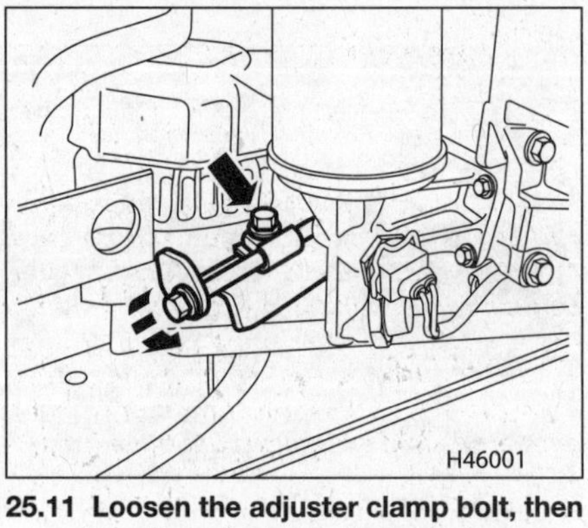

25.11 Loosen the adjuster clamp bolt, then turn the adjuster anti-clockwise

25.20 Release the belt tension using a spanner or socket, and insert a pin to hold it

25.30a Auxiliary drivebelt tensioner (belt removed) – fitting arrowed

25.30b Release the drivebelt from the alternator and power steering pump pulleys

spray such as WD-40 to free it (take care not to contaminate the drivebelt, if it is to be re-used).

12 Remove the drivebelt from the pulleys, noting how it is fitted and any direction-of-rotation markings.

13 Fit the new belt onto the two pulleys, ensuring it locates correctly in the grooves.

14 The belt tension will have to be set by feel – belt deflection is not quoted by MG Rover. Test the belt deflection midway between the pulleys on the bottom run of the belt – as a guide only, aim for a deflection of around 5 mm either way. Setting the belt tension too high may cause wear in the belt, and in the alternator bearings.

15 Use the adjuster bolt to set the belt tension, then lock it up using the clamp bolt. Tighten the adjustment bracket-to-engine bolt, and the pivot nut and bolt on top, then recheck the belt tension.

16 Turn the engine through a few complete revolutions, using a spanner or socket on the crankshaft pulley bolt. With the belt settled on its pulleys, recheck the belt tension and adjust if necessary.

17 Refit the power steering pump drivebelt as described previously in this Section.

18 If a new belt has been fitted, recheck the belt tension after (say) 500 miles, or earlier if there are signs that the belt is slipping. It is quite normal for a new belt to 'stretch' slightly in its first few miles of service (but don't overtension a new belt to compensate).

Alternator with air conditioning

19 Remove the power steering pump drivebelt as described previously in this Section.

20 The alternator/compressor drivebelt is removed in exactly the same way as the power steering drivebelt – a separate automatic tensioner is fitted, which is released using a 13 mm spanner on the hex fitting, and the tensioner can be pinned back using a small pin (or Allen key) **(see illustration)**.

21 Remove the drivebelt from the pulleys, noting how it is fitted and any direction-of-rotation markings.

22 Fit the new belt onto the pulleys, ensuring it locates correctly in the grooves.

23 Turn the tensioner slightly clockwise using the spanner on the hex fitting, and withdraw the holding pin. Release the spanner slowly and allow the tensioner to act on the belt.

24 Refit the power steering pump drivebelt as described previously in this Section.

All drivebelts

25 On completion, refit the engine undertray, wheel arch liner, and the right-hand roadwheel. Lower the car to the ground, and tighten the wheel bolts to the specified torque.

V6 models

26 Loosen the right-hand front wheel bolts. Raise the front of the car, and support it on axle stands (see *Jacking and vehicle support*). Remove the right-hand front wheel.

27 Remove the right-hand wheel arch liner as described in Chapter 11, Section 22.

28 Support the engine using a jack and block of wood under the sump.

29 Remove the engine right-hand mounting as described in Chapter 2B, then remove the four bolts and take off the engine mounting bracket from the engine. The drivebelt passes through the engine mounting, requiring that the mounting be split to remove it.

30 Using the 3/8-inch square drive from a suitable socket handle in the fitting provided on the tensioner, lift the tensioner and release the drivebelt, first from the alternator and then from the remaining pulleys **(see illustrations)**. If the belt is to be re-used, note any direction-of-rotation arrows.

31 Fit the new belt first to the crankshaft pulley.

32 Raise the tensioner as for removal, then fit the belt to the power steering pump, alternator and compressor pulleys, ensuring it locates correctly in the grooves. Release the tensioner slowly, and allow it to fully tension the belt.

33 Refit the engine right-hand engine mounting as described in Chapter 2B.

34 On completion, refit the wheel arch liner, and the right-hand roadwheel. Lower the car to the ground, and tighten the wheel bolts to the specified torque.

Every 2 years

26 Brake fluid renewal

Warning: Brake hydraulic fluid can harm your eyes and damage painted surfaces, so use extreme caution when handling and pouring it. Do not use fluid that has been standing open for some time, as it absorbs moisture from the air. Excess moisture can cause a dangerous loss of braking effectiveness.

1 The procedure is similar to that for bleeding the hydraulic system as described in Chapter 9, except that allowance should be made for the old fluid to be expelled when bleeding each section of the circuit.

2 Working as described in Chapter 9, open the first bleed screw in the sequence, and pump the brake pedal gently until the level in the reservoir is approaching the MIN mark. Top-up to the MAX level with new fluid, and continue pumping until only new fluid remains in the reservoir, and new fluid can be seen emerging from the bleed screw. Tighten the screw, and top the reservoir level up to the MAX level line.

3 Work through all the remaining bleed screws in the sequence until new fluid can be seen at all of them. Be careful to keep the master cylinder reservoir topped-up above the MIN level at all times, or air may enter the system. If this happens, further bleeding will be required, to remove the air.

HAYNES HiNT ***Old hydraulic fluid is invariably much darker in colour than the new, making it easy to distinguish the two.***

4 When the operation is complete, check that all bleed screws are securely tightened, and that their dust caps are refitted. Wash off all traces of spilt fluid, and recheck the master cylinder reservoir fluid level.

5 Check the operation of the brakes before taking the car on the road.

Every 4 years

27 Coolant renewal

Note: *The coolant used in the system from new is the Organic Acid Technology (OAT) type. This type of coolant should not be mixed with conventional antifreeze (normally blue/green in colour), even for topping-up. If the coolant is being changed to another type, flush the system through thoroughly with clean water before refilling.*

Cooling system draining

Warning: Wait until the engine is cold before starting this procedure. Do not allow antifreeze to come in contact with your skin, or with the painted surfaces of the car. Rinse off spills immediately with plenty of water. Never leave antifreeze lying around in an open container, or in a puddle in the driveway or on the garage floor. Children and pets are attracted by its sweet smell, but antifreeze can be fatal if ingested.

1 With the engine completely cold, remove the expansion tank filler cap. Turn the cap anti-clockwise, wait until any pressure remaining in the system is released, then unscrew it and lift it off.

1.8 litre engines

2 Place a suitable container under the heater return hose at the back of the engine (behind the timing belt cover). Release the hose clip, pull the hose off the engine, and allow the coolant to drain **(see illustration)**. On completion, refit the hose and secure with the hose clip – if preferred, update the spring clip with a Jubilee clip.

3 Remove the engine undertray, which is secured by a number of quick-release screw fasteners.

4 Position a larger container under the radiator bottom hose connection. Release the hose clip, then carefully work the bottom hose off the radiator (refer to Chapter 3, Section 2, if necessary) and allow the coolant to drain.

5 When the flow of coolant stops, refit the radiator hose and secure with the spring clip (or better still, fit a Jubilee clip). Refit the engine undertray.

6 If the coolant has been drained for a reason other than renewal, then provided it is clean and less than two years old, it can be re-used, though this is not recommended.

V6 engines

7 Remove the two bolts securing the engine top cover, then lift it off.

8 Remove the engine undertray, which is secured by a number of quick-release screw fasteners.

9 Position a suitable container under the cylinder block drain plug, which is on the front of the engine at the transmission end, next to the exhaust downpipe **(see illustration)**.

10 Remove the drain plug, and allow the coolant to drain.

11 Clean the drain plug, then apply a little thread-lock/sealant (such as Loctite 242) to the first three threads. When the flow of coolant stops, refit the plug and tighten to the specified torque.

12 Move the container under the radiator bottom hose connection. Release the hose clip, then carefully work the bottom hose off the radiator (refer to Chapter 3, Section 2, if necessary) and allow the coolant to drain **(see illustration)**.

13 When the coolant has drained, refit the radiator hose and secure with the spring clip (or better still, fit a Jubilee clip). Refit the engine undertray.

14 If the coolant has been drained for a reason other than renewal, then provided it is clean and less than two years old, it can be re-used, though this is not recommended.

Cooling system flushing

15 If coolant renewal has been neglected, or if the antifreeze mixture has become diluted, then in time, the cooling system may gradually lose efficiency, as the coolant passages become restricted due to rust, scale deposits, and other sediment. The cooling system efficiency can be restored by flushing the system clean.

16 The radiator should be flushed independently of the engine, to avoid unnecessary contamination.

Radiator flushing

17 Disconnect the top and bottom hoses and any other relevant hoses from the radiator, with reference to Chapter 3.

18 Insert a garden hose into the radiator top inlet. Direct a flow of clean water through the radiator, and continue flushing until clean water emerges from the radiator bottom outlet.

19 If after a reasonable period, the water still does not run clear, the radiator can be flushed with a good proprietary cleaning agent. It is important that their manufacturer's instructions are followed carefully. If the contamination is particularly bad, insert the hose in the radiator bottom outlet, and reverse-flush the radiator.

Engine flushing

20 Remove the thermostat as described in Chapter 3 then, if the radiator top hose has been disconnected from the engine, temporarily reconnect the hose.

21 With the top and bottom hoses disconnected from the radiator, insert a garden hose into the radiator top hose. Direct a clean flow of water through the engine, and continue flushing until clean water emerges from the radiator bottom hose.

27.2 Heater return hose – 1.8 litre engines

27.9 Cylinder block drain plug location – V6 engine

27.12a Release the spring clip . . .

27.12b . . . and pull off the radiator bottom hose

22 On completion of flushing, refit the thermostat and reconnect the hoses with reference to Chapter 3.

Antifreeze mixture

23 The antifreeze should always be renewed at the specified intervals. This is necessary not only to maintain the antifreeze properties, but also to prevent corrosion which would otherwise occur as the corrosion inhibitors become progressively less effective.

24 Always use an ethylene-glycol based antifreeze which is suitable for use in mixed-metal cooling systems. The quantity of antifreeze and levels of protection are given in the Specifications. The antifreeze recommended by MG Rover is specified at the beginning of this Chapter – this OAT type of coolant is known particularly for its long-lasting properties.

25 Before adding antifreeze, the cooling system should be completely drained, preferably flushed, and all hoses checked for condition and security.

26 After filling with antifreeze, a label should be attached to the expansion tank, stating the type and concentration of antifreeze used, and the date installed. Any subsequent topping-up should be made with the same type and concentration of antifreeze.

27 Do not use engine antifreeze in the windscreen/tailgate washer system, as it will cause damage to the paintwork. A screenwash additive should be added to the washer system in the quantities stated on the bottle.

Cooling system filling

28 Before attempting to fill the cooling system, make sure that all hoses and clips are in good condition, and that the clips are tight. Note that an antifreeze mixture must be used all year round, to prevent corrosion of the engine components.

HAYNES HiNT ***It is rare to ever drain the cooling system completely – a small quantity will remain. If the system has been extensively flushed with clean water, this remaining quantity will in fact be plain water. For this reason, some people will first fill the system with the required quantity of neat antifreeze (half the total system capacity, for a 50% mixture), and then complete the filling process with plain water. This ensures that the resulting coolant (once it has mixed inside the engine) is not 'diluted' by old coolant or water remaining in the system.***

1.8 litre engines

29 Release the hose clip and disconnect the hose from the bleed valve on the back of the engine (next to the engine oil dipstick tube).

30 Connect a suitable piece of hose to the bleed valve, and blow through it to ensure that the valve is not sticking.

31 Remove the temporary piece of hose, then refit the original and secure with the clip.

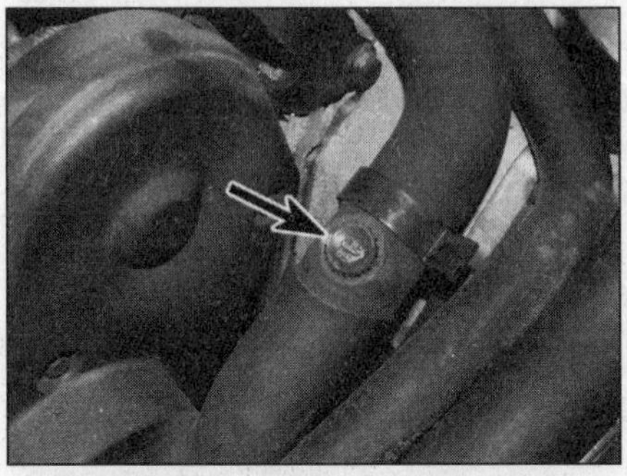

27.37 Remove the cooling system bleed screw

27.38 Disconnect the expansion tank bleed hose

27.39a Remove the expansion tank mounting bolt . . .

27.39b . . . then unhook the tank mounting pegs

32 Remove the bleed screw situated in the coolant hose which can be seen between the engine and the air cleaner.

33 Remove the expansion tank filler cap. If a funnel is available, use it to reduce the risk of spillage onto the paintwork under the bonnet.

34 Slowly fill the system, keeping the expansion tank full to just below the neck, until coolant emerges from the bleed hole in a steady stream.

35 Fit and securely tighten the bleed screw.

36 Continue filling the system until the level settles just below the expansion tank filler neck. Leave the expansion tank cap off for now.

V6 engines

37 Remove the bleed screw situated in the coolant hose which can be seen between the engine and the air cleaner **(see illustration)**.

38 Release the clip securing the expansion tank bleed hose to the top of the radiator **(see illustration)**.

39 Remove the single bolt securing the expansion tank to the radiator, then swing the tank backwards and unhook the side mounting pegs **(see illustrations)**.

40 The expansion tank must now be raised and supported as high as the hoses will allow (about 5 inches), but ensure none of the plastic hoses get kinked in the process. The tank only needs to be raised during initial filling, so could be held (with some difficulty) in one hand while filling with the other.

41 Slowly fill the system, keeping the expansion tank full to just below the neck, until coolant emerges from the bleed hole in a steady stream.

HAYNES HiNT ***Airlocks apparently form easily on the V6 engine, so take some time over filling and bleeding the system – also monitor the coolant level carefully for a few days after refilling.***

42 Fit and securely tighten the bleed screw.

43 With the tank still raised, continue filling the system until the level settles just below the expansion tank filler neck.

44 Lower the bottle into position, and secure with the single mounting bolt. Clip the bleed hose back onto the radiator top hose. Leave the expansion tank cap off for now.

45 Refit the engine top cover, and secure with the two bolts.

All engines

46 On models with air conditioning, ensure that the system is switched off before proceeding.

47 Start the engine, and have an assistant run it at a fast idle (1500 to 2500 rpm).

48 Be prepared to top-up the coolant in the expansion tank as the engine is started, and maintain the level just below the tank's filler neck. When the level starts to rise due to heat expansion, refit the expansion tank cap, and tighten it securely.

49 Keep the engine at fast idle until the cooling fan comes on, then reduce to normal idle until the fan cuts out. Switch off the engine, and allow it to cool, preferably overnight. Check the disturbed hose connections and bleed screw for signs of leakage.

50 With the engine completely cool, check the coolant level, and top-up if necessary to the MAX mark.

Airlocks

51 If, after draining and refilling the system, symptoms of overheating are found which did not occur previously, then the fault is almost certainly due to trapped air at some point in the system, causing an airlock and restricting the flow of coolant; usually, the air is trapped because the system was refilled too quickly.

52 If an airlock is suspected, first try gently squeezing all visible coolant hoses. A coolant hose which is full of air feels quite different to one full of coolant, when squeezed. After refilling the system, most airlocks will clear once the system has cooled, and been topped-up.

53 While the engine is running at operating temperature, switch on the heater and heater fan, and check for heat output. Provided there is sufficient coolant in the system, any lack of heat output could be due to an airlock in the system.

54 Airlocks can have more serious effects than simply reducing heater output – a severe airlock could reduce coolant flow around the engine. Check that the radiator top hose is hot when the engine is at operating temperature – a top hose which stays cold could be the result of an airlock (or a non-opening thermostat).

55 If the problem persists, stop the engine and allow it to cool down **completely**, before unscrewing the expansion tank filler cap or loosening the hose clips and squeezing the hoses to bleed out the trapped air. In the worst case, the system will have to be at least partially drained (this time, the coolant can be saved for re-use) and flushed to clear the problem.

Pressure (expansion tank) cap

56 Clean the pressure cap, and inspect the seal inside the cap for damage or deterioration. If there is any sign of damage or deterioration to the seal, fit a new pressure cap. If the cap is old, it is worth considering fitting a new one for peace of mind – they are not expensive.

Chapter 1 Part B:
Routine maintenance & servicing – diesel models

Contents

Degrees of difficulty

Easy, suitable for novice with little experience	**Fairly easy,** suitable for beginner with some experience	**Fairly difficult,** suitable for competent DIY mechanic	**Difficult,** suitable for experienced DIY mechanic	**Very difficult,** suitable for expert DIY or professional

Lubricants and fluids

Lubricants and fluids	Refer to *Weekly checks*

Capacities

Engine oil	
Including oil filter	6.75 litres
Cooling system	
Total capacity	8.2 litres
Transmission	
Oil/fluid change:	
Manual	1.4 litres
Automatic	4.0 litres
From dry:	
Manual	1.6 litres
Automatic	8.0 litres
Washer fluid reservoir	
All models	6.0 litres
Fuel tank	
All models	65.0 litres

Cooling system

Antifreeze mixture:	
50% antifreeze	Protection down to -48°C

Note: *Refer to antifreeze manufacturer for latest recommendations.*

Brakes

Friction material minimum thickness (nominal)	1.5 mm

Tyre pressures

See end of *Weekly checks* on page 0•18

Torque wrench settings

Torque wrench settings	Nm	lbf ft
Air conditioning compressor drivebelt:		
Belt tensioning torque:		
New belt	47	35
Used belt	38	28
Tensioner clamp and pivot bolts	24	18
Automatic transmission drain plug	45	33
Automatic transmission level plug	14	10
Engine block coolant drain plug	25	18
Engine oil drain plug	25	18
Front seat bolts	45	33
Oil filter housing cap	25	18
Manual transmission drain and filler/level plugs	35	26
Roadwheel bolts	125	92
Seat belts:		
Front belt pretensioner-to-seat bolt	30	22
Front belt-to-adjuster bolt	33	24
Mountings to vehicle body	50	37

The maintenance intervals in this manual are provided with the assumption that you, not the dealer, will be carrying out the work. These are the minimum maintenance intervals recommended by us for cars driven daily. If you wish to keep your car in peak condition at all times, you may wish to perform some of these procedures more often. We encourage frequent maintenance, because it enhances the efficiency, performance and resale value of your car.

If the car is driven in dusty areas, used to tow a trailer, or driven frequently at slow speeds (idling in traffic) or on short journeys, more frequent maintenance intervals are recommended.

When the car is new, it should be serviced by a factory-authorised dealer service department, in order to preserve the factory warranty.

Every 250 miles or weekly

- ☐ Refer to *Weekly checks*

Every 7500 miles or 6 months, whichever comes first

- ☐ Renew the engine oil and filter (Section 3)

Note: *MG Rover recommend that the engine oil and filter are changed every 15 000 miles or 12 months. However, oil and filter changes are good for the engine, and we recommend that the oil and filter are renewed more frequently, especially if the car is used on a lot of short journeys.*

Every 15 000 miles or 12 months, whichever comes first

- ☐ Reset the service indicator (Section 4)
- ☐ Check all components, pipes and hoses for fluid leaks (Section 5)
- ☐ Check the condition and tension of the auxiliary drivebelt (Section 6)
- ☐ Check the operation of all lights, wipers/washers and the horn (Section 7)
- ☐ Check the condition and operation of the seat belts (Section 8)
- ☐ Lubricate all hinges and locks (Section 9)
- ☐ Check the handbrake, and adjust if necessary (Section 10)
- ☐ Check the brake pads and discs for wear (Section 11)
- ☐ Check the steering and suspension components for condition and security (Section 12)
- ☐ Check the condition of the driveshaft gaiters (Section 13)
- ☐ Check the roadwheel bolts are tightened to the specified torque (Section 14)
- ☐ Check the braking system rubber hoses (Section 15)
- ☐ Carry out a road test (Section 16)

Every 30 000 miles or 2 years, whichever comes first

- ☐ Renew the pollen filter, where applicable (Section 17)
- ☐ Renew the air filter (Section 18)
- ☐ Check the transmission oil/fluid level (Section 19)
- ☐ Check the condition of all accessible engine/transmission mountings (Section 20)

Every 60 000 miles or 4 years, whichever comes first

- ☐ Renew the fuel filter (Section 21)
- ☐ Renew the automatic transmission fluid (Section 22)

Every 90 000 miles or 6 years, whichever comes first

- ☐ Renew the manual transmission oil (Section 23)
- ☐ Renew the auxiliary drivebelt (Section 24)

Every 2 years, regardless of mileage

- ☐ Renew the brake fluid (Section 25)

Every 4 years, regardless of mileage

- ☐ Renew the coolant (Section 26)

Underbonnet view

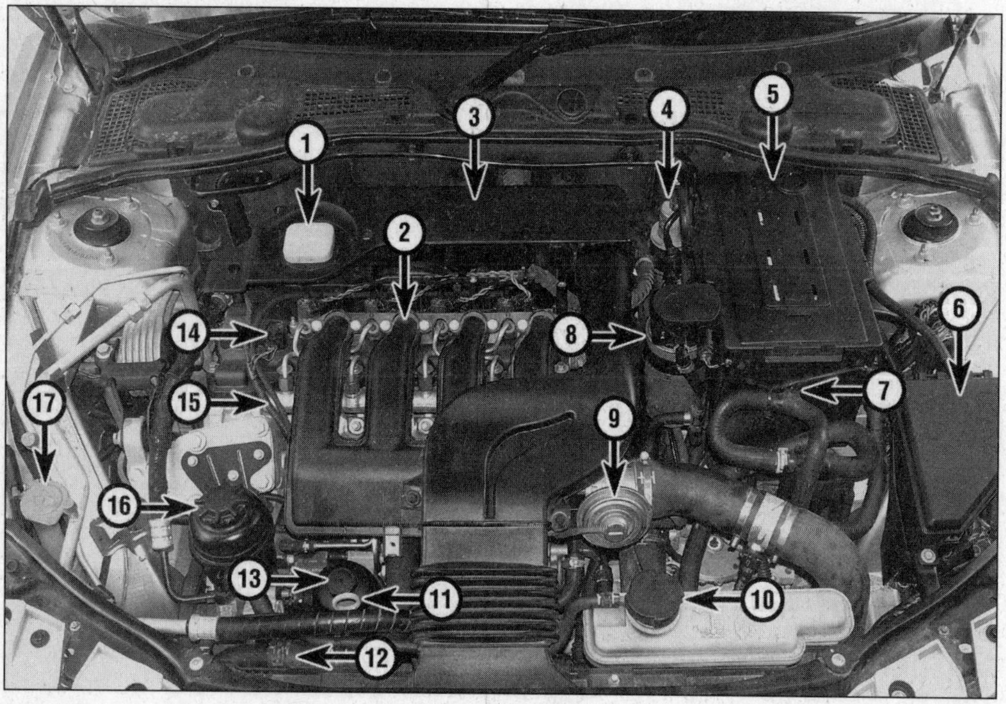

1 Engine oil filler cap
2 Inlet manifold
3 Air cleaner housing
4 Secondary fuel lift pump
5 Battery
6 Engine compartment fusebox
7 Cooling system bleed screw
8 Fuel filter assembly
9 EGR valve
10 Coolant expansion tank
11 Engine oil dipstick
12 Radiator top hose
13 Oil filter housing
14 Camshaft position sensor
15 Fuel rail
16 Power steering fluid reservoir
17 Washer fluid reservoir

Front underbody view

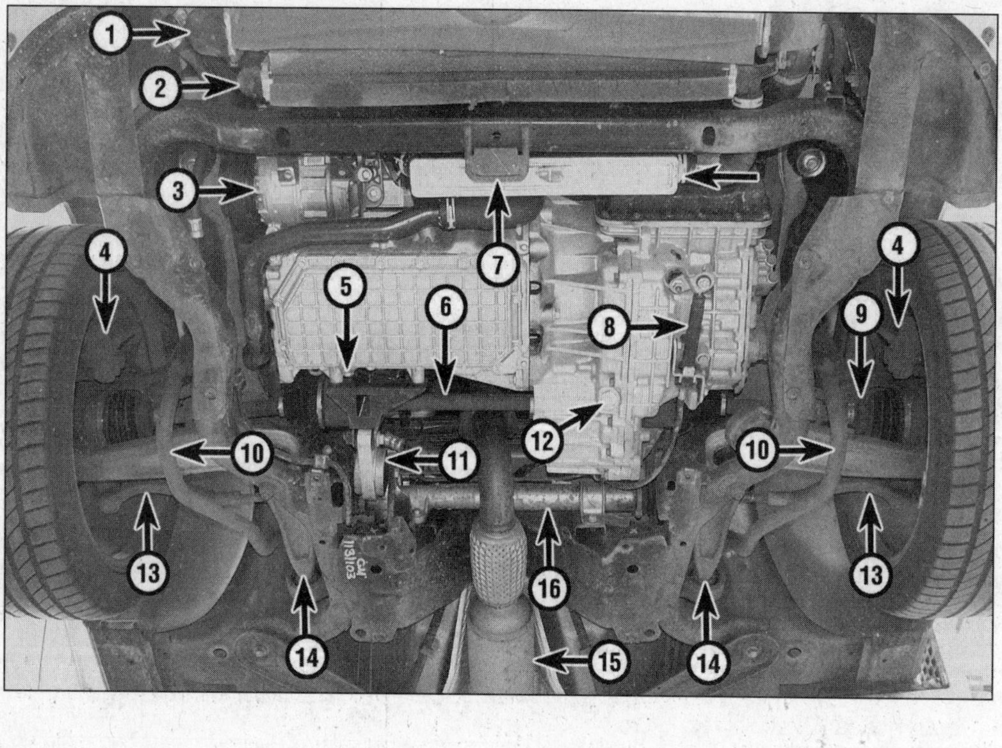

1 Intercooler
2 Radiator
3 Air conditioning compressor
4 Front brake caliper
5 Engine oil drain plug
6 Right-hand driveshaft
7 Front jacking/support point
8 Automatic transmission selector cable
9 Left-hand driveshaft
10 Front anti-roll bar
11 Engine rear mounting
12 Automatic transmission fluid drain plug
13 Track rod
14 Front suspension lower arm
15 Catalytic converter
16 Steering gear

Rear underbody view

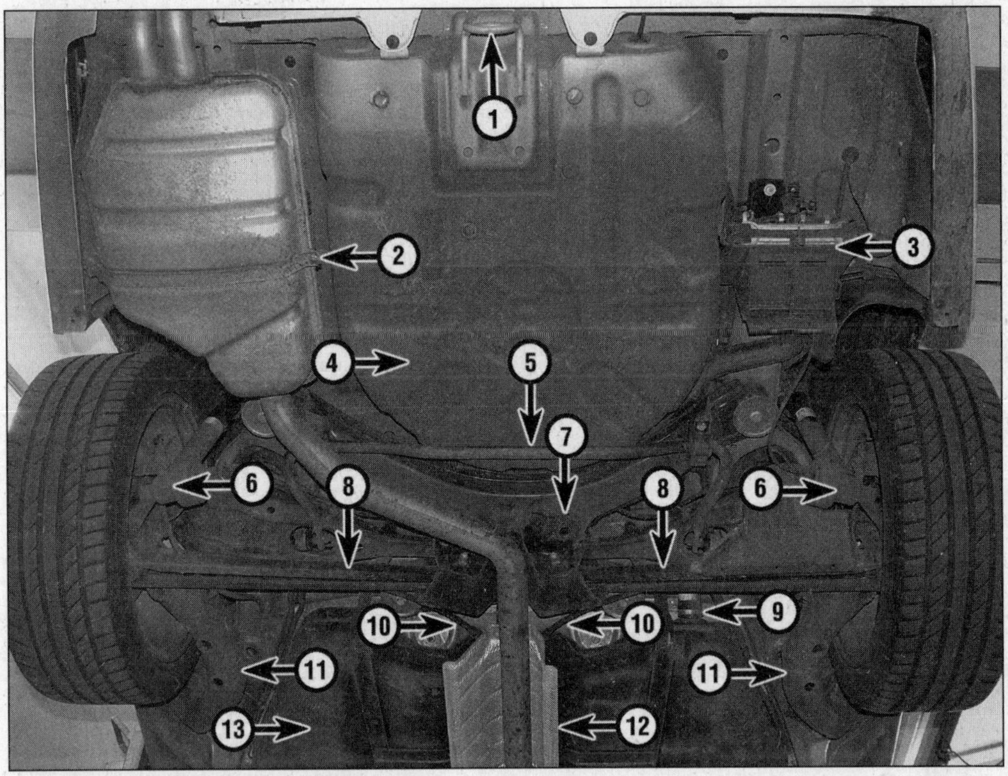

1 Rear jacking/support point
2 Exhaust rear silencer
3 Fuel cooler
4 Spare wheel well
5 Rear anti-roll bar
6 Rear shock absorber
7 Rear subframe
8 Rear lower arms
9 Fuel filler hose
10 Handbrake cables
11 Rear trailing arms
12 Heat shield
13 Fuel tank

1 General information

1 This Chapter is designed to help the home mechanic maintain his/her car for safety, economy, long life and peak performance.
2 The Chapter contains a master maintenance schedule, followed by Sections dealing specifically with each task in the schedule. Visual checks, adjustments, component renewal and other helpful items are included. Refer to the accompanying illustrations of the engine compartment and the underside of the car for the locations of the various components.
3 Servicing your car in accordance with the mileage/time maintenance schedule and the following Sections will provide a planned maintenance programme, which should result in a long and reliable service life. This is a comprehensive plan, so maintaining some items but not others at the specified service intervals, will not produce the same results.
4 As you service your car, you will discover that many of the procedures can – and should – be grouped together, because of the particular procedure being performed, or because of the proximity of two otherwise-unrelated components to one another. For example, if the car is raised for any reason, the exhaust can be inspected at the same time as the suspension and steering components.
5 The first step in this maintenance programme is to prepare yourself before the actual work begins. Read through all the Sections relevant to the work to be carried out, then make a list and gather all the parts and tools required. If a problem is encountered, seek advice from a parts specialist, or a dealer service department.

2 Regular maintenance

1 If, from the time the car is new, the routine maintenance schedule is followed closely, and frequent checks are made of fluid levels and high-wear items, as suggested throughout this manual, the engine will be kept in relatively good running condition, and the need for additional work will be minimised.
2 It is possible that there will be times when the engine is running poorly due to the lack of regular maintenance. This is even more likely if a used car, which has not received regular and frequent maintenance checks, is purchased. In such cases, additional work may need to be carried out, outside of the regular maintenance intervals.
3 If engine wear is suspected, a compression test (refer to Chapter 2C) will provide valuable information regarding the overall performance of the main internal components. Such a test can be used as a basis to decide on the extent of the work to be carried out. If, for example, a compression test indicates serious internal engine wear, conventional maintenance as described in this Chapter will not greatly improve the performance of the engine, and may prove a waste of time and money, unless extensive overhaul work is carried out first.
4 The following series of operations are those most often required to improve the performance of a generally poor-running engine:

Primary operations

a) Clean, inspect and test the battery (refer to 'Weekly checks').
b) Check all the engine-related fluids (refer to 'Weekly checks').
c) Check the condition and tension of the auxiliary drivebelt (Section 6).
d) Renew the fuel filter (Section 21).
e) Check the condition of the air filter, and renew if necessary (Section 18).
f) Check the condition of all hoses, and check for fluid leaks (Section 5).

5 If the above operations do not prove fully effective, carry out the following secondary operations:

Secondary operations

All items listed under *Primary operations*, plus the following:
a) Check the charging system (Chapter 5A).
b) Check the fuel system (Chapter 4C).

Every 7500 miles or 6 months

3 Engine oil and filter renewal

1 Frequent oil and filter changes are the most important preventative maintenance procedures which can be undertaken by the DIY owner. As engine oil ages, it becomes diluted and contaminated, which leads to premature engine wear.

2 Before starting this procedure, gather together all the necessary tools and materials. Also make sure that you have plenty of clean rags and newspapers handy, to mop-up any spills. Ideally, the engine oil should be warm, as it will drain more easily, and more built-up sludge will be removed with it. Take care not to touch the exhaust or any other hot parts of the engine when working under the car. To avoid any possibility of scalding, and to protect yourself from possible skin irritants and other harmful contaminants in used engine oils, it is advisable to wear gloves when carrying out this work.

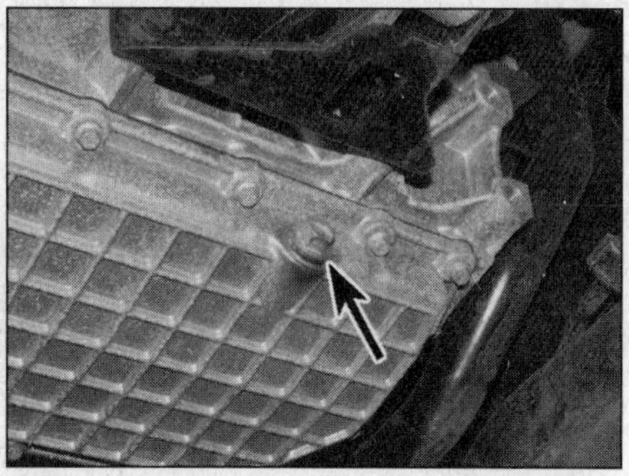

3.6 The engine oil drain plug is at the rear of the sump

3 Remove the oil filler cap.

4 Firmly apply the handbrake, then jack up the front of the car and support it on axle stands (see *Jacking and vehicle support*).

5 Remove the engine undertray, which is secured by a number of turn-buckle fasteners.

6 Using a spanner, or preferably a socket and bar, slacken the drain plug about half a turn. The drain plug is at the rear of the sump, on the driver's side. Position the draining container under the drain plug, then remove the plug completely **(see illustration)**.

HAYNES HiNT ***As the plug releases from the threads, move it away sharply, so that the stream of oil from the sump runs into the container, not up your sleeve.***

7 Allow some time for the oil to drain, noting that it may be necessary to reposition the container as the oil flow slows to a trickle.

8 After all the oil has drained, wipe the drain plug with a clean rag. Clean the area around the drain plug opening, then refit the plug, complete with a new washer, and tighten it to the specified torque **(see illustration)**.

9 Remove the old oil and all tools from under the car, refit the undertray, then lower the car to the ground.

10 The oil filter housing is at the front of the engine compartment, next to the power steering fluid reservoir **(see illustration)**. When working on the oil filter, care must be taken not to drip oil onto the nearby alternator – cover the alternator with clean rags or a plastic bag if possible before starting.

11 Unscrew the oil filter housing plastic cap (which has a 36 mm hex fitting on top) and discard the three O-ring seals inside **(see illustrations)**.

12 Lift out the oil filter element and discard it **(see illustration)**. Fit the new filter element, observing any direction-of-fitting markings.

13 Fit new O-ring seals, lubricated with clean oil, then refit the filter housing cap and tighten it securely (or to the specified torque) **(see illustration)**.

14 Fill the engine through the filler hole, using the correct grade and type of oil (refer to *Weekly checks* for details of topping-up). Pour in half the specified quantity of oil first, then wait a few minutes for the oil to drain into the sump. Continue to add oil, a small quantity at a time, until the level is up to the lower mark

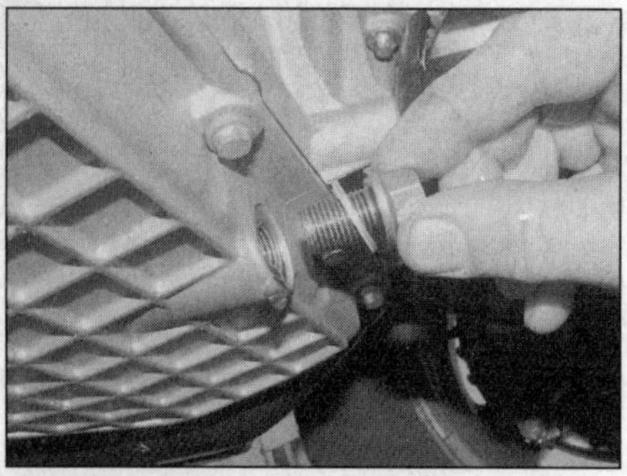

3.9 Refit the engine oil drain plug with a new sealing washer

3.10 The oil filter housing is next to the dipstick

3.11a Using a 36 mm socket and extension bar . . .

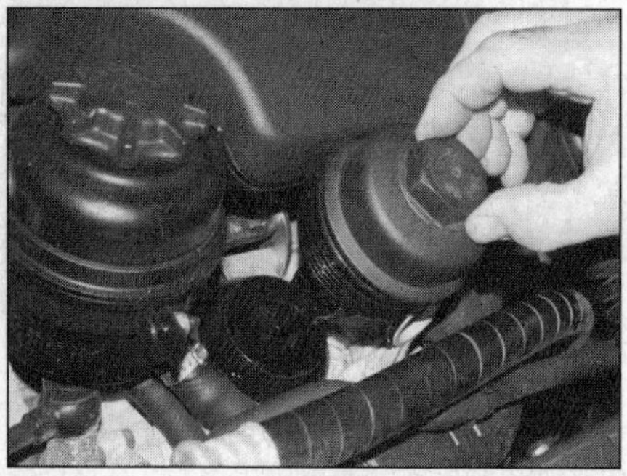

3.11b . . . unscrew and remove the oil filter housing cap

3.12 Withdraw the filter element – allow to drain before removing

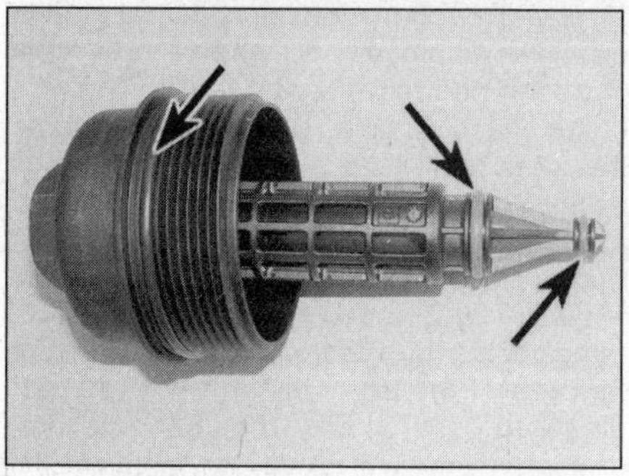

3.13 All three O-rings must be renewed before refitting the cap

on the dipstick **(see illustration)**. Adding approximately a further 1.0 litre will bring the level up to the upper mark on the dipstick.

15 Start the engine and run it for a few minutes, while checking for leaks around the oil filter seal and the sump drain plug. Note that there may be a delay of a few seconds before the oil pressure warning light goes out when the engine is first started, as the oil circulates through the new oil filter and the engine oil galleries before the pressure builds-up.

16 Stop the engine, and wait a few minutes for the oil to settle in the sump once more. With the new oil circulated and the filter housing now completely full, recheck the level on the dipstick, and add more oil as necessary.

17 Dispose of the used engine oil safely, with reference to *General repair procedures*.

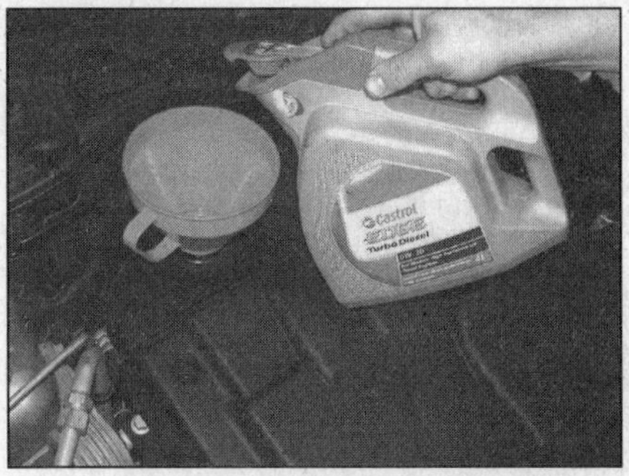

3.14 Add oil gradually, checking the dipstick often

Every 15 000 miles or 12 months

4 Service indicator resetting

1 The service indicator must be reset after each service, but this can only be done using the MG Rover Testbook, or equivalent resetting tool.

2 However, by temporarily bridging two of the pins in the diagnostic socket under the steering column, the display will reset.

Caution: It should be stressed that the following is NOT an official MG Rover procedure, and is undertaken at the owner's risk, but it does appear to work. If the wrong pins are used, apparently all that happens is a fuse blows, but we do not recommend testing this theory.

3 A bridging wire will be needed, to temporarily link two of the pins in the diagnostic socket. This need only be a short piece of stiff insulated wire, which should be stripped at each end as little as possible. Also, each bared end of this wire should be carefully twisted up, or ideally tinned with solder, to avoid stray strands from arcing other pins than those required. If a low-amp fuse can be incorporated into the bridging wire, this may help to avoid blowing the car's fuses if the wrong pins are used.

4 Turn the ignition switch to the second position (warning lights on).

5 Seen from under the steering column, the pin arrangement is as shown below:

16	15	14	13	12	11	10	09
08	07	06	05	**04**	03	02	01

6 Join pin number 8 to pin number 4 using the bridging wire, and hold in this position for up to 4 seconds. This should reset the oil service display. Holding the same pins for between 8 and 25 seconds will reset the inspection and time services.

7 This procedure may require more than one attempt to be successful. On completion, switch off the ignition.

HAYNES HiNT

A leak in the cooling system will usually show up as white- or rust-coloured deposits on the areas adjoining the leak.

5 Hose and fluid leak check

Coolant

Warning: Refer to the safety information given in 'Safety first!' and Chapter 3 before disturbing any of the cooling system components.

1 Carefully check the radiator and heater coolant hoses along their entire length. Renew any hose which is cracked, swollen or which shows signs of deterioration. Cracks will show up better if the hose is squeezed. Pay close attention to the clips that secure the hoses to the cooling system components. Hose clips that have been overtightened can pinch and puncture hoses, resulting in cooling system leaks.

5.6 Check fuel lines and connections under the car

2 Inspect all the cooling system components (hoses, joint faces, etc) for leaks. Where any problems of this nature are found on system components, renew the component or gasket with reference to Chapter 3.

3 A leak from the cooling system will usually show up as white or rust-coloured deposits on the area surrounding the leak **(see Haynes Hint)**.

Fuel

Warning: Refer to the safety information given in 'Safety first!' and Chapter 4C before disturbing any of the fuel system components.

4 Check all accessible fuel lines at their connections to the fuel filter, high-pressure pump and fuel rail.

5 Examine each fuel hose/pipe along its length for splits or cracks. Check for signs of leakage, which could be anything from a damp hose to an area of bodywork adjacent to the hose which seems especially clean (from being 'washed' by leaking fuel).

6 To identify fuel leaks between the fuel tank and the engine bay, the car should raised and securely supported on axle stands. Inspect the fuel tank and filler neck for punctures, cracks and other damage. The connection between the filler neck and tank is especially critical. Sometimes a rubber filler neck or connecting hose will leak due to loose retaining clamps or deteriorated rubber **(see illustration)**.

7 Carefully check all rubber hoses and metal fuel lines leading away from the fuel tank. Check for loose connections, deteriorated hoses, kinked lines, and other damage. Pay particular attention to the vent pipes and hoses, which often loop up around the filler neck and can become blocked or kinked, making tank filling difficult. Follow the fuel supply and return lines to the front of the car, carefully inspecting them all the way for signs of damage or corrosion. Renew damaged sections as necessary.

Engine oil

8 Inspect the area around the camshaft cover, cylinder head, oil filter and sump joint faces. Bear in mind that, over a period of time, some very slight seepage from these areas is to be expected – what you are really looking for is any indication of a serious leak caused by gasket failure. Engine oil seeping from the base of the timing belt/chain cover or the transmission bellhousing may be an indication of crankshaft or input shaft oil seal failure. Should a leak be found, renew the failed gasket or oil seal by referring to the appropriate Chapters in this manual.

Power-assisted steering fluid

9 Examine the hose running between the fluid reservoir and the power steering pump, and the return hose running from the steering rack to the fluid reservoir. Also examine the high pressure supply hose between the pump and the steering rack.

10 Check the hoses leading to the PAS fluid cooler at the front of the engine bay. Look for deterioration caused by corrosion and damage from grounding, or debris thrown up from the road surface.

11 Pay particular attention to crimped unions, and the area surrounding the hoses that are secured with adjustable worm-drive clips.

Air conditioning refrigerant

Warning: Refer to the safety information given in 'Safety first!' and Chapter 3, regarding the dangers of disturbing any of the air conditioning system components.

12 The air conditioning system is filled with a liquid refrigerant, which is retained under high pressure. If the air conditioning system is opened and depressurised without the aid of specialised equipment, the refrigerant will immediately turn into gas and escape into the atmosphere. If the liquid comes into contact with your skin, it can cause severe frostbite. In addition, the refrigerant contains substances which are environmentally damaging; for this reason, it should not be allowed to escape into the atmosphere.

13 Any suspected air conditioning system leaks should be immediately referred to a MG Rover dealer or air conditioning specialist. Leakage will be shown up as a steady drop in the level of refrigerant in the system.

14 Note that water may drip from the condenser drain pipe, underneath the car, immediately after the air conditioning system has been in use. This is normal, and should not be cause for concern.

Brake (and clutch) fluid

Warning: Refer to the safety information given in 'Safety first!' and Chapter 9, regarding the dangers of handling brake fluid.

15 With reference to Chapter 9, examine the area surrounding the brake pipe unions at the master cylinder for signs of leakage. Check the area around the base of fluid reservoir, for signs of leakage caused by seal failure. Also examine the brake pipe unions at the ABS hydraulic unit **(see illustration)**.

16 If fluid loss is evident, but the leak cannot be pinpointed in the engine bay, the brake calipers and underbody brake lines and should be carefully checked with the car raised and supported on axle stands. Leakage of fluid from the braking system is serious fault that must be rectified immediately.

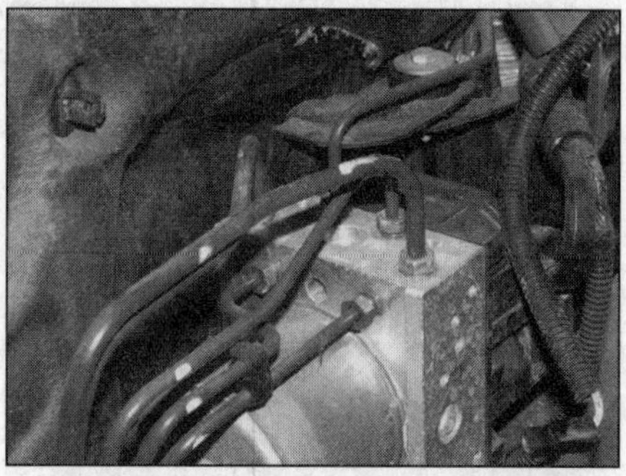

5.15 Check the ABS unit for fluid leaks

17 Refer to Chapter 6 and check for leakage around the hydraulic fluid line connections to the clutch master cylinder at the bulkhead, and to the clutch slave cylinder on the transmission.

18 Brake/clutch hydraulic fluid is a toxic substance with a watery consistency. New fluid is almost colourless, but it becomes darker with age and use.

Unidentified fluid leaks

19 If there are signs that a fluid of some description is leaking from the car, but you cannot identify the type of fluid or its exact origin, park the car overnight and slide a large piece of card underneath it. Providing that the card is positioned in roughly in the right location, even the smallest leak will show up on the card. Not only will this help you to pinpoint the exact location of the leak, it should be easier to identify the fluid from its colour. Bear in mind, though, that the leak may only be occurring when the engine is running!

Vacuum hoses

20 Although the braking system is hydraulically-operated, the brake servo unit amplifies the effort you apply at the brake pedal, using vacuum supplied by the vacuum pump (see Chapter 9). Vacuum is ported to the servo by means of a large-bore hose. Any leaks that develop in this hose will reduce the effectiveness of the braking system, and may affect engine running.

21 In addition, many of the underbonnet components, particularly the emission control components, are driven by vacuum supplied from the vacuum pump via narrow-bore hoses. A leak in a vacuum hose means that air is being drawn into the hose (rather than escaping from it) and this makes leakage very difficult to detect. One method is to use an old length of vacuum hose as a kind of stethoscope – hold one end close to (but not in) your ear and use the other end to probe the area around the suspected leak. When the end of the hose is directly over a vacuum leak, a hissing sound will be heard clearly through the hose. Care must be taken to avoid contacting hot or moving components, as the engine must be running when testing in this manner. Renew any vacuum hoses that are found to be defective.

6 Auxiliary drivebelt check

General

1 All models have a single main drivebelt on the right-hand side of the engine, with an automatic tensioner. Models with air conditioning have an additional drivebelt for the compressor, with a manually-adjusted tensioner.

Checking

2 Due to their function and material makeup, drivebelts are prone to failure after a long period of time, and should therefore be inspected regularly.

3 Since the drivebelt is located very close to the right-hand side of the engine compartment, it is possible to gain better access by raising the front of the car and removing the right-hand wheel. Also remove the engine top cover, which is secured by three bolts, and the right-hand front wheel arch liner as described in Chapter 11, Section 22.

4 With the engine stopped, inspect the full length of the drivebelt for cracks and separation of the belt plies. It will be necessary to turn the engine (using a spanner or socket and bar on the crankshaft pulley bolt) in order to move the belt from the pulleys so that the belt can be inspected thoroughly. Twist the belt between the pulleys so that both sides can be viewed. Also check for fraying, and glazing which gives the belt a shiny appearance. Check the pulleys for nicks, cracks, distortion and corrosion.

5 Small cracks in the belt ribs are not usually serious, but look closely to see whether the crack has extended into the belt plies. If the belt is in any way suspect, or is known to have seen long service, renew it as described in Section 24.

6 If the belt appears to be too slack (or has actually been slipping in service), this either indicates a problem with the belt tensioner, or may indicate external contamination of the belt (eg, by oil or water).

7 If the belt is satisfactory, refit the wheel arch liner and right-hand front wheel, and lower the car to the ground. Tighten the wheel bolts to the specified torque, and refit the engine top cover.

Renewal and adjustment

8 If the belts require renewal or adjustment, refer to Section 24.

7 Electrical equipment check

1 Check the operation of all electrical equipment, ie, lights, direction indicators, horn, etc. Refer to the appropriate Sections of Chapter 12 for details if any of the circuits are found to be inoperative.
2 Note that stop-light switch adjustment is described in Chapter 9.
3 Visually check all accessible wiring connectors, harnesses and retaining clips for security, and for signs of chafing or damage. Rectify any faults found.

8 Seat belt check

1 Check the seat belts for satisfactory operation and condition. Pull sharply on the belt to check that the locking mechanism engages correctly.
2 Pull each belt out fully, and inspect the entire length of webbing for fraying and cuts. Check that the belts retract smoothly and without binding into their reels.
3 Check that the seat belt mounting bolts are tight, and if necessary tighten them to the specified torque wrench settings.
4 Also check the front seats for signs of excessive movement, and if necessary retighten the seat mounting bolts.

9 Hinge and lock lubrication

1 Work around the car and lubricate the hinges of the bonnet, doors and tailgate with light oil.
2 Lightly lubricate the bonnet release mechanism with a smear of grease.
3 Check carefully the security and operation of all hinges, latches and locks, adjusting them where required. Check the operation of the central locking system.
4 Check the condition and operation of the boot lid or tailgate struts, renewing them if either is leaking or no longer able to support the boot lid or tailgate securely when raised.

10 Handbrake check and adjustment

Checking

1 The handbrake should be fully applied (and capable of holding the car on a slope) after approximately three clicks of the ratchet. The operating cables will stretch over time, and adjustment will be needed.
2 The handbrake is a conventional design, having separate cables for the two rear wheels, and a front cable with an equaliser plate which operates both rear cables equally. The handbrake is adjusted by means of a nut attached to the front cable.
3 With the rear of the car raised and supported (see *Jacking and vehicle support*), check that the rear wheels are free to turn with the handbrake fully released.
4 Apply the handbrake one click at a time, and check whether the rear wheels can still be turned. If the handbrake does not appear to be working equally on both wheels, this may indicate a problem with either the rear cable or the handbrake shoes on the less-operative side (see Chapter 9 for more details).

Adjustment

Note: *This simplified procedure is intended only to compensate for stretch in existing cables. If the limit of adjustment mentioned below is reached, the more elaborate procedure described in Chapter 9 should be followed, to compensate for wear in the handbrake shoes.*
5 If the handbrake appears to be working evenly, but requires an excessive amount of lever movement to operate, the front cable should be adjusted as follows. First, unclip and remove the gaiter around the handbrake lever **(see illustration)**.
6 With the lever released, tighten the adjuster nut by half a turn, then recheck the operation of the handbrake and repeat if necessary **(see illustration)**. Do not over-adjust, as this may accelerate the stretching of the front cable – the length of exposed thread above the adjuster nut should **not** exceed 25 mm. When the handbrake operation is satisfactory, check that the rear wheels are free to turn when the handbrake is fully released.
7 On completion, lower the car to the ground. Refit the handbrake gaiter to the centre console.

11 Brake pad and disc wear check

1 Apply the handbrake, then jack up the front of the car and support it securely on axle stands (see *Jacking and vehicle support*). Remove the front roadwheels.
2 The brake pad thickness, and the condition of the disc, can be assessed roughly with just the wheels removed **(see Haynes Hint)**. For a comprehensive check, the brake pads should be removed and cleaned. The operation of the caliper can then also be checked, and the condition of the brake disc itself can be fully examined on both sides. Refer to Chapter 9 for further information.
3 On completion, refit the roadwheels and lower the car to the ground.
4 Similarly, with the front wheels chocked, jack up the rear of the car, release the handbrake, and check the rear brake pads and discs.

12 Steering and suspension check

Front suspension and steering

1 Raise the front of the car, and securely support it on axle stands (see *Jacking and vehicle support*).
2 Visually inspect the balljoint dust covers and the steering rack-and-pinion gaiters for splits,

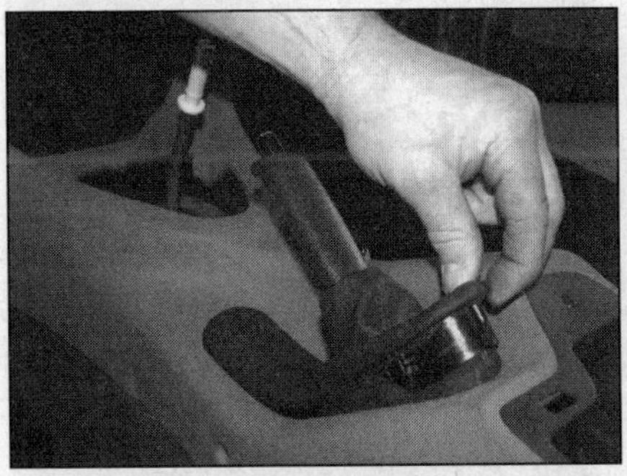

10.5 Unclip the handbrake lever gaiter from the centre console

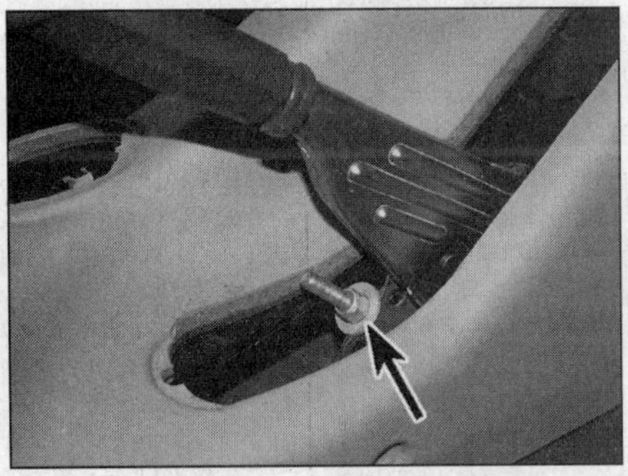

10.6 Handbrake cable adjuster nut

The pad thickness check can be carried out via the inspection hole at the front of the caliper.

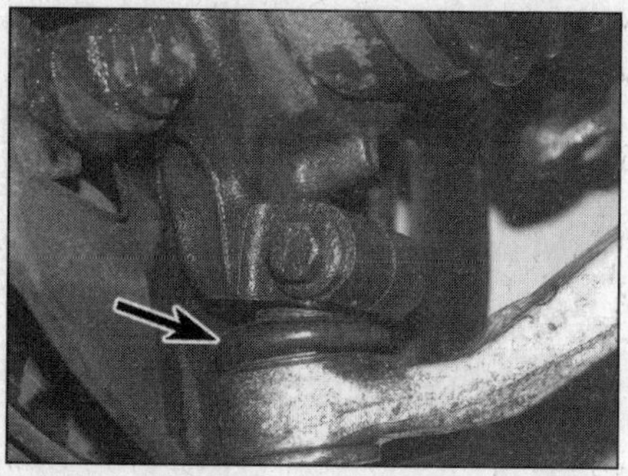

12.2a Check the lower balljoint dust covers . . .

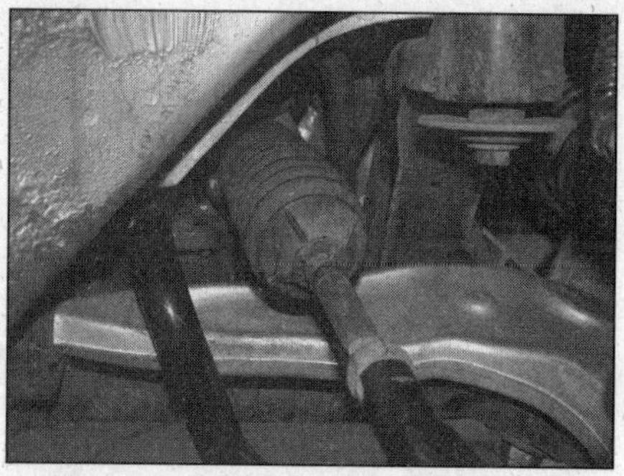

12.2b . . . and the steering rack gaiters for signs of damage

12.4 Grasp the roadwheel top and bottom, and try to rock it

chafing or deterioration **(see illustrations)**. Any wear of these components will cause loss of lubricant, together with dirt and water entry, resulting in rapid deterioration of the balljoints or steering gear.

3 Check the power steering fluid hoses for chafing or deterioration, and the pipe and hose unions for fluid leaks. Also check for signs of fluid leakage under pressure from the steering gear rubber gaiters, which would indicate failed fluid seals within the steering gear.

4 Grasp the roadwheel at the 12 o'clock and 6 o'clock positions, and try to rock it **(see illustration)**. Very slight free play may be felt, but if the movement is appreciable, further investigation is necessary to determine the source. Continue rocking the wheel while an assistant depresses the footbrake. If the movement is now eliminated or significantly reduced, it is likely that the hub bearings are at fault. If the free play is still evident with the footbrake depressed, then there is wear in the suspension joints or mountings.

5 Now grasp the wheel at the 9 o'clock and 3 o'clock positions, and try to rock it as before. Any movement felt now may again be caused by wear in the hub bearings or the steering track rod balljoints. If the outer balljoint is worn, the visual movement will be obvious. If the inner joint is suspect, it can be felt by placing a hand over the rack-and-pinion rubber gaiter and gripping the track rod. If the wheel is now rocked, movement will be felt at the inner joint if wear has taken place.

6 Using a large screwdriver or flat bar, check for wear in the suspension mounting bushes by levering between the relevant suspension component and its attachment point. Some movement is to be expected, as the mountings are made of rubber, but excessive wear should be obvious. Also check the condition of any visible rubber bushes, looking for splits, cracks or contamination of the rubber.

7 With the car standing on its wheels, have an assistant turn the steering wheel back-and-forth, about an eighth of a turn each way. There should be very little, if any, lost movement between the steering wheel and roadwheels. If this is not the case, closely observe the joints and mountings previously described. In addition, check the steering column universal joints for wear, and also check the rack-and-pinion steering gear itself.

Rear suspension

8 Chock the front wheels, then jack up the rear of the car and support securely on axle stands (see *Jacking and vehicle support*).

9 Working as described previously for the front suspension, check the rear hub bearings, the suspension bushes and the shock absorber mountings for wear.

Shock absorbers

10 Check for any signs of fluid leakage around the shock absorber body, or from the rubber gaiter around the piston rod. Should any fluid be noticed, the shock absorber is defective internally, and should be renewed. **Note:** *Shock absorbers should always be renewed in pairs on the same axle.*

11 The efficiency of the shock absorber may be checked by bouncing the car at each corner. Generally speaking, the body will return to its normal position and stop after being depressed. If it rises and returns on a rebound, the shock absorber is probably suspect. Also examine the shock absorber upper and lower mountings for any signs of wear.

13 Driveshaft gaiter check

1 With the car raised and securely supported on stands, turn the steering onto full lock, then slowly rotate the roadwheel. Inspect the condition of the outer constant velocity (CV) joint rubber gaiters while squeezing the gaiters to open out the folds. Check for signs of cracking, splits or deterioration of the rubber which may allow the grease to escape and lead to water and grit entry into the joint. Also check the security and condition of the retaining clips. Repeat these checks on the inner CV joints **(see illustrations)**. If any damage or deterioration is found, the gaiters should be renewed as described in Chapter 8.

13.1a Though splits appear most often in the outer CV gaiters . . .

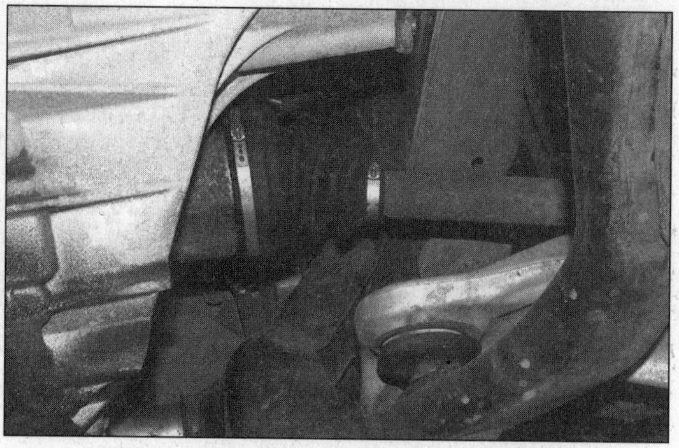

13.1b . . . it also pays to check the inner gaiters

14 Roadwheel bolt tightness check

1 Remove the wheel trims or alloy wheel centre covers, and slacken the roadwheel bolts slightly.
2 Tighten the bolts to the specified torque, using a torque wrench.

15 Braking system rubber hose check

1 Position the car over an inspection pit, on car ramps, or jack it up one wheel at a time (see *Jacking and vehicle support*).
2 Inspect the braking system rubber hoses fitted to each brake caliper **(see illustration)**. Look for perished, swollen or hardened rubber, and any signs of cracking, especially at the metal end fittings. If there's any doubt as to the condition of any hose, renew it as described in Chapter 9.

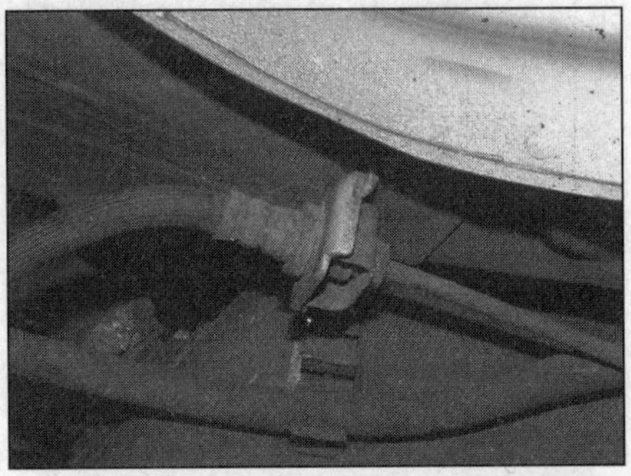

15.2 Check the condition of the brake flexible hoses

16 Road test

Instruments and facia switches

1 Check the operation of all instruments and electrical equipment.
2 Make sure that all instruments read correctly, and switch on all electrical equipment in turn, to check that it functions properly.

Steering and suspension

3 Check for any abnormalities in the steering, suspension, handling or road 'feel'.
4 Drive the car, and check that there are no unusual vibrations or noises.
5 Check that the steering feels positive, with no excessive 'sloppiness', or roughness, and check for any suspension noises when cornering and driving over bumps.

Drivetrain

6 Check the performance of the engine, clutch, transmission and driveshafts.
7 Listen for any unusual noises from the engine, clutch and transmission.
8 Make sure that the engine runs smoothly when idling, and that there is no hesitation when accelerating.
9 Check that, where applicable, the clutch action is smooth and progressive, that the drive is taken up smoothly, and that the pedal travel is not excessive. Also listen for any noises when the clutch pedal is depressed.
10 Check that all gears can be engaged smoothly without noise, and that the gear lever action is smooth and not abnormally vague or 'notchy'.
11 Listen for a metallic clicking sound from the front of the car, as the car is driven slowly in a circle with the steering on full-lock. Carry out this check in both directions. If a clicking noise is heard, this indicates wear in a driveshaft joint (see Chapter 8).

Braking system

12 Make sure that the car does not pull to one side when braking, and that the wheels do not lock when braking hard.
13 Check that there is no vibration through the steering when braking.
14 Check that the handbrake operates correctly, without excessive movement of the lever, and that it holds the car stationary on a slope.
15 Test the operation of the brake servo unit as follows. Depress the footbrake four or five times to exhaust the vacuum, then start the engine. As the engine starts, there should be a noticeable 'give' in the brake pedal as vacuum builds-up. Allow the engine to run for at least two minutes, and then switch it off. If the brake pedal is now depressed again, it should be possible to detect a hiss from the servo as the pedal is depressed. After about four or five applications, no further hissing should be heard, and the pedal should feel considerably harder.

Exhaust system

16 Listen carefully for any unusual noises from the system, which might indicate that it has started blowing, or that the mountings may be deteriorated, allowing the system to hit the underside of the car.
17 If any noises are detected, inspect the system with the car raised and supported on axle stands (see *Jacking and vehicle support*). Leaks are often accompanied by sooty stains, and are most common at the joints, and at welded sections, where pipes enter silencer boxes. Check the condition of the rubber mountings – if they are cracked or perished, fit new ones.

Every 30 000 miles or 2 years

17 Pollen filter renewal

Note: *If the pollen filter is wet when removed, this is a sign that its housing may be filling up with water, due to blocked drain channels. Since the engine control module shares this housing, any sign of this problem should be investigated without delay, to avoid possible ECM damage. Only models with air conditioning appear to be fitted with a pollen filter. Those without have a restrictor plate fitted instead, to limit the ram effect of incoming air – if wished, this plate can apparently be removed and a pollen filter fitted.*
1 Pull off the rubber weather strip at the front of the windscreen cowl panel.
2 Remove the two windscreen cowl panels, each of which is secured by two clips at the front edge.
3 Remove the windscreen wiper arms as described in Chapter 12.
4 Remove two screw/clips at the front corners, and a row of seven clips along the back edge, then lift out the cowl panel frame – collect the splash shield from the passenger side as it is removed.
5 Using a slim screwdriver between the ECM box and the bulkhead access panel, release the upper tab securing the ECM box, and lift the box up off its dovetail fitting. Move the box to one side **without** disconnecting the wiring plug.
Caution: If the ECM wiring plug has to be disconnected, this should only be done once the battery has also been disconnected, otherwise there is a risk of ECM damage.
6 Release the two clips, and lift the pollen filter out straight upwards.
7 Ensure that the filter housing is clean (and dry – refer to the note at the start of this Section). While the filter is removed, check that the drain holes in its housing are clear. Fit the new filter, observing any direction-of-fitting markings.
8 Refit the removed components in the reverse order of removal.

18 Air filter element renewal

1 The air cleaner is located at the rear of the engine.

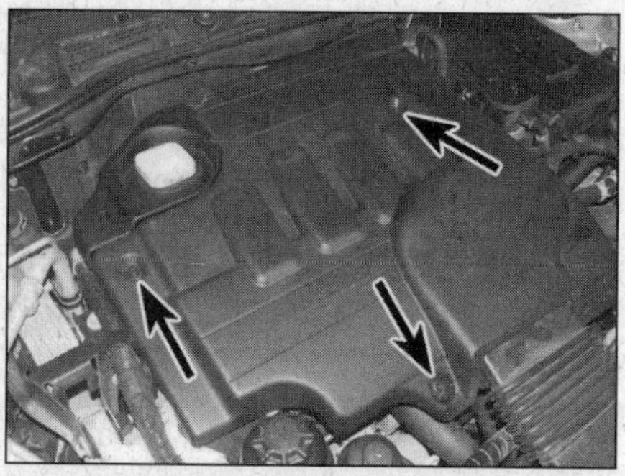

18.2a Unscrew the three bolts . . .

18.2b . . . and lift off the engine top cover

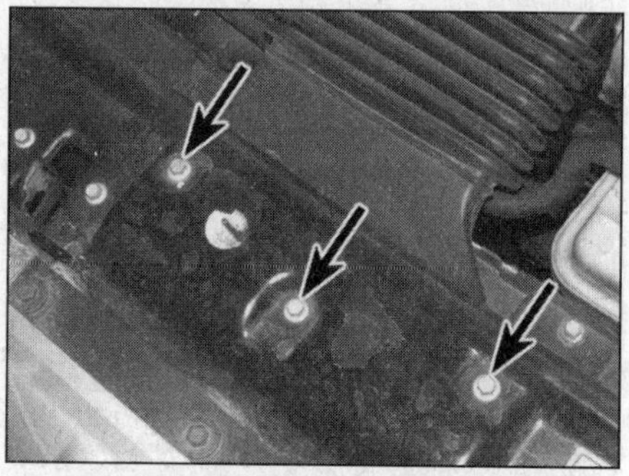

18.3a Remove the three bolts at the front . . .

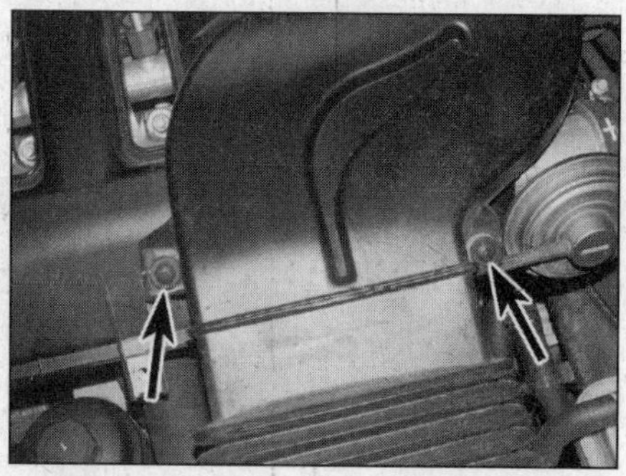

18.3b . . . and two screws securing the inlet duct to the manifold . . .

18.3c . . . then release the duct at the rear, and remove it

2 Remove the engine top cover, which is secured by three bolts **(see illustrations)**.

3 Remove the three bolts and two screws securing the air intake duct to the bonnet lock platform and the inlet manifold. Release the duct at the rear, and lift it off the engine **(see illustrations)**.

4 Remove the oil filler cap, and (as a precaution against any screws falling inside) cover the opening, or stuff it with clean rag.

5 Remove the five 5 mm Allen screws securing the air cleaner cover, and lift it out. The two rear screws, at the corners, are awkward to reach, due to limited access **(see illustrations)**.

6 Lift off the cover, then unhook the air filter element, and lift it out **(see illustrations)**.

7 Wipe clean the interior surfaces of the cover and base.

8 Fit the new element, engaging the locating peg, then refit the cover, tightening the Allen screws securely. Refit the oil filler cap.

9 Refit the air intake duct, engaging it first with the air cleaner cover, then secure with the three bolts and two screws.

10 Refit the engine top cover with the three bolts to complete.

19 Transmission oil/fluid level check

1 If possible, leave the car on the ground for this check – if the car is raised for better access underneath, it must be level to ensure accurate refilling.

Manual transmission

2 Remove the engine undertray, which is secured by a number of quick-release screw fasteners.

3 Clean the area around the filler/level plug, which is located on the end face of the

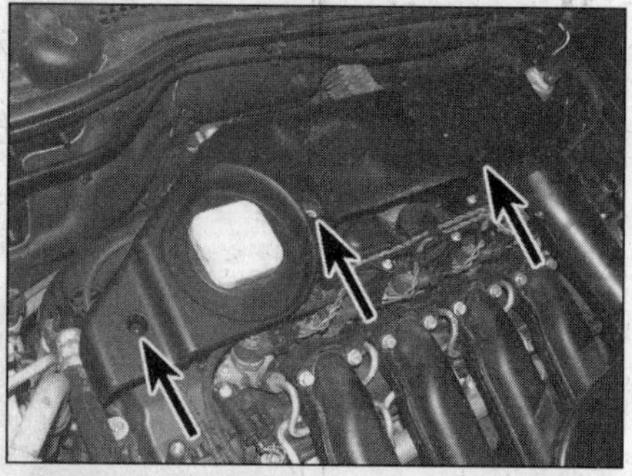

18.5a Three of the five air cleaner cover screws are easy to see . . .

18.5b . . . but there's another on the passenger rear corner . . .

18.5c . . . and the other rear corner screw needs an extension to reach

18.6a Lift off the cover . . .

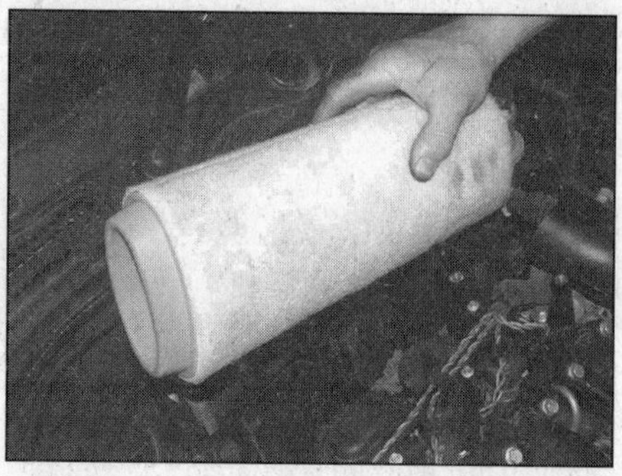

18.6b . . . then unhook and remove the filter element

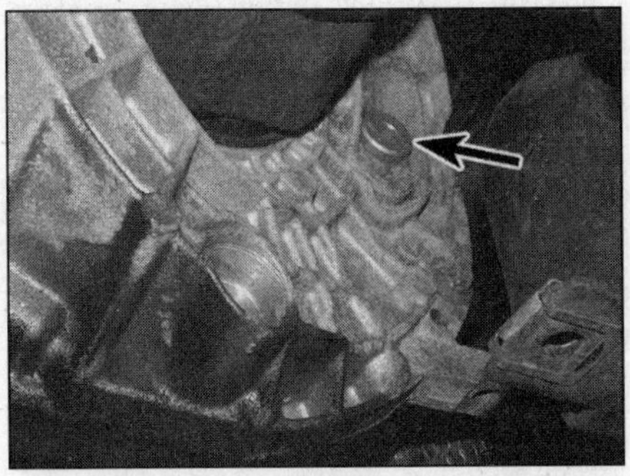

19.3 Manual transmission oil filler/level plug

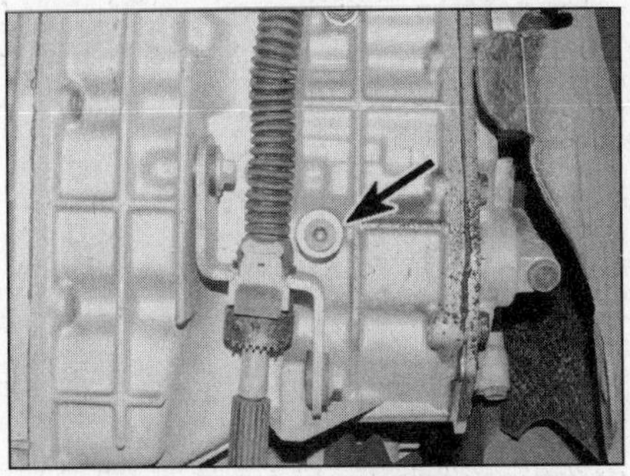

19.10 Unscrew the level plug, and allow excess fluid to drain

transmission, directly behind the right-hand driveshaft **(see illustration)**.

4 Unscrew the filler/level plug, which will probably be very tight.

5 The level must be just below the bottom edge of the filler/level plug hole (use a cranked tool such as an Allen key to check the level). If necessary, top-up the level with the specified grade of oil (see *Lubricants and fluids*) until the oil just starts to run out. Allow any excess oil to flow out until the level stabilises **(see illustration)**.

6 When the level is correct, clean and refit the filler/level plug, then tighten it to the specified torque.

7 Refit the engine undertray on completion.

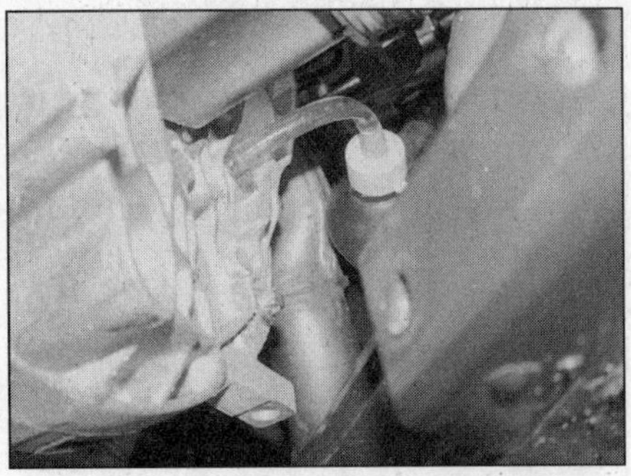

19.5 Top-up until the oil just starts to run out

19.15 Automatic transmission filler plug (arrowed)

Automatic transmission

Warning: The transmission fluid may be extremely hot.

8 Remove the engine undertray, which is secured by a number of quick-release fasteners.

9 The fluid level is checked with the transmission at operating temperature, and with the engine running. Starting at P, and with the footbrake firmly pressed, move the selector lever through each position. Pause in each position for a few seconds, then return to position P.

10 Clean the area around the level plug, which is located next to the selector cable **(see illustration)**.

11 Using a 5 mm Allen key, unscrew the filler/level plug, which will probably be very tight. Recover the sealing ring – a new one will be needed when refitting.

12 The level must be just below the bottom edge of the level plug hole (use a cranked tool such as an Allen key to check the level). With the engine running, allow any excess fluid to drain.

13 If the level is correct, refit the plug using a new sealing washer, and tighten it to the specified torque. Switch off the engine.

14 If topping-up is required, switch off the engine.

15 Clean around the filler pipe on top of the transmission – it is vital that no dirt enters the transmission at any stage. Pull out the filler plug **(see illustration)**.

16 Start the engine, then slowly add clean fluid of the specified type (see *Lubricants and fluids*). Add small amounts at a time, until fluid starts to flow from the level plug hole, then refit the filler plug firmly into its pipe.

17 Move the selector lever through all positions as described in paragraph 9, and allow any excess fluid to run out.

18 When the level stabilises, stop the engine. Refit and tighten the level plug (with a new sealing washer) to the specified torque.

19 Refit the engine undertray on completion.

20 Engine mounting check

1 Check the condition of the rubber sections of the engine left- and right-hand mountings, and examine the right-hand mounting (which has a hydraulic mount) for signs of fluid leakage.

2 As far as possible, check that the engine mounting bolts are fully tight, with reference to Chapter 2C.

3 Jack up the front of the car, and support it on axle stands (see *Jacking and vehicle support*).

4 Check the condition and security of the engine rear mounting link.

Every 60 000 miles or 4 years

21 Fuel filter renewal

1 The fuel filter is located next to the battery **(see illustration)**. Before starting work, position some absorbent rag around the filter head.

2 Loosen the fuel filter clamp bolt – access is a little tight between the bolt head and the battery **(see illustration)**.

21.1 The fuel filter is next to the battery

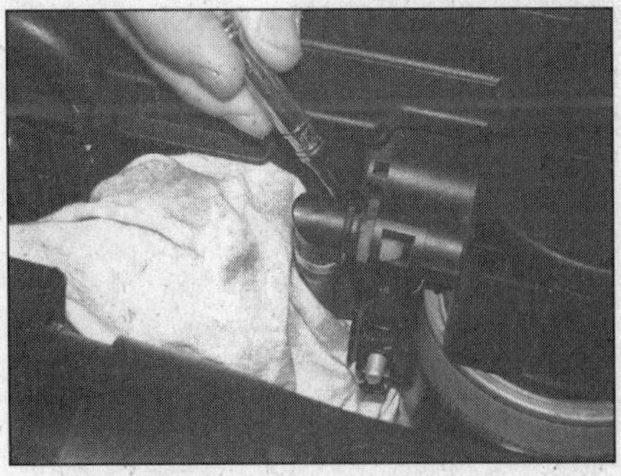

21.2 Loosen the filter clamp bolt

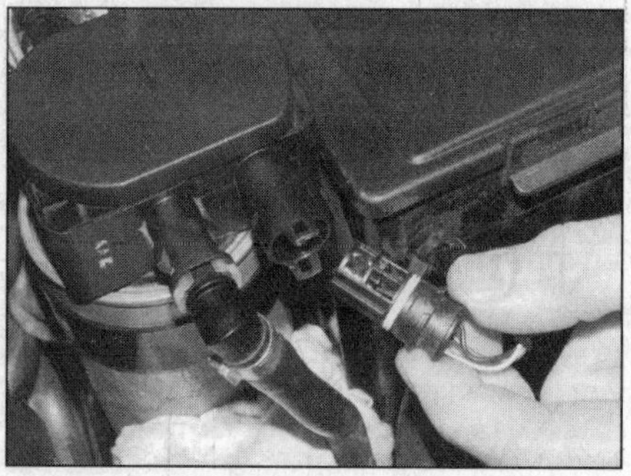
21.3 Disconnect the filter head wiring plug

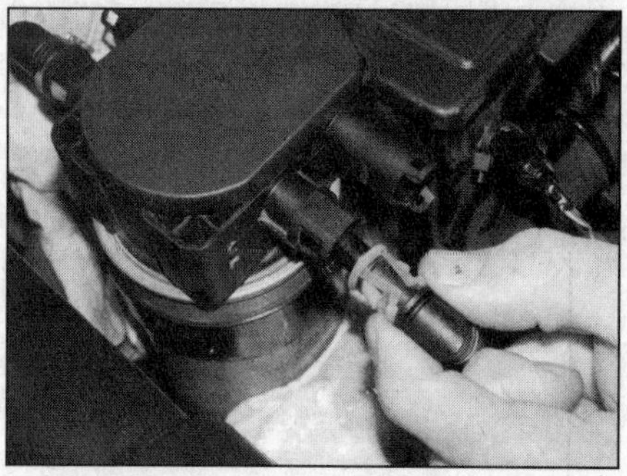
21.4a Disconnect the fuel hose from the front . . .

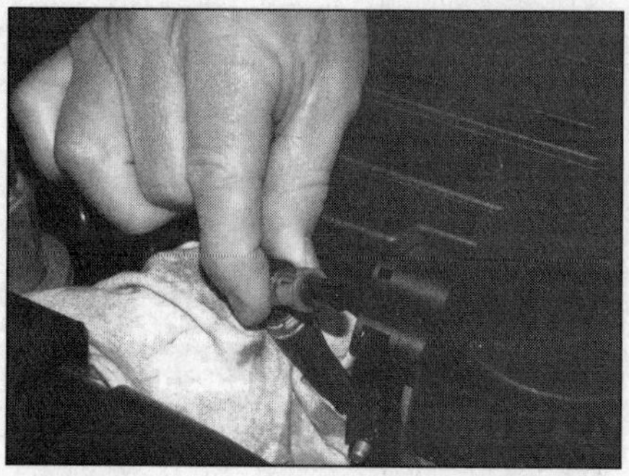
21.4b . . . and rear of the filter head

3 Disconnect the wiring plug from the fuel filter head **(see illustration)**.

4 Note the fitted positions of the fuel hoses, then depress the clips and disconnect the hoses from the filter head – anticipate some fuel spillage as this is done **(see illustration)**.

5 If the fuel pipes are to be left disconnected for long, it is advisable to plug them, or wrap them with tape, to prevent dirt entry.

6 Lift out the filter and the head as an assembly **(see illustration)**. Keep it as upright as possible, as it will be brim-full of fuel – have a clean bowl ready to place the assembly in.

7 Unscrew the filter from the head, and discard it – remember it will be full of fuel **(see illustration)**.

8 Clean the mating face on the filter head, and lubricate the new filter sealing ring with clean fuel.

9 Screw the new filter onto the filter head until it just seats, then tighten by a further half-turn.

10 Offer the filter and head assembly into the mounting clamp, and tighten the clamp bolt to hold it.

11 Reconnect the fuel hoses to their original locations, and reconnect the filter head wiring plug.

12 Switch on the 'ignition' to prime the filter with fresh fuel. Start the engine and check for signs of fuel leaks. Remember that the engine may take longer to start than usual, as the new filter must fill up first.

22 Automatic transmission fluid renewal

Warning: The transmission fluid may be extremely hot.

1 The fluid should ideally be drained with the transmission at operating temperature. For this reason, it is advisable to wear gloves for this procedure, to protect your hands from hot fluid and surrounding components.

2 Pull out the plug from the fluid filler pipe on top of the transmission **(see illustration 19.15)**.

3 Park the car on level ground, and remove the engine undertray, which is secured by a number of quick-release screw fasteners. If possible, leave the car on the ground – if the car is raised for better access underneath, it must be level to ensure accurate refilling.

4 Position a container (of at least 4.0 litre capacity) under the transmission drain plug, which is a hex-headed bolt at the rear of the housing **(see illustration)**. Clean the area around the drain plug.

5 Remove the drain plug, and recover the sealing washer – a new one should be obtained for refitting.

6 When the fluid has finished draining, refit the drain plug with a new washer, and tighten it to the specified torque.

7 Clean around the filler pipe on top of the transmission – it is vital that no dirt enters the transmission at any stage.

8 Slowly add 3.5 to 4.0 litres of clean fluid of the specified type (see *Lubricants and fluids*) through the filler pipe, then clean and refit the filler plug.

9 Start the engine. With the footbrake firmly pressed, move the selector lever through each position. Pause in each position for a few seconds, then return to position P.

10 Clean the area around the level plug, which is located next to the selector cable **(see illustration 19.10)**. Position a container under the level plug.

11 Using a 5 mm Allen key, unscrew the filler/level plug, which will probably be very tight. Recover the sealing ring – a new one will be needed when refitting.

12 Allow any excess fluid to run out. If none emerges, add a little fluid through the filler pipe on top of the transmission, until it just runs from the level hole. Move the selector through all its positions, finishing at P, then wait for the excess fluid to run out.

13 When the level stabilises, stop the engine. Refit and tighten the level plug (with a new sealing washer) to the specified torque.

14 Refit the engine undertray on completion.

21.6 Lift out the filter and head, keeping it upright

21.7 Unscrew the filter from the head

22.4 Automatic transmission fluid drain plug

Every 90 000 miles or 6 years

23 Manual transmission oil renewal

1 The oil is best drained when the transmission is hot, after a run, but this is not essential. If the oil is drained hot, take precautions against scalding from hot oil, and against burning yourself on hot components.
2 Position the car over an inspection pit, on car ramps, or jack it up, but make sure that it is level.
3 Remove the engine undertray, which is secured by a number of quick-release screw fasteners.
4 Clean the area around the filler/level plug, which is located on the end face of the transmission, directly behind the right-hand driveshaft.
5 Unscrew the filler/level plug, which will probably be very tight.
6 Similarly, clean around the drain plug, which is also on the right-hand end of the housing, but below and in front of the driveshaft, and surrounded by a collar **(see illustration)**.
7 Position a suitable container below the drain plug, then unscrew the plug and allow the oil to drain **(see illustration)**.
8 When the oil has finished draining, refit the drain plug, and tighten it to the specified torque.
9 Ensuring that the car is as level as possible, fill the transmission using the specified grade of oil (see *Lubricants and fluids*) via the filler hole. This can be an awkward operation, especially if the car has been lowered to the ground to get it level **(see Haynes Hint)**.
10 When the level is correct, clean and refit the filler/level plug, then tighten it to the specified torque.

24 Auxiliary drivebelt renewal

Main drivebelt

1 Remove the engine top cover, which is secured by three bolts.
2 Loosen the right-hand front wheel bolts. Raise the front of the car, and support it on axle stands (see *Jacking and vehicle support*). Remove the right-hand front wheel.
3 Remove the right-hand front wheel arch liner as described in Chapter 11, Section 22.
4 Using a suitable spanner on its central nut, turn the tensioner anti-clockwise to release the belt tension, and remove the belt from the pulleys **(see illustration)**. Clearance is tight between the engine and the inner wing, and there is a special MG Rover tool used to release the belt tension. However, all this amounts to is a long-handled slim spanner – provided a suitable alternative is available, there should be no real difficulty. Access to the tensioner is better from below.
5 As far as possible, check that all the pulleys are clean. This should only really be a problem if the old belt was obviously contaminated, in which case, every effort should be made not only to clean the affected pulleys, but also to trace and rectify the source of the leak.
6 Fit the new belt first to the power steering pump pulley (top front), then the idler, alternator and crankshaft pulley **(see illustration)**. If possible, have an assistant hold the tensioner in the released position, then fit the belt around it and the remaining (coolant pump) pulley.
7 Ensure that the belt is located correctly in all the pulley grooves, then release the tensioner slowly.
8 On completion, refit the wheel arch liner and right-hand front wheel, and lower the car to the ground. Tighten the wheel bolts to the specified torque, and refit the engine top cover.

Air conditioning drivebelt

9 Remove the main drivebelt as described previously in this Section.
10 Loosen the tensioner pivot and clamp

HAYNES HiNT

Take a piece of hosepipe (half a metre should be enough), and insert a smaller section of metal or plastic pipe which is a close fit in the filler/level hole. With a funnel on the other end, the transmission can be filled quite easily – add the oil in small amounts at a time when the transmission is almost full.

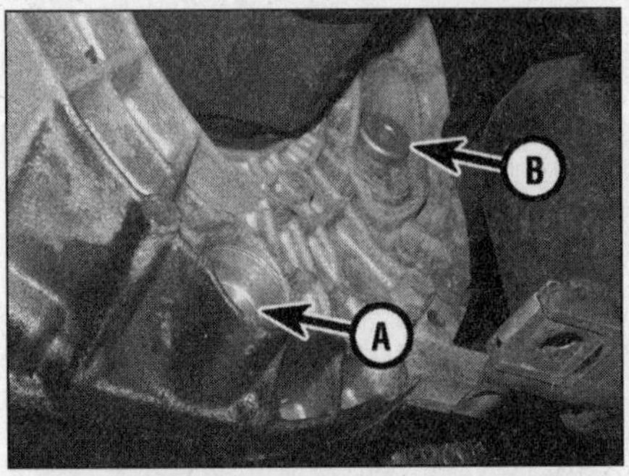

23.6 Manual transmission drain plug (A) and filler/level plug (B)

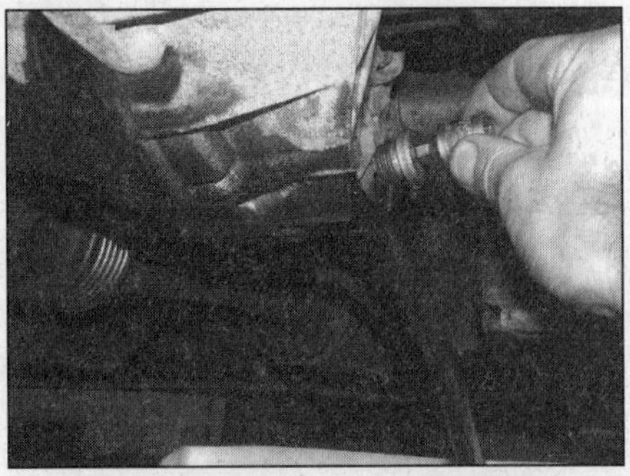

23.7 Draining the transmission oil

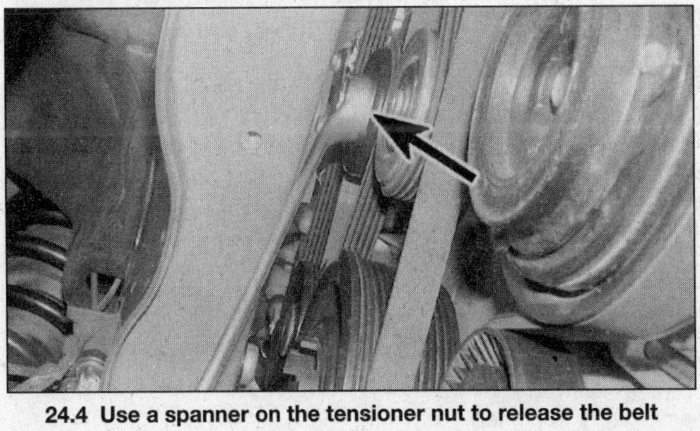

24.4 Use a spanner on the tensioner nut to release the belt

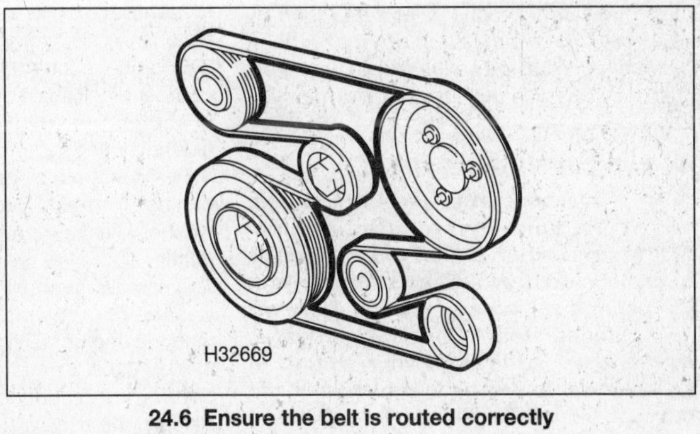

24.6 Ensure the belt is routed correctly

bolts, and slip the air conditioning compressor drivebelt from the pulleys **(see illustration)**.

11 Manoeuvre the belt into position around the compressor and crankshaft inner pulleys, routing it over the tensioner pulley. Ensure that the tensioner's pivot and clamp bolts are loose enough to allow the tensioner free movement.

12 Apply the specified torque (anti-clockwise) to the tensioner's large hex fitting (outside the pivot bolt), and tighten the tensioner clamp bolt to hold it **(see illustration)**. With the tensioner secured, tighten the clamp and pivot bolts to the specified torque.

13 Fit the main drivebelt as described previously in this Section.

24.10 Loosen the pivot and clamp bolts – also note the large hex fitting (arrowed)

24.12 Using a torque wrench, apply the correct tension to the belt

Every 2 years

25 Brake fluid renewal

Warning: Brake hydraulic fluid can harm your eyes and damage painted surfaces, so use extreme caution when handling and pouring it. Do not use fluid that has been standing open for some time, as it absorbs moisture from the air. Excess moisture can cause a dangerous loss of braking effectiveness.

1 The procedure is similar to that for bleeding the hydraulic system as described in Chapter 9, except that allowance should be made for the old fluid to be expelled when bleeding each section of the circuit.

2 Working as described in Chapter 9, open the first bleed screw in the sequence, and pump the brake pedal gently until the level in the reservoir is approaching the MIN mark. Top-up to the MAX level with new fluid, and continue pumping until only new fluid remains in the reservoir, and new fluid can be seen emerging from the bleed screw. Tighten the screw, and top the reservoir level up to the MAX level line.

3 Work through all the remaining bleed screws in the sequence until new fluid can be seen at all of them. Be careful to keep the master cylinder reservoir topped-up above the MIN level at all times, or air may enter the system. If this happens, further bleeding will be required, to remove the air.

HAYNES HiNT ***Old hydraulic fluid is invariably much darker in colour than the new, making it easy to distinguish the two.***

4 When the operation is complete, check that all bleed screws are securely tightened, and that their dust caps are refitted. Wash off all traces of spilt fluid, and recheck the master cylinder reservoir fluid level.

5 Check the operation of the brakes before taking the car on the road.

Every 4 years

26 Coolant renewal

Note: *The coolant used in the system from new is the Organic Acid Technology (OAT) type. This type of coolant should not be mixed with conventional antifreeze (normally blue/green in colour), even for topping-up. If the coolant is being changed to another type, flush the system through thoroughly with clean water before refilling.*

Cooling system draining

Warning: Wait until the engine is cold before starting this procedure. Do not allow antifreeze to come in contact with your skin, or with the painted surfaces of the car. Rinse off spills immediately with plenty of water. Never leave antifreeze lying around in an open container, or in a puddle in the driveway or on the garage floor. Children and pets are attracted by its sweet smell, but antifreeze can be fatal if ingested.

1 With the engine completely cold, remove the expansion tank filler cap. Turn the cap anti-clockwise, wait until any pressure remaining in the system is released, then unscrew it and lift it off.

2 Remove the engine undertray, which is secured by a number of turn-buckle fasteners.

3 Position a suitable container under the cylinder block drain plug, which is on the front of the engine, above the turbo-to-exhaust downpipe flange.

4 Remove the block drain plug, and allow the coolant to drain. Discard the plug's sealing washer – a new one should be used when refitting.

5 Clean the drain plug, and fit a new sealing washer. When the flow of coolant stops, refit the plug and tighten to the specified torque.

6 Move the container under the radiator bottom hose connection **(see illustration)**. Release the hose clip, then carefully work the bottom hose off the radiator (refer to Chapter 3, Section 2, if necessary) and allow the coolant to drain.

7 When the coolant has drained, refit the radiator hose and secure with the spring clip (or better still, fit a Jubilee clip). Refit the engine undertray.

8 If the coolant has been drained for a reason

26.6 Radiator bottom hose connection

other than renewal, then provided it is clean and less than two years old, it can be re-used, though this is not recommended.

Cooling system flushing

9 If coolant renewal has been neglected, or if the antifreeze mixture has become diluted, then in time, the cooling system may gradually lose efficiency, as the coolant passages become restricted due to rust, scale deposits, and other sediment. The cooling system efficiency can be restored by flushing the system clean.

10 The radiator should be flushed independently of the engine, to avoid unnecessary contamination.

Radiator flushing

11 Disconnect the top and bottom hoses and any other relevant hoses from the radiator, with reference to Chapter 3.

12 Insert a garden hose into the radiator top inlet. Direct a flow of clean water through the radiator, and continue flushing until clean water emerges from the radiator bottom outlet.

13 If after a reasonable period, the water still does not run clear, the radiator can be flushed with a good proprietary cleaning agent. It is important that their manufacturer's instructions are followed carefully. If the contamination is particularly bad, insert the hose in the radiator bottom outlet, and reverse-flush the radiator.

Engine flushing

14 Remove the thermostat as described in Chapter 3 then, if the radiator top hose has been disconnected from the engine, temporarily reconnect the hose.

15 With the top and bottom hoses disconnected from the radiator, insert a garden hose into the radiator top hose. Direct a clean flow of water through the engine, and continue flushing until clean water emerges from the radiator bottom hose.

16 On completion of flushing, refit the thermostat and reconnect the hoses with reference to Chapter 3.

Antifreeze mixture

17 The antifreeze should always be renewed at the specified intervals. This is necessary not only to maintain the antifreeze properties, but also to prevent corrosion which would otherwise occur as the corrosion inhibitors become progressively less effective.

18 Always use an ethylene-glycol based antifreeze which is suitable for use in mixed-metal cooling systems. The quantity of antifreeze and levels of protection are given in the Specifications. The antifreeze recommended by MG Rover is specified at the beginning of this Chapter – this OAT type of coolant is known particularly for its long-lasting properties.

19 Before adding antifreeze, the cooling system should be completely drained, preferably flushed, and all hoses checked for condition and security.

20 After filling with antifreeze, a label should be attached to the expansion tank, stating the type and concentration of antifreeze used, and the date installed. Any subsequent topping-up should be made with the same type and concentration of antifreeze.

21 Do not use engine antifreeze in the windscreen/tailgate washer system, as it will cause damage to the paintwork. A screenwash additive should be added to the washer system in the quantities stated on the bottle.

Cooling system filling

22 Before attempting to fill the cooling system, make sure that all hoses and clips are in good condition, and that the clips are tight. Note that an antifreeze mixture must be used all year round, to prevent corrosion of the engine components.

HAYNES HiNT ***It is rare to ever drain the cooling system completely – a small quantity will remain. If the system has been extensively flushed with clean water, this remaining quantity will in fact be plain water. For this reason, some people will first fill the system with the required quantity of neat antifreeze (half the total system capacity, for a 50% mixture), and then complete the filling process with plain water. This ensures that the resulting coolant (once it has mixed inside the engine) is not 'diluted' by old coolant or water remaining in the system.***

23 Remove the engine top cover, which is secured by three bolts.

24 Remove the bleed screw situated in the small-diameter heater hose in front of the battery **(see illustration)**.

25 Slowly fill the system, keeping the expansion tank full to just below the neck, until coolant emerges from the bleed hole in a steady stream.

26 Fit and securely tighten the bleed screw, and refit the engine top cover.

27 Continue filling the system until the level settles just below the expansion tank filler neck.

26.24 Cooling system bleed screw

28 On models with air conditioning, ensure that the system is switched off before proceeding.

29 Start the engine, and have an assistant run it at 2000 to 3000 rpm.

30 Be prepared to top-up the coolant in the expansion tank as the engine is started, and maintain the level just below the tank's filler neck. When the level starts to rise due to heat expansion, refit the expansion tank cap, and tighten it securely.

31 Keep the engine at 2000 to 3000 rpm until the cooling fan comes on, then reduce to normal idle until the fan cuts out. Switch off the engine, and allow it to cool, preferably overnight. Check the disturbed hose connections and bleed screw for signs of leakage.

32 With the engine completely cool, check the coolant level, and top-up if necessary to the MAX mark.

Airlocks

33 If, after draining and refilling the system, symptoms of overheating are found which did not occur previously, then the fault is almost certainly due to trapped air at some point in the system, causing an airlock and restricting the flow of coolant; usually, the air is trapped because the system was refilled too quickly.

34 If an airlock is suspected, first try gently squeezing all visible coolant hoses. A coolant hose which is full of air feels quite different to one full of coolant, when squeezed. After refilling the system, most airlocks will clear once the system has cooled, and been topped-up.

35 While the engine is running at operating temperature, switch on the heater and heater fan, and check for heat output. Provided there is sufficient coolant in the system, any lack of heat output could be due to an airlock in the system.

36 Airlocks can have more serious effects than simply reducing heater output – a severe airlock could reduce coolant flow around the engine. Check that the radiator top hose is hot when the engine is at operating temperature – a top hose which stays cold could be the result of an airlock (or a non-opening thermostat).

37 If the problem persists, stop the engine and allow it to cool down **completely**, before unscrewing the expansion tank filler cap or loosening the hose clips and squeezing the hoses to bleed out the trapped air. In the worst case, the system will have to be at least partially drained (this time, the coolant can be saved for re-use) and flushed to clear the problem.

Pressure (expansion tank) cap

38 Clean the pressure cap, and inspect the seal inside the cap for damage or deterioration. If there is any sign of damage or deterioration to the seal, fit a new pressure cap. If the cap is old, it is worth considering fitting a new one for peace of mind – they are not expensive.

Chapter 2 Part A: 1.8 litre engine in-car repair procedures

Contents

Degrees of difficulty

Easy, suitable for novice with little experience	**Fairly easy,** suitable for beginner with some experience	**Fairly difficult,** suitable for competent DIY mechanic	**Difficult,** suitable for experienced DIY mechanic	**Very difficult,** suitable for expert DIY or professional

Specifications

General

Engine type	Four-cylinder in-line, twin overhead cam 16-valve
Designation	K16 or K1.8
Bore	80.00 mm
Stroke	89.30 mm
Capacity	1796 cc
Firing order	1-3-4-2 (No 1 cylinder at timing belt end)
Direction of crankshaft rotation	Clockwise (seen from right-hand side of car)
Compression ratio:	
Non-turbo models	10.5:1
Turbo models	9.2:1
Compression pressure (typical)	10.0 bar minimum
Compression pressure difference between cylinders (typical)	1.5 bar maximum

Camshafts

General	Direct-acting on hydraulic tappets, bearings line-bored in cylinder head
Drive	Toothed belt from crankshaft, automatic tensioner
Bearing journal running clearance:	
Standard	0.060 to 0.094 mm
Service limit	0.150 mm
Camshaft endfloat:	
Standard	0.060 to 0.190 mm
Service limit	0.300 mm
Hydraulic tappet outside diameter	32.959 to 32.975 mm

Lubrication system

Oil pressure:	
Non-turbo models	1.0 bar at idle, 3.75 bar at 2500 rpm (hot)
Turbo models	4.0 to 4.2 bar at 1000 rpm
Relief valve opening pressure:	
Non-turbo models	4.1 bar
Turbo models	5.4 to 6.5 bar
Low oil pressure warning light comes on	0.2 to 0.6 bar
Pressure relief valve spring free length	38.9 mm
Oil pump clearances:	
Outer rotor-to-body clearance	0.28 to 0.36 mm
Inner rotor tip-to-outer rotor clearance	0.05 to 0.13 mm
Rotor endfloat	0.02 to 0.06 mm

Torque wrench settings

Torque wrench settings	Nm	lbf ft
Big-end bearing cap bolts*:		
Stage 1	20	15
Stage 2	Angle-tighten a further 45°	
Camshaft bearing carrier bolts	10	7
Camshaft cover bolts	10	7
Camshaft oil seal cover plate bolts	25	18
Camshaft position sensor bolt	6	4
Camshaft sprocket bolts	65	48
Coolant outlet elbow	9	7
Coolant rail bracket	24	18
Crankshaft pulley bolt	205	151
Cylinder head bolts:		
Stage 1	20	15
Stage 2	Angle-tighten a further 180°	
Stage 3	Angle-tighten a further 180°	
Dipstick tube mounting bolt	9	7
Engine oil drain plug	25	18
Engine/transmission mountings:		
Left-hand mounting through-bolt	100	74
Left-hand mounting to body	85	63
Left-hand mounting to transmission	85	63
Lower mounting bracket bolts:		
To subframe	85	63
To sump	45	33
Lower mounting through-bolts	100	74
Right-hand hydramount to body	85	63
Right-hand mounting bracket to engine	100	74
Right-hand mounting bracket-to-hydramount nut	85	63
Right-hand mounting steady (upper) bracket bolts	85	63
Right-hand mounting to body	85	63
Flywheel cover plate bolts	9	7
Flywheel/driveplate bolts*	80	59
Main bearing ladder-to-cylinder block bolts*:		
Stage 1	5	4
Stage 2	30	22
Oil pick-up pipe/strainer	12	9
Oil pressure switch	12	9
Oil pump bolts*	9	7
Oil pump pressure relief plug	25	18
Oil rail-to-main bearing ladder bolts	9	7
Oil temperature sensor	14	10
Power steering drivebelt tensioner bolts	9	7
Roadwheel bolts	125	92
Spark plugs	25	18
Sump bolts:		
Sump to main bearing ladder:		
M8 x 25	25	18
M8 x 60	30	22
Sump to transmission/transmission to sump	45	33
Timing belt tensioner bolt*	25	18

** Use new bolts*

1 General information and precautions

How to use this Chapter

This Part of the Chapter describes those repair procedures that can reasonably be carried out on the engine whilst it remains in the car. If the engine has been removed from the car and is being dismantled as described in Part D of this Chapter, any preliminary dismantling procedures can be ignored.

Note that whilst it may be possible physically to overhaul items such as the piston/connecting rod assemblies with the engine in the car, such tasks are not usually carried out as separate operations and usually require the execution of several additional procedures (not to mention the cleaning of components and of oilways). For this reason, all such tasks are classed as major overhaul procedures and are described in Part D of this Chapter.

Engine description

The 1.8 litre engine is from the long-running K-Series engine family, and is a four-cylinder, in-line unit, mounted transversely at the front of the car with the clutch and transmission on the left-hand end. The engine is of double overhead camshaft 16-valve design.

The main structure of the engine consists of three major castings – the cylinder head, the cylinder block/crankcase, and the crankshaft main bearing ladder.

The three major castings are made from aluminium alloy, and are clamped together by ten long cylinder head bolts; the bolts also perform the task of crankshaft main bearing bolts, as they screw into the main bearing ladder. An oil rail is fitted under the main bearing ladder, and to avoid disturbing the bottom end of the engine when removing the cylinder head bolts, the oil rail is secured independently to the main bearing ladder (by two nuts), and the main bearing ladder is secured to the cylinder block/crankcase (by ten bolts).

The crankshaft runs in five main bearings. Thrustwashers are fitted to the centre main bearing (upper half) to control crankshaft endfloat.

The connecting rods rotate on horizontally-split bearing shells at their big-ends. The pistons are attached to the connecting rods by gudgeon pins which are an interference fit in the connecting rod small-end eyes. The aluminium alloy pistons are fitted with three piston rings, comprising two compression rings and an oil control ring.

The cylinder bores are formed by renewable liners which locate in the cylinder block/crankcase at their top ends. The liners are known as 'damp' liners. To prevent the coolant escaping into the sump, the base of each liner is sealed with sealing compound.

The inlet and exhaust valves are each closed by coil springs and operate in guides pressed into the cylinder head. The valve seat inserts are pressed into the cylinder head and can be renewed separately if worn.

The camshafts are driven by a toothed timing belt, and operate the valves via self-adjusting hydraulic tappets. The camshafts rotate in bearings which are line-bored directly into the cylinder head and the (bolted-on) bearing carrier. This means that the bearing carrier and cylinder head are matched, and cannot be renewed independently. The water pump is driven by the timing belt. The fuel pump is electrically-operated.

Lubrication is by means of an eccentric-rotor type pump driven directly from the right-hand (timing belt end) of the crankshaft. The pump draws oil through a strainer located in the sump. It then forces it through an externally-mounted full-flow cartridge-type oil filter into galleries in the oil rail and the cylinder block/crankcase, from where it is distributed to the crankshaft (main bearings) and camshafts. The big-end bearings are supplied with oil via internal drillings in the crankshaft, while the camshaft bearings and the tappets receive a pressurised supply via drillings in the cylinder head. The camshaft lobes and valves are lubricated by oil splash, as are all other engine components.

Operations with engine in car

The following work can be carried out with the engine in the car:

a) Compression pressure – testing.
b) Camshaft cover – removal and refitting.
c) Crankshaft pulley – removal and refitting.
d) Timing belt covers – removal and refitting.
e) Timing belt – removal, refitting and adjustment.
f) Timing belt tensioner and sprockets – removal and refitting.
g) Camshaft oil seals – renewal.
h) Camshafts and tappets – removal, inspection and refitting.
i) Cylinder head – removal and refitting.
j) Cylinder head and pistons – decarbonising.
k) Sump – removal and refitting.
l) Oil pump – removal, overhaul and refitting.
m) Crankshaft oil seals – renewal.
n) Engine/transmission mountings – inspection and renewal.
o) Flywheel – removal, inspection and refitting.

Caution: Note that a side-effect of the K-Series engine design is that the crankshaft cannot be rotated once the cylinder head bolts have been slackened. During any servicing or overhaul work, the crankshaft must always be rotated to the desired position before the cylinder head bolts are disturbed.

2 Compression test – description and interpretation

Note: *A suitable compression tester will be required for this test.*

1 When engine performance is down, or if misfiring occurs which cannot be attributed to the ignition or fuel systems, a compression test can provide diagnostic clues as to the engine's condition. If the test is performed regularly it can give warning of trouble before any other symptoms become apparent.

2 The engine must be fully warmed-up to normal operating temperature, the battery must be fully charged and the spark plugs must be removed (see Chapter 1A). The aid of an assistant will be required.

3 The fuel pump must be disabled by removing the fuel pump relay from the fusebox.

4 Fit a compression tester to the No 1 cylinder spark plug hole. The type of tester which screws into the plug thread is preferred.

5 Have the assistant hold the throttle wide open and crank the engine on the starter motor. After one or two revolutions, the compression pressure should build-up to a maximum figure and then stabilise. Record the highest reading obtained.

6 Repeat the test on the remaining cylinders, recording the pressure in each.

7 All cylinders should produce very similar pressures; a difference of more than 2 bars between any two cylinders indicates a fault. Note that the compression should build-up quickly in a healthy engine; low compression on the first stroke, followed by gradually-increasing pressure on successive strokes, indicates worn piston rings. A low compression reading on the first stroke, which does not build-up during successive strokes, indicates leaking valves or a blown head gasket (a cracked head could also be the cause). Deposits on the undersides of the valve heads can also cause low compression.

8 Although MG Rover do not specify exact compression pressures, as a guide, any cylinder pressure of below 10 bar can be considered as less than healthy. Refer to an engine specialist if in doubt as to whether a particular pressure reading is acceptable.

9 If the pressure in any cylinder is significantly low, carry out the following test to isolate the cause. Introduce a teaspoonful of clean oil into that cylinder through its spark plug hole and repeat the test.

10 If the addition of oil temporarily improves the compression pressure, this indicates that bore or piston wear is responsible for the pressure loss. No improvement suggests that leaking or burnt valves, or a blown head gasket, may be to blame.

11 A low reading from two adjacent cylinders is almost certainly due to the head gasket having blown between them and the presence of coolant in the engine oil will confirm this.

12 If one cylinder is about 20 percent lower

3.8a Set the sprocket EXHAUST and IN marks, and align the timing marks (A) with the rear cover mark (B)

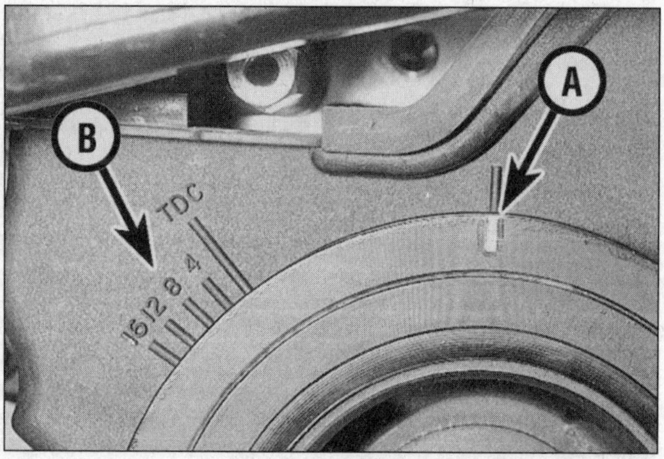

3.8b Align the crankshaft pulley timing notch with the mark (A) on the timing belt lower cover

Ignore the timing marks (B) on the cover (where present)

than the others and the engine has a slightly rough idle, a worn camshaft lobe could be the cause.

13 If the compression reading is unusually high, the combustion chambers are probably coated with carbon deposits. If this is the case, the cylinder head should be removed and decarbonised.

14 On completion of the test, refit the spark plugs (see Chapter 1A), reconnect the ignition coil(s) and refit the fuel pump relay.

3 Engine assembly/valve timing marks – general information and usage

Caution: Note that a side-effect of the K-Series engine design is that the crankshaft cannot be rotated once the cylinder head bolts have been slackened. During any servicing or overhaul work, the crankshaft must always be rotated to the desired position before the cylinder head bolts are disturbed.

1 The crankshaft pulley, crankshaft and camshaft sprockets all have timing marks which align when the crankshaft is at 90° BTDC. This positions the pistons half-way up the bores, ensuring there is no danger of the valves contacting the pistons when refitting the cylinder head/timing belt.

2 Disconnect the battery negative terminal (see *Disconnecting the battery*). If necessary, remove all the spark plugs as described in Chapter 1A to enable the engine to be easily turned over.

3 To gain access to the camshaft sprocket timing marks, remove the timing belt upper cover as described in Section 6.

4 Loosen the right-hand front wheel bolts. Firmly apply the handbrake, then jack up the front of the car and support it securely on axle stands (see *Jacking and vehicle support*). Remove the right-hand front wheel to improve access to the crankshaft pulley.

5 Remove the engine undertray, which is secured by a number of quick-release screw fasteners.

6 Remove the right-hand wheel arch liner as described in Chapter 11, Section 22.

7 Using a socket and extension bar on the crankshaft pulley bolt, turn the crankshaft whilst keeping an eye on the camshaft sprockets.

8 Rotate the crankshaft until the EXHAUST mark is at the rear (inlet manifold side) of each camshaft sprocket and the IN mark is at the front, and all timing marks are correctly aligned with the mark on the timing belt rear cover (representing the cylinder head upper surface). Once the camshaft sprocket marks are correctly positioned, the notch on the crankshaft pulley rim should align with the mark on the lower timing belt cover **(see illustrations)**.

9 With the crankshaft pulley and camshaft sprocket timing marks positioned as described, the engine can safely be dismantled.

4 Camshaft cover – removal and refitting

Removal

1 Disconnect the battery negative lead (see *Disconnecting the battery*).

2 Release the retaining clips and disconnect the breather hoses from the rear of the camshaft cover **(see illustration)**.

3 Disconnect the camshaft position sensor/coil supply wiring plug at the transmission end of the engine. Unscrew the two bolts securing the wiring harness bracket to the cylinder head, and move the bracket clear – note that these two bolts also secure the camshaft end cover, which may come off too, with the risk of a little oil spillage.

4 Remove the three bolts and lift off the spark plug cover **(see illustration)**. Undo the retaining bolts and remove the ignition coils, then disconnect the conventional HT leads from the remaining spark plugs.

5 Unscrew the single bolt securing the camshaft position sensor at the front of the head. Withdraw the sensor and lay it to one side. Recover the sensor's rubber O-ring – if in poor condition, a new one should be used when refitting.

6 Working progressively and in the **reverse** of the tightening sequence **(see illustration 4.10)**, slacken and remove the fifteen camshaft cover retaining bolts.

7 Carefully remove the cover, complete

4.2 Disconnect the breather hoses from the rear of the camshaft cover

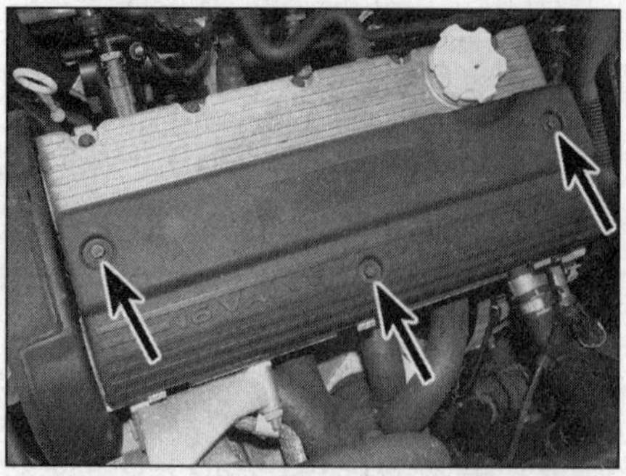

4.4 Spark plug cover bolts

with the gasket. Check the gasket for signs of damage or deterioration, and renew it if damaged. **Note:** *Do not separate the camshaft cover and gasket unless the gasket is to be renewed.*

Refitting

8 If the gasket has been removed from the cover, remove the crankcase ventilation system filters, wash them in solvent then dry them before refitting them to the cover. Ensure the cover is clean and dry, then fit the new gasket, making sure its EXHAUST MAN SIDE marking is pointing towards the exhaust manifold.

9 Make sure the mating surfaces are clean and dry, then refit the cover to the cylinder head, ensuring that the gasket remains correctly seated.

10 Refit the cover retaining bolts and tighten them all by hand. Once all bolts are in position, go around in the specified sequence and tighten them to the specified torque setting **(see illustration)**.

11 The remainder of refitting is a reversal of removal, noting the following points:

a) If the camshaft end cover came off with the wiring harness bracket, apply a thin film of sealant to the cover when refitting it.

b) Apply a little oil to the camshaft sensor's O-ring seal when refitting.

5 Crankshaft pulley – removal and refitting

Removal

1 Loosen the right-hand front wheel bolts. Firmly apply the handbrake, then jack up the front of the car and support it securely on axle stands (see *Jacking and vehicle support*). To improve access, remove the right-hand front wheel.

2 Remove the engine undertray, which is secured by a number of quick-release screw fasteners.

3 Remove the right-hand wheel arch liner as described in Chapter 11, Section 22.

5.8 Align the crankshaft pulley notch with the sprocket lug (arrowed) then refit the bolt and washer

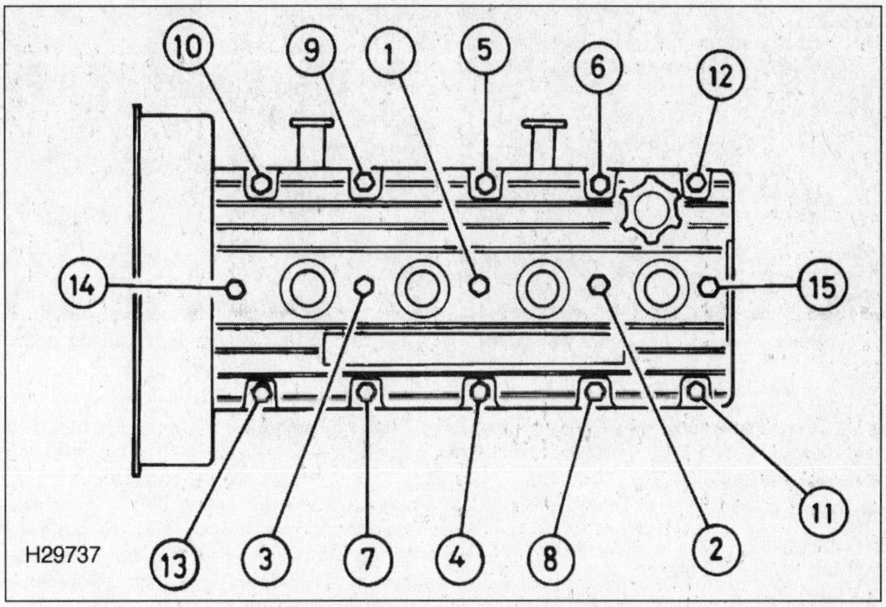

4.10 Camshaft cover bolt tightening sequence

4 If further dismantling is to be carried out, align the engine assembly/valve timing marks as described in Section 3.

5 Remove the auxiliary drivebelt(s) as described in Chapter 1A.

6 Slacken the crankshaft pulley retaining bolt. To prevent crankshaft rotation, have an assistant select top gear and apply the brakes firmly. If the engine is removed from the car, it will be necessary to lock the flywheel (see Section 17).

7 Unscrew the pulley bolt and washer, noting which way around the washer is fitted, then remove the pulley from the crankshaft.

Refitting

8 Fit the pulley to the crankshaft, aligning the notch in the pulley with the locating lug on the sprocket, then refit the retaining bolt and washer **(see illustration)**. Make sure that the tapered face of the washer is facing away from the pulley.

9 Lock the crankshaft using the method used on removal, and tighten the pulley retaining bolt to the specified torque setting.

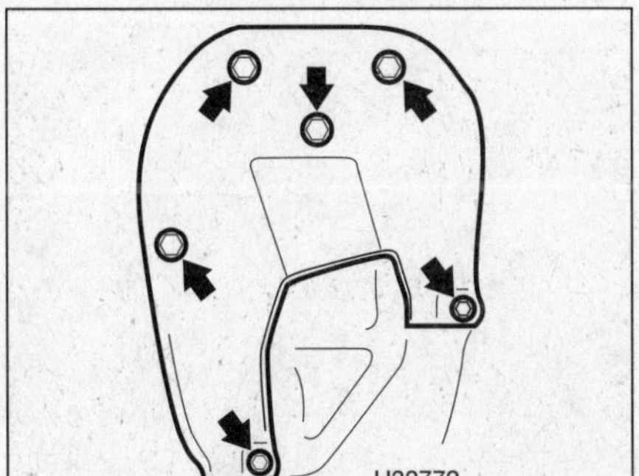

6.1 Unscrew the upper timing cover retaining bolts (arrowed)

10 Refit and tension the auxiliary drivebelt(s) as described in Chapter 1A.

11 The remainder of refitting is a reversal of removal. Tighten the wheel bolts to the specified torque.

6 Timing belt covers – removal and refitting

Upper cover

Removal

1 Slacken the lower bolts securing the upper cover to the engine then unscrew the upper bolts securing it to the rear cover **(see illustration)**.

2 Free the upper cover from the rear cover and remove it from the engine, taking care not to lose the seal which is fitted around the engine mounting bracket. Inspect the seal for signs of damage or deterioration and renew if necessary.

Refitting

3 Refitting is a reversal of removal. Ensure that the rubber seal is positioned correctly and tighten the cover bolts securely.

Lower cover

Removal

4 Remove the crankshaft pulley as described in Section 5.

5 Remove the upper timing belt cover as described previously in this Section.

6 Remove the two bolts securing the power steering drivebelt tensioner, and withdraw the tensioner from the engine.

7 Unscrew the three bolts and remove the

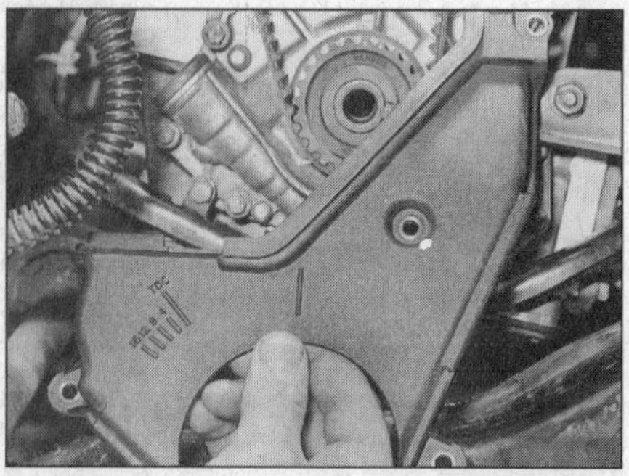

6.7 Remove the timing belt lower cover

6.12 Timing belt rear cover retaining bolts (arrowed)

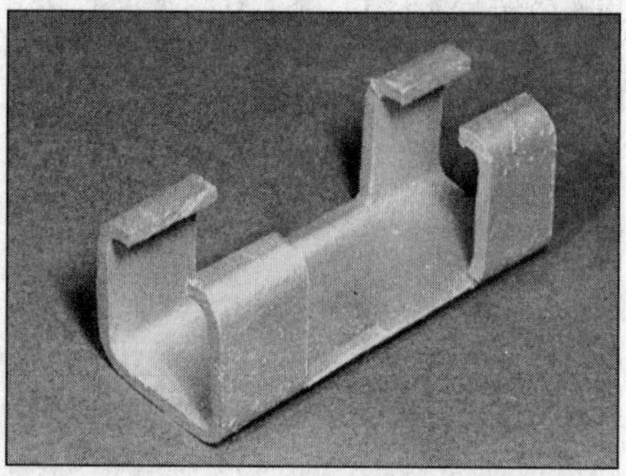

7.6a A sprocket locking tool can be made by cutting a square-section tube . . .

lower cover **(see illustration)**. Check the cover seals for signs of damage or deterioration and renew if necessary.

Refitting

8 Refitting is the reverse of removal ensuring that the seals are correctly fitted. Tighten all bolts securely.

Rear cover

Removal

9 Remove the timing belt as described in Section 7.

10 Remove the camshaft sprockets as described in Section 8.

11 Remove the bolt securing the dipstick support bracket, and the longer bolt which secures the rear cover to the water pump.

12 Undo the remaining three bolts securing the cover to the cylinder head/block, and remove the cover from the engine **(see illustration)**.

Refitting

13 Refitting is a reversal of removal, refitting the timing belt tensioner, sprockets and belt as described in Sections 7 and 8.

7 Timing belt – removal and refitting

Note: *Whenever the timing belt is disturbed, it is recommended that the belt be renewed as a matter of course, regardless of its apparent condition.*

Removal

1 Disconnect the battery negative lead (see *Disconnecting the battery*).

2 Align the engine assembly/valve timing marks as described in Section 3.

3 Remove the crankshaft pulley as described in Section 5, ensuring that all timing marks remain correctly aligned.

4 Remove the timing belt upper and lower covers as described in Section 6.

5 Place a jack, with a block of wood on its head, under the engine to support its weight. The engine right-hand mounting must now be removed for access to the timing belt – refer to Section 18.

6 Ideally, a suitable tool should be used to lock the camshaft sprockets together, as they usually move slightly under valve spring pressure when the timing belt is removed. Experienced mechanics may be able to manage without this tool (it is not essential), provided care is taken to re-align the sprocket marks as the belt is fitted. Special tool 18G 1570 slots in between the sprocket teeth, but an acceptable substitute can be fabricated from a length of steel square-section tube cut to fit as closely as possible around the sprocket spokes **(see illustrations)**. Ready-made substitutes for this tool may be available from motor factors.

7 Remove and discard the timing belt tensioner bolt – a new one should be used when refitting.

8 Disengage the tensioner index spring, whilst removing the tensioner. **Note:** *MG Rover recommend that the tensioner should be renewed every 100 000 miles – timing belt 'kits' are usually available, which include the belt and tensioner.*

9 Carefully slide the timing belt off its sprockets and remove it from the engine. **Do not** rotate the crankshaft or camshafts until the timing belt has been refitted. If the locking tool described in paragraph 6 is not used, note how the camshaft sprockets move when the belt is taken off – this movement will have to be reversed when the belt is fitted.

10 Due to the low cost of a new belt, it is recommended that the belt be renewed as a matter of course, regardless of its apparent condition. MG Rover state that a belt which has covered more than 45 000 miles should never be refitted. If signs of oil contamination are found, trace the source of the oil leak and rectify it, then wash down the engine timing belt area and all related components to remove all traces of oil. **Note:** *The sprockets used on this engine are sintered, rather than cast, which results in a lighter, but more porous, component. If the sprockets are heavily contaminated with oil, they should be soaked in solvent, then washed again with clean solvent before fitting, or they will contaminate the new belt.*

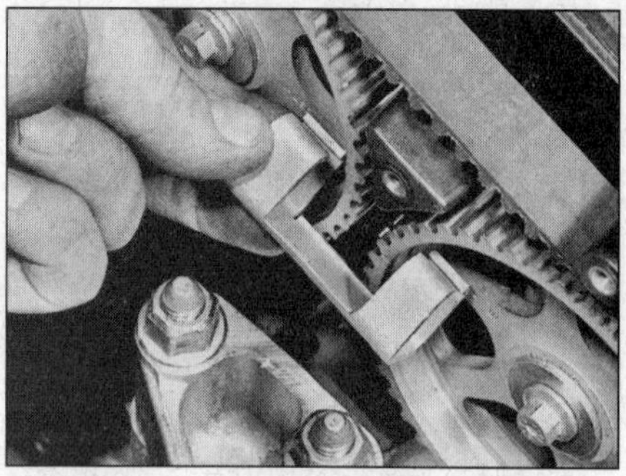

7.6b . . . so that it engages with the sprocket spokes and locks the sprockets together

Refitting

11 Thoroughly clean and dry the timing belt sprockets and check that the camshafts and crankshaft are still correctly positioned. The camshaft sprocket timing marks must still be aligned with the cylinder head surface (see Section 3) and the crankshaft sprocket timing dots must be positioned on each side of the raised rib on the oil pump housing **(see illustration)**.

12 Using a new bolt, refit the tensioner to the engine, ensuring that the index spring is positioned over the pillar bolt, and the tensioner arm is at the 9 o'clock position **(see illustration)**. Tighten the bolt only to the point where it is just possible to move the tensioner arm.

13 Fit the timing belt over the crankshaft, and then the front and rear camshaft sprockets, ensuring that the belt front run is taut (ie, all slack is on the tensioner side of the belt). Finally, fit the belt over the water pump sprocket and

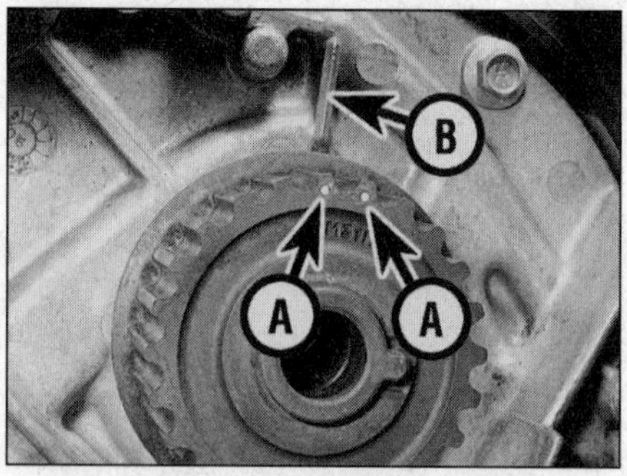

7.11 The crankshaft sprocket timing dots (A) should be either side of the oil pump housing rib (B)

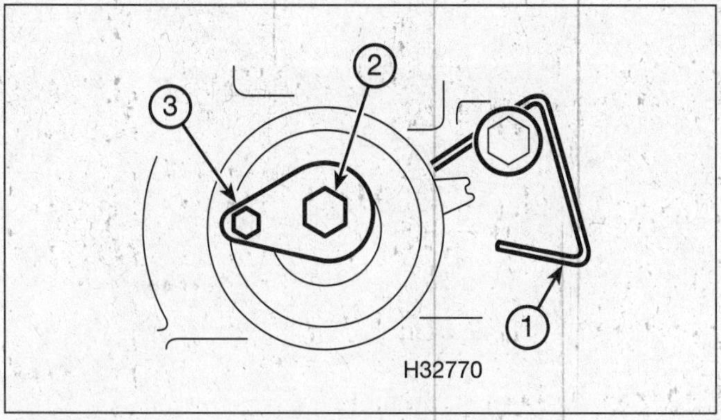

7.12 Index spring (1) hooked over the pillar bolt, tensioner arm (3) at 9 o'clock, and tensioner bolt (2)

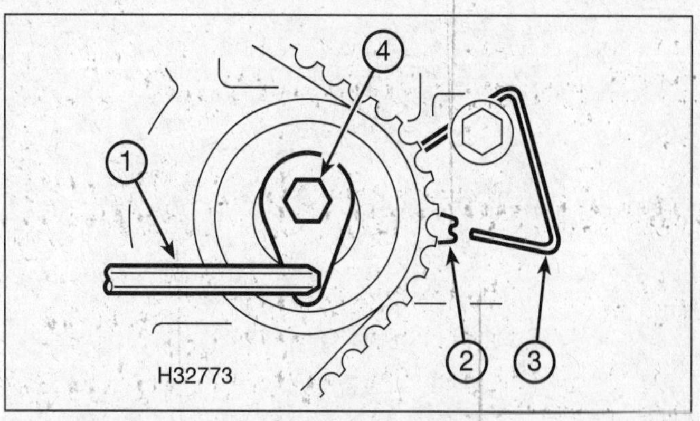

7.15 With an Allen key (1), turn tensioner arm anti-clockwise until pointer (2) aligns with index spring (3). Tighten tensioner bolt (4) to the specified torque

tensioner pulley. Do not twist the belt sharply while refitting it. Ensure that the belt teeth are correctly seated centrally in the sprockets, and that the timing marks remain in alignment.

14 If the camshaft locking tool described in paragraph 6 was not used, it will be necessary to turn the two sprockets slightly as the belt is fitted. With the help of an assistant, turn the front sprocket back into the alignment position – it should only have to move a few degrees to achieve this. MG Rover state that the sprocket bolts must not be used for turning, so a suitable tool will have to be used on the sprocket spokes. Fit the belt onto the front sprocket so that the belt is taut on the front run, and keep pressure on the belt to hold the sprocket. Turn the rear sprocket into the alignment position, and engage the belt teeth. Again, keep pressure on the belt to stop it jumping off the sprockets, until the belt is fitted around the water pump and tensioner.

15 Using an Allen key, rotate the tensioner arm anti-clockwise until the pointer to the right of the tensioner aligns with the end of the index spring. Tighten the tensioner bolt to the specified torque **(see illustration)**. **Note:** *Ensure that the pointer only approaches the index spring from above. If the pointer goes past the spring, release the tension completely and repeat the tensioning procedure.*

16 Refit the right-hand engine mounting components as described in Section 18. Tighten the bolts/nuts to the specified torque. Remove the jack1 and block of wood from under the engine.

17 With reference to Section 6, refit the lower timing belt cover, ensuring its sealing strips are correctly positioned and tighten the securing bolts.

18 Refit the crankshaft pulley, aligning the notch in the pulley with the locating lug on the sprocket. Refit the retaining bolt and washer, ensuring the tapered face of the washer is facing away from the pulley, but only hand-tighten the pulley bolt at this stage. Remove the tool used to lock the camshaft sprockets together, and rotate the crankshaft clockwise two complete revolutions using a spanner or socket on the crankshaft pulley bolt.

19 Check the sprocket timing marks are still correctly aligned. If adjustment is necessary, release the tensioner again then disengage the belt from the sprockets and make any necessary adjustments.

20 Tighten the crankshaft pulley retaining bolt to the specified torque, as described in Section 5.

21 Refit the timing belt upper cover, ensuring the seal is correctly positioned, and tighten its retaining bolts.

22 Refit the auxiliary drivebelts as described in Chapter 1A.

23 Refit the roadwheel, and lower the car to the ground, and tighten the wheel bolts to the specified torque. Reconnect the battery negative lead.

8.2 Using a home-made tool to hold a camshaft sprocket

8.7 Engage the exhaust camshaft locating pin with the EX cut-out and the inlet camshaft locating pin in the IN cut-out

8 Timing belt tensioner and sprockets – removal and refitting

Camshaft sprockets

Removal

1 Remove the timing belt as described in Section 7.

2 Slacken and remove each camshaft sprocket retaining bolt, along with the washer. To stop the camshaft turning, use a locking tool which fits between the sprocket spokes, which can be fabricated from two lengths of steel strip (one long, the other short) and three nuts and bolts. One nut and bolt should form the pivot of the forked tool, with the remaining two nuts and bolts at the tips of the forks to engage with the sprocket spokes **(see illustration)**.

3 Both sprockets are identical, but it is still a good idea to mark them for position before removal. Remove the sprockets from the camshafts, taking care not to lose the sprocket locating pins. If a pin is a loose fit in the end of the camshaft, remove it and store it with the sprocket for safe-keeping.

4 Check the sprockets for signs of wear or damage and renew if necessary.

Refitting

5 Prior to refitting, check the oil seals for signs of damage or leakage. If necessary, renew as described in Section 9.

6 Ensure the locating pins are in position in the camshaft ends. Note that the pins should be fitted with the split facing inwards.

7 Both inlet and exhaust camshaft sprockets are the same, but each one is equipped with two locating pin cut-outs. If the sprocket is being fitted to the inlet camshaft, engage the locating pin in the IN cut-out, and if the sprocket is being fitted to the exhaust camshaft, engage the locating pin in the EX cut-out **(see illustration)**. Ensure the camshaft locating pin is engaged in the correct sprocket cut-out then refit the washer and retaining bolt.

9.4 Use a socket to tap a camshaft oil seal into position

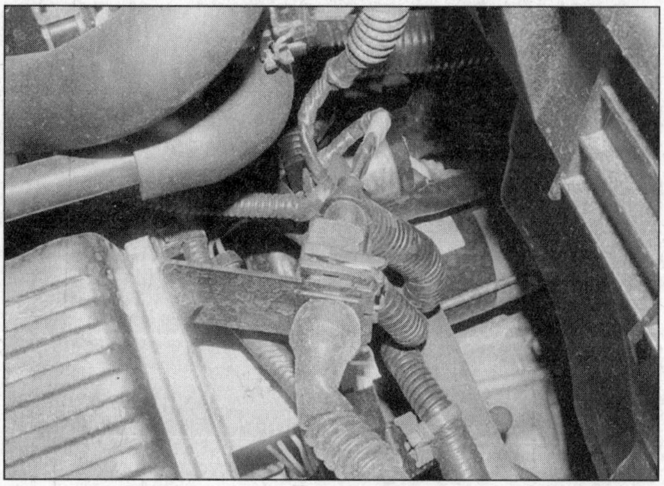

9.10 Disconnect the camshaft position sensor wiring plug

8 On all engines, retain the sprockets by the method used on removal, and tighten the retaining bolts to the specified torque setting.

9 Ensure the crankshaft pulley mark is still correctly aligned with the mark on the lower cover and the camshaft sprocket marks are correctly aligned with the cylinder head upper surface (see Section 3).

10 Refit the timing belt as described in Section 7.

Crankshaft sprocket

Removal

11 Remove the timing belt as described in Section 7.

12 Slide the sprocket off from the end of the crankshaft, noting which way around it is fitted.

Refitting

13 Refit the sprocket to the crankshaft, engaging it with the crankshaft flattened section. Check that the sprocket timing marks align – the two dots on the sprocket must be positioned on each side of the raised rib on the oil pump body.

14 Refit the timing belt as described in Section 7.

Tensioner assembly

15 The automatic tensioner is secured by one bolt though the pulley, and incorporates an index spring. This spring provides constant tension to press the pulley against the belt, and a reference point to enable the tensioner to be set initially. Whenever the automatic tensioner mounting bolt is disturbed, it must be renewed.

Removal and refitting

16 As the timing belt must be renewed whenever the tensioner is disturbed, follow the procedure given in Section 7 of this Chapter detailing the timing belt renewal procedure.

9 Camshaft oil seals – renewal

Timing belt end seals

1 Remove the camshaft sprockets as described in Section 8.

2 Punch or drill two small holes opposite each other in the oil seal(s). Screw a self-tapping screw into each hole, and pull on the screws with pliers to extract the seal.

3 Clean the seal housing, and polish off any burrs or raised edges which may have caused the seal to fail.

4 The new seal has a waxed outer surface, and should **not** be lubricated further prior to fitting. Just drive it into position, using a suitable tubular drift, such as a socket, which bears only on the hard outer edge of the seal **(see illustration)**. Take care not to damage the seal lips during fitting, and note that the seal lips should face inwards.

5 Refit the camshaft sprocket(s) as described in Section 8.

Flywheel end seals

6 Remove the air cleaner assembly as described in Chapter 4A and proceed as described under the relevant sub-heading.

Exhaust camshaft

7 Slacken and remove the two bolts securing the exhaust camshaft end cover plate to the cylinder head, and remove the plate. Be prepared for a small amount of oil spillage.

8 Renew the oil seal as described in paragraphs 2 to 4, noting again that the oil seal lips **must not** be oiled.

9 Ensure the mating surfaces are clean and dry, and apply a smear of sealant to the cover plate. Refit the plate, tightening the retaining bolts to the specified torque.

Inlet camshaft

10 Disconnect the camshaft position sensor/coil supply wiring plug at the transmission end of the engine **(see illustration)**. Unscrew the two bolts securing the wiring harness bracket to the cylinder head, and move the bracket clear – these two bolts also secure the end cover plate.

11 Remove the cover plate from the cylinder head – though the two bolts have just been removed, it should still be stuck in place with a little sealant. Be prepared for a small amount of oil spillage.

12 Renew the oil seal as described in paragraphs 2 to 4, noting that the oil seal lips **must not** be oiled.

13 Ensure the mating surfaces are clean and dry, and apply a smear of sealant to the cover plate. Refit the plate tightening the bolts to the specified torque.

10 Camshafts and tappets – removal, inspection and refitting

Note: *MG Rover produce a sealant kit which consists of a plastic scraper, gasket removing compound and the recommended sealant for the camshaft carrier joint. It is recommended that this kit is used during the following procedure. New camshaft oil seals will also be required.*

Removal

1 Remove the camshaft cover as described in Section 4.

2 Remove the air cleaner assembly with reference to Chapter 4A.

3 Slacken and remove the two bolts securing each camshaft end cover plate to the cylinder head, and remove the plates. Be prepared for a small amount of oil spillage.

4 Remove the camshaft sprockets as described in Section 8.

5 Remove the timing belt rear cover as described in Section 6.

6 Working in sequence, slacken the camshaft

bearing carrier retaining bolts progressively, by one turn at a time, to gradually release the pressure of the valve springs **(see illustration)**.

Caution: If the bearing carrier bolts are carelessly slackened, the carrier might break. If the carrier is broken, the complete cylinder head assembly must be renewed; the carrier is matched to the head and is not available separately.

7 Lift the camshaft bearing carrier away from the cylinder head, noting the correct fitted positions of the locating dowels. If the dowels are loose, remove them and store them with the bearing carrier for safe-keeping.

8 Carefully lift the camshafts from the cylinder head. Remove the oil seals and discard them; new ones should be used on refitting. Mark the camshafts for identification – the exhaust camshaft is the front one.

9 If necessary, obtain sixteen small, clean plastic containers, and label them for identification. Alternatively, divide a larger container into compartments. Using a sucker or magnet, withdraw each tappet in turn, and place it upright in its respective container, which should then be filled with clean engine oil **(see illustration)**.

Caution: Do not interchange the tappets, and do not allow the tappets to lose oil, as they will take a long time to refill with oil on restarting the engine, which could result in incorrect valve clearances. Absolute cleanliness is essential at all times when handling the tappets.

Inspection

10 Examine the camshaft bearing surfaces and cam lobes for signs of wear ridges and scoring. Renew the camshaft if any of these conditions are apparent. Examine the condition of the bearing surfaces both on the camshaft journals and in the cylinder head. If the head bearing surfaces are worn excessively, the cylinder head will need to be renewed.

11 Examine the tappet bearing surfaces which contact the camshaft lobes for wear ridges and scoring. Check the tappets and their bores in the cylinder head for signs of wear or damage. If a micrometer is available, measure the outside diameter of each tappet and compare it to the values given in the Specifications. If the engine's valve clearances have sounded noisy, particularly if the noise persists after initial start-up from cold, then there is reason to suspect a faulty tappet. If any tappet is thought to be faulty or is visibly worn it should be renewed.

Refitting

12 Liberally oil the camshaft bearings and tappets, then refit the tappets to their original locations in the cylinder head.

13 Lay the camshafts in position. Position the camshafts so that the camshaft sprocket locating pins are positioned as shown **(see illustration)**. When viewed from the right-hand end of the engine, the inlet camshaft sprocket pin should be in the 4 o'clock position and the exhaust camshaft sprocket pin should be in the 8 o'clock position.

14 Ensure the mating surfaces of the camshaft bearing carrier and cylinder head are clean and dry. Apply a 2 mm bead of sealant (such as Loctite 518 or 5205) to the bearing carrier mating surface **(see illustration)**. Spread the sealant in an even film, taking care not to allow any sealant to enter the oilway grooves.

15 Ensure that the locating dowels are in position, then refit the camshaft bearing carrier to the cylinder head. Ensure the carrier is correctly located then refit the retaining bolts, tightening them all by hand only at this stage.

16 Working in a diagonal sequence, evenly and progressively tighten the retaining bolts to draw the bearing carrier squarely down

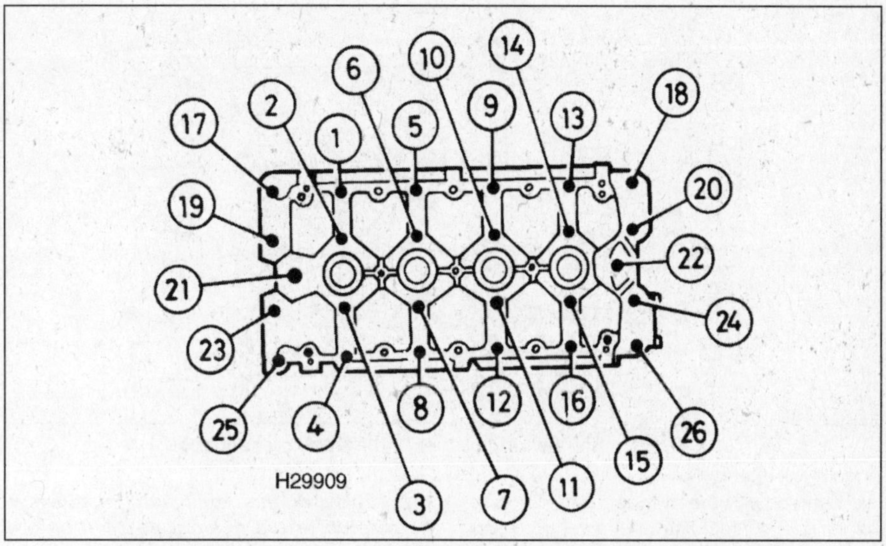

10.6 Camshaft bearing carrier retaining bolt slackening sequence

10.9 Use a sucker or magnet to remove the camshaft followers

10.13 Position the camshaft sprocket locating pins (arrowed) as shown

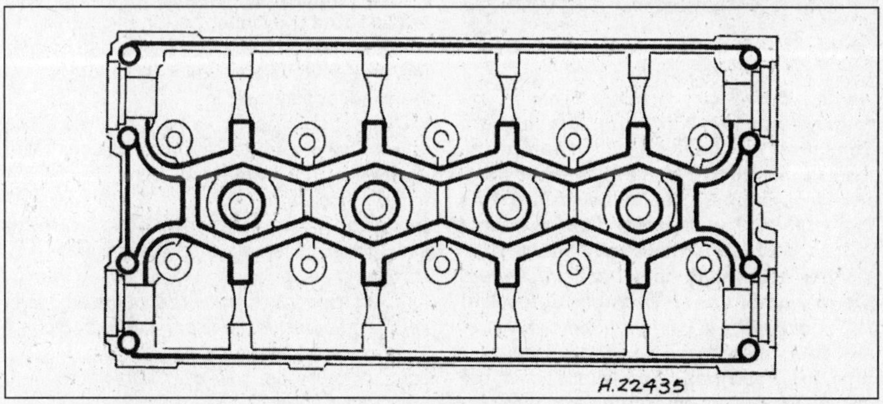

10.14 Apply a bead of sealant to the highlighted area of the bearing carrier mating surface

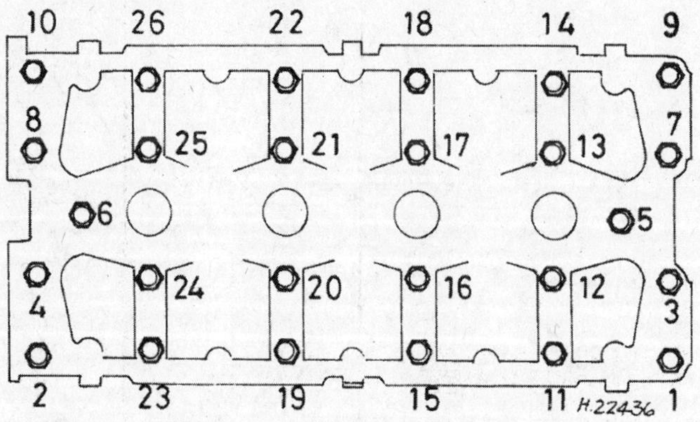

10.16 Camshaft bearing carrier bolt tightening sequence

into contact with the cylinder head. Once the carrier is in contact with the head, go around in the specified sequence and tighten the retaining bolts to the specified torque **(see illustration)**.

Caution: If the bearing carrier bolts are carelessly tightened, the carrier might break. If the carrier is broken then the complete cylinder head assembly must be renewed; the carrier is matched to the head and is not available separately.

17 Fit new camshaft oil seals as described in Section 9.

18 Ensure the mating surfaces are clean and dry, and apply a smear of sealant to the camshaft end cover plates. Refit the plates to the left-hand end of the cylinder head, and tighten the retaining bolts to the specified torque.

19 Refit the timing belt rear cover to the cylinder head, and tighten the bolts securely.

20 Refit the camshaft sprockets as described in Section 8.

21 Refit the camshaft cover as described in Section 4.

22 Refit the timing belt as described in Section 7.

11 Cylinder head – removal and refitting

Caution: Before commencing any servicing or overhaul work on the engine, the crankshaft must always be rotated to the desired position before the cylinder head bolts are disturbed. Due to the design of the engine, it will become very difficult, almost impossible, to turn the crankshaft once the cylinder head bolts have been slackened. The manufacturer accordingly states that the crankshaft will be 'tight' and should not be rotated more than absolutely necessary once the head has been removed. If the crankshaft cannot be rotated, then it must be removed for overhaul work to proceed. With this in mind, during any servicing or overhaul work, the crankshaft must always be rotated to the desired position before the bolts are disturbed.

Removal

1 Depressurise the fuel system and remove the air cleaner housing as described in Chapter 4A.

2 Disconnect the battery negative lead (see *Disconnecting the battery*).

3 Drain the cooling system as described in Chapter 1A.

4 Remove the timing belt as described in Section 7.

5 Remove the exhaust manifold as described in Chapter 4A. However, if no work is to be carried out on the cylinder head, the head can be removed complete with the manifold once the exhaust front pipe has been unbolted and the oxygen sensor wiring connector has been disconnected (see Chapter 4A).

6 Release the retaining clips and disconnect the coolant hoses from the outlet elbow on the front, left-hand end of the cylinder head. Disconnect the wiring connectors from the coolant temperature sensor(s) which are screwed into the elbow.

7 Disconnect the camshaft position sensor/coil supply wiring plug at the transmission end of the engine **(see illustration 9.10)**. Unscrew the two bolts securing the wiring harness bracket to the cylinder head, and move the bracket clear – these two bolts also secure the end cover plate, which should also be removed for safe-keeping.

8 Disconnect the coolant hoses from the outlet elbow, noting their fitted positions. Also disconnect the wiring plug from the coolant temperature sensor.

9 Disconnect the following engine management system wiring connectors:

a) Power steering pressure sensor (in the fluid supply line at the rear of the engine).
b) Throttle position sensor (in front of the throttle body).
c) Injector wiring multi-plug (behind the throttle body).
d) Inlet air temperature sensor (on top of the engine).
e) Idle air control valve (next to the oil filler cap)

10 Place absorbent rags below the fuel supply line in front of the throttle body. Depress the plastic collar on the fuel pipe and disconnect the pipe – plug the open connections.

11 Release the spring clip and pull off the charcoal canister hose from the throttle housing.

12 Unscrew the adjuster nut and slide out the accelerator cable from the mounting bracket on the throttle body. Unclip the accelerator cable from the inlet manifold.

13 Depress the locking collar, and pull off the brake servo vacuum hose from the inlet manifold.

14 Release the spring clip and disconnect the expansion tank hose from the inlet manifold.

15 Remove the alternator as described in Chapter 5A.

16 On models with air conditioning, remove the three compressor mounting bolts and tie the compressor to one side without straining any of the hoses.

17 Unbolt and remove the alternator heat shield.

18 Remove the camshaft cover as described in Section 4.

19 Working in the **reverse** of the tightening sequence shown later in this Section, progressively loosen cylinder head bolts 1 to 6, then remove them. Store the bolts in order, so that they can be refitted in their original locations. The bolts can be stored by pushing them through a clearly-marked cardboard template.

20 Remove the locking tool from the camshaft sprockets (if used), then turn both the sprockets clockwise to gain access to bolts 7 and 8. MG Rover state that the sprocket bolts must not be used for turning, so a suitable tool will have to be used on the sprocket spokes.

21 Continuing the sequence started in paragraph 19, progressively loosen cylinder head bolts 7 to 10, then remove and store them in their fitted order. Once all the bolts have been removed, no attempt should be made to turn the crankshaft until the cylinder liner clamps have been fitted (as described later in this Section).

22 Remove the camshaft sprockets as described in Section 8.

23 Remove the timing belt rear cover as described in Section 6.

24 The joint between the cylinder head and gasket and the cylinder block/crankcase must now be broken without disturbing the cylinder liners. Although these liners are better located and sealed than some wet-liner engines, there is still a risk of coolant and foreign matter leaking into the sump if the cylinder head is lifted carelessly. If care is not taken and the liners are moved, there is also a possibility of their seals being disturbed, causing leakage after refitting the head.

25 To break the joint, obtain two L-shaped metal bars which fit into the cylinder head bolt holes and gently rock the cylinder head free towards the front of the car **(see illustration)**.

Caution: Do not try to swivel the head on the cylinder block/crankcase, as it is located by dowels as well as by the tops of the liners.

26 When the joint is broken, lift the cylinder head away, using assistance if possible as it is a heavy assembly, especially if complete with the manifolds. Remove the gasket and discard it. Support the cylinder head on wooden blocks or stands – do not rest the lower face of the cylinder head on the work surface. Note the fitted positions of the two locating dowels, and remove them for safe-keeping if they are loose.

27 Note that further to the warnings given at the beginning of this Section, **do not** attempt to rotate the crankshaft with the cylinder head removed, otherwise the liners may be displaced. Operations that require the rotation of the crankshaft (eg, cleaning the piston crowns) can be carried out after fitting cylinder liner clamps **(see illustration)**.

> **HAYNES HiNT** *Liner clamps can be improvised using large washers and tubular spacers.*

28 If the cylinder head is to be dismantled, remove the camshafts, as described in Section 10, then refer to the relevant Sections of Part D of this Chapter.

Preparation for refitting

29 The mating faces of the cylinder head and cylinder block/crankcase must be perfectly clean before refitting the head. Use a hard plastic or wood scraper to remove all traces of gasket and carbon. Also clean the piston crowns. Take particular care, as the soft aluminium alloy is damaged easily.

30 Make sure that the carbon is not allowed to enter the oil and water passages – this is particularly important for the lubrication system, as carbon could block the oil supply to any of the engine components. Using adhesive tape and paper, seal the water, oil and bolt holes in the cylinder block/crankcase. To prevent carbon entering the gap between

11.35 Ensure the locating dowels (arrowed) are in position then fit the new head gasket . . .

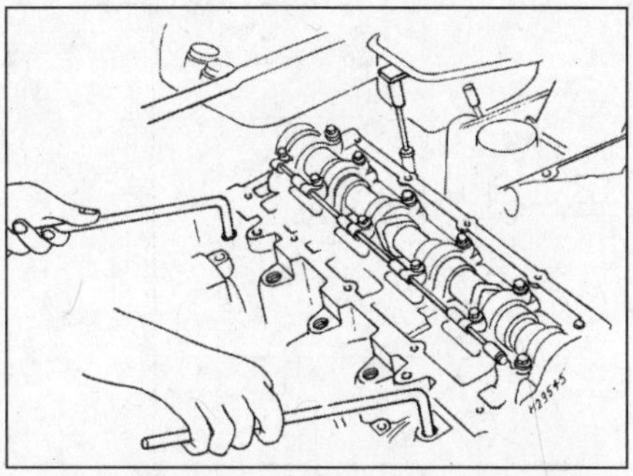

11.25 Use two L-shaped bars to break the cylinder head joint by rocking

the pistons and bores, smear a little grease in the gap. After cleaning each piston, use a small brush to remove all traces of grease and carbon from the gap, then wipe away the remainder with a clean cloth. Clean all the pistons in the same way. Take great care not to move the pistons during this procedure.

31 Check the mating surfaces of the cylinder block/crankcase and the cylinder head for nicks, deep scratches and other damage. If slight, they may be removed carefully with a file, but if excessive, machining may be the only alternative to renewal.

32 If warpage of the cylinder head gasket surface is suspected, use a straight-edge to check it for distortion. Refer to Part D of this Chapter if necessary.

33 Check the condition of the cylinder head bolts, particularly their threads. Keeping all bolts in their correct fitted order, wash them and wipe dry. Check each bolt for any sign of visible wear or damage, renewing as necessary. Note that if cylinder head bolts have been used to secure the cylinder liner clamps, each bolt and clamp should be removed one at a time for checking, and refitted immediately the bolt has been inspected. Although not specified by the manufacturer, we recommend that the bolts are renewed as a complete set, regardless of their apparent condition – this is particularly recommended if the bolts have seen long service, or are known to have already been re-used once.

Refitting

34 Remove the cylinder liner clamps (where

11.36 . . . making sure the TOP mark is upwards and the FRONT arrow points towards the timing belt end

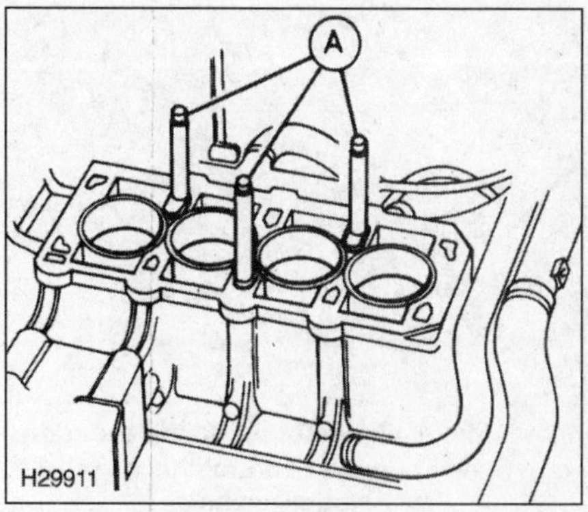

11.27 Cylinder liner clamps (A) in position on the cylinder block

fitted) and wipe clean the mating surfaces of the cylinder head and cylinder block/ crankcase.

35 Ensure that the two locating dowels are in position at each end of the cylinder block/ crankcase surface **(see illustration)**.

36 Position a new gasket on the cylinder block/crankcase surface so that its TOP mark is uppermost and the FRONT arrow points to the timing belt end **(see illustration)**.

37 Carefully refit the cylinder head, locating it on the dowels.

38 Keeping all the cylinder head bolts in their correct fitted order, lightly oil under the head and on the threads of each bolt, then carefully enter it into its original hole and screw it in, by hand only, until finger-tight. **Do not** drop the bolts into their holes.

39 In order to turn the camshafts for access to the head bolts, temporarily refit the camshaft sprockets, referring to Section 8.

40 Working progressively and in sequence, first tighten all the cylinder head bolts to the Stage 1 torque setting **(see illustration)**.

41 Once all bolts have been tightened to the Stage 1 torque, again working in the sequence shown, tighten each bolt through its specified Stage 2 angle, using a socket and extension bar. It is recommended that an angle-measuring gauge is used during this stage of tightening, to ensure accuracy. Prior to tightening, use a felt-tip pen or similar to make alignment marks between the radial

11.40 Cylinder head bolt tightening sequence

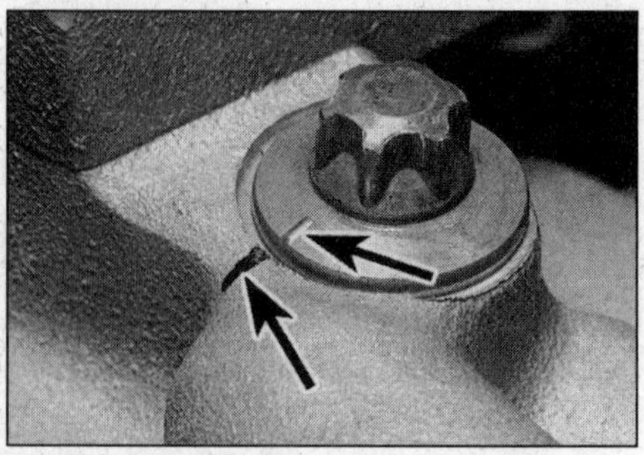

11.41 Make alignment marks between the bolt flange and the head to check correct bolt tightening

mark on each bolt head and the cylinder head **(see illustration)**. The second stage torque can then be achieved by tightening each bolt through half-a-turn so that the mark on the bolt head faces away from the corresponding mark on the cylinder head.

42 Finally go around in the specified sequence again and tighten all bolts through the specified Stage 3 angle. Each bolt head radial mark should now be realigned with the corresponding mark on the cylinder head again. If any bolt is overtightened beyond the mark on the cylinder head, slacken the bolt by a quarter-turn, then retighten until the marks align.

43 Remove the camshaft sprockets once more.

44 Refit the camshaft cover (Section 4).

45 Further refitting is a reversal of removal, noting the following points:

- *a) Use new gaskets/seals, as applicable.*
- *b) Tighten all fasteners to the specified torque.*
- *c) Adjust the accelerator cable as described in Chapter 4A.*
- *d) Fit a new timing belt as described in Section 7.*
- *e) Refill the cooling system as described in Chapter 1A.*

12 Sump – removal and refitting

Removal

1 Drain the engine oil (with reference to Chapter 1A if necessary), then clean and refit the engine oil drain plug with a new washer, tightening it to the specified torque wrench setting. If the engine is nearing the service interval when the oil and filter are due for renewal, it is recommended that the filter is also removed and a new one fitted. After reassembly, the engine can then be refilled with fresh engine oil.

2 Apply the handbrake, then jack up the front of the car and support it securely on axle stands (see *Jacking and vehicle support*).

3 Disconnect the exhaust front pipe as described in Chapter 4A.

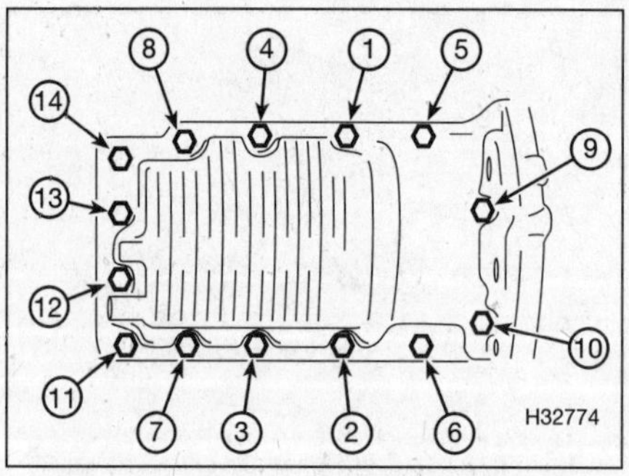

12.15 Sump bolt tightening sequence

4 Remove the front through-bolt from the engine lower mounting, referring to Section 18 if necessary.

5 Remove the four bolts securing the lower mounting bracket to the sump, and take it off.

6 Remove the two bolts securing the sump to the transmission casing, and the single transmission-to-sump bolt.

7 Progressively slacken and remove the fourteen bolts securing the sump to the base of the main bearing ladder – note the fitted locations of the two longer bolts.

8 Break the sump sealant joint by striking the sump with the palm of the hand. It is not advisable to prise between the mating faces, as this could result in a leak. If the sump is stuck, remove the drain plug, then use a sturdy screwdriver (wrapped in a rag or card to protect the drain plug threads) in the drain plug hole as a prising tool. Lower the sump away from the engine, holding the exhaust to the side as necessary.

9 While the sump is removed, take the opportunity to check the oil pump pick-up/strainer for signs of clogging or splitting. If necessary, unbolt the pick-up/strainer and remove it from the engine along with its sealing ring. The strainer can then be cleaned easily in solvent. Inspect the strainer mesh for signs of clogging or splitting and renew if necessary.

Refitting

10 Clean all traces of sealant from the mating surfaces of the cylinder block/crankcase and sump, then use a clean rag to wipe out the sump and the engine interior.

11 Where necessary, fit a new sealing ring to oil pump pick-up/strainer groove then carefully refit the pipe, tightening its retaining bolts to the specified torque setting.

12 Apply a 2 mm bead of suitable sealant (such as Loctite 518 or 5205) to the sump mating surface, then spread this to an even film using a roller.

13 Offer up the sump to the cylinder block/crankcase, and use the two longer bolts in their original locations to align it. Refit the remaining sump-to-main bearing ladder bolts, and tighten all bolts finger-tight only.

14 Insert the two sump-to-transmission bolts, and the single transmission-to-sump bolt, and tighten them finger-tight only at this stage.

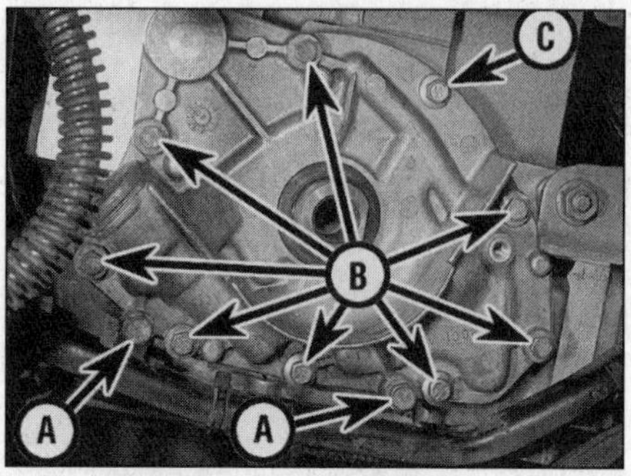

13.4 Oil pump fixings

A Engine harness guide bolts
B Oil pump retaining bolts (long)
C Oil pump retaining bolt (short)

15 Working in sequence, tighten the sump-to-main bearing ladder bolts to the specified torque setting **(see illustration)**. Note that the two longer bolts are tightened to a higher torque than the rest.

16 Tighten the sump-to-transmission/transmission-to-sump bolts to the specified torque.

17 Refit the engine lower mounting bracket to the sump, tightening the bolts to the specified torque. Refit the lower mounting using the through-bolt, also tightened to the specified torque.

18 Refit the exhaust front pipe as described in Chapter 4A.

19 Lower the car to the ground, and refill the engine with oil as described in Chapter 1A.

13 Oil pump – removal and refitting

Removal

1 Remove the crankshaft sprocket as described in Section 8.

2 Drain the engine oil, then clean and refit the engine oil drain plug with a new washer, tightening it to the specified torque wrench setting. If the engine is nearing the service interval when the oil and filter are due for renewal, it is recommended that the filter is also removed and a new one fitted. After reassembly, the engine can then be refilled with fresh engine oil (see Chapter 1A).

3 Unscrew the two lower bolts securing the engine wiring harness guide to the oil pump, and position the guide clear.

4 Slacken and remove the oil pump retaining bolts, noting the correct fitted location of the shorter bolt **(see illustration)**. Discard the bolts – new ones should be used when refitting.

5 Remove the timing belt rear cover lower bolt to facilitate removal of the pump – pull the cover clear as the pump is removed.

6 Free the oil pump from the cylinder block, then slide it off the end of the crankshaft. Note the correct fitted locations of the pump locating

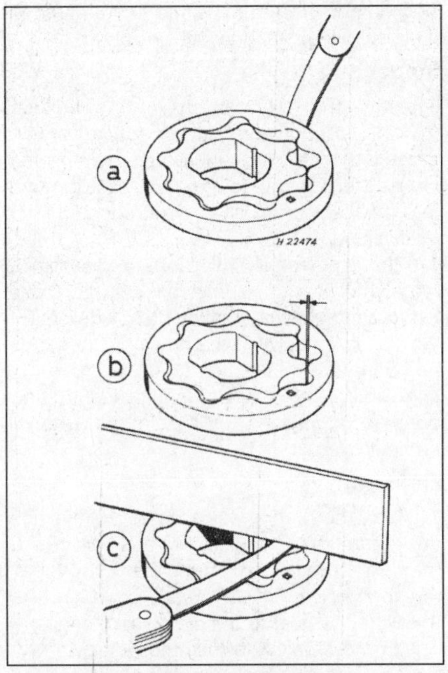

14.6 Oil pump checking

a *Outer rotor-to-pump body clearance*
b *Inner rotor tip-to-outer rotor clearance*
c *Rotor endfloat*

dowels; if the dowels are loose, remove them and store with the pump for safe-keeping. Remove the gasket and discard it.

Refitting

7 Ensure the mating surfaces of the oil pump and cylinder block are clean and dry. Clean all traces of locking compound from the pump mounting holes on the engine. Clean the oil seal surface on the crankshaft.

8 Ensure the locating dowels are in position, then fit a new gasket to the cylinder block.

9 Carefully manoeuvre the oil pump into position, and engage the inner rotor with the crankshaft end. Locate the pump on the dowels.

10 Fit the new oil pump bolts (with the short one in its previously-noted position), and tighten progressively in a diagonal sequence to the specified torque.

11 Genuine crankshaft oil seals should come with a fitting sleeve, which sits over the crankshaft nose. If one is not available, wrap a little tape round the sharp edge to protect the seal lips as it is fitted.

12 Fit the new oil seal (note that it should **not** be lubricated), ensuring its sealing lip is facing inwards, and ease it over the end of the crankshaft. Press it squarely into the housing using a tubular drift which bears only on the hard outer edge of the seal. Press the seal into position so that it is flush with the housing. Remove the oil seal guide or the tape on completion.

13 Refit the timing belt rear cover lower bolt, and tighten securely.

14 Secure the engine wiring harness guide to the oil pump with the two bolts.

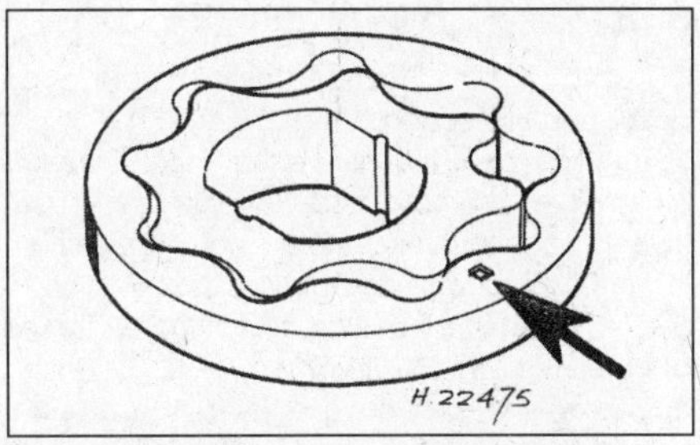

14.11 On reassembly, ensure the identification mark on the outer rotor (arrowed) faces outwards

15 Refit the crankshaft sprocket as described in Section 8.

16 On completion, refill the engine with oil as described in Chapter 1A.

14 Oil pump – dismantling, inspection and reassembly

Note: *If oil pump wear is suspected, check the cost and availability of new parts (only available in the form of a repair kit) against the cost of a new pump. Examine the pump as described in this Section and then decide whether renewal or repair is the best course of action.*

Dismantling

1 Remove the oil pump as described in Section 13.

2 Unscrew the retaining screws and remove the pump cover plate and sealing ring.

3 Note the identification marks on the outer rotor, then remove both the rotors from the body.

4 To dismantle the valve, slacken and remove the threaded plug and washer, then recover the valve spring and plunger.

Inspection

5 Inspect the rotors for obvious signs of wear or damage and renew if necessary. If the pump body or cover plate is scored or damaged, then the complete oil pump assembly must be renewed.

6 Refit the rotors to the body and, using feeler blades of the appropriate thickness, measure the clearance between the outer rotor and the pump body, then between the inner rotor tip

15.3 Oil pressure warning light switch location

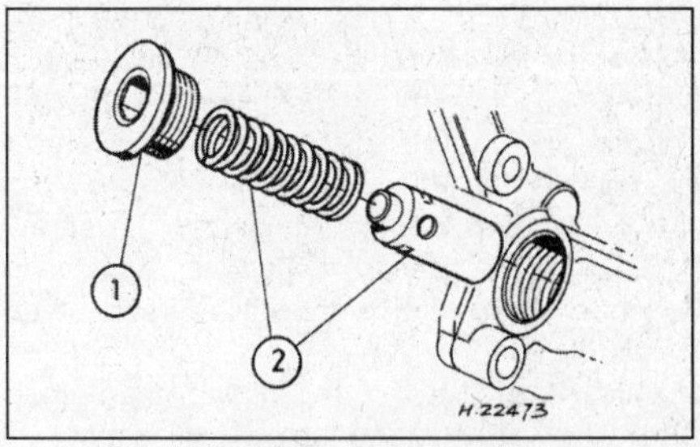

14.14 Oil pump pressure relief valve components

1 *Threaded plug and sealing washer*
2 *Plunger and spring*

and the outer rotor **(see illustration)**.

7 Using feeler blades and a straight-edge placed across the top of the pump body and the rotors, measure the rotor endfloat.

8 If any measurement is outside the specified limits, the complete pump assembly must be renewed.

9 If the pressure relief valve plunger is scored, or if it does not slide freely in the pump body bore, then it must be renewed, using all the components from the repair kit.

10 Thoroughly clean the threads of the pump cover plate securing screws and renew the cover sealing ring and relief valve washer, if damaged.

Reassembly

11 Lubricate the pump rotors with clean engine oil and refit them to the pump body, ensuring that the identification mark on the outer rotor faces outwards (ie, towards the pump cover) **(see illustration)**.

12 Fit the sealing ring to the pump body and refit the cover plate. Apply thread-locking compound to the threads of the cover plate screws then refit the screws, tightening them securely.

13 Check that the pump rotates freely, then prime it by injecting oil into its passages and rotating it. If a long time elapses before the pump is refitted to the engine, prime it again before installation.

14 Refit the oil pressure relief valve plunger, ensuring that it is the correct way up, then install the spring **(see illustration)**. Fit the sealing washer to the threaded plug and tighten the plug securely.

15 Oil pressure switch – removal and refitting

1 Firmly apply the handbrake, then jack up the front of the car and support it securely on axle stands (see *Jacking and vehicle support*).

2 Remove the engine undertray, which is secured by a number of quick-release screw fasteners.

3 The oil pressure switch is mounted near the oil filter, and is almost horizontal – do not confuse it with the vertically-mounted oil temperature switch, which is closer to the oil filter **(see illustration)**.

4 Disconnect the switch wiring plug.
5 Place a drain container under the switch – the amount of oil lost should only be whatever's in the oil filter, not the entire contents of the sump.
6 Anticipating oil spillage, slowly unscrew the switch and remove it. Recover the sealing washer – a new one should be used when refitting.
7 Allow the oil to finish draining, then clean the switch threads and the switch location.
8 Fit the switch using a new sealing washer, and tighten it to the specified torque. Reconnect the wiring plug, then refit the undertray and lower the car to the ground.

16 Crankshaft oil seals – renewal

Right-hand seal

1 Remove the crankshaft sprocket as described in Section 8.
2 Carefully punch or drill two small holes opposite each other in the oil seal. Screw a self-tapping screw into each, and pull on the screws with pliers to extract the seal.
Caution: Great care must be taken to avoid damage to the oil pump.
3 Clean the seal housing and polish off any burrs or raised edges which may have caused the seal to fail in the first place.
4 The new seal has a waxed outer surface, and should **not** be lubricated prior to fitting. Ease the new seal into position on the end of the shaft. Press the seal squarely into position until it is flush with the housing. If necessary, a suitable tubular drift, such as a socket, which bears only on the hard outer edge of the seal can be used to tap the seal into position. Take great care not to damage the seal lips during fitting and ensure that the seal lips face inwards; if a genuine MG Rover seal is being installed, use the seal protector supplied to protect the seal during fitting and remove the protector once the seal is correctly located.
5 Wash off any traces of oil, then refit the crankshaft sprocket as described in Section 8.

Left-hand oil seal

6 Remove the flywheel or driveplate as described in Section 17.
7 Taking care not to mark either the crankshaft or any part of the cylinder block/crankcase, lever the seal evenly out of its housing, using a large flat-bladed screwdriver or similar tool.
8 Clean the seal housing, removing all traces of oil or sealant. Polish off any burrs or raised edges which may have caused the original seal to fail.
9 Apply a 1.5 mm bead of sealant around the edge of the seal, then offer into place – note that the seal should **not** be lubricated. Ease the sealing lip of the seal over the crankshaft shoulder, by hand only, then press the seal evenly into its housing until its outer flange seats evenly on the housing lip **(see illustration)**. If necessary, a soft-faced mallet can be used to tap the seal gently into place. Ideally, a large socket or tube should be used to drive the seal in squarely.
10 Allow the sealant to cure fully before turning the crankshaft or topping-up the oil level.
11 Refit the flywheel/driveplate as described in Section 17.

17 Flywheel/driveplate – removal, inspection and refitting

Flywheel

Removal

1 Remove the clutch assembly as described in Chapter 6.
2 As a precaution, unbolt the crankshaft position sensor from the cylinder block (see Chapter 4A, Section 11) to prevent possible damage as the flywheel is removed.
3 Prevent the flywheel from turning by locking the ring gear teeth **(see illustration 17.9)**. Alternatively, bolt a strap between the flywheel and the cylinder block/crankcase. Make alignment marks between the flywheel and crankshaft using paint or a suitable marker pen.
4 Slacken and remove the retaining bolts and remove the flywheel. **Do not** drop it, as it is very heavy. Discard the bolts – they must be renewed whenever they are disturbed.

Inspection

5 If the flywheel clutch mating surface is deeply scored, cracked or otherwise damaged, then the flywheel must be renewed, unless it is possible to have it surface-ground. Seek the advice of an engine reconditioning specialist.
6 If the ring gear is badly worn or has missing teeth, then it must be renewed. This job is best left to an engine reconditioning specialist. The temperature to which the new ring gear must be heated for installation (350°C – shown by an even light blue colour) is critical and, if not done accurately, the hardness of the teeth will be destroyed.

Refitting

7 Clean the mating surfaces of the flywheel and crankshaft, and remove all traces of locking compound from the crankshaft threaded holes.
8 Fit the flywheel to the crankshaft, engaging it with the crankshaft locating dowel, and fit the new retaining bolts **(see illustration)**.
9 Lock the flywheel using the method employed on dismantling then, working in a diagonal sequence, evenly and progressively tighten the retaining bolts to the specified torque wrench setting **(see illustration)**.
10 Refit the crankshaft position sensor and tighten its retaining bolt to the specified torque (see Chapter 4A, Section 11).
11 Refit the clutch assembly (see Chapter 6).

Driveplate

12 All procedures are essentially the same as described for the flywheel, disregarding references to the clutch. To access the driveplate, remove the automatic transmission as described in Chapter 7B.

18 Engine/transmission mountings – inspection and renewal

Inspection

1 If improved access is required, raise the front of the car and support it securely on

16.9 Offer the new seal over the crankshaft shoulder, and drive it into position

17.8 Position the flywheel over the locating dowel and fit the new retaining bolts

17.9 Lock the flywheel, then tighten the retaining bolts to the specified torque

18.8 Unclip the coolant hose from the upper steady bracket

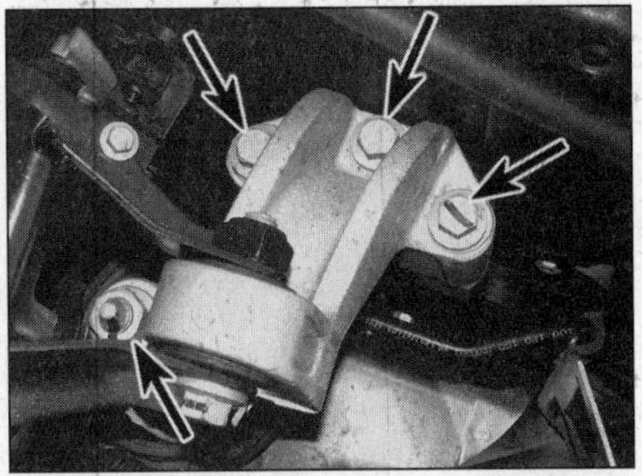

18.10 Engine mounting bracket nut and three bolts

18.12 The hydramount can be unscrewed if required

axle stands (see *Jacking and vehicle support*). Remove the engine undertray, which is secured by a number of quick-release screw fasteners.

2 Check the mounting rubber to see if it is cracked, hardened or separated from the metal at any point. Renew the mounting if any such damage or deterioration is evident.

3 Check that all mounting fasteners are securely tightened. Use a torque wrench to check, if possible.

4 Using a large screwdriver or a pry bar, check for wear in the mountings by carefully levering against it to check for free play. Where this is not possible, enlist the aid of an assistant to move the engine/gearbox unit back-and-forth or from side-to-side while you watch the mountings. While some free play is to be expected even from new components, excessive wear should be obvious. If excessive free play is found, check first that the fasteners are correctly secured, then renew any worn components as described below.

Right-hand mounting

5 Firmly apply the handbrake, then jack up the front of the car and support securely on axle stands (see *Jacking and vehicle support*). Undo the fasteners and remove the engine undertray.

6 Support the weight of the engine/ transmission using a trolley jack with a block of wood placed on its head. Position the jack underneath the engine and raise the engine slightly to remove all load from the mounting.

7 Where applicable, remove the two bolts securing the air conditioning hose to the engine right-hand mounting and bonnet lock platform. Release the hose from the mounting clips in the engine compartment as necessary, and move it clear as far as possible without disconnecting or straining it.

8 Unclip the small coolant hose from the upper steady bracket **(see illustration)**.

9 Remove the three bolts securing the upper steady bracket, and lift it off.

10 To remove the engine mounting bracket, unscrew the nut securing it to the hydramount, then remove the three further bolts securing it to the engine **(see illustration)**.

11 The right-hand mounting bracket on the inner wing is secured by a total of four bolts, and can be removed if required.

12 If required, the hydramount can be unscrewed from the wing, using MG Rover tool LRT-12-169 (which engages in the three slots around the mounting), or using a strap/ chain wrench around the circumference of the mounting **(see illustration)**.

13 Refitting is a reversal of removal. Tighten all fasteners to the specified torque – in the case of the hydramount, torque tightening may be impossible without the special tool, so tighten securely using the same method as for removal.

Left-hand mounting

14 Remove the air cleaner assembly as described in Chapter 4A.

15 For improved access, remove the battery and its tray as described in Chapter 5A.

16 Firmly apply the handbrake, then jack up the front of the car and support securely on axle stands (see *Jacking and vehicle support*). Undo the fasteners and remove the engine undertray.

17 Support the weight of the engine/ transmission using a trolley jack with a block of wood placed on its head. Position the jack underneath the transmission and raise it slightly to remove all load from the mounting.

18 To separate the mounting, unscrew and remove the through-bolt **(see illustration)**.

19 Once the through-bolt is removed, lower the transmission on the jack until the mounting is separated. If required, the two mounting brackets can now be unbolted from the body and transmission – each is secured by four bolts **(see illustrations)**.

20 Refitting is a reversal of removal. Tighten all fasteners to the specified torque.

Lower mounting

21 Firmly apply the handbrake, then jack up the front of the car and support securely on axle stands (see *Jacking and vehicle support*). Remove the engine undertray, which is secured by a number of quick-release screw fasteners.

22 Unscrew the two through-bolts from the lower mounting to release it, and withdraw it from the mounting brackets. Though removing the lower mounting will increase the amount of engine movement, provided they have not been disturbed, the engine will remain safely supported on its right- and left-hand mountings.

23 If required, the lower mounting brackets can be unbolted from the sump and subframe.

24 Refitting is a reversal of removal. Tighten all fasteners to the specified torque.

18.18 Left-hand mounting through-bolt

18.19a Left-hand mounting bracket on the inner wing – bolts arrowed

18.19b Left-hand mounting bracket on transmission

Chapter 2 Part B:
V6 engine in-car repair procedures

Contents

Degrees of difficulty

Easy, suitable for novice with little experience	**Fairly easy,** suitable for beginner with some experience	**Fairly difficult,** suitable for competent DIY mechanic	**Difficult,** suitable for experienced DIY mechanic	**Very difficult,** suitable for expert DIY or professional

Specifications

General

Engine type	Six-cylinders in a vee, twin overhead camshafts per bank, 24-valve
Designation	KV6
Bore	80.0 mm
Stroke:	
2.0 litre engine	66.2 mm
2.5 litre engine	82.8 mm
Capacity:	
2.0 litre engine	1997 cc
2.5 litre engine	2497 cc
Firing order	1-6-5-4-3-2 (No 1 cylinder at primary timing belt end, front bank)
Direction of crankshaft rotation	Clockwise (seen from right-hand side of car)
Compression ratio	10.25:1
Compression pressure (typical)	10.0 bar minimum
Compression pressure difference between cylinders (typical)	1.5 bar maximum

Camshafts

General	Direct-acting on hydraulic tappets, bearings line-bored in cylinder head
Drive	Toothed primary belt from crankshaft to inlet camshafts, automatic tensioner; two secondary toothed belts drive exhaust camshafts from rear of inlet camshafts
Bearing journal running clearance:	
Standard	0.025 to 0.059 mm
Service limit	0.100 mm
Camshaft endfloat:	
Standard	0.060 to 0.190 mm
Service limit	0.300 mm
Hydraulic tappet outside diameter	32.959 to 32.975 mm

Lubrication system

Oil pressure	1.0 bar at idle, 3.0 bar at 3000 rpm (hot)
Relief valve opening pressure	4.1 bar
Low oil pressure warning light comes on	0.3 to 0.5 bar
Oil pump clearances:	
Outer rotor-to-body clearance	0.13 to 0.23 mm
Rotor endfloat	0.04 to 0.09 mm

Torque wrench settings

	Nm	lbf ft
Auxiliary drivebelt top cover	25	18
Big-end bearing cap bolts*:		
Stage 1	20	15
Stage 2	Angle-tighten a further 70°	
Camshaft bearing carrier bolts	10	7
Camshaft cover bolts	9	7
Camshaft sprocket bolts*:		
Stage 1	27	20
Stage 2	Angle-tighten a further 90°	
Crankshaft flywheel end oil seal bolts*	9	7
Crankshaft pulley bolt	160	118
Cylinder head bolts:		
Stage 1	25	18
Stage 2 (see text)	25	18
Stage 3	Angle-tighten a further 90°	
Stage 4	Angle-tighten a further 90°	
Dipstick tube mounting bolt	9	7
Driveplate bolts	100	74
Engine front plate (primary timing belt end):		
Top bolts (x3)	45	33
Lower (end) bolts:		
M10 studs (x2)	45	33
M12 bolts (x5)	85	63
Engine/transmission mountings:		
Left-hand mounting through-bolt	100	74
Left-hand mounting to body	85	63
Left-hand mounting to transmission	85	63
Lower mounting bolts	100	74
Right-hand hydramount to body	85	63
Right-hand lower mounting bracket to engine plate	45	33
Right-hand mounting steady (upper) bracket bolts	85	63
Right-hand mounting to body	85	63
Right-hand mounting upper cross-brace	25	18
Right-hand upper mounting bracket bolts	100	74
Right-hand upper mounting bracket-to-hydramount nut	85	63
Exhaust front support bracket bolts	25	18
Exhaust manifold-to-downpipe flange nuts	75	55
Flywheel bolts	80	59
Idler pulley bolt	45	33
Inlet manifold	25	18
Lower crankcase-to-block bolts:		
M5 bolts	9	7
M8 bolts (and nut, where fitted)	35	26
Main bearing ladder-to-cylinder block bolts*:		
Stage 1	20	15
Stage 2	Angle-tighten a further 90°	
Oil cooler:		
Cooler-to-sump bolts	45	33
Pipe unions	26	19
Oil pick-up pipe/strainer	25	18
Oil pressure switch	14	10
Oil pump bolts*	25	18
Oil pump pressure relief plug	25	18
Sump bolts	35	26
Timing belt backplate bolts**	9	7
Timing belt tensioner mounting bolts**	25	18
Timing belt tensioner pulley bolt	45	33

** Use new bolts*

*** Use locking compound*

1 General information and precautions

How to use this Chapter

This Part of the Chapter describes those repair procedures that can reasonably be carried out on the engine whilst it remains in the car. If the engine has been removed from the car and is being dismantled as described in Part D of this Chapter, any preliminary dismantling procedures can be ignored.

Note that whilst it may be possible physically to overhaul items such as the piston/connecting rod assemblies with the engine in the car, such tasks are not usually carried out as separate operations and usually require the execution of several additional procedures (not to mention the cleaning of components and of oilways). For this reason, all such tasks are classed as major overhaul procedures and are described in Part D of this Chapter.

Engine description

The KV6 engine is derived from the long-running K-Series engine family, and is a V6 unit mounted transversely at the front of the car with the clutch and transmission on the left-hand end. The engine has double overhead camshafts on each bank of cylinders, and is a 24-valve design.

The main structure of the engine consists of several major castings – the cylinder heads, the cylinder block/crankcase, the crankshaft main bearing ladder, lower crankcase and sump. All the castings are of aluminium alloy, with the exception of the main bearing ladder, which is made of a special aero-industry-standard alloy.

Unlike the four-cylinder K-series engines, the KV6 does not have the extra-long cylinder head bolts which extend into the main bearing ladder. However, the more-conventional head bolts still extend into the block by 70 mm, for increased structural stiffness. The main bearing ladder is secured to the base of the block by sixteen bolts, with a cast alloy lower crankcase section below that for extra stiffness, and a cast sump 'pan' fitted below that.

The crankshaft runs in four main bearings. Thrustwashers are fitted to the rear main bearing to control crankshaft endfloat.

The connecting rods rotate on horizontally-split bearing shells at their big-ends. The pistons are attached to the connecting rods by gudgeon pins which are an interference fit in the connecting rod small-end eyes. The aluminium alloy pistons are fitted with three piston rings, comprising two compression rings and an oil control ring.

The cylinder bores are formed by renewable liners which locate in the cylinder block/crankcase at their top ends. The liners are known as 'damp' liners. To prevent the coolant escaping into the sump, the base of each liner is sealed with sealing compound.

The inlet and exhaust valves are each closed by coil springs and operate in guides pressed into the cylinder heads. The valve seat inserts are pressed into the cylinder head and can be renewed separately if worn.

Both inlet camshafts are driven by a single primary toothed timing belt, and the exhaust camshafts are each driven by a smaller secondary toothed belt from a sprocket on the rear of each inlet camshaft. The camshafts operate the valves via self-adjusting hydraulic tappets. The camshafts rotate in bearings which are line-bored directly into the cylinder head and the (bolted-on) bearing carrier. This means that the bearing carriers and cylinder heads are matched, and cannot be renewed independently. The water pump is driven by the main timing belt.

Lubrication is by means of an eccentric-rotor type pump driven directly from the right-hand (primary timing belt end) of the crankshaft. The pump draws oil through a strainer located in the sump. It then forces it through an externally-mounted full-flow cartridge-type oil filter into galleries in the oil rail and the cylinder block/crankcase, from where it is distributed to the crankshaft (main bearings) and camshafts. The big-end bearings are supplied with oil via internal drillings in the crankshaft, while the camshaft bearings and the tappets receive a pressurised supply via drillings in the cylinder heads. The camshaft lobes and valves are lubricated by oil splash, as are all other engine components. On models with air conditioning, a coolant-fed oil cooler is mounted externally on the sump, and oil circulates through two pipes to and from the oil filter housing.

Cylinder numbering

The KV6 engine is a transversely-mounted V6 unit. It will be necessary throughout this and other Chapters in the manual to refer to the cylinder head and piston positions, and this is less easy than an in-line engine. For the purposes of this manual, and hopefully for clarity, we have adopted the convention that since the 'left-hand' bank of three cylinders is the one at the front of the car, it will be called the 'front bank'. Similarly, the 'right-hand' bank, which is at the rear in the car, is the 'rear bank'.

There are timing belts at both ends of the engine, but we will maintain the convention that the 'timing belt end' refers to the KV6's primary timing belt end (opposite the transmission). When referring to the KV6's three timing belts, the 'primary' or 'main' belt is the one which drives the inlet camshafts from the crankshaft; the 'secondary' belts are the two smaller belts at the transmission end of the engine.

Using our adopted convention, No 1 cylinder is at the timing belt end on the front bank, with cylinders 3 and 5. The rear bank cylinders are numbered 2, 4 and 6 from the timing belt end.

Operations with engine in car

The following work can be carried out with the engine in the car:

a) Compression pressure – testing.
b) Camshaft covers – removal and refitting.
c) Crankshaft pulley – removal and refitting.
d) Timing belt covers – removal and refitting.
e) Timing belts – removal, refitting and adjustment.
f) Timing belt tensioner and sprockets – removal and refitting.
g) Camshaft oil seals – renewal.
h) Camshafts and tappets – removal, inspection and refitting.
i) Cylinder heads – removal and refitting.
j) Cylinder heads and pistons – decarbonising.
k) Sump – removal and refitting.
l) Oil pump – removal, overhaul and refitting.
m) Crankshaft oil seals – renewal.
n) Engine/transmission mountings – inspection and renewal.
o) Flywheel – removal, inspection and refitting.

2 Compression test – description and interpretation

Note: *A suitable compression tester will be required for this test.*

1 When engine performance is down, or if misfiring occurs which cannot be attributed to the ignition or fuel systems, a compression test can provide diagnostic clues as to the engine's condition. If the test is performed regularly it can give warning of trouble before any other symptoms become apparent.

2 The engine must be fully warmed-up to normal operating temperature, the battery must be fully-charged and the spark plugs must be removed (see Chapter 1A). The aid of an assistant will be required.

3 The fuel pump must be disabled by removing the fuel pump relay from the fusebox.

4 Fit a compression tester to the No 1 cylinder spark plug hole. The type of tester which screws into the plug thread is preferred.

5 Have the assistant hold the throttle wide open and crank the engine on the starter motor. After one or two revolutions, the compression pressure should build-up to a maximum figure and then stabilise. Record the highest reading obtained.

6 Repeat the test on the remaining cylinders, recording the pressure in each.

7 All cylinders should produce very similar pressures; a difference of more than 2 bars between any two cylinders indicates a fault. Note that the compression should build-up quickly in a healthy engine; low compression on the first stroke, followed by gradually-increasing pressure on successive strokes, indicates worn piston rings. A low compression reading on the first stroke, which does not build-up during successive

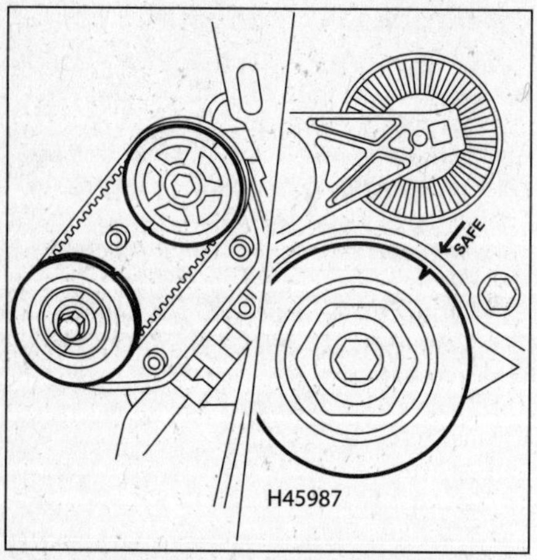

3.7 Crankshaft pulley notch aligned with SAFE arrow, and camshaft rear sprockets

strokes, indicates leaking valves or a blown head gasket (a cracked head could also be the cause). Deposits on the undersides of the valve heads can also cause low compression.

8 Although MG Rover do not specify exact compression pressures, as a guide, any cylinder pressure of below 10 bar can be considered as less than healthy. Refer to an engine specialist if in doubt as to whether a particular pressure reading is acceptable.

9 If the pressure in any cylinder is significantly low, carry out the following test to isolate the cause. Introduce a teaspoonful of clean oil into that cylinder through its spark plug hole and repeat the test.

10 If the addition of oil temporarily improves the compression pressure, this indicates that bore or piston wear is responsible for the pressure loss. No improvement suggests that leaking or burnt valves, or a blown head gasket, may be to blame.

11 A low reading from two adjacent cylinders is almost certainly due to the head gasket having blown between them and the presence of coolant in the engine oil will confirm this.

12 If one cylinder is about 20 percent lower than the others and the engine has a slightly rough idle, a worn camshaft lobe could be the cause.

13 If the compression reading is unusually high, the combustion chambers are probably coated with carbon deposits. If this is the case, the cylinder head should be removed and decarbonised.

14 On completion of the test, refit the spark plugs (see Chapter 1A), reconnect the ignition coil(s) and refit the fuel pump relay.

3 Engine assembly/valve timing marks – general information and usage

1 The crankshaft pulley and camshaft rear sprockets have timing marks which align when the crankshaft is positioned so there is no danger of the valves contacting the pistons when refitting the cylinder heads/timing belts.

2 Disconnect the battery negative terminal (see *Disconnecting the battery*). If necessary, remove all the spark plugs as described in Chapter 1A to enable the engine to be easily turned over.

3 To gain access to the camshaft sprocket timing marks, remove the secondary timing belt covers, as described in Section 6.

4 Loosen the right-hand front wheel bolts. Firmly apply the handbrake, then jack up the front of the car and support it securely on axle stands (see *Jacking and vehicle support*). Remove the right-hand front wheel to improve access to the crankshaft pulley.

5 Remove the engine undertray, which is secured by a number of quick-release screw fasteners.

6 Remove the right-hand wheel arch liner as described in Chapter 11, Section 22.

7 Using a socket and extension bar on the crankshaft pulley bolt, turn the crankshaft until the notch in the pulley is aligned with the SAFE arrow. At this point, the notches in both pairs of camshaft rear sprockets should be aligned facing each other **(see illustration)**.

8 With the engine in this position, it should also be possible to lock the flywheel (driveplate on automatic transmission models) using a timing pin. The pin should be inserted through a hole in the lower crankcase flange, and it engages in a hole in the flywheel or driveplate – the MG Rover tool is 18G 1746A, but an alternative can be made from a 10 mm bolt. The critical sizes are as follows:

1) *7.4 mm diameter for the first 12 mm length (to fit inside the flywheel or driveplate hole).*
2) *9.7 mm diameter for the next 36 mm length (to fit the hole in the crankcase lower flange).*

9 Insert the tool in the relevant hole – use the inner hole to lock the driveplate, or the hole which is further out to lock the flywheel. If it will not fit immediately, turn the engine very slightly forwards or backwards from the SAFE position until it engages the flywheel/driveplate hole **(see illustrations)**.

10 If the pin is not used, a degree of safety can be achieved (on manual transmission models) by applying the handbrake firmly and engaging a gear.

11 With the crankshaft pulley and camshaft sprocket timing marks positioned as described, the engine can safely be dismantled.

3.9a Insert the timing pin . . .

3.9b . . . and ensure it engages fully

4 Camshaft covers – removal and refitting

Front bank

Removal

1 Remove the engine top cover, which is secured by two bolts. Recover the washers and rubber grommets from the bolt holes, and store them for refitting **(see illustrations)**.

2 Depress the locking collars and release the

4.1a Remove the two mounting bolts . . .

4.1b . . . and lift off the engine top cover

4.2 Removing one of the two breather hoses

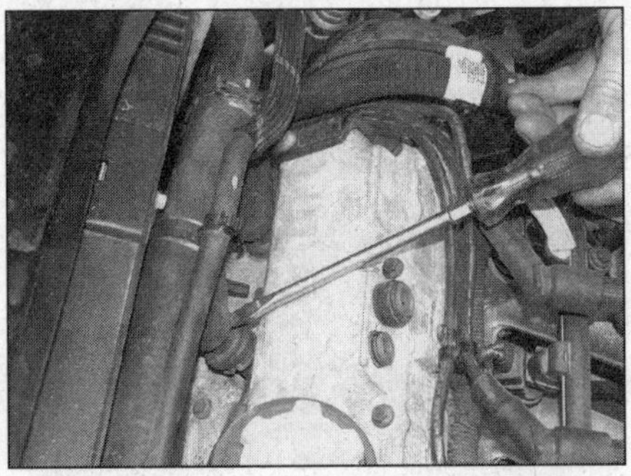

4.3a Carefully prise the HT lead end fittings upwards off the plugs. . .

4.3b . . . and unclip them from the camshaft cover

two breather hoses from the cover, noting their fitted positions **(see illustration)**.

3 Check to see whether the spark plug HT leads are marked for position. Confusion when refitting is unlikely, as they are of different lengths, but if required, label the leads 1, 3 and 5 from the timing belt end. Disconnect the leads from their plugs, and unclip them from the camshaft cover **(see illustrations)**.

4 Unbolt the HT lead guide clip from the camshaft cover **(see illustration)**.

5 At the transmission end of the cover, disconnect the camshaft position sensor wiring plug, and release the plug from the mounting bracket. Unscrew the bolt securing the bracket, and remove it **(see illustrations)**.

6 To make room for the camshaft cover to be removed, remove the single bolt securing the radiator hose support bracket **(see illustration)**. Unhook the top hose. The coolant elbow at the top of the radiator hinders access to some of the cover bolts, but removing this would mean draining the coolant.

7 Progressively loosen and remove the fourteen bolts securing the camshaft cover, and lift it off with its gasket **(see illustrations)**. Discard the gasket – a new one should be used when refitting.

Refitting

8 Clean the mating surfaces of the cover and camshaft carrier. Also clean inside the cover – if necessary, wash the oil separator mesh in a suitable solvent and allow to dry **(see illustration)**.

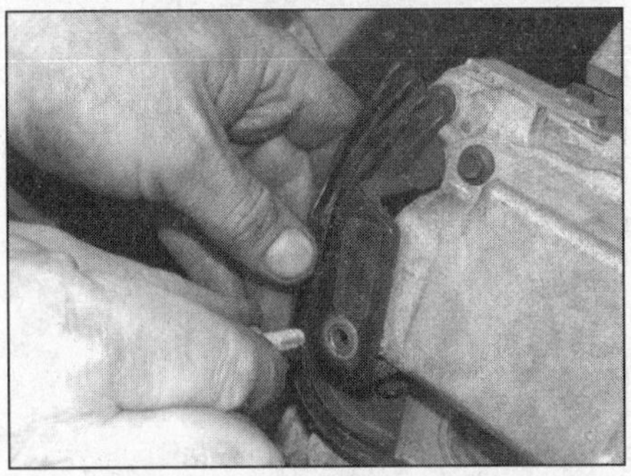

4.4 Unbolt and remove the HT lead guide clip

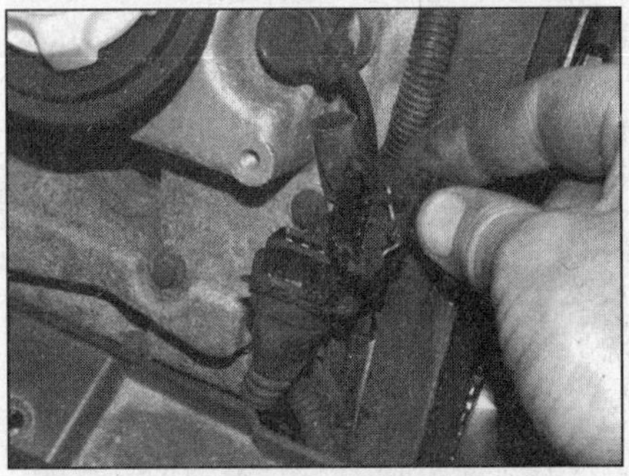

4.5a Disconnect the camshaft position sensor wiring plug . . .

4.5b . . . then unbolt and remove the wiring plug bracket

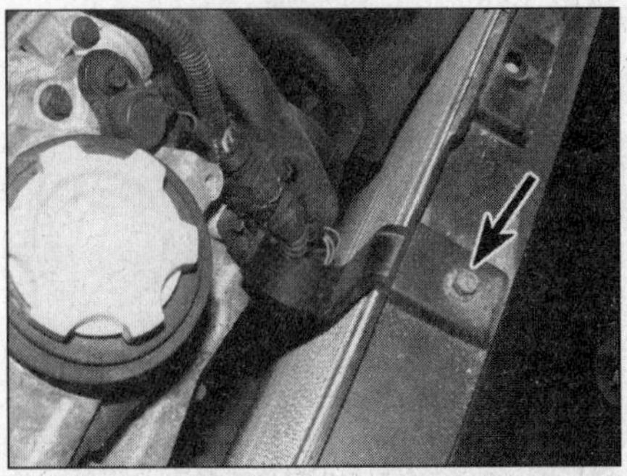

4.6 Remove the radiator top hose support bracket

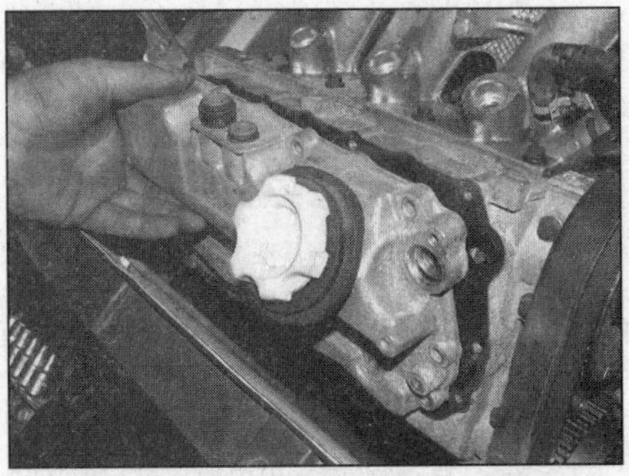

4.7a Unbolt and lift off the camshaft cover . . .

4.7b . . . and recover the metal gasket

4.8 Ensure that the oil separator meshes are clean

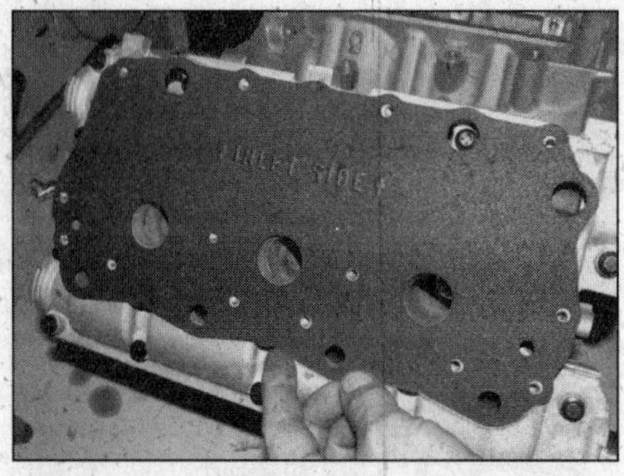
4.9 Observe the direction-of-fitting marks on the new gasket

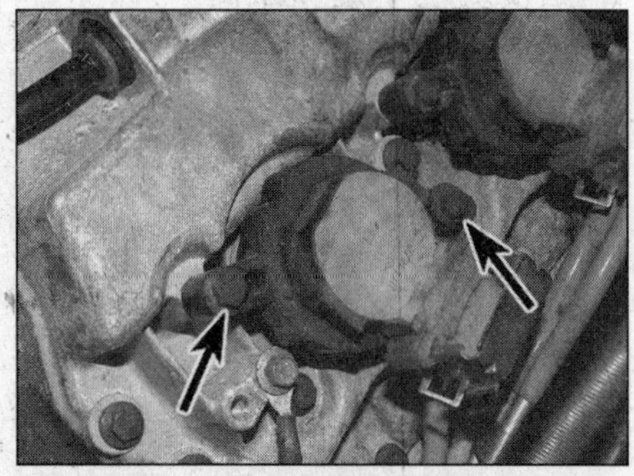
4.14a Unscrew the two bolts from each coil . . .

9 Fit the new gasket, observing any direction-of-fitting markings. The fitted position should be evident, but any arrows should point towards the inlet manifold **(see illustration)**.

10 Refit the cover, and secure with the fourteen bolts, which should be tightened progressively in sequence to the specified torque **(see illustration)**.

11 Further refitting is a reversal of removal. Refit the breather hoses by pushing them firmly home.

Rear bank

Removal

12 Remove the upper section of the inlet manifold as described in Chapter 4B.

13 Peel up the rubber weatherseal at the rear of the engine compartment. Remove the four nuts securing the central soundproofing panel, then lift it off the wiring harness which passes through the bulkhead. Remove the two bolts and take out the access panel behind the soundproofing (refer to Chapter 1A, Section 22).

4.15 Unscrew the bolt securing the earth lead

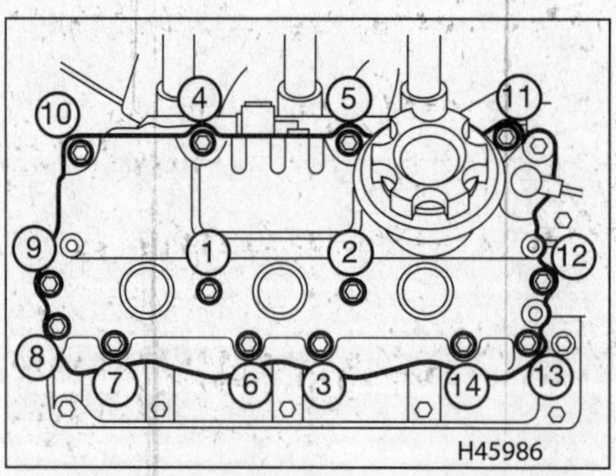

4.10 Camshaft front cover bolt tightening sequence

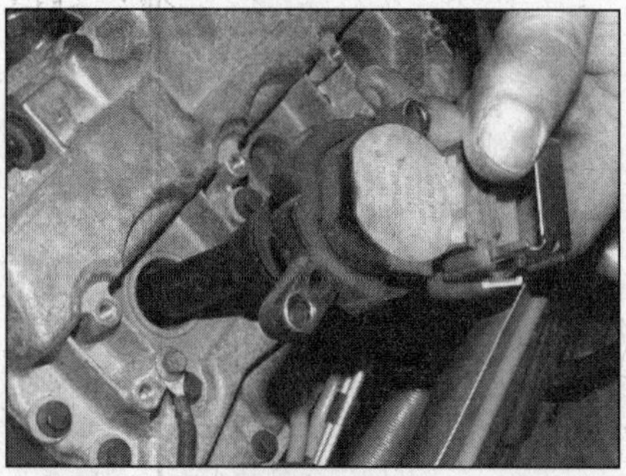
4.14b . . . then lift them off the plugs

14 Release the locking clips and disconnect the wiring plugs from the three ignition coils. Though not essential, it may be wise to mark the coils for position before removing them. Remove the two bolts securing each coil, and lift them off their respective spark plugs **(see illustrations)**.

15 Remove the bolt from the earth lead, and move the lead clear **(see illustration)**.

16 Depress the locking collar and release the breather hose from the cover **(see illustration)**.

17 Release the coil wiring harness from the two clips on the inlet manifold mounting bracket, and move the wiring clear.

18 Progressively loosen and remove the fourteen bolts securing the camshaft cover, and lift it off with its gasket. Discard the gasket – a new one should be used when refitting.

4.16 Disconnect the breather hose

Refitting

19 Clean the mating surfaces of the cover and camshaft carrier. Also clean inside the cover – if necessary, wash the oil separator mesh in a suitable solvent and allow to dry.

20 Fit the new gasket, observing any direction-of-fitting markings. The fitted position should be evident, but any arrows should point towards the inlet manifold.

21 Refit the cover, and secure with the fourteen bolts, which should be tightened progressively in sequence to the specified torque **(see illustration)**.

22 Further refitting is a reversal of removal. Refit the breather hose by pushing it firmly home.

5 Crankshaft pulley – removal and refitting

Removal

1 Loosen the right-hand front wheel bolts. Firmly apply the handbrake, then jack up the front of the car and support it securely on axle stands (see *Jacking and vehicle support*). To improve access, remove the right-hand front wheel.

2 Remove the engine undertray, which is secured by a number of quick-release screw fasteners.

3 Remove the right-hand wheel arch liner as described in Chapter 11, Section 22.

4 If further dismantling is to be carried out, align the engine assembly/valve timing marks as described in Section 3. However, the timing pin or bolt should be removed before loosening the crankshaft pulley bolt, as there is a risk of it shearing off otherwise. Reset the timing marks and refit the pin once the pulley has been removed, if necessary.

5 Remove the auxiliary drivebelt as described in Chapter 1A.

6 Slacken the crankshaft pulley retaining bolt. To prevent crankshaft rotation, have an assistant select top gear (manual transmission) and apply the brakes firmly. If the engine is

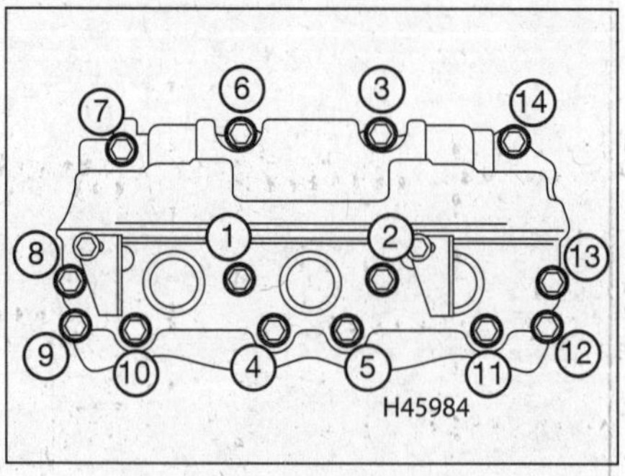

4.21 Camshaft rear cover bolt tightening sequence

5.7 Removing the crankshaft pulley

6.7 Loosen the power steering pump pulley bolts with the belt fitted

6.9 Removing the power steering pump pulley

removed from the car, it will be necessary to lock the flywheel/driveplate (see Section 19).

7 Unscrew the pulley bolt and washer, noting which way around the washer is fitted, then remove the pulley from the crankshaft **(see illustration)**.

Refitting

8 Fit the pulley to the crankshaft, aligning the notch in the pulley with the locating lug on the sprocket, then refit the retaining bolt and washer. Make sure that the tapered face of the washer is facing away from the pulley.

9 Lock the crankshaft using the method used on removal, and tighten the pulley retaining bolt to the specified torque setting.

10 Refit and tension the auxiliary drivebelt as described in Chapter 1A.

11 The remainder of refitting is a reversal of removal. Tighten the wheel bolts to the specified torque.

6 Timing belt covers – removal and refitting

1 If the timing belts are to be removed, then if not already done, set the engine to the safe position as described in Section 3.

Primary belt

Front bank upper cover

2 Remove the engine top cover, which is secured by two bolts. Recover the washers and rubber grommets from the bolt holes, and store them for refitting.

3 Loosen the right-hand front wheel bolts. Firmly apply the handbrake, then jack up the front of the car and support it securely on axle stands (see *Jacking and vehicle support*). To improve access, remove the right-hand front wheel.

4 Remove the engine undertray, which is secured by a number of quick-release screw fasteners.

5 Remove the right-hand wheel arch liner as described in Chapter 11, Section 22.

6 If both front covers are to be removed, unbolt the engine right-hand mounting as described in Section 20.

6.10 Removing the auxiliary drivebelt idler pulley

7 Loosen the three Torx bolts securing the power steering pump pulley **(see illustration)**. Do not remove them at this stage – loosening is done now to make removing the pulley easier once the drivebelt has been removed.

8 Using the 3/8-inch square drive from a suitable socket handle in the fitting provided on the tensioner, lift the tensioner and release the drivebelt, first from the alternator and then from the remaining pulleys. If the belt is to be re-used, note any direction-of-rotation arrows.

9 Remove the three previously-loosened bolts, and take off the power steering pump pulley **(see illustration)**.

10 Unscrew the single centre Torx bolt, and take off the auxiliary drivebelt idler pulley **(see illustration)**.

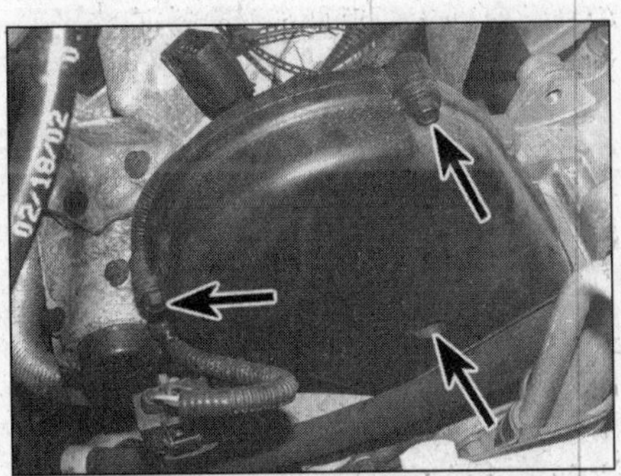

6.14a Rear bank upper cover bolts

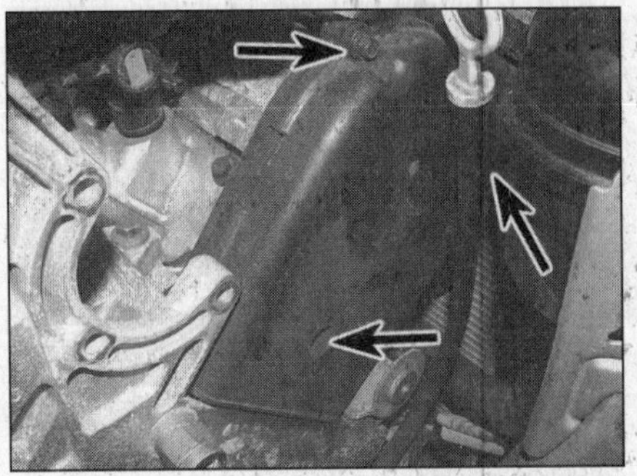

6.11 Front bank upper cover bolts

11 Remove the three bolts securing the belt cover, and lift it off **(see illustration)**.

12 Refitting is a reversal of removal. Tighten all fasteners to the specified torque, where given (fit the power steering pump pulley bolts hand-tight initially, and tighten fully once the auxiliary drivebelt has been refitted).

Rear bank upper cover

13 Remove the engine right-hand mounting as described in Section 20.

14 Remove the three bolts securing the belt cover, and lift it off **(see illustrations)**.

15 Refitting is a reversal of removal. Tighten all fasteners to the specified torque, where given.

Lower cover

16 Remove the crankshaft pulley as described in Section 5.

6.14b Removing the rear bank upper cover

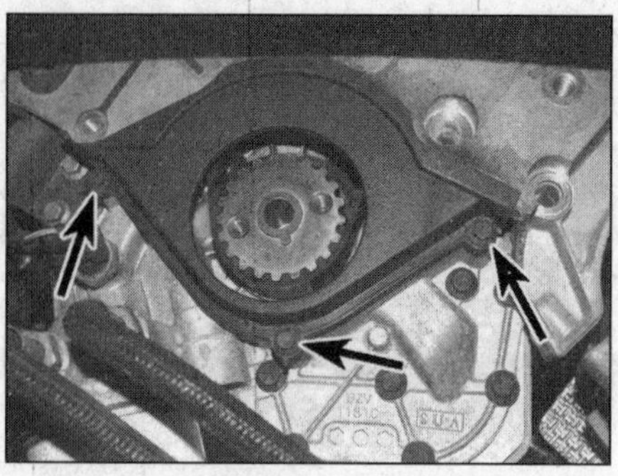

6.17a Remove the three bolts . . .

6.17b . . . and take off the lower cover

6.24 Removing the secondary belt rear bank cover

17 Remove the three bolts securing the belt cover, and lift it off **(see illustrations)**.

18 Refitting is a reversal of removal. Tighten all fasteners to the specified torque, where given.

Secondary belts

Front bank cover

19 Remove the air cleaner as described in Chapter 4B.

20 Remove the three bolts securing the belt cover, and lift it off.

21 Refitting is a reversal of removal.

Rear bank cover

22 Remove the battery and its tray as described in Chapter 5A.

23 Remove the inlet manifold upper section as described in Chapter 4B.

7.6a Remove the three mounting bolts . . .

7.7 Removing the auxiliary belt tensioner

24 Remove the three bolts securing the belt cover, and lift it out **(see illustration)**.

25 Refitting is a reversal of removal.

7 Timing belts – removal and refitting

Primary belt

Note: *To fit the new belt as the manufacturers say requires the use of special camshaft locking tools which are difficult to fabricate. We have provided two procedures which should both prove satisfactory – one using the special tools and one which does not (though some home-made tools are still needed). Clearly, if the special tools can be obtained, they should be used. The primary belt's inlet sprockets are not keyed to the camshafts, so if the special tools are not available, the sprocket bolts should not be disturbed if possible. Proceed according to the relevant headings which follow.*

7.6b . . . and lift the pump off the engine front plate

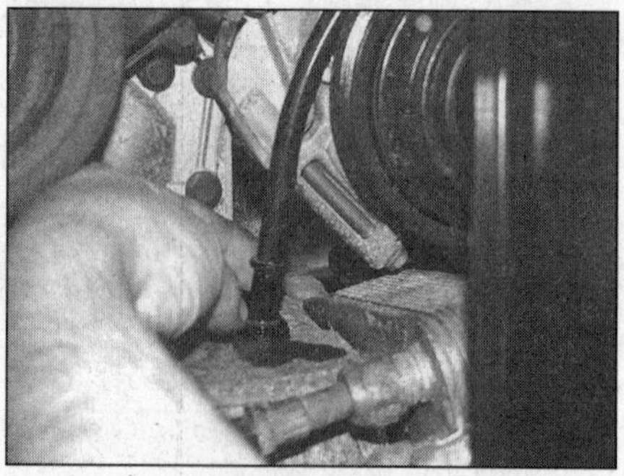

7.8 Press the collar and pull out the dipstick tube

1 Disconnect the battery negative lead (see *Disconnecting the battery*).

2 Align the engine assembly/valve timing marks as described in Section 3.

3 Remove the belt covers as described in Section 6.

4 Remove the auxiliary drivebelt as described in Chapter 1A – this will include removal of the engine right-hand mounting, which is also necessary for other parts of this procedure. **Note:** *If the engine is to be supported using the rear lifting eye, note that the eye will have to be removed when the engine front plate is removed later on.*

5 Remove the alternator as described in Chapter 5A.

6 Remove the three bolts securing the power steering pump, and move it away from its mounting bracket (which is the engine front plate), without disconnecting the hoses **(see illustrations)**.

7 Remove the auxiliary drivebelt tensioner, which is secured by two bolts **(see illustration)**.

8 Drain the engine oil as described in Chapter 1A. Remove the single bolt securing the oil dipstick tube to the block, then depress the locking collar at the base and pull the tube out of the sump (if the oil is not drained, oil spillage will result when the tube is removed) **(see illustration)**.

9 On models with air conditioning, using the information in Section 17, unbolt the oil cooler from the front of the sump – it should not be necessary to disconnect any hoses. This is necessary in order to access the air conditioning compressor mounting bolts later on.

10 On models with air conditioning, remove the three mounting bolts, then move the compressor to one side without disconnecting the hoses **(see illustrations)**. Recover the compressor heat shield, noting how it is fitted. If the oil cooler is now loosely bolted back in position, the compressor will rest on it so that the hoses are not under strain.

11 Remove the three top bolts from the engine front plate (which also serves as the

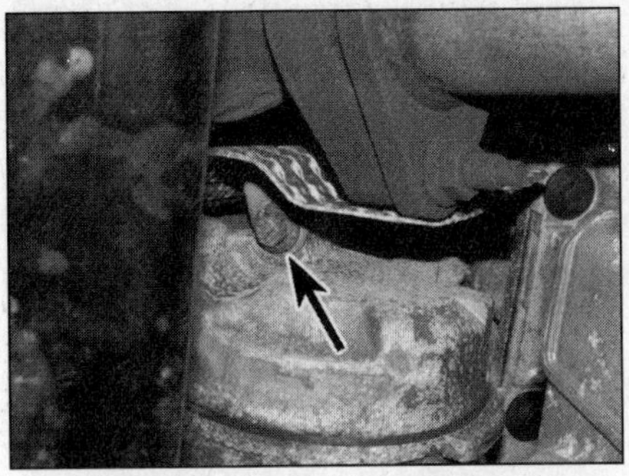

7.10a One of the three compressor mounting bolts

alternator mounting bracket), noting that the rearmost bolt is also used to secure the engine rear lifting eye. Noting their locations, unscrew the two mounting boss/bolts and five bolts from the end face of the front plate. Release and remove the plate **(see illustrations)**.

12 Unclip the rubber rear cover from the timing belt tensioner (where fitted). Loosen the two tensioner mounting bolts (**do not** loosen the Allen screw securing the tensioner pulley) **(see illustrations)**. The tensioner mounting bolts will be very stiff, due to the use of threadlock – ensure a good-quality, close-fitting socket is used.

13 Release the belt tension by turning the tensioner pulley clockwise using a suitable Allen key in the hole provided. Holding the tensioner pulley in the released position, remove the two mounting bolts and take off the tensioner **(see illustration)**. **Note:** *MG Rover recommend that the tensioner should be renewed every 100 000 miles – timing belt 'kits' are usually available, which include the belts and tensioner.*

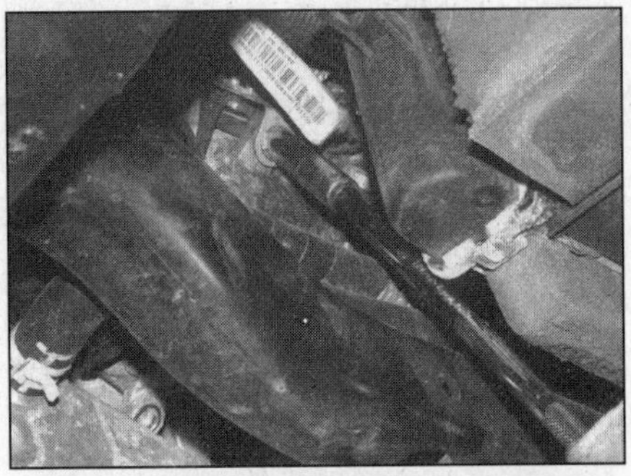

7.10b A long extension will be needed for this compressor bolt

7.11b . . . the two boss/bolts . . .

14 Make sure the timing marks are aligned as described in Section 3, and (if removed) refit the timing pin or bolt. Before removing the belt, paint accurate camshaft sprocket alignment marks between the inlet camshaft sprockets and the timing belt backplates, to make refitting easier – this is particularly important if the special camshaft locking tools are not available **(see illustrations)**.

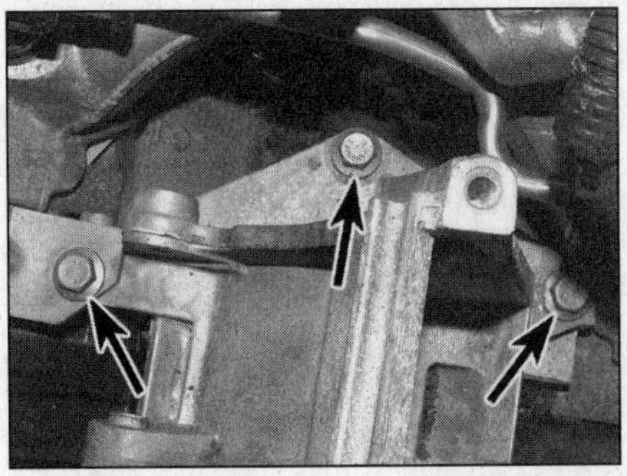

7.11a Unscrew the three top bolts . . .

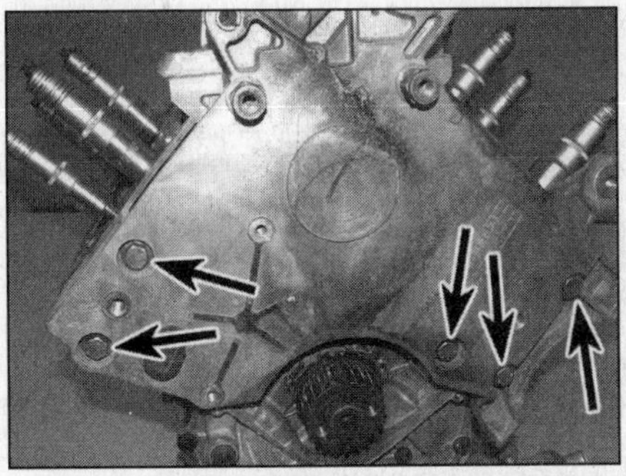

7.11c . . . five lower bolts (arrowed) . . .

7.11d . . . and remove the engine front plate

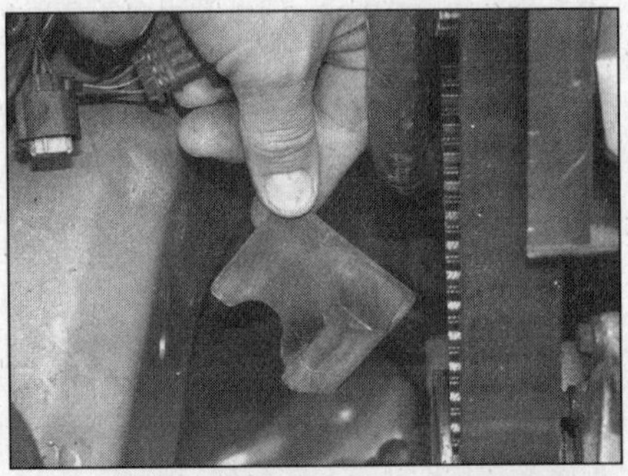

7.12a Remove the tensioner's rubber rear cover

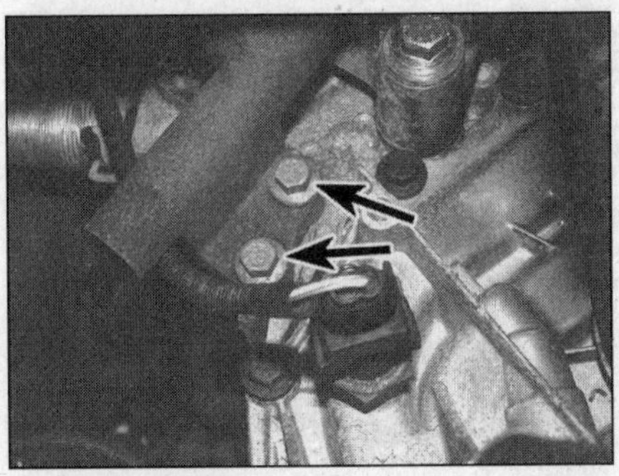

7.12b Loosen the tensioner body bolts

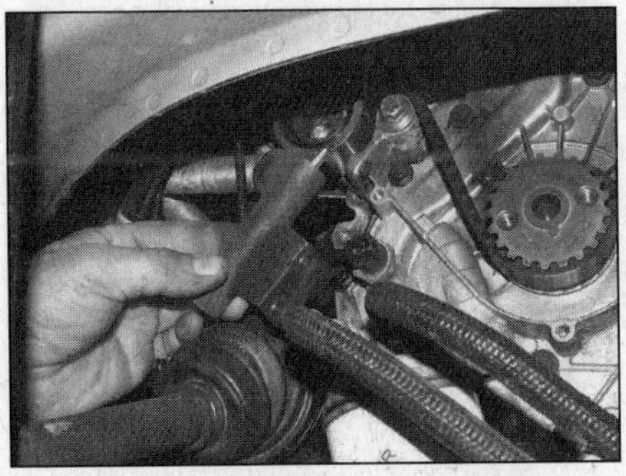

7.13 Removing the tensioner

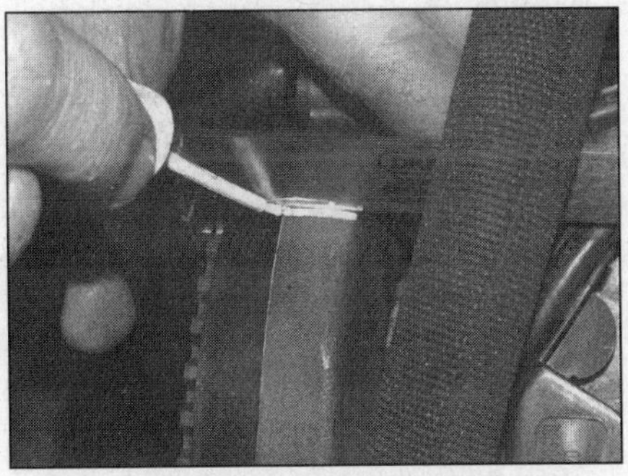

7.14a Use a straight-edge across the backplate and sprocket . . .

7.14b . . . and make alignment marks between the two

7.15a Note the routing of the belt before removal

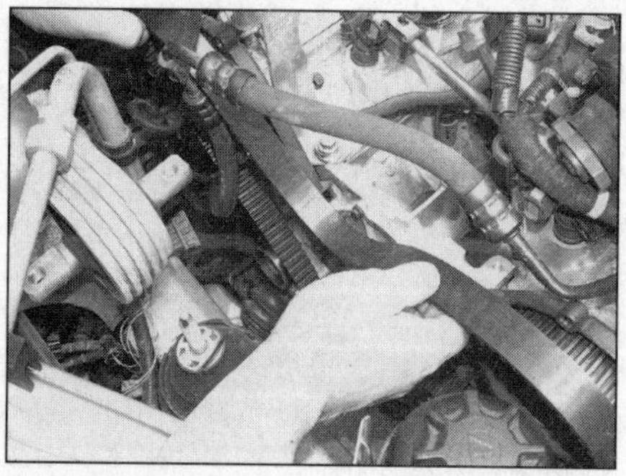

7.15b Removing the primary timing belt

7.15c The inlet camshaft sprockets will move towards each other

15 If the timing belt is to be refitted, mark its direction of rotation. Ease the belt off the sprockets, noting its fitted routing. **Do not** rotate the crankshaft or camshafts until the timing belt has been refitted. The sprockets will move slightly, due to the pressure of the valve springs, as the belt is removed – note how they move, as thls movement will have to be reversed when the new belt is fitted **(see illustrations)**.

16 Due to the low cost of a new belt, it is recommended that the belt be renewed as a matter of course, regardless of its apparent condition. MG Rover state that a belt which has covered more than 45 000 miles should **never** be refitted. If signs of oil contamination are found, trace the source of the oil leak and rectify it, then wash down the engine timing belt area and all related components to remove all traces of oil.

7.19 Fit the camshaft sprocket and new bolt

With special tools

17 Slacken and remove each inlet camshaft sprocket retaining bolt. If the special tools are fitted as described in paragraphs 21 and 22, they can be used to hold the sprocket while the bolt is loosened – otherwise, use a home-made forked tool like the one depicted elsewhere in this procedure. Discard the sprocket bolts – new ones should be used when refitting.

18 Remove the sprockets and their centres/hubs, noting how the centres are fitted. Clean all removed components thoroughly.

19 Fit the centres/hubs to the sprockets, then fit the sprockets to the camshafts, using new bolts **(see illustration)**. Tighten the bolts by hand so that the sprockets are still just able to turn on their own.

20 Fit the new belt loosely into place around the sprockets **(see illustration)**. It does not have to be engaged with the sprockets in any way yet, but must be in place before the special tools are fitted.

7.20 Fit the timing belt loosely around the sprockets to begin with

21 Tap off the end cap seals from both exhaust camshafts (next to the inlet camshaft sprockets, at the primary timing belt end) **(see illustration)**. This is to allow the fitting of the special tools. Note that new caps should be used when refitting – however, if care is taken in their removal, this may not be necessary.

22 Fit the relevant special tools to the end of each exhaust camshaft, and engage the locating pegs in the inlet camshaft sprocket centres **(see illustration)**.

2.0 litre engine – Tool number 12-187.
2.5 litre engine – Tool number 18G 1747-2.
190 models – Tool number 12R208.

23 Turn the inlet camshaft sprockets as far clockwise (viewed from the primary belt end of the engine) as they will go **(see illustration)**.

24 Fit the timing belt to the crankshaft sprocket, then round the front idler pulley and onto the front sprocket. Turn the sprocket as little as possible anti-clockwise to make the belt fit. Feed the belt under the water pump pulley, then onto the rear sprocket, keeping the belt as taut as possible, and again not turning the sprocket more than necessary from the fully-clockwise position.

25 MG Rover recommend fitting a wedge of some kind to stop the timing belt coming off the crankshaft sprocket as the tensioner is fitted. Alternatively, have an assistant on hand to hold the belt in place.

26 Using a vice with protected jaws, carefully compress the timing belt tensioner plunger

7.21 Remove the exhaust camshaft end caps

7.22 Engage the special tool into the exhaust camshaft and inlet sprocket

7.23 Turn the sprockets fully clockwise

7.26a Mount the tensioner in a vice with protected jaws . . .

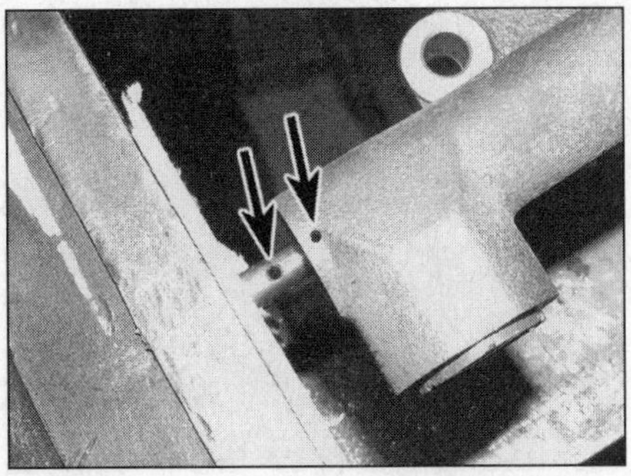

7.26b . . . and slowly compress the plunger until the two holes are in line . . .

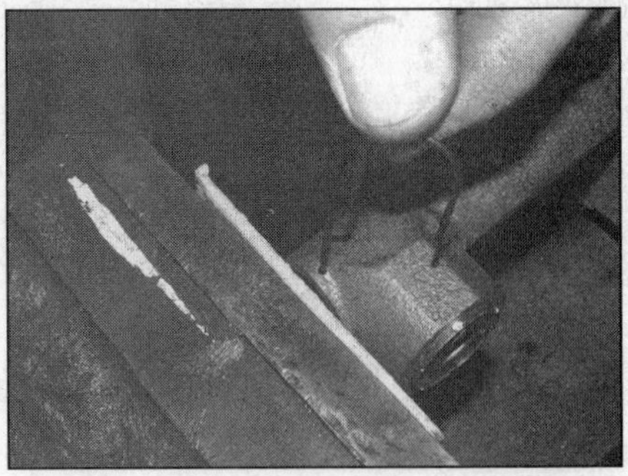

7.26c . . . then insert a pin through the body to lock the plunger

until a pin (approximately 1.5 mm diameter) can be inserted through the tensioner body and plunger to lock it **(see illustrations)**.

27 Clean the two tensioner mounting bolts, then apply a little threadlocking compound (such as Loctite 242) to their threads.

28 Turn the tensioner pulley clockwise using an Allen key (or have an assistant turn it by hand), then offer the tensioner up behind the belt and fit the two bolts. Tighten the bolts to the specified torque, then release the pulley, remove the locking pin, and allow the tensioner to act on the belt **(see illustrations)**.

29 Tighten the two inlet camshaft sprocket bolts to the specified torque, then remove the special tools (and the wedge holding the belt on the crankshaft sprocket, if fitted) **(see illustrations)**.

Without special tools

30 Fit the timing belt around the crankshaft sprocket, then behind the front idler pulley. Using a spanner, have an assistant turn the front camshaft sprocket slightly as required to bring the timing marks into alignment (either use your own marks, or have an assistant view those on the secondary belt sprockets). Hold the sprocket in this position, and engage the belt on the sprocket teeth, keeping it as taut as possible **(see illustration)**.

31 The front sprocket will have to be held in the aligned position while the belt is fed under the water pump pulley, then the rear sprocket must be turned into alignment and

7.28a Turn the pulley clockwise, then offer the tensioner into place . . .

7.28b . . . fit and tighten the two bolts . . .

7.28c . . . then withdraw the plunger locking pin

7.29a Timing belt refitted, with special tools in place

7.29b Tighten the camshaft sprocket bolts to the specified torque . . .

7.29c . . . then through the specified angle

7.30 The front sprocket can be turned into alignment with a spanner . . .

7.31 . . . but the rear sprocket must be turned using a home-made forked tool

held while the belt engages with the sprocket teeth. A spanner should **not** be used on the rear sprocket, as this may loosen the bolt – instead, use a home-made forked tool (or equivalent). Note that considerable pressure will be needed **(see illustration).**

32 Once the belt is fully fitted around the tensioner pulley, the camshaft sprockets can be released slowly (to ensure the belt does not jump off, or jump a tooth). Check that the timing marks are in alignment before proceeding, as it is possible to fit the belt exactly one tooth out.

33 Carry out the operations described in

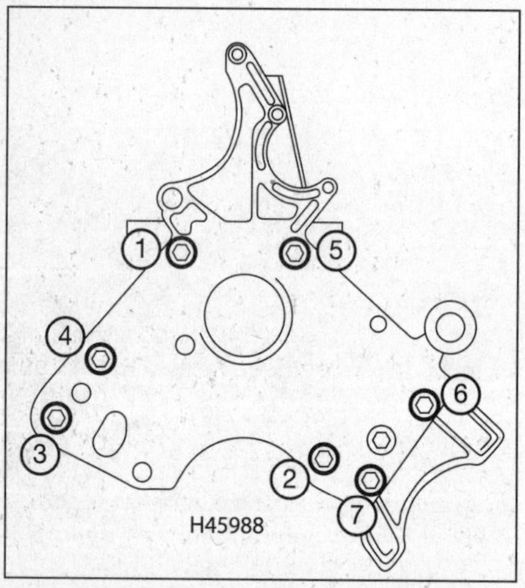

7.35 Engine front plate bolt tightening sequence

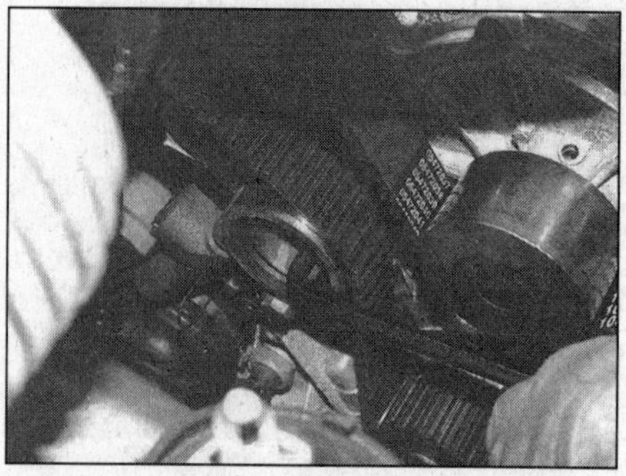

7.33a Turning the tensioner pulley using an Allen key

paragraphs 25 to 28. Owing to the limited access, this is a job for two people – one to turn the pulley, and one to fit the tensioner **(see illustrations).**

34 On completion, remove the wedge (if used) and any locking pins from the flywheel. Temporarily refit the crankshaft pulley, then turn the engine clockwise using a spanner or socket on the crankshaft pulley bolt through two complete revolutions. Check that all the sprocket marks come back into alignment (if not, the belt will have to be removed and the procedure repeated). If the secondary belts are also to be renewed, refit the flywheel locking pin.

All models

35 Offer up the engine front plate, and fit the front (end) bolts and two boss/bolts at the top. Tighten the bolts to their specified torques, working in sequence **(see illustration).**

7.39a Use a straight-edge . . .

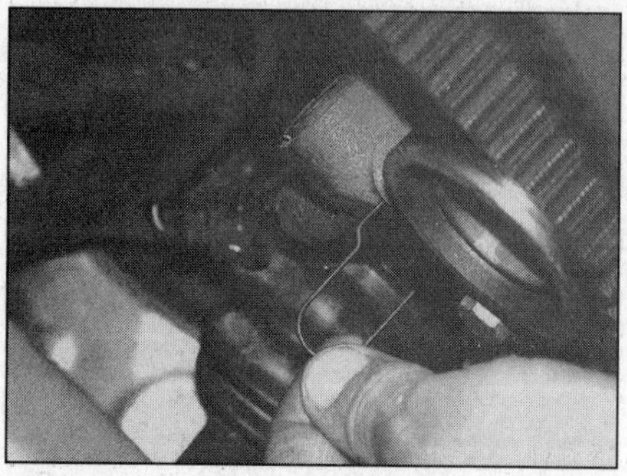

7.33b Removing the tensioner locking pin

36 Refit the top three bolts to the engine front plate, remembering that one of the bolts is also used to secure the engine rear lifting eye. Tighten the bolts to the specified torque.

37 If a new primary timing belt has been fitted, fit new secondary belts as described later in this Section.

Secondary belts

Note: *The secondary belt sprockets are keyed to the camshafts, unlike the inlet sprockets at the primary belt end. Providing the primary timing belt is fitted, and its alignment marks are in the correct position, the secondary sprockets can safely be removed – the inlet camshaft alignment will be preserved.*

38 If not already done, align the engine assembly/valve timing marks as described in Section 3.

39 Although the secondary belt sprockets have their own marks already, they can be hard to see, so it is helpful to make extra ones on the belt backplate. Extra marks **must** be made if the special tools are not available – refer to paragraph 41 **(see illustrations).**

Without special tools

40 Using a forked tool similar to that described in Section 8, hold the inlet camshaft sprocket (the spoked one) and loosen the bolt **(see illustration).** Do not attempt to loosen the sprocket bolt without such a tool, or excess load will be transferred though the inlet camshaft to the primary timing belt.

41 Before proceeding, check that accurate marks have been made between both sprockets and the belt backplate. A little

7.39b . . . to make marks on the rear inlet sprocket

7.39c Also mark the backplate and exhaust sprocket cut-out

7.40 Loosen the inlet sprocket bolt, using a forked sprocket-holding tool

7.42a Remove the sprocket bolt . . .

7.42b . . . then remove the inlet sprocket . . .

7.42c . . . and take the belt off the exhaust sprocket

paint (or typist's correction fluid) can be used to make a mark between the notch in the exhaust sprocket and the backplate. Similarly, a second line appears on the front face of the inlet sprocket, and a mark can be made on the edge of the backplate.

42 Discard the sprocket bolt (a new one is used when refitting), then remove the sprocket and slip off the belt **(see illustrations)**. **Do not** rotate the crankshaft or camshafts until the timing belt has been refitted. The exhaust camshaft will turn under pressure from the valve springs – note which way it moves, as it must be turned back when the belt is refitted.

43 If the timing belt is to be refitted, mark its direction of rotation.

44 Due to the low cost of a new belt, it is recommended that the belt be renewed as a matter of course, regardless of its apparent condition. MG Rover state that a belt which has covered more than 45 000 miles should never be refitted. If signs of oil contamination are found, trace the source of the oil leak and rectify it, then wash down the engine timing belt area and all related components to remove all traces of oil.

45 Two home-made tools must be made up to allow refitting of the belt, as described in the following paragraphs.

46 The first tool should be made from flat bar, at least 3 mm thick, and approximately 48 mm wide – this will fit in the slots on the end of the exhaust sprocket and, with a pair of pliers, can be used (by an assistant) to turn the exhaust sprocket so the timing marks line up.

47 The second tool is a tapered pin, to fit in the end of the inlet camshaft, and used to guide the sprocket into place. The pin is approximately 10 mm diameter, 100 mm long, and should be tapered down to about 8 mm at one end.

48 Fit the new belt around the exhaust sprocket **(see illustration)**.

49 Have an assistant turn back the sprocket using the tool described in paragraph 46, until the previously-made marks come into alignment. Hold the sprocket in this position while the other sprocket is refitted. Fit the inlet sprocket inside the belt, in such a way that the alignment marks will be correctly positioned when the sprocket is fitted. Insert the tapered pin tool into the end of the inlet camshaft.

50 Slide the sprocket over the pin, and engage the key on the back of the sprocket with the corresponding notch in the end of the camshaft. This will require some effort, to overcome the tension of a new belt, but there will be a definite 'click' when the sprocket engages **(see illustrations)**.

51 Check that the timing marks made previously are in alignment, then withdraw the tapered pin and fit the new sprocket bolt, tightened by hand initially. Gently release the tool from the exhaust sprocket.

52 When all is satisfactory, tighten the new bolt (using a forked tool to hold the sprocket) to the specified torque and angle **(see illustrations)**.

53 Repeat the procedure for the remaining secondary belt.

With special tools

54 If not already done, remove the exhaust

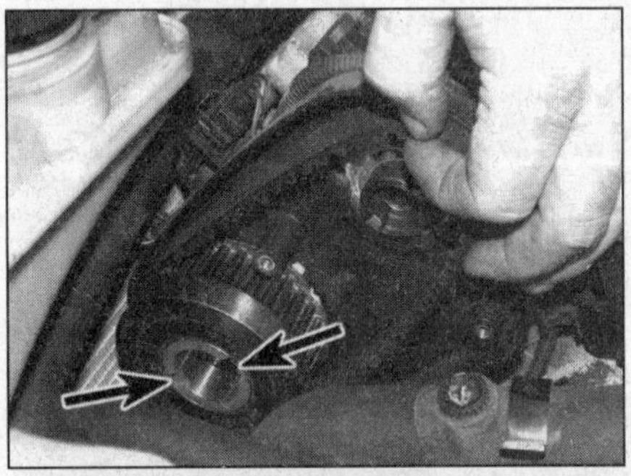

7.48 Fit the new belt round the exhaust sprocket

Slots in exhaust sprocket, for fitting home-made tool, arrowed

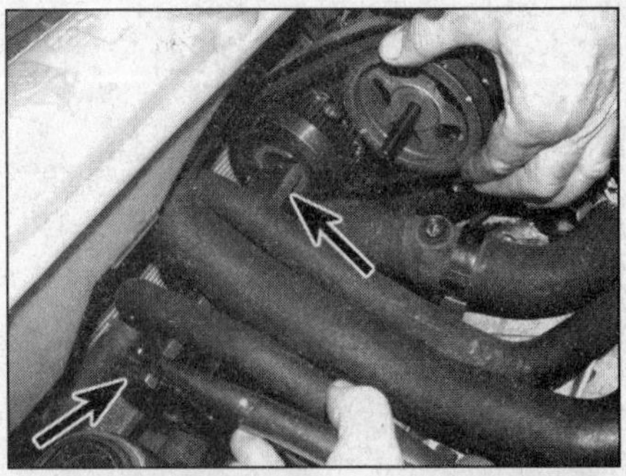

7.50a Flat bar inserted in exhaust sprocket, turned using pliers to align marks

7.50b Fit the inlet sprocket over the tapered pin until the key engages

7.52a Tighten the inlet sprocket bolt to the specified torque . . .

7.52b . . . then to the specified angle

7.58 Place the sprockets face down, and fit the new belt round them

7.59 Force the sprockets apart using special tool 18G 1747-1

camshaft end caps at the primary timing belt end (new caps should be used when refitting). Make an alignment mark between the exhaust camshafts and the primary belt end of each head, to use when fitting the new belt.

55 Using the special tool (12-175) placed over the sprockets to hold them, loosen the bolt from each one. Do not attempt to loosen the sprocket bolts without such a tool, or excess load will be transferred though the inlet camshaft to the primary timing belt.

56 Remove and discard the sprocket bolts (new ones are used when refitting), then remove the two sprockets and belt as an assembly. **Do not** rotate the crankshaft or camshafts until the timing belt has been refitted.

57 If the timing belt is to be refitted, mark its direction of rotation. Take the belt off the sprockets.

58 Place the two sprockets face down on a flat surface, so that both the keys are facing upwards, and directly opposite each other. Fit the belt around the sprockets **(see illustration)**.

59 A new belt will make the sprockets hard to fit over the camshaft ends, so the sprockets must be forced apart prior to fitting. The MG Rover tool for this is 18G 1747-1 **(see illustration)**.

60 Insert the two alignment pins (18G 1747-5) insert into the two camshaft threaded holes **(see illustration)**.

61 The exhaust camshaft will have to be turned back into alignment as the sprockets are refitted. A slot is provided in the camshaft end at the primary timing belt end, into which special tool 18G 1747-4 fits to turn the camshaft when required **(see illustration)**.

62 Turn the sprocket/belt assembly over, and place special tool 12-175 into position. Offer the sprockets and belt as an assembly over the alignment pins. The inlet sprocket's key should be felt to locate in the camshaft end **(see illustrations)**.

63 Have an assistant turn the exhaust camshaft slightly, to the previously-made alignment mark made at the primary belt end, then the exhaust sprocket should engage **(see illustration)**.

64 Withdraw the alignment pins, then fit the new camshaft sprocket bolts, and tighten by hand. Check that the sprocket marks are correctly aligned with each other before proceeding to tighten the bolts to the specified torque – hold the sprockets

7.60 Fit the alignment pins into the camshafts

7.61 Fit tool 18G 1747-4 into the exhaust camshaft, at the primary belt end

7.62a Place special tool 12-175 over the sprockets . . .

7.62b . . . then fit the assembly over the alignment pins

7.63 Turn the exhaust camshaft into alignment, from the primary end

7.64a Fit the new camshaft sprocket bolt . . .

7.64b . . . then tighten it to the specified torque . . .

7.64c . . . and through the specified angle

using the same method as removal **(see illustrations)**.

65 Repeat the procedure for the remaining secondary belt.

Final refitting

66 Refit all removed components using a reversal of the removal procedure, noting the following points:

a) *Clean the recesses in the ends of the exhaust camshafts, and fit new end cap seals (where necessary).*

b) *Tighten all fasteners to the specified torque.*

c) *Refer to Chapter 5A when refitting the alternator, and to Chapter 10 for the power steering pump.*

8 Timing belt tensioner and sprockets – removal and refitting

Camshaft sprockets

Primary belt

Note: *It is not advisable to remove the inlet camshaft sprockets from the primary timing belt end unless a full set of special tools are available to re-align them – the sprockets at the primary timing belt end are not keyed to the camshafts. It may be possible to re-align the sprockets if enough accurate marks are made beforehand, however – the secondary belt sprockets are both keyed to their camshafts, and this could be used to provide a reference.*

1 Remove the primary timing belt as described in Section 7.

2 Slacken and remove each camshaft sprocket retaining bolt, along with the centre/hub. To stop the camshaft turning, use a locking tool which fits between the sprocket spokes, which can be fabricated from two lengths of steel strip (one long, the other short) and three nuts and bolts. One nuts and bolt should form the pivot of the forked tool, with the remaining two nuts and bolts at the tips of the forks to engage with the sprocket spokes **(see illustration)**.

3 Mark the sprockets for position (front or rear bank) before removal. Remove the sprockets from the camshafts **(see illustration)**.

4 Check the sprockets for signs of wear or damage and renew if necessary.

5 Prior to refitting, check the oil seals for signs of damage or leakage. If necessary, renew as described in Section 9.

6 Refit the primary belt using the special tools as described in Section 7. Ensure that the sprockets are refitted to their original camshafts.

Secondary belt

7 The secondary belt sprockets are removed as an assembly with the belt, as described in Section 7.

8 Prior to refitting, check the oil seals for signs of damage or leakage. If necessary, renew as described in Section 9.

9 Refit the secondary belt as described in Section 7.

Crankshaft sprocket

10 Remove the primary timing belt as described in Section 7.

11 Slide the sprocket off from the end of the crankshaft, noting which way around it is fitted **(see illustration)**.

12 Refit the sprocket to the crankshaft, engaging it with the crankshaft flattened section.

13 Refit the timing belt as described in Section 7.

Tensioner body

14 The automatic tensioner is secured by two bolts, and incorporates spring plunger. This spring provides constant tension to press the pulley against the belt.

15 Gain access to the tensioner using the information in Section 7. The timing belt does not have to be removed to fit a new tensioner, though it is a good idea to fit a new belt at the same time. If the tensioner pulley is worn, or has seized, this will have damaged the belt, and a new belt should be fitted.

16 Unclip the rubber blanking plug from the rear of the timing belt tensioner. Loosen the two tensioner mounting bolts (**do not** loosen the Allen screw securing the tensioner pulley). Release the belt tension by turning the tensioner pulley clockwise using a suitable Allen key in the hole provided. Holding the tensioner in the released position, remove the mounting bolts and take off the tensioner.

8.2 Use a home-made tool to hold the sprocket

8.3 Removing the primary belt camshaft sprockets

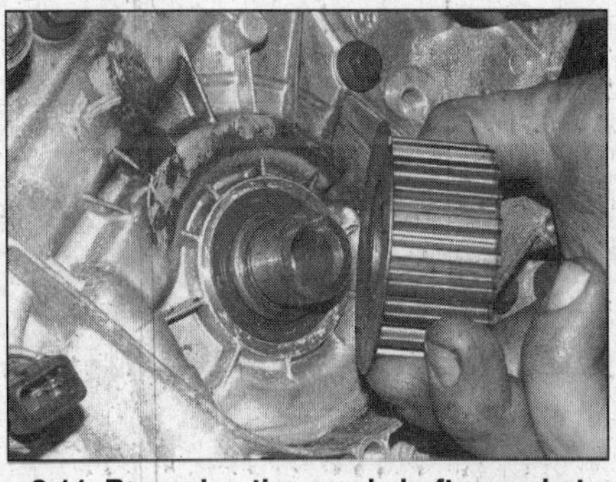
8.11 Removing the crankshaft sprocket

8.22a Unscrew the pulley mounting bolt . . .

8.22b . . . and recover the washer

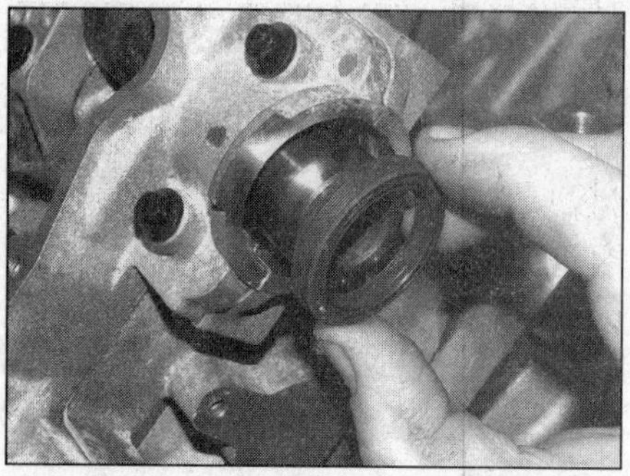

9.5a Offer the (black) seal into position . . .

17 Using a vice with protected jaws, carefully compress the timing belt tensioner plunger until a pin (approximately 1.5 mm diameter) can be inserted through the tensioner body and plunger to lock it.

18 Clean the two tensioner mounting bolts, then apply a little threadlocking compound (such as Loctite 242) to their threads.

19 Turn the tensioner pulley clockwise using an Allen key, then offer the tensioner up behind the belt and fit the two bolts. Tighten the bolts to the specified torque, then release the pulley, remove the locking pin, and allow the tensioner to act on the belt. Refit the tensioner's rubber plug.

20 Refit the components removed to access the tensioner, as described in Section 7.

Tensioner pulley

21 Remove the tensioner body as described previously in this Section.

22 Unscrew the pulley mounting bolt – this is below the pulley itself – and withdraw the pulley. Recover the washer fitted behind the pulley bracket **(see illustrations)**.

23 MG Rover state that the tensioner and pulley should be renewed after 100 000 miles. It's considered good practice to renew all timing belt-related pulleys, etc, during routine belt renewal – many parts suppliers sell timing belt 'kits', which contain all the relevant items.

24 If the tensioner pulley is visibly damaged, or rough when spun by hand, a new one should be fitted.

25 Fit the tensioner, ensuring that the washer is fitted between the pulley bracket and the engine, and tighten the bolt to the specified torque.

26 Refit the tensioner body as described previously in this Section.

9 Camshaft oil seals – renewal

Primary belt end seals

1 Remove the camshaft sprockets as described in Section 8.

2 Punch or drill two small holes opposite each other in the oil seal(s). Screw a self-tapping screw into each hole, and pull on the screws with pliers to extract the seal.

3 Clean the seal housing, and polish off any burrs or raised edges which may have caused the seal to fail.

4 The new (black) seal has a waxed outer surface, and should **not** be lubricated further prior to fitting. Genuine seals may be supplied with a cone-shaped fitting tool, which slides onto the end of the camshaft. If this is not available, tape the end of the camshaft to protect the seal lips.

5 Carefully offer the seal over the camshaft and into position. Drive it into position, using a suitable tubular drift, such as a socket, which bears only on the hard outer edge of the seal **(see illustrations)**. Take care not to damage the seal lips during fitting, and note that the seal lips should face inwards.

6 Refit the camshaft sprockets as described in Section 8.

Secondary belt end seals

7 Remove the camshaft sprockets as described in Section 8.

8 Punch or drill two small holes opposite each other in the oil seal(s). Screw a self-tapping screw into each hole, and pull on the screws with pliers to extract the seal.

9 Clean the seal housing, and polish off any burrs or raised edges which may have caused the seal to fail.

10 The new (red) seal has a waxed outer surface, and should **not** be lubricated further prior to fitting. Genuine seals may be supplied with a cone-shaped fitting tool, which slides onto the end of the camshaft. If this is not available, tape the end of the camshaft to protect the seal lips.

11 Carefully offer the seal over the camshaft and into position. Drive it into position, using a suitable tubular drift, such as a socket, which bears only on the hard outer edge of the seal **(see illustrations)**. Take care not to damage the seal lips during fitting, and note that the seal lips should face inwards.

12 Refit the camshaft sprockets as described in Section 8.

10 Camshafts and tappets – removal, inspection and refitting

1 Remove the primary timing belt as described in Section 7. If both camshafts are being removed, also take off the two

9.5b . . . then tap it fully home using a suitable socket

9.11a Carefully fit the new seal over the camshaft . . .

9.11b . . . and drive it home using a socket

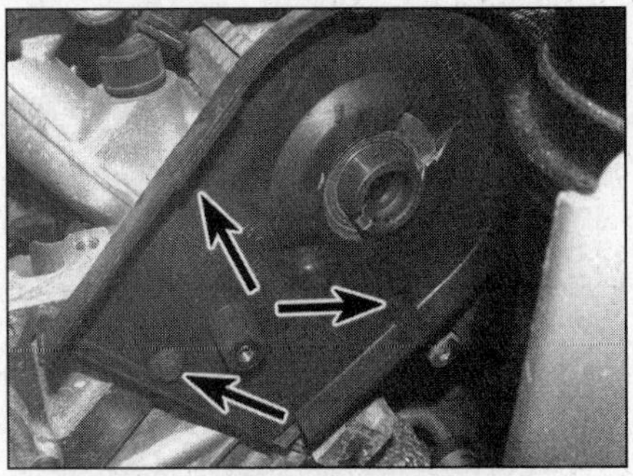

10.4a Remove the bolts . . .

10.4b . . . and lift out the primary belt backplates

10.5 Removing a secondary belt backplate

secondary belts (otherwise, only the belt from the relevant bank need be disturbed).

2 Remove the inlet camshaft sprockets as described in Section 8 – pay attention to the note at the start of that Section, regarding aligning the sprockets when refitting.

3 Remove the camshaft covers as described in Section 4.

4 Unscrew the bolts securing each inlet camshaft timing belt backplate, and remove them **(see illustrations)**. Each backplate may be secured by three or four bolts, depending on year of manufacture.

5 Similarly remove the backplates behind the secondary timing belt, which are secured by two bolts each **(see illustration)**.

6 Working in the **reverse** of the tightening sequence, progressively loosen the twenty-two camshaft carrier bolts on each bank, until the pressure from the valve springs is released. Remove the bolts, then lift the carriers off, noting that they are located on dowels.

7 Carefully lift the camshafts from the cylinder head **(see illustration)**. Remove the oil seals and discard them; new ones should be used on refitting. Mark the camshafts for identification – the inlet camshafts are the inner ones.

8 Obtain twenty-four small, clean plastic containers, and label them for identification. Alternatively, divide a larger container/tray into compartments. Using a sucker or magnet, withdraw each tappet in turn and place it upright in its respective container, which should then be filled with clean engine oil **(see illustration)**.

10.7 Lifting out one of the exhaust camshafts

10.8 Using a suction tool to withdraw the hydraulic tappets

Caution: Do not interchange the tappets, and do not allow the tappets to lose oil, as they will take a long time to refill with oil on restarting the engine, which could result in incorrect valve clearances. Absolute cleanliness is essential at all times when handling the tappets.

Inspection

9 Examine the camshaft bearing surfaces and cam lobes for signs of wear ridges and scoring. Renew the camshaft if any of these conditions are apparent. Examine the condition of the bearing surfaces both on the camshaft journals and in the cylinder head. If the head bearing surfaces are worn excessively, the cylinder head will need to be renewed.

10 Examine the tappet bearing surfaces which contact the camshaft lobes for wear ridges and scoring. Check the tappets and their bores in the cylinder head for signs of wear or damage. If a micrometer is available, measure the outside diameter of each tappet and compare it to the values given in the Specifications. If the engine's valve clearances have sounded noisy, particularly if the noise persists after initial start-up from cold, then there is reason to suspect a faulty tappet. If any tappet is thought to be faulty or is visibly worn it should be renewed.

Refitting

11 Liberally oil the camshaft bearings and tappets, then refit the tappets to their original locations in the cylinder head **(see illustration)**.

12 Lay the camshafts in position. Position the camshafts so that the camshaft sprocket locating notches at the secondary belt end are facing each other, at approximately 4 o'clock and 8 o'clock positions **(see illustration)**.

10.11 Oil the camshaft bearings in the cylinder head

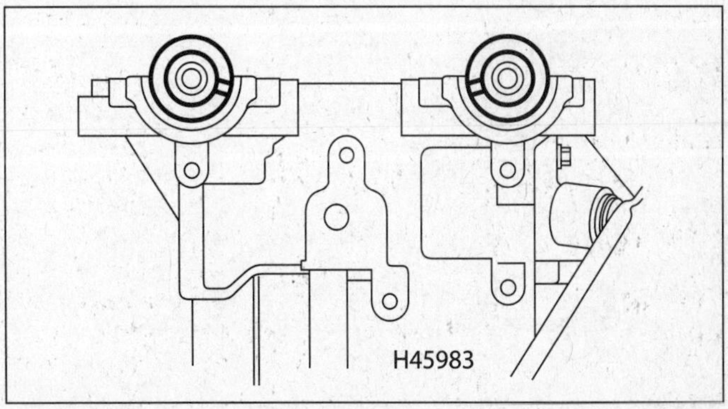

10.12 Set the camshafts so the rear sprocket notches are as shown

10.13a Clean the bearing carrier and cylinder head surfaces . . .

10.13b . . . then apply the sealant . . .

10.13c . . . and spread to a thin, even film using a roller (or a brush)

10.14 Refit the camshaft carrier onto the locating dowels

13 Ensure the mating surfaces of the camshaft bearing carrier and cylinder head are clean and dry. Apply several beads of sealant (part number GUG 705963GM) to the bearing carrier mating surface. Spread the sealant in an even film, taking care not to allow any sealant to enter the oilway grooves **(see illustrations)**.

14 Ensure that the locating dowels are in position, then refit the camshaft bearing carrier to the cylinder head **(see illustration)**. Ensure the carrier is correctly located then refit the retaining bolts, tightening them all by hand only at this stage.

15 Working in sequence, evenly and progressively tighten the retaining bolts to draw the bearing carrier squarely down into contact with the cylinder head. Once the carrier is in contact with the head, go around in sequence and tighten the retaining bolts to the specified torque **(see illustrations)**.

Caution: If the bearing carrier bolts are carelessly tightened, the carrier might break. If the carrier is broken, the complete cylinder head assembly must be renewed; the carrier is matched to the head, and is not available separately.

16 Fit new camshaft oil seals as described in Section 9.

17 Clean the timing belt backplate bolts, then apply a little threadlocking fluid (such as Loctite 242) to the threads, and tighten them to the specified torque.

18 Refit the camshaft covers as described in Section 4.

19 Fit the secondary timing belt(s) as described in Section 7.

20 Refit the inlet camshaft sprockets as described in Section 8. If the secondary timing belts have been correctly fitted, the camshafts should be in the correct positions.

21 Fit the primary timing belt as described in Section 7.

11 Cylinder heads - removal and refitting

Note: *Before removing the cylinder heads, ensure that the timing belt special tools described in Section 7 are available. The inlet camshaft sprockets have to be removed, so the camshaft timing will be lost, which means the tools are essential.*

1 Depressurise the fuel system as described in Chapter 4B.

2 Disconnect the battery negative lead (see *Disconnecting the battery*).

3 Drain the cooling system as described in Chapter 1A. Be sure to drain the cylinder block as well as removing the radiator bottom hose.

4 Remove the upper section of the inlet manifold as described in Chapter 4B.

5 Remove the primary timing belt as described in Section 7. When the primary timing belt is removed as part of a cylinder head removal procedure, a new belt **must** be fitted on reassembly.

Front bank

6 Remove the inlet camshaft sprocket as described in Section 8.

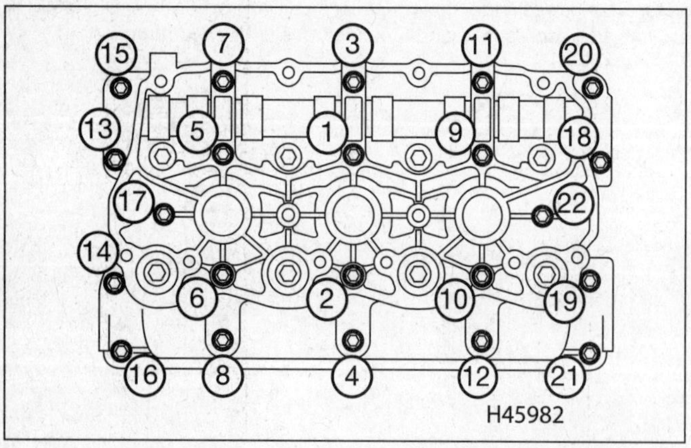

10.15a Camshaft bearing carrier bolt tightening sequence

10.15b Tightening the camshaft carrier bolts to the specified torque

11.7 Removing the timing belt backplate

11.8a Disconnect the expansion tank hose from the radiator . . .

11.8b . . . and from the T-piece on top of the inlet manifold

7 Remove the bolts securing the timing belt backplate, and lift it away **(see illustration)**.
8 Release the hose clips and disconnect the expansion tank bleed hoses from the tank (or the T-piece on top of the inlet manifold) and the radiator **(see illustrations)**.
9 Remove the expansion tank mounting bolt, then unhook the tank mounting pegs and move the tank to one side **(see illustrations)**.
10 Disconnect the radiator top hose, then release the hose from its support bracket and move to one side. Unbolt the radiator hose support bracket and remove it. Also unbolt and remove the radiator top hose connection elbow **(see illustrations)**.
11 Remove the camshaft cover from the front bank as described in Section 4.
12 Mark the ignition coils and HT leads for position. Pull back the locking collar and disconnect each coil's wiring plug. Remove the three mounting nuts and bolts from the three ignition coils serving the front bank – note that the nut for No 1 cylinder's coil also secures the earth lead. Disconnect the HT leads and remove the coils **(see illustrations)**.
13 Disconnect the coolant bleed hose from the inlet manifold, and move the hose clear.

11.9a Remove the expansion tank bolt . . .

11.9b . . . then disengage the tank mounting pegs

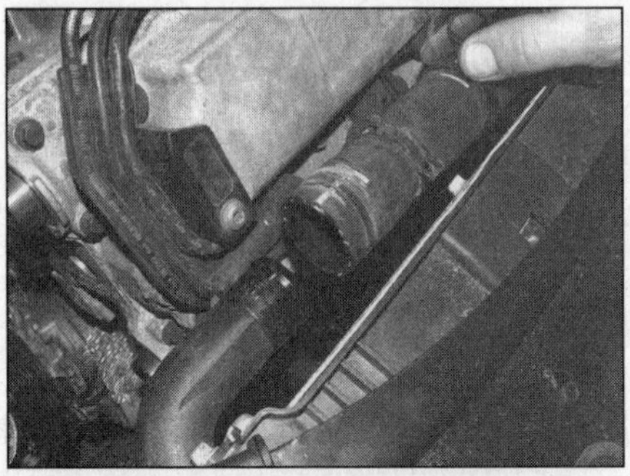

11.10a Disconnect the radiator top hose . . .

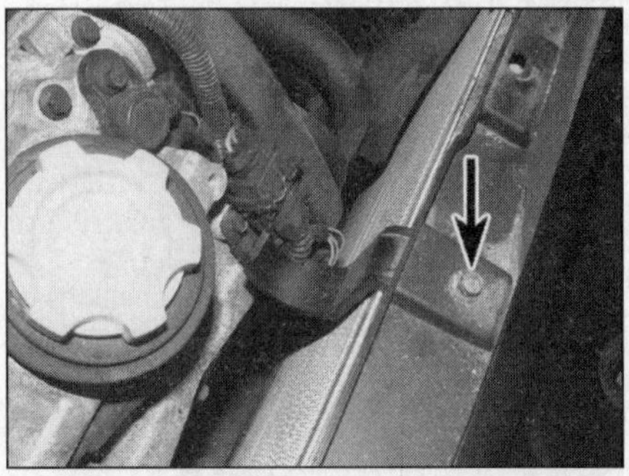

11.10b . . . then unbolt the hose support bracket . . .

11.10c . . . and the radiator coolant elbow

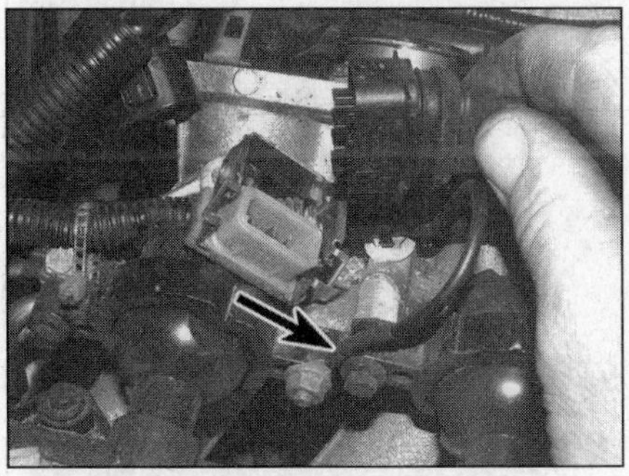

11.12a Disconnect the wiring plug – note earth lead (arrowed)

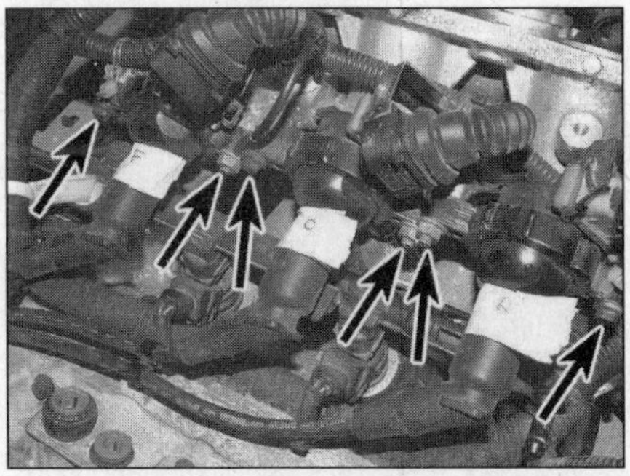

11.12b Mark the HT leads for position. Coil mounting nuts/bolts arrowed

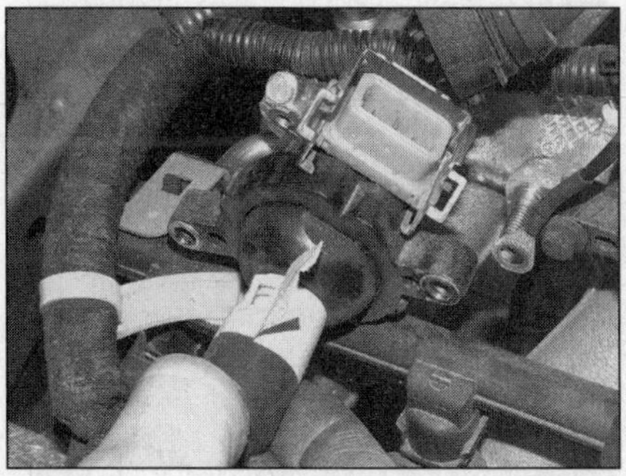

11.12c Disconnect the HT leads and remove the coils

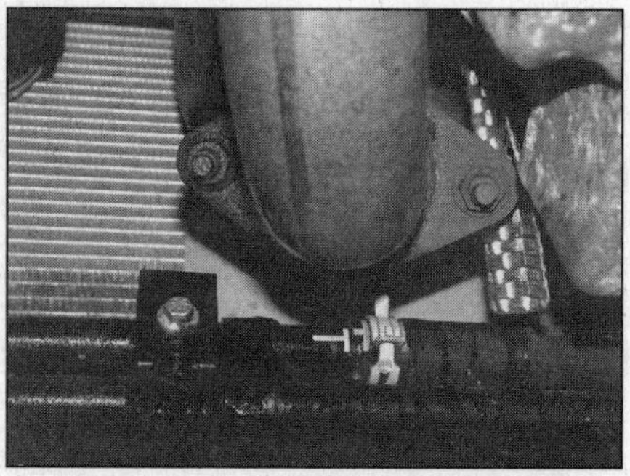

11.15 Unscrew the manifold-to-front downpipe nuts

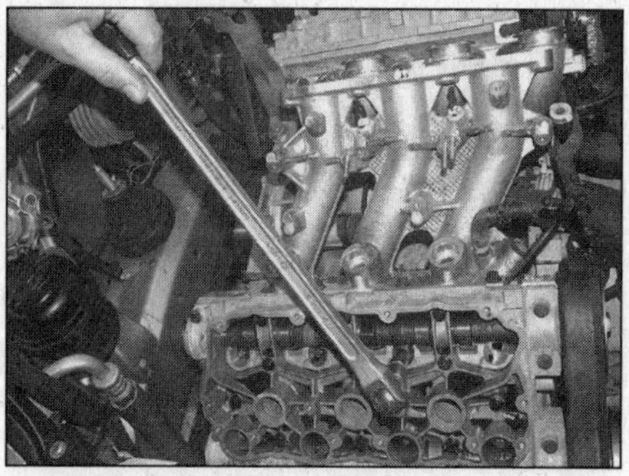

11.17a Loosen the head bolts in sequence

11.17b The rear row of bolts will come out . . .

11.17c . . . but the front ones won't – note card protecting radiator

11.20 Lifting off the head – note front bolts wrapped up with tape

HAYNES HiNT

Liner clamps can be improvised using large washers and tubular spacers, such as suitable deep sockets.

14 Remove the fuel rails and injectors as described in Chapter 4B, Section 11.

15 Working under the car, remove the two exhaust manifold-to-downpipe flange nuts, and separate the pipe **(see illustration)**.

16 Before removing the front cylinder head, it's advisable to protect the radiator from possible damage – this is most easily done by taping a large piece of card over its inner face.

17 Working in the **reverse** order of the tightening sequence, progressively loosen the eight cylinder head bolts, then remove the four rear bolts. The front row of four bolts won't come out, but they can be lifted far enough to clear the head-to-block joint – by lifting them this far, then wrapping some tape around all four, the head can be lifted off **(see illustrations)**.

18 The joint between the cylinder head and gasket and the cylinder block/crankcase must now be broken without disturbing the cylinder liners. Although these liners are better located and sealed than some wet-liner engines, there is still a risk of coolant and foreign matter leaking into the sump if the cylinder head is lifted carelessly. If care is not taken and the liners are moved, there is also a possibility of their seals being disturbed, causing leakage after refitting the head.

19 To break the joint, obtain two L-shaped metal bars which fit into the cylinder head bolt holes and gently rock the cylinder head free towards the front of the car.

Caution: Do not try to swivel the head on the cylinder block/crankcase, as it is located by dowels as well as by the tops of the liners.

20 When the joint is broken, lift the cylinder head away, using assistance if possible as it is a heavy assembly, especially if complete with the manifolds **(see illustration)**. Remove the gasket and discard it. Support the cylinder head on wooden blocks or stands – do not rest the lower face of the cylinder head on the work surface. Note the fitted positions of the two locating dowels, and remove them for safe-keeping if they are loose.

21 If the head bolts are to be re-used, store the bolts in order, so that they can be refitted in their original locations. The bolts can be stored by pushing them through a clearly-marked cardboard template.

22 Note that further to the warnings given at the beginning of this Section, **do not** attempt to rotate the crankshaft with the cylinder head removed, otherwise the liners may be displaced. Operations that require the rotation of the crankshaft (eg, cleaning the piston crowns) can be carried out after fitting cylinder liner clamps **(see Haynes Hint)**.

23 If the cylinder head is to be dismantled, remove the camshafts, as described in Section 10, then refer to the relevant Sections of Part D of this Chapter.

Rear bank

24 If only the head from the rear bank is being removed, proceed as described for the front bank, with the following differences:

a) Remove the camshaft cover from the rear bank as described in Section 4.

b) Ignore paragraphs 8 to 10, as the expansion tank and radiator top hose do not have to be disturbed.

c) There is no need to protect the radiator, as described in paragraph 16.

*d) There are several wiring plug brackets attached to the rear head – go round the head and disconnect the various plugs. In most cases, the wiring brackets must also be unbolted before the head is removed **(see illustration)**.*

e) Disconnect the breather pipe and coolant

11.24a Disconnect the wiring plugs and unbolt the brackets from the rear head

11.24b Depress the collar and remove the breather pipe . . .

11.24c . . . then release the clip and disconnect the coolant hose

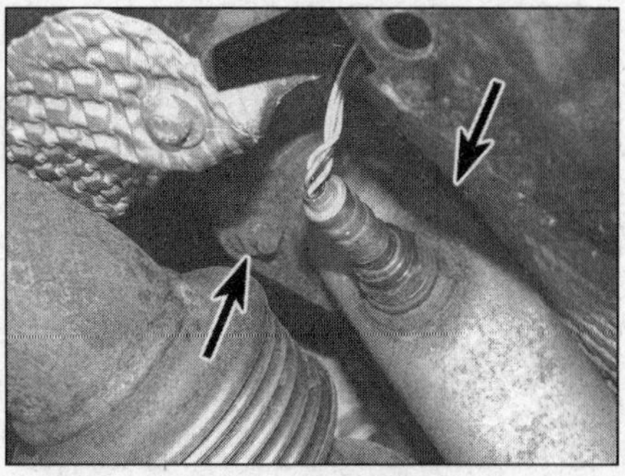

11.24d The rear manifold-to-downpipe nuts are hard to reach

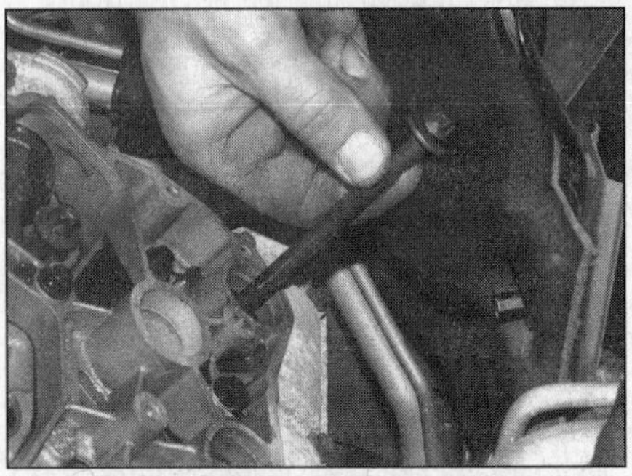

11.24e The driver's-side rear head bolt won't come out . . .

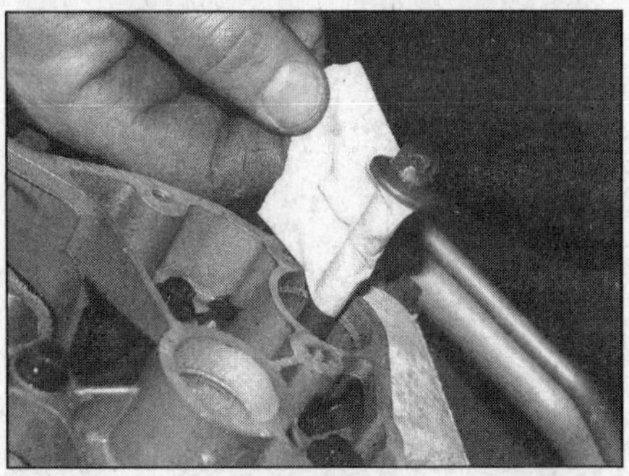

11.24f . . . so wrap some tape round it to stop it falling down

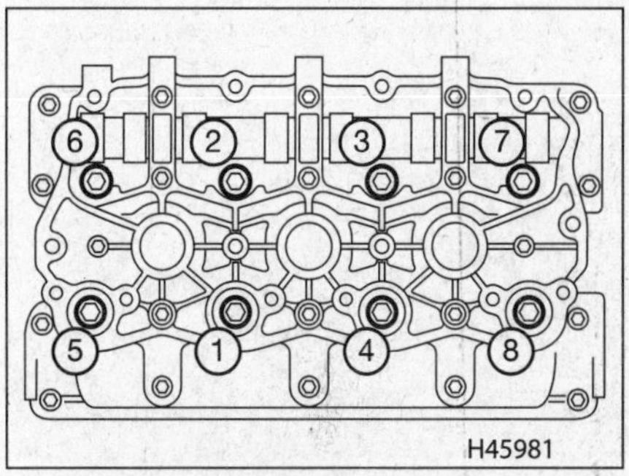

11.37 Cylinder head bolt tightening sequence

hose from the rear inlet manifold ***(see illustrations)****.*

f) *The rear exhaust manifold-to-downpipe nuts are tricky to reach – a long extension will be needed* ***(see illustration)****.*

g) *Only one cylinder head bolt (driver's-side rear) cannot be withdrawn before the head itself is removed. Lift the bolt up, then wrap enough tape around it to prevent it dropping back down, before removing the head* ***(see illustrations)****.*

Preparation for refitting

25 The mating faces of the cylinder head and cylinder block/crankcase must be perfectly clean before refitting the head. Use a hard plastic or wood scraper to remove all traces of gasket and carbon. Also clean the piston crowns. Take particular care, as the soft aluminium alloy is damaged easily.

26 Make sure that the carbon is not allowed to enter the oil and water passages – this is particularly important for the lubrication system, as carbon could block the oil supply to any of the engine components. Using adhesive tape and paper, seal the water, oil and bolt holes in the cylinder block/crankcase. To prevent carbon entering the gap between the pistons and bores, smear a little grease in the gap. After cleaning each piston, use a small brush to remove all traces of grease and carbon from the gap, then wipe away the remainder with a clean cloth. Clean all the pistons in the same way. Take great care not to move the pistons during this procedure.

27 Check the mating surfaces of the cylinder block/crankcase and the cylinder head for nicks, deep scratches and other damage. If slight, they may be removed carefully with a file, but if excessive, machining may be the only alternative to renewal.

28 If warpage of the cylinder head gasket surface is suspected, use a straight-edge to check it for distortion. Refer to Part D of this Chapter if necessary.

29 Check the condition of the cylinder head bolts, particularly their threads. Keeping all bolts in their correct fitted order, wash them and wipe dry. Check each bolt for any sign of visible wear or damage, renewing as necessary. Note that if cylinder head bolts have been used to secure the cylinder liner clamps, each bolt and clamp should be removed one at a time for checking, and refitted immediately the bolt has been inspected. Although not specified by the manufacturer, we recommend that the bolts are renewed as a complete set, regardless of their apparent condition – this is particularly recommended if the bolts have seen long service, or are known to have already been re-used once.

Refitting

30 Remove the cylinder liner clamps (where fitted) and wipe clean the mating surfaces of the cylinder head and cylinder block/crankcase.

31 Ensure that the two locating dowels are in position at each end of the cylinder block/crankcase surface.

32 Position a new gasket on the cylinder block/crankcase surface so that its TOP mark is uppermost.

33 Keeping all the cylinder head bolts in their correct fitted order, lightly oil under the head and on the threads of each bolt.

34 Before offering the head into position, fit the bolts which could not be withdrawn with the head in place. There's one bolt so affected on the rear head, and all four front bolts on the front head. As for removal, tape the bolts up so that they do not protrude below the gasket surface.

35 Carefully refit the cylinder head, locating it on the dowels.

36 Remove the tape from the bolts as applicable. Screw each bolt in, by hand only, until finger-tight. **Do not** drop the bolts into their holes.

37 Working progressively and in the sequence shown, first tighten all the cylinder head bolts to the Stage 1 torque setting **(see illustration)**.

38 Once all bolts have been tightened to the Stage 1 torque, again working in sequence, tighten each bolt to the specified Stage 2 torque. **Note:** *This setting is exactly the same as the Stage 1 value, but must be carried out as described. The head gasket is of metal laminate construction, and compresses when first tightened – if Stage 2 tightening is not completed to confirm the initial torque setting, subsequent angle-tightening may be inaccurate, giving an unevenly-tightened head.*

39 Once all bolts have been tightened to the Stage 2 torque, again working in sequence, tighten each bolt through its specified Stage 3 angle, using a socket and extension bar. It is recommended that an angle-measuring gauge is used during this stage of tightening, to ensure accuracy. Alternatively, prior to tightening, use a felt-tip pen or similar to make alignment marks between each bolt head and the cylinder head.

40 Finally go around in the specified sequence again and tighten all bolts through the specified Stage 4 angle. If the bolt heads were marked prior to angle-tightening, each bolt head mark should now be directly opposite the corresponding mark on the cylinder head.

41 Refit the removed components using a reversal of the removal procedure, noting the following points:

a) Use new gaskets/seals, as applicable.
b) Tighten all fasteners to the specified torque.
c) Fit a new primary timing belt as described in Section 7. If the camshafts have not been removed, new secondary belts do not have to be fitted.
d) Refill the cooling system as described in Chapter 1A.

12 Sump – removal and refitting

Removal

1 Drain the engine oil (with reference to Chapter 1A if necessary), then clean and refit the engine oil drain plug with a new washer, tightening it to the specified torque wrench setting. If the engine is nearing the service interval when the oil and filter are due for renewal, it is recommended that the filter is also removed and a new one fitted. After reassembly, the engine can then be refilled with fresh engine oil.

2 Apply the handbrake, then jack up the front of the car and support it securely on axle stands (see *Jacking and vehicle support*).

3 Remove the right-hand front wheel arch liner, as described in Chapter 11, Section 22.

4 Remove the single bolt securing the oil dipstick tube to the block, then depress the locking collar at the base and pull the tube out of the sump **(see illustration)**.

5 Unscrew the front and rear manifold-to-downpipe nuts, and separate the joints. Remove the exhaust front pipe support bracket, which is secured by two bolts **(see illustrations)**. If care is taken, it should now be possible to move the exhaust sufficiently to access the sump mounting bolts – if not, the complete system will have to be lowered, as described in Chapter 4B.

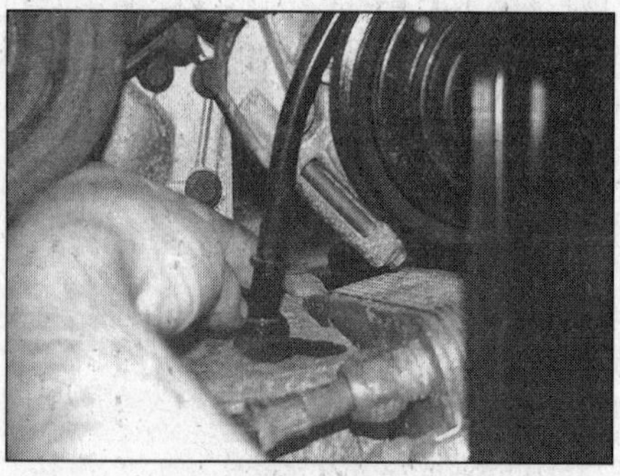

12.4 Depress the locking collar, and pull out the dipstick tube

12.5a Unscrew the exhaust front pipe support bracket bolts

6 Remove the engine lower mounting as described in Section 20.

7 Where applicable, unscrew the two oil cooler mounting bolts at the front of the sump, and tie the cooler forwards of the sump without disconnecting it **(see illustration)**.

8 Progressively slacken and remove the ten bolts securing the sump to the base of the lower crankcase **(see illustration)**.

9 Break the sump sealant joint by striking the sump with the palm of the hand. It is not advisable to prise between the mating faces, as this could result in a leak. If the sump is stuck, remove the drain plug, then use a sturdy screwdriver (wrapped in a rag or card to protect the drain plug threads) in the drain plug hole as a prising tool. Lower the sump away from the engine.

10 While the sump is removed, take the opportunity to check the oil pump pick-up/strainer for signs of clogging or splitting. If necessary, unbolt the pick-up/strainer and remove it from the engine along with its sealing ring. The strainer can then be cleaned easily in solvent. Inspect the strainer mesh for signs of clogging or splitting and renew if necessary.

Refitting

11 Clean all traces of sealant from the mating surfaces of the cylinder block/crankcase and sump, then use a clean rag to wipe out the sump.

12 Where necessary, fit a new sealing ring to oil pump pick-up/strainer groove then carefully refit the pipe, tightening its retaining bolt to the specified torque setting **(see illustrations)**.

12.5b Exhaust front manifold-to-downpipe nuts

12.7 Unbolt and move the oil cooler clear of the sump

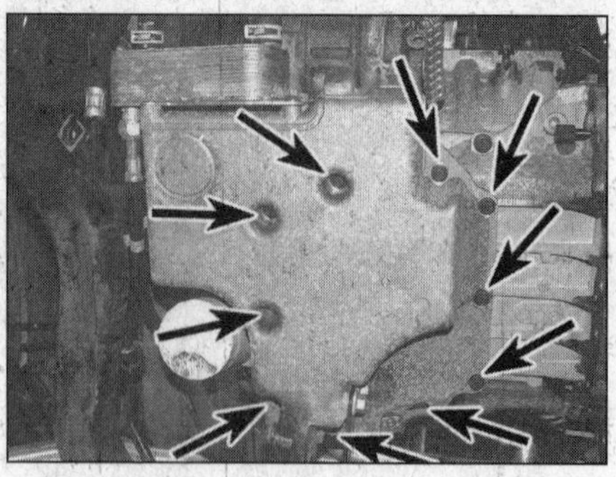

12.8 Sump bolts – seen from below

12.12a Fit a new O-ring to the groove . . .

12.12b . . . then oil and refit the oil pump pick-up

12.13a Apply sealant to the sump mating surface . . .

12.13b . . . and spread evenly with a roller or brush

12.14 Offer the sump into place, and fit the bolts finger-tight

13 Apply a 2 mm bead of suitable sealant (part number GUG 705963GM) to the sump mating surface, then spread this to an even film using a roller or brush **(see illustrations)**.

14 Offer up the sump to the cylinder block/crankcase, and tighten all bolts finger-tight only **(see illustration)**.

15 Working in sequence, tighten the sump bolts to the specified torque setting **(see illustration)**.

16 Refit the oil cooler to the front of the sump, and tighten the bolts to the specified torque.

17 Refit the engine lower mounting as described in Section 20.

18 Refit the exhaust front pipe mounting bracket, tightening the bolts to the specified torque. Refit the exhaust front pipes, using a new gasket on the rear pipe, and tighten the nuts to the specified torque.

19 Clean and refit the oil dipstick tube.

20 Lower the car to the ground, and refill the engine with oil as described in Chapter 1A.

13 Oil pump pressure relief valve – removal and refitting

Removal

1 Loosen the right-hand front wheel bolts. Firmly apply the handbrake, then jack up the front of the car and support it securely on axle stands (see *Jacking and vehicle support*). Remove the right-hand front wheel.

2 Remove the engine undertray, which is secured by a number of quick-release screw fasteners.

3 Remove the right-hand front wheel arch liner as described in Chapter 11, Section 22.

4 Place a drain container under the oil filter, then unscrew and remove the filter, referring to Chapter 1A if necessary. If the filter is not due to be changed, it can be refitted – in this case, store it upright so the oil is not lost.

5 Slacken and disconnect the two oil cooler unions. Recover and discard the O-ring seals – new ones should be fitted on reassembly.

6 Using a suitable Allen key or bit, unscrew and remove the relief valve plug – this will probably be quite tight, as threadlock is used when fitting **(see illustration)**. Remove the plug, and recover the spring and valve.

Refitting

7 Clean the plug, removing all traces of threadlock. Also clean the valve, spring and the valve seating, then lubricate the valve and seating with clean oil.

8 Apply a little threadlocking fluid (such as Loctite 542) to the plug threads. Fit the valve and spring, then fit and tighten the plug to the specified torque.

9 Clean around the oil cooler unions. Reconnect the unions using new O-rings lubricated with clean engine oil, and tighten the unions to the specified torque.

10 Fit the oil filter, and tighten by hand only, referring to Chapter 1A if necessary.

11 Refit the wheel arch liner, engine undertray, and right-hand front wheel, then lower the car to the ground. Tighten the wheel bolts to the specified torque.

14 Oil pump – removal and refitting

Removal

1 Remove the crankshaft sprocket as described in Section 8.

2 Drain the engine oil, then clean and refit the engine oil drain plug with a new washer, tightening it to the specified torque.

3 Disconnect the oil pressure switch multi-plug at the rear of the pump **(see illustration)**.

4 Place a drain container under the oil filter. Where applicable, slacken and disconnect the two oil cooler unions. Recover and discard the O-ring seals – new ones should be fitted on reassembly.

5 Unscrew and remove the oil filter – a new one should be obtained for refitting.

6 Loosen and remove the sixteen oil pump mounting bolts, then release the pump from its locating dowels and remove it with the gasket **(see illustrations)**. The gasket and bolts should both be discarded, and new ones used when refitting.

7 Remove the crankshaft oil seal from the oil

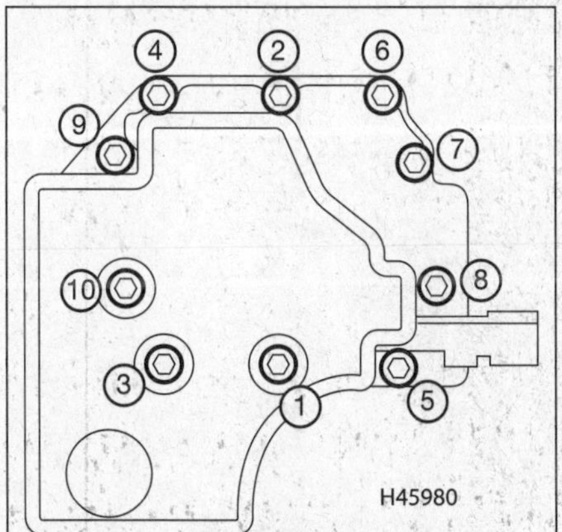

12.15 Sump bolt tightening sequence

13.6 Oil pump pressure relief valve plug

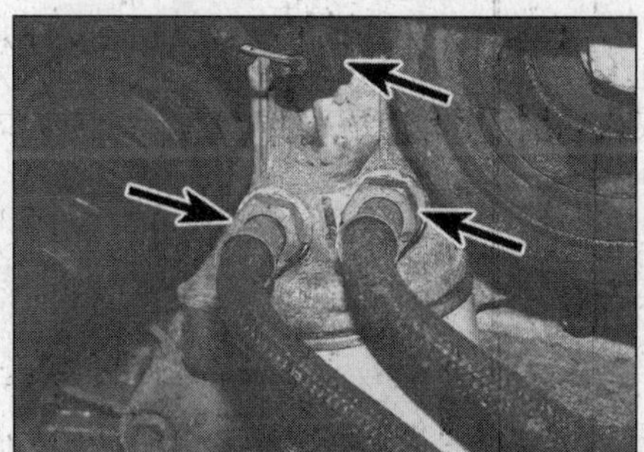

14.3 Oil pressure switch wiring plug and oil cooler unions

14.6a Remove the sixteen oil pump mounting bolts . . .

14.6b . . . then withdraw the pump . . .

14.6c . . . and recover the gasket

14.7 Prising out the crankshaft oil seal from the oil pump

14.9 Fit the new oil pump gasket

14.10 Locate the oil pump into place over the dowels

pump, and obtain a new one for refitting **(see illustration)**.

Refitting

8 Ensure the mating surfaces of the oil pump and cylinder block are clean and dry. Clean all traces of locking compound from the pump mounting holes on the engine. Clean the oil seal surface on the crankshaft, and the area around the oil cooler unions.

9 Ensure the locating dowels are in position, then fit a new gasket to the cylinder block **(see illustration)**.

10 Carefully manoeuvre the oil pump into position, aligning the flats on the pump drivegear with those on the crankshaft end. Locate the pump on the dowels **(see illustration)**.

11 Fit the new oil pump bolts, and tighten progressively in sequence to the specified torque **(see illustrations)**.

14.11a Fit the new bolts . . .

12 Genuine crankshaft oil seals should come with a fitting sleeve, which sits over the crankshaft nose **(see illustration)**. If one is

14.11b . . . then tighten them to the specified torque . . .

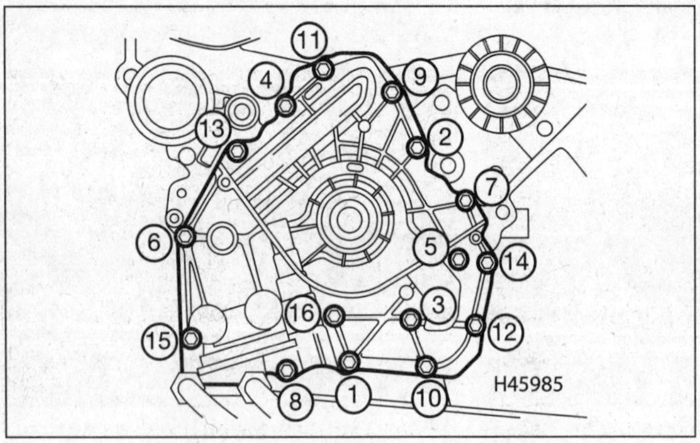

14.11c . . . using this tightening sequence

14.12 Fit the oil seal fitting sleeve in place

14.13a Ease the new oil seal into place . . .

not available, wrap a little tape round the sharp edge to protect the seal lips as it is fitted.

13 Fit the new oil seal (note that it should **not** be lubricated), ensuring its sealing lip is facing inwards, and ease it over the end of the crankshaft. Press it squarely into the housing using a tubular drift (such as a socket) which bears only on the hard outer edge of the seal **(see illustrations)**. Press the seal into position so that it is flush with the housing. Remove the oil seal guide or the tape on completion.

14 Reconnect the oil cooler pipe unions using new O-rings lubricated with clean engine oil, and tighten the unions to the specified torque.

15 Reconnect the oil pressure switch wiring plug.

16 Refit the crankshaft sprocket as described in Section 8.

17 On completion, refill the engine with oil and fit a new oil filter as described in Chapter 1A.

15 Oil pump – dismantling, inspection and reassembly

Note: *If oil pump wear is suspected, check the cost and availability of new parts (only available in the form of a repair kit) against the cost of a new pump. Examine the pump as described in this Section and then decide whether renewal or repair is the best course of action. The oil pressure relief valve can be removed with the oil pump in place, as described in Section 13.*

14.13b . . . and drive it home using a suitable socket

Dismantling

1 Remove the oil pump as described in Section 14.

2 Unscrew the retaining screws and remove the pump cover plate and sealing ring **(see illustration)**.

3 Note the identification marks on the outer rotor, then remove both the rotors from the body **(see illustration)**.

4 To dismantle the pressure relief valve, slacken and remove the threaded plug and washer, then recover the valve spring and plunger.

Inspection

5 Inspect the rotors for obvious signs of wear or damage and renew if necessary. If the pump body or cover plate is scored or damaged, then the complete oil pump assembly must be renewed.

6 Refit the rotors to the body and, using feeler blades of the appropriate thickness, measure the clearance between the outer rotor and the pump body **(see illustration)**.

7 Using feeler blades and a straight-edge placed across the top of the pump body and the rotors, measure the rotor endfloat **(see illustration)**.

8 If any measurement is outside the specified limits, the complete pump assembly must be renewed.

9 If the pressure relief valve plunger is scored, or if it does not slide freely in the pump body bore, then it must be renewed, using all the components from the repair kit.

10 Thoroughly clean the threads of the pump cover plate securing screws and renew the cover sealing ring and relief valve washer, if damaged.

Reassembly

11 Lubricate the pump rotors with clean engine oil and refit them to the pump body, ensuring that the identification mark on the outer rotor faces outwards (ie, towards the pump cover) **(see illustration)**.

12 Fit the sealing ring to the pump body and refit the cover plate. Apply threadlocking

15.2 Remove the pump cover plate screws

15.3 Remove the oil pump rotors

15.6 Measure the outer rotor-to-body clearance

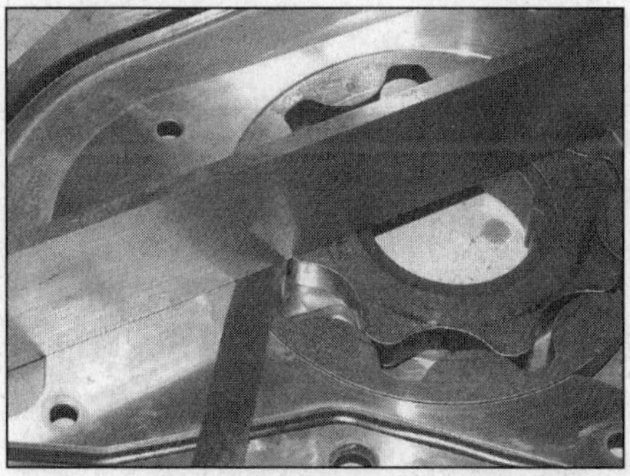

15.7 Check the rotor endfloat with a feeler blade and straight-edge

15.11 Lubricate the pump rotors before fitting them

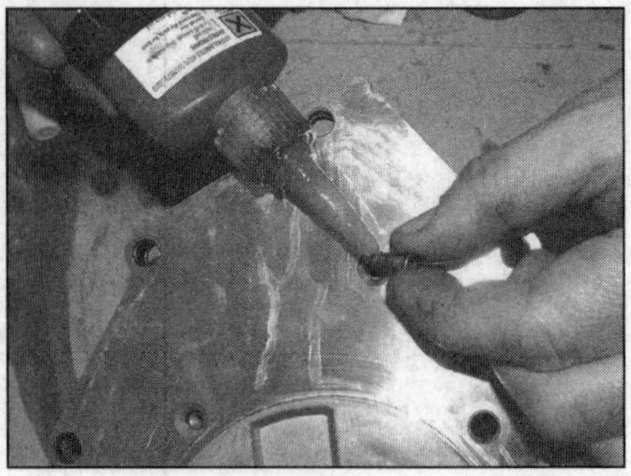

15.12 Thread-lock the oil pump cover screws

compound to the threads of the cover plate screws then refit the screws, tightening them securely **(see illustration)**.

13 Check that the pump rotates freely, then prime it by injecting oil into its passages and rotating it. If a long time elapses before the pump is refitted to the engine, prime it again before installation.

14 Refit the oil pressure relief valve plunger, ensuring that it is the correct way up, then install the spring. Fit the sealing washer to the threaded plug and tighten the plug securely.

16 Oil pressure switch – removal and refitting

1 The oil pressure switch is a vital early warning of low oil pressure. The switch operates the oil warning light on the instrument panel – the light

16.7 The oil pressure switch is above the oil filter

should come on with the ignition, and go out almost immediately when the engine starts.

2 If the light does not come on, there could be a fault on the instrument panel, the switch wiring, or the switch itself. If the light does not go out, low oil level, worn oil pump (or sump pick-up blocked), blocked oil filter, or worn main bearings could be to blame – or again, the switch may be faulty.

3 If the light comes on while driving, the best advice is to turn the engine off immediately, and not to drive the car until the problem has been investigated – ignoring the light could mean expensive engine damage.

Removal

4 Loosen the right-hand front wheel bolts. Firmly apply the handbrake, then jack up the front of the car and support it securely on axle stands (see *Jacking and vehicle support*). Remove the right-hand front wheel.

5 Remove the engine undertray, which is secured by a number of quick-release screw fasteners.

6 Remove the right-hand front wheel arch liner as described in Chapter 11, Section 22.

7 The oil pressure switch is mounted above the oil filter (and, where applicable, above the oil cooler hoses) **(see illustration)**.

8 Disconnect the switch wiring plug.

9 Place a drain container under the switch – the amount of oil lost should be quite small.

10 Anticipating oil spillage, slowly unscrew the switch and remove it. Recover the sealing washer – a new one should be used when refitting.

11 Allow the oil to finish draining, then clean the switch threads and the switch location.

Refitting

12 Fit the switch using a new sealing washer, and tighten it to the specified torque.

13 Reconnect the wiring plug, then refit the undertray, wheel arch liner and right-hand wheel, and lower the car to the ground. Tighten the wheel bolts to the specified torque.

17 Oil cooler – removal and refitting

Note: *The oil cooler is only fitted to models with air conditioning.*

HAYNES HiNT ***The oil cooler is a heat exchanger, which has engine oil and coolant running through it. If the cooler fails, this will either allow oil and coolant to mix, or will cause an external leak. Check the oil and coolant levels regularly (as described in 'Weekly checks') and also look for signs of oil/ water contamination – something which normally indicates cylinder head gasket failure.***

Removal

1 Drain the engine oil and coolant, and remove the auxiliary drivebelt, as described in Chapter 1A.

2 Place a drain container under the oil filter. Slacken and disconnect the two oil cooler unions on the oil pump. Recover and discard the O-ring seals – new ones should be fitted on reassembly **(see illustrations)**.

3 Remove the single bolt securing the oil dipstick tube to the block, then depress the locking collar at the base and pull the tube out of the sump **(see illustration)**.

4 Release the spring-type clips, and disconnect the two coolant hoses from the oil cooler.

5 Unscrew the two oil cooler mounting bolts, and withdraw the cooler from in front of the sump – note that it may be necessary to raise the engine on a jack to create clearance for removal **(see illustration)**.

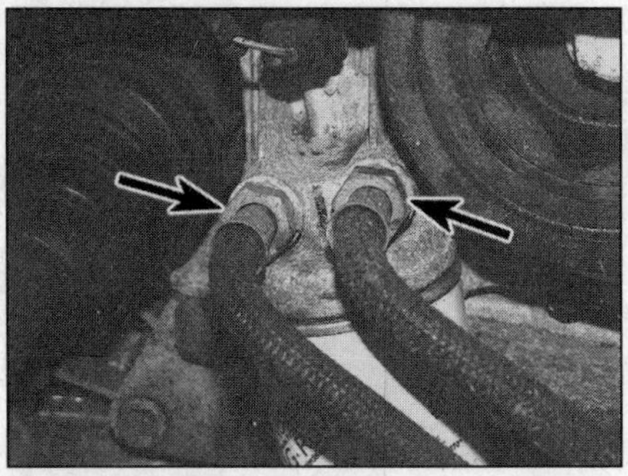

17.2a Disconnect the oil cooler unions at the oil pump . . .

17.2b . . . and recover the O-rings

17.3 Depress the collar, and pull out the dipstick tube

17.5 Oil cooler coolant hoses and mounting bolts

18.7a Unscrew the five mounting bolts . . .

18.7b . . . and remove the old oil seal

18.9 Fit the protector sleeve over the crankshaft

6 Noting their fitted positions, loosen the unions and disconnect the pipes from the cooler. Remove and discard the O-ring seals.

Refitting

7 Clean around the oil cooler unions on the cooler body and oil pump.
8 Reconnect the pipe unions to their original locations on the oil cooler, using new O-rings lubricated with clean engine oil, and tighten the unions to the specified torque.
9 Offer up the cooler to the sump, then refit the mounting bolts and tighten to the specified torque.
10 Reconnect the coolant hoses to the oil cooler, and secure with the hose clips. For preference, update the spring clips with Jubilee clips.
11 Clean and refit the oil dipstick tube.
12 Reconnect the pipe unions to the oil pump using new O-rings lubricated with clean engine oil, and tighten the unions to the specified torque.
13 Refit the auxiliary drivebelt, refill the cooling system and engine oil, as described in Chapter 1A.

18 Crankshaft oil seals - renewal

Primary timing belt end

Note: *On our project car, this oil seal was fitted after removing and refitting the oil pump - refer to Section 14.*

1 Remove the crankshaft sprocket as described in Section 8.
2 Carefully punch or drill two small holes opposite each other in the oil seal. Screw a self-tapping screw into each, and pull on the screws with pliers to extract the seal.
Caution: Great care must be taken to avoid damage to the oil pump.
3 Clean the seal housing and polish off any burrs or raised edges which may have caused the seal to fail in the first place.
4 The new seal has a waxed outer surface, and should **not** be lubricated prior to fitting. Ease the new seal into position on the end of the shaft. Press the seal squarely into position until it is flush with the housing. If necessary, a suitable tubular drift, such as a socket, which bears only on the hard outer edge of the seal can be used to tap the seal into position. Take great care not to damage the seal lips during fitting and ensure that the seal lips face inwards; if a genuine MG Rover seal is being installed, use the seal protector supplied to protect the seal during fitting and remove the protector once the seal is correctly located.
5 Wash off any traces of oil, then refit the crankshaft sprocket as described in Section 8.

Flywheel end

6 Remove the flywheel or driveplate as described in Section 19.
7 Remove the five bolts securing the oil seal to the engine. Discard the seal and the bolts, as new ones must be used **(see illustrations)**.
8 Clean the seal housing, removing all traces of oil. Polish off any burrs or raised edges which may have caused the original seal to fail.
9 Genuine oil seals may be supplied with a protector sleeve for fitting - if not, wrap a little tape around the end of the crankshaft to protect the oil seal lips during fitting **(see illustration)**.
10 Offer the seal into place - note that it must **not** be lubricated. Ease the sealing lip of the seal over the crankshaft shoulder, by hand only, then press the seal evenly into its housing until its outer flange seats evenly **(see illustration)**. If necessary, a soft-faced mallet can be used to tap the seal gently into place.
11 Fit the five new bolts, and tighten them evenly to draw the seal fully into position **(see illustration)**. Finally, tighten the bolts to the specified torque.
12 Refit the flywheel/driveplate as described in Section 19.

19 Flywheel/driveplate - removal, inspection and refitting

Flywheel

Removal

1 Remove the clutch assembly as described in Chapter 6.
2 Prevent the flywheel from turning by locking the ring gear teeth **(see illustration)**.

18.10 Fit the new seal over the sleeve, and press home

18.11 Use five new bolts to secure the seal

19.2 Home-made tool for locking the flywheel ring gear

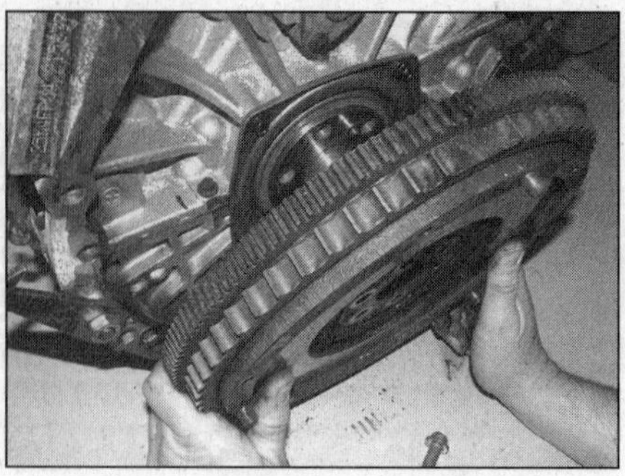

19.3 Removing the flywheel

19.7a Engage the flywheel on its locating dowel . . .

19.7b . . . then fit the bolts . . .

Alternatively, bolt a strap between the flywheel and the cylinder block/crankcase. Make alignment marks between the flywheel and crankshaft using paint or a suitable marker pen.

3 Slacken and remove the six retaining bolts and remove the flywheel **(see illustration). Do not** drop it, as it is very heavy.

Inspection

4 If the flywheel clutch mating surface is deeply scored, cracked or otherwise damaged, then the flywheel must be renewed, unless it is possible to have it surface-ground. Seek the advice of an engine reconditioning specialist.

5 If the ring gear is badly worn or has missing teeth, then it must be renewed. This job is best left to an engine reconditioning specialist. The temperature to which the new ring gear must be heated for installation (350°C – shown by an even light blue colour) is critical and, if not done accurately, the hardness of the teeth will be destroyed.

Refitting

6 Clean the mating surfaces of the flywheel and crankshaft, and remove all traces of locking compound from the crankshaft threaded holes.

7 Fit the flywheel to the crankshaft, engaging it with the crankshaft locating dowel, and fit the retaining bolts **(see illustrations)**.

8 Lock the flywheel using the method employed on dismantling then, working in a diagonal sequence, evenly and progressively tighten the retaining bolts to the specified torque wrench setting **(see illustration)**.

9 Refit the clutch assembly (see Chapter 6).

Driveplate

10 All procedures are essentially the same as described for the flywheel, disregarding references to the clutch. To access the driveplate, remove the automatic transmission as described in Chapter 7B. Note that driveplate bolts are tightened to a higher torque than flywheel bolts.

20 Engine/transmission mountings – inspection and renewal

Inspection

1 If improved access is required, raise the front of the car and support it securely on axle stands (see *Jacking and vehicle support*). Remove the engine undertray, which is secured by a number of quick-release screw fasteners.

2 Check the mounting rubber to see if it is cracked, hardened or separated from the metal at any point. Renew the mounting if any such damage or deterioration is evident.

3 Check that all mounting fasteners are securely tightened. Use a torque wrench to check, if possible.

4 Using a large screwdriver or a pry bar, check for wear in the mountings by carefully levering against it to check for free play. Where this is not possible, enlist the aid of an assistant to move the engine/gearbox unit back-and-forth or from side-to-side while you watch the mountings. While some free play is to be expected even from new components, excessive wear should be obvious. If excessive free play is found, check first that the fasteners are correctly secured, then renew any worn components as described below.

Right-hand mounting

5 Firmly apply the handbrake, then jack up the front of the car and support securely on axle stands (see *Jacking and vehicle support*). Undo the fasteners and remove the engine undertray.

6 Support the weight of the engine/transmission, preferably using a hoist. Alternatively, use a trolley jack with a block of wood placed on its head, positioned underneath the engine (if this method is used, make sure the oil cooler coolant hoses are not strained or distorted as the engine is raised). Raise the engine slightly to remove all load from the mounting.

7 Remove the two bolts securing the upper cross-brace, noting that one of the bolts also secures an engine earth lead. Lift off the cross-brace **(see illustrations)**.

8 Remove the two auxiliary drivebelt upper

19.8 . . . and tighten to the specified torque

20.7a Unscrew the two cross-brace mounting bolts . . .

20.7b . . . and lift it off, noting the earth lead

20.8a Remove the two bolts . . .

20.8b . . . and lift off the drivebelt upper cover

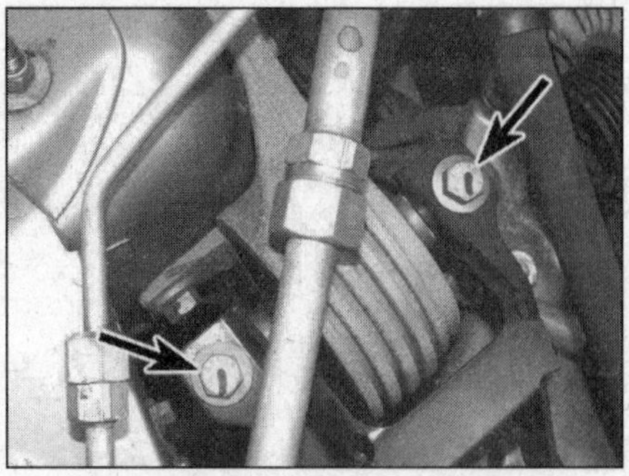
20.9a Steady bracket rear bolts . . .

cover bolts, and lift off the cover **(see illustrations)**.

9 The upper steady bracket is secured by three bolts – two at the rear, and a through-bolt at the front **(see illustrations)**. However, the through-bolt will not come out – it hits the inner wing. Therefore, the steady bracket must be removed with the upper mounting bracket.

10 To remove the engine upper mounting bracket, unscrew the nut securing it to the hydramount, then remove the four further bolts securing it to the lower mounting bracket **(see illustrations)**.

11 The lower mounting bracket is bolted to the engine front (end) plate by four bolts, and can be removed if required **(see illustrations)**.

12 The right-hand mounting bracket on the inner wing is secured by a total of four bolts, and can be removed if required **(see illustrations)**. First, where applicable, remove the two bolts securing the air conditioning

20.9b . . . and front through-bolt

20.10a Upper mounting bracket nut and bolts

hose to the engine right-hand mounting and bonnet lock platform. Release the hose from the mounting clips in the engine compartment as necessary, and move it clear as far as possible without disconnecting or straining it.

13 If required, the hydramount can be unscrewed from the wing, using MG Rover tool LRT-12-169 (which engages in the three slots around the mounting), or using a strap/chain wrench around the circumference of the mounting **(see illustration)**.

14 Refitting is a reversal of removal. Tighten

20.10b Removing the upper mounting bracket and steady bracket

20.11a Engine lower mounting bracket bolts

20.11b Removing the engine lower mounting bracket

20.12a Two of the right-hand mounting bracket bolts . . .

20.12b . . . and a third, seen from the right-hand front wheel arch

20.13 The hydramount can be unscrewed if required

20.20 Left-hand mounting through-bolt

all fasteners to the specified torque – in the case of the hydramount, torque tightening may be impossible without the special tool, so tighten securely using the same method as for removal.

Left-hand mounting

15 Remove the engine top cover, which is secured by two bolts.

20.24a Prise out the clip . . .

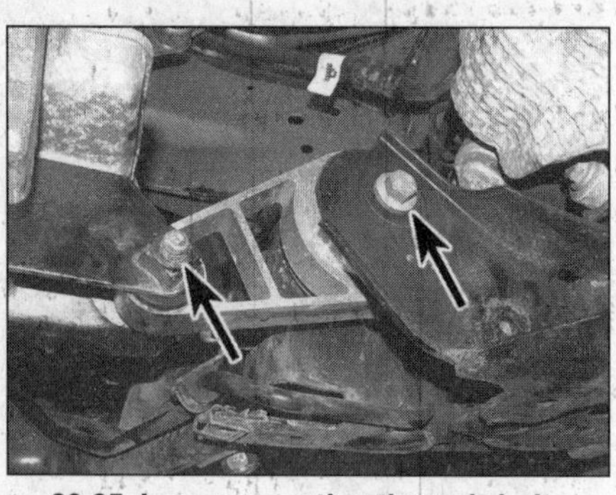

20.25 Lower mounting through-bolts

20.21a Left-hand mounting bracket on the inner wing – bolts arrowed

16 Remove the air cleaner assembly as described in Chapter 4B.

17 Remove the battery and its tray as described in Chapter 5A.

18 Firmly apply the handbrake, then jack up the front of the car and support securely on axle stands (see *Jacking and vehicle support*). Undo the fasteners and remove the engine undertray.

19 Support the weight of the engine/

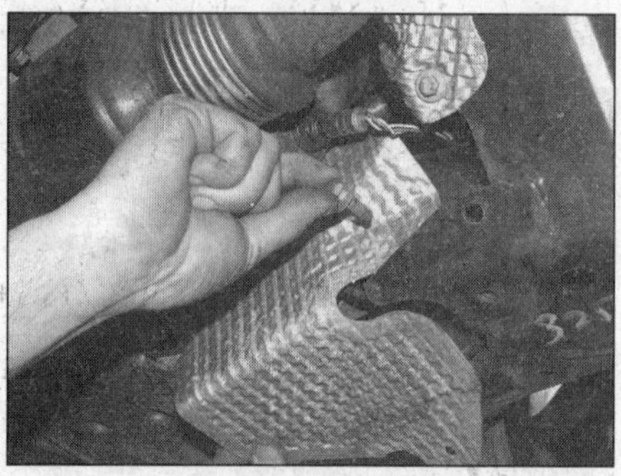

20.24b . . . then remove the bolt and take off the heat shield

20.26 The lower mounting bracket is secured to the sump by two bolts

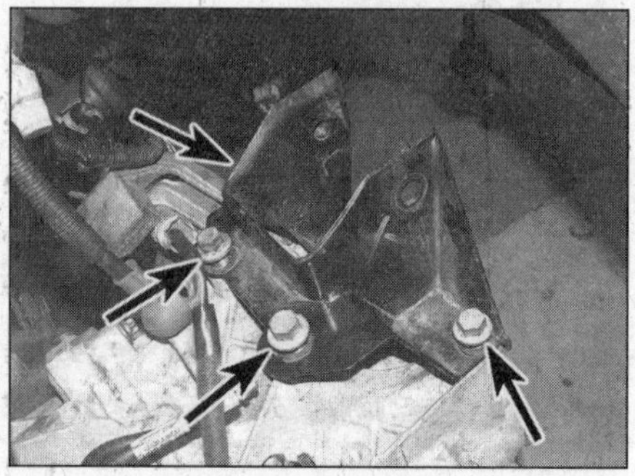

20.21b Left-hand mounting bracket on transmission

transmission, preferably using a hoist. Alternatively, use a trolley jack with a block of wood placed on its head, positioned underneath the transmission (if this method is used, make sure the oil cooler coolant hoses are not strained or distorted as the engine is raised). Raise the engine slightly to remove all load from the mounting.

20 To separate the mounting, unscrew and remove the through-bolt **(see illustration)**.

21 Once the through-bolt is removed, lower the transmission until the mounting is separated (again, check the oil cooler coolant hoses). If required, the two mounting brackets can now be unbolted from the body and transmission – each is secured by four bolts **(see illustrations)**.

22 Refitting is a reversal of removal. Tighten all fasteners to the specified torque.

Lower mounting

23 Firmly apply the handbrake, then jack up the front of the car and support securely on axle stands (see *Jacking and vehicle support*). Remove the engine undertray, which is secured by a number of quick-release screw fasteners.

24 Remove the single bolt and release the clip securing the heat shield fitted at one side of the lower mounting, and withdraw it **(see illustrations)**.

25 Unscrew the two through-bolts from the lower mounting to release it, and withdraw it from the mounting brackets **(see illustration)**. Though removing the lower mounting will increase the amount of engine movement, provided they have not been disturbed, the engine will remain safely supported on its right- and left-hand mountings.

26 If required, the lower mounting bracket can be unbolted from the sump **(see illustration)**.

27 Refitting is a reversal of removal. Tighten all fasteners to the specified torque.

Chapter 2 Part C:
Diesel engine in-car repair procedures

Contents

Degrees of difficulty

Easy, suitable for novice with little experience	**Fairly easy,** suitable for beginner with some experience	**Fairly difficult,** suitable for competent DIY mechanic	**Difficult,** suitable for experienced DIY mechanic	**Very difficult,** suitable for expert DIY or professional

Specifications

General

Engine type	Four-cylinder in-line, double overhead camshaft, 16-valve, four-stroke
Designation	M47R
Bore	84.0 mm
Stroke	88.0 mm
Capacity	1950 cc
Firing order	1-3-4-2 (No 1 cylinder at timing belt end)
Direction of crankshaft rotation	Clockwise (seen from right-hand side of car)
Compression ratio	18.0:1

Camshafts

Bearing journal running clearance	0.011 to 0.034 mm
Camshaft endfloat	0.15 to 0.33 mm

Lubrication system

Minimum system pressure	1.5 bar at idle, 3.0 to 4.5 bar at 3500 rpm (hot)
Pressure relief valve opening pressure	4.2 bar
Low oil pressure warning light comes on	0.2 to 0.5 bar
Oil pump outer rotor-to-body clearance	0.08 to 0.158 mm

Torque wrench settings

Torque wrench settings	Nm	lbf ft
Air conditioning compressor and mounting bracket	25	18
Big-end bearing cap bolts:		
Stage 1	5	4
Stage 2	25	18
Stage 3	Angle-tighten a further 70°	
Camshaft bearing cap bolts	10	7
Camshaft cover bolts	10	7
Camshaft sprocket bolts*:		
Stage 1	20	15
Stage 2	Angle-tighten a further 35°	
Coolant rail:		
Lower rail-to-sump bolts	10	7
Rail-to-cylinder head bolts	20	15
Rail-to-exhaust manifold bolts	20	15
Rail to thermostat housing	8	6
Crankshaft flywheel end oil seal housing bolts:		
M6	10	7
M8	22	16
Crankshaft pulley bolt*:		
Stage 1	100	74
Stage 2	Angle-tighten a further 60°	
Stage 3	Angle-tighten a further 60°	
Stage 4	Angle-tighten a further 30°	
Cylinder block reinforcing (baffle) plate	22	16
Cylinder head bolts*:		
Stage 1	80	59
Stage 2	Slacken 180°	
Stage 3	50	37
Stage 4	Angle-tighten a further 90°	
Stage 5	Angle-tighten a further 90°	
Stage 6 (41 mm long bolt in position 12 only)	110	81
Cylinder head-to-timing cover Allen screws	15	11
Dipstick tube-to-oil filter housing bolt	10	7
Driveplate bolts*	115	85
EGR cooler to cylinder head	25	18
Engine lifting eye	20	15
Engine oil drain plug	25	18
Engine/transmission mountings:		
Left-hand mounting through-bolt	100	74
Left-hand mounting to body	85	63
Left-hand mounting to transmission	85	63
Lower mounting bracket bolts:		
To subframe	85	63
To sump	10	7
Lower mounting through-bolts	100	74
Right-hand hydramount to body	85	63
Right-hand mounting bracket to engine	100	74
Right-hand mounting bracket-to-hydramount nut	85	63
Right-hand mounting steady (upper) bracket bolts	85	63
Right-hand mounting to body	85	63
Flywheel bolts*	110	81
Fuel injection pump drive chain lower guide Allen screw*	24	18
Fuel injection pump sprocket retaining nut	65	48
Fuel pipe union nuts	30	22
Fuel rail Allen screws	24	18
Main bearing cap bolts*:		
Stage 1	20	15
Stage 2	Angle-tighten a further 70°	
Oil cooler-to-oil filter housing bolts	22	16
Oil feed guide rail bolts	10	7
Oil filter cap	25	18
Oil filter housing bolts	25	18
Oil pressure switch	38	28
Oil pump:		
Drive sprocket-to-driveshaft Torx bolt	25	18
Mounting bolts	22	16
Pick-up/strainer bolts	10	7

Torque wrench settings (continued)

Torque wrench settings (continued)	Nm	lbf ft
Oil spray jet bolt*	10	7
Roadwheel bolts	125	92
Sump bolts:		
M6	10	7
M8	28	21
Sump plate bolts	10	7
Timing chain cover bolts	15	11
Timing chain guide Allen screw*	20	15
Timing chain guides support pins	20	15
Timing chain lubrication jet bolt	10	7
Timing chain tensioner:		
Access plug	30	22
Tensioner bolts	10	7
Turbocharger-to-exhaust manifold bolts	45	33
Vacuum pump bolts*	22	16

** Use new bolts*

1 General information and precautions

How to use this Chapter

This Part of the Chapter describes those repair procedures that can reasonably be carried out on the engine whilst it remains in the car. If the engine has been removed from the car and is being dismantled as described in Part D of this Chapter, any preliminary dismantling procedures can be ignored.

Note that whilst it may be possible physically to overhaul items such as the piston/connecting rod assemblies with the engine in the car, such tasks are not usually carried out as separate operations and usually require the execution of several additional procedures (not to mention the cleaning of components and of oilways). For this reason, all such tasks are classed as major overhaul procedures and are described in Part D of this Chapter.

Engine description

The 2.0 litre diesel engine is of BMW origin, and is a four-cylinder, double overhead camshaft, 16-valve, in-line unit, mounted transversely at the front of the car with the clutch (where applicable) and transmission on the left-hand end.

The cast-iron cylinder block is of the dry-liner type. The crankshaft is supported within the cylinder block on five shell-type main bearings. Thrustwashers are integral with the No 4 main bearing shells to control crankshaft endfloat.

The cylinder head is a double overhead camshaft, 16-valve design – two inlet and two exhaust valves per cylinder. The valves are operated by one inlet camshaft and one exhaust camshaft, via rocker fingers. One end of each finger acts upon the valve stem, whilst the other end pivots on a support pillar. Valve clearances are maintained automatically by hydraulic compensation elements (tappets) incorporated within the support pillars. In order to achieve high levels of combustion efficiency, the cylinder head has two inlet ports for each cylinder – one port is tangential, whilst the other is helical, to promote swirl.

The connecting rods rotate on horizontally-split bearing shells at their big-ends. The pistons are attached to the connecting rods by gudgeon pins which are secured in position with circlips. The aluminium alloy pistons are fitted with three piston rings, comprising two compression rings and an oil control ring.

The inlet and exhaust valves are each closed by coil springs, and operate in guides pressed into the cylinder head. Valve guides cannot be renewed.

A simplex chain, driven by the crankshaft, drives the high-pressure fuel pump sprocket, which in turn drives the camshafts. The vacuum pump is fitted to the left-hand end of the cylinder head, and is driven by the exhaust camshaft. The water pump is driven by the auxiliary drivebelt.

Lubrication is by means of an eccentric-rotor type pump driven by the crankshaft via a simplex chain. The pump draws oil through a strainer located in the sump, and then forces it through an externally-mounted full-flow paper element type oil filter into galleries in the cylinder block/crankcase, from where it is distributed to the crankshaft (main bearings), timing chain (sprayed by a jet), and camshaft. The big-end bearings are supplied with oil via internal drillings in the crankshaft, while the camshaft bearings and the followers receive a pressurised supply via drillings in the cylinder head. The camshaft lobes and valves are lubricated by oil splash, as are all other engine components. An oil cooler (integral with the oil filter housing) is fitted to keep the oil temperature stable under arduous operating conditions.

Operations with engine in car

The following work can be carried out with the engine in the car:

a) Compression pressure – testing.
b) Camshaft cover – removal and refitting.
c) Crankshaft pulley – removal and refitting.
d) Camshaft oil seals – renewal.
e) Camshafts and rocker arms – removal, inspection and refitting.
f) Cylinder head – removal and refitting.
g) Cylinder head and pistons – decarbonising.
h) Sump – removal and refitting.
i) Oil pump – removal, overhaul and refitting.
j) Oil filter housing/cooler – removal and refitting.
k) Crankshaft oil seals – renewal.
l) Engine/transmission mountings – inspection and renewal.
m) Flywheel/driveplate – removal, inspection and refitting.

Note: *Although in theory it is possible to remove the timing cover and timing chains with the engine fitted, in practice access is extremely limited, special MG Rover tools are needed, and the cylinder head and sump must be removed. Consequently, it is recommended that the engine is removed prior to timing cover and chains removal.*

2 Compression test – description and interpretation

Compression test

Note: *A compression tester specifically designed for diesel engines must be used for this test.*

1 When engine performance is down, or if misfiring occurs which cannot be attributed to the fuel system, a compression test can provide diagnostic clues as to the engine's condition. If the test is performed regularly, it can give warning of trouble before any other symptoms become apparent.

2 The tester is connected to an adaptor which screws into the glow plug or injector hole. It is unlikely to be worthwhile buying such a tester for occasional use, but it may be possible to borrow or hire one – if not, have the test performed by a garage.

3 Unless specific instructions to the contrary are supplied with the tester, observe the following points:

a) The battery must be in a good state of charge, the air filter must be clean, and the engine should be at normal operating temperature.

b) All the injectors or glow plugs should be removed before starting the test (see Chapter 4C or 5C).

4 There is no need to hold the accelerator pedal down during the test, because the diesel engine air inlet is not throttled.

5 Crank the engine on the starter motor; after one or two revolutions, the compression pressure should build-up to a maximum figure, and then stabilise. Record the highest reading obtained.

6 Repeat the test on the remaining cylinders, recording the pressure in each.

7 All cylinders should produce very similar pressures; a difference of more than 2 bars between any two cylinders indicates a fault. Note that the compression should build-up quickly in a healthy engine; low compression on the first stroke, followed by gradually-increasing pressure on successive strokes, indicates worn piston rings. A low compression reading on the first stroke, which does not build-up during successive strokes, indicates leaking valves or a blown head gasket (a cracked head could also be the cause). Deposits on the undersides of the valve heads can also cause low compression. **Note:** *The cause of poor compression is less easy to establish on a diesel engine than on a petrol one. The effect of introducing oil into the cylinders ('wet' testing) is not conclusive, because there is a risk that the oil will sit in the swirl chamber or in the recess on the piston crown instead of passing to the rings.*

3.5 Pull out the blanking plug from the timing pin hole in the engine block

8 Although MG Rover do not specify exact compression pressures, as a guide, any cylinder pressure of below 20 bars can be considered as less than healthy. Refer to an engine specialist if in doubt as to whether a particular pressure reading is acceptable.

9 On completion of the test, refit the injectors or glow plugs as described in Chapter 4C or 5C.

Leakdown test

10 A leakdown test measures the rate at which compressed air fed into the cylinder is lost. It is an alternative to a compression test, and in many ways it is better, since the escaping air provides easy identification of where pressure loss is occurring (piston rings, valves or head gasket).

11 The equipment needed for leakdown testing is unlikely to be available to the home mechanic. If poor compression is suspected, have the test performed by a suitably-equipped garage.

3 Engine assembly/valve timing settings – general information and usage

Note: *An assistant will be required.*

Note: *MG Rover tool LRT-12-171 or suitable home-made equivalent will be required to lock the crankshaft in position, and access to MG Rover tool LRT-12-173 or home-made equivalent is required to position the camshafts.*

1 The flywheel is equipped with an indent which aligns with a hole in the engine block when Nos 1 and 4 pistons are at TDC (top dead centre). In this position, if No 1 piston is at TDC on its compression stroke, it will be possible to fit a MG Rover special tool (LRT-12-173) or home-made equivalent, over the square sections of the inlet and exhaust camshafts (with all four No 1 cylinder camshaft lobes pointing upwards).

2 Slacken the right-hand front roadwheel bolts, firmly apply the handbrake, then jack up the front of the car and support it securely on axle stands (see *Jacking and vehicle support*). Remove the front right-hand roadwheel.

3 Undo the retaining screws/clips and remove the engine undertray, and right-hand wheel arch liner.

4 Remove the camshaft cover and gasket, as described in Section 4.

5 Pull out the blanking plug from the timing pin hole in the engine block **(see illustration)**.

6 Using a socket and extension bar on the crankshaft pulley centre bolt, turn the crankshaft clockwise (viewed from the right-hand end of the engine whilst keeping an eye on the No 1 cylinder camshaft lobes. **Note:** *Do not turn the engine anti-clockwise.*

7 Rotate the crankshaft clockwise until the No 1 cylinder camshaft lobes approach the point where all four lobes are beginning to point up. Have an assistant insert MG Rover tool LRT-12-171 or a home-made equivalent into the timing pin hole, and press the pin gently against the flywheel. Continue to slowly turn the crankshaft slowly until the pin is felt to engage in the indent in the flywheel, and the crankshaft locks **(see illustrations)**.

8 With the crankshaft in this position, all four camshaft lobes of No 1 cylinder should be pointing upwards. Fit MG Rover tool LRT-12-173 over the inlet camshaft square section, adjacent to No 1 camshaft bearing cap. If the camshaft is timed correctly, the tool will contact both sides of the camshaft cover gasket face on the cylinder head. If the tool is not available, it is possible to fabricate

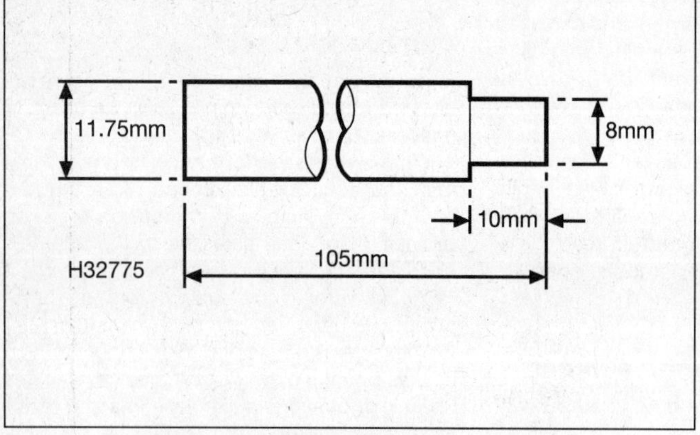

3.7a Crankshaft locking pin dimensions

3.7b Insert the locking pin through the block and into the flywheel indent

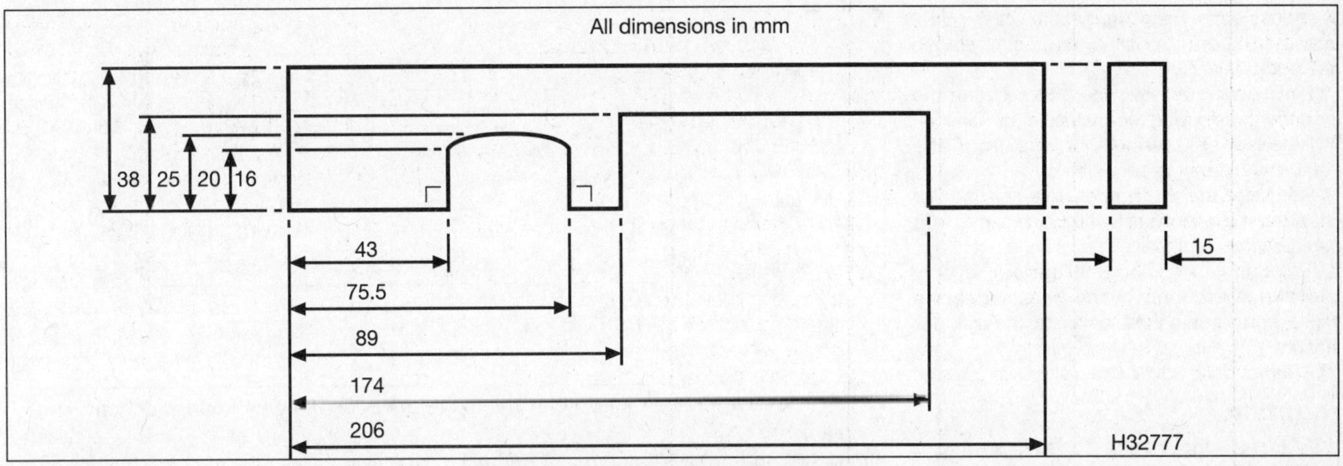

3.8a Camshaft positioning tool dimensions

3.8b The tool should contact both sides of the camshaft cover gasket face on the cylinder head

4.2a Unscrew the three bolts . . .

4.2b . . . and lift off the engine top cover

a home-made equivalent **(see illustrations)**. **Note:** *When fabricating the home-made tool, it is absolutely essential that the dimensions are accurately followed where the tool slides over the square section of the camshaft.*

9 Remove the tool from the inlet camshaft, and position it over the square section of the exhaust camshaft. Again, the tool will contact both sides of the camshaft cover gasket face on the cylinder head if the camshaft is timed correctly.

4 Camshaft cover – removal and refitting

Removal

1 Disconnect the battery negative lead (see *Disconnecting the battery*).

2 Unscrew the three bolts and remove the engine top cover **(see illustrations)**.

3 With reference to Chapter 4C, remove the fuel injectors.

4 Remove the engine oil filler cap, undo the five Allen screws and remove the air cleaner cover. Lift the air cleaner element from the housing (refer to Chapter 1B if necessary).

5 Disconnect the wiring plugs from the camshaft position, and mass airflow/intake air temperature sensors **(see illustrations)**.

6 Using a screwdriver, prise open the two clips securing the turbocharger air duct to

4.5a Disconnect the wiring plugs from the camshaft position sensor . . .

4.5b . . . and the mass airflow sensor

the mass airflow sensor, disconnect the duct breather pipe to the air cleaner, and remove the duct.

7 Slacken and remove the bolt securing the breather pipe clip to the mass airflow sensor.

8 Release the wiring harness from the retaining clip on the camshaft cover.

9 Remove the bolt securing the power steering pipe support clip to the cylinder head.

10 Working in a diagonal pattern, evenly slacken and remove the fourteen bolts securing the camshaft cover to the cylinder head.

11 Remove the cover and discard its gasket.

Refitting

12 Ensure the mating surfaces are clean and dry, then fit the new gasket to the cover.

13 Refit the engine breather pipe connector to the air cleaner housing.

14 Apply a 2 mm bead of sealant to the cylinder head mating surface **(see illustration)**.

15 Refit the cover to the cylinder head, ensuring that the gasket remains correctly seated.

16 Insert the cover retaining bolts, and tighten them in a diagonal sequence to the specified torque.

17 The remainder of refitting is a reversal of removal.

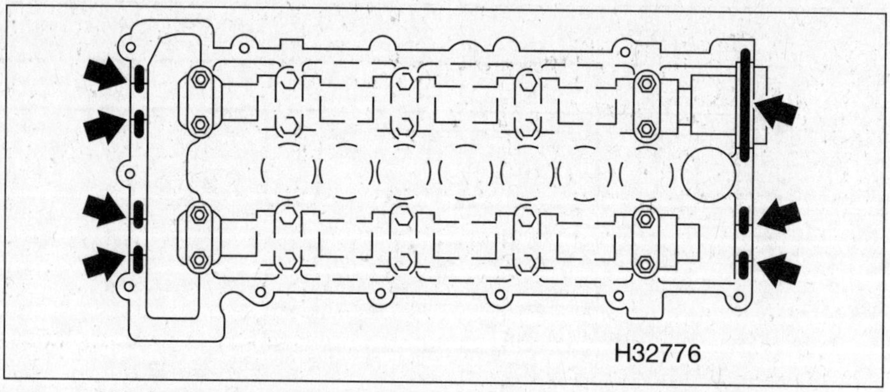

4.14 Apply a 2 mm bead of sealant to the cylinder head mating surface

5 Crankshaft pulley – removal and refitting

Removal

1 Undo the three bolts, and remove the engine top cover.

2 Firmly apply the handbrake, then slacken the right-hand front roadwheel bolts. Jack up the front of the car and support it securely on axle stands (see *Jacking and vehicle support*). Unscrew the bolts and remove the right-hand front roadwheel.

3 Remove the auxiliary drivebelt and (where applicable) the air conditioning compressor drivebelt as described in Chapter 1B.

4 If further dismantling is to be carried out, align the engine assembly/valve timing settings as described in Section 3.

5 Slacken the crankshaft pulley retaining bolt. To prevent crankshaft rotation (the pulley retaining bolt is extremely tight) remove the starter motor as described in Chapter 5A to expose the flywheel ring gear, and have an assistant insert a wide-bladed screwdriver between the ring gear teeth and the transmission bellhousing whilst the pulley retaining bolt is slackened. If the engine is removed from the car, it will be necessary to lock the flywheel (see Section 14).

Caution: Do not be tempted to use the crankshaft locking pin (see Section 3) to prevent rotation as the centre bolt is slackened.

6 Unscrew the retaining bolt and washer, and remove the pulley from the crankshaft **(see illustrations)**.

Refitting

7 Fit the pulley to the crankshaft and screw in the retaining bolt with the washer fitted.

8 Lock the crankshaft by the method used on removal, and tighten the pulley retaining bolt to the specified Stage 1 torque setting, then angle-tighten the bolt through the specified Stages 2, 3 and 4 angles, using a socket and extension bar. It is recommended that an angle-measuring gauge is used during the final stages of the tightening, to ensure accuracy. If a gauge is not available, use paint to make alignment marks between the bolt head and pulley prior to tightening; the marks can then be used to check that the bolt has been rotated through the correct angle **(see illustration)**.

9 Refit the auxiliary drivebelt and (where applicable) air conditioning compressor drivebelt as described in Chapter 1B.

10 Refit the roadwheel, then lower the car to the ground and tighten the wheel bolts to the specified torque.

11 Refit the engine top cover.

6 Camshafts, rocker arms and hydraulic tappets – removal, inspection and refitting

Removal

1 Set the crankshaft and camshafts to TDC on No 1 cylinder as described in Section 3.

2 Remove the auxiliary and air conditioning compressor drivebelts as described in Chapter 1B.

3 With reference to Section 15, remove the right-hand hydramount (engine mounting).

4 Using a 17 mm Allen key, remove the camshaft timing chain tensioner access plug from the timing chain cover. The plug is located adjacent to the water pump pulley.

5 With a spanner on its hexagonal section, rotate the exhaust camshaft slightly clockwise (viewed from the right-hand end of the engine) to fully compress the plunger into the

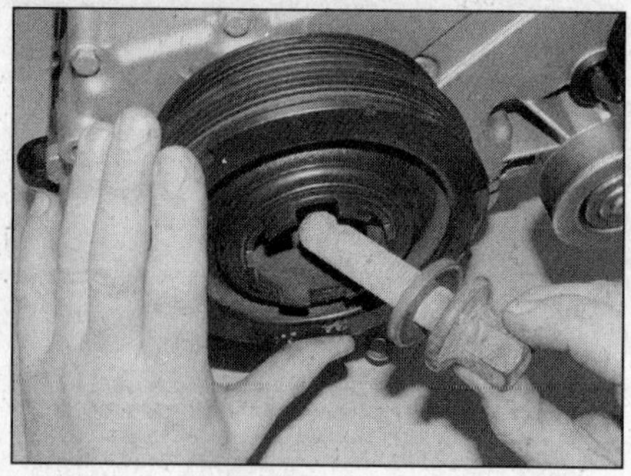

5.6a Unscrew the retaining bolt and washer . . .

5.6b . . . and remove the crankshaft pulley

5.8 Use paint to make alignment marks between the bolt head and pulley prior to tightening

6.5a With a spanner on its hexagonal section, rotate the exhaust camshaft slightly clockwise . . .

6.5b . . . and insert a 4 mm drill bit to lock the tensioner plunger

6.6 Remove the oil feed guide rail from between the camshafts

tensioner. Holding the cam in this position, insert MG Rover tool LRT-12-172 through the timing cover access hole into the tensioner body, to lock the plunger in place. If the tool is not available, a 4 mm drill bit or rod will make a suitable substitute **(see illustrations)**.

6 Undo the two retaining bolts, and remove the oil feed guide rail from between the camshafts **(see illustration)**. Discard the seal.

7 Hold the camshafts with a spanner on their hexagonal sections, and slacken the camshaft sprocket Torx screws.

8 Withdraw the crankshaft locking pin, and rotate the engine 45° backwards (anti-clockwise) using a spanner or socket on the crankshaft pulley. This is to prevent accidental valve-to-piston contact.

9 Completely unscrew the sprocket retaining bolts, and release the sprockets from the camshafts. Discard the bolts, as new ones must be fitted.

10 Identify the camshaft bearing caps, to ensure they are refitted to their original positions. The exhaust camshaft is marked A, so mark the exhaust camshaft bearing caps as A1, A2, A3, etc, starting with the cap nearest the timing chain. The inlet camshaft is marked E, so repeat the procedure for the inlet camshaft starting with E1 adjacent to the timing chain **(see illustration)**.

11 Evenly and progressively slacken and remove the retaining bolts, and remove the camshaft bearing caps.

12 Remove the camshafts from the cylinder head, disengaging the vacuum pump coupling from the left-hand end of the exhaust camshaft as it is withdrawn.

13 Lift the rocker arms from the cylinder head, and lay them out in order on a clean surface, so that they can be fitted into their original positions – if they are to be re-used.

14 If necessary, obtain sixteen small, clean plastic containers, and label them for identification. Alternatively, divide a larger container into compartments. Withdraw each tappet in turn, and place it upright in its respective container, which should then be filled with clean engine oil **(see illustration)**. ***Caution: Do not interchange the tappets, and do not allow the tappets to lose oil, as they will take a long time to refill with oil on restarting the engine, which could result in incorrect valve clearances. Absolute cleanliness is essential at all times when handling the tappets.***

Inspection

15 Examine the camshaft bearing surfaces and cam lobes for signs of wear ridges and scoring. Renew the camshaft if any of these conditions are apparent. Examine the condition of the bearing surfaces both on the camshaft journals and in the cylinder head. If the head bearing surfaces are worn excessively, the cylinder head will need to be renewed.

16 Examine the rocker bearing surfaces which contact the camshaft lobes for wear ridges and scoring. If the engine's valve clearances have sounded noisy, particularly if the noise persists after initial start-up from cold, then there is reason to suspect a faulty tappet. If any tappet is thought to be faulty or is visibly worn, it should be renewed.

Refitting

17 Where removed, lubricate the tappets with clean engine oil and carefully insert each one into its original location in the cylinder head **(see illustration)**.

18 Refit the rocker arms to their original locations, ensuring that they are correctly orientated **(see illustration)**.

19 Ensure that the crankshaft is still at the 45° before TDC position, liberally oil the camshaft bearings and rocker arms, then refit

6.10 Identify the camshaft bearing caps, to ensure they are refitted to their original positions (see text)

6.14 Withdraw each hydraulic tappet in turn, invert it to prevent oil loss

6.17 Lubricate the tappets with clean engine oil and carefully insert each one into its original location

6.18 Refit the rocker arms

6.19a Position the shafts so that the camshaft lobes for No 1 cylinder are pointing upwards

6.19b Engage the left-hand end of the exhaust camshaft with the vacuum pump coupling

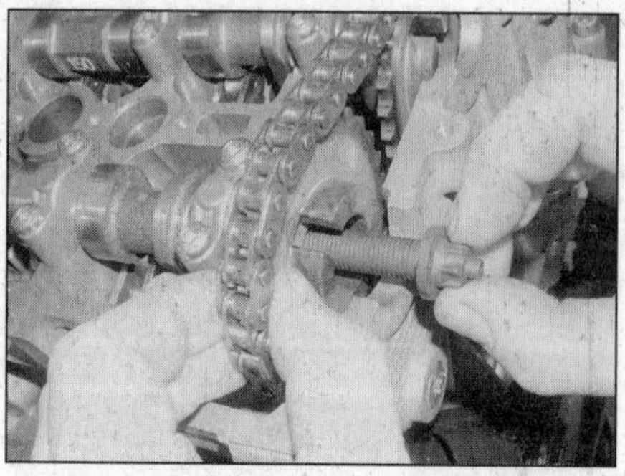

6.23 Fit the new sprocket retaining bolts, finger tighten them only

the camshafts to the cylinder head. Position the shafts so that the camshaft lobes for No 1 cylinder are pointing upwards. Engage the left-hand end of the exhaust camshaft with the vacuum pump coupling as the camshaft is fitted **(see illustrations)**.

20 Lubricate the camshaft bearing journals with clean engine oil. Refit the camshaft bearing caps to the cylinder head, ensuring that they are fitted to their original positions.

21 Screw in the bearing cap retaining bolts, tightening them all by hand only at this stage.

22 Evenly and progressively tighten the retaining bolts to draw the bearing caps squarely down into contact with the cylinder head. Once the caps are in contact with the head, tighten the retaining bolts to the specified torque.

Caution: If the bearing caps bolts are carelessly tightened, the caps might break. If the caps are broken then the complete cylinder head assembly must be renewed; the caps are matched to the head and are not available separately.

23 Engage the camshaft sprockets with the timing chain, and position them on the end of the camshafts. Fit the new sprocket bolts, finger-tight only at this stage – it must be possible to rotate the sprockets independently of the camshafts **(see illustration)**.

24 Clean the mating surfaces, and fit the oil feed guide rail, with a new seal, to the cylinder head between the camshafts. Tighten the bolts to the specified torque.

25 Whilst holding the exhaust camshaft stationary with a spanner on its hexagonal section, temporarily tighten the exhaust camshaft sprocket bolt sufficiently to stop the sprocket rotating independently of the camshaft.

26 With the spanner still on the hexagonal section, rotate the exhaust camshaft clockwise a little, to compress the plunger of the chain tensioner. Remove the tensioner locking pin from the timing cover access plug. Allow the camshaft to return to its previous position, and the tensioner to take up any slack in the chain.

27 Slacken the exhaust camshaft sprocket retaining bolt, to allow the sprocket to rotate.

28 Using a spanner or socket on the crankshaft pulley bolt, rotate the crankshaft 45° in the normal direction of rotation (clockwise viewed from the right-hand end of the engine), until the crankshaft locking pin can be inserted through the timing hole in the block and into the locating hole in the flywheel). In this position the crankshaft should be locked at TDC for No 1 cylinder.

29 Clean and refit the timing chain access plug to the chain cover, and tighten it to the specified torque.

30 Slide MG Rover tool LRT-12-173, or home-made equivalent (see Section 3, paragraph 8), over the square section of the inlet camshaft (adjacent to the No 1 bearing cap). Using a spanner on the hexagonal section, rotate the camshaft until both sides of the tool contact the cylinder head-to-camshaft cover mating surface **(see illustration)**. Check that the crankshaft is still locked in the TDC position. If possible, have an assistant available to keep the camshaft alignment tool in place, and to hold the camshaft with the spanner.

31 Tighten the camshaft sprocket retaining bolt to the specified Stage 1 torque setting, then tighten it to the Stage 2 angle using an angle-measuring gauge **(see illustration)**.

32 Repeat the procedure detailed in paragraphs 30 and 31 for the exhaust camshaft.

33 Withdraw the crankshaft locking pin, and camshaft aligning tool. Using a spanner on the crankshaft pulley bolt, rotate the crankshaft

6.30 Slide the positioning tool over the square section of the inlet camshaft

6.31 Holding the camshaft in this position with the spanner on the hexagonal section, tighten the camshaft sprocket retaining screw

7.3 Disconnect the fuel pressure sensor wiring plug

7.5 Disconnect the engine coolant temperature sensor wiring plug (arrowed)

clockwise two complete revolutions, until the locking pin can be inserted again through the timing hole at the front of the block, into the flywheel indent.

34 Following the procedure in paragraphs 30 and 31, check that the camshafts are still aligned correctly. If necessary slacken the camshaft sprocket retaining bolts, and repeat the alignment procedure.

35 With the camshafts and crankshaft correctly aligned, remove the locking pin and

7.6 Remove the fuel pipe from the fuel pump to the common rail

alignment tool, and refit the blanking plug to the timing hole in the block.

36 With reference to Section 15, refit the right-hand hydramount.

37 Refit the camshaft cover as described in Section 4.

38 Refer to Chapter 1B and refit the auxiliary and air conditioning compressor (where applicable) drivebelt.

39 Refit the right-hand wheel arch liner, undertray and roadwheel, lower the car to the ground, and tighten the roadwheel bolts to the specified torque.

7 Cylinder head – removal and refitting

Removal

1 Remove the camshafts, rocker arms and tappets as described in Section 6.

2 Drain the cooling system, as described in Chapter 1B.

3 Disconnect the fuel pressure sensor wiring plug, and release the harness grommet from the cylinder head **(see illustration)**.

4 Gently pull the connectors from the glow plugs.

5 Disconnect the engine coolant temperature sensor wiring plug **(see illustration)**.

6 Undo the fuel union nuts and remove the fuel pipe from the fuel pump to the common rail **(see illustration)**. Be prepared for fuel spillage, and collect the fuel pipe support bush. Plug or cover the rail and pump apertures to prevent contamination.

> **HAYNES HiNT** ***Cut the fingertips from an old pair of rubber gloves and secure them over the fuel ports with elastic bands.***

7 Unscrew the two Allen screws and remove the common fuel rail from the cylinder head **(see illustration)**.

8 Slacken and remove the two retaining bolts, and remove the vacuum pump from the left-hand end of the cylinder head. Discard the O-ring seal and bolts, new ones must be fitted.

9 Undo the three retaining bolts, and pull the coolant elbow away from the cylinder head **(see illustration)**.

7.7 Unscrew the two bolts and remove the common fuel rail (arrowed)

7.9 Undo the three retaining bolts (arrowed), and pull the coolant hose connector away from the cylinder head

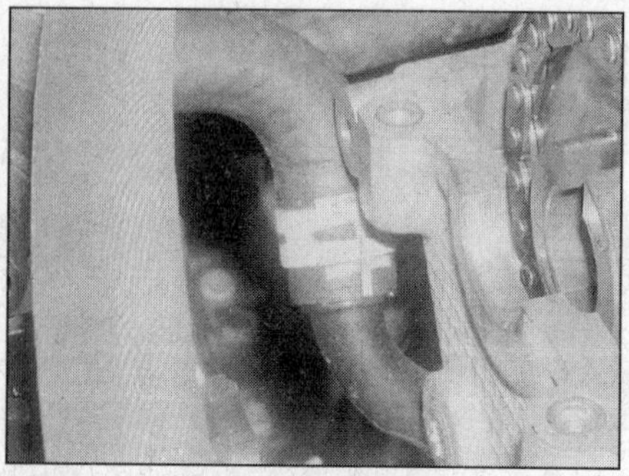

7.10 Disconnect the expansion tank hose from the coolant rail

7.11a Unscrew the bolt securing the coolant rail to the fuel pipe (arrowed) . . .

7.11b . . . the cylinder head (arrowed) . . .

7.11c . . . and the exhaust manifold (arrowed)

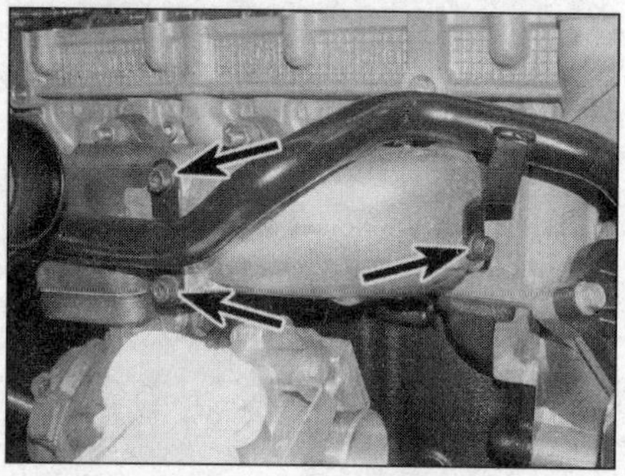

7.14 Undo the three Allen screws securing the coolant rail heat shield (arrowed)

10 Release the retaining clip, and disconnect the expansion tank hose from the coolant rail at the right-hand end of the cylinder head **(see illustration)**.

11 Unscrew the bolts securing the coolant rail to the fuel pipe, cylinder head, and exhaust manifold **(see illustrations)**.

12 Release the retaining clips and remove the turbocharger outlet hose.

13 On automatic models, slacken the clamp screw securing the EGR (exhaust gas recirculation) pipe to the cooler, and release the clamp. Remove the three retaining bolts and remove the EGR cooler.

14 Undo the three Allen screws securing the coolant rail heat shield **(see illustration)**.

15 Slacken and remove the bolt securing the coolant rail to the thermostat housing, and remove the heat shield.

16 Unscrew the three bolts securing the turbocharger to the exhaust manifold, and discard the gasket.

17 Remove the bolts securing the engine lifting eye to the power steering pipe clip and cylinder head.

18 Disengage the camshaft sprockets from the timing chain.

19 Using a Torx key, unscrew and discard the timing chain guide pins. New ones must be fitted **(see illustration)**.

20 Remove the rear chain guide. The front chain guide is easier to remove once the cylinder head has been removed.

21 Unscrew the five Allen screws and single cylinder head bolt securing the cylinder head to the timing cover **(see illustration)**.

22 Make a final check to ensure that all relevant hoses, pipes and wires, etc, have been disconnected.

23 Working in the **reverse** of the tightening sequence **(see illustration 7.41)**, progressively slacken the cylinder head bolts by a third of a turn at a time until all bolts can be unscrewed by hand. Note that bolt 12 in the sequence has already been removed. Withdraw and discard the bolts – new ones must be fitted.

24 Lift the cylinder head from the cylinder block. If necessary, tap the cylinder head gently with a soft-faced mallet to free it from the block, but **do not** lever at the mating faces.

25 When the joint is broken, lift the cylinder head away then remove the gasket. Note the fitted positions of the two locating dowels, and remove them for safe-keeping if they are loose. Keep the gasket for identification purposes (see paragraph 32).

7.19 Unscrew and discard the timing chain guide pins. New ones must be fitted

7.21 Unscrew the bolts securing the cylinder head to the timing cover (arrowed)

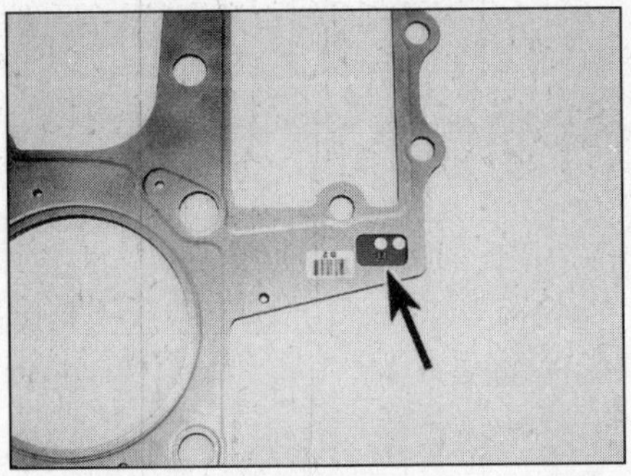

7.32 Gasket identification holes – see text

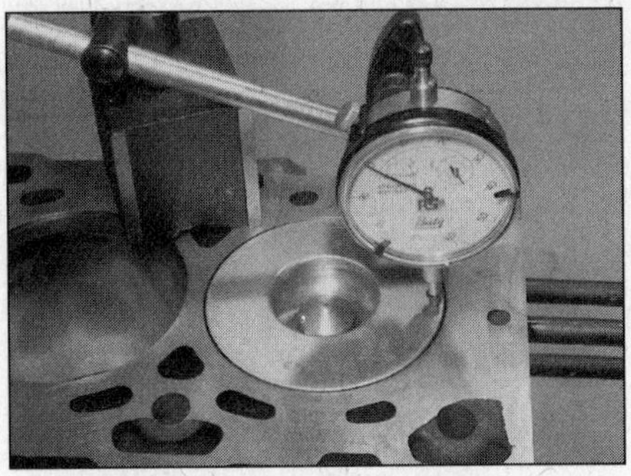

7.34 Measuring piston protrusion

7.37 Ensure that the locating dowels are in place

Caution: Do not lay the head on its lower mating surface; support the head on wooden blocks, ensuring each block only contacts the head mating surface, not the glow plugs. The glow plugs protrude from the bottom of the head, and they will be damaged if the head is placed directly onto a bench.

26 If the cylinder head is to be dismantled, refer to the relevant Sections of Part D of this Chapter.

Preparation for refitting

27 The mating faces of the cylinder head and block must be perfectly clean before refitting the head. Use a scraper to remove all traces of gasket and carbon, and also clean the tops of the pistons. Take particular care with the aluminium surfaces, as the soft metal is damaged easily.

28 Make sure that debris is not allowed to enter the oil and water channels – this is particularly important for the oil circuit, as carbon could block the oil supply to the camshaft or crankshaft bearings. Using adhesive tape and paper, seal the water, oil and bolt holes in the cylinder block. To prevent carbon entering the gap between the pistons and bores, smear a little grease in the gap. After cleaning the piston, rotate the crankshaft so that the piston moves down the bore, then wipe out the grease and carbon with a cloth rag. Clean the piston crowns in the same way.

29 Check the block and head for nicks, deep scratches and other damage. If slight, they may be removed carefully with a file. More serious damage may be repaired by machining, but this is a specialist job.

30 If warpage of the cylinder head gasket surface is suspected, use a straight-edge to check it for distortion. Refer to Part D of this Chapter if necessary.

31 Ensure that the cylinder head bolt holes in the crankcase are clean and free of oil. Syringe or soak up any oil left in the bolt holes. This is most important in order that the correct bolt tightening torque can be applied and to prevent the possibility of the block being cracked by hydraulic pressure when the bolts are tightened.

32 On this engine, the cylinder head-to-piston clearance is controlled by fitting different thickness head gaskets. The piston protrusion is matched by the number of holes in the gasket next to the timing chain area **(see illustration)**.

Gasket holes	Piston protrusion
One hole	*Up to 0.91 mm*
Two holes	*0.92 to 1.03 mm*
Three holes	*Over 1.03 mm*

Select the new gasket which has the same thickness/number of holes as the original, unless new piston and connecting rod assemblies have been fitted. In that case, the correct thickness of gasket required is selected by measuring the piston protrusions as follows.

33 Remove the locking pin from the flywheel and mount a dial test indicator securely on the block so that its pointer can be easily pivoted between the piston crown and block mating surface.

34 Ensure the piston is at exactly TDC, then zero the dial test indicator on the gasket surface of the cylinder block. Carefully move the indicator over No 1 piston, taking measurements in line with the gudgeon pin axis, measure the protrusion on both the left-hand and right-hand side of the piston **(see illustration)**. Repeat this procedure on No 4 piston.

35 Rotate the crankshaft half-a-turn to bring Nos 2 and 3 pistons to TDC. **Note:** *When turning the crankshaft, ensure that the timing chain does not jam in the timing cover.* Ensure the crankshaft is accurately positioned, then measure the protrusions of Nos 2 and 3 pistons, taking two measurements for each piston. Once both pistons have been measured, rotate the crankshaft through half-a-turn to bring Nos 1 and 4 pistons back to TDC and lock the crankshaft in position again.

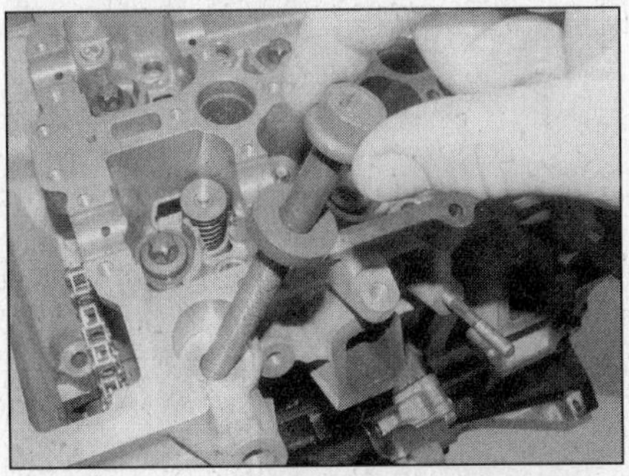

7.40 Ensure that the slightly shorter bolt (with the Torx socket head) is fitted to position 11

36 Use the table in paragraph 32 to select the appropriate gasket for the maximum protrusion.

Refitting

37 Wipe clean the mating faces of the head and block, and ensure that the two locating dowels are in position at each end of the cylinder block/crankcase surface **(see illustration)**.

38 Fit the new gasket to the cylinder block, ensuring that it fits correctly over the locating dowels.

39 Carefully refit the cylinder head, locating it on the dowels. Make sure the timing chain can be pulled up through the cylinder head tunnel.

40 Lightly oil under the head and on the threads of each new bolt, carefully enter bolts 1 to 11 into the holes and screw them in, by hand only, until finger-tight **(see illustration)**. Ensure that the slightly shorter bolt (with the different Torx head) is fitted into position 11.

Caution: Do not drop the bolts into their holes.

41 Working progressively and in sequence, first tighten cylinder head bolts 1 to 11 to the Stage 1 torque setting **(see illustration)**. Note that bolt number 12 is tightened separately, at the end.

42 Slacken bolts 1 to 11 half a turn, then

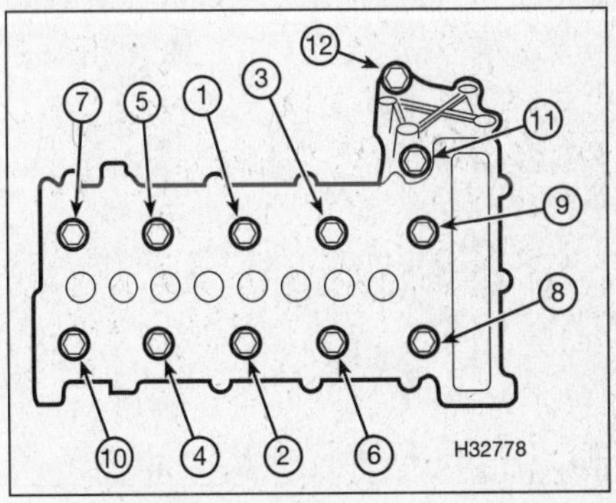

7.41 Cylinder head bolt tightening sequence

7.43 Angle-tightening the cylinder head bolts

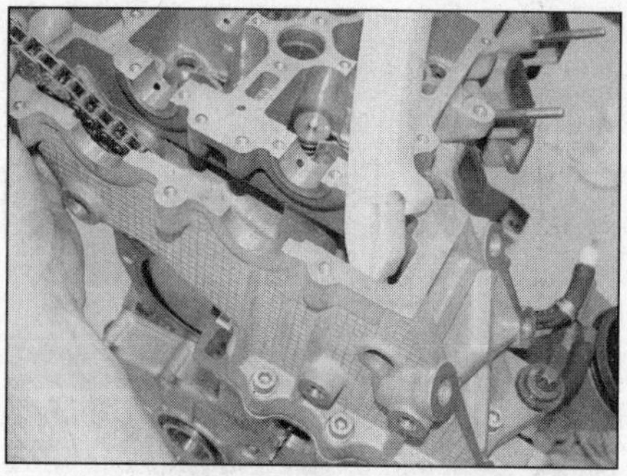

7.47 Make sure that the front guide is located correctly on its lower support pin

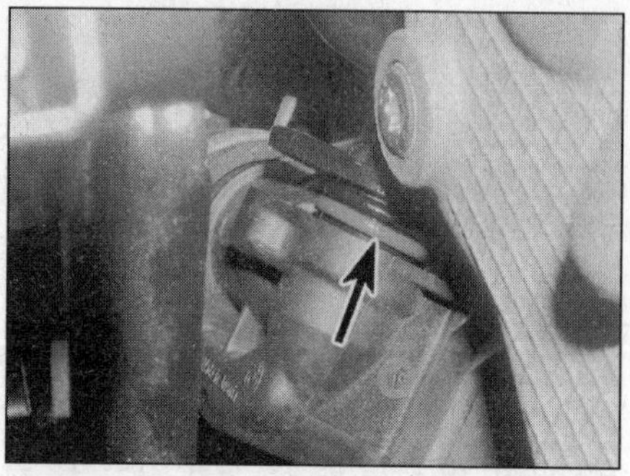

7.51 With a new seal (arrowed), fit the coolant rail to the thermostat housing

tighten them in sequence to the Stage 3 setting.

43 Once the eleven bolts have been tightened to the Stage 3 torque, again working in the sequence shown, tighten each bolt through its specified Stage 4 angle, using a socket and extension bar. It is recommended that an angle-measuring gauge is used during this stage of tightening, to ensure accuracy **(see illustration)**. Alternatively, prior to tightening, use a felt-tip pen or similar to make alignment marks between each bolt head and the cylinder head.

44 Finally go around in the specified sequence again and tighten the eleven bolts through the specified Stage 5 angle. If the bolt heads were marked prior to angle-tightening, each bolt head mark should now be directly opposite the corresponding mark on the cylinder head.

45 Fit and tighten the 41 mm bolt in position 12 to the specified torque **(see illustration 7.41)**.

46 Refit and tighten the five Allen screws securing the cylinder head to the timing cover to the specified torque. **Note:** *Take great care not to drop the inner screw down the timing chain tunnel* **(see illustration 7.21)**.

47 Ensure that the timing chain guides are in good condition, and refit them into place. Make sure that the front guide is located correctly on its lower support pin. Fit the new upper guide pins and tighten them to the specified torque **(see illustration)**.

48 Clean the camshaft sprockets, and engage them with the timing chain.

49 Refit the lifting eye to the cylinder head and the power steering pipe clip, and tighten the bolts securely.

50 Fit the new gasket, and reconnect the turbocharger to the exhaust manifold. Tighten the bolts to the specified torque.

51 Clean the coolant rail and thermostat housing mating surfaces, fit the heat shield, and with a new seal, fit the coolant rail to the thermostat housing. Tighten the bolt to the specified torque **(see illustration)**.

52 Tighten the Allen screws securing the heat shield securely.

53 On automatic models, align the EGR cooler and coolant rail and tighten the bolts to the specified torque. Refit and tighten the EGR pipe clamp.

54 Refit and tighten the coolant rail-to-cylinder head and exhaust manifold bolts to the specified torque. Tighten the rail-to-fuel pipe bolt securely.

55 Fit the turbocharger outlet pipe and tighten the retaining clips.

56 Reconnect the expansion tank hose to the coolant rail, and tighten the retaining clip.

57 Clean the coolant elbow mating surface, with a new seal, fit it to the cylinder head. Tighten the bolts securely.

58 Ensure that the vacuum pump mating surface is clean, and refit it with a new seal and new bolts. Tighten the bolts to the specified torque.

59 Refit the common fuel rail to the cylinder head and tighten the Allen screws to the specified torque.

60 Connect the fuel pipe to the pump and fuel rail, and tighten the unions to the specified torque.

61 Reconnect the wiring plugs to the engine coolant temperature sensor, fuel pressure sensor and glow plugs.

62 With reference to Section 6, refit the tappets, rocker arms and camshafts.

63 Refill the cooling system as described in Chapter 1B.

8 Sump – removal and refitting

Main sump casting

Removal

1 Disconnect the battery negative lead.

2 Slacken the right-hand front roadwheel bolts, apply the handbrake, then jack up the front of the car and support it securely on axle stands (see *Jacking and vehicle support*). Remove the fasteners and lower out the engine undertray. Remove the front right-hand roadwheel and wheel arch liner.

3 Drain the engine oil and remove the oil filter as described in Chapter 1B. Refit the sump plug with a new washer and tighten the plug to the specified torque.

4 Slacken and remove the bolt securing the dipstick tube to the oil filter housing, pull the tube out and discard the seal **(see illustration)**.

5 On models with air conditioning, remove the two retaining bolts and remove the compressor drivebelt tensioner.

6 Undo the three bolts securing the coolant rail to the sump and cylinder block **(see illustration)**.

7 On models with air conditioning, undo the retaining bolts, and move the compressor to one side. Do **not** disconnect the refrigerant hoses. Undo the three retaining bolts and remove the compressor mounting bracket.

8 Slacken the through-bolt securing the engine lower mounting to the subframe, then remove the through-bolt securing the mounting to the sump bracket.

9 Undo the five bolts securing the lower mounting bracket to the sump.

8.4 Slacken and remove the bolt securing the dipstick tube to the oil filter housing

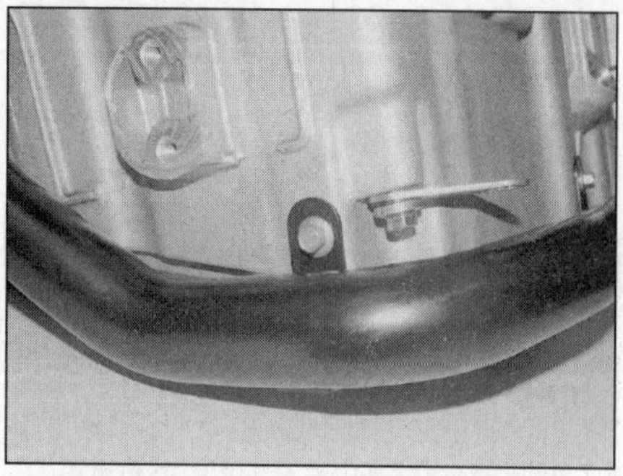

8.6 Undo the bolts securing the coolant rail to the sump and cylinder block

8.11 Two bolts accessible through the cut-outs in the flywheel

8.13 Unscrew the pick-up/strainer bolts (arrowed)

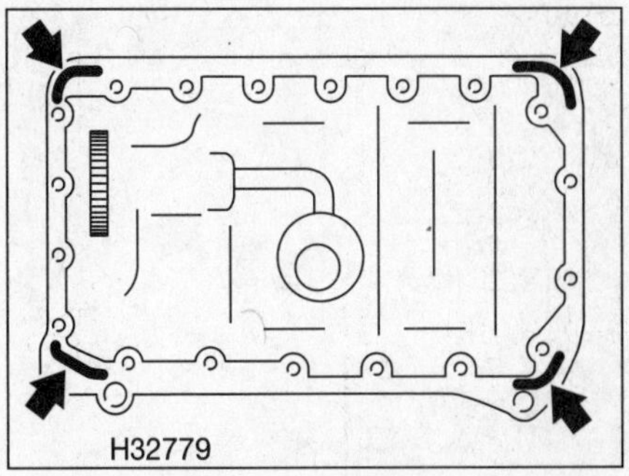

8.16 Apply a bead of suitable sealant to the areas shown

10 Slacken and remove the three bolts securing the transmission casing to the sump.

11 Progressively slacken and remove the nineteen bolts securing the sump to the base of the cylinder block **(see illustration)**. Two of these bolts, accessed through the transmission housing, secure the sump to the crankshaft flywheel end oil seal housing.

12 Break the sump sealant joint by striking the sump with the palm of the hand. It is not advisable to prise between the mating faces, as this could result in a leak. If the sump is stuck, remove the drain plug, then use a sturdy screwdriver (wrapped in a rag or card to protect the drain plug threads) in the drain plug hole as a prising tool. Lower the sump away from the engine. Remove the gasket and discard it – a new one should be used on refitting.

13 While the sump is removed, take the opportunity to check the oil pump pick-up/strainer. If necessary, unbolt the pick-up/strainer, and remove it from the engine along with its gasket **(see illustration)**. The strainer can then be cleaned easily in solvent. Inspect the strainer mesh for signs of clogging or splitting and renew if necessary. If the pick-up/strainer bolts are damaged, they must be renewed.

Refitting

14 Clean all traces of gasket from the mating surfaces of the cylinder block and sump, then use a clean rag to wipe out the sump and the engine interior.

15 Where necessary, fit a new gasket to the oil pump pick-up/strainer then carefully refit the pipe. Refit the retaining bolts, and tighten them to the specified torque setting.

16 Apply a 2 mm bead of suitable sealant (such as Three Bond 1209) to the cylinder block/crankcase mating surface **(see illustration)**.

17 Fit the gasket to the sump then offer up the sump to the cylinder block/crankcase. Refit the sump retaining bolts, and tighten the bolts finger-tight only.

18 Fit the bolts securing the sump to the transmission. In order to align the sump rear flange with the transmission, lightly tighten the bolts, then slacken them. If the sump is being refitted to the engine with the transmission removed, use a straight-edge to ensure that the sump casting is flush with the end of the engine block **(see illustration)**.

19 Tighten the sump-to-engine block bolts, and then the sump-to-transmission bolts to the specified torque. Note that the two bolts accessed through the transmission housing are smaller, and tightened to a lower setting, than the others.

20 Position the engine lower mounting bracket against the sump, refit the tighten the retaining bolts to the specified torque.

21 Refit the lower mounting, and tighten the bolts to the specified torque.

22 On models with air conditioning, refit the compressor mounting bracket, and the compressor, tightening the bolts to the specified torque.

23 Position the lower coolant rail against the sump, and tighten the bolts to the specified torque.

24 On models with air conditioning, refit the compressor drivebelt tensioner and drivebelt. Carry out the tensioning procedure described in Chapter 1B.

25 Refit the oil dipstick tube, with a new O-ring, and tighten the bolt to the specified torque.

26 Fit the engine undertray, wheel arch liner, and right-hand roadwheel. Lower the car to the ground and tighten the roadwheel bolts to the specified torque.

27 Fit a new oil filter, and fill the engine with the correct quantity of new oil as described in Chapter 1B.

28 Reconnect the battery negative lead.

Lower sump plate

Removal

29 Apply the handbrake, then jack up the front of the car and support it securely on axle stands (see *Jacking and vehicle support*). Remove the fasteners and lower out the engine undertray.

30 Drain the engine oil and remove the oil filter as described in Chapter 1B. Refit the sump plug with a new washer and tighten the plug to the specified torque.

31 Unscrew the sixteen sump plate retaining bolts **(see illustration)**.

32 Break the sump plate joint by striking the plate with the palm of the hand, then lower the plate away from the sump. Remove the gasket and discard it – a new one should be used on refitting.

Refitting

33 Ensure the plate and sump mating surfaces are clean and dry, and fit the new gasket **(see illustration)**.

8.18 Use a straight-edge to ensure the sump is flush with the end of the block

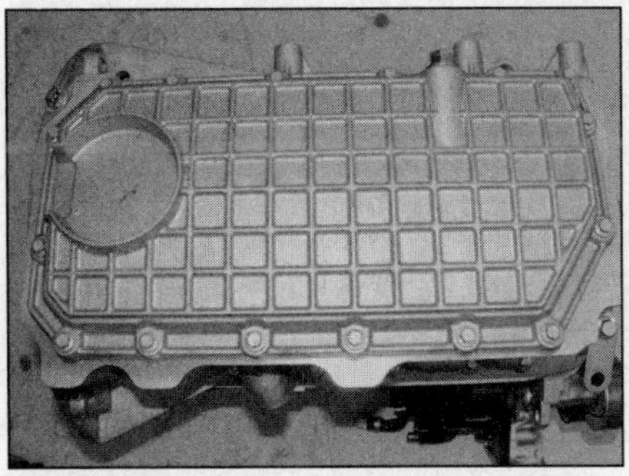

8.31 Unscrew the sump plate retaining bolts

8.33 Fit the new sump plate gasket

9.4 Remove the oil pump from the cylinder block

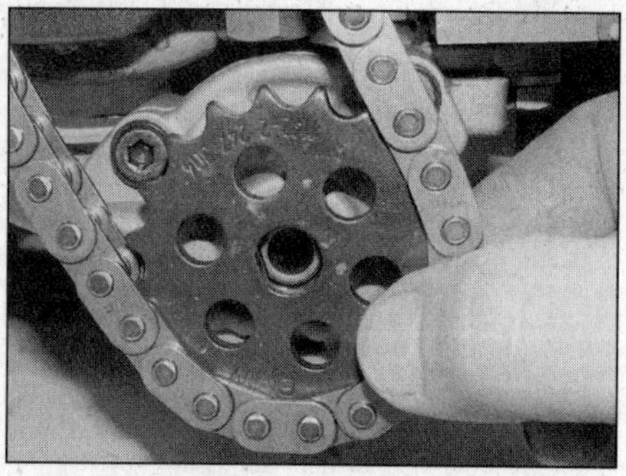

9.8 Align the 'flat' on the pump shaft with the 'flat' in the sprocket centre

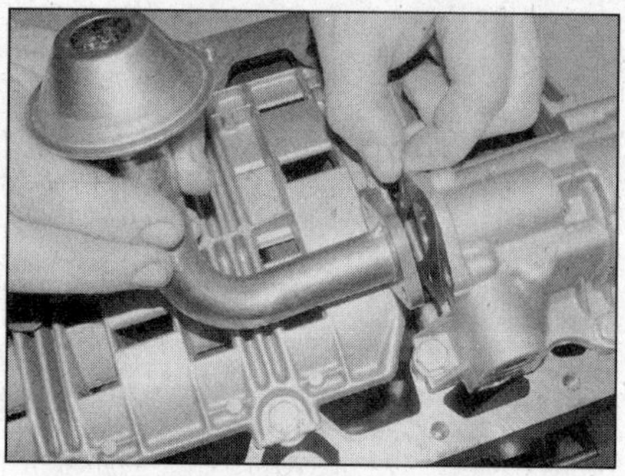

9.9 Refit the pick-up tube with a new gasket

34 Refit the plate and evenly tighten the bolts to the specified torque.

35 Refit the engine undertray, and lower the car to the ground.

36 Fit a new oil filter, and fill the engine with the correct quantity of new oil, as described in Chapter 1B.

9 Oil pump – removal and refitting

Removal

1 Remove the main sump casting as described in Section 8.

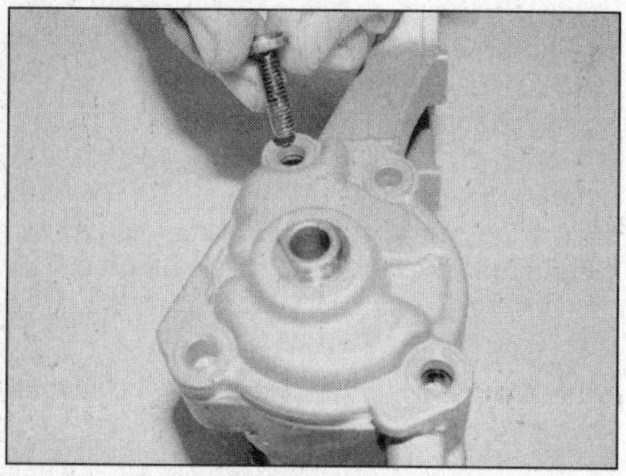

10.2 Undo the bolts and remove the oil pump cover

2 Unscrew the three retaining bolts, and remove the oil pump pick-up pipe and strainer **(see illustration 8.13)**. Discard the gasket.

3 Undo the Torx bolt securing the sprocket to the pump driveshaft, and slide the sprocket and chain from the pump.

4 Slacken and remove the four bolts securing the oil pump to the cylinder block **(see illustration)**.

5 Carefully ease the pump down and release it from the locating dowels.

Refitting

6 Ensure the mating surfaces of the oil pump and cylinder block are clean and dry. Make sure the locating dowels are in position.

7 Position the oil pump on the locating dowels. Tighten the bolts to the specified torque.

8 Engage the sprocket with the chain, align the sprocket with the 'flat' machined into the oil pump driveshaft, and tighten the Torx bolt to the specified torque setting **(see illustration)**.

9 Using a new gasket, refit the oil pick-up pipe and strainer to the oil pump, and tighten the bolts to the specified torque **(see illustration)**.

10 Refit the sump main casting as described in Section 8.

10 Oil pump – dismantling, inspection and reassembly

Dismantling

1 Remove the oil pump and drive sprocket as described in Section 9.

2 Undo the bolts and remove the pump cover **(see illustration)**.

3 Note the identification marks on the inner and outer rotors to ensure they are fitted the same way around on reassembly. Remove both the rotors from the body **(see illustration)**.

Inspection

4 Inspect the rotors for obvious signs of wear or damage and renew if necessary. If the pump body or cover plate is scored or damaged, then the complete oil pump assembly must be renewed.

5 Refit the rotors to the body and, using feeler blades of the appropriate thickness, measure the clearance between the outer rotor and the pump body **(see illustration)**.

6 If the measurement is outside the specified limits, the complete pump assembly must be renewed. **Note:** *Although the oil pressure relief valve can be dismantled, at the time of writing, no information was available concerning the fitted depth of the plunger*

10.3 Note the rotor markings must face out

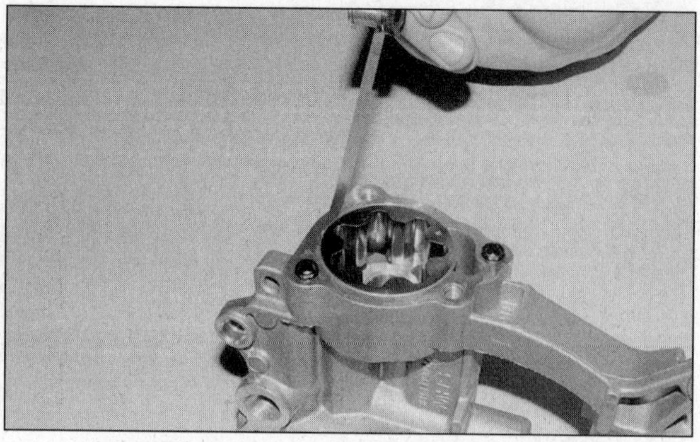

10.5 Measure the outer rotor-to-body clearance

retaining plug. The position of the plug is critical to the performance of the valve. Consequently, consult an MG Rover specialist before attempting to dismantle the valve ***(see illustrations)****.*

Reassembly

7 Remove all traces of locking compound from the threads of the body and cover screws.
8 Lubricate the pump rotors with clean engine oil and refit them to the pump body, using the identification marks to ensure they are fitted the correct way around **(see illustration)**.
9 Refit the cover to the pump body.
10 Ensure the threads of the cover screws are clean and dry, and apply a drop of thread-locking compound to each screw. Refit the screws and tighten them securely.
11 Check that the pump rotates freely, then prime it by injecting oil into its passages and rotating it. If a long time elapses before the pump is refitted to the engine, prime it again before installation.
12 Refit the pump as described in Section 9.

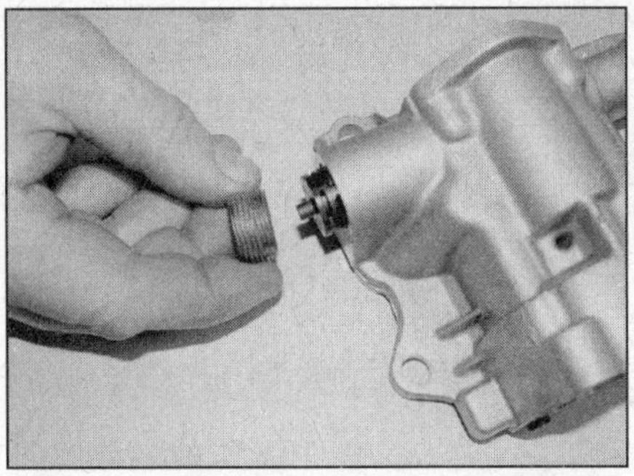

10.6a Unscrew the plunger retaining plug . . .

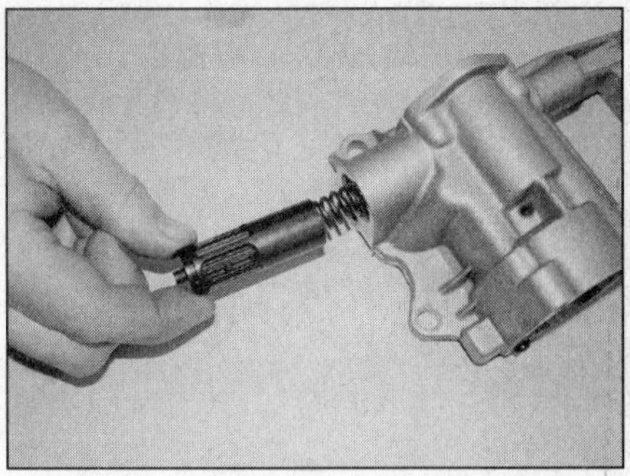

10.6b . . . followed by the plunger

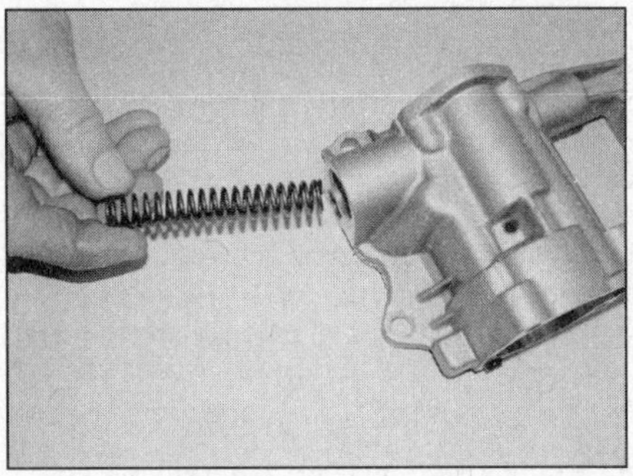

10.6c . . . and spring

10.8 Refit the rotors into the pump body

11 Oil cooler – removal and refitting

Removal

1 Drain the engine coolant and engine oil, and remove the oil filter as described in Chapter 1B.
2 With reference to Chapter 4C, remove the inlet manifold.
3 Remove the starter motor as described in Chapter 5A.
4 Release the securing clip, and disconnect the hose from the oil cooler.
5 Unscrew the three Torx screws and remove the oil cooler from the oil filter housing. Discard the gasket. Be prepared for fluid spillage **(see illustrations)**.

Refitting

6 Ensure the mating surfaces of the oil cooler and oil filter housing are clean and dry, and with a new gasket, fit the cooler to the housing. Tighten the Torx screws to the specified torque.
7 Reconnect the hose to the cooler, and tighten the retaining clip.
8 With reference to Chapter 5A, refit the starter motor.
9 Refit the inlet manifold with reference to Chapter 4C.
10 With reference to Chapter 1B, replenish the engine coolant, fit a new oil filter, and fill the engine with the correct quantity of new engine oil.

12 Oil pressure switch – removal and refitting

1 The oil pressure switch is a vital early warning of low oil pressure. The switch operates the oil warning light on the instrument panel – the light should come on with the ignition, and go out almost immediately when the engine starts.
2 If the light does not come on, there could be a fault on the instrument panel, the switch wiring, or the switch itself. If the light does not go out, low oil level, worn oil pump (or sump pick-up blocked), blocked oil filter, or worn main bearings could be to blame – or again, the switch may be faulty.
3 If the light comes on while driving, the best advice is to turn the engine off immediately, and not to drive the car until the problem has been investigated – ignoring the light could mean expensive engine damage.

Removal

4 Disconnect the battery negative lead, and move the lead away from the battery (see *Disconnecting the battery*).
5 Remove the starter motor as described in Chapter 5A.
6 The oil pressure switch is fitted behind the oil cooler **(see illustration)**. Place a drain container underneath (the amount of oil lost

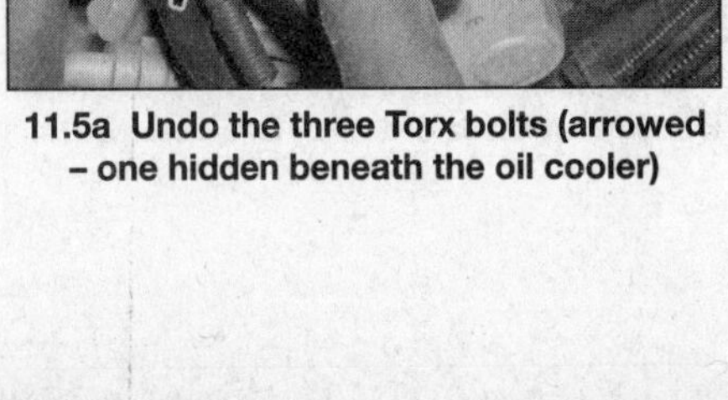

11.5a Undo the three Torx bolts (arrowed – one hidden beneath the oil cooler)

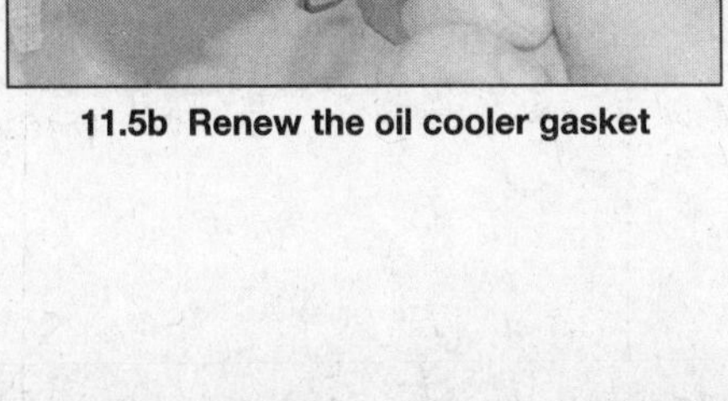

11.5b Renew the oil cooler gasket

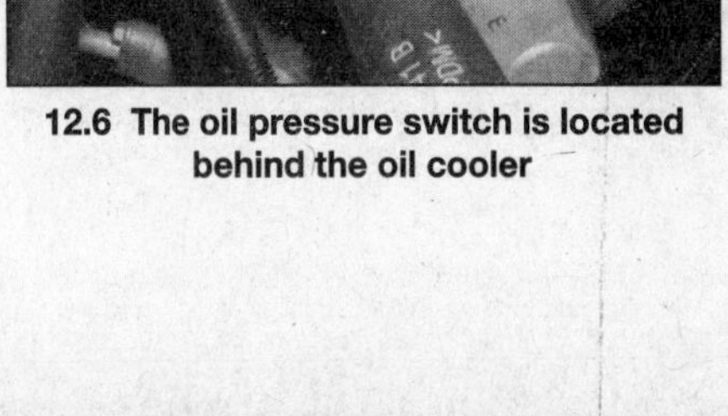

12.6 The oil pressure switch is located behind the oil cooler

13.2 Remove the crankshaft oil seal using a self-tapping screw

should be quite small). Disconnect the wiring plug, then unscrew and remove the switch – discard the sealing washer, as a new one should be used when refitting.

Refitting

7 Clean the switch threads, and fit a new sealing washer.

8 Fit and tighten the switch, if possible to the specified torque. Reconnect the switch multi-plug.

9 Refit the starter motor as described in Chapter 5A.

13 Crankshaft oil seals – renewal

Timing chain end

1 Remove the crankshaft pulley as described in Section 5.

2 Very carefully punch or drill two small holes opposite each other in the oil seal. Screw a self-tapping screw into each and pull on the screws with pliers to extract the seal **(see illustration)**.

Caution: Great care must be taken to avoid damage to the crankshaft.

3 Clean the seal housing and polish off any burrs or raised edges which may have caused the seal to fail in the first place.

4 Lubricate the lips of the new seal with clean engine oil and ease it into position on the end of the shaft. Press the seal squarely into position until it is flush with the housing. If necessary, a suitable tubular drift, such as a socket, which bears only on the hard outer edge of the seal can be used to tap the seal into position. Take great care not to damage the seal lips during fitting and ensure that the seal lips face inwards.

5 Wash off any traces of oil, then refit the crankshaft pulley as described in Section 5.

13.12 With the seal protector over the end of the crankshaft, ease the oil seal and housing into place

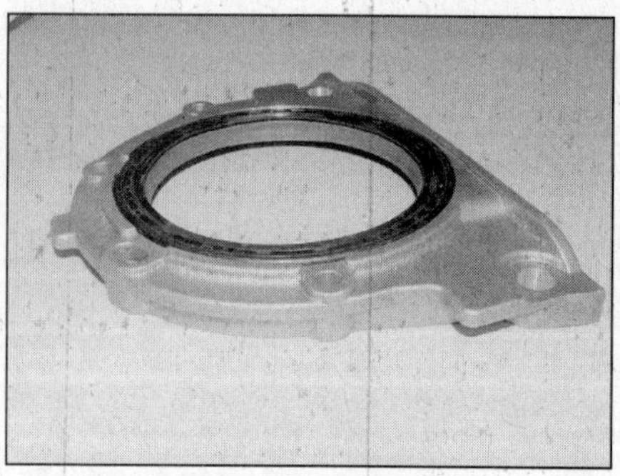

13.10 Press the seal in until it's flush with the housing

Flywheel/driveplate end

6 Remove the flywheel or driveplate as described in Section 14.

7 With reference to Section 8, remove the main sump casting.

8 Undo the retaining bolts and remove the oil seal housing. Using a punch, drive the oil seal from the housing.

9 Clean the seal housing and polish off any burrs or raised edges which may have caused the seal to fail.

10 Press the seal evenly into the housing, until its outer flange is flush with the housing lip **(see illustration)**. If necessary, a soft-faced mallet can be used to tap the seal gently into place.

11 Position a new gasket over the locating dowels **(see illustration)**.

12 Fit the seal protector (supplied with the genuine MG Rover seal) over the end of the crankshaft, and ease the seal and housing over the crankshaft shoulder **(see illustration)**.

13 Refit the oil seal housing bolts, and tighten them to the specified torque.

14.2 Lock the flywheel ring gear with a home-made tool

13.11 Position the new gasket over the locating dowels

14 Refit the main sump casting as described in Section 8.

15 Wash off any oil, then refit the flywheel/driveplate as described in Section 14.

14 Flywheel/driveplate – removal, inspection and refitting

Flywheel

Note: *New flywheel retaining bolts must be used on refitting.*

Removal

1 Remove the clutch assembly as described in Chapter 6.

2 Prevent the flywheel from turning by locking the ring gear teeth with a similar arrangement to that shown **(see illustration)**. Alternatively, bolt a strap between the flywheel and the cylinder block/crankcase.

3 Slacken and remove the retaining bolts and remove the flywheel, noting its locating dowel **(see illustration)**. **Do not** drop it, as it is very heavy. Discard the bolts – they must be renewed whenever they are disturbed.

Inspection

4 If the flywheel-to-clutch mating surface is deeply scored, cracked or otherwise damaged, then the flywheel must be renewed, unless it is possible to have it surface ground. Seek the advice of an engine reconditioning specialist.

14.3 Slacken and remove the flywheel bolts, then discard them – new ones must be fitted

14.7 The one larger flywheel bolt hole engages with the locating dowel (arrowed)

5 If the ring gear is badly worn or has missing teeth, then it must be renewed. This job is best left to an engine reconditioning specialist.

Refitting

6 Clean the mating surfaces of the flywheel and crankshaft, and remove all traces of locking compound from the crankshaft threaded holes.

7 Fit the flywheel to the crankshaft, engaging it with the crankshaft locating dowel, and fit the new retaining bolts **(see illustration)**. **Note:** *If the new bolts are not supplied precoated with locking compound, apply a few drops prior to fitting the bolts.*

8 Lock the flywheel using the method employed on dismantling then, working in a diagonal sequence, tighten all the retaining bolts to the specified torque setting.

9 Refit the clutch assembly as described in Chapter 6.

Driveplate

Note: *New driveplate retaining bolts must be used on refitting.*

Removal

10 Remove the automatic transmission and torque converter as described in Chapter 7B.

11 Prevent the driveplate from turning by locking the ring gear teeth with a similar arrangement to that shown **(see illustration 14.2)**. Alternatively, bolt a strap between the driveplate and the cylinder block/ crankcase.

12 Slacken and remove the retaining bolts and remove the driveplate, noting its locating dowel. Discard the bolts – they must be renewed whenever they are disturbed.

Inspection

13 If the ring gear is badly worn or has missing teeth, then it must be renewed. This job is best left to an engine reconditioning specialist.

Refitting

14 Clean the mating surfaces of the driveplate and crankshaft and remove all traces of locking compound from the crankshaft threaded holes.

15 Fit the driveplate to the crankshaft, engaging it with the crankshaft locating dowel, and fit the new retaining bolts. **Note:** *If the new bolts are not supplied precoated with locking compound, apply a few drops prior to fitting the bolts.*

16 Lock the driveplate using the method employed on dismantling then, working in a diagonal sequence, tighten all the retaining bolts to the specified torque setting.

17 Refit the torque converter and automatic transmission as described in Chapter 7B.

15 Engine/transmission mountings – inspection and renewal

Inspection

1 If improved access is required, raise the front of the car and support it securely on axle stands (see *Jacking and vehicle support*). Remove the engine undertray, which is secured by a number of quick-release screw fasteners.

2 Check the mounting rubber to see if it is cracked, hardened or separated from the metal at any point. Renew the mounting if any such damage or deterioration is evident.

3 Check that all mounting fasteners are securely tightened. Use a torque wrench to check, if possible.

4 Using a large screwdriver or a pry bar, check for wear in the mountings by carefully levering against it to check for free play. Where this is not possible, enlist the aid of an assistant to move the engine/gearbox unit back-and-forth or from side-to-side while you watch the mountings. While some free play is to be expected even from new components, excessive wear should be obvious. If excessive free play is found, check first that the fasteners are correctly secured, then renew any worn components as described below.

Right-hand mounting

5 Firmly apply the handbrake, then jack up the front of the car and support securely on axle stands (see *Jacking and vehicle support*). Undo the fasteners and remove the engine undertray.

6 Remove the engine top cover, which is secured by three bolts.

7 Support the weight of the engine/ transmission, preferably using a hoist. Alternatively, use a trolley jack with a block of wood placed on its head, positioned underneath the engine. Raise the engine slightly to remove all load from the mounting.

8 Where applicable, remove the two bolts securing the air conditioning hose to the engine right-hand mounting and bonnet lock platform. Release the hose from the mounting clips in the engine compartment as necessary, and move it clear as far as possible without disconnecting or straining it.

9 Remove the three bolts securing the upper steady bracket, and lift it off **(see illustration)**.

10 To remove the engine upper mounting bracket, first remove the three bolts securing the power steering fluid reservoir to the bracket, and move the reservoir aside without disconnecting the hoses. Unscrew the nut securing the bracket to the hydramount, then remove the four further bolts securing it to the engine **(see illustrations)**.

11 The right-hand mounting bracket on the inner wing is secured by a total of four bolts, and can be removed if required.

12 If required, the hydramount can be unscrewed from the wing, using MG Rover tool LRT-12-169 (which engages in the three slots around the mounting), or using a strap/ chain wrench around the circumference of the mounting.

13 Refitting is a reversal of removal. Tighten all fasteners to the specified torque – in the case of the hydramount, torque tightening may be impossible without the special tool, so

15.9 One of the three upper steady bracket bolts

15.10a View of the engine upper mounting bracket

15.10b Engine upper mounting bracket-to-hydramount nut

15.21 Removing the left-hand mounting through-bolt

tighten securely using the same method as for removal.

Left-hand mounting

14 Remove the engine top cover, which is secured by three bolts.

15 Remove the fuel filter as described in Chapter 1B.

16 Remove the battery and its tray as described in Chapter 5A.

17 Remove a total of three bolts and two screws securing the air intake duct to the bonnet lock platform and inlet manifold. Unclip and remove the air intake duct.

18 Remove the bolt securing the fuel lift pump to its mounting bracket, and move the pump to one side. Noting how they are routed, unclip the pump wiring, brake servo pipe and battery lead from the pump mounting bracket. On models with the fuel-burning heater, unclip the fuel pipe/hoses from the bracket. Unbolt and remove the pump bracket.

19 Firmly apply the handbrake, then jack up the front of the car and support securely on axle stands (see *Jacking and vehicle support*).

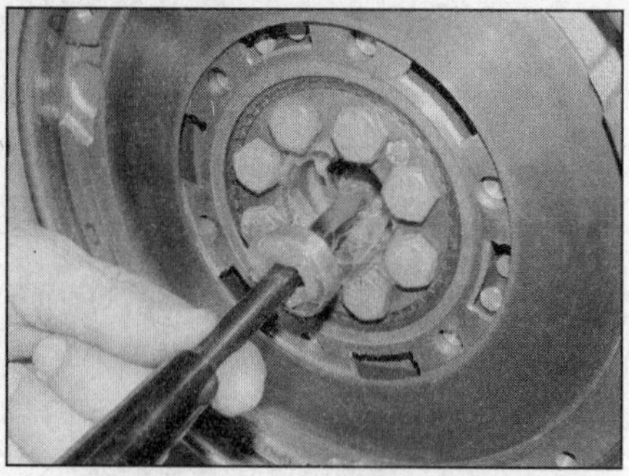

16.5 It may be necessary to repack the bearing with grease to release it

15.25 Engine lower mounting through-bolts

Undo the fasteners and remove the engine undertray.

20 Support the weight of the engine/transmission, preferably using a hoist. Alternatively, use a trolley jack with a block of wood placed on its head, positioned underneath the transmission. Raise the engine slightly to remove all load from the mounting.

21 To separate the mounting, unscrew and remove the through-bolt **(see illustration)**.

22 Once the through-bolt is removed, lower the transmission until the mounting is separated. If required, the two mounting brackets can now be unbolted from the body and transmission – each is secured by four bolts.

23 Refitting is a reversal of removal. Tighten all fasteners to the specified torque.

Lower mounting

24 Firmly apply the handbrake, then jack up the front of the car and support securely on axle stands (see *Jacking and vehicle support*). Remove the engine undertray, which is secured by a number of quick-release screw fasteners.

25 Unscrew the two through-bolts from the lower mounting to release it, and withdraw it from the mounting brackets **(see illustration)**. Though removing the lower mounting will increase the amount of engine movement, provided they have not been disturbed, the engine will remain safely supported on its right- and left-hand mountings.

26 If required, the lower mounting bracket can be unbolted from the sump.

27 Refitting is a reversal of removal. Tighten all fasteners to the specified torque.

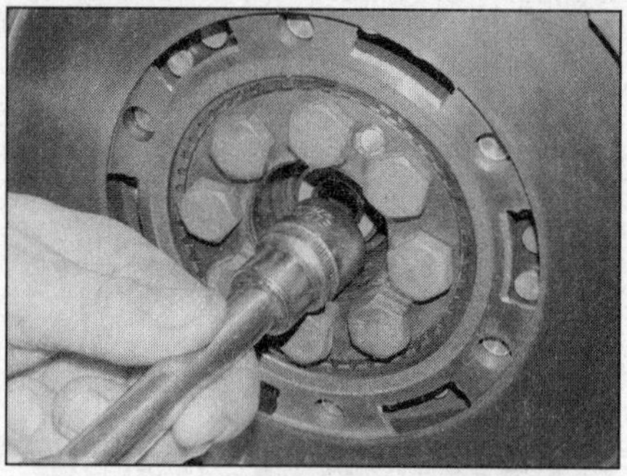

16.6 Use a tubular drift, or socket, that bears only on the outer edge of the bearing

16 Crankshaft pilot bearing – inspection, removal and refitting

Inspection

1 The pilot bearing is fitted to the end of the crankshaft, and provides support for the free end of the transmission input shaft on manual transmission models. It can only be examined once the clutch has been removed. Using a finger, rotate the inner race of the bearing and check for any roughness, binding or looseness in the bearing. If any of these conditions are evident, the bearing must be renewed.

Removal

2 Remove the clutch as described in Chapter 6.

3 Using a flat-bladed screwdriver or similar, pack grease through the centre hole of the bearing, until the space between the bearing and the crankshaft, and the centre bearing hole, is completely filled.

4 Select a socket and extension, or rod, that just fits into the centre hole of the bearing. The idea is to tap the tool into the centre hole of the bearing, compress the grease, and force the bearing from the crankshaft; the tool must be a snug fit in the bearing centre hole, or the grease will escape past it.

5 It may be necessary to repack the bearing with grease several times before the bearing is released **(see illustration)**.

Refitting

6 Using a suitable socket that bears only on the hard outer edge of the bearing, drive the new bearing into the crankshaft until it contacts the shoulder **(see illustration)**.

7 Refit the clutch as described in Chapter 6.

Chapter 2 Part D:
Engine removal and overhaul procedures

Contents

Degrees of difficulty

Easy, suitable for novice with little experience	**Fairly easy,** suitable for beginner with some experience	**Fairly difficult,** suitable for competent DIY mechanic	**Difficult,** suitable for experienced DIY mechanic	**Very difficult,** suitable for expert DIY or professional

Specifications

Petrol engines

Cylinder head(s)

Height	118.95 to 119.05 mm
Reface limit	0.20 mm
Maximum acceptable gasket face distortion	0.05 mm
Valve seat width:	
Inlet	1.2 mm
Exhaust	1.6 mm

Valves, valve springs and guides

Valve stem diameter:	
Inlet	5.952 to 5.967 mm
Exhaust	5.947 to 5.962 mm
Valve stem installed height:	
New	38.93 to 39.84 mm
Service limit	40.10 mm
Valve guide inside diameter	6.000 to 6.025 mm
Valve stem-to-guide clearance:	
Inlet:	
Standard	0.033 to 0.063 mm
Service limit	0.07 mm
Exhaust:	
Standard	0.038 to 0.078 mm
Service limit	0.11 mm
Valve guide installed height	6.0 mm
Valve spring free length	50.0 mm

Petrol engines (continued)

Cylinder block

Cylinder liner bore diameter:	
Grade A (Red)	80.000 to 80.015 mm
Grade B (Blue)	80.016 to 80.030 mm

Pistons and rings

Piston diameter:	
Grade A (Red)	79.975 to 79.990 mm
Grade B (Blue)	79.991 to 80.005 mm
Piston-to-bore clearance	0.010 to 0.040 mm
Piston ring fitted end gaps:	
Top compression ring	0.2 to 0.35 mm
Second compression ring	0.28 to 0.48 mm
Oil control ring	0.15 to 0.4 mm
Piston ring-to-groove clearance:	
Top compression ring	0.04 to 0.072 mm
Second compression ring	0.03 to 0.062 mm
Oil control ring	0.01 to 0.18 mm

Crankshaft – 1.8 litre

Main bearing journal diameter	47.986 to 48.007 mm
Main bearing journal size grades:	
Grade 1	48.000 to 48.007 mm
Grade 2	47.993 to 48.000 mm
Grade 3	47.986 to 47.993 mm
Big-end (crankpin) journal diameter	47.986 to 48.007 mm
Big-end (crankpin) journal size grades:	
Grade A	48.000 to 48.007 mm
Grade B	47.993 to 48.000 mm
Grade C	47.986 to 47.993 mm
Maximum journal ovality	0.01 mm
Main bearing running clearance	0.013 to 0.043 mm
Big-end bearing running clearance	0.021 to 0.049 mm
Crankshaft endfloat:	
Standard	0.1 to 0.25 mm
Service limit	0.34 mm
Thrustwasher thickness	2.61 to 2.65 mm

Crankshaft – V6 engine

Main bearing journal diameter	67.731 to 67.749 mm
Main bearing journal size grades:	
Grade 1	67.743 to 67.749 mm
Grade 2	67.737 to 67.743 mm
Grade 3	67.731 to 67.737 mm
Main bearing ladder diameters:	
Grade A	71.600 to 71.593 mm
Grade B	71.593 to 71.586 mm
Grade C	71.586 to 71.579 mm
Big-end (crankpin) journal diameter	54.037 to 54.055 mm
Big-end (crankpin) journal size grades:	
Grade A	54.049 to 54.055 mm
Grade B	54.043 to 54.049 mm
Grade C	54.037 to 54.043 mm
Big-end housing size grades:	
Grade A	57.677 to 57.671 mm
Grade B	57.671 to 57.665 mm
Grade C	57.665 to 57.659 mm
Maximum journal ovality	0.01 mm
Main bearing running clearance	0.021 to 0.039 mm
Big-end bearing running clearance	0.022 to 0.040 mm
Crankshaft endfloat:	
Standard	0.10 to 0.30 mm
Service limit	0.40 mm
Thrustwasher thickness	2.61 to 2.65 mm

Torque wrench settings

Refer to Chapter 2A or 2B Specifications

Diesel engines

Cylinder head

Maximum acceptable gasket face distortion	0.03 mm

Refacing of the cylinder head is not permitted

Valves, valve springs and guides

Valve stem diameter	5.97 ± 0.01 mm
Valve head recess below cylinder head surface (maximum):	
Inlet	0.73 ± 0.1 mm
Exhaust	0.56 ± 0.1 mm
Valve stem-to-guide clearance	0.025 to 0.054 mm
Valve spring free length	47.5 mm

Valve guides cannot be renewed
Valve seats must not be recut

Cylinder block

Cylinder bore diameter:	
Standard	84.0 to 84.018 mm
Wear limit	84.04 mm
Intermediate	84.08 to 84.098 mm
Wear limit	84.12 mm
1st oversize	84.25 to 84.268 mm
Wear limit	84.29 mm
Cylinder block ovality (maximum)	0.04 mm
Cylinder block taper (maximum)	0.04 mm

Pistons and rings

Piston diameter (measured 12 mm from base, 90° to gudgeon pin):	
Standard	83.95 ± 0.009 mm
Intermediate	84.03 ± 0.009 mm
1st oversize	84.2 ± 0.009 mm
Piston-to-bore clearance	0.036 to 0.15 mm
Piston ring fitted end gaps:	
Top compression ring	0.2 to 0.35 mm
Second compression ring	0.3 to 0.45 mm
Oil control ring	0.2 to 0.4 mm
Piston ring-to-groove clearance:	
Top compression ring	0.108 to 0.137 mm
Second compression ring	0.05 to 0.09 mm
Oil control ring	0.03 to 0.07 mm

Crankshaft

Big-end (crankpin) journal diameter	44.975 to 45.009 mm
Big-end bearing running clearance	0.020 to 0.055 mm
Crankshaft endfloat	0.09 to 0.19 mm
Main bearing journal ground sizes:	
Standard:	
Yellow	59.977 to 59.983 mm
Green	59.970 to 59.976 mm
White	59.964 to 59.970 mm
1st undersize (0.25 mm):	
Yellow	59.727 to 59.733 mm
Green	59.720 to 59.726 mm
White	59.714 to 59.720 mm
2nd undersize (0.50 mm):	
Yellow	59.477 to 59.483 mm
Green	59.470 to 59.476 mm
White	59.464 to 59.469 mm
Main bearing running clearance	0.027 to 0.063 mm
Maximum journal ovality*	0.01 mm

** This is a suggested figure – no exact measurements are quoted by MG Rover. Seek the advice of a MG Rover dealer or engine overhaul specialist before condemning components*

Torque wrench settings

Refer to Chapter 2C Specifications

1 General information

Included in this Part of Chapter 2 are details of removing the engine/transmission from the car and general overhaul procedures for the cylinder head, cylinder block and all other engine internal components.

The information given ranges from advice concerning preparation for an overhaul and the purchase of new parts, to detailed step-by-step procedures covering removal, inspection, renovation and refitting of engine internal components.

After Section 6, all instructions are based on the assumption that the engine has been removed from the car. For information concerning in-car engine repair, as well as the removal and refitting of those external components necessary for full overhaul, refer to the relevant in-car repair procedure section (Chapter 2A to 2C) of this Chapter and to Section 6. Ignore any preliminary dismantling operations described in the relevant in-car repair sections that are no longer relevant once the engine has been removed.

Apart from torque wrench settings, which are given at the beginning of the relevant in-car repair procedure Chapter (2A to 2C), all specifications relating to engine overhaul are at the beginning of this Part of Chapter 2.

2 Engine overhaul – general information

It is not always easy to determine when, or if, an engine should be completely overhauled, as a number of factors must be considered.

High mileage is not necessarily an indication that an overhaul is needed, while low mileage does not preclude the need for an overhaul. Frequency of servicing is probably the most important consideration. An engine which has had regular and frequent oil and filter changes, as well as other required maintenance, should give many thousands of miles of reliable service. Conversely, a neglected engine may require an overhaul very early in its life.

Excessive oil consumption is an indication that piston rings, valve seals and/or valve guides are in need of attention. Make sure that oil leaks are not responsible before deciding that the rings and/or guides are worn. Perform a compression test, as described in the relevant Part of this Chapter, to determine the likely cause of the problem.

Check the oil pressure with a gauge fitted in place of the oil pressure switch, and compare it with that specified. If it is extremely low, the main and big-end bearings, and/or the oil pump, are probably worn out.

Loss of power, rough running, knocking or metallic engine noises, excessive valve gear noise, and high fuel consumption may also point to the need for an overhaul, especially if they are all present at the same time. If a complete service does not remedy the situation, major mechanical work is the only solution.

An engine overhaul involves restoring all internal parts to the specification of a new engine. During an overhaul, the pistons and the piston rings are renewed. New main and big-end bearings are generally fitted; if necessary, the crankshaft may be renewed, to restore the journals. The valves are also serviced as well, since they are usually in less-than-perfect condition at this point. While the engine is being overhauled, other components, such as the starter and alternator, can be overhauled as well. The end result should be an as-new engine that will give many trouble-free miles. **Note:** *Critical cooling system components such as the hoses, thermostat and coolant pump should be renewed when an engine is overhauled. The radiator should be checked carefully, to ensure that it is not clogged or leaking. Also, it is a good idea to renew the oil pump whenever the engine is overhauled.*

Before beginning the engine overhaul, read through the entire procedure, to familiarise yourself with the scope and requirements of the job. Overhauling an engine is not difficult if you follow carefully all of the instructions, have the necessary tools and equipment, and pay close attention to all specifications. It can, however, be time-consuming. Plan on the car being off the road for a minimum of two weeks, especially if parts must be taken to an engineering works for repair or reconditioning. Check on the availability of parts and make sure that any necessary special tools and equipment are obtained in advance. Most work can be done with typical hand tools, although a number of precision measuring tools are required for inspecting parts to determine if they must be renewed. Often the engineering works will handle the inspection of parts and offer advice concerning reconditioning and renewal. **Note:** *Always wait until the engine has been completely dismantled, and until all components (especially the cylinder block and the crankshaft) have been inspected, before deciding what service and repair operations must be performed by an engineering works. The condition of these components will be the major factor to consider when determining whether to overhaul the original engine, or to buy a reconditioned unit. Do not, therefore, purchase parts or have overhaul work done on other components until they have been thoroughly inspected.* As a general rule, time is the primary cost of an overhaul, so it does not pay to fit worn or sub-standard parts.

As a final note, to ensure maximum life and minimum trouble from a reconditioned engine, everything must be assembled with care, in a spotlessly-clean environment.

3 Engine removal – methods and precautions

If you have decided that the engine must be removed for overhaul or major repair work, several preliminary steps should be taken.

Locating a suitable place to work is extremely important. Adequate work space, along with storage space for the car, will be needed. If a workshop or garage is not available, at the very least, a flat, level, clean work surface is required.

Cleaning the engine compartment and engine/transmission before beginning the removal procedure will help keep tools clean and organised.

An engine hoist or A-frame will also be necessary. Make sure the equipment is rated in excess of the combined weight of the engine and transmission. Safety is of primary importance, considering the potential hazards involved in lifting the engine/transmission out of the car.

On all models, the engine and transmission are removed as a unit by lifting out from above. In the case of the 1.8 litre engine, lifting eyes have to be made up which can be bolted to the cylinder head – ensure these are made from quality steel (it may even be possible to obtain something suitable from other engines, at a scrapyard).

If this is the first time you have removed an engine, an assistant should ideally be available. Advice and aid from someone more experienced would also be helpful. There are many instances when one person cannot simultaneously perform all of the operations required when lifting the engine out of the car.

Plan the operation ahead of time. Read through the entire procedure before starting work, and arrange for the hire of or obtain all of the tools and equipment you will need. Some of the equipment necessary to perform engine/transmission removal and installation safely and with relative ease (in addition to an engine hoist) is as follows: a heavy duty trolley jack, complete sets of spanners and sockets as described in the rear of this manual, wooden blocks, and plenty of rags and cleaning solvent for mopping-up spilled oil, coolant and fuel. If the hoist must be hired, make sure that you arrange for it in advance, and perform all of the operations possible without it beforehand. This will save you money and time.

Plan for the car to be out of use for quite a while. An engineering works will be required to perform some of the work which the do-it-yourselfer cannot accomplish without special equipment. These places often have a busy schedule, so it would be a good idea to consult them before removing the engine, in order to accurately estimate the amount of time required to rebuild or repair components that may need work.

Always be extremely careful when removing and refitting the engine/transmission. Serious injury can result from careless actions. Plan ahead and take your time, and a job of this nature, although major, can be accomplished successfully.

4 Petrol engine and transmission – removal, separation and refitting

1 Park the car on firm, level ground.
2 Drain the cooling system as described in Chapter 1A.
3 Depressurise the fuel system and remove the air cleaner as described in Chapter 4A or 4B.
4 Remove the battery and its tray as described in Chapter 5A.
5 Remove the bonnet as described in Chapter 11.

1.8 litre models

6 Cut the cable-ties securing the wiring harness and earth lead to the air cleaner mounting bracket. Unscrew the three bolts, and take off the mounting bracket.
7 Release the hose clips, and disconnect the following coolant hoses:
a) Hoses on the engine coolant elbow.
b) Hose to the coolant rail.
c) Heater hose to the engine block.
d) Expansion tank hose to the inlet manifold.
8 Depress the collar at the base, then pull out the vacuum pipe from the inlet manifold.
9 Referring to Chapter 5A if necessary, disconnect the starter motor wiring.
10 Unscrew the bolt securing the earth strap to the transmission.
11 Open the engine compartment fusebox, then disconnect the main wiring multi-plug and the bolt securing the battery lead.
12 Disconnect the engine harness to main harness multi-plug, located behind the engine compartment fusebox.
13 Disconnect the wiring plug from the canister purge solenoid valve (behind the throttle body), then trace the pipe from the valve to the inlet manifold, and disconnect it.
14 Squeeze the tabs to release the connector, and disconnect the fuel supply hose from the fuel rail.
15 Remove the bolt securing the power steering support bracket to the coolant rail.
16 Where applicable, disconnect the clutch fluid supply pipe from the slave cylinder, as described in Chapter 6.
17 On manual transmission models, referring to Chapter 7A if necessary, disconnect the gearchange cables from the selector levers and support brackets. Disconnect the reversing light switch wiring plug above the left-hand driveshaft.
18 Remove the windscreen cowl panels as described in Chapter 11. Slide the ECM wiring plug locking clip to the side, and disconnect the plug – feed the ECM wiring harness back into the engine compartment.
19 Refer to Chapter 10 and disconnect the fluid supply flange and return hose from the power steering pump – anticipate some loss of fluid. Plug or cover the open connections to keep them clean. Also disconnect the power steering pressure switch wiring plug.
20 Unscrew the three nuts securing the power steering fluid reservoir to the bulkhead, and move the reservoir to one side.
21 Unscrew the accelerator cable adjuster nut slightly, then unclip the cable outer from the throttle body bracket by sliding it out sideways. Unhook the inner cable from the throttle cam, and disconnect it completely.
22 If not already done, loosen the front wheel bolts, then jack up the front of the car and support it on axle stands. Remove the front wheels.
23 Drain the transmission oil or fluid as described in Chapter 1A.
24 Where applicable, remove the air conditioning compressor auxiliary drivebelt as described in Chapter 1A. Remove the three mounting bolts and tie the compressor to one side, without disconnecting the hoses.
25 Unscrew the two exhaust manifold-to-downpipe flange nuts, and separate the pipe. Discard the gasket – a new one will be needed for refitting.
26 Remove the two through-bolts from the engine lower mounting.
27 Working in the front wheel arches, unclip the front caliper brake hose, and the ABS and pad wear sensor wiring, from the support clip. Disconnect the pad wear sensor wiring plug. Repeat this process on the other front wheel.
28 With reference to Chapter 10, disconnect the track rod ends and lower arm balljoints from the front hubs.
29 Unscrew the three bolts securing the right-hand driveshaft bearing support bracket to the back of the engine.
30 Prise the left-hand driveshaft out of the transmission, while an assistant pulls the left-hand front wheel outwards. Recover the circlip from the end of the shaft, and obtain a new one for refitting. Tie the driveshaft to one side.
31 Similarly, pull out the right-hand driveshaft from the transmission (in this case, no prising should be required), and tie it to one side.
32 Make up suitable engine lifting eyes which can be bolted to the cylinder head (see Section 3). MG Rover suggest bolting one eye to a point behind the engine oil dipstick, and after removing the end cover plate from the exhaust camshaft, using the two bolt holes to attach another eye.
33 Attach the engine hoist, and raise it so that the weight of the engine is taken evenly off the mountings.
34 With the engine supported, remove the three bolts securing the right-hand mounting's upper steady bracket, and lift it off. Also unscrew the nut securing the right-hand mounting's lower bracket to the hydramount.
35 Remove the left-hand mounting through-bolt, then unbolt the left-hand mounting and bracket from the transmission and inner wing (four bolts each).
36 Make a final check that all necessary components have been removed, disconnected, or moved sufficiently clear. With the help of an assistant, manoeuvre the engine and transmission up and out of the engine compartment. When clear of the car, lower it to the ground. Be prepared to steady the engine when it touches down, to stop it toppling over. If the engine is lowered onto some old carpet or card, this will protect it, and make it easier to drag around as necessary.

V6 models

37 Unscrew the three bolts, and remove the air cleaner mounting bracket **(see illustrations)**.

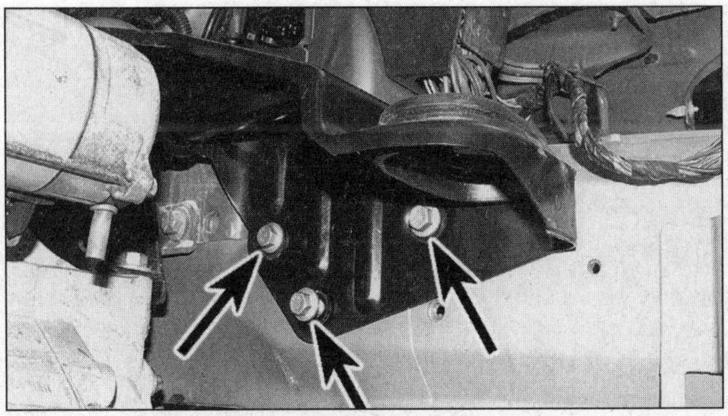

4.37a Unscrew the three mounting bolts . . .

4.37b . . . and remove the air cleaner mounting bracket

4.38a Disconnect the expansion tank hoses . . .

4.38b . . . then remove the mounting bolt . . .

38 Release the hose clips at each end, and disconnect the bleed hose from the radiator and expansion tank. Remove the single

4.38c . . . and unhook the expansion tank mounting lugs

mounting bolt, then unhook the mounting lugs and free the expansion tank from the radiator **(see illustrations)**. Release the hose clip, and disconnect the lower hose from the expansion tank, after which the tank can be removed completely.

39 Release the radiator top hose clip, and detach the hose from the radiator. Lift the hose out of its support clip, then unbolt the support clip and remove it from the radiator **(see illustration)**.

40 Referring to Chapter 5A if necessary, disconnect the starter motor wiring. Also remove the starter motor mounting bolt which secures the engine earth strap **(see illustration)**.

41 Open the engine compartment fusebox, then disconnect the main wiring multi-plug and the bolts securing the battery leads **(see illustrations)**.

42 Disconnect the two engine harness wiring connectors behind the engine compartment fusebox – these connectors are effectively 'screw-type', in that they unscrew from each other **(see illustration)**.

43 Release the clip and disconnect the hose from the canister-purge solenoid valve. Trace the hose from the valve, and disconnect it at the fuel rail.

44 Release the hose clips and disconnect the hoses from the coolant elbow on top of the engine **(see illustration)**.

45 Where applicable, disconnect the clutch fluid supply pipe from the slave cylinder, as described in Chapter 6.

46 On manual transmission models, referring

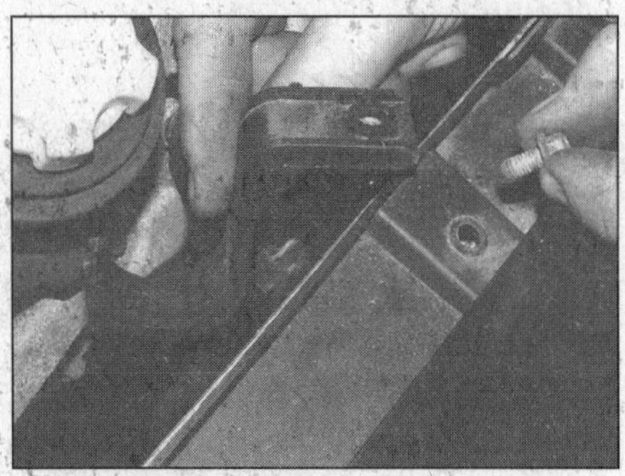

4.39 Unbolt and remove the top hose support bracket

4.40 Remove the starter motor bolt securing the earth strap

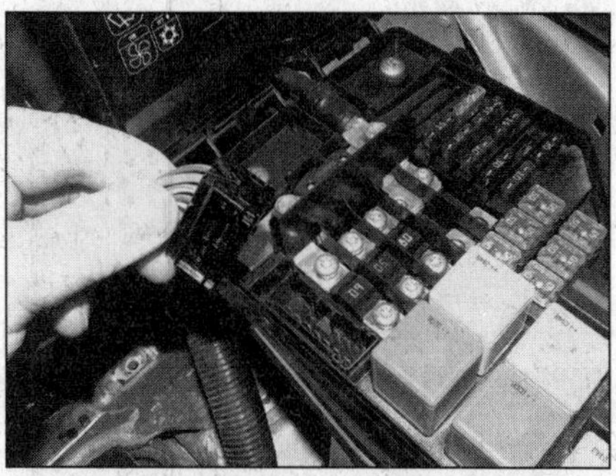

4.41a Disconnect the fusebox wiring plug . . .

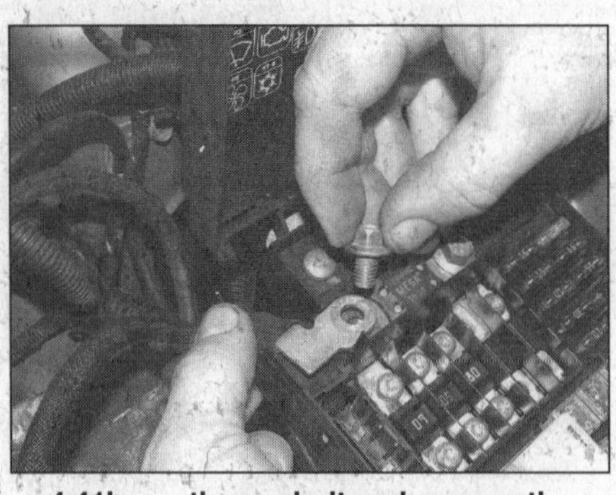

4.41b . . . then unbolt and remove the battery leads

4.42 Unscrew the engine harness connector plugs

4.44 Disconnect the three hoses from the coolant elbow

4.46a Prise off the gearchange cables

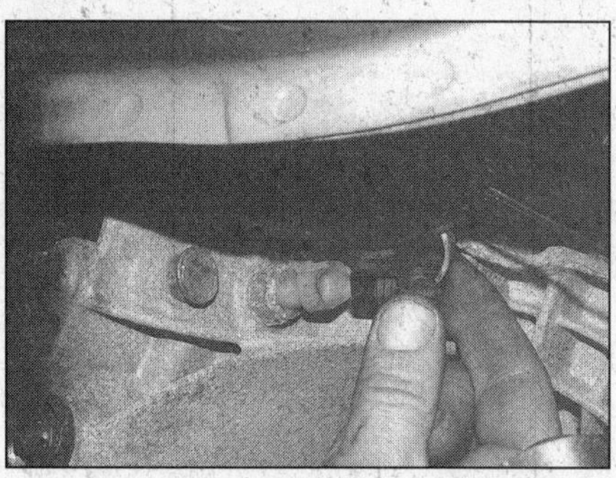
4.46b Disconnect the reversing light switch

4.47 Disconnect the ECM wiring plug

to Chapter 7A if necessary, disconnect the gearchange cables from the selector levers and support brackets. Disconnect the reversing light switch wiring plug above the left-hand driveshaft **(see illustrations)**.

47 Remove the windscreen cowl panels as described in Chapter 11. Slide the ECM wiring plug locking clip to the side, and disconnect the plug – feed the ECM wiring harness back into the engine compartment **(see illustration)**.

48 Unbolt and remove the power steering pump – move the pump to one side, without disconnecting the fluid hoses.

49 If not already done, loosen the front wheel bolts, then jack up the front of the car and support it on axle stands. Remove the front wheels.

50 Drain the transmission oil or fluid as described in Chapter 1A.

51 On models with air conditioning, carry out the following:

a) Remove the auxiliary drivebelt as described in Chapter 1A.

b) Remove the Torx bolt securing the drivebelt idler pulley.

c) Remove the oil cooler as described in Chapter 2B.

d) Remove the three mounting bolts, and tie the air conditioning compressor to one side, without disconnecting the hoses.

52 Disconnect the oil pressure switch wiring plug (behind the crankshaft pulley).

53 Unscrew the front and rear manifold-to-downpipe nuts, and separate the joints. Remove the exhaust front pipe support bracket, which is secured by two bolts **(see illustrations)**.

54 Remove the engine lower mounting as described in Chapter 2B.

55 Working in the front wheel arches, unclip the front caliper brake hose, and the ABS and pad wear sensor wiring, from the support clip. Disconnect the pad wear sensor wiring plug. Repeat this process on the other front wheel.

56 With reference to Chapter 10, disconnect the track rod ends and lower arm balljoints from the front hubs.

57 Unscrew the two bolts securing the right-hand driveshaft bearing support bracket to the back of the engine.

58 Prise the left-hand driveshaft out of the transmission, while an assistant pulls the left-hand front wheel outwards. Recover the circlip from the end of the shaft, and obtain a new one for refitting. Tie the driveshaft to one side.

59 Similarly, pull out the right-hand driveshaft from the transmission (in this case, no prising should be required), and tie it to one side.

60 The engine is removed by lifting it out. Although this is possible without removing the radiator, clearance is tight – we recommend that the radiator's rear surface is protected with a sheet of card before proceeding further. Refitting the engine is made much easier if the radiator is removed as described in Chapter 3, but this itself is quite an involved procedure.

61 Attach the engine hoist, and raise it so that the weight of the engine is taken evenly off the mountings.

62 With the engine supported, remove the right-hand mounting completely as described in Chapter 2B.

63 Remove the left-hand mounting through-bolt, then unbolt the left-hand mounting and bracket from the transmission and inner wing (four bolts each).

64 Raise the engine slightly on the hoist, until the heater hose on the rear of the block is accessible. Release the clip and disconnect the hose.

65 Make a final check that all necessary components have been removed, disconnected, or moved sufficiently clear. With the help of an assistant, manoeuvre the engine and transmission up and out of the engine compartment **(see illustration)**. When clear of the car, lower it to the ground. Be prepared to steady the engine when it touches down, to stop it toppling over. If the engine is lowered onto some old carpet or card, this will protect it, and make it easier to drag around as necessary.

Separation

66 With the engine/transmission assembly removed, support the assembly on suitable blocks of wood, on a workbench (or failing that, on a clean area of the workshop floor).

67 To separate the transmission from the engine, first remove the starter motor with reference to Chapter 5A.

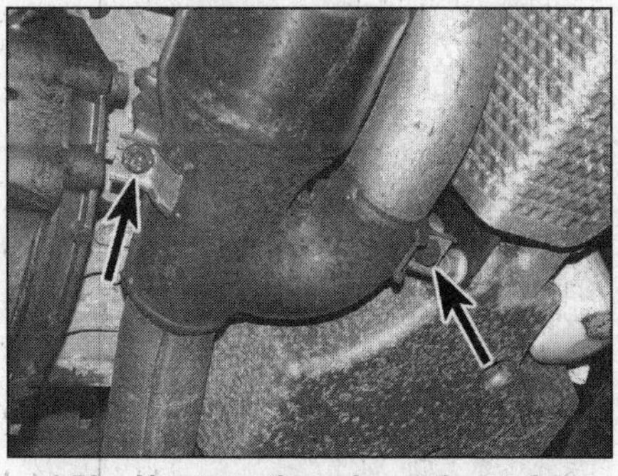
4.53a Unscrew the exhaust front pipe support bracket bolts

4.53b Exhaust front manifold-to-downpipe nuts

4.65 Removing the V6 engine/transmission

Manual transmission models

68 Progressively unscrew and remove the transmission-to-engine bolts, noting where each one goes, and the location of any brackets attached, for guidance when refitting.

69 With the help of an assistant, withdraw the transmission directly from the engine, making sure that its weight is not allowed to bear on the input shaft. Note that there are two locating dowels used.

Automatic transmission models

70 The torque converter is attached to the driveplate by four bolts which are accessed through an aperture on the end face of the transmission. Remove the single securing bolt, then withdraw the grommet from the access hole. Turn the engine as required to position each bolt in the aperture in turn, then unscrew and remove them.

71 Slacken and remove the bolts securing the transmission to the engine. Note the correct fitted positions of each bolt, and the necessary brackets, as they are removed to use as a reference on refitting.

72 Carefully prise the transmission off the engine, to free its locating dowels. As the transmission is removed, make sure the torque converter is kept pushed fully onto the transmission shaft.

73 Once the transmission is free, secure the torque converter in position by bolting a length of metal bar to one of the housing holes.

Refitting

74 Refitting is a reversal of removal, noting the following additional points:

a) Make sure that all mating faces are clean, and use new gaskets where necessary.
b) Tighten all nuts and bolts to the specified torque setting, where given.
c) If the transmission was removed, refit it to the engine as described in Chapter 7A or 7B, as applicable.
d) If the radiator is not removed on V6 models (see paragraph 60), take care to avoid damage to it as the engine is refitted.
e) Delay fully tightening the engine left- and right-hand mountings until the engine has settled into place.
f) Fit a new circlip to the groove in the inner end of the left-hand driveshaft, and ensure it fully engages as the shaft is fitted into the transmission.
g) On manual transmission models, check the operation of the clutch on completion – the system should not require bleeding, or even topping-up, but only in theory (see 'Weekly checks' and Chapter 6).
h) Refill the transmission oil or fluid, with reference to Chapter 1A.
i) Refill the cooling system as described in Chapter 1A.
j) Where applicable, use new washers when reconnecting the power steering pump, then fill and bleed the system as described in Chapter 10.

5 Diesel engine and transmission – removal, separation and refitting

1 Park the car on firm, level ground.

2 Remove the engine top cover, which is secured by three bolts.

3 Drain the cooling system as described in Chapter 1B. Leave the radiator bottom hose disconnected.

4 Remove the battery and its tray as described in Chapter 5A.

5 Where applicable, remove the fuel-burning heater and its mounting bracket as described in Chapter 3.

6 Remove the bonnet as described in Chapter 11.

7 Release the hose clips and remove the radiator top hose – note that the clip at the radiator is released by pulling out the wire clip.

8 Loosen the clips and disconnect the intake hose from the EGR valve, and the intercooler hose from the turbocharger.

9 Release the clips and remove the expansion tank hose and heater hose from the coolant rail.

10 Remove the fuel filter as described in Chapter 1B. Release the clip and disconnect the fuel return hose from the pipe.

11 Release the clip and disconnect the vacuum hose from the vacuum pump.

12 Remove the transmission-to-engine bolt at the top which also secures an earth lead – move the lead to one side.

13 Referring to Chapter 5A if necessary, disconnect the starter motor wiring.

14 Pull off the rubber weather strip at the front of the windscreen cowl panel, and remove the two windscreen cowl panels, each of which is secured by two clips at the front edge. Remove the windscreen wiper arms as described in Chapter 12. Remove two screw/clips at the front corners, and a row of seven clips along the back edge, then lift out the cowl panel frame – collect the splash shield from the passenger side as it is removed.

15 Release the upper tab securing the ECM box inside the housing, then remove the cover and disconnect the two multi-plugs by swinging the locking levers to one side. Disconnect the wiring plugs for the glow plug controller and the main engine harness, and withdraw the wiring into the engine compartment.

16 Where applicable, disconnect the clutch fluid supply pipe from the slave cylinder, as described in Chapter 6.

17 On manual transmission models, referring to Chapter 7A if necessary, disconnect the gearchange cables from the selector levers and support brackets. Disconnect the reversing light switch wiring plug above the left-hand driveshaft.

18 Refer to Chapter 10 and disconnect the fluid return hose and banjo union from the power steering pump – anticipate some loss of fluid. Plug or cover the open connections to keep them clean.

19 Remove the bolt securing the power steering pipe support bracket to the cylinder head.

20 If not already done, loosen the front wheel bolts, then jack up the front of the car and support it on axle stands. Remove the front wheels.

21 Drain the transmission oil or fluid as described in Chapter 1B.

22 On models with air conditioning, carry out the following:

a) Remove the auxiliary drivebelts as described in Chapter 1B.
b) Remove the three mounting bolts, and tie the air conditioning compressor to one side, without disconnecting the hoses.

23 Unscrew the three turbo-to-downpipe flange nuts, and separate the pipe – recover and discard the gasket, as a new one must be used when refitting.

24 Remove the two through-bolts from the engine lower mounting.

25 Working in the front wheel arches, unclip the front caliper brake hose, and the ABS and pad wear sensor wiring, from the support clip. Disconnect the pad wear sensor wiring plug. Repeat this process on the other front wheel.

26 With reference to Chapter 10, disconnect the track rod ends and lower arm balljoints from the front hubs.

27 Unscrew the two bolts securing the right-hand driveshaft bearing support bracket to the back of the engine.

28 Prise the left-hand driveshaft out of the transmission, while an assistant pulls the left-hand front wheel outwards. Recover the circlip from the end of the shaft, and obtain a new one for refitting. Tie the driveshaft to one side.

29 Similarly, pull out the right-hand driveshaft from the transmission (in this case, no prising should be required), and tie it to one side.

30 Attach the engine hoist, and raise it so that the weight of the engine is taken evenly off the mountings.

31 With the engine supported, remove the three bolts securing the right-hand mounting's upper steady bracket, and lift it off. Also unscrew the nut securing the right-hand mounting's lower bracket to the hydramount.

32 Unbolt the air conditioning pipe support bracket (where applicable), then remove the four bolts securing the engine right-hand mounting to the inner wing, and lift it out.

33 Remove the left-hand mounting through-bolt, then unbolt the left-hand mounting and bracket from the transmission and inner wing (four bolts each).

34 Make a final check that all necessary components have been removed, disconnected, or moved sufficiently clear. With the help of an assistant, manoeuvre the engine and transmission up and out of the engine compartment. When clear of the car, lower it to the ground. Be prepared to steady the engine when it touches down, to stop it toppling over. If the engine is lowered onto some old carpet or card, this will protect it, and make it easier to drag around as necessary.

Separation

35 With the engine/transmission assembly removed, support the assembly on suitable blocks of wood, on a workbench (or failing that, on a clean area of the workshop floor).

36 To separate the transmission from the engine, first remove the starter motor with reference to Chapter 5A.

Manual transmission models

37 Progressively unscrew and remove the transmission-to-engine bolts, noting where each one goes, and the location of any brackets attached, for guidance when refitting.

38 With the help of an assistant, withdraw the transmission directly from the engine, making sure that its weight is not allowed to bear on the input shaft. Note that there are two locating dowels used.

Automatic transmission models

39 The torque converter is attached to the driveplate by four bolts which are accessed through an aperture on the end face of the transmission. Remove the single securing bolt, then withdraw the grommet from the access hole. Turn the engine as required to position each bolt in the aperture in turn, then unscrew and remove them.

40 Slacken and remove the bolts securing the transmission to the engine. Note the correct fitted positions of each bolt, and the necessary brackets, as they are removed to use as a reference on refitting.

41 Carefully prise the transmission off the engine, to free its locating dowels. As the transmission is removed, make sure the torque converter is kept pushed fully onto the transmission shaft.

42 Once the transmission is free, secure the torque converter in position by bolting a length of metal bar to one of the housing holes.

Refitting

43 Refitting is a reversal of removal, noting the following additional points:

a) Make sure that all mating faces are clean, and use new gaskets where necessary.
b) Tighten all nuts and bolts to the specified torque setting, where given.
c) If the transmission was removed, refit it to the engine as described in Chapter 7A or 7B, as applicable.
d) Delay fully tightening the engine left- and right-hand mountings until the engine has settled into place.
e) Fit a new circlip to the groove in the inner end of the left-hand driveshaft, and ensure it fully engages as the shaft is fitted into the transmission.
f) When reconnecting the power steering pump pipe/hose, use new sealing washers and O-rings as applicable. Top-up and bleed the power steering system as described in Chapter 10.
g) On manual transmission models, top-up and bleed the clutch hydraulic system as described in Chapter 6.
h) Refill the transmission oil or fluid, with reference to Chapter 1B.
i) Refill the cooling system as described in Chapter 1B.

6 Engine overhaul – dismantling sequence

1 It is much easier to dismantle and work on the engine if it is mounted on a portable engine stand. These stands can often be hired from a tool hire shop. Before the engine is mounted on a stand, the flywheel/driveplate should be removed, so that the stand bolts can be tightened into the end of the cylinder block.

2 If a stand is not available, it is possible to dismantle the engine with it blocked up on a sturdy workbench, or on the floor. Be extra careful not to tip or drop the engine when working without a stand.

3 If you are going to obtain a reconditioned engine, all the external components must be removed first, to be transferred to the new engine (just as they will if you are doing a complete engine overhaul yourself). These components include the following:

a) Inlet and exhaust manifolds (relevant part of Chapter 4).
b) Alternator/power steering pump/air conditioning compressor bracket(s) (as applicable).
c) Coolant pump (Chapter 3).
d) Fuel system components (relevant part of Chapter 4).
e) Wiring harness and all electrical switches and sensors.
f) Oil filter (relevant part of Chapter 1).
g) Flywheel/driveplate (relevant part of this Chapter).
h) Brake vacuum pump – diesel models (Chapter 9).
i) Dipstick and tube, where applicable.
j) Oil cooler, where applicable (Chapter 2B or 2C)
k) Engine mounting brackets (relevant part of Chapter 2).

Note: *When removing the external components from the engine, pay close attention to details that may be helpful or important during refitting. Note the fitted position of gaskets, seals, spacers, pins, washers, bolts, and other small items.*

4 If you are obtaining a 'short' engine (which consists of the engine cylinder block, crankshaft, pistons and connecting rods all assembled), then the cylinder head, sump, oil pump, and timing belt/chains (as applicable) will have to be removed also.

5 If you are planning a complete overhaul, the engine can be dismantled, and the internal components removed, in the order given below, referring to the relevant Part of this Chapter unless otherwise stated.

a) Inlet and exhaust manifolds (relevant part of Chapter 4).
b) Timing belt(s), sprockets and tensioner – petrol engines.
c) Cylinder head(s).
d) Flywheel/driveplate.
e) Sump.
f) Oil pump.
g) Timing chains and sprockets – diesel engine only.
h) Piston/connecting rod assemblies.
i) Crankshaft.

6 Before beginning the dismantling and overhaul procedures, make sure that you have all of the correct tools necessary. Refer to the *Tools and working facilities* Section of this manual for further information.

7 Timing chain cover (diesel engine) – removal and refitting

Removal

1 Refer to Chapter 2C, and remove the cylinder head, oil pump and crankshaft pulley.

2 With reference to Chapter 5A, remove the alternator.

3 Undo the Allen screw, and remove the auxiliary drivebelt idler pulley from the timing cover **(see illustration)**.

4 Slacken and remove the retaining nut, and remove the auxiliary drivebelt tensioner arm from the spring housing. Discard the seal, a new one must be fitted **(see illustrations)**.

5 Undo the two retaining bolts and remove the lower coolant rail support bracket from the timing cover.

6 The timing cover is held by fourteen bolts. Undo the bolts and remove the timing cover.

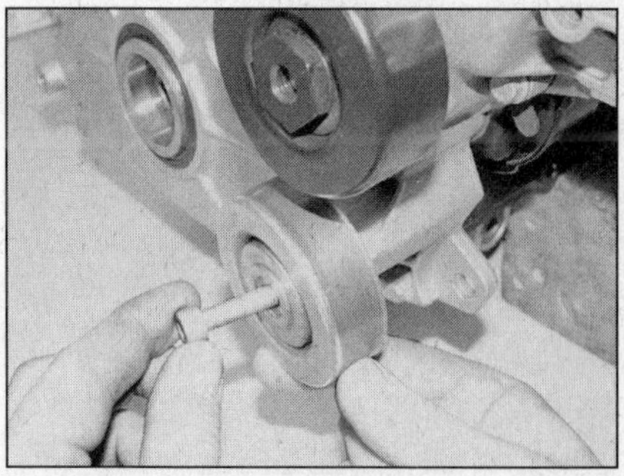

7.3 Undo the Allen screw, and remove the auxiliary drivebelt idler pulley

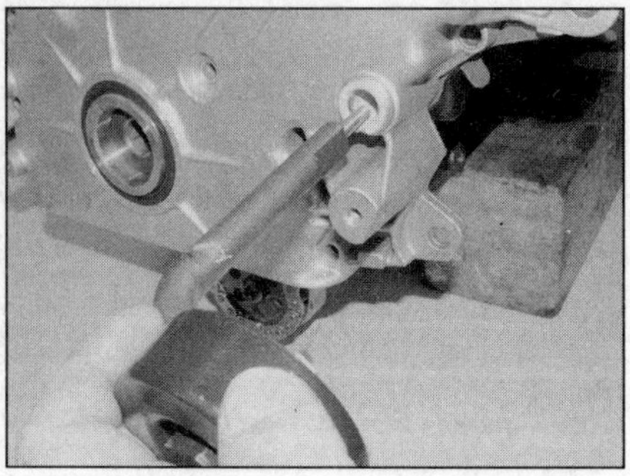

7.4a Slacken and remove the retaining nut, and remove the auxiliary drivebelt tensioner arm . . .

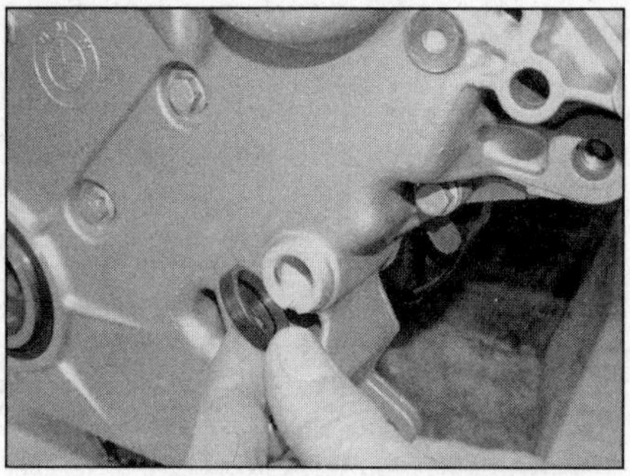

7.4b . . . and discard the seal – a new one must be fitted

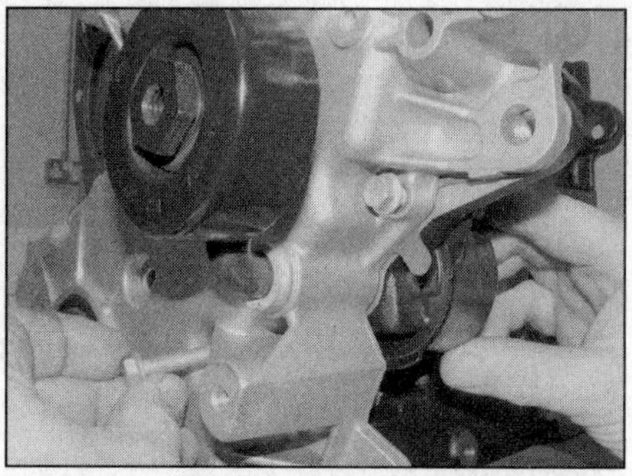

7.6 The removal of the timing cover bolts will release the auxiliary drivebelt tensioner

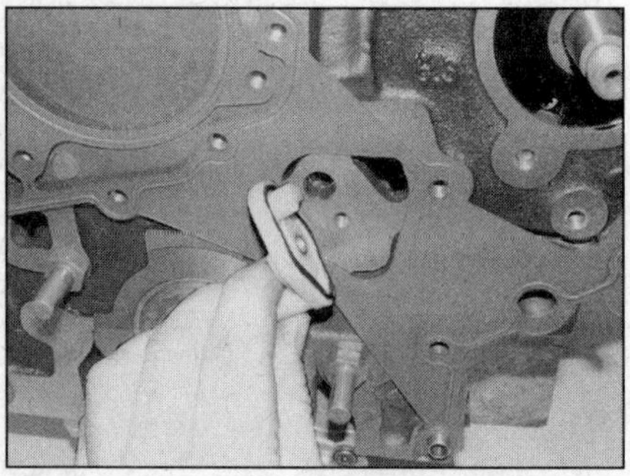

7.8 Undo the retaining bolt and remove the chain lubrication jet

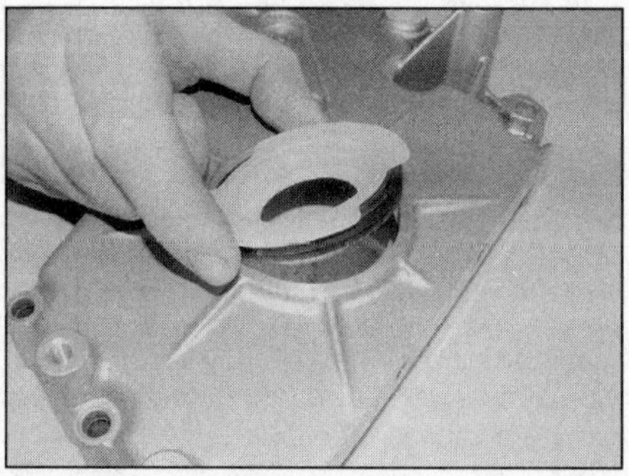

7.10a Use the seal protector supplied with the new seal . . .

The removal of the bolts will release the auxiliary drivebelt tensioner **(see illustration)**.

7 In order to remove the old gasket and fit the new one, the fuel injection pump drive chain, tensioner and sprocket, and crankshaft sprocket must be removed as described in Section 8.

8 Undo the retaining bolt and remove the chain lubrication jet **(see illustration)**. Discard the oil seal – a new one must be used.

9 Remove the timing cover gasket.

Refitting

10 Prior to refitting the timing cover, prise out the old crankshaft oil seal, and drive a new one into the cover, using a suitable tubular drift or socket **(see illustrations)**.

11 Ensure that the mating faces of the timing cover and engine block are clean and dry, and fit the new timing cover gasket to the engine block **(see illustration)**.

12 Check to make sure the mating faces are clean, then refit the chain lubrication jet (with the new seal in place), tightening the retaining bolt to the specified torque.

13 Refit the fuel pump drive chain, sprocket, crankshaft sprocket and tensioner as described in Section 8.

14 Fit the camshaft drive chain to the fuel pump sprocket.

15 Position the timing cover in place against the engine block, and temporarily fit the auxiliary drivebelt tensioner pulley arm to align the tensioner.

16 Evenly and progressively tighten the timing cover retaining bolts to the specified torque.

17 Remove the auxiliary drivebelt tensioner pulley arm, fit the new seal, refit the arm and tighten the retaining nut to the specified torque **(see illustration 7.4a)**.

18 Fit the auxiliary drivebelt idler pulley, and tighten the Allen screw to the specified torque.

19 Carry out the following operations:

a) Refit the alternator (Chapter 5A).
b) Refit the oil pump (Chapter 2C).
c) Refit the crankshaft pulley (Chapter 2C).
d) Refit the cylinder head (Chapter 2C).
e) Refit the air conditioning and auxiliary drivebelts (Chapter 1B).

8 Timing chains and components (diesel engine) – removal, inspection and refitting

Removal

Camshaft timing chain

1 Remove the timing chain cover as described in Section 7 of this Chapter.

2 Disengage the timing chain from the fuel pump sprocket.

Timing chain tensioner and guides

3 Remove the timing chain cover as described in Section 7 of this Chapter.

4 Press the lower chain tensioner plunger fully into the tensioner body, and insert MG Rover tool LRT-12-172 into the body to lock the plunger in place. If the tool is not available, a 4 mm drill bit or rod will make a suitable substitute **(see illustration)**.

7.10b . . . and drive the seal in until it is flush with the cover

7.11 Fit the new timing cover gasket to the engine block

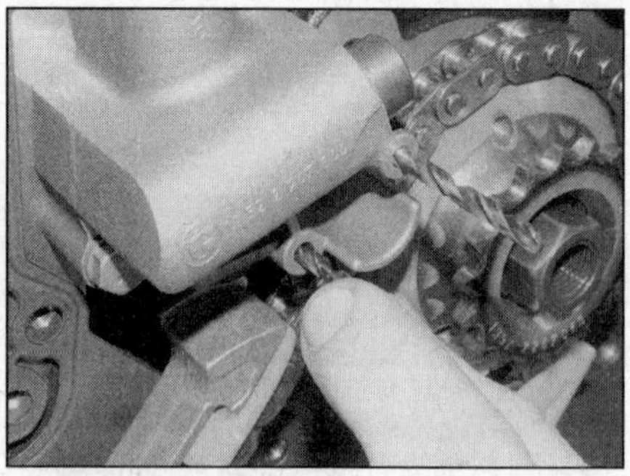

8.4 Insert a 4 mm drill bit to lock the timing chain tensioner plunger in place

8.5 Undo the three bolts (arrowed) and remove the tensioner from the engine block

8.6a Slide the rear chain guide from the its locating pin (arrowed)

8.6b Undo the Allen screw and lift the front chain guide from its locating pin

5 Undo the three bolts and remove the tensioner from the engine block **(see illustration)**.

6 Slide the rear chain guide from the its locating pin. Undo the Allen screw and remove the front chain guide from its locating pin **(see illustrations)**. Discard the Allen screw, a new one must be fitted.

Fuel pump and crankshaft sprockets and chain

7 Remove the timing chain cover as described in Section 7 of this Chapter.

8 Disengage the camshaft timing chain from the fuel injection pump sprocket.

9 As described in paragraphs 4 to 6 of this Section, remove the chain tensioner and guides.

10 Undo the fuel injection pump central retaining nut. Use a strap wrench (or similar) to prevent the sprocket from rotating **(see illustration)**.

11 Using a suitable two- or three-legged puller, remove the fuel injection pump sprocket from the pump shaft **(see illustration)**.

12 As the fuel pump sprocket is withdrawn, slide the sprocket from the crankshaft. Recover the key from the crankshaft if it is loose. Disengage the sprockets from the chains.

13 Undo the retaining bolt, and remove the chain lubrication jet.

Inspection

14 Examine the teeth on the camshafts, fuel injection pump and crankshaft sprockets for any sign of wear or damage such as chipped or hooked teeth. If there is any sign of wear or damage on either sprocket, *all* sprockets and timing chains should be renewed as a set.

15 Inspect the links of the timing chains for signs of wear or damage on the rollers. The extent of wear can be judged by checking the amount by which the chain can be bent sideways; a new chain will have very little sideways movement. If there is an excessive amount of side play in either timing chain, it must be renewed.

16 Note that it is a sensible precaution to renew the timing chains, regardless of their apparent condition, if the engine has covered a high mileage, or if it has been noted that the chain(s) have sounded noisy with the engine running. Although not strictly necessary, it is always worth renewing the chains and sprockets as a matched set, since it is false economy to run a new chain on worn sprockets and *vice-versa*. If there is any doubt about the condition of the timing chains and sprockets, seek the advice of an engine reconditioning specialist.

17 Examine the chain guides for signs of wear or damage to their chain contact faces, renewing any which are badly marked.

Refitting

18 Remove the remains of the timing cover gasket from the engine block, and ensure the mating surfaces of the block and timing cover are clean and dry.

19 Position the new timing cover gasket on the engine block, and refit the chain lubrication jet (with a new O-ring seal), tightening its retaining bolt to the specified torque.

20 Engage the crankshaft and fuel injection pump sprockets with the oil pump and fuel injection pump drive chains. The oil pump chain is fitted to the inside row of teeth on the crankshaft sprocket, and the drive chain is fitted to the inside row of teeth on the fuel injection pump sprocket **(see illustration)**. **Note:** *Due to the common rail design of the fuel injection system, there is no need to 'time' the fuel injection pump to the crankshaft position.*

21 Align the keyway in the crankshaft sprocket with the key in the crankshaft, and slide the sprocket onto the crankshaft. Fit the sprocket to the fuel injection pump at the same time **(see illustration)**.

8.10 Use a strap wrench (or similar) to prevent the fuel pump sprocket from rotating

8.11 Using a suitable two- or three-legged puller, remove the fuel injection pump sprocket

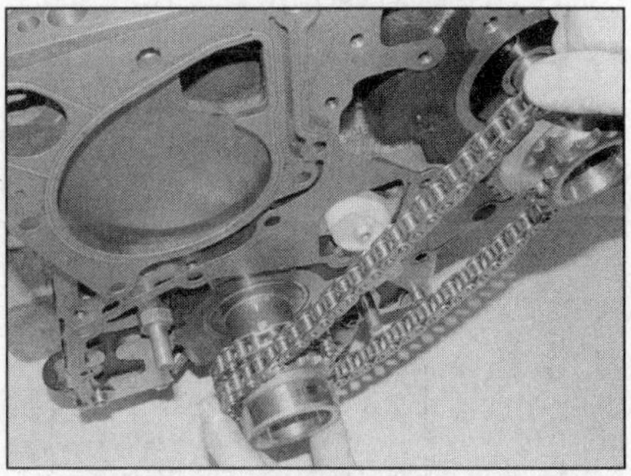

8.20 The oil pump chain fits on the crankshaft sprocket's inside teeth, with the pump chain on the pump sprocket's inside teeth

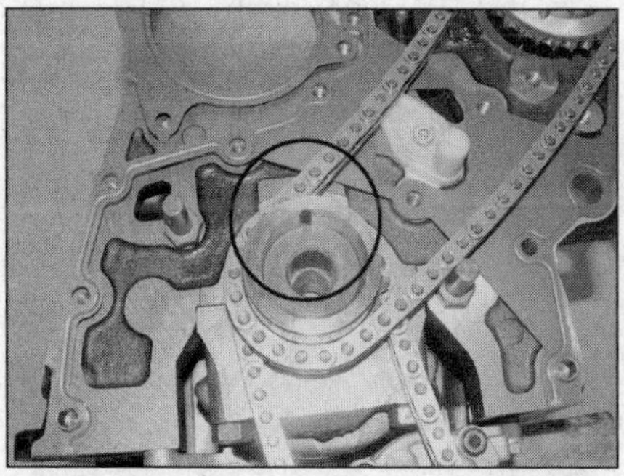

8.21 Align the keyway in the crankshaft sprocket with the key in the crankshaft

8.22 Tighten the fuel injection pump sprocket retaining nut to the specified torque

9.3a Use a valve spring compressor to compress a valve spring

9.3b Carefully remove the stem oil seal from the valve guide

22 Tighten the fuel injection pump sprocket retaining nut to the specified torque, using a strap wrench (or similar) to prevent the sprocket from rotating **(see illustration)**.

23 Fit the front chain guide to the locating pin, and tighten the new Allen screw to the specified torque **(see illustration 8.6b)**.

24 Refit the rear chain guide to its locating pin **(see illustration 8.6a)**.

25 Ensure that the tensioner body mating surface, and oilways are clean, and fit the tensioner to the engine block, tightening the retaining bolts to the specified torque.

26 Press the lower tensioner plunger into tensioner body, and withdraw the locking tool/rod/drill bit (as applicable).

27 Engage the camshaft drive chain with the fuel injection pump sprocket.

28 Refit the timing chain cover as described in Section 7 of this Chapter.

9 Cylinder head – dismantling

Note: *New and reconditioned cylinder heads are available from the manufacturer, and from engine overhaul specialists. Be aware that some specialist tools are required for the dismantling and inspection procedures, and new components may not be readily available. It may therefore be more practical and economical for the home mechanic to purchase a reconditioned head, rather than dismantle, inspect and recondition the original head.*

1 On petrol engines, referring to Part A or B of this Chapter, remove the camshafts and followers, then remove the cylinder head(s) from the engine. Remove the spark plugs (see Chapter 1A).

2 On diesel engines, remove the glow plugs (Chapter 5C) and injectors (Chapter 4C). Remove the camshafts, rockers and tappets, then remove the cylinder head as described in Part C of this Chapter.

3 On all engines, using a valve spring compressor, compress each valve spring in turn until the split collets can be removed. Release the compressor, and lift off the spring retainer and spring. Using a pair of pliers, carefully extract the valve stem seal from the valve guide **(see illustrations)**.

4 If, when the valve spring compressor is screwed down, the spring retainer refuses to free and expose the split collets, gently tap the top of the tool, directly over the retainer, with a light hammer. This will free the retainer.

5 Withdraw the valve through the combustion chamber. It is essential that each valve is stored together with its collets, retainer and spring. The valves should also be kept in their correct sequence, unless they are so badly worn that they are to be renewed **(see Haynes Hint)**.

HAYNES HiNT

If the components are to be refitted, place each valve and its associated components in a labelled polythene bag or similar small container, and mark the bag/container with the relevant valve number to ensure that it is refitted in its original location.

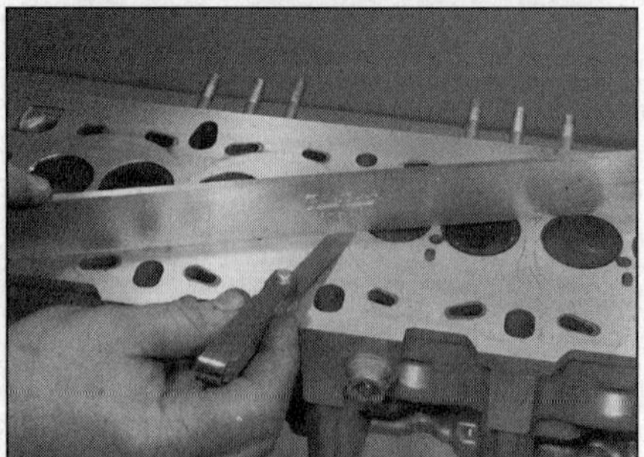

10.6 Use a straight-edge and feeler blade to check the cylinder head surface for distortion

10 Cylinder head and valves – cleaning and inspection

1 Thorough cleaning of the cylinder head and valve components, followed by a detailed inspection, will enable you to decide how much valve service work must be carried out during the engine overhaul. **Note:** *If the engine has been severely overheated, it is best to assume that the cylinder head is warped – check carefully for signs of this.*

Cleaning

2 Scrape away all traces of old gasket material from the cylinder head.

3 Scrape away the carbon from the combustion chambers and ports, then wash the cylinder head thoroughly with paraffin or a suitable solvent.

4 Scrape off any heavy carbon deposits that may have formed on the valves, then use a power-operated wire brush to remove deposits from the valve heads and stems.

Inspection

Note: *Be sure to perform all the following inspection procedures before concluding that the services of a machine shop or engine overhaul specialist are required. Make a list of all items that require attention.*

Cylinder head

5 Inspect the head very carefully for cracks, evidence of coolant leakage, and other damage. If cracks are found, a new cylinder head should be obtained.

6 Use a straight-edge and feeler blade to check that the cylinder head surface is not distorted **(see illustration)**. If it is, it may be possible to resurface it (petrol engines only), provided that the cylinder head is not reduced to less than the minimum specified height.

7 Examine the valve seats in each of the combustion chambers. If they are severely pitted, cracked or burned, then they will need to be renewed or recut by an engine overhaul

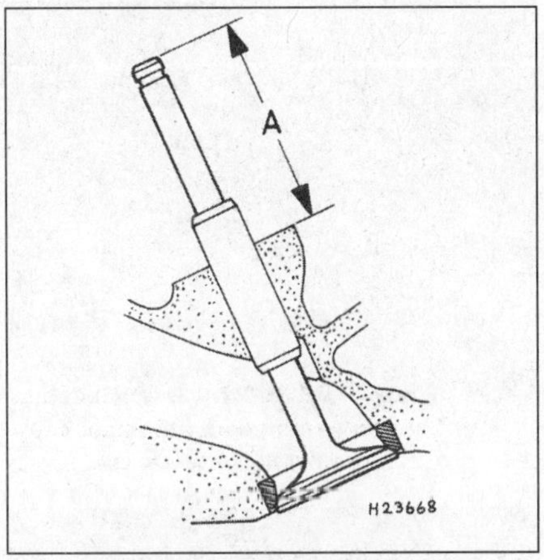

10.8a Valve stem installed height measurement (A) – petrol engine

specialist (petrol engines only). If they are only slightly pitted, this can be removed by grinding-in the valve heads and seats with fine valve-grinding compound, as described below.

8 Check valve seat wear by inserting each valve into its relevant guide. On petrol engines, measure the projected height of the valve stem above the cylinder head surface and on diesel engines, using a straight-edge and feeler blades, measure the valve head recess from the cylinder head mating surface **(see illustrations)**. If any measurement exceeds the specified limit, repeat the check with a new valve. If the measurement still exceeds the specified limit, then the valve seat is excessively worn and must be renewed. The valve seats can only be renewed on petrol engines, on diesel engines, the cylinder head must be renewed.

9 If the valve guides are worn (indicated by a side-to-side motion of the valve, and accompanied by excessive blue smoke in the exhaust when running) new guides must be fitted. Measure the diameter of the existing valve stems (see below) and the bore of the guides, then calculate the clearance and compare the result with the specified value. If the clearance is not within the specified limits, renew the valves and/or guides as necessary. The valve guides can only be renewed on

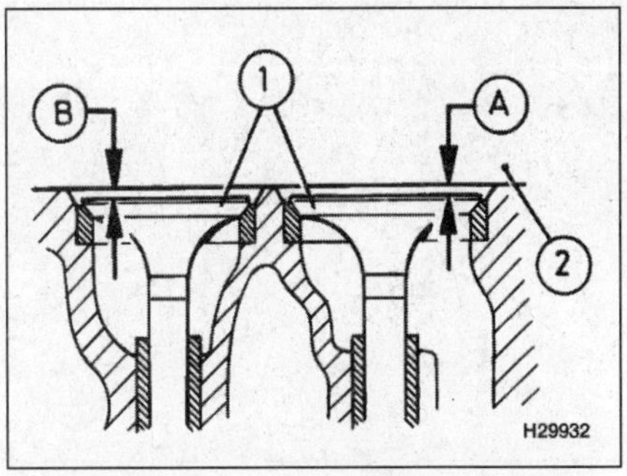

10.8b Valve head recess measurement – diesel engine

1 Valves — *A Inlet valve*
2 Straight-edge — *B Exhaust valve*

petrol engines – on diesel engines, the cylinder head must be renewed.

10 The renewal of valve guides is best carried out by an engine overhaul specialist. If the work is to be carried out at home, however, on petrol engines, use a stepped, double-diameter drift to drive out the worn guide towards the combustion chamber. Drive the guide into position until it projects the specified amount above the cylinder head surface **(see illustration)**.

HAYNES HiNT ***Haynes hint: When fitting the new guide, place it first in a deep-freeze for one hour, then drive it into its cylinder head bore from the camshaft side.***

11 If the valve seats are to be recut this must be done only after the guides have been renewed.

Valves

12 Examine the head of each valve for pitting, burning, cracks and general wear, and check the valve stem for scoring and wear ridges. Rotate the valve, and check for any obvious indication that it is bent. Look for pitting and excessive wear on the tip of each valve stem. Renew any valve that shows any such signs of wear or damage.

13 If the valve appears satisfactory at this stage, measure the valve stem diameter at several points using a micrometer **(see illustration)**. Any significant difference in the readings obtained indicates wear of the valve stem. Should any of these conditions be apparent, the valve(s) must be renewed.

14 If the valves are in satisfactory condition, they should be ground (lapped) into their respective seats, to ensure a smooth gas-tight seal. If the seat is only lightly pitted, or if it has been recut, fine grinding compound **only** should be used to produce the required finish. Coarse valve-grinding compound should **not** be used unless a seat is badly burned or deeply pitted; if this is the case, the cylinder head and valves should be inspected by an expert to decide whether seat recutting, or even the renewal of the valve or seat insert, is required.

15 Valve grinding is carried out as follows. Place the cylinder head upside-down on a bench.

16 Smear a trace of the appropriate grade of valve-grinding compound on the seat face, and press a suction grinding tool onto the valve head. With a semi-rotary action, grind the valve head to its seat, lifting the valve occasionally to redistribute the grinding compound **(see illustration)**. A light spring placed under the valve head will greatly ease this operation.

17 If coarse grinding compound is being used, work only until a dull, matt even surface is produced on both the valve seat and the valve, then wipe off the used compound and repeat the process with fine compound. When a smooth unbroken ring of light grey matt finish is produced on both the valve and seat, the grinding operation is complete. **Do not** grind in the valves any further than absolutely necessary, or the seat will be prematurely sunk into the cylinder head.

18 When all the valves have been ground-in, carefully wash off all traces of grinding compound using paraffin or a suitable solvent before reassembly of the cylinder head.

Valve components

19 Examine the valve springs for signs of damage and discoloration. The condition of each spring can be judged by measuring

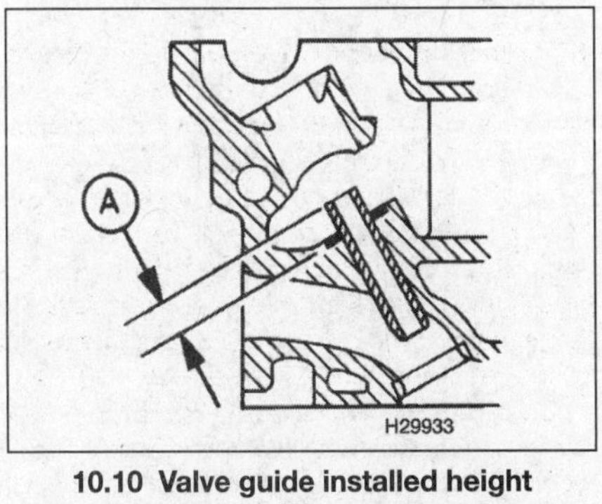

10.10 Valve guide installed height measurement (A) – petrol engine

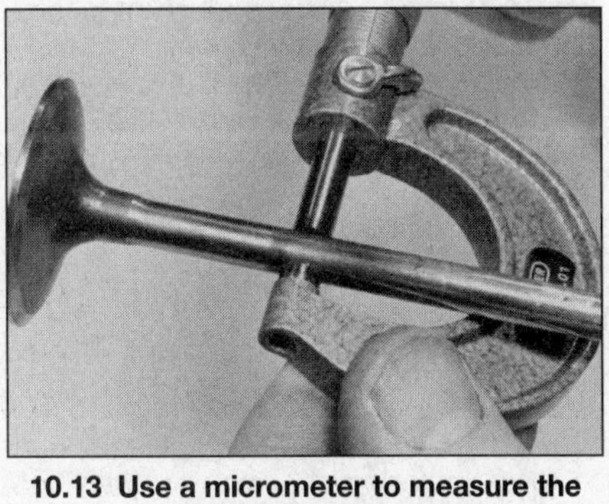

10.13 Use a micrometer to measure the valve stem diameter

10.16 Grinding-in a valve seat

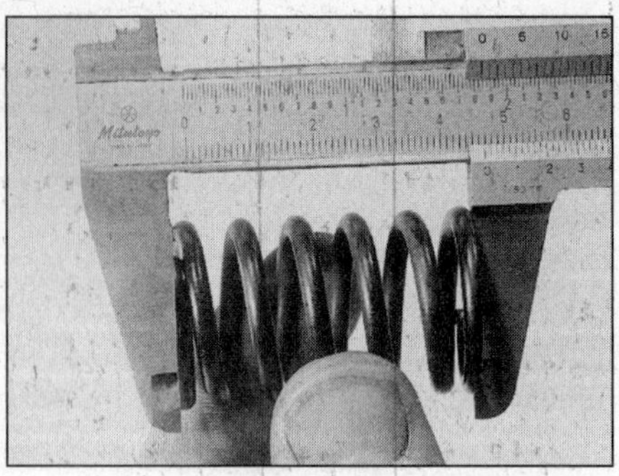

10.19 Measure the valve spring free length

its free length **(see illustration)**. Stand each spring on a flat surface, and check it for squareness. If any of the springs are less than the specified free length or are damaged or distorted, obtain a complete new set of springs.

11 Cylinder head – reassembly

1 Lubricate the stems of the valves, and insert them into their original locations **(see illustration)**. If new valves are being fitted, insert them into the locations to which they have been ground.

2 Working on the first valve, fit the seal protector (where supplied), dip the new valve stem seal in fresh engine oil, then carefully locate it over the valve and onto the guide.

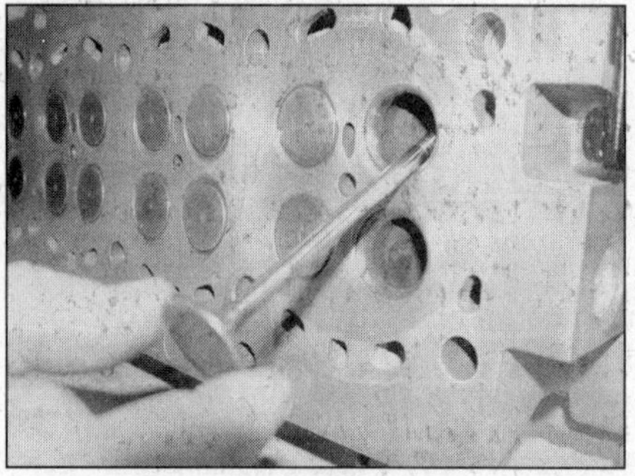

11.1 Insert the valves into their original locations

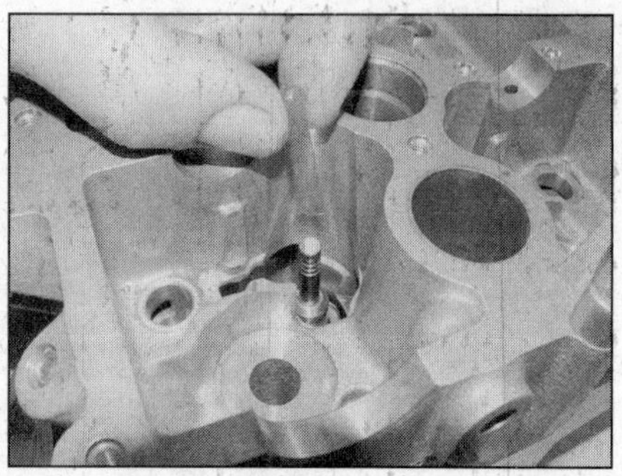

11.2a Where supplied, fit the seal protector over the valve stem . . .

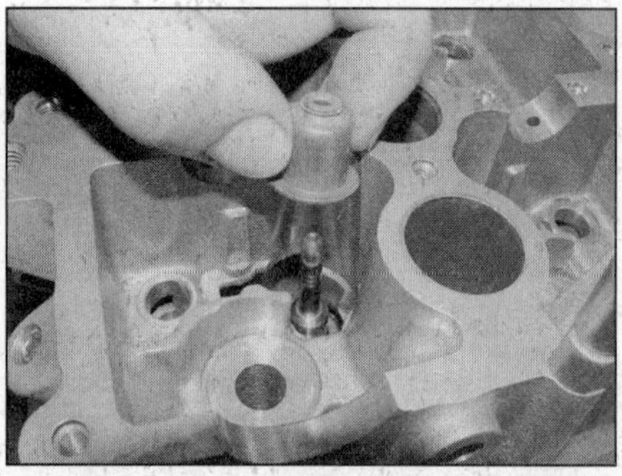

11.2b . . . then locate the seal over the guide . . .

11.2c . . . and using a socket (or similar) press the seal into place

Take care not to damage the seal as it is passed over the valve stem. Use a suitable socket or metal tube to press the seal firmly onto the guide **(see illustrations)**.

3 Locate the spring over the seal and fit the spring retainer **(see illustrations)**.

4 Compress the valve spring, and locate the split collets in the recess in the valve stem **(see illustrations and Haynes Hint)**. Release the compressor, then repeat the procedure on the remaining valves.

5 With all the valves installed, using a hammer and interposed block of wood, lightly tap the end of each valve stem to settle the components.

6 On petrol engines, working as described in Part A or B, refit the cylinder head to the engine and install the followers and camshafts.

7 On diesel engines, working as described in Part C, refit the cylinder head to the engine and install the followers, rockers, tappets and camshafts. Refit the injectors and glow plugs as described in Chapters 4C and 5C.

11.3a Fit the valve spring . . .

11.3b . . . followed by the retainer

11.4a Compress the valve spring and retainer . . .

11.4b . . . and locate the collets in position

HAYNES HiNT

Use a dab of grease to hold the collets in position on the valve stem whilst the spring compressor is released.

12.4 Remove the oil rail from the base of the main bearing ladder

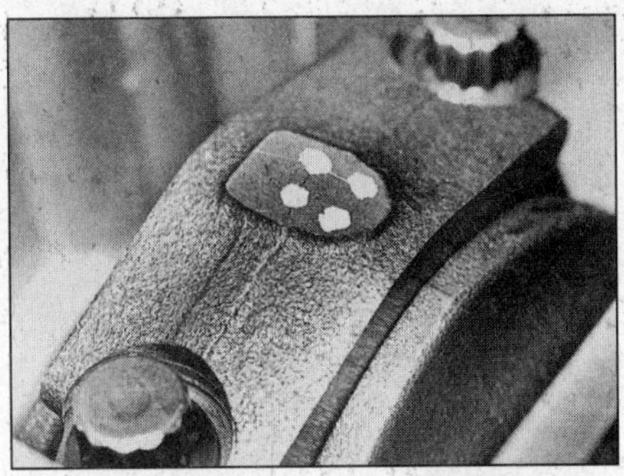

12.5 Mark each connecting rod big-end bearing cap with its respective cylinder number prior to removal

12.14 Mark the liner positions relative to the block, using paint

12 Piston/connecting rod assembly – removal

1.8 litre engine

Note: *Due to the design of the engine, it will become very difficult, almost impossible, to turn the crankshaft once the cylinder head bolts have been slackened. The manufacturer accordingly states that the crankshaft will be 'tight', and should not be rotated more than absolutely necessary once the head has been removed. If the crankshaft cannot be rotated, then it must be removed for overhaul work to proceed. With this in mind, during any servicing or overhaul work, the crankshaft must always be rotated to the desired position before the bolts are disturbed.*

1 Remove the camshafts and followers, then remove the sump and oil pump pick-up/strainer as described in Part A of this Chapter.

2 Rotate the crankshaft until Nos 1 and 4 cylinder pistons are at the top of their stroke, then remove the cylinder head and clamp the liners securely in position as described in Part A (the liner clamps will have to be moved slightly later, to allow the piston to pass). The crankshaft should not be rotated once the head has been removed.

3 Slacken and remove the dipstick tube retaining bolts and remove the tube from the cylinder block/crankcase.

4 Unscrew the two retaining nuts and remove the oil rail from the base of the main bearing ladder **(see illustration)**.

5 Using a hammer and centre-punch, paint or similar, mark each connecting rod big-end bearing cap with its respective cylinder number on the flat, machined surface provided **(see illustration)**. If the engine has been dismantled before, note carefully any identifying marks made previously. Note that No 1 cylinder is at the timing belt end of the engine.

6 Unscrew and remove the big-end bearing cap bolts and withdraw the cap, complete with bearing shell, from the connecting rod. If only the bearing shells are being attended to, push the connecting rod up and off the crankpin, ensuring that the connecting rod big-ends do not mark the cylinder bore walls, then remove the upper bearing shell. Keep the cap, bolts and (if they are to be refitted) the bearing shells together in their correct sequence.

7 With Nos 2 and 3 cylinder big-ends disconnected, repeat the procedure (exercising great care to prevent damage to any of the components) to remove Nos 1 and 4 cylinder bearing caps.

8 Remove the ridge of carbon from the top of each cylinder bore, and reposition the liner clamps as necessary to allow each piston to pass (for safety, ensure each liner is still clamped in two places, at least while its piston is being removed).

9 Push each piston/connecting rod assembly up and remove it from the top of the bore, and ensure that the connecting rod big-ends do not mark the cylinder bore walls.

10 Note that the number stamped by you on each bearing cap should match the cylinder number stamped on the front of each connecting rod (the letter on the rod is the weight code and the number on the front of bearing cap is the big-end bore size code). If any connecting rod number does not match its correct cylinder, mark or label it immediately so that each piston/connecting rod assembly can be refitted to its original bore. Fit the bearing cap, shells and bolts to each removed piston/connecting rod assembly, so that they are all kept together as a matched set.

V6 engine

11 Remove the cylinder heads, crankshaft oil seal, sump and oil pump as described in Part B of this Chapter.

12 Remove the single bolt securing the oil pump pick-up strainer. Withdraw it from the base of the engine, and recover the O-ring – a new one should be used when refitting.

13 Unscrew a total of eleven bolts securing the lower crankcase, noting the positions of the two smaller bolts. Some early models may have a stud and nut at the flywheel end. Remove the lower crankcase, noting that sealant is used during assembly – if possible, do not prise between the mating surfaces to free it.

14 The cylinder liners have to be removed with each piston/rod assembly – the big ends will not pass up through the liners. Therefore, unless new liners are being fitted, mark the fitted position of each liner in the block, using paint **(see illustration)**.

15 Position the crankshaft so that the first connecting rod is accessible (it may be possible to remove the rods in pairs, if wished).

16 Using a hammer and centre-punch, paint or similar, mark each connecting rod big-end bearing cap with its respective cylinder number. On our car, the caps were numbered already, with the numbers were facing inwards. If the engine has been dismantled before, note carefully any identifying marks made previously. Refer to Chapter 2B, Section 1, for details on cylinder numbering.

17 Unscrew and remove the big-end bearing cap bolts and withdraw the cap, complete with bearing shell, from the connecting rod.

18 If only the bearing shells are being attended to, push the connecting rod up and off the crankpin, ensuring that the connecting rod big-ends do not mark the cylinder bore walls, then remove the upper bearing shell. Keep the cap, bolts and (if they are to be refitted) the bearing shells together in their correct sequence.

19 Repeat the procedure (exercising great care to prevent damage to any of the components) to remove the remaining bearing caps.

20 Using a suitable wooden drift, carefully tap the cylinder liners upwards and out of the block **(see illustrations)**. Fit the bearing cap, shells and bolts to each removed piston/

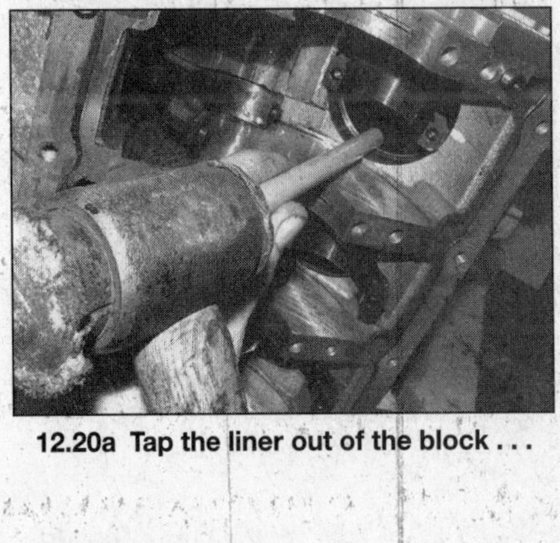

12.20a Tap the liner out of the block . . .

12.20b . . . and withdraw it from the engine

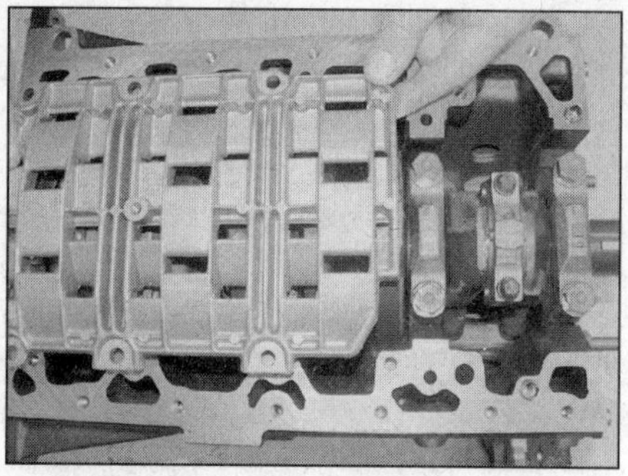

12.23 Unscrew the six retaining bolts, and remove the reinforcing plate from the cylinder block

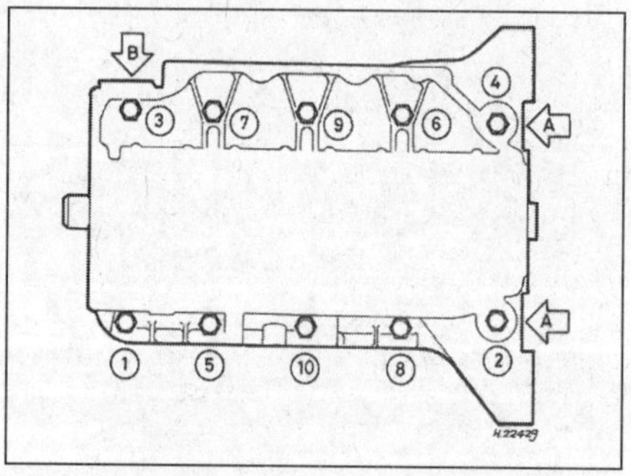

13.4a Main bearing ladder slackening sequence – petrol engine

A Bolts hidden in ladder flanges
B Location of longer bolt

connecting rod assembly, so that they are all kept together as a matched set.

21 As required, the piston and connecting rod assemblies can be withdrawn from the bottom of the liner. Before doing so, however, mark the liner with its cylinder number .

Diesel engine

22 Referring to Part C of this Chapter, remove the cylinder head and sump, then unbolt the pick-up/strainer and oil pump from the base of the cylinder block.

23 Unscrew the six retaining bolts, and remove the reinforcing plate from the cylinder block **(see illustration)**.

24 If there is a pronounced wear ridge at the top of any bore, it may be necessary to remove it with a scraper or ridge reamer, to avoid piston damage during removal. Such a ridge indicates excessive wear of the cylinder bore.

25 Using a hammer and centre-punch, paint or similar, mark each connecting rod and its bearing cap with its respective cylinder number on the flat machined surface provided; make the marks in such a way that there is no possibility in fitting the caps the wrong way around on refitting. If the engine has been dismantled before, note carefully any identifying marks made previously. Note that No 1 cylinder is at the timing belt end of the engine.

26 Turn the crankshaft to bring pistons 1 and 4 to BDC (bottom dead centre).

27 Unscrew the nuts/bolts (as applicable) from No 1 piston big-end bearing cap. Take off the cap and recover the bottom half bearing shell. If the bearing shells are to be re-used, tape the cap and the shell together. **Note:** *The big-end caps are located on the connecting rods by dowels. Do not tap the caps sideways in an attempt to remove them.*

28 Using a hammer handle, push the piston up through the bore, and remove it from the top of the cylinder block. Recover the bearing shell, and tape it to the connecting rod for safe-keeping.

29 Loosely refit the big-end cap to the connecting rod, and secure with the nuts/bolts – this will help to keep the components in their correct order.

30 Remove No 4 piston assembly in the same way.

31 Turn the crankshaft through 180° to bring pistons 2 and 3 to BDC (bottom dead centre), and remove them in the same way.

13 Crankshaft – removal

1.8 litre engine

1 Remove the cylinder head, sump, oil pump and flywheel as described in Part A of this Chapter.

2 Slacken and remove the dipstick tube retaining bolts and remove the tube from the cylinder block/crankcase.

3 Unscrew the two retaining nuts and remove the oil rail from the base of the main bearing ladder.

4 Working in sequence, progressively unscrew the main bearing ladder retaining bolts by a turn at a time, then withdraw the ladder. Note the two locating dowels and the main bearing shells, which should be removed from the ladder and stored in their correct fitted order **(see illustrations)**.

5 Remove the piston and connecting rod assemblies as described in Section 12 **(see illustration)**. If no work is to be done on the pistons and connecting rods, unbolt the caps and push the pistons far enough up the bores so that the connecting rods are positioned clear of the crankshaft journals.

6 Check the crankshaft endfloat as described in Section 16, then remove the crankshaft **(see illustration)**.

7 Withdraw the two thrustwashers from the No 3 main bearing upper location. Noting the position of the grooved shells, remove the upper main bearing shells, which must be kept with their correct respective partners from the main bearing ladder so that all shells can be identified and (if necessary) refitted in their original locations.

V6 engine

8 Remove the cylinder heads, sump, oil pump and flywheel as described in Part B of this Chapter.

13.4b Removing the main bearing ladder – note the fitted locations of the dowels (arrowed)

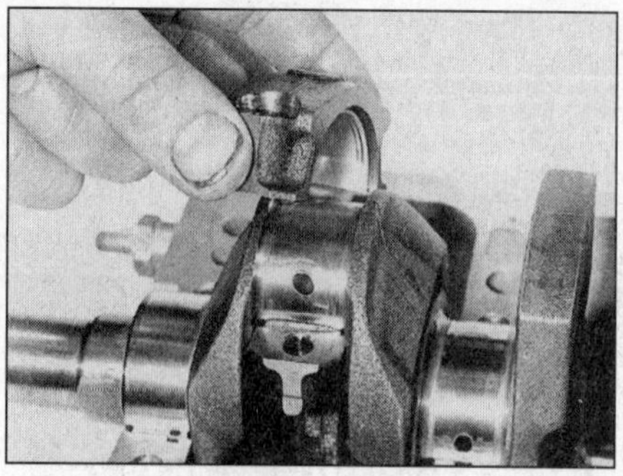

13.5 Remove the No 1 cylinder big-end bearing cap and shell

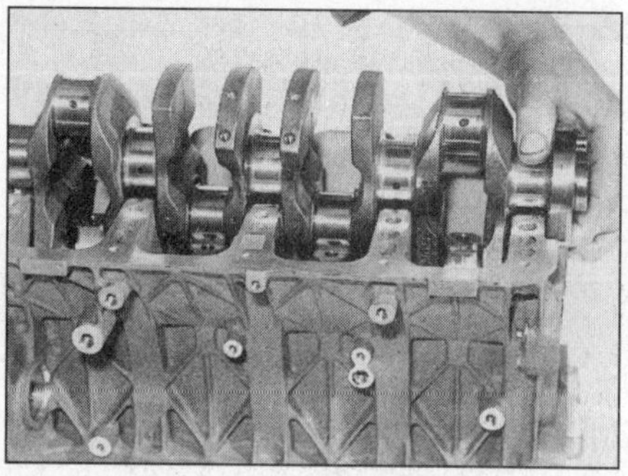

13.6 Remove the crankshaft

9 Remove the liners, piston and connecting rod assemblies as described in Section 12. If no work is to be done on the pistons and connecting rods, unbolt the caps and push the pistons far enough up the liners so that the connecting rods are positioned clear of the crankshaft journals.

10 Progressively unscrew the main bearing ladder retaining bolts by a turn at a time, noting that the eight shorter bolts are fitted to the outside edges. Withdraw the ladder, noting that it is located on dowels.

11 Check the crankshaft endfloat as described in Section 16, then remove the crankshaft.

12 Withdraw the thrustwashers from the No 4 main bearing location. Noting the position of the grooved shells, remove the upper main bearing shells, which must be kept with their correct respective partners from the main bearing ladder so that all shells can be identified and (if necessary) refitted in their original locations.

Diesel engine

13 Referring to Part C of this Chapter, remove the oil pump, flywheel and crankshaft flywheel end oil seal housing.

14 Remove the piston and connecting rod assemblies as described in Section 12. If no work is to be done on the pistons and connecting rods, the cylinder head can be left in position – unbolt the caps and push the pistons far enough up the bores so that the connecting rods are positioned clear of the crankshaft journals.

15 Check the crankshaft endfloat as described in Section 16, then proceed as follows.

16 The main bearing caps should be numbered 1 to 5 from the timing chain end of the engine and the arrow on each cap should point towards the timing chain end of the engine. If the bearing caps are not marked, using a hammer and punch or a suitable marker pen, number the caps from 1 to 5 from the timing chain end of the engine and mark each cap to indicate its correct fitted direction to avoid confusion on refitting.

17 Working in a diagonal sequence, evenly and progressively slacken the ten main bearing cap retaining bolts by half a turn at a time until all bolts are loose. Remove all bolts, keeping them in the correct fitted order.

18 Carefully remove each cap from the cylinder block, ensuring that the lower main bearing shell remains in position in the cap **(see illustration)**. Note the No 4 main bearing cap shell incorporates thrustwashers.

19 Carefully lift out the crankshaft, taking care not to displace the upper main bearing shells.

20 Recover the upper bearing shells from the cylinder block and tape them to their respective caps for safe-keeping. Note that the No 4 main bearing upper shell incorporates thrustwashers.

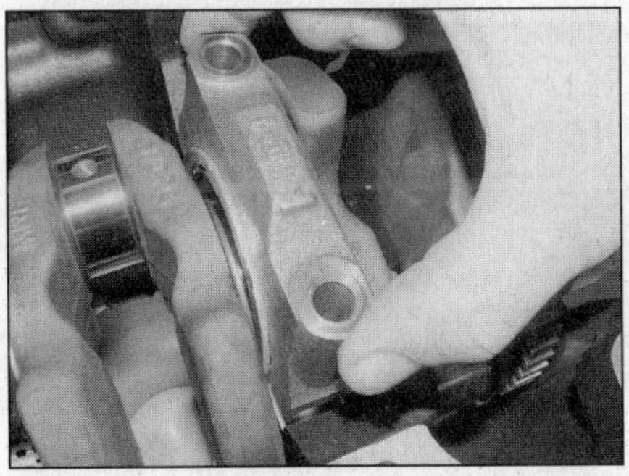

13.18 Carefully remove each cap from the cylinder block

14 Cylinder block – cleaning and inspection

Cleaning

1 Remove all external components and electrical switches/sensors from the block. For complete cleaning, the core plugs should ideally be removed. Drill a small hole in the plugs, then insert a self-tapping screw into the hole. Pull out the plugs by pulling on the screw with a pair of grips, or by using a slide hammer.

2 On petrol engines, remove the liners as described in paragraph 13.

3 On diesel engines, undo the retaining bolts and remove each piston oil jet spray tube from inside the cylinder block **(see illustration)**. Discard the retaining bolts – new ones must be used on refitting.

4 On all engines, scrape all traces of gasket from the cylinder block/crankcase, and from the main bearing ladder/caps (as applicable), taking care not to damage the gasket/sealing surfaces.

5 Remove all oil gallery plugs (where fitted). The plugs are usually very tight – they may have to be drilled out, and the holes retapped. Use new plugs when the engine is reassembled.

6 If any of the castings are extremely dirty, all should be steam-cleaned.

14.3 Unscrew the retaining bolts and remove the piston oil jet spray tubes – diesel engine

7 After the castings are returned, clean all oil holes and oil galleries one more time. Flush all internal passages with warm water until the water runs clear. Dry thoroughly, and apply a light film of oil to all mating surfaces, to prevent rusting. Also oil the cylinder bores. If you have access to compressed air, use it to speed up the drying process, and to blow out all the oil holes and galleries.

Warning: Wear eye protection when using compressed air.

8 If the castings are not very dirty, you can do an adequate cleaning job with hot (as hot as you can stand), soapy water and a stiff brush. Take plenty of time, and do a thorough job. Regardless of the cleaning method used, be sure to clean all oil holes and galleries very thoroughly, and to dry all components well. Protect the cylinder bores as described above, to prevent rusting.

9 All threaded holes must be clean, to ensure accurate torque readings during reassembly. To clean the threads, run the correct-size tap into each of the holes to remove rust, corrosion, thread sealant or sludge, and to restore damaged threads. If possible, use compressed air to clear the holes of debris produced by this operation. A good alternative is to inject aerosol-applied water-dispersant lubricant into each hole, using the long spout usually supplied.

Warning: Wear eye protection when cleaning out these holes in this way.

10 Apply suitable sealant to the new oil gallery plugs, and insert them into the holes in the block. Tighten them securely.

11 On diesel engines, apply a drop of threadlocking compound to the threads of the oil jet spray tube new retaining bolts, ensuring that the bolt oil holes are not obstructed. Refit the piston oil jet spray tubes to the cylinder block, then fit the new retaining bolts, tightening them to the specified torque setting.

12 If the engine is not going to be reassembled right away, cover it with a large plastic bag to keep it clean; protect all mating surfaces and the cylinder bores as described above, to prevent rusting.

Inspection

Petrol engine

13 Remove the liner clamps (where used), then use a hard wood drift to tap out each liner from the inside of the cylinder block. When all the liners are released, remove each liner from the top of the block. As each liner is removed, stick masking tape on its left-hand (flywheel side) face, and write the cylinder number on the tape. On 1.8 litre engines, No 1 cylinder is at the timing belt end of the engine; refer to Chapter 2B, Section 1, for cylinder numbering details on the V6 engine.

14 Check each cylinder liner for scuffing and scoring. Check for signs of a wear ridge at

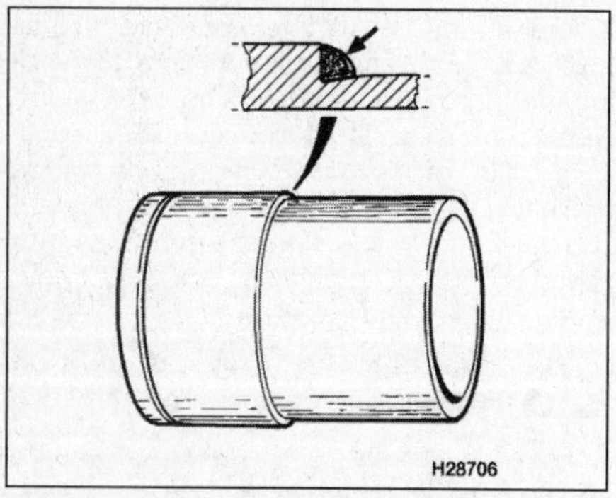

14.21 Apply a continuous 2.0 mm bead of sealant around the liner locating shoulder

14.22 Using a hammer and a block of wood, tap each liner lightly but fully onto its locating shoulder

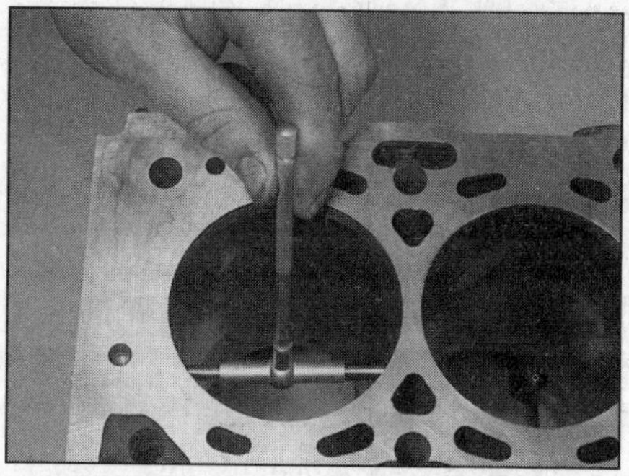

14.27 Use an internal micrometer to measure cylinder bore diameter

the top of the liner, indicating that the bore is excessively worn.

15 If the necessary measuring equipment is available, measure the bore diameter of each cylinder bore. The measurement should be taken 65 mm down from the top of the bore. Take two measurements, one parallel to the crankshaft axis and the other at right-angles to the crankshaft axis. Compare the results with the figures given in the Specifications.

16 If the liner wear exceeds the permitted tolerances at any point, or if the cylinder liner walls are badly scored or scuffed, then renewal of the relevant liner assembly will be necessary. If there is any doubt about the condition of the cylinder bores, seek the advice of an engine reconditioning specialist. If the bores are in reasonably good condition and not worn to the specified limits, then the piston rings should be renewed but according to MG Rover, the bores should **not** be honed.

17 If renewal is necessary, new liners should be obtainable from MG Rover parts suppliers, or an engine specialist. New piston/connecting rod assemblies will also be required. Note that the pistons are only supplied as assemblies complete with the connecting rods.

18 To allow for manufacturing tolerances, pistons and liners are separated into two size groups. The size group of each piston is indicated by a letter (A or B) stamped onto its crown, and the size group of each liner is indicated by a paint marking; Red for size group A and Blue for size group B. Ensure that each piston and its respective liner are both of the same size group. It is permissible to have different size group piston and liner assemblies fitted to the same engine, but never fit a piston of one size group to a liner in a different group.

19 The liners are also available in two 'step heights', denoted by the letter V or Z. All liners should be the same step height in one engine, and any new liners should also be the same step height as those removed.

20 Prior to installing the liners, thoroughly clean the liner mating surfaces in the cylinder block, and use fine abrasive paper to polish away any burrs or sharp edges which hinder installation.

21 Ensure the liner and block mating surfaces are clean and dry. Apply a continuous bead of sealant (MG Rover part no GGC 102) approximately 2.0 mm thick around the locating shoulder on the liner **(see illustration)**.

22 Carefully insert the liner squarely into the cylinder block and press it fully into position. If the original liners are being refitted, use the marks made on removal to ensure that each is refitted the correct way round, and is inserted into its original bore. Insert each liner into the cylinder block and press it home as far as possible by hand. Using a hammer and a block of wood, tap each liner lightly but fully onto its locating shoulder **(see illustration)**. Wipe clean, then lightly oil, all exposed liner surfaces, to prevent rusting. If possible, clamp the liners in position.

23 Check the condition of the cylinder head bolts, and particularly their threads, whenever they are removed.

24 Keeping all the bolts in their correct fitted order, wash them and wipe dry, then check each for any sign of visible wear or damage. Renew any bolt if necessary. As a precaution, we recommend that the bolts are renewed as a complete set, regardless of their apparent condition. On 1.8 litre engines, note that if any of the cylinder head bolt threads in the oil rail are found to be damaged, then the oil rail must be renewed – helicoils (thread inserts) are not an acceptable repair in this instance.

Diesel engine

25 Visually check the castings for cracks and corrosion. Look for stripped threads in the threaded holes. If there has been any history of internal water leakage, it may be worthwhile having an engine overhaul specialist check the cylinder block/crankcase with special equipment. If defects are found, have them repaired if possible, or renew the assembly.

26 Check each cylinder bore for scuffing and scoring. Check for signs of a wear ridge at the top of the cylinder, indicating that the bore is excessively worn.

27 If the necessary measuring equipment is available, measure the bore diameter of each cylinder bore. The measurement should be taken 70 mm down from the top of the bore. Take two measurements, one parallel to the crankshaft axis and the other at right-angles to the crankshaft axis **(see illustration)**. Compare the results with the figures given in the Specifications.

28 Oversize pistons are available, and it should be possible to have the cylinder block rebored and fit the oversize pistons. Seek the advice of an engine reconditioning specialist on the best course of action.

29 If the bores are in reasonably good condition and not worn to the specified limits, then the piston rings should be renewed. If this is the case, the bores should be honed to allow the new rings to bed in correctly and provide the best possible seal.

30 The conventional type of hone has spring-loaded stones, and is used with a power drill. You will also need some paraffin (or honing oil) and rags. The hone should be moved up-and-down the bore to produce a crosshatch pattern, and plenty of honing oil should be used. Ideally, the crosshatch lines should intersect at approximately a 60° angle. Do not take off more material than is necessary to produce the required finish.

31 If new pistons are being fitted, the piston manufacturers may specify a finish with a different angle, so their instructions should be followed. Do not withdraw the hone from the bore while it is still being turned – stop it first. After honing a bore, wipe out all traces of the honing oil.

32 If equipment of this type is not available, or if you are not sure whether you are competent to undertake the task yourself, an engine overhaul specialist will carry out the work at moderate cost.

15 Piston/connecting rod assembly – inspection

1 Before the inspection process can begin, the piston/connecting rod assemblies must be cleaned, and the original piston rings removed from the pistons.

2 Carefully expand the old rings over the top of the pistons. The use of two or three old feeler blades will be helpful in preventing the rings dropping into empty grooves. Be careful

15.2a The oil control ring consists of two side rails . . .

15.2b . . . and an expander ring

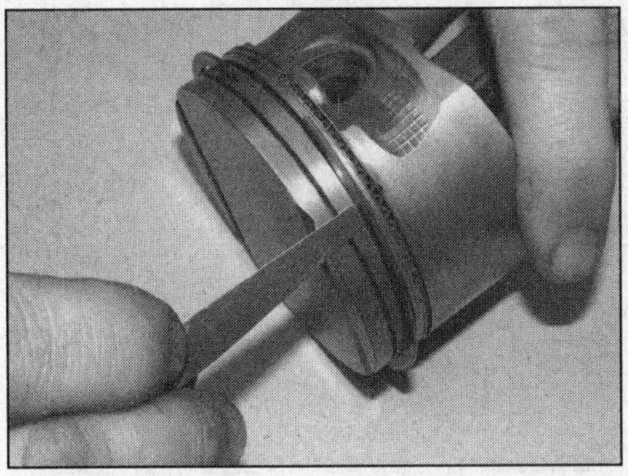

15.2c Use a feeler blade to remove a piston ring

not to scratch the piston with the ends of the ring. The rings are brittle, and will snap if they are spread too far. They're also very sharp – protect your hands and fingers. Note that the third (oil control) ring may consist of a spacer and two side rails, or a one-piece ring **(see illustrations)**. Always remove the rings from the top of the piston. Keep each set of rings with its piston if the old rings are to be re-used.

3 Scrape away all traces of carbon from the top of the piston. A hand-held wire brush (or a piece of fine emery cloth) can be used, once the majority of the deposits have been scraped away. The piston identification markings should now be visible.

4 Remove the carbon from the ring grooves in the piston, using an old ring. Break the ring in half to do this (be careful not to cut your fingers – piston rings are sharp). Be careful to remove only the carbon deposits – do not remove any metal, and do not nick or scratch the sides of the ring grooves.

5 Once the deposits have been removed, clean the piston/connecting rod assembly with paraffin or a suitable solvent, and dry thoroughly. Make sure that the oil return holes in the ring grooves are clear.

6 If the cylinder bores are not damaged or worn excessively (see Section 14), check the piston/connecting rods as follows.

Petrol engine

Note: *Pistons and connecting rods are only supplied as an assembly.*

7 Carefully inspect each piston for cracks around the skirt, around the gudgeon pin holes, and at the piston ring 'lands' (between the ring grooves).

8 Look for scoring and scuffing on the piston skirt, holes in the piston crown, and burned areas at the edge of the crown. If the skirt is scored or scuffed, the engine may have been suffering from overheating, and/or abnormal combustion which caused excessively high operating temperatures. The cooling and lubrication systems should be checked thoroughly. Scorch marks on the sides of the pistons show that blow-by has occurred.

9 A hole in the piston crown, or burned areas at the edge of the piston crown, indicates that abnormal combustion (pre-ignition, knocking, or detonation) has been occurring. If any of these problems exist, the causes must be investigated and corrected, or the damage will occur again. The causes may relate to the ignition system (spark plugs or ignition timing), or a weak mixture (faulty injector, air leak, etc).

10 Corrosion of the piston, in the form of pitting, indicates that coolant has been leaking into the combustion chamber and/or the crankcase. Again, the cause must be corrected, or the problem may persist in the rebuilt engine.

11 Measure the piston diameter at right-angles to the gudgeon pin axis, 8 mm up from the base of the piston skirt, and compare the results with the Specifications at the beginning of this Chapter **(see illustration)**. Note that there are two piston size groups to allow for manufacturing tolerances; the size group marking is stamped on the piston crown.

12 To measure the piston-to-bore clearance, measure the bore diameter at right-angles to the crankshaft axis, 20 mm up from the base of the bore (see Section 14). Calculate the clearance by subtracting the piston diameter from the bore measurement. Alternatively, insert each piston into its original bore, then select a feeler blade and slip it into the bore along with the piston. The piston must be aligned exactly in its normal attitude, and the feeler blade must be between the piston and bore, on one of the thrust faces, 20 mm from the bottom of the bore. If the clearance is excessive, a new piston will be required. If the piston binds at the lower end of the bore and is loose towards the top, the bore is tapered. If tight spots are encountered as the piston/feeler blade is rotated in the bore, the bore is out-of-round.

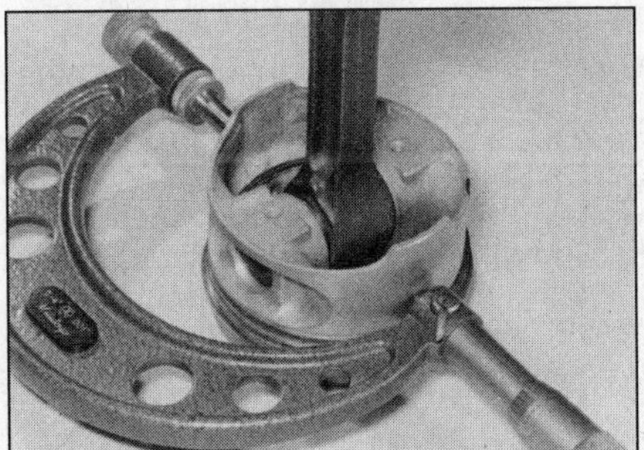

15.11 Measure the piston diameter at right-angles to the gudgeon pin axis

13 Repeat this procedure for the remaining pistons and cylinder bores. Any piston which is worn beyond the specified limits must be renewed.

14 Examine each connecting rod carefully for signs of damage, such as cracks around the big-end and small-end bearings. Check that the rod is not bent or distorted. Damage is highly unlikely, unless the engine has been seized or badly overheated. Detailed checking of the connecting rod assembly can only be carried out by an engine repair specialist with the necessary equipment.

15 The gudgeon pins are an interference fit in the connecting rod small-end bearings, and MG Rover state that the pistons and connecting rods must not be dismantled. MG Rover only supply pistons and connecting rods as an assembly; it is not possible to purchase them separately. Therefore, if either the piston or connecting rod is damaged, both must be renewed as an assembly.

16 Inspect the connecting rod big-end cap bolts closely for signs of wear or damage, and check that they screw easily into the connecting rods. Renew any bolt which shows visible signs of damage or does not screw easily into position.

Diesel engine

17 Carry out the checks described in paragraphs 7 to 10.

18 Measure the piston diameter at right angles to the gudgeon pin axis, 12 mm up from the base of the piston skirt, and compare the results with the Specifications at the beginning of this Chapter.

19 To measure the piston-to-bore clearance, measure the bore diameter at 45° to the crankshaft axis, at the top, centre, and bottom of the bore. Re-measure the bore diameter at 90° to the first measurement. Calculate the clearance by subtracting the piston diameter from the bore measurement. If the clearance is excessive, a rebore and new pistons may be required.

20 Repeat this procedure for the remaining pistons and cylinder bores. Any piston which

15.22 Using a small screwdriver, remove the circlips from the piston

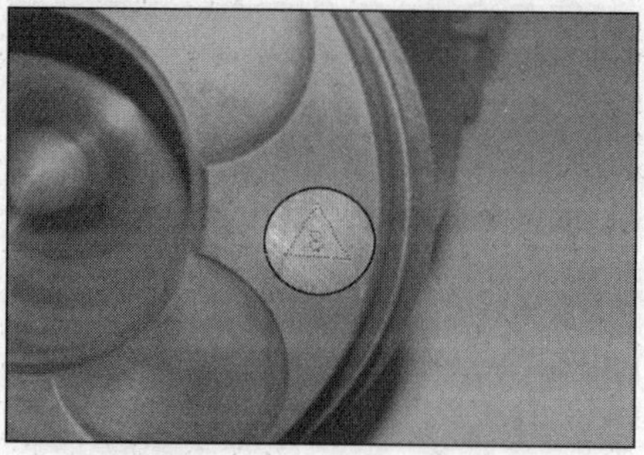

15.26a The arrow on the piston crown (highlighted) must face the timing chain end . . .

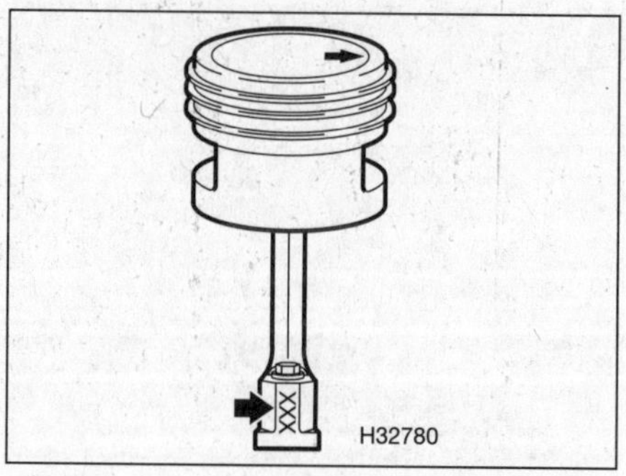

15.26b . . . with the grade number on the connecting rod positioned as shown

is worn beyond the specified limits must be renewed.

21 Examine each connecting rod carefully for signs of damage, such as cracks around the big-end and small-end bearings. Check that the rod is not bent or distorted. Damage is highly unlikely, unless the engine has been seized or badly overheated. Detailed checking of the connecting rod assembly can only be carried out by an engine repair specialist with the necessary equipment. The pistons and connecting rods can be separated as follows.

22 Using a small screwdriver, remove the circlips from the piston, then push out the gudgeon pin **(see illustration)**. Hand pressure should be sufficient to remove the pin. Identify the piston and rod to ensure correct reassembly. Discard the circlips – new ones **must** be used on refitting.

23 Examine the gudgeon pin and connecting rod small-end bearing for signs of wear or damage. Wear will require the renewal of both the pin and connecting rod.

24 The connecting rods themselves should not be in need of renewal, unless seizure or some other major mechanical failure has occurred. Check the alignment of the connecting rods visually, and if the rods are not straight, take them to an engine overhaul specialist for a more detailed check.

25 Examine all components, and obtain any new parts from your MG Rover parts supplier. If new pistons are purchased, they will be supplied complete with gudgeon pins and circlips. Circlips can also be purchased individually.

16.2 Check the endfloat using a dial gauge in contact with the end of the crankshaft

26 Assemble the piston and connecting rod so that if the arrow on the piston crown is pointing towards the timing chain end, the grade number cast into the side of the connecting rod, is on the right-hand side **(see illustrations)**.

27 Apply a smear of clean engine oil to the gudgeon pin. Slide it into the piston and through the connecting rod small-end. Check that the piston pivots freely on the rod, then secure the gudgeon pin in position with two new circlips, ensuring that each circlip is correctly located in its groove in the piston.

28 Inspect the connecting rod big-end cap bolts closely for signs of wear or damage, and check that they screw easily into the connecting rods. Renew any bolt which shows visible signs of damage or does not screw easily into position.

16 Crankshaft - inspection

Checking endfloat

1 If the crankshaft endfloat is to be checked, this must be done when the crankshaft is still installed in the cylinder block, but is free to move (see Section 13). On 1.8 litre engines, this means checking the endfloat with the connecting rods released from the crankshaft, but the cylinder head still in place and the cylinder head bolts still securing the main bearing ladder.

2 Check the endfloat using a dial gauge in contact with the end of the crankshaft. Push the crankshaft fully one way, and then zero the gauge. Push the crankshaft fully the other way, and check the endfloat **(see illustration)**. The result can be compared with the specified amount, and will give an indication as to whether new thrustwasher halves are required.

16.3 Using feeler blades to measure the crankshaft endfloat

3 If a dial gauge is not available, feeler blades can be used. First push the crankshaft fully towards the flywheel end of the engine, then use feeler blades to measure the gap between the web of the crankpin and the side of thrustwasher **(see illustration)**. On 1.8 litre petrol engines, the thrustwashers are only fitted to the sides of the upper centre (No 3) main bearing shell, V6 engines have thrustwashers on the left (No 4) main bearing, whilst on diesel engines, they are integral with the No 4 main bearing shells.

Inspection

4 Clean the crankshaft using paraffin or a suitable solvent, and dry it, preferably with compressed air if available. Be sure to clean the oil holes with a pipe cleaner or similar probe, to ensure that they are not obstructed.

Warning: Wear eye protection when using compressed air.

5 Check the main and big-end bearing journals for uneven wear, scoring, pitting and cracking.

6 Big-end bearing wear is accompanied by distinct metallic knocking when the engine is running (particularly noticeable when the engine is pulling from low speed) and some loss of oil pressure.

7 Main bearing wear is accompanied by severe engine vibration and rumble – getting progressively worse as engine speed increases – and again by loss of oil pressure.

8 Check the bearing journal for roughness by running a finger lightly over the bearing surface. Any roughness (which will be accompanied by obvious bearing wear) indicates that the crankshaft requires regrinding (where possible) or renewal.

9 Check for burrs around the crankshaft oil holes (the holes are usually chamfered, so burrs should not be a problem unless regrinding has been carried out carelessly).

16.10 Measure the crankshaft main bearing journal diameter

Remove any burrs with a fine file or scraper, and thoroughly clean the oil holes as described previously.

10 Using a micrometer, measure the diameter of the main and big-end bearing journals (see Sections 20 and 21 for size group marking information on petrol engines), and compare the results with the Specifications **(see illustration)**. By measuring the diameter at a number of points around each journal's circumference, you will be able to determine whether or not the journal is out-of-round. Take the measurement at each end of the journal, near the webs, to determine if the journal is tapered. Compare the results obtained with those given in the Specifications.

11 Check the oil seal contact surfaces at each end of the crankshaft for wear and damage. If the seal has worn a deep groove in the surface of the crankshaft, consult an engine overhaul specialist; repair may be possible, but otherwise a new crankshaft will be required.

12 At the time of writing, it appears that MG Rover do not produce undersize bearing shells for the petrol engines. Therefore, if the crankshaft has worn beyond the specified limits, it will have to be renewed. Undersize bearings are available for the diesel engine. Consult your MG Rover parts supplier or engine specialist for further information on parts availability.

17 Main and big-end bearings - inspection

1 Even though the main and big-end bearings should be renewed during the engine overhaul, the old bearings should be retained for close examination, as they may reveal valuable information about the condition of the engine.

2 Bearing failure can occur due to lack of lubrication, the presence of dirt or other foreign particles, overloading the engine, or corrosion **(see illustration)**. Regardless of the cause of bearing failure, the cause must be corrected (where applicable) before the engine is reassembled, to prevent it from happening again.

3 When examining the bearing shells, remove them from the cylinder block, the main bearing caps, the connecting rods and the connecting rod big-end bearing caps. Lay them out on a clean surface in the same general position as their location in the engine. This will enable you to match any bearing problems with the corresponding crankshaft journal.

4 Dirt and other foreign matter gets into the engine in a variety of ways. It may be left in the engine during assembly, or it may pass through filters or the crankcase ventilation system. It may get into the oil, and from there into the bearings. Metal chips from machining operations and normal engine wear are often present. Abrasives are sometimes left in engine components after reconditioning, especially when parts are not thoroughly cleaned using the proper cleaning methods.

5 Whatever the source, foreign objects often end up embedded in the soft bearing material, and are easily recognised. Large particles will not embed in the bearing, and will score or gouge the bearing and journal. The best prevention for this cause of bearing failure is to clean all parts thoroughly, and keep everything spotlessly-clean during engine assembly. Frequent and regular engine oil and filter changes are also recommended.

6 Lack of lubrication (or lubrication breakdown) has a number of interrelated causes. Excessive heat (which thins the oil), overloading (which squeezes the oil from the bearing face) and oil leakage (from excessive bearing clearances, worn oil pump or high engine speeds) all contribute to lubrication breakdown. Blocked oil passages, which usually are the result of misaligned oil holes in a bearing shell, will also oil-starve a bearing, and destroy it. When lack of lubrication is the cause of bearing failure, the bearing material is wiped or extruded from the steel backing of the bearing. Temperatures may increase to the point where the steel backing turns blue from overheating.

7 Driving habits can have a definite effect on bearing life. Full-throttle, low-speed operation (labouring the engine) puts very high loads on bearings, tending to squeeze out the oil film. These loads cause the bearings to flex, which produces fine cracks in the bearing face (fatigue failure). Eventually, the bearing material will loosen in pieces, and tear away from the steel backing.

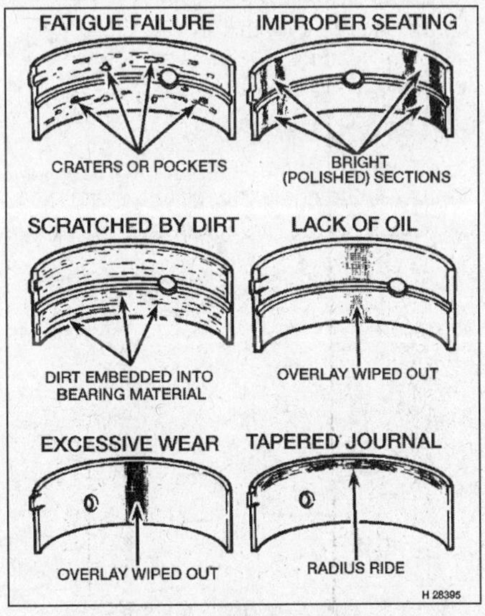

17.2 Typical bearing shell failures

8 Short-distance driving leads to corrosion of bearings, because insufficient engine heat is produced to drive off the condensed water and corrosive gases. These products collect in the engine oil, forming acid and sludge. As the oil is carried to the engine bearings, the acid attacks and corrodes the bearing material.

9 Incorrect bearing installation during engine assembly will lead to bearing failure as well. Tight-fitting bearings leave insufficient bearing running clearance, and will result in oil starvation. Dirt or foreign particles trapped behind a bearing shell result in high spots on the bearing, which lead to failure.

10 As mentioned at the beginning of this Section, the bearing shells should be renewed as a matter of course during engine overhaul; to do otherwise is false economy.

18 Engine overhaul - reassembly sequence

1 Before reassembly begins, ensure that all new parts have been obtained, and that all necessary tools are available. Read through the entire procedure to familiarise yourself with the work involved, and to ensure that all items necessary for reassembly of the engine are at hand. In addition to all normal tools and materials, threadlocking compound will be needed. A good quality tube of liquid sealant will also be required for the joint faces that are fitted without gaskets.

2 In order to save time and avoid problems, engine reassembly can be carried out in the following order:

a) Crankshaft.
b) Piston/connecting rod assemblies.
c) Oil pump.
d) Sump.
e) Flywheel.
f) Cylinder head.
g) Timing belt/chain tensioner and sprockets, and belts/chains.
h) Inlet and exhaust manifolds (relevant part of Chapter 4).
i) Engine external components.

3 At this stage, all engine components should be absolutely clean and dry, with all faults repaired. The components should be laid out (or in individual containers) on a completely clean work surface.

19 Piston rings - refitting

1 Before fitting new piston rings, the ring end gaps must be checked as follows.

19.4 Position the piston ring as described then measure the end gap using feeler blades

2 Lay out the piston/connecting rod assemblies and the new piston ring sets, so that the ring sets will be matched with the same piston and cylinder during the end gap measurement and subsequent engine reassembly.

3 Insert the top ring into the first cylinder, and push it down the bore using the top of the piston. This will ensure that the ring remains square with the cylinder walls. Push the ring down into the bore until it is positioned 20 mm down from the top edge of the bore on petrol engines, and 30 mm down from the top of the bore on diesel engines. Withdraw the piston.

4 Measure the end gap using feeler blades, and compare the measurements with the figures given in the Specifications **(see illustration)**.

5 If the gap is too small (unlikely if genuine MG Rover parts are used), it must be enlarged, or the ring ends may contact each other during engine operation, causing serious damage. Ideally, new piston rings providing the correct end gap should be fitted. As a last resort, the end gap can be increased by filing the ring ends very carefully with a fine file. Mount the file in a vice with soft jaws, slip the ring over the file with the ends contacting the file face, and slowly move the ring to remove material from the ends. Take care, as piston rings are sharp, and are easily broken.

6 With new piston rings, it is unlikely that the end gap will be too large. If the gaps are too large, check that you have the correct rings

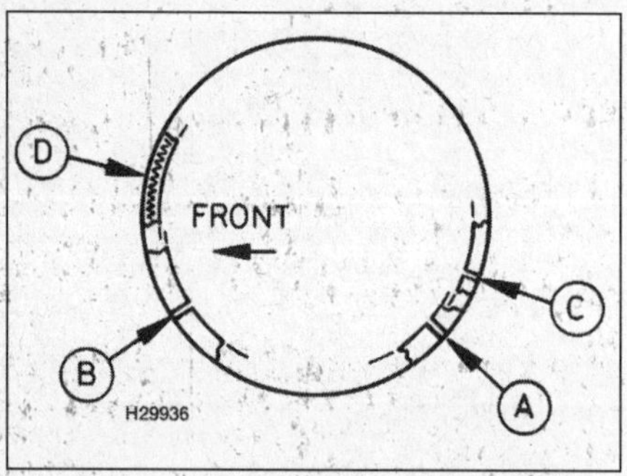

19.10 Piston ring end gap locations – petrol engine

A Top compression ring
B Second compression ring
C Oil control ring
D Oil control ring expander

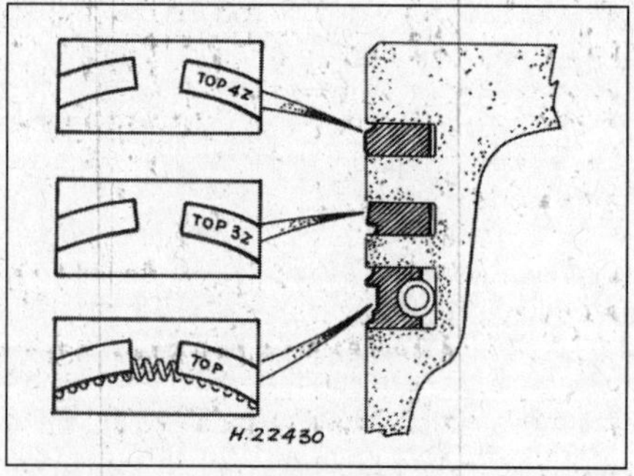

19.9 Piston ring identification – petrol engine

for your engine and for the particular cylinder bore size.

7 Repeat the checking procedure for each ring in the first cylinder, and then for the rings in the remaining cylinders. Remember to keep rings, pistons and cylinders matched up.

8 Once the ring end gaps have been checked and if necessary corrected, the rings can be fitted to the pistons as follows, using the same technique as for removal.

Petrol engines

9 Fit the oil control ring expander first (it will be easier if the end gap is correctly positioned at this point), then fit the ring, making sure its identification (eg, TOP) marking is uppermost **(see illustration)**. The second and top rings are different and can be identified by their cross-sections. The second ring is thicker. Fit the second and top compression rings, ensuring that each ring is fitted the correct way up with its identification (TOP) mark uppermost. **Note:** *Always follow any instructions supplied with the new piston ring sets – different manufacturers may specify different procedures. Do not mix up the top and second compression rings.*

10 Check that each ring is free to rotate easily in its groove, then measure the ring-to-groove clearance of each ring, using feeler blades. If the clearance is within the specified range, position the ring end gaps as shown **(see illustration)**.

Diesel engine

11 Fit the oil control ring expander first then carefully fit the ring to the piston, the ring has no identification marking and can be fitted either way up.

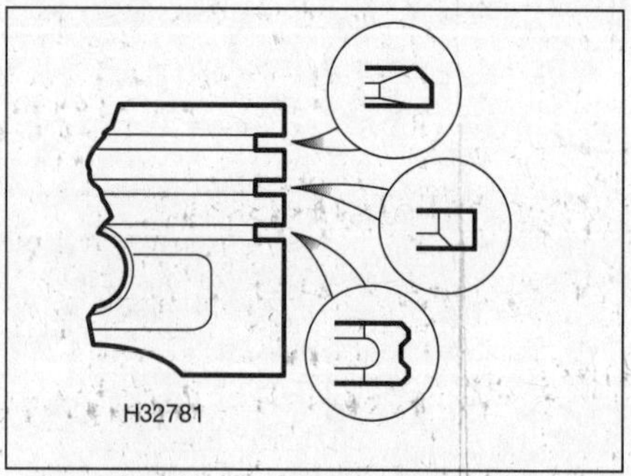

19.12 Piston ring identification – diesel engine

12 The second and top rings are different and can be identified by their cross-sections **(see illustrations)**. Fit the second and top compression rings ensuring that each ring is fitted the correct way up with its identification (TOP) mark uppermost. **Note:** *Always follow any instructions supplied with the new piston ring sets – different manufacturers may specify different procedures. Do not mix up the top and second compression rings.*

13 Check that each ring is free to rotate easily in its groove, then measure the ring-to-groove clearance of each ring, using feeler blades. If the clearance is within the specified range, space the ring end gaps at 120° intervals making sure no end gap is in line with the piston thrust (front and rear) faces.

20 Crankshaft – refitting

Note: *It is recommended that new main bearing shells are fitted, regardless of the condition of the original ones. Refer to an engine reconditioning specialist for assistance in selecting the appropriate shells.*

1 Crankshaft refitting is the first major step in engine reassembly. It is assumed at this point that the cylinder block/crankcase and crankshaft have been cleaned, inspected and repaired or reconditioned as necessary. Position the engine upside-down.

2 If temporarily refitted, remove the main bearing cap bolts, and lift out the caps. Lay the caps out in the proper order, to ensure correct installation.

3 If they are still in place, remove the old bearing shells from the block and the main bearing caps. Wipe the bearing recesses with a clean, lint-free cloth. They must be kept spotlessly clean.

1.8 litre engine

4 Clean the backs of the bearing shells, and the bearing locations in both the cylinder block/crankcase and the main bearing ladder. If new shells are being fitted, ensure that all traces of the protective grease are cleaned off using paraffin. Wipe dry the shells and connecting rods with a lint-free cloth.

5 Press the bearing shells into their locations, ensuring that the tab on each shell engages in the notch in the cylinder block/crankcase or main bearing ladder location. Take care not to touch any shell bearing surface with your fingers.

6 Press the bearing shells into their locations, ensuring that the tab on each shell engages in the notch in the cylinder block or main bearing cap, noting the following:

a) Make sure that the grooved bearing shells are fitted in the upper (cylinder block) locations of Nos 2, 3 and 4 main bearings.
b) If bearing shells of different grades are being fitted to the same bearing, ensure

20.9a Tighten the big-end cap bolts to the specified Stage 1 torque . . .

20.9b . . . then through the specified Stage 2 angle

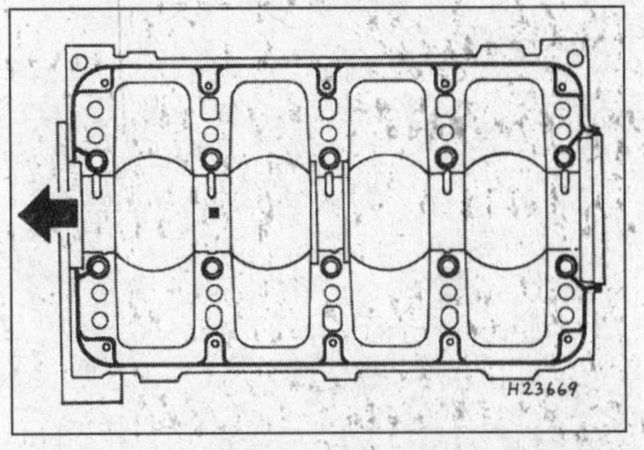

20.10 Apply sealant (as shown by the thick lines) to the cylinder block/bearing ladder mating surfaces

that the thicker shell is fitted in the lower (main bearing ladder) location.

c) If the original bearing shells are being re-used, ensure they are refitted in their original locations.

7 Using a little grease, stick the thrustwashers to each side of the centre (No 3) main bearing upper location. Ensure that the oilway grooves on each thrustwasher face outwards.

8 Liberally lubricate each bearing shell in the cylinder block/crankcase, then lower the crankshaft into position. Check the crankshaft endfloat as described in Section 16.

9 Refit the piston/connecting rod assemblies to the crankshaft as described in Section 21 and position the crankshaft so the pistons are half-way up the bores **(see illustrations)**.

10 Thoroughly degrease the mating surfaces of the cylinder block and the main bearing ladder. Apply a continuous bead of sealant (part no GUG 705963GM) to the mating surface of the cylinder block/crankcase as shown, then spread the sealant to an even film **(see illustration)**. Carefully follow the instructions supplied with the sealant.

11 Ensure the lower bearing shells are correctly fitted to the bearing ladder, and lubricate them with clean engine oil.

12 Ensure the locating dowels are in position then refit the main bearing ladder to the cylinder block, taking care to ensure that the shells are not displaced. Once the ladder is correctly located on the dowels, refit the retaining bolts, tightening them all by hand only.

13 Working in the specified sequence, go around and tighten all bolts to the specified Stage 1 torque setting, then go around again in the specified sequence and tighten them to the specified Stage 2 torque setting **(see illustration)**. **Note:** *The crankshaft cannot now be rotated until the cylinder head has been refitted.*

14 Thoroughly degrease the mating surfaces of the oil rail and the main bearing ladder. Apply the same sealant (paragraph 10) to the oil rail mating surface as shown **(see illustration)**.

15 Refit the oil rail to the main bearing ladder and tighten its retaining nuts to the specified torque.

16 Refit the dipstick tube, using a new gasket, and securely tighten its retaining bolts.

17 Working as described in Part A of this Chapter, carry out the following procedures in order.

a) Refit the oil pump, pick-up/strainer and sump.

b) Fit a new left-hand oil seal to the crankshaft and refit the flywheel.

c) Refit the cylinder head and camshafts.

d) Refit the timing belt sprockets and belt.

18 On completion, remove the spark plugs then fit a torque wrench to the crankshaft pulley bolt and rotate the crankshaft in the normal direction of rotation. The crankshaft must rotate smoothly, without any sign of binding, and the amount of force required to rotate the crankshaft should not exceed 31 Nm (23 lbf ft). If the effort required is greater than this, the engine should be dismantled again to trace and rectify the cause. This value takes into account the increased friction of a new engine and is much higher than the actual pressure required to rotate a run-in engine, so do not make allowances for tight components.

V6 engine

19 Clean the backs of the bearing shells, and the bearing locations in both the cylinder block/crankcase and the main bearing ladder. If new shells are being fitted, ensure that all traces of the protective grease are cleaned off using paraffin. Wipe dry the shells and connecting rods with a lint-free cloth.

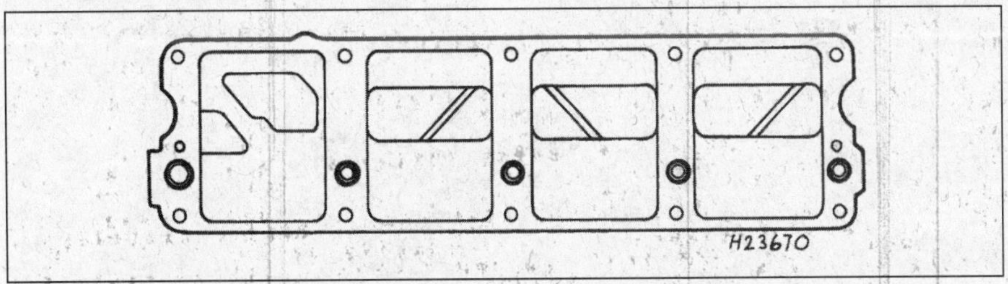

20.14 Apply circles of sealant (as shown by thick black lines) to the oil rail

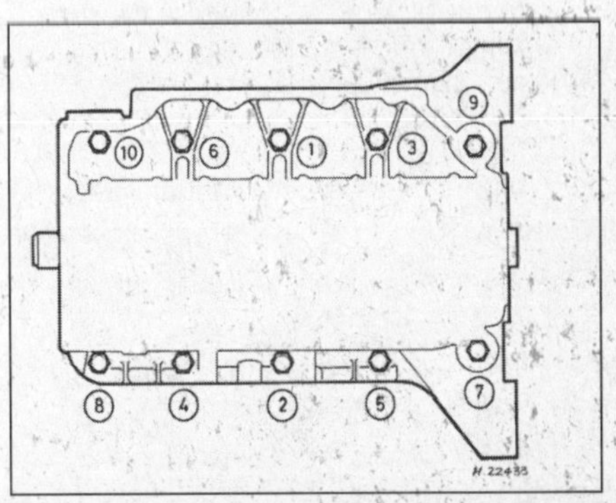

20.13 Crankshaft main bearing ladder bolt tightening sequence

20 Press the bearing shells into their locations, ensuring that the tab on each shell engages in the notch in the cylinder block/crankcase or main bearing ladder location. Take care not to touch any shell bearing surface with your fingers.

21 Press the bearing shells into their locations, ensuring that the tab on each shell engages in the notch in the cylinder block or main bearing cap, noting the following:

*a) Make sure that the grooved bearing shells are fitted in the upper (cylinder block) locations **(see illustration)**.*

b) If bearing shells of different grades are being fitted to the same bearing, ensure

20.21 Engage the bearing shell tab into its location

20.22 Use grease to hold the thrustwashers – note oilway grooves

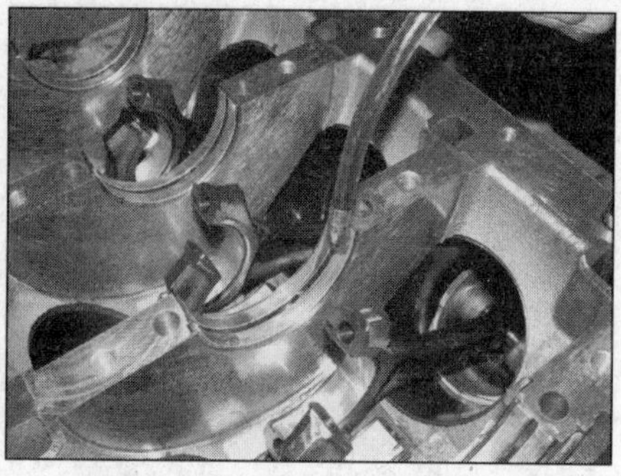

20.23a Oil the bearing shells . . .

20.23b . . . then lay the crankshaft in position

that the thicker shell is fitted in the lower (main bearing ladder) location.

c) *If the original bearing shells are being re-used, ensure they are refitted in their original locations.*

22 Using a little grease, stick the thrustwashers to the left (No 4) main bearing upper location. Ensure that the oilway grooves on each thrustwasher face outwards **(see illustration)**.

23 Liberally lubricate each bearing shell in the cylinder block/crankcase, then lower the crankshaft into position **(see illustrations)**. Check the crankshaft endfloat as described in Section 16.

24 Refit the liner/piston/connecting rod assemblies to the crankshaft as described in Section 21, and position the crankshaft so that none of the pistons is at the top of its bore.

25 Thoroughly degrease the mating surfaces of the cylinder block and the main bearing ladder. Apply a bead of sealant (part no GUG 705963GM) to the mating surface of the cylinder block/crankcase, then spread the sealant to an even film. Carefully follow the instructions supplied with the sealant.

26 Ensure the lower bearing shells are correctly fitted to the bearing ladder, and lubricate them with clean engine oil **(see illustrations)**.

27 Using a little grease, stick the thrustwashers to the No 4 main bearing ladder location. Ensure that the oilway grooves on each thrustwasher face outwards **(see illustration)**.

28 Ensure the locating dowels are in position, then refit the main bearing ladder to the cylinder block, taking care to ensure that the shells are not displaced. Once the ladder is correctly located on the dowels, refit the retaining bolts, tightening them all by hand only. Note that the eight shorter bolts are fitted to the outer positions **(see illustrations)**.

29 Working in the specified sequence, go around and tighten all bolts to the specified Stage 1 torque setting, then go around again in the specified sequence and tighten them to the specified Stage 2 angle **(see illustration)**.

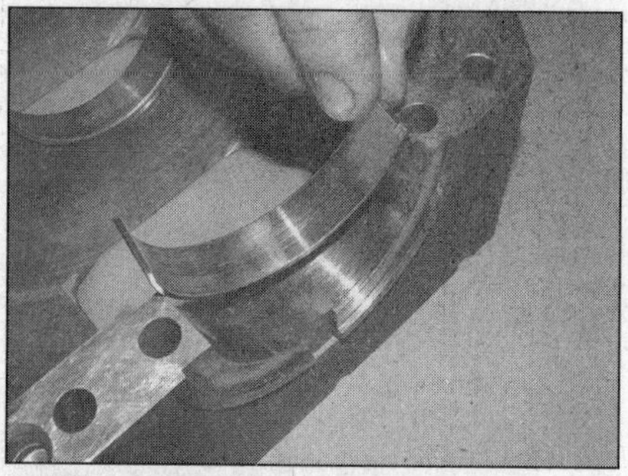

20.26a Fit the lower bearing shells into the ladder, locating the tabs

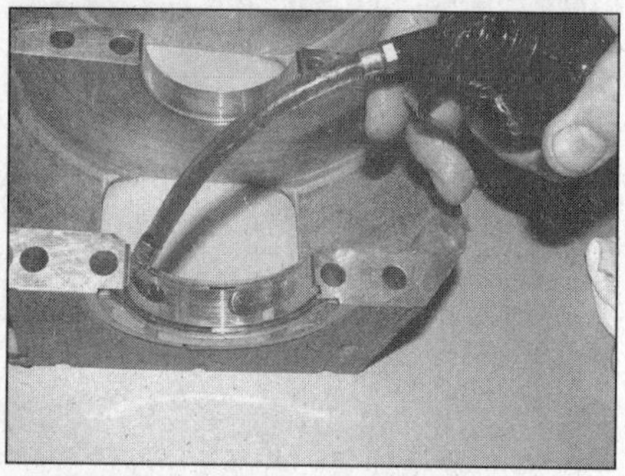

20.26b Lubricate the bearing shells

20.27 Stick on the thrustwashers, ensuring the oil grooves face outwards

20.28a Locate the main bearing ladder in position on the dowels . . .

20.28b . . . then fit the bolts, noting that two different types are used

20.29a Tighten the main bearing ladder bolts to the specified torque . . .

20.29b . . . then to the specified angle

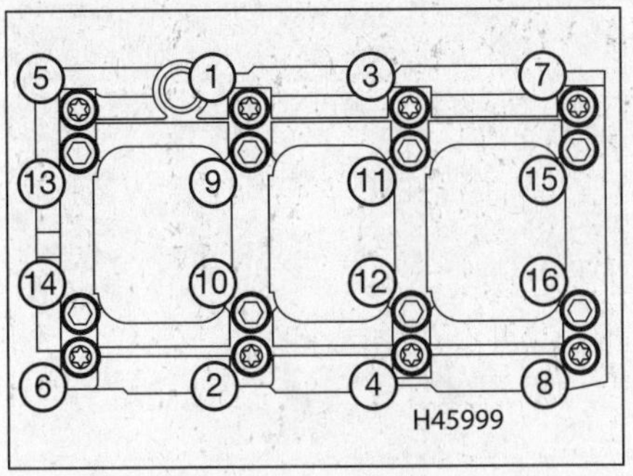

20.29c V6 engine main bearing ladder bolt tightening sequence

30 Thoroughly degrease the mating surfaces of the cylinder block and the lower crankcase. Apply the same sealant (paragraph 25) to the lower crankcase mating surface as shown **(see illustration)**.

31 Refit the lower crankcase, inserting the two smaller bolts in their previously-noted positions. Working in sequence, tighten the retaining bolts (and nut, on early models) to the specified torque **(see illustration)**.

32 On completion of tightening, wait one minute, then go around again and retighten the M8 bolts (and nut, where fitted) to the specified torque.

33 Working as described in Part B of this

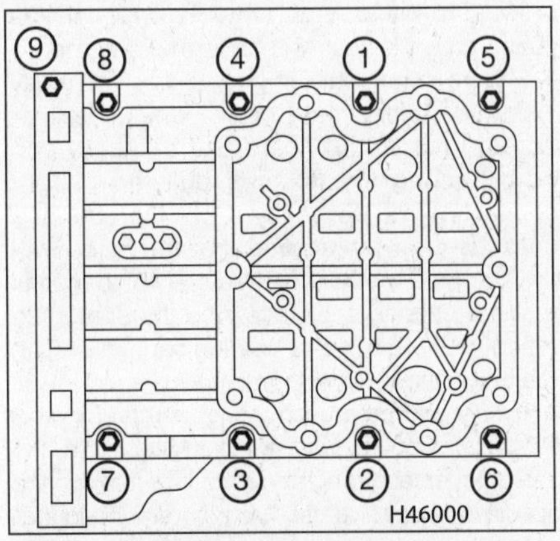

20.31b V6 engine lower crankcase bolt tightening procedure

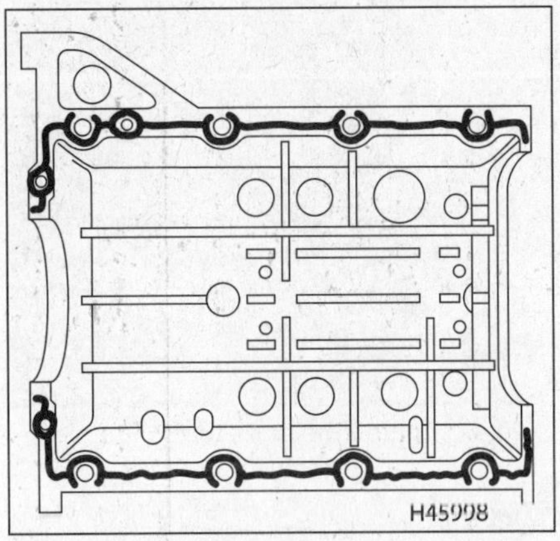

20.30 Apply sealant as shown to the lower crankcase

Chapter, carry out the following procedures in order:

a) Refit the oil pump, pick-up/strainer and sump.
b) Fit a new flywheel end oil seal to the crankshaft, and refit the flywheel/ driveplate.
c) Refit the cylinder heads and camshafts.
d) Refit the timing belt sprockets and belts.

34 On completion, remove the spark plugs and rotate the crankshaft in the normal direction of rotation. The crankshaft must rotate smoothly, without any sign of binding.

Diesel engine

35 Clean the backs of the bearing shells

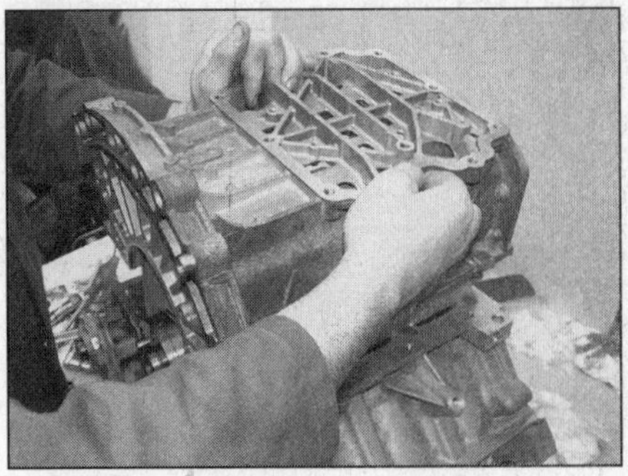

20.31a Fitting the lower crankcase

and the bearing locations in both the cylinder block and the main bearing caps. Ensure that all traces of the protective grease are cleaned off the new shells, using paraffin. Wipe dry the shells and caps with a lint-free cloth. The original bearing shells should never be re-used.

36 Press the bearing shells into their locations, ensuring that the tab on each shell engages in the notch in the cylinder block or main bearing cap; on shells with no locating tab, ensure the shell is positioned centrally. Fit the grooved bearing shells in the upper (cylinder block) locations and fit the plain shells in the lower (bearing cap) locations **(see illustrations)**. Note that the No 4 main bearing shell incorporates the thrustwashers.

37 Lubricate the upper shells with clean engine oil, then lower the crankshaft into position **(see illustrations)**.

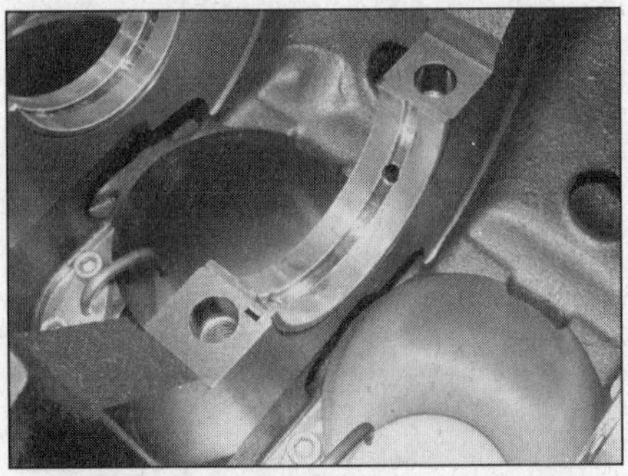

20.36a Fit the shells with the grooves to the cylinder block . . .

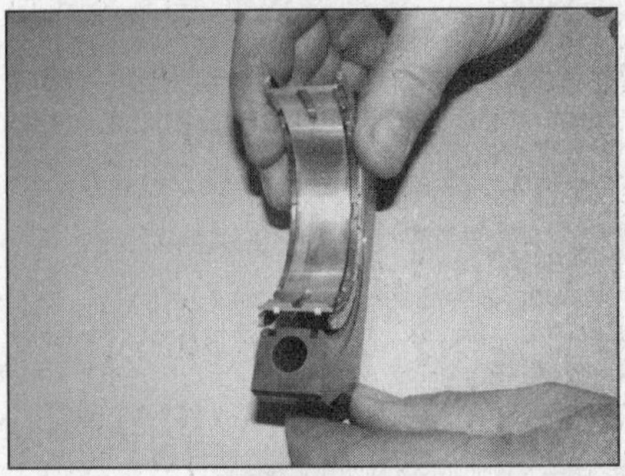

20.36b . . . and the plain shells to the main bearing cap

20.36c No 4 main bearing shell incorporates the thrustwashers

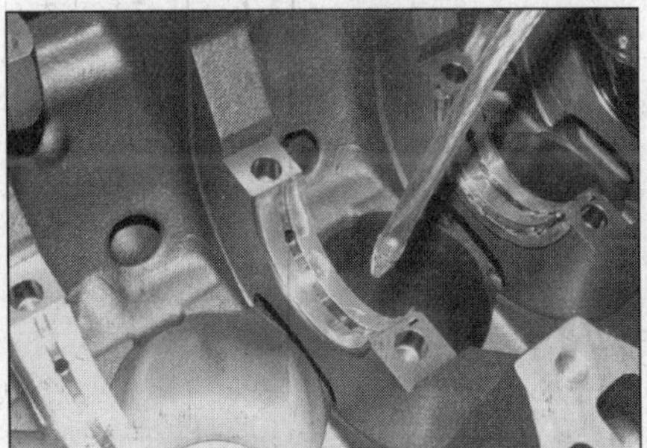

20.37a Lubricate the shells bearings . . .

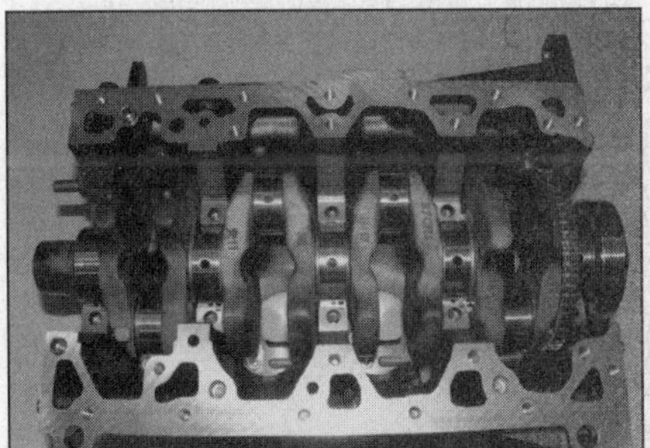

20.37b . . . and carefully lower the crankshaft into place

20.38 Bearing cap identification number (arrowed) is on the rear (turbo) side of the block

20.40 Tighten the bolts to the Stage 1 torque . . .

20.41 . . . then to the Stage 2 angle

38 Ensure the bearing shells are correctly located in the caps. Refit the caps to the cylinder block. Ensure the caps are fitted in their correct locations, with No 1 cap at the timing chain end, and are fitted the correct way around so that the identification number is on the rear (turbocharger) side of the engine block **(see illustration)**.

39 Apply a smear of clean engine to oil to the threads and underneath the heads of the new main bearing cap bolts. Fit the bolts, tightening them all by hand.

40 Working in a diagonal sequence from the centre outwards, tighten the main bearing cap bolts evenly and progressively to the specified Stage 1 torque setting **(see illustration)**.

41 Using an angle-measuring gauge, tighten the bolts in the same sequence to the Stage 2 angle **(see illustration)**.

42 Check that the crankshaft is free to rotate smoothly; if excessive pressure is required to turn the crankshaft, investigate the cause before proceeding further.

43 Check the crankshaft endfloat as described in Section 16.

44 Refit/reconnect the piston connecting rod assemblies to the crankshaft as described in Section 21.

45 Working as described in Part C of this Chapter, carry out the following procedures in order:

a) Refit the oil pump and pick-up/strainer.
b) Cylinder block reinforcing plate.
c) Fit a new left-hand oil seal to the crankshaft and refit the flywheel/driveplate.
d) Refit the cylinder head and camshafts.
e) Refit the timing chains, sprockets and tensioner.

21 Piston/connecting rod assembly – refitting

Note: *It is recommended that new piston rings and big-end bearing shells are fitted regardless of the condition of the original ones. Refer to an engine reconditioning specialist for assistance in selecting the appropriate shells.*

1.8 litre engine

1 Note that the following procedure assumes that the cylinder liners have been refitted to the cylinder block/crankcase and that the crankshaft and main bearing ladder are in place. It is of course possible to refit the piston/connecting rod assemblies to the cylinder bores, to refit the crankshaft and to reassemble the piston/connecting rods on the crankshaft before refitting the main bearing ladder (see Section 20).

2 Clean the backs of the bearing shells and the bearing recesses in both the connecting rod and the big-end bearing cap. Ensure that all traces of the protective grease are cleaned off using paraffin. Wipe dry the shells and connecting rods with a lint-free cloth.

3 Press the bearing shells into their locations, ensuring that the tab on each shell engages in the notch in the connecting rod or big-end bearing cap and taking care not to touch any shell's bearing surface with your fingers. If bearing shells of differing grades are to be fitted to the same connecting rod, the thicker shell must always be fitted in the lower (bearing cap) location.

4 Lubricate the cylinder bores, the pistons and piston rings, then lay out each piston/connecting rod assembly in its respective position.

5 Starting with assembly No 1, make sure that the piston rings are still correctly spaced (see Section 19) then clamp them in position with a piston ring compressor.

6 Insert the piston/connecting rod assembly into the top of liner No 1, ensuring that the arrow (or FRONT marking) on the piston crown faces the timing belt end of the engine. Note that the stamped marks on the connecting rod and big-end bearing cap should face the front of the engine **(see illustrations)**. Using a block of wood or hammer handle against the piston crown, tap the assembly into the liner until the piston crown is flush with the top of the liner.

7 Ensure that the bearing shell is still correctly installed. Taking care not to mark the liner bores, liberally lubricate the crankpin and both bearing shells, then pull the piston/connecting rod assembly down the bore and onto the crankpin. Noting that the faces with the stamped marks must match (which means that the bearing shell locating tabs abut each other), refit the big-end bearing cap, tightening the bolts finger-tight at first.

8 Evenly and progressively tighten the big-end bearing cap bolts to the specified Stage 1 torque setting, then angle-tighten each bolt through the specified Stage 2 angle. It is recommended that an angle-measuring gauge is used during this stage of the tightening, to ensure accuracy **(see illustration)**.

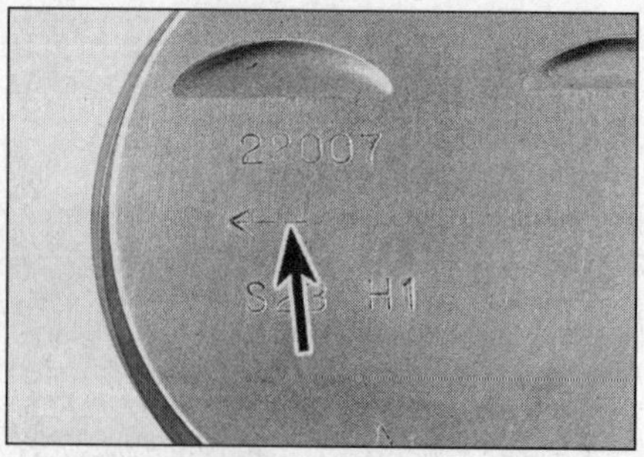

21.6a The arrow (or FRONT marking) on the piston crown must face the (main) timing belt end

21.6b Use a piston ring compressor to refit a piston/connecting rod assembly

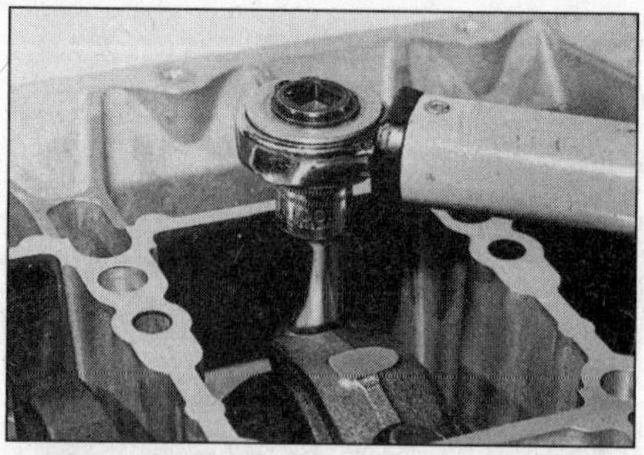

21.8 Tighten the big-end bearing cap bolts to the Stage 1 torque, then through the Stage 2 angle

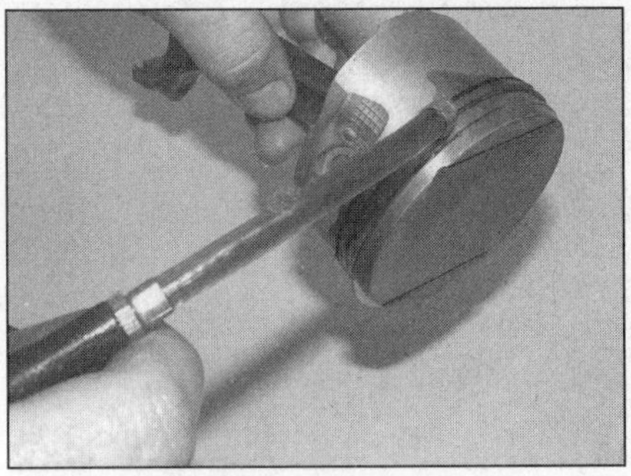

21.10a Lubricate the rings . . .

21.10b . . . then fit the piston into the ring compressor

21.11 Tap the piston into the liner

9 Repeat the procedure for the remaining piston/connecting rod assemblies. On 1.8 litre engines, do not attempt to rotate the crankshaft.

V6 engine

10 Lubricate the piston rings, then fit the piston into a suitable ring compressor **(see illustrations)**.

11 Fit the compressor to the base of the relevant liner, then carefully tap the piston until it is fully fitted inside the bore **(see illustrations)**.

12 The cylinder number positions are clearly marked on the cylinder block, to avoid confusion **(see illustration)**.

13 Carefully clean the liner shoulders, and their seating positions in the block – it is essential that a good seal is made when the liners are refitted – if the seal fails, the engine oil and coolant will mix **(see illustrations)**.

14 Apply a continuous bead of suitable sealant to the liner shoulder **(see illustration)**. The MG Rover specialists we spoke to recommended Blue Hylomar for this – check with your specialist or parts supplier for confirmation, however.

15 Remembering that the big-end numbers are fitted facing inwards, insert each liner/piston assembly into its original location, and ensure that the painted alignment marks line up. Seat the liner fully up to its shoulder, then ensure that it does not move, to allow the sealant to cure **(see illustration)**.

16 Refit the liner clamps used prior to dismantling – otherwise, the liners will be displaced when the big-ends are refitted to the crankshaft.

17 Lubricate the bearing and journal, then fit the first connecting rod onto the crankshaft – ensure that the liner is clamped, and move the piston as little as possible.

18 Ensure that the big-end bearing shells are in place, then lubricate and refit the big-end bearing caps to their original locations **(see illustration)**. The manufacturer's markings should face inwards (or use those made prior to removal).

19 Lubricate the threads of the new big-end bolts with clean engine oil, then screw them into position in the connecting rod, tightening them by hand. Evenly and progressively tighten the bolts to the specified Stage 1 torque setting, followed by angle-tightening each bolt through the specified Stage 2 angle. It is recommended that an angle-measuring gauge is used

21.12 Cylinder numbers are cast into the block

21.13a Clean the liner shoulders . . .

21.13b . . . and the seating positions in the block

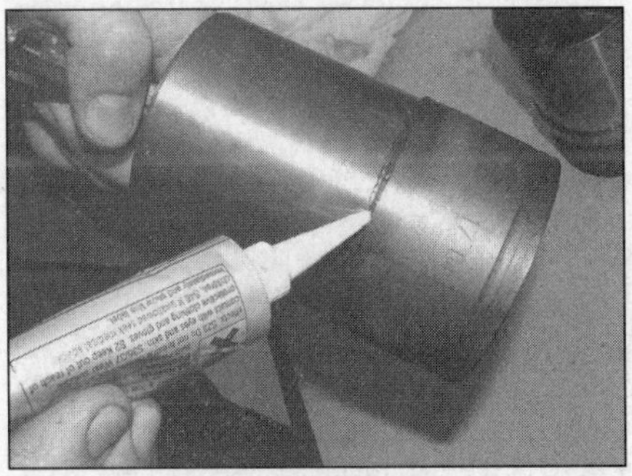

21.14 Apply a bead of sealant to the liner shoulder

21.15 Refit each liner/piston assembly fully into the block

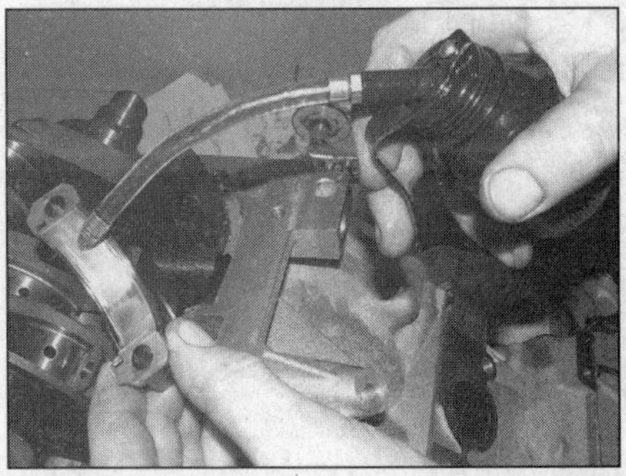

21.18 Lubricate the big-end bearing caps

21.19a Lightly oil and fit the new bolts . . .

21.19b . . . then tighten them to the specified torque . . .

21.19c . . . and through the specified angle

during this stage of the tightening, to ensure accuracy **(see illustrations)**.

20 Refit the remaining big-end caps in the same way.

21 Before turning the crankshaft, make absolutely certain that all the liners are clamped. Rotate the crankshaft, and check that it turns freely, with no signs of binding or tight spots.

22 Refit the main bearing ladder and lower crankcase, as described in Section 20.

Diesel engine

23 Clean the backs of the bearing shells and the bearing recesses in both the connecting rod and the big-end bearing cap. Ensure that all traces of the protective grease are cleaned off using paraffin. Wipe dry the shells and connecting rods with a lint-free cloth.

24 Press the bearing shells into their locations, ensuring that the tab on each shell engages in the notch in the connecting rod and big-end bearing cap. Note that the bearing shell fitted to the connecting rod is of the 'Sputter' type, identified by the letter S or a series of XXX-marks on the outside of the shell **(see illustrations)**.

21.24a Note the bearing shell markings – a letter S or a series of XXX-marks on the outside

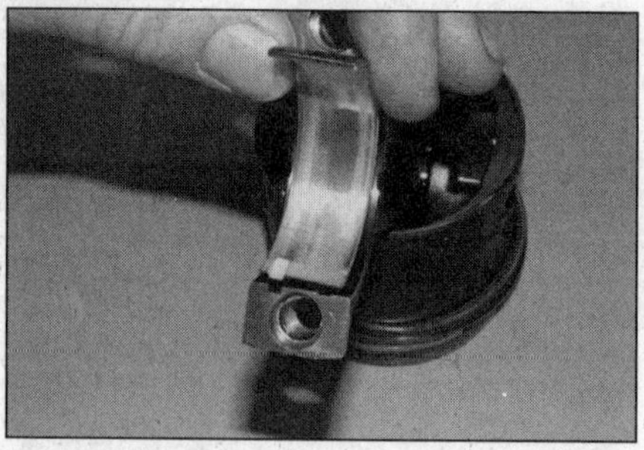

21.24b The tab on each shell engages in the notch in the connecting rod and big-end bearing cap

25 Lubricate the bores, the pistons and piston rings then lay out each piston/connecting rod assembly in its respective position.

26 Starting with assembly No 1, make sure that the piston rings are still spaced as described in Section 19, then clamp them in position with a piston ring compressor.

27 Insert the piston/connecting rod assembly into the top of cylinder No 1, ensuring that the arrow marking on the piston crown is pointing towards the timing chain end of the engine **(see illustration 15.26a)**.

28 Using a block of wood or hammer handle against the piston crown, tap the assembly into the cylinder until the piston crown is flush with the top of the cylinder.

29 Taking care not to mark the cylinder bore, liberally lubricate the crankpin and both bearing shells, then pull the piston/connecting rod assembly down the bore and onto the crankpin. Refit the big-end bearing cap using the markings made prior to removal to ensure it is fitted the correct way around; the connecting rod and bearing cap shell locating notches (where fitted) should abut each other **(see illustration)**.

30 Lubricate the threads of the bolts with clean engine oil then screw them into position in the connecting rod, tightening them both by hand. Evenly and progressively tighten the bolts to the specified Stage 1 torque setting, then the Stage 2 torque setting, followed by angle-tightening each bolt through the specified Stage 3 angle. It is recommended that an angle-measuring gauge is used during this stage of the tightening, to ensure accuracy.

21.29 The connecting rod and bearing cap shell locating notches (arrowed) should abut each other

31 Refit the remaining three piston and connecting rod assemblies in the same way.

32 Rotate the crankshaft, and check that it turns freely, with no signs of binding or tight spots.

33 Refit the cylinder block reinforcing plate, oil pump and strainer, sump and the cylinder head as described in Part C of this Chapter.

22 Engine – initial start-up after overhaul

With the engine refitted in the car, double-check the engine oil and coolant levels (see *Weekly checks*). Make a final check that everything has been reconnected, and that there are no tools or rags left in the engine compartment.

On petrol engine models, remove the spark plugs (see Chapter 1A). Turn the engine on the starter until the oil pressure warning light goes out, then stop and refit the spark plugs.

On diesel engine models, switch on the 'ignition' and immediately turn the engine with the starter motor (without allowing the glow plugs to heat up) until the oil pressure warning light goes out.

On all models, start the engine as normal noting that this may take a little longer than usual, due to the fuel system components having been disturbed.

While the engine is idling, check for fuel, water and oil leaks. Don't be alarmed if there are some odd smells and smoke from parts getting hot and burning off oil deposits.

Assuming all is well, keep the engine idling until hot water is felt circulating through the top hose, then switch off the engine.

Allow the engine to cool then recheck the oil and coolant levels as described in *Weekly checks*, and top-up as necessary.

If new pistons, rings or crankshaft bearings have been fitted, the engine must be treated as new, and run-in for the first 500 miles. *Do not* operate the engine at full-throttle, or allow it to labour at low engine speeds in any gear. It is recommended that the oil and filter be changed at the end of this period.

Chapter 3
Cooling, heating and ventilation systems

Contents

Degrees of difficulty

Easy, suitable for novice with little experience	**Fairly easy,** suitable for beginner with some experience	**Fairly difficult,** suitable for competent DIY mechanic	**Difficult,** suitable for experienced DIY mechanic	**Very difficult,** suitable for expert DIY or professional

Specifications

General

System type	Pressurised, pump-assisted with front-mounted radiator and ECM-controlled electric cooling fan
Expansion tank cap pressure:	
Petrol engines	1.0 bar
Diesel engines	1.4 bar

Thermostat

Type	Wax	
Operating temperatures:	**Starts to open**	**Fully open**
1.8 litre engines	88°C	102°C
V6 engines	88 ± 2°C	96°C
Diesel engines	88 ± 2°C	Not available

Air conditioning system

Refrigerant	R134a
Refrigerant charge quantity	450 ± 50g
Compressor:	
Pressure (high side)	35.3 bar
Pressure (low side)	16.7 bar
Lubricating oil	Nippon Denso ND-8
Lubricating oil quantity (new)	120 ± 10 cc

Torque wrench settings

	Nm	lbf ft
Cooling system		
Petrol engines:		
Coolant elbow to cylinder head:		
1.8 litre engines	9	7
V6 engines	18	13
Water pump cover	10	7
Water pump to cylinder block	10	7
Coolant rail to block	9	7
Cooling fan housing to radiator	6	4
Cooling fan to housing	6	4
Engine block drain plug	20	15
Engine coolant temperature sensor	15	11
Thermostat housing:		
1.8 litre engines	9	7
V6 engines	18	13
Diesel engines:		
Coolant hose connector to cylinder head	9	7
Water pump to cylinder block	10	7
Coolant rail-to-cylinder head bolts	24	18
Coolant rail to exhaust manifold	24	18
Engine coolant temperature sensor	15	11
Fuel-burning heater bracket bolts	45	33
Lower coolant rail support bracket bolts	15	11
Thermostat housing to water pump	9	7
Upper coolant rail-to-thermostat housing bolts	9	7
Air conditioning system		
Compressor bracket to cylinder block	25	18
Compressor drivebelt tensioner clamp/pivot bolt (diesel engines)	24	18
Compressor to bracket	25	18
Condenser pipe to compressor	9	7
Condenser to fan housing	9	7
Cooling fan to housing	9	7
Drier housing Allen-headed plug	12	9
Engine oil cooler mounting bolts (V6 engines)	45	33
Evaporator pipe to compressor	9	7
Refrigerant pipe flange bolts:		
At bulkhead or condenser	9	7
At compressor	25	18
Sump support strap bolt (diesel engines)	25	18
Trinary switch	10	7

1 General information and precautions

General information

The cooling system is of pressurised type, comprising a front-mounted radiator, an expansion tank mounted at the front of the engine compartment, electric cooling fan(s) mounted on the rear of the radiator, a thermostat and a centrifugal water pump.

The cooling fan is controlled by the engine management electronic control module, through the fan control unit. The thermostat is located in the water pump inlet on the rear right-hand side of the cylinder block on 1.8 litre engines, in a coolant elbow between the cylinder banks at the transmission end on V6 engines, and on the water pump housing on the right-hand end of the engine on diesel engines. On 1.8 litre engines, the water pump is located on the right-hand rear end of the cylinder block and is driven by the timing belt. The V6 engines' water pump is driven by the primary timing belt, and located between the cylinder banks. On diesel engines, the water pump is located on the right-hand end of the engine, and is driven by the auxiliary drivebelt.

The system functions as follows. With the engine cold, the thermostat is closed and circulation is restricted to the cylinder block, cylinder head and heater matrix; there is no circulation through the radiator. When the coolant reaches a predetermined temperature, the thermostat opens and the coolant is allowed to flow freely through the top hose to the radiator. As the coolant circulates through the radiator, it is cooled by the inrush of air when the car is in forward motion. Airflow is supplemented by the action of the electric cooling fan when necessary. Upon reaching the bottom of the radiator, the coolant is now cooled and the cycle is repeated.

With the engine at normal operating temperature, the coolant expands, and some of it is displaced into the expansion tank. This coolant collects in the tank and is returned to the radiator when the system cools.

The operation of the radiator cooling fan is controlled by the engine management electronic control module, which receives engine temperature data from the engine coolant temperature sensor. At a predetermined temperature, the ECM energises the relay box which operates the cooling fan. On models with air conditioning, the same fan is used to maintain airflow through the condenser where necessary (see Section 10).

Precautions

Cooling system

- Do not attempt to remove the expansion tank filler cap or to disturb any part of the cooling system with the engine hot, as there is a risk of scalding. If the expansion tank

2.3a Hoses may be secured by worm-drive clips . . .

2.3b . . . spring type clips . . .

2.4 . . . or have quick-release couplings

filler cap must be removed before the engine and radiator have fully cooled down (even though this is not recommended) the pressure in the cooling system must first be released. Cover the cap with a thick layer of cloth, to avoid scalding, and slowly unscrew the filler cap until a hissing sound can be heard. When the hissing has stopped, showing that the pressure is released, slowly unscrew the filler cap until it can be removed. If more hissing sounds are heard, wait until they have stopped before unscrewing the cap completely. At all times keep well away from the filler opening.

- Do not allow antifreeze to come in contact with your skin or painted surfaces of the car. Rinse off spills immediately with plenty of water. Never leave antifreeze lying around; as it can be fatal if ingested.
- If the engine is hot, the electric cooling fan may start rotating even if the engine is not running, so be careful to keep hands, hair and loose clothing well clear when working in the engine compartment.

Air conditioning system

- On models with an air conditioning system, it is necessary to observe special precautions whenever dealing with any part of the system, its associated components and any items which necessitate disconnection of the system. If for any reason the system must be disconnected, entrust this task to a refrigeration engineer.
- Refrigerant must not be allowed to come in contact with a naked flame, otherwise a poisonous gas will be created. **Do not** allow the fluid to come in contact with the skin or eyes.

2 Cooling system hoses – disconnection and renewal

Note: *Refer to the warnings given in Section 1 of this Chapter before proceeding. Hoses should only be disconnected once the engine has cooled sufficiently to avoid scalding.*

1 The number, routing and pattern of hoses will vary according to model, but the same basic procedure applies. Before commencing work, make sure that the new hoses are to hand, along with new hose clips if needed. It is good practice to renew the hose clips at the same time as the hoses.

2 Drain the cooling system, as described in Chapter 1A or 1B, saving the coolant if it is fit for re-use. Squirt a little penetrating oil onto the hose clips if they are rusty.

3 Release the hose clips from the hose concerned. Almost all the standard clips fitted at the factory are the spring type, released by squeezing its tangs together with pliers, at the same time working the clip away from the hose stub **(see illustrations)**. These clips can be awkward to use, can pinch old hoses, and may become less effective with age, so may have been updated with Jubilee clips (released by turning the screw).

4 On the diesel engine especially, some of the larger hoses have a different clip arrangement, of 'quick-release' type. To release these hoses, prise out the retaining wire clip a little until it is felt to come to a stop, then pull the hose from the connection **(see illustration)**. Push the clip back in again before refitting.

5 Unclip any wires, cables or other hoses which may be attached to the hose being removed. Make notes for reference when reassembling if necessary.

6 Note that the coolant unions are fragile (most are made of plastic); do not use excessive force when attempting to remove the hoses. If a hose proves to be difficult to remove, try to release it by rotating the hose ends before attempting to free it – if this fails, try gently prising up the end of the hose with a small screwdriver to 'break' the seal.

HAYNES HiNT ***If the hose is stiff, use a little soapy water as a lubricant, or soften the hose by soaking it with hot water. If all else fails, cut the coolant hose with a sharp knife, then slit it so that it can be peeled off in two pieces. Although this may prove expensive if the hose is otherwise undamaged, it is preferable to buying a new radiator.***

7 Before fitting the new hose, smear the stubs with washing-up liquid or a suitable rubber lubricant to aid fitting. **Do not** use oil or grease, which may attack the rubber.

8 Fit the hose clips over the ends of the hose, then fit the hose over its stubs. When refitting hose clips, give some thought to how easy they will be to remove in the future – make sure the screw fitting or spring tangs will be accessible.

9 Work each hose end fully onto its outlet, check that the hose is settled correctly and is properly routed, then slide each clip along the hose until it is behind the outlet flared end before tightening it securely. Spring-type clips must have the ends squeezed together, and the clip positioned over the outlet flared end, then released. 'Quick-release' clips are simply pushed over the outlet until they are heard, or felt, to click into place.

10 Refill the cooling system as described in Chapter 1A or 1B. Run the engine, and check that there are no leaks.

11 Recheck the tightness of the hose clips on any new hoses after a few hundred miles.

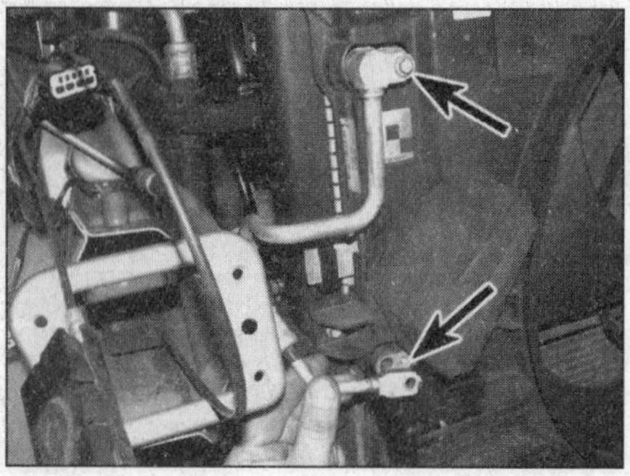

3.3a Unbolt the condenser pipe flanges . . .

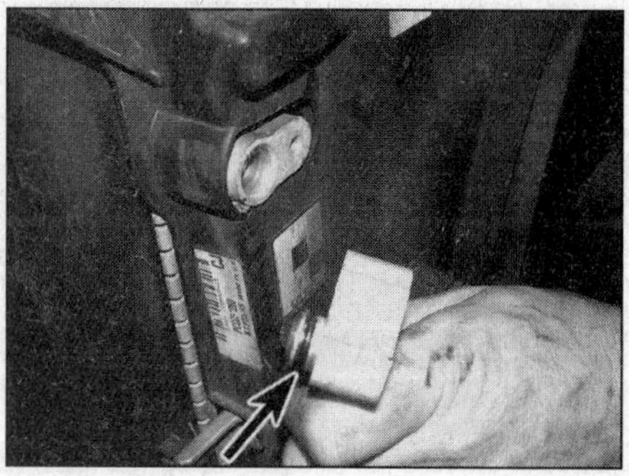

3.3b . . . and recover the O-rings

3.4 Disconnect the two wiring plugs on the left-hand chassis leg

3 Radiator and expansion tank – removal, inspection and refitting

Radiator removal

Petrol engines

1 Drain the cooling system (see Chapter 1A).

2 Except on 1.8 litre models with manual transmission, remove the bonnet lock platform as described in Chapter 11.

3 On models with air conditioning, have the system professionally discharged. Unbolt and disconnect the two condenser pipes in front of the radiator, recovering the O-ring seals (which must be renewed when refitting) **(see illustration)**. Plug or tape over the open connections.

4 Disconnect the two cooling fan wiring plugs on the left-hand chassis leg – note that one plug is clipped to the top of the other **(see illustration)**.

5 Release the clips and disconnect the top hose from the engine and radiator. Remove the bolt securing the top hose support bracket **(see illustrations)**.

6 Remove the expansion tank as described later in this Section.

7 On models with automatic transmission, remove the bolt on the right-hand side securing the transmission fluid cooler to the radiator. Unhook the cooler from the two clips on the left, and move the fluid cooler to one side.

8 Release the radiator from its mountings, and remove it from the car **(see illustration)**.

9 Where applicable, unbolt and unhook the condenser, using the information in Section 11.

10 Unscrew the two side bolts and two lower metal clips securing the fan cowl to the front of the radiator, then separate the radiator from the fan cowl **(see illustrations)**.

11 Remove the two radiator mounting bolts from the bonnet lock platform, and recover the upper mounting brackets.

12 If a new radiator is being fitted, transfer the upper mounting brackets and lower mounting bushes to the new radiator. Foam sealing strips are fitted to the base and sides of the radiator, and it is likely that new ones will also be needed.

Diesel engines

13 Drain the cooling system as described in Chapter 1B.

14 Remove the bonnet lock platform as described in Chapter 11.

15 On models with air conditioning, remove the condenser as described in Section 11.

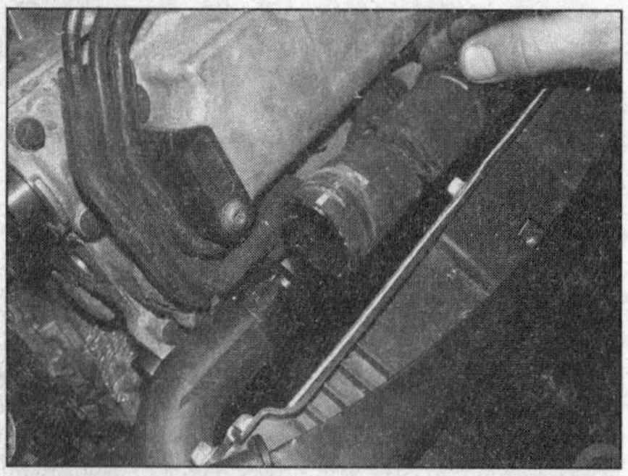

3.5a Disconnecting the radiator top hose

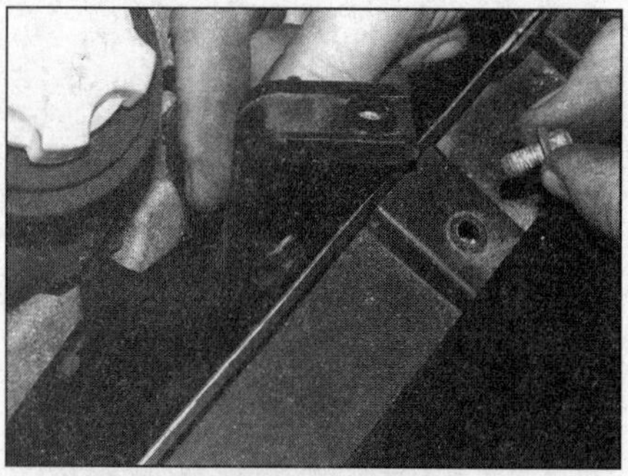

3.5b Unbolt and remove the top hose support bracket

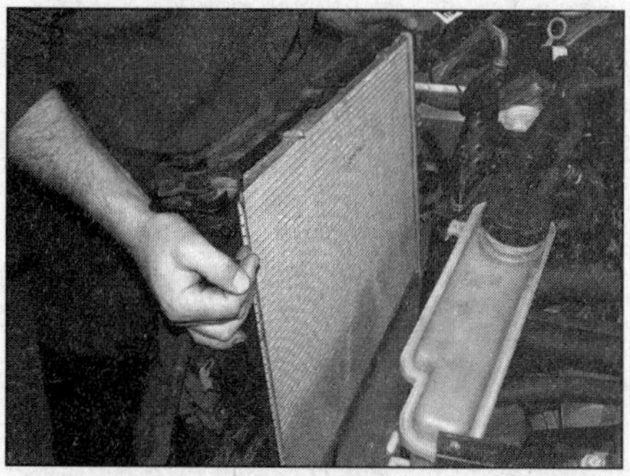

3.8 Removing the radiator

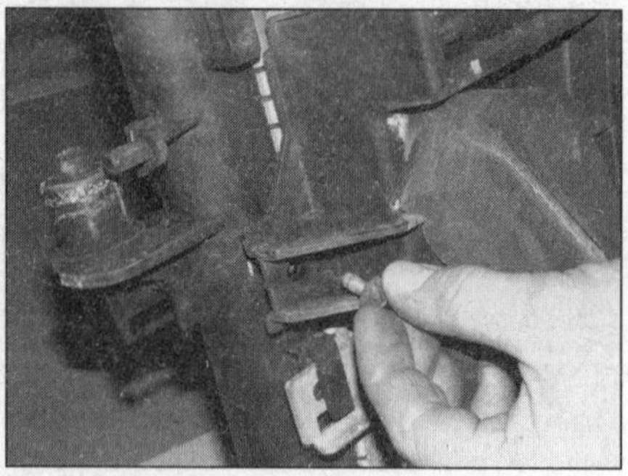

3.10a Remove the bolt each side . . .

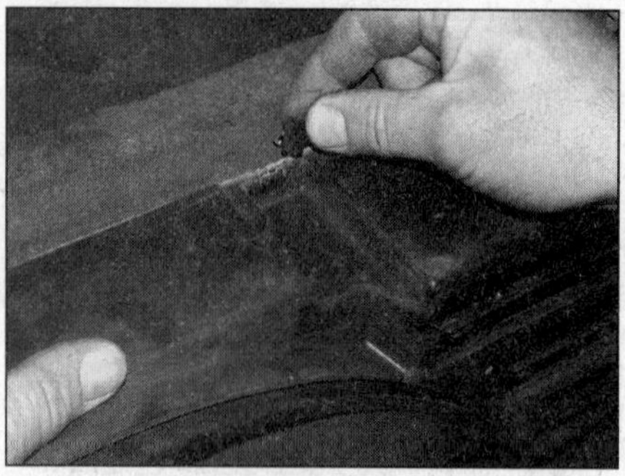

3.10b . . . and the metal clips on the base . . .

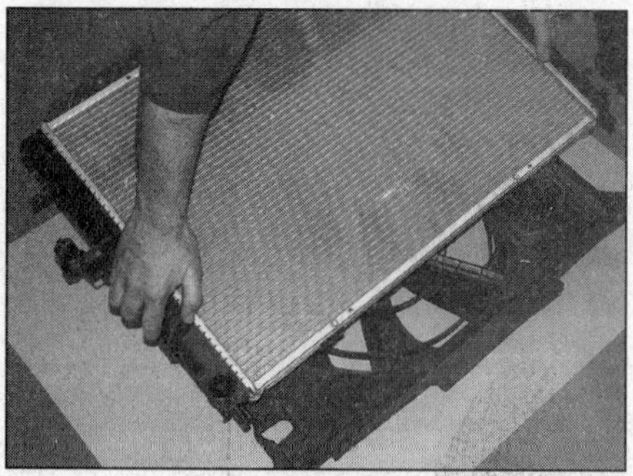

3.10c . . . then separate the radiator from the fan cowl

16 Release the clips and disconnect the top hose from the engine and radiator.

17 Remove the expansion tank as described later in this Section.

18 Remove the two radiator upper mounting bolts, and recover the upper mounting brackets.

19 Disconnect the two cooling fan wiring plugs on the left-hand side of the radiator.

20 Unscrew the four bolts securing the fan cowl to the front of the radiator, then ease the fan cowl off the radiator upper mounting rubbers.

21 Remove the intercooler right-hand mounting bolt from the radiator, then unscrew the intercooler pipe mounting bolt on the left-hand side. Release the intercooler mounting clips either side, and withdraw it from the radiator as far as possible.

22 Release the radiator from its mountings, and remove it from the car.

23 If a new radiator is being fitted, remove the two fan cowl bolts and ease the cowl off the top mountings. Transfer the upper mounting brackets and lower mounting bushes to the new radiator. Foam sealing strips are fitted to the base and sides of the radiator, and it is likely that new ones will also be needed.

Radiator inspection

24 If the radiator was removed because of clogging (causing overheating) then try reverse flushing or, in severe cases, use a radiator cleanser strictly in accordance with the manufacturer's instructions. Refer to Chapter 1A or 1B for further information

25 Use a soft brush and an air line or garden hose to clear the radiator matrix of leaves, insects, etc.

26 Major leaks or extensive damage should be repaired by a specialist. If the radiator is old, a new or reconditioned one should be obtained.

27 Examine the mounting rubbers for signs of damage or deterioration, and renew if necessary.

Radiator refitting

28 Refitting is a reversal of removal, noting the following points:

a) Tighten all nuts and bolts to the specified torque, where given.

b) Where applicable, refit the bonnet lock platform as described in Chapter 11.

c) On completion, refill the cooling system as described in Chapter 1A or 1B.

Expansion tank

Removal

29 With the engine cold, unscrew and remove the filler cap from the expansion tank.

30 Place a suitable container under the expansion tank to collect the drained coolant.

31 Loosen the clip and disconnect the bleed hose from the top of the expansion tank.

32 Release the retaining clip and disconnect the coolant feed hose from the bottom of the tank.

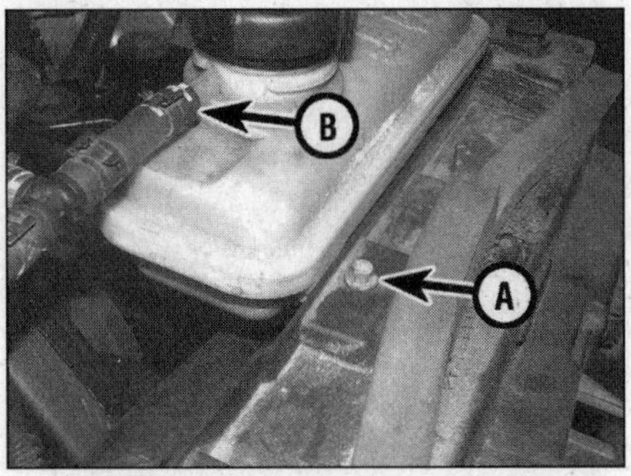

3.33a Expansion tank mounting bolt (A) and bleed hose (B)

3.33b Unhook the tank mounting lugs

33 Undo the single mounting bolt, then slide the expansion tank mounting lugs out of the radiator **(see illustrations)**.

Inspection

34 Empty any remaining coolant from the tank, and flush it with fresh water to clean it. If the tank is leaking, it must be renewed.

35 The expansion tank cap should be cleaned and checked whenever it is removed. Check that its sealing surfaces and threads are clean and undamaged.

36 The cap's performance can only be checked by using a cap pressure-tester (cooling system tester) with a suitable adaptor. On applying pressure, the cap's pressure relief valve should hold until the specified pressure is reached, at which point the valve should open.

37 If there is any doubt about the cap's performance, then it must be renewed. Ensure that the new unit is of the correct type and rating.

Refitting

38 Refitting is a reversal of removal, but tighten the expansion tank mounting bolt securely and top up the cooling system with reference to *Weekly checks*.

4 **Thermostat** – removal, testing and refitting

1 As the thermostat ages, it will become slower to react to changes in water temperature ('lazy'). Ultimately, the unit may stick in the open or closed position, and this causes problems. A thermostat which is stuck open will result in a very slow warm-up; a thermostat which is stuck shut will lead to rapid overheating.

2 Before assuming the thermostat is to blame for a cooling system problem, check the coolant level. If the system is draining due to a leak, or has not been properly filled, there may be an airlock in the system (refer to the coolant renewal procedure in Chapter 1A or 1B).

3 If the engine seems to be taking a long time to warm-up (based on heater output), the thermostat could be stuck open. Don't necessarily believe the temperature gauge reading – some gauges never seem to register very high in normal driving.

4 A lengthy warm-up period might suggest that the thermostat is missing – it may have been removed or inadvertently omitted by a previous owner or mechanic. Don't drive the car without a thermostat – the engine management system's ECU will then stay in warm-up mode for longer than necessary, causing emissions and fuel economy to suffer.

5 If the engine runs hot, use your hand to check the temperature of the radiator top hose. If the hose isn't hot, but the engine clearly is, the thermostat is probably stuck closed, preventing the coolant inside the engine from escaping to the radiator – renew the thermostat. Again, this problem may also be due to an airlock (refer to the coolant renewal procedure in Chapter 1A or 1B).

6 If the radiator top hose is hot, it means that the coolant is flowing (at least as far as the radiator) and the thermostat is open. Consult the *Fault diagnosis* section at the end of this manual to assist in tracing possible cooling system faults, but a lack of heater output would now definitely suggest an airlock or a blockage.

7 To gain a rough idea of whether the thermostat is working properly when the engine is warming-up, without dismantling the system, proceed as follows.

8 With the engine completely cold, start the engine and let it idle, while checking the temperature of the radiator top hose. Periodically check the temperature indicated on the coolant temperature gauge – if overheating is indicated, switch the engine off immediately.

9 The top hose should feel cold for some time as the engine warms-up, and should then get warm quite quickly as the thermostat opens.

10 The above is not a precise or definitive test of thermostat operation, but if the system does not perform as described, remove and test the thermostat as described below.

Removal

11 Drain the cooling system (see Chapter 1A or 1B).

1.8 litre engines

12 Remove the air cleaner as described in Chapter 4A.

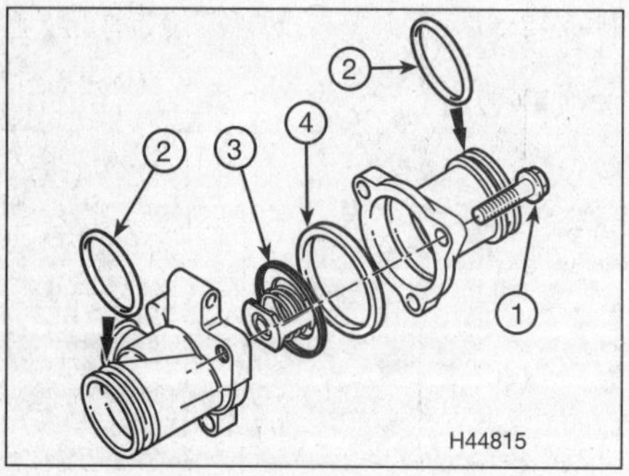

4.18 Thermostat components – 1.8 litre engines

1 Bolt
2 O-ring seals
3 Thermostat
4 Rubber seal

4.22 Release the three hoses from the housing

4.23a Remove the mounting bolt . . .

13 The thermostat is located on the rear right-hand side of the cylinder block.

14 Loosen the clip and disconnect the heater hose from the thermostat housing located on the rear of the cylinder block.

15 Unscrew the two bolts securing the coolant rail to the rear of the cylinder block, then ease the rail from the thermostat housing using a twisting action.

16 Unscrew the bolt securing the thermostat housing to the cylinder block. Ease the thermostat housing from the water pump with a twisting action and withdraw.

17 Remove the O-ring seals from the grooves in the housing inlet and outlet stubs using a small screwdriver.

18 Unscrew the three bolts and separate the cover from the thermostat housing **(see illustration)**.

19 Remove the thermostat from the housing noting which way round it is fitted, then remove the rubber seal from the periphery of the thermostat.

V6 engines

20 Remove the air cleaner and inlet manifold upper section as described in Chapter 4B.

21 Release the two clips securing the engine wiring harness to the engine lifting eye and the rear cylinder head, and move the harness aside.

22 Note the position of the three hoses on the coolant elbow/thermostat housing, then release the hose clips and disconnect the hoses **(see illustration)**.

23 Unscrew the single bolt securing the coolant elbow and thermostat housing. Prise out and remove the coolant elbow, recovering the O-ring seal, which must be renewed when refitting **(see illustrations)**.

24 Twist and release the thermostat housing from the cylinder block, then release the rigid coolant pipe from the housing and withdraw it **(see illustration)**. Note that the two plastic clips on the rigid pipe do not have to be disturbed to remove the pipe.

25 Recover all the O-ring seals from the housing – new ones must be used when refitting.

Diesel engine

26 The thermostat can only be renewed once the water pump has been removed. Refer to Section 5 and remove the water pump.

27 Undo the four retaining bolts and remove the thermostat housing from the water pump **(see illustration)**.

28 Note how the thermostat is fitted, and remove it from the housing **(see illustrations)**.

4.23b . . . then carefully prise out the housing . . .

4.23c . . . and recover the O-ring

4.24 Release the housing from the rigid pipe

4.27 Undo the four retaining bolts (arrowed) and remove the thermostat housing

4.28a To remove the thermostat, press down, rotate it anti-clockwise . . .

4.28b . . . and lift it from the housing

4.35 Renew the thermostat seal(s)

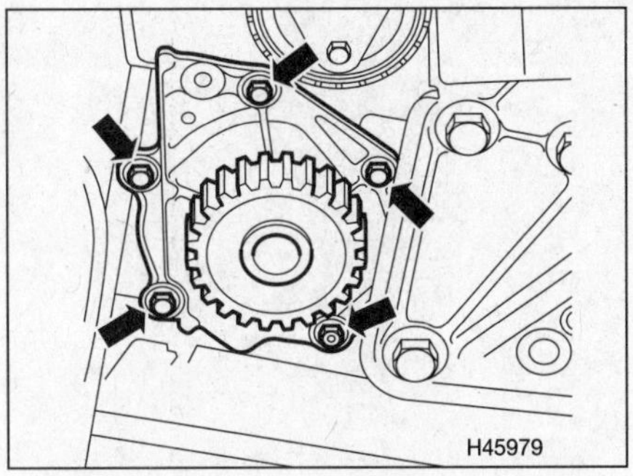

5.7 Water pump mounting bolts – 1.8 litre engines

5.11 Water pump bolts – V6 engines

Testing

Note: *Frankly, if there is any question about the operation of the thermostat, it's best to renew it – they are not expensive items. Testing involves heating in, or over, an open pan of boiling water, which carries with it the risk of scalding. A thermostat which has seen more than five years' service may well be past its best already.*

29 If the thermostat remains in the open position at room temperature, it is faulty, and must be renewed as a matter of course.

30 Check to see if there's a open temperature marking stamped on the thermostat.

31 Using a thermometer and container of water, heat the water until the temperature corresponds with the temperature marking stamped on the thermostat. If no marking is found, start the test with the water hot, and heat slowly until it boils.

32 Suspend the (closed) thermostat on a length of string in the water, and check that maximum opening occurs within two minutes, or before the water boils.

33 Remove the thermostat and allow it to cool down; check that it closes fully.

34 If the thermostat does not open and close as described, or if it sticks in either position, it must be renewed.

Refitting

35 Refitting is a reversal of removal, but note the following additional points:

a) Clean all mating surfaces thoroughly before reassembly.

b) Renew all seals and gaskets, and smear O-rings with a little rubber grease to aid seating ***(see illustration)****.*

c) Tighten all bolts to their specified torque wrench settings (where given).

d) Ensure the coolant hose clips are positioned so that they do not foul any other components, and so they can easily be removed in future, then tighten them securely.

e) Refill the cooling system (see Chapter 1A or 1B).

5 Water pump – removal and refitting

Removal

1 Water pump failure is usually indicated by coolant leaking from the gland behind the pump bearing, or by rough and noisy operation, usually accompanied by excessive pump spindle play. If the pump shows any of these symptoms then it must be renewed as follows.

2 Drain the cooling system (see Chapter 1A or 1B).

1.8 litre engines

3 The water pump is at the rear of the engine, at the timing belt end.

4 Remove the timing belt as described in Chapter 2A.

5 Unscrew the bolt securing the dipstick tube support bracket to the thermostat housing.

6 Remove the bolt securing the timing belt backplate to the water pump.

7 Unscrew the five water pump mounting bolts **(see illustration)**.

8 Withdraw the water pump from the cylinder block, noting that it is located on two dowels. Prise out the O-ring seal from the groove in the rear mating face – discard the seal and obtain a new one.

V6 engines

9 The water pump is located at the primary timing belt end of the cylinder block, between the cylinder banks.

10 Remove the primary timing belt as described in Chapter 2B.

11 Remove the seven water pump mounting bolts, and discard them – new bolts must be used when refitting **(see illustration)**.

12 Release the pump from its location, and recover the large O-ring seal – a new one will be needed for refitting **(see illustrations)**.

Diesel engine

13 The water pump is at the rear of the engine, at the timing chain end.

14 Remove the engine right-hand mounting and hydramount as described in Chapter 2C.

15 Remove the auxiliary drivebelt and air cleaner element as described in Chapter 1B.

16 Release the wire clips securing the turbo air duct to the mass airflow sensor, and take off the duct, recovering the breather pipe connecting sleeve.

17 Remove the bolt securing the power steering fluid pipe support bracket to the cylinder head.

18 Release the two spring clips and disconnect the hoses from the thermostat housing and lower coolant rail **(see illustration)**.

5.12a Withdraw the water pump . . .

5.12b . . . and recover the O-ring

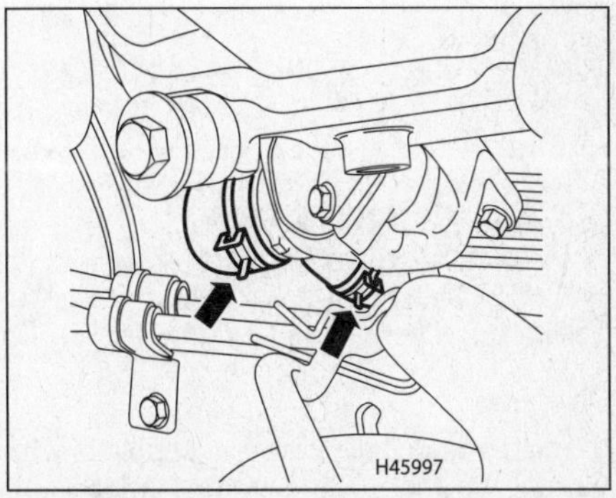

5.18 Release the two spring clips from the thermostat and lower coolant rail (arrowed)

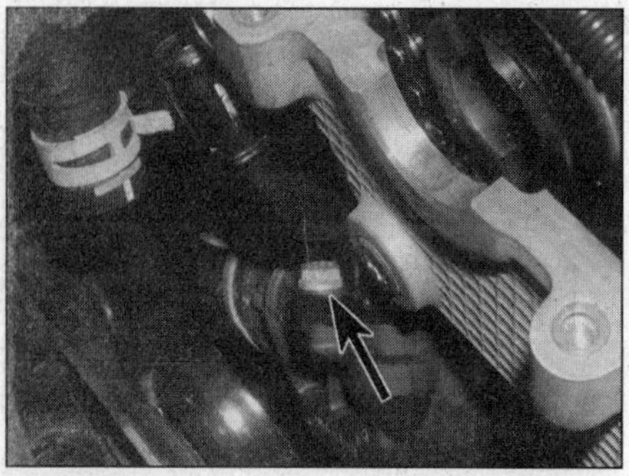

5.20 Remove the bolt securing the coolant rail to the thermostat housing (arrowed)

5.21 Unscrew the four bolts (arrowed) and remove the coolant pump

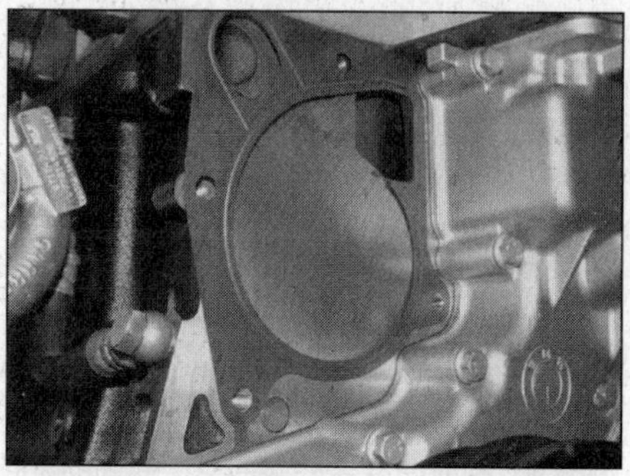

5.22 If necessary, cut the coolant pump section of the timing cover gasket away

19 On models with air conditioning, remove the single bolt securing the refrigerant pipe to the inner wing, and move the pipe clear as far as possible.

20 Slacken and remove the bolt securing the coolant rail to the thermostat housing **(see illustration)**. Separate the flange from the housing, and recover the O-ring seal (discard the seal – a new one must be fitted).

21 Using the jack, adjust the height of the engine for access to the water pump bolts. Unscrew the four bolts, and remove the water pump **(see illustration)**.

22 If this is the first time the pump has been removed, the water pump gasket will not come away, as it is attached to the timing cover gasket at the three 'corners', and must be cut through at three points to remove it **(see illustration)**. Once removed, discard the gasket.

Refitting

23 Refitting is a reversal of removal, but note the following additional points:

a) Clean all mating surfaces thoroughly before reassembly.
b) Renew all seals and gaskets, and smear O-rings with a little rubber grease to aid seating.
c) On V6 engines, fit new bolts.
d) Tighten all bolts to their specified torque wrench settings (where given).
e) Ensure the coolant hose clips are positioned so that they do not foul any other components, and so they can easily be removed in future, then tighten them securely.
f) Refill the cooling system as described in Chapter 1A or 1B.

6 Electric cooling fan assembly – testing, removal and refitting

Testing

1 The cooling fan motor is supplied with current via the ignition switch, a fuse and the cooling fan relay (inside the fan control unit). The relay is energised by the engine management ECM (electronic control module).

2 If the fan does not appear to work, first check that the fuse is in good condition and not blown (see Chapter 12). Check all relevant wiring and connectors. For more information on the fan control unit, refer to Section 11.

3 To check the motor itself, disconnect the wiring loom from the motor, and connect a 12 volt supply directly to it. If the motor does not work, then it must be renewed. Further investigation and diagnosis is only possible using dedicated test equipment which can interrogate the engine management ECM for any stored fault codes.

Removal

4 Disconnect the battery negative (earth) lead (see *Disconnecting the battery*).

5 Remove the radiator as described in Section 3.

6 Hold the centre nut on the fan motor spindle, then turn the fan itself clockwise to unscrew it. The manufacturers state that, once removed, the original fan should not be refitted.

7 To remove the fan control unit, unclip it and the wiring harness from the fan cowl. On models with air conditioning, the fan control unit has a dual role – see Section 11.

Refitting

8 Refitting is a reversal of removal, noting the following points:

a) Ensure that the wiring plugs are securely reconnected, and that the wiring harness is also routed and secured as before.
b) The manufacturers state that a new cooling fan must be used when refitting. Hold the spindle nut and turn the fan anti-clockwise until secure.
c) Refit the radiator as described in Section 3.

7 Cooling system temperature sensor – testing, removal and refitting

Refer to the relevant Part of Chapter 4. The sensor performs a vital role in the engine management system, besides providing the feed for the temperature gauge.

8 Heating and ventilation system – general information

The heating/ventilation system consists of a blower motor (housed in the heater distribution box in the centre of the facia), face level vents in the centre and at each end of the facia, and air ducts to the front and rear footwells.

The control unit is located in the centre of the facia, and the controls operate flap valves to deflect and mix the air flowing through the various parts of the heating/ventilation system. The flap valves are contained in the air distribution housing, which acts as a central distribution unit, passing air to the various ducts and vents.

Cold air enters the system through the grille at the rear of the engine compartment, and (on models with air conditioning) is filtered by a pollen filter, to remove particulates – see Chapter 1A or 1B. If required, the airflow is boosted by the blower fan, and then flows through the various ducts, according to the settings of the controls. Stale air is expelled through ducts at the rear of the car. If warm air is required, the cold air is passed over the heater matrix, which is heated by the engine coolant.

A recirculation switch enables the outside air supply to be closed off, while the air inside the car is recirculated. This can be useful to prevent unpleasant odours entering from outside the car, but should only be used briefly, as the recirculated air inside the car will soon become stale.

Diesel models are equipped with a fuel-burning heater (FBH), an auxiliary heating system that compensates for the relatively low coolant temperatures inherent in the diesel engine. At low ambient temperatures, the system heats the coolant supply to the heater assembly, and maintains it within the temperature range required for good in-car heating performance. The system consists of an ambient air temperature sensor, an FBH fuel pump and an FBH unit. Fuel for the FBH system is taken from the fuel tank, and supplied via the FBH fuel pump at the rear of the car to the FBH unit, mounted on the lower left-hand side of the engine compartment.

In the FBH unit, the fuel is burned and the resultant heat output is used to heat the coolant. An ECU integrated into the FBH unit controls the operation of the system. Models with the system may also have a parking heater, which is essentially a timer, allowing the FBH to be programmed to come on automatically – for example, to warm the car prior to driving.

9 Heating and ventilation system components – removal and refitting

Heater control panel

1 Remove the audio/navigation unit as described in Chapter 12.
2 Carefully unclip the heater control surround panel – it is secured by a total of seven clips. On lower-specification models without a row of switches below the heater control panel, a blanking plate can be removed first, making unclipping the heater control surround easier **(see illustrations)**.
3 Unscrew the two screws either side of the control panel, and withdraw it from the facia **(see illustrations)**.
4 Disconnect the two wiring multi-plugs from the back of the panel **(see illustration)**.
5 On models without air conditioning, noting their fitted positions, unhook the end fittings and disconnect the two heater control cables from the panel.
6 Remove the heater control panel from the car.

9.2a Where applicable, the blanking plate can be unclipped . . .

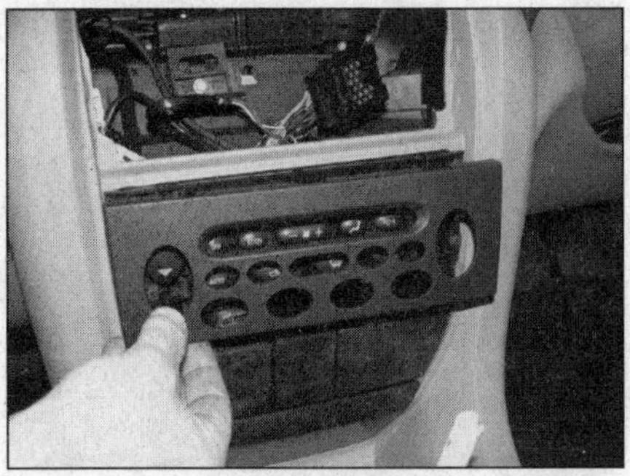

9.2b . . . to make unclipping the heater control surround easier

7 Refitting is a reversal of removal, noting the following points:

a) Where applicable, ensure the cables are correctly refitted – once connected, check their operation before the panel is finally fitted.
b) Refit the audio/navigation unit as described in Chapter 12.

Heater bypass control

8 Remove the driver's side facia veneer trim panel as described in Chapter 11, Section 25.
9 On the rear of the trim panel, unscrew the Torx screws securing the two centre vents, and remove them **(see illustrations)**.
10 Noting how they are fitted, carefully remove the trim panel securing clips as necessary from the back of the panel.
11 Unclip the bypass control from the back of the panel, and remove it with the cable **(see illustration)**.
12 Refitting is a reversal of removal. Refit the facia trim panel as described in Chapter 11.

Centre vents

13 Remove the driver's side facia veneer trim panel as described in Chapter 11, Section 25.
14 On the rear of the trim panel, unscrew the eight Torx screws securing the two centre vents, and remove them **(see illustrations 9.9a and 9.9b)**.
15 Refitting is a reversal of removal. Refit the facia trim panel as described in Chapter 11.

Facia end vents

Driver's side

16 Remove the driver's side facia veneer trim panel as described in Chapter 11, Section 25.
17 On the rear of the trim panel, unscrew the two Torx screws securing the end vent.

9.3a Remove a total of four screws . . .

9.3b . . . and withdraw the heater control panel

9.4 Disconnect the wiring from the panel

9.9a Remove the Torx screws . . .

9.9b . . . and lift out the centre vents

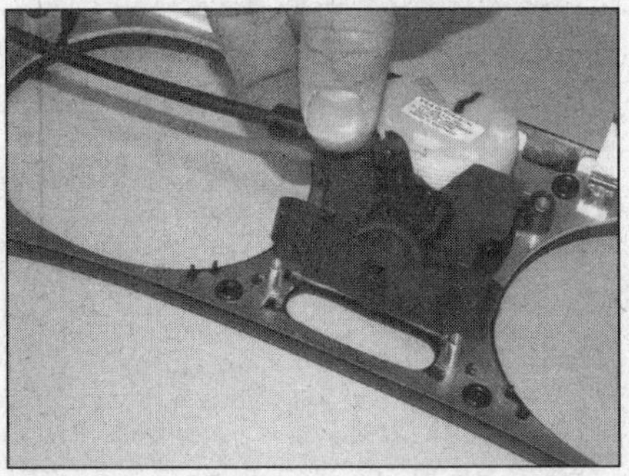

9.11 Removing the heater bypass control

9.20a Pull the vent out at the base . . .

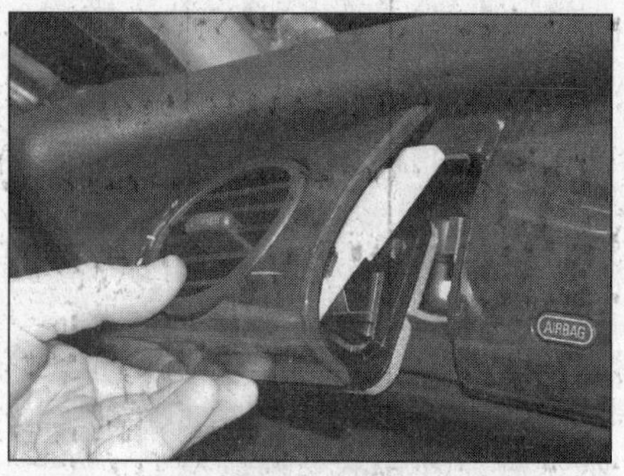

9.20b . . . then slide towards the centre of the car, and remove

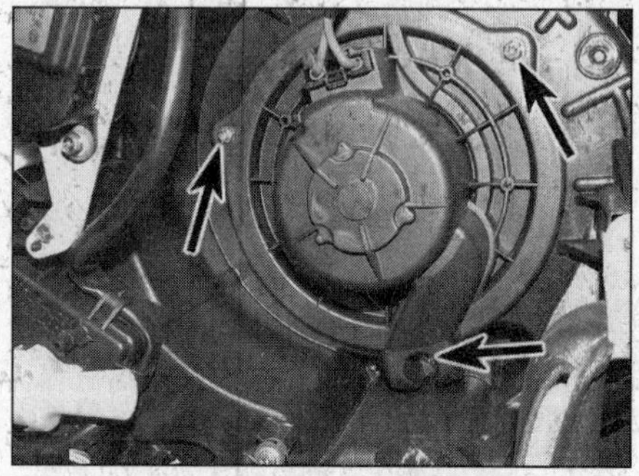
9.32 Blower motor mounting screws

Remove the vent and the trim panel end clip, noting how it is fitted.

18 Refitting is a reversal of removal. Refit the facia trim panel as described in Chapter 11.

Passenger's side

19 Close the vent before attempting to remove it.

20 Pull the vent trim veneer panel out and downwards at the bottom edge to release it from the facia. Pull the vent panel towards the centre of the car to release the end clip, and remove it **(see illustrations)**.

21 On the rear of the trim panel, unscrew the three Torx screws securing the end vent and trim panel mounting bracket. Remove the vent, bracket and the trim panel clips, noting how they are fitted.

22 Refitting is a reversal of removal. Offer in the assembled trim panel at the top edge first, then press in the lower edge to secure it.

9.33a Disconnect the wiring plug . . .

9.36 Blower motor resistor unit

Temperature cable

23 Remove the heater control panel as described previously in this Section.

24 Working in the passenger footwell, release the two turn-buckle fasteners at the top, and the two push-fasteners at the bottom, then drop down the passenger lower facia trim panel.

25 Unhook the cable end fitting from the lever on the heater assembly. Release the clip securing the cable outer, so the cable is free to be withdrawn.

26 Refitting is a reversal of removal. Check the cable operation before finally refitting the control panel.

Air distribution cable

27 Remove the heater control panel as described previously in this Section.

28 Working in the driver's footwell, remove the trim panel fitted above the pedals, which is secured by two screws at the top, and two push-fasteners at the bottom.

29 Unhook the cable end fitting from the lever on the heater assembly. Release the clip securing the cable outer, so the cable is free to be withdrawn.

30 Refitting is a reversal of removal. Check the cable operation before finally refitting the control panel.

9.33b . . . then withdraw the blower motor

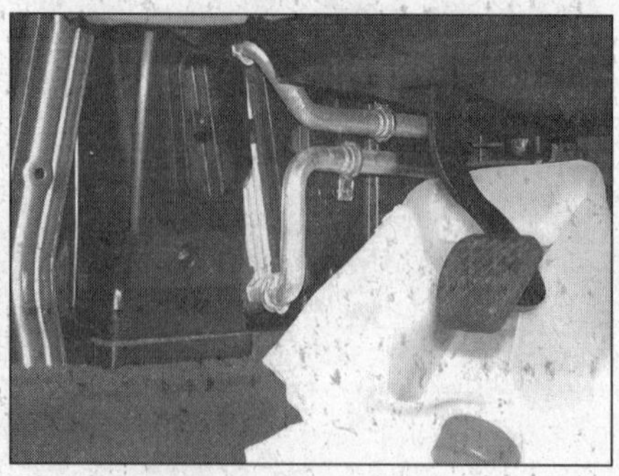
9.40 Position a container under the two supply pipes

Blower motor

31 Remove the pedal box as described in Chapter 9.

32 Working in the driver's footwell, remove the three blower motor mounting screws **(see illustration)**.

33 Disconnect the blower motor wiring plug, then withdraw the motor from the heater unit **(see illustrations)**.

34 Refitting is a reversal of removal.

Blower motor resistor unit

35 The blower motor resistor unit is located on the left-hand side of the heater unit – remove the passenger footwell right-hand side trim panel for access, as described in Chapter 11, Section 25.

36 Disconnect the wiring plug on top of the unit, then remove the screws and withdraw the unit **(see illustration)**.

37 Refitting is a reversal of removal.

Heater matrix

38 Drain the cooling system as described in Chapter 1A or 1B, or alternatively clamp the heater hoses at the bulkhead in the engine compartment using purpose-made hose clamps.

39 Remove the driver's footwell left-hand trim panel and the facia closing panel above the foot pedals, as described in Chapter 11, Section 25.

40 Place a waterproof sheet inside the car, below the heater matrix, to protect the carpet from coolant spillage. Have ready a shallow container to catch the coolant which will be lost when the heater pipes are disconnected (this applies even if the cooling system was drained, as coolant will remain in the matrix) **(see illustration)**.

41 Remove the screw from the pipe support

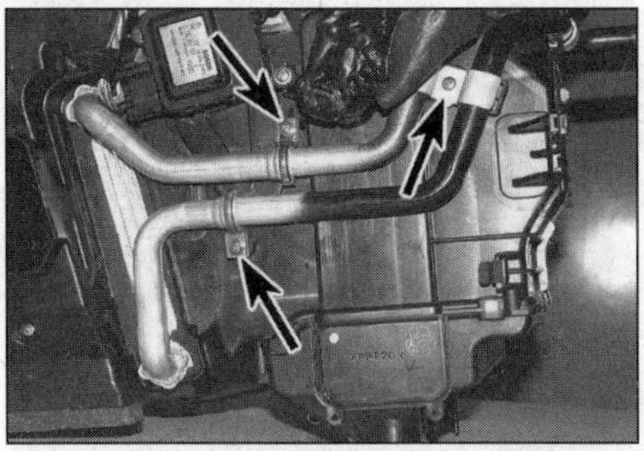

9.41a Heater matrix details (heater unit removed) – pipe clips and support bracket arrowed

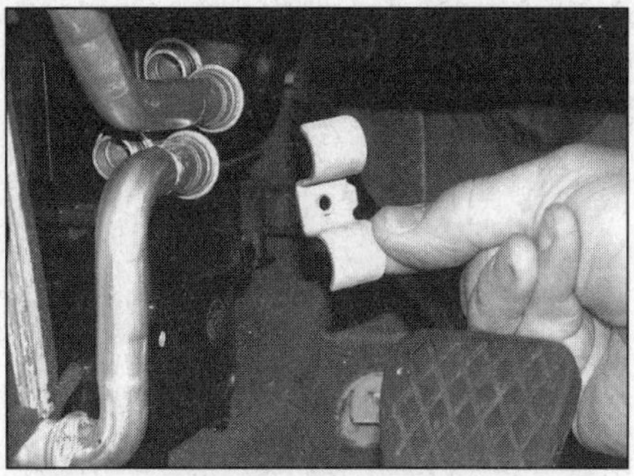

9.41b Remove the pipe support bracket at the front . . .

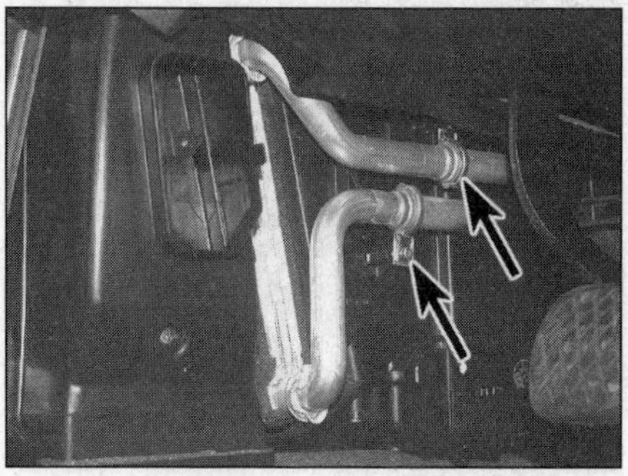

9.41c . . . then remove the pipe clips . . .

bracket at the front, then remove the screw securing each pipe to the side of the heater assembly. Anticipating some coolant spillage, separate the pipes and recover the O-ring seals **(see illustrations)**.

42 Slide out the matrix from the heater unit, keeping it upright to minimise further coolant loss **(see illustration)**.

43 Refitting is a reversal of removal, noting the following points:

a) Use new O-ring seals on the heater matrix coolant pipes.

b) Refill or top-up the cooling system, as applicable.

Heater unit

44 Drain the cooling system as described in Chapter 1A or 1B, or alternatively clamp the heater hoses at the bulkhead in the engine compartment using purpose-made hose clamps, after removing the bulkhead access panels as described in paragraph 47.

45 Have the air conditioning system professionally discharged, on models so equipped.

46 Remove the windscreen cowl panels as described in Chapter 11.

47 Remove the four nuts securing the bulkhead central soundproofing panel, then lift it off the wiring harness which passes through the bulkhead. Remove the two bolts and take out the access panel behind the soundproofing (refer to Chapter 1A, Section 22).

48 Release the two spring-type hose clips, and disconnect the heater hoses where they pass through the bulkhead **(see illustration)**. If the system has not been drained, turn the hose ends upwards afterwards to minimise coolant loss.

49 On models with air conditioning, there are two refrigerant pipes to disconnect, each secured by a single bolt **(see illustration)**. **Do not** disturb the pipes unless the system has been discharged first (see Section 10) – for maximum personal safety, have these pipes disconnected by the engineer who discharges the system for you, and ensure the system is kept switched off afterwards. Each pipe has an O-ring seal fitted, which must be renewed when reconnecting. Plug the open pipes to prevent contamination of the system.

50 With reference to Chapter 11, remove the facia and the crossmember behind.

51 Support the heater assembly, then remove the six bolts securing it to the body **(see illustration)**.

52 Disconnect the two drain hoses from the bottom of the housing **(see illustration)**.

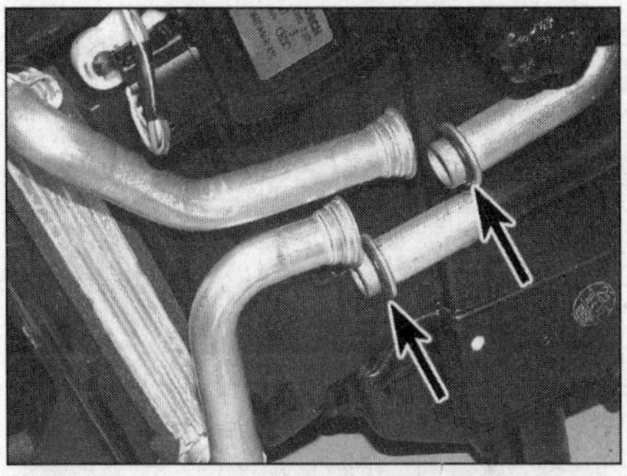

9.41d . . . separate the pipes, and recover the O-rings

9.42 Removing the heater matrix

9.48 Heater coolant hoses and air conditioning pipes

9.49 Disconnecting an air conditioning pipe

9.51 Three of the six heater unit mounting bolts

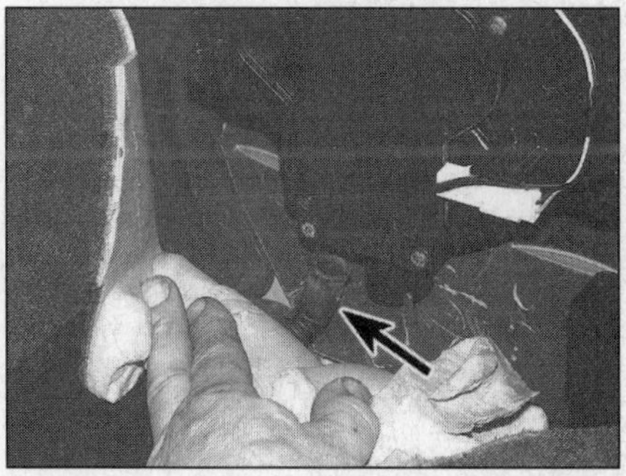

9.52 Disconnect the drain hoses at the base of the heater unit

9.53 Disconnect the heater unit wiring harness plug

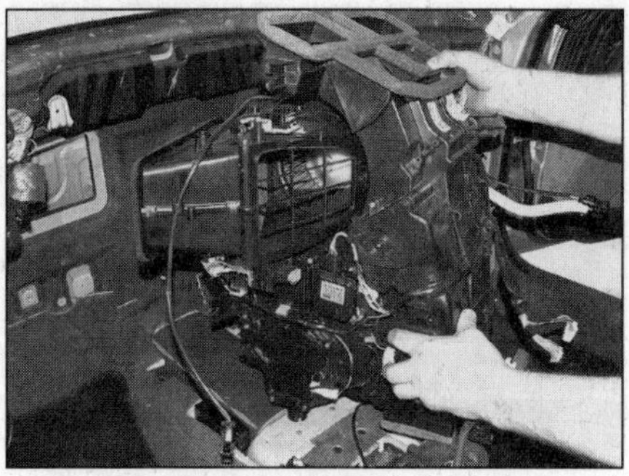

9.55 Removing the heater unit

53 Disconnect the wiring plug from the unit **(see illustration)**.

54 Place a waterproof sheet inside the car, below the heater matrix, to protect the carpet from coolant spillage (this applies even if the cooling system was drained, as coolant will remain in the matrix).

55 Release the heater assembly from the air inlet in the bulkhead, and from the ducting leading back to the centre console. Lift the unit out of the car – try to keep it level, to minimise coolant loss from the matrix **(see illustration)**.

56 Refitting is a reversal of removal, noting the following points:

a) Refit the facia and crossmember as described in Chapter 11.

b) On completion, fill and bleed the cooling system as described in Chapter 1A or 1B.

c) On models with air conditioning, have the refrigerant pipes reconnected (using new O-ring seals) and the system recharged by a specialist.

Fuel-burning heater (FBH)

57 Drain the cooling system as described in Chapter 1B.

58 Loosen the large hose clip and disconnect the large-diameter hose from the EGR valve.

59 Cut the cable-ties securing the FBH intake hose, coolant hose and fuel filter harness to the battery tray.

60 Anticipating some loss of fuel and coolant, release the hose clips and disconnect the fuel supply and coolant hoses from the FBH – note their fitted positions. Plug the fuel pipe to reduce fuel loss and prevent dirt entry.

61 Disconnect the two wiring plugs from the top of the FBH.

62 Remove the nut securing the FBH exhaust pipe to the heater mounting bracket. Unscrew the three bolts securing the heater to its mounting bracket, and lift it out (only one of the three bolts need be removed, as the other two have slotted fixings). Loosen the exhaust pipe clamp bolt on the base of the heater, and separate the pipe from the heater.

63 Refitting is a reversal of removal, noting the following points:

a) Reconnect the fuel and coolant hoses correctly and securely.

b) On completion, fill and bleed the cooling system as described in Chapter 1B. Check the operation of the heater, and for signs of leaks from the disturbed connections.

Fuel-burning heater pump

64 The fuel pump which supplies the fuel-burning heater is mounted under the rear of the car on the right-hand side.

65 Chock the front wheels, then jack up the rear of the car, and support it on axle stands (see *Jacking and vehicle support*).

66 Disconnect the wiring multi-plug from the pump.

67 Anticipating some fuel spillage, release the clips and disconnect the hoses from the pump. Plug or cap the hoses to reduce further fuel loss, and to prevent dirt entry.

68 Release the pump from its rubber mountings, or remove the two nuts and take it off with its mounting bracket.

69 Refitting is a reversal of removal.

10 Air conditioning system – general information and precautions

General information

An air conditioning system is fitted to several models. The system enables the temperature of incoming air to be lowered, and it also dehumidifies the air, which makes for rapid demisting and increased comfort.

The cooling side of the system works in the same way as a domestic refrigerator. Refrigerant gas is drawn into a belt-driven compressor, and passes into a condenser mounted on the front of the radiator, where it loses heat and becomes liquid. The liquid passes through an expansion valve to an evaporator, where it changes from liquid under high pressure to gas under low pressure. This change is accompanied by a drop in temperature, which cools the evaporator. The refrigerant returns to the compressor, and the cycle begins again.

The radiator cooling fan is operated through the fan control unit where necessary (for example, when the car is stationary) to maintain airflow over the condenser. Air blown through the evaporator passes to the air distribution unit and then into the passenger compartment.

The heating side of the system works in the same way as on models without air conditioning.

The system is electronically-controlled. Any problems with the system should be referred to an automotive air conditioning specialist **(see Tool tip)**.

TOOL TiP

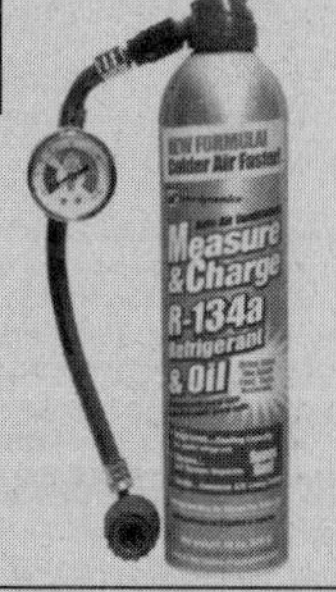

Many car accessory shops sell one-shot air conditioning recharge aerosols. These generally contain refrigerant, compressor oil, leak sealer and system conditioner. Some also have a dye to help pinpoint leaks.

Warning: These products must only be used as directed by the manufacturer, and do not remove the need for regular maintenance.

Precautions

• With an air conditioning system, it is necessary to observe special precautions whenever dealing with any part of the system, or its associated components. If for any reason the system must be disconnected, entrust this task to a refrigeration engineer.

Warning: The refrigeration circuit contains a liquid refrigerant which is potentially dangerous, and should only be handled by qualified persons. If it is splashed onto the skin, it can cause frostbite. It is not itself poisonous, but in the presence of a naked flame (including a cigarette), it forms a poisonous gas. Uncontrolled discharging of the refrigerant is dangerous, and potentially damaging to the environment. For all these reasons, it is dangerous to disconnect any part of the system without specialised knowledge and equipment.

• Do not operate the air conditioning system if it is known to be short of refrigerant, as this may damage the compressor.

11 Air conditioning system components – removal and refitting

Warning: The air conditioning system must be professionally discharged before carrying out most of the following work. Cap or plug the pipe lines as soon as they are disconnected to prevent the entry of moisture.

Compressor

1 Have the air conditioning system discharged by a qualified refrigeration engineer.
2 Remove the auxiliary drivebelt(s) as described in Chapter 1A or 1B.

1.8 litre engines

3 Loosen and remove the pipe flange bolts, and separate the two pipes from the compressor. Recover the O-ring seals – new ones must be used when refitting. Plug or tape over the open connections.
4 Disconnect the compressor wiring plug.
5 Remove the three compressor mounting bolts, then manoeuvre the compressor out and down through the wheel arch.
6 Refitting is a reversal of removal, noting the following points:

a) If a new compressor is being fitted, it should be supplied filled with refrigerant oil – if not, consult a refrigeration specialist and have it filled before fitting.
b) Use new O-ring seals on the refrigerant pipes, lubricated with a little refrigerant oil, and tighten the flange bolts to the specified torque.
c) Tighten the compressor mounting bolts to the specified torque.
d) Refit the auxiliary drivebelts as described in Chapter 1A.
e) The manufacturers recommend that a new desiccant pack is fitted whenever the system is opened – this procedure is described later in this Section.
f) Have the system professionally recharged on completion.

V6 engines

7 Remove the engine undertray, which is secured by a number of quick-release screw fasteners.
8 Remove the oil cooler's two mounting bolts, and release the cooler from the sump – this should provide access to the compressor mounting bolts from below **(see illustration)**.
9 Disconnect the compressor wiring plug.
10 Remove the two compressor upper mounting bolts, which also secure the compressor heat shield. Note how the heat shield is fitted as it is removed.
11 Loosen and remove the pipe flange bolts, and separate the two pipes from the compressor. Recover the O-ring seals – new ones must be used when refitting. Plug or tape over the open connections.

11.8 Unscrew the oil cooler mounting bolts

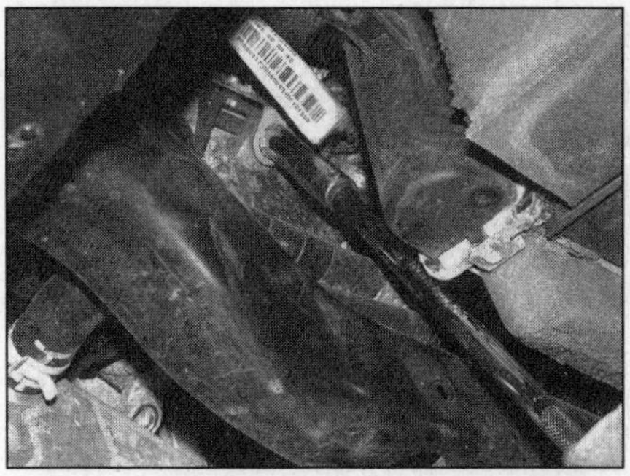

11.12 Removing the compressor lower mounting bolt

12 Remove the compressor lower mounting bolt **(see illustration)**, then manoeuvre the compressor out and down through the wheel arch.
13 Refitting is a reversal of removal, noting the following points:

a) If a new compressor is being fitted, it should be supplied filled with refrigerant oil – if not, consult a refrigeration specialist and have it filled before fitting.
b) Use new O-ring seals on the refrigerant pipes, lubricated with a little refrigerant oil, and tighten the flange bolts to the specified torque.
c) Tighten the compressor mounting bolts and oil cooler bolts to the specified torque.
d) Refit the auxiliary drivebelt as described in Chapter 1A.
e) The manufacturers recommend that a new desiccant pack is fitted whenever the system is opened – this procedure is described later in this Section.
f) Have the system professionally recharged on completion.

Diesel engines

14 Loosen and remove the pipe flange bolts, and separate the two pipes from the compressor. Recover the O-ring seals – new ones must be used when refitting. Plug or tape over the open connections.
15 Loosen the bolt securing the compressor support strap to the sump.
16 Remove the three mounting bolts, and remove the compressor from its mounting bracket. Move the sump support strap to one side, then disconnect the wiring plug and remove the unit.
17 Refitting is a reversal of removal, noting the following points:

a) If a new compressor is being fitted, it should be supplied filled with refrigerant oil – if not, consult a refrigeration specialist and have it filled before fitting.
b) Use new O-ring seals on the refrigerant pipes, lubricated with a little refrigerant oil, and tighten the flange bolts to the specified torque.
c) Tighten the compressor mounting bolts and sump support strap bolt to the specified torque.
d) Refit the auxiliary drivebelts as described in Chapter 1B.
e) The manufacturers recommend that a new desiccant pack is fitted whenever the system is opened – this procedure is described later in this Section.
f) Have the system professionally recharged on completion.

Condenser

18 Have the air conditioning system discharged by a qualified refrigeration engineer.
19 Remove the radiator as described in Section 3.
20 Remove the two bolts (petrol engines) or four bolts (diesel engines) from the fan cowl. Release the two metal clips on the base, and separate the radiator from the cowl.
21 Remove the two upper bolts securing the condenser to the radiator, then lift it off its mountings and remove it **(see illustrations)**.

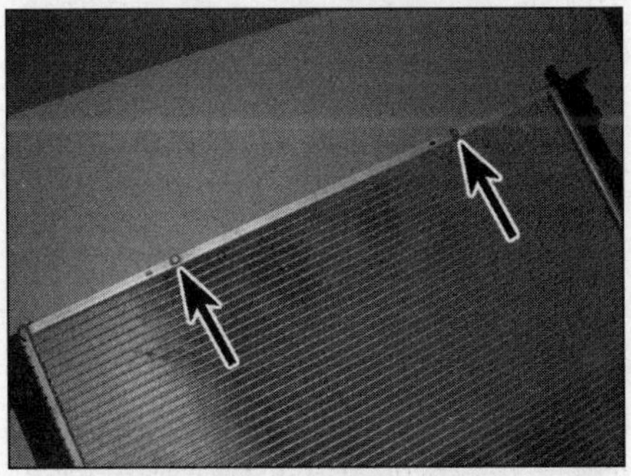

11.21a Condenser-to-radiator mounting bolts

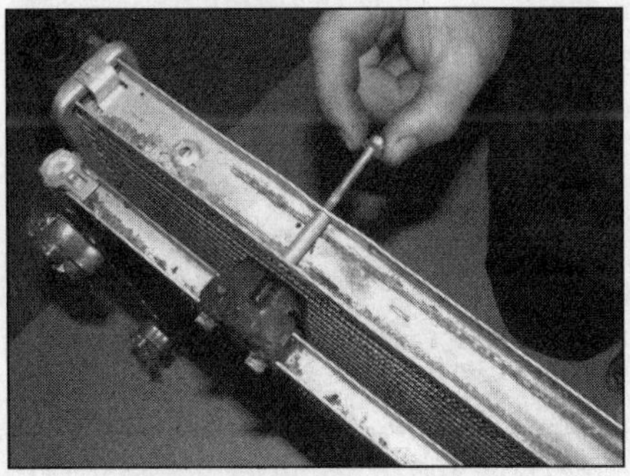

11.21b Remove the bolts . . .

11.21c . . . and lift off the condenser

11.24a Using a suitable Allen key or socket . . .

11.24b . . . unscrew the desiccant pack access plug

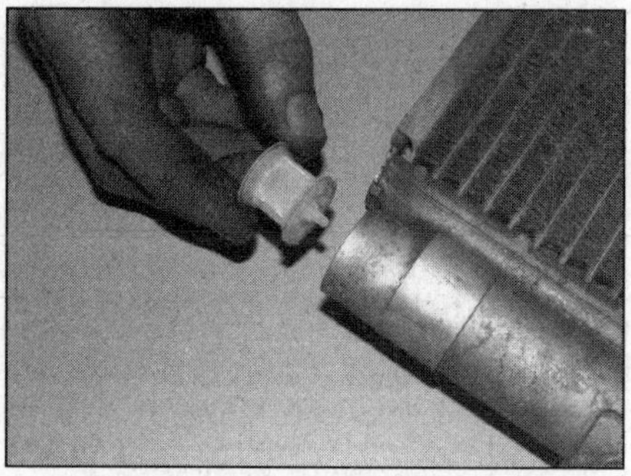

11.25a Extract the filter . . .

22 Refitting is a reversal of removal, noting the following points:

a) The manufacturers recommend that a new desiccant pack is fitted whenever the system is opened – this procedure is described later in this Section.

b) Use new O-ring seals on the refrigerant pipes, lubricated with a little refrigerant oil, and tighten the flange bolts to the specified torque.

c) Refit the radiator as described in Section 3.

d) Have the system professionally recharged on completion.

Desiccant pack

23 Remove the condenser as described previously in this Section.

24 Unscrew the Allen-headed plug from the base of the drier housing on the right-hand side of the condenser **(see illustration)**. Recover the O-ring seals – new ones should be used when refitting.

25 Extract the filter and the desiccant pack from the drier housing – note which way up the desiccant pack is fitted **(see illustrations)**.

26 Do not remove the new desiccant pack from its packaging until just prior to fitting.

27 Insert the new pack into the housing, with the double-layer thickness at the bottom **(see illustration)**.

28 Fit the new filter.

29 Lubricate the new O-rings with a little refrigerant oil, then fit them to the plug, and tighten the plug to the specified torque.

30 Further refitting is a reversal of removal. On completion, have the air conditioning system recharged by a refrigeration specialist.

Trinary pressure switch

31 The switch is located in the refrigerant pipe at the right-hand rear corner of the engine compartment, near the bulkhead (right as seen from the driver's seat) **(see illustration)**.

32 Have the air conditioning system discharged by a qualified refrigeration engineer.

33 Disconnect the wiring plug on top of the switch.

34 Unscrew the switch using a suitable deep socket, and recover the O-ring – a new one will be needed for refitting. Plug or tape over the open connection.

35 Refitting is a reversal of removal, noting the following points:

a) Use a new O-ring, lubricated with a little refrigerant oil.

b) Tighten the switch to the specified torque.

c) Have the system professionally recharged on completion.

Exterior temperature sensor

36 Jack up the front of the car, and support it on axle stands (see *Jacking and vehicle support*).

37 Remove the fasteners from the front of the engine undertray, and lower the tray for access to the sensor.

38 The sensor is fitted below the front bumper, behind the lower grille **(see illustration)**.

39 The sensor slides onto a moulded tab, and is released using a small screwdriver. Disconnect the wiring plug and remove the sensor **(see illustration)**.

40 Refitting is a reversal of removal.

11.25b . . . and the old desiccant pack

11.27 Fitting the new desiccant pack

11.31 Trinary pressure switch location

11.38 The exterior temperature sensor is mounted behind the bumper grille

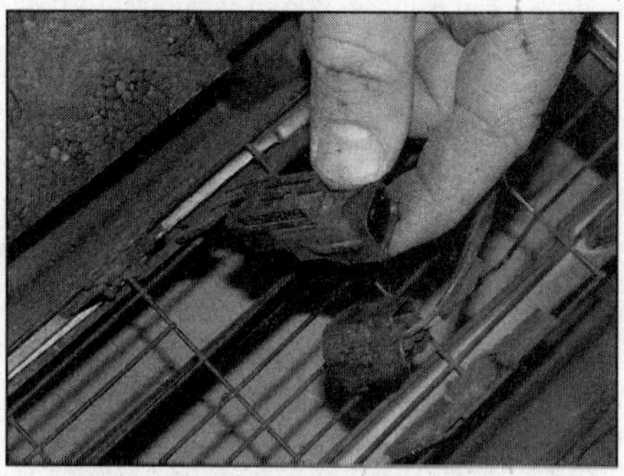

11.39 Removing the temperature sensor

11.45 Disconnecting the temperature control motor

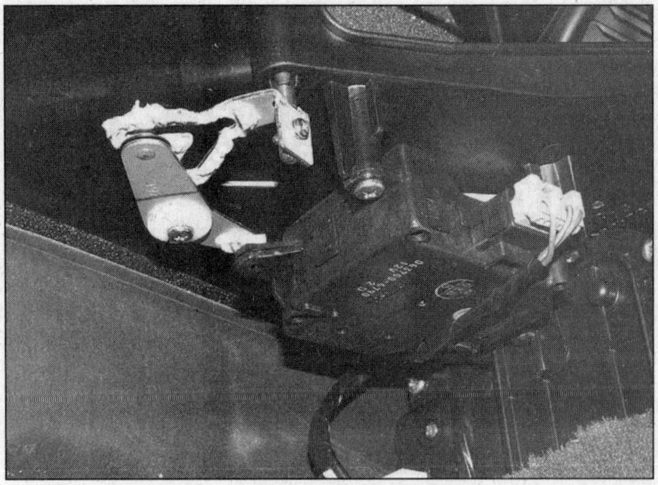

11.46 Recirculation control motor

Cabin sun sensor

41 The sun sensor has a domed cover, and is fitted to the top of the facia, between the windscreen vents.

42 Using a small screwdriver, and taking care not to damage the sensor or the facia, carefully prise the sensor either side to release the clips, and lift it out.

43 Disconnect the wiring plug from the sensor. Use tape to secure the plug to the facia, otherwise it will fall down inside the facia, and be difficult to retrieve.

44 Refitting is a reversal of removal.

Control motors

Temperature motor

45 The temperature motor is located on the right-hand side of the heater unit, above the matrix, and is accessed after removing the driver's footwell left-hand trim panel, as described in Chapter 11, Section 25 **(see illustration)**.

Recirculation motor

46 The recirculation motor is on the same side as the temperature motor, but is fitted vertically underneath the heater unit **(see illustration)**.

Distribution motor

47 The distribution motor is on the right-hand side of the heater unit – remove the driver's footwell left-hand trim panel as described in Chapter 11, Section 25 **(see illustration)**.

All motors

48 Removal and refitting details are almost identical for all the motors **(see illustrations)**:

a) *Disconnect the wiring plug.*
b) *Remove the three mounting screws.*
c) *Withdraw the motor, unhooking the operating rod from the lever.*
d) *Refitting is a reversal of removal. Check for correct operation before refitting any removed trim.*

Evaporator

49 Have the air conditioning system discharged by a qualified refrigeration engineer.

50 Remove the windscreen cowl panels as described in Chapter 11.

51 Disconnect the two refrigerant pipes at the bulkhead – each is secured by a single bolt. **Do not** disturb the pipes unless the system has been discharged first (see Section 10) – for maximum personal safety, have these pipes disconnected by the engineer who discharges the system for you, and ensure the system is kept switched off afterwards. Each pipe has an O-ring seal fitted, which must be renewed when reconnecting. Plug the open pipes to prevent contamination of the system.

52 Remove the side trim and the facia closing panel from both front footwells, as described in Chapter 11, Section 25, to give access to both sides of the heater unit.

53 Remove the screw securing the pipe assembly for the thermostatic expansion valve, on the right-hand side of the heater unit. Unwrap the insulation, then unscrew the two

11.47 Distribution motor

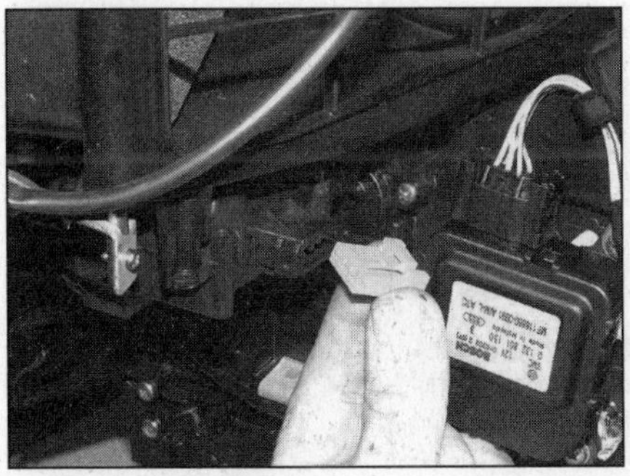

11.48a Disconnect the wiring plug . . .

11.48b . . . then remove the mounting screws . . .

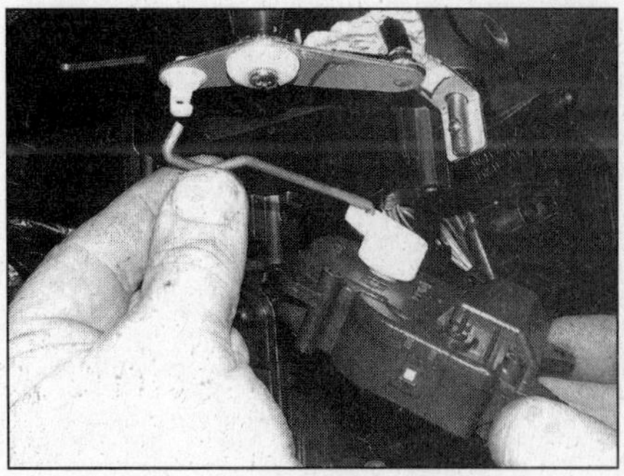

11.48c . . . and unhook the motor operating rod

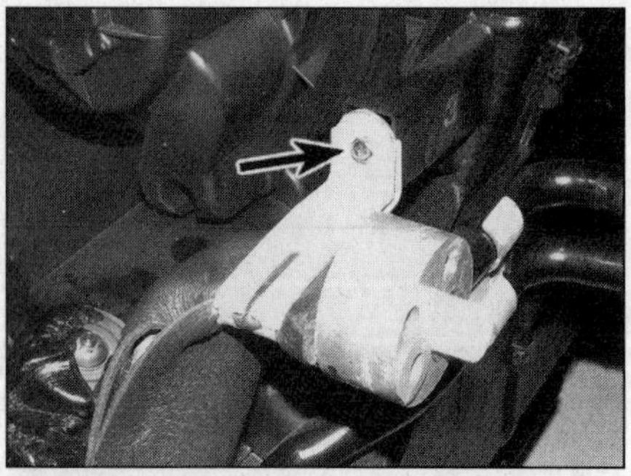

11.53a Remove the pipe support bracket screw . . .

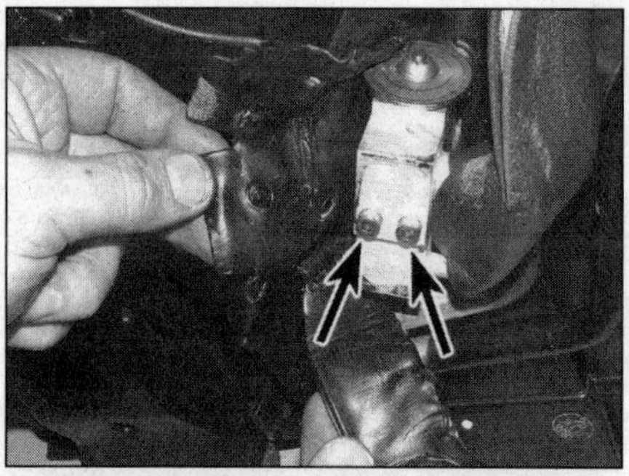

11.53b . . . then unwrap the insulation to access the two lower bolts . . .

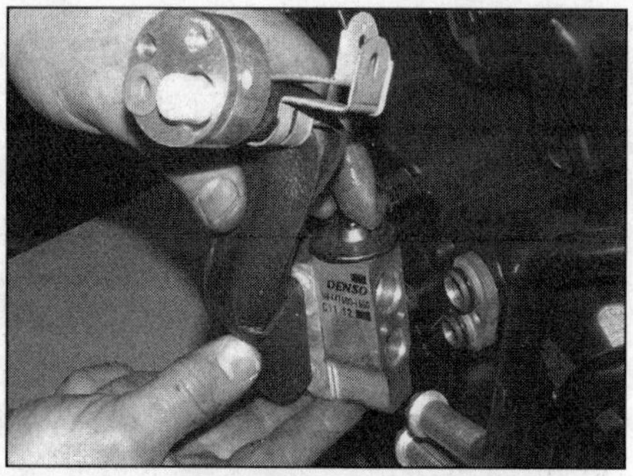

11.53c . . . and remove the thermostatic expansion valve

11.53d Renew the O-rings (arrowed)

Allen bolts securing the pipe assembly to the evaporator. Withdraw the pipes, recovering the O-rings (which must be renewed on reassembly) and the thermostatic expansion valve **(see illustrations)**.

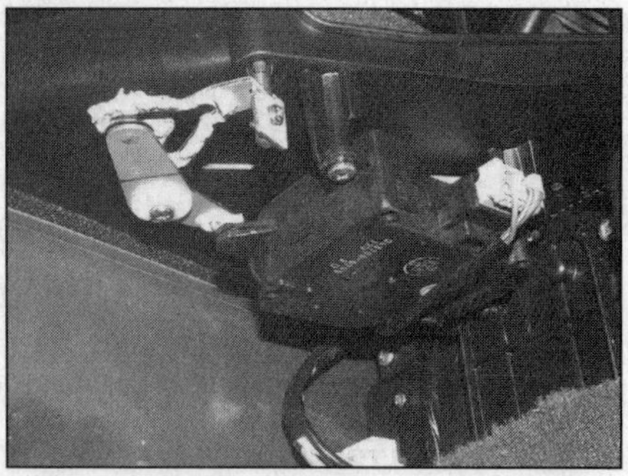

11.55 Unbolt and remove the recirculation control motor

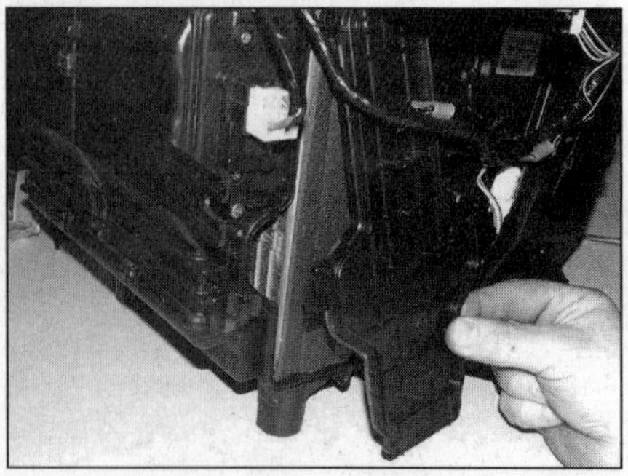

11.58 Unscrew and remove the evaporator access panel

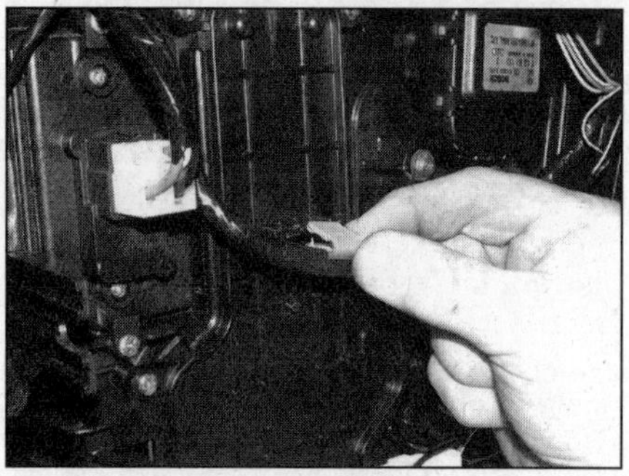

11.54 Unclip the wiring from the evaporator access panel

54 Unclip the heater wiring harness where it passes in front of the evaporator access panel **(see illustration)**.

55 Remove the three screws securing the air recirculation control motor to the underside of the heater unit. Move the motor to one side **(see illustration)**.

56 On models with automatic transmission or cruise control, unscrew the two bolts securing the ECU mounting bracket under the heater unit, and move the ECU clear.

57 Unclip and disconnect the evaporator temperature sensor wiring plug **(see illustration)**.

58 Remove the six screws securing the evaporator access panel, and remove it **(see illustration)**.

59 Slide out the evaporator, noting that the temperature sensor is clipped to the back of it. Recover the O-rings from the inner end and discard them – new ones should be used when refitting. If a new evaporator is being fitted, unclip the temperature sensor, and transfer it to the new unit **(see illustrations)**.

60 Refitting is a reversal of removal, noting the following points:

a) The manufacturers recommend that a new desiccant pack is fitted whenever the system is opened – this procedure is described earlier in this Section.

b) Use new O-ring seals on the evaporator, refrigerant pipes and thermostatic expansion valve, lubricated with a little refrigerant oil. Tighten the flange bolts to the specified torque.

c) Have the system professionally recharged on completion.

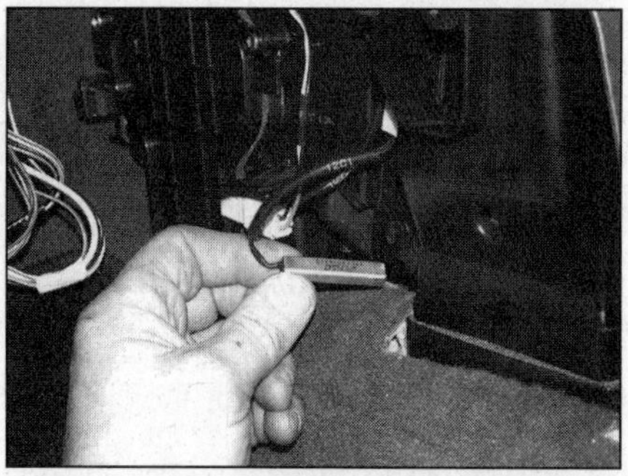

11.57 Disconnect the evaporator temperature sensor

11.59a Slide out the evaporator . . .

Auxiliary heater

61 This is an electric heater element fitted to the base of the main heater assembly.

11.59b . . . and unclip the temperature sensor from it

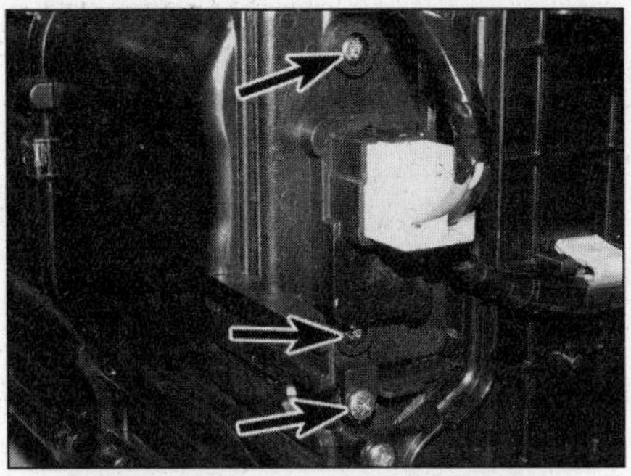
11.63a Remove the end cover screws . . .

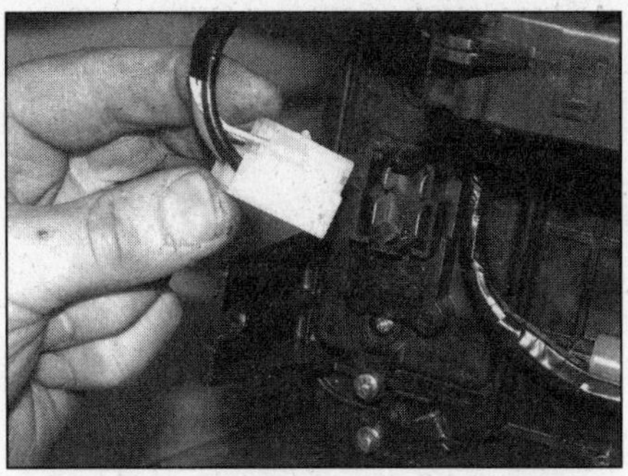
11.63b . . . then disconnect the wiring plug . . .

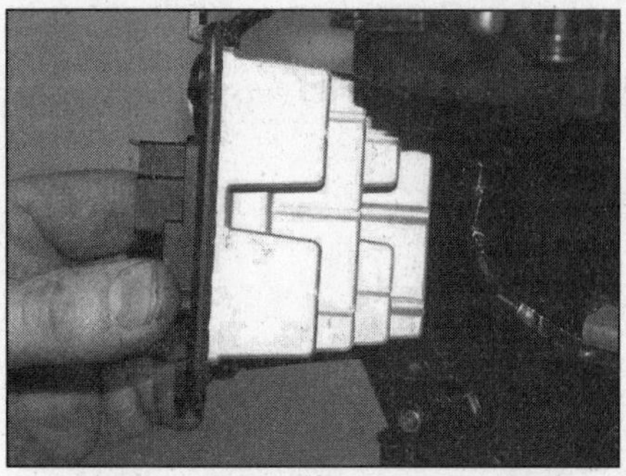
11.63c . . . and withdraw the auxiliary heater

It provides 'instant' heat from cold when required, and will also be employed to supplement the heat from the main heater matrix as necessary, to maintain the selected cabin temperature.

62 The auxiliary heater is located just in front of the evaporator. Remove the passenger footwell side trim and facia closing panels as described in Chapter 11, Section 25.

63 Remove the end cover screws, then disconnect the wiring plug, and withdraw the heater into the footwell **(see illustrations)**.

64 Refitting is a reversal of removal.

Fan control unit

65 The radiator cooling fan is used by the air conditioning system to maintain the flow of cool air into the car when stationary. A control unit is fitted to the rear of the radiator fan cowl.

66 Remove the radiator as described in Section 3, and separate it from the fan cowl.

67 Squeeze the two clips at the top, and release the control unit from the fan cowl **(see illustration)**. Trace the wiring harness back, unclipping it from the cowl, and finally remove the unit.

68 Unclipping the unit cover gives access to the wiring and relays inside **(see illustrations)**. At the time of writing, it appears that the unit it only available complete.

69 Refitting is a reversal of removal.

11.67 Squeeze the top clips to release the unit

11.68a Prise the lugs to release the cover . . .

11.68b . . . for access to the wiring and relays inside

Chapter 4 Part A:
Fuel & exhaust systems – 1.8 litre engines

Contents

Degrees of difficulty

Easy, suitable for novice with little experience	**Fairly easy,** suitable for beginner with some experience	**Fairly difficult,** suitable for competent DIY mechanic	**Difficult,** suitable for experienced DIY mechanic	**Very difficult,** suitable for expert DIY or professional

Specifications

General

System type	Motorola modular engine management system (MEMS 3) sequential multi-point fuel injection system, returnless fuel rail, integrated with ignition system

Fuel pump

Type	Electric roller vane pump in fuel tank
Operating pressure:	
Non-turbo models	3.5 bar
Turbo models	4.45 bar

Turbocharger

Type	Garrett GT2052LS

Idle settings (for reference only)

Idle speed	750 ± 50 rpm
Idle mixture (CO content)	Less than 0.5 %

Torque wrench settings

Torque wrench settings	Nm	lbf ft
Air cleaner mounting bracket	45	33
Air conditioning compressor mounting bolts	25	18
Alternator heat shield bolts	45	33
Alternator mounting bracket bolts	25	18
Camshaft position sensor bolt	10	7
Engine lower mounting through-bolts	100	74
Engine oil temperature sensor	14	10
Exhaust clamp nuts	48	35
Exhaust cross-brace bolts	25	18
Exhaust front pipe flange nuts	75	55
Exhaust manifold nuts	45	33
Exhaust support strap nuts/bolts	22	16
Fuel rail-to-manifold bolts	9	7
Fuel tank mounting bolts	24	18
Fuel tank unit locking ring	38	28
Inlet manifold nuts/bolts	17	13
Oxygen sensors	55	41
Power steering pressure switch	24	18
Rear subframe mounting bolts	100	74
Throttle body-to-inlet manifold bolts	9	7
Turbocharger-to-manifold nuts	45	33
Turbocharger oil feed pipe banjo bolt	18	13

1 General information and precautions

General information

The fuel and ignition systems are controlled by the Modular Engine Management System (MEMS 3). For more information on the ignition side of the system, refer to Chapter 5B, but note that most of the system sensors are deemed to have a dual role, and will be covered in this Chapter.

Fuel is supplied from the rear-mounted fuel tank by an electric pump mounted in the tank, via a tank-mounted pressure regulator and fuel filter, to the fuel rail. Unlike many earlier injection systems, no fuel return system is fitted. The fuel rail acts as a reservoir for the four fuel injectors, which inject fuel onto the back of the inlet valves. A pressure damper is fitted to the rail, to minimise the effect of pressure fluctuations.

The injectors operate sequentially in firing order, with fuel being injected during each cylinder's induction stroke. The injectors are electronically controlled by the Engine Control Module (ECM). Each injector has a solenoid which, when energised by a pulse from the ECM, lifts the injector needle and fuel is sprayed into the cylinder. The duration of the pulse determines the length of time the needle is lifted and, therefore, the amount of fuel injected. Pulse duration is calculated by the ECM, and is constantly varying to match engine operating and ambient conditions.

The fuelling and ignition timing calculation is based on information supplied to the ECM by the following sensors:

a) *Throttle position sensor (TP) – mounted on the throttle body, the sensor provides a signal representing the amount and rate of throttle opening – ie, driver demand.*
b) *Crankshaft position sensor (CKP) – supplies a signal representing the speed and angular position of the crankshaft.*
c) *Camshaft position sensor (CMP) – attached to the camshaft cover, the sensor provides a signal representing the angular position of the camshaft, in relation to the angular position of the crankshaft.*
d) *Manifold absolute pressure (MAP) – located in the intake manifold, supplies a signal representing the air pressure in the inlet manifold, which is used to determine the amount of air entering the cylinders. Turbo models have a TMAP sensor, which additionally provides air temperature information.*
e) *Inlet air temperature (IAT) – only fitted to non-turbo models, this provides inlet air temperature information.*
f) *Engine coolant temperature (ECT) – located in the coolant outlet elbow from the cylinder head. The sensor provides a coolant temperature signal.*
g) *Engine oil temperature – (EOT) located on the oil filter housing, the sensor supplies an oil temperature signal.*
h) *Oxygen sensors – one is located in the exhaust manifold, upstream of the catalytic converter, with later models having a second sensor located in the exhaust pipe, downstream of the converter. The sensors provide signals representing the amount of oxygen in the exhaust gas, and allow the ECM to precisely control the air/fuel ratio around the ideal combustion ratio of 14.7:1.*

Idle speed is controlled by the ECM via an Idle Air Control Valve (IACV), which varies the amount of air bypassing the throttle valve.

On turbocharged models, an ECM-controlled solenoid valve mounted on the airbox regulates the turbo boost pressure.

Information on engine loads, such as the power steering and air conditioning systems, is provided by the power steering pressure sensor and by the ambient air temperature sensor. Vehicle speed information is provided to the ECM from the four ABS wheel sensors

Failure of certain sensors – either complete loss of signal, or sending an abnormal signal, will cause the ECM to default to preprogrammed values. In most cases this will be noticeable as poor or erratic engine performance, and the engine management warning light on the instrument panel will come on. If the crankshaft position (CKP) sensor signal is lost, the engine will not run. Whenever a sensor fault occurs, a fault code is stored in a memory of the ECM. Using specialist diagnostic equipment, the codes can be extracted so that the problem can be isolated.

All models are fitted with a fuel inertia cut-off switch (see Section 11), which cuts off the fuel supply in the event of the car being involved in an impact – the interior lights will be on all the time until the switch is reset. The engine cannot be started if the switch is activated – the switch must be reset manually.

Precautions

- Before disconnecting any fuel lines, or working on any part of the fuel system, the system must be depressurised as described in Section 7.
- Care must be taken when disconnecting the fuel lines. When disconnecting a fuel union or hose, loosen the union or clamp screw slowly, to avoid sudden uncontrolled fuel spillage. Take adequate fire precautions.
- When working on fuel system components,

scrupulous cleanliness must be observed, and care must be taken not to introduce any foreign matter into fuel lines or components.

- After carrying out any work involving disconnection of fuel lines, it is advisable to check the connections for leaks; pressurise the system by switching the ignition on and off several times.
- Before disconnecting any wiring, or removing components, always ensure at least that the ignition is switched off – better still, disconnect the battery. If this is not done, and a component is disconnected when 'live', it could be damaged – or a fault code may be stored, which would then have to be cleared to regain normal operation.
- Do not attempt to improvise fault diagnosis procedures using a test light or multi-meter, as irreparable damage could be caused to the module.

Warning: Many of the procedures in this Chapter require the disconnection of fuel line connections, and the removal of components, which may result in some fuel spillage. Before carrying out any operation on the fuel system, refer to the precautions given in 'Safety first!' at the beginning of this manual, and follow them implicitly. Petrol is a highly-dangerous and volatile liquid, and the precautions necessary when handling it cannot be overstressed.

2 Air cleaner assembly – removal and refitting

Non-turbo models

1 Remove the two screws at the back of the air cleaner cover, then lift the cover and take out the filter element.

2 Release the large hose clip and disconnect the throttle body inlet hose from the air cleaner cover – note that this clip may be a toothed plastic type, which may prove difficult to refit afterwards (use a Jubilee clip if preferred) **(see illustration)**. Release the cover at the front, and lift it off.

3 The air cleaner base can now be lifted out. It is located in two grommets at the rear, and must be released from the air intake duct at the front.

4 Refitting is a reversal of removal. Ensure that the hose clips are tightened securely, otherwise this will produce an air leak.

Turbo models

5 Pull off the small hose which supplies the boost control solenoid valve, then unclip and remove the valve from the air cleaner – if preferred, it can be removed completely (see Section 11).

6 Loosen the large hose clip on the front of the assembly, and disconnect the air inlet hose leading to the turbocharger **(see illustration)**. If the hose will be left disconnected for any length of time, plug the end with some clean rag – if foreign objects of any size fall inside, they may enter the turbo vanes, causing damage.

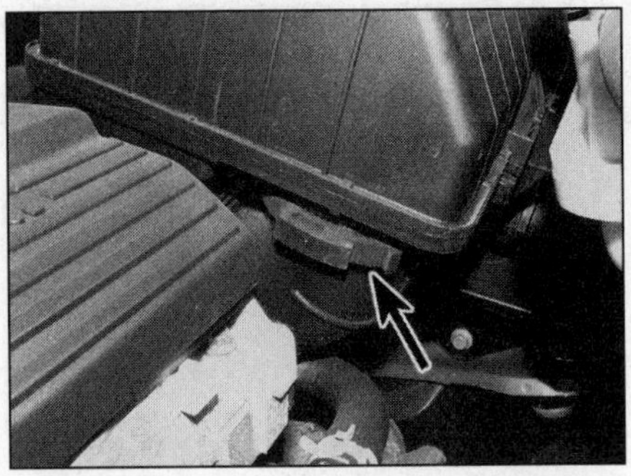

2.2 Air inlet hose clip may be of toothed plastic type

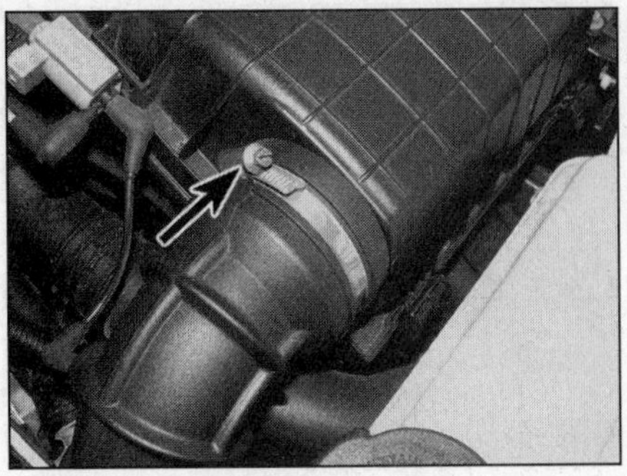

2.6 Air inlet hose clip – turbo models

7 The air cleaner can now be lifted out. It is located in two grommets at the rear, and must be released from the air intake duct at the front.

8 Refitting is a reversal of removal. Ensure that the hose clips are tightened securely, otherwise this will produce an air leak.

3 Fuel tank and filler neck – removal, inspection and refitting

Warning: This procedure should be carried out in a well-ventilated area, and it is vital to take adequate fire precautions – refer to 'Safety first!' for further details.

Fuel tank

Removal

1 Disconnect the battery negative lead, and move the lead away from the battery (see *Disconnecting the battery*).

2 Chock the front wheels, then jack up the rear of the car and support securely on axle stands (see *Jacking and vehicle support*).

3 Clearly, this operation is best performed when the fuel level in the tank is as low as possible. Working under the car, disconnect an accessible fuel line connection at the tank, and drain the remaining fuel into a suitable container – note that a tamperproof cover is fitted over the hose clip screw heads.

4 Using the information in Chapter 9, disconnect the handbrake cables at the front. Release them from under the car, and move them clear of the fuel tank.

5 Working as described in Section 17, either remove completely (or at least lower) the exhaust system for access to the tank.

6 If not already done, remove the hose clip's tamperproof cover, and loosen the clip at the base of the fuel filler hose where it joins the tank **(see illustration 3.24)**. Have a container ready to catch any fuel spillage, then disconnect the hose, recovering the two spacers. To avoid further fuel spillage as the tank is removed (and to prevent dirt entry), plug the open stub on the tank.

7 Place a trolley jack under the fuel tank, with a block of wood between the jack and the tank. If possible, try not to trap the fuel tank support cradle, so that this can be removed once the bolts have been unscrewed.

8 Progressively unscrew the four tank support cradle bolts (two in front, two behind) until the cradle is released from the car floor, and the tank is supported by the jack **(see illustration)**.

9 Lower the tank slightly, until access can be gained to its top surface. Disconnect the fuel pump multi-plug, then release a total of four clips from the rear edge which secure the breather and vent hoses. Trace the hoses to their tank connections, and disconnect them.

10 Unclip the fuel feed and charcoal canister pipes behind the tank **(see illustration)**.

3.8 One of the fuel tank support cradle bolts (arrowed)

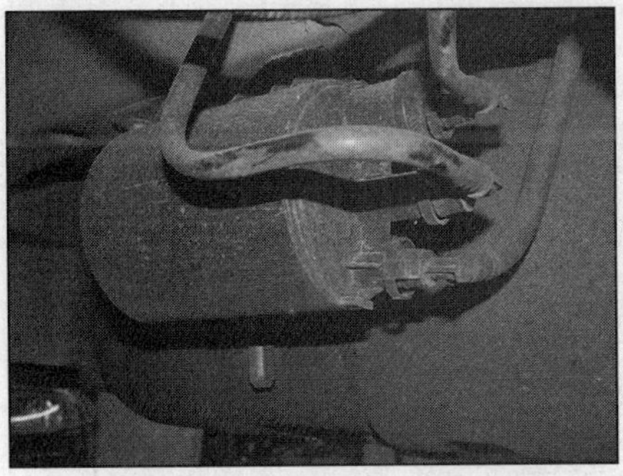

3.10 Disconnect the hoses from the charcoal canister behind the tank

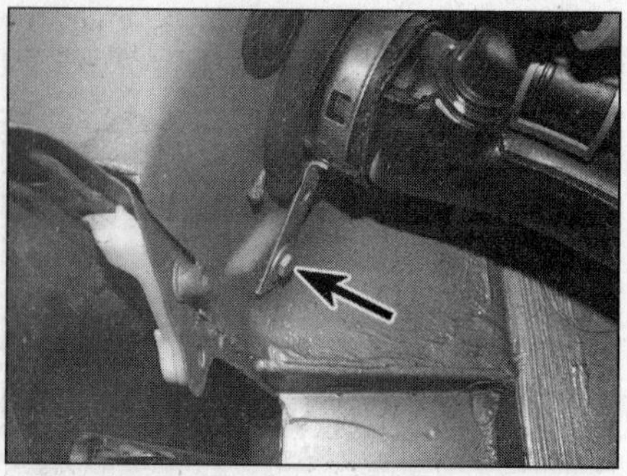

3.18a Remove the bolt from the grommet support collar

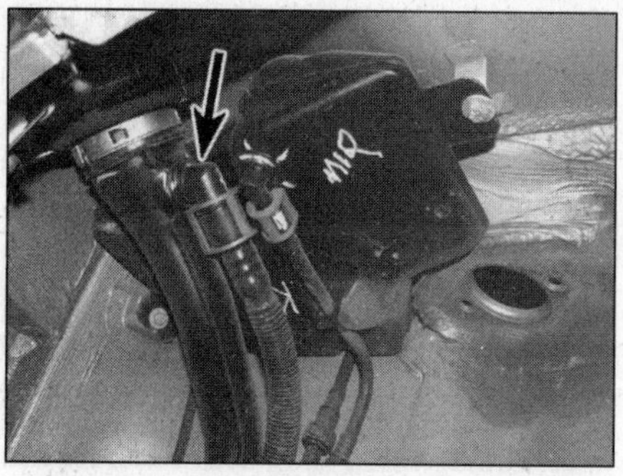

3.18b Disconnect the filler neck breather hose

3.20 One of the filler neck mounting bolts

3.24 Filler neck hose clip at fuel tank

11 Lower the tank further, checking all the while that nothing is still attached. If possible, have an assistant on hand to steady the tank on the jack as it is lowered, and to help manoeuvre the tank out from under the car.

Inspection

12 If the tank contains sediment or water, it may be cleaned out using two or three rinses with paraffin. Shake vigorously using several changes of paraffin, but before doing so remove the fuel pump/gauge sender unit (see Section 8).

13 Any repairs to the fuel tank should be carried out by a professional. Do not under any circumstances attempt to weld or solder a fuel tank. Removal of residual fuel vapour requires several hours of specialist cleaning.

Refitting

14 Refitting is a reversal of removal, but ensure that all hoses are reconnected to their correct locations as noted before removal, and use new hose clips if necessary.

Fuel filler neck

Removal

15 Disconnect the battery negative lead, and move the lead away from the battery (see *Disconnecting the battery*).

16 Loosen the right-hand rear wheel bolts. Chock the front wheels, then jack up the rear of the car and support securely on axle stands (see *Jacking and vehicle support*). Remove the right-hand rear roadwheel.

17 Remove the left-hand rear wheel arch liner as described in Chapter 11, Section 22.

18 From inside the wheel arch, remove the small bolt securing the filler neck grommet support collar. Disconnect the main breather hose from the filler neck **(see illustrations)**.

19 Remove the fuel filler cap, then release the filler neck's rubber grommet.

20 Unscrew the remaining bolt securing the filler neck to the wheel arch **(see illustration)**.

21 Using a suitable trolley jack with a block of wood on top, support the weight of the rear suspension subframe.

22 Loosen the single bolt at the rear of the subframe on each side, until the bolts are only in by a few threads. Lower the jack supporting the subframe until the filler neck's two lower bolts are accessible.

23 Unscrew and remove the filler neck's two lower bolts, and release the neck.

24 Have a container ready below the filler neck to catch any fuel spillage. Remove the tamperproof cap from each of the two filler neck hose clips, then loosen the clips and disconnect the hose from the tank – the filler neck can now be removed completely **(see illustration)**. Where applicable, recover the hose spacers.

Refitting

25 Refitting is a reversal of removal, noting the following points:

a) Tighten the hose clips securely – use new ones if necessary.

b) Tighten the rear subframe bolts to the specified torque.

4 Fuel filler flap release solenoid – removal and refitting

1 Remove the right-hand trim panel from the boot as described in Chapter 11, Section 25.

2 Open the fuel filler flap, then pull off the rubber collar from the plastic nut. Turn the plastic nut a quarter-turn, and remove it **(see illustrations)**.

3 Back in the boot, the solenoid can now be turned anti-clockwise to release the bayonet fitting, and the solenoid can be withdrawn into the boot **(see illustration)**.

4 Disconnect the wiring plug, and remove the solenoid.

5 Refitting is a reversal of removal. Fit the mounting nut loosely, then offer the solenoid back into position. Locate the nut in its slotted hole, then tighten it securely from outside.

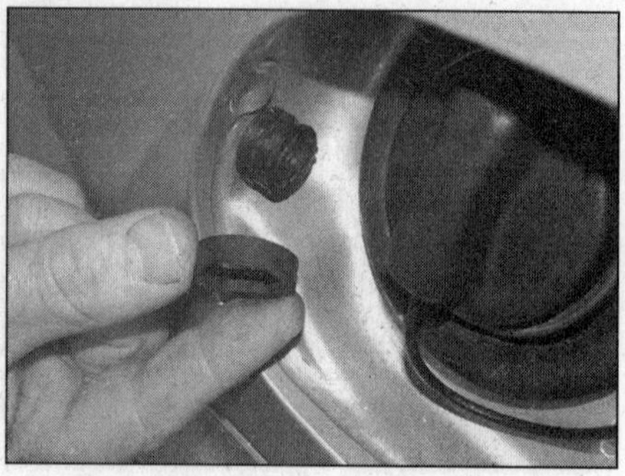

4.2a Pull off the rubber collar . . .

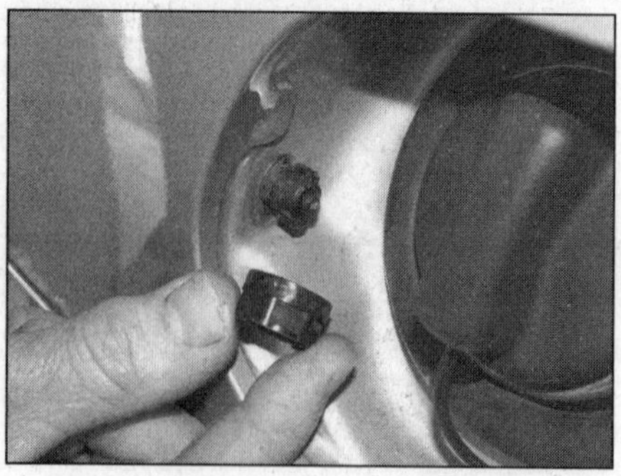

4.2b . . . then unscrew the plastic nut

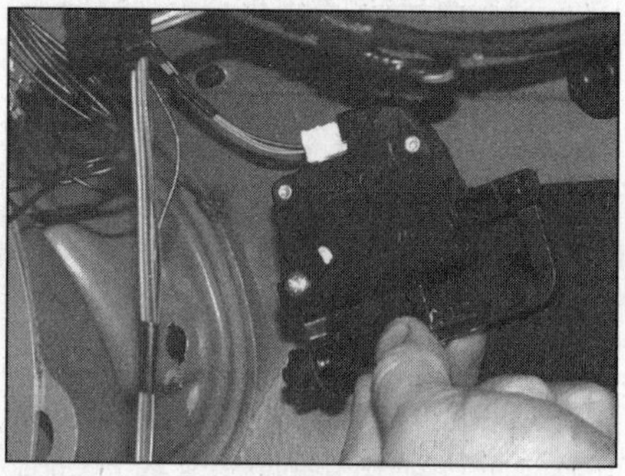

4.3 Turn the solenoid to release the fitting, and remove

5.1 Accelerator cable adjuster on the inlet manifold

5 Accelerator cable – removal, refitting and adjustment

Removal

1 Slide the cable adjuster from the bracket on the throttle body/inlet manifold **(see illustration)**.

2 Slide the cable end fitting from the groove in the throttle lever, and disconnect the cable from the lever.

3 Release the cable from the clip on the inlet manifold.

4 Working at the engine compartment bulkhead, turn the collar on the accelerator cable through 90°, and release the cable from the bulkhead.

5 Remove the trim panel fitted above the pedals, which is secured by two screws at the top, and two push-fasteners at the bottom.

6 Reach up under the facia, and pull the end of the cable forwards from the pedal, then squeeze the securing lugs and remove the plastic cable securing clip from the end of the pedal. Release the end of the cable from the pedal **(see illustration)**.

7 Pull the cable through the bulkhead into the engine compartment, and withdraw the cable from the car.

Refitting

8 Refitting is a reversal of removal, but smear the bulkhead grommet with rubber grease and, on completion, check the cable adjustment as described in the following paragraphs.

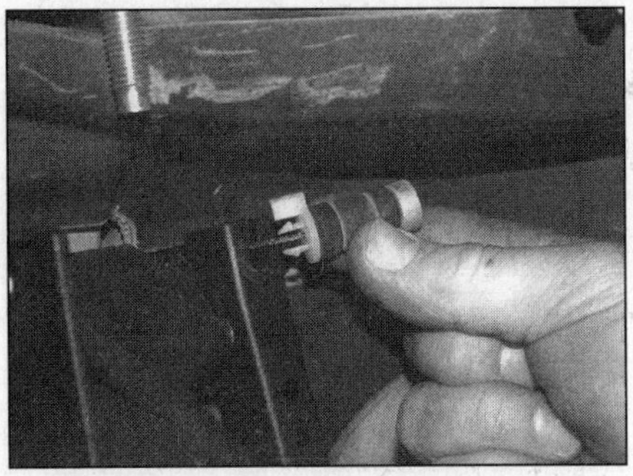

5.6 Pull out the cable end fitting, and unhook from the pedal

Adjustment

9 Slide the cable adjuster from the bracket on the inlet manifold/throttle body, then position the cable's square adjuster against the rear of the bracket.

10 Hold the throttle lever on the throttle body in the fully closed position, ensuring that the cam on the throttle lever rests against the throttle stop screw.

11 Turn the cable adjuster as necessary until all freeplay is removed from the cable, without moving the throttle lever.

12 Slide the adjuster back into position in the bracket.

13 Have an assistant fully depress the throttle pedal, and check that the throttle lever moves to the fully open position, and returns to the fully closed position when the pedal is released.

6 Accelerator pedal – removal and refitting

Removal

1 Remove the trim panel fitted above the pedals, which is secured by two screws at the top, and two push-fasteners at the bottom.

2 Disconnect the end of the accelerator cable from the pedal as described in Section 5.

3 Using a suitable pair of pliers, unhook the return spring from the pedal **(see illustration)**.

4 Working at the left-hand side of the pedal pivot shaft, prise off the securing clip, then slide the pedal assembly from the mounting bracket towards the right-hand side of the car, until it can be removed **(see illustrations)**.

Refitting

5 Refitting is a reversal of removal, but make sure that the securing clip is securely refitted.

7 Fuel injection system – depressurising

Warning: The following procedure will merely relieve the pressure in the fuel system – remember that fuel will still be present in the system components, and take precautions accordingly before disconnecting any of them.

1 The fuel system referred to in this Chapter is defined as the fuel tank and tank-mounted fuel pump/fuel gauge sender unit, the fuel injectors, and the metal pipes and flexible hoses of the fuel lines between these components. All these contain fuel, which will be under pressure while the engine is running and/or while the ignition is switched on.

2 The pressure will remain for some time after the ignition has been switched off, and must be relieved before any of these components is disturbed for servicing work.

3 The simplest depressurisation method is to disconnect the fuel pump electrical supply by removing the fuel pump fuse (make sure the ignition is off – typically, it's fuse number 20) and starting the engine. Allow the engine to idle until it stops through lack of fuel. If it won't start, turn the engine over once or twice on the starter to ensure that all pressure is released. Switch off the ignition on completion. Remember to refit the fuse when work is complete – the ignition must be off when this is done.

4 Before opening the fuel system, **always** disconnect the battery negative lead, and move the lead away from the battery (see *Disconnecting the battery*).

5 When opening any high-pressure fuel union, wrap absorbent cloth around the union, then **slowly** slacken the union nut. Allow the fuel

6.3 Unhook the accelerator pedal return spring

6.4a Prise off the pivot shaft clip . . .

6.4b . . . then slide the pedal off sideways

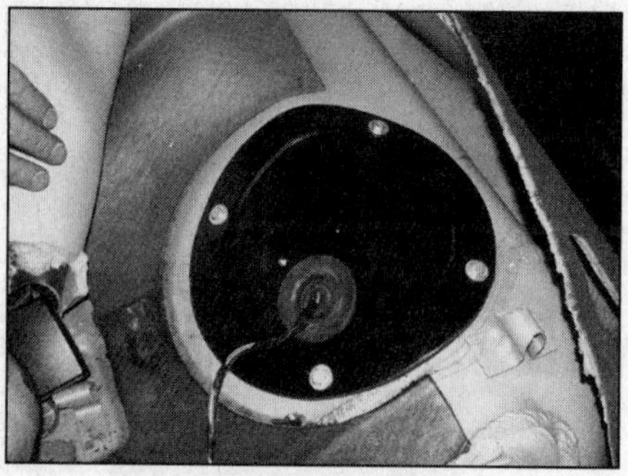

8.4a Pull back the carpet and soundproofing, then remove four screws . . .

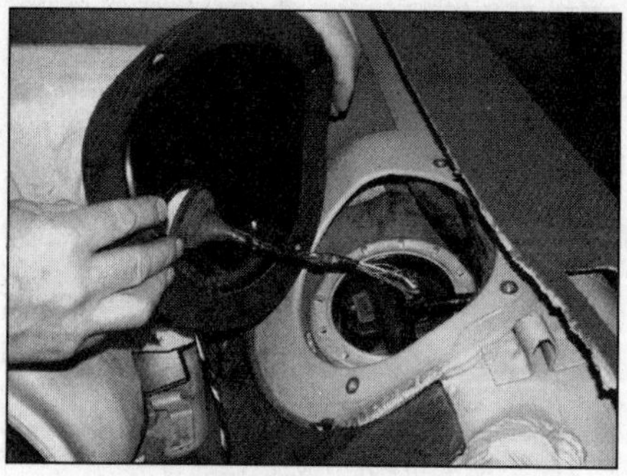

8.4b . . . and lift up the access plate, releasing the wiring grommet

8.5 Disconnect the wiring plug from the top of the pump

pressure to dissipate, then retighten the union nut.

6 Note that, once the fuel system has been depressurised and drained (even partially), it will take significantly longer to restart the engine – perhaps several seconds of cranking – before the system is refilled and pressure restored. To avoid this, the system can be 'primed' before starting by switching the ignition on a few times – each time this is done, the fuel pump should be heard running for a short time. If the pump does not stop running, this may indicate a leak in the system – investigate before starting the engine.

8 Fuel pump/fuel gauge sender unit – removal and refitting

Note: *Refer to the precautions in Section 1 before proceeding.*

Pump/sender unit

Note: *The procedure given below is that suggested by MG Rover. When we tried to use the procedure in our workshop, we were unsuccessful. The problem is one of access, in that the unit will not come out as described, partly due to the two pipes attached to its base, which run across inside the tank to the filter unit on the opposite side. It appeared to be necessary to disconnect these pipes inside the tank before the unit would lift out, not afterwards as MG Rover suggest.*

Removal

1 Disconnect the battery negative lead (refer to *Disconnecting the battery* in the Reference Section).

2 Remove the rear seat cushion as described in Chapter 11 for access to the fuel pump cover.

3 Pull back the carpet and the soundproofing beneath the seat on the driver's side.

4 Remove the four screws, then release the wiring grommet and take out the floor access plate **(see illustrations)**.

5 Release the locking catch and disconnect the pump/sender wiring connector **(see illustration)**.

6 Protect the area around the access plate with clean cloth or newspaper, as a precaution against fuel dripping from the pump/sender unit when it is removed.

7 Check for alignment arrows on the locking ring or cover, to indicate its correct fitted position – if none are visible, make your own.

8 Unscrew the locking ring and remove it from the tank. This can be accomplished by using a screwdriver on the raised ribs of the locking ring – carefully tap the screwdriver to turn the ring anti-clockwise until it can be unscrewed by hand. Alternatively, a removal tool can be fabricated out of metal bar and two bolts **(see illustrations)**.

9 Carefully lift the pump assembly out of the fuel tank, taking great care not to damage the fuel level gauge sender arm, or to spill fuel in the interior of the car **(see illustration)**.

10 Remove the rubber sealing ring and check it for deterioration; if it is in good condition, it may be re-used.

11 Drain the fuel tank, either by using the method described in Section 3, or by syphoning the fuel directly through the pump/sender unit aperture.

12 Working through the pump/sender unit aperture, release the fuel pipe adaptor retaining clip at the base of the tank. Disconnect the pump/sender unit wiring plug, then remove the clip and disconnect the fuel pump hose from the adaptor.

13 If required, the fuel pump can be separated from the assembly, as follows. Cut the cable-ties securing the wiring harness, then remove the three mounting screws and disconnect the spade terminals.

Refitting

14 Refitting is a reversal of removal, noting the following points:

a) Make sure all hose and wiring connections are securely remade.
b) Use a new sealing ring if necessary.
c) Tighten the locking ring securely.

Filter/sender unit

Removal

15 Disconnect the battery negative lead (refer to *Disconnecting the battery* in the Reference Section).

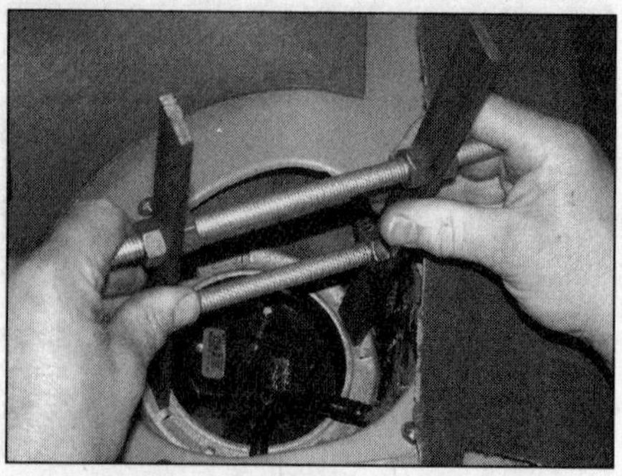

8.8a Using a fabricated tool in the raised ribs . . .

8.8b . . . unscrew and remove the locking ring

8.9 Lift the sender unit out of the tank

8.18 Remove the filter unit access plate

8.19 Disconnect the fuel pipe

8.20 Unscrew the filter unit locking ring

16 Remove the rear seat cushion as described in Chapter 11 for access to the fuel pump cover.
17 Pull back the carpet and the soundproofing beneath the seat on the passenger's side.
18 Remove the four screws, and take out the floor access plate **(see illustration)**.
19 Disconnect the fuel pipe from the top of the unit **(see illustration)**.
20 Unscrew the filter unit locking ring, using one of the methods described in paragraph 8 **(see illustration)**.
21 Carefully lift the filter unit out of the fuel tank, taking great care not to damage the fuel level gauge sender arm, or to spill fuel in the interior of the car **(see illustration)**.
22 If required, the sender unit can be separated after releasing the securing clips **(see illustration)**.
23 To fit a new filter (note that this is not a service item), release the three securing clips and withdraw the filter. Recover the two O-rings – new ones should be used when refitting.

Refitting

24 Refitting is a reversal of removal, noting the following points:
a) Make sure all hose and wiring connections are securely remade.
b) Use a new sealing ring if necessary ***(see illustration).***
c) Tighten the locking ring securely.

9 Fuel injection system – testing and adjustment

Testing

1 If a fault appears in the fuel injection system, first ensure that all the system wiring connectors are securely connected and free from corrosion. Ensure that the fault is not due to poor maintenance; ie, check that the air cleaner filter element is clean, that the spark plugs are in good condition and correctly gapped (see Chapter 1A), that the cylinder compression pressures are correct (see Chapter 2A), and that the engine breather hoses are clear and undamaged (see Chapter 4D).
2 If the engine will not start, check that the fuel inertia cut-off switch has not operated (see Section 11). Push the switch button behind the glovebox to reset if necessary.
3 If these checks fail to reveal the cause of the problem, the car should be taken to a garage with diagnostic equipment for testing. A wiring connector is provided under the steering column, into which a special electronic diagnostic tester can be plugged. The tester should locate the fault quickly and simply, avoiding the need to test all the system components individually, which is time-consuming, and also carries a risk of damaging the ECM.

Adjustment

4 Experienced home mechanics with access to a tachometer and an accurately-calibrated exhaust gas analyser may be able to check the exhaust CO level and the idle speed. However, if either of these settings is found to be in need of adjustment, the car must be taken to a garage with diagnostic equipment for further testing.
5 No manual adjustment of the exhaust CO level or idle speed is possible.

10 Throttle body – removal and refitting

Note: *On completion, the throttle body may need to be set up using diagnostic equipment, in order to function correctly. This is particularly the case if a new or secondhand unit is being fitted.*

Removal

1 Ensure that the ignition is switched off (take out the key).
2 Loosen the hose clip and disconnect the air inlet hose from the throttle body. Though not essential, removing the battery as described in Chapter 5A will provide more working room.
3 Disconnect the (upper) hose from the idle air control valve.

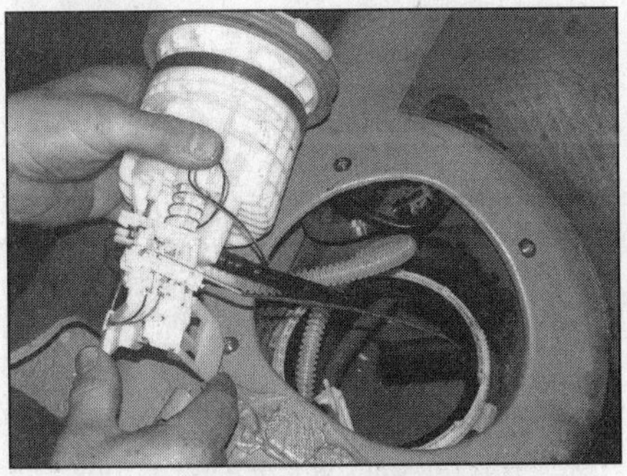
8.21 Lift out the filter unit, avoiding damage to the float arm

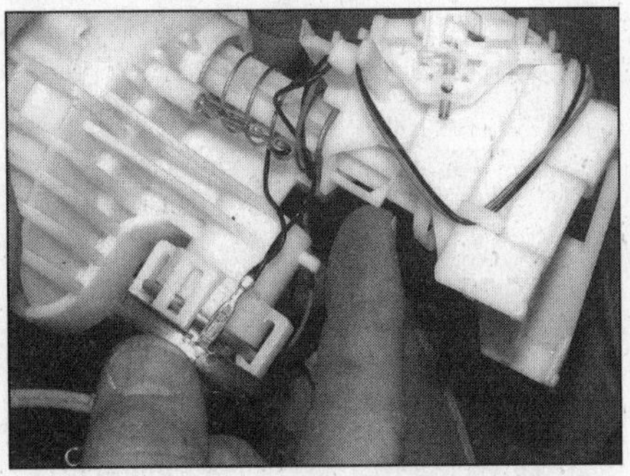
8.22 Release the sender unit clips

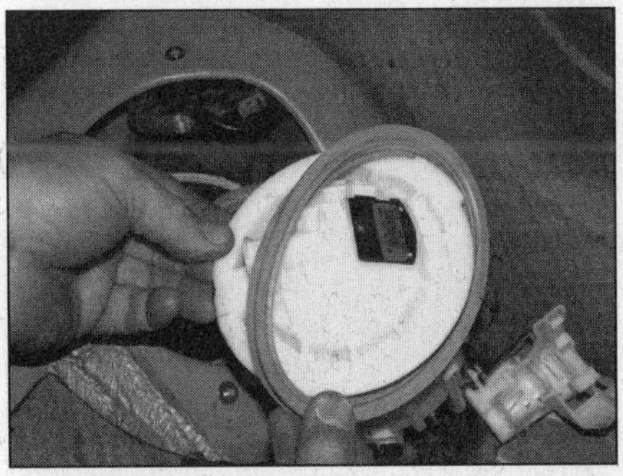
8.24 Check the condition of the filter unit sealing ring

10.4 Disconnect the throttle position sensor wiring plug

4 Disconnect the wiring plug from the throttle position sensor (TPS) **(see illustration)**.

5 Release the hose clip(s), and disconnect the (lower) breather hose from the throttle body.

6 Slide out the accelerator cable's square adjuster from the bracket on the inlet manifold/throttle body, then slide the cable end fitting from the groove in the throttle lever, and disconnect the cable from the lever.

7 Unscrew the four securing bolts, and withdraw the throttle body from the inlet manifold. Recover the O-ring and discard it.

Refitting

8 Clean the mating faces of the throttle body and inlet manifold.

9 Lubricate a new O-ring with silicone grease, and fit it to the throttle body.

10 Locate the throttle body on the inlet manifold, then fit and lightly tighten the four bolts.

11 Working in sequence, use a torque wrench to tighten the bolts as follows **(see illustration)**:

1) *Tighten to 4 Nm (3 lbf ft).*
2) *Back off one flat.*
3) *Tighten to 9 Nm (7 lbf ft).*

12 The remaining refitting is a reversal of the removal procedure.

13 If the engine does not run properly on completion (after a reasonable period has been given for the engine to 'relearn' its settings), it may be necessary to have the engine set up using diagnostic equipment, at a suitably-equipped garage.

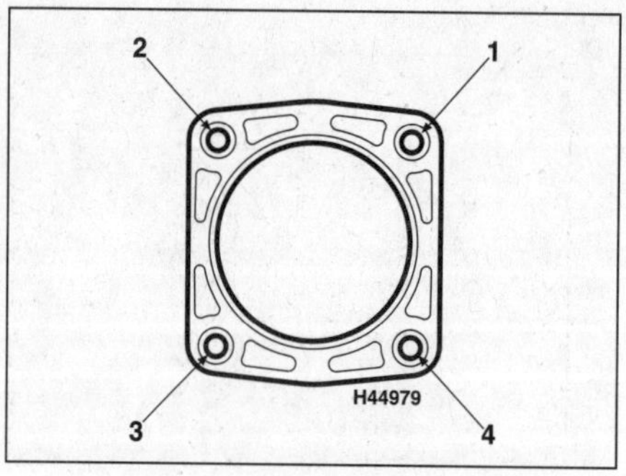

10.11 Throttle body bolt tightening sequence

11 Fuel injection system components – removal and refitting

1 Before disconnecting any fuel injection wiring plugs, ensure that the ignition is switched off (take out the key). If any component is disconnected 'live', it could introduce a fault code in the ECM memory. Better still, disconnect the battery negative lead, and move the lead away from the battery (see *Disconnecting the battery*).

Fuel rail and injectors

2 Depressurise the fuel system as described in Section 7.

3 Remove the engine oil dipstick.

4 Release the clip, then disconnect the vacuum hose on top of the fuel pressure damper located at the right-hand end of the fuel rail (right as seen from the driver's seat) **(see illustration)**.

5 Pack absorbent cloth under the fuel rail. Disconnect the fuel supply hose from the fuel rail by squeezing the quick-release connection's tabs. Plug the pipe connections.

6 Remove two bolts securing the fuel rail to the inlet manifold **(see illustration)**. Carefully pull the fuel rail and injectors squarely upwards from the inlet manifold (there will be resistance from the O-rings), and remove the injector spacers.

7 Disconnect the injector multi-plugs, then remove the fuel rail complete with injectors.

8 Release the spring clips securing the injectors to the fuel rail, and remove the injectors.

9 Remove and discard two O-rings from each injector. Cover both ends of each injector with a protective cap.

10 Refitting is a reversal of the removal procedure, noting the following points:

a) *Use new injector O-rings, lubricated with a little light oil before fitting them to the injectors.*
b) *Tighten the fuel rail bolts to the specified torque.*

Fuel pressure damper

11 The fuel pressure damper is mounted on the fuel rail, and is intended to reduce the effects of pressure variations in the fuel supplied from the tank-mounted pump.

12 Depressurise the fuel system as described in Section 7.

13 Release the clip, then disconnect the vacuum hose on top of the fuel pressure damper, which is located at the right-hand end of the fuel rail (right as seen from the driver's seat).

14 The damper is secured to the fuel rail by a flat circular clip, which is released by turning it anti-clockwise – this can be accomplished using the tip of a small screwdriver.

15 Withdraw the damper from its location, and recover the O-ring seal – a new seal should be used when refitting.

16 Refitting is a reversal of removal, noting the following points:

a) *Use a new damper O-ring seal.*
b) *Secure the damper using the metal clip, turned fully clockwise.*

Idle air control valve

17 The idle air control valve is located on the inlet manifold, behind the oil filler cap.

18 Disconnect the wiring plug from the valve **(see illustration)**.

19 Disconnect the control valve's air bypass hose (upper) and the breather hose (lower) from the throttle body.

20 Remove the four Torx screws securing the valve to the inlet manifold, then withdraw

11.4 Release the clip and disconnect the vacuum hose on top of the fuel pressure damper

11.6 Undo the two fuel rail mounting bolts (arrowed)

11.18 Disconnect the idle air control valve plug (arrowed)

the valve from the manifold **(see illustration)**. Recover the O-ring and discard it.

21 Refitting is a reversal of removal. Use a new O-ring, lubricated with a little silicone grease, and tighten the valve securing screws securely.

Inlet air temperature sensor

Note: *This sensor is fitted to non-turbo models only.*

22 The IAT sensor is located at the left-hand rear of the inlet manifold, under the throttle body.

23 Remove the air cleaner as described in Section 2.

24 To access the sensor multi-plug, unclip the oxygen sensor plug from its mounting bracket, and move it to one side.

25 Disconnect the temperature sensor multi-plug, then unscrew the sensor from the inlet manifold.

26 Refitting is a reversal of removal. Prior to refitting, clean the sensor threads and mating faces, then fit the sensor to the inlet manifold and tighten securely.

Engine coolant temperature sensor

27 The ECT sensor is screwed into the front of the coolant outlet elbow, next to the radiator top hose connection.

28 Have a container positioned under the switch – only a very small amount of coolant should be lost.

29 Disconnect the sensor multi-plug, then unscrew and remove the switch from the coolant elbow **(see illustration)**.

30 Refitting is a reversal of the removal procedure, noting the following points:

a) Clean and degrease the sensor threads, and apply a smear of thread sealant (such as Loctite 577).

b) Tighten the sensor securely.

c) Top-up the coolant level as described in 'Weekly checks'.

Throttle position sensor

Note: *Whenever the sensor is removed or renewed, a 'throttle initialisation' procedure must be carried out, to ensure correct operation afterwards – also see paragraph 33. As this requires the use of diagnostic equipment, it may be advisable to have work involving this sensor carried out by a suitably-equipped garage or specialist.*

31 The sensor is mounted on the side of the throttle body.

32 To improve access to the sensor, disconnect the air bypass (upper) hose from the throttle body.

33 Disconnect the multi-plug from the sensor **(see illustration)**.

34 Remove and discard two Torx screws and wave washers securing the sensor to the throttle housing – discard the washers and

11.20 Two of the four idle air control valve Torx screws

screws, as new ones should be used when refitting.

35 Remove the sensor specification plate, and pull the sensor from the throttle spindle without twisting it.

36 The sensor's inner section should not be turned while it is removed – if the same unit is being refitted, this minimises the need for the sensor to be 'initialised' on completion.

Caution: The sensor can easily be damaged, especially during fitting – handle it with care. Ensure, for example, that the machined flat on the throttle spindle is accurately aligned with the corresponding one inside the sensor. If nothing has been moved, and the original sensor is being refitted, it should only be necessary to align the mounting screw holes.

37 Clean the mating faces of the throttle housing and sensor.

38 Align the flat on the sensor with the flat on the throttle spindle, and push the sensor gently onto the spindle. If a new sensor is being fitted, rotate the sensor in an anti-clockwise direction to align the screw holes – **do not** turn it clockwise, nor beyond its internal stop. If possible, set the new sensor to the same position as the one just removed.

39 Fit the specification plate, with new wave washers and Torx screws. Tighten the screws securely.

40 Connect the multi-plug to the sensor, then refit the air bypass hose to the throttle body.

41 Operate the throttle linkage by hand a few times, and check that both idle and full-throttle positions appear to be available.

11.33 Disconnect the wiring plug (1) then remove the two Torx screws (2)

11.29 Disconnect the wiring plug, and unscrew the sensor

42 Run the engine and test the operation of the sensor. If the idle quality has suffered, and does not improve even after giving the system time to 'relearn' its values, throttle initialisation may be required – this requires diagnostic equipment.

Manifold absolute pressure sensor

Note: *This procedure also applies to the TMAP sensor fitted to turbo models.*

43 The sensor is located near the centre of the inlet manifold – disconnect the multi-plug from the sensor.

44 Remove two Torx screws, and withdraw the sensor from the inlet manifold **(see illustration)**.

45 Refitting is a reversal of removal. Clean the sensor and manifold mating faces prior to fitting.

Oxygen sensor

46 Refer to Chapter 4D.

Camshaft position sensor

47 Remove the spark plug cover from the top of the engine – this is secured by three screws.

48 Unclip the sensor multi-plug from its bracket at the transmission end of the engine, and disconnect the plug.

49 Release the sensor wiring from the clip on top of the engine.

11.44 Disconnect the MAP sensor wiring plug, then remove the two Torx screws

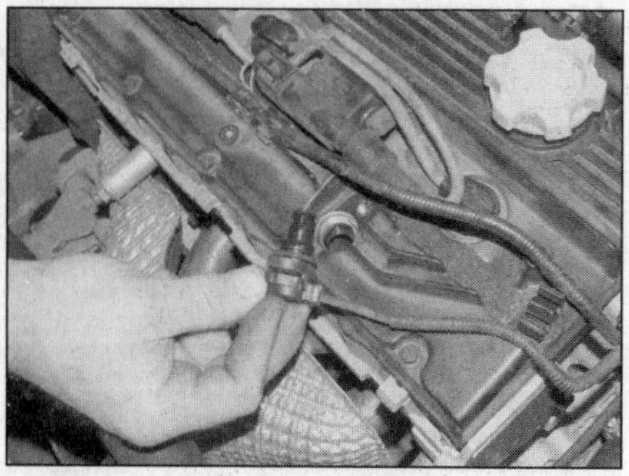

11.50 Remove the single bolt, and withdraw the camshaft position sensor

50 Remove the single bolt securing the sensor to the camshaft cover, then withdraw the sensor **(see illustration)**.

51 Refitting is a reversal of removal. Clean the mating faces of the sensor and camshaft cover, and tighten the bolt securely.

Inertia (fuel cut-off) switch

52 The inertia switch is mounted to the left of the front passenger footwell. Access to the switch itself is hampered by the wiring harness which runs in front of it.

53 Working as described in Chapter 11, Section 25, remove the glovebox, the passenger's facia closing trim panel, and the footwell left-hand trim panel.

54 Disconnect the multi-plug from the base of the switch **(see illustration)**.

55 Remove the two mounting screws, and withdraw the switch from the footwell.

11.58 Disconnect the wiring plug . . .

11.69 Power steering pressure switch

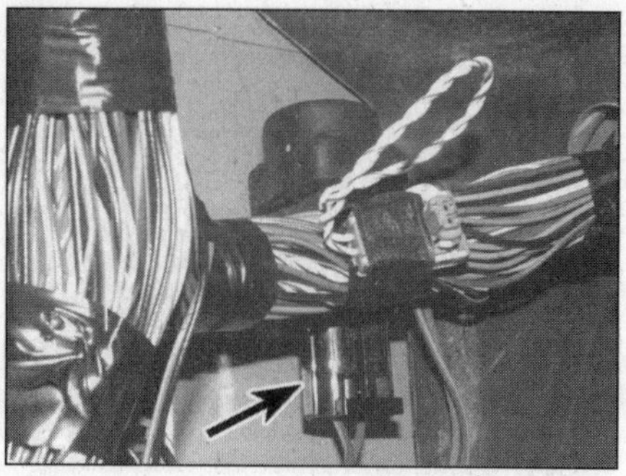

11.54 Disconnect the inertia switch wiring plug

56 Refitting is a reversal of removal, but ensure that the switch is reset by pressing the button on the top of the switch.

Crankshaft position sensor

57 The sensor is mounted at the front of the transmission bellhousing (at the left-hand end of the engine) **(see illustration)**. To improve access to the sensor, apply the handbrake, then jack up the left-hand front wheel and support securely on axle stands (see *Jacking and vehicle support*).

58 Disconnect the wiring plug above the sensor **(see illustration)**.

59 Unscrew the single bolt securing the sensor to the bellhousing, then remove the sensor **(see illustration)**.

60 Thoroughly clean the mating faces on the sensor and housing, then refit the sensor using a reversal of the removal procedure.

11.59 . . . then withdraw the sensor from the transmission

11.76 The exterior temperature sensor is mounted behind the bumper grille

11.57 The crankshaft position sensor is on the front of the transmission

Engine oil temperature sensor

61 Firmly apply the handbrake, then jack up the front of the car and support it securely on axle stands (see *Jacking and vehicle support*).

62 Remove the engine undertray, which is secured by a number of quick-release screw fasteners.

63 The oil temperature sensor is mounted near the oil filter, and is almost vertical – do not confuse it with the horizontally-mounted oil pressure switch, which is further from the oil filter.

64 Disconnect the sensor wiring plug.

65 Place a drain container under the switch – the amount of oil lost should only be whatever's in the oil filter, not the entire contents of the sump.

66 Anticipating oil spillage, slowly unscrew the switch and remove it.

67 Allow the oil to finish draining, then clean the switch threads and the switch location.

68 Fit the switch and tighten securely. Reconnect the wiring plug, then refit the undertray and lower the car to the ground.

Power steering pressure switch

69 The switch is located at the rear of the power steering pump **(see illustration)**.

70 Disconnect the multi-plug from the switch.

71 Position a container under the switch to catch any lost fluid.

72 Unscrew the switch, and remove it. Recover the O-ring – a new one should be used when refitting.

73 Refitting is a reversal of removal. Use a new O-ring, lubricated with power steering fluid, and tighten the switch to the specified torque – counterhold the union with another spanner as this is done.

Exterior temperature sensor

74 Jack up the front of the car, and support it on axle stands (see *Jacking and vehicle support*).

75 Remove the fasteners from the front of the engine undertray, and lower the tray for access to the sensor.

76 The sensor is fitted below the front bumper, behind the lower grille **(see illustration)**.

77 The sensor slides onto a moulded tab, and is released using a small screwdriver.

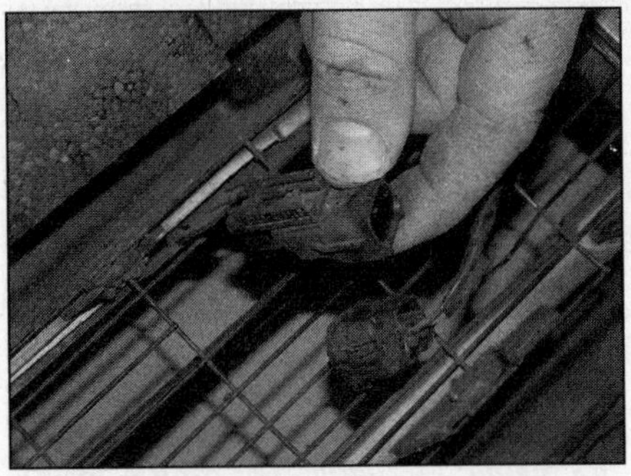

11.77 Removing the temperature sensor

Disconnect the wiring plug and remove the sensor **(see illustration)**.

78 Refitting is a reversal of removal.

Boost control solenoid valve

79 The valve is mounted on the side of the air cleaner **(see illustration)**.

80 Disconnect the wiring plug at the back of the valve.

81 There are three hoses to disconnect from the valve – mark each one's fitted position, perhaps by wrapping a label (or a piece of masking tape) round each hose. Disconnect the air intake hose, and the ones leading to the turbo housing and wastegate capsule.

82 Unclip the valve from the side of the air cleaner, and remove it.

83 Refitting is a reversal of removal.

Canister purge valve

84 Refer to Chapter 4D.

Engine control module (ECM)

Note: *If a new module is to be fitted, it will need to be programmed with the code from the anti-theft security unit before the engine can be started. This can only be done using diagnostic equipment, and it may therefore be advisable to have this work carried out by a suitably-equipped garage or specialist.*

85 Disconnect the battery negative lead, and move the lead away from the battery (see *Disconnecting the battery*). This is **essential** – if the ECM wiring plug is disconnected (or reconnected) 'live', the module could be damaged.

11.89 Lift out the ECM

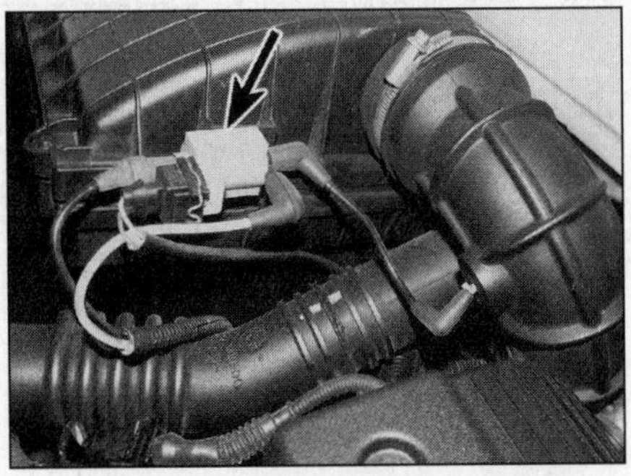

11.79 Boost control solenoid valve and hoses

86 Release and lift off the passenger-side half of the windscreen outer grille panel, which is secured by two tabs at the front edge.

87 Pull off the rubber weatherstrip at the front of the windscreen cowl panel on the passenger side.

88 Remove the three clips at the rear, and the single screw/clip at the front, then carefully lift up the passenger side of the windscreen cowl panel frame. Slide out the water shield panel **(see illustration)**.

89 Release the ECM securing clips either side, and lift it out **(see illustration)**.

90 Slide the ECM wiring plug locking clips to the sides, then disconnect them and remove the module **(see illustration)**.

91 While the module is removed, check that the drain holes inside the housing are clear, as they can become blocked, which may lead to ECM damage.

92 Refitting is a reversal of removal. Ensure that the module wiring plugs are securely reconnected.

12 Manifolds – removal and refitting

Inlet manifold

1 Depressurise the fuel system as described in Section 7.

2 Disconnect the battery negative lead, and move the lead away from the battery (see *Disconnecting the battery*).

11.90 Slide the locking clips sideways, and disconnect the wiring plug

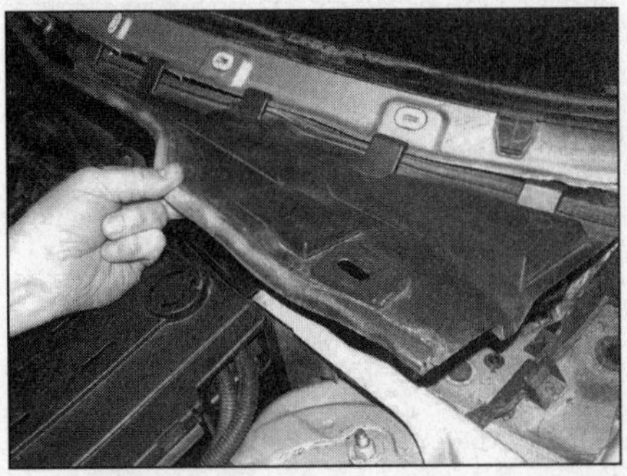

11.88 Slide out the water shield panel

3 Drain the cooling system – see Chapter 1A.

4 Remove the air cleaner as described in Section 2.

5 Noting their fitted positions, disconnect the following from the inlet manifold:

a) Purge valve hose (behind the throttle body).
b) Breather hose (behind the oil filler cap).
c) Brake servo vacuum hose (at the rear – depress the collar to release).

6 Disconnect the following from the throttle body:

a) Idle air control valve bypass (upper) hose.
b) Wiring plug from the throttle position sensor.
c) Breather hose (lower).
d) Accelerator cable – slide the square adjuster from the bracket, then slide the cable end fitting from the groove in the throttle lever, and disconnect the cable from the lever.

7 Disconnect the power steering pressure switch (behind the power steering pump).

8 Remove the spark plug cover from the top of the engine – this is secured by three bolts.

9 Unscrew the two mounting bolts from the right-hand ignition coil (right as seen from the driver's seat). Disconnect the coil multi-plugs, and release the wiring from the retaining clips.

10 Release the hose clips and disconnect the coolant hose from the inlet manifold (timing belt end, rear).

11 Unclip the injector wiring harness multi-plug from the bracket at the transmission end of the engine. Lift the locking catch and disconnect the wiring plug. Unclip the engine wiring harness from the same bracket.

12 On non-turbo models, disconnect the wiring plug from the inlet air temperature sensor.

13 Place absorbent cloth under the fuel supply connection to the fuel rail (next to the throttle body). Squeeze the two tabs on the quick-release fitting, and disconnect the supply pipe. Plug or tape over the open connections.

14 Working in the **reverse** of the tightening sequence, progressively loosen the inlet manifold's three nuts and four bolts (or seven nuts, depending on model). Free the manifold from the cylinder head, and remove it with

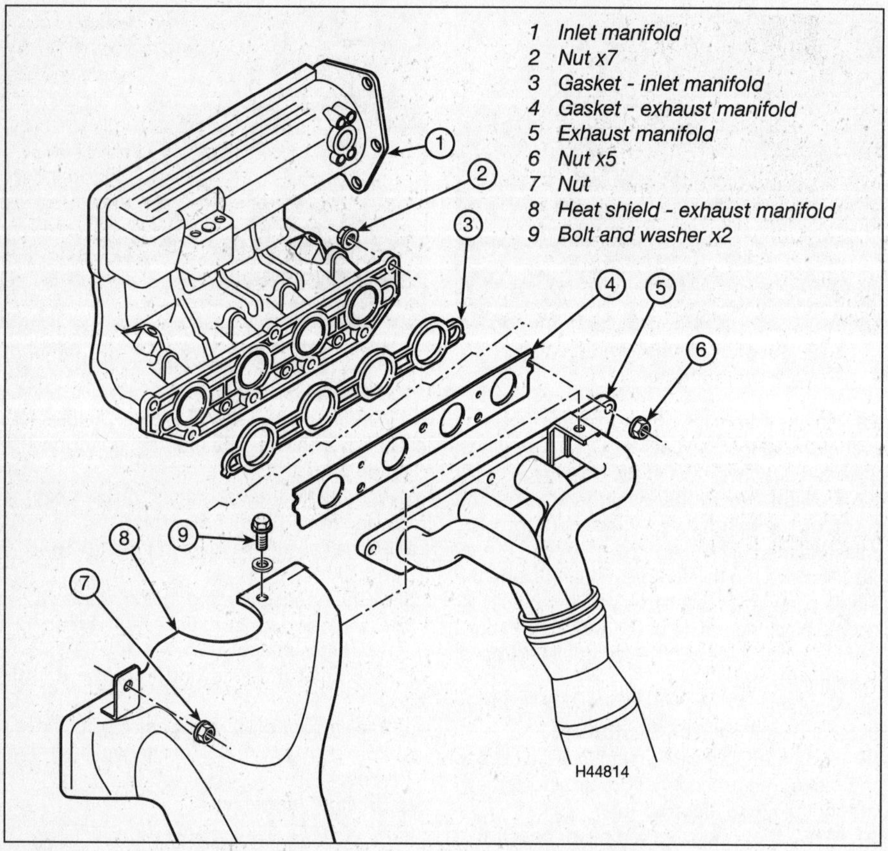

12.14 Manifold components – non-turbo models

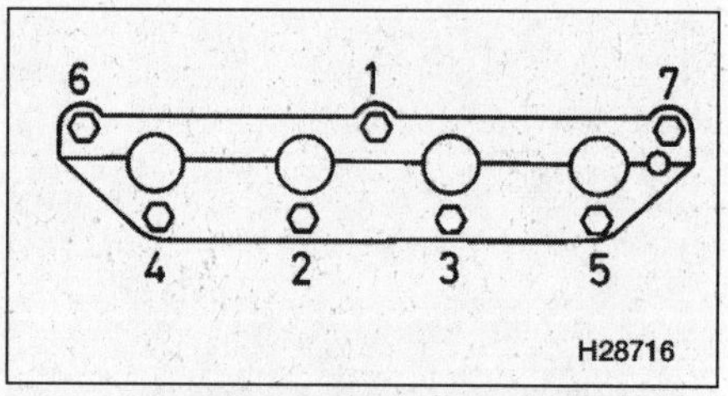

12.16 Inlet manifold nut and bolt tightening sequence

its gasket – a new gasket will be needed for reassembly **(see illustration)**.

15 Clean the mating faces of the manifold and cylinder head, and ensure that metal inserts are fitted in the inlet manifold stud and bolt holes.

16 Using a new gasket, locate the manifold against the cylinder head, and fit the nuts/bolts. Use a torque wrench to tighten the nuts/bolts, in sequence, to the specified torque **(see illustration)**.

17 The remaining refitting is a reversal of the removal procedure, noting the following points:

a) *Adjust the accelerator cable if necessary, as described in Section 5.*
b) *Top-up the cooling system as described in 'Weekly checks'.*

Exhaust manifold

Non-turbo models

18 Jack up the front of the car, and support it on axle stands (see *Jacking and vehicle support*).

19 Remove the engine undertray, which is secured by a number of quick-release screw fasteners.

20 Loosen and remove the two manifold-to-downpipe flange nuts, then separate the joint and recover the gasket – a new one will be needed for refitting. If wished, the car can now be lowered back to the ground.

21 Remove the air cleaner as described in Section 2.

22 Unclip the oxygen sensor wiring plug from the bracket at the transmission end of the engine, and disconnect the plug. Trace the wiring back to the coolant elbow at the front of the engine, and cut the cable-tie securing it to the elbow.

23 Unscrew the two retaining bolts, and remove the exhaust manifold heat shield. It's likely that these bolts may be in very poor condition, having suffered corrosion damage – make sure the spanner or socket used to remove them is a good fit, and spray the bolts with penetrating lubricant before trying to remove them. If the bolts are found to be in poor condition, it is advisable to obtain new bolts for reassembly.

24 Starting with the outer nuts and working inwards, progressively loosen and remove the five nuts securing the manifold to the head.

25 Withdraw the manifold from the studs, taking care that the oxygen sensor wiring does not get trapped. Recover the gasket – a new one must be used when refitting. If the manifold nuts are in poor condition, new ones should be obtained for reassembly – in this case, also consider fitting new studs.

Caution: The exhaust manifold fitted to later models may include a 'starter' catalytic converter, upstream of the main converter – for this reason, do not handle the manifold roughly, nor drop it, or the converter may be damaged.

26 If any studs were removed with the nuts, these can be refitted to the head using two nuts tightened against each other. If any studs have to be refitted (or renewed, if their threads are in poor condition), apply a little threadlocking fluid to their threads before screwing them into the head.

27 Clean the mating faces of the manifold and cylinder head, and fit a new gasket to the studs in the cylinder head.

28 Locate the manifold against the cylinder head, feed the oxygen sensor wiring into place, and fit the nuts. Working from the centre nut outwards, tighten the nuts to the specified torque.

29 The remainder of refitting is a reversal of the removal procedure.

Turbo models

30 Drain the cooling system as described in Chapter 1A.

31 Unclip the oxygen sensor wiring plug from the bracket at the transmission end of the engine, and disconnect the plug. Trace the wiring back to the coolant elbow at the front of the engine, and cut the cable-tie securing it to the elbow.

32 Jack up the front of the car, and support it on axle stands (see *Jacking and vehicle support*).

33 Remove the engine undertray, which is secured by a number of quick-release screw fasteners.

34 Unscrew and remove the oxygen sensor from the downpipe – tie the sensor up clear of the exhaust **(see illustration)**. Recover the washer – a new one should be used when refitting.

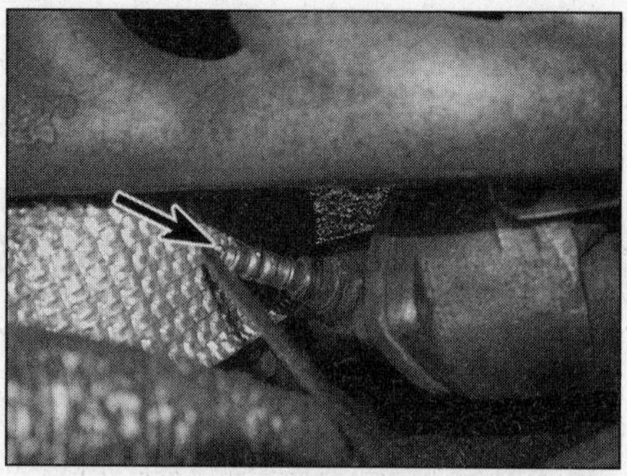

12.34 Unscrew and remove the oxygen sensor

12.35 Turbo-to-downpipe flange nuts (three visible from above)

35 Loosen and remove the four turbo-to-downpipe flange nuts – three accessible from above, one from below **(see illustration)**.

36 Loosen and remove the three downpipe-to-intermediate pipe flange nuts, then remove the single bolt securing the downpipe to the sump.

37 Remove the two through-bolts from the engine lower mounting, to allow extra movement for the downpipe to be removed.

38 Lower out the downpipe, and recover both the flange gaskets – new ones will be needed for refitting.

39 Remove the alternator as described in Chapter 5A.

40 Where applicable, remove the three mounting bolts, then tie the air conditioning compressor to one side, without disconnecting the hoses.

41 Remove the remaining bolt securing the alternator heat shield to the engine, and withdraw the shield.

42 Unscrew the two bolts at each end, and remove the oil drain pipe from the turbo and from the engine – anticipate a small amount of oil loss as this is done. Recover the gaskets from each end of the pipe – new ones should be used when refitting.

43 Loosen the large hose clip and disconnect the turbo air inlet hose **(see illustration)**. If wished, the hose can be removed completely, after slackening the hose clip at the air cleaner.

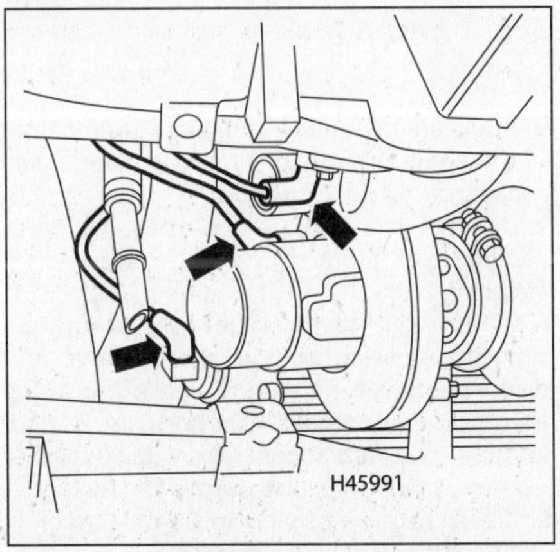

12.44 Mark the fitted positions of the turbo boost pressure control hoses

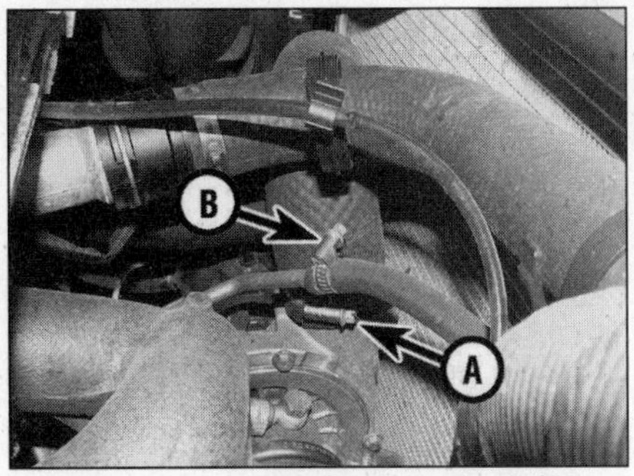

12.43 Turbo air inlet hose clip (A) and coolant hose clip (B)

44 There are now three boost pressure control hoses to remove from the turbo and wastegate – mark each one's fitted position, perhaps by wrapping a label (or a piece of masking tape) round each hose **(see illustration)**. Disconnect the hoses, and move them clear.

45 Loosen the hose clip securing the turbo's coolant supply hose, and disconnect it. If wished, the car can now be lowered back to the ground.

46 On top of the turbo, unscrew the oil supply banjo bolt, and recover the two washers – new washers should be used on reassembly. Also release the clip and disconnect the upper coolant hose from the turbo **(see illustration)**.

47 Unscrew the nut and bolt from the alternator mounting bracket, and remove the bracket from the front of the engine.

48 Remove the spark plug cover from the top of the engine – this is secured by three screws.

49 Release the radiator top hose clip, and disconnect the hose.

50 Starting with the outer nuts and working inwards, progressively loosen and remove the five nuts securing the manifold to the head.

51 Taking care not to damage the radiator, and with the help of an assistant, withdraw the manifold and turbo from the cylinder head studs – take care that the oxygen sensor wiring does not become trapped. Recover the manifold gasket – a new one must be used when refitting. If the manifold nuts are in poor condition, new ones should be obtained for reassembly – in this case, also consider fitting new studs.

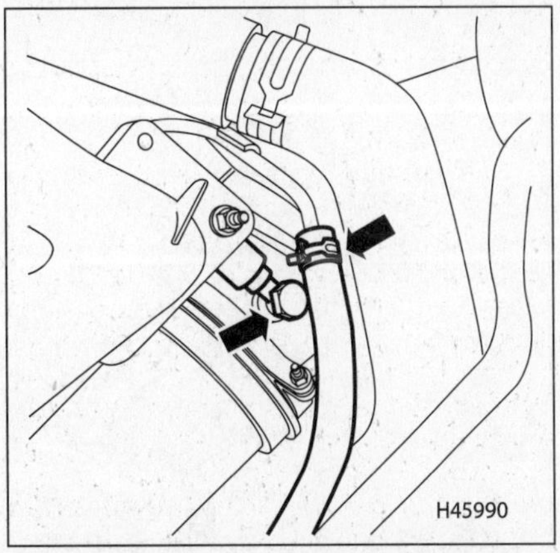

12.46 Unscrew the oil supply banjo bolt, and disconnect the upper coolant hose

52 If any studs were removed with the nuts, these can be refitted to the head using two nuts tightened against each other. If any studs have to be refitted (or renewed, if their threads are in poor condition), apply a little thread-locking fluid to their threads before screwing them into the head.

53 If required, the turbo can be separated from the manifold, as described in Section 14.

54 Clean the mating faces of the manifold and cylinder head, and fit a new gasket to the studs in the cylinder head.

55 Locate the manifold against the cylinder head, feed the oxygen sensor wiring into place, and fit the nuts. Working from the centre nut outwards, tighten the nuts to the specified torque.

56 The remainder of refitting is a reversal of the removal procedure, noting the following points:

a) Use new gaskets, and tighten all fasteners to the specified torque.

b) Use new sealing washers on the turbo oil feed pipe banjo bolt, and on the oxygen sensor, where applicable.

c) Ensure that all hoses are securely refitted, and in particular those relating to the turbo.

d) When refitting the alternator heat shield, only fit the lower retaining bolt until the alternator and compressor have been refitted.

e) Refit the alternator as described in Chapter 5A.

f) Refill the cooling system as described in Chapter 1A.

13 Turbocharger – general information and precautions

General information

1 A turbocharger increases engine efficiency by raising the pressure in the inlet manifold above atmospheric pressure. Instead of the air simply being sucked into the cylinders, it is forced in. Additional fuel is supplied in proportion to the increased air intake.

2 Energy for the operation of the turbocharger comes from the exhaust gas. The gas flows through a specially-shaped housing (the turbine housing) and in so doing, spins the turbine wheel. The turbine wheel is attached to a shaft, at the end of which is another vaned wheel known as the compressor wheel. The compressor wheel spins in its own housing and compresses the inducted air on the way to the inlet manifold.

3 Between the turbocharger and the inlet manifold, the compressed air passes through an intercooler. This is an air-to-air heat exchanger, mounted behind the front bumper.

The purpose of the intercooler is to remove, from the inducted air, some of the heat gained in being compressed. Because cooler air is denser, removal of this heat further increases engine efficiency.

4 Boost pressure (the pressure in the inlet manifold) is limited by a wastegate, which diverts the exhaust gas away from the turbine wheel in response to a pressure-sensitive actuator. Turbocharging pressure is controlled by a boost control solenoid valve mounted on the air cleaner – refer to Section 11.

5 The turbo shaft is pressure-lubricated by an oil feed pipe from the main oil gallery. The shaft 'floats' on a cushion of oil. A drain pipe returns the oil to the sump.

Precautions

- The turbocharger operates at extremely high speeds and temperatures. Certain precautions must be observed to avoid premature failure of the turbo or injury to the operator.
- Do not race the engine immediately after start-up, especially if it is cold. Give the oil a few seconds to circulate.
- Always allow the engine to return to idle speed before switching it off – do not blip the throttle and switch off, as this will leave the turbo spinning without lubrication.
- Allow the engine to idle for several minutes before switching off after a high-speed run.
- Observe the recommended intervals for oil and filter changing, and use a reputable oil of the specified quality. Neglect of oil changing, or use of inferior oil, can cause carbon formation on the turbo shaft and subsequent failure.

Warning: Do not operate the turbo with the air hoses or exhaust downpipe removed. Foreign objects falling onto the rotating vanes could cause excessive damage and (if ejected) personal injury.

14 Turbocharger – removal and refitting

Removal

1 The turbo is removed with the exhaust manifold, as described in Section 12. Once removed, the turbo can be separated from the manifold by unscrewing the four mounting nuts. Recover the gasket – a new one must be used when refitting **(see illustration)**. If the turbo-to-manifold nuts are in less-than-perfect condition, new ones should be obtained.

Refitting

2 Clean the turbo and manifold mating surfaces, wire-brush the turbo-to-manifold studs, and fit a new gasket.

3 Tighten the turbo-to-manifold nuts to the specified torque.

4 Refit the exhaust manifold as described in Section 12.

15 Turbocharger – examination and overhaul

With the turbocharger removed, inspect the housing for cracks or other visible damage.

Spin the turbine or the compressor wheel to verify that the shaft is intact, and to feel for excessive shake or roughness. Some play is normal, since in use the shaft is 'floating' on a film of oil. Check that the wheel vanes are undamaged.

The wastegate and actuator are integral with the turbocharger, and cannot be checked or renewed separately. Consult a turbocharger specialist if the wastegate is thought to be faulty.

If the exhaust or induction passages are oil-contaminated, the turbo shaft oil seals have probably failed. (On the induction side, this will also have contaminated the intercooler, which if necessary should be flushed with a suitable solvent.)

No DIY repair of the turbo is possible. A new or reconditioned unit may be available on an exchange basis.

16 Intercooler – removal and refitting

Removal

1 The intercooler is mounted in front of the radiator.

2 Remove the front bumper as described in Chapter 11.

3 Though access to the intercooler may be hindered by the radiator cooling fan, it should not be necessary to remove it.

4 Release the hose clips from the two intercooler air hoses, and disconnect them.

5 Unscrew the mounting bolt at either end, then remove the intercooler from the car.

6 If required, the intercooler hoses can now be removed, after disconnecting the other ends from the turbo and throttle body.

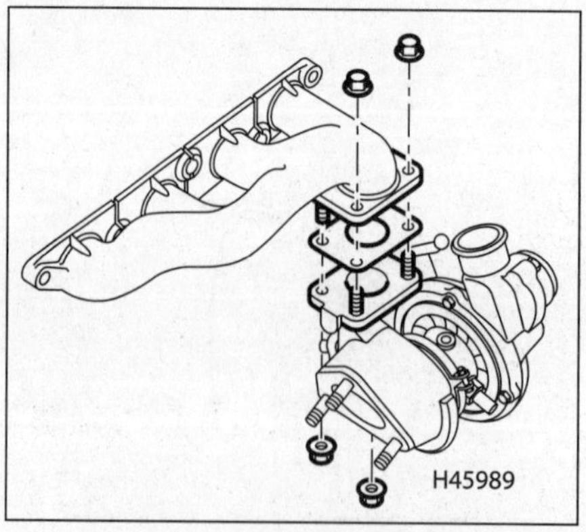

14.1 Turbo-to-exhaust manifold mounting nuts and gasket

Refitting

7 Before refitting the intercooler, check inside the duct connection stubs for significant amounts of oil. If present, this can be cleaned out with a suitable solvent, but it does indicate that the turbocharger oil seals have failed – the turbo should be removed for inspection as described in Section 14.

8 Refitting is a reversal of removal, but tighten all hose clips securely, to avoid air leaks. Refit the bumper as described in Chapter 11.

17 Exhaust system – general information and component renewal

1 The exhaust system fitted at the factory is a one-piece item on non-turbo models, with a catalytic converter and two silencer boxes. Some models additionally have a 'starter' catalytic converter incorporated into the exhaust manifold.

2 Turbo models have the exhaust in two sections, separated at a flanged joint, with a flexible section, catalytic converter, and three silencer boxes.

3 Repair sections are available for the centre and tail silencer boxes, but to fit them on the factory original system requires that the pipe is cut at precisely the right point – for this reason, owners may prefer to have exhaust work carried out by an exhaust specialist. Where these repair sections have been fitted previously, references to cutting can be ignored, as the pipes can be separated by loosening the clamps.

4 The front pipe, which connects to the exhaust manifold (or turbo), includes a catalytic converter, and on later models, one or more oxygen sensors.

5 The intermediate/tail section incorporates two or more silencers, which contain baffle plates and expansion chambers designed to reduce engine exhaust noise.

Front pipe

Non-turbo models

6 Apply the handbrake, then jack up the front of the car and support it on axle stands (see *Jacking and vehicle support*).

7 Remove the engine undertray, which is secured by a number of quick-release screw fasteners.

8 Where applicable, trace the wiring up from the post-catalyst oxygen sensor, and disconnect it at the plug. Release the wiring from any clips or ties. Unscrew the sensor from the pipe, and recover the sealing washer – a new washer must be used when refitting.

9 Clean the area of pipe to be cut, which is just behind the catalytic converter.

10 Either offer up the new pipe as a guide for cutting, or measure back 1063 mm from the centreline of the flange holes, and mark the pipe for cutting **(see illustration)**.

11 Cut the pipe through squarely, using a proper pipe-cutting tool if available.

12 Unscrew the two flange nuts, and remove the front pipe.

13 De-burr the cut pipe on the rear section, then fit the pipe clamp loosely in position **(see illustration)**.

14 Offer up the new pipe into the pipe clamp, and (using a new gasket) onto the manifold studs. Secure with the flange nuts, tightened by hand only at this stage.

15 Ensure that the pipe is 'settled' into position, then tighten the clamps securely. Tighten the flange nuts to the specified torque.

16 Where applicable, refit the rear oxygen sensor using a new washer, and tighten it securely (if possible, to the specified torque). Plug the sensor back in, and ensure the wiring is routed and clipped in as before.

17 Refit the engine undertray, then lower the car to the ground.

Turbo models

18 Unclip the oxygen sensor wiring plug from the bracket at the transmission end of the engine, and disconnect the plug. Trace the wiring back to the coolant elbow at the front of the engine, and cut the cable-tie securing it to the elbow.

19 Jack up the front of the car, and support it on axle stands (see *Jacking and vehicle support*).

20 Remove the engine undertray, which is secured by a number of quick-release screw fasteners.

21 Unscrew and remove the oxygen sensor from the downpipe – tie the sensor up clear of the exhaust **(see illustration)**.

22 Loosen and remove the three turbo-to-downpipe flange nuts.

23 Loosen and remove the three downpipe-to-intermediate pipe flange nuts, then remove the single bolt securing the downpipe to the sump.

24 Remove the two through-bolts from the engine lower mounting, to allow extra movement for the downpipe to be removed.

25 Lower out the downpipe, and recover both the flange gaskets – new ones will be needed for refitting.

26 Refitting is a reversal of removal, noting the following points:

a) Use new flange gaskets, and a new oxygen sensor sealing washer, where applicable.

b) Tighten the flange nuts (and, if possible) the oxygen sensor to the specified torque.

Intermediate pipe

27 Apply the handbrake, then jack up the car and support it on axle stands (see *Jacking and vehicle support*). For the best access, if enough axle stands are available, the car should be raised front and rear.

28 Remove the engine undertray, which is secured by a number of quick-release screw fasteners.

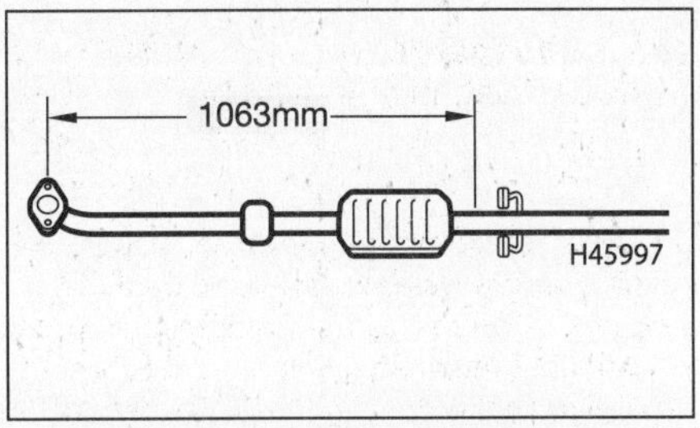

17.10 Cutting point for exhaust front pipe renewal

29 On non-turbo models, cut the front pipe as described in paragraphs 8 to 11.

30 On turbo models, loosen and remove the three downpipe-to-intermediate pipe flange nuts, remove the two through-bolts from the engine lower mounting, then separate the flange joint and recover the gasket – have a new one ready for refitting.

31 In the centre of the car, unscrew a total of ten bolts and remove the three cross-braces fitted below the exhaust **(see illustrations)**.

32 Unhook the exhaust from its rubber mountings, and lower it to the floor.

33 On non-turbo models, de-burr the cut pipe on the front section, then fit the pipe clamp loosely in position.

34 Offer the new section into place (with a new gasket on turbo models), and hook it onto the rubber mountings. With the system 'settled' in place (and not touching the floor or suspension components), tighten the clamp nuts or flange nuts to the specified torque.

35 Refit the three cross-braces, and tighten the bolts to the specified torque.

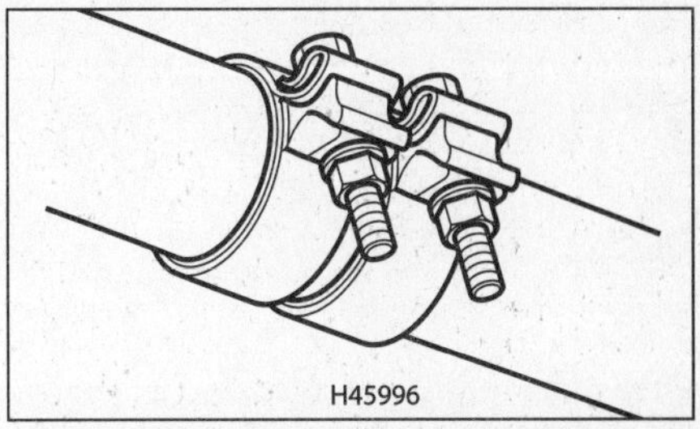

17.13 Exhaust clamp used to join the two sections of pipe

36 Refit the engine undertray, then lower the car to the ground.

Tail pipe

37 Jack up the rear of the car, and support it on axle stands (see *Jacking and vehicle support*).

38 Offer up the new section, and mark the pipe for cutting (if the tail section has been renewed previously, loosen the clamp nuts).

39 Where applicable, cut the pipe through squarely, using a proper pipe-cutting tool if available.

40 Unscrew the nut and bolt each side securing the silencer support strap, then lower the strap and silencer **(see illustration)**.

41 Where applicable, de-burr the cut end of pipe, and fit the clamp loosely in to place.

42 Offer in the new section, and hand-tighten the clamp nuts.

43 Refit the support strap, and tighten the nuts/bolts to the specified torque.

44 With the new section 'settled' in place, tighten the clamp nuts to the specified torque.

45 Lower the car to the ground to complete.

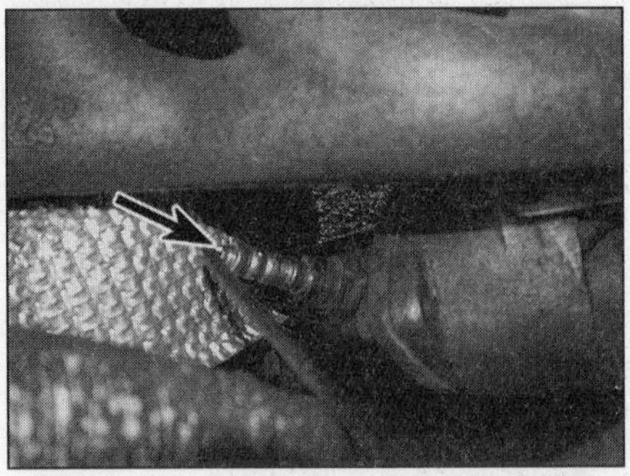

17.21 Unscrew the oxygen sensor from the downpipe

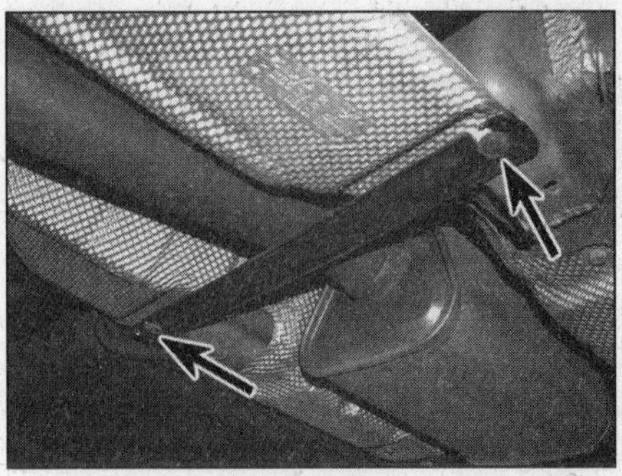

17.31a The front cross-brace is secured by two bolts . . .

17.31b . . . but the two further back have four bolts each

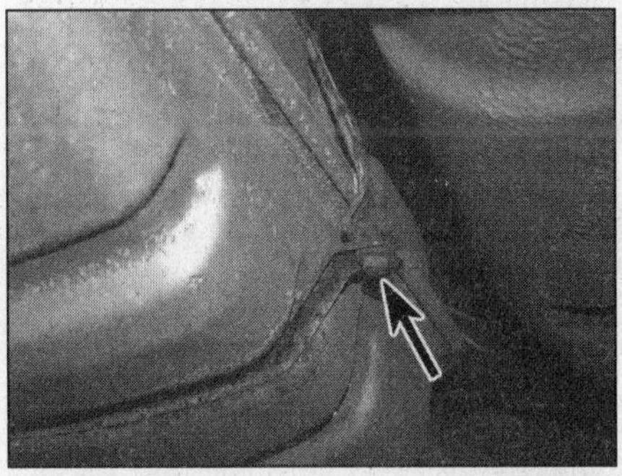

17.40 Unbolt the silencer support strap

Chapter 4 Part B: Fuel & exhaust systems – V6 engines

Contents

Degrees of difficulty

Easy, suitable for novice with little experience	**Fairly easy,** suitable for beginner with some experience	**Fairly difficult,** suitable for competent DIY mechanic	**Difficult,** suitable for experienced DIY mechanic	**Very difficult,** suitable for expert DIY or professional

Specifications

General

System type	Siemens engine management system, sequential multi-point fuel injection system, variable inlet manifold geometry, integrated with ignition system

Fuel pump

Type	Electric roller vane pump in fuel tank
Operating pressure	3.5 bar

Idle settings (for reference only)

Idle speed	750 ± 50 rpm
Idle mixture (CO content)	Less than 0.5 %

Torque wrench settings

Torque wrench settings	Nm	lbf ft
Air cleaner mounting bracket	45	33
Air conditioning compressor mounting bolts	25	18
Camshaft position sensor bolt	10	7
Engine coolant temperature sensor	17	13
Engine lower mounting through-bolts	100	74
Engine right-hand mounting upper cross-brace	25	18
Exhaust clamp nuts	48	35
Exhaust cross-brace bolts	25	18
Exhaust flange-to-manifold nuts	75	55
Exhaust manifold-to-head nuts	45	33
Exhaust pipe-to-manifold nuts	40	30
Exhaust support strap nuts/bolts	22	16
Fuel rail-to-manifold bolts	9	7
Fuel tank mounting bolts	24	18
Fuel tank unit locking ring	38	28
Inlet manifold-to-head bolts	25	18
Inlet manifold upper section bolts	18	13
Knock sensor mounting bolts	25	18
Oxygen sensors	55	41
Power steering pressure switch	24	18
Rear subframe mounting bolts	100	74

1 General information and precautions

General information

The fuel and ignition systems are controlled by the Siemens engine management system. For more information on the ignition side of the system, refer to Chapter 5B, but note that most of the system sensors are deemed to have a dual role, and will be covered in this Chapter.

Fuel is supplied from the rear-mounted fuel tank by an electric pump mounted in the tank, via a tank-mounted fuel filter, to the two plastic fuel rails. The rail serving the rear bank has a pressure damper, and a steel crossover tube joins the two rails. Unlike many earlier injection systems, no fuel return system is fitted. The fuel rails act as a reservoir for the six fuel injectors, which inject fuel onto the back of the inlet valves.

The injectors operate sequentially in firing order, with fuel being injected during each cylinder's induction stroke. The injectors are electronically controlled by the Engine Control Module (ECM). Each injector has a solenoid which, when energised by a pulse from the ECM, lifts the injector needle and fuel is sprayed into the cylinder. The duration of the pulse determines the length of time the needle is lifted and, therefore, the amount of fuel injected. Pulse duration is calculated by the ECM, and is constantly varying to match engine operating and ambient conditions.

The fuelling and ignition timing calculation is based on information supplied to the ECM by the following sensors:

a) Throttle position sensor (TP) – mounted on the throttle body, the sensor provides a signal representing the amount and rate of throttle opening – ie, driver demand.

b) Crankshaft position sensor (CKP) – supplies a signal representing the speed and angular position of the crankshaft.

c) Camshaft position sensor (CMP) – attached to the camshaft cover on the front bank, the sensor provides a signal representing the angular position of the camshaft, in relation to the angular position of the crankshaft.

d) Manifold absolute pressure (MAP) – located on the throttle body, supplies a signal representing the air pressure in the inlet manifold, which is used to determine the amount of air entering the cylinders. Built-in air temperature sensor monitors inlet air temperature.

e) Engine coolant temperature (ECT) – located in the top of the engine block. The sensor provides a coolant temperature signal.

f) Oxygen sensors – one is located in each front pipe, upstream of the 'starter' catalytic converter, with later models having a third sensor located in the exhaust pipe, downstream of the main converter. The sensors provide signals representing the amount of oxygen in the exhaust gas, and allow the ECM to precisely control the air/fuel ratio around the ideal combustion ratio of 14.7:1.

g) Knock sensors – one per bank, located between the two banks. Detects combustion 'knock' or 'pinking', typically caused by over-advanced ignition timing.

Idle speed is controlled by the ECM via an Idle Air Control Valve (IACV), which varies the amount of air bypassing the throttle valve. Fine control of idle speed is further achieved by small variations in ignition timing.

Information on engine loads, such as the power steering and air conditioning systems, is provided by the power steering pressure sensor and by the ambient air temperature sensor. Vehicle speed information is provided to the ECM from the four ABS wheel sensors

Failure of certain sensors – either complete loss of signal, or sending an abnormal signal, will cause the ECM to default to preprogrammed values. In most cases this will be noticeable as poor or erratic engine performance, and the engine management warning light on the instrument panel will come on. If the crankshaft position (CKP) sensor signal is lost, the engine will not run. Whenever a sensor fault occurs, a fault code is stored in a memory of the ECM. Using specialist diagnostic equipment, the codes can be extracted so that the problem can be isolated.

All models are fitted with a fuel inertia cut-off switch (see Section 11), which cuts off the fuel supply in the event of the car being involved in an impact – the interior lights will be on all the time until the switch is reset. The engine cannot be started if the switch is activated – the switch must be reset manually.

The inlet manifold features variable-length inlet tracts, for optimum torque at all engine speeds and loads. The system is controlled by the ECM – for more details, see Section 13.

Precautions

- Before disconnecting any fuel lines, or working on any part of the fuel system, the system must be depressurised as described in Section 7.
- Care must be taken when disconnecting the fuel lines. When disconnecting a fuel union or hose, loosen the union or clamp screw slowly, to avoid sudden uncontrolled fuel spillage. Take adequate fire precautions.
- When working on fuel system components, scrupulous cleanliness must be observed, and care must be taken not to introduce any foreign matter into fuel lines or components.
- After carrying out any work involving disconnection of fuel lines, it is advisable to check the connections for leaks; pressurise the system by switching the ignition on and off several times.
- Before disconnecting any wiring, or removing components, always ensure at least that the ignition is switched off – better still, disconnect the battery. If this is not done, and a component is disconnected when 'live', it could be damaged – or a fault code may be stored, which would then have to be cleared to regain normal operation.
- Do not attempt to improvise fault diagnosis procedures using a test light or multi-meter, as irreparable damage could be caused to the module.

Warning: Many of the procedures in this Chapter require the disconnection of fuel line connections, and the removal of components, which may result in some fuel spillage. Before carrying out any operation on the fuel system, refer to the precautions given in 'Safety first!' at the beginning of this manual, and follow them implicitly. Petrol is a highly-dangerous and volatile liquid, and the precautions necessary when handling it cannot be overstressed.

2 Air cleaner assembly – removal and refitting

1 Remove the two screws at the back of the air cleaner cover, then lift the cover and take out the filter element **(see illustrations)**.

2 Loosen the large hose clip and disconnect the throttle body inlet hose from the air cleaner

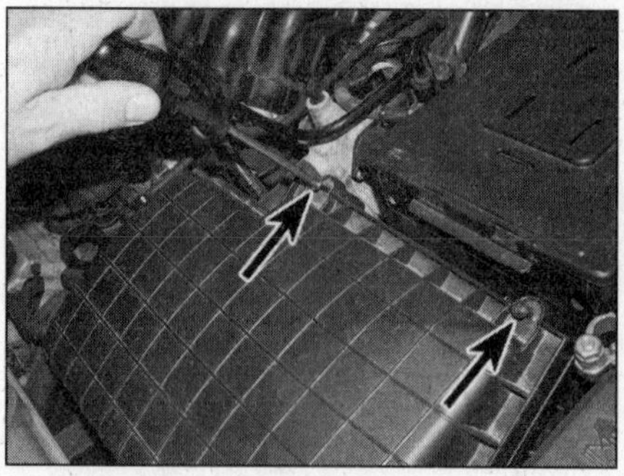

2.1a Remove the two screws . . .

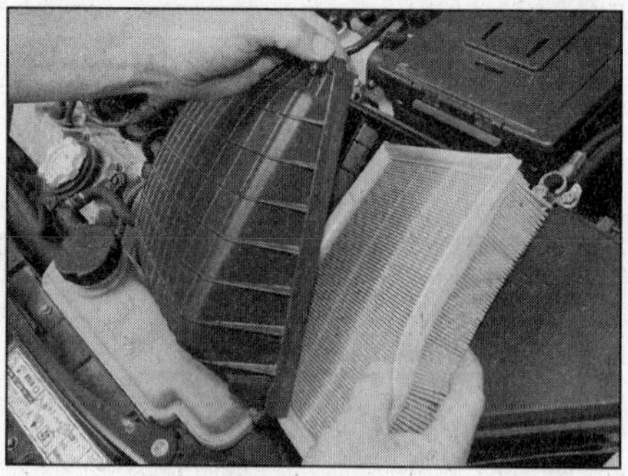

2.1b . . . then lift the air cleaner cover and remove the element

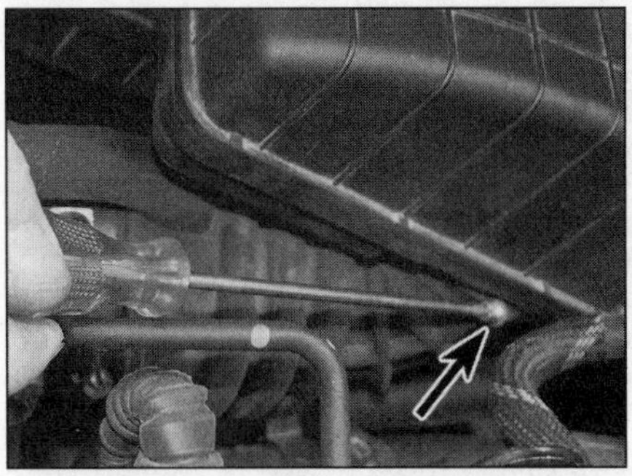

2.2a Loosen the hose clip underneath . . .

2.2b . . . and lift off the air cleaner cover

2.3 Release the air cleaner base from the rear grommets

cover. Release the cover at the front, and lift it off **(see illustrations)**.

3 The air cleaner base can now be lifted out. It is located in two grommets at the rear, and must be released from the air intake duct at the front **(see illustration)**.

4 Refitting is a reversal of removal. Ensure that the hose clips are tightened securely, otherwise this will produce an air leak.

3 Fuel tank and filler neck – removal, inspection and refitting

Refer to Chapter 4A.

4 Fuel filler flap release solenoid – removal and refitting

Refer to Chapter 4A.

5 Accelerator cable – removal, refitting and adjustment

Note: *On models with traction control, this procedure applies only to the primary cable. Refer to Section 15 for information on the secondary cable.*

Removal

1 Slide the cable end fitting from the groove in the throttle lever, and disconnect the cable from the lever **(see illustration)**.

2 Slide the cable adjuster from the bracket on the throttle body/inlet manifold **(see illustration)**.

3 Release the cable from the clip on the inlet manifold **(see illustration)**.

4 Working at the engine compartment bulkhead, turn the collar on the accelerator cable through 90°, and release the cable from the bulkhead.

5 Remove the trim panel fitted above the pedals, which is secured by two screws at the top, and two push-fasteners at the bottom.

6 Reach up under the facia, and pull the end of the cable forwards from the pedal, then squeeze the securing lugs and remove the plastic cable securing clip from the end of the pedal. Release the end of the cable from the pedal **(see illustration)**.

7 Pull the cable through the bulkhead into the engine compartment, and withdraw the cable from the car.

Refitting

8 Refitting is a reversal of removal, but smear the bulkhead grommet with rubber grease and, on completion, check the cable adjustment as described in the following paragraphs.

Adjustment

9 Slide the cable adjuster from the bracket on the inlet manifold/throttle body, then position the cable's square adjuster against the rear of the bracket.

10 Hold the throttle lever on the throttle body in the fully closed position, ensuring that the cam on the throttle lever rests against the throttle stop screw.

11 Turn the cable adjuster as necessary until all freeplay is removed from the cable, without moving the throttle lever.

12 Slide the adjuster back into position in the bracket.

13 Have an assistant fully depress the throttle pedal, and check that the throttle lever moves to the fully open position, and returns to the fully closed position when the pedal is released.

6 Accelerator pedal – removal and refitting

Refer to Chapter 4A.

5.1 Slide out and unhook the cable end fitting

5.2 Lift out the cable adjuster

5.3 Unclip the cable from the inlet manifold

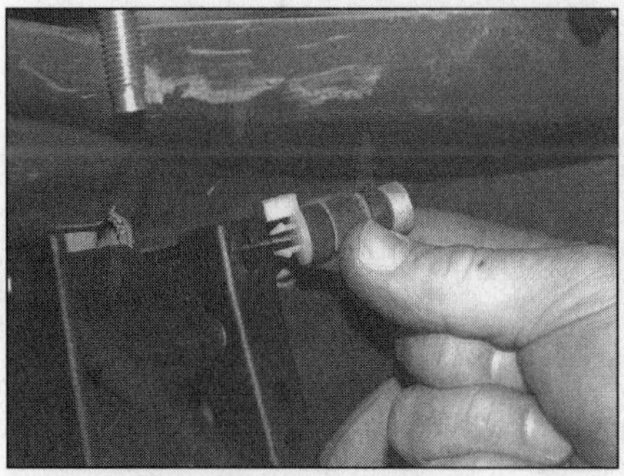

5.6 Pull out the cable end fitting, and unhook from the pedal

7 Fuel injection system – depressurising

Warning: The following procedure will merely relieve the pressure in the fuel system – remember that fuel will still be present in the system components, and take precautions accordingly before disconnecting any of them.

1 The fuel system referred to in this Chapter is defined as the fuel tank and tank-mounted fuel pump/fuel gauge sender unit, the fuel injectors, fuel pressure damper, and the metal pipes and flexible hoses of the fuel lines between these components. All these contain fuel, which will be under pressure while the engine is running and/or while the ignition is switched on.

2 The pressure will remain for some time after the ignition has been switched off, and must be relieved before any of these components is disturbed for servicing work.

3 The simplest depressurisation method is to disconnect the fuel pump electrical supply by removing the fuel pump fuse (make sure the ignition is off – typically, it's fuse number 20) and starting the engine. Allow the engine to idle until it stops through lack of fuel. If it won't start, turn the engine over once or twice on the starter to ensure that all pressure is released. Switch off the ignition on completion. Remember to refit the fuse when work is complete – the ignition must be off when this is done.

4 Before opening the fuel system, **always** disconnect the battery negative lead, and move the lead away from the battery (see *Disconnecting the battery*).

5 When opening any high-pressure fuel union, wrap absorbent cloth around the union, then **slowly** slacken the union nut. Allow the fuel pressure to dissipate, then retighten the union nut.

6 Note that, once the fuel system has been depressurised and drained (even partially), it will take significantly longer to restart the engine – perhaps several seconds of cranking – before the system is refilled and pressure restored. To avoid this, the system can be 'primed' before starting by switching the ignition on a few times – each time this is done, the fuel pump should be heard running for a short time. If the pump does not stop running, this may indicate a leak in the system – investigate before starting the engine.

8 Fuel pump/fuel gauge sender unit – removal and refitting

Refer to Chapter 4A.

9 Fuel injection system – testing and adjustment

Testing

1 If a fault appears in the fuel injection system, first ensure that all the system wiring connectors are securely connected and free from corrosion. Ensure that the fault is not due to poor maintenance; ie, check that the air cleaner filter element is clean, that the spark plugs are in good condition and correctly gapped (see Chapter 1A), that the cylinder compression pressures are correct (see Chapter 2B), and that the engine breather hoses are clear and undamaged (see Chapter 4D).

2 If the engine will not start, check that the fuel inertia cut-off switch has not operated (see Section 11). Push the switch button behind the glovebox to reset if necessary.

3 If these checks fail to reveal the cause of the problem, the car should be taken to a garage with diagnostic equipment for testing. A wiring connector is provided under the steering column, into which a special electronic diagnostic tester can be plugged. The tester should locate the fault quickly and simply, avoiding the need to test all the system components individually, which is time-consuming, and also carries a risk of damaging the ECM.

Adjustment

4 Experienced home mechanics with access to a tachometer and an accurately-calibrated exhaust gas analyser may be able to check the exhaust CO level and the idle speed. However, if either of these settings is found to be in need of adjustment, the car must be taken to a garage with diagnostic equipment for further testing.

5 No manual adjustment of the exhaust CO level or idle speed is possible.

10 Throttle body – removal and refitting

Note: *On completion, the throttle body may need to be set up using diagnostic equipment, in order to function correctly. This is particularly the case if a new or secondhand unit is being fitted.*

Removal

1 Ensure that the ignition is switched off (take out the key).

2 Remove the air cleaner as described in Section 2.

3 Loosen the hose clip on the throttle body, and remove the inlet air duct, pulling off the smaller hose from the idle air control valve at the same time **(see illustration)**.

4 Depress the locking collars, and pull out the breather and vacuum pipes from the throttle body and idle air control valve, noting their fitted positions **(see illustrations)**.

5 Slide out the accelerator cable's square adjuster from the bracket on the inlet manifold/throttle body, then slide the cable end fitting from the groove in the throttle lever, and disconnect the cable from the lever – refer to Section 5 if necessary.

6 On models with traction control, release the secondary accelerator cable from its bracket and the throttle cam (refer to Section 15 if necessary). Disconnect the multi-plug from the secondary throttle position sensor.

7 On models with cruise control, disconnect the vacuum hose from the cruise control actuator.

8 Disconnect the wiring plugs from the

10.3 Removing the inlet air duct

10.4a Disconnect the vacuum hose from the idle control valve . . .

10.4b . . . and pull the breather from the throttle body

10.8 **Disconnect the throttle sensor and air valve wiring plugs**

10.9a **Throttle body upper . . .**

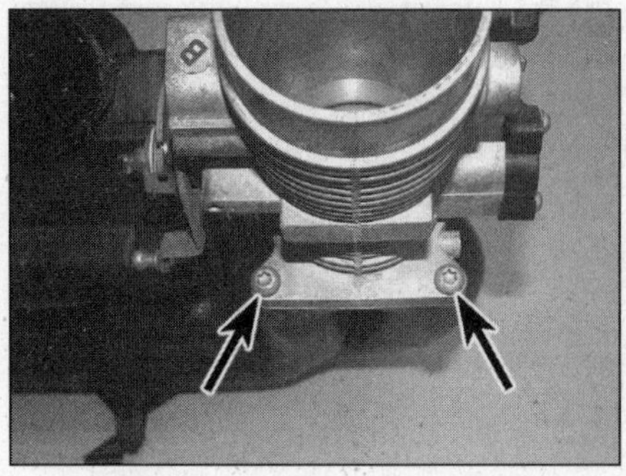

10.9b **. . . and lower Torx screws**

primary throttle position sensor and idle air control valve **(see illustration)**.

9 Unscrew the four Torx bolts, and withdraw the throttle body from the inlet manifold **(see illustrations)**. Recover the seal from the inlet manifold and discard it.

10 If a new throttle body is being fitted, the following components should be removed from it, and transferred to the new unit:

a) Cruise control actuator (Section 14).
b) Secondary throttle position sensor and secondary accelerator cable bracket – models with traction control (Section 15).
c) Primary throttle position sensor (Section 11).
d) Idle air control valve (Section 11).

Refitting

11 Clean the mating faces of the throttle body and inlet manifold.

12 Fit a new seal to the throttle body.

13 Locate the throttle body on the inlet manifold, then fit and securely tighten the four bolts.

14 The remaining refitting is a reversal of the removal procedure.

15 If the engine does not run properly on completion (after a reasonable period has been given for the engine to 'relearn' its settings), it may be necessary to have the engine set up using diagnostic equipment, at a suitably-equipped garage.

11 Fuel injection system components – removal and refitting

1 Before disconnecting any fuel injection wiring plugs, ensure that the ignition is switched off (take out the key). If any component is disconnected 'live', it could introduce a fault code in the ECM memory. Better still, disconnect the battery negative lead, and move the lead away from the battery (see *Disconnecting the battery*).

Fuel rails and injectors

2 Depressurise the fuel system as described in Section 7.

3 Remove the inlet manifold upper section as described in Section 12.

4 Disconnect the fuel pipe from the front fuel rail – this will require careful use of a small screwdriver to release its retaining clip **(see illustration)**.

5 Mark the ignition coils for position. Remove the three mounting nuts and bolts from the three ignition coils serving the front bank – note that one of the bolts also secures the earth lead. Lift out the coils and place to one side **(see illustrations)**.

6 Where applicable, release the two clips and two bolts securing the fuel injector protection plate, and lift the plate out – the two bolts are also used to secure the rear fuel rail.

7 Disconnect the injector multi-plugs, noting that one of the rear injectors is fitted the 'wrong' way round. Unscrew the two bolts from

11.4 **Use a small screwdriver to release the fuel rail rigid pipe**

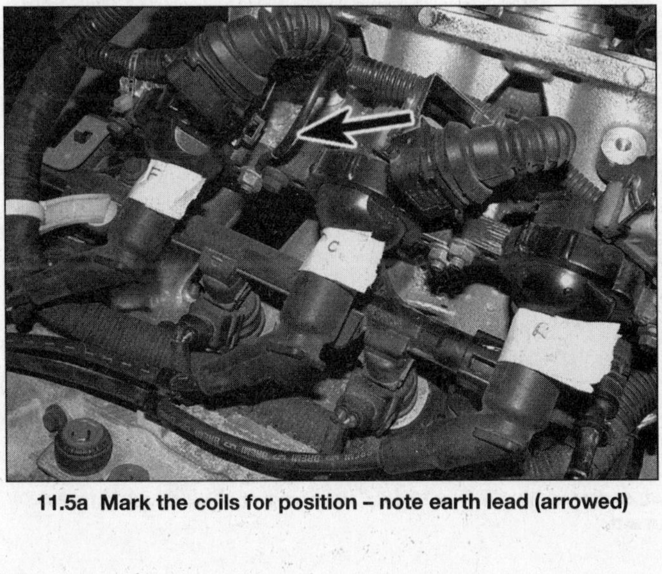

11.5a **Mark the coils for position – note earth lead (arrowed)**

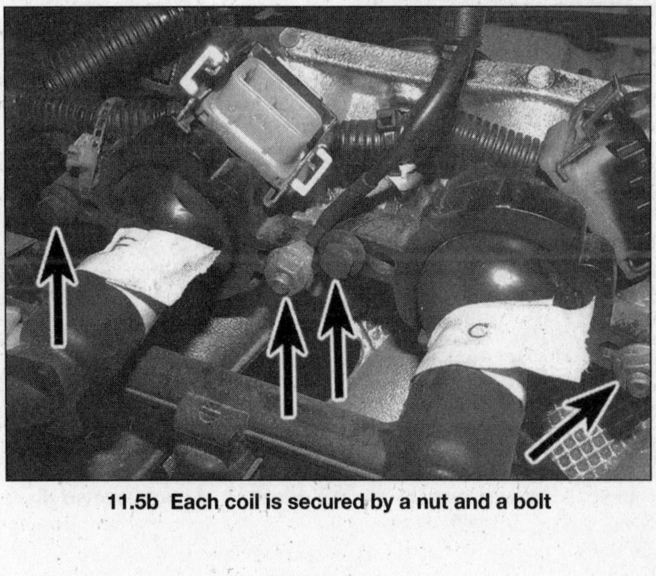

11.5b **Each coil is secured by a nut and a bolt**

11.7a Disconnect the injector wiring plugs

11.7b One of the rear injectors is reversed

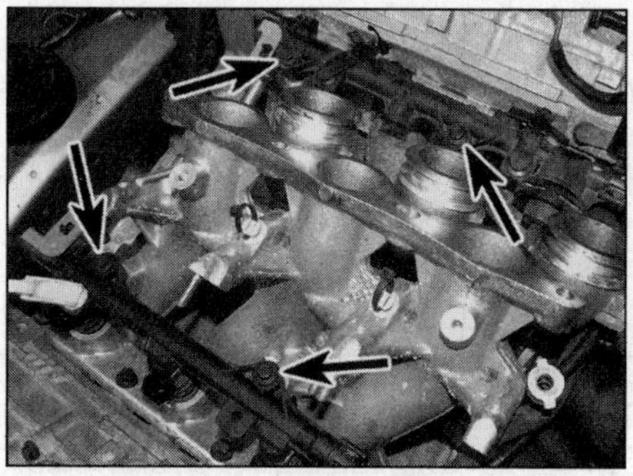

11.7c Front and rear fuel rail bolts

the front fuel rail, and two more from the rear rail, if not already done **(see illustrations)**.

8 Disconnect the vacuum pipe from the fuel pressure damper, and cut the clips securing the injector wiring harness to the rear fuel rail. Ease out the two fuel rails, noting that there will be resistance from the injector O-rings. Note the crossover pipe fitted between the rails, which means the two rails must be lifted out evenly, to avoid damage. Place the two fuel rail and injector assemblies carefully to one side **(see illustrations)**.

9 Release the spring clips securing the injectors to the fuel rail, and remove the injectors. Remove and discard the three O-rings from each injector **(see illustrations)**. Cover both ends of each injector with a protective cap.

10 Refitting is a reversal of the removal procedure, noting the following points:

a) Use new injector O-rings, lubricated with a little light oil before fitting them to the injectors ***(see illustration)****.*

b) Tighten the fuel rail bolts to the specified torque, noting that those for the rear bank also secure the injector protection plate.

Fuel pressure damper

Note: *On later models, the damper is an integral part of the rear fuel rail, and cannot be removed.*

11 The fuel pressure damper is mounted on the fuel rail serving the rear bank, and is intended to reduce the effects of pressure variations in the fuel supplied from the tank-mounted pump.

12 Depressurise the fuel system as described in Section 7.

13 Remove the inlet manifold upper section as described in Section 12.

14 Mark the ignition coils for position. Remove the three mounting nuts and bolts from the three ignition coils serving the front bank – note that one of the bolts also secures the earth lead. Lift out the coils and place to one side.

15 Where applicable, release the two clips and two bolts securing the fuel injector protection plate, and lift the plate out – the two bolts are also used to secure the rear fuel rail.

16 Disconnect the pressure damper vacuum pipe. The damper is retained by a large spring clip – squeeze together the legs

11.8a Carefully cut the clips securing the fuel rail wiring harness . . .

11.8b . . . then ease out the rails evenly, and remove them as a pair

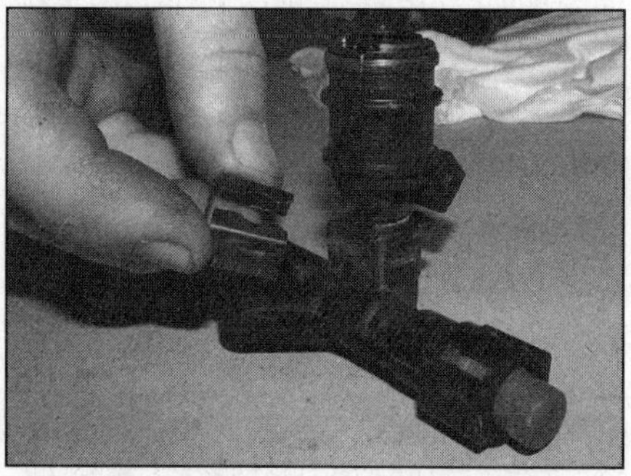

11.9a Pull off the spring clip . . .

11.9b . . . then ease each injector out of the fuel rail

11.9c Recover the O-ring seals – new ones must be used

11.10 Each injector should have three new O-rings

11.16 Removing the pressure damper retaining clip

11.21 Disconnect the idle air valve vacuum hose

11.22 Idle air control valve Allen screws

at one side of the clip, and withdraw it **(see illustration)**.

17 Anticipating some fuel spillage, pull the damper out of the fuel rail, and recover the O-rings.

18 Refitting is a reversal of removal. Use new O-rings, and ensure the damper is securely clipped into the fuel rail.

Idle air control valve

19 The idle air control valve is located on top of the throttle body.

20 Disconnect the wiring plug from the valve.

21 Depress the locking collar, and pull out the control valve's vacuum hose **(see illustration)**. The air bypass hose, which is part of the main air inlet duct, just pulls off.

22 Remove the two Allen screws securing the valve to the throttle body, then withdraw the valve from the manifold **(see illustration)**. Recover the gasket and discard it.

23 Refitting is a reversal of removal, using a new gasket and tightening the valve securing screws securely.

Engine coolant temperature sensor

24 The ECT sensor is screwed into the top of the engine.

25 Remove the air cleaner and inlet manifold upper section as described in Chapter 4B.

26 Disconnect the sensor multi-plug, then unscrew and remove the switch **(see illustrations)**. Recover the sealing washer – a new one should be obtained for refitting.

11.26a Disconnect the wiring plug next to the thermostat housing . . .

27 Refitting is a reversal of the removal procedure, noting the following points:

a) Clean the sensor and the mating face on the block, and use a new sealing washer.

b) Tighten the sensor to the specified torque.

c) Refit the thermostat as described in Chapter 3.

Crankshaft position sensor

28 The sensor is mounted at the front of the transmission bellhousing (at the left-hand end of the engine) **(see illustration)**.

29 Release the front edge of the engine undertray, which is secured by a number of quick-release screw fasteners.

30 Disconnect the wiring plug above the sensor **(see illustration)**.

31 Unscrew the single bolt securing the sensor to the bellhousing, then remove the sensor **(see illustration)**.

11.26b . . . then unscrew and remove the coolant temperature sensor

32 Thoroughly clean the mating faces on the sensor and housing, then refit the sensor using a reversal of the removal procedure.

Throttle position sensor

Note: *Whenever the sensor is removed or renewed, a 'throttle initialisation' procedure must be carried out, to ensure correct operation afterwards – also see paragraph 38. As this requires the use of diagnostic equipment, it may be advisable to have work involving this sensor carried out by a suitably-equipped garage or specialist.*

33 The sensor is mounted on the side of the throttle body.

34 Remove the battery and its tray as described in Chapter 5A.

35 Disconnect the multi-plug from the sensor.

36 Remove and discard two Torx screws and wave washers securing the sensor to the

11.28 The crankshaft position sensor is on the front of the transmission

11.30 Disconnect the wiring plug . . .

11.31 . . . then withdraw the sensor from the transmission

11.36 Throttle position sensor wiring plug and Torx screws (arrowed)

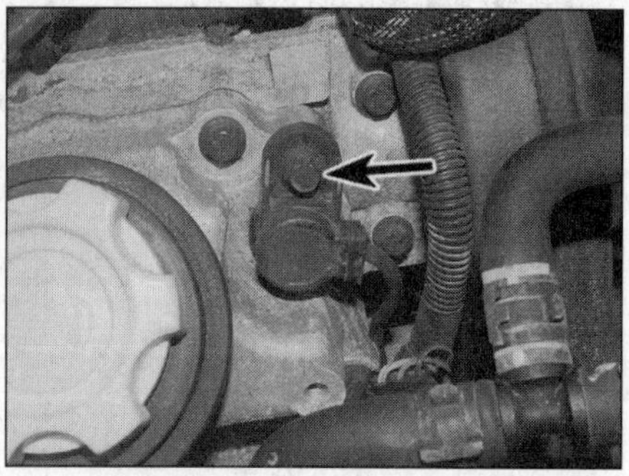

11.46 Camshaft position sensor location

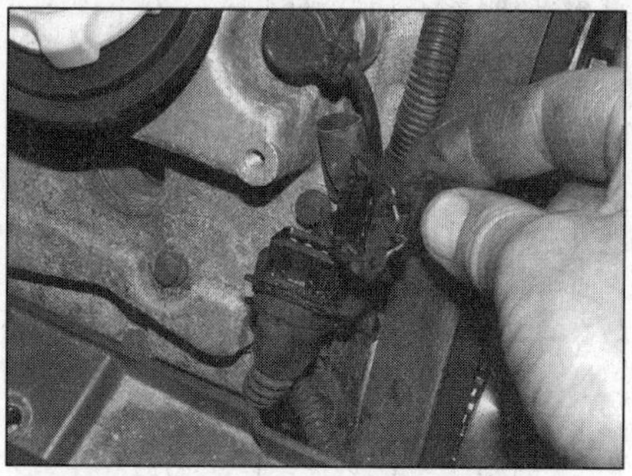

11.47a Disconnect one half of the wiring plug . . .

throttle housing – discard the washers and screws, as new ones should be used when refitting **(see illustration)**.

37 Remove the sensor specification plate, and pull the sensor from the throttle spindle without twisting it.

38 The sensor's inner section should not be turned while it is removed – if the same unit is being refitted, this minimises the need for the sensor to be 'initialised' on completion.

Caution: The sensor can easily be damaged, especially during fitting – handle it with care. Ensure, for example, that the machined flat on the throttle spindle is accurately aligned with the corresponding one inside the sensor. If nothing has been moved, and the original sensor is being refitted, it should only be necessary to align the mounting screw holes.

39 Clean the mating faces of the throttle housing and sensor.

40 Align the flat on the sensor with the flat on the throttle spindle, and push the sensor gently onto the spindle. If a new sensor is being fitted, rotate the sensor in an anti-clockwise direction to align the screw holes – **do not** turn it clockwise, nor beyond its internal stop. If possible, set the new sensor to the same position as the one just removed.

41 Fit the specification plate, with new wave washers and Torx screws. Tighten the screws securely.

42 Connect the multi-plug to the sensor.

43 Operate the throttle linkage by hand a few times, and check that both idle and full-throttle positions appear to be available.

44 Run the engine and test the operation of the sensor. If the idle quality has suffered, and does not improve even after giving the system time to 'relearn' its values, throttle initialisation may be required – this requires diagnostic equipment.

Camshaft position sensor

45 Remove the two bolts and unclip the engine top cover. Recover the washers and rubber grommets from the bolt holes, and store them for refitting.

46 The sensor is screwed into the front bank of the engine, and is located next to the oil filler cap **(see illustration)**. Trace the sensor wiring to the end of the cylinder head, to the wiring plug.

47 Disconnect the wiring plug, then unscrew the single bolt securing the sensor in position, and withdraw it from the cylinder head **(see illustrations)**. Recover the sensor's O-ring seal – a new one should be used when refitting.

48 To remove the sensor completely, slide the other half of the wiring plug out of the bracket, then unscrew the bolt securing the bracket to the head, and remove it to free the sensor wiring behind **(see illustrations)**.

49 Refitting is a reversal of removal, noting the following points:

a) *Clean the mating faces of the sensor and cylinder head.*
b) *Lubricate a new seal with engine oil, and tighten the bolt securely.*
c) *Ensure that the sensor wiring is routed as before, behind the wiring plug bracket.*

Manifold absolute pressure sensor

Note: *This sensor has a built-in inlet air temperature sensor.*

50 The MAP sensor is located behind the idle air control valve **(see illustration)**.

11.47b . . . then unbolt and remove the camshaft position sensor

11.48a Slide out the wiring plug . . .

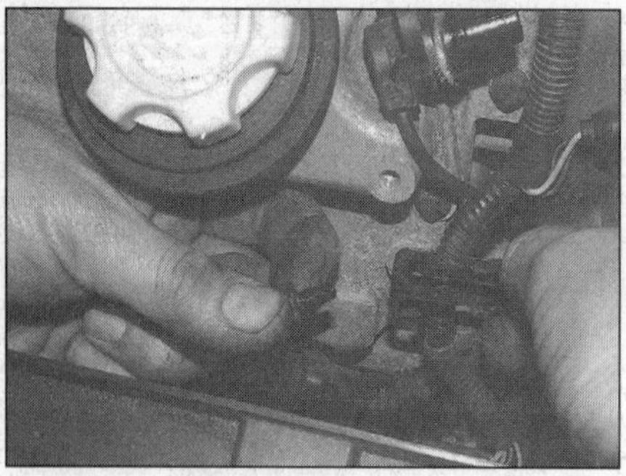

11.48b . . . then unbolt and remove the bracket

11.50 The MAP sensor is behind the idle air control valve – screws arrowed

11.51 Disconnecting the MAP sensor wiring plug

11.57 Disconnect the inertia switch wiring plug

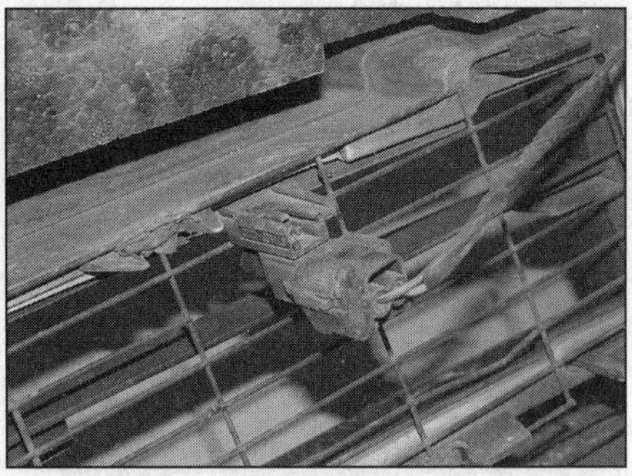

11.67 The exterior temperature sensor is mounted behind the bumper grille

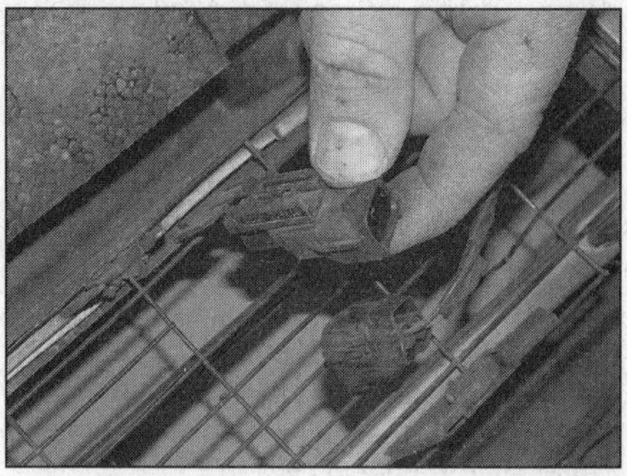

11.68 Removing the temperature sensor

51 Disconnect the sensor wiring plug **(see illustration)**.

52 Remove the two screws and lift the sensor off.

53 Refitting is a reversal of removal. Clean the sensor and manifold mating faces prior to fitting.

Oxygen sensors

54 Refer to Chapter 4D.

Inertia (fuel cut-off) switch

55 The inertia switch is mounted to the left of the front passenger footwell. Access to the switch itself is hampered by the wiring harness which runs in front of it.

56 Working as described in Chapter 11, Section 25, remove the glovebox, the passenger's facia closing trim panel, and the footwell left-hand trim panel.

57 Disconnect the multi-plug from the base of the switch **(see illustration)**.

58 Remove the two mounting screws, and withdraw the switch from the footwell.

59 Refitting is a reversal of removal, but ensure that the switch is reset by pressing the button on the top of the switch.

Power steering pressure switch

60 The switch is located at the rear of the power steering pump.

61 Remove the two bolts, and lift off the engine right-hand mounting's upper cross-brace.

62 Disconnect the multi-plug from the switch.

63 Position a container under the switch to catch any lost fluid. Unscrew the switch, and remove it. Recover the O-ring – a new one should be used when refitting.

64 Refitting is a reversal of removal, noting the following points:

a) Use a new O-ring, lubricated with power steering fluid.

b) Tighten the switch to the specified torque – counterhold the union with another spanner as this is done.

c) Tighten the engine mounting cross-brace bolts to the specified torque.

Exterior temperature sensor

65 The sensor is fitted below the front bumper, behind the lower grille.

66 Remove the fasteners from the front of the engine undertray, and lower the tray for access to the sensor.

67 Disconnect the wiring plug from the sensor **(see illustration)**.

68 The sensor slides onto a moulded tab, and is released using a small screwdriver **(see illustration)**. Remove the sensor from under the car.

69 Refitting is a reversal of removal.

Canister purge valve

70 Refer to Chapter 4D.

Engine control module

Note: *If a new module is to be fitted, it will need to be programmed with the code from the anti-theft security unit before the engine can be started. This can only be done using diagnostic equipment, and it may therefore be advisable to have this work carried out by a suitably-equipped garage or specialist.*

71 Disconnect the battery negative lead, and move the lead away from the battery (see *Disconnecting the battery*). This is **essential** – if the ECM wiring plug is disconnected (or reconnected) 'live', the module could be damaged.

72 Release and lift off the passenger-side half of the windscreen outer grille panel, which is secured by two tabs at the front edge.

73 Pull off the rubber weather strip at the front of the windscreen cowl panel on the passenger side.

74 Remove the three clips at the rear, and the single screw/clip at the front, then carefully lift up the passenger side of the windscreen cowl panel frame. Slide out the water shield panel **(see illustration)**.

75 Release the ECM securing clips either side, and lift it out **(see illustration)**.

76 Slide the ECM wiring plug locking clips to the sides, then disconnect them and remove the module **(see illustration)**.

77 While the module is removed, check that the drain holes inside the housing are clear, as they can become blocked, which may lead to ECM damage.

78 Refitting is a reversal of removal. Ensure that the module wiring plugs are securely reconnected.

11.74 Slide out the water shield panel

11.75 Lift out the ECM

11.76 Slide the locking clips sideways, and disconnect the wiring plug

12 Manifolds – removal and refitting

Inlet manifold

Upper chamber

1 Remove the two bolts and unclip the engine top cover. Recover the washers and rubber grommets from the bolt holes, and store them for refitting.

2 Remove the air cleaner as described in Section 2.

3 Remove the battery and its tray as described in Chapter 5A.

4 Disconnect the two hoses and the wiring plug from the canister purge valve **(see illustrations)**.

5 Depress the locking collars, and pull out the breather and vacuum pipes from the throttle body and idle air control valve, noting their fitted positions. Similarly disconnect the brake servo vacuum hose from the inlet manifold **(see illustrations)**.

6 Referring to Section 11 as necessary, disconnect the wiring plugs from the throttle position sensor(s), idle air control valve and MAP sensor **(see illustrations)**. Unclip the wiring harness and move it clear.

7 Where applicable, disconnect the vacuum hose from the cruise control actuator, and unclip it from the manifold.

8 Referring to Section 5, disconnect the accelerator cable(s) from the throttle body.

12.4a Disconnect the two hoses, noting their fitted positions . . .

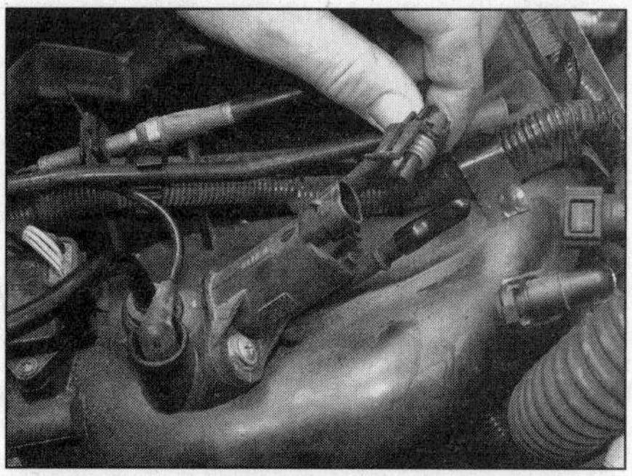

12.4b . . . and the wiring plug from the purge valve

12.5a Depress the locking collars, and remove the breathers . . .

12.5b . . . and vacuum pipes from the throttle body . . .

9 Noting how they are routed, unclip the vacuum and breather hoses from the top of the engine, removing them as a complete assembly with the T-piece. Also disconnect the hoses from the front cylinder head **(see illustrations)**.

10 Disconnect the wiring plugs from the variable induction system motors on the right-

12.5c . . . and disconnect the brake servo vacuum hose

12.6a Disconnect the wiring plugs from the throttle body . . .

12.6b . . . and from the MAP sensor

12.9a Disconnect the breather hoses from the front . . .

12.9b . . . and rear cylinder heads . . .

12.9c . . . and remove them as an assembly where possible

12.10 Disconnect the VIS motor wiring plugs

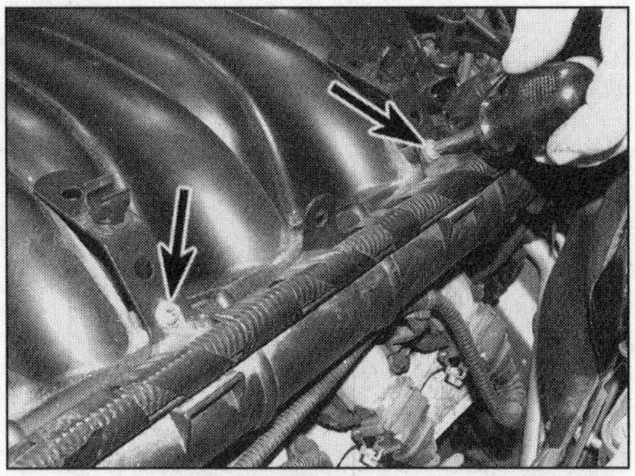

12.11 Remove the screws securing the wiring harness

12.12 Unscrew the bolts from the two manifold rear support brackets

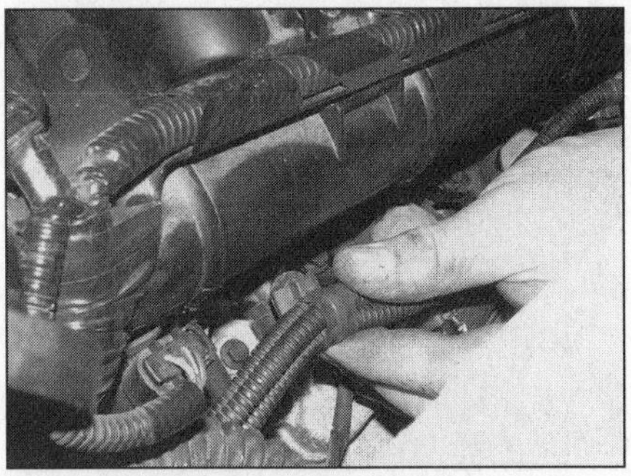

12.13 Unclip the rear ignition coil wiring harness from the manifold

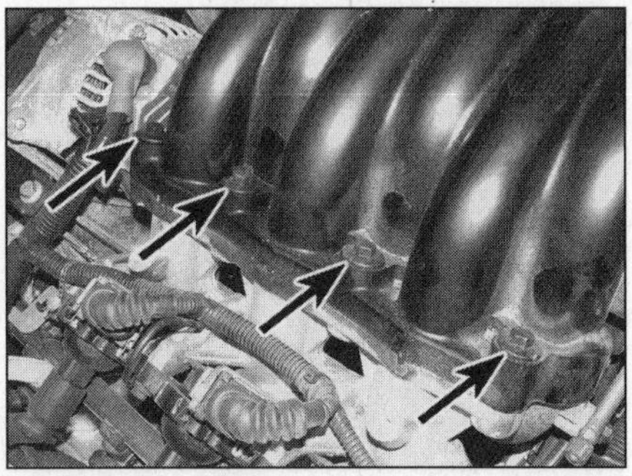

12.14 Unscrew the four manifold mounting bolts

hand side of the manifold **(see illustration)**. Remove the screws securing the wiring harness brackets.

11 Remove the two screws securing the wiring harness to the back of the manifold, and move the harness clear **(see illustration)**.

12 Unscrew the bolt securing each manifold support bracket to the rear bank's camshaft cover – there are two, but they are quite hard to reach **(see illustration)**.

13 Release the two clips securing the rear bank's ignition coil wiring harness to the upper manifold mounting brackets **(see illustration)**.

14 Progressively loosen and remove the four bolts securing the upper manifold to the front inlet manifold **(see illustration)**.

15 Lift the upper section off the front and rear manifolds, this is made very difficult, due to resistance from the three large O-rings – prise the upper section carefully, and pack progressively larger (non-metal) wedges in the resulting gap until the O-rings release **(see illustrations)**.

16 Remove the upper manifold seals and the O-rings from the rear inlet manifold – new seals and O-rings will be needed for refitting **(see illustrations)**.

17 Refitting is a reversal of removal, noting the following points:

*a) Clean the mating surfaces, and fit new seals and O-rings **(see illustration)**.*

12.15a Carefully prise the manifold at each end, and insert wedges . . .

12.15b . . . until the manifold is freed from the large O-rings . . .

12.15c . . . and can be lifted off

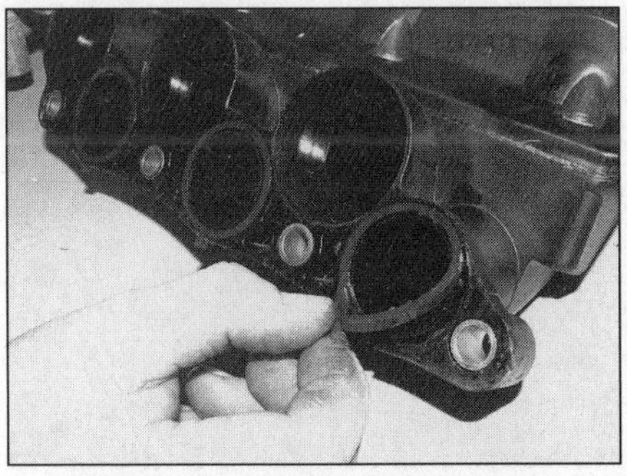

12.16a Remove the upper manifold seals . . .

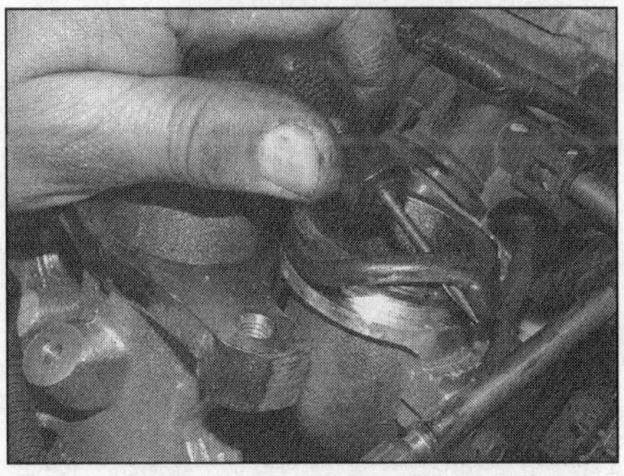

12.16b . . . and the O-rings

12.17 Fit new seals and O-rings when refitting

b) *Align the upper chamber with the manifolds, then fit and tighten the four bolts to the specified torque.*
c) *Ensure that all hoses are correctly routed and reconnected as noted before removal.*
d) *Adjust the accelerator cable(s) if necessary, as described in Section 5.*

Front

18 Drain the cooling system as described in Chapter 1A.
19 Remove the fuel rail as described in Section 11.
20 Depress the locking collar and pull out the breather hose from the front inlet manifold.
21 Release the hose clip and disconnect the coolant hose from the manifold.
22 Progressively loosen and remove the seven bolts securing the front inlet manifold to the head **(see illustration)**.
23 Lift off the inlet manifold, and recover the gasket – a new one will be needed for refitting.
24 Refitting is a reversal of removal, noting the following points:
a) *Clean the mating surfaces, and fit a new gasket.*
b) *Starting from the centre and working outwards, progressively tighten the manifold bolts to the specified torque.*
c) *Refill the cooling system as described in Chapter 1A.*

Rear

25 Drain the cooling system as described in Chapter 1A.
26 Remove the fuel rail as described in Section 11.
27 Depress the locking collar and pull out the vacuum hose from the rear inlet manifold.
28 Release the hose clip and disconnect the coolant hose from the manifold.
29 Progressively loosen and remove the seven bolts securing the front inlet manifold to the head.
30 Lift off the inlet manifold, and recover the gasket – a new one will be needed for refitting. Remove the bolt securing the hose bracket to the manifold.
31 Refitting is a reversal of removal, noting the following points:
a) *Clean the mating surfaces, and fit a new gasket* ***(see illustrations)****.*

12.22 Four of the seven front inlet manifold bolts

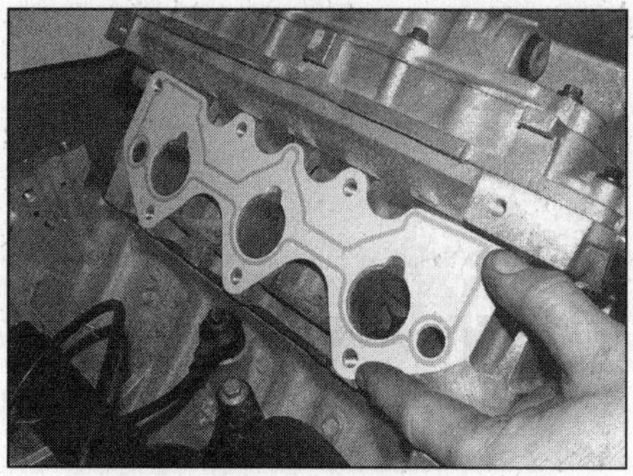

12.31a Fit a new gasket . . .

12.31b . . . then refit the rear manifold, and tighten the bolts

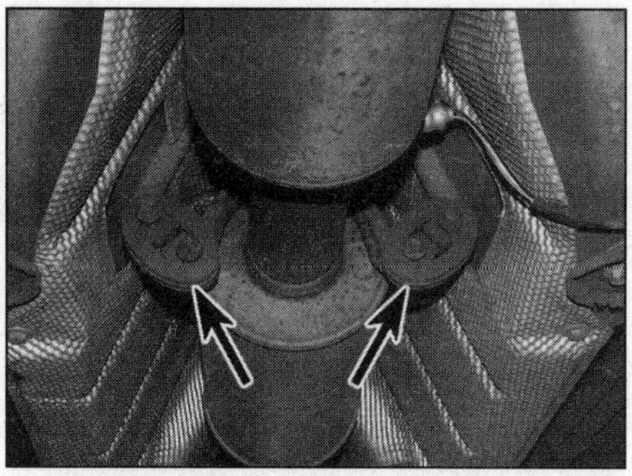

12.34 Unhook the exhaust from the front rubber mountings

b) *Starting from the centre and working outwards, progressively tighten the manifold bolts to the specified torque.*
c) *Refill the cooling system as described in Chapter 1A.*

Exhaust manifolds

32 Jack up the front of the car, and support it on axle stands (see *Jacking and vehicle support*).
33 Remove the engine undertray, which is secured by a number of quick-release screw fasteners.
34 Unhook the front section of the exhaust from its rubber mountings **(see illustration)**.
35 Remove the two bolts securing the front downpipe to the support bracket under the engine **(see illustration)**.
36 Remove the two nuts from each of the manifold-to-downpipe flanges, and separate the joints **(see illustration)**. Discard the flange gaskets – new ones must be used when refitting. Lower the downpipe clear, but support it so the pipe is not under strain.
37 If removing the front manifold on models with air conditioning, remove the oil cooler as described in Chapter 2B. Unscrew the three air conditioning compressor mounting bolts, and tie the compressor to one side without disconnecting the hoses.
38 Progressively loosen and remove the four nuts securing the front or rear manifold to the cylinder head **(see illustration)**. Remove the manifold from the studs, and recover the gasket – a new one must be used when refitting. If the manifold nuts are in poor condition, new ones should be obtained for reassembly – in this case, also consider fitting new studs.
39 If any studs were removed with the nuts, these can be refitted to the head using two nuts tightened against each other. If any

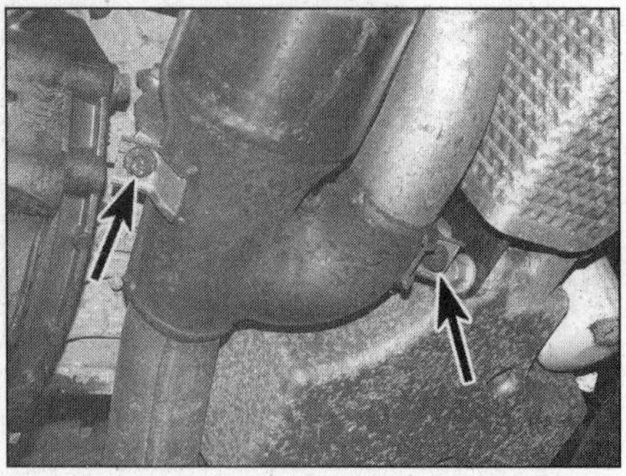

12.35 Remove the two exhaust support bracket bolts

12.36 Remove the manifold-to-downpipe nuts

12.38 Exhaust manifold mounting nuts

12.40a Fit a new manifold gasket . . .

12.40b . . . then refit the manifold and tighten the nuts

studs have to be refitted (or renewed, if their threads are in poor condition), apply a little threadlocking fluid to their threads before screwing them into the head.

40 Refitting is a reversal of removal, noting the following points:

a) *Clean the mating surfaces, and fit a new manifold gasket **(see illustration).***
b) *Progressively tighten the manifold nuts to the specified torque **(see illustration).***
c) *Fit new downpipe flange gaskets, and tighten their nuts to the specified torque.*
d) *Tighten the two downpipe-to-support bracket bolts to the specified torque.*
e) *On completion, run the engine and check for exhaust leaks from the disturbed joints.*

13 Variable induction system – general information and component renewal

General information

1 The inlet manifold features variable-length inlet tracts, for optimum torque at all engine speeds and loads.

2 Variable Induction System (VIS) valves, known as the balance valve and the power valves, are operated via the ECM by two motors on the right-hand side of the inlet manifold.

3 From the throttle body, a Y-shaped section feeds air into the two plenum chambers which serve each bank of three cylinders. At the end of the two plenum chambers is the balance valve, which allows the chambers to be connected together, giving an inlet tract length of up to 500 mm. The tract in each plenum chamber also has a power valve fitted 350 mm along its length which, when opened, diverts the air to a third plenum, thus shortening the inlet tract. One motor can operate all six power valves simultaneously, by means of a rod.

4 In the event of a failure in part of the system, the engine will typically lack bottom-end torque. Apparently, the most likely reason for failure will be one of the VIS motors, which can be renewed quite easily as described in the following paragraphs.

VIS motors

Removal

5 Disconnect the multi-plug from the motor to be removed **(see illustration)**.

6 Remove the four mounting screws, and lift the motor from the inlet manifold upper chamber **(see illustrations)**. Recover the seal fitted to each motor – if they are in good condition, they can be re-used.

Refitting

7 Clean the motor and inlet manifold mating faces, and check that the seal is fitted to the motor.

8 Locate the motor drive pin into the groove, and make sure the seal is correctly located on the manifold.

9 Fit and securely tighten the motor mounting screws, then reconnect the multi-plug.

14 Cruise control – general information and component renewal

1 The cruise control system fitted to some models offers the means of automatically maintaining any speed selected by the driver (from 22 to 125 mph), without using the accelerator pedal. This is useful for long periods of motorway cruising, and/or as a means of avoiding speeding convictions.

2 The system works via a vacuum actuator attached to the throttle cam, operated by a vacuum pump via its own ECU. When the facia master switch is pressed, the system becomes active. Once the desired speed has been reached, using the SET+ control on the steering wheel, the speed can be selected, and then increased. Once this has been done, the speed is controlled by the vacuum actuator, which opens and closes the throttle automatically in response to changing road conditions – information on the current vehicle speed is provided by the ABS wheel sensors. The system can be deactivated by pressing the brake or clutch (or on automatic transmission models, by selecting N), or by using the RES steering wheel control – afterwards, the RES control can be used to have the system resume the previously-set speed.

Vacuum actuator

3 Remove the two bolts and unclip the engine top cover. Recover the washers and rubber grommets from the bolt holes, and store them for refitting.

4 Remove the air cleaner as described in Section 2.

5 Disconnect the vacuum hose from the actuator on the side of the throttle body.

6 Unscrew the mounting nut, then detach the operating rod from the throttle cam and remove the actuator.

7 Refitting is a reversal of removal. Check the condition of the vacuum hose before refitting it – any cracks or splits will result in partial or non-operation of the system.

Vacuum pump

8 The vacuum pump is located on the left-hand inner wing (left as seen from the driver's seat).

13.5 Disconnect the VIS motor wiring plug

13.6a Remove the mounting screws . . .

13.6b . . . and lift off the motor

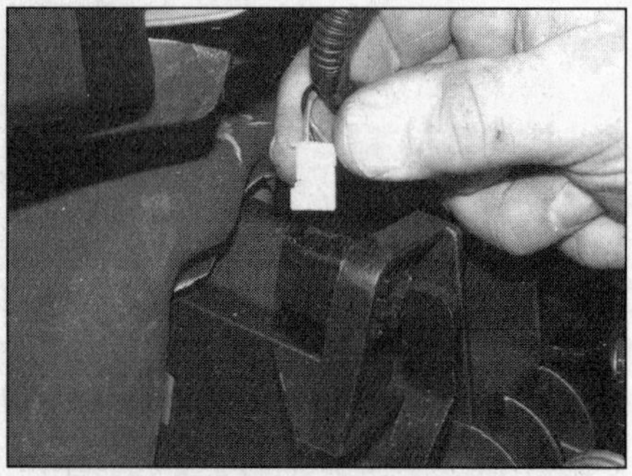

14.20a Disconnect the clutch switch wiring plug . . .

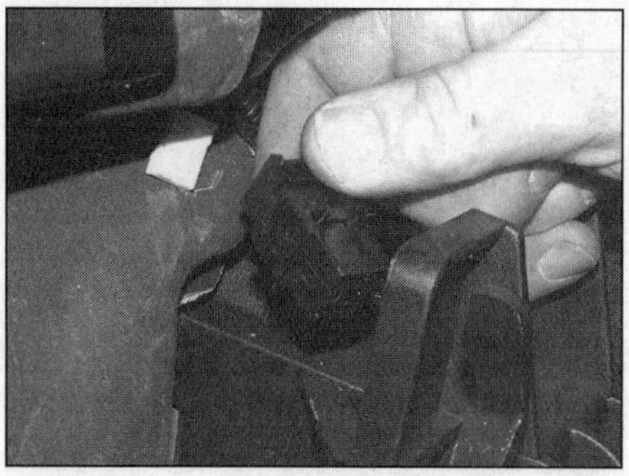

14.20b . . . then pull the switch from its bracket

9 Jack up the front of the car, and support it on axle stands (see *Jacking and vehicle support*).

10 Remove the engine undertray, which is secured by a number of turn-buckle fasteners.

11 Disconnect the pump motor wiring plug, and the vacuum supply hose.

12 Unscrew the two mounting bolts and remove the pump from the car, together with its mounting bracket.

13 The pump is attached to its bracket by three rubber mountings – release these to remove the pump completely.

14 Refitting is a reversal of removal. Check the condition of the vacuum hose before refitting it – any cracks or splits will result in partial or non-operation of the system.

Master switch

15 Taking care not to mark the facia, prise out the trim panel which sits over the central row of switches – this is secured by four clips.

16 Unclip the switch from the facia, then disconnect the wiring plug behind and remove it.

17 Refitting is a reversal of removal.

Steering wheel switches

18 The steering wheel switches for the cruise control are removed with the horn switches, as described in Chapter 12, Section 4.

Clutch switch

19 Remove the trim panel fitted above the pedals, which is secured by two screws at the top, and two push-fasteners at the bottom.

20 Disconnect the wiring plug, then pull out the clutch switch from the pedal bracket, and remove it **(see illustrations)**.

21 Refitting is a reversal of removal. Fully depress the clutch pedal and hold it down, then manoeuvre the switch into position. Slide the switch as far as it will go into the bracket, then **slowly** release the clutch pedal and allow it to return to its starting position. **Note:** *If the pedal is released too quickly, the switch will be incorrectly adjusted.*

ECU and interface

22 Ensure that the ignition is switched off (take out the key).

23 Remove the glovebox as described in Chapter 11, Section 25.

24 The ECU is a small unit to the left of the fuse panel, secured by two bolts; the interface unit is smaller still, and mounted above it.

25 Swing the required unit's wiring plug locking lever to the left, and disconnect the wiring multi-plug.

26 If removing the ECU, unscrew the two mounting bolts, and withdraw the unit.

27 To remove the interface unit, release the clip securing it to the mounting bracket, and remove it.

28 Refitting is a reversal of removal.

15 Traction control system – general information and component renewal

1 The traction control system fitted to some V6 models is intended to reduce the tendency for the front wheels to spin under hard acceleration, or when driving on slippery surfaces. The system is largely a feature of the anti-lock braking system (ABS) – see Chapter 9. From the wheel sensors, the ABS ECU checks for wheelspin by comparing the speed of each front (driven) wheel with the rear (non-driven) wheel on the same side. If required, the front brakes are applied lightly and evenly, until the front wheel speeds normalise.

2 In addition, when the wheelspin condition is detected, engine power is reduced by the engine control module (ECM), or by the traction control ECU, in one of three ways:

1) *First, the ignition is retarded by the ECM.*
2) *A secondary throttle system is used, to progressively restrict the airflow into the engine. A second throttle plate is fitted inside the throttle body, operated via cable by an actuator controlled by the traction control ECU. The plate is fully-open by default, but can be closed as required.*
3) *If further reduction in power is required, the ECM alters the fuelling.*

3 The system is active every time the engine is started, but can be switched off using a facia-mounted switch if the driver prefers.

Secondary throttle position sensor

4 The procedure is identical to the (primary) throttle position sensor, described in Section 11.

Secondary accelerator cable

Removal

5 Remove the air cleaner assembly as described in Section 2.

6 Slide the cable adjuster from the bracket on the throttle body/inlet manifold.

7 Slide the cable end fitting from the groove in the throttle lever, and disconnect the cable from the lever.

8 Noting its routing, unclip the cable from the top of the inlet manifold, and trace it back to the actuator.

9 Unclip and open the access flap on the top of the actuator, then unhook the cable end fitting from the drivegear.

10 Release the clip and detach the outer cable from the actuator, and remove it.

Refitting

11 Refitting is a reversal of removal.

Adjustment

12 If not already done, remove the air cleaner as described in Section 2.

13 Slide the cable adjuster from the bracket on the throttle body, then position the cable's square adjuster against the rear of the bracket.

14 Ensure the secondary throttle plate is in the fully-open position, and that the cam on the throttle lever rests against the stop.

15 Turn the cable adjuster as necessary until all freeplay is removed from the cable, without moving the throttle lever.

16 Slide the adjuster back into position in the bracket.

17 Refit the air cleaner as described in Section 2.

Secondary throttle actuator

Removal

18 Remove the secondary accelerator cable as described previously in this Section.

19 Disconnect the multi-plug from the base of the actuator.

20 Unscrew the three nuts securing the actuator mounting bracket to the bulkhead, and withdraw it.

21 If required, the actuator can be separated from the mounting bracket after unscrewing the two bolts.

Refitting

22 Refitting is a reversal of removal. Refit and adjust the cable as described previously in this Section.

16 Exhaust system – general information and component renewal

1 The exhaust system fitted at the factory is a one-piece item, with two catalytic converters and three silencer boxes. A three-branch manifold is fitted to each bank of cylinders, and the two manifolds merge into a single pipe ahead of the 'starter' catalytic converter,

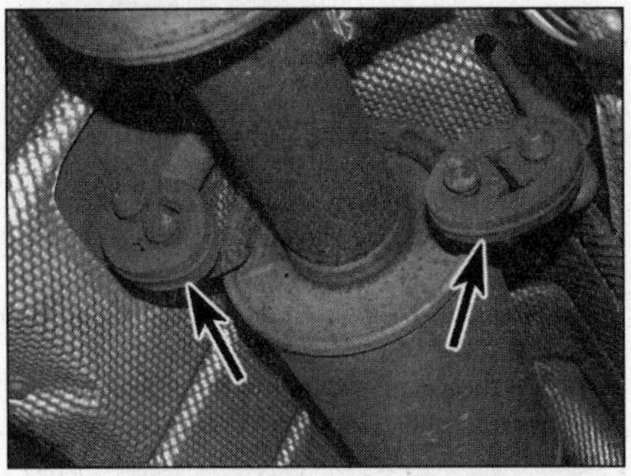

16.11 Unhook the exhaust front mountings

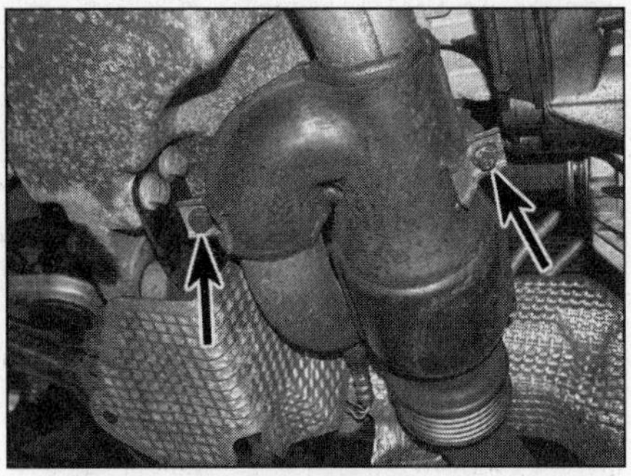

16.12 Unbolt the exhaust support from the bottom of the engine

16.13 One of the oxygen sensor wiring plugs at the driver's-side rear of the engine

which is fitted upstream of the main catalytic converter.

2 Repair sections are available for the centre and tail silencer boxes, but to fit them on the factory original system requires that the pipe is cut at precisely the right point – for this reason, owners may prefer to have exhaust work carried out by an exhaust specialist. Where these repair sections have been fitted previously, references to cutting can be ignored, as the pipes can be separated by loosening the clamps.

3 The front pipe, which connects to the exhaust manifolds, includes the two catalytic converters, and three oxygen sensors.

4 The intermediate/tail section incorporates three silencers, which contain baffle plates and expansion chambers designed to reduce engine exhaust noise.

5 In the first instance, establish which section needs to be renewed, and what service sections are available.

6 Renewal of each section involves essentially the same process – owners may prefer to remove the complete system initially, as this should make working on it easier.

Front pipe

7 Jack up the front of the car, and support it on axle stands (see *Jacking and vehicle support*).

8 Remove the engine undertray, which is secured by a number of quick-release screw fasteners.

9 Offer up the new pipe as a guide for cutting, then clean and mark the pipe for cutting.

10 Cut the pipe through squarely, using a proper pipe-cutting tool if available.

11 Unhook the front section of the exhaust from its rubber mountings **(see illustration)**.

12 Remove the two bolts securing the front downpipe to the support bracket under the engine **(see illustration)**.

13 Trace the wiring from the three oxygen sensors (one below each manifold flange, and another behind the main catalytic converter) back to the wiring connectors, and disconnect it so that the sensors can be removed with the front pipe. Typically, the wiring plugs are mounted high up on the engine **(see illustration)**.

14 Remove the two nuts from each of the manifold-to-downpipe flanges, and separate the joints **(see illustration)**. Discard the flange gaskets – new ones must be used when refitting. Lower the downpipe clear.

15 De-burr the cut pipe, then fit the pipe clamp loosely in position.

16 As necessary, unscrew and transfer the oxygen sensors to the new pipe section – note that, where applicable, new sealing washers should be used. If possible, tighten the sensors to the specified torque.

17 Offer up the new section into the pipe clamp, and set it in place.

18 Fit new flange gaskets, and tighten the flange nuts by hand.

19 Refit the two bolts underneath securing the downpipe to its support bracket, and tighten them to the specified torque.

20 Tighten the downpipe flange nuts and the pipe clamp nuts to the specified torque.

21 Reconnect the oxygen sensor wiring.

22 Refit the engine undertray, then lower the car to the ground.

Intermediate pipe

23 Apply the handbrake, then jack up the car and support it on axle stands (see *Jacking and vehicle support*). For the best access, if enough axle stands are available, the car should be raised front and rear.

24 Remove the engine undertray, which is secured by a number of quick-release screw fasteners.

25 Offer up the new pipe as a guide for cutting, then clean and mark the pipe for cutting.

26 Cut the pipe through squarely front and rear, using a proper pipe-cutting tool if available.

27 In the centre of the car, unscrew a total of ten bolts and remove the three cross-braces fitted below the exhaust **(see illustrations)**.

28 Unhook the exhaust from its rubber mountings, and lower it to the floor.

29 De-burr the cut pipes, then fit the pipe clamps loosely in position.

30 Offer the new section into place, and hook it onto the rubber mountings. With the system 'settled' in place (and not touching the floor or suspension components), tighten the clamp nuts to the specified torque.

31 Refit the three cross-braces, and tighten the bolts to the specified torque.

32 Refit the engine undertray, then lower the car to the ground.

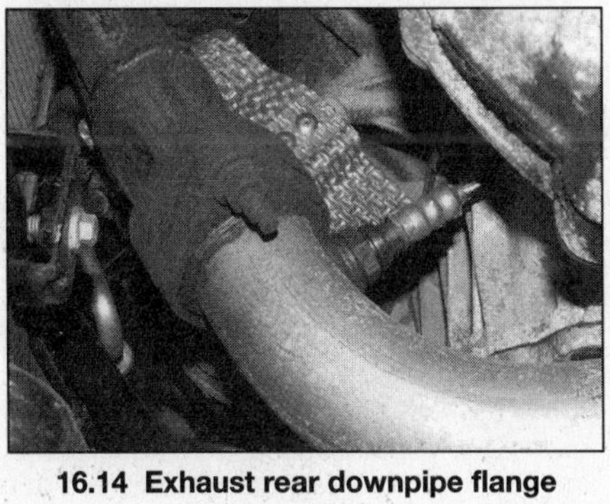

16.14 Exhaust rear downpipe flange

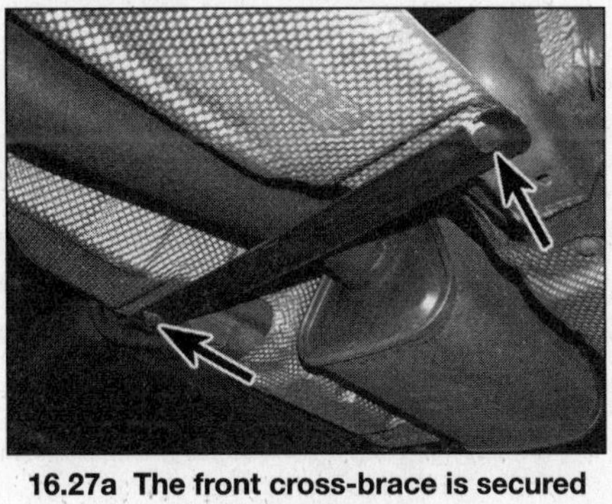

16.27a The front cross-brace is secured by two bolts . . .

16.27b . . . but the two further back have four bolts each

16.36 Unbolt the silencer support strap

Tail pipe

33 Jack up the rear of the car, and support it on axle stands (see *Jacking and vehicle support*).

34 Offer up the new section, and mark the pipe for cutting (if the tail section has been renewed previously, loosen the clamp nuts).

35 Where applicable, cut the pipe through squarely, using a proper pipe-cutting tool if available.

36 Unscrew the nut and bolt each side securing the silencer support strap, then lower the strap and silencer **(see illustration)**.

37 Where applicable, de-burr the cut end of pipe, and fit the clamp loosely in to place.

38 Offer in the new section, and hand-tighten the clamp nuts.

39 Refit the support strap, and tighten the nuts/bolts to the specified torque.

40 With the new section 'settled' in place, tighten the clamp nuts to the specified torque.

41 Lower the car to the ground to complete.

Chapter 4 Part C:
Fuel & exhaust systems – diesel engines

Contents

Degrees of difficulty

Easy, suitable for novice with little experience	**Fairly easy,** suitable for beginner with some experience	**Fairly difficult,** suitable for competent DIY mechanic	**Difficult,** suitable for experienced DIY mechanic	**Very difficult,** suitable for expert DIY or professional

Specifications

General

System type	Direct injection common rail with Bosch high-pressure delivery pump and Electronic Diesel Control with DDE 4.0 electronic control module
Fuel tank pump pressure	2.5 bar
Fuel injection pump	Bosch Cp1 3 x radial piston pump
Injection pressure	250 to 1350 bar
Turbocharger type	Mitsubishi MR1 TD025L3-08T-3.3
Turbocharger boost pressure	1.765 ± 0.03 bar (max)
Idle speed*	780 ± 50 rpm

** Not adjustable – controlled by engine control module (ECM)*

Torque wrench settings	Nm	lbf ft
EGR pipe bolts	22	16
Exhaust clamp nuts	48	35
Exhaust cross-brace bolts	25	18
Exhaust downpipe-to-elbow nuts	75	55
Exhaust manifold-to-head nuts	24	18
Exhaust outlet elbow-to-turbo nuts	75	55
Exhaust support strap nuts/bolts	22	16
Fuel high-pressure sensor	38	28
Fuel injection pump mounting nuts	24	18
Fuel injection pump sprocket retaining nut	65	48
Fuel injector clamp nuts/studs	10	7
Fuel pipe union nuts	20	15
Fuel rail-to-coolant rail bolts	10	7
Fuel rail-to-cylinder head bolts	24	18
Fuel tank mounting bolts	24	18
Fuel tank unit locking ring	38	28
Inlet manifold:		
M6 bolts	10	7
M7 nuts and bolt	15	11
Power steering pressure switch	24	18
Rear subframe mounting bolts	100	74
Timing cover access plug	30	22
Turbocharger mounting bolts	50	37
Turbocharger oil feed banjo bolts	22	16

1 General information and precautions

General information

The operation of the fuel injection system is described in more detail in Section 6.

Fuel is drawn from a tank under the rear of the car by a tank-immersed electric pump, then by an electrically-powered lift pump, and then forced through a filter to the injection pump. The chain-driven injection pump supplies very high pressure fuel to the common fuel rail, which is connected to each individual injector. The injectors are operated by solenoids controlled by the electronic control module (ECM), based on information supplied by various sensors. If the fuel temperature is sufficient, the returning fuel passes through a fuel cooling radiator mounted at the front of the engine compartment, and then returns to the fuel tank. The ECM also controls the preheating side of the system – refer to Chapter 5C for more details.

The engine management system is known as EDC (electronic diesel control), and incorporates a 'drive by wire' system, where the traditional accelerator cable is superceded by an accelerator pedal position sensor. The position and rate-of-change of the accelerator pedal is reported by the position sensor to the ECM, which then adjusts the fuel injectors to deliver the required amount of fuel, and optimum combustion efficiency

The exhaust system incorporates a turbocharger, and an exhaust gas recirculation system (EGR). Further detail of the emission control systems can be found in Chapter 4D.

Precautions

- When working on fuel system components, scrupulous cleanliness must be observed, and care must be taken not to introduce any foreign matter into fuel lines or components.
- After carrying out any work involving disconnection of fuel lines, it is advisable to check the connections for leaks; pressurise the system by cranking the engine several times.
- Electronic control units are very sensitive components, and certain precautions must be taken to avoid damage to these units as follows.
- When carrying out welding operations on the car using electric welding equipment, the battery and alternator should be disconnected.
- Although the underbonnet-mounted modules will tolerate normal underbonnet conditions, they can be adversely affected by excess heat or moisture. If using welding equipment or pressure-washing equipment in the vicinity of an electronic module, take care not to direct heat, or jets of water or steam, at the module. If this cannot be avoided, remove the module from the car, and protect its wiring plug with a plastic bag.
- Before disconnecting any wiring, or removing components, always ensure at least that the ignition is switched off – better still, disconnect the battery. If this is not done, and a component is disconnected when 'live', it could be damaged – or a fault code may be stored, which would then have to be cleared to regain normal operation.
- Do not attempt to improvise fault diagnosis procedures using a test light or multi-meter, as irreparable damage could be caused to the module.
- After working on fuel injection/engine management system components, ensure that all wiring is correctly reconnected before reconnecting the battery or switching on the ignition.

2 Air cleaner assembly – removal and refitting

The air cleaner housing is integral with the camshaft cover, and cannot be removed separately (see Chapter 2C). To remove the air cleaner top cover and element, refer to Chapter 1B.

3 Fuel tank – removal and refitting

Refer to Chapter 4A.

4 Fuel filler flap release solenoid – removal and refitting

Refer to Chapter 4A.

5 Accelerator pedal – removal and refitting

Removal

1 Remove the trim panel fitted above the pedals, which is secured by two screws at the top, and two push-fasteners at the bottom.

2 Unscrew the nut, and disconnect the pedal position sensor lever from the accelerator pedal.

3 Prise off the retaining clip, and slide the pedal pivot to one side. Disconnect the return spring, and remove the pedal.

4 The accelerator pedal mounting bracket is part of the brake and clutch pedal mounting bracket. In order to remove the bracket, refer to Chapter 9.

Refitting

5 Reconnect the return spring and position the pedal in the mounting bracket.

6 Slide the pivot into place, and secure it with a new retaining clip.

7 With the throttle pedal in the closed position, refit the sensor lever.

6 Fuel injection system – general information

The system is under the overall control of the Electronic Diesel Control (EDC) system, which also controls the preheating system (see Chapter 5C).

Fuel is supplied from the rear-mounted fuel tank by an electric pump mounted in the tank, to a secondary low-pressure pump by the battery tray, and fuel filter, to the high-pressure fuel injection pump. The fuel injection pump supplies fuel under high pressure to the common fuel rail. The fuel rail provides a reservoir of fuel under pressure ready for the injectors to deliver direct to the combustion chamber. The individual fuel injectors incorporate solenoids which, when operated, allow the high-pressure fuel to be injected. The solenoids are controlled by the ECM – the fuel injection pump merely provides high-pressure fuel, and performs no timing function. The timing and duration of the injection is controlled by the ECM, based on the information received from the various sensors. In order to increase combustion efficiency and reduce combustion noise (diesel 'knock'), a small amount of fuel is injected before the main injection takes place – this is known as pre- or pilot-injection.

Additionally, the control module activates the preheating system, and the exhaust gas recirculation (EGR) system (see Chapter 4D).

The system uses the following sensors:

a) *Crankshaft sensor – informs the ECM of the crankshaft speed and position.*
b) *Coolant temperature sensor – informs the ECM of engine temperature.*
c) *Mass airflow/intake temperature sensor – informs the ECM of the mass and temperature of air entering the intake tract.*
d) *Anti-lock braking system (ABS) wheel sensor signal – informs the ECM of the vehicle speed.*
e) *Throttle position sensor – informs the ECM of throttle position, and the rate of throttle opening/closing.*
f) *Fuel high-pressure sensor – informs the ECM of the pressure of the fuel in the common rail.*
g) *Fuel low pressure sensor – informs the ECM of the pressure of the fuel in the filter.*
h) *Fuel pressure regulator – controls the pressure produced by the high-pressure fuel pump.*
i) *Camshaft position sensor – informs the ECM of the camshaft position so that the engine firing sequence can be established.*
j) *Stop-light switch – informs the ECM when the brakes are being applied*

k) Turbocharger boost pressure sensor – informs the ECM of the boost pressure generated by the turbocharger.

On all models, a 'drive-by-wire' throttle control system is used. The accelerator pedal is not physically connected to the fuel injection pump, but instead is connected by a cable to a throttle position sensor, mounted in the engine compartment, which provides the engine control module (ECM) with a signal relating to accelerator pedal movement.

The signals from the various sensors are processed by the ECM, and the optimum fuel quantity and injection timing settings are selected for the prevailing engine operating conditions.

A catalytic converter and an exhaust gas recirculation (EGR) system are fitted, to reduce harmful exhaust gas emissions. Details of this and other emissions control system equipment are given in Chapter 4C.

If there is an abnormality in any of the readings obtained from any sensor, the ECM enters its back-up mode. In this event, the ECM ignores the abnormal sensor signal, and assumes a preprogrammed value which will allow the engine to continue running (albeit at reduced efficiency). If the ECM enters this back-up mode, the warning light on the instrument panel will come on, and the relevant fault code will be stored in the ECM memory.

If the warning light comes on, the car should be taken to a diagnostic specialist at the earliest opportunity. A complete test of the Electronic Diesel Control (EDC) system can then be carried out, using a special electronic test unit which is simply plugged into the system's diagnostic connector (under the steering column).

7 Fuel system – priming and bleeding

1 Unlike earlier diesel engines, the common-rail system is self-priming.

2 Depress the accelerator pedal to the floor, then start the engine as normal (this may take longer than usual, especially if the fuel system has been allowed to run dry – operate the starter in ten-second bursts, with five seconds' rest in between each operation). Run the engine at a fast idle speed for a minute or so to purge any remaining trapped air from the fuel lines. After this time, the engine should idle smoothly at a constant speed.

3 If the engine idles roughly, then there is still some air trapped in the fuel system. Increase the engine speed again for another minute or so then recheck the idle speed. Repeat this procedure as necessary until the engine is idling smoothly.

8 Fuel pump/fuel gauge sender unit – removal and refitting

Refer to Chapter 4A. Note that on diesel models, there will be a fuel return hose, and possibly a supply hose for the fuel-burning heater, to disconnect on top of the unit. Plug or tape over the pipe ends, to reduce fuel loss, and to prevent dirt entry.

9 Fuel system – testing and adjustment

Testing

1 If a fault appears in the fuel system, first ensure that all the system wiring connectors are securely connected and free from corrosion. Ensure that the fault is not due to poor maintenance; ie, check that the air cleaner filter element is clean, that the cylinder compression pressures are correct (see Chapter 2C), and that the engine breather hoses are clear and undamaged (see Chapter 4D).

2 If the engine will not start, check the condition of the glow plugs (see Chapter 5C).

3 If these checks fail to reveal the cause of the problem, the car should be taken to a diagnostic specialist for testing using special electronic equipment which is plugged into the diagnostic connector (see Section 6). The tester should locate the fault quickly and simply, avoiding the need to test all the system components individually, which is time-consuming, and also carries a risk of damaging the ECM.

Adjustment

4 The engine idle speed, maximum speed and fuel injection pump timing are all controlled by the ECM. Whilst in theory it is possible to check the settings, if they are found to be in need of adjustment, the car will have to be taken to a suitably-equipped diagnostic specialist. They will have access to the necessary equipment required to test and (where possible) adjust the settings.

10 Fuel injection pump – removal and refitting

Caution: Be careful not to allow dirt into the injection pump or injector pipes during this procedure.

Removal

1 Disconnect the battery negative lead, and move the lead away from the battery (see *Disconnecting the battery*).

2 Remove the engine top cover, which is secured by three bolts.

3 Remove the inlet manifold as described in Section 20.

4 Remove the starter motor as described in Chapter 5A.

5 Referring to Chapter 2C, remove the engine right-hand mounting, including the hydramount.

6 With reference to Chapter 1B, remove the auxiliary drivebelt.

7 Using a 17 mm Allen key, unscrew the large access plug in the timing chain cover **(see illustration)**. Discard the seal, a new one must be fitted.

8 Slacken and remove the fuel pump sprocket nut.

9 Screw special tool 12-178/1 into the timing chain cover, then screw special tool 12-178 into the fuel pump drive sprocket. Carefully tighten the centre bolt of the tool, and free the sprocket from the pump shaft – do not remove the puller from the sprocket until the pump is refitted **(see illustrations)**. If the special tools are not available, the only other alternative is to remove the timing chains and

10.7 Unscrew the large access plug in the timing chain cover

10.9a Screw tool 12-178/1 into the timing chain cover . . .

10.9b . . . then screw tool 12-178 into the fuel pump drive sprocket

10.11 Remove the bolt (arrowed) securing the fuel pipe bracket to the oil filter housing

10.13 Release the retaining clips and disconnect the fuel hoses (arrowed)

10.14 Remove the high-pressure fuel pipe from the pump to the common fuel rail

pull the sprocket from the shaft as described in Chapter 2D – this necessitates the remove of the engine and transmission. Although in theory it would be possible to free the sprocket from the shaft using a drift or similar, the position of the sprocket, and therefore the tension of the timing chains, would be lost.

10 Disconnect wiring plug from the fuel pump.

11 Unscrew and remove the bolt securing the fuel pipe bracket to the oil filter housing **(see illustration)**.

12 Remove the bolt securing the fuel pipe to the coolant rail.

13 Place a wad of absorbent cloth under the fuel pump, then release the retaining clips and disconnect the fuel hoses from the pump **(see illustration)**.

14 Undo the two union nuts, and remove the high-pressure fuel pipe from the pump to the common fuel rail **(see illustration)**.

15 Disconnect the wiring plugs from Nos 1 and 2 glow plugs.

16 Undo the three mounting nuts and remove the fuel pump **(see illustration)**. Discard the gasket – a new one must be fitted.

Refitting

17 Ensure that the mating surfaces of the pump and engine are clean and dry, and fit the new pump gasket.

18 Position the fuel pump, and tighten the mounting nuts to the specified torque.

19 Refit the glow plug wiring connectors.

20 Ensure that the high-pressure fuel pipe unions are clean, and refit the pipe. Tighten the unions to the specified torque.

21 Reconnect the fuel hoses to the pump, and secure them in place with the retaining clips.

22 Refit the bolts securing the fuel pipes to oil filter housing and coolant rail.

23 Reconnect the wiring plug to the fuel pump.

24 If the special tools were used to release the fuel pump drive sprocket hold the sprocket in position, unscrew the tools, fit and tighten the sprocket retaining nut to the specified torque. If the tools were not available, refit the timing chains, sprockets and covers, as described in Chapter 2D.

25 Ensure that the timing cover access plug is clean, and tighten it to the specified torque.

26 With reference to Chapter 1B, refit the auxiliary drivebelt.

27 Referring to Chapter 2C, refit the engine right-hand mounting.

28 With reference to Chapter 5A, refit the starter motor.

29 Refit the inlet manifold as described in Section 20.

30 Refit the engine top cover, and reconnect the battery negative lead.

31 Depress the accelerator pedal to the floor, then start the engine as normal (this may take longer than usual – operate the starter in ten-second bursts with five seconds' rest in between each operation). Run the engine at a fast idle speed for a minute or so, to purge any remaining trapped air from the fuel lines. After this time the engine should idle smoothly at a constant speed.

11 Fuel injectors – removal and refitting

Caution: Be careful not to allow dirt into the injection pump or injector pipes during this procedure.

Removal

1 Disconnect the battery negative lead, and move the lead away from the battery (see *Disconnecting the battery*).

2 Remove the inlet manifold as described in Section 20.

3 Release the clips from the injector pipes, slacken the pipe unions (where possible, counterhold the union on the common fuel rail and the injector), and remove the relevant injector pipe **(see illustration)**.

4 Free the injector fuel return hose from the clip on the camshaft cover.

5 In order to remove No 1 injector (nearest the timing chain), remove the oil filler cap, undo the five screws and remove the air cleaner cover.

6 Disconnect the wiring plugs from the injectors, and if removing injector Nos 2, 3 or 4, undo the retaining bracket screws and move the wiring harness to one side **(see illustration)**.

7 Push in the closed end of the clips, and remove the fuel return hoses from the injectors

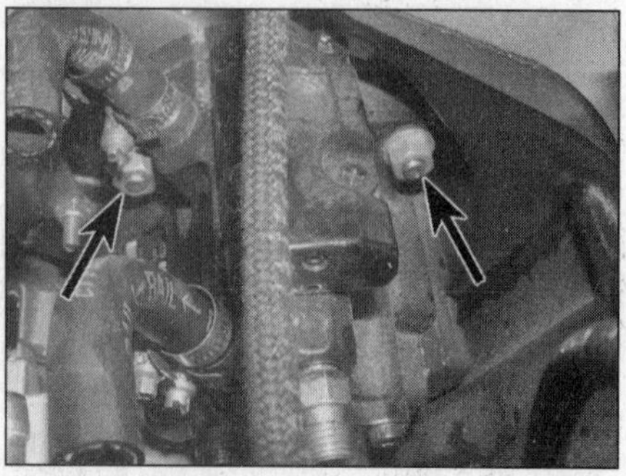

10.16 Undo the three mounting nuts (two arrowed, lower one hidden) and remove the fuel pump

11.3 Release the clips and slacken the pipe unions

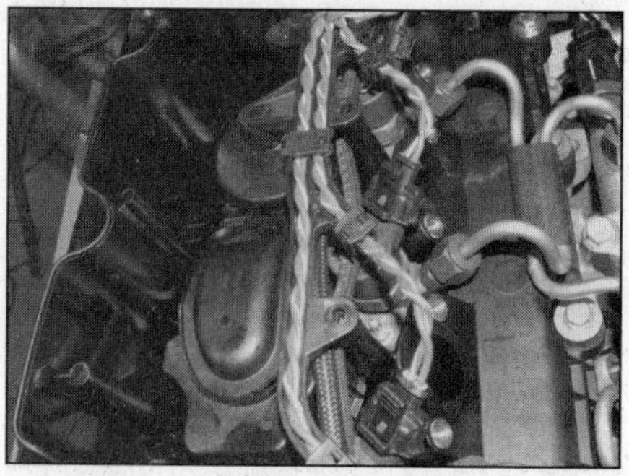

11.6 Disconnect the wiring plugs from the injectors

11.7 Push in the closed end of the clips, and remove the fuel return hoses

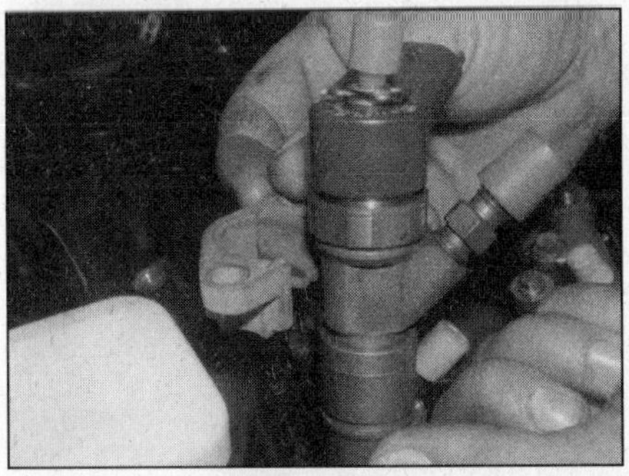

11.8b . . . until the injectors and clamps can be removed

(see illustration). Discard the return hose seals, new ones must be fitted.

8 Unscrew the two nuts securing each injector clamp and, using a Torx socket, unscrew the injector clamp studs until the injectors and clamps can be removed **(see illustrations)**. Discard the sealing washers – new ones must be fitted.

Refitting

9 Ensure that the injectors and seats in cylinder head are clean and dry.

10 Refit the clamp studs, tightening them to the specified torque.

11 Fit new sealing washers to the injectors, and refit them with the clamps **(see illustration)**. Tighten the clamp nuts to the specified torque.

12 With new seals fitted, squeeze together the closed ends of the clips and refit the fuel return hoses to the injectors.

13 If injector Nos 2, 3 or 4 were removed, reposition the wiring harness, and secure the harness brackets in place with the screws.

14 If No 1 injector was removed, refit the air cleaner cover, and tighten the retaining screws securely.

15 Secure the fuel return hose to the camshaft cover using the retaining clip.

16 Reconnect the wiring plugs to the injectors.

17 Refit the injection pipes, and tighten the unions to the specified torque. Refit the pipe retaining clips.

18 Refit the inlet manifold as described in Section 20.

19 Reconnect the battery negative lead.

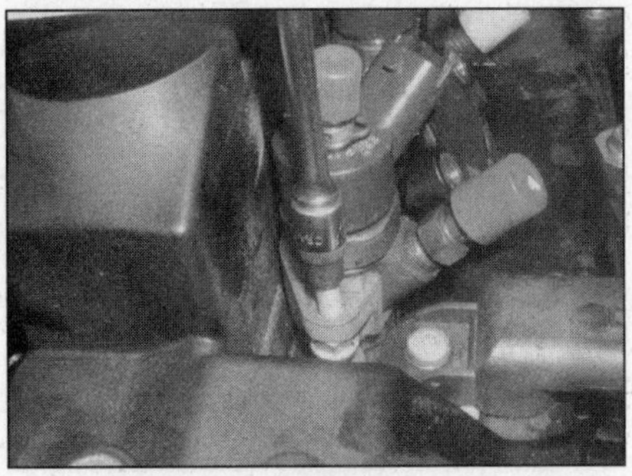

11.8a Unscrew the injector clamp studs . . .

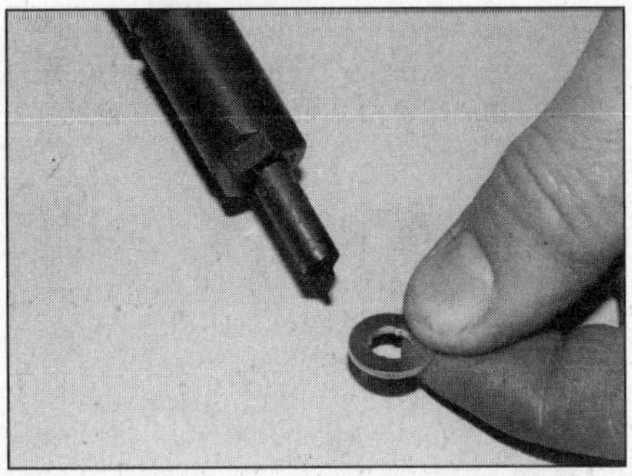

11.11 Fit new sealing washers to the injectors

12 Fuel rail – removal and refitting

Caution: Be careful not to allow dirt into the injector pipes or fuel rail during this procedure.

Removal

1 Disconnect the battery negative lead, and move the lead away from the battery (see *Disconnecting the battery*).

2 Remove the inlet manifold as described in Section 20.

3 Release the clips from the injector pipes, slacken the pipe unions (where possible, counterhold the union on the fuel rail and the injector), and remove the injector pipes. Note the fitted positions of the pipes – if necessary, label the pipes.

4 Disconnect the wiring plug from the fuel high-pressure sensor at the end of the fuel rail. Place absorbent rags underneath, then unscrew and remove the sensor. Recover the sealing washer – a new one should be used when refitting.

5 Loosen the unions on the fuel feed pipe, and disconnect it from the fuel rail.

6 Unscrew the two Allen bolts, then carefully lift out the fuel rail **(see illustration)**. Particularly if the fuel rail will be removed for some time, tape over the open connections, or wrap it up to prevent dirt entry.

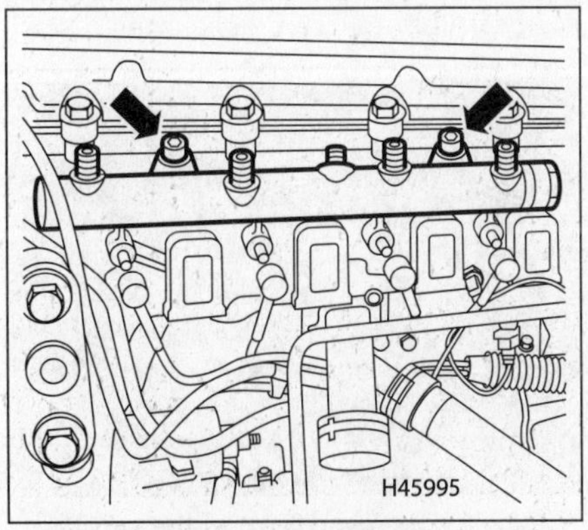

12.6 Remove the two Allen bolts, and lift out the fuel rail

Refitting

7 Refitting is a reversal of removal, noting the following points:

a) Clean the fuel pipe unions and high-pressure sensor before fitting.

b) Tighten the fuel rail bolts, pipe unions and pressure sensor to the specified torque.

c) Check for signs of fuel leakage from the disturbed unions when the engine is next run.

13 Electronic Diesel Control (EDC) system components – removal and refitting

1 Before disconnecting any fuel injection wiring plugs, ensure that the ignition is switched off (take out the key). If any component is disconnected 'live', it could introduce a fault code in the ECM memory. Better still, disconnect the battery negative lead, and move the lead away from the battery (see *Disconnecting the battery*).

Crankshaft sensor

2 The sensor is mounted on the front face of the engine block, at the flywheel end. To gain access, remove the starter motor as described in Chapter 5A.

3 Disconnect the wiring connector from the sensor.

4 Unscrew the Allen bolt and carefully remove the sensor from the engine **(see illustration)**. Recover the seal – a new one should be used when refitting.

13.4 Crankshaft position sensor

13.11 Coolant temperature sensor

5 Refitting is the reverse of removal, using a new seal and tightening the retaining bolt securely.

Coolant temperature sensor

6 The coolant temperature sensor is screwed into the front of the cylinder head, between two of the inlet ports.

7 Drain the cooling system as described in Chapter 1B. However, if the new sensor can be fitted quickly to minimise loss of coolant, this can be omitted.

8 Remove the engine top cover, which is secured by three bolts.

9 Remove a total of five screws securing the air intake duct (two to the inlet manifold, and three to the bonnet lock platform). Release and lift out the air intake duct.

10 Disconnect the wiring plug from the sensor.

11 Using a deep socket, unscrew and remove the sensor **(see illustration).** If better access is required, or if a suitable deep socket is not available, remove the inlet manifold as described in Section 20. Recover the sensor seal – a new one should be used when refitting.

12 Refitting is a reversal of removal. Use a new seal, and tighten the sensor securely. Top-up or refill the cooling system as necessary.

Throttle pedal position sensor

13 The sensor is secured to the accelerator pedal bracket.

14 Remove the trim panel fitted above the pedals, which is secured by two screws at the top, and two push-fasteners at the bottom.

15 Release the throttle sensor wiring plug from its bracket, then disconnect the wiring plug.

16 Prise the sensor's operating linkage off the top of the pedal. If required, the linkage can be removed completely, after unscrewing the nut from the end of the sensor body.

17 Unscrew the two mounting bolts, then remove the sensor **(see illustration).**

18 Refitting is the reverse of removal. **Note:** *If the pedal operation is unsatisfactory after fitting a new sensor, have the sensor operation confirmed by means of dedicated test equipment – consult a diagnostic specialist.*

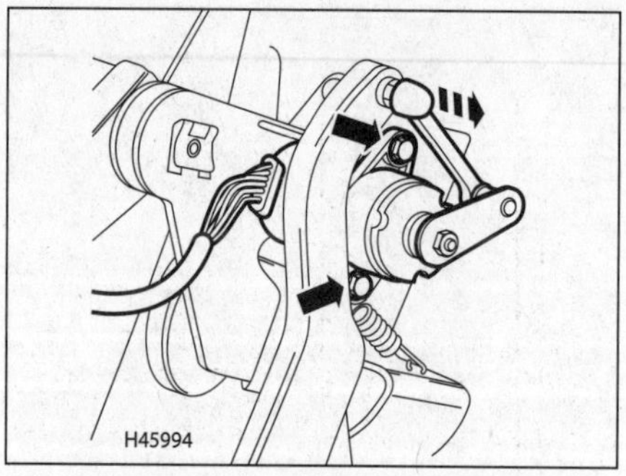

13.17 Prise off the arm (arrowed) then remove the sensor mounting bolts

Mass airflow/ inlet air temperature sensor

19 Remove the air filter element as described in Chapter 1B.

20 Free the vacuum hose and wiring harness from the turbocharger duct.

21 Release the two over-centre wire clips and disconnect the turbocharger duct from the sensor **(see illustration).** Recover the duct seal and engine breather tube connector.

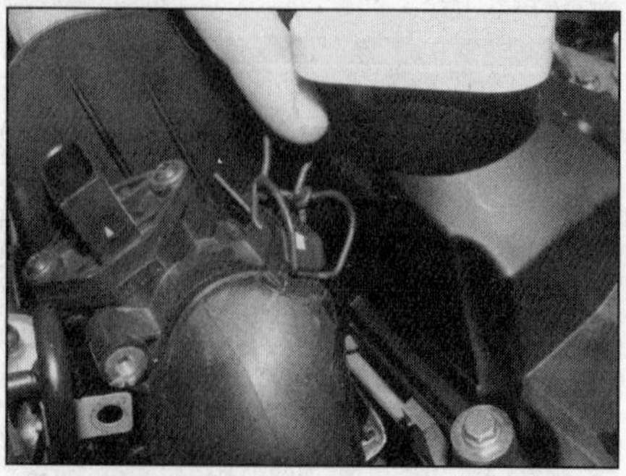

13.21 Release the two retaining clips and disconnect the turbocharger duct from the sensor

22 Unscrew the breather pipe retaining bracket bolt and move the pipe to one side.

23 Slacken and remove the two Torx screws, and withdraw the sensor **(see illustration).**

13.23 Slacken and remove the two Torx screws (arrowed), and withdraw the sensor

24 Refitting is a reversal of removal.

Stop-light switch

25 The engine control module receives a signal from the stop-light switch which indicates when the brakes are being applied. Stop-light switch removal and refitting details can be found in Chapter 9.

Engine control module

Note: *If a new module is to be fitted, it will need to be programmed with the code from the anti-theft security unit before the engine can be started. This can only be done using diagnostic equipment, and it may therefore be advisable to have this work carried out by a suitably-equipped garage or specialist.*

26 Disconnect the battery negative lead, and move the lead away from the battery (see *Disconnecting the battery*). This is essential – if the ECM wiring plugs are disconnected (or reconnected) 'live', the module could be damaged.

27 Pull off the rubber weather strip at the front of the windscreen cowl panel.

28 Remove the two windscreen cowl panels, each of which is secured by two clips at the front edge.

29 Remove the windscreen wiper arms as described in Chapter 12.

30 Remove two screw/clips at the front corners, and a row of seven clips along the back edge, then lift out the cowl panel frame – collect the splash shield from the passenger side as it is removed.

31 Using a slim screwdriver between the ECM box and the bulkhead access panel, release the upper tab securing the ECM box. Lift the box up and off the dovetail fitting.

32 Release the four clips and take off the top of the ECM box, for access to the wiring plugs.

33 Swing the plug locking levers to the side, then disconnect the five wiring plugs from the ECM.

34 Remove the module from the box.

35 While the module is removed, check that the drain holes inside the housing are clear, as they can become blocked, which may lead to ECM damage.

36 Refitting is a reversal of removal. Ensure that the module wiring plugs are securely reconnected.

Relays

37 The fuel pump relay is located in the passenger compartment fusebox below the glovebox.

38 Release the two turn-buckle fasteners at the top, and drop down the lower facia trim panel. To remove the panel completely, take out the two push-fasteners at the bottom.

39 Carefully pull the relay from the holder. The fuel pump relay is the larger of the two centrally-mounted relays.

40 Refitting is a reversal of removal.

Inertia (fuel cut-off) switch

41 Remove the glovebox as described in Chapter 11, Section 25.

42 Release the two turn-buckle fasteners at the top, and drop down the lower facia trim panel. To remove the panel completely, take out the two push-fasteners at the bottom.

13.48 Turbo boost pressure sensor is mounted on the right-hand end of the inlet manifold

43 Disconnect the multi-plug from the base of the switch.
44 Remove the two mounting screws, and withdraw the switch from the footwell.
45 Refitting is a reversal of removal, but ensure that the switch is reset by pressing the button on the top of the switch.

Turbocharger boost pressure sensor

46 Remove the engine top cover, which is secured by three bolts.
47 Release the wiring harness and the fuel return hose from the retaining clips on the inlet manifold, adjacent to the right-hand engine mounting bracket.
48 Disconnect the wiring plug, undo the retaining bolt, and remove the sensor **(see illustration)**. Recover the seal – a new one must be used when refitting.
49 Ensure that the mating surfaces of the sensor and manifold are clean and dry. Using a new seal, refit the sensor to the manifold, and tighten the securing bolt securely.
50 The remainder of refitting is a reversal of removal.

Turbocharger boost temperature sensor

51 The boost temperature sensor is located in the intercooler air duct, at the front of the engine **(see illustration)**.

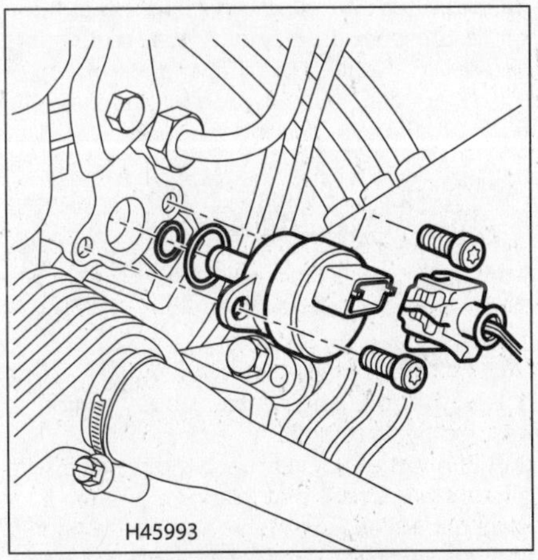

13.63 Fuel pressure regulator details – note the two seals

13.51 Turbocharger boost temperature sensor

52 Disconnect the wiring plug from the sensor, then unscrew and remove it from the housing. Recover the seal – a new one should be used when refitting.
53 Refitting is a reversal of removal. Use a new seal, and tighten the sensor securely.

Fuel high-pressure sensor

54 Remove the engine top cover, which is secured by three bolts.
55 Remove the five bolts securing the air intake duct to the bonnet lock platform and the inlet manifold. Release the duct at the rear, and lift it off the engine.
56 Disconnect the wiring plug from the fuel high-pressure sensor, which is at the end of the fuel rail **(see illustration)**. Place absorbent rags underneath, then unscrew and remove the sensor, using a deep socket. Recover the sealing washer – a new one should be used when refitting. Plug the port on the common rail to prevent contamination.
57 Ensure that the mating surfaces of the sensor and common rail are clean and dry, and refit the sensor with a new seal, tightening the sensor to the specified torque.
58 The remainder of refitting is a reversal of removal.

Fuel low-pressure sensor

59 The low pressure sensor is integral with the fuel filter head, and cannot be removed separately. If faulty, the complete filter should be renewed.

13.66 Camshaft position sensor location – screw arrowed

13.56 The fuel pressure sensor is in the left-hand end of the common fuel rail

Fuel pressure regulator

60 The fuel pressure regulator is fitted to the left-hand end of the injection pump (left as seen from the driver's seat).
61 Remove the starter motor as described in Chapter 5A.
62 Disconnect the wiring plug from the regulator, then place absorbent rags underneath.
63 Undo the two Torx screws and remove the regulator. Discard the two seals – new ones must be fitted **(see illustration)**.
64 Refitting is a reversal of removal, noting the following points:

a) *Ensure the pump and regulator mating faces are clean, and use new seals.*
b) *Refit the starter motor as described in Chapter 5A.*

Camshaft position sensor

65 Undo the three retaining bolts and remove the plastic cover from the top of the engine.
66 Disconnect the wiring plug from the sensor, located on the right-hand side of the camshaft cover **(see illustration)**.
67 Undo the Torx screw and remove the sensor **(see illustration)**. Discard the seal – a new one must be fitted.
68 Refitting is a reversal of removal. Ensure the mating face of the camshaft cover and sensor are clean, and fit the new seal.

13.67 Remove the camshaft position sensor, and recover the O-ring

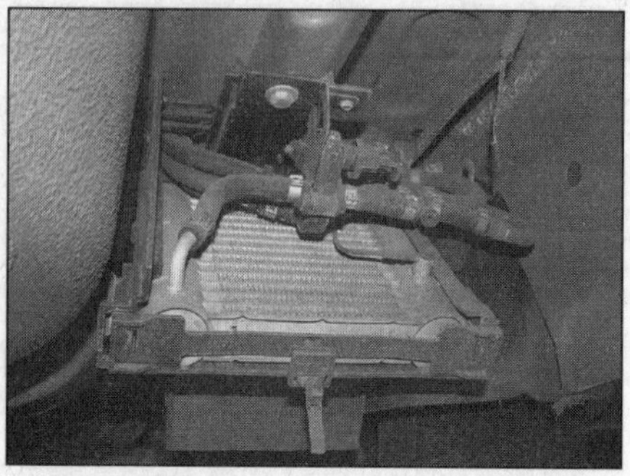

14.1 Fuel cooler location, behind right-hand rear wheel

15.1 The secondary fuel lift pump is mounted next to the battery

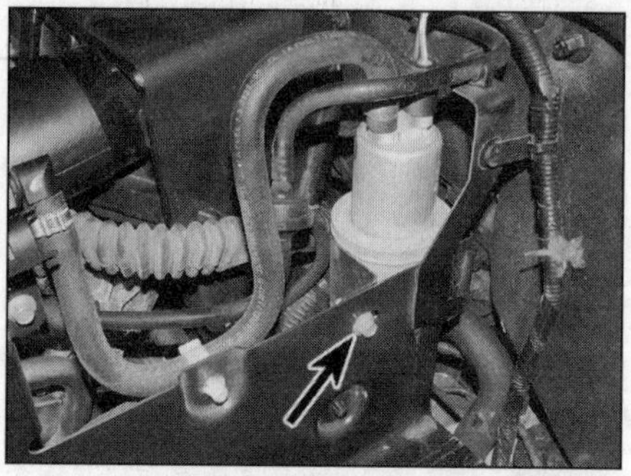

15.4 Secondary fuel lift pump mounting clamp bolt (arrowed)

14 Fuel cooler matrix – removal and refitting

Removal

1 The fuel cooler is mounted under the rear of the car, on the right-hand side **(see illustration)**. Its function is to cool fuel returned from the injection pump and fuel rail before it is returned to the tank.

2 Disconnect the battery negative lead, and move the lead away from the battery (see *Disconnecting the battery*).

3 Jack up the left-hand rear wheel, and support the car on an axle stand (see *Jacking and vehicle support*).

4 Clean around the cooler before proceeding, then place a container underneath to catch any fuel spillage.

5 Remove the two bolts securing the cooler to the chassis, and lower it slightly.

6 Clean thoroughly around the cooler's four fuel unions – it is vital that no dirt enters the system.

7 Release the four fuel unions, noting their fitted positions, and lower the cooler from under the car.

Refitting

8 Refitting is a reversal of removal. Clean the unions before reconnecting. On completion, start the engine and check for fuel leakage.

15 Secondary fuel lift pump – removal and refitting

Removal

1 The secondary fuel lift pump is mounted in a clamp on the battery tray mounting plate **(see illustration)**.

2 Remove the battery and its tray as described in Chapter 5A.

3 Disconnect the wiring plug on the top of the pump.

4 Loosen the fuel pump mounting clamp bolt, and slide the pump upwards for access to both hose clips **(see illustration)**.

5 Place absorbent cloth underneath the pump to catch any fuel spillage.

6 Release the hose clips and disconnect the hoses, then remove the pump. Plug the open connections to reduce further fuel loss, and to prevent dirt entry.

Refitting

7 Refitting is a reversal of removal, ensuring that the hose connections are clean prior to reconnection. The fuel system should self-prime when the engine is next started – see Section 7.

16 Turbocharger – description and precautions

Description

A turbocharger increases engine efficiency by raising the pressure in the inlet manifold above atmospheric pressure. Instead of the air simply being sucked into the cylinders, it is forced in. Additional fuel is supplied by the injection pump in proportion to the increased air intake.

Energy for the operation of the turbocharger comes from the exhaust gas. The gas flows through a specially-shaped housing (the turbine housing) and in so doing, spins the turbine wheel. The turbine wheel is attached to a shaft, at the end of which is another vaned wheel known as the compressor wheel. The compressor wheel spins in its own housing and compresses the inducted air on the way to the inlet manifold.

The compressed air passes through an intercooler. This is an air-to-air heat exchanger, mounted with the radiator at the front of the car. The purpose of the intercooler is to remove from the inducted air some of the heat gained in being compressed. Because cooler air is denser, removal of this heat further increases engine efficiency.

The turbocharger has nine adjustable guide vanes controlling the flow of exhaust gas into the turbine. The vanes are swivelled by the ECM (see Section 13). At lower engine speeds, the vanes close together, giving a smaller exhaust gas entry port, and therefore higher gas speed, which increases boost pressure at low engine speed. At high engine speed, the vanes are turned to give a larger exhaust gas entry port, and therefore lower gas speed, effectively maintaining a reasonably constant boost pressure over the engine rev range. This is known as a variable nozzle turbocharger.

The turbo shaft is pressure-lubricated by an oil feed pipe from the main oil gallery. The shaft 'floats' on a cushion of oil. A drain pipe returns the oil to the sump.

Precautions

- The turbocharger operates at extremely high speeds and temperatures. Certain precautions must be observed to avoid premature failure of the turbo or injury to the operator.
- **Do not** operate the turbo with any parts exposed. Foreign objects falling onto the rotating vanes could cause excessive damage and (if ejected) personal injury.
- **Do not** race the engine immediately after start-up, especially if it is cold. Give the oil a few seconds to circulate.
- **Always** allow the engine to return to idle speed before switching it off – do not blip the throttle and switch off, as this will leave the turbo spinning without lubrication.
- **Allow the engine to idle for several minutes before switching off after a high-speed run.**
- **Observe the recommended intervals for oil and filter changing, and use a reputable oil of the specified quality (see** *Lubricants and fluids*). Neglect of oil changing, or use of inferior oil, can cause carbon formation on the turbo shaft and subsequent failure.

17 Turbocharger – removal and refitting

Removal

1 Remove the engine top cover, which is secured by three bolts.

2 Remove the five bolts securing the air intake duct to the bonnet lock platform and the inlet manifold. Release the duct at the rear, and lift it off the engine.

3 Remove the engine oil filler cap, unscrew the five Allen screws and remove the air

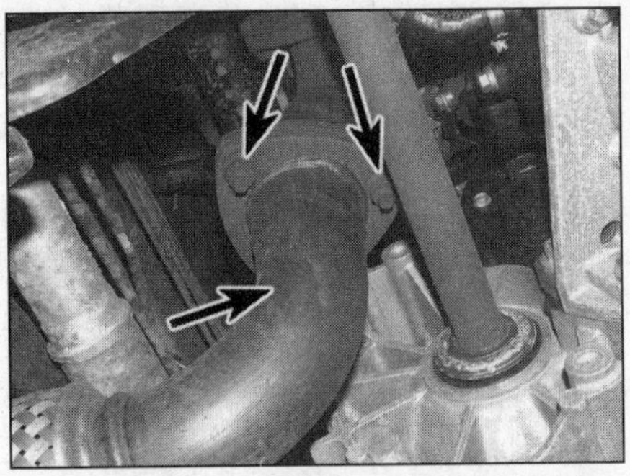

17.7 Turbo-to-downpipe flange nuts (one hidden)

17.12 Slacken the two retaining clips and remove the turbocharger outlet hose

cleaner cover. Remove the air filter element, and refit the oil filler cap.

4 Jack up the front of the car, and support it on axle stands (see *Jacking and vehicle support*).

5 Remove the engine undertray, which is secured by a number of quick-release screw fasteners.

6 Unhook the front section of the exhaust from its rubber mountings.

7 Remove the three nuts from the turbo-to-downpipe flanges, and separate the joints **(see illustration)**. Discard the flange gasket – a new one must be used when refitting. Lower the downpipe clear, but ensure the exhaust is not placed under strain. Check the condition of the nuts, and obtain new ones if necessary.

8 Unscrew the three nuts and remove the exhaust outlet elbow from the turbocharger. Recover and discard the gasket – a new one will be needed for refitting. Again, check the condition of the nuts, and obtain new ones if necessary.

9 Unscrew the two bolts and disconnect the oil drain pipe flange from the base of the turbo. Discard the gasket – a new one must be used on reassembly.

10 Unscrew the turbo oil feed banjo bolt from the engine block, and recover the two washers (new ones should be used when refitting).

11 Release the two over-centre wire clips and disconnect the turbocharger duct from the mass airflow sensor. Recover the duct seal and engine breather tube connector.

12 Slacken the two retaining clips and remove the turbocharger outlet hose **(see illustration)**.

17.14 Press down the rearmost holes in the heat shield access plate, and slide the plate to the rear

13 Prise out the three rubber access plugs from the base of the air cleaner housing.

14 Working in the base of the air cleaner housing, press down the rearmost holes in the heat shield access plate, and slide the plate to the rear to expose the turbocharger-to-manifold bolts **(see illustration)**.

15 Unscrew the three mounting bolts through the base of the air cleaner housing, and remove the turbocharger. Discard the gasket – a new one must be fitted.

16 If required, note the fitted positions of the turbocharger oil feed and return pipes, undo the bolts and remove them from the turbo. Discard the sealing washers/gaskets – new ones must be fitted.

Refitting

17 Refitting is a reversal of removal, noting the following points:

a) Ensure all mating surfaces are clean and dry.

b) Renew all O-rings, seals and gaskets.

c) Tighten all fasteners to the specified torque where given.

d) Prior to starting the engine, remove the fuel pump relay as described in Section 13, and operate the starter until the oil pressure warning light extinguishes. Refit the relay, start the engine and check for leaks.

18 Turbocharger – examination and overhaul

With the turbocharger removed, inspect the housing for cracks or other visible damage.

Spin the turbine or the compressor wheel to verify that the shaft is intact, and to feel for excessive shake or roughness. Some play is normal, since in use the shaft is 'floating' on a film of oil. Check that the wheel vanes are undamaged.

The wastegate and actuator are integral with the turbocharger, and cannot be checked or renewed separately. Consult a turbocharger specialist if the wastegate is thought to be faulty.

If the exhaust or induction passages are oil-contaminated, the turbo shaft oil seals have probably failed. (On the induction side, this will also have contaminated the intercooler, which if necessary should be flushed with a suitable solvent.)

No DIY repair of the turbo is possible. A new or reconditioned unit may be available on an exchange basis.

19 Intercooler – removal and refitting

Removal

1 With reference to Chapter 11, remove the bonnet lock platform.

2 Loosen the hose clip and disconnect the air inlet hose from the intercooler.

3 Unscrew the bolt securing the intercooler outlet pipe stub to the radiator. Carefully pull the pipe stub upwards and remove it from the intercooler, recovering the two large O-ring seals – new seals will be needed for refitting.

4 Remove the two bolts at the base of the radiator fan cowl, and a further nut and bolt from the passenger side of the cowl.

5 On the driver's side of the intercooler, remove the bolt securing it to the radiator.

6 Carefully pull the intercooler forwards off the radiator mounting lugs, then slide it to the passenger side to clear the mountings. Pull the fan cowl forwards slightly and remove the intercooler.

Refitting

7 Before refitting the intercooler, check inside the duct connection stubs for significant amounts of oil. If present, this can be cleaned out with a suitable solvent, but it does indicate that the turbocharger oil seals have failed – the turbo should be removed for inspection as described in Section 17.

8 Refitting is the reverse of removal, noting the following points:

a) Ensure the intercooler hoses are securely reconnected, to prevent air leaks.

b) Refit the bonnet lock platform as described in Chapter 11.

20 Manifolds – removal and refitting

Inlet manifold

1 Ensure that the ignition is switched off (take out the key). If any component is disconnected 'live', it could introduce a fault code in the ECM memory. Better still, disconnect the battery negative lead, and move the lead away from the battery (see *Disconnecting the battery*).

2 Remove the engine top cover, which is secured by three bolts.

3 Remove the five bolts securing the air intake duct to the bonnet lock platform and the inlet

20.7 Completely unscrew the EGR pipe retaining clip

manifold. Release the duct at the rear, and lift it off the engine.

4 Release the wiring harness and fuel return hose from the retaining clips on the inlet manifold.

5 Disconnect the wiring plug from the turbocharger boost pressure sensor.

6 Loosen the hose clip and disconnect the air intake hose from the EGR valve.

7 Completely unscrew the retaining clip, and disconnect the EGR pipe from the EGR valve **(see illustration)**.

8 Disconnect the EGR valve vacuum hose.

9 Undo the nine bolts and four nuts, and remove the inlet manifold. Recover the spacers and washers, noting how they are fitted – if the same manifold is being refitted, try not to disturb them. Discard the eight inlet manifold seals.

10 Ensure the manifold and cylinder head mating surfaces are clean and dry, and position new seals on the inlet manifold **(see illustration)**.

11 Refit the manifold to the cylinder head, and evenly tighten the bolts and nuts to the specified torque.

12 The remainder of refitting is a reversal of removal.

Exhaust manifold

13 Drain the cooling system as described in Chapter 1B.

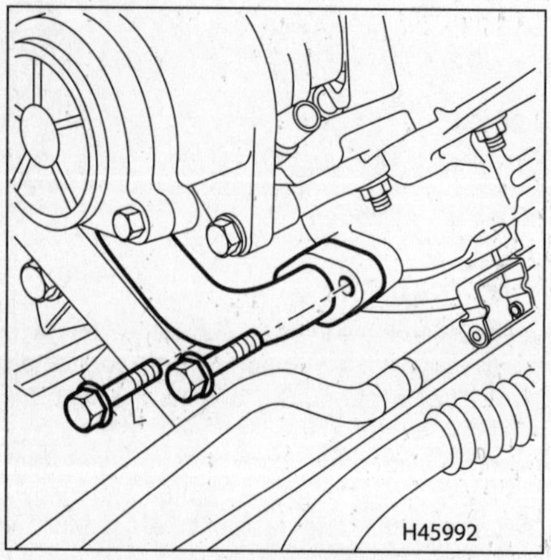

20.18 Remove the two EGR pipe bolts

20.10 Position new seals on the inlet manifold

14 With reference to Chapter 2C, remove the camshaft cover.

15 Remove the turbocharger as described in Section 17.

16 Remove the three bolts and one nut securing the coolant rail and intercooler pipe at the side of the engine **(see illustration)**.

17 Remove the bolt and disconnect the coolant rail from the thermostat housing. Recover the seal – a new one should be used when refitting.

18 Remove the two EGR pipe flange bolts from the manifold, and move the pipe aside **(see illustration)**.

19 Progressively loosen and remove the eight nuts securing the manifold to the cylinder head. Remove the manifold from the studs, and recover the gaskets – new ones must be used when refitting **(see illustration)**. If the manifold nuts are in poor condition, new ones should be obtained for reassembly – in this case, also consider fitting new studs.

20 If any studs were removed with the nuts, these can be refitted to the head using two nuts tightened against each other. If any studs have to be refitted (or renewed, if their threads are in poor condition), apply a little thread-locking fluid to their threads before screwing them into the head.

21 Ensure the mating surfaces of the exhaust manifold and cylinder head are clean and dry. Position new gaskets, and refit the exhaust manifold to the cylinder head. Tighten the nuts to the specified torque.

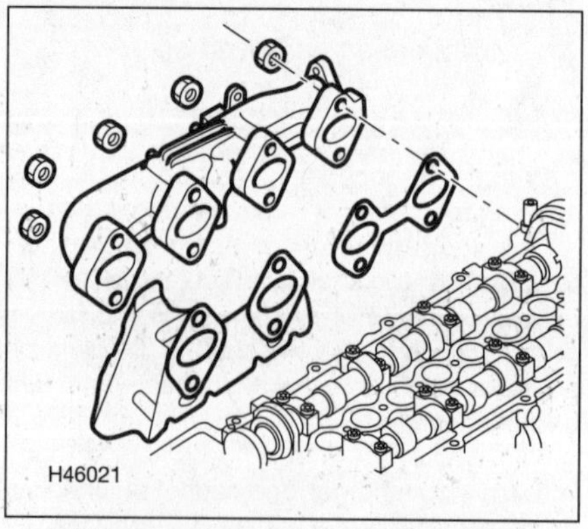

20.19 Exhaust manifold and gaskets

20.16 Undo the bolt securing the coolant rail to the manifold

22 The remainder of refitting is a reversal of removal, noting the following points:

a) Tighten all fasteners to their specified torque where given.

b) Refill the cooling system as described in Chapter 1B.

c) Check and, if necessary, top-up the oil level as described in 'Weekly checks'.

d) Before restarting the engine, remove the fuel pump relay (see Section 13) then turn the engine over on the starter until the oil pressure warning light goes out; this will allow oil to be circulated around the turbocharger bearings before the engine is started. Refit the relay and start the engine as normal.

21 Exhaust system – general information and component renewal

1 The exhaust system fitted at the factory is a one-piece item, with a catalytic converter and a single rear silencer box. An outlet elbow (with a built-in flexible section to allow for engine vibration and movement) links the turbocharger to the main system, with a flanged joint at each end.

2 Repair sections are available for the front and tail silencer boxes, but to fit them on the factory original system requires that the pipe is cut at precisely the right point – for this reason, owners may prefer to have exhaust work carried out by an exhaust specialist. Where these repair sections have been fitted previously, references to cutting can be ignored, as the pipes can be separated by loosening the clamps.

3 In the first instance, establish which section needs to be renewed, and what service sections are available.

4 Renewal of each section involves essentially the same process – owners may prefer to remove the complete system initially, as this should make working on it easier.

Outlet elbow

5 Jack up the front of the car, and support it on axle stands (see *Jacking and vehicle support*).

6 Remove the engine undertray, which is

secured by a number of quick-release screw fasteners.
7 Unhook the front section of the exhaust from its rubber mountings.
8 Remove the three nuts from the turbo-to-downpipe flanges, and separate the joints. Discard the flange gasket – a new one must be used when refitting. Lower the downpipe clear, but ensure the exhaust is not placed under strain. Check the condition of the nuts, and obtain new ones if necessary.
9 Unscrew the three nuts and remove the exhaust outlet elbow from the turbocharger. Recover and discard the gasket – a new one will be needed for refitting. Again, check the condition of the nuts, and obtain new ones if necessary.
10 Refitting is a reversal of removal, noting the following points:

- *a) Clean the mating faces on the elbow, turbo and exhaust front pipe.*
- *b) Using new gaskets (and nuts if necessary), fit the elbow and tighten the nuts to the specified torque.*

Front pipe

11 Jack up the front of the car, and support it on axle stands (see *Jacking and vehicle support*).
12 Remove the engine undertray, which is secured by a number of quick-release screw fasteners.
13 Offer up the new pipe as a guide for cutting, then clean and mark the pipe for cutting.
14 Cut the pipe through squarely, using a proper pipe-cutting tool if available.
15 Unhook the front section of the exhaust from its rubber mountings.
16 Remove the three nuts from the outlet elbow-to-downpipe flange, and separate the joint **(see illustration 17.7)**. Discard the flange gasket – a new one must be used when refitting. Lower the downpipe clear.
17 De-burr the cut pipe, then fit the pipe clamp loosely in position.
18 Offer up the new section into the pipe clamp, and set it in place.
19 Fit a new flange gasket, and tighten the flange nuts by hand.
20 Settle the new section into place, then tighten the downpipe flange nuts and the pipe clamp nuts to the specified torque.
21 Refit the engine undertray, then lower the car to the ground.

Centre pipe and rear silencer

22 Apply the handbrake, then jack up the car and support it on axle stands (see *Jacking and vehicle support*). For the best access, if enough axle stands are available, the car should be raised front and rear.
23 Remove the engine undertray, which is secured by a number of quick-release screw fasteners.
24 Offer up the new pipe as a guide for cutting, then clean and mark the pipe for cutting.
25 Cut the pipe through squarely, using a proper pipe-cutting tool if available.
26 In the centre of the car, unscrew a total of ten bolts and remove the three cross-braces fitted below the exhaust.
27 Unhook the exhaust from its rubber mountings, and lower it to the floor.
28 De-burr the cut pipe, then fit the pipe clamp loosely in position.
29 Offer the new section into place, and hook it onto the rubber mountings. With the system 'settled' in place (and not touching the floor or suspension components), tighten the clamp nuts to the specified torque.
30 Refit the three cross-braces, and tighten the bolts to the specified torque.
31 Refit the engine undertray, then lower the car to the ground.

Chapter 4 Part D:
Emissions control systems

Contents

Degrees of difficulty

Easy, suitable for novice with little experience	**Fairly easy,** suitable for beginner with some experience	**Fairly difficult,** suitable for competent DIY mechanic	**Difficult,** suitable for experienced DIY mechanic	**Very difficult,** suitable for expert DIY or professional

Specifications

Torque wrench settings	**Nm**	**lbf ft**
Exhaust gas recirculation (EGR) valve/pipe bolts:		
M6 bolts	10	7
M8 bolts	25	18
Oxygen sensors	55	41

1 General information

All petrol engine models use unleaded petrol and also have various other features built into the fuel system to help minimise harmful emissions. All models are equipped with a crankcase emission control system, a 'starter' catalytic converter (two on V6 engines) and main closed-loop converter, and an evaporative emission control system to keep fuel vapour/exhaust gas emissions down to a minimum.

All diesel engine models are also designed to meet strict emission requirements. All models are fitted with a crankcase emission control system, an oxidising open-loop catalytic converter and an exhaust gas recirculation (EGR) system to keep exhaust emissions down to a minimum.

The emission control systems function as follows.

Petrol models

Crankcase emission control

To reduce the emission of unburned hydrocarbons from the crankcase into the atmosphere, the engine is sealed, and the blow-by gases and oil vapour are drawn from inside the crankcase, through a wire mesh oil separator, into the inlet tract to be burned by the engine during normal combustion.

Under conditions of high manifold depression (idling, deceleration) the gases will be sucked positively out of the crankcase through a small diameter pipe and into the inlet tract 'downstream' of the throttle valve. A larger diameter pipe, 'upstream' of the throttle valve, allows fresh air to be drawn back into the crankcase, and mix with the crankcase gases. Under conditions of low manifold depression (acceleration, full-throttle running) the gases are forced out of the crankcase by the (relatively) higher crankcase pressure; and drawn through both pipes 'upstream and downstream' of the throttle valve.

Exhaust emission control

To minimise the amount of pollutants which escape into the atmosphere, all models are fitted with a catalytic converter in the exhaust system. The system is of the closed-loop type, in which an oxygen sensor in the exhaust system supplies a voltage signal to the engine management system ECM, enabling the ECM to adjust the mixture to provide the best possible conditions for the converter to operate. Most models are fitted with two oxygen sensors – one fitted to the exhaust manifold(s) (pre-catalyst sensor), and one 'downstream' of the catalytic converter (post-catalyst sensor), to monitor the converter's efficiency. Each oxygen sensor has a built-in heating element which is controlled by the ECM; the heating element is used to warm the sensor when the engine is cold to bring it quickly up to an efficient operating temperature.

The oxygen sensor's tip is sensitive to oxygen and sends the ECM a varying voltage depending on the amount of oxygen in the exhaust gases; the leaner the air/fuel mixture, the higher the oxygen content, and the lower the voltage from the sensor(s). If the intake air/fuel mixture is too rich, the exhaust gases are low in oxygen so the sensor sends a higher-voltage signal.

Peak conversion efficiency of all major pollutants occurs if the intake air/fuel mixture is maintained at the chemically-correct ratio for the complete combustion of petrol of 14.7 parts (by weight) of air to 1 part of fuel (the 'stoichiometric' ratio). The sensor output voltage alters in a large step at this point, the ECM using the signal change as a reference point and correcting the intake air/fuel mixture accordingly by altering the fuel injector pulse width.

Evaporative emission control

To minimise the escape into the atmosphere of unburned hydrocarbons, an evaporative emissions control system is also fitted to all petrol models. The fuel tank filler cap is sealed, a vapour separator is fitted in the fuel tank filler neck, and a charcoal canister is mounted under the rear offside of the car. The canister collects the petrol vapours generated in the tank when the car is parked, and stores them until they can be cleared from the canister (under the control of the engine management system ECM) via the purge valve into the inlet tract, to be burned by the engine during normal combustion.

To ensure that the engine runs correctly when it is cold and/or idling and to protect the catalytic converter from the effects of an over-rich mixture, the purge control valve is not opened by the ECM until the engine has warmed-up, and the engine is under load; the valve solenoid is then modulated on and off to allow the stored vapour to pass into the inlet tract.

Diesel models

Crankcase emission control

To reduce the emission of unburned hydrocarbons from the crankcase into the atmosphere, the engine is sealed and the blow-by gases and oil vapour are drawn from inside the crankcase, through a wire mesh oil separator, into the inlet tract to be burned by the engine during normal combustion. Crankcase gases are drawn via a depression limiting valve. The valve closes progressively as the engine speed increases, so limiting the maximum depression in the crankcase.

Exhaust emission control

To minimise the level of exhaust pollutants released into the atmosphere, a catalytic converter is fitted in the exhaust system.

The catalytic converter consists of a canister containing a fine mesh impregnated with a catalyst material, over which the hot exhaust gases pass. The catalyst speeds up the oxidation of harmful carbon monoxide, unburned hydrocarbons and soot, effectively reducing the quantity of harmful products released into the atmosphere via the exhaust gases.

Exhaust gas recirculation system

This system is designed to recirculate small quantities of exhaust gas into the inlet tract, and therefore into the combustion process. This process reduces the level of unburnt hydrocarbons present in the exhaust gas before it reaches the catalytic converter. The system is controlled by the engine management system ECM, using the information from its various sensors, via the EGR valve which is fitted to the metal pipe connecting the inlet and exhaust manifolds. The exhaust gases are cooled prior to entering the inlet manifold by passing through a cooler mounted on the side of the EGR valve. Engine coolant circulates through the cooler. The EGR valve is vacuum-operated, and is switched on and off by an electrical solenoid valve.

2 Petrol engine emission control systems - testing and component renewal

Crankcase emission control

1 The components of this system require no attention other than to check that the hoses are clear and undamaged at regular intervals.

Evaporative emission control

2 If the system is thought to be faulty, disconnect the hoses from the charcoal canister and purge control valve and check that they are clear by blowing through them. Full testing of the system can only be carried out using specialist electronic equipment which is connected to the engine management system diagnostic wiring connector (see Chapter 4A or 4B). If the purge control valve or charcoal canister are thought to be faulty, they must be renewed.

Charcoal canister

3 The canister is located under the right-hand side of the car, bolted to the chassis, just behind the right-hand rear roadwheel **(see illustration)**. Working underneath the car, unscrew the retaining bolt at the rear of the canister and unhook the canister bracket from the chassis at the front.

4 Note the fitted locations of the pipes. Squeeze together the union lugs and disconnect the tank, air and purge pipes from the canister.

5 Refitting is a reverse of the removal procedure, ensuring the hoses are correctly and securely reconnected.

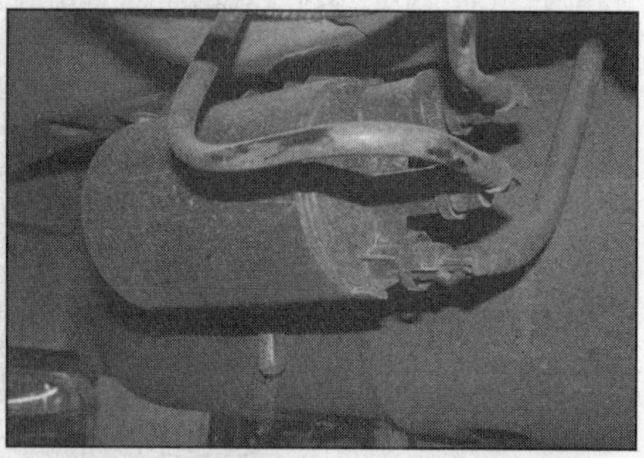

2.3 The charcoal canister is to the right-hand side of the spare wheel well

2.6 Canister purge valve location - 1.8 litre models

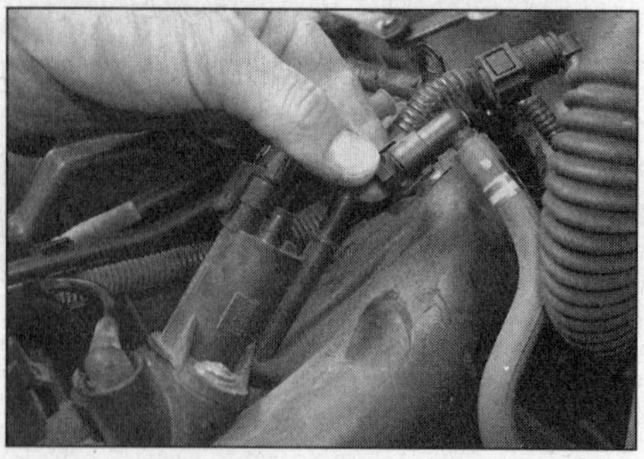

2.11 Note the fitted positions of the hoses, then disconnect them

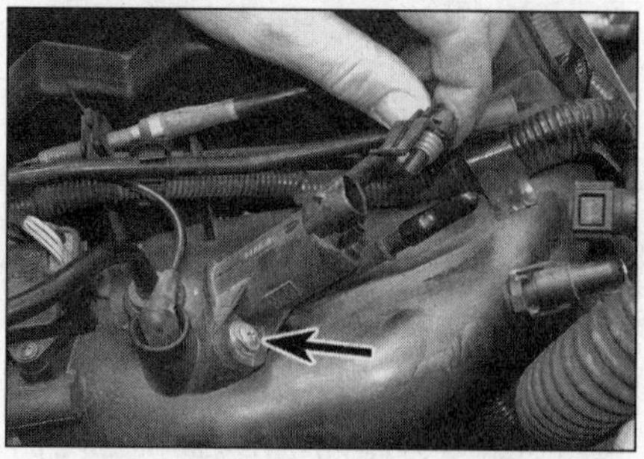

2.12 Disconnecting the purge valve - note mounting screw (arrowed)

Purge valve

1.8 litre engines

6 The valve is located on the battery tray **(see illustration)**.

7 Ensure the ignition is switched off, and disconnect the wiring plug from the valve.

8 Squeeze the top hose quick-release connector, and release the hose.

9 Disconnect the lower hose from the valve, and remove it.

V6 engines

10 On V6 engines, the valve is mounted on the inlet manifold, behind the throttle body.

11 Noting their fitted positions, squeeze and release the connections on the two hoses **(see illustration)**.

12 Disconnect the wiring plug from the valve **(see illustration)**.

13 Remove the single screw and washer, and withdraw the valve, noting its sealing ring, which should be renewed when refitting.

All engines

14 Refitting is a reversal of removal. Ensure the hose connections are securely made, using a new seal where applicable on V6 engines.

Exhaust emission control

15 The performance of the catalytic converter can be checked only by measuring the exhaust gases using a good-quality, carefully-calibrated exhaust gas analyser.

16 If the CO level at the tailpipe is too high, the car should be taken to a specialist so that the complete fuel injection and ignition systems, including the oxygen sensor(s), can be thoroughly checked using diagnostic equipment. Note that exhaust system leaks can cause inaccurate readings, so ensure that the exhaust system is in good condition. Once these have been checked and are known to be free from faults, a fault is indicated in the catalytic converter.

Catalytic converter

17 The main converter is part of the exhaust system – refer to the relevant Section of Chapter 4A or 4B. The 'starter' converter is an integral part of the exhaust manifold(s)

Oxygen sensor

Note: *The oxygen sensor is delicate, and will not work if it is dropped or knocked, if its power supply is disrupted, or if any cleaning materials are used on it.*

Exhaust manifold sensor

18 Ensure the ignition is switched off, then trace the wiring back from the oxygen sensor. Free the connector from its retaining clip and disconnect the two halves of the connector **(see illustration)**.

19 To gain access to the sensor, on some 1.8 litre models, unscrew the two bolts from the exhaust manifold heat shield, and remove it.

2.18 Trace the oxygen sensor wiring back to the connector

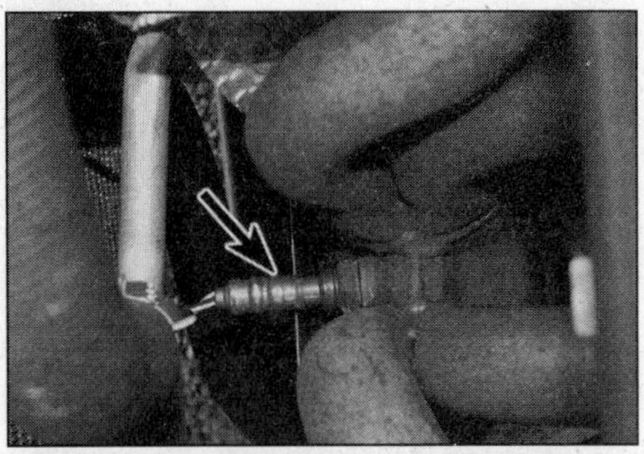

2.20a Non-turbo 1.8 litre engines have the oxygen sensor in the manifold . . .

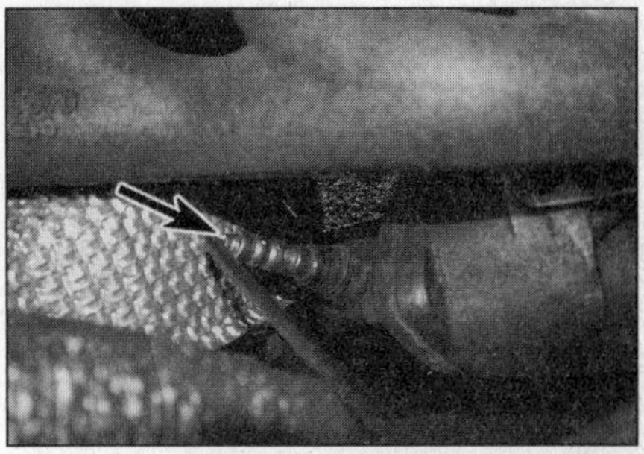

2.20b . . . while turbo models have it next to the turbocharger

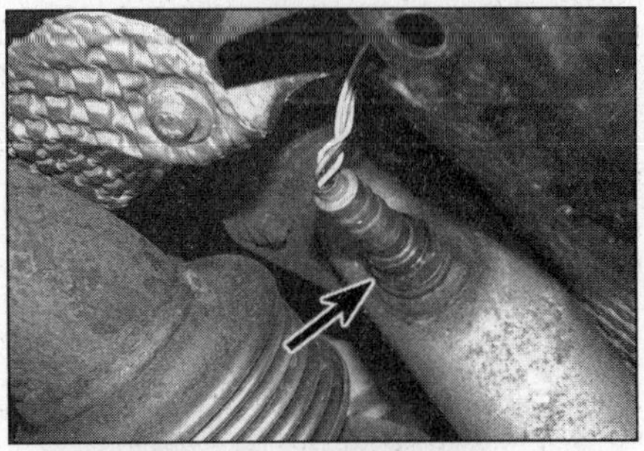

2.20c Oxygen sensor location in rear downpipe (V6 engine)

2.24 Unscrew the post-catalyst sensor from the exhaust

On V6 models, jack up the front of the car, and remove the engine undertray.

20 Unscrew the sensor and remove it from the manifold or downpipe **(see illustrations)**. Note that the use of a special deep, split socket is recommended – otherwise, a spanner must be used (a normal deep socket may damage the sensor wiring). Note that the sensor will be very tight – use good-quality, close-fitting tools, and protect your hands from damage. Where applicable, recover the sensor sealing washer and discard it; a new one must be used on refitting.

21 Refitting is a reverse of the removal procedure, using a new sealing washer where applicable. Tighten the sensor to the specified torque (if possible) and ensure that the wiring is correctly routed and in no danger of contacting either the exhaust manifold or the engine.

Post-catalyst sensor

22 Ensure the ignition is switched off, then jack up the front of the car, and support it on axle stands (see *Jacking and vehicle support*).

23 Release the oxygen sensor wiring plug from its support bracket, and disconnect it.

24 Unscrew the sensor from the rear of the catalytic converter **(see illustration)**. Note that the use of a special deep, split socket is recommended – otherwise, a spanner must be used (a normal deep socket may damage the sensor wiring). Note that the sensor will be very tight – use good-quality, close-fitting tools, and protect your hands from damage.

25 Refitting is a reverse of the removal procedure. Tighten the sensor to the specified torque (if possible), and ensure the wiring is correctly routed and in no danger of contacting the exhaust system.

3 Diesel engine emission control systems – testing and component renewal

Crankcase emission control

1 The components of this system require no attention other than to check that the hoses are clear and undamaged at regular intervals. If the system is thought to be faulty, renew the crankcase pressure limiting valve as follows.

Pressure limiting valve

2 With reference to Chapter 1B, remove the air cleaner cover.

3 Disconnect the injector wiring plugs, unscrew the three retaining screws, and move the injector harness to one side.

4 Unscrew the four Allen screws, and remove the depression limiting valve complete with filter **(see illustration)**. Check the condition of the two seals – these can be re-used if undamaged.

5 Ensure the mating surfaces are clean and dry, refit the valve housing, using new seals if necessary. Tighten the Allen screws securely.

6 The remainder of refitting is a reversal of removal.

Exhaust emission control

7 The performance of the catalytic converter can be checked only by measuring the exhaust gases using a good-quality, carefully-calibrated exhaust gas analyser.

8 Before assuming that the catalytic converter is faulty, it is worth checking whether the problem is not due to a faulty injector(s). Refer to a diagnostic specialist for further information.

Catalytic converter

9 The main converter is part of the exhaust system – refer to the relevant Section of Chapter 4C.

Exhaust gas recirculation

10 Comprehensive testing of the system can only be carried out using specialist electronic equipment which is connected to the injection system diagnostic wiring connector (see Chapter 4C). If the EGR valve or solenoid valve are thought to be faulty, they must be renewed as follows.

EGR valve

11 Remove the engine top cover, which is secured by three screws.

12 Remove the air intake duct, which is secured by three screws at the front to the bonnet lock platform, and with two further screws to the inlet manifold.

13 Disconnect the vacuum hose from the EGR valve **(see illustration)**.

3.4 Remove the depression limiting valve complete with filter

3.13 Disconnect the vacuum hose from the EGR valve

14 Slacken the hose clips and disconnect the EGR pipe and intercooler duct from the valve **(see illustration)**.
15 Unscrew the four Allen bolts, and remove the EGR valve. Discard the seal – a new one should be used when refitting.
16 Refitting is a reversal of removal, using a new seal and tightening the valve retaining bolts securely.

EGR solenoid valve

17 Remove the engine top cover, which is secured by three screws.
18 Remove the air intake duct, which is secured by three screws at the front to the bonnet lock platform, and with two further screws to the inlet manifold.
19 Disconnect the wiring plug from the solenoid, which is located at the front of the engine **(see illustration)**.
20 Unscrew the two bolts securing the solenoid bracket to the cylinder block. Note their fitted locations, then disconnect the vacuum hoses. If necessary, the solenoid can be separated from the mounting bracket by unscrewing the two retaining nuts.
21 Refitting is a reversal of removal.

3.14 Slacken the EGR pipe and intercooler duct hose clips

3.19 EGR solenoid valve wiring plug

4 Catalytic converter – general information and precautions

General information

1 The catalytic converter reduces harmful exhaust emissions by chemically converting the more poisonous gases to ones which (in theory at least) are less harmful. The chemical reaction is known as an 'oxidising' reaction, or one where oxygen is 'added'.
2 Inside the converter is a honeycomb structure, made of ceramic material and coated with the precious metals palladium, platinum and rhodium (the 'catalyst' which promotes the chemical reaction). The chemical reaction generates heat, which itself promotes the reaction – therefore, once the car has been driven several miles, the body of the converter will be very hot.
3 The ceramic structure contained within the converter is understandably fragile, and will not withstand rough treatment. Since the converter runs at a high temperature, driving through deep standing water (in flood conditions, for example) is to be avoided, since the thermal stresses imposed when plunging the hot converter into cold water may well cause the ceramic internals to fracture, resulting in a 'blocked' converter – a common cause of failure. A converter which has been damaged in this way can be checked by shaking it (do not strike it) – if a rattling noise is heard, this indicates probable failure.

Precautions

4 The catalytic converter is a reliable and simple device which needs no maintenance in itself, but there are some facts of which an owner should be aware if the converter is to function properly for its full service life.

Petrol models

a) DO NOT use leaded petrol (or lead-replacement petrol, LRP) in a car equipped with a catalytic converter – the lead (or other additives) will coat the precious metals, reducing their converting efficiency and will eventually destroy the converter.
b) Always keep the ignition and fuel systems well-maintained in accordance with the manufacturer's schedule (see Chapter 1A).
c) If the engine develops a misfire, do not drive the car at all (or at least as little as possible) until the fault is cured.
d) DO NOT push or tow start the car – this will soak the catalytic converter in unburned fuel, causing it to overheat when the engine does start.
e) DO NOT switch off the ignition at high engine speeds – ie do not 'blip' the throttle immediately before switching off the engine.
f) DO NOT use fuel or engine oil additives – these may contain substances harmful to the catalytic converter.
g) DO NOT continue to use the car if the engine burns oil to the extent of leaving a visible trail of blue smoke.
h) Remember that the catalytic converter operates at very high temperatures. DO NOT, therefore, park the car on dry undergrowth, over long grass or piles of dead leaves after a long run.
i) As mentioned above, driving through deep water should be avoided if possible. The sudden cooling effect may fracture the ceramic honeycomb, damaging it beyond repair.
j) Remember that the catalytic converter is FRAGILE – do not strike it with tools during servicing work, and take care handling it when removing it from the car for any reason.
k) In some cases, a sulphurous smell (like that of rotten eggs) may be noticed from the exhaust. This is common to many catalytic converter-equipped cars, and has more to do with the sulphur content of the brand of fuel being used than the converter itself.
l) If a substantial loss of power is experienced, remember that this could be due to the converter being blocked. This can occur simply as a result of high mileage, but may be due to the ceramic element having fractured and collapsed internally (see paragraph 3). A new converter is the only cure in this instance.
m) The catalytic converter, used on a well-maintained and well-driven car, should last at least 100 000 miles – if the converter is no longer effective, it must be renewed.

Diesel models

5 The catalytic converter fitted to diesel models is simpler than that fitted to petrol models, but it still needs to be treated with respect to avoid problems:

a) DO NOT use fuel or engine oil additives – these may contain substances harmful to the catalytic converter.
b) DO NOT continue to use the car if the engine burns (engine) oil to the extent of leaving a visible trail of blue smoke.
c) Remember that the catalytic converter operates at very high temperatures. DO NOT, therefore, park the car in dry undergrowth, over long grass or piles of dead leaves after a long run.
d) As mentioned above, driving through deep water should be avoided if possible. The sudden cooling effect will fracture the ceramic honeycomb, damaging it beyond repair.
e) Remember that the catalytic converter is FRAGILE – do not strike it with tools during servicing work, and take care handling it when removing it from the car for any reason.
f) If a substantial loss of power is experienced, remember that this could be due to the converter being blocked. This can occur simply as a result of high mileage, but may be due to the ceramic element having fractured and collapsed internally (see paragraph 3). A new converter is the only cure in this instance.
g) The catalytic converter, used on a well-maintained and well-driven car, should last at least 100 000 miles – if the converter is no longer effective, it must be renewed.

Chapter 5 Part A:
Starting and charging systems

Contents

Degrees of difficulty

Easy, suitable for novice with little experience	**Fairly easy,** suitable for beginner with some experience	**Fairly difficult,** suitable for competent DIY mechanic	**Difficult,** suitable for experienced DIY mechanic	**Very difficult,** suitable for expert DIY or professional

Specifications

System type	12 volt, negative-earth	
Battery		
Type	Lead-acid, 'maintenance-free'	
Charge condition:		
Poor	11.5 volts	
Normal	12.0 volts	
Good	12.5 volts	
Alternator		
Type:		
Petrol engines	Denso 105 A	
Diesel engines	Valeo 115 A	
Starter motor		
Type	Denso, 1.0 to 2.0 kW depending on model	
Torque wrench settings	**Nm**	**lbf ft**
Alternator mountings:		
M8 bolts	24	18
M10 bolts	47	35
Battery tray Torx bolts	24	18
Starter motor mounting bolts	45	33

1 General information and precautions

General information

The engine electrical system consists mainly of the charging and starting systems. Because of their engine-related functions, these components are covered separately from the body electrical devices such as the lights, instruments, etc (which are covered in Chapter 12). On petrol engine models, refer to Part B for information on the ignition system, and on diesel models, refer to Part C for information on the preheating system.

The electrical system is of the 12 volt negative-earth type.

The original-equipment battery is of the 'maintenance-free' (sealed for life) type, and is charged by the alternator, which is belt-driven from the crankshaft pulley.

The starter motor is of the pre-engaged type, incorporating an integral solenoid. On starting, the solenoid moves the drive pinion into engagement with the flywheel ring gear before the starter motor is energised. Once the engine has started, a one-way clutch prevents the motor armature being driven by the engine until the pinion disengages from the flywheel.

Precautions

- It is necessary to take extra care when working on the electrical system to avoid damage to semi-conductor devices (diodes and transistors), and to avoid the risk of personal injury. In addition to the precautions given in *Safety first!* at the beginning of this manual, observe the following when working on the system:
- *Always remove rings, watches, etc, before working on the electrical system.* Even with the battery disconnected, capacitive discharge could occur if a component's live terminal is earthed through a metal object. This could cause a shock or nasty burn.
- *Do not reverse the battery connections.* Components such as the alternator, electronic control units, or any other components having semi-conductor circuitry could be irreparably damaged.
- If the engine is being started using jump leads and a slave battery, connect the batteries *positive-to-positive* and *negative-to-negative* (see *Jump starting*). This also applies when connecting a battery charger.
- Never disconnect the battery terminals, the alternator, any electrical wiring or any test instruments when the engine is running.
- Do not allow the engine to turn the alternator when the alternator is not connected.
- Never 'test' for alternator output by 'flashing' the output lead to earth.
- Never use an ohmmeter of the type incorporating a hand-cranked generator for circuit or continuity testing.
- Always ensure that the battery negative lead is disconnected when working on the electrical system.
- Before using electric-arc welding equipment on the car, disconnect the battery, alternator and components such as the fuel injection/ignition electronic control unit to protect them from the risk of damage.

Battery disconnection

Refer to the precautions listed in *Disconnecting the battery*, in the Reference section of this manual.

2 Electrical fault finding - general information

Refer to Chapter 12.

3 Battery - testing and charging

Testing

Low-maintenance battery

1 If the car covers a small annual mileage, it is worthwhile checking the specific gravity of the electrolyte every three months to determine the state of charge of the battery. Use a hydrometer to make the check and compare the results with the following table. Note that the specific gravity readings assume an electrolyte temperature of 15°C (60°F); for every 10°C (18°F) below 15°C (60°F) subtract 0.007. For every 10°C (18°F) above 15°C (60°F) add 0.007.

	Ambient temperature	
	Above 25°C	**Below 25°C**
Fully-charged	*1.210 to 1.230*	*1.270 to 1.290*
70% charged	*1.170 to 1.190*	*1.230 to 1.250*
Discharged	*1.050 to 1.070*	*1.110 to 1.130*

2 If the battery condition is suspect, first check the specific gravity of electrolyte in each cell. A variation of 0.040 or more between any cells indicates loss of electrolyte or deterioration of the internal plates.

3 If the specific gravity variation is 0.040 or more, the battery should be renewed. If the cell variation is satisfactory but the battery is discharged, it should be charged as described later in this Section.

Maintenance-free battery

4 In cases where a 'sealed for life' maintenance-free battery is fitted, topping-up and testing of the electrolyte in each cell is not possible. The condition of the battery can therefore only be tested using a battery condition indicator or a voltmeter.

All battery types

5 If testing the battery using a voltmeter, connect the voltmeter across the battery and compare the result with those given in the Specifications under 'charge condition'. The test is only accurate if the battery has not been subjected to any kind of charge for the previous six hours. If this is not the case, switch on the headlights for 30 seconds, then wait four to five minutes before testing the battery after switching off the headlights. All other electrical circuits must be switched off, so check that the doors and tailgate/boot lid are fully shut when making the test.

6 If the voltage reading is less than 12.0 volts, then the battery is discharged.

7 If the battery is to be charged, remove it from the car (Section 4) and charge it as described later in this Section.

Charging

Note: *The following is intended as a guide only. Always refer to the manufacturer's recommendations (often printed on a label attached to the battery), and always disconnect both terminal leads before charging a battery.*

Low-maintenance battery

8 It is advisable to remove the cell caps or covers if possible during charging, but note that the battery will be giving off potentially-explosive hydrogen gas while it is being charged. Small amounts of acidic electrolyte may also escape as the battery nears full charge. Removing the cell caps will allow you to check whether all six cells are receiving charge – after a while, the electrolyte should start to bubble. If any cell does not bubble, this may indicate that it has failed, and the battery is no longer fit for use.

9 Charge the battery at a rate of 3.5 to 4 amps, and continue to charge the battery at this rate until no further rise in specific gravity is noted over a four-hour period.

10 Alternatively, a trickle charger charging at the rate of 1.5 amps can safely be used overnight.

11 Specially rapid 'boost' charges which are claimed to restore the power of the battery in 1 to 2 hours are not recommended, as they can cause serious damage to the battery plates through overheating.

12 While charging the battery, note that the temperature of the electrolyte should never exceed 37.8°C (100°F).

Maintenance-free battery

13 This battery type takes considerably longer to fully recharge than the standard type, the time taken being dependent on the extent of discharge, but it can take anything up to three days.

14 A constant-voltage type charger is required, to be set, when connected, to 13.9 to 14.9 volts with a charger current below 25 amps. Using this method, the battery should be usable within three hours, giving a voltage reading of 12.5 volts, but this is for a partially-discharged battery and, as mentioned, full charging can take considerably longer.

15 If the battery is to be charged from a fully-discharged state (condition reading less than 12.2 volts), have it recharged by your local automotive electrician, as the charge rate is higher and constant supervision during charging is necessary.

4.2 Unclip the battery top cover

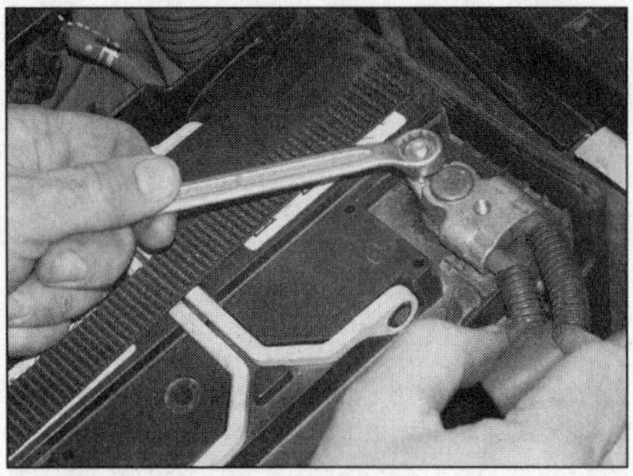
4.3 Disconnecting the battery positive lead

4.4a Unscrew the clamp bolt at the front . . .

4 Battery – removal and refitting

Note: *Refer to the precautions given in 'Safety first!' and in Section 1 of this Chapter.*

Battery

1 The battery is located on the left-hand side of the engine compartment.

2 Unclip the battery top cover, and lift it off **(see illustration)**.

3 Slacken the battery terminal clamps, and disconnect the leads, negative first **(see illustration)**.

4 Remove the bolt from the battery clamp at the front, and lift it out with the webbing strap **(see illustrations)**.

5 Lift out the battery, using the handles provided on top where applicable **(see illustration)**. Particularly on diesel models, the battery is heavy.

6 Refitting is a reversal of removal. Smear petroleum jelly on the battery terminals after reconnecting the leads, to reduce corrosion. Always reconnect the positive lead first, and the negative lead last.

Battery tray

7 Cut the cable-ties at the front securing the battery leads to the battery tray – depending on model, there will be several sections of wiring loom to unclip and disconnect **(see illustrations)**. On diesel models especially, removing the battery tray is quite an involved task. Models with the 1.8 litre petrol engine have the charcoal canister purge valve mounted on the battery tray – refer to Chapter 4D if necessary.

8 Unscrew the four Torx bolts in the base of the tray, and lift it out. On diesel models, unclip the hoses from the base of the tray, noting their fitted positions **(see illustrations)**.

9 Refitting is a reversal of removal. Tighten the Torx bolts to the specified torque.

5 Charging system – testing

Note: *Refer to the precautions given in 'Safety first!' and in Section 1 of this Chapter.*

1 If the no-charge warning light fails to illuminate when the ignition is switched on, first check the alternator wiring connections for security. If satisfactory, check the instrument panel itself, though modern panels no longer contain conventional bulbs, and instead are

4.4b . . . then lift the clamp out with the webbing strap

4.5 Lifting out the battery

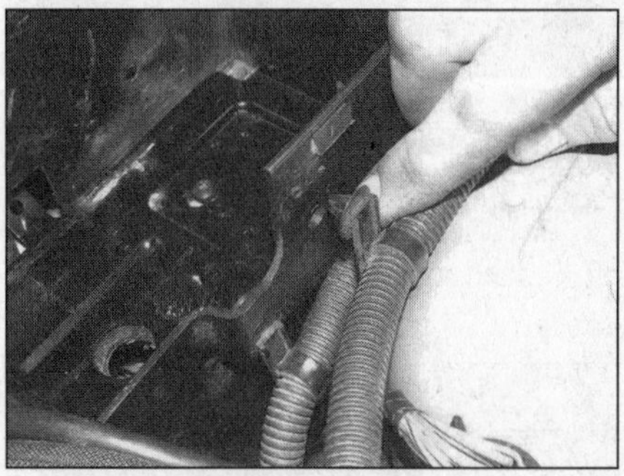
4.7a Unclip the wiring harness , , ,

4.7b . . . and wiring loom from the battery tray

4.8a Remove the four bolts . . .

4.8b . . . and lift out the battery tray

'solid-state' items with LEDs (see Chapter 12). If the light still fails to illuminate, check the continuity of the warning light feed wire from the alternator to the instrument panel. If all is satisfactory, the alternator is at fault, and should be renewed or taken to an auto-electrician for testing and repair.

2 If the ignition warning light illuminates when the engine is running, stop the engine and check that the drivebelt is correctly tensioned (see Chapter 1A or 1B) and that the alternator connections are secure. If all is so far satisfactory, have the alternator checked by an auto-electrician for testing and repair.

3 If the alternator output is suspect even though the warning light functions correctly, the regulated voltage may be checked as follows.

4 Connect a voltmeter across the battery terminals and start the engine.

5 Increase the engine speed until the voltmeter reading remains steady; the reading should be between 13.2 and 14.8 volts.

6 Switch on as many electrical accessories (eg, the headlights, heated rear window and heater blower) as possible, and check that the alternator maintains the regulated voltage between 13.2 and 14.8 volts.

7 If the regulated voltage is not as stated, the fault may be due to worn brushes, weak brush springs, a faulty voltage regulator, a faulty diode, a severed phase winding, or worn or damaged slip-rings. The alternator should be renewed or taken to an auto-electrician for testing and repair.

7.10 Battery supply cable nut is under a rubber cover

8 If the battery keeps going flat, it is more likely to be a faulty battery than any alternator trouble. Typically, a battery will fail if one or more of the six cells 'dies' – this will result in a battery voltage of only 10 volts, and can happen overnight. If the battery has removable cell covers, this can be proved by removing the battery and charging it – after a while, the good cells will start to bubble.

6 Alternator – testing

If the alternator is thought to be suspect, it should be removed from the vehicle and taken to an auto-electrician for testing. Most auto-electricians will be able to supply and fit brushes at a reasonable cost. However, check on the cost of repairs before proceeding, as it may prove more economical to obtain a new or exchange alternator.

7 Alternator – removal and refitting

1.8 litre engine

Without air conditioning

1 Disconnect the battery negative lead, and move the lead away from the battery (see *Disconnecting the battery*).

2 Remove the auxiliary drivebelts as described in Chapter 1A.

3 Unscrew the nut securing the battery supply cable, and move the cable to one side.

4 Unclip and disconnect the alternator multi-plug.

5 Working underneath, remove the drivebelt adjuster clamp bolt.

6 Support the alternator, then unscrew and remove the upper mounting bolt. Free the alternator from the mounting bracket, and remove it.

7 Refitting is a reversal of removal, noting the following points:

a) Fit the alternator in position, but leave the mounting and clamp bolts loose until the drivebelt has been refitted.

b) Refit the auxiliary drivebelts as described in Chapter 1A.

With air conditioning

8 Disconnect the battery negative lead, and move the lead away from the battery (see *Disconnecting the battery*).

9 Remove the auxiliary drivebelts as described in Chapter 1A.

10 Lift the rubber cap, unscrew the nut securing the battery supply cable, and move the cable to one side **(see illustration)**.

11 Unclip and disconnect the alternator multi-plug **(see illustration)**.

12 Remove the upper nut and bolt securing the alternator to the top mounting bracket. Recover the washer **(see illustration)**.

13 Remove the two lower mounting bolts and washers.

14 Move the refrigerant hose, expansion tank hose and wiring harness clear of the alternator.

15 Unscrew the two nuts securing the upper mounting bracket to the cylinder head.

16 Remove the alternator from the car.

17 Refitting is a reversal of removal, noting the following points:

a) Offer in the alternator, and fit it loosely to the lower bracket. Fit the upper bracket to the head, then fit and tighten the upper nut and bolt. Finally, tighten the lower bolts to the specified torque.

b) Refit the auxiliary drivebelts as described in Chapter 1A.

7.11 Disconnect the alternator wiring plug

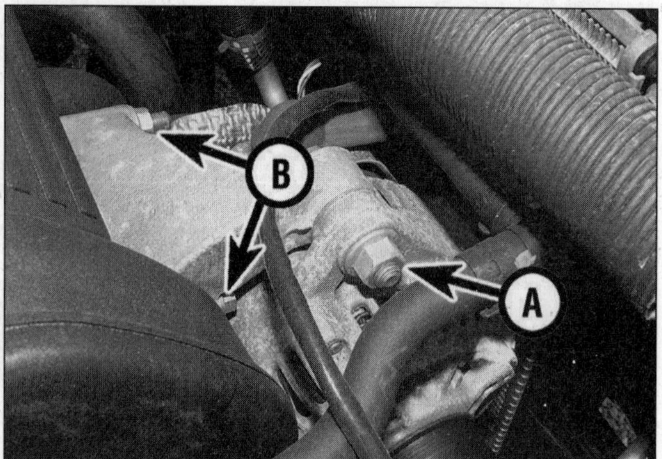

7.12 Alternator upper mounting nut/bolt (A) and bracket-to-head nuts (B)

7.21a Unclip the cover, then unscrew the nut . . .

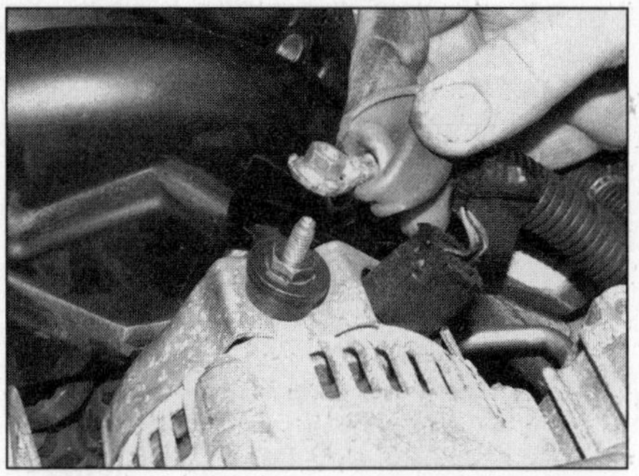

7.21b . . . and lift off the battery supply cable

7.22 Disconnect the alternator multi-plug

7.23a Unscrew the alternator upper . . .

7.23b . . . and lower bolt . . .

7.23c . . . and lift out the alternator

V6 engines

18 Disconnect the battery negative lead, and move the lead away from the battery (see *Disconnecting the battery*).

19 Remove the auxiliary drivebelt as described in Chapter 1A. **Note:** *This includes removing the engine right-hand mounting, which is essential to allow removal of the alternator lower mounting bolt.*

20 Remove the engine top cover, which is secured by two bolts. Recover the washers and rubber grommets from the bolt holes, and store them for refitting.

21 Unclip the cover, then unscrew the nut securing the battery supply cable, and move the cable to one side **(see illustrations)**.

22 Unclip and disconnect the alternator multi-plug **(see illustration)**.

23 Unscrew the two mounting bolts, and lift off the alternator **(see illustrations)**.

24 Refitting is a reversal of removal, noting the following points:

a) Tighten the alternator mounting bolts to the specified torque..

b) Refit the auxiliary drivebelt as described in Chapter 1A.

Diesel engines

25 Disconnect the battery negative lead, and move the lead away from the battery (see *Disconnecting the battery*).

26 Remove the auxiliary drivebelt(s) as described in Chapter 1B. Prior to removing the main drivebelt, just loosen (do not remove) the three power steering pump pulley bolts.

27 Remove the radiator as described in Chapter 3.

28 Unscrew the nut securing the battery supply cable, and move the cable to one side.

29 Unclip and disconnect the alternator multi-plug.

30 Remove the three bolts and take off the power steering pump pulley.

31 Unscrew the three alternator mounting bolts (two from the side, one from the front), and manoeuvre out the alternator.

32 Refitting is a reversal of removal, noting the following points:

a) Tighten the alternator mounting bolts to the specified torque.

b) Refit the radiator as described in Chapter 3.

c) Refit the auxiliary drivebelt(s) as described in Chapter 1B.

8 Starting system – testing

Note: *Refer to the precautions given in 'Safety first!' and in Section 1 of this Chapter before starting work.*

1 If the starter motor fails to operate, the following may be the possible causes:

a) The battery is faulty.

b) The electrical connections between the ignition switch, solenoid, battery and starter motor are somewhere failing to pass the necessary current from the battery through the starter to earth.

c) The solenoid is faulty.

d) The starter motor is mechanically or electrically defective.

2 To check the battery, switch on the headlights. If they dim after a few seconds, this indicates that the battery is discharged – recharge (see Section 3) or renew the battery. If the headlights glow brightly, turn the key and observe the lights. If they dim, then this indicates that current is reaching the starter motor, therefore the fault must lie in the starter motor. If the lights continue to glow brightly (and no clicking sound can be heard from the starter motor solenoid), this indicates that there is a fault in the circuit or solenoid – see the following paragraphs. If the starter motor turns slowly when operated, but the battery is in good condition, then this indicates that either the starter motor is faulty, or there is considerable resistance somewhere in the circuit.

3 If a fault in the circuit is suspected, disconnect the battery leads (including the earth connection to the body), the starter/solenoid wiring and the engine/transmission earth strap. Thoroughly clean the connections, and reconnect the leads and wiring, then use a voltmeter or test light to check that full battery voltage is available at the battery positive lead connection to the solenoid, and that the earth is sound. Smear petroleum jelly around the battery terminals to prevent corrosion – corroded connections are amongst the most frequent causes of electrical system faults.

4 If the battery and all connections are in good condition, check the circuit by disconnecting

9.3 Starter motor details – 1.8 litre models

A Solenoid spade connector
B Battery cable
C Upper mounting bolt

the wire from the solenoid blade terminal. Connect a voltmeter or test light between the wire end and a good earth (such as the battery negative terminal), and check that the wire is live when the ignition key is turned. If it is, then the circuit is sound – if not the circuit wiring can be checked as described in Chapter 12.

5 The solenoid contacts can be checked by connecting a voltmeter or test light between the battery positive feed connection on the starter side of the solenoid and earth. When the ignition key is turned, there should be a reading or lighted bulb, as applicable. If there is no reading or lighted bulb, the solenoid is faulty and should be renewed.

6 If the circuit and solenoid are proved sound, the fault must lie in the starter motor. In this event, it may be possible to have the starter motor overhauled by a specialist, but check on the cost of spares before proceeding, as it may prove more economical to obtain a new or exchange motor.

9 Starter motor – removal and refitting

1.8 litre engines

1 Disconnect the battery negative lead, and

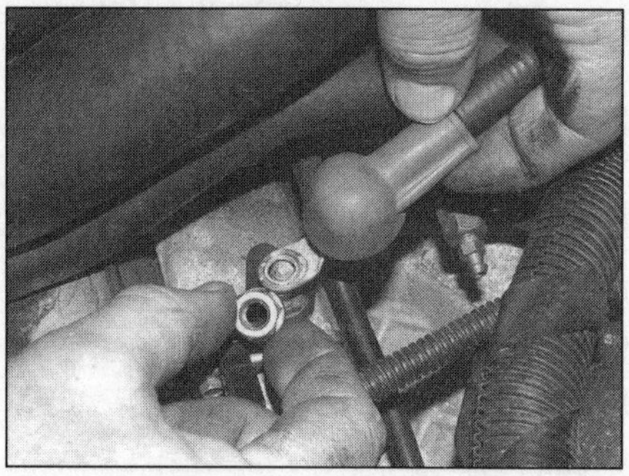

9.9 Unscrew the nut and disconnect the starter's battery lead

move the lead away from the battery (see *Disconnecting the battery*).

2 Firmly apply the handbrake, then jack up the front of the vehicle and support it on axle stands (see *Jacking and vehicle support*).

3 The starter motor is at the rear of the engine. Disconnect the spade connector from the starter solenoid **(see illustration)**.

4 Pull off the protective cap, then unscrew the nut securing the battery cable, and move the cable clear.

5 Unscrew the two starter motor mounting bolts, and withdraw the starter from under the car.

6 Refitting is a reversal of removal. Tighten the starter mounting bolts to the specified torque.

V6 engines

Manual transmission

7 Disconnect the battery negative lead, and move the lead away from the battery (see *Disconnecting the battery*).

8 Remove the air cleaner as described in Chapter 4B.

9 Unclip the cover, then unscrew the nut securing the battery cable, and move the cable clear **(see illustration)**.

10 Disconnect the spade connector from the starter solenoid **(see illustration)**.

11 Unscrew the two starter motor mounting bolts, noting that the upper bolt also secures an engine earth lead, while the lower bolt also holds a wiring plug bracket. Withdraw the starter from the car **(see illustrations)**.

12 Refitting is a reversal of removal. Tighten the starter mounting bolts to the specified torque.

Automatic transmission

13 Remove the air cleaner as described in Chapter 4B.

14 Remove the battery and its tray as described in Section 4.

15 Cut the cable-tie securing the engine wiring harness to the air cleaner support bracket, and move the harness clear.

16 Disconnect the spade connector from the starter solenoid.

17 Unscrew the nut securing the battery cable, and move the cable clear.

18 Unscrew the three starter motor mounting bolts, noting that the upper bolt also secures an engine earth lead, while the left-hand lower bolt also holds a wiring plug bracket. Withdraw the starter from the car.

19 Refitting is a reversal of removal. Tighten the starter mounting bolts to the specified torque.

Diesel engines

20 Disconnect the battery negative lead, and move the lead away from the battery (see *Disconnecting the battery*).

21 Remove the engine top cover, which is secured by three bolts.

22 Remove the three bolts securing the air intake duct to the bonnet lock platform, and two more from the inlet manifold. Release the duct at the rear, and lift it off the engine.

23 Disconnect the spade connector from the starter solenoid.

24 Unscrew the nut securing the two battery cables, and move the cables clear.

25 Unscrew the two starter motor mounting bolts (some models may have a lower nut and bolt), noting that the upper bolt also secures an engine earth lead. Withdraw the starter from the car.

26 Refitting is a reversal of removal. Tighten the starter mounting bolts to the specified torque.

9.10 Disconnect the starter solenoid wire

9.11a Starter motor upper mounting bolt also secures earth lead

9.11b Removing the starter motor

Chapter 5 Part B:
Ignition system – petrol models

Contents

Degrees of difficulty

Easy, suitable for novice with little experience	**Fairly easy,** suitable for beginner with some experience	**Fairly difficult,** suitable for competent DIY mechanic	**Difficult,** suitable for experienced DIY mechanic	**Very difficult,** suitable for expert DIY or professional

Specifications

General

System type:	
1.8 litre engines	Rover/Motorola Modular Engine Management System 3 (MEMS 3)
V6 engines	Siemens engine management system
Firing order:	
1.8 litre engines	1-3-4-2 (No 1 cylinder at timing belt end)
V6 engines	1-6-5-4-3-2 (No 1 cylinder at primary timing belt end, front bank)

Ignition coil

Type:	
1.8 litre engines	2x twin-output plug top-mounted coils, serving cylinders 1&4, 2&3, Nippon Denso NEC 100730
V6 engines	6x coils, three plug-top mounted, three remote-mounted, BREMR
Primary resistance:	
1.8 litre engines	0.7 ohms
V6 engines	Not stated
Secondary resistance:	
1.8 litre engines	10 ohms
V6 engines	Not stated

Ignition timing	Controlled by the ECM

Torque wrench settings

Torque wrench settings	Nm	lbf ft
Ignition coil retaining nuts/bolts	8	6
Knock sensors	25	18
Spark plugs	25	18

1 General information and precautions

The ignition system is integrated with the fuel injection system to form a combined engine management system under the control of one ECM (See Chapter 4A or 4B for further information).

The MEMS 3 system fitted to 1.8 litre engines has two dual-output coils fitted to the camshaft cover – one above No 1 spark plug, and the other above No 3 spark plug. Whilst one output from each coil goes directly to the spark plug below it, the other output is sent via an HT lead to another spark plug. The coil over No 1 spark plug connects to No 4 spark plug, and the coil above No 3 spark plug connects to No 2 spark plug. Each coil fires both spark plugs simultaneously. The engine management ECM uses inputs from the various sensors to calculate the required ignition advance setting.

On the Siemens system fitted to V6 engines, six separate ignition coils are used, each ignition coil supplying a single cylinder. Plug-top ignition coils are used on the rear bank of cylinders, whilst the front bank of cylinders are fed through HT leads from ignition coils mounted on the inlet manifold. V6 engines also have two knock sensors located in the vee of the engine. One sensor is used for each engine bank, to detect combustion knock. Combustion knock (also known as 'pinking', pre-ignition, or detonation) is caused by pressure waves from the uncontrolled, spontaneous combustion of gases in the cylinder. The knock sensors contain piezo-ceramic crystals that oscillate to create a voltage signal. When knock occurs, the frequency of crystal oscillation increases which alters the signal output to the ECM. If combustion knock is detected, the ECM retards the ignition timing until it stops. If no more pre-ignition is detected, the timing is gradually advanced to the original setting.

Precautions

The following precautions must be observed, to prevent damage to the ignition system components and to reduce risk of personal injury.

a) *Ensure the ignition is switched off before disconnecting any of the ignition wiring.*
b) *Ensure that the ignition is switched off before connecting or disconnecting any ignition test equipment, such as a timing light.*
c) *Do not earth the coil primary or secondary circuits.*

Warning: Voltages produced by an electronic ignition system are considerably higher than those produced by conventional ignition systems. Extreme care must be taken when working on the system with the ignition switched on. Persons with surgically-implanted cardiac pacemaker devices should keep well clear of the ignition circuits, components and test equipment

2 Ignition system – testing

1 If a fault appears in the engine management (fuel injection/ignition) system first ensure that the fault is not due to a poor electrical connection or poor maintenance; ie, check that the air cleaner filter element is clean, the spark plugs are in good condition and correctly gapped, that the engine breather hoses are clear and undamaged, referring to Chapter 1A for further information. Also check that the accelerator cable is correctly adjusted as described in Chapter 4A or 4B. If the engine is running very roughly, check the compression pressures as described in Chapter 2A or 2B.

2 If these checks fail to reveal the cause of the problem, the car should be taken to a suitably-equipped specialist for testing. A wiring block connector is incorporated in the engine management circuit, into which a special electronic diagnostic tester can be plugged. The tester will locate the fault quickly and simply alleviating the need to test all the system components individually, which is a time-consuming operation that carries a high risk of damaging the ECM.

3 The only ignition system checks which can be carried out by the home mechanic are those described in Chapter 1A, relating to the spark plugs and HT leads. If necessary, the system wiring and wiring connectors can be checked as described in Chapter 12, ensuring that the ECM wiring connector(s) have first been disconnected.

3 Ignition HT coils – removal and refitting

1.8 litre engines

1 Disconnect the battery negative lead, and move the lead away from the battery (see *Disconnecting the battery*).

2 Unscrew the three retaining screws and remove the coil/lead cover **(see illustration)**.

3 Disconnect the two HT leads from the spark plugs serving cylinders 2 and 4, and release them from the retaining clips, noting how they are routed **(see illustration)**.

4 If the coils are not marked for position, it may be advisable to label them before removal. However, it would appear they are identical, and that no harm would come from not refitting them in their original positions.

5 Disconnect the wiring plugs from the two coils, which are fitted above cylinders 1 and 3. Undo the two retaining bolts, and pull upwards to release each coil from the spark plug underneath it **(see illustration)**.

6 Refitting is the reverse of removal, tightening the coil retaining bolts to the specified torque. Ensure the HT lead(s) and wiring connectors are correctly and securely reconnected.

V6 engines

7 Remove the two bolts and unclip the engine top cover. Recover the washers and rubber grommets from the bolt holes, and store them for refitting.

Front bank

8 If the coils are not marked for position, it may be advisable to label them before removal. However, it would appear they are all identical, and that no harm would come from not refitting them in their original positions.

9 Mark the leads for position by wrapping a piece of labelled masking tape around (we

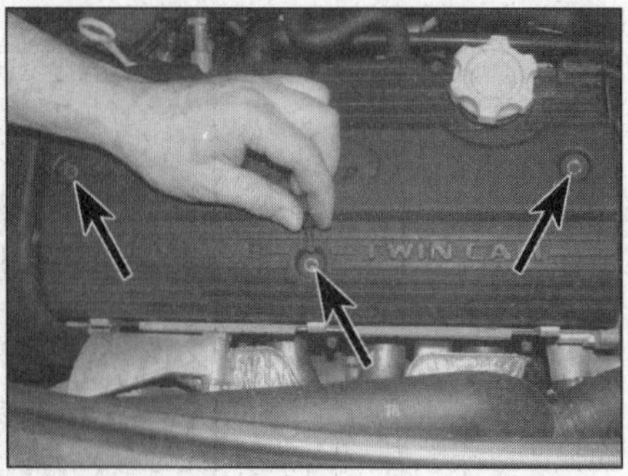

3.2 Unscrew the three retaining screws (arrowed) and remove the coil lead cover

3.3 Disconnect the HT leads by pulling up the cap – not the leads

3.5 Undo the retaining bolts and release the coils from the spark plugs

3.9 Mark the HT leads for position

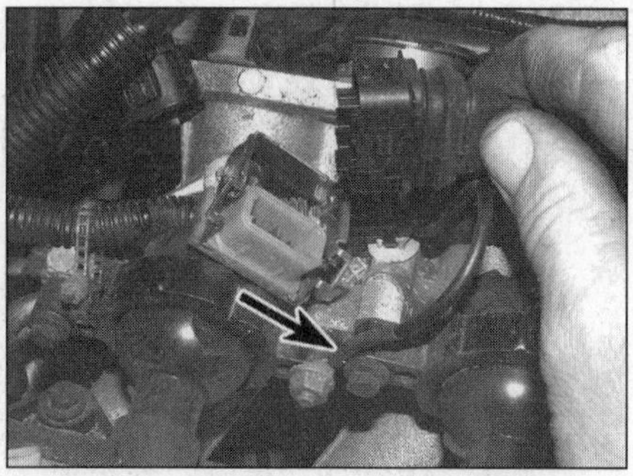

3.10 Disconnect the coil wiring plug – note earth lead under coil mounting nut

3.11 Disconnect the HT leads, and remove the front coils

marked ours F, C and R, for Front, Centre and Rear) **(see illustration)**.

10 Release the locking catch, and disconnect the wiring multi-plug from each of the three coils. Unscrew the mounting bolt and nut from each coil, noting that the bolt from the first coil is also used for the coil earth lead **(see illustration)**.

11 Disconnect the HT leads, and withdraw the coils from the inlet manifold **(see illustration)**.

12 Refitting is the reverse of removal, tightening the coil retaining nuts and bolts to the specified torque. Ensure the HT leads and wiring connectors are correctly and securely reconnected.

Rear bank

13 Peel up the rubber weatherseal at the rear of the engine compartment **(see illustration)**.

14 Remove the four nuts securing the central soundproofing panel, then lift it off the wiring harness which passes through the bulkhead **(see illustrations)**.

3.13 Peel up the rubber seal from the rear bulkhead

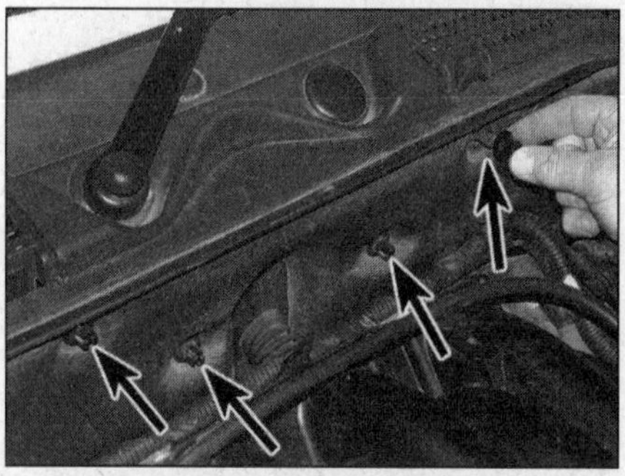

3.14a Remove the plastic nuts . . .

15 Remove the two bolts and take out the access panel behind the soundproofing **(see illustrations)**.

16 If the coils are not marked for position, it may be advisable to label them before removal. However, it would appear they are all identical, and that no harm would come from not refitting them in their original positions.

17 Lift the locking clips and disconnect the wiring plug from each of the three ignition coils. Remove the two bolts securing each coil, then lift them off the spark plugs **(see illustrations)**.

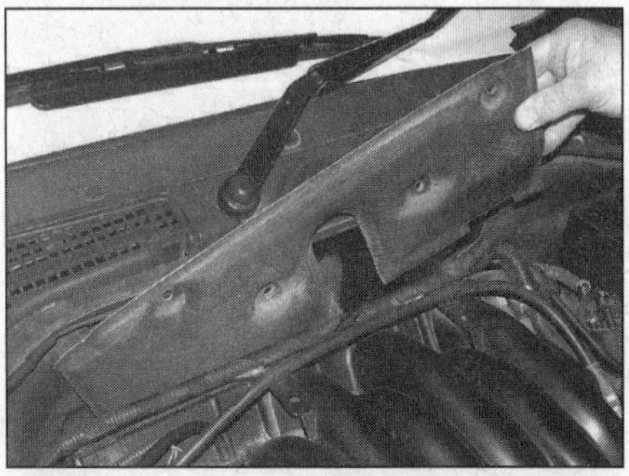

3.14b . . . and take off the soundproofing panel

3.15a Remove the two bolts . . .

3.15b . . . and lift out the metal access panel

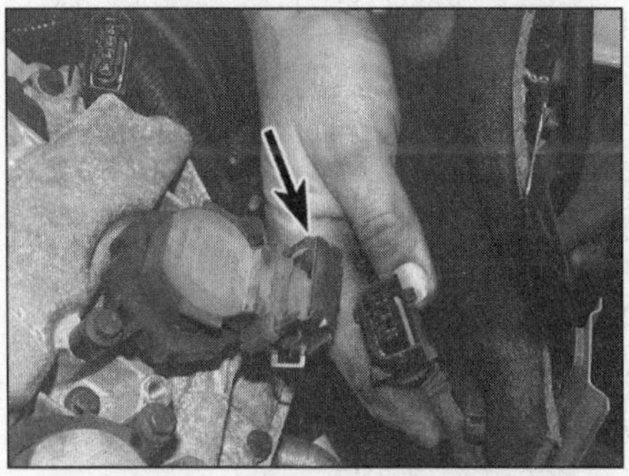

3.17a Lift the locking clip (arrowed) and disconnect the coil wiring plugs . . .

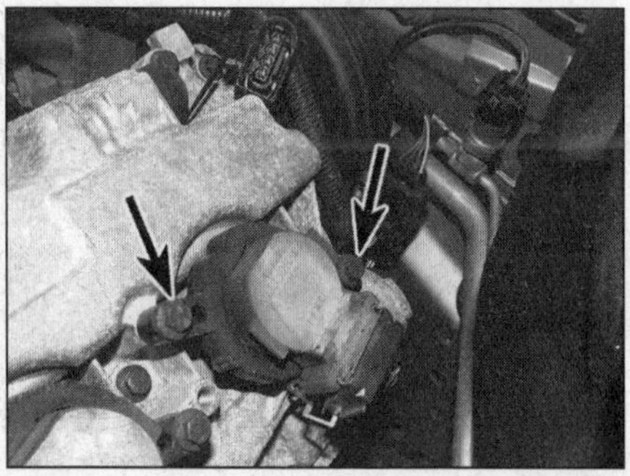

3.17b . . . then unscrew the two bolts from each coil . . .

3.17c . . . and lift them off the spark plugs

4.5a Unscrew the mounting bolts . . .

4.5b . . . and remove the knock sensor

18 Refitting is the reverse of removal, tightening the coil retaining bolts to the specified torque. Ensure the wiring connectors are correctly and securely reconnected.

4 Knock sensors (V6 engines) – removal and refitting

Removal

1 The knock sensors are located in the vee of the engine (between the front and rear banks of cylinders).

2 Ensure that the ignition is switched off (take out the key).

3 Remove the inlet manifold upper chamber and the front inlet manifold as described in Chapter 4B.

4 Trace the wiring back from the two sensors to the single wiring multi-plug above the transmission, and disconnect it. Note how the wiring is routed.

5 Unscrew the bolt securing each sensor, and remove them from the engine **(see illustrations)**.

Refitting

6 Refitting is a reversal of removal. Ensure that the sensors and their mating faces on the engine are completely clean. Tighten the sensor to the specified torque wrench setting. It is essential that these measures are scrupulously observed, as if the sensor is not correctly secured to a clean mating surface, it may not be able to detect the impulses caused by pre-ignition. If this were to happen, the correction of ignition timing would not take place, with the consequent risk of severe engine damage.

5 Ignition timing – checking and adjustment

The timing is constantly being monitored and adjusted by the engine management ECM. The only way in which the ignition timing can be checked and (where possible) adjusted is by using special electronic test equipment, connected to the engine management system diagnostic connector (refer to Chapter 4A or 4B). Refer to a diagnostic specialist for further information.

Chapter 5 Part C: Preheating system – diesel models

Contents

Degrees of difficulty

Easy, suitable for novice with little experience	**Fairly easy,** suitable for beginner with some experience	**Fairly difficult,** suitable for competent DIY mechanic	**Difficult,** suitable for experienced DIY mechanic	**Very difficult,** suitable for expert DIY or professional

Specifications

Torque wrench settings	**Nm**	**lbf ft**
Glow plugs	20	15
Inlet manifold:		
M6 bolts	10	7
M7 nuts and bolt	15	11

1 General information

To assist cold-starting, diesel engine models are fitted with a preheating system, which comprises a control unit and four glow plugs. The system is controlled by the Electronic Diesel Control (EDC) system (see Chapter 4C).

The glow plugs are miniature electric heating elements, encapsulated in a metal case with a probe at one end, and an electrical connection at the other. The four combustion chambers each have a glow plug threaded into them. When the glow plug is energised, it heats up rapidly, causing the temperature of the air charge drawn into each of the combustion chambers to rise. Each glow plug probe is positioned directly in line with the incoming spray of fuel from the injector. Hence the fuel passing over the glow plug probe is also heated, allowing its optimum combustion temperature to be achieved more readily.

The duration of the preheating period is governed by the Electronic Diesel Control (EDC) system control module (ECM) using information provided by the coolant temperature sensor. The ECM alters the preheating time (the length for which the glow plugs are supplied with current) to suit the prevailing conditions.

A warning light informs the driver that preheating is taking place. The light extinguishes when sufficient preheating has taken place to allow the engine to be started, but power will still be supplied to the glow plugs for a further period until the engine is started (post-heating). If no attempt is made to start the engine, the power supply to the glow plugs is switched off to prevent battery drain and glow plug burn-out.

2 Preheating system – testing

1 Full testing of the system can only be carried out using specialist diagnostic equipment which is connected to the engine management system diagnostic wiring connector (see Chapter 4C). If the preheating system is thought to be faulty, some preliminary checks of the glow plug operation may be made as described in the following paragraphs.

2 Connect a voltmeter or 12 volt test light between the glow plug supply cable, and a good earth point on the engine.

Caution: Make sure that the live connection is kept well clear of the engine and bodywork.

3 Have an assistant activate the preheating system by turning the ignition key to the second position, and check that battery voltage is applied to the glow plug electrical connection. **Note:** *The supply voltage will be less than battery voltage initially, but will rise and settle as the glow plug heats-up. It will then drop to zero when the preheating period ends and the safety cut-out operates.*

4 If no supply voltage can be detected at the glow plug, then the glow plug relay or the supply cable may be faulty.

5 To locate a faulty glow plug, first operate the preheating system to allow the glow plugs to reach working temperature, then disconnect the battery negative cable and position it away from the battery terminal (see *Disconnecting the battery*).

6 Refer to Section 3, and remove the supply cable from No 2 glow plug terminal. Measure the electrical resistance between the glow plug terminal and the engine earth. A reading of anything more than a few ohms indicates that the glow plug is defective.

7 As a final check, remove the glow plugs and inspect them visually, as described in Section 3.

8 If no problems are found, take the car to a suitably-equipped garage for testing using the appropriate diagnostic equipment.

3 Glow plugs – removal, inspection and refitting

Removal

1 Ensure that the ignition is switched off (take out the key).

2 With reference to Chapter 4C, remove the inlet manifold.

3 Squeeze together the lugs at the end of the connectors and pull them from the glow plugs **(see illustration)**.

4 Using a deep socket, unscrew and remove the glow plugs **(see illustration)**.

Inspection

5 Inspect the glow plugs for signs of damage. Burnt or eroded glow plug tips can be caused by a bad injector spray pattern. Have the injectors checked if this sort of damage is found.

6 If the glow plugs are in good condition, check them electrically, as described in Section 2.

7 The glow plugs can be energised by applying 12 volts to them to verify that they heat up evenly and in the required time. Observe the following precautions:

a) *Support the glow plug by clamping it carefully in a vice or self-locking pliers. Remember it will be red-hot.*

b) *Make sure that the power supply or test lead incorporates a fuse or overload trip to protect against damage from a short-circuit.*

c) *After testing, allow the glow plug to cool for several minutes before attempting to handle it.*

8 A glow plug in good condition will start to glow red at the tip after drawing current for 5 seconds or so. Any plug which takes much longer to start glowing, or which starts glowing in the middle instead of at the tip, is probably defective.

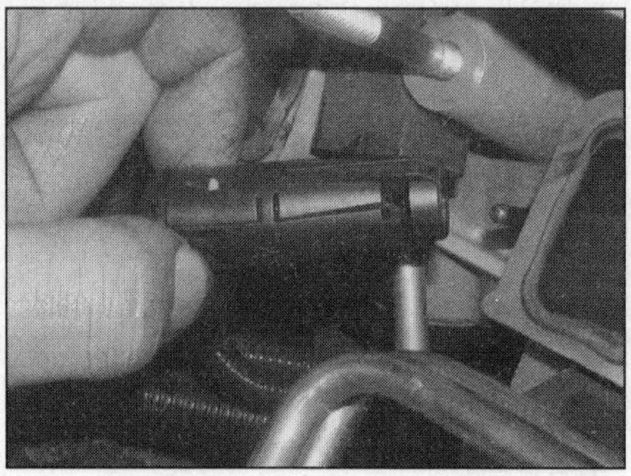

3.3 Squeeze the end of the connector, and pull it from the glow plug

Refitting

9 Thoroughly clean the glow plugs, and the glow plug seating areas in the cylinder head.

10 Apply a smear of copper-based anti-seize compound to the glow plug threads, then refit the glow plug and tighten it to the specified torque.

3.4 Unscrew the glow plugs with a deep socket, and remove them

11 Reconnect the wiring to the glow plug. The connectors are a push-fit.

12 Refit the inlet manifold as described in Chapter 4C.

4 Glow plug control unit – removal and refitting

Removal

1 Disconnect the battery negative lead, and move the lead away from the battery (see *Disconnecting the battery*).

2 Remove the engine management ECM as described in Chapter 4C.

3 Release the securing tab at the side of the control unit, and slide the unit up off its mounting guides.

4 Unscrew the nut and disconnect the glow plug supply lead from the unit.

5 Disconnect the unit wiring multi-plug, and remove it.

Refitting

6 Refitting is a reversal of removal.

Chapter 6
Clutch

Contents

Degrees of difficulty

Easy, suitable for novice with little experience	**Fairly easy,** suitable for beginner with some experience	**Fairly difficult,** suitable for competent DIY mechanic	**Difficult,** suitable for experienced DIY mechanic	**Very difficult,** suitable for expert DIY or professional

Specifications

General

Clutch type	Single dry plate with diaphragm spring, hydraulically-operated by concentric slave cylinder/release bearing

Friction disc

Diameter:	
1.8 litre non-turbo models	215 mm
All other models	228 mm
Friction material-to-rivet head depth:	
New (approximate)	1.0 mm
Service limit	0.25 mm
Thickness:	
New	6.9 to 7.4 mm
Service limit	5.9 mm
Run-out	0.4 mm maximum

Torque wrench settings

Torque wrench settings	Nm	lbf ft
Master cylinder mounting bolts	10	7
Pressure plate retaining bolts	25	18

1 General information

The clutch consists of a friction disc, a pressure plate assembly, a release bearing and the release mechanism; all of these components are contained in the large cast-aluminium alloy bellhousing, sandwiched between the engine and the transmission. The clutch release mechanism is hydraulically-operated.

The friction disc is fitted between the engine flywheel and the clutch pressure plate, and is allowed to slide on the transmission input shaft splines.

The pressure plate assembly is bolted to the engine flywheel. When the engine is running, drive is transmitted from the crankshaft, via the flywheel, to the friction disc (these components being clamped securely together by the pressure plate assembly) and from the friction disc to the transmission input shaft.

To interrupt the drive, the spring pressure must be relaxed. Depressing the pedal pushes on the master cylinder pushrod, and the hydraulic pressure causes the centrally-mounted slave cylinder/release bearing to act against the pressure plate fingers. This causes the springs to deform and releases the clamping force on the pressure plate. The hydraulic clutch is self-adjusting and requires no manual adjustment.

All manual transmission models are fitted with a dual-mass flywheel. As the name implies, a dual-mass flywheel comprises two major components – a primary mass (essentially replacing the conventional flywheel) and an additional secondary mass which, via the clutch, transmits drive to the transmission. The secondary mass is supported on the primary mass via a roller bearing, and the drive connection between the primary and secondary mass is achieved by a coil-sprung torsional damper. The primary function of the dual-mass flywheel is to insulate the transmission from uneven loads produced by the engine, giving a much better input into the transmission, and a corresponding improvement in drivetrain refinement.

The master cylinder, and the slave cylinder and connecting pipework, are only available as complete assemblies, pre-filled with hydraulic fluid, and are intended to be 'sealed for life'.

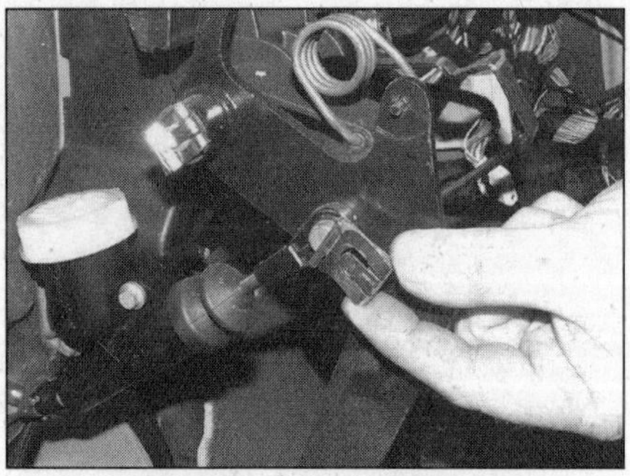

3.5 Removing the master cylinder pushrod-to-pedal spring clip

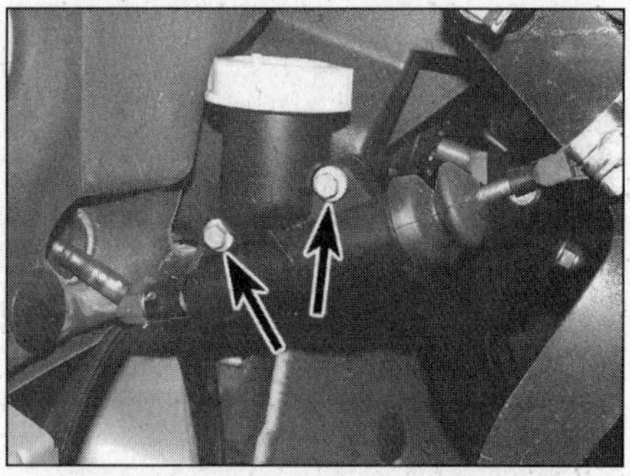

3.6 Master cylinder mounting bolts

2 Clutch pedal – removal and refitting

Refer to the pedal box removal procedure in Chapter 9.

3 Clutch master cylinder – removal and refitting

Removal

1 Remove the battery and its tray as described in Chapter 5A.

2 Separate the fluid pipe from the front of the master cylinder. This is a self-sealing 'quick-release' connection, which should just pull apart with the help of a small screwdriver – there is an MG Rover special tool, simply a flat piece of metal with a vee cut in it, which could easily be made in case of difficulty.

3 Remove the driver's lower facia panel, as described in Chapter 11, Section 25.

4 Remove the trim panel fitted above the pedals, which is secured by two screws at the top, and two push-fasteners at the bottom.

5 Prise off the spring clip, and release the master cylinder pushrod from the pedal **(see illustration)**.

6 Unscrew the two master cylinder mounting bolts, and free it from the pedal box **(see illustration)**.

7 Release the bulkhead grommets around the clutch fluid pipe, then withdraw the master cylinder into the car. If a new master cylinder is being fitted, recover the bulkhead grommets and fit them to the new unit.

Refitting

8 Refitting is a reversal of removal. Check the operation of the clutch pedal. The clutch hydraulic system is sealed, and should not need bleeding – however, a bleed screw is provided if necessary **(see illustration)**.

4 Clutch slave cylinder – removal and refitting

Removal

1 With reference to Chapter 7A, remove the transmission.

2 Carefully prise out the grommet sealing the slave cylinder pipes into the top of the transmission housing **(see illustration)**.

3 Pull the release bearing from the guide tube, and manoeuvre the bearing and pipes from the transmission housing **(see illustration)**.

4 Check that the release bearing contact surface rotates smoothly and easily, with no sign of noise or roughness. Also check that the surface itself is smooth and unworn, with no signs of cracks, pitting or scoring. If there is any doubt about its condition, the

3.8 Clutch hydraulic system bleed screw on top of the transmission

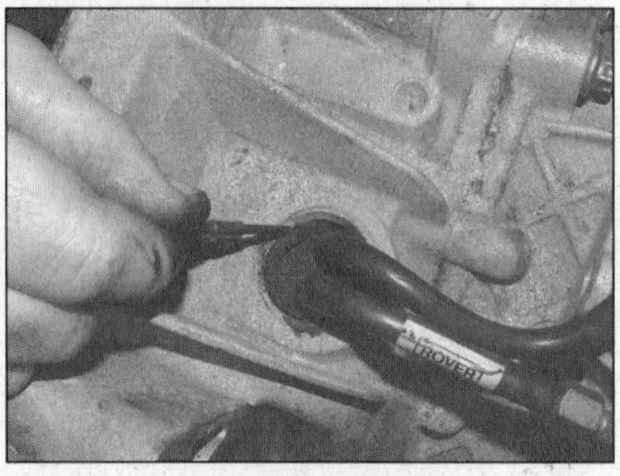

4.2 Prise out the grommet from the slave cylinder pipes

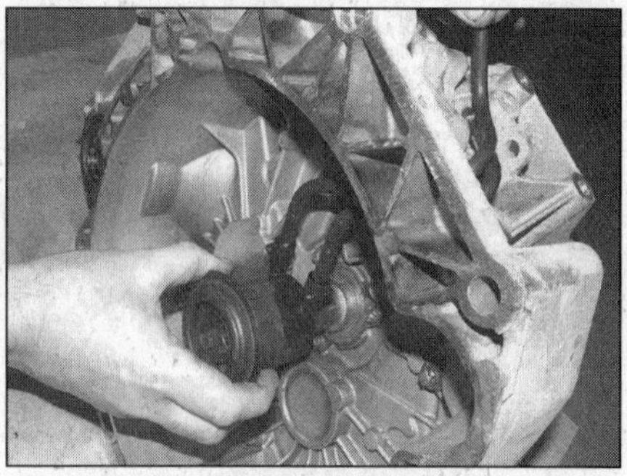

4.3 Pull the release bearing from the guide tube, and feed the pipes through

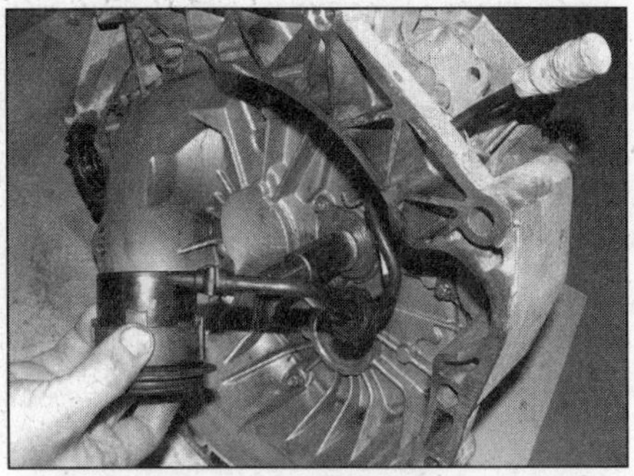

4.6 Offering the release bearing and pipes into place

bearing must be renewed along with the slave cylinder.

Refitting

5 Clean the release bearing and the guide tube, then lubricate the running surfaces with a little molybdenum disulphide grease.

6 Manoeuvre the slave cylinder pipes through the transmission casing hole, so the slave cylinder and release bearing are positioned over the guide tube **(see illustration)**. Fit the slave cylinder to the guide tube by pressing it into place.

7 Refit the sealing grommet to the transmission casing and slave cylinder pipes.

8 Refit the transmission as described in Chapter 7A.

5 Clutch hydraulic system - bleeding

The clutch hydraulic system is a sealed system, and (in theory) never requires topping-up or bleeding. If a problem develops, it suggests either the master cylinder or slave cylinder is faulty, and renewal is the only option.

However, a bleed screw is provided on top of the transmission **(see illustration 3.8)**. No procedure for bleeding is given by MG Rover, but a suggested procedure is given below:

1) Open the bleed screw, and top-up the reservoir until a steady flow of fluid emerges.

2) Connect a one-man brake bleeding kit to the bleed screw (see Chapter 9 for bleeding the brakes), and gently operate the clutch pedal until fluid free of air bubbles emerges.

3) On completion, tighten the bleed screw securely. Wash off any spilt fluid, and top-up the reservoir.

6 Clutch assembly - removal, inspection and refitting

Warning: Dust created by clutch wear and deposited on the clutch components may contain asbestos, which is a health hazard. DO NOT blow it out with compressed air, or inhale any of it. DO NOT use petrol or petroleum-based solvents to clean off the dust. Brake system cleaner or methylated spirit should be used to flush the dust into a suitable receptacle. After the clutch components are wiped clean with rags, dispose of the contaminated rags and cleaner in a sealed, marked container.

Note: *Although some friction materials may no longer contain asbestos, it is safest to assume that they do, and to take precautions accordingly.*

Removal

1 Unless the complete engine/transmission unit is to be removed from the car and separated for major overhaul (see the appropriate part of Chapter 2), the clutch can be reached by removing the transmission as described Chapter 7A.

2 Before disturbing the clutch, use chalk or a marker pen to mark the relationship of the pressure plate assembly to the flywheel.

3 Hold the flywheel to prevent it turning as the pressure plate bolts are loosened – this can be achieved using a home-made tool engaged in the flywheel ring gear, or by bolting a strap between the engine and flywheel.

4 Working in a diagonal sequence, slacken the six pressure plate bolts by half a turn at a time, until spring pressure is released and the bolts can be unscrewed by hand **(see illustration)**.

5 Prise the pressure plate assembly off its locating dowels, and collect the friction disc, noting which way round the friction disc is fitted **(see illustration)**.

Inspection

Note: *Due to the amount of work necessary to remove and refit clutch components, it is usually considered good practice to renew the clutch friction disc, pressure plate assembly and release bearing as a matched set, even if only one of these is actually worn enough to require renewal. It is also worth considering the renewal of the clutch components on a preventive basis if the engine and/or transmission have been removed for some other reason.*

6 Remove the clutch assembly.

7 When cleaning clutch components, read first the warning at the beginning of this Section; remove dust using a clean, dry cloth, and working in a well-ventilated atmosphere.

8 Check the friction disc facings for signs of wear, damage or oil contamination. If the friction material is cracked, burnt, scored or damaged, or if it is contaminated with oil or grease (shown by shiny black patches), the friction disc must be renewed. Measure the friction disc thickness and check the depth of the rivets below the friction material surface **(see illustration)**. If the friction disc thickness or the depth of any rivet is equal to, or less than, the service limit given in the Specifications, then the friction disc must be renewed.

9 If the friction material is still serviceable, check that the centre boss splines are unworn, that the torsion springs are in good condition and securely fastened, and that all the rivets are tight. If any wear or damage is found, the friction disc must be renewed.

10 If the friction material is fouled with oil, this must be due to an oil leak from the crankshaft left-hand oil seal, from the sump-to-cylinder block joint, or from the transmission input shaft. Renew the seal or repair the joint, as appropriate, as described in the appropriate part of Chapter 2 or 7A, before installing the new friction disc.

11 Check the pressure plate assembly for obvious signs of wear or damage; shake it to check for loose rivets or worn or damaged

6.4 Working in a diagonal sequence, slacken the pressure plate bolts by half a turn at a time

6.5 Remove the clutch pressure plate and friction disc from the flywheel

6.8 Use a vernier to measure the friction disc rivet head depth below the friction material

6.15a Offer the friction disc into position . . .

6.15b . . . with the GEARBOX marking facing away from the flywheel

6.17 A typical clutch aligning tool

fulcrum rings, and check that the drive straps securing the pressure plate to the cover do not show signs of overheating (such as a deep yellow or blue discoloration). Check the diaphragm spring fingers for signs of wear or damage and check that the height of each finger above the pressure plate machined face. If the diaphragm spring is worn or damaged, or if its pressure is in any way suspect, the pressure plate assembly should be renewed.

12 Examine the machined bearing surfaces of the pressure plate and of the flywheel; they should be clean, completely flat, and free from scratches or scoring. If either is discoloured from excessive heat, or shows signs of cracks, it should be renewed – although minor damage of this nature can sometimes be polished away using emery paper. Using a straight-edge, check the pressure plate surface for warpage at several points around its diameter, if the warpage is excessive the plate must be renewed.

13 Check that the release bearing contact surface rotates smoothly and easily, with no sign of noise or roughness. Also check that the surface itself is smooth and unworn, with no signs of cracks, pitting or scoring. If there is any doubt about its condition, the bearing must be renewed.

6.18a Fit the pressure plate onto its locating dowels . . .

Refitting

14 On reassembly, ensure that the friction surfaces of the flywheel and pressure plate are completely clean, smooth, and free from oil or grease. Use solvent to remove any protective grease from new components.

15 Fit the friction disc so that its spring hub assembly faces away from the flywheel; there may also be a marking showing which way round the plate is to be refitted. On some genuine clutches, the friction disc should be fitted with the GETRIEBESEITE (GEARBOX SIDE) marking facing away from the flywheel, or SCHWUNGRADSEITE (FLYWHEEL SIDE) towards the flywheel **(see illustrations)**.

16 The friction disc must now be centralised, so that when the transmission is refitted its input shaft will pass through the splines at the centre of the friction disc.

17 Centralisation can be achieved by passing a screwdriver or other long bar through the friction disc and into the hole in the crankshaft; the friction disc can then be moved around until it is centred on the crankshaft hole. Alternatively, a clutch-aligning tool can be used to eliminate the guesswork; these can be obtained from most accessory shops **(see illustration)**.

6.18b . . . and fit the bolts, tightened by hand only at this stage

18 Refit the pressure plate assembly, aligning the marks made on dismantling (if the original pressure plate is re-used), and locating the pressure plate on its locating dowels. Fit the pressure plate bolts, but tighten them only finger-tight, so that the friction disc can still be moved **(see illustrations)**.

HAYNES HiNT ***A home-made aligning tool can be fabricated from a length of metal rod or wooden dowel which fits closely inside the crankshaft hole, and has insulating tape wrap around it to match the diameter of the friction disc splined hole.***

19 When the friction disc is centralised, tighten the pressure plate bolts evenly and in a diagonal sequence to the specified torque setting. Ensure the pressure plate is drawn squarely onto the flywheel, to prevent the pressure plate being distorted.

20 Refit the transmission as described in Chapter 7A.

7 Clutch release bearing – removal, inspection and refitting

The release bearing is integral with the clutch slave cylinder, and can only be renewed as a complete unit. Refer to Section 4.

Chapter 7 Part A: Manual transmission

Contents

Degrees of difficulty

Easy, suitable for novice with little experience	**Fairly easy,** suitable for beginner with some experience	**Fairly difficult,** suitable for competent DIY mechanic	**Difficult,** suitable for experienced DIY mechanic	**Very difficult,** suitable for expert DIY or professional

Specifications

General

Type	Getrag 283, five forward speeds and one reverse, cable-operated. Synchromesh on all speeds	
Ratios:	**Petrol**	**Diesel**
First	3.577 : 1	3.577 : 1
Second	2.022 : 1	2.022 : 1
Third	1.348 : 1	1.292 : 1
Fourth	1.029 : 1	0.919 : 1
Fifth	0.809 : 1	0.686 : 1
Reverse	3.308 : 1	3.308 : 1
Final drive ratio:		
1.8 litre non-turbo engine, and 2.0 litre V6 engine	4.410 : 1	
1.8 litre turbo engine, and 2.5 litre V6 engine	3.947 : 1	
Diesel engines	3.737 : 1	

Lubrication

Recommended oil	See *Lubricants and fluids*
Capacity:	
From dry	1.6 litres
Drain and refill	1.4 litres

Torque wrench settings

Torque wrench settings	Nm	lbf ft
Drain plug	35	26
Engine/transmission mountings:		
Left-hand mounting through-bolt	100	74
Left-hand mounting to body	85	63
Left-hand mounting to transmission	85	63
Lower mounting through-bolts	100	74
Filler/level plug	35	26
Gearchange mechanism-to-floor Torx bolts	9	7
Release bearing sleeve bolts	12	9
Reversing light switch	25	18
Transmission mounting bracket bolts	85	63
Transmission rear cover Torx bolts*	25	18
Transmission-to-engine/sump bolts	85	63

* *Use new bolts*

1 General information

The transmission is equipped with five forward gears, one reverse gear and a final drive differential, incorporated in one casing bolted to the left-hand end of the engine.

Drive is transmitted from the crankshaft via the clutch to the input shaft which rotates in sealed ball-bearings, and has a splined extension to accept the clutch friction disc. From the input shaft, drive is transmitted to the output shaft, which rotates in a roller bearing at its right-hand end, and a sealed ball-bearing at its left-hand end. From the output shaft, drive is transmitted to the differential crown wheel, which rotates with the differential case and planetary gears, thus driving the side gears and driveshafts. The rotation of the planetary gears on their shaft allows the inner roadwheel to rotate at a slower speed than the outer roadwheel when the car is cornering.

The input and output shafts are arranged side-by-side, parallel to the crankshaft and driveshafts, so that their gear pinion teeth are in constant mesh. In the neutral position, the output shaft gear pinions rotate freely, so that drive cannot be transmitted to the final drive gear.

Gear selection is via a floor-mounted lever and selector cable mechanism. The selector cable causes the appropriate selector fork to move its respective synchro-sleeve along the shaft, to lock the gear pinion to the synchro-hub. Since the synchro-hubs are splined to the output shaft, this locks the pinion to the shaft, so that drive can be transmitted. To ensure that gearchanging can be made quickly and quietly, a synchromesh system is fitted to all gears (including reverse gear), consisting of baulk rings and spring-loaded fingers, as well as the gear pinions and synchro-hubs. The synchromesh cones are formed on the mating faces of the baulk rings and gear pinions.

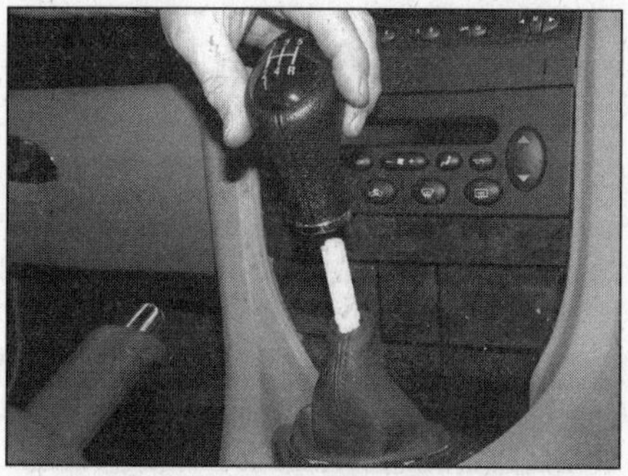

3.2 Pull the gear knob sharply upwards to detach it

2 Transmission oil – draining and refilling

Refer to Chapter 1A or 1B.

3 Gearchange mechanism and cables – removal and refitting

Removal

1 When removing the gearchange mechanism, the gear lever should be in neutral.

2 Pull up sharply to disengage the gear knob's securing tab, and remove the gear knob **(see illustration)**.

3 Unclip the gear lever gaiter trim panel from the centre console, and lift it off the gear lever **(see illustration)**. For the best access, remove the centre console as described in Chapter 11.

4 Remove the battery and its tray as described in Chapter 5A.

5 Working under the bonnet, prise off the gearchange cable end fittings from the ball-studs on the transmission selector levers **(see illustration)**.

6 Compress the retaining springs and slide the two cables out of their support bracket **(see illustration)**.

7 Referring to the relevant Part of Chapter 4, either lower the front half of the exhaust system, or (for the best access) remove the

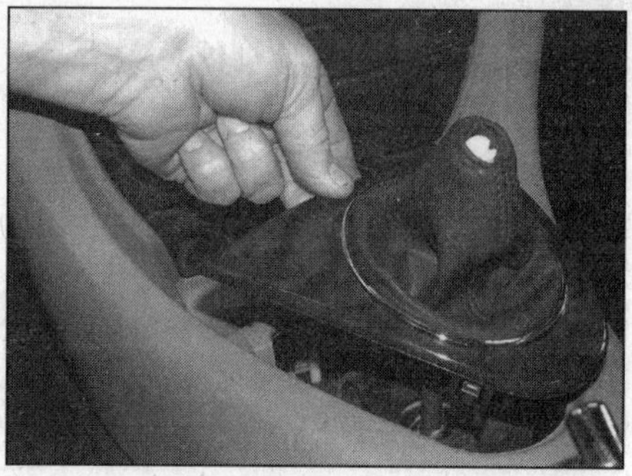

3.3 Unclip and remove the gear lever trim panel

whole system. The exhaust's central heat shield must be removed for access to the gearchange mechanism.

8 Remove the bolts securing the centre heat shield (nine bolts on petrol models, or five on diesel models), and remove the heat shield from under the car.

9 Unscrew the four Torx bolts securing the gearchange mechanism to the underside of the car. Lower the mechanism through the floor, and remove it from under the car.

Refitting

10 Refitting is a reversal of removal. Check that the gears can be selected (without starting the engine) before finally refitting the exhaust.

4 Oil seals – renewal

Driveshaft seals

1 Working as described in Chapter 8, remove the driveshaft on the side concerned.

2 Carefully prise the oil seal out of the transmission using a large flat-bladed screwdriver **(see illustration)**.

3 Remove all traces of dirt from the area around the oil seal aperture. The new seal has a waxed outer surface, and should **not** be lubricated prior to fitting. Ensure the seal is correctly positioned, with its sealing lip facing inwards, and drive it squarely into position, using a suitable tubular drift (such as a socket)

3.5 Using a large pair of pliers to prise off the gearchange cable end fittings

3.6 Compress the spring and disconnect the cables

4.2 Prise the oil seal out of the gearbox using a large flat-bladed screwdriver

4.3 Ensure the seal is correctly positioned, with its sealing lip facing inwards

4.7a Undo the three bolts securing the clutch release bearing guide sleeve in position . . .

4.7b . . . slide the guide off the input shaft . . .

which bears only on the hard outer edge of the seal **(see illustration)**.

4 Ensure the seal is correctly located in the transmission housing, then refit the driveshaft as described in Chapter 8.

5 Refill the transmission with the specified type of oil (see *Lubricants and fluids*) as described in the appropriate Part of Chapter 1.

Input shaft seal

6 Remove the transmission from the car, and slide off the clutch release bearing/slave cylinder (see Chapter 6).

7 Undo the three bolts securing the clutch release bearing guide sleeve in position, and slide the guide off the input shaft. Discard the O-ring seal **(see illustrations)**. **Note:** *The bearing guide sleeve contains an oil seal. However, this seal is only supplied complete with the guide sleeve.*

8 Ensure that the release bearing sleeve and mating face are clean.

9 Using a new O-ring, refit the bearing sleeve to the transmission casing. Apply locking compound to the threads and tighten the retaining bolts to the specified torque.

10 Refit the release bearing/slave cylinder as described in Chapter 6.

Gearchange selector shaft seal

11 Chock the rear wheels, apply the handbrake, then jack up the front of the car and support it on axle stands (see *Jacking and vehicle support*).

12 Remove the engine undertray, which is secured by a number of quick-release screw fasteners.

13 With reference to Chapter 5A, remove the battery and its tray.

14 Remove the left-hand front wheel arch liner as described in Chapter 11, Section 22.

15 On diesel models, unbolt the secondary fuel lift pump and the fuel filter bracket, with reference to Chapters 4C and 1B.

16 Remove the two bolts securing the battery tray mounting bracket, and lift it out.

17 Disconnect the wiring plug from the ABS unit.

18 Inside the car, move the gear lever into neutral, then in the engine compartment, prise off the gearchange cable end fittings from the ball-studs on the transmission selector levers.

19 Compress the retaining springs and slide the two cables out of their support bracket. Move the cables to one side.

20 Working through the wheel arch, unscrew the Torx bolt above the transmission end cover.

21 Unscrew the five Torx bolts securing the selector mechanism to the back of the transmission, and lift it off **(see illustration)**. New bolts should be used when refitting.

22 Drive out the roll pin securing the two sections of the selector mechanism, and separate them. With the lever removed, prise out and discard the oil seal from the gearchange cover.

23 Clean the seal recess, then drive the new seal in squarely. Lubricate the gearchange cover bearing with clean transmission oil, and apply a 1 mm bead of silicone sealant to the gearchange cover **(see illustration)**.

24 Refit the cover to the transmission, and tighten the new Torx screws to the specified torque.

25 Position the lever on the selector shaft, and drive in a new roll pin. Check the operation of the selector mechanism.

26 Further refitting is a reversal of removal.

5 Reversing light switch – testing, removal and refitting

Testing

1 The reversing light circuit is controlled by a plunger-type switch that is screwed into the top of the transmission casing, above the left-hand driveshaft. If a fault develops in the circuit, first ensure that the circuit fuse has not blown (see Chapter 12).

2 To test the switch, disconnect the wiring connector. Use a multimeter (set to the resistance function) or a battery-and-bulb test circuit to check that there is continuity between the switch terminals only when reverse gear is selected. If this is not the case, and there are no obvious breaks or other damage to the wires, the switch is faulty and must be renewed.

Removal

3 Loosen the left-hand front wheel bolts. Firmly apply the handbrake, then jack up the

4.7c . . . then remove the O-ring seal

4.21 Unscrew the five Torx screws and remove the gearchange cover

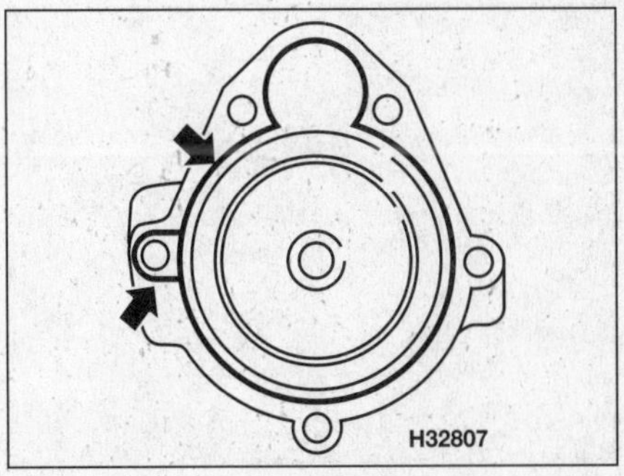

4.23 Apply a 1 mm bead of silicone sealant to the gearchange cover

front of the car and support it on axle stands (see *Jacking and vehicle support*).

4 Remove the engine undertray, which is secured by a number of quick-release screw fasteners.

5 Remove the left-hand front wheel arch liner, as described in Chapter 11, Section 22.

6 Disconnect the wiring connector from the switch **(see illustration)**.

7 Wipe clean the area around the switch, then unscrew it and remove it from the transmission **(see illustration)**.

Refitting

8 Refitting is a reversal of removal.

6 Speedometer drive – removal and refitting

All models are fitted with an electrically-operated speedometer which is operated by the ABS control unit and wheel speed sensors.

7 Transmission – removal and refitting

Caution: The transmission is a heavy and awkward assembly, and care should be taken to avoid personal injury during its removal. It is recommended that this task is only undertaken with the help of an assistant. Read through the entire procedure before starting work.

1 Park the car on firm, level ground.

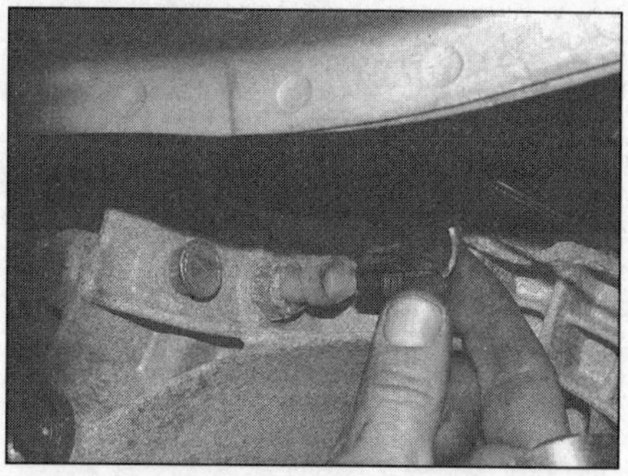

5.6 Disconnecting the reversing light switch

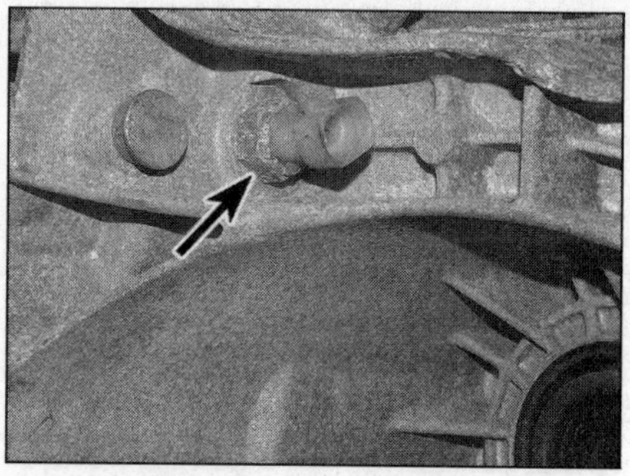

5.7 Reversing light switch location

1.8 litre engines

2 Remove the air cleaner as described in Chapter 4A. Cut the cable-ties securing the wiring to the air cleaner support bracket, then remove the three bolts and lift out the bracket.

3 Remove the battery and its tray, and the starter motor, as described in Chapter 5A.

4 Remove the bonnet as described in Chapter 11.

5 Inside the car, move the gear lever into neutral then, in the engine compartment, prise off the gearchange cable end fittings from the ball-studs on the transmission selector levers.

6 Compress the retaining springs and slide the two cables out of their support bracket. Move the cables to one side.

7 Using a suitable flat-bladed screwdriver, carefully prise apart the clutch fluid pipe quick-release fitting on top of the transmission.

8 Unscrew the transmission-to-engine bolt also used to secure the engine earth lead, and the bolt next to it which holds the crankshaft position sensor wiring plug mounting bracket. Move the earth lead and bracket clear. Unscrew the crankshaft position sensor mounting bolt from the front of the transmission, and withdraw the sensor.

9 Unscrew the three bolts, and withdraw the curved closing plate from the front of the transmission. At the back, remove two further bolts, and withdraw the stepped closing plate above the right-hand driveshaft.

V6 engines

10 Remove the air cleaner and throttle body as described in Chapter 4B.

11 Remove the battery and its tray, and the starter motor, as described in Chapter 5A.

12 Remove the bonnet as described in Chapter 11.

13 Inside the car, move the gear lever into neutral then, in the engine compartment, prise off the gearchange cable end fittings from the ball-studs on the transmission selector levers **(see illustration)**.

14 Compress the retaining springs and slide the two cables out of their support bracket **(see illustration)**. Move the cables to one side.

15 Using a suitable flat-bladed screwdriver, carefully prise apart the clutch fluid pipe quick-release fitting on top of the transmission **(see illustrations)**.

16 Unscrew the crankshaft position sensor mounting bolt from the front of the transmission, and withdraw the sensor **(see illustration)**.

17 Remove the two bolts, and withdraw the

7.13 Using a large pair of pliers to prise off the gearchange cable end fittings

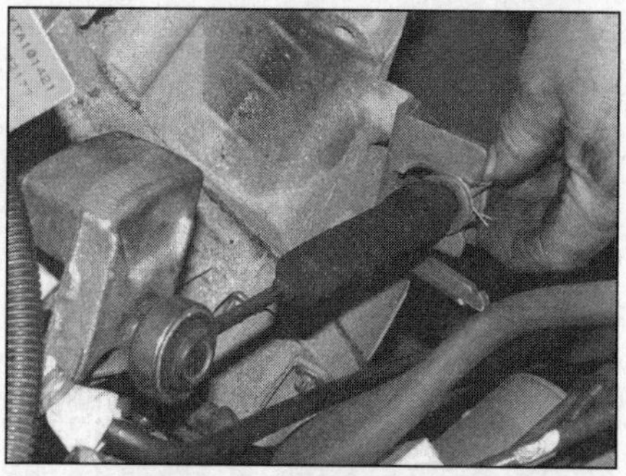

7.14 Compress the spring and disconnect the cables

7.15a Using a small screwdriver, carefully prise apart . . .

7.15b . . . and disconnect the clutch fluid pipe

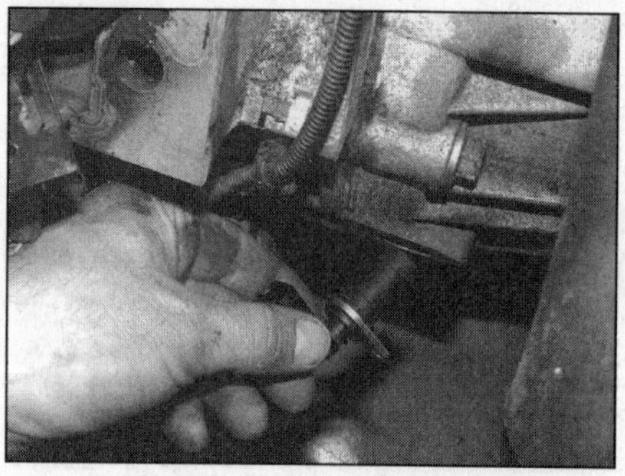

7.16 Remove the crankshaft position sensor from the front of the transmission

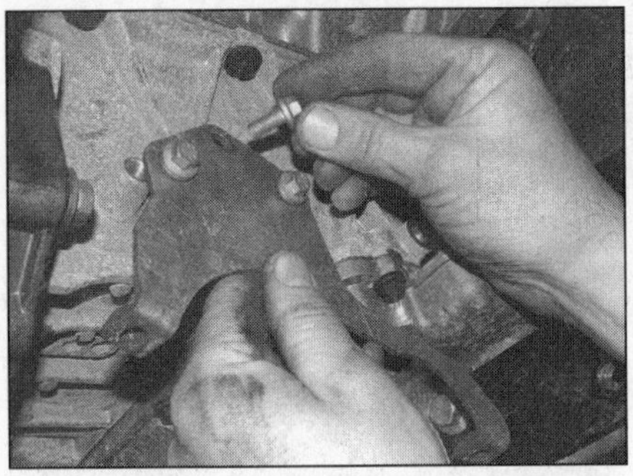

7.17 Removing the exhaust front support bracket

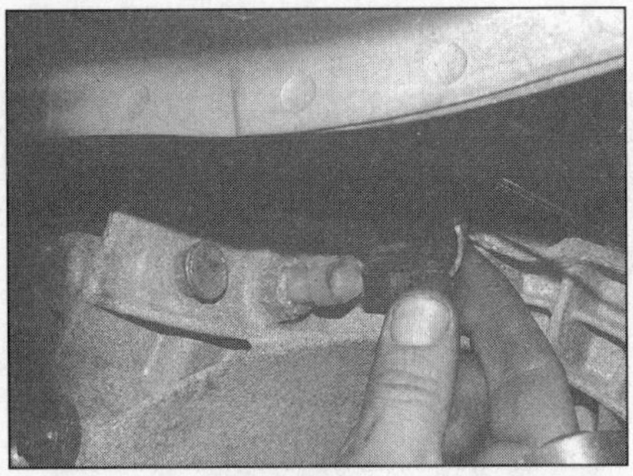

7.28 Disconnecting the reversing light switch

7.29a Removing a transmission-to-engine bolt

stepped closing plate above the right-hand driveshaft. Next to it, remove three more bolts from the exhaust front bracket, and separate the bracket from the transmission **(see illustration)**.

Diesel engines

18 Remove the battery and its tray, and the starter motor, as described in Chapter 5A.

19 Remove the bonnet as described in Chapter 11.

20 Where applicable, remove the fuel-burning heater as described in Chapter 3.

21 Inside the car, move the gear lever into neutral then, in the engine compartment, prise off the gearchange cable end fittings from the ball-studs on the transmission selector levers.

22 Compress the retaining springs and slide the two cables out of their support bracket. Move the cables to one side.

23 Using a suitable flat-bladed screwdriver, carefully prise apart the clutch fluid pipe quick-release fitting on top of the transmission.

24 Remove the single bolt securing the cover plate above the right-hand driveshaft.

All engines

25 Bolt a suitable lifting eye to a convenient point on the transmission casing. Alternatively, the transmission can be removed just by supporting it from below.

26 Remove the front subframe as described in Chapter 10. Raise the front of the car sufficiently to allow the transmission to be lowered out and withdrawn from underneath.

27 Remove the driveshafts as described in Chapter 8.

28 Disconnect the reversing light switch wiring plug **(see illustration)**.

29 Loosen all of the transmission-to-engine bolts by half a turn only – some less-accessible ones can be removed if wished, but do not remove them all. There are seven in total – on petrol engine models, one or more of these bolts will have been removed earlier in the procedure. V6 models have a nut and bolt at the front **(see illustrations)**.

30 Support the transmission from below using a substantial jack with a flat piece of wood on top of it. Another jack will be required to support the engine – alternatively, use an engine support bar for this, located in the bonnet side channels on the inner wings.

31 Make a final check from below and above that there is nothing left attached to the transmission, nor anything in the way which would prevent the unit from being lowered out.

32 Loosen and remove the engine/transmission left-hand mounting through-bolt, then remove the four bolts securing the mounting bracket to the top of the transmission **(see illustrations)**.

33 Lower the engine on the jack, and remove the transmission mounting bracket. If a lifting eye was fitted to the transmission, attach the lifting equipment to it, and take the weight.

> **HAYNES HiNT** ***Before removing the transmission from the engine, it is helpful for refitting to paint or scratch an alignment mark or two across the engine/transmission, so that the transmission can be offered up in approximately the right alignment to engage the dowels.***

34 With the help of an assistant to steady the transmission, remove the bolts securing it to the engine. Note that the unit is also mounted on two dowels – if necessary, carefully prise the transmission away from the engine to free it.

35 Withdraw the transmission off the engine, taking care that its weight is not allowed to hang on the input shaft. Once it is free, while an assistant keeps it steady on the jack, lower it to the ground (or, if a hoist is used, the jack can be removed before lowering) **(see illustration)**. With the help of your assistant, remove it from under the car.

36 The clutch components can now be inspected with reference to Chapter 6,

7.29b V6 engine models have a transmission-to-engine front nut and bolt

7.32a Remove the left-hand mounting through-bolt . . .

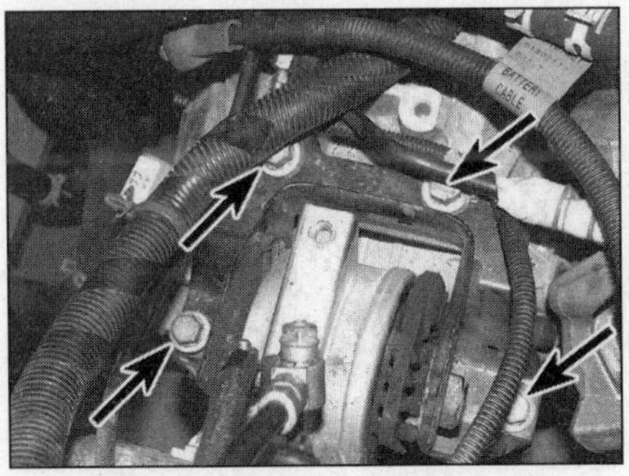

7.32b . . . then remove the four transmission mounting bracket bolts

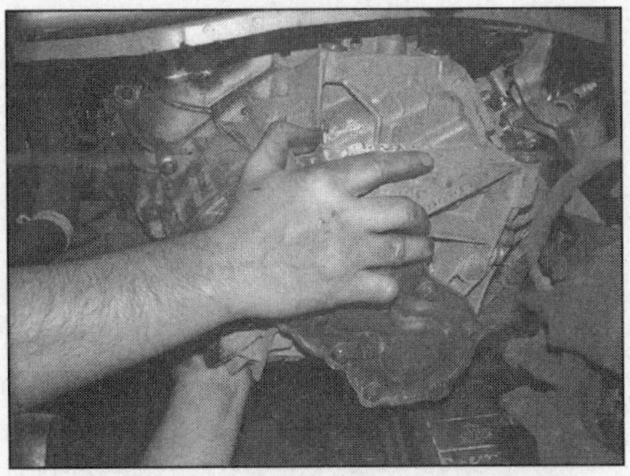

7.35 Have an assistant steady the transmission on the jack as it is lowered

and renewed if necessary. Unless they are virtually new, it is worth renewing the clutch components as a matter of course, even if the transmission has been removed for some other reason.

Refitting

37 The transmission is refitted using a reversal of the removal procedure, bearing in mind the following points:

a) *Apply a smear of molybdenum disulphide grease to the clutch release bearing, fork and guide sleeve contact surfaces and check the operation of the clutch release mechanism (see Chapter 6). Also apply a smear of grease to the transmission input shaft splines; but do not apply too much grease, otherwise the clutch friction disc may be contaminated.*

b) *Ensure the locating dowels are correctly positioned prior to installation.*

c) *Tighten all nuts and bolts to the specified torque (where given).*

d) *Renew the driveshaft oil seals (see Section 4) then refit the driveshafts as described in Chapter 8, renewing the inner joint circlips prior to refitting.*

e) *Renew all roll pins.*

f) *On completion, refill the transmission with the specified type and quantity of lubricant (see 'Lubricants and fluids') then check the oil level as described in the appropriate Part of Chapter 1.*

8 Transmission overhaul – general information

Overhauling a manual transmission is a difficult and involved job for the DIY home mechanic. In addition to dismantling and reassembling many small parts, clearances must be precisely measured and, if necessary, changed by selecting shims and spacers. Internal transmission components are also often difficult to obtain, and in many instances, extremely expensive. Because of this, if the transmission develops a fault or becomes noisy, the best course of action is to have the unit overhauled by a specialist repairer, or to obtain an exchange reconditioned unit.

Nevertheless, it is not impossible for the more experienced mechanic to overhaul the transmission, provided the special tools are available, and the job is done in a deliberate step-by-step manner, so that nothing is overlooked.

The tools necessary for an overhaul include internal and external circlip pliers, bearing pullers, a slide hammer, a set of pin punches, a dial test indicator, and possibly a hydraulic press. In addition, a large, sturdy workbench and a vice will be required.

During dismantling of the transmission, make careful notes of how each component is fitted, to make reassembly easier and more accurate.

Before dismantling the transmission, it will help if you have some idea what area is malfunctioning. Certain problems can be closely related to specific areas in the transmission, which can make component examination and renewal easier. Refer to the *Fault finding* Section of this manual for more information.

Chapter 7 Part B: Automatic transmission

Contents

Degrees of difficulty

Easy, suitable for novice with little experience	**Fairly easy,** suitable for beginner with some experience	**Fairly difficult,** suitable for competent DIY mechanic	**Difficult,** suitable for experienced DIY mechanic	**Very difficult,** suitable for expert DIY or professional

Specifications

General

Type	Jatco, five forward speeds and reverse
Ratios:	
Except 2.5 litre V6 engines:	
First	3.801 : 1
Second	2.131 : 1
Third	1.364 : 1
Fourth	0.935 : 1
Fifth	0.685 : 1
2.5 litre V6 engines:	
First	3.474 : 1
Second	1.948 : 1
Third	1.247 : 1
Fourth	0.854 : 1
Fifth	0.685 : 1
Final drive ratio:	
1.8 litre engine, and 2.0 litre V6 engine	4.15 : 1
2.5 litre V6 engine	3.89 : 1
Diesel engines	3.45 : 1

Torque wrench settings	Nm	lbf ft
Engine/transmission mountings:		
Left-hand mounting through-bolt	100	74
Left-hand mounting to body	85	63
Left-hand mounting to transmission	85	63
Lower mounting through-bolts	100	74
Fluid cooler (diesel models):		
Hose unions to cooler	25	18
Mounting bolts to subframe	22	16
Mounting nut	15	11
Fluid drain plug	45	33
Fluid filler/level plug	14	10
Fluid hose unions to transmission	18	13
Fluid pan bolts	7	5
Selector cable bracket to transmission	25	18
Selector housing-to-floor Torx bolts	9	7
Selector lever-to-transmission selector shaft nut	25	18
Torque converter access plate bolts	9	7
Torque converter-to-driveplate bolts	45	33

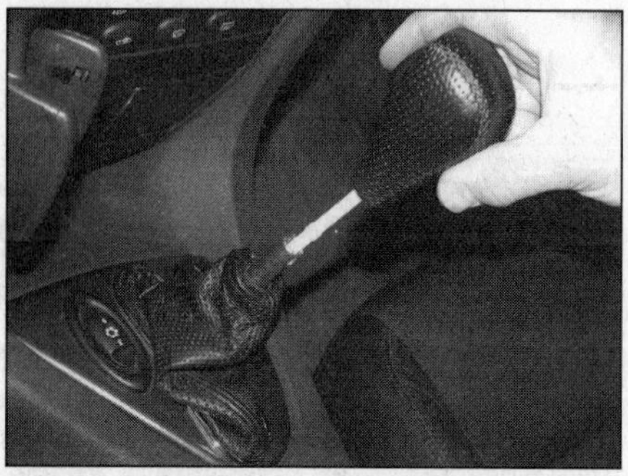

2.1 Pull up sharply to remove the selector lever knob

1 General information

A 5-speed fully-automatic transmission is available as an option on all models. The transmission consists of a torque converter, an epicyclic geartrain, and hydraulically-operated clutches and brakes.

The torque converter provides a fluid coupling between the engine and transmission, acts as an automatic 'clutch', and also provides a degree of torque multiplication when accelerating. To improve economy, the torque converter has a 'lock-up' facility under low-load conditions (such as when cruising), which eliminates the small degree of slip which would otherwise be present. Unlike other transmissions which offer this facility only in top gear, the Jatco unit fitted to the 75 and ZT has this available in all forward gears except 1st.

Three modes of operation are available: Normal (economy), Sport or Snow, displayed by symbols in the instrument panel, and selected using the mode switch next to the selector lever. In Sport mode, the software programme makes the transmission more responsive, and allows upshifts to happen at higher engine speeds for better acceleration. The Snow mode, designed for winter driving, makes starting off easier in slippery conditions (2nd gear is used), and the transmission upshifts at lower engine speeds to reduce wheelspin.

Sophisticated adaptive software programming

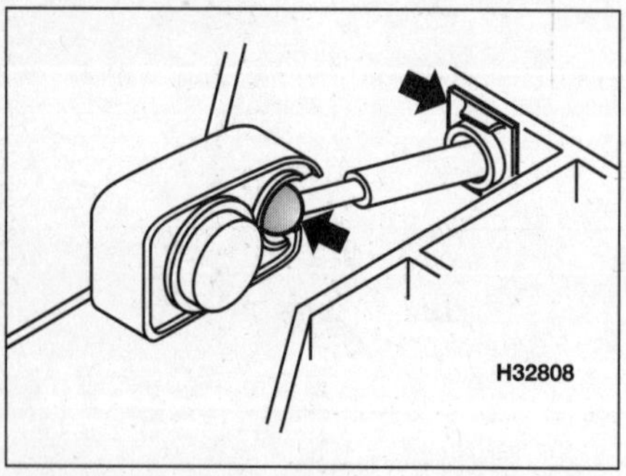

2.6 Selector inner cable end fitting at the selector lever, and outer cable clip (arrowed)

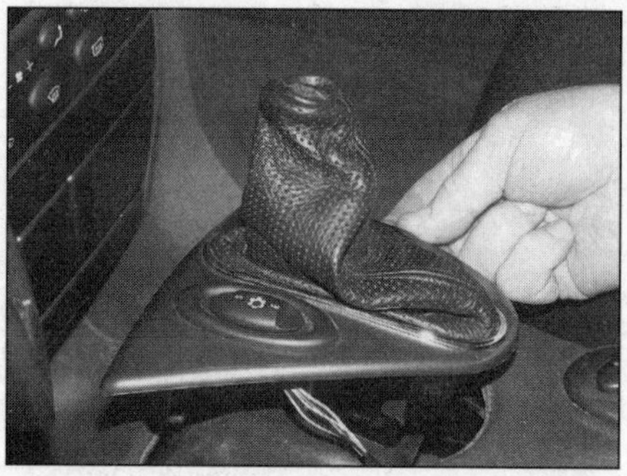

2.2a Unclip the selector lever gaiter panel . . .

of the transmission control unit enables it to recognise driving situations such as towing, downhill overrun, steep mountain roads, etc, and select the optimum shift strategies for each.

Due to the complexity of the automatic transmission, any repair or overhaul work must be entrusted to a suitably-qualified transmission specialist, with the necessary specialist equipment and knowledge for fault diagnosis and repair. Refer to the *Fault finding* Section at the end of this manual for further information.

2 Selector mechanism – removal and refitting

Removal

1 With the lever in neutral (N), pull up sharply to disengage the selector knob's securing tab, and remove the selector knob **(see illustration)**.

2 Unclip the selector lever gaiter trim panel from the centre console, then disconnect two wiring plugs and lift the panel and gaiter off the selector lever **(see illustrations)**.

3 Referring to the relevant Part of Chapter 4, either lower the front half of the exhaust system, or (for the best access) remove the whole system. The exhaust's central heat shield must be removed for access to the selector mechanism.

4 Remove the bolts securing the centre heat

3.4a Slacken the selector inner cable clamp nut (arrowed) at the transmission end of the cable . . .

2.2b . . . then turn it over and disconnect the wiring plugs

shield (nine bolts on petrol models, or five on diesel models), and remove the heat shield from under the car.

5 Unscrew the four Torx bolts securing the selector mechanism to the underside of the car. Lower the mechanism through the floor.

6 Pull off the rubber boot from the selector mechanism. Slide the barrelled end of the inner cable from the selector lever, pull out the retaining clip and release the outer cable from the selector housing **(see illustration)**.

Refitting

7 Refitting is a reversal of removal. Adjust the selector cable as described in Section 3 on completion.

3 Selector cable – removal, refitting and adjustment

Removal

1 Remove the selector mechanism as described in Section 2.

2 Release the selector cable from the retaining clips on the car body.

3 Where applicable, unscrew the two bolts and remove the cable support bracket from the transmission.

4 Slacken the selector inner cable clamp nut at the transmission end of the cable, and remove the outer cable-to-transmission bracket retaining clip **(see illustrations)**. Remove the cable.

3.4b . . . and remove the outer cable-to-transmission bracket retaining clip (arrowed)

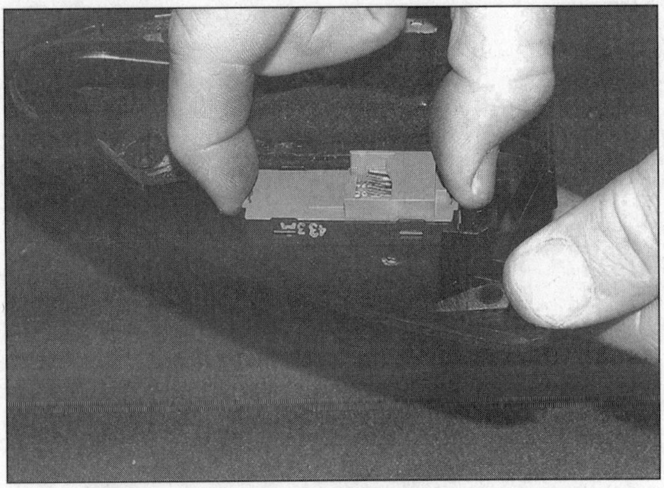

4.2a Squeeze the tabs under the indicator panel . . .

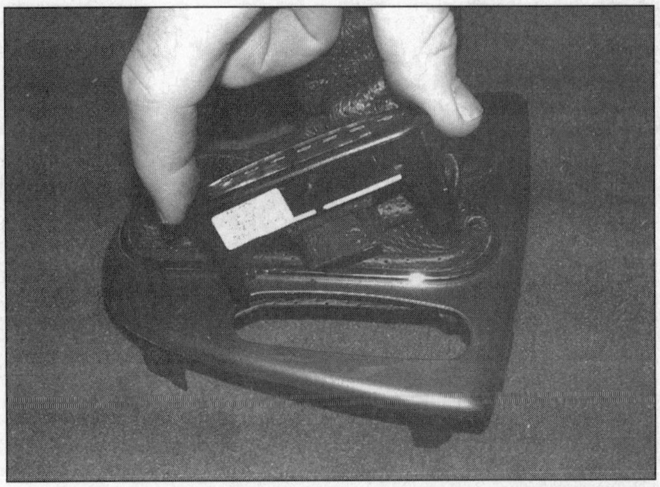

4.2b . . . and lift it out of the selector lever trim panel

Refitting

5 Refitting is a reversal of removal. Adjust the cable as described below.

Adjustment

6 Park the car on level ground, switch off the ignition, and apply the handbrake firmly. Jack up the front of the car and support it securely on axle stands (see *Jacking and vehicle support*).

7 Remove the engine undertray, which is secured by a number of quick-release screw fasteners.

8 Slacken the selector inner cable clamp nut at the transmission end of the cable **(see illustration 3.4a)**.

9 Move the selector lever in the passenger compartment into position P.

10 Move the selector lever on the transmission fully clockwise to engage the P position.

11 At the transmission end, gently pull the inner cable to eliminate any slack, and then tighten the inner cable clamp nut securely.

12 Check that all selector lever operation is correct, and that the engine can only be started in positions P and N.

13 Refit the engine undertray, and lower the car to the ground.

4 Selector indicator – removal and refitting

Removal

1 Remove the selector lever trim panel as described in Section 2, paragraphs 1 and 2. It is possible to prise the indicator out from above, but it's arguably safer to press it out from below.

2 Squeeze the tabs on the underside, and lift the indicator out of the panel **(see illustrations)**.

Refitting

3 Refitting is a reversal of removal.

5 Inhibitor switch – description, removal, refitting and adjustment

Description

1 The starter inhibitor switch is screwed into the top of transmission casing. The function of the switch ensures that the engine can only be started with the selector lever in either the N or the P positions, therefore preventing the engine from being started with the transmission in gear. If at any time it is noted that the engine can be started with the selector lever in any position other than N or P, then it is likely that the inhibitor function of the switch is faulty, or the selector cable adjustment is incorrect (see Section 3).

Removal

2 On petrol engine models, remove the air cleaner as described in Chapter 4A or 4B.

3 Park the car on level ground, switch off the ignition, and apply the handbrake firmly. Jack up the front of the car and support it securely on axle stands (see *Jacking and vehicle support*).

4 Remove the engine undertray, which is secured by a number of quick-release screw fasteners.

5 Move the selector lever to position N.

6 Release the inhibitor switch wiring plug from the retaining clip on the transmission fluid pan, and disconnect it **(see illustration)**.

7 Unscrew the two retaining bolts and remove the switch from the transmission casing.

Refitting

8 Commence refitting by cleaning the switch, and the switch mating face in the transmission casing.

9 Align the internal lugs with the mark on the inhibitor switch.

10 Align the two lugs of the switch with the machined grooves in the selector lever shaft, and fit the switch. Do not tighten the switch bolts at this stage.

11 Reconnect the switch wiring plug, and refit the connector to the retaining clip.

12 Carry out the adjustment procedure.

Adjustment

13 On petrol engine models, if not already done, remove the air cleaner as described in Chapter 4A or 4B.

14 Ensure the selector lever is in position N.

15 Slacken the inhibitor switch bolts.

16 Fit special tool 44-018 over the selector lever shaft, and rotate the switch so that the tool alignment pin can be inserted through

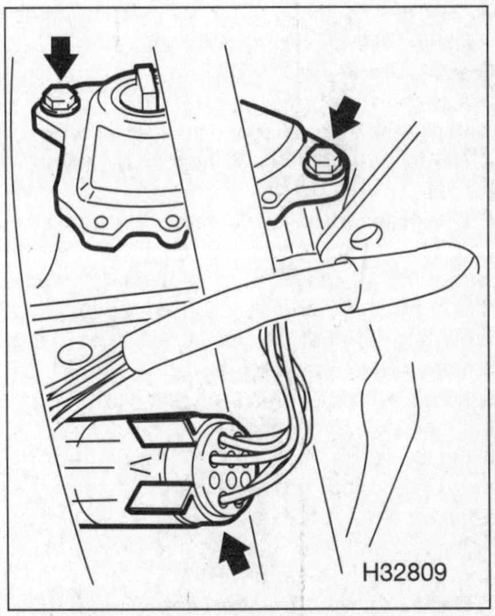

5.6 Release the inhibitor switch wiring plug from the clip, and undo the two bolts (arrowed)

5.16a MG Rover inhibitor switch aligning tools

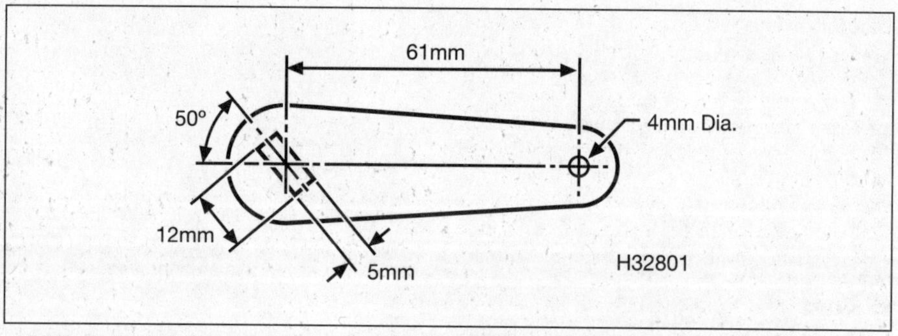

5.16b If the MG Rover tool is not available, make an equivalent using the dimensions shown

the tool lever, and into the inhibitor switch. If the special tool is not available, a suitable home-made equivalent can be fabricated **(see illustrations)**.

17 Tighten the inhibitor switch bolts securely, and remove the alignment tool.

18 Check the inhibitor switch operation by attempting to start the engine with the selector lever in positions other than P or N.

6 Automatic transmission – removal and refitting

Caution: The transmission is a heavy and awkward assembly, and care should be taken to avoid personal injury during its removal. It is recommended that this task is only undertaken with the help of an assistant. Read through the entire procedure before starting work.

1 Park the car on firm, level ground.

1.8 litre engines

2 Remove the air cleaner as described in Chapter 4A. Cut the cable-ties securing the wiring to the air cleaner support bracket, then remove the three bolts and lift out the bracket.

3 Remove the battery and its tray, and the starter motor, as described in Chapter 5A.

4 Remove the bonnet as described in Chapter 11.

5 Unscrew the transmission-to-engine bolt also used to secure the engine earth lead, and the bolt next to it which holds the crankshaft position sensor wiring plug mounting bracket. Move the earth lead and bracket clear. Unscrew the crankshaft position sensor mounting bolt from the front of the transmission, and withdraw the sensor.

6 Unscrew the three bolts, and withdraw the curved closing plate from the front of the transmission. At the back, remove two further bolts, and withdraw the stepped closing plate above the right-hand driveshaft.

7 Unclip the two transmission wiring multi-plugs from the brackets on the front of the transmission, then disconnect them by twisting them apart.

V6 engines

8 Remove the air cleaner and throttle body as described in Chapter 4B.

9 Remove the battery and its tray, and the starter motor, as described in Chapter 5A.

10 Remove the bonnet as described in Chapter 11.

11 Unclip the two transmission wiring multi-plugs from the brackets on the front of the transmission, then disconnect them by twisting them apart.

12 Disconnect the crankshaft position sensor wiring plug, then unscrew the sensor mounting bolt from the front of the transmission, and withdraw the sensor.

13 Remove the two bolts, and withdraw the stepped closing plate above the right-hand driveshaft.

Diesel engines

14 Remove the battery and its tray, and the starter motor, as described in Chapter 5A.

15 Cut the cable-ties securing the bonnet earth strap to the left-hand bonnet support strut (left as seen from the driver's seat). Have an assistant support the bonnet, then prise out the spring clip at the top and disconnect the tops of the struts. On the left-hand strut, unscrew the ball-stud to release the earth strap. Protect the windscreen, then tie the bonnet back to allow the maximum room for engine removal. Alternatively, remove the bonnet as described in Chapter 11.

16 Remove the fuel-burning heater as described in Chapter 3.

17 Unclip the two transmission wiring multi-plugs from the brackets on the inner wing, then disconnect them by twisting them apart.

18 Remove the single bolt securing the cover plate above the right-hand driveshaft, then prise out the grommet from the torque converter access hole.

All engines

19 Bolt two suitable lifting eyes to the transmission casing. Alternatively, the transmission can be removed just by supporting it from below.

20 Remove the front subframe as described in Chapter 10. Raise the front of the car sufficiently to allow the transmission to be lowered out and withdrawn from underneath.

5.16c Aligning tool and pin fitted

21 Remove the driveshafts as described in Chapter 8.

22 Slacken the selector inner cable clamp nut at the transmission end of the cable, and remove the outer cable-to-transmission bracket retaining clip. Where applicable, remove the two bolts from the cable support bracket on the transmission. Move the selector cable clear.

23 Turn the engine so that the first of the four torque converter bolts is accessible in the aperture above the right-hand driveshaft – on diesel models, there may be a grommet to prise out for access **(see illustration)**. On models with the 1.8 litre engine, it may be necessary to access the torque converter bolts from the aperture at the front of the transmission.

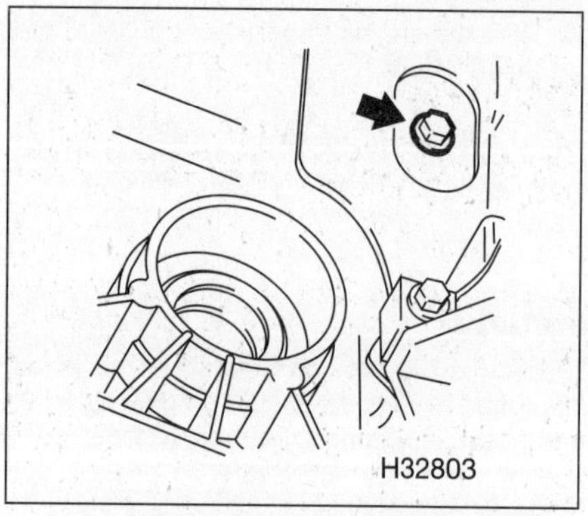

6.23 Prise out the grommet in the cover plate to gain access to the torque converter bolts

24 Mark the relationship of the driveplate to the torque converter, to aid refitment. Rotate the crankshaft using a spanner or socket on the crankshaft pulley to access, and unscrew the four torque converter bolts one at a time.
25 Loosen all of the transmission-to-engine bolts by half a turn only. There are seven in total – on petrol engine models, one or more of these bolts will have been removed earlier in the procedure. V6 models have a nut and bolt at the front.
26 On diesel engine models, loosen the union nuts, then disconnect the two fluid cooler unions from the transmission – note their positions for refitting. Recover the O-rings (new ones will be needed for refitting) and plug or tape over the open connections.
27 On petrol engine models, squeeze the quick-release collars on the fluid cooler hoses, and disconnect them from the transmission. The connections should be self-sealing, but it may still be advisable to tape over them to avoid contamination.
28 Support the transmission from below using a substantial jack with a flat piece of wood on top of it. Another jack will be required to support the engine – alternatively, use an engine support bar for this, located in the bonnet side channels on the inner wings.
29 Make a final check from below and above that there is nothing left attached to the transmission, nor anything in the way which would prevent the unit from being lowered out.
30 Loosen and remove the engine/transmission left-hand mounting through-bolt, then remove the four bolts securing the mounting bracket to the top of the transmission.
31 Lower the engine on the jack, and remove the transmission mounting bracket.
32 If lifting eyes were fitted to the transmission, unbolt and remove the transmission mounting bracket from the inner wing, then attach the lifting equipment to them, and take the weight.

HAYNES HiNT ***Before removing the transmission from the engine, it is helpful for refitting to paint or scratch an alignment mark or two across the engine/transmission, so that the transmission can be offered up in approximately the right alignment to engage the dowels.***

33 With the help of an assistant to steady the transmission, remove the bolts securing it to the engine. Note that the unit is also mounted on two dowels – if necessary, carefully prise the transmission away from the engine to free it.
34 Withdraw the transmission off the engine, taking care that its weight is not allowed to hang on the input shaft. Once it is free, while an assistant keeps it steady on the jack, lower it to the ground (or, if a hoist is used, the jack can be removed before lowering). With the help of your assistant, remove it from under the car.

Refitting

35 The transmission is refitted using a reversal of the removal procedure, bearing in mind the following points:

a) If required, the torque converter fluid seal can be renewed as described in Section 9.
b) Make sure that the torque converter is correctly fitted to the transmission input shaft (see Section 9).
c) Ensure the locating dowels are correctly positioned prior to installation.
d) Align the torque converter with the driveplate, and tighten the securing bolts to the specified torque. If the original torque converter and driveplate components are being refitted, ensure that the marks made on the torque converter and the driveplate before removal are aligned.
e) Tighten all nuts and bolts to the specified torque (where given).
f) Refit the driveshafts as described in Chapter 8, renewing the inner joint circlips prior to refitting.
g) On diesel engine models, fit new O-rings to the fluid cooler hoses, and tighten the unions to the specified torque.
h) On completion, refill the transmission with the specified type and quantity of fluid (see 'Lubricants and fluids') as described in Chapter 1A or 1B.

7 Automatic transmission overhaul – general information

In the event of a fault occurring on the transmission, it is first necessary to determine whether it is of an electrical, mechanical or hydraulic nature, and to achieve this, special test equipment is required. It is therefore essential to have the work carried out by a suitably-equipped specialist if a transmission fault is suspected.

Do not remove the transmission from the car for possible repair before professional fault diagnosis has been carried out, since most tests require the transmission to be in the car.

8 Fluid cooler – removal and refitting

Petrol engine models

1 Remove the radiator as described in Chapter 3.
2 Carefully prise apart the two quick-release hose connections at the fluid cooler, and disconnect them, noting their fitted positions.
3 Remove the fluid cooler from the car.
4 Refitting is a reversal of removal. On completion, check and top-up the transmission fluid level as described in Chapter 1A.

Diesel engine models

5 Remove the front bumper as described in Chapter 11.
6 Loosen the nut securing the fluid cooler pipe inner clamp.
7 Behind the fluid cooler fan, remove the bolt securing the fluid pipe mounting bracket. Remove the bracket and recover the two rubber sleeves.
8 Disconnect the multi-plugs from the fluid cooler temperature sensor and cooling fan. Release the wiring harness from the mounting bracket clips.
9 Position a suitable container under the fluid cooler connections. Loosen the fluid cooler unions, but leave them connected at this stage.
10 Remove the two screws securing the fluid cooler to the intercooler air duct, then release the air duct from the two posts on the cooler, and move the duct to one side.
11 Remove the three fluid cooler-to-subframe bolts.
12 At the left-hand rear of the fluid cooler fan, unscrew the nut and recover the washer from the fluid cooler mounting bracket.
13 Unscrew the fluid cooler union nuts fully (anticipate some loss of fluid as this is done), and recover the O-rings – new ones will be needed for refitting. Plug or tape over the open connections. Manoeuvre the cooler assembly out of the car.
14 If a new cooler is being fitted, remove the three mounting bushes and washers from the mounting bracket. Unscrew the four mounting nuts, and take off the cooler fan. Unscrew the fluid temperature sensor, and recover the sealing washer – a new one will be needed when refitting.
15 Refitting is a reversal of removal, noting the following points:

a) If the fluid temperature sensor was removed, use a new sealing washer.
b) Clean the fluid cooler unions, and fit new O-rings, lubricated with transmission fluid.
c) Tighten the unions and mounting bolts/nut to the specified torque.
d) On completion, check and top-up the transmission fluid level as described in Chapter 1B.

9 Fluid seals – renewal

Torque converter fluid seal

1 Remove the transmission as described in Section 6, and slide the torque converter from the transmission input shaft.
2 Discard the O-ring seal from the input shaft and, using a flat-bladed screwdriver, prise the

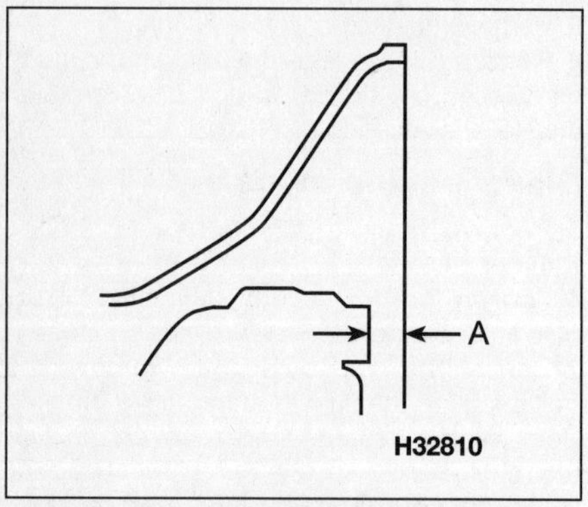

9.5 Showing the torque converter fitted depth (A)

fluid seal from the input shaft housing. Note the fitted depth of the seal.

3 Ensure that the fluid seal recess in the transmission and the torque converter spigot are clean and dry. Lubricate the new fluid seal with clean transmission fluid, and fit it to the transmission. Use a tubular drift that bears only on the hard outer edge of the seal. Fit the seal squarely into the housing, with the inner lip facing the transmission.

4 Fit a new O-ring to the transmission input shaft.

5 Position the torque converter over the input shaft, and check that it is fully located **(see illustration)**. The correct fitted depth, by engine type, is shown below:

a) 1.8 litre engines – 5 mm.
b) V6 engines – 4 mm.
c) Diesel engines – 27 mm.

Driveshaft fluid seals

6 Working as described in Chapter 8, remove the driveshaft on the side concerned.

7 Carefully prise the seal out of the transmission using a large flat-bladed screwdriver.

8 Remove all traces of dirt from the area around the seal aperture. The new seal has a waxed outer surface, and should **not** be lubricated prior to fitting. Ensure the seal is correctly positioned, with its sealing lip facing inwards, and drive it squarely into position, using a suitable tubular drift (such as a socket) which bears only on the hard outer edge of the seal.

9 Ensure the seal is correctly located in the transmission housing, then refit the driveshaft as described in Chapter 8.

10 Refill the transmission with the specified type of fluid (see *Lubricants and fluids*) as described in Chapter 1A or 1B.

10 Transmission ECU – removal and refitting

Removal

1 Disconnect the battery negative lead, and move the lead away from the battery (see *Disconnecting the battery*).

2 Working in the passenger's front footwell, release the two turn-buckle fasteners at the top, and drop down the lower facia trim panel. To remove the panel completely, take out the two push-fasteners at the bottom.

3 Release the locking lever, and disconnect the ECU multi-plug.

4 Unscrew the two mounting bolts and remove the ECU from its location.

Refitting

5 Refitting is a reversal of removal.

Chapter 8
Driveshafts

Contents

Section number

Degrees of difficulty

Easy, suitable for novice with little experience	**Fairly easy,** suitable for beginner with some experience	**Fairly difficult,** suitable for competent DIY mechanic	**Difficult,** suitable for experienced DIY mechanic	**Very difficult,** suitable for expert DIY or professional

Specifications

General

Driveshaft type	Solid steel shafts, splined to inner and outer constant velocity joints, vibration damper fitted to both driveshafts

Torque wrench settings

Torque wrench settings	Nm	lbf ft
Driveshaft retaining nut*	350	258
Driveshaft support bearing bolts	25	18
Lower balljoint nut/bolt	45	33
Roadwheel bolts	125	92
Track rod end balljoint nut*	30	22

** Use new nuts*

1 General information

Drive is transmitted from the differential to the front wheels by means of two, unequal-length driveshafts.

Each driveshaft is fitted with an inner and outer constant velocity (CV) joint. The inner constant velocity joint is of the tripode type, fixed to the shaft, and the outer joint is of the ball-and-cage type, secured by a circlip. Each outer joint is splined to engage with the wheel hub, and is threaded so that it can be fastened to the hub by a large nut. The inner joint is also splined to engage with the differential sunwheel, and the left-hand shaft is secured into the transmission with a circlip.

On the right-hand driveshaft, the inner constant velocity (CV) joint is located approximately halfway along the shaft length, and the joint is supported by the rear of the cylinder block via a support bearing bracket.

2 Driveshaft – removal and refitting

Removal

1 Drain the manual transmission oil or automatic transmission fluid as described in Chapter 1A or 1B. If this is not done, anticipate a large amount of oil or fluid being lost when the driveshaft is withdrawn.

2.3 Use a hammer and chisel to knock back the staking in the driveshaft nut

2 Slacken the wheel bolts. If it is possible to access the driveshaft nut with the wheel on (by removing the wheel trim or alloy wheel centre cap), it is preferable to loosen the nut with the car resting on its wheels.

3 Use a hammer and chisel to knock back the staking (depression) in the driveshaft nut's outer collar **(see illustration)**. Loosen but do not remove the nut.

Warning: The driveshaft nut is done up extremely tight, and considerable effort will be required to loosen it. Do not use poor-quality, badly-fitting tools for this task, due to the risk of personal injury.

4 Chock the rear wheels, then with the handbrake applied, jack up the front of the car and support it on axle stands (see *Jacking and vehicle support*). Remove the appropriate front roadwheel.

5 If the driveshaft nut was not slackened with

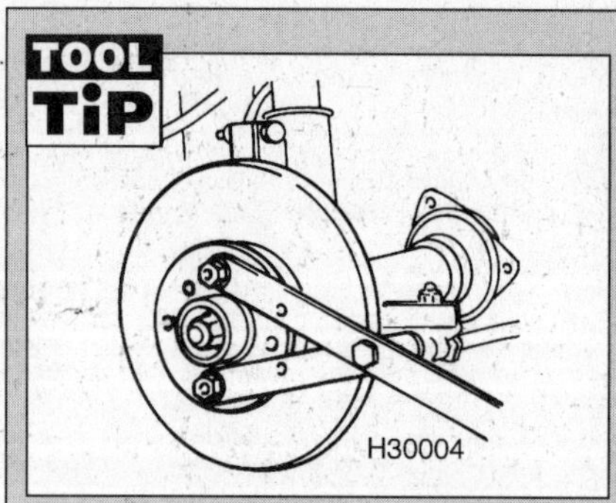

Using a fabricated tool to hold the front hub stationary whilst the driveshaft nut is slackened.

the wheels on the ground (see paragraph 2), refit at least two roadwheel bolts to the front hub, tightening them securely, then have an assistant firmly depress the brake pedal to prevent the front hub from rotating, whilst you slacken and remove the driveshaft retaining nut. Alternatively, a tool can be fabricated from two lengths of steel strip (one long, one short) and a nut and bolt; the nut and bolt forming the pivot of a forked tool **(see Tool Tip)**.

6 Remove the wheel arch liner on the side concerned, as described in Chapter 11, Section 22.

7 Release the brake flexible hose, brake pad wear wire and ABS sensor harness from the support clip on the suspension strut **(see illustration)**.

8 Slacken the nut securing the steering gear track rod end balljoint to the swivel hub, but

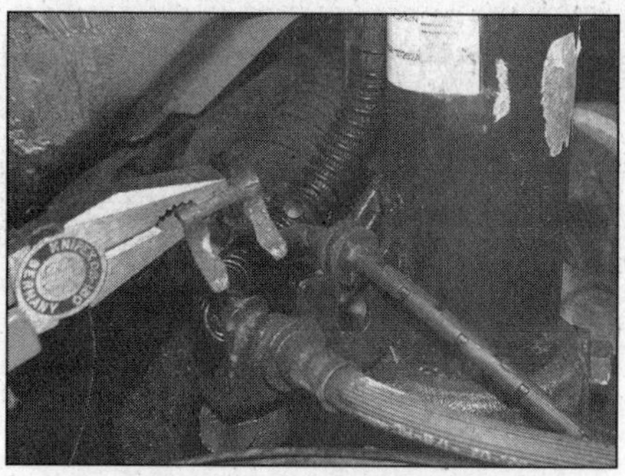

2.7 Pull out the brake hose clip, and release the other wiring from the strut

leave the nut attached by just a few threads. Release the balljoint tapered shank using a universal balljoint separator, then unscrew the nut completely and separate the joint **(see illustrations)**.

9 Unscrew and remove the lower balljoint retaining nut, and tap out the bolt **(see illustration)**.

10 The lower balljoint must now be separated by pulling the lower arm downwards. This may prove difficult, due to corrosion between the balljoint and the hub. Apply plenty of penetrating spray to begin with. We used a long pole, fitted into a wooden block under the car, with a chain wrapped around the end of the lower arm, to provide sufficient leverage. Tapping in a tapered punch between the 'jaws' for the balljoint on the hub also proved useful **(see illustrations)**.

11 Once the lower balljoint has been separated, the balljoint rubber is vulnerable

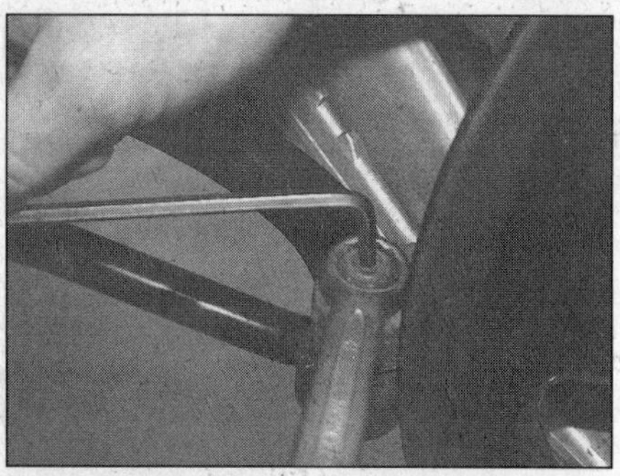

2.8a Unscrew the track rod end nut, using an Allen key to hold the stud . . .

2.8b . . . then use a balljoint separator tool . . .

2.8c . . . to free the track rod

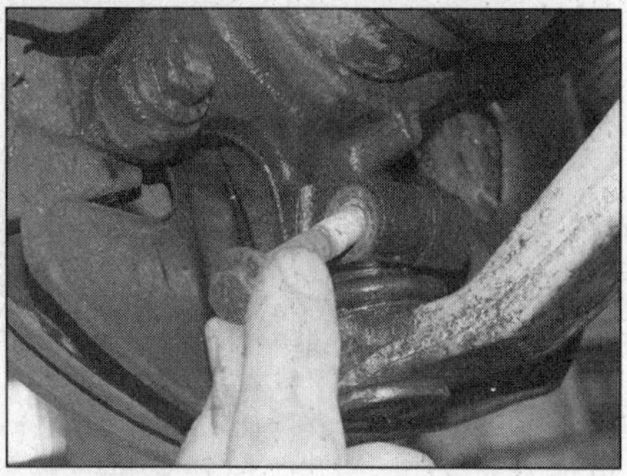

2.9 Removing the lower balljoint bolt

2.10a Lever down the lower arm . . .

2.10b . . . and open the balljoint 'jaws' to free the balljoint

2.14 Pull the hub outwards, and withdraw the driveshaft

to damage. To prevent this, try wrapping masking tape (or similar) around the balljoint while it is disconnected, and remove it just prior to refitting.

12 The splined end of the driveshaft now has to be released from its location in the hub. It's likely that the splines will be very tight (corrosion may even be a factor, if the driveshaft has not been disturbed for some time), and considerable force may be needed. Tap the end of the shaft with a plastic or hide mallet only – if an ordinary hammer is used, place a small piece of wood over the end of the driveshaft – and leave the old nut loosely in place on the end to avoid damaging the splines.

13 Once the splines have been released, remove the driveshaft nut and discard it – the nut is only intended to be used once.

14 Pull the disc/hub outwards, and turn it to allow the driveshaft to be withdrawn through the hub **(see illustration)**. It's helpful to have an assistant on hand here, to pull the hub outwards, while you slide out the driveshaft.

15 The inner end of the left-hand driveshaft must now be pulled out of the transmission. This is likely to prove difficult, as the inner end of the shaft is secured using a circlip. The MG Rover method of removal involves using a specially-shaped prising tool (54-023) with a thin curved end, inserted between the inner joint and the transmission. If such a tool is not available, a large flat-bladed screwdriver may be used, noting that this may damage the oil seal if care is not taken. Alternatively, if the driveshaft nut is refitted by hand, it may be possible to release the inner circlip by pulling outwards on the suspension strut – this may damage the driveshaft outer joint, however. **Note:** *The risk of damaging the driveshaft oil seal is increased if the inner shaft is not pulled out horizontally.*

16 To remove the right-hand driveshaft on V6 engine models, remove the single bolt and release the clip securing the heat shield next to the engine lower mounting, and withdraw it **(see illustrations)**.

17 On the right-hand driveshaft, unscrew the two bolts (three on 1.8 litre engines) securing the driveshaft support bearing to the back of the engine **(see illustration)**. These bolts require a twelve-point socket to unscrew them – a type which is commonly found in most socket sets – a six-sided hex socket will not fit.

2.16a On V6 models, prise out the clip . . .

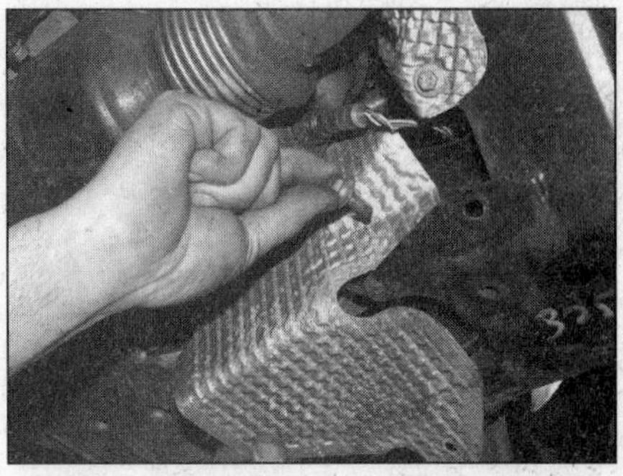

2.16b . . . then remove the bolt and take down the engine mounting heat shield

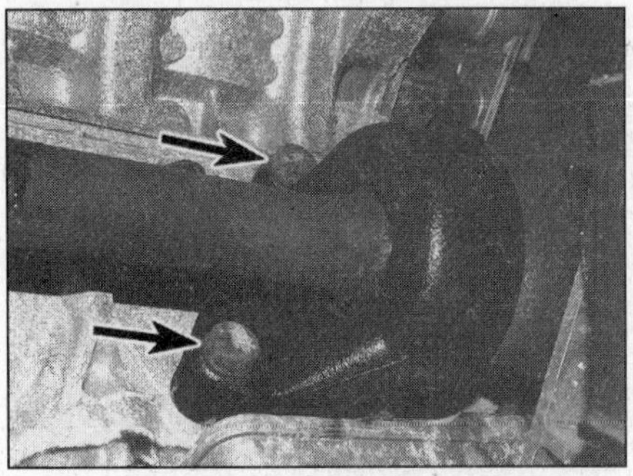

2.17 Remove the two bolts and take off the support bearing bracket

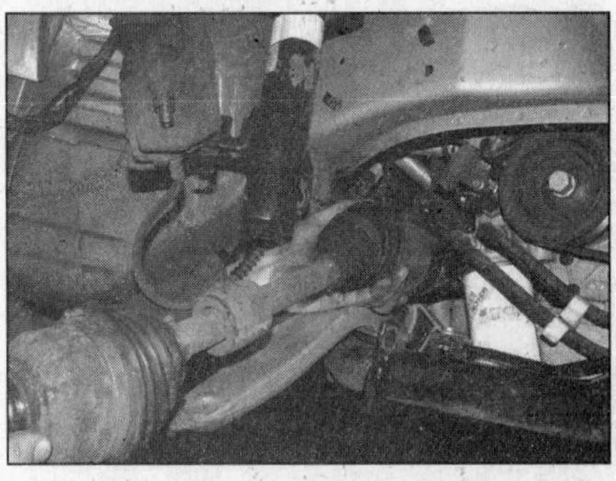

2.18 Removing the right-hand driveshaft

18 Pull the driveshaft out of the transmission, and remove it, ensuring that neither of the CV joints is bent excessively during the procedure **(see illustration)**. Also take care that the joint gaiters do not suffer unnecessary damage during removal. Recover the dust seal from the inner end of the right-hand driveshaft.

Refitting

19 Refitting is a reversal of removal, noting the following points:

a) *Whenever a driveshaft is removed, the driveshaft oil seals in the transmission should be inspected, and if necessary, new ones fitted as described in Chapter 7A or 7B.*
b) *Fit a new circlip to the groove in the left-hand driveshaft.*
c) *Apply a little grease to the driveshaft splines.*
d) *Tighten all nuts and bolts to the specified torque.*
e) *Once the driveshaft has been re-inserted in the hub, tighten the new driveshaft nut as fully as possible by hand initially – delay tightening to the specified torque until the car is resting back on its wheels. Finally, use a chisel to stake the nut's collar into the groove on the end of the driveshaft.*

3 Driveshaft gaiters – renewal

Outer joint

1 Remove the driveshaft as described in Section 2. It may be useful to mount the driveshaft in a vice, but this is not essential.

2 Note the fitted location of both of the outer joint gaiter retaining clips, then release the clips from the gaiter, and slide the gaiter back along the driveshaft a little way. It's quite likely that the original-equipment clips will have to be cut off **(see illustrations)**.

3.2a It's likely that the old clips will have to be cut . . .

3.2b . . . in order to release them

3.3 Cut off the old gaiter

3.4a Using a soft-metal drift on the inner collar . . .

3.4b . . . tap off the driveshaft joint

3.6 Slide the new gaiter and inner clip onto the shaft

3.7 Fit a new circlip to the driveshaft

HAYNES HiNT

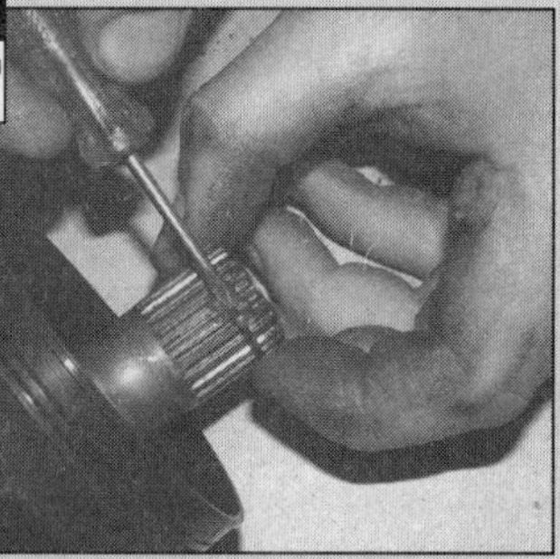

Use a little grease to help keep the circlip central in its groove – if it hangs to one side, the joint will be more difficult to fit.

3.8 Fit the joint over the end of the shaft

3 The easiest way to remove the old gaiter is to cut it off **(see illustration)**. Clean up the shaft and wipe off the joint.

4 Using a wood or soft-metal drift, carefully drive the outer CV joint from the splines on the driveshaft. Initial resistance will be felt until the internal circlip is released. Take care not to damage the bearing cage **(see illustrations)**.

5 Remove the circlip from the groove on the driveshaft – a new one should be used when refitting. Clean the shaft and wipe the old grease out of the joint. Unless the joint is contaminated with grit (which would quickly destroy it), it is not recommended that any solvent is used. If the joint is washed out with solvent, it must be given time to dry before applying fresh grease.

6 Slide the new gaiter (together with a new inner clip) onto the driveshaft **(see illustration)**.

7 Fit a new circlip to the groove in the end of the driveshaft **(see illustration and Haynes hint)**.

8 Locate the CV joint on the driveshaft so that the splines are aligned, then push the joint until the internal circlip is fully engaged **(see illustration)**.

9 Pack the joint with fresh grease, working it well into the bearings. Take care that the fresh grease does not become contaminated with dirt or grit as it is being applied. Put any excess left over into the gaiter **(see illustration)**.

10 Locate the larger end of the gaiter onto the groove on the joint housing, and secure with the clip, ensuring that it does not become twisted. Similarly, secure the inner end of the gaiter with its clip to complete **(see illustrations)**.

11 Refit the driveshaft as described in Section 2.

3.9 Pack fresh grease into the joint

3.10a Secure the gaiter's larger end to the housing . . .

3.10b . . . and pinch up the inner clip

3.13a Cut through the raised section of the clip . . .

3.13b . . . in order to release it

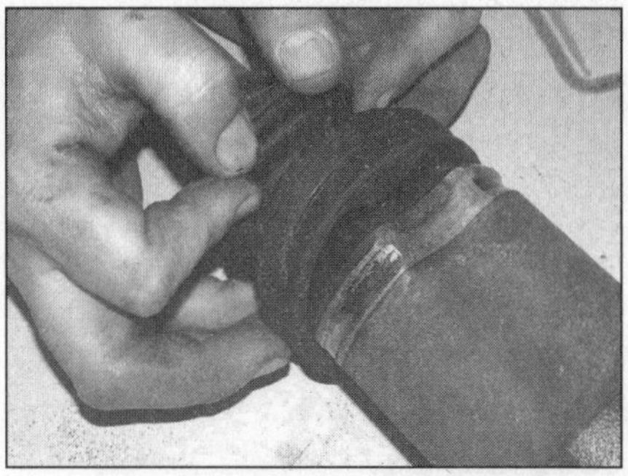

3.13c Release the gaiter by pulling the lips out of the housing groove

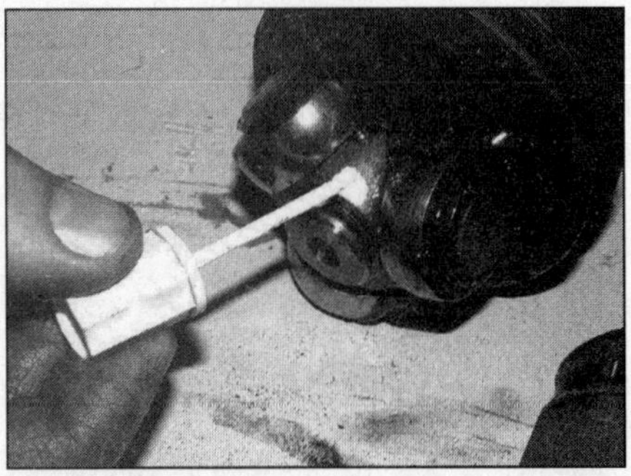

3.14a Mark the tripode joint to the shaft

3.14b Three line marks on the end of the shaft

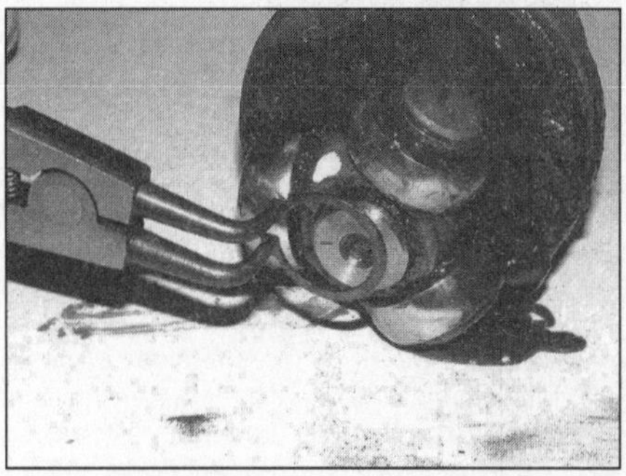

3.15 Extract the retaining circlip . . .

Inner joint

12 Remove the driveshaft as described in Section 2. It may be useful to mount the driveshaft in a vice, but this is not essential.

13 Note the fitted location of both of the outer joint gaiter retaining clips, then release the clips from the gaiter, and slide the gaiter back along the driveshaft a little way. It's quite likely that the original-equipment clips will have to be cut off **(see illustrations)**.

14 Mark the position of the tripode joint to the shaft, using paint (or carefully scratch marks across the two) – our driveshaft had three line marks on the end, which appear to line up with each part of the bearing **(see illustrations)**.

15 Using circlip pliers, extract the clip from the end of the driveshaft **(see illustration)**.

16 Tap off the tripode joint, using a wood or soft-metal drift **(see illustration)**.

17 Slide the old gaiter off the shaft **(see illustration)**.

18 Clean the shaft and wipe the old grease out of the joint. Unless the joint is contaminated with grit (which would quickly destroy it), it is not recommended that any solvent is used. If the joint is washed out with solvent, it must be given time to dry before applying fresh grease.

19 Slide the new gaiter (together with a new inner clip) onto the driveshaft **(see illustration)**.

20 Locate the joint on the driveshaft so that the marks are aligned, and tap it home using a wood or soft-metal drift **(see illustrations)**.

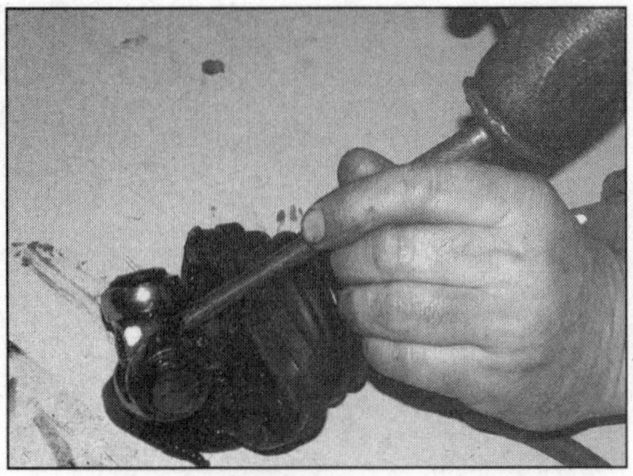

3.16 . . . then tap off the tripode joint

3.17 Slide off the old gaiter

3.19 Slide the new gaiter into position

3.20a Locate the joint onto the shaft . . .

3.20b . . . and tap it into place

3.21 Fit a new clip using circlip pliers

3.22 Fit the large clip over the joint housing

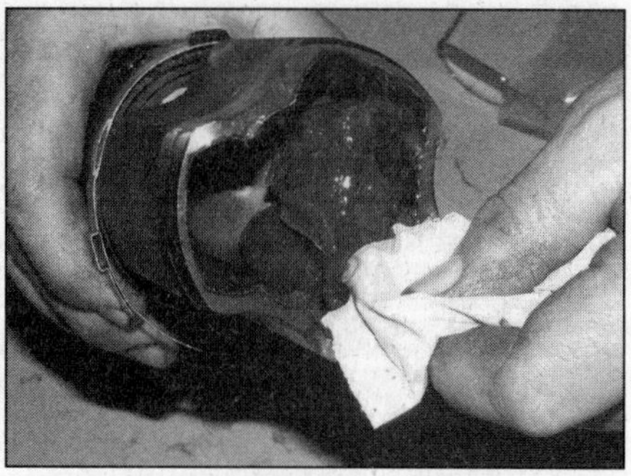

3.23a Pack the grease into the joint housing . . .

21 Fit a new circlip to the groove, using suitable pliers **(see illustration)**.
22 Fit the larger gaiter retaining clip over the joint housing **(see illustration)**.
23 Pack the joint housing with fresh grease, and apply some to the joint, working it well into the bearings. Take care that the fresh grease does not become contaminated with dirt or grit as it is being applied. Put any excess grease into the new gaiter **(see illustrations)**.
24 Fit the joint into its housing, and secure with the two gaiter clips **(see illustrations)**.
25 Refit the driveshaft as described in Section 2.

4 Driveshaft overhaul – general information

If any of the checks described in Chapter 1A or 1B reveal wear in a driveshaft joint, first remove the roadwheel trim, centre cap or the complete wheel (as required) and check that the driveshaft retaining nut is still correctly tightened; if in doubt, use a torque wrench to check it. Refit the centre cap or trim, and repeat the check on the other driveshaft.

Road test the car, and listen for a metallic clicking from the front as the car is driven slowly in a circle on full-lock. If a clicking noise is heard, this indicates wear in the outer constant velocity joint.

If vibration, consistent with roadspeed, is felt through the car when accelerating, there is a possibility of wear in the inner constant velocity joints.

Check with your parts supplier on the availability of spare parts. In theory, gaiter kits and the outer joint should all be available separately, as required.

3.23b . . . and put the excess into the gaiter

3.24a Fit the joint into the housing . . .

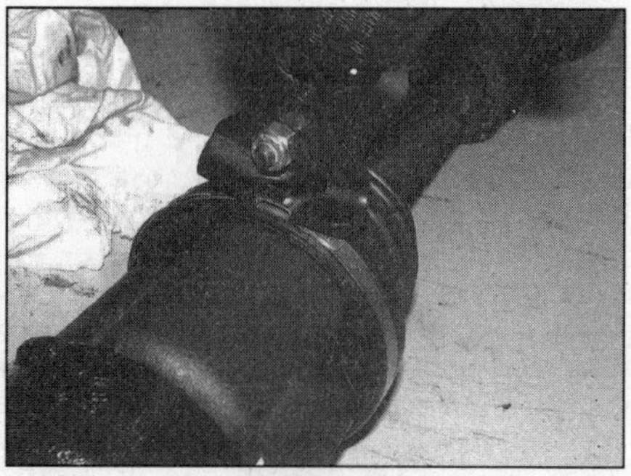

3.24b . . . and secure with the gaiter clips

Chapter 9
Braking system

Contents

Degrees of difficulty

Easy, suitable for novice with little experience	**Fairly easy,** suitable for beginner with some experience	**Fairly difficult,** suitable for competent DIY mechanic	**Difficult,** suitable for experienced DIY mechanic	**Very difficult,** suitable for expert DIY or professional

Specifications

Front brakes

Disc diameter:	
MG 190 bhp models	325 mm
All other models	284 mm
Disc minimum thickness (stamped on disc):	
MG 190 bhp models	22.8 mm
All other models	19.0 mm
Maximum disc run-out	0.06 mm
Brake pad friction material minimum thickness	2.0 mm

Rear brakes

Disc diameter:	
MG 190 bhp models	276 mm
All other models	280 mm
Disc minimum thickness (stamped on disc):	
MG 190 bhp models	16.4 mm
All other models	8.0 mm
Maximum disc run-out	0.06 mm
Brake pad friction material minimum thickness	2.0 mm
Handbrake shoe friction material minimum thickness	1.5 mm

Torque wrench settings

	Nm	lbf ft
ABS unit top mounting bolt	9	7
ABS wheel sensor retaining bolts	9	7
Brake disc shield bolt	9	7
Brake disc Torx screw	33	24
Brake hose/pipe unions	16	12
Front brake caliper:		
Guide pins	28	21
Mounting bracket bolts	100	74
Master cylinder mounting nuts*	25	18
Pedal box nuts/bolts	22	16
Rear brake caliper:		
Guide pins	28	21
Mounting bracket bolts	64	47
Roadwheel bolts	125	92
Servo unit mounting nuts	22	16
Steering column lower mounting bolts	18	13
Vacuum pump mounting bolts*	22	16

** Use new nuts/bolts*

1 General information

The braking system is of the servo-assisted, dual-circuit hydraulic type. Under normal circumstances, both circuits operate in unison. However, if there is hydraulic failure in one circuit, full braking force will still be available at two wheels.

All models are fitted with front and rear disc brakes. Bosch 5.7 ABS is fitted as standard to all models, with Electronic Brake force Distribution (EBD) – refer to Section 19 for further information on ABS operation. **Note:** *On models equipped with Electronic Traction Control (ETC), the ABS also forms part of the traction control system.*

The ventilated front disc brakes are actuated by single-piston sliding type calipers, which ensure that equal pressure is applied to each disc pad.

All models are fitted with rear disc brakes, actuated by single-piston sliding calipers, whilst a separate drum brake arrangement is fitted in the centre of the brake disc to provide a separate means of handbrake application.

The vacuum servo unit uses inlet manifold depression (generated only when a petrol engine is running) to boost the effort applied by the driver at the brake pedal and transmits this increased effort to the master cylinder pistons. Because there is no throttling of the inlet manifold on a diesel engine, it is not a suitable source of vacuum for brake servo operation. Vacuum is therefore derived from a separate vacuum pump, driven via a pushrod operated by an eccentric on the camshaft.

Precautions

The car's braking system is one of its most important safety features. When working on the brakes, there are a number of points to be aware of to ensure that your health (or even your life) is not being put at risk.

Warning: Brake fluid is poisonous. Take care to keep it off bare skin, and in particular not to get splashes in your eyes. The fluid also attacks paintwork and plastics – wash off spillages immediately with cold water. Finally, brake fluid is highly inflammable, and should be handled with the same care as petrol.

- ***Make sure the ignition is off (take out the key) before disconnecting any braking system hydraulic union, and do not switch it on until after the hydraulic system has been bled. Failure to do this could lead to air entering the ABS hydraulic unit. If air enters the hydraulic unit pump, it will prove very difficult (in some cases impossible) to bleed the unit.***
- ***When servicing any part of the system, work carefully and methodically – do not take short-cuts; also observe scrupulous cleanliness when overhauling any part of the hydraulic system.***
- ***Always renew components in axle sets, where applicable – this means renewing brake pads on BOTH sides, even if only one set of pads is worn (for example). In the instance of uneven brake wear, the cause should be investigated and fixed (sticking caliper pistons is a likely problem).***
- ***Use only genuine MG Rover parts, or at least those of known good quality.***
- ***Although genuine MG Rover brake pads are asbestos-free, the dust created by wear of non-genuine parts may contain asbestos, which is a health hazard. Never blow it out with compressed air, and don't inhale any of it.***
- ***DO NOT use petroleum-based solvents to clean brake parts; use brake cleaner or methylated spirit only.***
- ***DO NOT allow any brake fluid, oil or grease to contact the brake pads or disc.***

2 Brake hydraulic system – bleeding

Note: *Refer to the precautions in Section 1 before proceeding.*

General

1 The correct operation of any hydraulic system is only possible after removing all air from the components and circuit; this is achieved by bleeding the system.

2 During the bleeding procedure, add only clean, unused hydraulic fluid of the recommended type; never re-use fluid that has already been bled from the system. Ensure that sufficient fluid is available before starting work.

3 If there is any possibility of incorrect fluid being already in the system, the brake components and circuit must be flushed completely with uncontaminated, correct fluid, and new seals should be fitted to the various components.

4 If hydraulic fluid has been lost from the system, or air has entered because of a leak, ensure that the fault is cured before continuing further.

5 Park the car on level ground, switch off the engine, remove the ignition key and select first or reverse gear (or P on automatic transmission models). Chock the wheels and release the handbrake.

6 Check that all pipes and hoses are secure, unions tight and bleed screws closed. Clean any dirt from around the bleed screws with a small wire brush – if they have not been opened for some time, apply a maintenance spray such as WD-40, and allow time for it to soak in.

7 Unscrew the master cylinder reservoir cap, and top the master cylinder reservoir up to the MAX level line; refit the cap loosely, and remember to maintain the fluid level at least above the MIN level line throughout the procedure, or there is a risk of further air entering the system.

8 There is a number of one-man, do-it-yourself brake bleeding kits currently available from motor accessory shops. It is recommended that one of these kits is used whenever possible, as they greatly simplify the bleeding operation, and reduce the risk of expelled air and fluid being drawn back into the system. If such a kit is not available, the basic (two-man) method must be used, which is described in detail below.

9 If a kit is to be used, prepare the car as described previously, and follow the kit manufacturer's instructions, as the procedure may vary slightly according to the type being used; generally, they are as outlined below in the relevant sub-section.

10 Whichever method is used, the same sequence must be followed (paragraphs 11 and 12) to ensure the removal of all air from the system.

Bleeding

Sequence

11 If the system has been only partially disconnected, and suitable precautions were taken to minimise fluid loss, it should be necessary only to bleed that part of the system.

12 If the complete system is to be bled, then it should be done working in the following sequence:

a) Left-hand rear brake.
b) Right-hand rear brake.
c) Left-hand front brake.
d) Right-hand front brake.

Basic (two-man) method

13 Collect a clean glass jar, a suitable length of plastic or rubber tubing which is a tight fit over the bleed screw, and a ring spanner to fit the screw. The help of an assistant will also be required.

14 Remove the dust cap from the first screw in the sequence. Fit the spanner and tube to the screw, place the other end of the tube in the jar, and pour in sufficient fluid to cover the end of the tube.

15 Ensure that the master cylinder reservoir fluid level is maintained at least above the MIN level line throughout the procedure.

16 Have the assistant fully depress the brake pedal several times to build-up pressure, then maintain it on the final downstroke.

17 While pedal pressure is maintained, unscrew the bleed screw (approximately one turn) and allow the compressed fluid and air to flow into the jar. The assistant should maintain pedal pressure, following it down to the floor if necessary, and should not release it until instructed to do so. When the flow stops, tighten the bleed screw again, have the assistant release the pedal slowly, and recheck the reservoir fluid level.

18 Repeat the steps in paragraphs 16 and 17 until the fluid emerging from the bleed screw is free from air bubbles. If the master cylinder has been drained and refilled, and air is being bled from the first screw in the sequence, allow about 5 seconds between cycles for the master cylinder passages to refill.

19 When no more air bubbles appear, tighten the bleed screw securely, remove the tube and spanner, and refit the dust cap. Do not overtighten the bleed screw.

20 Repeat the procedure on the remaining screws in the sequence, until all air is removed from the system and the brake pedal feels firm again.

Using a one-way valve kit

21 As their name implies, these kits consist of a length of tubing with a one-way valve fitted, to prevent expelled air and fluid being drawn back into the system; some kits include a translucent container, which can be positioned so that the air bubbles can be more easily seen flowing from the end of the tube.

22 The kit is connected to the bleed screw, which is then opened **(see illustration)**. The user returns to the driver's seat, depresses the brake pedal with a smooth, steady stroke, and slowly releases it; this is repeated until the expelled fluid is clear of air bubbles.

23 Note that these kits simplify work so much that it is easy to forget the master cylinder reservoir fluid level; ensure that this is maintained at least above the MIN level line at all times.

Using a pressure-bleeding kit

24 These kits are usually operated by the reservoir of pressurised air contained in the spare tyre. However, note that it will probably be necessary to reduce the pressure to a lower level than normal; refer to the instructions supplied with the kit. **Note:** *A pressure of 2 bar (29 psi) should not be exceeded.*

25 By connecting a pressurised, fluid-filled container to the master cylinder reservoir, bleeding can be carried out simply by opening each screw in turn (in the specified sequence), and allowing the fluid to flow out until no more air bubbles can be seen in the expelled fluid.

26 This method has the advantage that the large reservoir of fluid provides an additional safeguard against air being drawn into the system during bleeding.

2.22 Connect up a one-man kit, and open the bleed screw

27 Pressure-bleeding is particularly effective when bleeding 'difficult' systems, or when bleeding the complete system at the time of routine fluid renewal.

All methods

28 When bleeding is complete, and firm pedal feel is restored, wash off any spilt fluid, tighten the bleed screws securely, and refit their dust caps.

29 Check the hydraulic fluid level in the master cylinder reservoir, and top-up if necessary (see *Weekly checks*).

30 Discard any hydraulic fluid that has been bled from the system; it will not be fit for re-use.

31 Check the feel of the brake pedal. If it feels at all spongy, air must still be present in the system, and further bleeding is required. Failure to bleed satisfactorily after a reasonable repetition of the bleeding procedure may be due to worn master cylinder seals.

3 Brake pipes and hoses – renewal

Note: *Refer to the precautions in Section 1 before proceeding.*

1 If any pipe or hose is to be renewed, minimise fluid loss by removing the master cylinder reservoir cap and then tightening it down onto a piece of polythene (taking care not to damage the sender unit) to obtain an airtight seal. Alternatively, flexible hoses can be sealed, if required, using a proprietary brake hose clamp; metal brake pipe unions can be plugged (if care is taken not to allow dirt into the system) or capped immediately they are disconnected. Place a wad of rag under any union that is to be disconnected, to catch any spilt fluid.

2 If a flexible hose is to be disconnected, unscrew the brake pipe union nut before removing the spring clip which secures the hose to its mounting bracket.

3 To unscrew the union nuts, it is preferable to obtain a brake pipe spanner of the correct size; these are available from most large motor accessory shops. Failing this, a close-fitting open-ended spanner will be required, though if the nuts are tight or corroded, their flats may be rounded-off if the spanner slips. In such a case, using self-locking pliers is often the only way to unscrew a stubborn union, but it follows that the pipe and the damaged nuts must be renewed on reassembly. Always clean a union and surrounding area before disconnecting it. If disconnecting a component with more than one union, make a careful note of the connections before disturbing any of them.

4 If a brake pipe is to be renewed, it can be obtained, cut to length and with the union nuts and end flares in place, from your MG Rover parts supplier. All that is then necessary is to bend it to shape, following the line of the original, before fitting it to the car. Alternatively, most motor accessory shops can make up brake pipes from kits, but this requires very careful measurement of the original, to ensure that the new one is of the correct length. The safest answer is usually to take the original to the shop as a pattern.

5 On refitting, do not overtighten the union nuts. It is not necessary to exercise brute force to obtain a sound joint.

6 Ensure that the pipes and hoses are correctly routed, with no kinks, and that they are secured in the clips or brackets provided. After fitting, remove the polythene from the reservoir, and bleed the hydraulic system as described in Section 2. Wash off any spilt fluid, and check carefully for fluid leaks.

4 Front brake pads – renewal

Note: *Refer to the precautions in Section 1 before proceeding. Always renew the pads on both front brakes, never just on one side.*

1 Loosen the front wheel bolts. With the handbrake applied, jack up the front of the car and support it on axle stands (see *Jacking and vehicle support*). Remove the front roadwheels.

2 On the right-hand side only, work round the wheel arch and release the pad wear sensor wiring (noting its routing) from its various clips. Slide the brake pad wear sensor from the brake pad and remove it from the caliper aperture – note the retaining clip, which should be removed for safekeeping **(see illustrations)**.

3 Using a screwdriver, carefully unclip the retaining spring from the side of the brake caliper, noting its correct fitted position **(see illustrations)**.

4 Remove the two plastic plugs from the back of the caliper to gain access to the guide pins **(see illustrations)**.

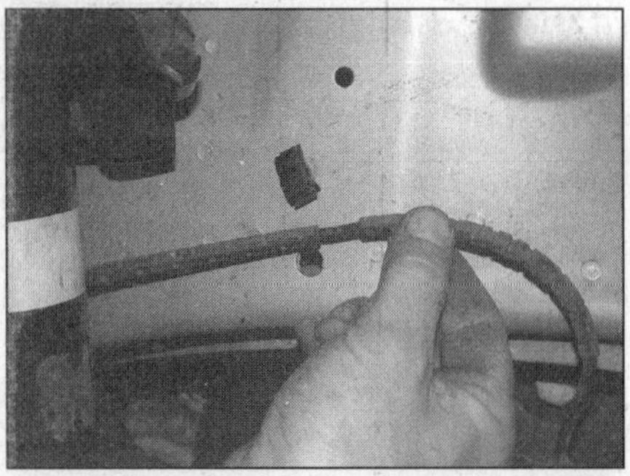

4.2a Release the pad wear sensor wiring from the clips . . .

4.2b . . . including the one next to the bleed screw . . .

4.2c . . . then pull off the connector on the brake pad . . .

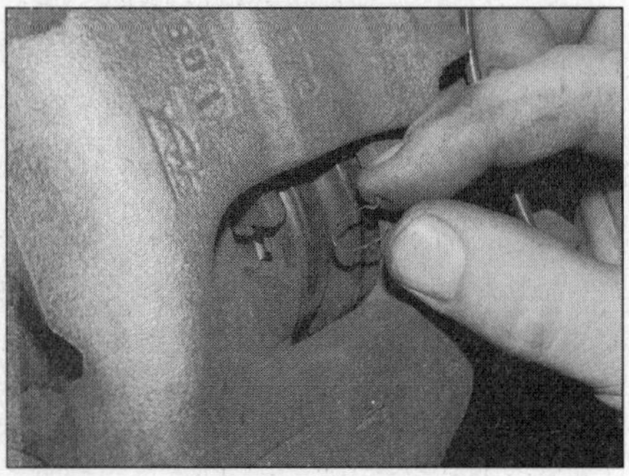

4.2d . . . and recover its retaining clip

4.3a Using a small screwdriver . . .

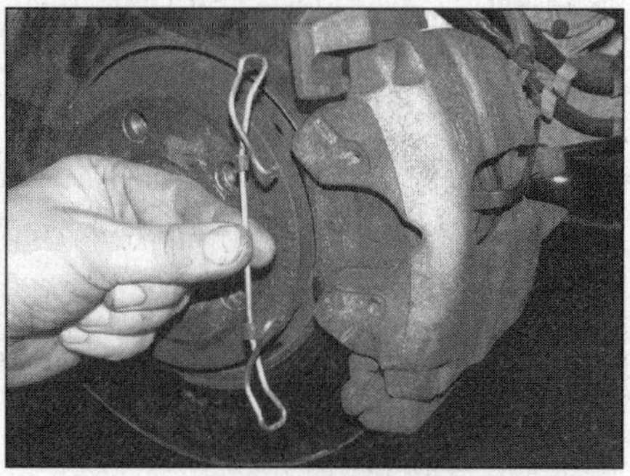

4.3b . . . release and remove the pad retaining clip

4.4a Prise out the two plugs . . .

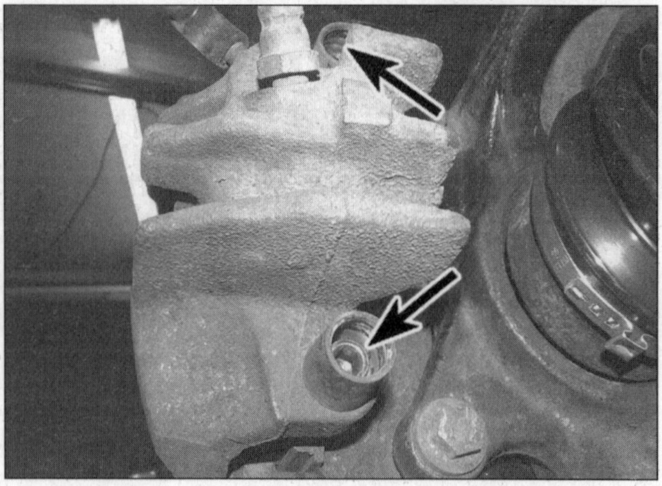

4.4b . . . to access the guide pins on the rear

5 Slacken and remove the two guide pins, noting that a suitable Allen key will be needed. Lift the caliper away from the caliper mounting bracket, and tie it to the suspension strut using a suitable piece of wire **(see illustrations)**. Do not allow the caliper to hang unsupported on the flexible brake hose.

6 Unclip the inner brake pad from the caliper piston, and withdraw the outer pad from the caliper mounting bracket **(see illustrations)**.

7 First measure the thickness of each brake pad's friction material. If either pad is worn at any point to the specified minimum thickness or less, all four front pads must be renewed. Also, the pads should be renewed if any are fouled with oil or grease; there is no satisfactory way of degreasing friction material, once contaminated. If any of the brake pads are worn unevenly, or are fouled with oil or grease, trace and rectify the cause before reassembly.

> **HAYNES HiNT** ***If the pads are wearing unevenly, the calipers are probably seized, which will also wear the discs prematurely. Just removing the pads and pushing the piston fully back into its bore (see paragraph 11) may unseize the piston enough to restore correct operation. If not, remove and overhaul the calipers as described in Section 8.***

8 If the brake pads are still serviceable, carefully clean them using a clean, fine wire brush or similar, paying particular attention to the sides and back of the metal backing. Clean out the grooves in the friction material (where applicable), and pick out any large embedded particles of dirt or debris. Carefully clean the pad locations in the caliper body/mounting bracket.

9 Prior to fitting the pads, check that the guide pins are a light, sliding fit in the caliper body bushes, with little sign of free play. If any of the guide pins appear to worn or damaged, renew them all. Brush the dust and dirt from the caliper and piston, but *do not* inhale it, as it may be a health hazard. Inspect the dust seal around the piston for damage, and the piston for evidence of fluid leaks, corrosion or damage. If attention to any of these components is necessary, refer to Section 8.

10 The caliper piston must be pushed back into the caliper to make room for the new pads – this may require considerable effort. Either use a G-clamp, sliding-jaw (water pump) pliers, or suitable pieces of wood as levers **(see illustration)**.

Caution: Pushing back the piston causes a reverse-flow of brake fluid, which has been known to 'flip' the master cylinder rubber seals, resulting in a total loss of braking. To avoid this, clamp the caliper flexible hose and open the bleed screw – as the piston is pushed back, the fluid can be directed into a suitable container using a hose attached to the bleed screw. Close the screw just before the piston is pushed fully back, to ensure no air enters the system.

11 If the recommended method of opening a bleed screw before pushing back the piston is not used, the fluid level in the reservoir will

4.5a Unscrew the guide pins using an Allen key . . .

4.5b . . . then lift off the caliper . . .

4.5c . . . and hang it up using a piece of wire

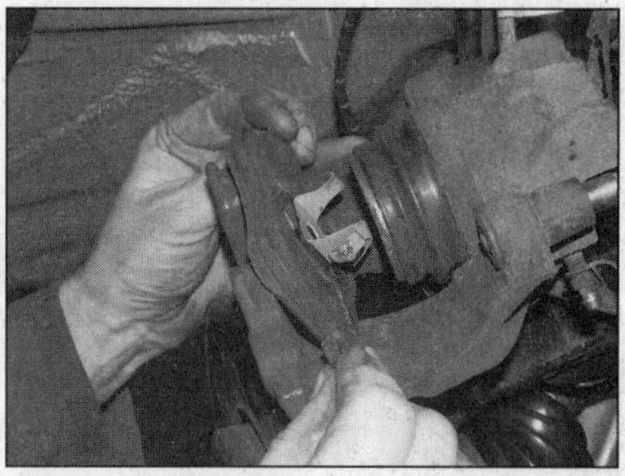

4.6a Unclip the inner brake pad from the caliper . . .

4.6b . . . and withdraw the outer pad from the mounting bracket

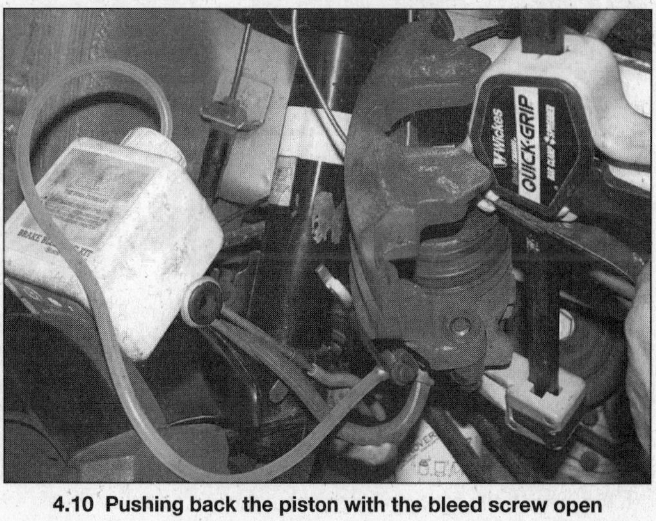

4.10 Pushing back the piston with the bleed screw open

4.13a Fit the outer pad to the mounting bracket . . .

4.13b . . . and peel off the backing paper (where applicable)

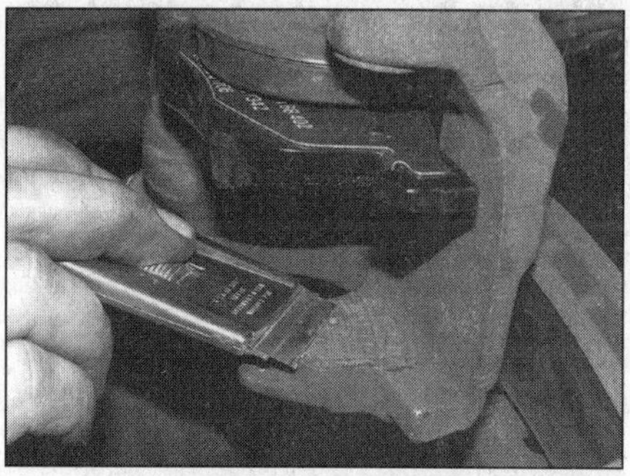

4.13c Clean off any old adhesive or brake dust inside the caliper

rise, and possibly overflow. Make sure that there is sufficient space in the brake fluid reservoir to accept the displaced fluid and, if necessary, syphon some off first. Any brake fluid spilt on paintwork should be washed off with clean water, without delay – brake fluid is also a highly-effective paint-stripper.

12 Except on genuine MG Rover pads (which have their own special adhesive backing) apply a smear of copper brake grease to the backing plate of each pad, and the pad backing plate contact points on the caliper bracket; do not apply excess grease, nor allow the grease to contact the friction material.

13 Fit the outer pad to the caliper mounting bracket, ensuring that its friction material is against the brake disc. On genuine MG Rover pads, peel off the paper from the adhesive backing, and clean any old backing from the caliper inner surfaces **(see illustrations)**.

14 Clip the inner pad into the caliper piston, and manoeuvre the caliper assembly into position **(see illustrations)**. If the caliper will not fit properly, the piston has not been pushed back far enough (see paragraph 10).

15 Install the caliper guide pins, and tighten them to the specified torque setting. Refit the plugs to the ends of the caliper guide pins.

16 On the right-hand caliper, attach the spring clip and push the pad wear sensor back into position in the outer pad. Feed the wiring back into position around the wheel arch **(see illustrations)**.

17 Clip the retaining spring into position in the caliper **(see illustration)**. Depress the brake pedal repeatedly, until the pads are pressed into firm contact with the brake disc, and normal (non-assisted) pedal pressure is restored.

18 Repeat the above procedure on the remaining front brake caliper.

4.14a Clip the inner pad into the caliper piston

4.14b Offer the caliper into position

19 Refit the roadwheels, then lower the car to the ground and tighten the wheel bolts to the specified torque.

20 Check the hydraulic fluid level as described in *Weekly checks*.

21 Turn the ignition key to position I, and leave it there for at least 30 seconds without starting the engine. This clears the brake pad wear warning fault stored in the ECM, and turns out the brake pad wear warning light in the instrument cluster.

22 If new pads have been fitted, full braking efficiency will not be obtained until the linings have bedded-in. Be prepared for longer stopping distances, and avoid harsh braking as far as possible for the first hundred miles or so after fitting new pads.

5 Rear brake pads – renewal

Note: *Refer to the precautions in Section 1 before proceeding. Always renew the pads on both rear brakes, never just on one side.*

1 The rear brake calipers are virtually identical to those fitted at the front. Refer to the procedures in Section 4 in addition.

2 Loosen the rear wheel bolts. Chock the front wheels, then jack up the rear of the car and support it on axle stands (see *Jacking and vehicle support*). Remove the rear roadwheels.

3 On the right-hand caliper, unclip the pad

4.16a Attach the spring clip to the wiring connector . . .

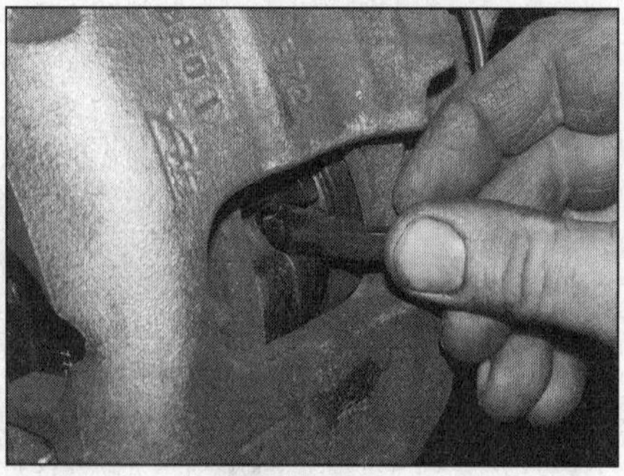

4.16b . . . then push it onto the pad wear sensor

4.17 Use pliers to clip the retaining spring back in place

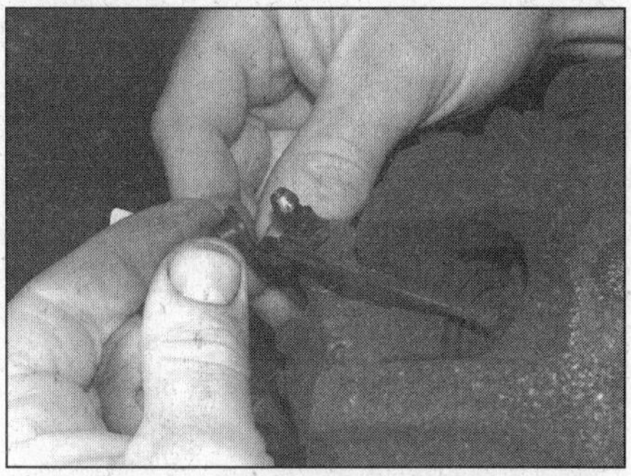

5.3a Release the pad wear sensor wiring under the bleed screw cap . . .

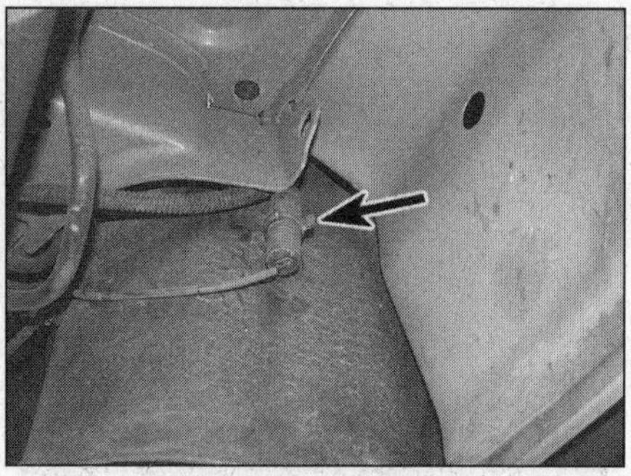

5.3b . . . then trace it to the plug behind the arch liner . . .

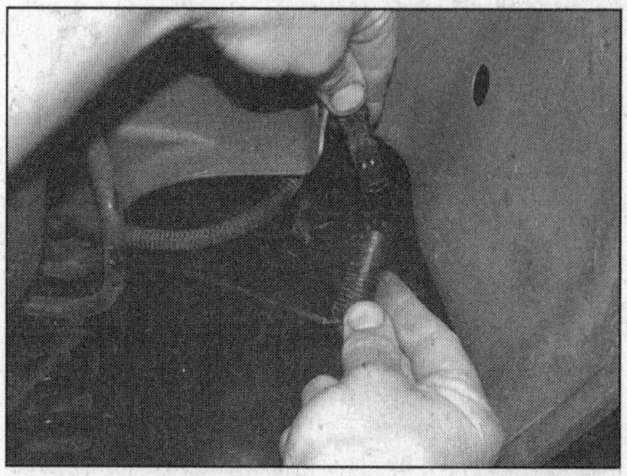

5.3c . . . and disconnect it

wear wiring, noting how it is routed. Trace the wiring to the back of the wheel arch liner, and disconnect the wiring plug **(see illustrations)**.

4 Follow the accompanying photo sequence, keeping in order **(see illustrations)**.

Caution: Pushing back the piston causes a reverse-flow of brake fluid, which has been known to 'flip' the master cylinder rubber seals, resulting in a total loss of braking. To avoid this, clamp the caliper flexible hose and open the bleed screw – as the piston is pushed back, the fluid can be directed into a suitable container using a hose attached to the bleed screw. Close the screw just before the piston is pushed fully back, to ensure no air enters the system.

5 Tighten the guide pins to the specified torque, then refit the plastic plugs.

6 Where applicable, connect the pad wear wiring to the new pad, and feed the wiring back round the wheel arch. Finally, reconnect

5.4a Unclip the pad retaining clip . . .

the wiring plug, and clip it to the back of the wheel arch liner as before.

7 Repeat this procedure on the other rear caliper.

8 Refit the roadwheels, then lower the car to

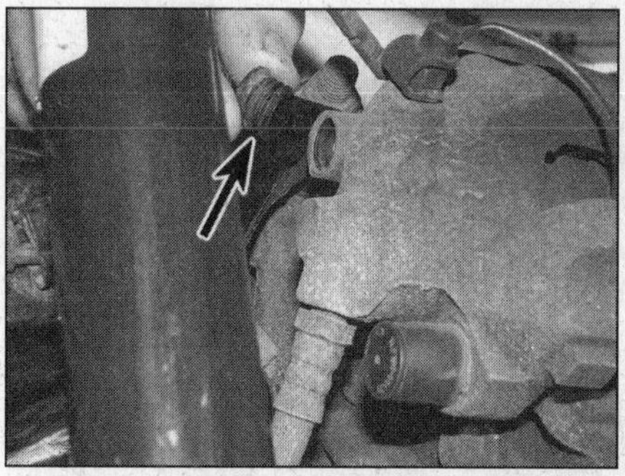

5.4b . . . then prise out the plugs on the back . . .

the ground and tighten the wheel bolts to the specified torque.

9 Check the hydraulic fluid level as described in *Weekly checks*.

10 Turn the ignition key to position I, and

5.4c . . . and unscrew the guide pins

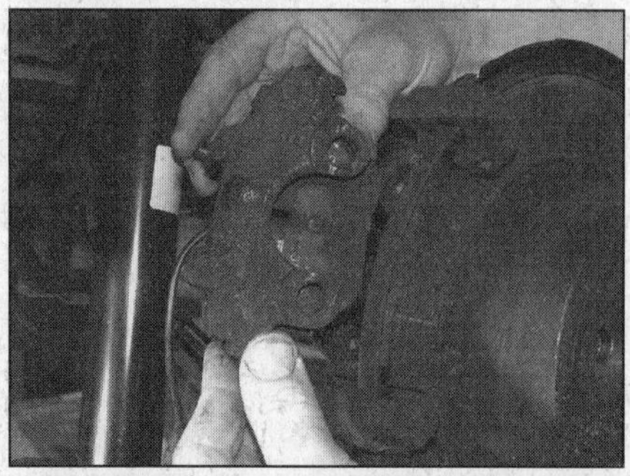

5.4d Slide off the caliper, and remove the old pads

5.4e Push the piston back using a suitable tool

5.4f Clip the inner pad into the piston . . .

5.4g . . . and the outer pad into the bracket

5.4h Slide the caliper into place over the new pads

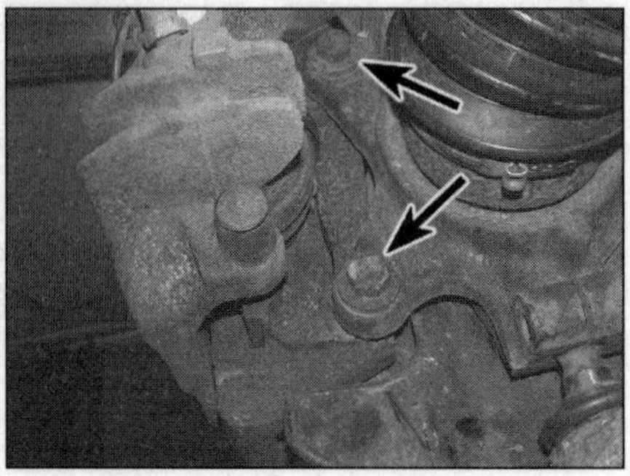

6.6a Unscrew the two caliper mounting bolts . . .

6.6b . . . and withdraw the caliper from the disc

leave it there for at least 30 seconds without starting the engine. This clears the brake pad wear warning fault stored in the ECM, and turns out the brake pad wear warning light in the instrument cluster.

11 If new pads have been fitted, full braking efficiency will not be obtained until the linings have bedded-in. Be prepared for longer stopping distances, and avoid harsh braking as far as possible for the first hundred miles or so after fitting new pads.

6 Front brake disc – inspection, removal and refitting

Note: *Refer to the precautions in Section 1 before proceeding.*

Inspection

1 Loosen the front wheel bolts. Apply the handbrake, then jack up the front of the car and support it on axle stands. Remove the front wheels.

2 Slowly rotate the brake disc so that the full area of both sides can be checked; remove the brake pads if better access is required to the inboard surface (see Section 4). Light scoring is normal in the area swept by the brake pads, but if heavy scoring or cracks are found, the disc must be renewed.

3 It is normal to find a lip of rust and brake dust around the disc's perimeter; this can be scraped off if required. If, however, a lip has formed due to excessive wear of the brake pad swept area, then the disc's thickness must be measured using a micrometer. Take measurements at several places around the disc, at the inside and outside of the pad swept area; if the disc has worn at any point to the specified minimum thickness or less, the discs must be renewed.

4 If the disc is thought to be warped, it can be checked for run-out. Either use a dial gauge mounted on any convenient fixed point, while the disc is slowly rotated, or use feeler blades to measure (at several points all around the disc) the clearance between the disc and a fixed point, such as the caliper mounting bracket. If the measurements obtained are at the specified maximum or beyond, the disc is excessively warped, and must be renewed; however, it is worth checking first that the hub bearing is in good condition (Chapter 10). If the run-out is excessive, the discs must be renewed.

5 Check the disc for cracks, especially around the wheel bolt holes, and any other wear or damage, and renew if necessary.

Removal

6 Unscrew the two bolts securing the brake caliper mounting bracket to the hub carrier, then slide the caliper assembly off the disc **(see illustrations)**. Using a piece of wire or string, tie the caliper to the front suspension coil spring, to avoid placing any strain on the hydraulic brake hose.

7 Remove the Torx screw securing the brake disc to the hub, and take off the disc **(see illustrations)**. If the disc is tight, lightly tap its rear face with a hide or plastic mallet.

Refitting

8 Refitting is the reverse of the removal procedure, noting the following points:

a) Ensure that the mating surfaces of the disc and hub are clean and flat.

b) Align (if applicable) the marks made on removal, and tighten the disc retaining screw to the specified torque.

c) If a new disc has been fitted, use a suitable solvent to wipe any preservative coating from the disc, before refitting the caliper.

d) Slide the caliper into position over the disc, making sure the pads pass either side of the disc. Tighten the caliper mounting bolts to the specified torque setting.

e) Refit the roadwheel, then lower the car to the ground and tighten the roadwheel bolts to the specified torque. On completion, repeatedly depress the brake pedal until normal (non-assisted) pedal pressure returns.

7 Rear brake disc – inspection, removal and refitting

Note: *Refer to the precautions in Section 1 before proceeding.*

Inspection

1 Loosen the rear wheel bolts. Firmly chock the front wheels, then jack up the rear of the car and support it on axle stands. Remove the appropriate rear wheel. Release the handbrake.

2 Inspect the disc as described in Section 6.

Removal

3 Unscrew the two bolts securing the brake caliper mounting bracket to the trailing arm, then slide the caliper assembly off the disc **(see illustration)**. Using a piece of wire or string, tie the caliper to the rear suspension coil spring, to avoid placing any strain on the hydraulic brake hose. If necessary unclip the rubber brake hose from the lower mounting bracket to provide enough slack to manoeuvre the caliper and bracket.

6.7a Remove the Torx retaining screw . . .

6.7b . . . and withdraw the disc from the hub

7.3 Remove the two caliper mounting bolts

4 Slacken and remove the brake disc Torx screw **(see illustration)**.

5 It should now be possible to withdraw the brake disc from the stub axle by hand **(see illustration)**. If it is tight, lightly tap its rear face with a hide or plastic mallet. If the handbrake shoes are binding, first check that the handbrake is fully released, then continue as follows.

6 Referring to Section 14 for further details, fully slacken the handbrake adjustment to obtain maximum free play in the cable.

7 Insert a screwdriver through one of the wheel bolt holes in the brake disc, and rotate the adjuster knurled wheel on the upper pivot to retract the shoes. The brake disc can then be withdrawn.

Refitting

8 If a new disc is been fitted, use a suitable solvent to wipe any preservative coating from the disc.

9 Align (if applicable) the marks made on removal, then fit the disc and tighten the retaining screw to the specified torque.

10 Slide the caliper into position over the disc, making sure the pads pass either side of the disc. Tighten the caliper bracket mounting bolts to the specified torque setting.

11 Adjust the handbrake shoes and cable as described in Section 14.

12 Refit the roadwheel, then lower the car to the ground, and tighten the roadwheel bolts to the specified torque. On completion, repeatedly depress the brake pedal until normal (non-assisted) pedal pressure returns. Recheck the handbrake adjustment.

7.4 Remove the rear brake disc securing screw

7.5 Removing the rear brake disc

8 Front brake caliper – removal, overhaul and refitting

Note: *Refer to the precautions in Section 1 before proceeding.*

Removal

1 Loosen the relevant front wheel bolts. Apply the handbrake, then jack up the front of the car and support it on axle stands (see *Jacking and vehicle support*). Remove the appropriate roadwheel.

2 Minimise fluid loss by using a brake hose clamp, a G-clamp or a similar tool to clamp the flexible hose.

3 Clean the area around the union, then loosen the brake hose union on the caliper.

4 Remove the brake pads (see Section 4).

5 Unscrew the caliper from the end of the brake hose, and remove it from the car.

Overhaul

6 With the caliper on the bench, wipe away all traces of dust and dirt, but *avoid inhaling the dust, as it is a health hazard.*

7 Withdraw the partially-ejected piston from the caliper body, and remove the dust seal **(see illustration)**. **Note:** *If the piston cannot be withdrawn by hand, it can be pushed out by applying compressed air to the brake hose union hole. Only low pressure should be required, such as is generated by a foot pump. As the piston is expelled, take great care not to trap your fingers between the piston and caliper.*

8 Using a small screwdriver, extract the piston hydraulic seal, taking great care not to damage the caliper bore **(see illustration)**.

9 Thoroughly clean all components, using only methylated spirit, isopropyl alcohol or clean hydraulic fluid as a cleaning medium. Never use mineral-based solvents such as petrol or paraffin, as they will attack the hydraulic system's rubber components. Dry the components immediately, using compressed air or a clean, lint-free cloth. Use compressed air to blow clear the fluid passages.

10 Check all components, and renew any that are worn or damaged. Check particularly the cylinder bore and piston; these should be renewed (note that this means the renewal of the complete body assembly) if they are scratched, worn or corroded in any way. Similarly check the condition of the guide pins and their bushes; both pins should be

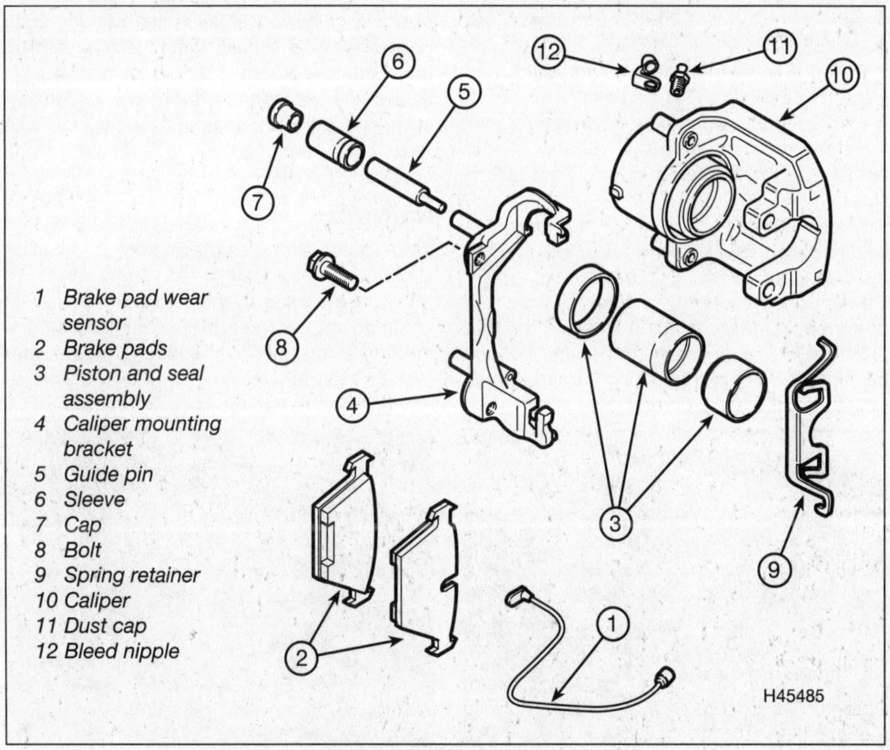

8.7 Front brake caliper

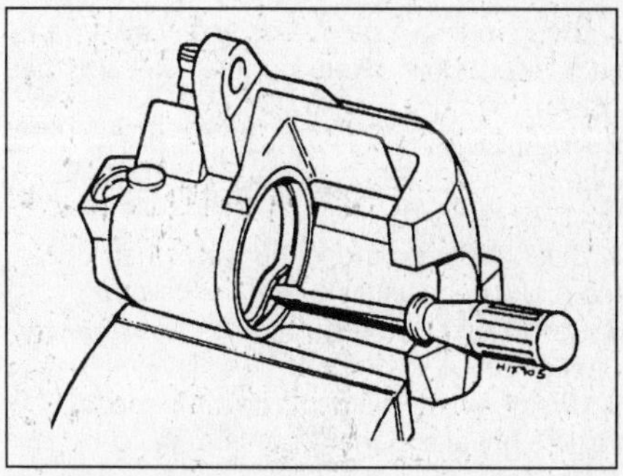

8.8 Extract the piston seal – take care not to scratch the surface of the bore

undamaged and (when cleaned) a reasonably tight sliding fit in the bushes. If there is any doubt about the condition of any component, renew it.

11 If the assembly is fit for further use, obtain the appropriate repair kit; the components should be available from your parts supplier in various combinations. All rubber seals should be renewed as a matter of course; these should never be re-used.

12 On reassembly, ensure that all components are clean and dry.

13 Soak the piston and the new piston (fluid) seal in clean hydraulic fluid. Smear clean fluid on the cylinder bore surface.

14 Fit the new piston (fluid) seal, using only your fingers (no tools) to manipulate it into the cylinder bore groove.

15 Fit the new dust seal to the piston. Locate the rear of the seal in the recess in the caliper body, and refit the piston to the cylinder bore using a twisting motion. Ensure that the piston enters squarely into the bore, and press it fully into the bore.

Refitting

16 Screw the caliper fully onto the flexible hose union.

17 Refit the brake pads (see Section 4).

18 Securely tighten the brake pipe union nut.

19 Remove the brake hose clamp or polythene, as applicable, and bleed the hydraulic system as described in Section 2. Note that, providing the precautions described were taken to minimise brake fluid loss, it should only be necessary to bleed the relevant front brake.

20 Refit the roadwheel, then lower the car to the ground and tighten the wheel bolts to the specified torque. On completion, check the hydraulic fluid level as described in *Weekly checks*.

9 Rear brake caliper – removal, overhaul and refitting

Note: *Refer to the precautions in Section 1 before proceeding.*

Removal

1 Loosen the rear wheel bolts. Chock the front wheels, then jack up the rear of the car and support on axle stands (see *Jacking and vehicle support*). Remove the relevant rear wheel.

2 Minimise fluid loss by using a brake hose clamp, a G-clamp or a similar tool to clamp the flexible hose.

3 Clean the area around the union, then loosen the brake hose union nut on the caliper.

4 Remove the brake pads as described in Section 5.

5 Unscrew the caliper from the end of the flexible hose, and remove it from the car.

Overhaul

6 Refer to Section 8.

Refitting

7 Screw the caliper fully onto the flexible hose union.

8 Refit the brake pads (refer to Section 5).

9 Securely tighten the brake pipe union nut.

10 Remove the brake hose clamp or polythene, as applicable, and bleed the hydraulic system as described in Section 2. Note that, providing the precautions described were taken to minimise brake fluid loss, it should only be necessary to bleed the relevant rear brake.

11 Refit the roadwheel, then lower the car to the ground and tighten the roadwheel bolts to the specified torque. On completion, check the hydraulic fluid level as described in *Weekly checks*.

10 Master cylinder – removal, overhaul and refitting

Note: *Refer to the precautions in Section 1 before proceeding.*

Removal

1 Pack some clean absorbent rag around the master cylinder, to absorb any fluid spillage. If possible, syringe out as much fluid from the reservoir as possible before starting – or use kitchen towel to 'soak out' the fluid. Alternatively, open any convenient bleed screw in the system, and gently pump the brake pedal to expel the fluid through a plastic tube connected to the screw until the level of fluid drops below that of the reservoir (see Section 2).

2 Remove the windscreen wiper motor and linkage as described in Chapter 12.

3 On V6 models with traction control, remove the three nuts securing the traction control actuator to the bulkhead, and move it to one side.

4 On 1.8 litre models, remove the three nuts securing the power steering fluid reservoir to the bulkhead, and move it to one side.

5 Peel up the rubber weatherseal at the rear of the engine compartment. Remove the four plastic nuts securing the central soundproofing panel, then lift it off the wiring harness which passes through the bulkhead. Remove the two bolts and take out the access panel behind the soundproofing **(see illustrations)**.

6 Unscrew the three nuts securing the soundproofing to the driver's-side bulkhead access panel, and pull the soundproofing.

7 Remove the driver's-side bulkhead access panel, which is secured by five bolts.

8 Disconnect the wiring plug from the brake fluid low level indicator switch.

9 At the base of the reservoir, unscrew and remove the Torx screw which secures the reservoir to the master cylinder.

10 Anticipating some loss of fluid (substantial loss, if the reservoir wasn't drained as described in paragraph 1), carefully ease the reservoir out of the master cylinder – it is located on two rubber seals. The seals should be renewed when refitting.

11 Wipe clean the area around the brake pipe unions on the side of the master cylinder, and place absorbent rags beneath the pipe unions to catch any surplus fluid. Make a note of the correct fitted positions of the unions, then undo the union nuts. Plug or tape over the pipe ends and master cylinder orifices, to minimise the loss of brake fluid, and to prevent the entry of dirt into the system. Wash off any spilt fluid immediately with cold water.

12 Unscrew and remove the two nuts and washers securing the master cylinder to the servo. Discard the nuts – new ones must be used when refitting.

Overhaul

13 If the master cylinder is faulty, it must be renewed. At the time of writing, repair kits are not likely to be available, so the cylinder must be treated as a sealed unit. Check with your parts supplier or motor factors for overhaul kit availability before purchasing a new master cylinder. Renew the master cylinder reservoir seals and mounting nuts regardless of their apparent condition.

Refitting

14 Remove all traces of dirt from the master cylinder and servo unit mating surfaces.

15 Fit the master cylinder to the servo unit, ensuring that the servo unit pushrod enters the master cylinder bore centrally. Fit the new master cylinder retaining nuts and washers, and tighten them to the specified torque.

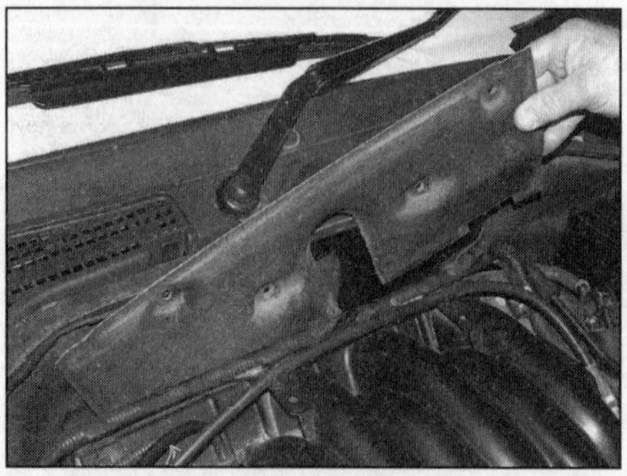

10.5a Remove the four nuts and take out the soundproofing panel . . .

10.5b . . . then remove two more bolts and lift out the bulkhead access panel

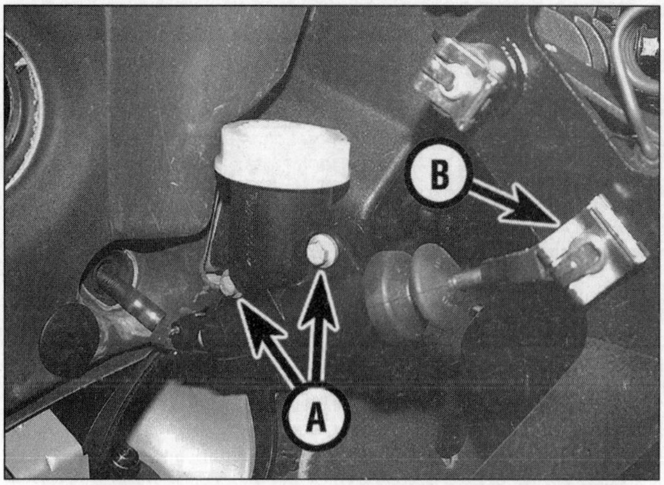

11.4 Clutch master cylinder mounting bolts (A) and clip (B)

11.5 Brake pedal-to-servo pushrod clip (A) and pedal box/servo mounting nuts (B)

16 The remainder of the procedure is a reversal of removal noting the following points:

a) Wipe clean the brake pipe unions, then refit them to the master cylinder ports and tighten them securely.

b) Press the new reservoir seals firmly into the master cylinder ports, then ease the reservoir into position. Tighten the reservoir retaining bolt securely. Reconnect the fluid hose(s) to the reservoir, and reconnect the wiring connector(s).

c) Refill the master cylinder reservoir with new fluid, and bleed the complete hydraulic system as described in Section 2.

11 Pedal box – removal and refitting

Removal

1 Remove the driver's lower facia trim panel as described in Chapter 11, Section 25.

2 Remove the trim panel fitted above the pedals, which is secured by two screws at the top, and two push-fasteners at the bottom.

3 Remove the four bolts and two screws securing the steering column to its support bracket, and lower the column into the footwell.

4 On manual transmission models, prise off the clip and release the clutch master cylinder pushrod from the pedal. Unscrew the two mounting bolts, and move the cylinder to one side **(see illustration)**.

5 Prise off the clip and withdraw the clevis pin securing the brake pedal to the servo pushrod **(see illustration)**.

6 On petrol models, unhook the accelerator cable from the top of the pedal **(see illustration)**.

7 Remove the two bolts and four nuts securing the pedal box assembly to the bulkhead **(see illustration)**. Disconnect the multi-plug(s) and remove the assembly.

8 On diesel models, unscrew the nut securing the throttle position sensor to the pedal, then unscrew the two mounting bolts and remove the sensor.

9 On manual transmission models, unhook the clutch pedal return spring, then prise off the clip and slide the clutch pedal off the pivot shaft **(see illustration)**.

10 On automatic transmission models, prise off the clip from the end of the brake pedal pivot shaft.

11 Hold the brake pedal, then slide out the pivot shaft and remove the brake pedal. Collect the return spring.

12 On petrol models, unhook the return spring, then prise off the clip, slide out the pivot shaft and remove the pedal.

13 If a new pedal box is being fitted, pull out the brake stop-light switch from the bracket on the pedal box, then unclip the bracket itself from the pedal box. On models with cruise control, remove the clutch switch using the same method.

14 Carefully clean and inspect all components, renewing any that are worn or damaged

Refitting

15 Refitting is a reversal of removal, noting the following points:

a) Apply a little grease to the pivot shafts and clevis pin.

b) Tighten the pedal box and steering column fasteners to the specified torque.

c) Refit the brake stop-light switch (and clutch switch, where applicable) using the method described in Section 18.

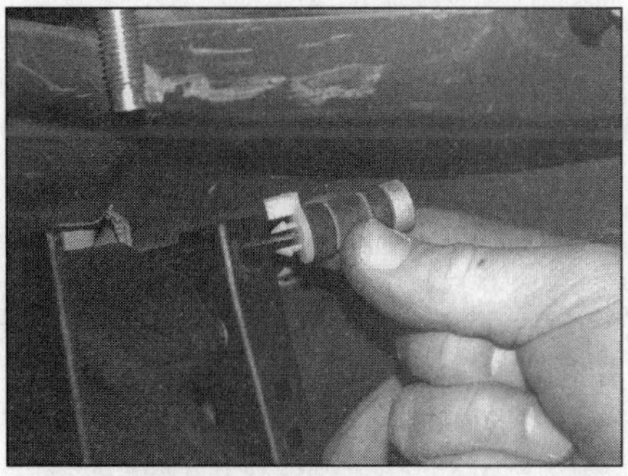

11.6 Unhook the accelerator cable at the top

11.7 Remove the two pedal box mounting bolts

11.9 Clutch pedal return spring and pivot shaft clip

12 Vacuum servo unit – testing, removal and refitting

Testing

1 To test the operation of the servo unit, depress the footbrake several times to exhaust the vacuum, then start the engine whilst keeping the pedal firmly depressed. As the engine starts, there should be a noticeable 'give' in the brake pedal as the vacuum builds-up. Allow the engine to run for at least two minutes, then switch it off. If the brake pedal is now depressed it should feel normal, but further applications should result in the pedal feeling firmer, with the pedal stroke decreasing with each application.
2 If the servo does not operate as described, first inspect the servo unit check valve as described in Section 13. On diesel models, the fault may lie with the vacuum pump – see Section 21.
3 If the servo unit still fails to operate satisfactorily, the fault lies within the unit itself. Repairs to the unit are not possible – if faulty, the servo unit must be renewed.

Removal

4 Remove the master cylinder as described in Section 10.
5 Prise out the vacuum and check valve from the front of the servo unit, and collect the seal.
6 Remove the driver's lower facia trim panel as described in Chapter 11, Section 25.
7 Remove the trim panel fitted above the

13.2 Servo unit check valve – 1.8 litre engine shown

pedals, which is secured by two screws at the top, and two push-fasteners at the bottom.
8 Prise off the clip and withdraw the clevis pin securing the brake pedal to the servo pushrod **(see illustration 11.5)**.
9 Unscrew and remove the four nuts behind the brake pedal securing the servo to the bulkhead.
10 Back in the engine compartment, ease the servo away from the bulkhead, and recover the gasket behind it – a new gasket will be needed when refitting.

Refitting

11 Refitting is the reverse of removal, noting the following points:

a) Use a new gasket.
b) Tighten the mounting nuts to the specified torque.
c) Check the servo unit check valve seal for signs of damage or deterioration, and renew if necessary.
d) Apply a smear of grease to the servo pushrod clevis pin, and secure it in position with the retaining clip.
e) Refit the master cylinder as described in Section 10 of this Chapter.
f) On completion, start the engine and check for air leaks at the vacuum hose-to-servo unit connection; check the operation of the braking system.

13 Vacuum servo unit check valve – removal, testing and refitting

Removal

1 Before starting, depress the brake pedal several times, to collapse any vacuum in the servo.
2 Working in the engine compartment, unclip the hoses to and from the check valve and remove it **(see illustration)**.

Testing

3 Examine the check valve for signs of damage, and renew if necessary.
4 The valve may be tested by blowing through it in both directions; air should flow through the valve in one direction only – when blown through from the servo unit end of the valve. Renew the valve if this is not the case.

Refitting

5 Reconnect the vacuum hoses securely to the valve, using new clips.

14 Handbrake – adjustment

Note: *A simple adjustment procedure to compensate for stretch in existing cables will be found in Chapter 1A or 1B. If this proves unsatisfactory, or if new handbrake components have been fitted, the full procedure described below should be followed.*
1 First, unclip and remove the gaiter around the handbrake lever **(see illustrations)**.
2 Loosen the handbrake adjuster nut right to the end of the adjuster threads.
3 Chock the front wheels, and loosen the rear wheel bolts. Jack up the rear of the car, and support it on axle stands (see *Jacking and vehicle support*). Remove the rear wheels.
4 Turn each rear disc until one wheel bolt hole is aligned with the brake shoe toothed adjuster **(see illustration)**.
5 Using a thin, flat-bladed screwdriver through the wheel bolt hole, turn each adjuster until the rear disc cannot be turned **(see illustration)**. Now unscrew the adjuster by five notches, and check that the disc is free to turn.
6 Apply and release the handbrake fully about five times, to settle the cables and shoes. Leave the handbrake released on completion.
7 Inside the car, tighten the handbrake adjuster nut until between 23 and 25 mm of

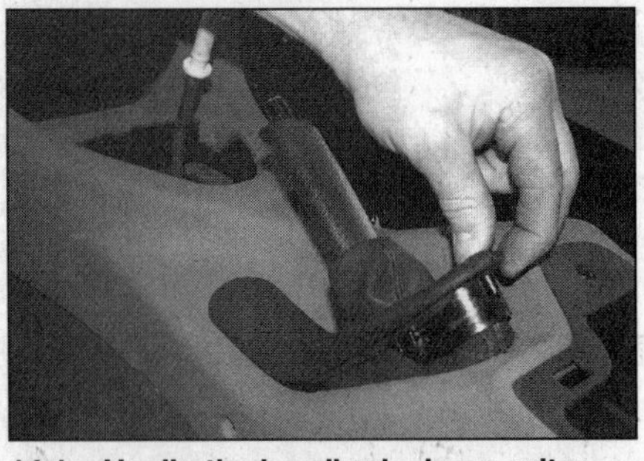

14.1a Unclip the handbrake lever gaiter . . .

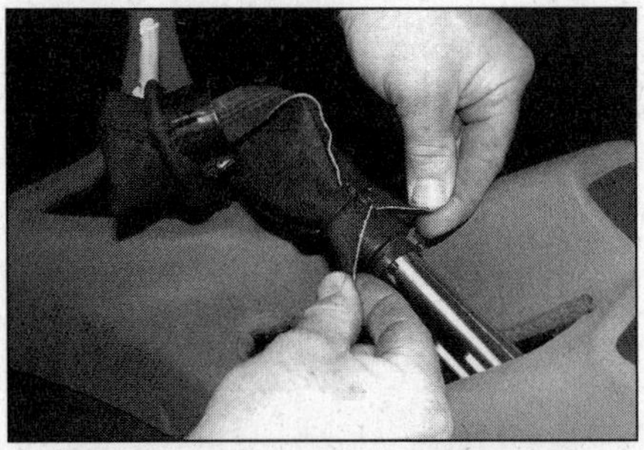

14.1b . . . then turn it inside-out and remove over the lever

14.4 Turn the disc so that one wheel bolt hole aligns with the adjuster

14.5 Adjusting the handbrake – seen with disc removed for clarity

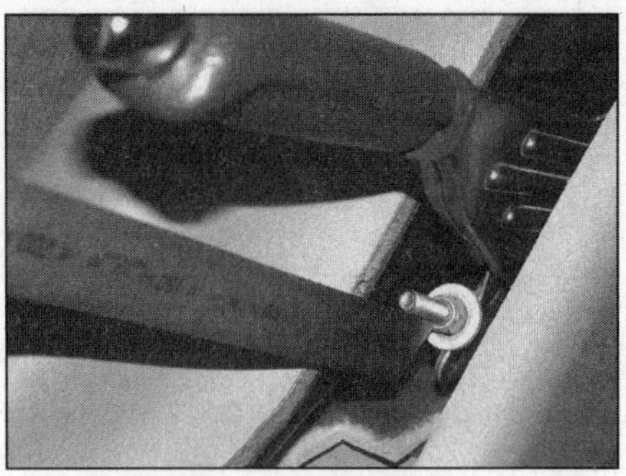

14.7 Tighten the handbrake adjuster nut as described in the text

thread is showing above the upper surface of the nut **(see illustration)**. Do not tighten the adjuster nut beyond the point where 25 mm is showing, as this may lead to damage.

8 Apply and release the handbrake, then apply it by two 'clicks'.

9 Check the force required to turn the rear discs – turning should be possible, with light resistance, indicating that the handbrake is coming on. The amount of effort should be similar on both sides – if necessary, adjust the shoes slightly using the shoe adjuster.

10 Release the handbrake, and check that the discs are free to turn.

11 Switch on the ignition to position II (warning lights on).

12 Apply the handbrake one click at a time, and check its operation and that of the instrument panel warning light, as follows:

a) First click – brake discs still turn without resistance, and the warning light may be on or off.

b) Second click – brake discs turn with some resistance, warning light on.

c) Third click – brake discs locked, warning light on.

13 Switch off the ignition, then refit the handbrake lever gaiter to the centre console.

14 Refit the rear wheels, then lower the car to the ground and tighten the wheel bolts to the specified torque.

15 Handbrake lever – removal and refitting

Removal

1 Remove the centre console as described in Chapter 11 to gain access to the handbrake lever.

2 Disconnect the spade connector from the handbrake warning light switch behind the handbrake. Alternatively, unclip the warning light switch from the back of the lever **(see illustration)**.

3 Behind the handbrake, squeeze together the legs and pull out the retaining peg to release the handbrake cable from the compensator.

4 Unscrew and remove the three Torx mounting bolts (lift the carpet for access), and lift out the handbrake lever **(see illustration)**.

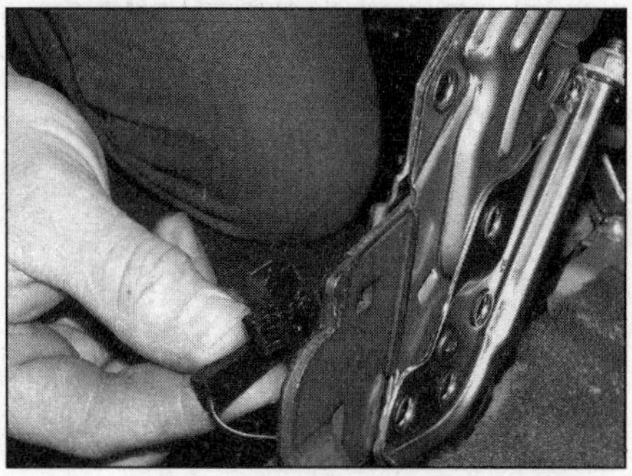

15.2 Unclip the warning light switch from the handbrake lever

5 If a new lever is being fitted, unclip the warning light switch from it, and transfer it to the new lever.

Refitting

6 Refitting is a reversal of the removal. Prior to refitting the centre console, adjust the handbrake as described in Section 14.

16 Handbrake cables – removal and refitting

Removal

1 Unclip the handbrake lever gaiter from the centre console.

2 Loosen the handbrake adjuster nut right to the end of the adjuster threads.

3 Remove the exhaust system as described in the relevant Part of Chapter 4.

4 Remove the fuel tank's exhaust heat shield, which is secured by two bolts.

5 Remove the bolts securing the centre heat shield (nine bolts on petrol models, or five on diesel models), and remove the heat shield from under the car.

6 Directly below the handbrake, prise out the large grommet in the floor for access to the handbrake compensator.

7 Squeeze together the legs and pull out the retaining peg to release the handbrake front cable from the compensator.

8 Unhook the two rear cables from the compensator – if required, the compensator can now be removed.

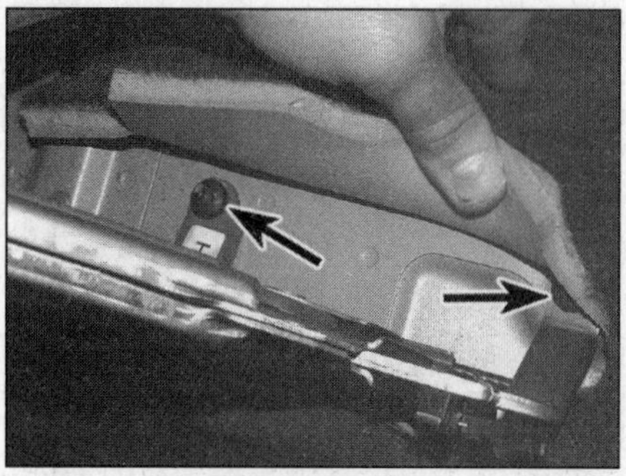

15.4 Two of the three handbrake lever mounting bolts

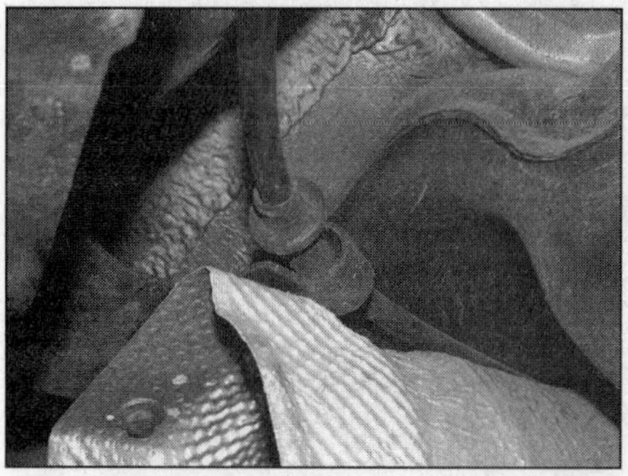

16.11 Release the handbrake cable from its various underbody clips

9 The rear cable front fittings must now be released from the floor bracket, and this is not as easy as it first appears. The fittings have legs which come through the floor bracket, and the legs must be squeezed together to free them. Working through the floor grommet, use a screwdriver to compress the clips, while pulling gently on the cable.

10 Remove the single bolt securing the cable front support bracket from the floor.

11 Work back along the length of the cable, noting its correct routing, and free it from all the relevant retaining clips **(see illustration)**.

12 Remove the rear discs as described in Section 7.

13 Slide the inner cable in the direction of the hub flange up to the stop, and manoeuvre the cable end fitting from the expander assembly. If the outer cable is seized in the casing, apply some penetrating fluid and twist the fitting using a pair of self-grip pliers **(see illustrations)**.

16.13a Slide the inner cable towards the hub flange, and free it from the expander assembly

16.13b If the outer cable is seized, use penetrating spray, and carefully twist it

17.3 Press and turn to remove the shoe retaining pins and springs

17.4 Remove the shoes from the backplate as an assembly

17.5a Unhook the upper return spring, and take out the adjuster

Refitting

14 Insert the cable into the brake carrier/ guard plate, and push it in up to the stop on the cable outer sleeve.

15 Grip the sleeve of the cable end, and push it into the expander until it snaps into place.

16 Refitting is a reversal of the removal procedure. Prior to refitting the centre console, adjust the handbrake as described in Section 14.

17 Handbrake shoes – removal and refitting

Removal

1 Remove the rear brake discs as described in Section 7, then remove the rear hubs as described in Chapter 10.

2 Make a note of the correct fitted position of all components before starting.

> **HAYNES HiNT** *Only work on one rear brake assembly at a time, so that the other is available as a pattern for reference.*

3 Release the shoe retaining pins using an Allen key by depressing them and rotating them through 90°, then remove the pins and springs **(see illustration)**.

4 Remove both handbrake shoes, complete with the return springs, adjuster and expander **(see illustration)**.

5 Noting their fitted positions, unhook and remove the return springs. Collect the adjuster and expander, noting how they are fitted **(see illustrations)**.

17.5b Unhook the lower spring and the expander

17.8 Apply brake grease to the shoe contact points on the backplate

6 Inspect the handbrake shoes for wear or contamination, and renew if necessary. It is recommended that the return springs are renewed as a matter of course.

7 While the shoes are removed, clean and inspect the condition of the shoe adjuster and expander mechanisms – renew them if they show signs of wear or damage. If all is well, apply a fresh coat of copper-based brake grease to the threads of the adjuster and sliding surfaces of the expander mechanism. Do not allow the grease to contact the shoe friction material.

Refitting

8 Prior to installation, clean the backplate, and apply a thin smear of high-temperature brake grease or anti-seize compound to all those surfaces of the backplate which bear on the shoes **(see illustration)**. Do not allow the lubricant to foul the friction material.

9 Reconnect the handbrake cable to the expander **(see illustration)**.

10 Fit the shoes onto the expander at the base, and reconnect the lower return spring. Secure one of the shoes in position on the backplate, using the pin and spring **(see illustrations)**.

11 Fit the adjuster to the tops of the shoes, and hook on the upper return spring **(see illustrations)**.

12 Fit the other retaining pin and spring to complete **(see illustration)**.

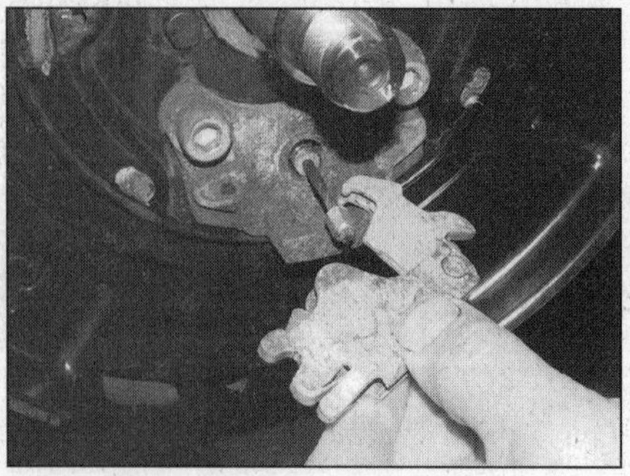

17.9 Engage the handbrake cable end fitting in the expander

17.10a Refit the shoes and lower return spring . . .

17.10b . . . then secure one shoe with the retaining pin and spring

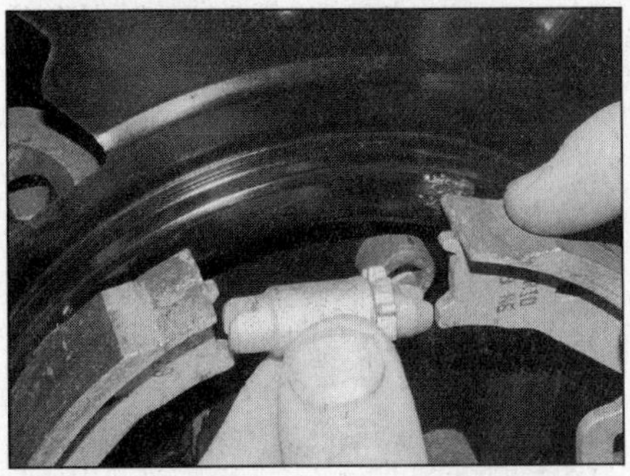

17.11a Fit the adjuster to the tops of the shoes . . .

17.11b . . . then hook on the upper spring

17.12 Handbrake shoes correctly refitted

13 Refit the hubs as described in Chapter 10.

14 Centralise the handbrake shoes, and refit the brake discs as described in Section 7.

15 Prior to refitting the roadwheels, adjust the handbrake as described in Section 14.

16 Refit the wheels, then lower the car to the ground and tighten the wheel bolts to the specified torque.

17 Where new handbrake shoes have been fitted, MG Rover recommend bedding-in the shoes as follows, after adjusting the handbrake. Drive the car at walking pace, then gradually apply the handbrake to five clicks, keeping the car moving at walking pace for approximately 100 yards. Release the handbrake, then recheck its operation and re-adjust if necessary.

18 Stop-light switch – removal and refitting

Removal

1 The stop-light switch is located on the pedal box, behind the brake pedal.

2 Remove the driver's lower facia trim panel as described in Chapter 11, Section 25.

3 Remove the trim panel fitted above the pedals, which is secured by two screws at the top, and two push-fasteners at the bottom.

4 Disconnect the wiring connector from the switch **(see illustration)**.

5 Pull the switch from its mounting bracket, and remove it – it is held by the plastic 'teeth' either side. If required, squeeze together the sides of the clips and withdraw the switch mounting sleeve from the pedal bracket **(see illustration)**.

Refitting

6 Fully depress the brake pedal and hold it down, then manoeuvre the switch into position. Slide the switch as far as it will go into the sleeve, then **slowly** release the brake pedal and allow it to return to its starting position. **Note:** *If the pedal is released too quickly, the switch will be incorrectly adjusted.*

7 Reconnect the wiring connector, and check the operation of the stop-lights.

8 On completion, refit the trim panel above the pedals, and driver's lower facia panel.

19 Anti-lock braking system (ABS) – general information

The purpose of the system is to prevent the wheel(s) locking during heavy braking. This is achieved by automatic release of the brake on the relevant wheel before it can lock up, followed by rapid reapplication of the brake.

The main components of the system are four wheel sensors (one per wheel), and a modulator block which contains the ABS computer, the hydraulic solenoid valves and accumulators, and an electrically-driven return pump.

The solenoids are controlled by the computer, which receives signals from the wheel sensors. The sensors detect the speed of rotation of a reluctor ring, attached to the wheel hub. By comparing the speed signals from the four wheels, the computer can determine when a wheel is decelerating at an abnormal rate, and can therefore predict when a wheel is about to lock. During normal operation, the system functions in the same way as a non-ABS braking system does.

If the computer senses that a wheel is about to lock, the ABS enters the 'pressure-maintain' phase. The computer operates the relevant solenoid valve in the modulator block; this isolates the brake on the wheel in question from the master cylinder, effectively sealing-in the hydraulic pressure.

If the speed of rotation of the wheel continues to decrease at an abnormal rate, the ABS then enters the 'pressure-decrease'

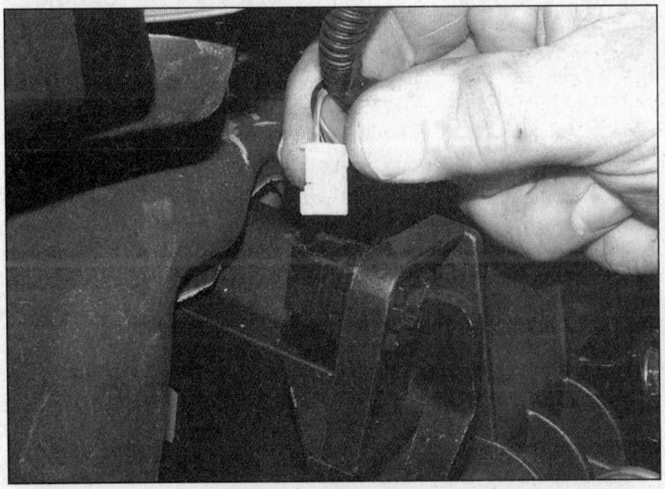

18.4 Disconnect the switch wiring plug (clutch switch shown, stop-light switch similar)

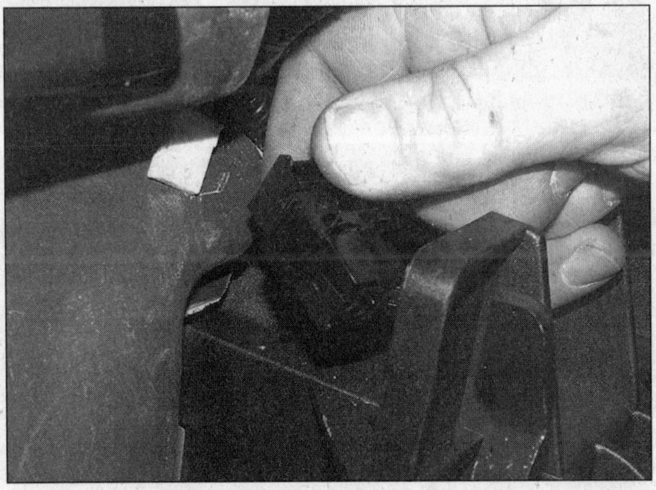

18.5 Either pull the switch out, or remove it with the mounting sleeve phase. The return pump operates and pumps the hydraulic fluid back into the master cylinder, releasing pressure on the brake. When the speed of rotation of the wheel returns to an acceptable rate, the pump stops and the solenoid valve opens, allowing hydraulic pressure to return and reapply the brake. This cycle can be carried out at up to 10 times a second.

The action of the solenoid valves and return pump creates pulses in the hydraulic circuit. When the ABS is functioning, these pulses can be felt through the brake pedal.

The 75/ZT is equipped with an additional safety feature built into the ABS, called EBD (Electronic Brake force Distribution), which automatically apportions braking effort between the front and rear wheels. The EBD function is built into the system's software, and the intention is to limit braking effort (fluid pressure) to the rear wheels, to prevent them locking up under heavy braking.

On models with electronic traction control (ETC), the ABS hydraulic unit also works the traction control system. From the wheel sensors, the ABS ECU checks for wheelspin by comparing the speed of each front (driven) wheel with the rear (non-driven) wheel on the same side. If the wheels start to spin, the front brakes are applied lightly and evenly, until the front wheel speeds normalise. In addition, engine power is reduced by the engine management system (see Chapter 4B).

The operation of the ABS is entirely dependent on electrical signals. To prevent the system responding to any inaccurate signals, a built-in safety circuit monitors all signals received by the computer. If an inaccurate signal or low battery voltage is detected, the ABS is automatically shut down, and the warning light on the instrument panel is illuminated to inform the driver that the ABS is not operational. Normal braking is unaffected, apart from the loss of the Electronic Brake force Distribution function (which may result in premature rear wheel lock-up under braking).

If a fault does develop in the ABS, the car must be taken to a suitably-equipped specialist for fault diagnosis and repair. Check first, however, that the problem is not due to loose, damaged or dirty wiring connections, or badly-routed wiring picking up spurious signals from the ignition system.

20 Anti-lock braking system (ABS) components – removal and refitting

Hydraulic unit (modulator)

1 Remove the battery and its tray as described in Chapter 5A.

2 Pack some clean absorbent rag around the hydraulic unit, to absorb any fluid spillage.

3 Slide back the locking clip, then disconnect the hydraulic unit wiring connector.

4 Clean thoroughly around all six brake pipe unions on the unit – it is essential that no dirt is allowed to enter the system.

5 Unscrew the unions and disconnect the two fluid inlet pipes at the side of the unit. Note the fitted positions of the four unions on top, and disconnect these also. Plug or tape over the open connections, to reduce fluid loss and to prevent dirt entry.

6 Unscrew the top bolt securing the unit to its mounting bracket, then release the unit from its two lower grommets, and remove it from the car. If required, the mounting bracket can be removed completely by unscrewing two further bolts.

7 Refitting is a reversal of removal.

a) *Reconnect the pipes to their original locations, and tighten the unions to the specified torque.*

b) *On completion, top-up and bleed the hydraulic system as described in Section 2.*

c) *Especially if a new unit is being fitted, note that fault codes may be introduced in the fitting process (or afterwards), which would have to be cleared by a suitably-equipped garage or specialist.*

Electronic control unit (ECU)

8 To remove the ECU, the hydraulic unit must be removed as described previously in this Section. The ECU is screwed to the side of the ABS hydraulic unit.

Front wheel sensor

9 Loosen the relevant front wheel bolts, then firmly apply the handbrake, jack up the front of the car and support on axle stands (see *Jacking and vehicle support*). Remove the appropriate front wheel.

10 Release the lead and grommet from the retaining bracket on the suspension strut, then unclip the sensor wiring and release it from the grommet in the wheel arch liner **(see illustration)**.

11 Draw the sensor wiring from the engine compartment into the wheel arch, and separate the (blue) wiring connector **(see illustrations)**.

12 Slacken and remove the single bolt securing the sensor to the hub carrier, and remove the sensor and lead assembly from the car. It's likely that it won't be that easy, however – when we tried removing the sensor during the wheel bearing renewal procedure (with the hub carrier removed), we had to soak the sensor with penetrating fluid, then carefully press it out of the hub using slip-joint pliers and a screwdriver **(see illustrations)**.

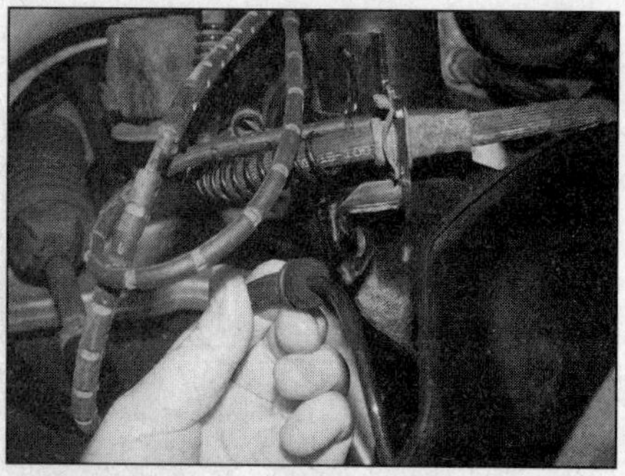

20.10 Unclip the sensor wiring from the suspension strut

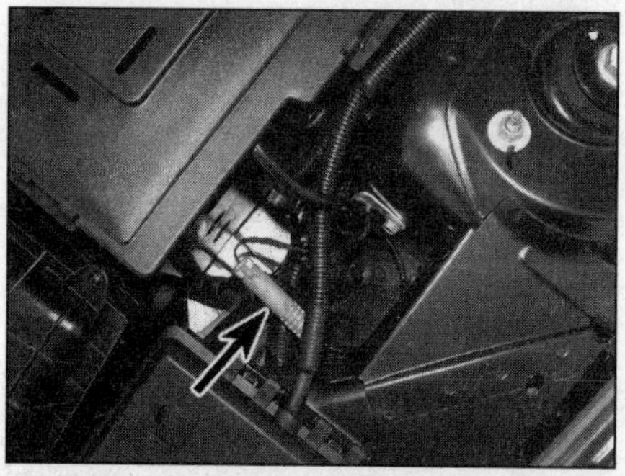

20.11a The sensor wiring plug is located on the inner wing

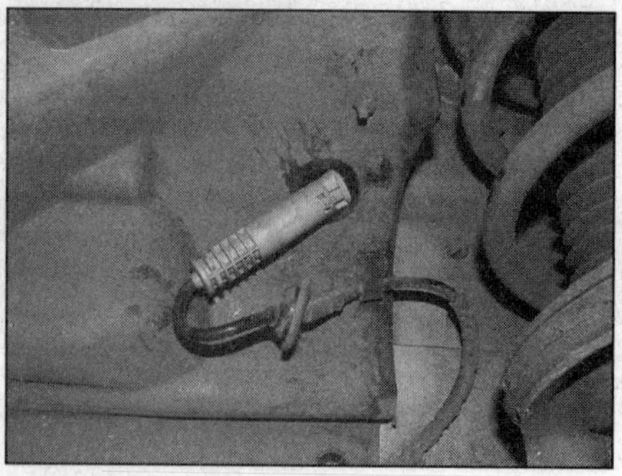

20.11b Pull the sensor wiring into the wheel arch . . .

20.11c . . . and separate the connector

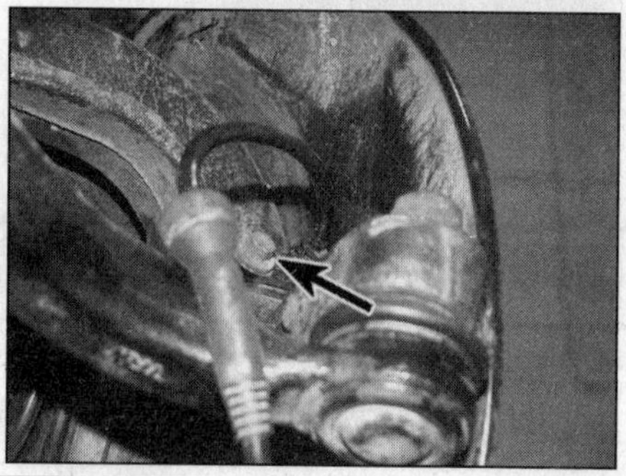

20.12a Unscrew the sensor mounting bolt

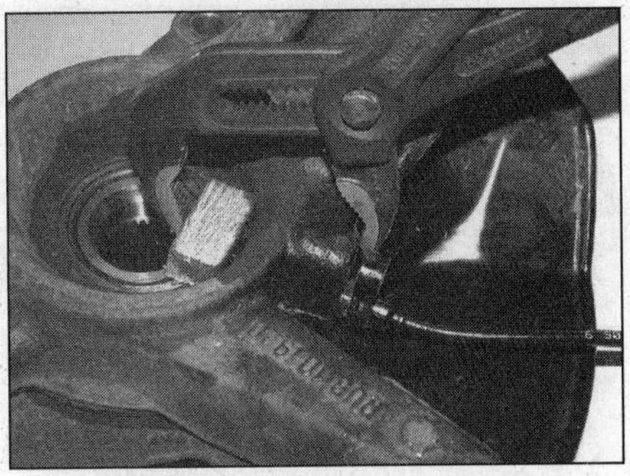

20.12b Press the sensor out using slip-joint pliers, protecting its end face . . .

20.12c . . . and prise out with a screwdriver

20.12d Withdrawing the sensor from the hub

13 Ensure that the sensor and hub carrier sealing faces are clean. Prior to refitting, apply a thin coat of multi-purpose grease to the sensor tip, and to the hub mating surfaces.
14 Fit the sensor to the hub. Refit the retaining bolt and tighten it to the specified torque.
15 Ensure that the sensor wiring is correctly routed and retained by all the necessary clips, and reconnect it to its wiring connector.
16 Refit the wheel, then lower the car to the ground and tighten the wheel bolts to the specified torque.

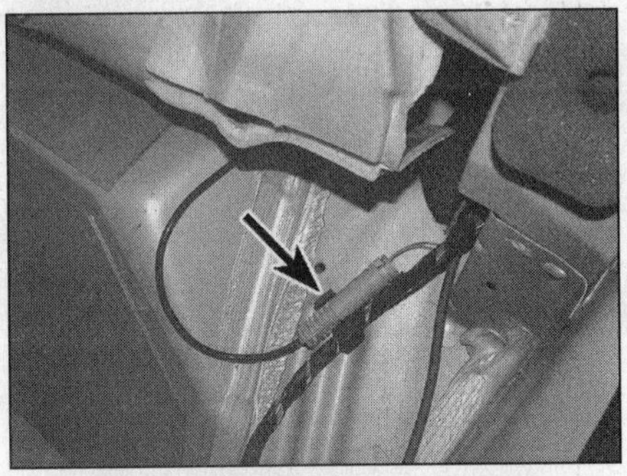

20.19a unclip the connector from its location . . .

Rear wheel sensor

17 Loosen the relevant rear wheel bolts. Chock the front wheels, then jack up the rear of the car and support it on axle stands (see *Jacking and vehicle support*). Remove the appropriate rear wheel.
18 Remove the rear seat as described in Chapter 11.
19 Unclip and separate the (blue) wiring connector located behind the rear seat, then feed the wiring down through the grommet towards the rear wheel arch **(see illustrations)**.
20 Back in the wheel arch, release the sensor lead from the suspension arm, noting how it is routed.
21 Slacken and remove the single bolt securing the sensor to the hub, and remove the sensor and lead assembly from the car **(see illustration)**.
22 Refit the sensor as described above in paragraphs 13 to 16.

Reluctor rings

23 The front reluctor rings are integral with the wheel bearing oil seals. If the seals are damaged, the bearing must be renewed, with reference to Chapter 10.

21 Vacuum pump (diesel models) – removal, overhaul and refitting

Removal

1 The brake vacuum pump is driven from the exhaust camshaft, and is mounted on the transmission end of the engine.
2 Remove the engine top cover, which is secured by three bolts.
3 Remove a total of five screws securing the air intake duct (two to the inlet manifold, and three to the bonnet lock platform). Release and lift out the air intake duct.
4 Move the injector wiring harness clear of the vacuum pump, releasing any clips or cable-ties as necessary.
5 Release the spring clip, and disconnect the vacuum supply hose from the pump **(see illustration)**.
6 Unscrew the pump's two mounting bolts, and discard them – new ones should be used when refitting.
7 Withdraw the pump from the engine, noting how its drivegear engages with the end of the camshaft. Recover the pump's O-ring

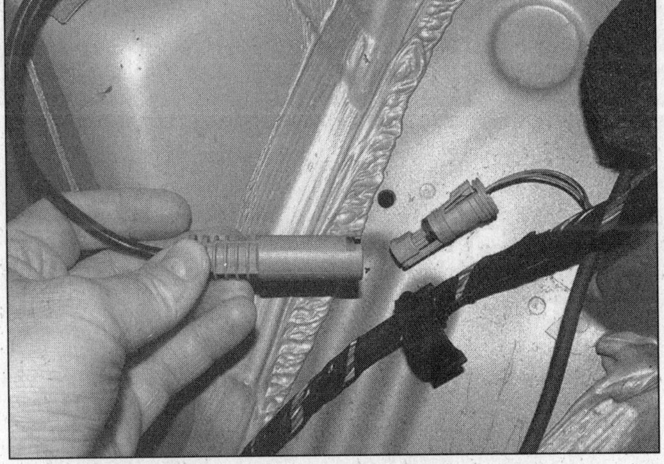

20.19b . . . then separate it and feed the wiring through

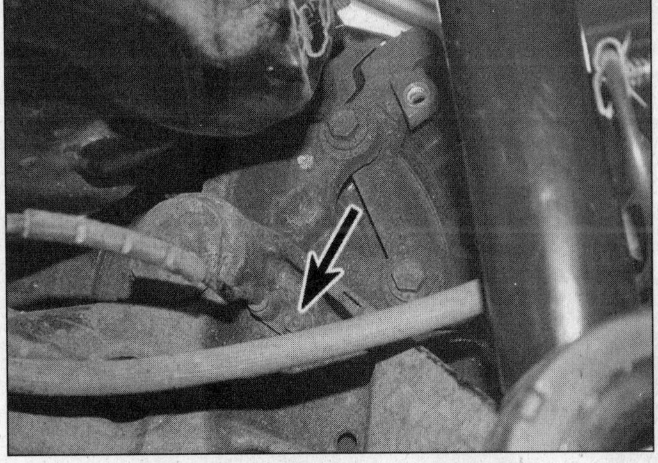

20.21 Rear wheel sensor mounting bolt

21.5 Release the clip and disconnect the vacuum hose from the pump

21.7 Recover the O-ring seal and discard it – use a new one when refitting

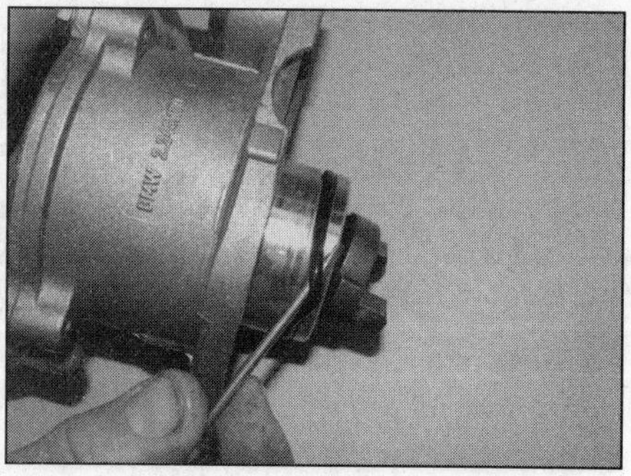

21.10 Note how the vacuum pump drive engages with the camshaft

– a new one will be needed for refitting **(see illustration)**.

Overhaul

8 If the pump is faulty, a complete new unit must be fitted. At the time of writing, no overhaul kits were available.

Refitting

9 Clean the mating faces of the vacuum pump and engine, then fit a new O-ring to the pump.

10 Offer the pump into position, turning the pump drivegear to align with the end of the camshaft **(see illustration)**.

11 Insert the two new mounting bolts, and tighten them to the specified torque.

12 Reconnect the vacuum hose, and secure with the hose clip.

13 Refit the air intake duct and engine top cover to complete. Test the operation of the servo as described in Section 12.

Chapter 10
Suspension and steering

Contents

Degrees of difficulty

Easy, suitable for novice with little experience	**Fairly easy,** suitable for beginner with some experience	**Fairly difficult,** suitable for competent DIY mechanic	**Difficult,** suitable for experienced DIY mechanic	**Very difficult,** suitable for expert DIY or professional

Specifications

Front suspension

Type	Independent, with MacPherson struts incorporating coil springs and telescopic shock absorbers, with rear-facing L-shaped lower arms and subframe. Anti-roll bar fitted to all models

Rear suspension

Type	Independent 'Z-axle', with trailing arms, lower arms and upper control arms, coil springs and shock absorbers, subframe-mounted. Self-levelling electro-pneumatic shock absorbers available as an option. Anti-roll bar fitted to most models

Steering

Type	Rack-and-pinion. Power assistance standard on all models

Wheel alignment and steering angles

Front wheel:	
Camber angle (unladen)	-0.33 ± 0.75°
Castor angle (unladen)	3.45 ± 1.0°
Kingpin inclination	12.55°
Toe setting (total, unladen)	0.17 ± 0.25°
Rear wheel:	
Camber angle (unladen)	-0.52 ± 0.75°
Toe setting (total, unladen)	0.37 ± 0.25°

Roadwheels

Types	Pressed-steel or aluminium alloy
Sizes	6J x 15, 6.5J x 15, 6.5J x 16, 7J x 17, 7.5J x 18

Tyres

Size	From 195/65 R 15 to 225/45 ZR 18, depending on model and wheel type*
Pressures	See *Weekly checks*

** Consult your handbook or a suitable tyre dealer for the correct size for your car*

Torque wrench settings

	Nm	lbf ft
Front suspension		
Anti-roll bar connecting link nuts	60	44
Anti-roll bar mounting clamp bolts**	25	18
Lower arm bush housing-to-subframe bolts*	150	111
Lower arm lower balljoint nut	45	33
Lower arm subframe balljoint nut	75	55
Strut mounting-to-body nuts	22	16
Strut piston rod nut*	30	22
Strut-to-hub carrier pinch-bolt	100	74
Subframe brace-to-body bolts*	23	17
Subframe-to-body bolts*	115	85
Rear suspension		
Anti-roll bar connecting link nuts and bolts	60	44
Anti-roll bar mounting clamp bolts	25	18
Hub nut*	210	155
Lower arm-to-subframe (inboard) bolt	120	89
Lower arm-to-trailing arm nut and bolt	100	74
Shock absorber lower mounting bolt	155	114
Shock absorber upper mounting-to-body nuts	22	16
Shock absorber piston rod locknut*	30	22
Subframe-to-body bolts	100	74
Trailing arm bracket and upper mounting bolts	100	74
Upper arm-to-subframe (inboard) bolt	120	89
Upper arm-to-trailing arm nut and bolt	100	74
Steering		
Power steering pressure sensor	24	18
Power steering pump banjo bolt	28	21
Power steering pump bracket bolts (1.8 litre engines)	45	33
Power steering pump mounting bolts:		
M6 bolts	9	7
M8 bolts	25	18
Power steering pump pipe flange bolts (diesel engines)	10	7
Power steering pump pulley bolts	9	7
Steering column lower pinch-bolt/locknut*	30	22
Steering column support bracket bolts	18	13
Steering rack fluid unions	25	18
Steering rack-to-subframe bolts	45	33
Steering wheel bolt	65	48
Track rod balljoint nut*	30	22
Track rod locknut	50	37
Driveshafts		
Driveshaft nut*	350	258
Roadwheels		
Roadwheel bolts	125	92

** Use new nuts/bolts*

*** Check torque setting twice – see text*

1 General information

The independent front suspension is of the MacPherson strut type, incorporating coil springs and integral telescopic shock absorbers. The MacPherson struts are located into the hub carriers, and secured using a pinch-bolt. The L-shaped forged aluminium lower arms are attached to the subframe at the rear by a cast housing and compliance bush, and pivot on inner balljoints which are also subframe-mounted. At their outer ends, another balljoint attaches the arms to the hub carriers, which house the wheel bearings and carry the brake disc/caliper assemblies. A front anti-roll bar is fitted to all models – this is mounted to the subframe and attached to the strut lower spring plates by connecting links.

The rear suspension is of the fully-independent type, derived from a BMW design known as the 'Z-axle'. This is a multi-link design, mounted on a subframe attached to the rear floor using rubber mountings designed to allow a degree of 'rear steering' effect. The trailing arms are mounted to the body using brackets which allow for rear toe adjustment – the compliance bushes used in the brackets also control the 'rear steering' effect. The brake calipers and hubs are mounted on the trailing arm. The rear shock absorbers are also attached to the trailing arms at the bottom, with mountings to the body at the top. The lower arm is attached to the subframe and trailing arm, with pivot bushes either end. The upper arm is similarly attached, but also incorporates the coil spring lower seat – the spring upper seat is attached to the rear floor. The rear anti-roll bar is mounted on the subframe, with links connecting the bar ends to the suspension upper arms. Despite its complexity, the Z-axle is compact, and gives minimal intrusion into cabin and boot space.

The steering column is connected to the steering rack by an intermediate shaft, which incorporates a universal joint.

The steering rack is mounted onto the front subframe, and is connected by two track rods, with balljoints at their outer ends, to the steering arms projecting forwards from the hub carriers. The track rod ends are threaded, to facilitate adjustment.

Power-assisted steering is fitted as standard to all models. The hydraulic steering system is powered by a belt-driven pump, which is driven off the crankshaft pulley.

2 Front hub carrier – removal and refitting

Removal

1 Slacken the wheel bolts. If it is possible to access the driveshaft nut with the wheel on (by removing the wheel trim or alloy wheel centre cap), it is preferable to loosen the nut with the car resting on its wheels. Use a hammer and chisel to knock back the staking (depression) in the driveshaft nut's outer collar. Loosen but do not remove the nut (32 mm on our car).

Warning: The driveshaft nut is done up extremely tight, and considerable effort will be required to loosen it. Do not use poor-quality, badly-fitting tools for this task, due to the risk of personal injury.

2 Jack up the front of the car and support it on axle stands (see *Jacking and vehicle support*). Remove the front wheel.

3 Unclip the ABS and brake pad wear sensor wiring, and the brake hose, from the support clip on the suspension strut. The brake hose is retained by a metal clip, which should be lifted out using pliers **(see illustration)**.

4 Remove the front brake disc and ABS wheel sensor as described in Chapter 9.

5 Loosen the track rod end balljoint nut, unscrewing it almost to the end of its threads (if the nut will not unscrew, hold the balljoint stud on top using an Allen key). Use a balljoint separator tool to free the balljoint, then unscrew the nut completely, and disconnect the track rod from the hub carrier **(see illustrations)**. Note that a new balljoint nut will be needed for refitting.

6 Unscrew the nut from the lower balljoint bolt, then tap out the bolt and remove it **(see illustration)**.

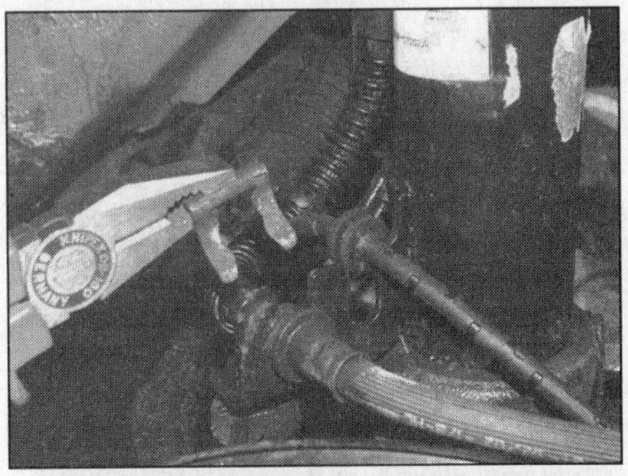

2.3 Remove the brake hose clip, and release the wiring from the strut

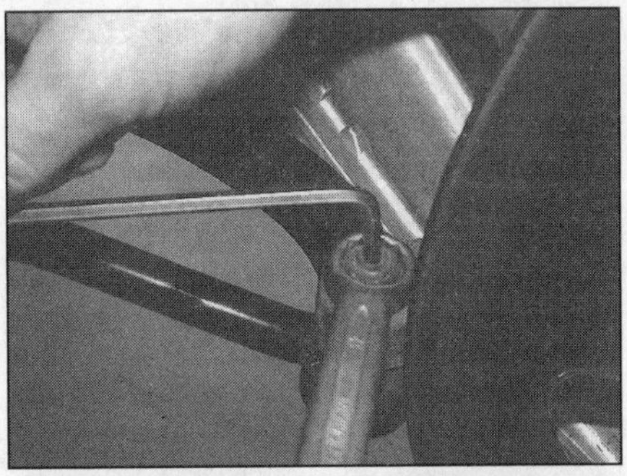

2.5a Unscrew the track rod balljoint nut, holding the stud if necessary . . .

2.5b . . . then use a balljoint splitter . . .

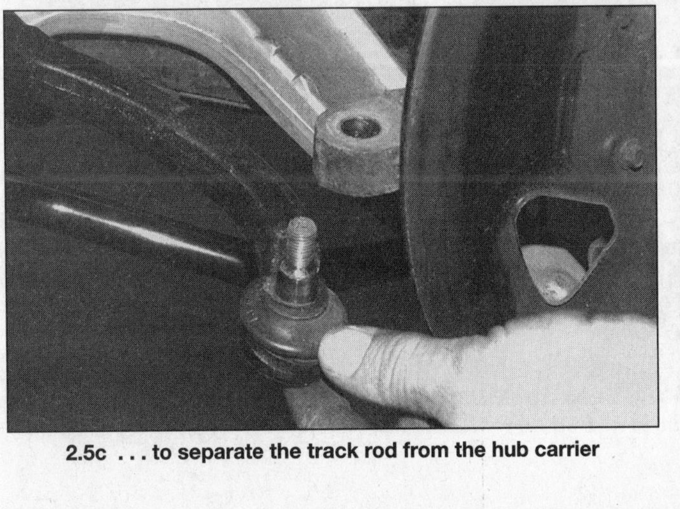

2.5c . . . to separate the track rod from the hub carrier

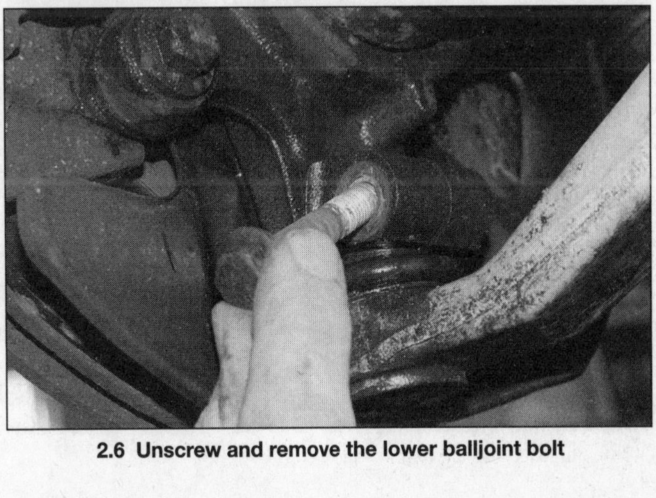

2.6 Unscrew and remove the lower balljoint bolt

2.7a Lever or pull the lower arm downwards . . .

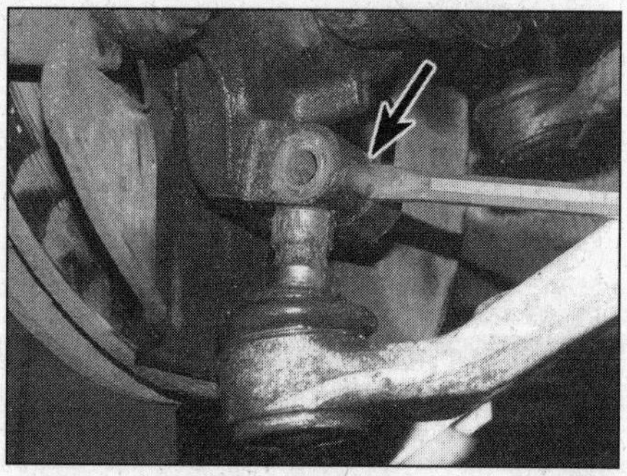

2.7b . . . and use a tapered punch to open the balljoint 'jaws'

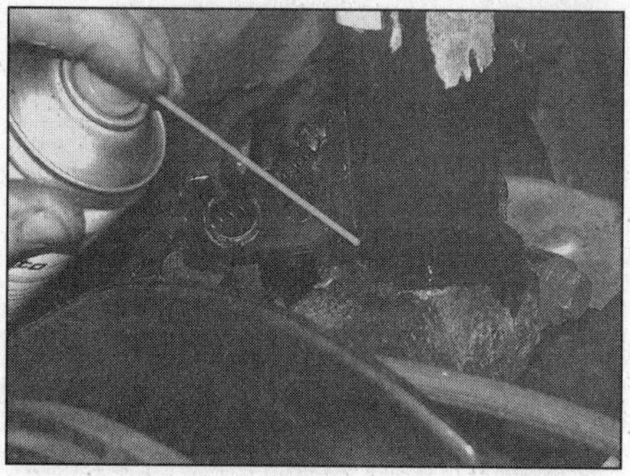

2.8 Apply penetrating spray to the top of the hub carrier

7 The lower balljoint must now be separated, by pulling the lower arm downwards. This may prove difficult, due to corrosion between the balljoint and the hub. Apply plenty of penetrating spray to begin with. Tap in a tapered punch (or use a large screwdriver) between the hub carrier 'jaws' to open them slightly, then lever down the suspension arm **(see illustrations)**.

8 At the top of the hub carrier, apply penetrating spray (such as WD-40) to the joint between the hub and the base of the strut **(see illustration)**.

9 Unscrew and remove the pinch-bolt from the base of the strut, noting which way round it is fitted **(see illustration)**. To ease removal, insert a large screwdriver into the slot on the back of the hub carrier and slightly spread the hub carrier clamp. Take care to spread the carrier clamp only as much as absolutely necessary, as excessive force will cause damage.

10 Using a hammer and block of wood if necessary, tap the hub downwards to separate it from the base of the strut **(see illustration)**.

11 The splined end of the driveshaft now has to be released from its location in the hub, and it's possible that the splines will be very tight (corrosion may even be a factor, if the driveshaft has not been disturbed for some time). Tap the end of the shaft with a plastic or hide mallet. If an ordinary hammer is used, place a small piece of wood over the end of the driveshaft – in addition to the loosened driveshaft nut, this will protect the threads from damage.

12 Pull the disc/hub outwards, and turn it to allow the driveshaft to be withdrawn through the hub **(see illustration)**. It's helpful to have an assistant on hand here, to pull the hub outwards, while you slide out the driveshaft.

13 With the driveshaft removed, take the hub carrier assembly off the car **(see illustration)**.

Refitting

14 Refitting is a reversal of removal, noting the following points:

a) *When offering the hub back up to the base of the strut, align the locating flange on the back of the strut with the slot in the top of the hub* ***(see illustration)****.*
b) *Lubricate the driveshaft splines with a little grease before inserting into the hub.*
c) *Use a new driveshaft nut, and a new track rod balljoint nut. Stake the driveshaft nut collar into the groove once it has been tightened.*
d) *Tighten all nuts/bolts to the specified torque, but delay tightening the driveshaft nut fully until the car it back on the ground.*
e) *Ensure that the brake hose and ABS/pad sensor wiring are routed correctly, and clipped into their respective brackets securely.*
f) *On completion, if new components have been fitted, it is advisable to have the wheel alignment checked.*

3 Front wheel bearings – checking, removal and refitting

Note: *The bearing is a sealed, pre-adjusted and pre-lubricated, double-row roller type, and is intended to last the car's entire service life without maintenance or attention. Do not attempt to remove the bearing unless absolutely necessary, as it will be damaged*

2.9 Unscrew and remove the strut-to-hub carrier pinch-bolt

2.10 Tap the hub carrier down off the base of the strut

2.12 Withdraw the driveshaft from the hub

2.13 Take off the hub carrier assembly

2.14 Align the strut flange with the hub carrier slot

3.6a By fitting a large bolt and washer, and using a large hammer . . .

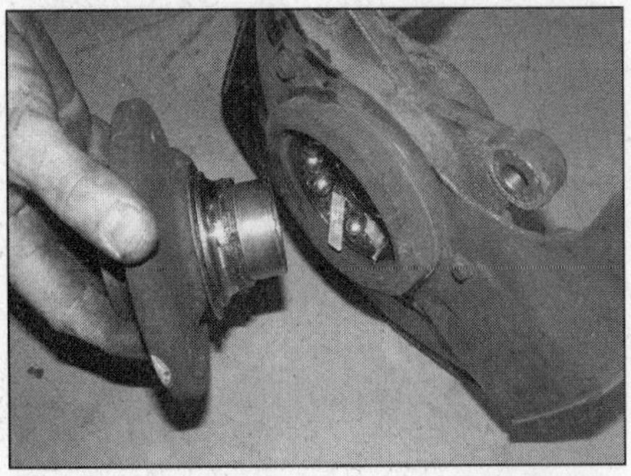
3.6b . . . we were able to drive out the hub flange

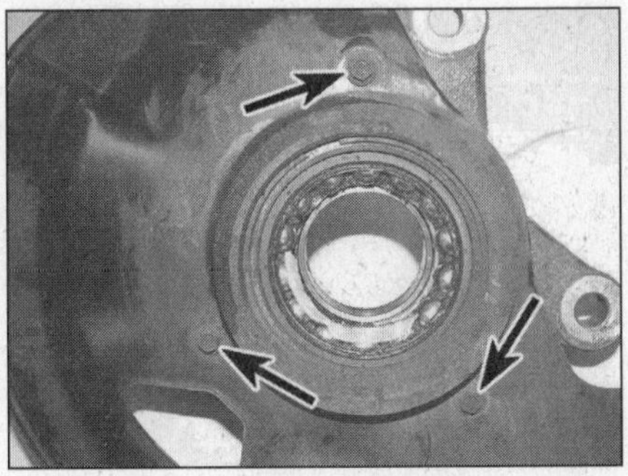
3.7a Remove the three bolts . . .

during the removal operation. Never overtighten the driveshaft nut in an attempt to 'adjust' the bearing.

Note: *A press will be required to dismantle and rebuild the assembly; if such a tool is not available, a large bench vice, big nuts/bolts and spacers (such as large sockets) will serve as an adequate substitute. A punch or chisel will also be needed to remove the bearing inner race from the hub flange.*

Checking

1 Wear in the front hub bearings can be checked for as described in Chapter 1A or 1B. However, the most common first symptom of bearing wear is a rumbling noise, noted at a particular road speed, or when the offending wheel is loaded-up during cornering. In this case, besides rocking the wheel, spin it and listen carefully, to distinguish between the sound of the brake pads rubbing the disc, and the rumble of bearing wear. Compare the sound with the other front wheel to confirm.

2 Wheel bearings do not have to be renewed in pairs. However, if the bearing on one side has worn, it may only be a short while before the other one needs renewal.

Removal

3 With the hub carrier removed as described in Section 2, proceed as follows.

4 Remove the ABS wheel sensor as described in Chapter 9.

5 The hub flange must first be removed from the carrier. It is preferable to use a press to do this, but it is possible to drive out the hub using a metal tube of suitable diameter. Alternatively, a suitable puller can be used.

6 Securely support the hub carrier, on two metal bars for instance, with the inner face uppermost then, using a metal bar or tube of suitable diameter, press or drive out the hub flange – we used a bolt and large washer (the same diameter as the end of the hub's splined end) **(see illustrations)**. Alternatively, use the puller to separate the hub flange from the bearing. Note that the bearing inner race will remain on the hub.

7 Remove the brake disc splash shield, which is secured by three bolts **(see illustrations)**.

8 The bearing inner race left on the hub flange must now be removed. To do this, grip the edge of the flange in a vice, and tap the race off with a chisel. Tap the race at the top and both sides (even turn the flange over in the vice) to stop it jamming as it comes off. Alternatively, use a knife-edge puller **(see illustrations)**.

9 To remove the bearing itself, the retaining circlip must first be removed, which requires the use of a pair of small flat-bladed screwdrivers – one to hook out the circlip end, and the other to slide the circlip from its groove **(see illustrations)**.

3.7b . . . and take off the brake disc splash shield

3.8a Either tap off the bearing inner race using a chisel . . .

3.8b . . . or use a knife-edge puller

3.8c Removing the bearing inner race

3.9a Using a pair of small screwdrivers . . .

3.9b . . . remove the bearing circlip

3.10a Mount the bearing in a vice, with a nut and threaded bar . . .

3.10b . . . and a number of washers and spacers

3.10c Tighten the nut, and tap with a hammer . . .

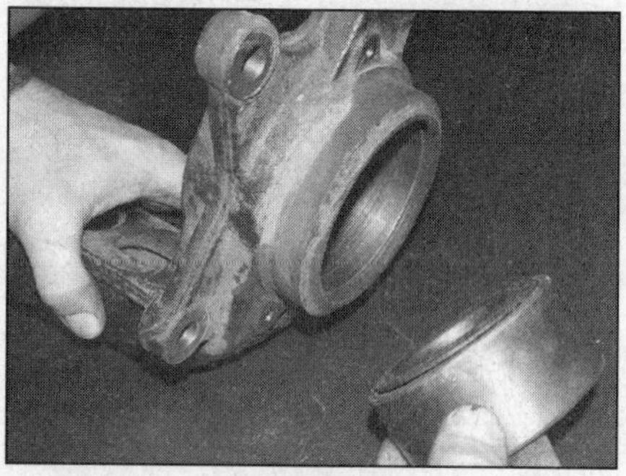

3.10d . . . to withdraw the bearing

10 Now the bearing itself must be removed. After applying a generous amount of spray lubricant, we were able to pull the bearing out, using another old bearing, together with a large nut and bolt, and several washers/spacers. Mount the hub carrier in a vice, then tighten the nut and bolt to apply pressure to the bearing – this, and a few hammer blows, should be enough to get the bearing moving, and extract it **(see illustrations)**.

11 Using emery paper, clean off any burrs or raised edges from the hub flange and hub, which might stop the components going back together. Clean and lightly lubricate the bearing location in the hub **(see illustrations)**.

12 The new bearing has a magnetic reluctor ring fitted to its inner face (for the ABS sensor), and should not be roughly handled during fitting. This means that, unlike a normal bearing, heavy hammer blows cannot be used to drive it into the hub carrier. It also means that the new bearing should be kept clean – do not remove its protective cover until just prior to fitting. Offer the bearing into place with its oil seal (black) side facing inwards **(see illustration)**.

13 As for removal, mount the hub carrier in a sturdy bench vice. First, start the bearing into position by gently tapping it squarely into the hub, using a small hammer and protective wooden block.

14 Using the same nut/bolt and spacers as for removal (or if possible, the old bearing), tighten the nut and bolt to press the bearing into place. Providing the bearing itself is protected, light taps from a hammer will also help install the bearing **(see illustrations)**.

15 The bearing is fully seated when the circlip groove is visible. If a new circlip has been provided with the new bearing, it should be fitted – otherwise, providing it is in good

3.11a Carefully clean the inner surfaces as necessary . . .

3.11b . . . and lubricate prior to fitting the new bearing

3.12 Only remove the bearing's cover just before fitting

3.14a The old bearing can be used as a spacer for fitting . . .

3.14b . . . together with the nut, washers and threaded bar

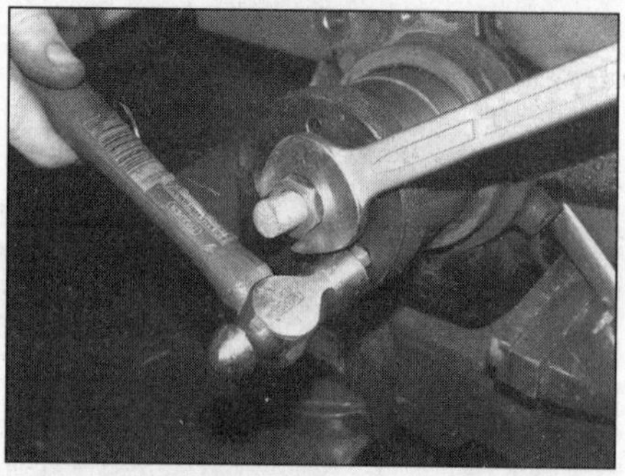

3.14c Tighten the nut, and tap lightly with a hammer

3.15a When the bearing is fully seated, the circlip groove will be visible

3.15b Fitting the new circlip can be achieved by hand

3.16 Refit the splash shield before pressing in the hub flange

condition, the old one may be re-used **(see illustrations)**.

16 Refit the brake disc splash shield, tightening the bolts securely **(see illustration)**.

17 The hub flange can be pressed into the new bearing using a very similar method to the one just used **(see illustrations)**.

18 On completion, refit the hub carrier as described in Section 2.

4 Front suspension strut – removal, overhaul and refitting

Removal

1 Loosen the relevant front wheel bolts, then jack up the front of the car and support it on axle stands *(see Jacking and vehicle support)*. Remove the appropriate roadwheel.

2 Unclip the ABS and brake pad wear sensor wiring, and the brake hose, from the support clip on the suspension strut. The brake hose is retained by a metal clip, which should be lifted out using pliers **(see illustration)**.

3 Unscrew the nut from the lower end of the anti-roll bar drop link, if necessary using an open-ended spanner on the flats provided to prevent the balljoint stud turning as this is done **(see illustration)**.

4 Unscrew the nut from the lower balljoint bolt, then tap out the bolt and remove it **(see illustration)**.

5 The lower balljoint must now be separated, by pulling the lower arm downwards. This may prove difficult, due to corrosion between the balljoint and the hub. Apply plenty of penetrating spray to begin with. Tap in a tapered punch (or use a large screwdriver) between the hub carrier 'jaws' to open them slightly, then lever down the suspension arm **(see illustrations)**.

3.17a Lubricate the hub flange . . .

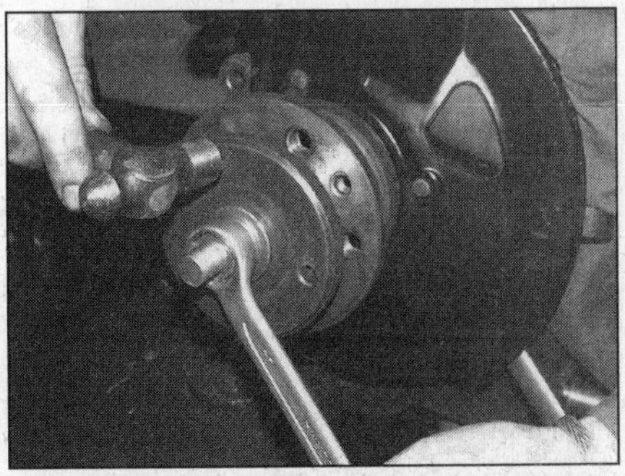
3.17b . . . then press it in place like the bearing

4.2 Remove the brake hose clip, and release the wiring from the strut

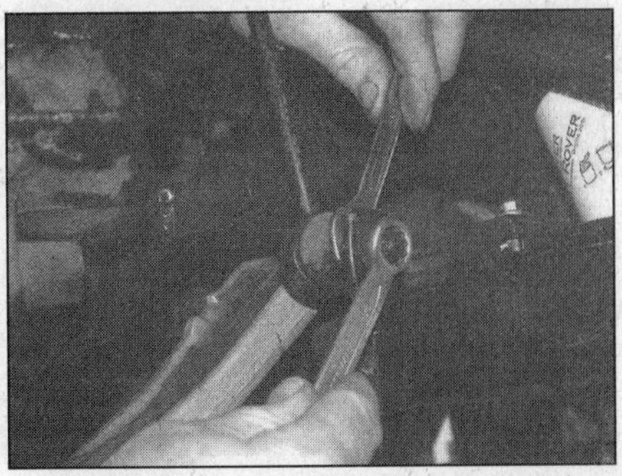
4.3 Unscrew the anti-roll bar drop link lower nut

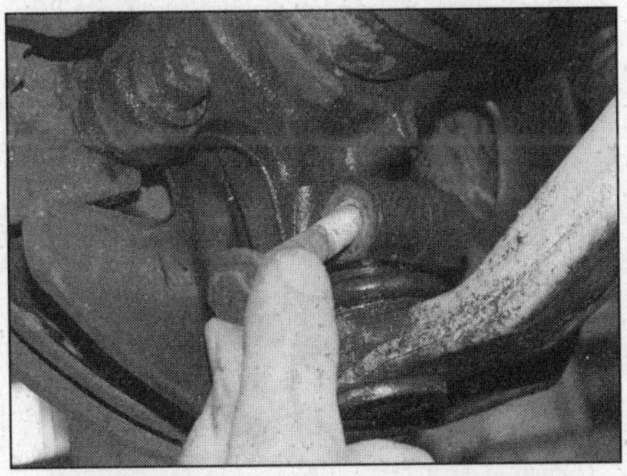
4.4 Unscrew and remove the lower balljoint bolt

4.5a Lever or pull the lower arm downwards . . .

4.5b . . . and use a tapered punch to open the balljoint 'jaws'

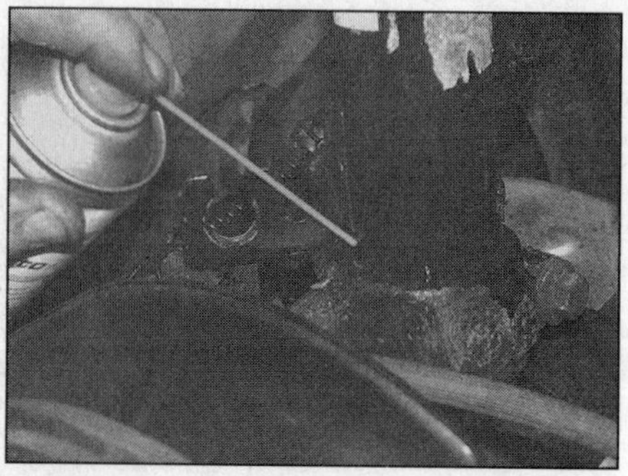

4.6 Apply penetrating spray to the top of the hub carrier

4.7 Unscrew and remove the strut-to-hub carrier pinch-bolt

4.8 Tap the hub carrier down off the base of the strut

6 At the top of the hub carrier, apply penetrating spray (such as WD-40) to the joint between the hub and the base of the strut **(see illustration)**.

7 Unscrew and remove the pinch-bolt from the base of the strut, noting which way round it is fitted **(see illustration)**. To ease removal, insert a large screwdriver into the slot on the back of the hub carrier and slightly spread the hub carrier clamp. Take care to spread the carrier clamp only as much as absolutely necessary, as excessive force will cause damage.

8 Using a hammer and block of wood if necessary, tap the hub downwards to separate it from the base of the strut **(see illustration)**. Take care to avoid damage to the gaiters for the lower balljoint and driveshaft outer CV joint as the hub is lowered.

9 Have an assistant support the strut from below, then unscrew and remove the three strut upper nuts – do not loosen the centre nut at this stage. Lower the strut assembly out from under the wheel arch **(see illustrations)**.

10 While the strut is removed, lift the hub assembly back onto the lower balljoint for support.

Overhaul

Warning: Before attempting to dismantle the front suspension strut, a suitable tool to hold the coil spring in compression must be obtained. Adjustable coil spring compressors are readily available, and are recommended for this operation. Any attempt to dismantle the strut without such a tool is likely to result in damage or personal injury.

11 With the strut removed from the car, clean away all external dirt. Unscrew the nut securing the anti-roll bar connecting link to the spring lower seat, and remove the link **(see illustrations)**.

12 Fit the spring compressors, and compress the coil spring until all tension is relieved from the upper spring seat – for safety, this is best done with the strut mounted in a vice **(see illustration)**.

13 Slacken the piston nut whilst retaining the strut piston with an Allen key **(see illustration)**. Note that a new piston rod nut must be used when reassembling.

14 Remove the nut and washer, followed

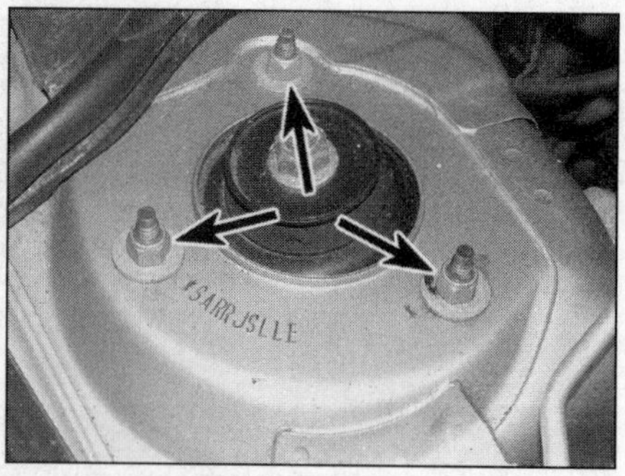

4.9a Remove the three strut upper mounting nuts . . .

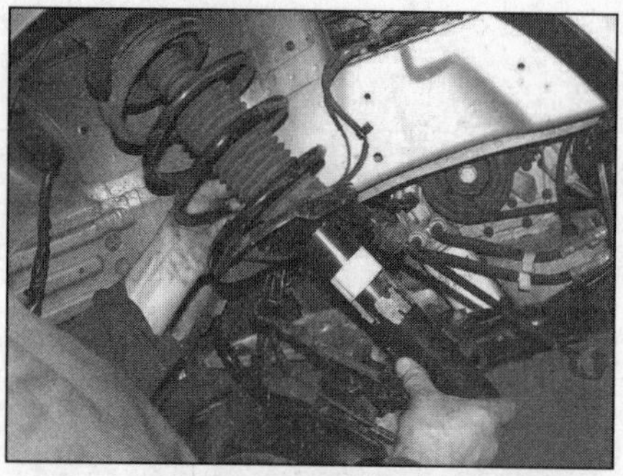

4.9b . . . then lower the strut out into the wheel arch

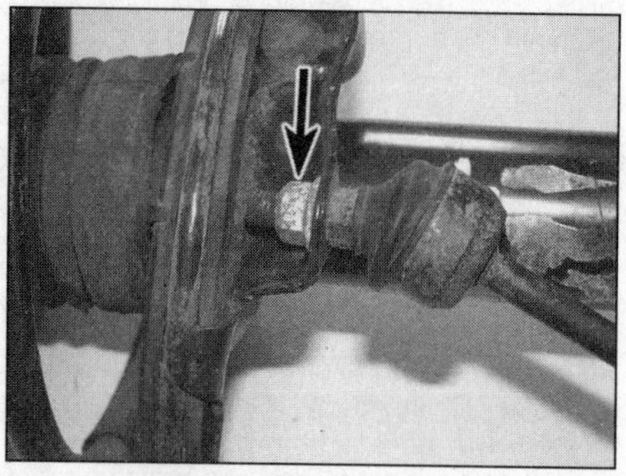

4.11a Unscrew the upper nut . . .

4.11b . . . and remove the anti-roll bar drop link from the strut

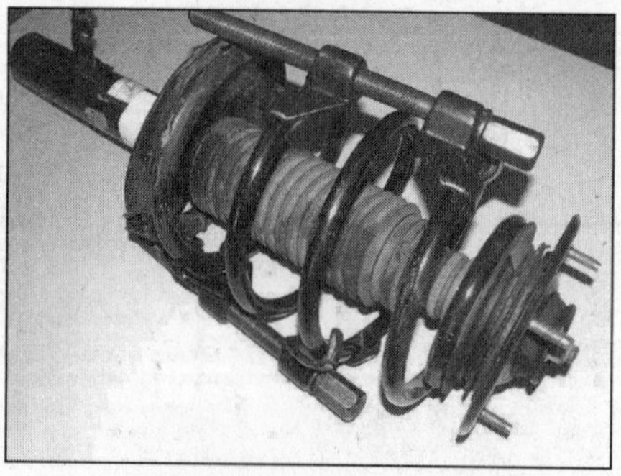

4.12 Compress the spring until pressure is released from the top seat

4.13 Use an Allen key to hold the strut piston while the nut is loosened

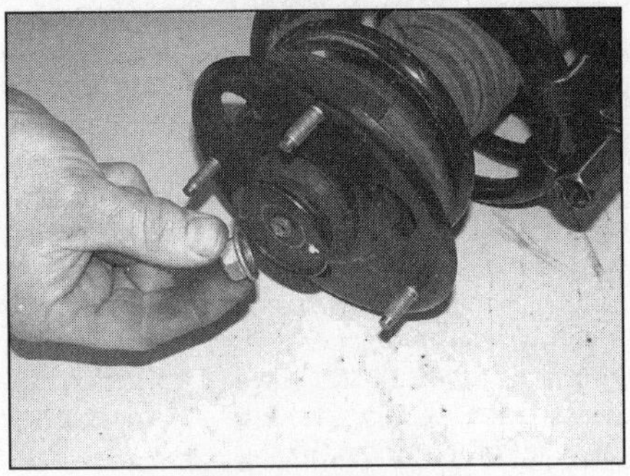

4.14a Remove the top nut . . .

4.14b . . . then the washer . . .

4.14c . . . top mounting plate . . .

4.14d . . . upper spring seat . . .

4.14e . . . and the compressed spring

by the top mounting plate/bearing, upper spring seat and the compressed spring **(see illustrations)**.

15 Lift off the bump stop washer, bump stop rubber and the gaiter, which has a securing clip at its base **(see illustrations)**.

16 With the strut assembly now completely dismantled, examine all the components for wear, damage or deformation, and check the upper mounting bearing for smoothness of operation.

17 Examine the strut for signs of fluid leakage. Check the strut piston for signs of pitting along its entire length, and check the strut body for signs of damage. While holding it in an upright position, test the operation of the strut by moving the piston up-and-down. Due to the design of the shock absorber, it will not be possible to move the piston through a full stroke by hand. However, the resistance felt should be smooth. If the resistance is jerky, or uneven, or if there is any visible sign of wear or damage to the strut, renewal is necessary.

18 If any doubt exists about the condition of the coil spring, carefully remove the spring compressors, and check the spring for distortion and signs of cracking. Renew the spring if it is damaged or distorted, or if there is any doubt as to its condition.

19 Inspect all other components for damage or deterioration, and renew any that are suspect.

20 Refit the anti-roll bar link to the spring lower seat, and tighten the nut to the specified torque, holding the link's ball-stud using an open-ended spanner on the flats provided.

21 Slide on the bump stop and gaiter onto the strut piston, followed by the bump stop washer.

22 Fit the coil spring onto the strut, making sure the spring end is correctly located.

23 Fit the spring upper seat, bearing, and top mounting plate. Ensure that the spring end is against the seat stop.

24 Fit the washer and new piston rod nut, then tighten it to the specified torque while holding the piston rod with an Allen key. A special 'cut-away' socket is available from good tool retailers that allows an Allen key to be inserted into the top of the piston rod whilst the torque wrench is fitted.

25 Ensure the spring ends and seats are correctly located, then carefully release the compressor and remove it from the strut.

Refitting

26 Refitting is a reversal of removal, noting the following points:

a) *Lightly lubricate the base of the strut where it enters the top of the hub carrier.*
b) *When offering the base of the strut into the hub, align the locating flange on the back of the strut with the slot in the top of the hub* ***(see illustration)****.*
c) *Tighten all nuts/bolts to the specified torque.*

5 Front lower arm – removal, overhaul and refitting

Removal

1 Loosen the relevant front wheel bolts. Chock the rear wheels, firmly apply the handbrake, then jack up the front of the car and support on axle stands (see *Jacking and*

4.15a Remove the bump stop washer . . .

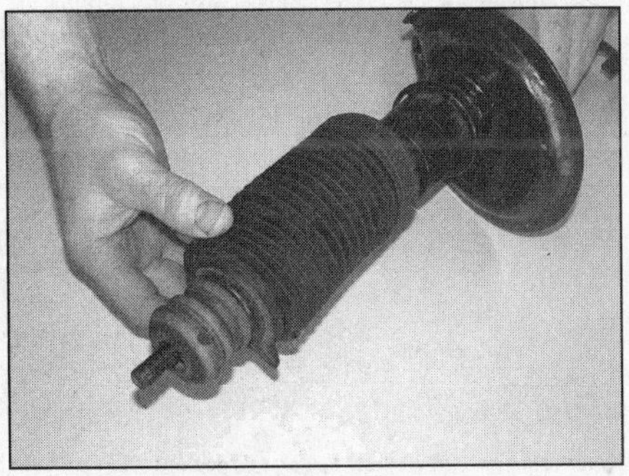

4.15b . . . followed by the bump stop rubber and gaiter

4.26 Align the strut flange with the hub carrier slot

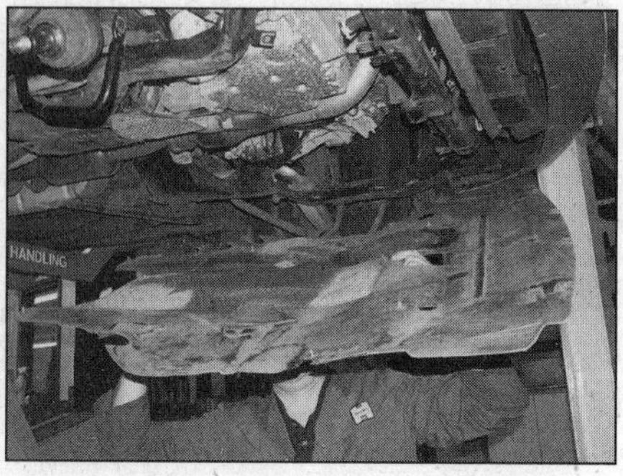

5.2 Removing the engine undertray

vehicle support). Remove the appropriate front roadwheel.

2 Remove the engine undertray, which is secured by a number of quick-release screw fasteners **(see illustration)**.

3 Unscrew the lower nut on the anti-roll bar connecting link, if necessary holding the ball-stud still using a spanner on the flats provided **(see illustration)**. Disconnect the link from the anti-roll bar.

4 On the side concerned, unscrew the two bolts securing the anti-roll bar mounting clamp to the subframe, and remove it. Access to the bolts is extremely limited, but the clamp has to be moved to gain access to the lower arm's rear mounting bolts **(see illustrations)**.

5 Unscrew the nut from the lower balljoint bolt, then tap out the bolt and remove it **(see illustration 4.4)**.

6 The lower balljoint must now be separated, by pulling the lower arm downwards. This

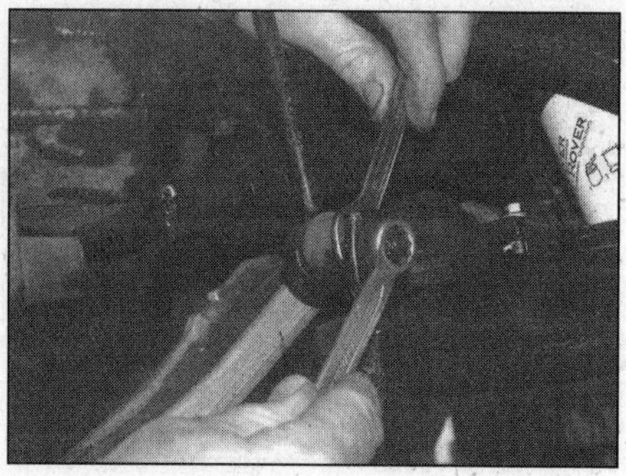

5.3 Unscrew the anti-roll bar drop link lower nut

may prove difficult, due to corrosion between the balljoint and the hub. Apply plenty of penetrating spray to begin with. Tap in a tapered punch (or use a large screwdriver) between the hub carrier 'jaws' to open them slightly, then lever down the suspension arm **(see illustrations 4.5a and 4.5b)**.

7 Move the anti-roll bar end to one side, for access to the two bolts securing the lower arm's rear bush housing to the subframe. Unscrew the bolts and separate the housing from the subframe – discard the bolts, as new ones must be used when refitting.

8 Unscrew the lower arm's balljoint nut underneath the subframe. Release the balljoint taper from the subframe mounting – if it is tight, temporarily refit the nut, and use a hammer and block of wood to free it. Remove the lower arm from under the car **(see illustrations)**.

Overhaul

9 Thoroughly clean the lower arm and the area around the arm mountings, removing all traces of dirt and underseal if necessary, then check carefully for cracks, distortion or any other signs of wear or damage, paying particular attention to the mounting bushes and balljoints. At the time of writing, only the bush is available separately. If either balljoint requires renewal, the lower arm should be renewed. Check with your MG Rover parts supplier or motor factors.

10 Renewal of the lower arm bush requires either a press, or the use of a bush/bearing puller, and the new bush must be aligned with the marks on the bush housing when refitting. Check parts availability and prices before removing the old bush, as it may be preferable to renew the lower arm complete.

11 If the outer balljoint gaiter has been damaged, it is possible that gaiter repair kits (consisting of the gaiter and two spring clips) will be available. Fitting is a fiddly operation, however. If the gaiter has been damaged for a long while, the balljoint may have suffered damage, meaning a new lower arm will still be needed.

Refitting

12 Offer in the lower arm, and loosely fit the two new bush housing bolts, tightening by hand only at this stage.

13 Fit the subframe balljoint nut, and tighten it to the specified torque. If necessary, hold the balljoint stud with an Allen key to stop it turning as the nut is tightened.

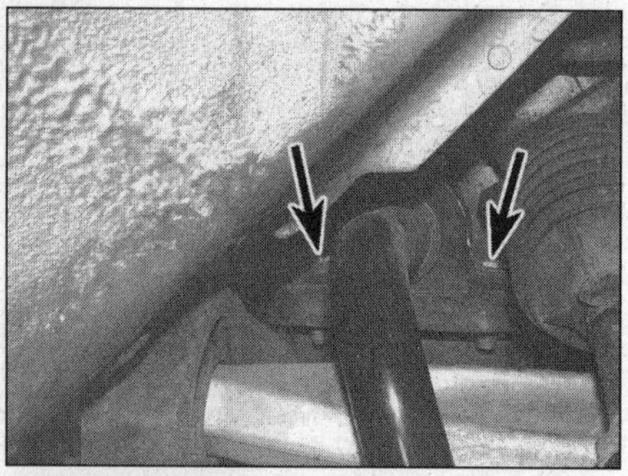

5.4a Anti-roll bar clamp bolts (arrowed)

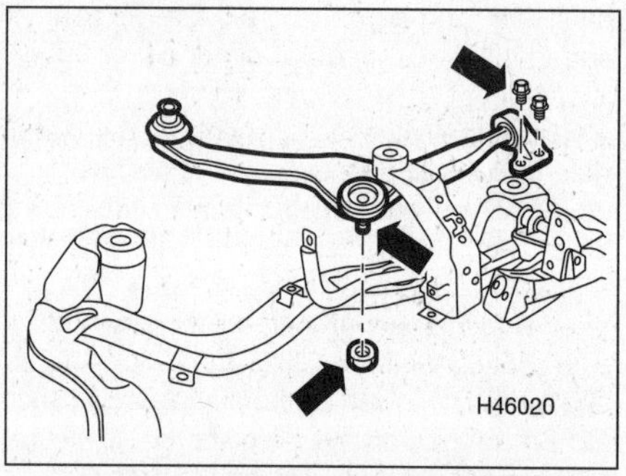

5.4b Front lower arm – rear bush housing bolts and inner balljoint nut

5.8a Holding the balljoint stud with an Allen key if necessary . . .

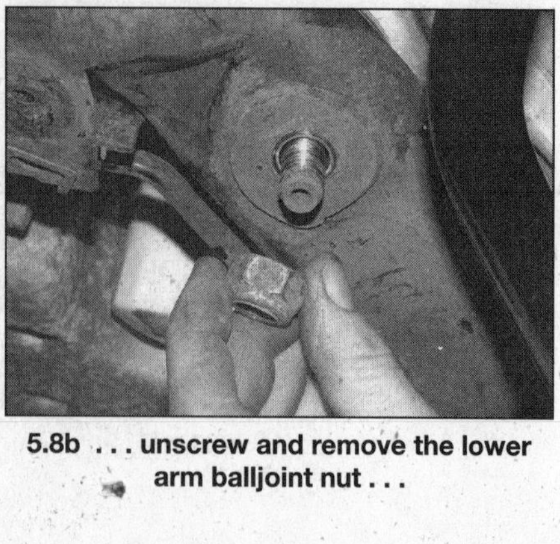

5.8b . . . unscrew and remove the lower arm balljoint nut . . .

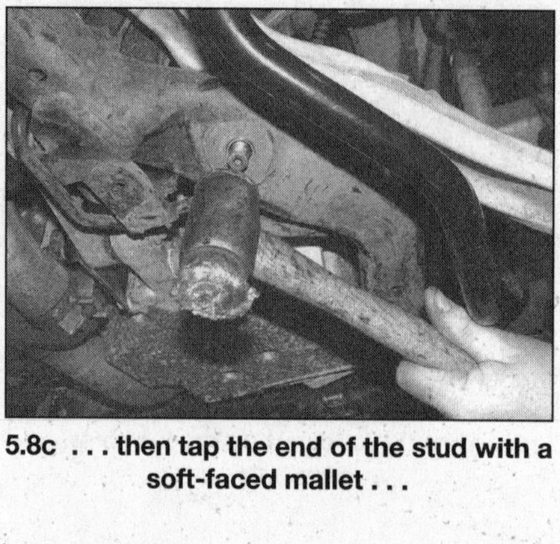

5.8c . . . then tap the end of the stud with a soft-faced mallet . . .

5.8d . . . to release the balljoint and remove the arm

14 Tighten the bush housing bolts to the specified torque.

15 Fit the anti-roll bar clamp, then fit the bolts and tighten to the specified torque. Ensure the two bolts are correctly tightened by checking them with the torque wrench again, set to the same torque as before.

16 Further refitting is a reversal of removal, noting the following points:

a) Tighten all nuts/bolts to the specified torque.

b) MG Rover recommend fitting the anti-roll bar lower link nuts hand-tight only, then tightening them to the specified torque once the car is resting on its wheels.

c) On completion, if new components have been fitted, it is advisable to have the wheel alignment checked.

6 Front anti-roll bar – removal and refitting

Removal

1 Loosen the front wheel bolts, then jack up the front of the car, and support it on axle stands (see *Jacking and vehicle support*). Remove the front wheels.

2 Unscrew the retaining nut, and free the connecting link from each end of the anti-roll bar, using a second spanner to counterhold the link balljoint stud **(see illustration 5.3)**.

3 Using the information in Section 8, unbolt and lower the front subframe sufficiently to gain access to the anti-roll bar clamps. It should not be necessary to disconnect the lower arms, however.

4 Unscrew the two bolts from each clamp, then remove the anti-roll bar from the subframe **(see illustration 5.4a)**. Manoeuvre the anti-roll bar out from under the car. Remove the mounting bushes from the bar.

5 Carefully examine the anti-roll bar components for signs of wear, damage or deterioration, paying particular attention to the mounting bushes. Renew worn components as necessary.

Refitting

6 Fit the rubber mounting bushes to the anti-roll bar, noting that no lubricant should be used.

7 Offer the bar into position. Fit the anti-roll bar clamps, then fit the bolts and tighten to the specified torque. Ensure the two bolts on each clamp are correctly tightened by checking them with the torque wrench again, set to the same torque as before.

8 Refit the subframe as described in Section 8.

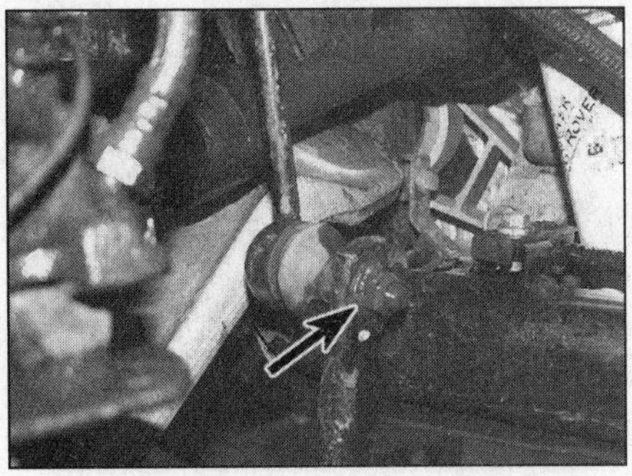

7.3 Anti-roll bar drop link lower nut

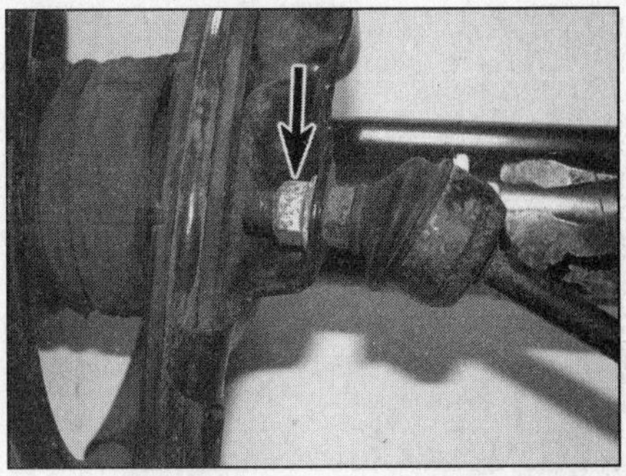

7.4 Unscrew the link upper nut (arrowed) – seen with strut removed

7 Front anti-roll bar connecting link – removal and refitting

1 Wear in the anti-roll bar connecting links (also known as the 'drop links') is typified by a knocking noise over certain types of bump. If the noise is noted on the (unloaded) passenger side of the car when the car is driven solo, this is further evidence of wear in the links. It is recommended that the links are renewed in pairs.

Removal

2 Loosen the relevant front wheel bolts, then jack up the front of the car, and support it on axle stands (see *Jacking and vehicle support*). Remove the appropriate front wheel, and turn the steering onto full lock.

3 Unscrew the retaining nut, and free the connecting link from the end of the anti-roll bar, using a second spanner to counterhold the link balljoint stud **(see illustration)**.

4 Similarly, unscrew the nut at the top of the link which secures it to the strut's spring lower plate – access to this nut is not easy **(see illustration)**. Manoeuvre the link out from under the wheel arch.

5 Check the connecting link balljoints for signs of wear. Check that each balljoint is free to move easily, and that the rubber gaiters are undamaged. If necessary renew the connecting link.

Refitting

6 Refitting is a reverse of the removal sequence. MG Rover recommend fitting the link lower nuts hand-tight only, then tightening them to the specified torque once the car is resting on its wheels.

8 Front subframe – removal and refitting

Removal

1 Loosen the front wheel bolts, then jack up the front of the car, and support it on axle stands (see *Jacking and vehicle support*). Remove the front wheels.

2 Remove the engine undertray, and the front wheel arch liners as described in Chapter 11, Section 22.

3 Remove the exhaust system (or at least lower the front part, where possible) as described in the relevant Part of Chapter 4.

4 Unscrew the retaining nut, and free the connecting link from each end of the anti-roll bar, using a second spanner to counterhold the link balljoint stud.

5 On the driver's side, remove the two bolts securing the power steering fluid pipe brackets to the subframe. At the front, remove the two bolts securing the radiator lower coolant pipe to the subframe **(see illustrations)**.

6 Using the information in the relevant Part of Chapter 2, remove the two through-bolts from the engine lower mounting.

8.5a One of the power steering fluid pipe mounting brackets

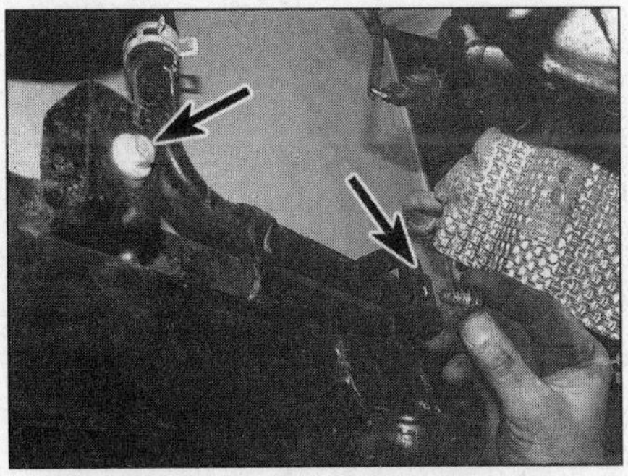

8.5b Remove the two bolts from the radiator lower coolant pipe brackets

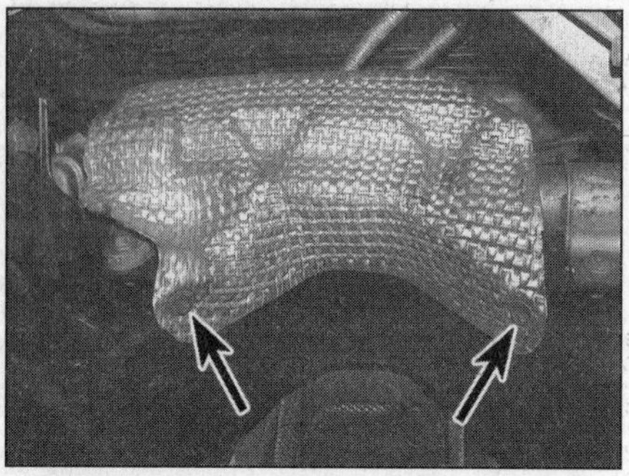

8.7 The steering rack heat shield is secured by two bolts

8.8 Two of the four steering rack mounting bolts

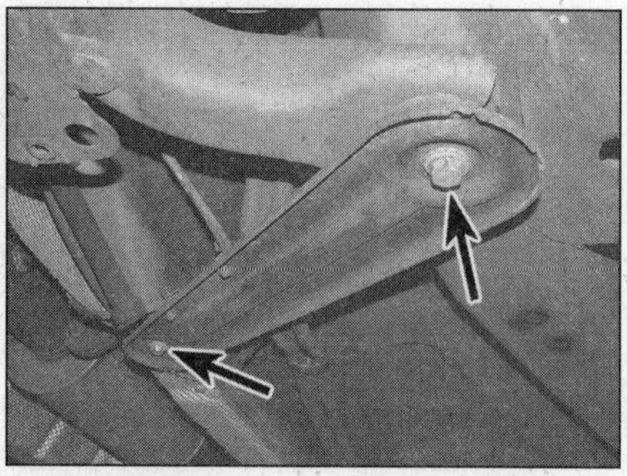

8.13 The subframe braces have a mounting bolt at each end

8.14 One of the subframe mounting bolts

7 Remove the two bolts securing the steering rack heat shield, and remove the shield **(see illustration)**.
8 Unscrew the four bolts securing the steering rack to the subframe, then tie the rack up clear of the subframe **(see illustration)**.
9 Unscrew the nut from each lower arm's lower balljoint bolt, then tap out the bolt and remove it.
10 The lower balljoints must now be separated, by pulling the lower arm downwards. This may prove difficult, due to corrosion between the balljoint and the hub. Apply plenty of penetrating spray to begin with. Tap in a tapered punch (or use a large screwdriver) between the hub carrier 'jaws' to open them slightly, then lever down the suspension arm.
11 Support the subframe from below using at least one substantial jack, and preferably with the help of an assistant.
12 If the existing subframe is being refitted, it may be helpful to make several alignment marks between the subframe and the car body, to make refitting easier. These marks are purely for convenience - it would appear to be impossible to refit the subframe misaligned.
13 Unscrew the two bolts from the two subframe braces **(see illustration)**. Discard the bolts – new ones should be used when refitting.
14 With the subframe supported, progressively unscrew and remove a total of six subframe mounting bolts **(see illustration)**. With the help of an assistant, lower the subframe to the ground. Recover the subframe braces and the four stepped locating washers. The subframe bolts are of different lengths and types, so note their fitted positions – note also that new ones should be obtained for refitting.
15 If a new subframe is being fitted, transfer the lower arms and anti-roll bar to it, using the information in Sections 5 and 6. Also move the engine undertray fixings to the new subframe.

Refitting

16 Refitting is a reversal of removal, noting the following points:

a) Use new subframe and subframe brace bolts. Note that the wider (front) ends of the subframe braces are secured by the rearmost subframe bolts.
b) Tighten all nuts and bolts to the specified torque, where given.
c) MG Rover recommend fitting the anti-roll bar lower link nuts hand-tight only, then tightening them to the specified torque once the car is resting on its wheels.
d) Refit the engine lower mounting as described in the relevant Part of Chapter 2.
e) Refit the exhaust system as described in the relevant Part of Chapter 4.
f) On completion, have the front wheel alignment checked.

9 Rear hub – removal and refitting

Removal

1 Remove the rear brake disc as described in Chapter 9.
2 Carefully prise out the hub centre cap. A new cap should ideally be used when refitting – however, if the old one has not been damaged, it could be re-used.
3 Use a hammer and chisel to knock back the staking (depression) in the hub nut's outer collar **(see illustration)**.
4 Ensure that the rear of the car is securely supported, then slacken the hub nut.

Warning: The hub nut is done up extremely tight, and considerable effort will be required to loosen it. Do not use poor-quality, badly-fitting tools for this task, due to the risk of personal injury.

5 Remove the hub nut and discard it – a new one should be used when refitting. Recover the toothed washer from the stub axle **(see illustration)**.
6 Remove the hub from the stub axle **(see illustration)**. The hub has a magnetic reluctor ring fitted to its inner face (for the ABS sensor), so it should not be roughly handled. It also means that the hub should be kept clean – if

9.3 Knock back the depression in the hub nut's collar

9.5 Unscrew the nut and take off the toothed washer

9.6 Withdraw the hub from the stub axle

a new one is being fitted, do not remove its protective cover until just prior to fitting.

Refitting

7 Clean the stub axle and the hub carrier, then fit the hub carrier, followed by the toothed washer and the new hub nut.

8 Once again check that the car is still securely supported, then tighten the hub nut to the specified torque **(see illustration)**.

9 Use a chisel to stake the hub nut's collar into the groove on the end of the stub axle **(see illustration)**.

10 Fit the hub centre cap, tapping it squarely into place.

11 Refit the rear brake disc as described in Chapter 9.

10 Rear wheel bearings – renewal

The rear wheel bearings are incorporated into the rear hubs, and are not available separately. Refer to Section 9 for rear hub removal and refitting.

11 Rear shock absorber – removal, testing, overhaul and refitting

Removal

1 Remove the boot side trim panels as described in Chapter 11, Section 25, to access the rear shock absorber upper mounting.

2 Loosen relevant the rear wheel bolts. Chock the front wheels, then jack up the rear of the car, and support it on axle stands (see *Jacking and vehicle support*). Remove the appropriate rear wheel.

3 Position a suitable jack (with a block of wood on its head) under the shock absorber lower mounting on the trailing arm. Raise the trailing arm slightly. Do not jack the rear suspension under the upper or lower arms, as damage may be caused.

4 Working in the luggage compartment, unscrew and remove the two shock absorber upper mounting nuts **(see illustrations)**.

5 Under the car, unscrew the shock absorber lower mounting bolt and washer. Withdraw the bolt, and take off the damper weight, noting how it is fitted **(see illustration)**.

9.8 Tighten the hub nut to the specified torque

9.9 Stake the hub nut collar into the stub axle groove

6 Withdraw the shock absorber down into the wheel arch. This may prove difficult, due to the top rubber cover inside the boot catching on the mounting hole. Pull the shock absorber down to release the cover, leaving it behind in the boot – the cover should be refitted before offering the unit back into place **(see illustration)**.

Testing

7 Examine the shock absorber for signs of fluid leakage. Check the piston for signs of pitting along its entire length, and check the body for signs of damage. While holding it in an upright position, test the operation by moving the piston up-and-down. Due to the design of the shock absorber, it will not be possible to move the piston through a full stroke by hand. However, the resistance felt should be smooth. If the resistance is jerky, or uneven, or if there is any visible sign of wear or damage, renewal is necessary.

8 Check the rubber mounting bushes for damage and deterioration. Renew the shock absorber complete if any damage or wear is evident; the mounting bushes are not available separately. Inspect the mounting nuts/bolts for signs of wear or damage, and renew as necessary. Shock absorbers should always be renewed in pairs.

Overhaul

9 If a new shock absorber is being fitted, the old one must be dismantled, and several components transferred to the new unit.

10 If not already done, remove the rubber cover from the top of the shock absorber.

11 Using an Allen key to hold the piston rod against rotation, unscrew and remove the shock absorber piston rod locknut **(see illustration)**. Discard the nut – a new one will be needed when refitting.

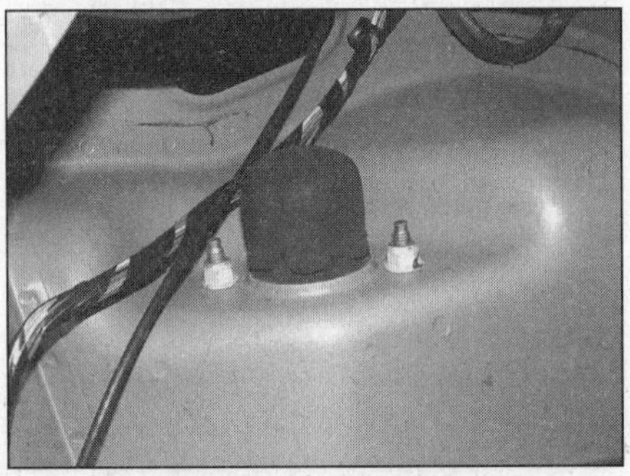

11.4a Rear shock absorber upper mounting nuts on the Saloon . . .

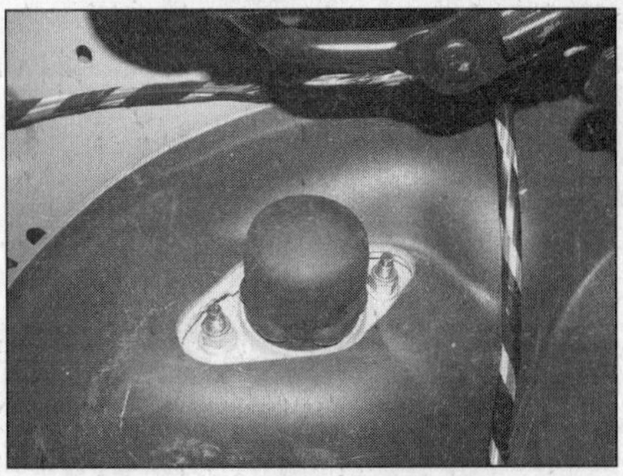

11.4b . . . and on the Tourer

11.5 Unscrew the lower mounting bolt, and take off the damper weight

11.6 Withdraw the shock absorber into the wheel arch

11.11 Hold the piston rod with an Allen key, and unscrew the top nut

12 Remove the upper washer, top mounting plate, bump stop plate, bump stop and gaiter, noting how they are fitted **(see illustration)**. If any of the components are in poor condition, new items should be obtained.

13 Transfer the removed components to the new shock absorber, retaining their fitted sequence.

14 Fit a new piston rod locknut, and tighten it (if possible, to the specified torque) while holding the piston rod with an Allen key. A special 'cut-away' socket is available from good tool retailers that allows an Allen key to be inserted into the top of the piston rod whilst the torque wrench is fitted. Refit the rubber cover to the top mounting on completion.

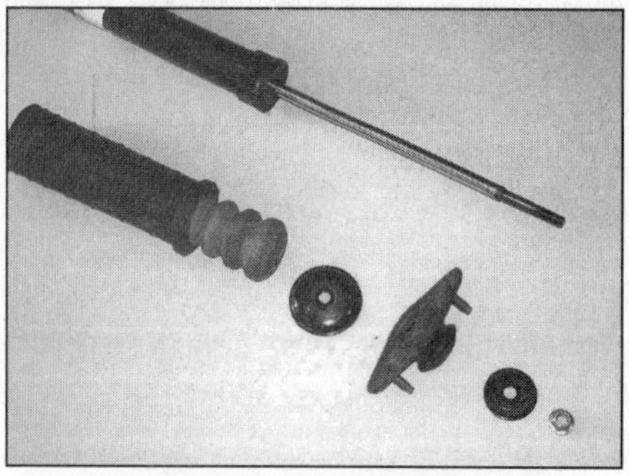

11.12 Dismantle the shock absorber, keeping the parts in fitted order

11.16 Refit the top rubber cover prior to refitting

Refitting

15 Clean the shock absorber upper mounting and body mating surfaces.

16 Offer the shock absorber into position. If the rubber cover came off during removal (or has since been removed), fit it over the top mounting now **(see illustration)**. Fit the upper mounting studs through the two holes in the body, then fit the two upper mounting nuts and tighten to the specified torque.

17 Either extend the shock absorber, or adjust the height of the trailing arm using the jack, until the lower mounting bolt and washer, and the damper weight, can be refitted.

18 Remove the jack from under the trailing arm, then tighten the lower mounting bolt to the specified torque.

19 Refit the roadwheel, then lower the car to the ground, and tighten the wheel bolts to the specified torque.

12 Rear coil spring – removal and refitting

Removal

1 Loosen the rear wheel bolts. Chock the front wheels, then jack up the rear of the car and support it on axle stands (see *Jacking and vehicle support*). Remove both roadwheels.

2 Remove the rear anti-roll bar, where applicable, as described in Section 16.

3 Position a suitable jack (with a block of wood on its head) under the lower bush on the trailing arm. Raise the trailing arm slightly. Do not jack the rear suspension under the upper or lower arms, as damage may be caused.

4 Loosen but do not remove the upper arm's inboard pivot bolt **(see illustration)**.

5 Unscrew and remove the lower arm's inboard pivot bolt, and the shock absorber lower mounting bolt and washer **(see illustration)**.

6 Lower the trailing arm on the jack. To avoid straining the rear brake hose, follow the hose towards the rear hub, and unclip it from the trailing arm **(see illustration)**.

7 Turn the coil spring 90° anti-clockwise to release the bayonet fitting on the base of the spring where it fits into the upper arm, and remove it from under the car **(see illustrations)**.

8 Inspect the spring closely for signs of

12.4 Loosen the upper arm inboard bolt

12.5 Unscrew and remove the lower arm inboard bolt

12.6 Unclip the rear brake hose from the trailing arm

12.7a At the base of the coil spring is a bayonet fitting . . .

12.7b . . . which, when turned through 90°, releases the spring . . .

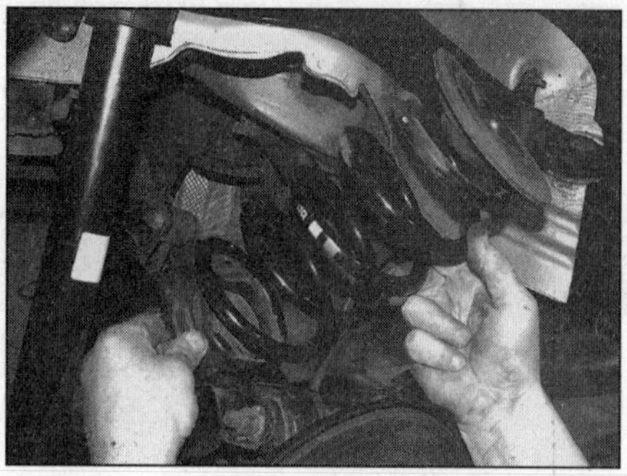

12.7c . . . which can then be removed

damage, such as cracking, and check the spring seats for signs of wear **(see illustration)**. Renew worn components as necessary.

9 If new springs are required, they should ideally be of the same type as originally fitted. Springs can be identified by the colour code painted on them. In addition, a label attached to the fuel tank access cover under the rear seat cushion gives details of the original springs **(see illustration)**.

12.8 Check the spring seats for wear

12.9 A label under the rear seat details the original springs

Refitting

10 Fit the upper and lower spring seats, if removed.

11 Apply a little grease to the spring end coils, then offer the spring into position on the upper arm. The bottom coil of the spring is greater in diameter than the upper coil, to help orientation. Turn the spring 90° clockwise to engage the bayonet fitting. Ensure the cut-outs in the spring seat are aligned with the drainage holes in the upper arm.

12 Raise the trailing arm on the jack, and engage the top end of the spring with the body mounting.

13 Refit the shock absorber lower mounting bolt/washer, hand-tight at this stage.

14 Refitting the lower arm's inboard pivot bolt is less easy, and is definitely a job for two people. The rear hub must be levered outwards, and a sturdy screwdriver will also be needed to align the inboard end of the arm, so that the bolt can be inserted. Once the bolt is pushed or tapped fully home, further alignment will be required before the bolt thread will bite in the captive nut. Do not tighten the bolt fully at this stage.

15 Remove the jack from under the trailing arm.

16 Refit the rear anti-roll bar as described in Section 16, where applicable.

17 Refit the rear wheels, then lower the car to the ground. Tighten the rear wheel bolts to the specified torque.

18 Tighten the upper and lower arm inboard pivot bolts, and the shock absorber lower mounting bolt, to their specified torques.

13 Rear trailing arm – removal and refitting

Removal

1 Remove the rear hub on the side concerned, as described in Section 9.

2 Remove the handbrake shoes as described in Chapter 9.

3 Unscrew the four Allen bolts and remove the backplate from the trailing arm **(see illustration)**.

4 Unscrew the bolt securing the ABS sensor, then withdraw the sensor and move it clear. Unclip the sensor wiring connector, which is clipped to the back of the wheel arch liner.

5 Remove the rear spring on the side concerned, as described in Section 12.

6 Unscrew the nuts and bolts securing the upper and lower arms to the trailing arm **(see illustrations)**.

7 Release the rear brake hose from the trailing arm **(see illustration)**.

8 Mark the trailing arm pivot bush for position to the mountings on the underside of the car – this is essential, to preserve the rear wheel toe setting.

9 Have an assistant support the trailing arm, then unscrew the three upper mounting bolts and lower out the trailing arm **(see illustration)**.

10 If a new arm is being fitted, first note its alignment to the old arm, then unscrew the nut and bolt securing the upper mounting bracket, and transfer it to the new arm. Align the bracket as noted, then fit and tighten the nut and bolt to the specified torque. Also unbolt and transfer the brake hose securing bracket.

11 Thoroughly clean the trailing arm and the area around the arm mountings, taking care not to remove any alignment markings. Check carefully for cracks, distortion or any other

13.3 The brake backplate's four mounting bolts

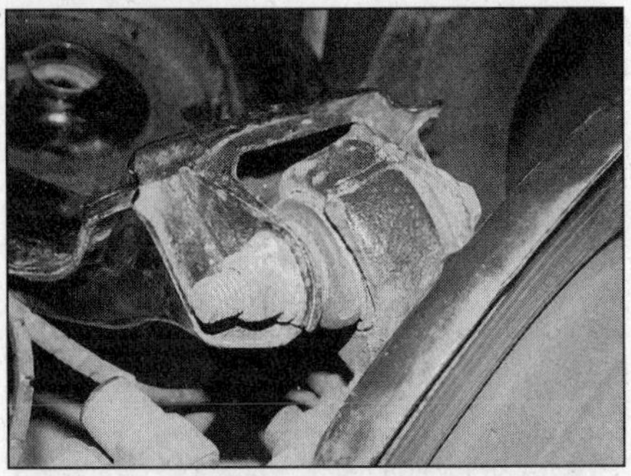

13.6a Unscrew the upper arm-to-trailing arm nut and bolt . . .

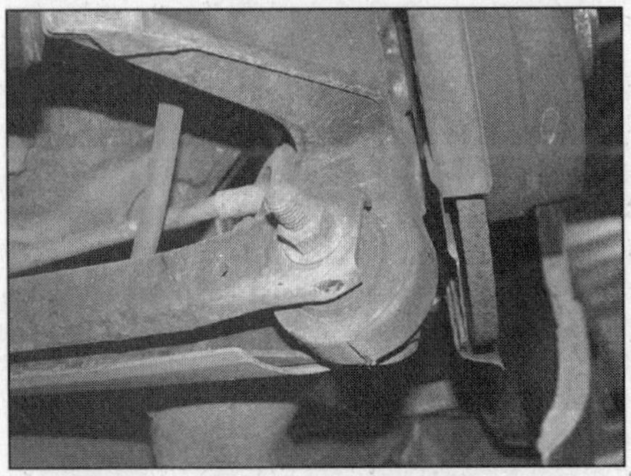

13.6b . . . and the one for the lower arm

13.7 Unclip the rear brake hose from the trailing arm

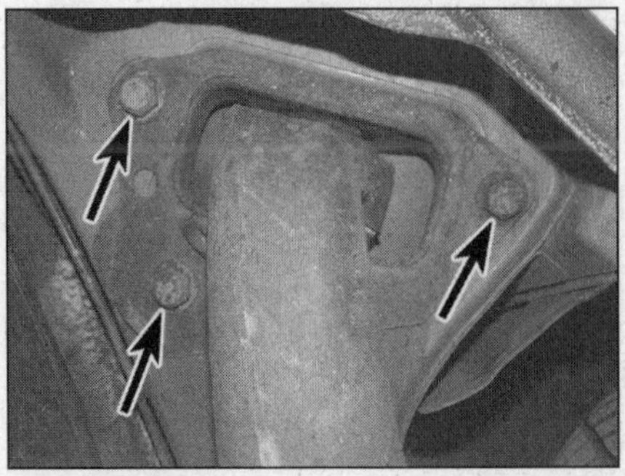

13.9 Trailing arm-to-floor mounting bolts

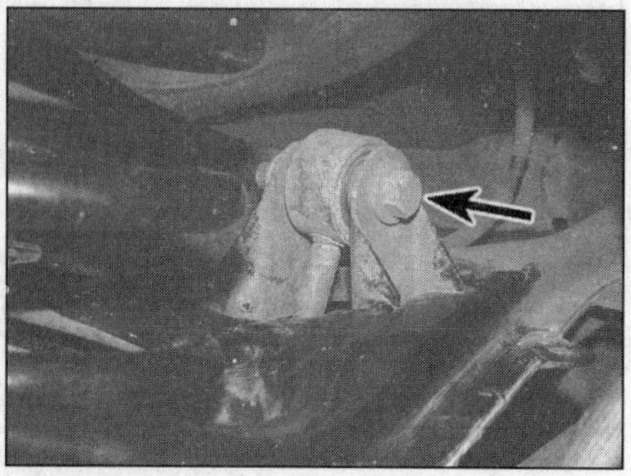
14.4 Anti-roll bar link upper mounting bolt

15.4a Remove the lower arm inboard pivot bolt . . .

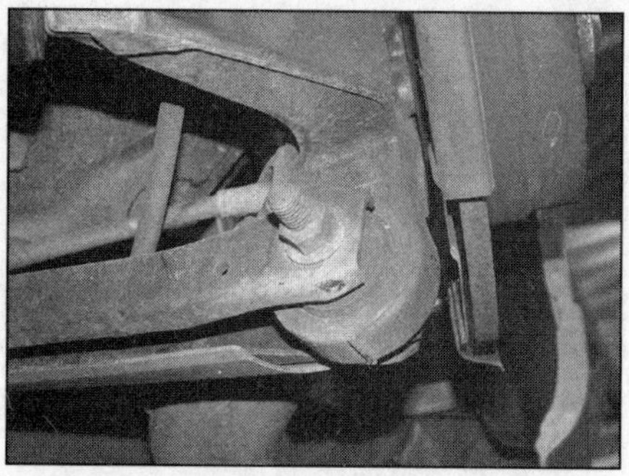
15.4b . . . and the lower arm-to-trailing arm nut and bolt

signs of wear or damage, paying particular attention to the mounting bushes. If the bushes are worn, refer to Section 18.

Refitting

12 Offer up the trailing arm to the body, align the marks made (where applicable), then fit and tighten the upper mounting bolts to the specified torque.
13 Fit the upper and lower arm nuts and bolts, but tighten them only hand-tight at this stage.
14 Refit the brake hose to the bracket.
15 Refit the rear spring as described in Section 12.
16 Refit the ABS wheel sensor, and tighten the bolt.
17 Clean the brake backplate and mating surfaces, then fit the Allen bolts and tighten them securely.
18 Refit the handbrake shoes as described in Chapter 9.
19 Refit the rear hub as described in Section 9.
20 Refit the wheel, then lower the car to the ground and tighten the wheel bolts to the specified torque.
21 With the car on its wheels, tighten the upper and lower arm nuts and bolts to the specified torque.
22 Particularly if a new trailing arm has been fitted, it is advisable to have the rear wheel toe setting checked on completion.

14 Rear upper arm – removal, overhaul and refitting

Removal

1 Remove the coil spring on the side concerned, as described in Section 12.
2 Release the ABS sensor wiring, and (on the right-hand arm) the pad wear sensor wiring, from the clips on the upper arm.
3 Unscrew and remove the nut and bolt securing the upper arm to the lower arm **(see illustration 13.6a)**.
4 Where applicable, unscrew and remove the nut and bolt from the anti-roll bar connecting link **(see illustration)**.
5 Remove the inboard pivot bolt, and free the upper arm from the subframe **(see illustration 12.4)**. Remove the upper arm from under the car.
6 If a new arm is being fitted, transfer the wiring harness clips to the new arm.

Overhaul

7 Thoroughly clean the arm and the area around the arm mountings, removing all traces of dirt and underseal if necessary, then check carefully for cracks, distortion or any other signs of wear or damage, paying particular attention to the mounting bushes. If the bushes are worn, refer to Section 18.
8 Inspect the pivot bolts for signs of wear or damage, and renew as necessary.

Refitting

9 Fit the anti-roll bar connecting link nut and bolt, upper-to-lower arm nut and bolt, and the upper arm pivot bolt, hand-tight only to begin with.
10 Clip the wiring back in place on the upper arm.
11 Refit the coil spring as described in Section 12.
12 Refit the rear wheel, then lower the car to the ground and tighten the wheel bolts to the specified torque.
13 With the car on its wheels, tighten the anti-roll bar connecting link nut and bolt, upper-to-trailing arm nut and bolt, and the upper arm inboard bolt, to their specified torques.

15 Rear lower arm – removal, overhaul and refitting

Removal

1 Loosen the relevant rear wheel bolts. Chock the front wheels, then jack up the rear of the car and support it on axle stands (see *Jacking and vehicle support*). Remove the appropriate rear roadwheel.
2 Position a suitable jack (with a block of wood on its head) under the shock absorber lower mounting on the trailing arm. Raise the trailing arm slightly. Do not jack the rear suspension under the upper or lower arms, as damage may be caused.
3 Unclip the protective cover from the lower arm, noting how it fits.
4 Remove the lower arm-to-trailing arm nut and bolt, and the inboard pivot bolt from the subframe **(see illustrations)**. Withdraw the lower arm from under the car.

Overhaul

5 Thoroughly clean the arm and the area around the arm mountings, removing all traces of dirt and underseal if necessary, then check carefully for cracks, distortion or any other signs of wear or damage, paying particular attention to the mounting bushes. If the bushes are worn, refer to Section 18.
6 Inspect the pivot bolts for signs of wear or damage, and renew as necessary.

Refitting

7 Offer up the arm, ensuring that the UP marking and arrow face upwards.
8 Fit the lower arm-to-trailing arm nut and bolt, and the inboard pivot bolt, but tighten them only hand-tight at this stage.
9 Refit the wheel, then lower the car to the ground and tighten the wheel bolts to the specified torque.
10 With the car on its wheels, tighten the lower arm-to-trailing arm nut and bolt, and the inboard pivot bolt, to their specified torques.
11 Clip the protective cover back on the arm to complete.

16 Rear anti-roll bar – removal and refitting

Removal

1 Loosen the rear wheel bolts. Chock the front wheels, then jack up the rear of the car and support it on axle stands (see *Jacking and vehicle support*). To improve access, remove the rear roadwheels.
2 Unscrew the nut securing the connecting link to each end of the anti-roll bar, if

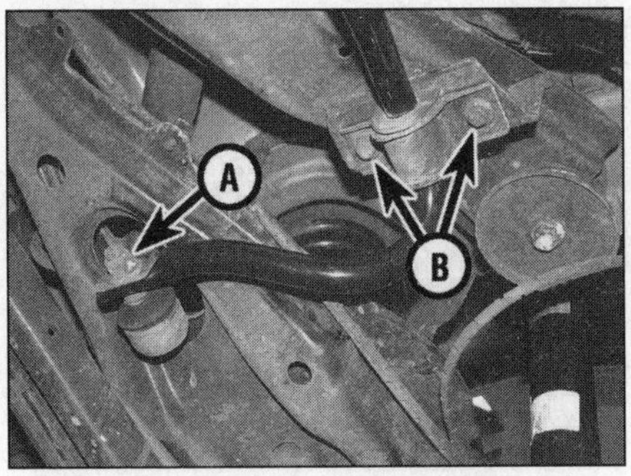

16.2a Rear anti-roll bar drop link nut (A) and mounting clamp (B)

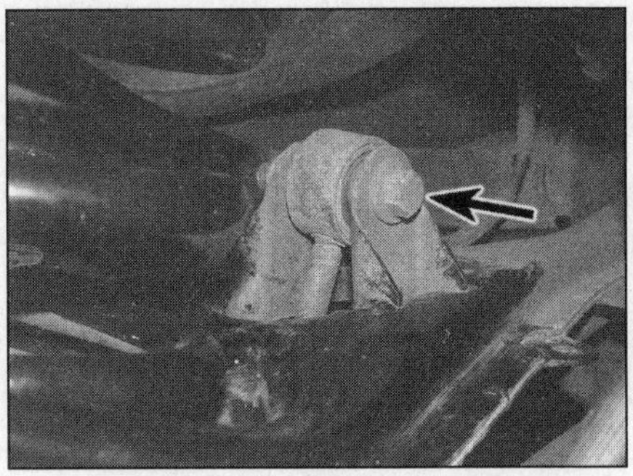

16.2b Drop link upper bolt (arrowed)

16.2c Counterhold the drop link stud while unscrewing the nut

necessary holding the connecting link ball-stud with a spanner on the flats provided **(see illustrations)**.

3 Unscrew the two bolts from each clamp, then remove the anti-roll bar from the subframe. Manoeuvre the anti-roll bar out from under the car. Remove the mounting bushes from the bar **(see illustrations)**.

4 Carefully examine the anti-roll bar components for signs of wear, damage or deterioration, paying particular attention to the mounting bushes. Renew worn components as necessary.

Refitting

5 Fit the rubber mounting bushes to the anti-roll bar, noting that no lubricant should be used.

6 Offer the bar into position. Fit the anti-roll bar clamps, then fit the bolts and tighten to the specified torque. Ensure the two bolts on each clamp are correctly tightened by checking them with the torque wrench again, set to the same torque as before.

7 Fit the connecting link nuts to the ends of the anti-roll bar, and tighten them by hand only at this stage.

8 Refit the roadwheels, then lower the car to the ground and tighten the wheel bolts to the specified torque.

9 With the car on its wheels, tighten the connecting link nuts to the specified torque, if necessary holding the ball-studs with a spanner as for removal.

17 Rear anti-roll bar connecting link – removal and refitting

1 Wear in the anti-roll bar connecting links (also known as the 'drop links') is typified by a knocking noise over certain types of bump. If the noise is noted on the (unloaded) passenger side of the car when the car is driven solo, this may be regarded as further evidence of wear in the links. It is recommended that the links are renewed in pairs.

Removal

2 Loosen the relevant rear wheel bolts. Chock the front wheels, then jack up the rear of the car and support it on axle stands (see *Jacking and vehicle support*). To improve access, remove the appropriate rear wheel.

3 Unscrew the nut securing the connecting link to the anti-roll bar, if necessary holding the connecting link ball-stud with a spanner on the flats provided **(see illustration 16.2c)**.

4 Unscrew and remove the nut and bolt securing the upper end of the link to the upper arm **(see illustration 16.2b)**.

5 Withdraw the link from under the car.

6 Check the connecting link balljoints for signs of wear. Check that each balljoint is free to move easily, and that the rubber gaiters are undamaged. If necessary renew the connecting link.

Refitting

7 Offer the link into position, noting that they are handed, and should be marked L or R.

8 Fit the upper nut and bolt to the upper arm, and the lower nut to the anti-roll bar, but tighten by hand only at this stage.

9 Refit the wheel, then lower the car to the ground and tighten the wheel bolts to the specified torque.

10 With the car on its wheels, tighten the connecting link lower nut to the specified torque, if necessary holding the ball-stud with a spanner as for removal. Also tighten the upper nut and bolt to the specified torque.

18 Rear suspension bushes – renewal

It appears that, when the car was new, all the rear suspension bushes were available separately – whether this is still the case is unclear at the time of writing. Check with your MG Rover parts supplier for the latest information. If the bushes can still be obtained, renewal may require either a press, or the use of a bush/bearing puller. In some cases, it is sufficient to have a selection of sockets and washers, some bolts or threaded bar, and a sturdy bench vice, to extract and press in the bushes. Most well-equipped local garages should be able to fit new bushes for you, for minimal cost.

19 Steering wheel – removal and refitting

Removal

1 Remove the airbag unit from the centre of the steering wheel, referring to Chapter 12.

2 Set the front wheels in the straight-ahead position.

3 Disconnect the wiring plug at the top of

16.3a Unbolt the mounting clamp and recover the (split) rubber bush

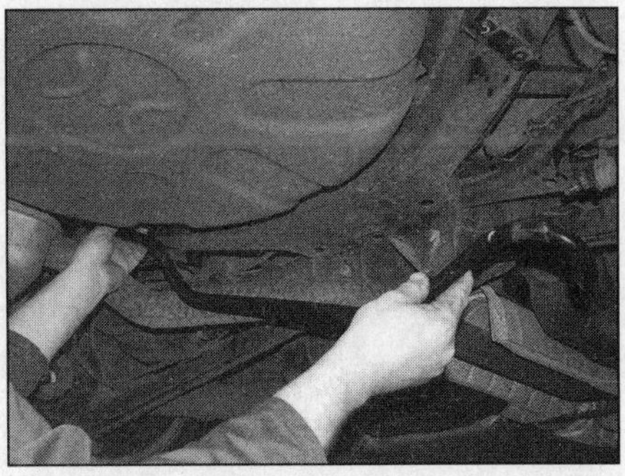

16.3b Remove the anti-roll bar from under the car

19.3 Disconnect the steering wheel harness plug

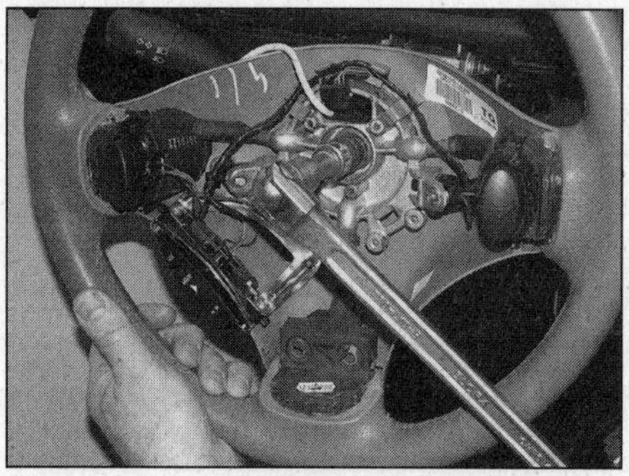

19.4 Hold the wheel rim while unscrewing the wheel bolt

19.5 Note the alignment notch between the wheel hub and steering column

19.6a Feed through the airbag wiring . . .

the wheel – this plug serves the horn, remote audio and (where applicable) cruise control switches **(see illustration)**.

4 Unscrew and remove the steering wheel bolt, holding the wheel rim with one hand, and loosening the bolt with the other – do not rely on the steering lock to prevent the wheel turning, otherwise it may be damaged **(see illustration)**.

5 Before removing the wheel, make your own alignment marks between the wheel and column with a pin punch or paint. Our car had an alignment notch at the base **(see illustration)**.

6 Refit the steering wheel bolt by a few threads, then pull the wheel all round the rim to free it from the splines. Feed through the airbag wiring as the wheel is removed. Once the wheel is free, unscrew the bolt and remove the wheel **(see illustrations)**.

7 Stick a piece of tape across the front and side of the airbag rotary coupler (clockspring), to ensure that it does not turn while the wheel is removed **(see illustration)**.

8 Check the position of the indicator cancelling cam, for refitting – unless the column and front wheels are disturbed, this should not move.

9 If a new wheel is being fitted, refer to Chapter 12 and remove the horn, remote audio and (where applicable) cruise control switches, then transfer them to the new wheel.

Refitting

10 Refitting is the reverse of removal, noting the following points:

a) Carefully remove the tape from the airbag clockspring. If the clockspring has been rotated significantly with the wheel removed, centralise it as described in Chapter 12.
b) Prior to refitting, ensure the indicator switch stalk is in the central (OFF) position. Failure to do so could lead to the steering wheel lug breaking the switch tab.
c) Check that the front wheels are in the straight-ahead position, and that the indicator cancelling cam is in the same position as noted on removal.
d) Engage the wheel with the column splines, aligning the marks made on removal. Tighten the steering wheel retaining bolt to the specified torque, holding the wheel rim as for removal.
e) Refit the airbag unit (see Chapter 12).

20 Steering column – removal, inspection and refitting

Removal

1 Remove the airbag rotary coupler (clockspring) as described in Chapter 12.

2 Remove the driver's facia lower trim panel as described in Chapter 11, Section 25.

3 Disconnect the wiring plugs from the ignition switch and the immobiliser reader coil (one plug either side of the column). Release

19.6b . . . then release the wheel and remove it

19.7 Tape up the airbag clockspring to stop it turning

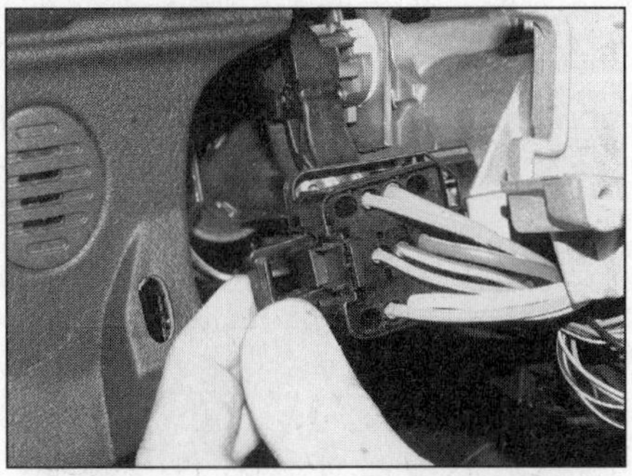

20.3a Disconnect the wiring plugs from the ignition switch . . .

20.3b . . . and the immobiliser reader coil . . .

20.3c . . . then unclip the wiring harness clips from the column

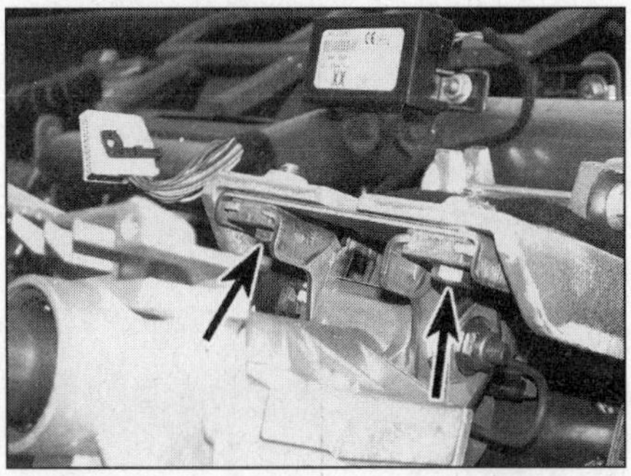

20.4a Remove the two upper . . .

20.4b . . . and two lower column mounting bolts

the wiring harness from the two clips under the column **(see illustrations)**.

4 Support the column, then unscrew and remove the four column mounting bolts below the column. Loosen the two column support screws, and release the column from the screw slots. Lower the column into the footwell, and recover the washers from the top face of the column **(see illustrations)**.

5 At the base of the column, unclip the protective boot for access to the universal joint. Unscrew and remove the locknut – note that a new nut must be used when refitting. Release the retaining clip from the pinch-bolt, and withdraw the bolt. Release the universal joint from the rack by pulling upwards. Remove the column from the car **(see illustrations)**.

Inspection

6 The steering column incorporates a telescopic safety feature. In the event of a front-end crash, the shaft collapses and prevents the steering wheel injuring the driver. Before refitting the steering column, examine the column and mountings for damage and deformation, and renew as necessary.

7 Check the steering shaft for signs of free play in the column bushes. If any damage or wear is found on the steering column bushes, the column should be overhauled. Overhaul of the column is a complex task requiring several

20.4c Loosen the two remaining support screws

20.4d Recover the two washers on top of the column

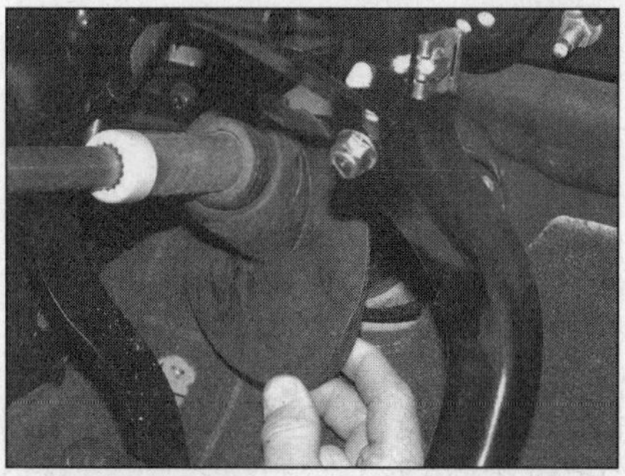

20.5a Unclip the rubber boot . . .

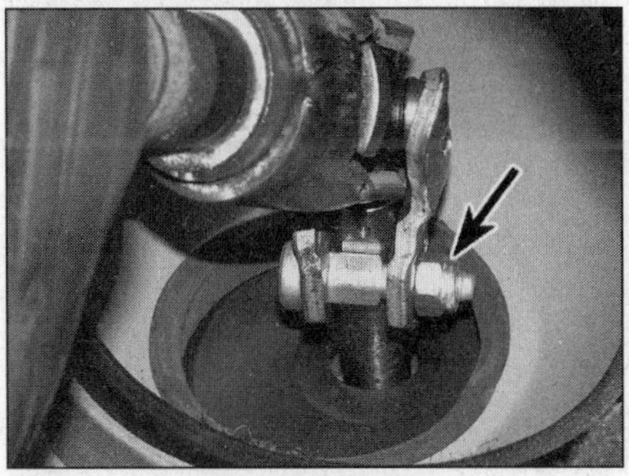

20.5b . . . then unscrew the universal joint pinch-bolt . . .

20.5c . . . and separate the joint

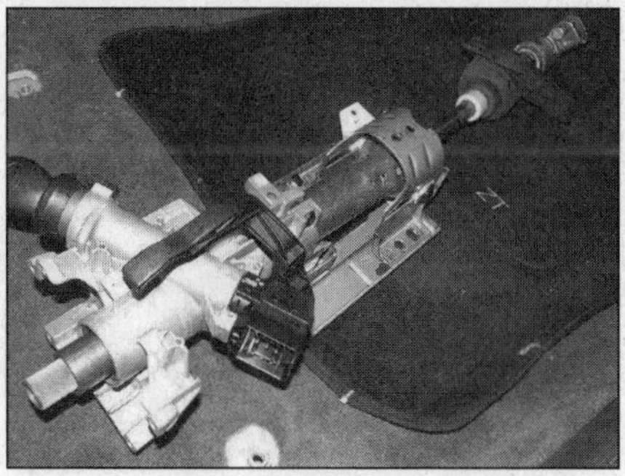

20.5d Withdraw the column into the footwell

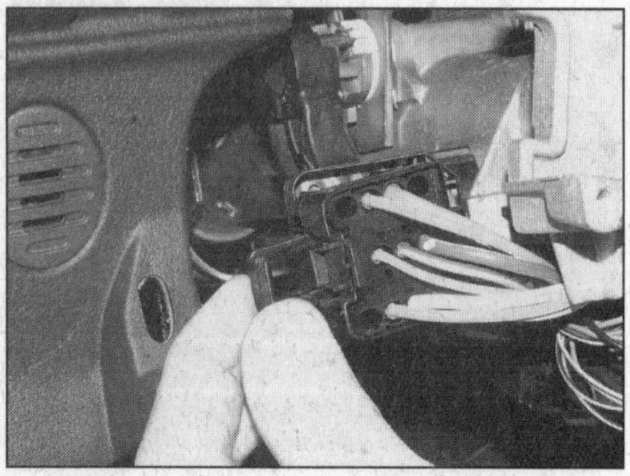

21.6 Slide out the locking clip to disconnect the wiring plug

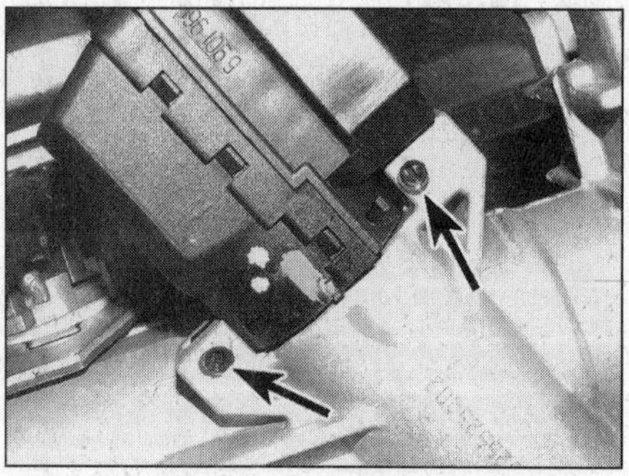

21.7a Unscrew the two grub screws underneath . . .

21.7b . . . and remove the ignition switch from the column

special tools, and should be entrusted to a suitably-equipped garage or specialist.

Refitting

8 Manoeuvre the column into position, and first locate it on the two support screws. Once in position, tighten the screws securely.

9 Ensure that the front wheels are still in the straight-ahead position, then locate the lower end of the column on the universal joint. Fit the pinch-bolt with a new self-locking nut, and tighten lightly. At the 12 o'clock position, check that there is a gap of 4 mm between the joint and the floor aperture – if the gap is less than this, lever the joint upwards. Finally, tighten the locknut and pinch-bolt to the specified torque. Clip the protective cover back in place.

10 Fit the column mounting bolts, and tighten them to the specified torque.

11 Clip the wiring harness back onto the steering column, then reconnect the wiring plugs to the immobiliser reader coil and ignition switch.

12 Refit the driver's facia lower trim panel as described in Chapter 11, Section 25.

13 Refit the airbag rotary coupler (clockspring) as described in Chapter 12.

21 Ignition switch/steering column lock – removal and refitting

Ignition switch

1 Disconnect the battery negative lead, and move the lead away from the battery (see *Disconnecting the battery*).

2 Remove the driver's facia lower trim panel as described in Chapter 11, Section 25.

3 Release the locking lever, and fully lower the steering column.

4 Remove the two screws from the column lower shroud.

5 Release the three clips either side, and separate the upper and lower column shrouds. Release the locking lever, and remove the lower shroud. Lift the upper shroud – note that it cannot be removed completely, as the trim is trapped behind the instrument panel.

6 Disconnect the wiring plug from the ignition switch by sliding out the locking clip sideways **(see illustration)**.

7 Undo the two grub screws and remove the switch block from the lock assembly **(see illustrations)**.

8 Refitting is the reverse of removal, noting the following points:

a) *Apply thread-locking fluid to the switch grub screws prior to refitting, to lock them in position.*

b) *Check the operation of the switch prior to refitting the steering column shrouds.*

Ignition lock barrel

9 Disconnect the battery negative lead, and move the lead away from the battery (see *Disconnecting the battery*).

10 Remove the driver's facia lower trim panel as described in Chapter 11, Section 25.

11 Release the locking lever, and fully lower the steering column.

12 Remove the two screws from the column lower shroud.

13 Release the three clips either side, and separate the upper and lower column shrouds. Release the locking lever, and remove the lower shroud. Lift the upper shroud – note that it cannot be removed completely, as the trim is trapped behind the instrument panel.

14 Disconnect the wiring plug from the immobiliser reader coil. Using two screwdrivers, carefully prise the coil over the end of the ignition switch housing **(see illustrations)**.

15 Turn the ignition key to the first position, then insert a suitable thin rod (eg, a straightened paper clip or small drill bit) into the hole in the housing and depress the

21.14a Disconnect the immobiliser reader coil wiring plug . . .

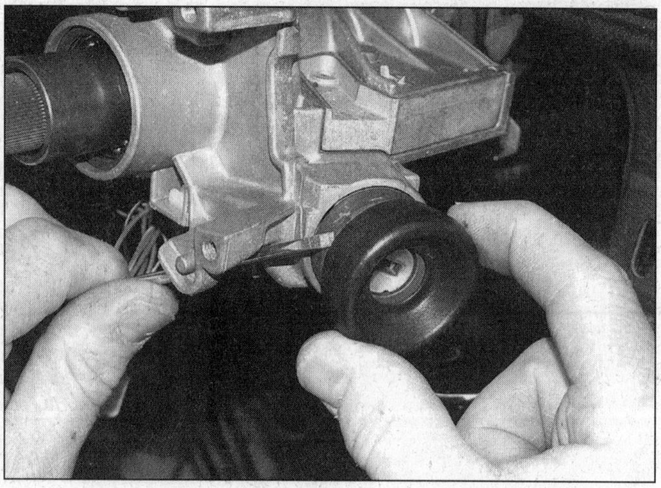

21.14b . . . then carefully prise the coil off the lock barrel

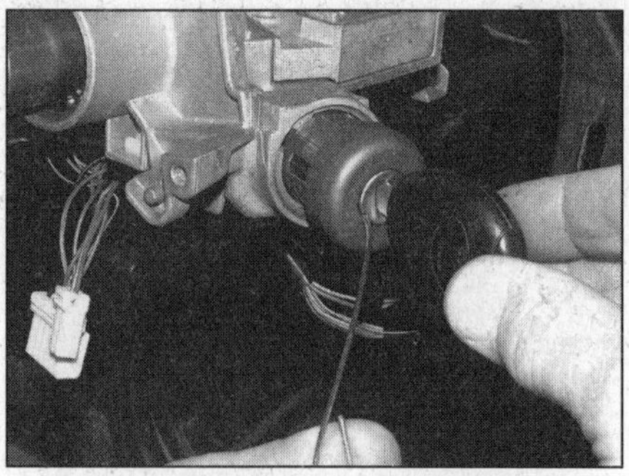

21.15a Insert a thin piece of wire as shown, and withdraw the lock barrel

21.15b Lock barrel removed, showing curved detent lever with small hole . . .

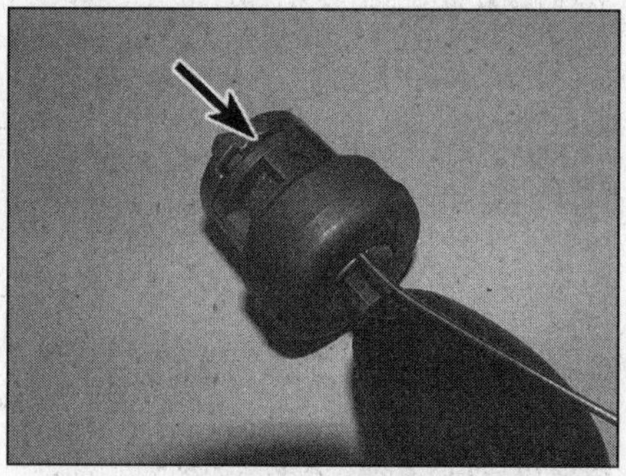

21.15c . . . with wire inserted into hole, curved detent lever retracts

lock cylinder detent. This will take a little experimentation and wiggling. Slide the lock cylinder out, noting its fitted alignment for use when refitting **(see illustrations)**.

16 Refitting is a reversal of removal, noting the following points:

a) *Position the lock cylinder as noted on removal, and insert the cylinder into the housing until it clicks in to position.*

b) *The immobiliser reader coil is a push-fit over the lock housing.*

Steering lock assembly

17 Renewal of the lock assembly requires the steering column to be dismantled. This task requires the use of several special tools, and for this reason should be entrusted to a suitably-equipped specialist.

22 Steering rack assembly – removal, overhaul and refitting

Removal

1 Working in the driver's footwell, at the base of the column, unclip the protective boot for access to the universal joint. Unscrew and remove the locknut – note that a new nut must be used when refitting. Release the retaining clip from the pinch-bolt, and withdraw the bolt. Release the universal joint from the rack by pulling upwards.

2 Loosen the front wheel bolts. Chock the rear wheels, firmly apply the handbrake, then jack up the front of the car and support on axle stands (see *Jacking and vehicle support*). Remove the front wheels.

3 Remove the engine undertray, which is secured by a number of quick-release screw fasteners.

4 Working on each side of the car in turn, loosen the track rod end balljoint nut, unscrewing it almost to the end of its threads (if the nut will not unscrew, hold the balljoint stud on top using an Allen key). Use a balljoint separator tool to free the balljoint, then unscrew the nut completely, and disconnect the track rod from the hub carrier **(see illustrations)**. Note that new balljoint nuts will be needed for refitting.

5 Working as described in the relevant Part of Chapter 4, unbolt the exhaust system from the manifold(s) or turbo, then release the front mountings and lower the system – if necessary, support it on a jack or axle stand.

6 Unscrew the two bolts and remove the heat shield from the steering rack **(see illustration)**.

7 On V6 engine models, remove the single bolt and release the clip securing the heat shield fitted at one side of the lower mounting, and withdraw it **(see illustrations)**.

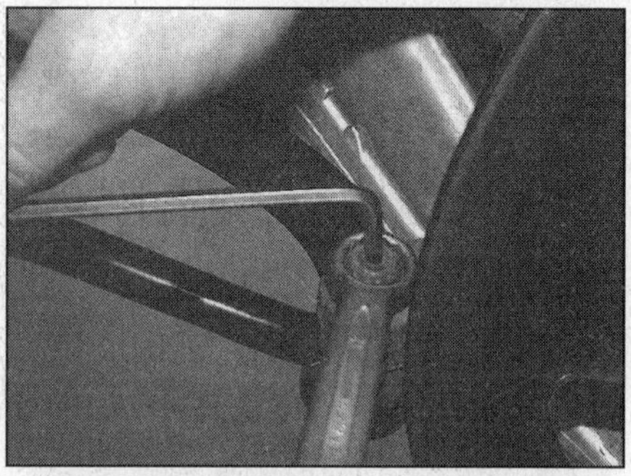

22.4a Unscrew the track rod end nut, holding the stud with an Allen key . . .

22.4b . . . then use a balljoint separator tool . . .

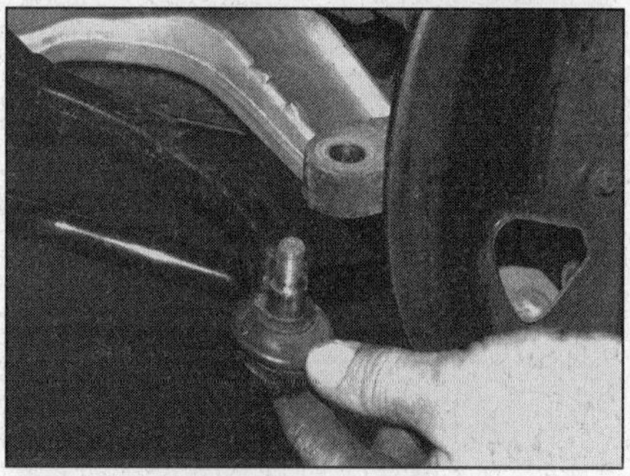

22.4c . . . to release the balljoint taper and disconnect the track rod

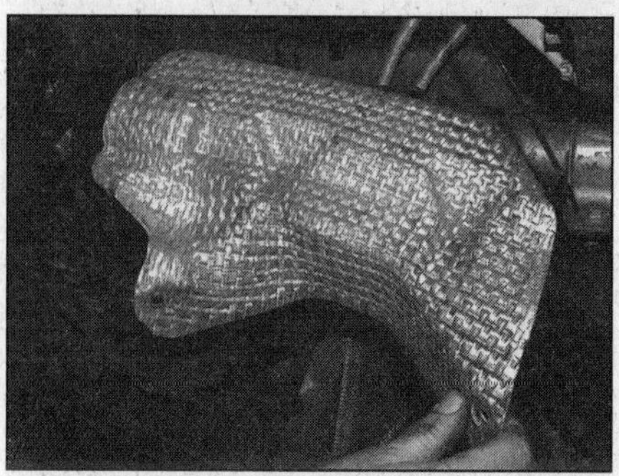

22.6 Remove the steering rack heat shield

22.7a Prise out the clip . . .

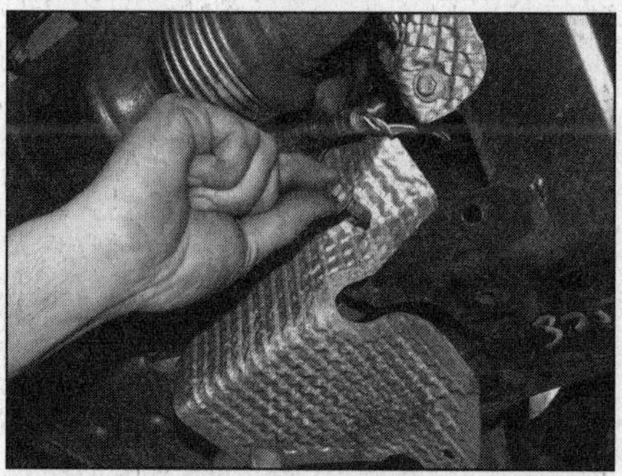

22.7b . . . then remove the bolt and take off the heat shield

8 Support the front subframe at the rear, using a substantial jack with a block of wood on its head.

9 Loosen the two bolts securing the subframe braces to the underbody **(see illustration)**.

10 Remove the two rearmost subframe bolts. Recover the stepped washers, and move the subframe braces clear.

11 Remove the two centre subframe bolts (on spars which reach up from the main subframe) and recover the stepped washers.

12 The subframe should now be supported only on the two front bolts (and the jack at the rear). Loosen the two front bolts by a few turns only – do not remove them. Slowly lower the jack at the rear, to lower the rear of the subframe – only lower sufficiently to gain access to the rack and pipework, ensuring that nothing is being placed under strain.

13 Note that all bolts removed from the subframe or braces must be renewed when refitting.

14 Remove the two steering fluid pipe support brackets from the subframe – each is secured by a single bolt.

15 Place a suitable container under the steering rack pipe connections. Noting their fitted positions, disconnect the fluid feed banjo union and the return pipe from the rack. Recover and discard the sealing washers and O-ring, as new ones must be used when refitting. If possible, plug or tape over the open connections, to prevent dirt entry into the system.

16 Unscrew and remove the four rack mounting bolts, then lower the rack to release the rubber grommet/gaiter fitted between the pinion and the floor aperture **(see illustration)**. Withdraw the rack from the driver's side of the car, and recover the pinion gaiter.

Overhaul

17 Examine the steering rack assembly for signs of wear or damage, and check that the rack moves freely throughout the full length of its travel, with no signs of roughness or excessive free play between the steering rack pinion and rack. It is not possible to overhaul the steering rack assembly housing components; if it is faulty, the assembly must be renewed. The only components which can be renewed individually are the steering rack gaiters, and the track rod balljoints. These procedures are covered later in this Chapter.

Refitting

18 Offer in the steering rack, engage the pinion gaiter/grommet, and insert the two lower mounting bolts first. Tighten the two lower bolts to the specified torque. Fit the rack upper mounting bolts, and tighten them to the specified torque.

19 Clean the fluid connections to the rack, then using new washers, reconnect the feed pipe banjo bolt and tighten to the specified torque. Reconnect the return union using a new O-ring, and tighten to the specified torque.

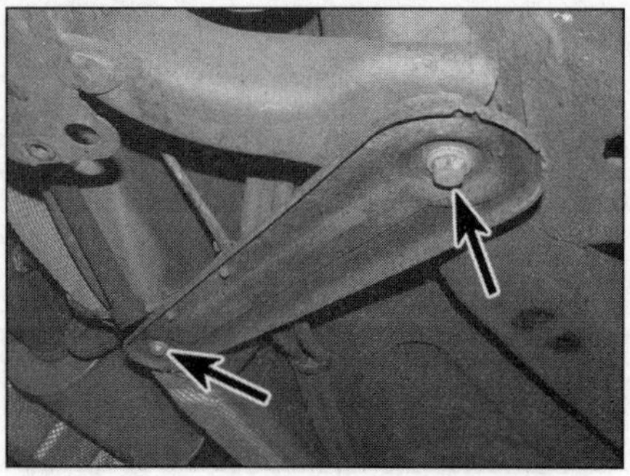

22.9 Remove the two bolts securing the subframe braces

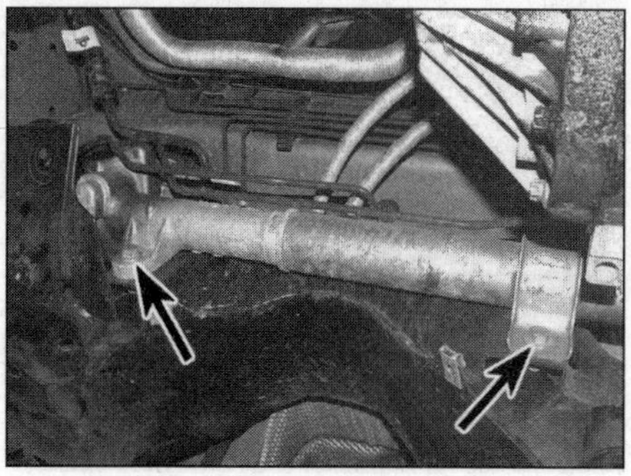

22.16 Two of the four steering rack mounting bolts

20 Reconnect the fluid pipe support brackets to the subframe, tightening their bolts securely.

21 Raise the subframe into position, and fit the new centre bolts with their stepped locating washers. Tighten the centre bolts to the specified torque.

22 Remove the subframe front bolts, making sure the stepped washers do not fall out, then fit the new bolts and tighten to the specified torque.

23 Fit the new subframe rear bolts (which also secure the front ends of the subframe braces), and tighten to the specified torque..

24 Fit and tighten the subframe braces' (smaller) new rear bolts to the specified torque.

25 Further refitting is a reversal of removal, noting the following points:

a) Use new track rod balljoint nuts.
b) Reconnect the exhaust pipe(s) as described in the relevant Part of Chapter 4.
c) Wait until the car is resting on its wheels before reconnecting the column universal joint, using a new locknut.
d) Top-up and bleed the power steering system as described in Section 25.
e) Have the front wheel alignment checked on completion.

23 Power steering pump – removal and refitting

1.8 litre engines

1 Disconnect the wiring plug from the fluid pressure sensor, which is located at the rear of the pump **(see illustration)**.

2 Anticipating some loss of fluid, loosen the banjo bolt and disconnect the fluid high-pressure pipe from the pump. Recover the sealing washers – new ones should be used when refitting. Plug or tape over the open connections.

3 Remove the clip from the fluid low-pressure hose, and disconnect the hose from the pump. The original crimp-type clip may have to be cut off, so a new clip will be needed for refitting – it is recommended that a Jubilee clip is used. Plug or tape over the open connections.

4 If possible, loosen (do not remove) the three bolts securing the power steering pump pulley before removing the auxiliary drivebelt.

5 Remove the power steering pump (auxiliary) drivebelt as described in Chapter 1A.

6 Unscrew the three bolts, and take off the power steering pump pulley. If the bolts were not previously loosened, this can be done using a screwdriver handle between two of the bolts to hold the pulley while the remaining bolt is loosened – repeat until all three are loose, and the pulley can be removed.

7 Remove the bolt securing the pump to the mounting bracket.

8 Support the pump, then unscrew and remove the two nuts and through-bolts, and remove the pump from the engine. Try to keep the pump upright, to reduce further fluid spillage.

9 Refitting is a reversal of removal, noting the following points:

a) Tighten the pump mountings to the specified torque.
b) Refit the pump pulley, and tighten the three bolts by hand only until the drivebelt is refitted.
c) Refit the drivebelt as described in Chapter 1A.
d) Tighten the pump pulley bolts to the specified torque.
e) Fit new washers to the pump high-pressure union, then fit the pipe and tighten the banjo bolt to the specified torque.
f) On completion, top-up and bleed the power steering system as described in Section 25.

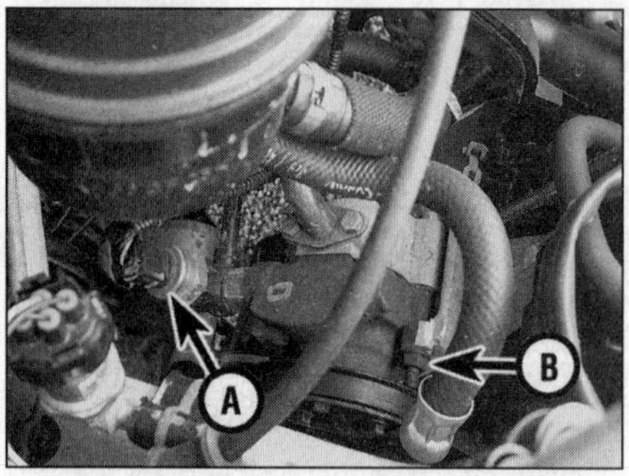

23.1 Power steering fluid pressure sensor (A) and through-bolt nut (B)

23.11 Loosen the power steering pump pulley bolts

23.13 Power steering pump high-pressure union

23.15 Take off the pump pulley

V6 engines

10 Remove the two bolts and unclip the engine top cover. Recover the washers and rubber grommets from the bolt holes, and store them for refitting.

11 Loosen (do not remove) the three bolts securing the power steering pump pulley before removing the auxiliary drivebelt **(see illustration)**.

12 Remove the auxiliary drivebelt as described in Chapter 1A. This includes removing the engine right-hand mounting, which is essential for access to the pump's lowest mounting bolt.

13 Anticipating some loss of fluid, loosen the banjo bolt and disconnect the fluid high-pressure pipe from the pump **(see illustration)**. Recover the sealing washers – new ones should be used when refitting. Plug or tape over the open connections.

14 Remove the clip from the fluid low-pressure hose, and disconnect the hose from the pump. The original crimp-type clip may have to be cut off, so a new clip will be needed for refitting – it is recommended that a Jubilee clip is used. Plug or tape over the open connections.

15 Unscrew the three bolts, and take off the power steering pump pulley **(see illustration)**. If the bolts were not previously loosened, this can be done using a screwdriver handle between two of the bolts to hold the pulley while the remaining bolt is loosened – repeat until all three are loose, and the pulley can be removed.

23.16a Unscrew the three mounting bolts . . .

16 Support the pump, then unscrew the three mounting bolts, and remove the pump from the engine **(see illustrations)**. Try to keep the pump upright, to reduce further fluid spillage.

17 Refitting is a reversal of removal, noting the following points:

- *a) Tighten the pump mountings to the specified torque.*
- *b) Refit the pump pulley, and tighten the three bolts by hand only until the drivebelt is refitted.*
- *c) Refit the drivebelt as described in Chapter 1A.*
- *d) Tighten the pump pulley bolts to the specified torque.*
- *e) Fit new washers to the pump high-pressure union, then fit the pipe and tighten the banjo bolt to the specified torque.*
- *f) On completion, top-up and bleed the power steering system as described in Section 25.*

Diesel engines

18 Remove the engine right-hand mounting, including the hydramount, as described in Chapter 2C.

19 Loosen (do not remove) the three bolts securing the power steering pump pulley before removing the auxiliary drivebelt.

20 Remove the main auxiliary drivebelt as described in Chapter 1B.

21 Cover the alternator with something like a plastic bag, as a precaution against fluid spillage.

23.16b . . . and withdraw the pump from the bracket

22 Lift the engine slightly, either using a hoist or the jack which is supporting the engine while the mounting is removed, so that the pump can be removed from the engine.

23 Unscrew the three bolts, and take off the power steering pump pulley. If the bolts were not previously loosened, this can be done using a screwdriver handle between two of the bolts to hold the pulley while the remaining bolt is loosened – repeat until all three are loose, and the pulley can be removed.

24 Unscrew the pump's banjo bolt, and separate the high-pressure pipe. Recover the sealing washers – new ones must be used when refitting. Plug or tape over the open connections.

25 Unscrew the two flange bolts, and disconnect the fluid low-pressure pipe flange from the pump – move the fluid reservoir aside. Recover the flange O-ring seal – a new one must be used when refitting. Plug or tape over the open connections.

26 Support the pump, then unscrew the three mounting bolts, and remove the pump from the engine. Try to keep the pump upright, to reduce further fluid spillage.

27 Refitting is a reversal of removal, noting the following points:

- *a) Tighten the pump mountings to the specified torque.*
- *b) Fit new washers to the pump high-pressure union, then fit the pipe and tighten the banjo bolt to the specified torque.*
- *c) Fit a new O-ring to the pump pipe flange, then fit the flange and tighten the two bolts to the specified torque.*
- *d) Refit the pump pulley, and tighten the three bolts by hand only until the drivebelt is refitted.*
- *e) Refit the drivebelt as described in Chapter 1B.*
- *f) Tighten the pump pulley bolts to the specified torque.*
- *g) Refit the engine right-hand mounting components as described in Chapter 2C.*
- *h) On completion, top-up and bleed the power steering system as described in Section 25.*

24.4 One of the power steering fluid cooler mounting bolts

26.4 Release the steering gaiter retaining clips

24 Power steering fluid cooler – removal and refitting

Removal

1 Remove the front bumper as described in Chapter 11.

2 Position a suitable container under the two connections on the side of the cooler.

3 Squeeze the quick-release connectors to disconnect the hoses, and let the fluid drain. When the flow of fluid stops, fit plugs or tape over the open connections.

4 Remove the two bolts securing the cooler to the front of the car, and remove it **(see illustration)**. Try to keep the ends uppermost, to keep further fluid loss to a minimum.

Refitting

5 Refitting is a reversal of removal. On completion, top-up and bleed the power steering system as described in Section 25.

25 Power steering system – bleeding

1 Clean and remove the fluid reservoir filler cap, then clean around the top of the reservoir. It is essential that no dirt is allowed to enter the system. Especially on diesel engines, also take care when filling the reservoir that no fluid spills onto the alternator – it may be wise to cover the alternator with (say) a plastic bag.

2 Referring to *Weekly checks* if necessary, top-up the reservoir to the upper mark on the fluid dipstick, which is incorporated in the filler cap.

3 Start the engine, and let it run at idle speed for about 10 seconds, then switch it off

4 Top-up the fluid level to the upper mark.

5 Start the engine, then slowly turn the steering fully to the left and right – do not hold on full-lock for longer than 10 seconds. Centre the steering, then switch off the engine.

6 Top-up the fluid level to the upper mark.

7 Repeat paragraph 5, but this time, keep turning the steering slowly fully left then right for approximately 2 minutes before switching off the engine.

8 If the fluid in the reservoir (or on the dipstick) appears aerated, wait until the fluid is free of bubbles before topping-up to the upper level. Refit the reservoir cap on completion.

9 If, after bleeding, the steering is noisy when turned, this may mean that air is still present in the system, and further bleeding is indicated. It may be sufficient to drive the car for a few miles in this case, and recheck the fluid level afterwards, after allowing time for the system to cool – remember that the level is normally checked when cold, and checking when hot could produce a falsely-high reading.

26 Steering rack rubber gaiters – renewal

1 Loosen the front wheel bolts. Chock the rear wheels, firmly apply the handbrake, then jack up the front of the car and support on axle stands (see *Jacking and vehicle support*). To improve access, remove the front wheels.

2 Remove the engine undertray, which is secured by a number of quick-release screw fasteners.

3 Remove the track rod balljoint as described in Section 27.

4 Note the correct fitted position of the gaiter on the track rod, then release the retaining clip(s) and slide the gaiter off the steering rack housing and track rod end **(see illustration)**.

5 Thoroughly clean the track rod and the steering rack housing, using fine abrasive paper to polish off any corrosion, burrs or sharp edges, which might damage the new gaiter's sealing lips on installation. Scrape off all the grease from the old gaiter, and apply it to the track rod inner balljoint. (This assumes that grease has not been lost or contaminated as a result of damage to the old gaiter. Use fresh grease if in doubt.)

6 Carefully slide the new gaiter onto the track rod end, and locate it on the steering rack housing. Position the outer edge of the gaiter on the track rod, as was noted prior to removal.

7 Make sure the gaiter is not twisted, then lift the outer sealing lip of the gaiter to equalise air pressure within the gaiter. Secure the gaiter in position with the new retaining clip(s).

8 Refit the track rod balljoint as described in Section 27.

27 Track rod balljoint – removal and refitting

Removal

1 Loosen the relevant front wheel bolts. Chock the rear wheels, firmly apply the handbrake, then jack up the front of the car and support on axle stands (see *Jacking and vehicle support*). Remove the appropriate front wheel.

2 Make a mark on the track rod and measure the distance from the mark to the centre of the balljoint. Note this measurement down, as it will be needed to ensure the wheel alignment remains correctly set when the balljoint is installed. Alternatively, count the number of exposed threads next to the track rod locknut, and ensure the same number are visible when refitting.

3 Loosen the track rod locknut **(see illustration)**.

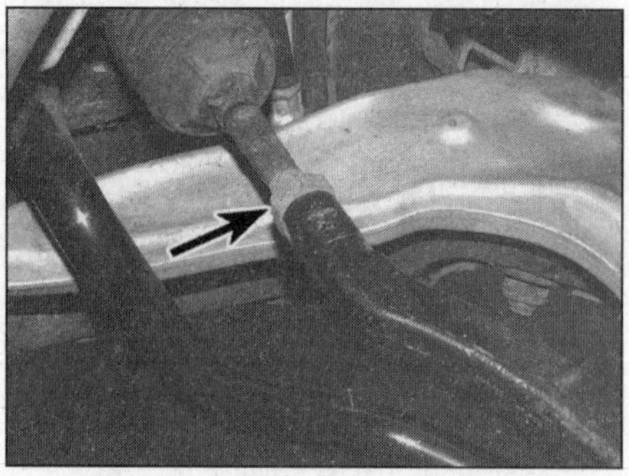

27.3 Loosen the track rod locknut (arrowed)

27.4 Separate the track rod from the hub carrier

Once loosened, screw the nut gently back up to the track rod balljoint by hand, and see that it does not move – in this position, it can be used as a reference point for refitting.

4 Loosen the track rod balljoint nut, unscrewing it almost to the end of its threads (if the nut will not unscrew, hold the balljoint stud on top using a small spanner). Use a balljoint separator tool to free the balljoint, then unscrew the nut completely and disconnect the track rod from the hub carrier **(see illustration)**. Note that a new balljoint nut will be needed for refitting.

5 Counting the exact number of turns necessary to do so, unscrew the balljoint from the track rod end.

6 Carefully clean the balljoint and the threads. Renew the balljoint if its movement is sloppy or too stiff, if excessively worn, or if damaged in any way; carefully check the stud taper and threads. If the balljoint gaiter is damaged, the complete balljoint assembly must be renewed – it is not possible to obtain the gaiter separately.

Refitting

7 Screw the balljoint onto the track rod by the number of turns noted on removal, up to the locknut. This should position the balljoint at the relevant distance from the track rod mark that was noted prior to removal.

8 Refit the balljoint shank to the hub carrier, then fit a new retaining nut and tighten it to the specified torque.

9 Tighten the track rod locknut to the specified torque.

10 Refit the roadwheel, then lower the car to the ground and tighten the roadwheel bolts to the specified torque.

11 It's recommended that the front wheel alignment is checked at the earliest opportunity,

28 Wheel alignment and steering angles – general information

Definitions

1 A car's steering and suspension geometry is defined in four basic settings – all angles are expressed in degrees; the steering axis is defined as an imaginary line drawn through the axis of the suspension strut, extended where necessary to contact the ground.

2 Camber is the angle between each roadwheel and a vertical line drawn through its centre and tyre contact patch, when viewed from the front or rear of the car. Positive camber is when the roadwheels are tilted outwards from the vertical at the top; negative camber is when they are tilted inwards.

3 The front camber angle is not adjustable, and is given for reference only (see paragraph 5). The rear camber angle is adjustable and can be adjusted using a camber angle gauge.

4 Castor is the angle between the steering axis and a vertical line drawn through each roadwheel's centre and tyre contact patch, when viewed from the side of the car. Positive castor is when the steering axis is tilted so that it contacts the ground ahead of the vertical; negative castor is when it contacts the ground behind the vertical.

5 Castor is not adjustable, and is given for reference only; while it can be checked using a castor checking gauge, if the figure obtained is significantly different from that specified, the car must be taken for careful checking by a professional, as the fault can only be caused by wear or damage to the body or suspension components.

6 Steering axis inclination/SAI – also known as **kingpin inclination/KPI** – is the angle between the steering axis and a vertical line drawn through each roadwheel's centre and tyre contact patch, when viewed from the front or rear of the car.

7 SAI/KPI is not adjustable, and is given for reference only.

8 Toe is the difference, viewed from above, between lines drawn through the roadwheel centres and the car's centre-line. 'Toe-in' is when the roadwheels point inwards, towards each other at the front, while 'toe-out' is when they splay outwards from each other at the front.

9 The front wheel toe setting is adjusted by screwing the track rods in or out of their balljoint, to alter the effective length of the track rod assembly.

10 Rear wheel toe setting is also adjustable, by loosening the three trailing arm-to-body bolts and turning the rear wheel as required.

Checking – general

11 Due to the special measuring equipment necessary to check the wheel alignment, and the skill required to use it properly, the checking and adjustment of these settings is best left to an expert. Most tyre-fitting centres now possess sophisticated checking equipment.

12 For accurate checking, the car must be at the kerb weight specified in *Dimensions and weights* in the Reference Section.

13 Before starting work, check first that the tyre sizes and types are as specified, then check tyre pressures and tread wear. Also check roadwheel run-out, the condition of the hub bearings, the steering wheel free play and the condition of the front suspension components (Chapter 1A or 1B). Correct any faults.

14 Park the car on level ground, with the front roadwheels in the straight-ahead position. Rock both ends to settle the suspension. Release the handbrake and roll the car backwards 1 metre (3 feet), then forwards again, to relieve any stresses in the steering and suspension components.

Front wheel toe setting

Checking

15 Normally, two methods are available to the home mechanic for checking the front wheel toe setting. One method is to use a gauge to measure the distance between the front and rear inside edges of the roadwheels. However, MG Rover do not quote toe settings in millimetres, so the measurement procedure cannot be used.

16 The alternative method is to use a scuff plate, in which each front wheel is rolled across a movable plate which records any deviation, or scuff, of the tyre from the straight-ahead position as it moves across the plate. Such gauges are available in relatively-inexpensive form from accessory outlets. It is up to the owner to decide whether the expense is justified, in view of the small amount of use such equipment would normally receive.

17 Prepare the car as described previously in paragraphs 12 to 14.

18 Roll the car backwards, check that the roadwheels are in the straight-ahead position, then roll it across the scuff plates so that each front roadwheel passes squarely over the centre of its respective plate. Note the angle recorded by the scuff plates. To ensure accuracy, repeat the check three times, and take the average of the three readings. If the roadwheels are running parallel, there will of course be no angle recorded; if a deviation value is shown on the scuff plates, compare the reading obtained for each wheel with that specified. If the value recorded is outside the specified tolerance, the toe setting is incorrect, and must be adjusted as follows.

Adjustment

19 With the handbrake applied, jack up the front of the car and support it securely on axle stands (see *Jacking and vehicle support*). Turn the steering wheel onto full-left lock, and record the number of exposed threads on the right-hand track rod end. Now turn the steering onto full-right lock, and record the number of threads on the left-hand side. If there are the same number of threads visible on both sides, then subsequent adjustment should be made equally on both sides. If there are more threads visible on one side than the other, it will be necessary to compensate for this during adjustment. **Note:** *It is important that, after adjustment, the same number of threads be visible on each track rod end.*

20 First clean the track rod threads; if they are corroded, apply penetrating fluid before starting adjustment. Release the rubber gaiter

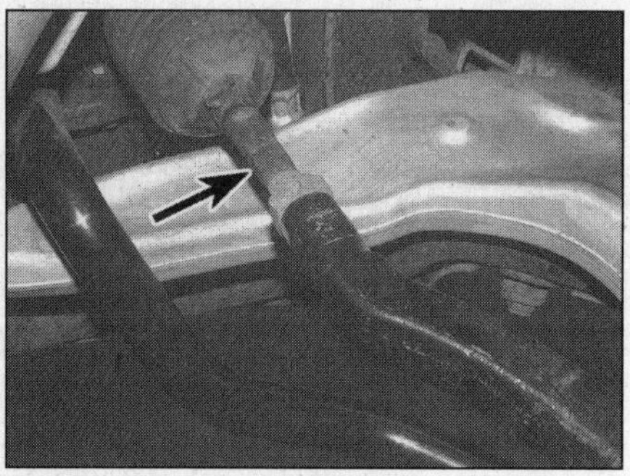

28.22 Use the flats (arrowed) on the track rod to turn it

outboard clips, then peel back the gaiters and apply a smear of grease, so that both gaiters are free and will not be twisted or strained as their respective track rods are rotated.

21 Use a straight-edge and a scriber or similar to mark the relationship of each track rod to its balljoint. Holding each track rod in turn, unscrew its locknut fully.

22 Alter the length of the track rods, bearing in mind the note in paragraph 19, by screwing them into or out of the balljoints. Rotate the track rod using an open-ended spanner fitted to the flats provided **(see illustration)**. Shortening the track rods (screwing them onto their balljoints) will reduce toe-in and increase toe-out. Each flat that the hex adjuster is turned effectively adjusts the toe setting by approximately 0.1°.

23 When the setting is correct, hold the track rods and securely tighten the balljoint locknuts or clamps. Check that the balljoints are seated correctly in their sockets, and count the exposed threads. If the number of threads exposed is not the same on both sides, then the adjustment has not been made equally, and problems will be encountered with tyre scrubbing in turns; also, the steering wheel spokes will no longer be horizontal when the wheels are in the straight-ahead position.

24 When the track rod lengths are the same, lower the car to the ground and recheck the toe setting; readjust if necessary. Ensure that the rubber gaiters are seated correctly and are not twisted or strained; secure them in position with new retaining clips.

Rear wheel toe setting

Checking

25 The procedure for checking the rear toe setting is similar to that described for the front wheels.

Adjustment

26 Adjusting the rear toe setting involves loosening the trailing arm mounting bolts, and turning the arm to reset the rear wheel position. This is not considered a DIY operation, and should only be attempted if the proper tools are available.

Chapter 11
Bodywork and fittings

Contents

Degrees of difficulty

Easy, suitable for novice with little experience	**Fairly easy,** suitable for beginner with some experience	**Fairly difficult,** suitable for competent DIY mechanic	**Difficult,** suitable for experienced DIY mechanic	**Very difficult,** suitable for expert DIY or professional

Specifications

Torque wrench settings	Nm	lbf ft
Bonnet hinge bolts	25	18
Boot lid hinge bolts	25	18
Door hinge bolts	30	22
Door lock striker Torx bolts	18	13
Facia crossmember bolts	22	16
Front bumper reinforcement bar nuts/bolts	22	16
Front seat belt adjuster bolts	22	16
Front seat belt upper mounting nut	33	24
Front seat mounting Torx bolts*	45	33
Front seat tensioner mounting bolts	30	22
Seat belt/buckle mountings to body	50	37
Steering column support bracket-to-crossmember nuts/bolts	18	13
Tailgate window securing Torx screws	9	7
Tailgate hinge bolts	25	18

** Use new bolts*

1 General information

The bodyshell and floorpan are manufactured from pressed-steel, and form an integral part of the car's structure (monocoque), without the need for a separate chassis. The 75/MG ZT is available in 4-door Saloon and 5-door Tourer (Estate) bodystyles. The bodyshell is very highly engineered, with innovative dual-thickness steels combining strength and lightness, resulting in a stiff shell with very tight shutlines.

Various areas of the structure are strengthened to provide for suspension, steering and engine mounting points, and load distribution.

Corrosion protection is applied to all models. Various anti-corrosion preparations are used, including galvanising, zinc phosphatisation, and PVC underseal. An 'anti-gravel' undercoat is applied to various exposed areas, to prevent corrosion and paint chipping caused by stones and other road debris hitting the car. Protective wax is injected into the box sections and other hollow cavities.

Extensive use is made of plastic for peripheral components, such as the radiator grille, bumpers and wheel trims, and for much of the interior trim. Plastic wheel arch liners are fitted, to protect the metal body panels against corrosion due to a build-up of road dirt.

2 Maintenance – bodywork and underframe

The general condition of a car's bodywork is the one thing that significantly affects its value. Maintenance is easy, but needs to be regular. Neglect, particularly after minor damage, can lead quickly to further deterioration and costly repair bills. It is important also to keep watch on those parts of the car not immediately visible, for instance the underside, inside all the wheel arches, and the lower part of the engine compartment.

The basic maintenance routine for the bodywork is washing – preferably with a lot of water, from a hose. This will remove all the loose solids which may have stuck to the car. It is important to flush these off in such a way as to prevent grit from scratching the finish. The wheel arches and underside need washing in the same way, to remove any accumulated mud which will retain moisture and tend to encourage rust. Strange as it sounds, the best time to clean the underside and wheel arches is in wet weather, when the mud is thoroughly wet and soft. In very wet weather, the underside is usually cleaned of large accumulations automatically, and this is a good time for inspection.

Periodically, except on cars with a wax-based underbody protective coating, it is a good idea to have the whole of the underframe of the car steam-cleaned, engine compartment included, so that a thorough inspection can be carried out to see what minor repairs and renovations are necessary. Steam-cleaning is available at many garages, and is necessary for the removal of the accumulation of oily grime, which sometimes is allowed to become thick in certain areas. If steam-cleaning facilities are not available, grease solvents are available, which can be brush-applied; the dirt can then be simply hosed off. Note that these methods should not be used on cars with wax-based underbody protective coating, or the coating will be removed. Such cars should be inspected annually, preferably just prior to Winter, when the underbody should be washed down, and any damage to the wax coating repaired. Ideally, a completely fresh coat should be applied. It would also be worth considering the use of such wax-based protection for injection into door panels, sills, box sections, etc, as an additional safeguard against rust damage, where such protection is not provided by the car manufacturer.

After washing the paintwork, wipe off with a chamois leather to give an unspotted clear finish. A coat of clear protective wax polish will give added protection against chemical pollutants in the air. If the paintwork sheen has dulled or oxidised, use a cleaner/polisher combination to restore the brilliance of the shine. This requires a little effort, but such dulling is usually caused because regular washing has been neglected. Care needs to be taken with metallic paintwork, as special non-abrasive cleaner/polisher is required to avoid damage to the finish. Always check that the door and ventilator opening drain holes and pipes are completely clear, so that water can be drained out. Brightwork should be treated in the same way as paintwork. Windscreens and windows can be kept clear of the smeary film which often appears, by the use of proprietary glass cleaner. Never use wax polish on glass, and particularly not on the windscreen.

3 Maintenance – upholstery and carpets

Mats and carpets should be brushed or vacuum-cleaned regularly, to keep them free of grit. If they are badly stained, remove them from the car for scrubbing or sponging, and make quite sure they are dry before refitting.

Cloth or velour seats and interior trim panels can be kept clean by wiping with a damp cloth. If they do become stained (which can be more apparent on light-coloured cloth or velour upholstery), use a little liquid detergent and a soft nail brush to scour the grime out of the grain of the material. Keep the headlining clean in the same way as the upholstery

In the case of leather upholstery, a whole range of different products exist to clean, feed and generally restore the leather, and it is recommended that these are used exclusively. Ordinary detergents should be avoided, as they will prematurely dry out leather, causing it to crack and split.

When using liquid cleaners inside the car, do not over-wet the surfaces being cleaned. Excessive damp could get into the seams and padded interior, causing stains, offensive odours or even rot. If the inside of the car gets wet accidentally, it is worthwhile taking some trouble to dry it out properly, particularly where carpets are involved. *Do not leave oil or electric heaters inside the car for this purpose.*

4 Minor body damage – repair

Repair of minor scratches

If the scratch is very superficial, and does not penetrate to the metal of the bodywork, repair is very simple. Lightly rub the area of the scratch with a paintwork renovator, or a very fine cutting paste, to remove loose paint from the scratch, and to clear the surrounding bodywork of wax polish. Rinse the area with clean water.

In the case of metallic paint, the most commonly-found scratches are not in the paint, but in the lacquer top coat, and appear white. If care is taken, these can sometimes be rendered less obvious by very careful use of paintwork renovator (which would otherwise not be used on metallic paintwork); otherwise, repair of these scratches can be achieved by applying lacquer with a fine brush. Also note that damage to the lacquer coat will show up worse if (white) polish residue collects in the chip or scratch – clean any suspected area thoroughly.

Apply touch-up paint to the scratch using a fine paint brush; continue to apply fine layers of paint (allowing each one time to dry) until the surface of the paint in the scratch is level with the surrounding paintwork. Allow the new paint at least two weeks to harden, then blend it into the surrounding paintwork by rubbing the scratch area with a paintwork renovator or a very fine cutting paste. Finally, apply wax polish.

Where the scratch has penetrated right through to the metal of the bodywork, causing the metal to rust, a different repair technique is required. Remove any loose rust from the bottom of the scratch with a penknife, then apply rust-inhibiting paint, to prevent the formation of rust in the future. Using a rubber or nylon applicator, fill the scratch with bodystopper paste. If required, this paste can be mixed with cellulose thinners, to provide a very thin paste which is ideal for filling narrow scratches. Before the stopper-paste in the scratch hardens, wrap a piece of smooth cotton rag around the top of a finger. Dip the finger in cellulose thinners, and quickly sweep it across the surface of the stopper-paste in the scratch; this will ensure that the surface of the stopper-paste is slightly hollowed. The scratch can now be painted over as described earlier in this Section.

Repair of dents

If the dent is shallow, and the paint has not been broken, it may be possible to have the dent repaired professionally, by one of the specialist mobile dent repair companies.

When deep denting of the car's bodywork has taken place, the first task is to pull the dent out, until the affected bodywork almost attains its original shape. There is little point in trying to restore the original shape completely, as the metal in the damaged area will have stretched on impact, and cannot be reshaped fully to its original contour. It is better to bring the level of the dent up to a point which is about 3 mm below the level of the surrounding bodywork. In cases where the dent is very shallow anyway, it is not worth trying to pull it out at all. If the underside of the dent is accessible, it can be hammered out gently from behind, using a mallet with a wooden or plastic head. Whilst doing this, hold a block of wood firmly against the outside of the panel, to absorb the impact from the hammer blows and thus prevent a large area of the bodywork from being 'belled-out'.

Should the dent be in a section of the bodywork which has a double skin, or some other factor making it inaccessible from behind, a different technique is called for. Drill several small holes through the metal inside the area – particularly in the deeper section. Then screw long self-tapping screws into the holes, just sufficiently for them to gain a good purchase in the metal. Now the dent can be pulled out by pulling on the protruding heads of the screws with a pair of pliers.

The next stage of the repair is the removal of the paint from the damaged area, and from an inch or so of the surrounding 'sound' bodywork. This is accomplished most easily by using a wire brush or abrasive pad on a power drill, although it can be done just as effectively by hand, using sheets of abrasive paper. To complete the preparation for filling, score the surface of the bare metal with a screwdriver or the tang of a file, or alternatively, drill small holes in the affected area. This will provide a really good 'key' for the filler paste.

To complete the repair, see the Section on filling and respraying.

Repair of rust holes or gashes

Remove all paint from the affected area, and from an inch or so of the surrounding 'sound' bodywork, using an abrasive pad or a wire brush on a power drill. If these are not available, a few sheets of abrasive paper will do the job most effectively. With the paint removed, you will be able to judge the severity of the corrosion, and therefore decide whether to renew the whole panel (if this is possible) or to repair the affected area. New body panels are not as expensive as most people think, and it is often quicker and more satisfactory to fit a new panel than to attempt to repair large areas of corrosion.

Remove all fittings from the affected area, except those which will act as a guide to the original shape of the damaged bodywork (e.g. light units). Then, using tin snips or a hacksaw blade, remove all loose metal and any other metal badly affected by corrosion. Hammer the edges of the hole inwards, in order to create a slight depression for the filler paste.

Wire-brush the affected area to remove the powdery rust from the surface of the remaining metal. Paint the affected area with rust-inhibiting paint; if the back of the rusted area is accessible, treat this also.

Before filling can take place, it will be necessary to block the hole in some way. This can be achieved by the use of aluminium or plastic mesh, or aluminium tape.

Aluminium or plastic mesh, or glass-fibre matting is probably the best material to use for a large hole. Cut a piece to the approximate size and shape of the hole to be filled, then position it in the hole so that its edges are below the level of the surrounding bodywork. It can be retained in position by several blobs of filler paste around its periphery.

Aluminium tape should be used for small or very narrow holes. Pull a piece off the roll, trim it to the approximate size and shape required, then pull off the backing paper (if used) and stick the tape over the hole; it can be overlapped if the thickness of one piece is insufficient. Burnish down the edges of the tape with the handle of a screwdriver or similar, to ensure that the tape is securely attached to the metal underneath.

Filling and respraying

Before using this Section, see the Sections on dent, deep scratch, rust holes and gash repairs.

Many types of bodyfiller are available, but generally speaking, those proprietary kits which contain a tin of filler paste and a tube of resin hardener are best for this type of repair. A wide, flexible plastic or nylon applicator will be found invaluable for imparting a smooth and well-contoured finish to the surface of the filler.

Mix up a little filler on a clean piece of card or board – measure the hardener carefully (follow the maker's instructions on the pack), otherwise the filler will set too rapidly or too slowly. Using the applicator, apply the filler paste to the prepared area; draw the applicator across the surface of the filler to achieve the correct contour and to level the surface. As soon as a contour that approximates to the correct one is achieved, stop working the paste – if you carry on too long, the paste will become sticky and begin to 'pick-up' on the applicator. Continue to add thin layers of filler paste at 20-minute intervals, until the level of the filler is just proud of the surrounding bodywork.

Once the filler has hardened, the excess can be removed using a metal plane or file. From then on, progressively-finer grades of abrasive paper should be used, starting with a 40-grade production paper, and finishing with a 400-grade wet-and-dry paper. Always wrap the abrasive paper around a flat rubber, cork, or wooden block – otherwise the surface of the filler will not be completely flat. During the smoothing of the filler surface, the wet-and-dry paper should be periodically rinsed in water. This will ensure that a very smooth finish is imparted to the filler at the final stage.

At this stage, the 'dent' should be surrounded by a ring of bare metal, which in turn should be encircled by the finely 'feathered' edge of the good paintwork. Rinse the repair area with clean water, until all of the dust produced by the rubbing-down operation has gone.

Spray the whole area with a light coat of – this will show up any imperfections in the surface of the filler. Repair these imperfections with fresh filler paste or bodystopper, and once more smooth the surface with abrasive paper. If bodystopper is used, it can be mixed with cellulose thinners, to form a really thin paste which is ideal for filling small holes. Repeat this spray-and-repair procedure until you are satisfied that the surface of the filler, and the feathered edge of the paintwork, are perfect. Clean the repair area with clean water, and allow to dry fully.

The repair area is now ready for final spraying. Paint spraying must be carried out in a warm, dry, windless and dust-free atmosphere. This condition can be created artificially if you have access to a large indoor working area, but if you are forced to work in the open, you will have to pick your day very carefully. If you are working indoors, dousing the floor in the work area with water will help to settle the dust which would otherwise be in the atmosphere. If the repair area is confined to one body panel, mask off the surrounding panels; this will help to minimise the effects of a slight mis-match in paint colours. Bodywork fittings (e.g. chrome strips, door handles etc) will also need to be masked off. Use genuine masking tape, and several thicknesses of newspaper, for the masking operations.

Before commencing to spray, agitate the aerosol can thoroughly, then spray a test area (an old tin, or similar) until the technique is mastered. Cover the repair area with a thick coat of primer; the thickness should be built up using several thin layers of paint, rather than one thick one. Using 400 grade wet-and-dry paper, rub down the surface of the primer until it is really smooth. While doing this, the work area should be thoroughly doused with water, and the wet-and-dry paper periodically rinsed in water. Allow to dry before spraying on more paint.

Spray on the top coat, again building up the thickness by using several thin layers of paint. Start spraying at the top of the repair area, and then, using a side-to-side motion, work downwards until the whole repair area and about 2 inches of the surrounding original paintwork is covered. Remove all masking material 10 to 15 minutes after spraying on the final coat of paint.

Allow the new paint at least two weeks to harden, then, using a paintwork renovator or a very fine cutting paste, blend the edges of the paint into the existing paintwork. Finally, apply wax polish.

Plastic components

With the use of more and more plastic body components by the car manufacturers (e.g. bumpers, spoilers, and in some cases major body panels), rectification of more serious damage to such items has become a matter of either entrusting repair work to a specialist in this field, or renewing complete components. Repair of such damage by the DIY owner is not really feasible, owing to the cost of the equipment and materials required for effecting such repairs. The basic technique involves making a groove along the line of the crack in the plastic, using a rotary burr in a power drill. The damaged part is then welded back together, using a hot air gun to heat up and fuse a plastic filler rod into the groove. Any excess plastic is then removed, and the area rubbed down to a smooth finish. It is important that a filler rod of the correct plastic is used, as body components can be made of a variety of different types (e.g. polycarbonate, ABS, polypropylene).

Damage of a less serious nature (abrasions, minor cracks etc) can be repaired by the DIY owner using a two-part epoxy filler repair. Once mixed in equal, this is used in similar fashion to the bodywork filler used on metal panels. The filler is usually cured in twenty to thirty minutes, ready for sanding and painting.

If the owner is renewing a complete component himself, or if he has repaired it with epoxy filler, he will be left with the problem of finding a suitable paint for finishing which is compatible with the type of plastic used. At one time, the use of a universal paint was not possible, owing to the complex range of plastics encountered in body component applications. Standard paints, generally speaking, will not bond to plastic or rubber satisfactorily, but suitable paints to match any plastic or rubber finish, can be obtained from dealers. However, it is now possible to obtain a plastic body parts finishing kit which consists of a pre-primer treatment, a primer and coloured top coat. Full instructions are normally supplied with a kit, but basically, the method of use is to first apply the pre-primer to the component concerned, and allow it to dry for up to 30 minutes. Then the primer is applied, and left to dry for about an hour before finally applying the special-coloured top coat. The result is a correctly-coloured component, where the paint will flex with the plastic or rubber, a property that standard paint does not normally possess.

5 Major body damage – repair

Where serious damage has occurred, or large areas need renewal due to neglect, it means that complete new panels will need welding-in, and this is best left to professionals. If the damage is due to impact, it will also be necessary to check completely the alignment of the bodyshell, and this can only be carried out accurately by an MG Rover-approved bodyshop using special jigs. If the body is left misaligned, it is primarily dangerous, as the car will not handle properly, and secondly, uneven stresses will be imposed on the steering, suspension and possibly transmission, causing abnormal wear, or complete failure, particularly to such items as the tyres.

6 Bumpers – removal and refitting

Front bumper

1 Open the bonnet, and remove a total of nine (black) bolts which secure the top edge of the bumper to the bonnet lock platform – five behind the grille, and two more above each headlight **(see illustrations)**.

2 Inside the wheel arch, remove a bumper-to-wheel arch liner screw, and a vertical bumper-to-wheel arch bolt, on each side **(see illustrations)**.

3 Underneath the bumper, remove the three cross-head screws at the front of each wheel arch which secure the bumper to the front brake air ducts **(see illustration)**.

4 Under the car, in the centre of the bumper, remove a total of four quick-release screw fasteners which secure the engine undertray to the bumper lower edge **(see illustration)**.

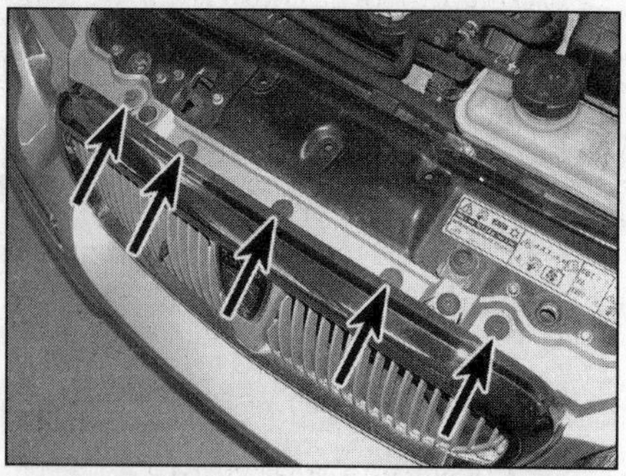

6.1a Remove the five bolts behind the grille . . .

6.1b . . . and two more above each headlight

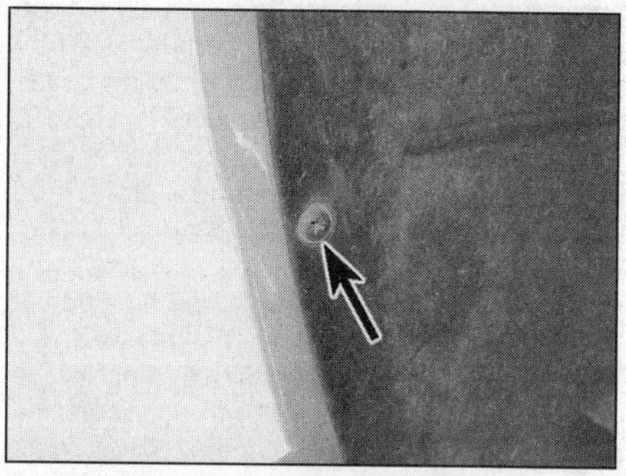

6.2a Remove the bumper-to-wheel arch screw . . .

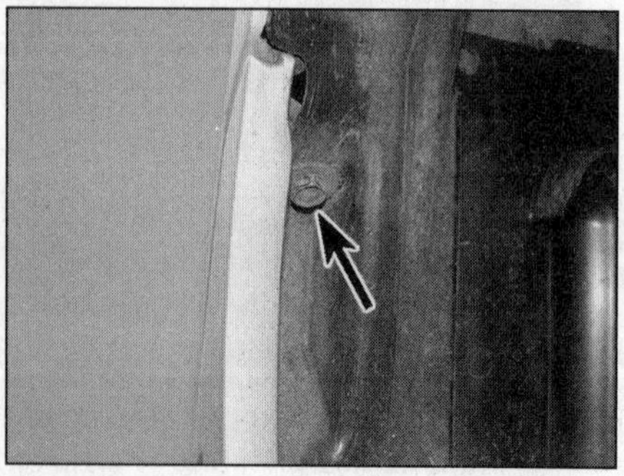

6.2b . . . and the vertically-mounted bolt (seen here from below)

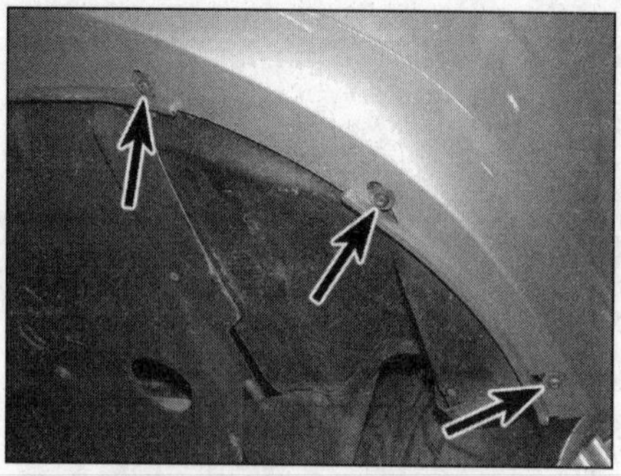

6.3 Underneath the bumper, remove the three screws each side . . .

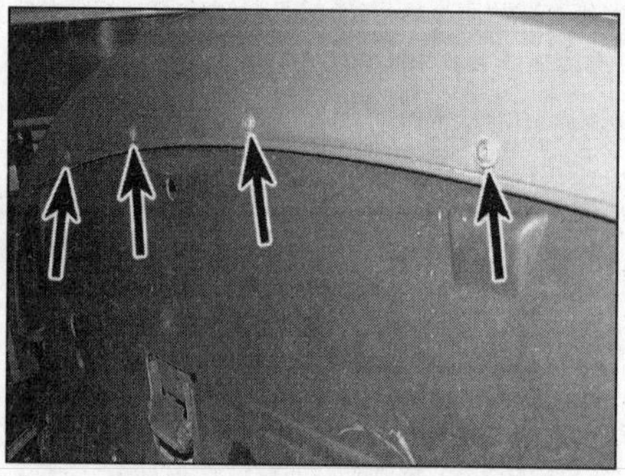

6.4 . . . and four more screws in the centre

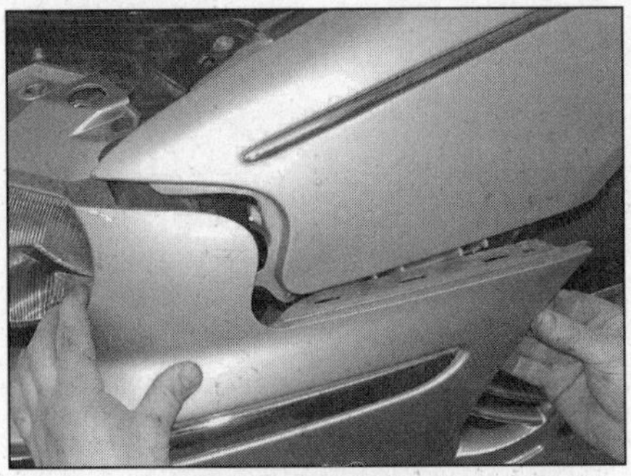
6.5 Lift the bumper ends, and pull outwards to unclip

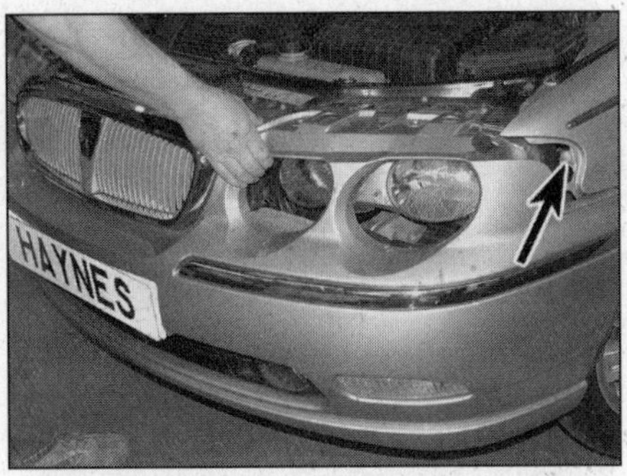

6.6 Release the 'fir-tree' clip each side (arrowed) and withdraw the bumper

6.7 Disconnect the bumper wiring harness plug under the headlight

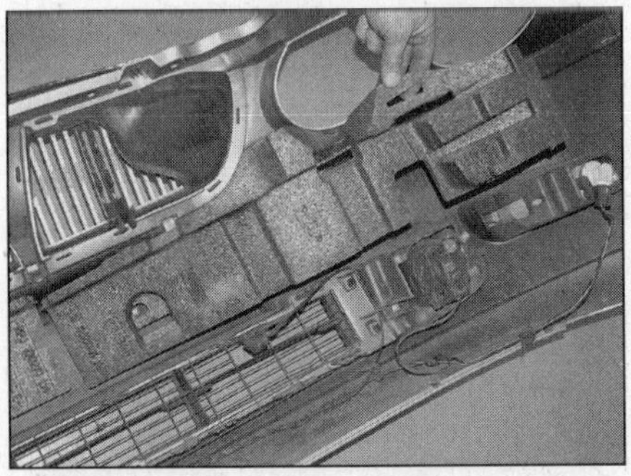
6.9a The bumper foam pieces may fall out as the bumper is refitted . . .

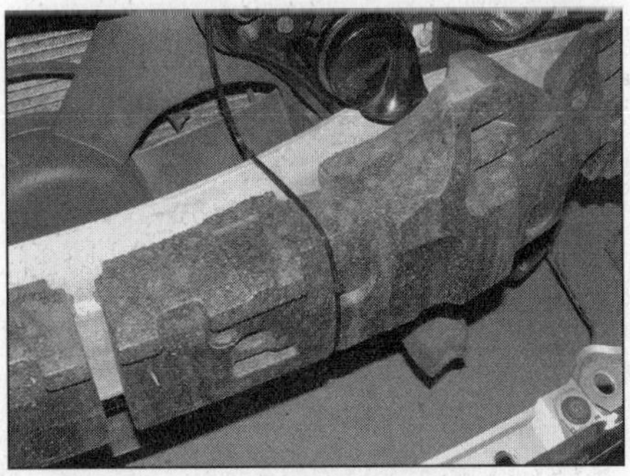
6.9b . . . so we cable-tied them to the bumper beam instead

6.9c Use pliers to release the 'fir-tree' clips from the wings . . .

5 With the help of an assistant, carefully lift and pull outwards the bumper ends, to detach them from the side mountings – this may take some effort, if the bumper has not previously been disturbed **(see illustration)**.

6 The bumper is now held by a single (yellow) push-in clip – known by MG Rover as a 'fir-tree' clip – on each side, at the front of the front wing. With the help of an assistant, carefully pull the bumper forwards to separate these two clips, and lower the bumper to the floor **(see illustration)**.

7 Disconnect the bumper wiring harness multi-plug, which is clipped under the left-hand headlight **(see illustration)**. On models with headlight washers, trace the washer hose back to the reservoir, then release the clip and disconnect the hose.

8 Check that nothing else remains attached to the bumper, then remove it completely.

9 Refitting is a reversal of removal, noting the following points:

a) *The bumper contains two large pieces of impact-absorbing polystyrene foam in the centre, which readily fall out. We found that attaching them to the bumper beam on the front of the car with cable-ties was better than them falling out of the bumper during fitting* ***(see illustrations)****.*

b) *The main body of each 'fir-tree' clip will remain in the wing, and must be removed prior to refitting the bumper. Use thin-nosed pliers to squeeze the clip legs, and pull them out. Press them back onto the sockets remaining in the bumper* ***(see illustrations)****.*

c) *Take care when refitting that the 'fir-tree' clips are accurately aligned with the holes at the front of the wings, and are pushed fully home* ***(see illustration)****. Also ensure that the side mountings engage properly.*

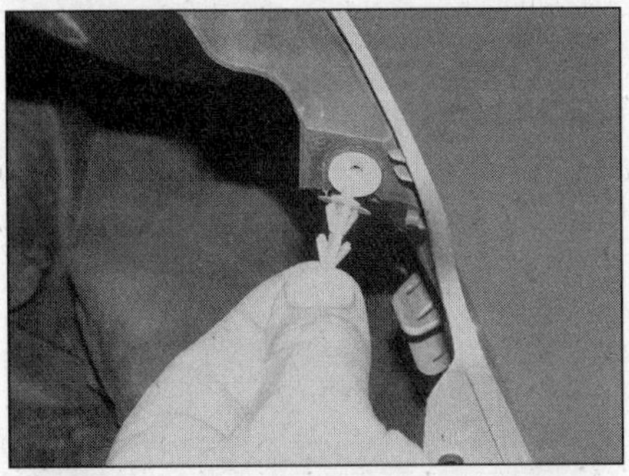
6.9d . . . and refit them to the bumper sockets

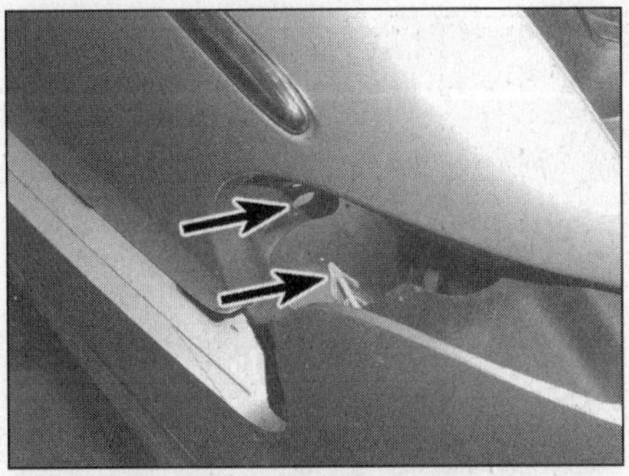
6.9e Align the clips with the wing holes, and press firmly home

Rear bumper

Saloon

10 Open the boot, and remove the five screw/clips (known as 'scrivets') from the top edge of the bumper **(see illustrations)**

6.10a Remove the five screws along the top edge of the bumper . . .

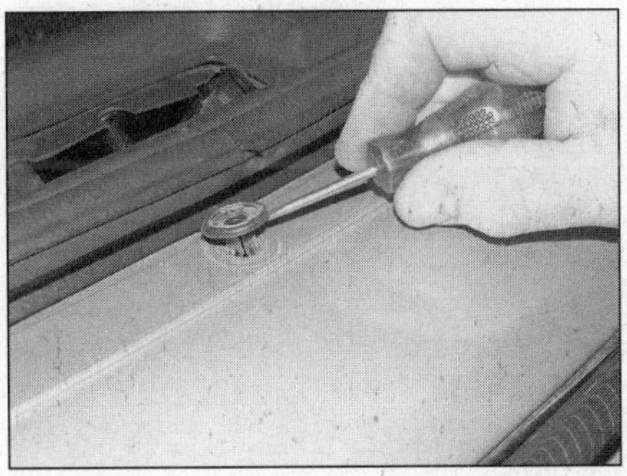
6.10b . . . and prise out the clips

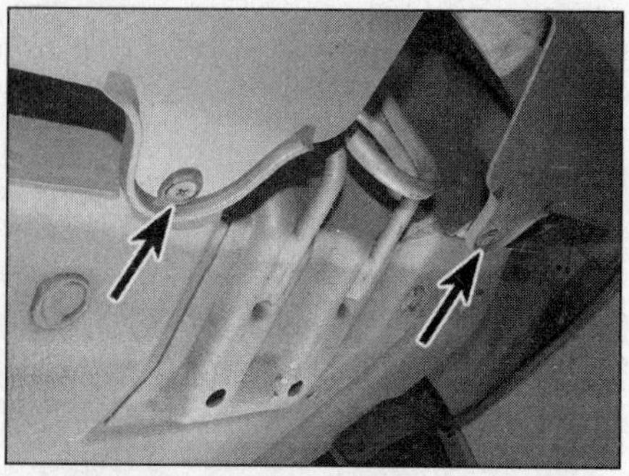

6.11 Remove the two screw/clips either side of the towing eye

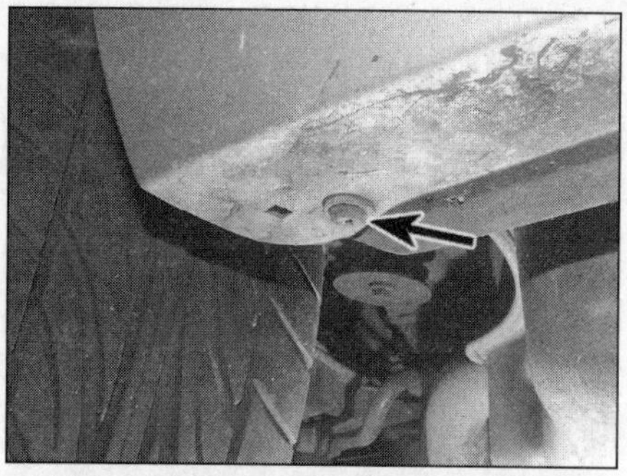

6.12 Remove the screw each side at the front end

6.13 Lift and pull the bumper ends to release the clips

6.18 Remove the bumper-to-wheel arch liner screw each side

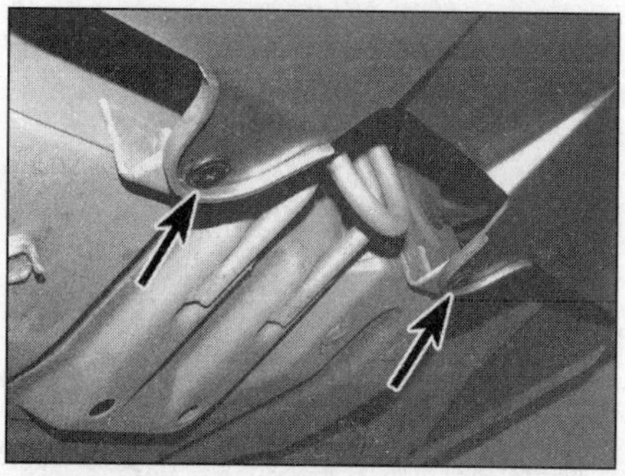

6.19 Remove the two 'scrivets' in the centre

11 From underneath, remove the screw/clip either side of the cut-out for the rear towing eye **(see illustration)**.

12 Remove the single screw securing each end of the bumper to the rear wheel arch liner **(see illustration)**.

13 With the help of an assistant, carefully lift and pull outwards the bumper ends, to detach them from the side mountings **(see illustration)** – the clips are quite stiff to release. Pull the bumper rearwards off the car.

14 On models with rear parking sensors, disconnect the sensor harness wiring plug.

15 Withdraw the bumper from the rear of the car, and remove it completely.

16 Where applicable, the four rear parking sensors can be removed after disconnecting each one's wiring plug. Each sensor is clipped into a holder, which is itself clipped to the bumper.

17 Refitting is a reversal of removal.

Tourer

18 Remove the single screw securing each end of the bumper to the rear wheel arch liner, under the car **(see illustration)**.

19 Also under the car, remove the two screw/clips (known as 'scrivets') securing the centre of the bumper to the spare wheel well **(see illustration)**. On models with rear parking sensors, reach up behind the bumper, just to the right of centre, and disconnect the wiring multi-plug for the bumper harness – alternatively, this can be left connected until the bumper is removed.

20 Remove the single bumper securing screw each side, just below the rear light cluster **(see illustration)**.

21 Unclip and remove the plastic 'tread plate' from the top of the bumper, just behind the tailgate aperture. Remove the five bumper retaining screws underneath the plate **(see illustration)**.

22 Carefully lift and pull outwards the bumper ends, to detach them from the side mountings – the clips are quite stiff to release. With the help of an assistant, pull the bumper rearwards off the car. If not already done, disconnect the wiring plug for the rear parking sensors, where applicable **(see illustrations)**.

6.20 Remove the screw each side, below the light cluster

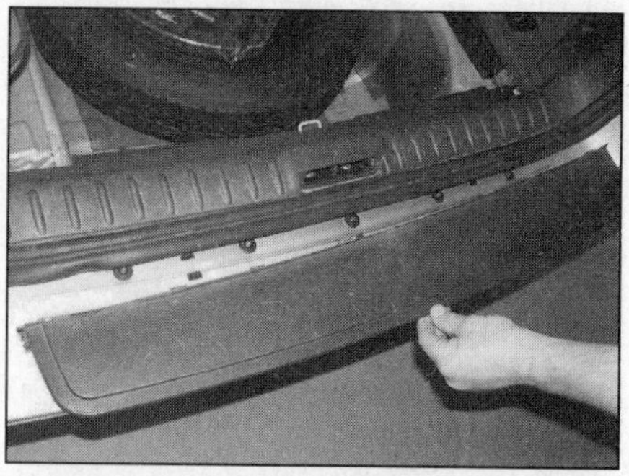

6.21 Unclip the 'tread plate' and remove the five screws beneath

6.22a Unclip the bumper ends . . .

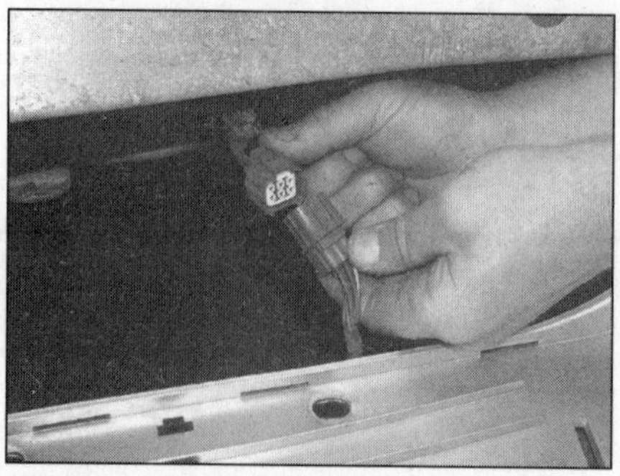

6.22b . . . then withdraw the bumper, and disconnect the parking sensor plug . . .

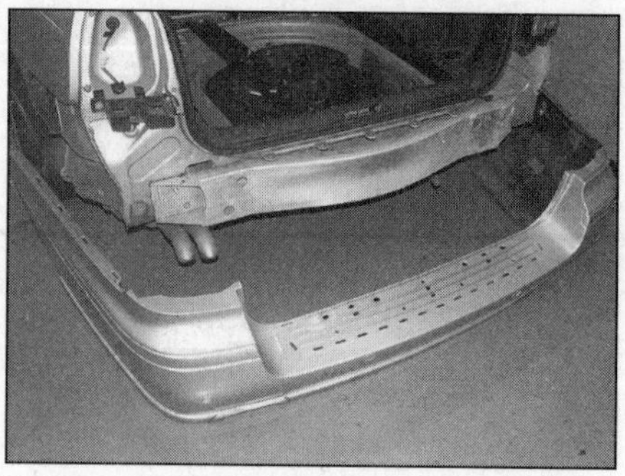

6.22c . . . before lowering the bumper to the floor

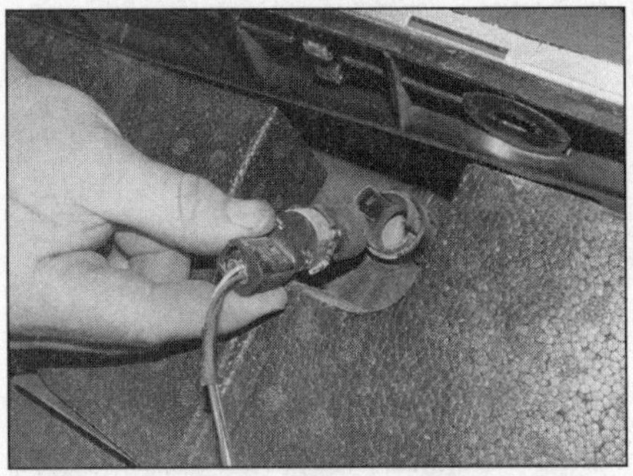

6.23 Removing one of the parking sensors from the rear bumper

23 The four rear parking sensors can be removed after disconnecting each one's wiring plug. Each sensor is clipped into a holder, and a further finisher is clipped to the bumper **(see illustration)**.

24 Refitting is a reversal of removal.

7 Radiator grille panel – removal and refitting

Rover 75 models

1 The grille is removed by unscrewing the two cross-head screws and prising out the clips (known as 'scrivets') visible behind the grille with the bonnet open **(see illustration)**.

2 With the scrivets removed, carefully unclip and remove the grille from the car **(see illustration)**.

3 Refitting is a reversal of removal. Take care that the bonnet safety catch operating lever is fed through the grille correctly.

MG ZT models

4 On MG models, the grille is part of the front bumper assembly, which is removed as described in Section 6.

8 Windscreen cowl panels – removal and refitting

Removal

1 Open the bonnet.

2 Each of the two panels is secured by two clips at the front edge – release the clips and

8.6a At the back edge of the panel, prise out . . .

7.1 Remove the screw and prise out the clip underneath . . .

remove the panels **(see illustration)**.

3 Pull off the rubber weather strip at the top of the bulkhead **(see illustration)**.

4 To remove the cowl panel frame, remove the windscreen wiper arms as described in Chapter 12.

8.2 Press the two clips at the front, and remove the access panels

8.5a At each front corner, remove the cross-head screw . . .

8.6b . . . and remove seven clips . . .

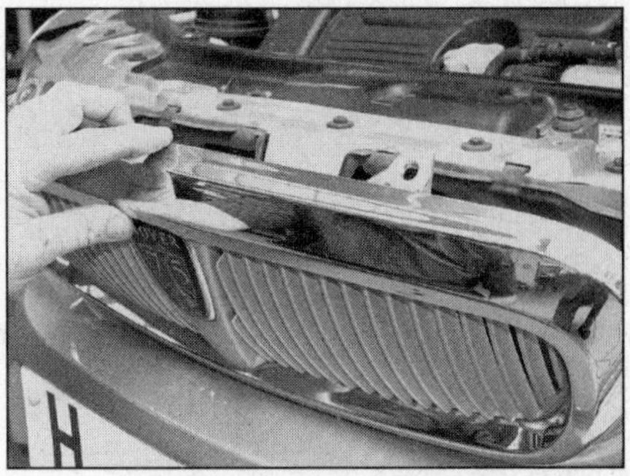

7.2 . . . then unclip and remove the grille

5 Remove the screw/clip at the front corners **(see illustrations)**.

6 Prise out the row of seven clips along the back edge, then lift out the cowl panel frame, unclipping the washer tube from it as it is removed **(see illustrations)**.

8.3 Pull off the rubber weatherstrip

8.5b . . . and prise out the clip

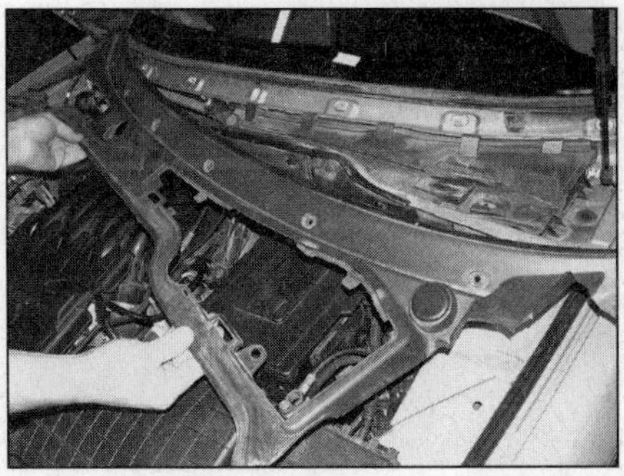

8.6c . . . then lift out the cowl panel frame

8.7 Unclip the splash shield from the passenger side

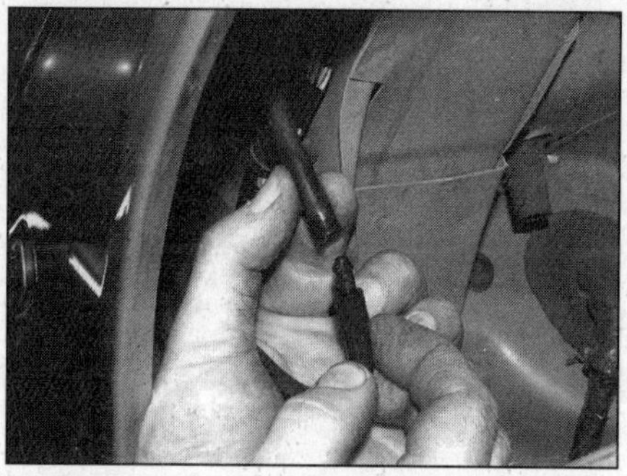

9.4 Disconnect the washer tube at the in-line connector

9.5 Release the washer tubing from the bonnet clip

7 If required, unclip the splash shield from the passenger side **(see illustration)**.

Refitting

8 Refitting is a reversal of removal. Before refitting the cowl panels, however, check for signs of water getting trapped in the plenum housing below due to blocked water drains, as this can lead to ECU problems.

9 Bonnet – removal and refitting

Removal

1 Open the bonnet, and let the struts support it for now – an assistant will be required later, to support the bonnet during removal.

2 On models with heated washer jets, prise out the ten clips used to retain the soundproofing panel to the underside of the bonnet, and remove the panel. Peel off the tape securing the wiring multi-plugs to the underside of the bonnet, then disconnect the plugs. Pull out and disconnect the wiring grommet on the passenger's side of the bonnet.

3 Remove the right-hand front wheel arch liner, as described in Section 22.

4 At the top of the wheel arch, disconnect the windscreen washer hose at the in-line connector **(see illustration)**.

5 Unclip the washer tube at the driver's side of the bonnet **(see illustration)**. Tie string or wire to the wiring harness and washer tubing, to make pulling it back into place when refitting easier. Withdraw the wiring and tubing through the driver's side of the bonnet, then untie the string and leave it in place.

6 Where applicable, unbolt and unclip the earth strap from the passenger-side bonnet hinge.

7 Have an assistant support the bonnet in the open position.

8 Pull out the spring clip at the top of the bonnet support struts, then pull the top of each strut off its ball-stud fitting **(see illustration)**.

9 If the original bonnet is to be refitted, mark the position of the hinges on the bonnet to aid alignment on refitting (a line can be drawn around the hinge using a suitable pen, or typist's correction fluid).

10 Remove the bolts securing the bonnet to the hinges (two bolts at each side), then carefully withdraw the bonnet from the car **(see illustration)**.

Refitting

11 Refitting is a reversal of removal, bearing in mind the following points:

a) *Where applicable, align the hinges with the marks made on the bonnet before removal.*
b) *Close the bonnet (carefully, in case it fouls the surrounding bodywork), and check the alignment with the surrounding body panels. Also check the alignment with the bonnet locks.*
c) *If necessary, the alignment of the bonnet can be adjusted by altering the position of the bonnet on the hinges, using the elongated holes provided. Tighten the hinge bolts to the specified torque on completion.*

10 Bonnet lock platform – removal and refitting

Removal

1 With reference to Section 6, remove the front bumper.

2 Remove the eight bolts and two nuts, and

9.8 Remove the clip, then pull off each bonnet support strut

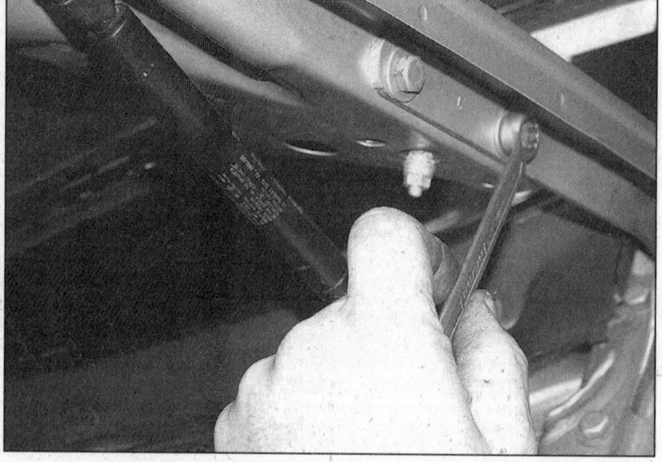

9.10 Loosening the bonnet hinge bolts

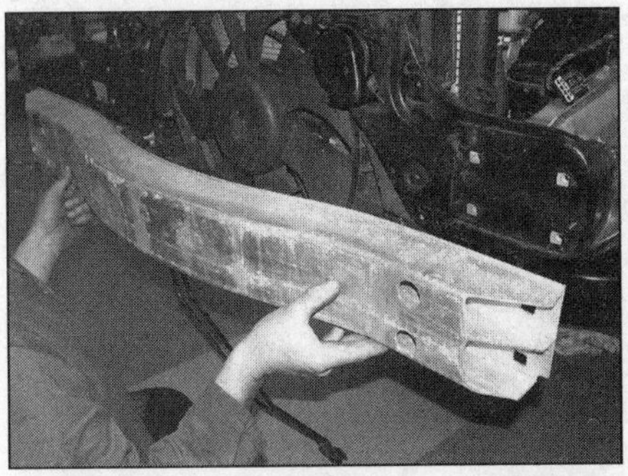

10.2 Removing the bumper reinforcement bar

10.4a Lock platform-to-wing bolt

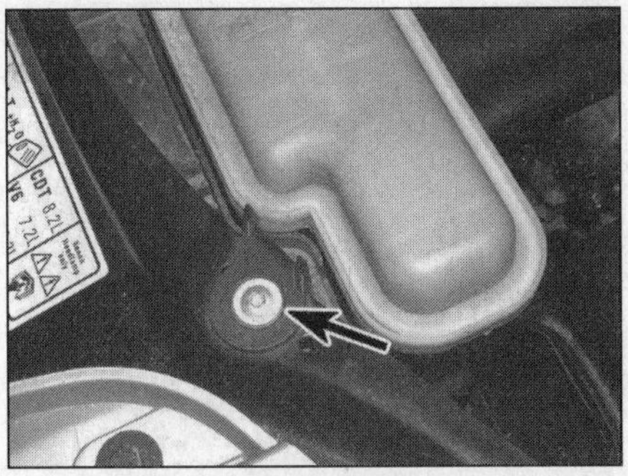

10.4b Radiator upper mounting bolt

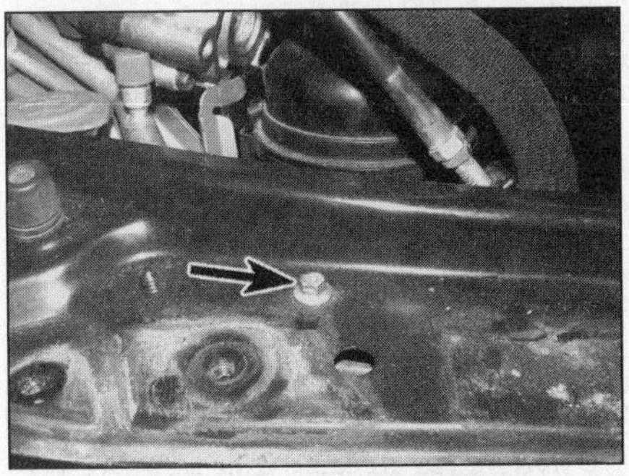

10.4c Refrigerant pipe bolt

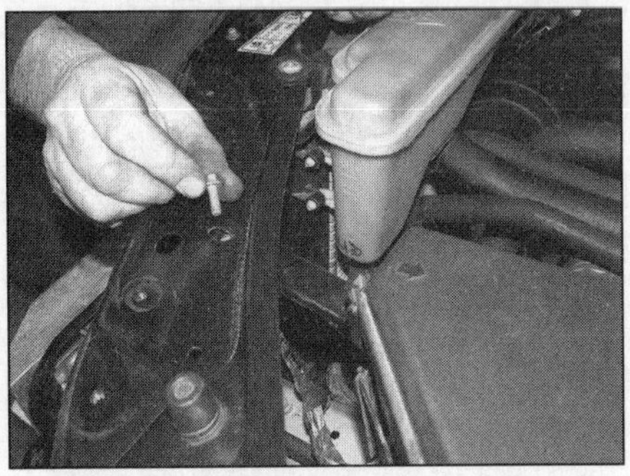

10.4d Removing the fusebox mounting bracket bolt

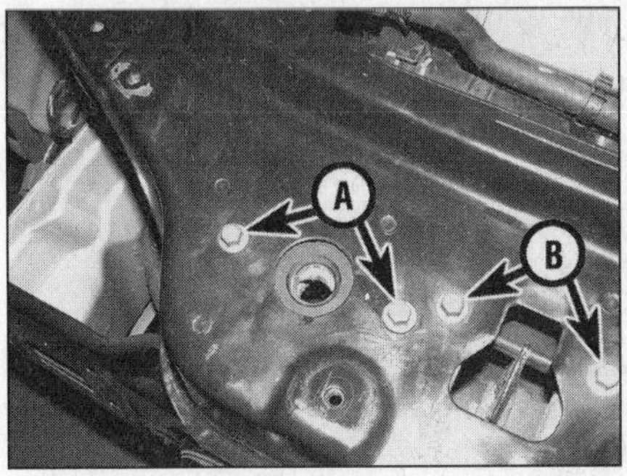

10.4e Bonnet lock bolts (A) and release catch bolts (B)

take off the bumper reinforcement bar **(see illustration)**.

3 Unscrew the four mounting bolts from each headlight, then disconnect the wiring plugs and remove the headlights completely.

4 Remove the following bolts from the bonnet lock platform **(see illustrations)**:

a) One bolt each side securing the platform to the wings.

b) The two radiator upper mounting bolts.

c) On diesel models, three bolts in the centre, securing the air intake duct.

d) On models with air conditioning, one bolt on the driver's side securing the refrigerant pipe.

e) On the passenger side, one bolt from the fusebox mounting bracket.

f) Two bolts from each bonnet lock, and two more from the release catch.

5 Release the bonnet lock platform from the front of the car, then disconnect the main wiring harness wiring plug on the driver's-side chassis leg. Release the bonnet lock cable from the clips, and remove the platform completely **(see illustrations)**.

Refitting

6 Refitting is a reversal of removal. Tighten all fasteners securely, or to the specified torque.

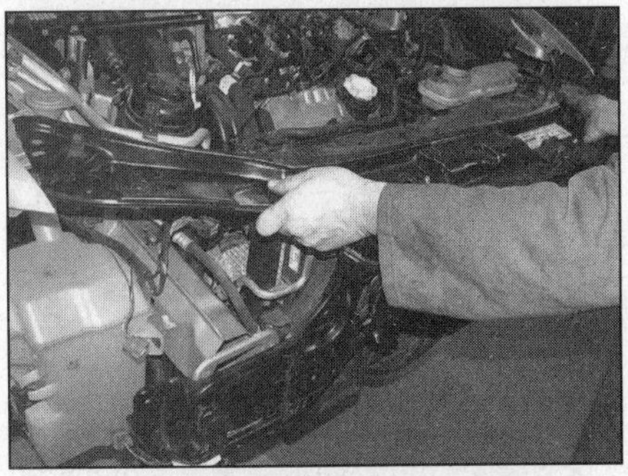

10.5a Withdraw the bonnet lock platform . . .

10.5b . . . then disconnect the wiring harness plug . . .

10.5c . . . and unclip the bonnet lock cables underneath

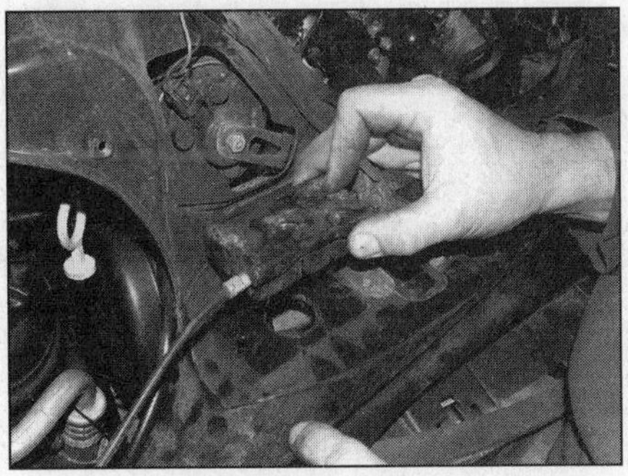

11.2 Removing the lock from under the lock platform

11 Bonnet lock components – removal and refitting

Lock assemblies

1 Remove the bonnet lock platform as described in Section 10.

2 Unhook the operating cable from the lock, then unscrew the two mounting bolts and remove it – note that two locks are fitted **(see illustration)**.

3 Refitting is a reversal of removal. Refit the bonnet lock platform as described in Section 10.

11.4 Bonnet lock cable coupling box location on right-hand inner wing

11.5 Unclip the top cover from the bonnet cable coupling box

Lock release cables

4 There are three cables fitted altogether – from the operating handle inside the car to a coupling box, then a separate cable for each of the two locks **(see illustration)**.

Handle cable

5 Unclip the bonnet release cable coupling box, located behind the driver's-side headlight on the inner wing **(see illustration)**.
6 Disconnect the handle cable from the coupling box **(see illustration)**.
7 Trace the cable back from the coupling box to the bulkhead, then release the cable grommet and feed the cable inside.
8 Inside the car, remove the driver's footwell trim panel as described in Section 25.
9 Remove the two bolts securing the operating handle, and turn it over. Unhook the cable end fitting from the back of the operating handle, then unclip and withdraw the cable **(see illustrations)**.
10 Refitting is a reversal of removal. Check that the cable is working correctly before closing the bonnet.

Lock cables

11 Remove the bonnet lock platform as described in Section 10.
12 Unhook the relevant operating cable from the lock(s).
13 For the driver's-side lock cable, unclip the bonnet release cable coupling box, located behind the driver's-side headlight on the inner wing **(see illustration 11.4)**. Disconnect the lock cable from the coupling box.
14 Refitting is a reversal of removal. Check that the cable is working correctly before closing the bonnet.

Safety catch

15 Remove the horn unit as described in Chapter 12.
16 Tie a long piece of string around the catch before removing it, and secure the other end to a convenient point in the engine compartment – this will make it easier to pull the catch back into position, as access is difficult.
17 Unscrew the two mounting bolts, and the catch will drop down – it will have to be retrieved from under the front bumper **(see illustration)**. Untie the string from the catch, leaving the string in place to pull the catch back up with.
18 Refitting is a reversal of removal. Pull the catch back into position, then secure with the two bolts. Refit the horn unit to complete.

11.6 Unhook the cable end fitting to disconnect it

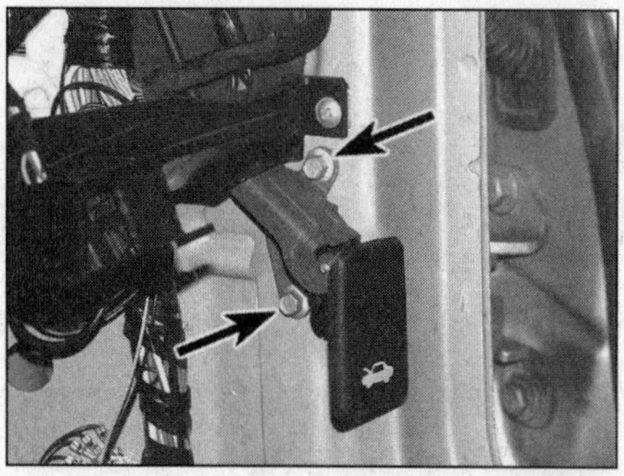

11.9a Remove the two operating handle bolts . . .

12 Doors – removal and refitting

Removal

1 To remove a door, open it fully, and support it under its lower edge on blocks or axle stands covered with pads of rag. Alternatively, have an assistant on hand to support the door.
2 Unscrew the single bolt at the front of the door check strap, and release it from the A-pillar (front door) or B-pillar (rear door) **(see illustration)**.

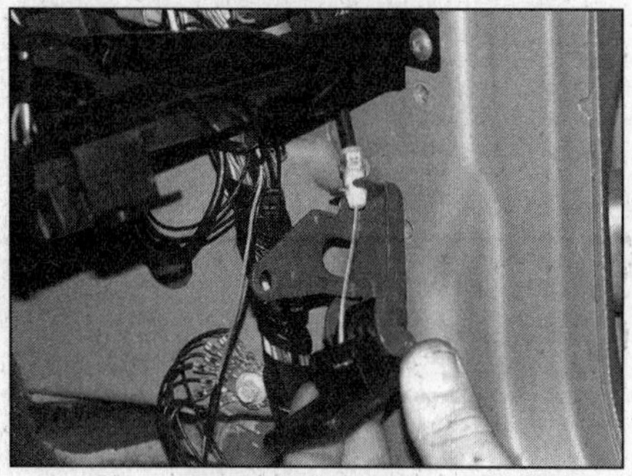

11.9b . . . then unclip and unhook the cable from the back

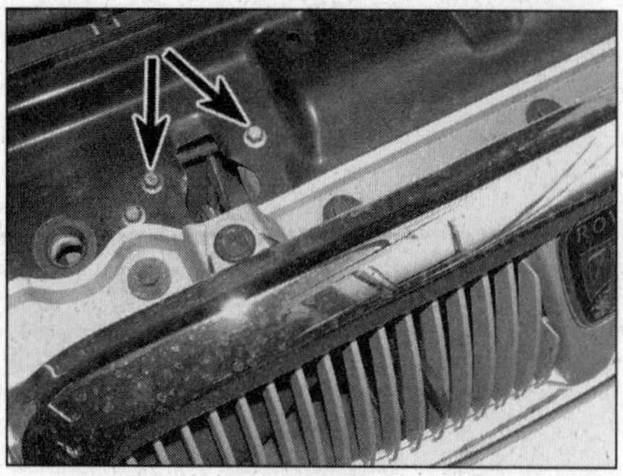

11.17 Bonnet safety catch mounting bolts (arrowed)

12.2 Unscrew the door check strap bolt

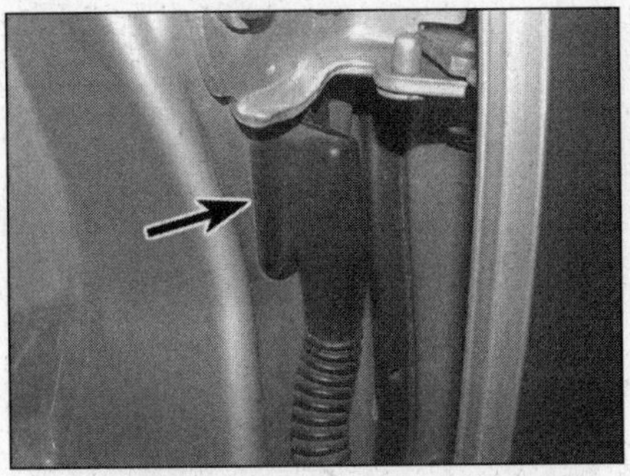

12.3a Prise out the door wiring harness grommet . . .

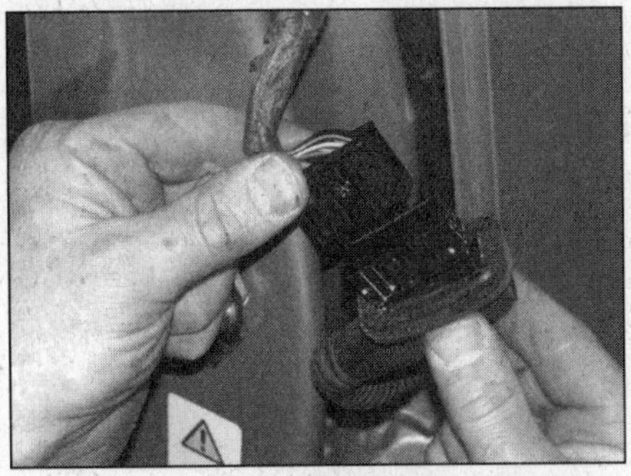

12.3b . . . and disconnect the connector plug

12.4 Carefully prise off the C-clip at the top of the hinge pins

3 Prise out the door wiring harness grommet from the door, then disconnect the wiring connector **(see illustrations)**.

4 Support the door, then prise off the C-clip from the top of each hinge pin (take care the clips do not fly off and get lost in the process) **(see illustration)**. Lift the door off the hinges and withdraw it from the car.

Refitting

5 Refitting is a reversal of removal. Fit new hinge C-clips if the old ones are in poor condition (or if they were lost during removal). Check the operation of the door. If the same doors are refitted, no adjustment should be required.

Adjustment

6 Door closure may be most easily adjusted by altering the position of the lock striker on the body pillar, after unscrewing the two Torx bolts **(see illustration)**. If the hinge pins are worn, causing the door to drop at the rear, this can be corrected by fitting new hinge pins.

7 The hinges are secured in position with bolts, and their position can be adjusted if required, though this method is not recommended unless absolutely necessary **(see illustration)**.

12.6 Adjust the door striker after loosening the Torx bolts

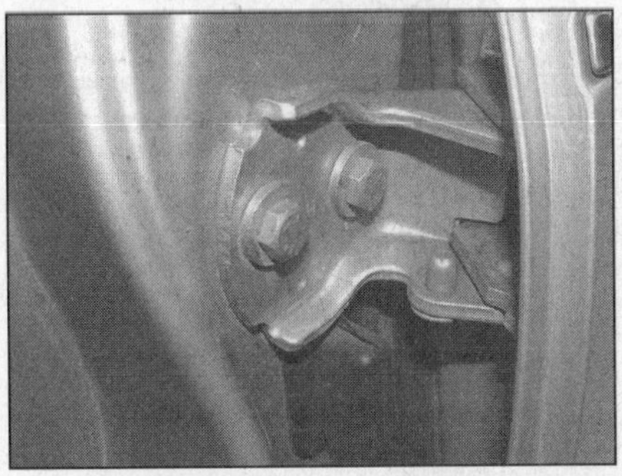

12.7 Door hinge mounting bolts

13 Door handle and lock components – removal and refitting

Door interior handle

1 Prise out the trim cover, and remove the single screw securing the door interior handle to the door **(see illustrations)**.

2 To prise out the handle (which is a tight fit in the panel), first push it backwards and unhook it at the front. Pull the handle forwards to clear the panel, turn it over, then unhook the operating cable from the rear of it **(see illustrations)**.

3 Refitting is a reversal of removal.

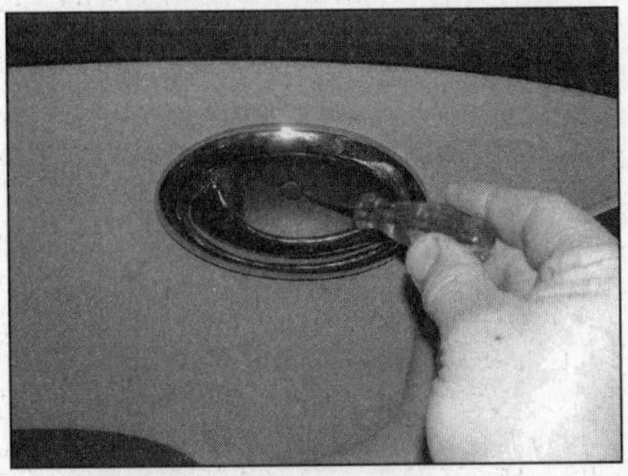

13.1a Prise out the screw cover . . .

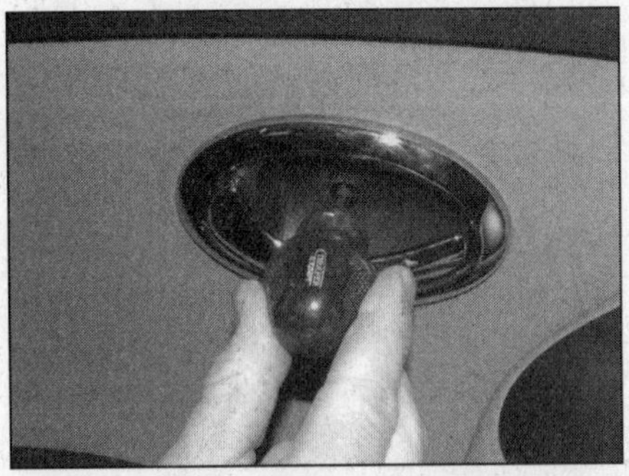

13.1b . . . and remove the cross-head screw behind

13.2a Push the handle rearwards, and unhook it at the front . . .

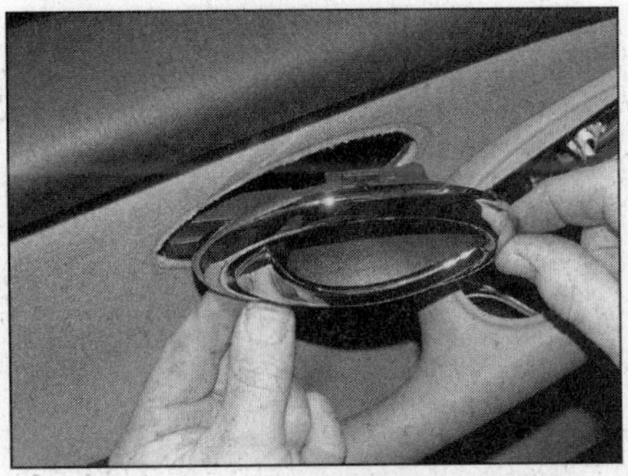

13.2b . . . pull it forwards as far as possible . . .

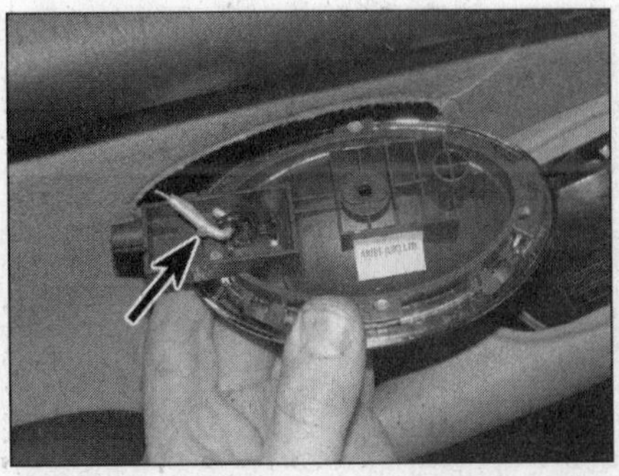

13.2c . . . then turn it over and unhook the operating cable

13.6a Use a screwdriver through the door top to push back the clip

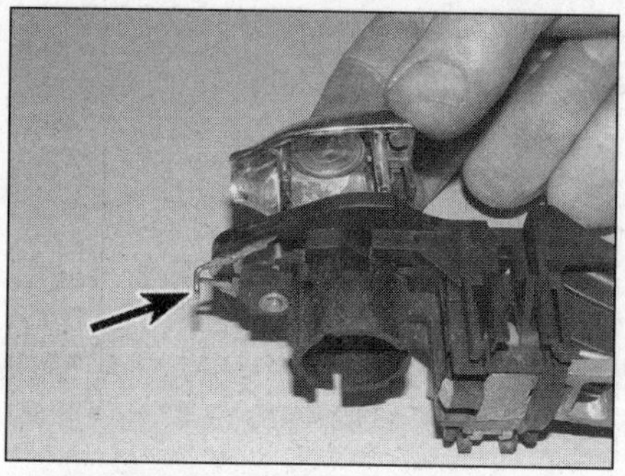

13.6b With the handle removed, the clip can be more easily seen

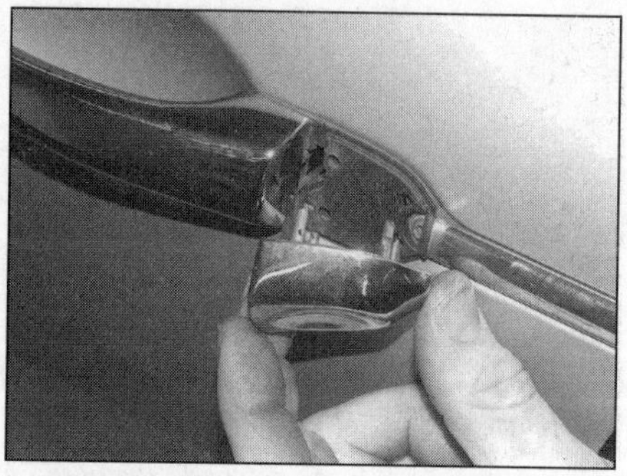

13.7 Removing the door handle rear trim

Door exterior handle

4 Remove the door trim panel as described in Section 14. Peel back the foam membrane at the rear upper corner.

5 On front doors, remove the lock as described later in this Section.

6 Look down inside the gap at the top of the door (an electric torch may be needed) to the inside of the handle. At the rear, a small metal tab should be visible – this has to be pushed rearwards to release the exterior handle's rear trim piece. Use a slim long-handled screwdriver to push the clip to the rear **(see illustrations)**.

7 Remove the door handle rear trim piece from the outside of the door **(see illustration)**.

8 Move the door handle rearwards to release it, then withdraw it from the door. Recover the gaskets fitted front and rear – obtain new ones if necessary for refitting **(see illustrations)**.

9 Loosen the two Torx screws securing the handle mounting plate, then slide the plate off the inside of the door **(see illustrations)**.

10 Refitting is a reversal of removal.

Door lock cylinder

11 Remove the door exterior handle and mounting plate as described previously in this Section.

12 The lock cylinder is clipped to the handle mounting plate – prise up the tab above the cylinder, and release it.

13 Refitting is a reversal of removal.

Door lock

14 Remove the door trim panel as described in Section 14. Peel back the foam membrane at the rear.

15 On front doors only, remove the door glass as described in Section 15. To improve access to the lock, loosen the top bolt, remove the lower bolt, and pull the glass rear guide channel forwards – it does not have to be removed completely **(see illustrations)**.

16 Disconnect the lock wiring plug at the base of the unit **(see illustration)**.

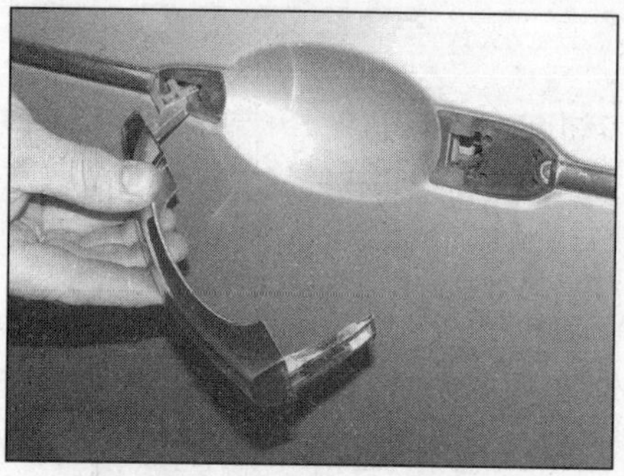

13.8a Take off the door handle . . .

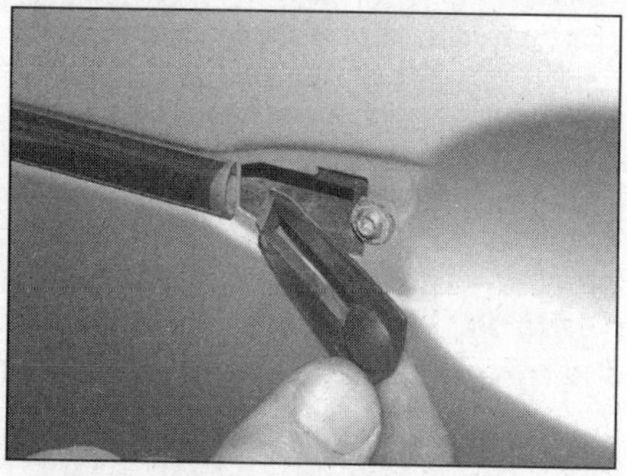

13.8b . . . and remove the gaskets, which cover the screws

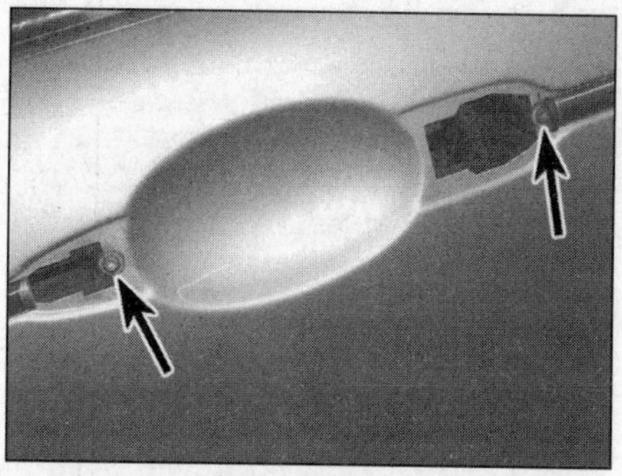

13.9a Loosen the two screws under the gaskets . . .

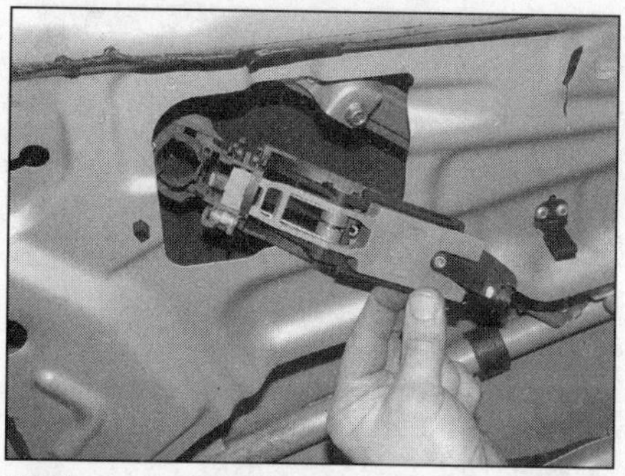

13.9b . . . and remove the handle mounting plate inside the door

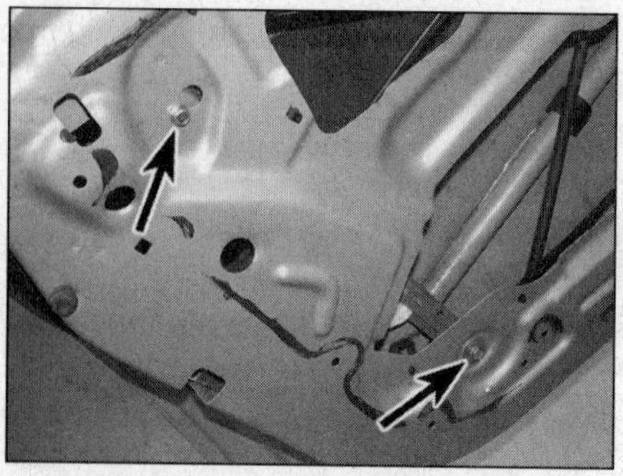

13.15a To improve access to the lock, remove the two bolts . . .

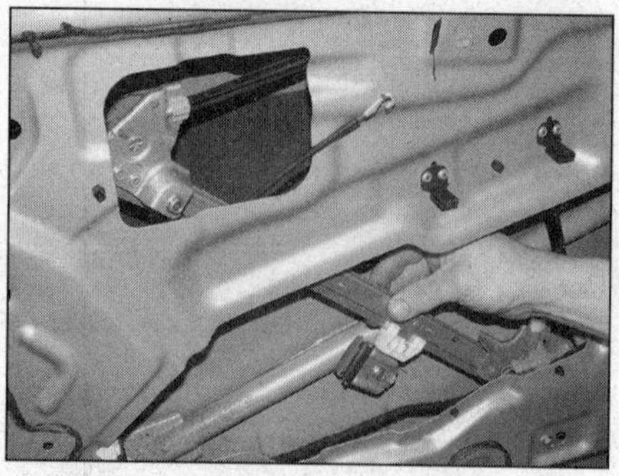

13.15b . . . and pull the glass rear guide channel forwards

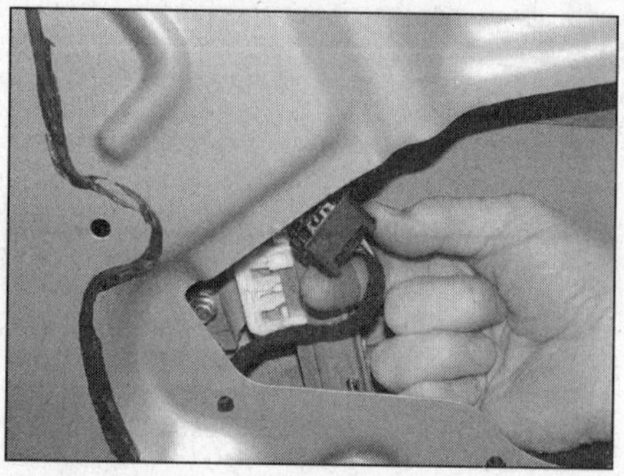

13.16 Disconnect the lock unit wiring plug

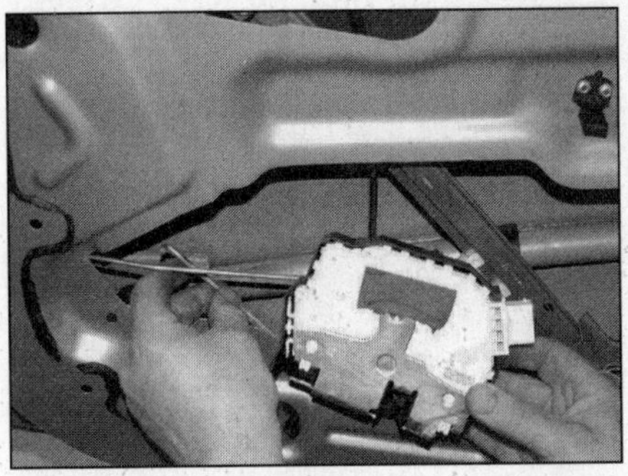

13.17 Lock partially removed, showing the two link rods

13.18 Remove the three lock mounting screws

13.19a Prise open the access panel . . .

17 Have an assistant hold open the exterior handle. Reaching inside the door to the rear of the lock, carefully release the clip and disconnect the link rod for the exterior handle, and the one for the door lock button **(see illustration)**.

18 At the rear edge of the door, remove the three lock mounting Torx screws **(see illustration)**. Lower the lock down, and remove it from the door.

19 If required, open the access panel on the lock unit, and fold the flap down to access the interior handle operating cable. Unhook the inner cable, then release the outer cable from the lock unit **(see illustrations)**.

20 Refitting is a reversal of removal.

Central locking components

21 Refer to Section 18.

14 Door trim panel – removal and refitting

Front door

1 Remove the door interior handle as described in Section 13.

2 Taking care not to mark the trim, prise out the window switch panel from the door pull/armrest. Disconnect the wiring plug(s) from below the switch panel, and remove it.

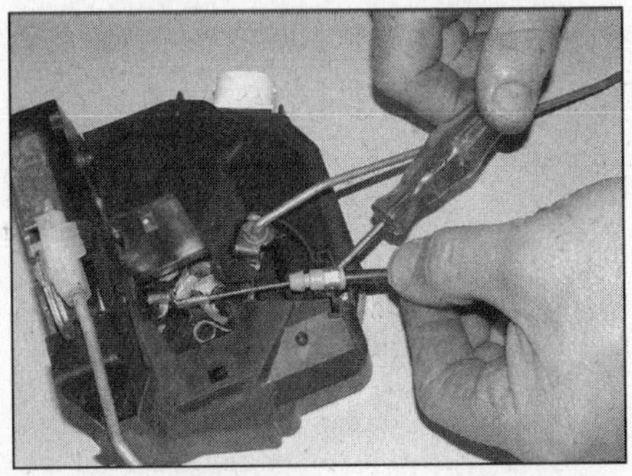

13.19b . . . then prise out the outer cable . . .

13.19c . . . and unhook the inner cable

3 Remove the single cross-head screw at the front of the panel, inside the duct for the side window vent **(see illustration)**.

4 The panel is secured by a number of clips, in the main around its edge, but with two more in the centre. Starting at the bottom corners, pull sharply on the panel to release the clips. Work along the base and up the sides of the panel, until all the side and bottom clips have been released **(see illustration)**.

5 The two clips holding the panel in the centre are metal spring clips, and very difficult to release. Simply pulling the panel will probably result in damage. We found that, by pulling the panel away at the base for access, we could press up the bottom of each clip using a long screwdriver, which helped to free the clips

6 Lift the panel at the rear, to clear the door lock button, and remove it from the door **(see illustration)**.

7 To access the door inner components, it

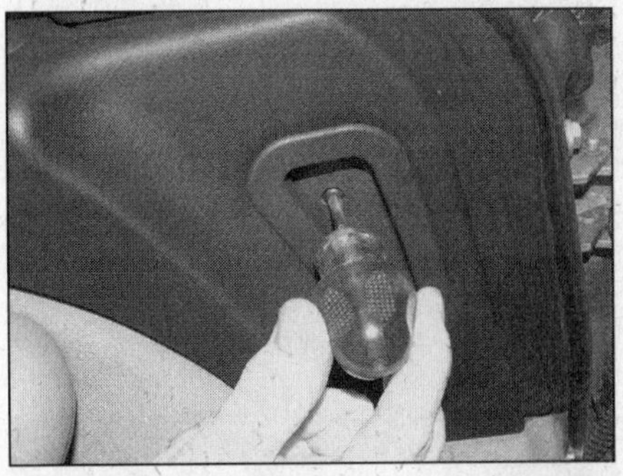

14.3 Remove the screw at the front of the panel

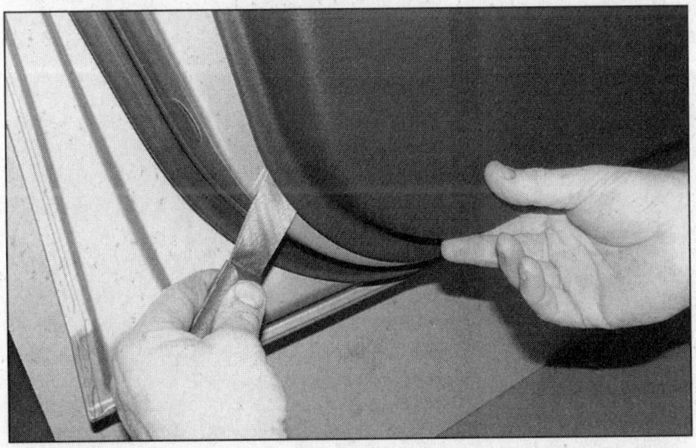

14.4 Use a flat-bladed tool to release the side and bottom clips

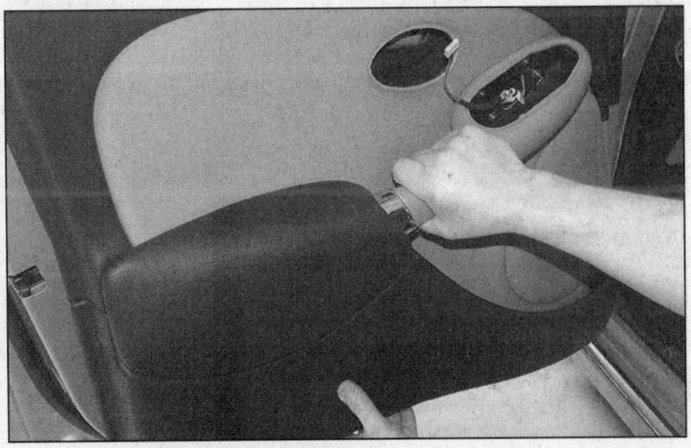

14.6 Lift the trim panel at the rear and remove it

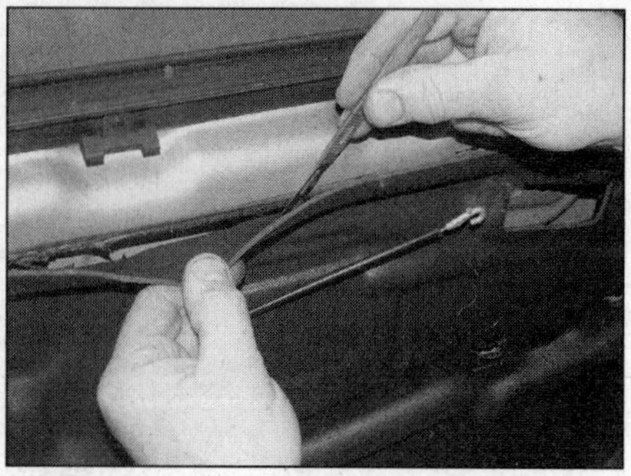

14.7a Slice along the bead of sealant . . .

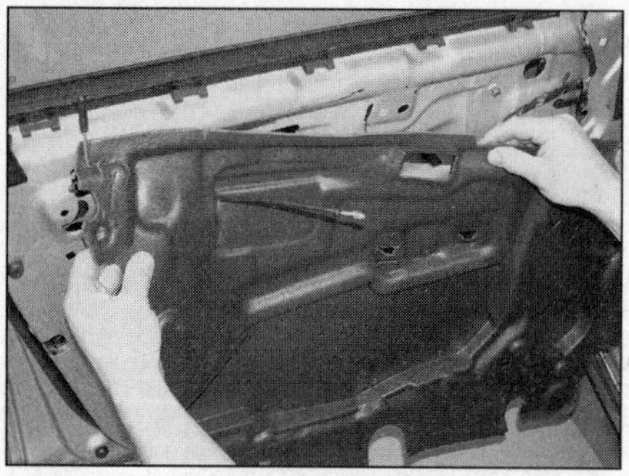

14.7b . . . and remove the foam membrane complete

14.11a Prise out the switch panel without marking the trim . . .

will usually be necessary to remove the foam membrane from the door. Slice along the bead of sealant using a sharp knife, as the panel will tear otherwise. To remove the membrane completely, also unscrew the door speaker mounting screws and disconnect the speaker wiring plug **(see illustrations)**.

8 Refitting is a reversal of removal, noting the following points:

a) Renew plastic clips which were lost or broken during removal.

b) Bearing in mind the difficulty releasing the metal centre clips, make very sure that the door lock and window components are working (if they have been disturbed) before clipping the panel back in place.

Rear door

9 Remove the door interior handle as described in Section 13.

10 On models with manual rear windows, use a hooked piece of wire to release the window regulator handle securing clip from the shaft. Tool companies such as Draper produce simple tools which can be used for this. If neither is available, see the **Haynes Hint**. Pull off the regulator handle, and recover the spring clip and the trim disc.

11 Where electric rear windows are fitted, taking care not to mark the trim, prise out the window switch panel from the door pull/armrest. Disconnect the wiring plug from below the switch panel, and remove it **(see illustrations)**.

12 The panel is secured by a number of clips, in the main around its edge, but with one more in the centre. Starting at the bottom corners, pull sharply on the panel to release the clips. Work along the base and up the sides of the panel, until all the side and bottom clips have been released **(see illustration)**.

13 The clip holding the panel in the centre is a metal spring type, and very difficult to release.

HAYNES HiNT ***Prise the winder handle to open a gap between it and the circular disc behind. Work the edge of a piece of (clean) cloth/rag into the gap behind the handle, either from the top or underneath. Using a 'sawing' action, work the cloth side-to-side, and also pull the ends of the cloth up (or down). It may take some time, but what you're trying to do is snag the ends of the spring clip holding the handle in place – when you do, the sawing action should work the clip off, allowing the handle to be pulled from the splines. A little patience is required, but it will work. Keep an eye on where the spring clip goes, though.***

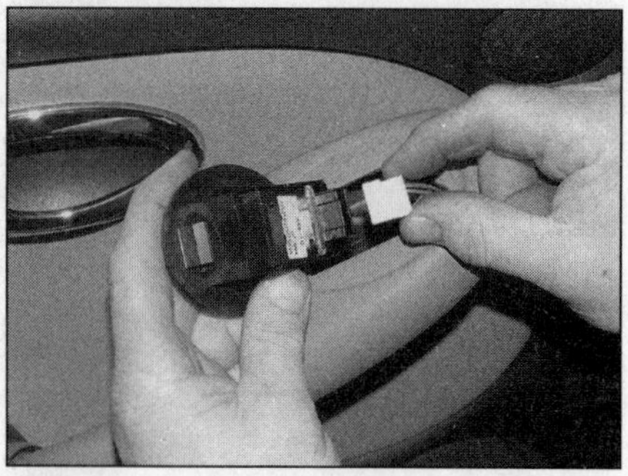

14.11b . . . and disconnect the wiring plug underneath

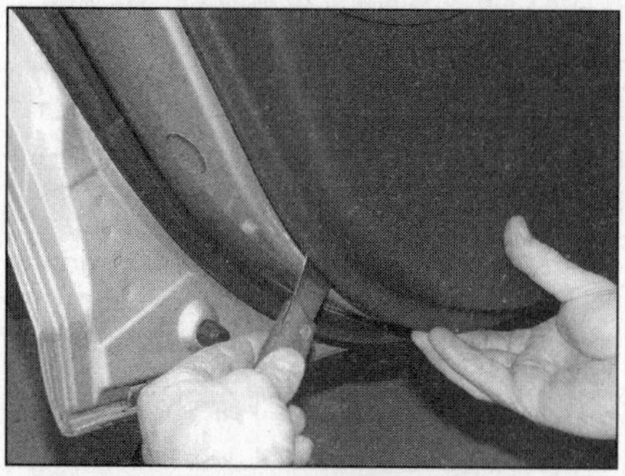

14.12 Carefully release the edges of the trim panel

Unlike the front door panel, we found no way to release the clip, other than by pulling very hard, which in our case pulled the riveted clip off the door **(see illustration)**.

14 Where applicable, disconnect the wiring plug from the rear tweeter speaker.

15 Lift the panel at the rear, to clear the door lock button, and remove it from the door **(see illustration)**.

16 To access the door inner components, it will usually be necessary to remove the foam membrane from the door. Slice along the bead of sealant using a sharp knife, as the panel will tear otherwise **(see illustration)**. To remove the membrane completely, unscrew the door speaker mounting screws and disconnect the speaker wiring plug.

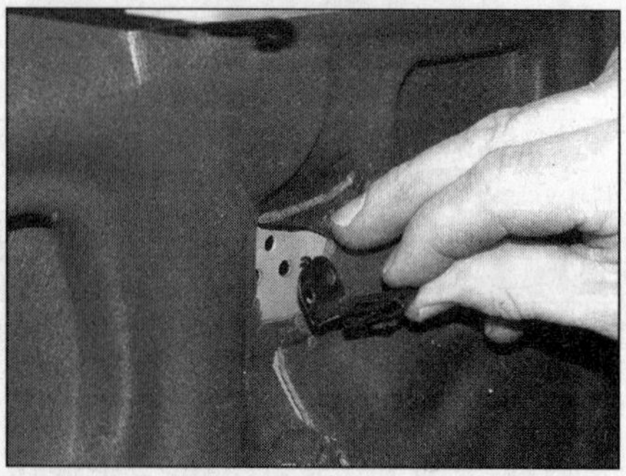

14.13 The central riveted spring clip came off during removal

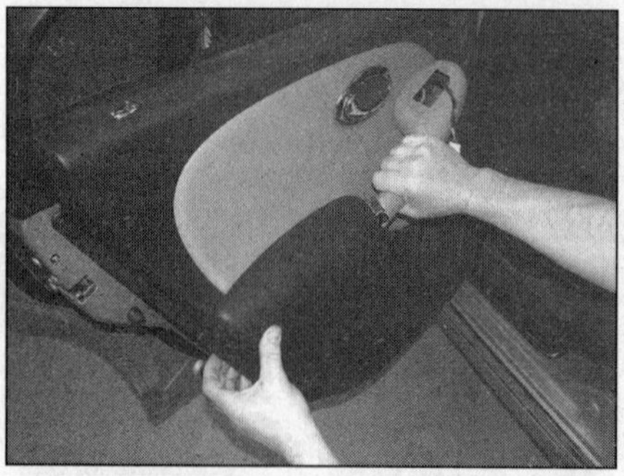

14.15 Lift and remove the door trim panel

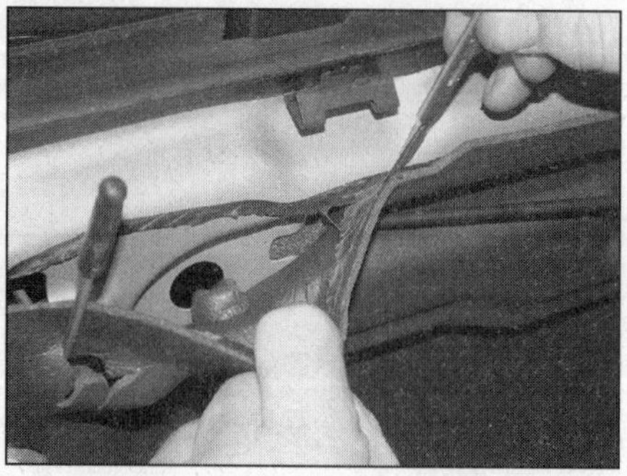

14.16 Slice through the sealant, not the foam membrane

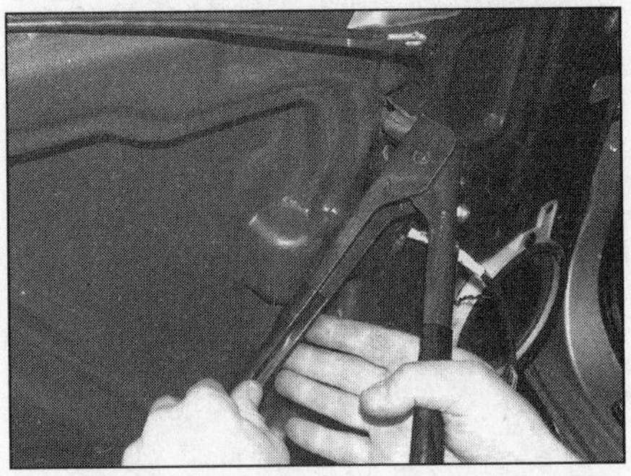

14.17 If necessary, rivet the centre spring clip back onto the door

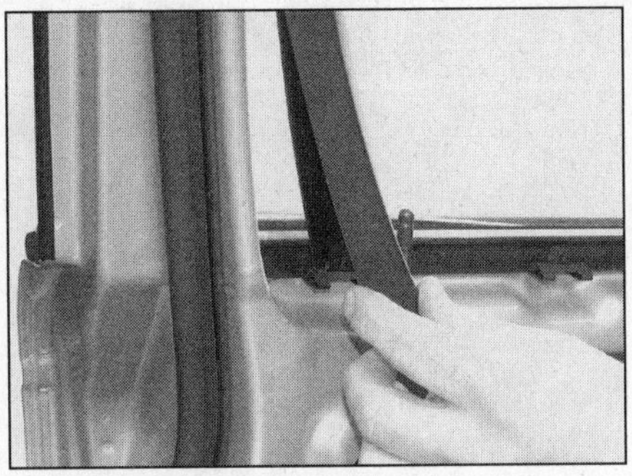

15.2a Start at the rear of the window frame, and unclip the trim . . .

15.2b . . . working to the front, and disconnect the speaker

17 Refitting is a reversal of removal, noting the following points:

a) *Renew plastic clips which were lost or broken during removal.*
b) *If necessary, re-attach the centre clip mounting bracket, using a pop-rivet gun* ***(see illustration).***
c) *Bearing in mind the difficulty releasing the metal centre clip, make very sure that the door lock and window components are working (if they have been disturbed) before clipping the panel back in place.*
d) *On models with manual rear windows, refit the spring clip to the handle. Ensure the window is closed, then fit the handle in the same position as the one on the other side of the car.*

15 Door window glass and regulator – removal and refitting

Front door

Door glass

1 Remove the door trim panel, as described in the previous Section.

2 Work around the inside edge of the window frame, and unclip the trim strip. At the front of the window trim, disconnect the wiring plugs for the electric window anti-trap sensor (where applicable), and for the tweeter speaker **(see illustrations)**.

3 Unclip and remove the window channel trim strip which runs along the base of the window aperture in the door **(see illustrations)**.

4 Temporarily reconnect the window switch, and move the glass so that the two glass-to-regulator clamp bolts are accessible through the door apertures **(see illustrations)**. Note the fitted positions of the clamps, to use as a guide when refitting.

5 Loosen the two clamp bolts, then lower the regulator using the switch, and lift the glass out of the door **(see illustration)**.

6 Refitting is a reversal of removal, noting the following points:

a) *Take care over the glass-to-regulator alignment, and check that the window opens and closes properly before refitting the window trim and door trim panel.*
b) *The window frame trim takes time to fit correctly. Use a small screwdriver to help 'feed' the trim under the rubber seal.*

Regulator

7 Remove the door trim panel, as described in the previous Section.

8 Temporarily reconnect the window switch, and move the glass so that the two glass-to-regulator clamp bolts are accessible through the door apertures. Note the fitted positions of the clamps, to use as a guide when refitting.

9 Loosen the two clamp bolts, then lift the glass up to the top of the door. Secure the glass to the top of the frame with some tape.

10 Disconnect the wiring plug from the

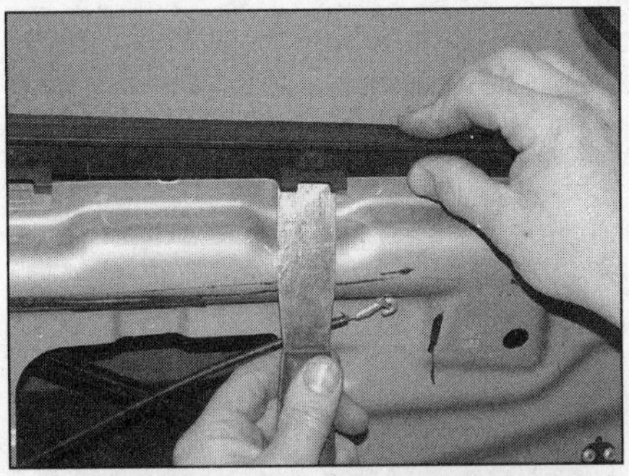

15.3a Prise up the clips securing the window channel strip . . .

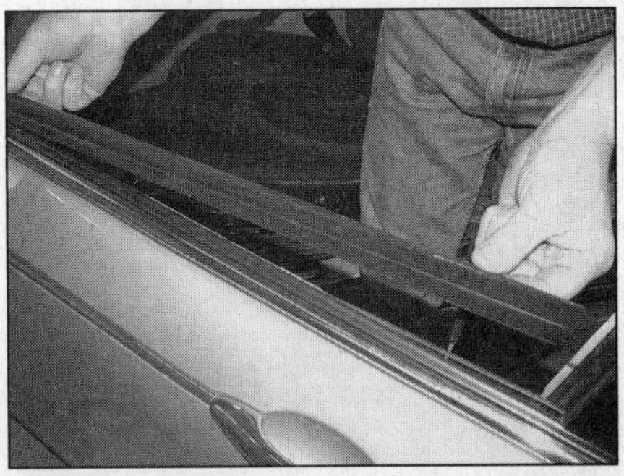

15.3b . . . and remove it from the door

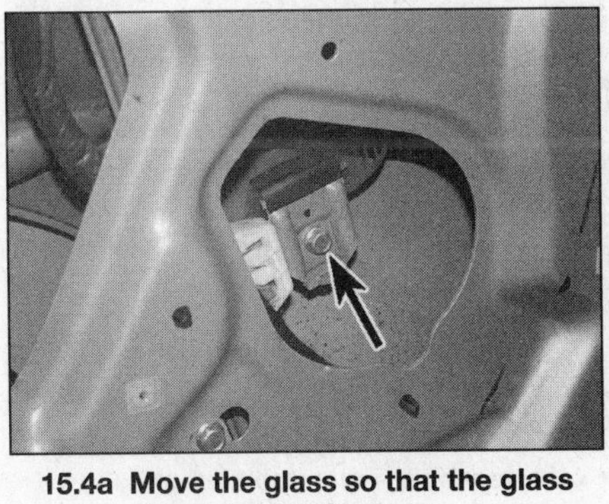

15.4a Move the glass so that the glass clamp bolt at the front . . .

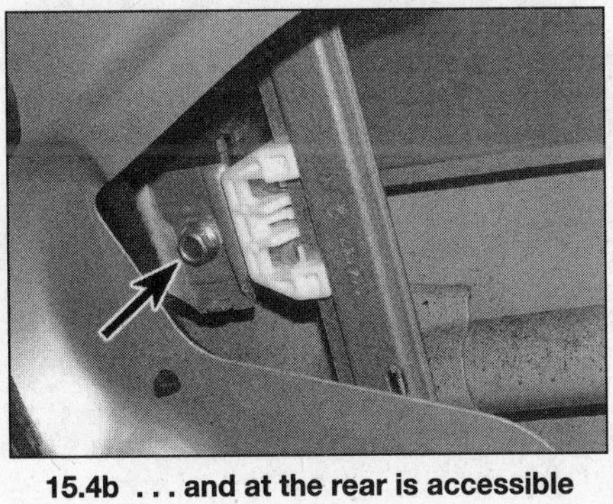

15.4b . . . and at the rear is accessible

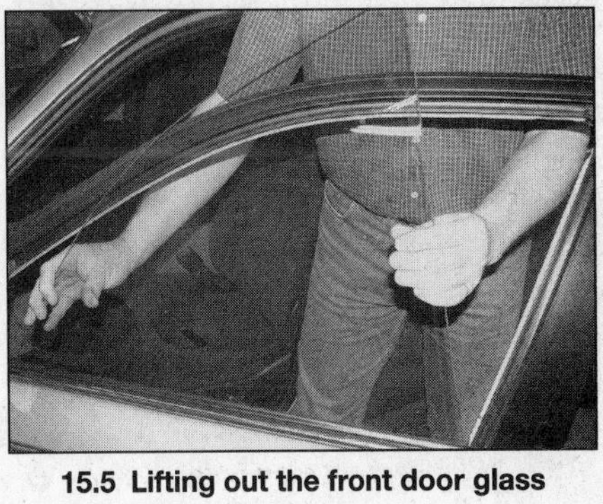

15.5 Lifting out the front door glass

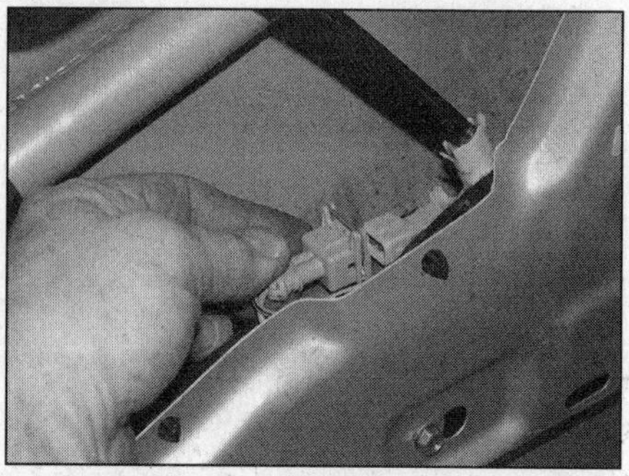
15.10 Disconnect the window motor wiring plug

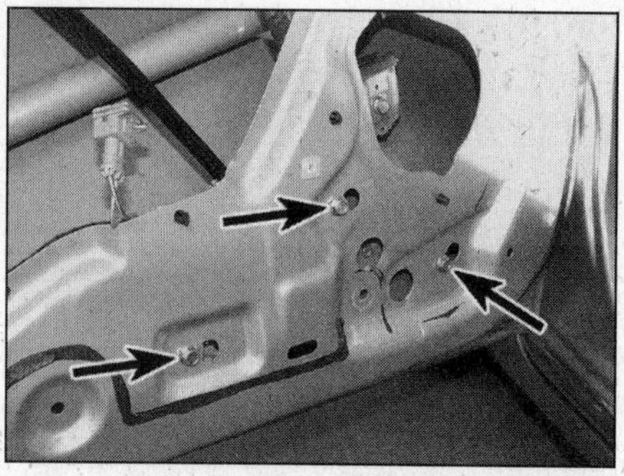
15.11a Three of the regulator bolts are at the base of the door . . .

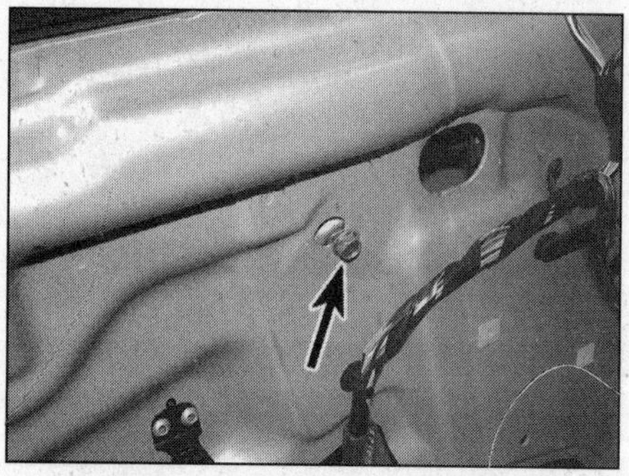
15.11b . . . with one more above . . .

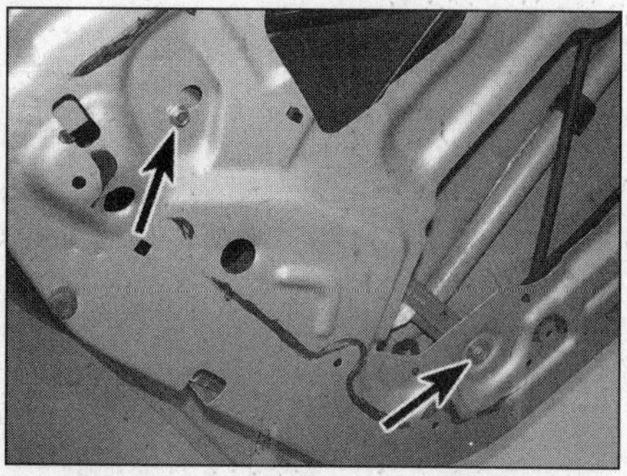
15.11c . . . and two more at the rear

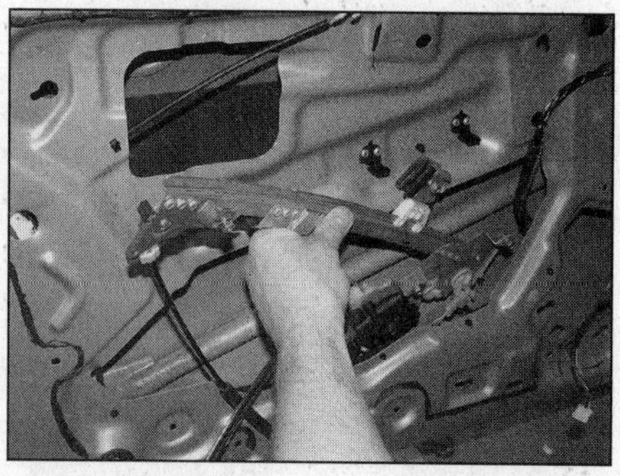
15.12 Removing the regulator assembly

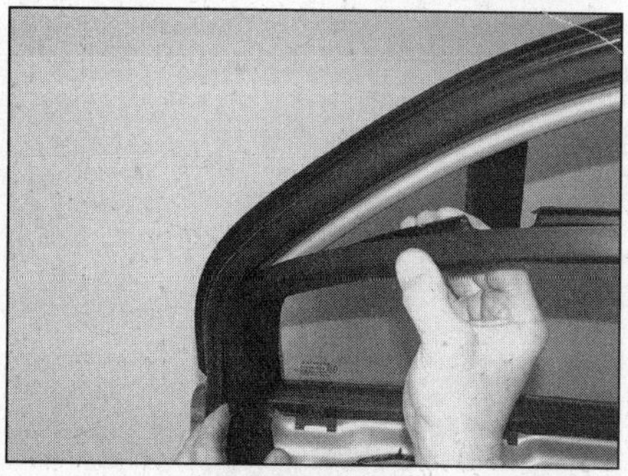
15.15 Unclip the trim strip from the window frame

window motor, which is at the base of the door **(see illustration)**.

11 Loosen a total of six bolts securing the regulator to the door – all except one are in slotted holes in the door, so removal of all the bolts is not necessary. There are three bolts at the base of the door, with one more above, with the final two on the window guide channel at the rear of the door **(see illustrations)**.

12 Reach in behind the regulator to release the central clip, then lift and manoeuvre it out through the aperture at the base of the door **(see illustration)**.

13 Refitting is a reversal of removal. Take care over the glass-to-regulator alignment, and check that the window opens and closes properly before refitting the window trim and door trim panel.

Rear door

Sliding glass

14 Remove the door trim panel, as described in the previous Section.

15 Work around the inside edge of the window frame, and unclip the trim strip **(see illustration)**.

16 Unclip and remove the window channel trim strip which runs along the base of the window aperture in the door, on the inside **(see illustration)**.

17 Temporarily reconnect the window switch (or refit the handle), and move the glass so that the two glass-to-regulator clamp bolts are accessible through the door apertures **(see illustration)**.

18 Loosen the two clamp bolts, then lower the regulator (using the switch or the handle).

19 Prise off the trim from the inside of the division bar which separates the sliding glass

15.16 Prise up the window channel strip

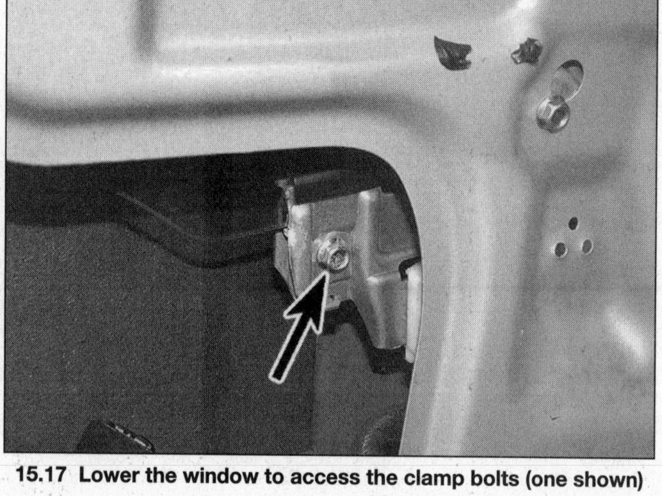
15.17 Lower the window to access the clamp bolts (one shown)

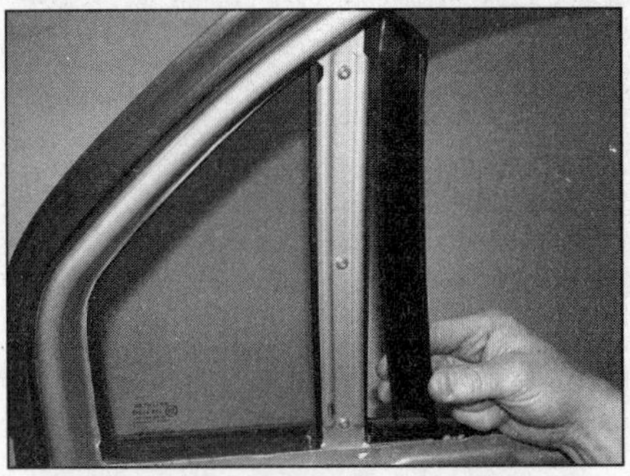

15.19a Prise off the division bar trim to access the three Torx screws . . .

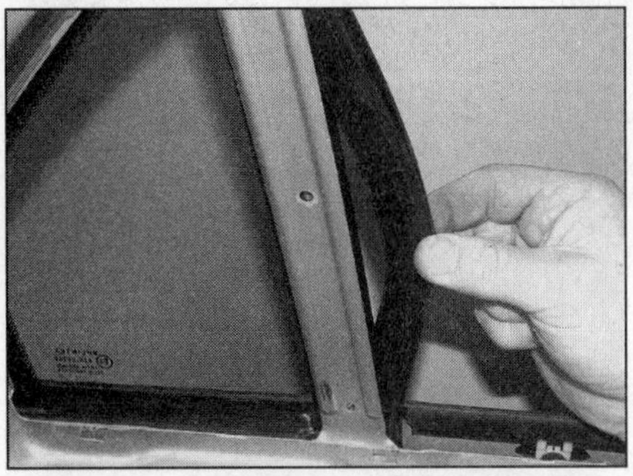

15.19b . . . remove the screws, then pull out the sealing strip . . .

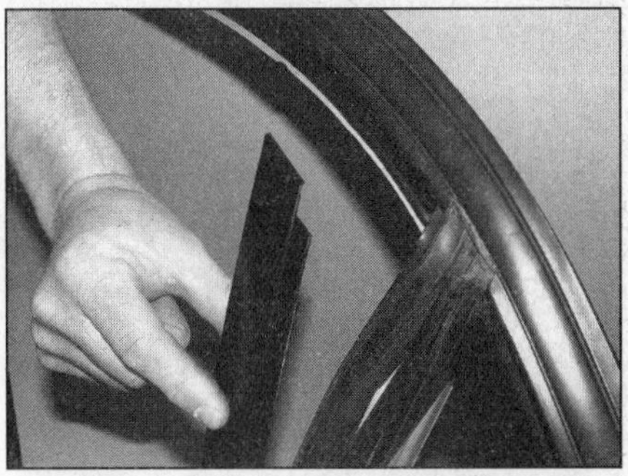

15.19c . . . and remove the division bar

from the fixed glass. Remove the three division bar securing screws. Prise out the window channel sealing strip from the division bar, then remove the bar from the window frame **(see illustrations)**.

20 Withdraw the sliding glass from the door **(see illustration)**.

21 Refitting is a reversal of removal. Check that the window opens and closes properly before refitting the window trim and door trim panel.

Fixed glass

22 Remove the sliding glass as described previously in this Section.

23 Pull the fixed glass out of the window frame seal **(see illustration)**.

24 Refitting is a reversal of removal.

Manual regulator

25 Remove the door trim panel as described in the previous Section.

26 Move the glass so that the two glass-to-regulator clamp bolts are accessible through the door apertures. Note the fitted positions of the clamps, to use as a guide when refitting.

27 Loosen the two clamp bolts, then lift the glass up to the top of the door. Secure the glass to the top of the frame with some tape.

28 Lower the regulator to the mid-way point.

29 Loosen the four regulator mounting bolts in the slotted holes, then unscrew and remove the remaining two mounting bolts.

30 Lift the regulator to release the four bolts from the slotted holes, then manoeuvre it out through the bottom of the door.

15.20 Removing the rear door sliding glass

31 Refitting is a reversal of removal. Check that the window opens and closes properly before refitting the window trim and door trim panel.

Electric regulator

32 Remove the door trim panel as described in the previous Section.

33 Temporarily reconnect the window switch, and move the glass so that the two glass-to-regulator clamp bolts are accessible through the door apertures. Note the fitted positions of the clamps, to use as a guide when refitting.

34 Loosen the two clamp bolts, then lift the glass up to the top of the door. Secure the glass to the top of the frame with some tape.

35 Lower the regulator to the mid-way point, then disconnect the wiring plug from the window motor **(see illustration)**.

36 Loosen the four regulator mounting bolts in the slotted holes, then unscrew and

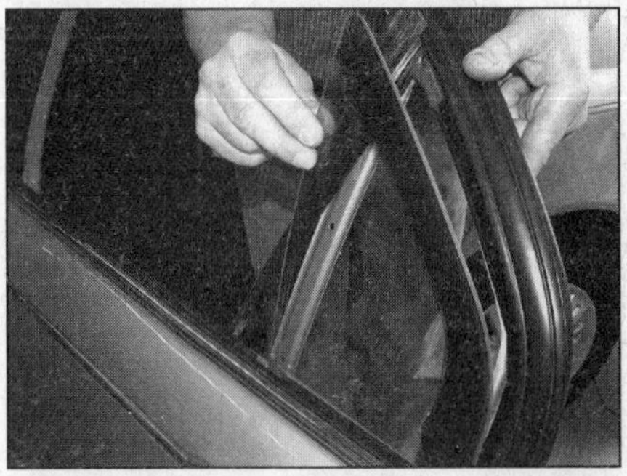

15.23 Pull the fixed glass out of the seal

remove the remaining mounting bolt **(see illustration)**.

37 Lift the regulator to release the four bolts from the slotted holes, then manoeuvre it out through the bottom of the door **(see illustration)**.

38 Refitting is a reversal of removal. Check that the window opens and closes properly before refitting the window trim and door trim panel.

16 Boot lid and related components – removal and refitting

Boot lid

1 Open the boot lid.

2 Remove the inner trim panel, which is

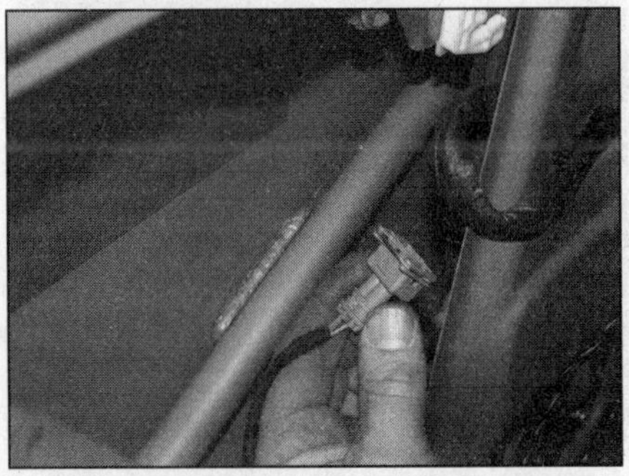

15.35 Disconnect the window motor wiring plug

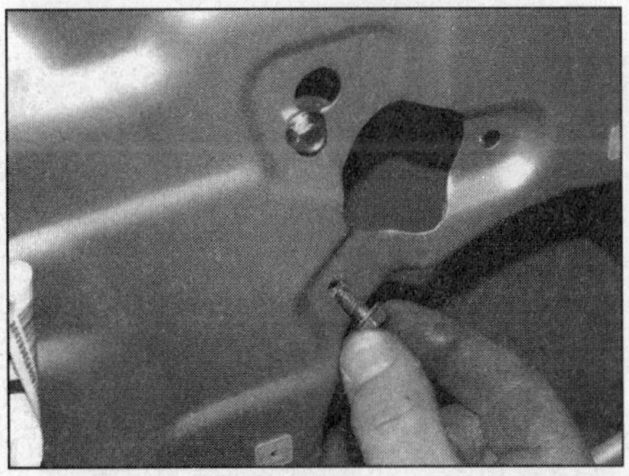

15.36 Four of the bolts are in slotted holes; one must be removed

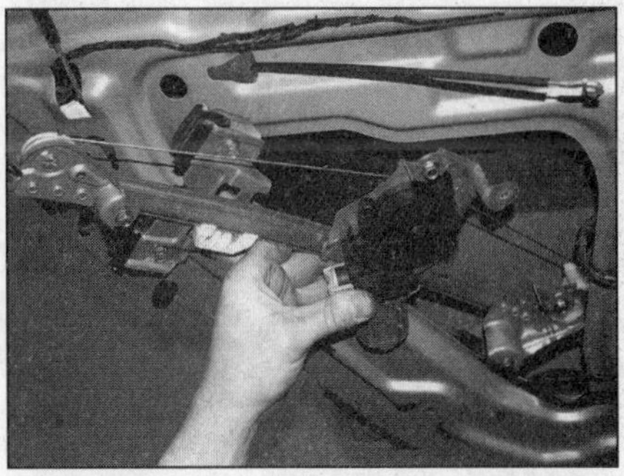

15.37 Removing the rear window regulator

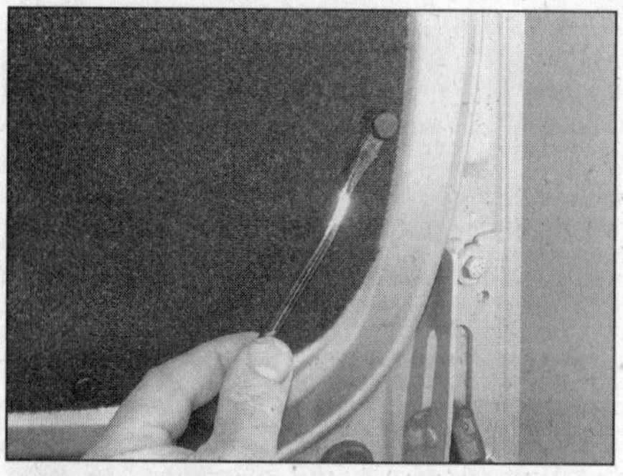

16.2a Prise out a total of fifteen clips around the edge . . .

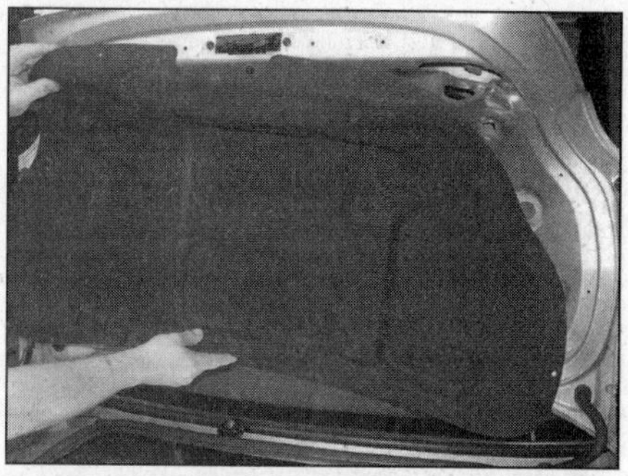

16.2b . . . and remove the boot lid trim panel

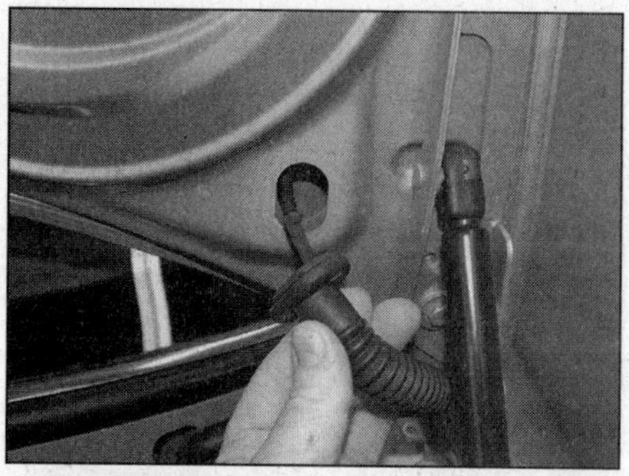

16.5 Free the wiring harness grommet/sleeve from the boot lid

secured by a total of fifteen clips around the edge **(see illustrations)**.

3 Disconnect the wiring from the central locking motor, and from the number plate light, referring where necessary to the relevant removal procedures. Release the wiring loom from any securing clips.

4 Unclip the wiring from its support clips and ties, then feed it down to the right-hand lower corner of the boot lid, noting its routing.

HAYNES HiNT *If string is tied to the end of the loom, it can be untied once the wiring is pulled through, and left in place to pull the wiring back through on refitting.*

5 Release the wiring grommet at the base of the boot lid, and pull the wiring clear **(see illustration)**.

6 Have an assistant support the boot lid, then pull out the spring clips and pull the ends of the support struts from the ball fittings **(see illustration)**.

7 Mark the positions of the hinges in relation to the boot lid. Again with the help of an assistant, unscrew the hinge bolts and lift the boot lid clear of the car **(see illustration)**.

8 Refitting is a reversal of removal.

Support struts

9 Open the boot lid, and prop it in the fully-open position – alternatively, have an assistant hold the boot lid open.

10 Disconnect the support strut from the boot lid by prising out the securing clip using a small screwdriver, then pull the end of the strut off the ball fitting **(see illustration)**.

11 Repeat the procedure for the clip securing the strut to the body, and withdraw the strut from the car.

12 Refitting is a reversal of removal.

Boot lid lock

13 Open the boot lid.

14 Remove the inner trim panel, which is secured by a total of fifteen clips around the edge.

15 Remove the three lock Torx screws, and partially withdraw the lock from the boot lid **(see illustration)**.

16 The link rod connecting the lock to the lock cylinder on the right-hand side must be unclipped at some point. Access to the rod on the lock isn't easy – we found it was simpler to unclip the rod from the lock cylinder, then withdraw the lock to unclip the other end of the rod **(see illustrations)**.

16.6 Prise out the spring clip from each support strut

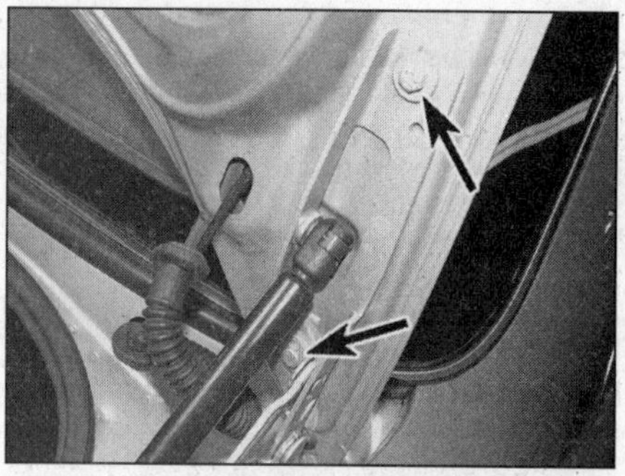

16.7 Unscrew the two hinge bolts each side

16.10 Use a small screwdriver to prise off the spring clip

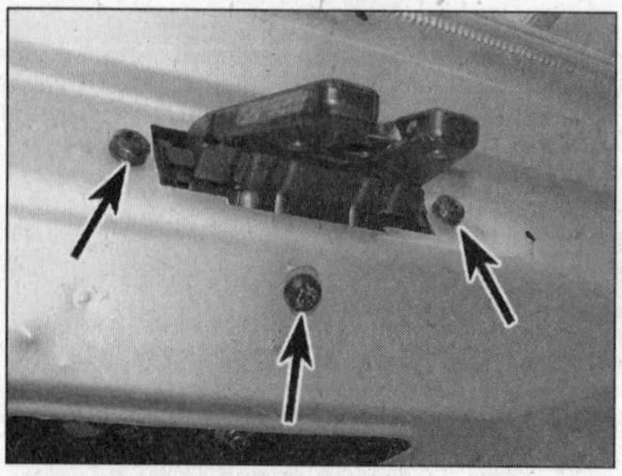

16.15 Remove the three Torx screws securing the lock

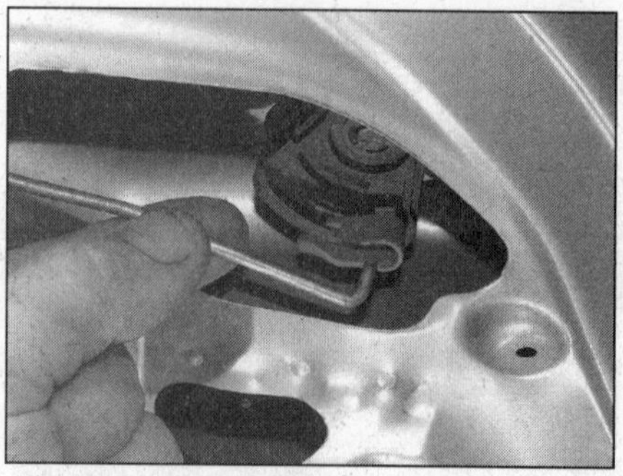

16.16a Unclip the link rod from the lock cylinder . . .

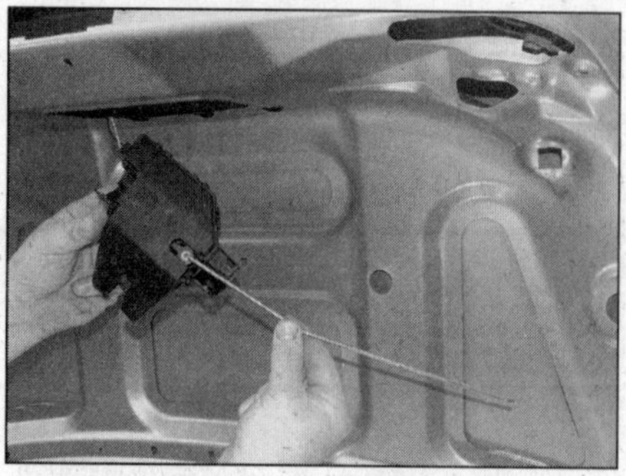

16.16b . . . then withdraw the lock and unclip the rod from it

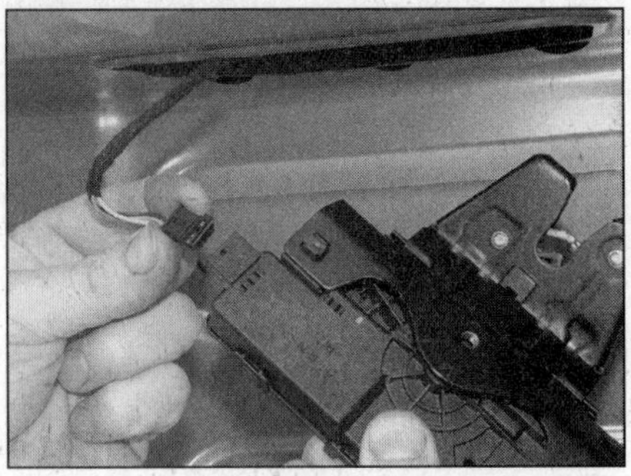

16.17 Disconnect the wiring plug from the lock

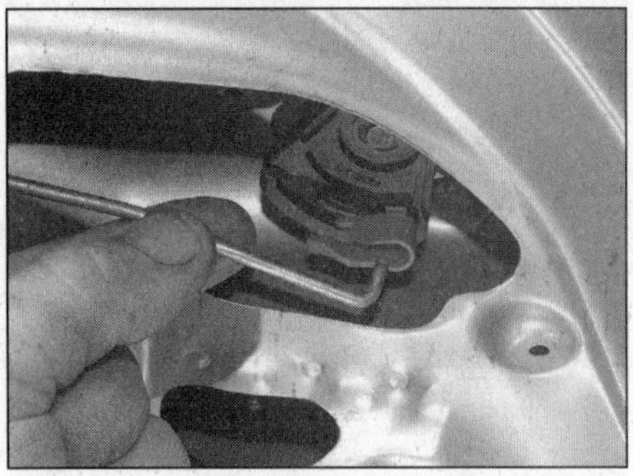

16.20a Unclip the lock cylinder link rod . . .

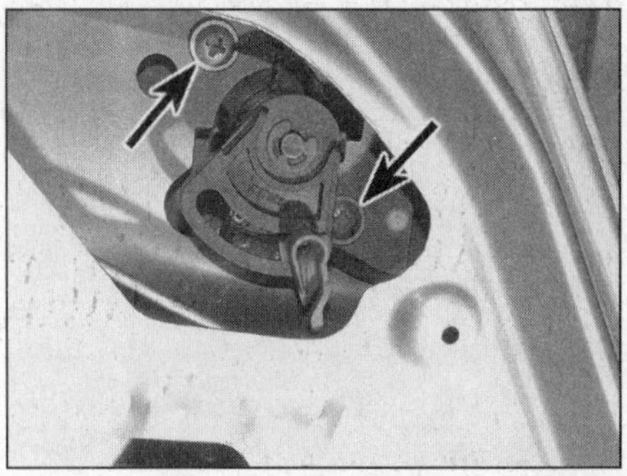

16.20b . . . then remove the two screws and withdraw the lock

17 Disconnect the wiring plug from the lock, and remove it completely **(see illustration)**.
18 Refitting is a reversal of removal.

Boot lid lock cylinder

19 Open the boot lid, and remove the inner trim panel, which is secured by a total of fifteen clips around the edge.
20 Carefully unclip the link rod, then remove the two mounting screws and twist the lock cylinder clockwise to remove it from the boot lid **(see illustrations)**.
21 Disconnect the wiring plug from the lock, and remove it completely **(see illustration)**.
22 Refitting is a reversal of removal.

Boot lid catch

23 The catch is secured by two Torx screws **(see illustration)**. The catch can be adjusted if required after loosening the screws.

Boot lid remote release switch

24 Inside the car, prise out the clip at the front, then carefully unclip the panel, which is secured by three clips.
25 Disconnect the switch wiring plug, then unclip and withdraw it from the back of the panel **(see illustrations)**.
26 Refitting is a reversal of removal.

Boot lid trim/handle

27 Open the boot lid, and remove the inner trim panel, which is secured by a total of fifteen clips around the edge.
28 The outer trim/handle is secured by four nuts on the inside. Unscrew the nuts, then release the panel from the boot lid – it may be a tight fit over the number plate light **(see illustrations)**.
29 The number plate light unit itself is

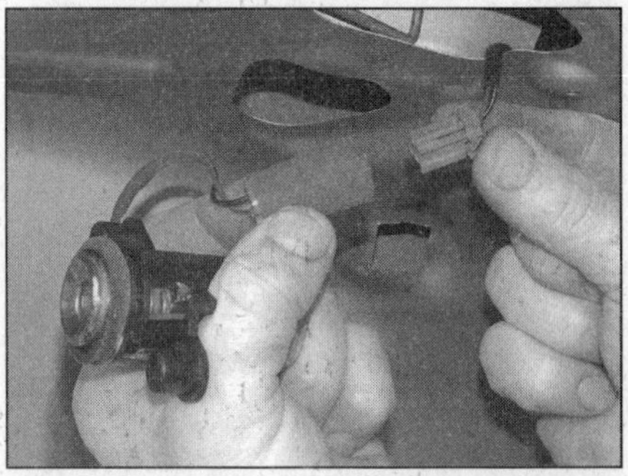

16.21 Disconnect the lock cylinder wiring plug

secured to the boot lid using double-sided tape – removal is described in Chapter 12, Section 7.
30 Refitting is a reversal of removal.

16.23 The boot lid catch is secured by two Torx screws

16.25a Disconnect the switch wiring plug . . .

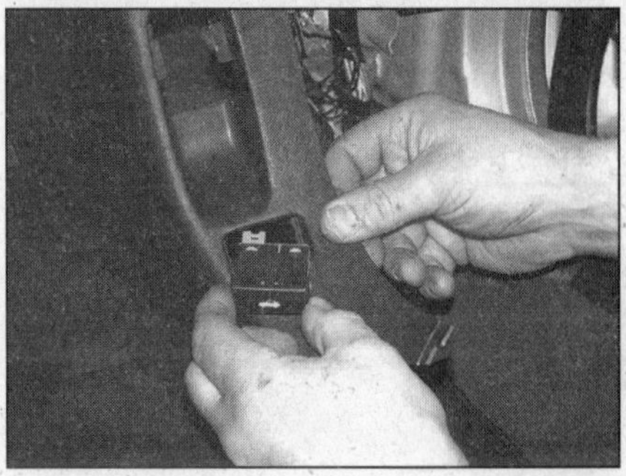

16.25b . . . then push the switch out of the panel

16.28a The boot lid trim panel is secured by four nuts . . .

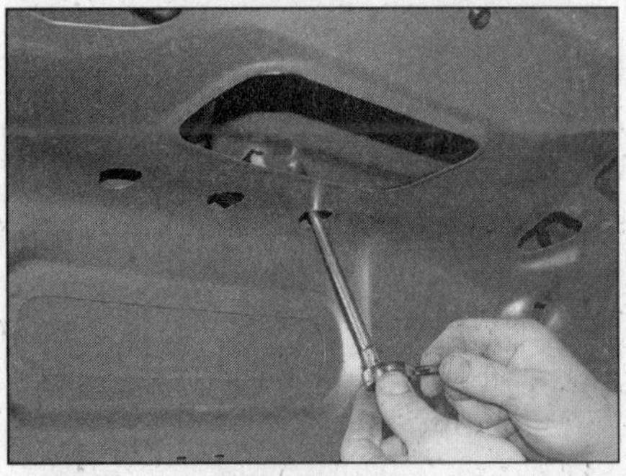

16.28b . . . accessed through holes inside the boot lid

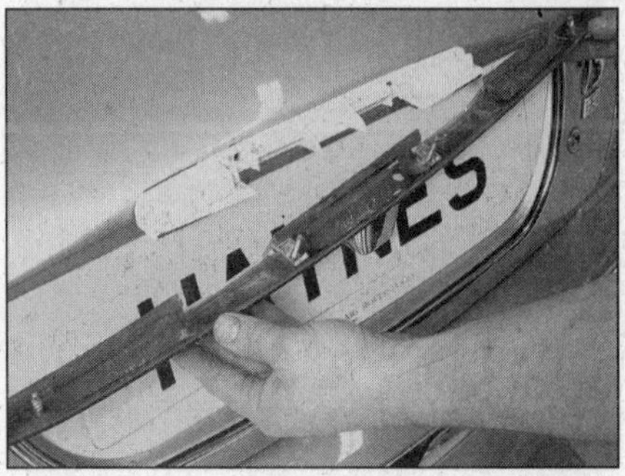

16.28c Unclip the trim panel in the centre, and remove it

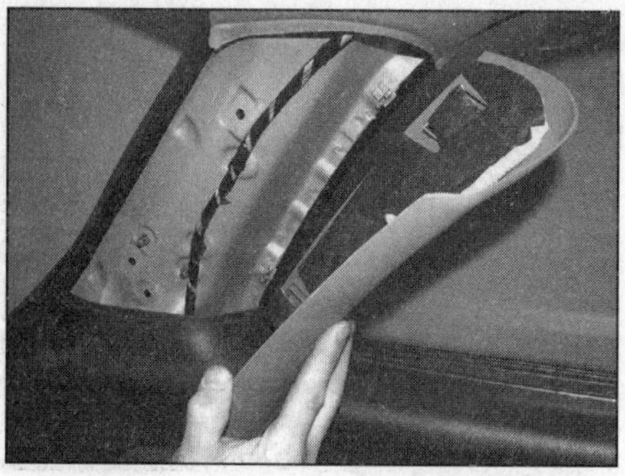

17.1 Unclip the D-pillar trim panel

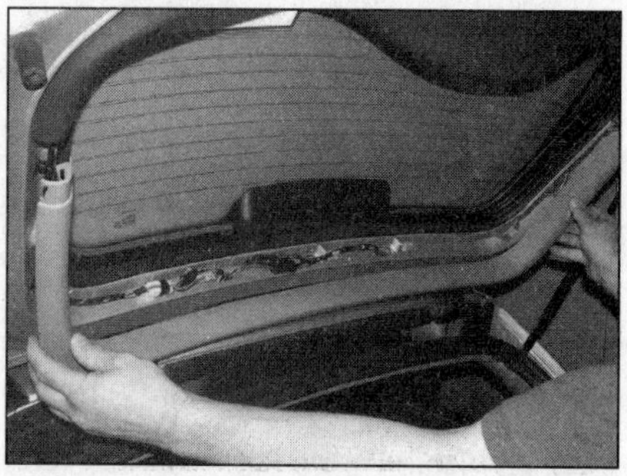

17.6a Unclip the tailgate window surround panel . . .

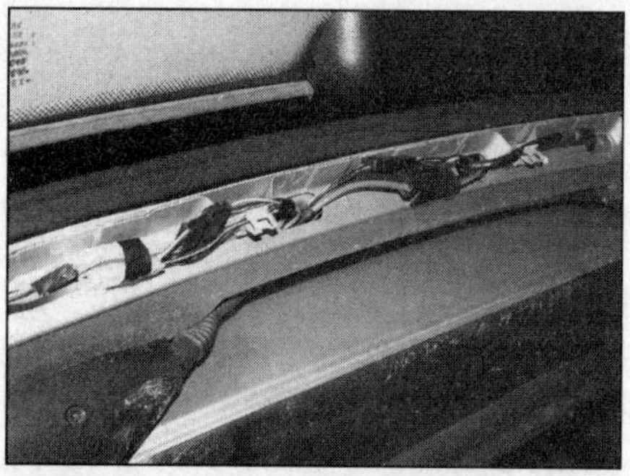

17.6b . . . and disconnect the wiring plugs beneath

Spoiler

31 The boot lid spoiler is secured by a nut and bolt at each end, and by strips of double-sided tape to the top of the boot lid.

32 Open the boot lid, and remove the rubber plug under the spoiler at each end.

33 Remove the nut and bolt at each end of the spoiler.

34 Close the boot lid, then carefully peel the spoiler off the top surface. Unless absolutely necessary, do not use a knife to cut through the tape – risk of damaging the paintwork.

35 Clean the tape off the boot lid and spoiler mating faces, then fit new tape – delay peeling off the backing until the spoiler is in position.

36 Offer the spoiler into position, and engage the two studs in the boot lid holes. Loosely fit the nuts and bolts, then peel off the backing and stick the spoiler to the boot lid. Tighten the nuts and bolts securely to complete.

17 Tailgate and related components – removal and refitting

Tailgate

1 Open the tailgate, and carefully prise off the D-pillar trim panels – each is secured by four clips. Also prise off the roof trim panel fitted across the top of the tailgate – this panel is secured by seven clips **(see illustration)**.

2 Prise out the lens from the boot light, then remove the two light unit mounting screws. Withdraw the light from the headlining, then disconnect the wiring plug and remove it.

3 Remove the single Torx screw each side, and take off the luggage net retainers from the headlining.

4 Carefully unclip the rear edge of the headlining, which is held by two clips – one either side of the boot light location. Take care not to damage or crease the headlining.

5 At the top of the tailgate next to the right-hand hinge, disconnect the tailgate washer tube, then unscrew the bolt securing the tailgate earth lead. Release the grommet and rubber boot from the tailgate, and pull through the washer tube and earth lead.

6 Carefully prise off the trim panel from the sides and top of the tailgate window. Next to the left-hand hinge, disconnect the four multi-plugs from the wiring harness. Release the left-hand grommet and rubber boot, and pull through the wiring harness **(see illustrations)**.

7 Remove the two screws securing each tailgate hinge cover, then unclip the covers and remove them.

8 Have an assistant support the tailgate, then pull out the spring clips and pull the ends of the support struts from the ball fittings.

9 Again with the help of an assistant, unscrew the hinge bolts and lift the tailgate clear of the car.

10 Refitting is a reversal of removal.

Tailgate support strut

11 Open the tailgate, and have an assistant support it in the fully-open position.

12 Disconnect the support strut from the tailgate by prising out the securing clip using a small screwdriver, then pull the end of the strut off the ball fitting **(see illustration)**.

13 Repeat the procedure for the clip securing the strut to the body, and withdraw the strut from the car.

14 Refitting is a reversal of removal.

Tailgate inner trim panel

15 Open the tailgate window, then prise out the two trim plugs and take off the trim panel surrounding the window catch **(see illustrations)**.

16 Open the tailgate, then release the two turn-buckle fasteners and open the compartment containing the warning triangle. Remove the four screws in the centre of the tailgate trim panel **(see illustration)**.

17 Carefully prise the off the panel, which is

17.12 Prise out the spring clip at he top of the support strut

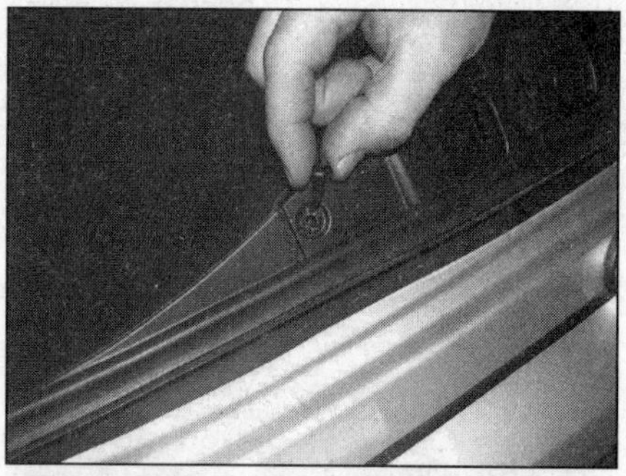

17.15a Prise out the two trim plugs . . .

17.15b . . . and take off the window catch trim

17.16 Remove the four screws behind the hinged panel

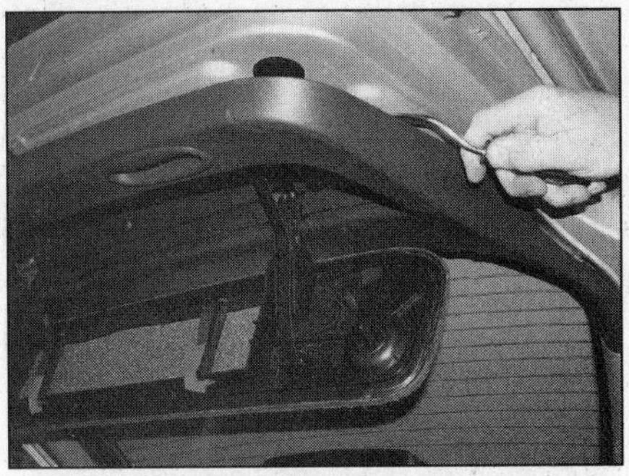

17.17a Carefully prise the panel to release the clips . . .

17.17b . . . and remove the panel from the tailgate

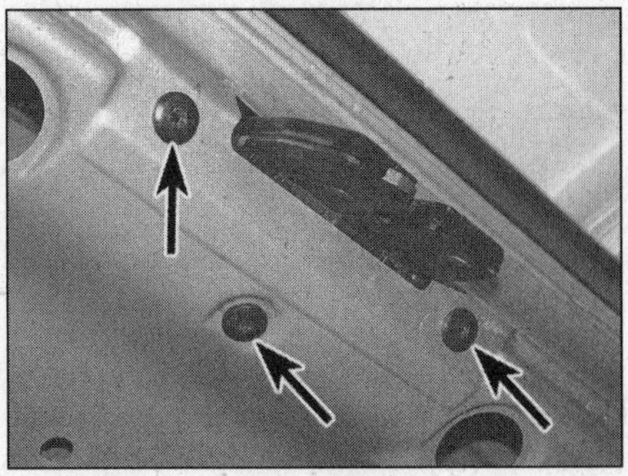

17.20 Remove the tailgate lock mounting screws . . .

secured by twelve clips **(see illustrations)**. At each side, separate the panel from the window surround panel (otherwise the window surround will try and come off with it). Remove the inner trim panel from the tailgate.

18 Refitting is a reversal of removal.

Tailgate lock

19 Remove the inner trim panel as described previously in this Section.

20 Remove the three Torx screws, and withdraw the lock from the tailgate **(see illustration)**.

21 Disconnect the wiring plug from the lock, and remove it completely **(see illustration)**.

22 Refitting is a reversal of removal.

Tailgate lock striker

23 Open the tailgate, then lift the spare wheel cover and unclip the trim panel at the rear of the spare wheel well **(see illustration)**.

24 The striker is secured by two Torx bolts **(see illustration)**. Prior to removal, mark its original position, to use as a reference for refitting.

25 Refitting is a reversal of removal. Check for satisfactory tailgate closing, and if necessary adjust the striker's position.

Tailgate outer trim

26 Remove the inner trim panel as described previously in this Section.

27 Unscrew the eight nuts on the inside of the tailgate, then release the five clips and take off the trim panel from outside the tailgate.

28 Refitting is a reversal of removal.

Tailgate release handle

29 Remove the inner trim panel as described previously in this Section.

30 Disconnect the number plate wiring plug **(see illustration)**.

31 Remove a total of four Torx screws (two each side of the number plate lights), and withdraw the handle **(see illustrations)**. Feed the wiring harness through the hole in the tailgate, and remove the handle completely. Note that the two outer screws have rubber washers fitted.

32 Refitting is a reversal of removal. Check the condition of the handle's rubber seal, and if necessary fit a new one.

Window release unit

33 Remove the inner trim panel as described previously in this Section.

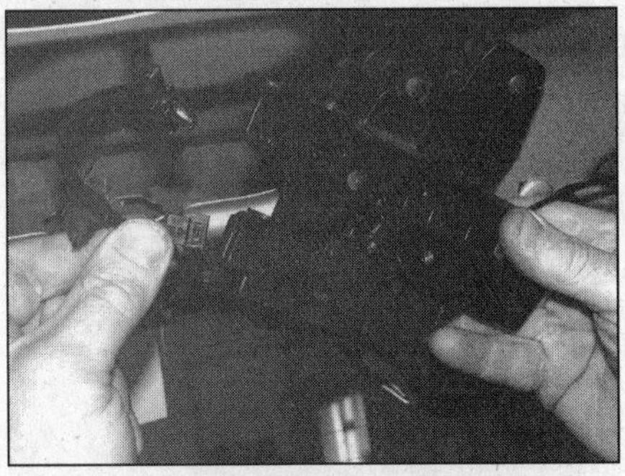

17.21 . . . then withdraw the lock and disconnect the wiring plug

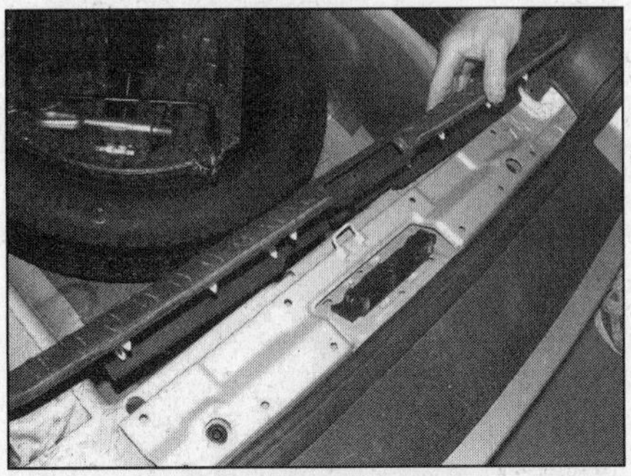

17.23 Unclip the trim panel from the rear of the spare wheel well

17.24 Tailgate lock striker bolts (arrowed)

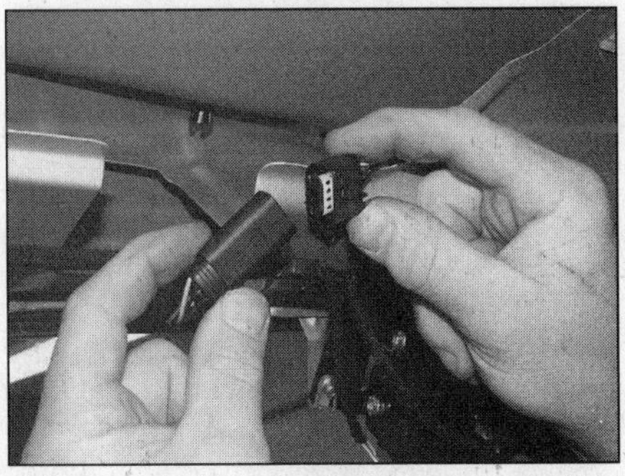

17.30 Disconnect the number plate wiring plug

17.31a Remove the four Torx screws . . .

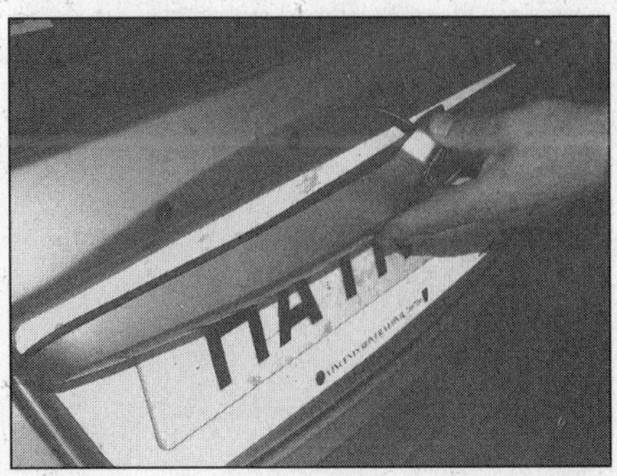

17.31b . . . then withdraw the handle from the tailgate

17.35 Disconnect the release unit wiring plug

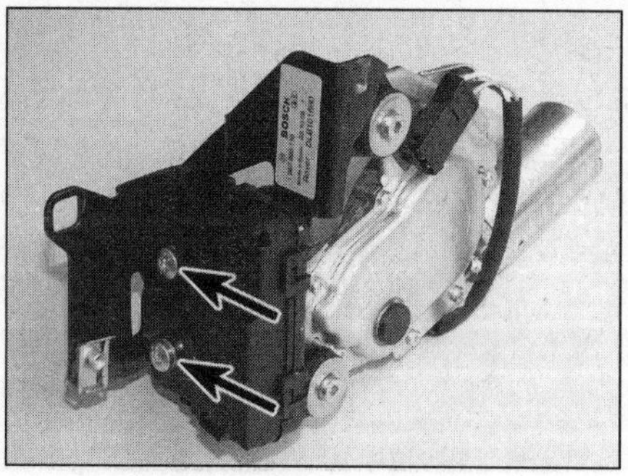

17.36 Release unit mounting screws

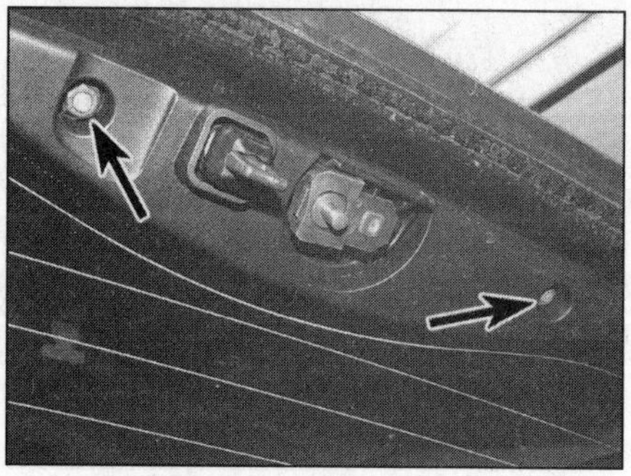

17.40a Unscrew the two nuts . . .

34 Close the tailgate and open the tailgate window.

35 Disconnect the wiring plug from the release unit **(see illustration)**.

36 Remove the two Torx screws securing the unit to the wiper motor mounting bracket, and remove it **(see illustration)**.

37 Refitting is a reversal of removal.

Window catch

38 Remove the tailgate wiper arm as described in Chapter 12.

39 Open the tailgate window.

40 Remove the nut at each end, and take off the catch cover **(see illustrations)**.

41 Disconnect the wiring plug from the catch **(see illustration)**.

42 Remove the inner mounting nut, then close the window and remove the nut from the wiper spindle. Ease the catch out of the glass, and recover the seal.

43 Refitting is a reversal of removal. Check the condition of the seal, and if necessary fit a new one.

Window support strut

44 Open the window, and have an assistant support it in the fully-open position.

45 Disconnect the support strut from the window by prising out the securing clip using a small screwdriver, then pull the end of the strut off the ball fitting **(see illustration)**.

46 Repeat the procedure for the clip securing the strut to the tailgate, and withdraw the strut from the car.

47 Refitting is a reversal of removal.

Tailgate window

48 Open the tailgate then, starting at one end, carefully prise off the window surround trim, which is secured by a total of seven clips **(see illustration)**.

49 Disconnect the washer tube and two multi-plugs under the trim panel just removed **(see illustration)**.

50 Close the tailgate, and open the window.

51 Remove the high-level brake light as described in Chapter 12, Section 7.

52 Release the grommets from the wiring harness, and pull the wiring through the window.

53 Have an assistant support the window.

54 Pull out the spring clip at the top of each support strut, and detach the struts from the window.

55 Unscrew and remove the four Torx screws securing the window to its hinges, and withdraw the window from the car **(see illustration)**.

56 Refitting is a reversal of removal, noting the following points:

a) *Fit the four Torx screws hand-tight only at first, until the struts, wiring and washer tubing have been reconnected.*

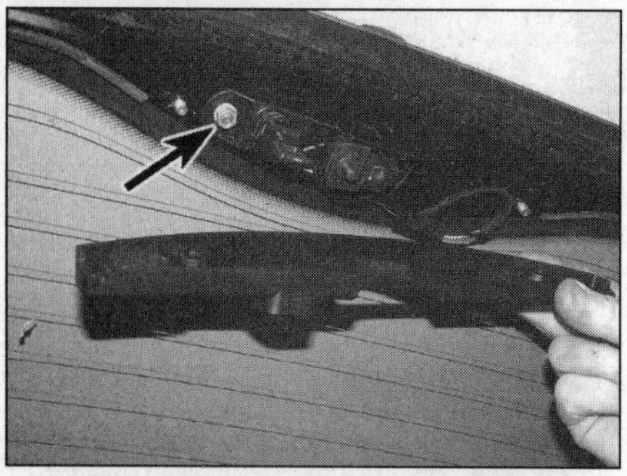

17.40b . . . and take off the catch cover – inner mounting nut arrowed

17.41 Disconnect the wiring plug from the catch

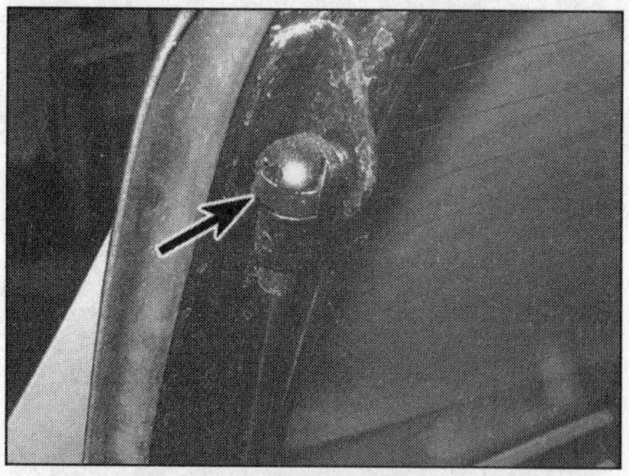

17.45 Prise out the spring clip from the window strut

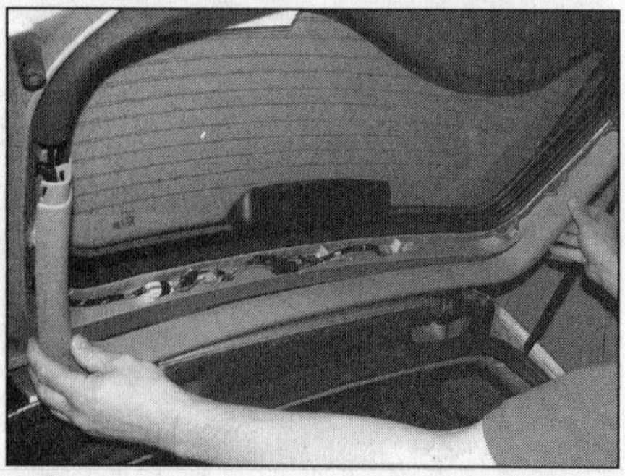

17.48 Unclip the window surround trim . . .

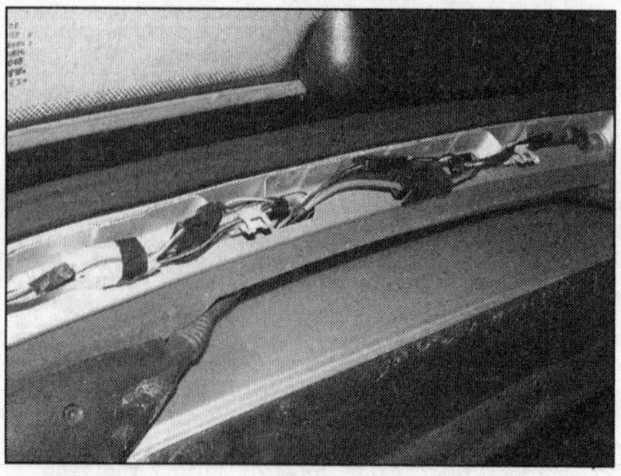

17.49 . . . for access to the wiring plugs underneath

17.55 Each tailgate window hinge has two Torx screws

b) Tighten the window securing screws to the specified torque.
c) Refit the high-level brake light as described in Chapter 12.

Spoiler

57 The tailgate spoiler is secured by a nut and bolt at each end, and by strips of double-sided tape to the top of the tailgate.
58 Open the tailgate, and remove the rubber plug under the spoiler at each end.
59 Remove the nut and bolt at each end of the spoiler.
60 Close the tailgate, then carefully peel the spoiler off the top surface. Unless absolutely necessary, do not use a knife to cut through the tape – risk of damaging the paintwork.
61 Clean the tape off the tailgate and spoiler mating faces, then fit new tape – delay peeling off the backing until the spoiler is in position.
62 Offer the spoiler into position, and engage the two studs in the tailgate holes. Loosely fit the nuts and bolts, then peel off the backing and stick the spoiler in place. Tighten the nuts and bolts securely to complete.

18 Central locking components - general information

1 The central locking is controlled by the body control unit (BCU), which also holds a number of relays. The BCU is located behind the glovebox – refer to Chapter 12, Section 3, for more details. If there is a fault with this unit, it will require checking with diagnostic equipment. The body control unit is part of the multiplex vehicle wiring system (or K-bus network) fitted to the 75 and ZT, and it is able to communicate with the other control units fitted to the car.
2 The door lock motors and switches are an integral part of the lock assemblies – see Sections 13, 16 and 17 of this Chapter.
3 The remote locking receiver unit is located under the centre console up to 2001 model year, or behind the instrument panel on models produced after that date **(see illustration)**. Remove either the centre console as described in Section 26, or the instrument panel as described in Chapter 12, then disconnect the wiring plug and unscrew the two mounting bolts to remove the unit.

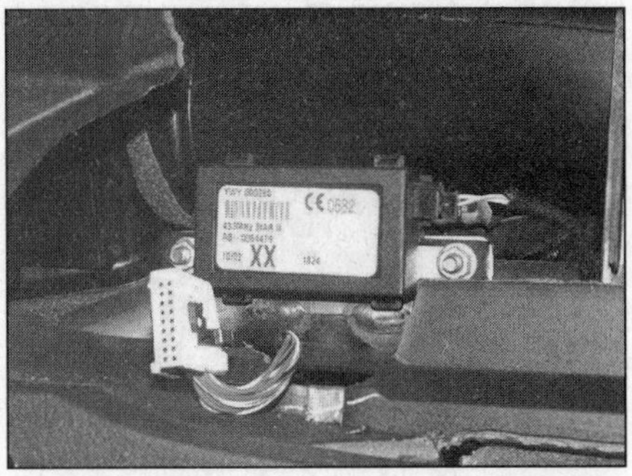

18.3 Remote locking receiver unit behind instrument panel (later models)

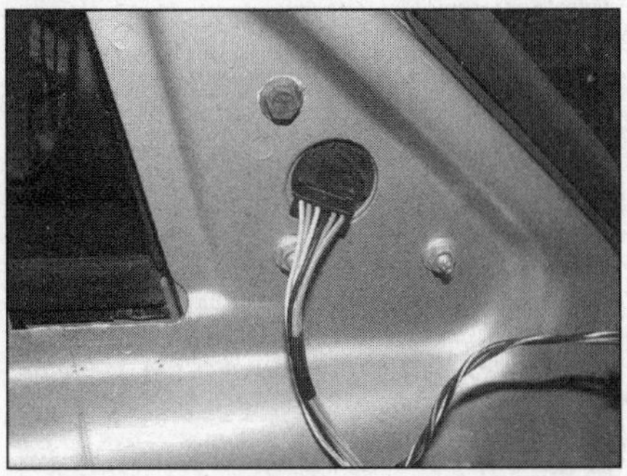

19.3 Mirror wiring plug, mounting bolt and nuts

19 Mirrors - removal, refitting and glass renewal

Door mirror

1 Remove the door trim panel as described in Section 14.
2 Work around the inside edge of the window frame, and unclip the trim strip. At the front of the window trim, disconnect the wiring plugs for the electric window anti-trap sensor (where applicable), and for the tweeter speaker **(see illustrations 15.2a and 15.2b)**.
3 Disconnect the mirror wiring plug. Support the mirror from outside, then unscrew the two mounting nuts and single bolt securing the mirror to the door **(see illustration)**.
4 Withdraw the mirror, and feed through the wiring. Recover the gasket fitted between the mirror and the door – renew it if necessary **(see illustration)**.
5 Refitting is a reversal of removal.

Glass renewal

Caution: If the glass is broken, wear thick gloves to protect your hands.

6 Using a flat-bladed tool, carefully prise behind the lower edge of the mirror glass – the glass is held in place by a total of eight plastic clips, in the centre. Support the glass, lever the tool forwards and the mirror glass will unclip from the mirror assembly **(see illustrations)**. Take care not to drop the glass as it is released.
7 Where applicable, disconnect the wiring connectors from the rear of the mirror glass **(see illustration)**.
8 To refit the glass, line it up and press it into position until it engages securely **(see illustration)**.

19.4 Withdrawing the door mirror from the door

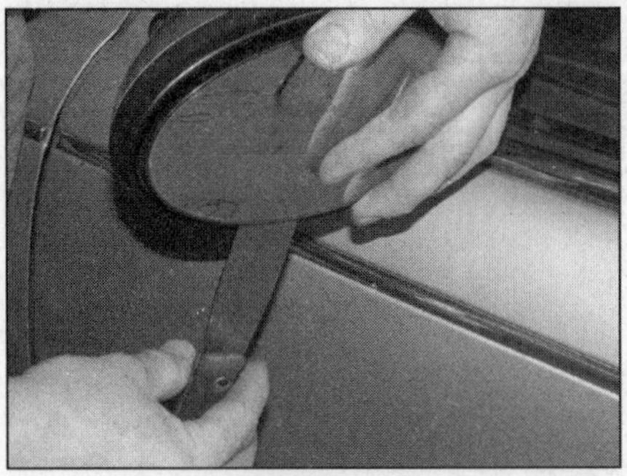

19.6a Carefully prise the glass off near the centre . . .

19.6b . . . to release the circle of clips behind

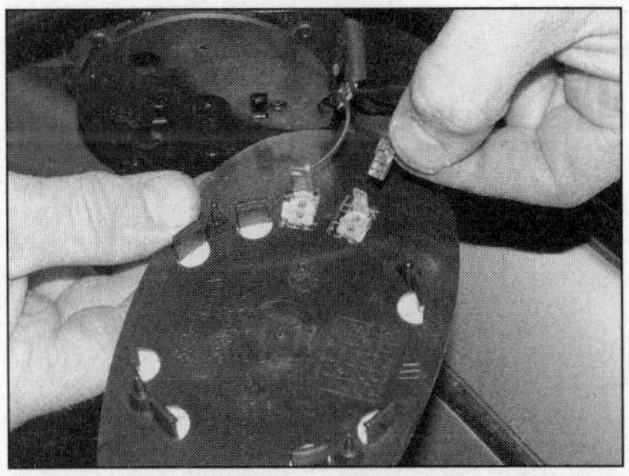

19.7 Disconnect the wiring plugs for the heating element

19.8 To refit the glass, press it evenly near the centre

Interior mirror

9 Using a small screwdriver, separate the two half-trims surrounding the mirror base.
10 Disconnect the wiring plug above the mirror.
11 The interior mirror is very firmly attached, but can be removed by turning it anti-clockwise, which will free it from the mounting.
12 Refitting is a reversal of removal.

20 Windscreen, rear window and fixed side glass - general information

These areas of glass are secured by the tight fit of the weatherseal in the body aperture, and are bonded in position with a special adhesive. Renewal of such fixed glass is a difficult, messy and time-consuming task, which is considered beyond the scope of the home mechanic. It is difficult, unless one has plenty of practice, to obtain a secure, waterproof fit. Furthermore, the task carries a high risk of breakage; this applies especially to the laminated glass windscreen. In view of this, owners are strongly advised to have this sort of work carried out by one of the many specialist windscreen fitters.

Removal of the rear door window fixed glass is covered in Section 15.

21 Sunroof components - removal and refitting

The sunroof is a complex piece of equipment, consisting of a large number of components. It is strongly recommended that the sunroof mechanism is not disturbed unless absolutely necessary. If the sunroof mechanism is faulty, or requires overhaul, consult a garage with experience of MG Rover cars for advice. Even removing the sunroof motor requires that the headlining be taken down, which is not a job to be taken on lightly.

Sunroof switch removal and refitting is described in Chapter 12, Section 4.

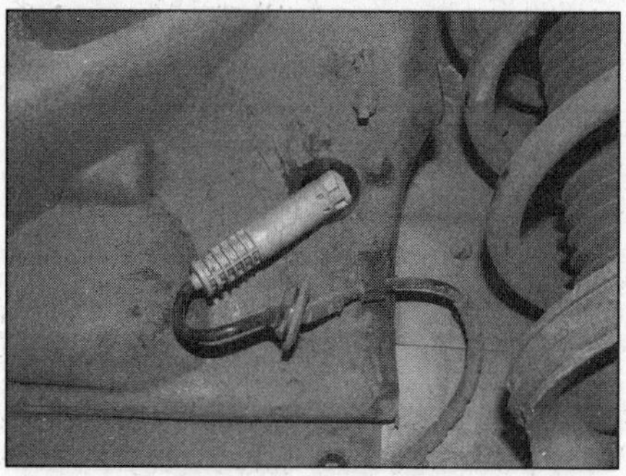
22.3a Prise out the grommet, and pull the wiring into the wheel arch

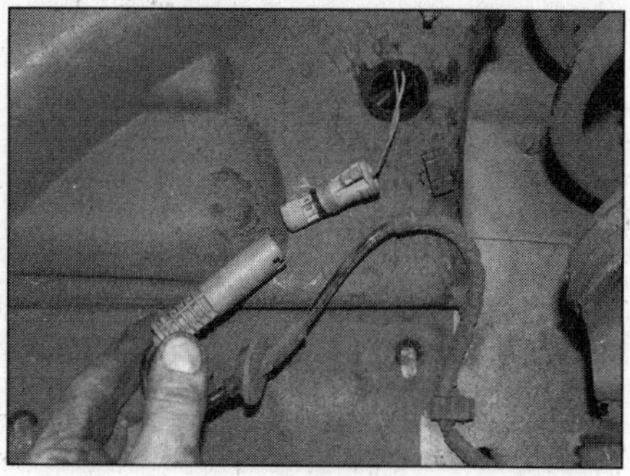
22.3b Separate the ABS sensor wiring connector

22 Body exterior fittings - removal and refitting

Wheel arch liners

Front

1 Loosen the relevant front wheel bolts, then jack up the front of the car, and support it on axle stands (see *Jacking and vehicle support*). Remove the appropriate front wheel.
2 Remove the engine undertray, which is secured by a number of quick-release screw fasteners.
3 Inside the wheel arch, unclip the sensor wiring harness from the wheel arch and the arch liner. Trace the wiring up to the grommet where it feeds through into the engine compartment, and prise out the grommet. Pull the wiring through into the wheel arch, and disconnect the plugs **(see illustrations)**.
4 Remove the screws securing the trim to the rear edge of the arch **(see illustration)**. Similarly, remove the air deflector at the front of the arch, which is secured by two screws.
5 Remove the vertical bolt which secures the liner to the front bumper, and the rearmost screw under the bumper's edge **(see illustrations)**.
6 The wheel arch liner itself is secured by six screw/clips (known as 'scrivets') – remove the screw from each, and pull out the clip. Remove all the clips, then withdraw the liner **(see illustrations)**.
7 Refitting is a reversal of removal.

Rear

8 Loosen the relevant rear wheel bolts. Chock the front wheels, then jack up the rear of the car, and support it on axle stands (see *Jacking*

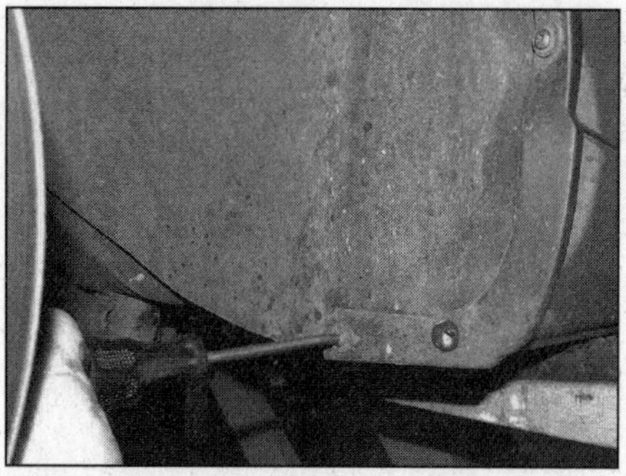
22.4 Remove the screws securing the rear arch trim

22.5a Remove the vertical liner-to-bumper bolt . . .

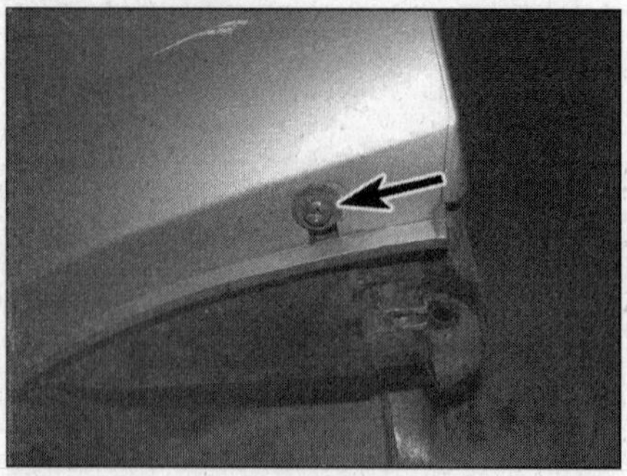
22.5b . . . and the rearmost screw on the bumper's lower edge

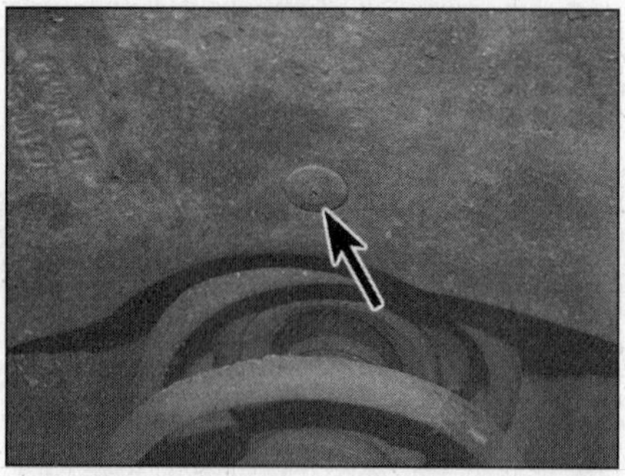
22.6a One of the liner securing screw/clips

22.6b Removing the front wheel arch liner

and vehicle support). Remove the appropriate rear wheel.

9 Remove the four plastic nuts and single screw (underneath the rear bumper) securing the liner to the wheel arch **(see illustrations)**.

10 Trace the ABS wiring harness around the rear of the liner, and unclip the wiring connector from the spring clip **(see illustration)**.

11 Unclip and remove the liner **(see illustration)**.

12 Refitting is a reversal of removal.

Trim strips

Note: *Take care not to damage the paintwork when removing the rubbing strips.*

13 The trim strips fitted down the sides and to the roof of the car are secured by numerous clips along their length. The exception is the trim strip fitted to the A-pillar and above the windows, which additionally has a screw at the front.

Boot lid trim

14 The boot lid trim doubles as the number plate light housing – refer to Chapter 12, Section 7, for number plate light unit removal.

Tailgate trim

15 On Tourer models, the tailgate trim also houses the tailgate release handle – refer to Section 17.

Badges

16 The various badges may be secured with adhesives. To remove them, either soften the adhesive using a hot-air gun or hairdryer (taking care to avoid damage to the paintwork), or separate the badge from the body by 'sawing' through the adhesive using a length of nylon cord. **Note:** *Some badges are located by pegs in plastic grommets – these will need to be carefully prised from the bodywork.*

17 Clean off all traces of adhesive using white spirit, then wash the area with warm soapy water to remove all traces of spirit, and allow to dry. Ensure that the surface to which the new badge is to be fastened is completely clean, and free from grease and dirt.

18 Use the hot-air gun to soften the adhesive on the new badge, then press it firmly into position.

Fuel filler flap

19 Refer to the relevant Part of Chapter 4.

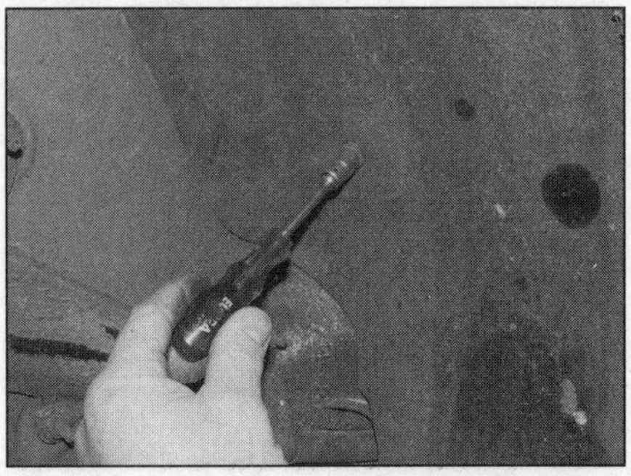

22.9a Remove the four plastic nuts inside the wheel arch . . .

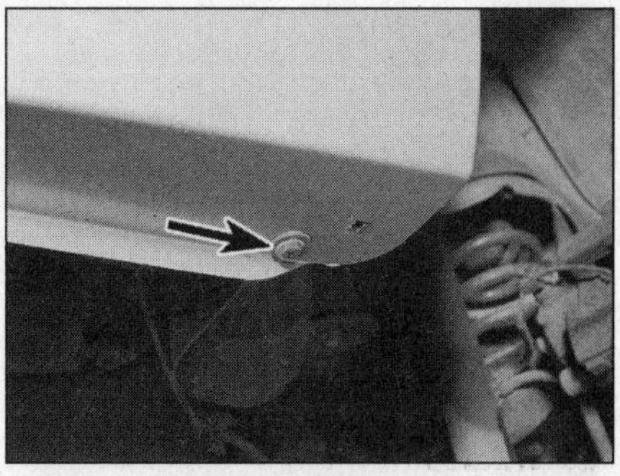

22.9b . . . and the single screw under the rear bumper

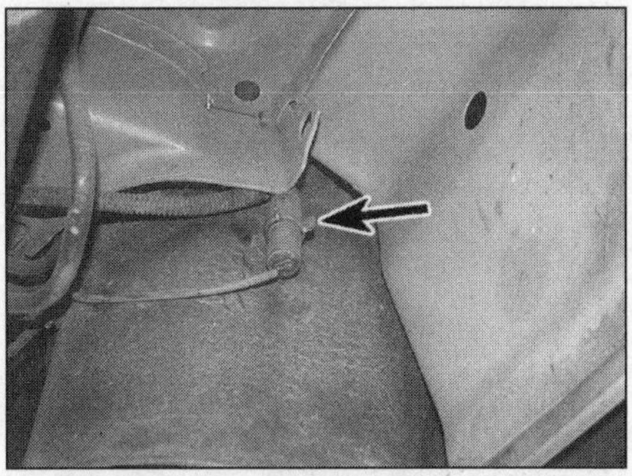

22.10 Unclip the ABS connector behind the liner

22.11 Removing the rear wheel arch liner

23 Seats – removal and refitting

Front seat

Warning: Remove the ignition key, disconnect both battery leads, negative first (see 'Disconnecting the battery'), then wait for 10 minutes before proceeding. If this waiting period is not observed, there is danger of activating the side airbags and seat belt tensioners.

1 On front seats with manual height adjustment (typically, this will only be the driver's seat), set the seat height to maximum. If this precaution is not taken, and the height adjustment mechanism is accidentally released while the seat is being removed, personal injury could result.

2 To make more room for manoeuvring the seat out later, remove the headrest.

3 Slide the seat fully to the rear, and unscrew the seat mounting Torx bolt at the front ends of the runners **(see illustration)**. These bolts should be discarded, and new ones obtained for refitting.

4 Slide the seat forwards, and unscrew the seat mounting Torx bolt at the rear of each runner. These two bolts should also be renewed when refitting.

5 Unhook the seat belt height adjusting cable from the side of the seat **(see illustration)**.

6 Disconnect the wiring plugs for the seat belt tensioner and the side airbag **(see illustration)**. On models with electric seat adjustment, also disconnect the main wiring harness plug under the seat.

7 Lift the seat out of the car – note that it is a heavy and awkward assembly to move, and that an assistant would be useful **(see**

23.3 Unscrew the seat mounting bolts

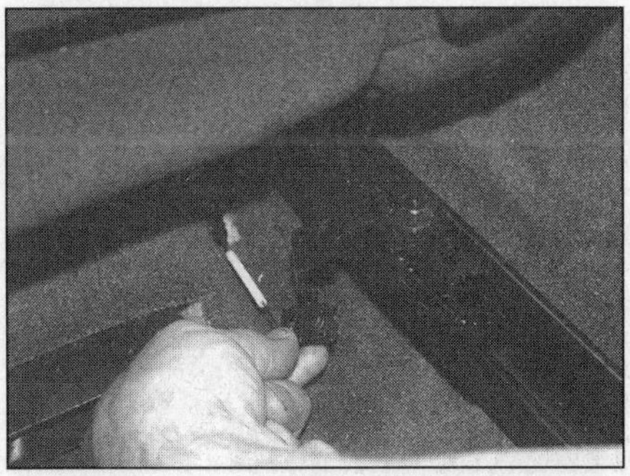

23.5 Unhook the seat belt height adjusting cable

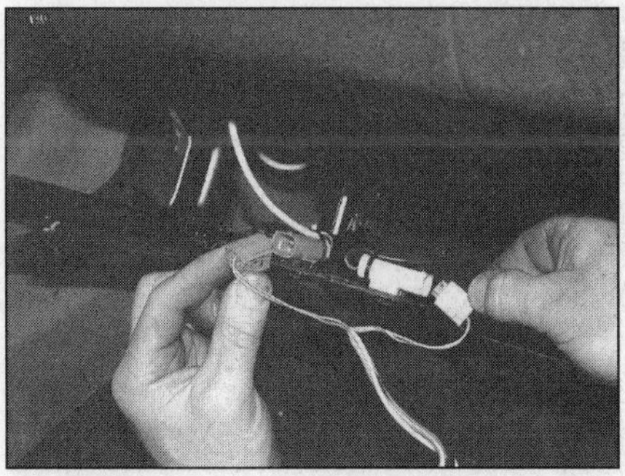

23.6 Disconnect the side airbag and seat belt tensioner wiring plugs

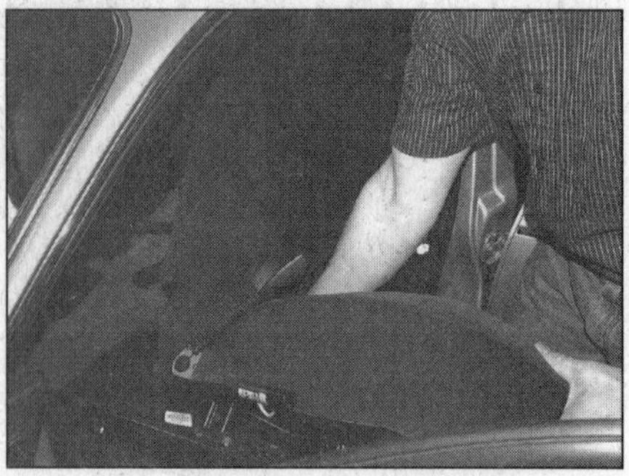

23.7 Lifting out the front seat

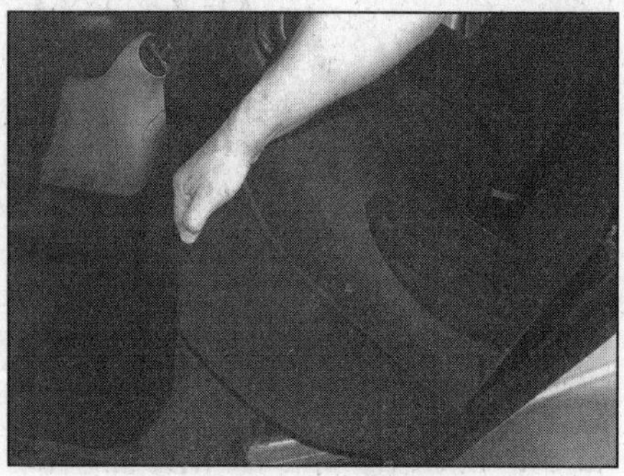

23.10 Pull up the front of the seat cushion to release the clips

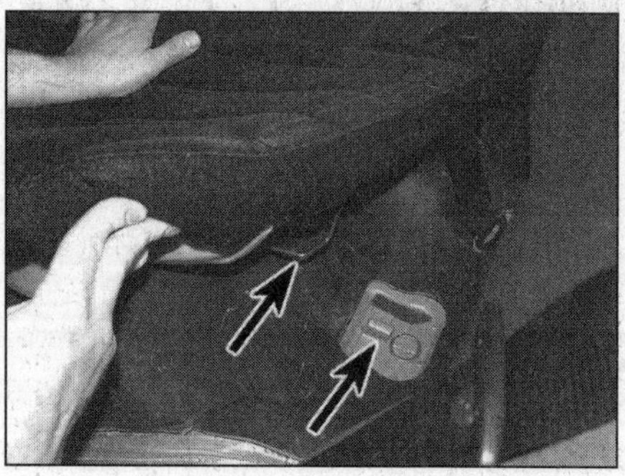

23.11 Unhook the seat cushion's rear clips from the floor

illustration). Also, be careful that the seat runners do not scratch any trim or paintwork as the seat is removed. Remember that the seat contains an airbag and seat belt tensioner – handle it gently.

8 Refitting is a reversal of removal, noting the following points:

a) *Use new seat mounting bolts, tightened to the specified torque. If for any reason new bolts are not available, clean the threads of the old ones, and apply a little threadlocking fluid before fitting.*

b) *Before reconnecting the tensioner and side airbag wiring plugs, make sure the battery is still disconnected. Ensure the plugs are securely reconnected, and that the wiring is not likely to become trapped in use.*

Rear seat cushion

9 Unclip the rear seat belts as necessary.

10 With the help of an assistant on the other end of the seat, pull the front of the cushion upwards to release the floor clips **(see illustration)**.

11 Once the front of the seat is free, push the cushion backwards, then lift the rear edge to unhook the rear clips **(see illustration)**.

12 Pull the cushion forwards, to access the lower seat belt mountings **(see illustration)**.

13 Unscrew the Torx bolt securing the centre seat belt mounting to the floor, then release the seat belt from the seat cushion **(see illustration)**.

14 Withdraw the seat cushion from the car **(see illustration)**.

15 Refitting is a reversal of removal, noting the following points:

a) *Tighten the seat belt mounting bolt to the specified torque, and ensure that the belt is not fitted twisted.*

b) *Ensure that all the seat mounting clips engage correctly, and that the seat is secure.*

Rear seat backrest

Saloon

16 Remove the seat cushion as described previously in this Section.

17 Where applicable, unclip and remove the bolsters from the sides of the backrest.

18 On models with fixed (non-folding) rear seats, use the pull straps provided to release the backrest clips, and pull the backrest forwards **(see illustration)**.

19 On models with folding rear seats, depress the release buttons and fold the backrest forwards.

20 Unhook the base of the backrest, and remove it from the car **(see illustrations)**.

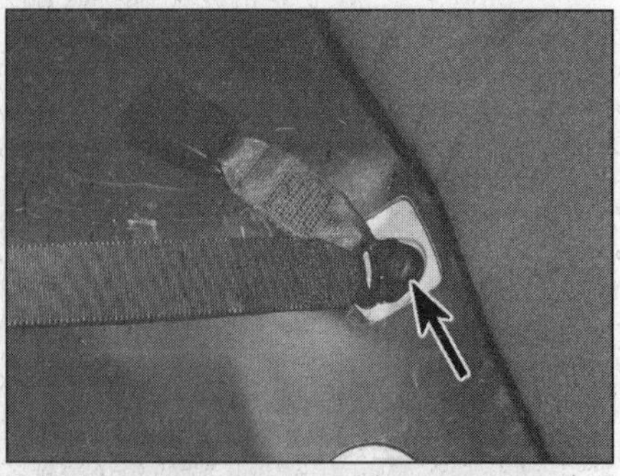

23.12 Move the cushion forwards to access the centre seat belt mounting

23.13 Feed the centre seat belt through the seat cushion

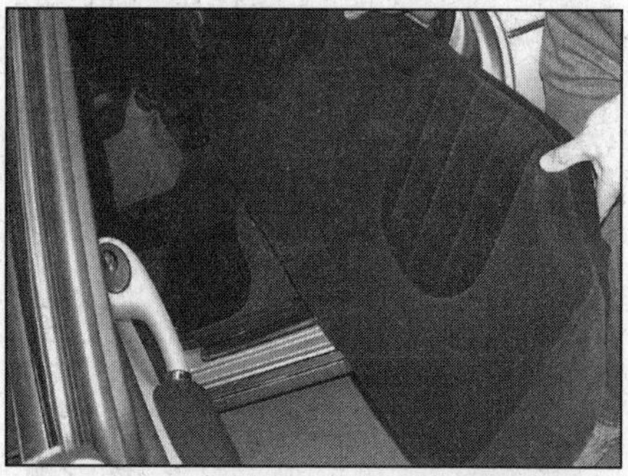

23.14 Removing the rear seat cushion

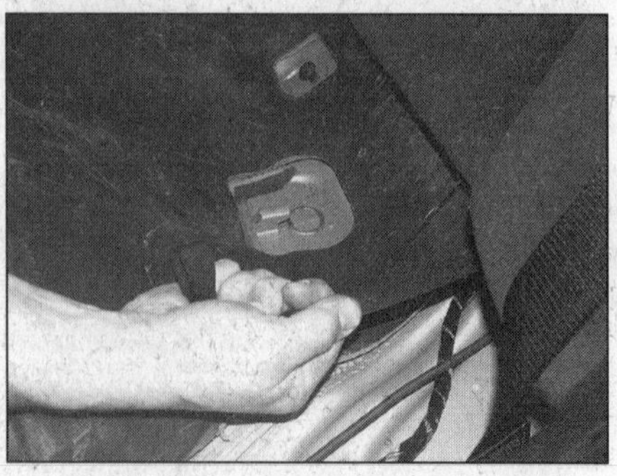

23.18 Pull the straps to release the backrest upper clips

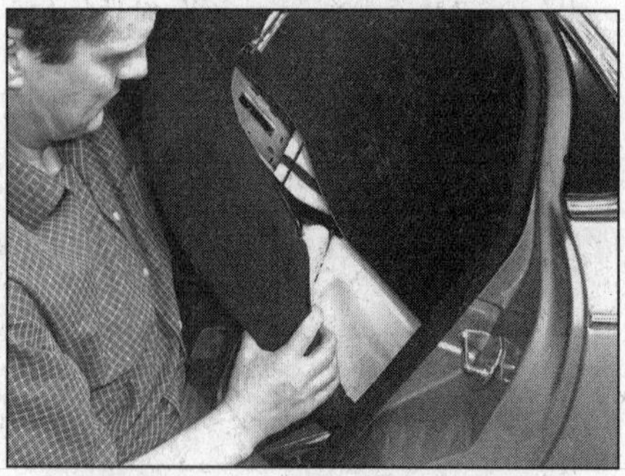

23.20a Unhook the backrest at the base . . .

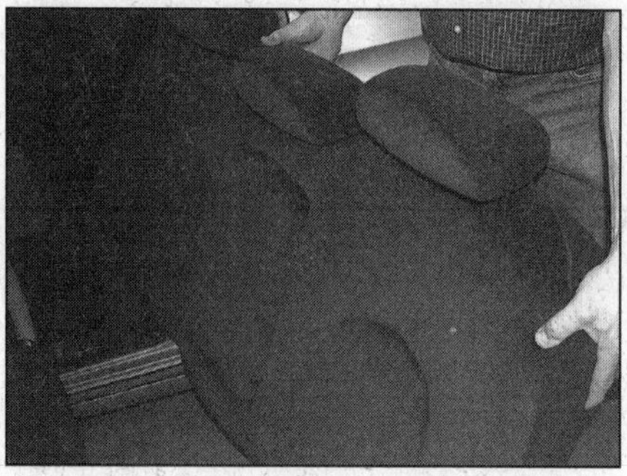

23.20b . . . and remove it from the car

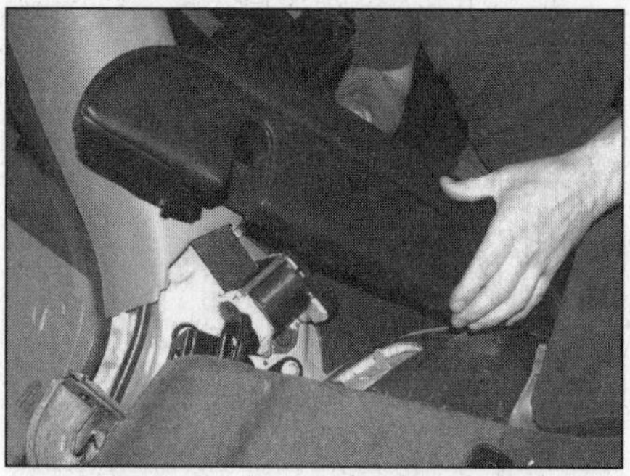

23.24 Unclip and remove the side bolsters

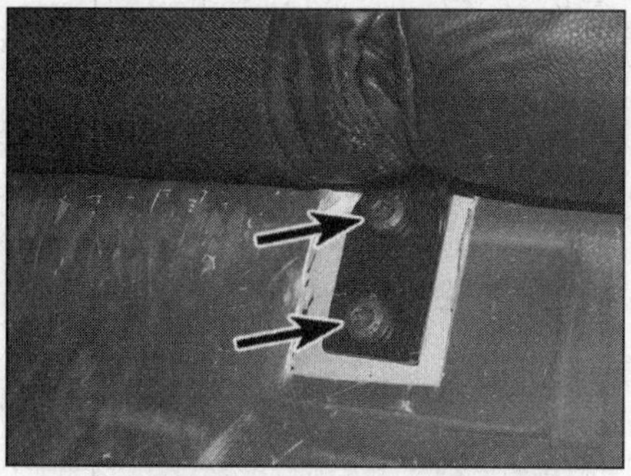

23.25 Unscrew the lower two bolts from the backrest central hinge

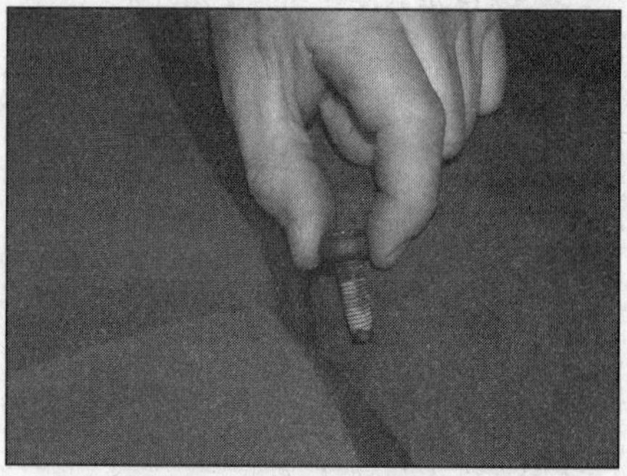

23.26 Remove the third bolt from the central hinge

21 Refitting is a reversal of removal.
22 Ensure the seat retaining clips engage properly, then refit the side bolsters (where fitted) and cushion as described previously in this Section.

Tourer

23 Remove the rear seat cushion as described previously in this Section.
24 Unclip and remove the seat end cushions (side bolsters), starting at the top, and pulling forwards. The bolsters have a hooked-over plastic clip at the top, and a wire clip at the base **(see illustration)**.
25 With the backrests still upright, the lower two central hinge mounting bolts can be unscrewed **(see illustration)**.
26 Fold the backrests flat, then reach in between the base of the seat and the boot floor, and remove the third bolt from the central hinge **(see illustration)**.
27 To release the backrests from the outer hinge points, use a screwdriver to press the spring-loaded collar on each outer locating 'peg' inwards. With the collar pressed in, lift the seat to detach it from the outer hinge point – the seat is now free to be removed from the car **(see illustrations)**.
28 Repeat the previous paragraph to remove the other section of the backrest.
29 Refitting is a reversal of removal, noting the following points:
a) *Engage the backrest locating pegs into the outer hinge points, and ensure the locking collars spring out to lock the seat in place. If necessary, help the collar to spring out, using a screwdriver.*
b) *Align the centre hinge with the bolt holes in the floor, using a screwdriver or similar tool. Insert the bolts, and tighten securely.*

24 Seat belt components – removal and refitting

Warning: Remove the ignition key, disconnect both battery leads, negative first (see 'Disconnecting the battery'), then wait for 10 minutes before proceeding. If this waiting period is not observed, there is danger of activating the seat belt tensioners.
Note: *If the car has been in an accident, all the affected seat belt components must be renewed.*

Seat belt tensioners

Information and precautions

1 Seat belt tensioners are fitted to remove any slack from the front and rear seat belts in the event of a frontal impact. The system is designed to reduce the chances of injury to the driver and passenger(s) in the event of an accident, by pulling their bodies back into the seat.
2 The system consists of a special seat belt tensioner/stalk assembly mounted directly on the front seats, or on the rear belt inertia reels, connected to the airbag control unit.
3 Each front seat tensioner/stalk assembly consists of a special buckle attached to a cable. The end of the cable is attached to a piston inside the tensioner cylinder.
4 In the event of a sufficiently-severe frontal impact, the seat belt tensioners will be triggered by the airbag control unit (for more information on the airbag system, refer to Chapter 12).
5 When a tensioner ignition module is triggered, a small capsule is energised, which rapidly releases gas into the tensioner cylinder. As the gas is released, the piston is forced along the cylinder, pulling the cable (approximately 70 mm) and hence the seat belt stalk, which in turn removes any slack from the seat belt, pulling the belt tight against the wearer.
6 The rear belt inertia reels have a similar system, except that the gas canister acts directly on the belt reel via a rack-and-pinion mechanism. The belt can be retracted by up to 180 mm when the tensioner is triggered.
7 Once a seat belt tensioner has been triggered, it must be renewed.
8 Take care, when working on the car, not to expose the tensioner system components to excess heat, impact, or even a magnetic field, as this may cause inadvertent triggering or a malfunction in an accident.

Front belt

9 Remove the plastic cap from the seat belt lower mounting bolt, then unscrew the bolt and detach the belt **(see illustration)**.
10 Remove the B-pillar upper trim panel as described in Section 25.
11 Unscrew and remove the seat belt upper

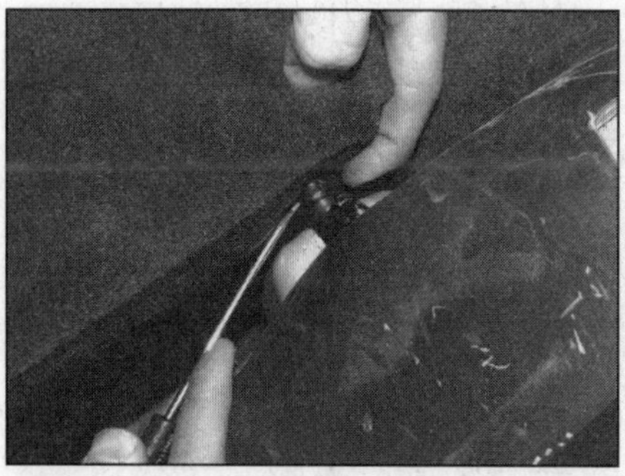

23.27a Use a screwdriver to depress the spring-loaded collar

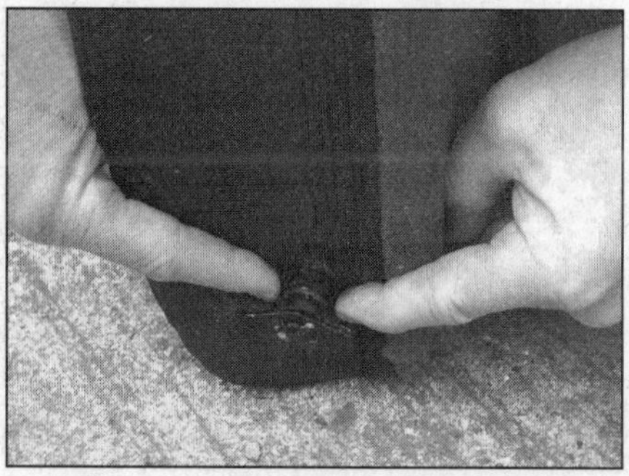

23.27b Backrest outer mounting seen removed from the car

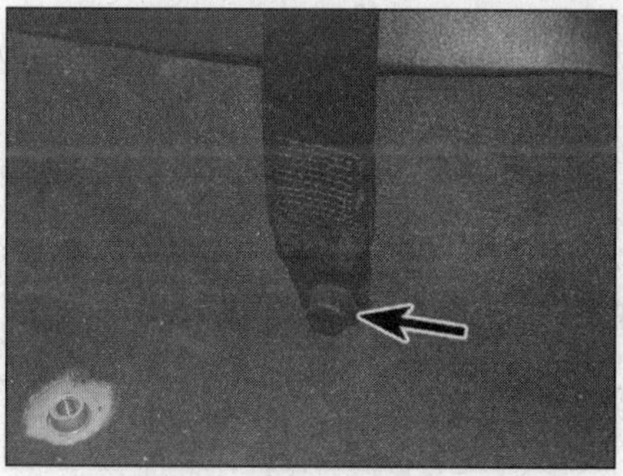

24.9 Remove the front seat belt lower mounting bolt

24.11 Unscrew the seat belt upper mounting nut

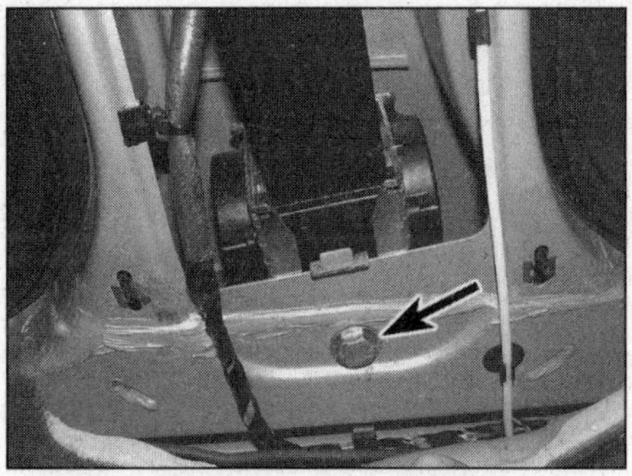

24.12 Remove the inertia reel bolt, and remove the seat belt

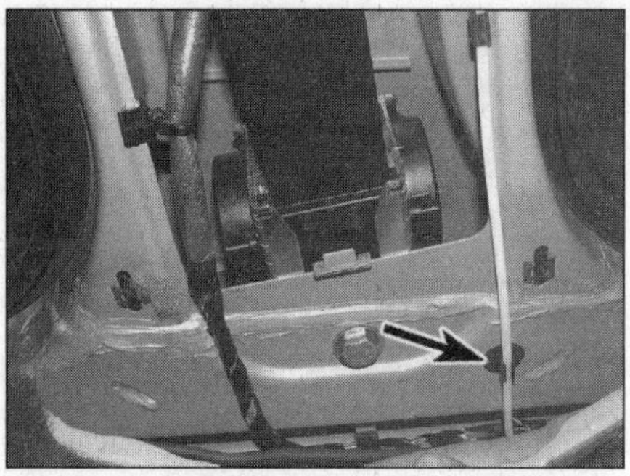

24.17a Unclip the outer cable from the B-pillar clips . . .

mounting nut, which secures the belt's D-loop to its adjuster mechanism **(see illustration)**.

12 Unscrew the seat belt reel mounting bolt, then withdraw the reel **(see illustration)**. Remove the seat belt from the car.

13 Refitting is a reversal of removal. Tighten all belt mountings to the specified torque.

Front belt height adjuster

14 Remove the relevant front seat as described in Section 23.

15 Remove the B-pillar upper and lower trim panels as described in Section 25.

16 Unscrew the seat belt upper mounting nut, and move the belt to one side.

17 Release the height adjuster cable from the four clips on the B-pillar. Unclip the cable end fitting from the adjuster, then unhook the inner cable **(see illustrations)**.

18 Unscrew the two Torx bolts securing the adjuster to the B-pillar **(see illustration)**.

19 Unclip the carpet at the base of the B-pillar, and lift it for access to the adjuster mechanism on the floor crossmember.

20 Release the pin securing the adjuster mechanism to the crossmember bracket, and remove it from the car.

21 Refitting is a reversal of removal. Tighten the adjuster bolts and seat belt upper mounting nut to the specified torque.

Front belt tensioners

22 Remove the relevant front seat as described in Section 23.

23 Under the seat, release the cable-tie clip securing the tensioner wiring to the seat frame.

24 Release the clip securing the tensioner's blue wiring connector to the seat. Similarly, where applicable, release the black connector for the seat belt warning light.

25 Unscrew the Torx bolt securing the tensioner to the side of the seat, then unhook it at the front and remove it **(see illustration)**.

26 Refitting is a reversal of removal, noting the following points:

- *a) Tighten the tensioner mounting bolt to the specified torque.*
- *b) Ensure that the wiring is securely clipped back into place, and cannot get trapped or damaged in use.*
- *c) Refit the front seat as described in Section 23.*

Rear seat belt

Saloon

27 Remove the parcel shelf as described in Section 25.

28 If removing one of the side belts, remove the rear wheel arch trim panel as described in Section 25, and unscrew the belt lower mounting Torx bolt **(see illustration)**.

29 Disconnect the wiring plug from the relevant inertia reel **(see illustration)**.

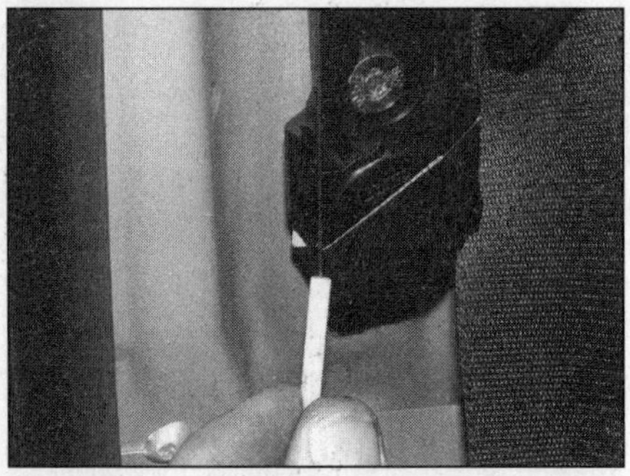

24.17b . . . then release it from the adjuster . . .

24.17c . . . and unhook the inner cable

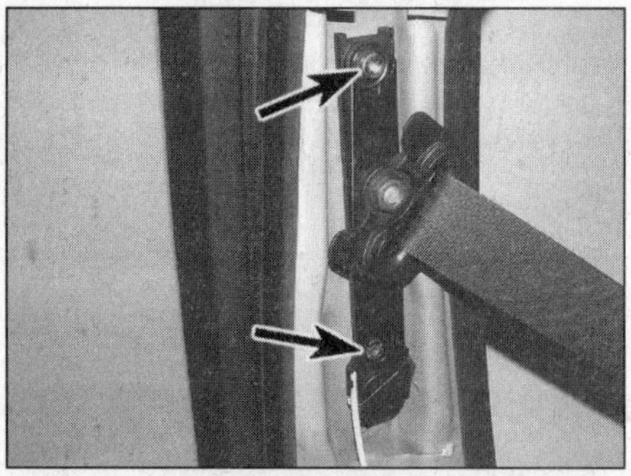

24.18 Unscrew the adjuster's two Torx bolts

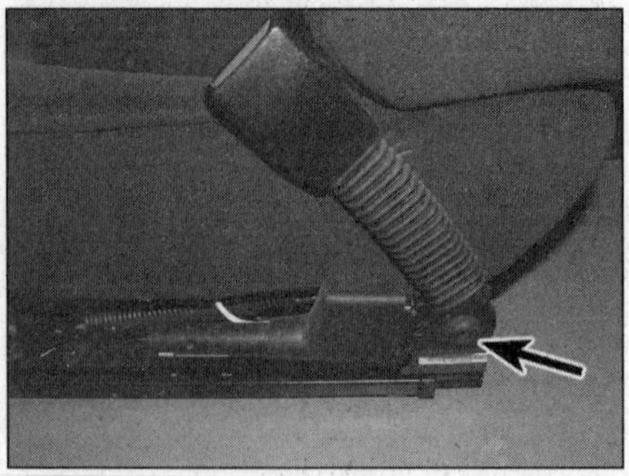

24.25 Front seat belt tensioner mounting bolt

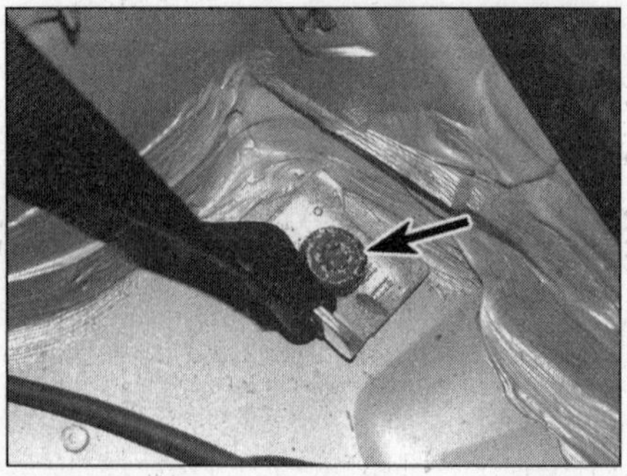

24.28 Rear side seat belt lower mounting bolt

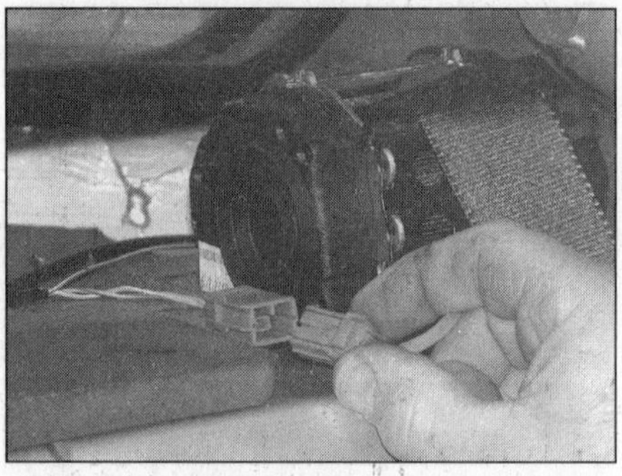

24.29 Disconnect the rear seat belt inertia reel wiring plug

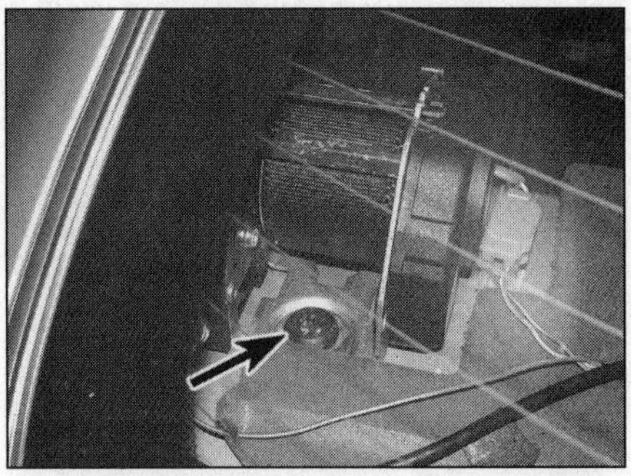

24.30 Rear inertia reel mounting bolt (seen through rear window)

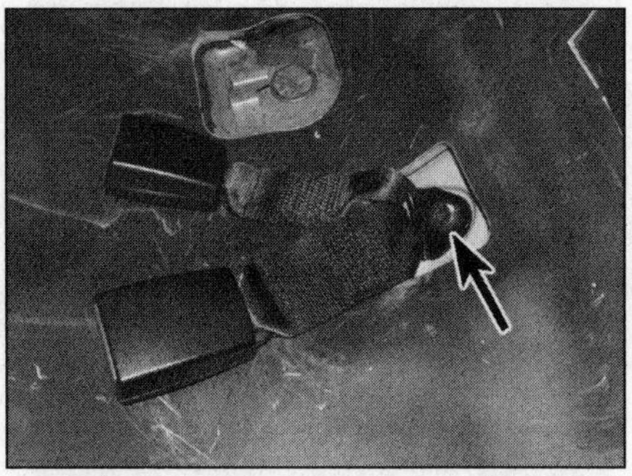

24.31 Rear seat belt buckle mounting bolt

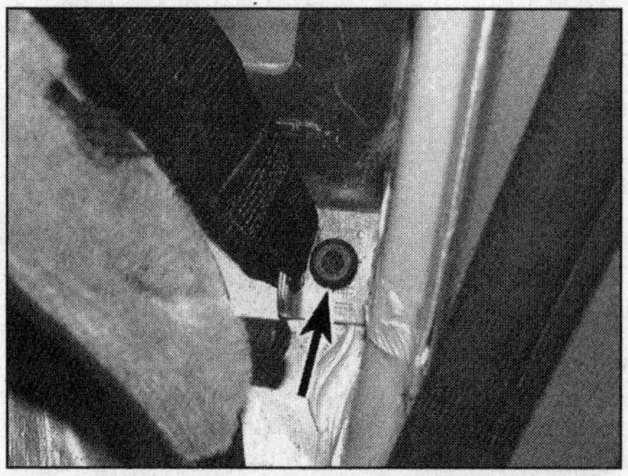

24.35 Rear seat belt lower mounting bolt - Tourer

30 Unscrew the Torx bolt securing the relevant inertia reel to the body **(see illustration)**, and remove the belt from the car.

31 If required, the belt buckles can be removed after unscrewing the Torx bolt securing them to the floor **(see illustration)**.

32 Refitting is a reversal of removal, noting the following points:

a) Tighten the seat belt/buckle mounting bolts to the specified torque.
b) Ensure that the inertia reel wiring plug is securely reconnected.
c) Refit the parcel shelf as described in Section 25.

Tourer

Note: *The centre belt's inertia reel is contained inside the seat backrest, requiring the backrest cover to be removed first – this is not considered a DIY operation. Any problems with the centre belt should be referred to a garage with experience of MG Rover vehicles, or perhaps to a car upholstery specialist in the first instance.*

33 Remove the rear wheel arch trim panel as described in Section 25.

34 Unclip the C-pillar trim panel, which is secured by two clips at its rear edge.

35 Unscrew and remove the Torx bolt from the seat belt lower mounting, and detach the end of the seat belt **(see illustration)**. Pass the seat belt through the C-pillar trim panel.

36 Disconnect the wiring plug from the inertia reel.

37 Unscrew and remove the seat belt Torx upper mounting bolt from the C-pillar, and the inertia reel mounting bolt **(see illustrations)**. Withdraw the seat belt from the car.

38 If required, the belt buckles can be removed after unscrewing the Torx bolt securing them to the floor.

39 Refitting is a reversal of removal, noting the following points:

a) Tighten the seat belt/buckle mounting bolts to the specified torque.
b) Ensure that the inertia reel wiring plug is securely reconnected.
c) Refit the removed trim panels as described in Section 25.

25 Interior trim panels - removal and refitting

General information

1 The interior trim panels are all secured using either plastic clips (some built into the panel), or screws. Note that the type and number of fasteners used often varies during the production run of a particular model, so differences may be found to the procedures provided.

2 Before removing a panel, study it carefully, noting how it is secured. Often, other panels or ancillary components (such as seat belt mountings, grab handles, etc) must be removed before a particular panel can be withdrawn.

3 Once any such components have been removed, check that there are no other panels overlapping the one to be removed. Usually, the sequence to be followed will become obvious on close inspection.

4 Remove all obvious fasteners, such as screws, which may have plastic covers fitted. If the panel cannot be freed, it is probably secured by hidden clips or fasteners on the rear of the panel. Such fasteners are usually situated around the edge of the panel, and can be prised up to release them. Note that plastic clips can break quite easily, so it is advisable to have a few new clips of the correct type available for refitting. Generally, the best way of releasing such clips is to use a wide flat-bladed tool, designed for the purpose – these are available from tool suppliers such as Draper. If this is not available, an old, broad-bladed screwdriver with the edges rounded-off and wrapped in insulating tape will serve as a good substitute.

5 When removing a panel, **never** use excessive force, or the panel may be damaged. Always check carefully that all fasteners have been removed or released before attempting to withdraw a panel.

6 When refitting, secure the fasteners by pressing them firmly into place. Ensure that all disturbed components are correctly secured, to prevent rattles.

Door trim panels

7 Refer to Section 14.

Facia (veneer) trim panels

Note: *These procedures apply equally to the wood-effect facia panels fitted to most Rover 75 models, and to the equivalent non-wood panels fitted to MG ZT models.*

Driver's side

8 Remove the driver's lower facia trim panel as described later in this Section.

9 Release the locking lever, and fully lower the steering column.

10 Remove the two screws from the column lower shroud **(see illustration)**.

11 Release the three clips either side, and separate the upper and lower column shrouds. Release the locking lever, and remove the lower shroud. Lift the upper shroud – note that removing the shroud will not be possible, as

24.37a Rear seat belt upper mounting bolt - Tourer

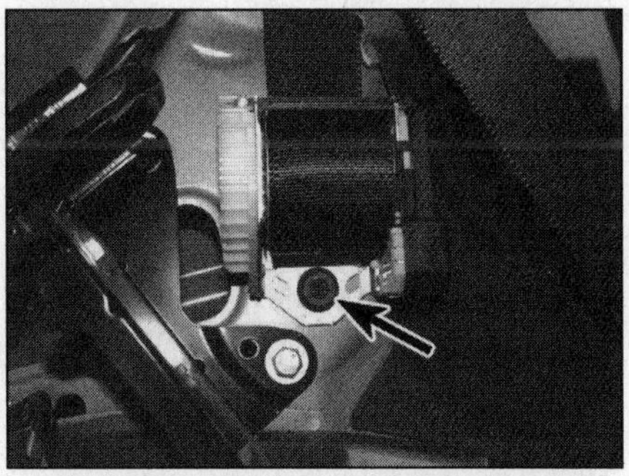

24.37b Rear belt inertia reel (Tourer) - mounting bolt arrowed

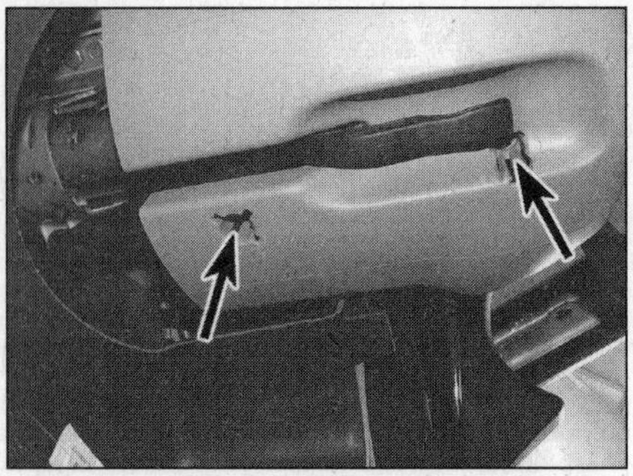

25.10 Steering column lower shroud screws

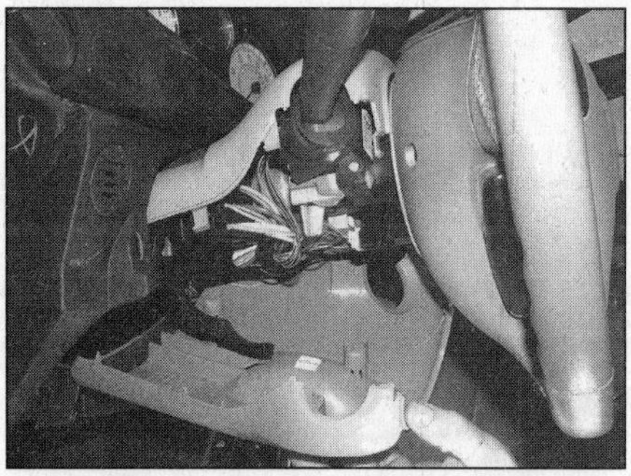

25.11a Unclip the shrouds, and remove the lower one

25.11b The upper shroud trim is trapped behind the instruments

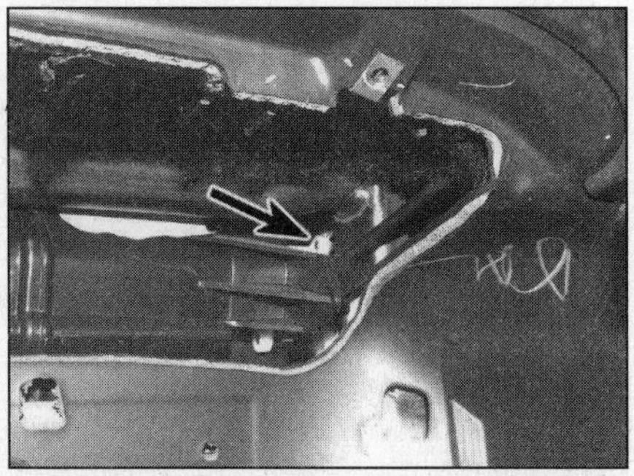

25.12a With the centre console removed, the vent control lever is visible

25.12b Unclip the vent control cable towards the steering wheel

the front trim is trapped behind the instrument panel **(see illustrations)**.

12 The centre vent control cable must now be disconnected. This is supposedly possible by reaching up behind the facia from the driver's footwell, but is far easier if the centre console is removed (Section 26) as this allows access from the front. The cable end fitting pulls off sideways from the white plastic lever on the heater assembly, then the cable's outer clip can also be released **(see illustrations)**.

13 Close the facia vents in the centre and on the driver's side.

14 Using only your fingers (no tools), carefully unclip the facia trim, starting below the instrument panel and working towards the centre of the car. Finally, release the clip at the driver's side **(see illustrations)**.

15 Disconnect the wiring plug from the back of the clock, and manoeuvre the trim panel out from behind the steering wheel **(see illustration)**.

16 Refitting is a reversal of removal.

Passenger's side

17 Carefully prise at the base of the panel to release the two lower clips – take care not to insert any prising tools too deeply, as the passenger airbag is located behind the panel **(see illustration)**.

18 Lift the panel out at the bottom edge, and withdraw it. Remove the seven Torx screws securing the veneer panel on the inside, and withdraw the panel. If required, the airbag cover panel can also be removed, after unhooking the metal plates at the ends of the webbing straps **(see illustrations)**.

19 Refitting is a reversal of removal.

Vent surround

20 The veneer panel surrounding the passenger-side vent is removed with the vent, as described in Chapter 3.

25.14a Unclip the panel. working towards the centre of the car . . .

25.14b . . . then release it at the driver's side

25.15 Disconnect the wiring plug from behind the clock

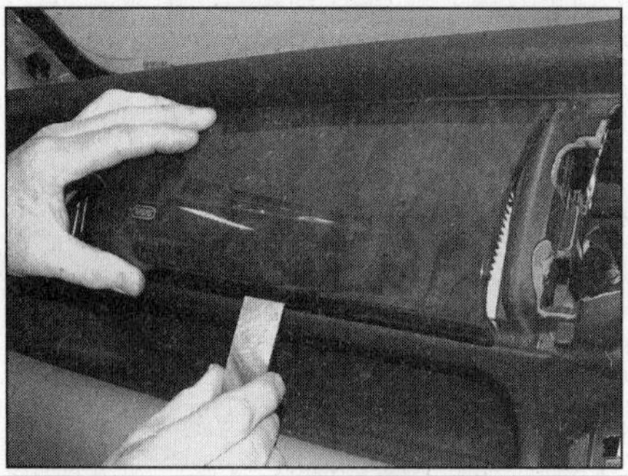

25.17 Carefully prise out the panel using a wide-bladed tool

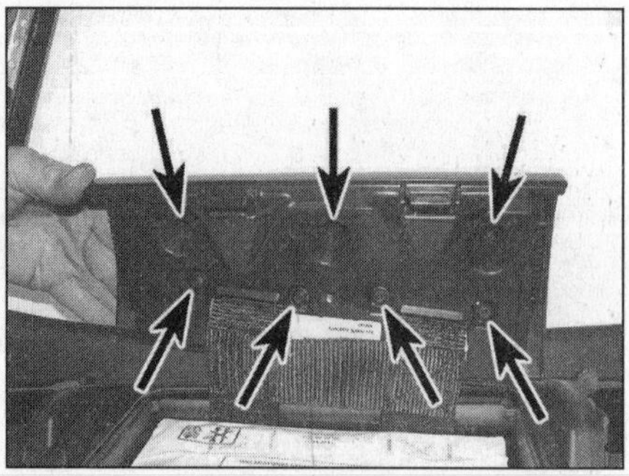

25.18a Remove seven Torx screws behind the panel . . .

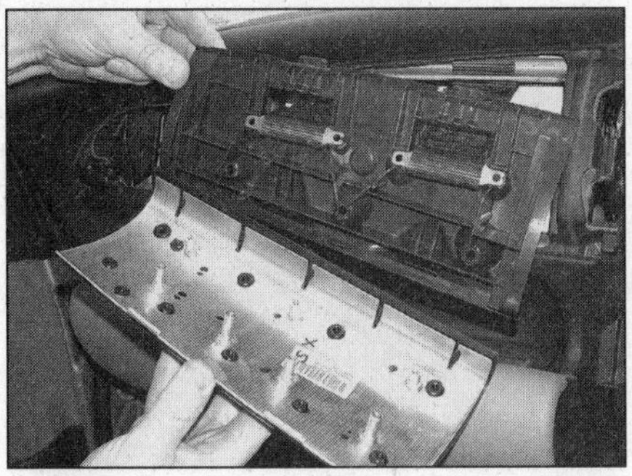

25.18b . . . and separate the veneer panel

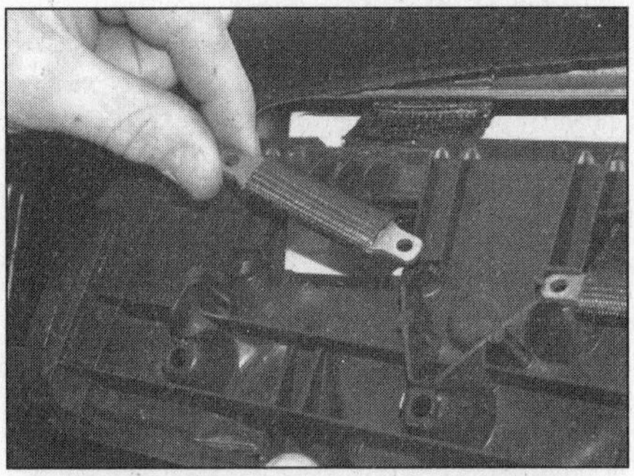

25.18c Remove the inner panel by unhooking the two metal plates . . .

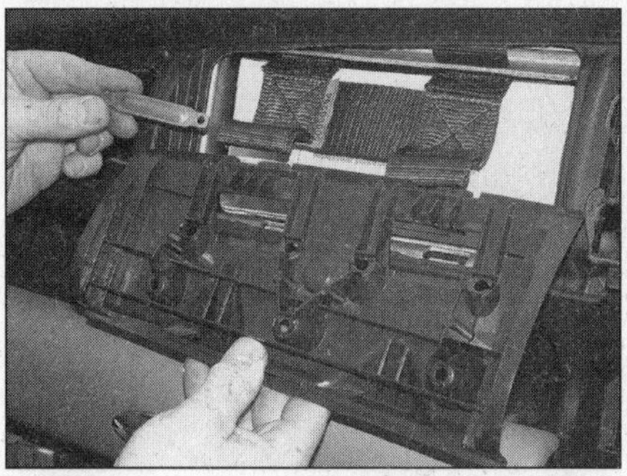

25.18d . . . then feed through the two webbing straps

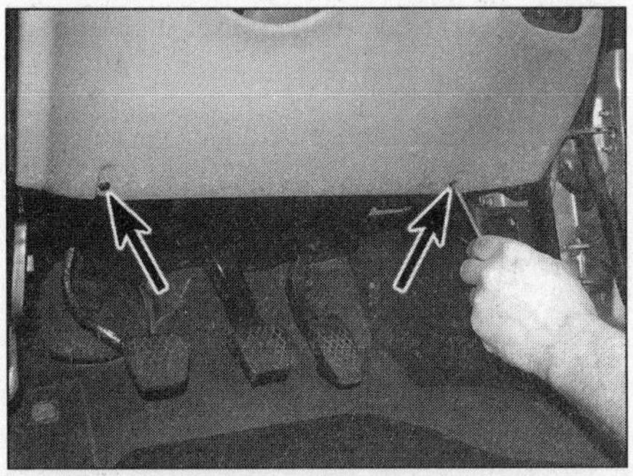

25.21a Remove the two screws (also used to secure the closing panel) . . .

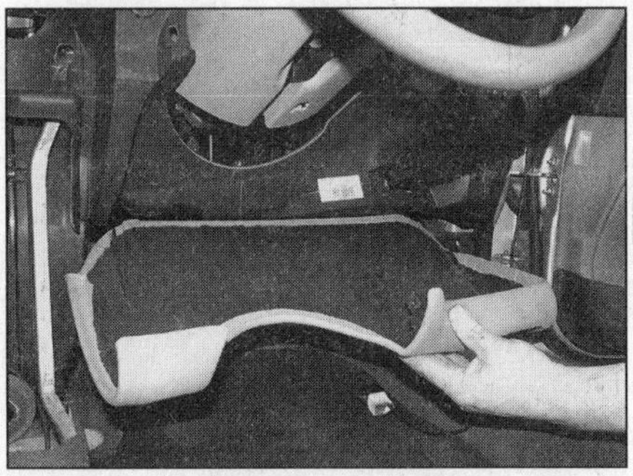

25.21b . . . and pull to release the upper row of three clips

Driver's lower facia panel

21 This panel, fitted below and to the right of the steering column, is secured by two screws underneath and three clips along the top edge. Remove the screws, pull the panel to release the clips, then withdraw the panel from the facia **(see illustrations)**. This will also release the facia closing panel above the pedals, which can easily be removed in addition.

22 Refitting is a reversal of removal.

Facia closing panels

23 A separate panel is fitted on each side of the facia, where the facia joins the carpet. In both cases, two push-clips are used at the base, which must be prised out. On the panel fitted above the pedals on the driver's side, two screws are used at the top corners; the panel under the glovebox on the passenger's side has two turn-buckle fasteners at the top **(see illustrations)**.

24 Refitting is a reversal of removal.

Glovebox

25 Open the glovebox, and carefully peel up the lining to reveal three of the Torx mounting screws **(see illustrations)**.

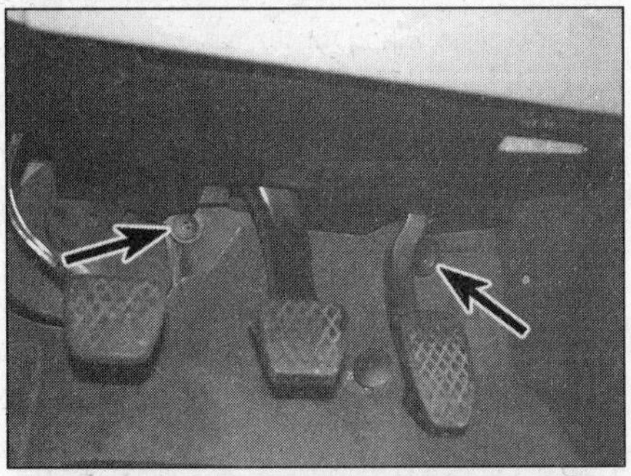

25.23a Prise out the two push-clips at the base . . .

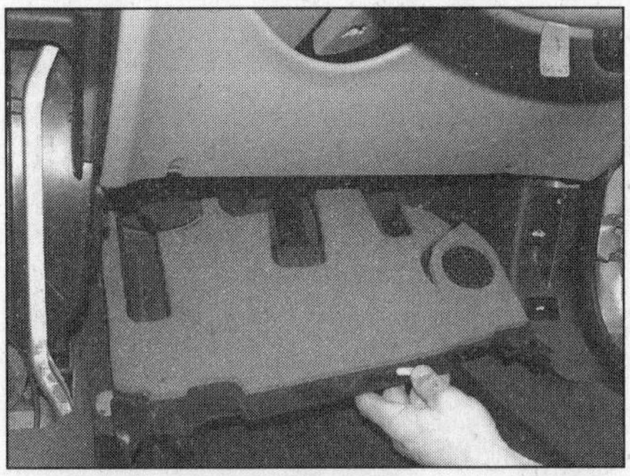

25.23b . . . then remove the two screws and lower the driver's panel . . .

25.23c . . . or use a coin to release the upper fasteners . . .

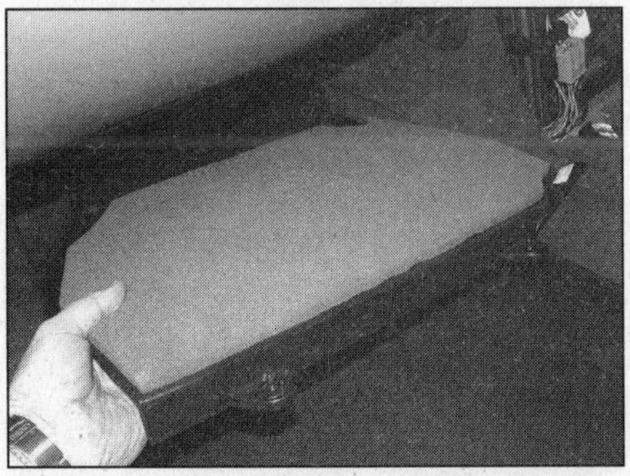

25.23d . . . and remove the passenger's panel

25.25a Starting at one corner, peel up the glovebox lining . . .

25.25b . . . to reveal a row of three Torx screws

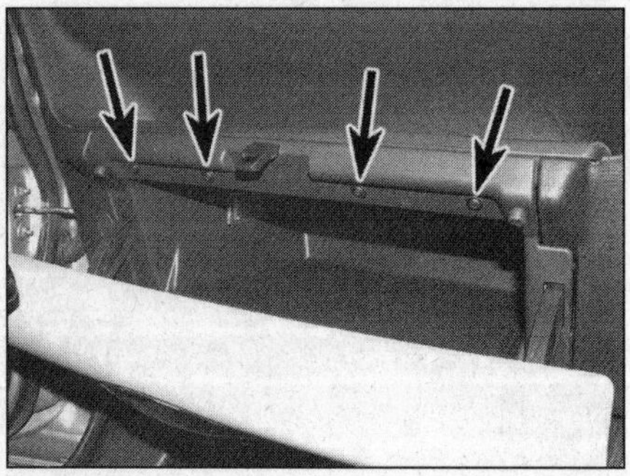

25.26a Remove four more screws from the top of the glovebox . . .

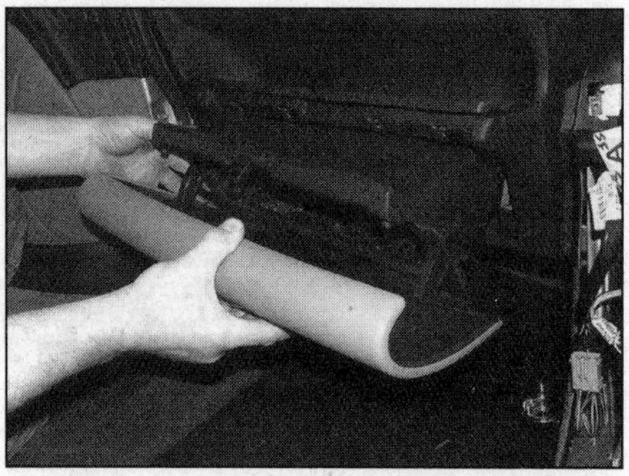

25.26b . . . and withdraw the glovebox from the facia

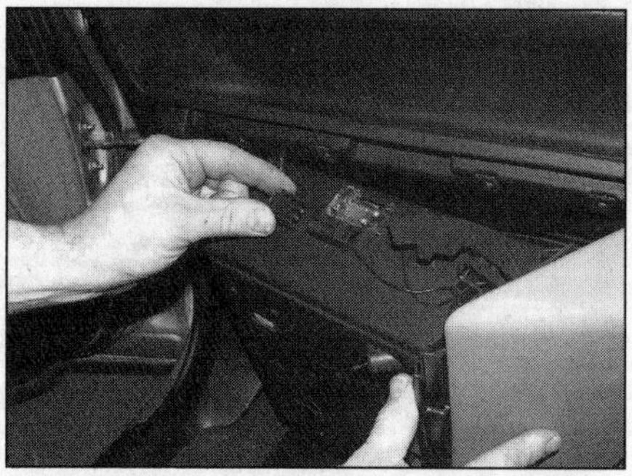

25.27 Disconnect the glovebox light

26 Remove a total of seven Torx screws, and release the glovebox from the facia **(see illustrations)**.

27 Disconnect the wiring plug for the glovebox light, and remove it completely **(see illustration)**. Where applicable, disconnect the multi-plugs on the left-hand side for the CD changer. If required, the CD changer can be separated from the glovebox after removing the four mounting nuts.

28 Refitting is a reversal of removal.

Steering column shrouds

29 Remove the driver's lower facia trim panel as described previously in this Section.

30 Release the locking lever, and fully lower the steering column. Remove the two screws from the column lower shroud **(see illustration)**.

31 Release the three clips either side, and separate the upper and lower column shrouds. Release the locking lever, and remove the lower shroud. Lift the upper shroud, noting that complete removal will be prevented by the flexible trim at the front – if removal is essential, remove the instrument panel as described in Chapter 12, and the trim can be slipped out **(see illustrations)**.

32 Refitting is a reversal of removal.

Sunvisors

33 Unclip the inner end of the sunvisor from its retaining clip.

34 At the hinged end, remove the two mounting screws, and withdraw the sunvisor from the headlining.

35 Where applicable, disconnect the wiring plugs, and remove the sunvisor completely.

36 Refitting is a reversal of removal.

Grab handles

37 Using a small screwdriver, prise out the cover at each end of the grab handle **(see illustration)**.

38 Remove the screw under each cover, then lower the grab handle from the headlining and remove it.

39 Refitting is a reversal of removal.

A-pillar trim panel

Warning: Remove the ignition key, disconnect both battery leads, negative first (see 'Disconnecting the battery'), then wait for 10 minutes before proceeding. This is a precaution against accidentally disconnecting the side curtain airbags, which (where fitted) are located behind and above the A-pillar trim panels.

40 The A-pillar trim panel is secured by three clips in the centre, along its length. Starting at the top, prise the panel carefully to unclip it, then unhook it from the facia at the bottom **(see illustration)**. On models with side curtain airbags, there is a danger of disconnecting or damaging the wiring for the airbag unit, which is located behind the A-pillar trim panel (and above the driver's door).

41 When the panel is free, release and remove it from the car. MG Rover recommend that, on models with side curtain airbags, a new trim panel should be fitted once the original has been disturbed.

42 Refitting is a reversal of removal.

Footwell trim panels

Plastic panels

43 Prise out the clip at the front, then carefully unclip the panel, which is secured by three

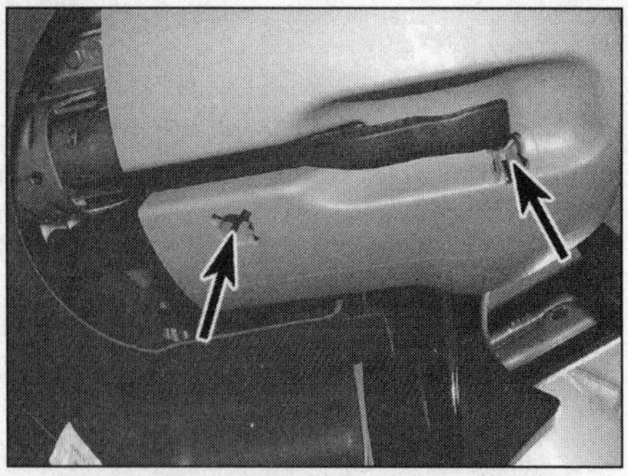

25.30 Steering column lower shroud screws

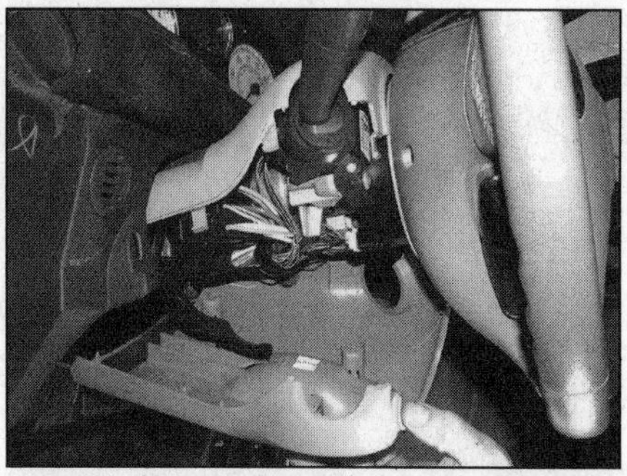

25.31a Unclip the shrouds, and remove the lower one

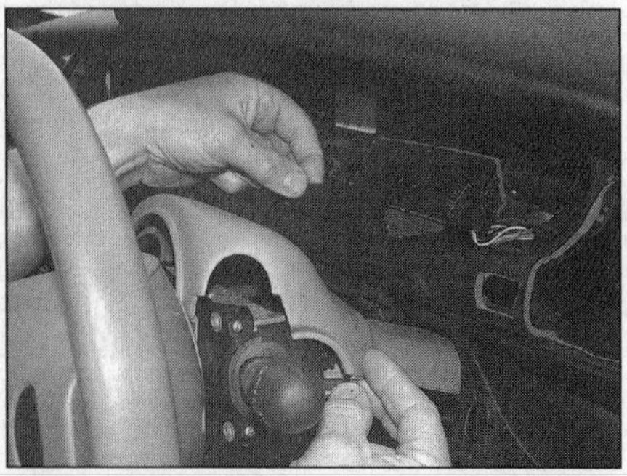

25.31b Without the instruments, the upper shroud trim slides out

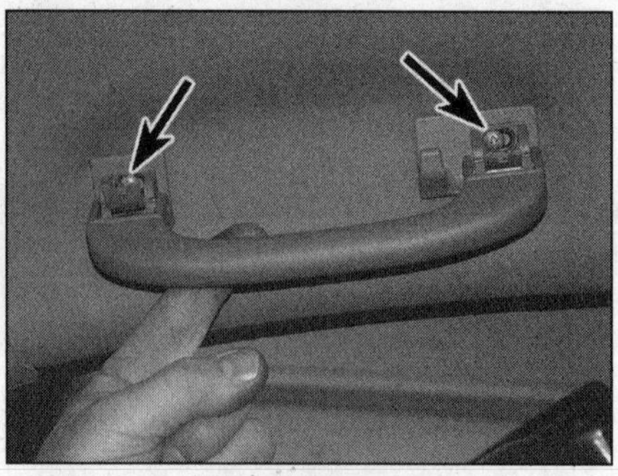

25.37 Prise out the end covers to access the grab handle screws

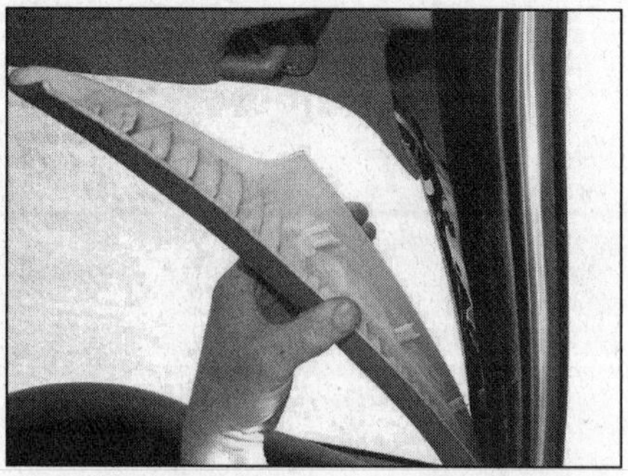

25.40 Release the three clips securing the A-pillar trim panel

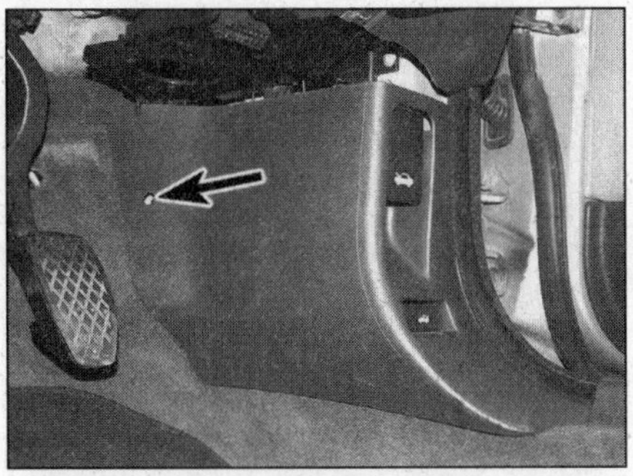

25.43a The footwell trim panel is secured by a clip at the front . . .

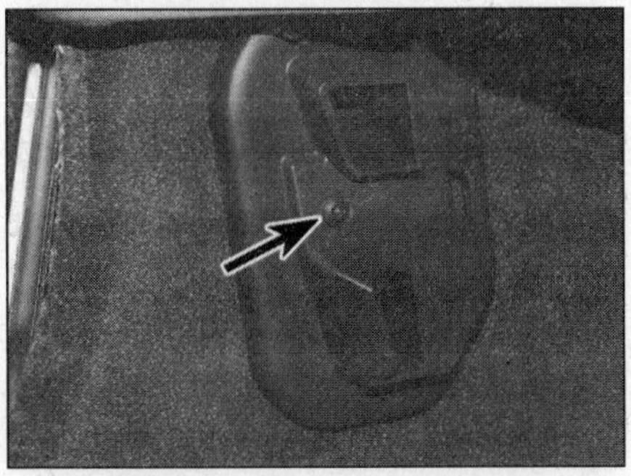

25.46a Remove the single screw . . .

clips. Peel back the door rubber seal if it will help removal **(see illustrations)**.

44 On the driver's side, disconnect the wiring plug from the boot lid/tailgate release switch **(see illustration)**.

45 Refitting is a reversal of removal.

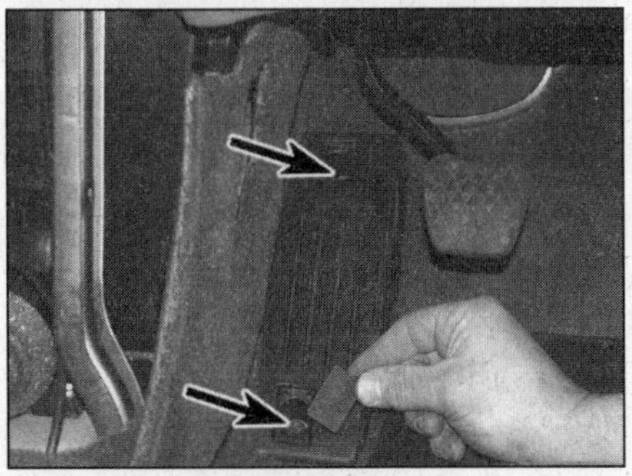

25.47a Prise out the screw covers, remove the two screws . . .

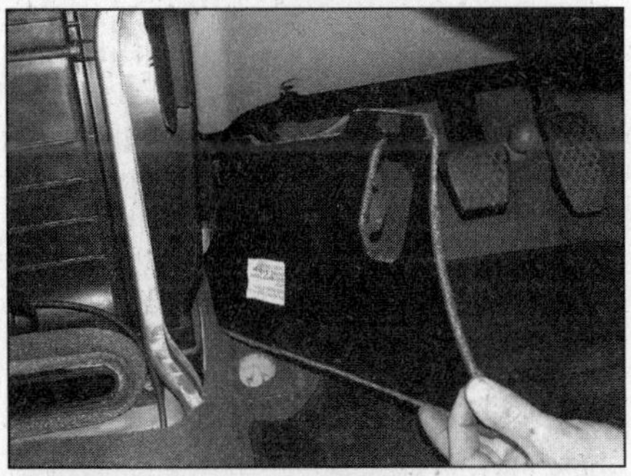

25.48 Unclip and remove the carpet panel from the footwell

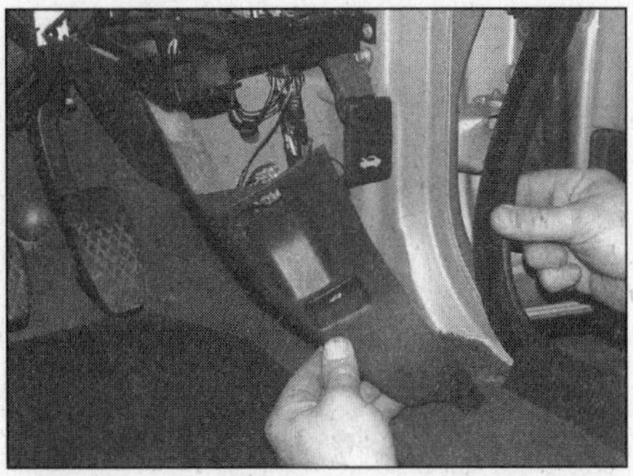

25.43b . . . and can then be unclipped from its location

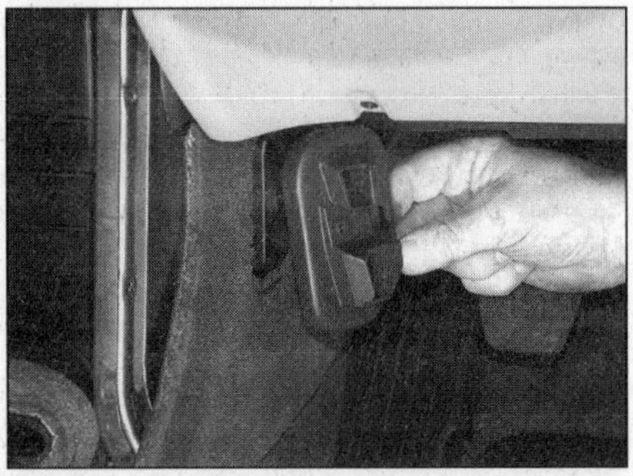

25.46b . . . and withdraw the footwell vent

Carpet panels

46 Remove the screw securing the footwell vent, and withdraw the vent from the panel **(see illustrations)**.

47 On the driver's side, prise out the screw covers, then remove the two screws and take out the left footrest (where applicable) **(see illustrations)**.

48 Unclip and remove the carpet panel from the footwell **(see illustration)**.

49 Refitting is a reversal of removal.

25.47b . . . then take out the driver's left footrest

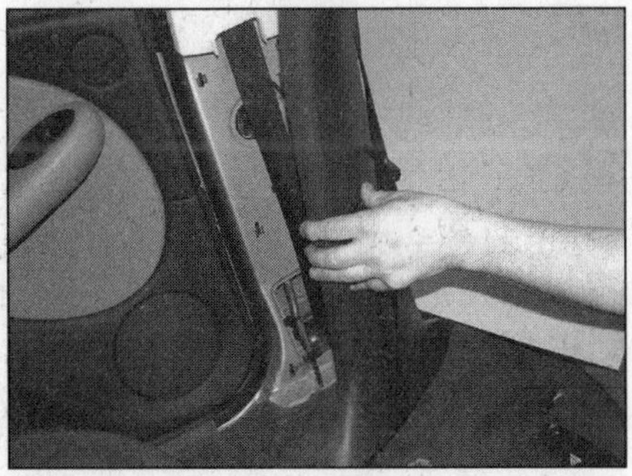

25.56 Unclip the lower half of the B-pillar trim panel

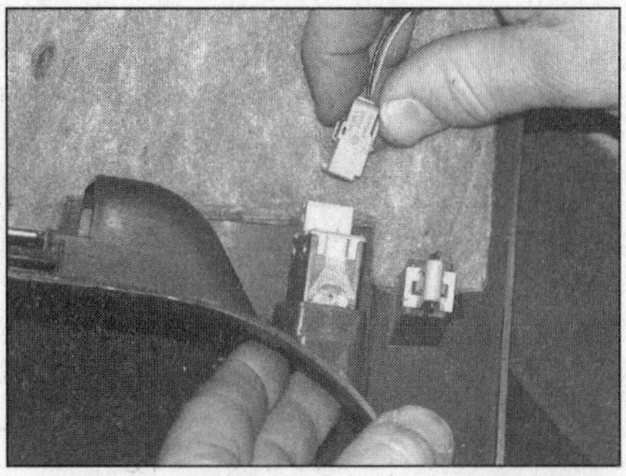

25.44 Disconnect the boot lid/tailgate release switch on the driver's side

Sill trim panels

Inner

50 Pull up the door rubber seal at the top of the panel.

51 Unclip and remove the inner trim, noting that it might also be necessary to ease out the panels at either end to remove it.

52 Refitting is a reversal of removal.

Outer

53 Pull up the door rubber seal at the top of the panel.

54 Carefully prise up the chrome panel, taking great care not to bend it, nor scratch the paintwork – the panel is attached to the sill with double-sided tape. Remove the panel from the car.

55 Refitting is a reversal of removal. Clean the trim panel and the mating surface on the door sill prior to fitting, and take care to align the panel accurately before peeling off the backing and sticking in position.

B-pillar trim panels

56 Unclip and remove the lower half of the trim panel, which is secured by two rows of three clips along the front and rear edges **(see illustration)**.

57 Unclip the upper half of the trim panel, which is secured by three clips **(see illustration)**. Feed

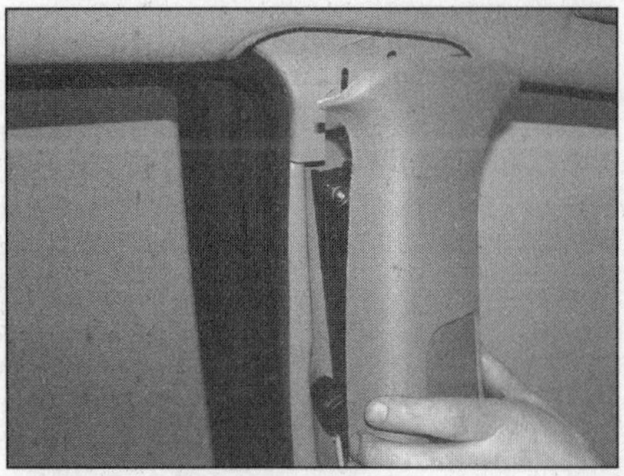

25.57 The upper half of the B-pillar trim also unclips

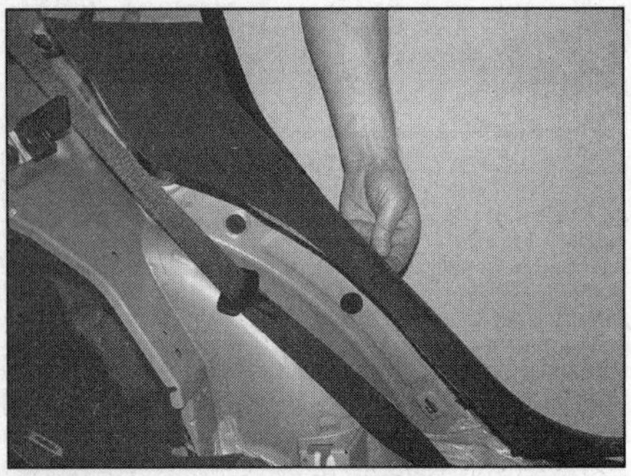

25.61 Unclip and remove the rear wheel arch trim panel

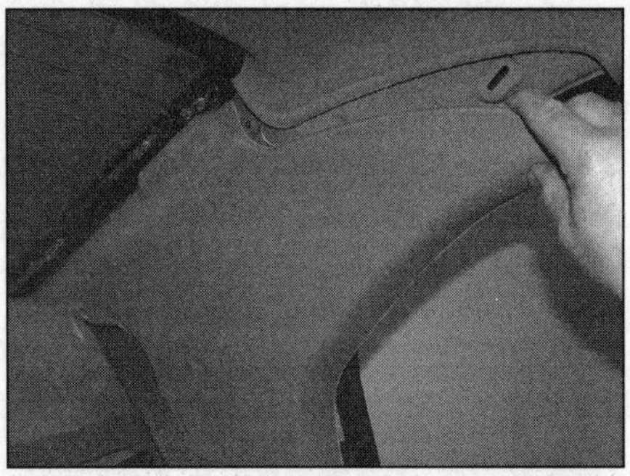

25.66 Carefully unclip the C-pillar trim panel

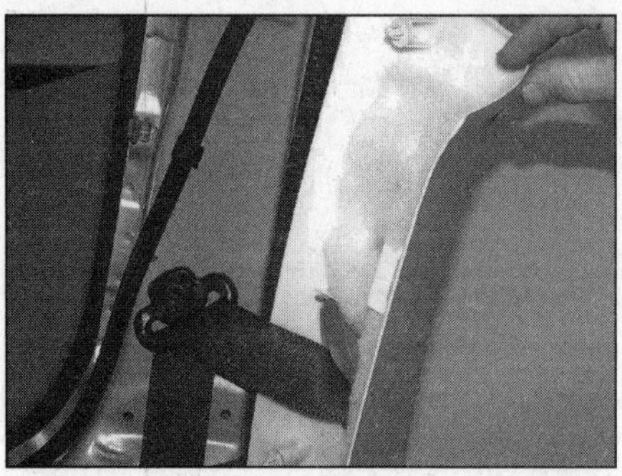

25.69 Removing the C-pillar trim panel on a Tourer

the seat belt through, then remove the panel completely.

58 Refitting is a reversal of removal.

Rear wheel arch trim panel

59 Pull up the door rubber seal along the edge of the panel – this is more for refitting than for removal.

Saloon

60 Remove the rear seat as described in Section 23.

61 Taking care not to damage the paintwork, carefully prise up the panel at one end. Release a total of four clips, and remove the panel from the car **(see illustration)**.

62 Refitting is a reversal of removal.

Tourer

63 Fold the rear seat forwards, then unclip and remove the rear seat side bolster, starting at the top, and pulling forwards. The bolsters have a hooked-over plastic clip at the top, and a wire clip at the base.

64 Prise out the two trim panel retaining clips, and remove the panel.

65 Refitting is a reversal of removal.

C-pillar trim panel

Saloon

66 The C-pillar trim panel is secured by three clips – carefully prise the panel away, and remove it **(see illustration)**.

67 Refitting is a reversal of removal.

Tourer

68 Remove the rear wheel arch trim panel as described previously in this Section.

69 Unclip the C-pillar trim panel, which is secured by two clips at its rear edge **(see illustration)**.

70 Unscrew and remove the Torx bolt from the seat belt lower mounting, and detach the end of the seat belt. Pass the seat belt through the C-pillar trim panel, and the trim panel can be removed.

Parcel shelf – Saloon

71 Remove the rear seat as described in Section 23.

72 Where applicable, remove the rear subwoofer speaker as described in Chapter 12, Section 21.

73 Carefully unclip and remove the C-pillar trim panels – each is secured by three clips.

74 Carefully prise out a total of eight plastic clips securing the two foam strips in front of the shelf – these clips also secure the shelf's front edge.

75 Unclip the seat belt trims from the shelf **(see illustration)**. It's a good idea to leave them on the seat belts, so they don't get lost.

76 Either from inside the car, or through the boot, push up and release the central plastic clip which secures the back of the shelf – on our project car, this clip was bright red **(see illustration)**.

77 Pass the centre seat belt through the parcel shelf, unhook the side belts from each end, and remove the shelf from the car **(see illustration)**.

78 On models with a rear sunblind, disconnect the wiring plug from the blind, then the shelf can be removed completely. To remove the rear sunblind, first unclip the two end pieces, then remove the three screws and release the assembly from the three locating clips.

79 Refitting is a reversal of removal.

Boot trim panels – Saloon

80 On models with satellite navigation, if removing the right-hand panel, use the removal tools (similar to audio unit removal tools) to release the unit, then pull it out of the side trim panel and disconnect the wiring plugs.

81 For complete removal, the trim panel at the rear of the boot must be removed first – the carpet side panel rear edges are trapped under the rear trim panel. Prise the panel up at the top to release a row of four clips, and pull forwards to remove **(see illustration)**.

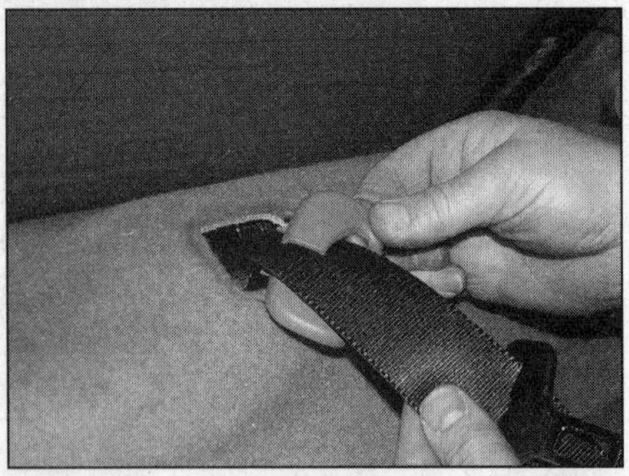

25.75 Unclip the seat belt trims from the parcel shelf

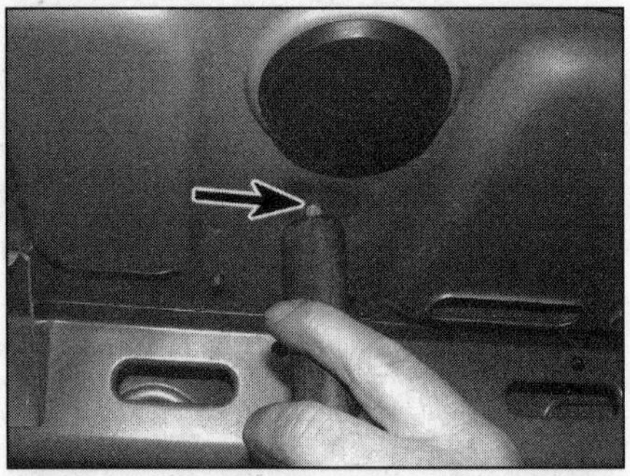

25.76 Using a hammer handle to push up the parcel shelf rear clip

25.77 Removing the parcel shelf

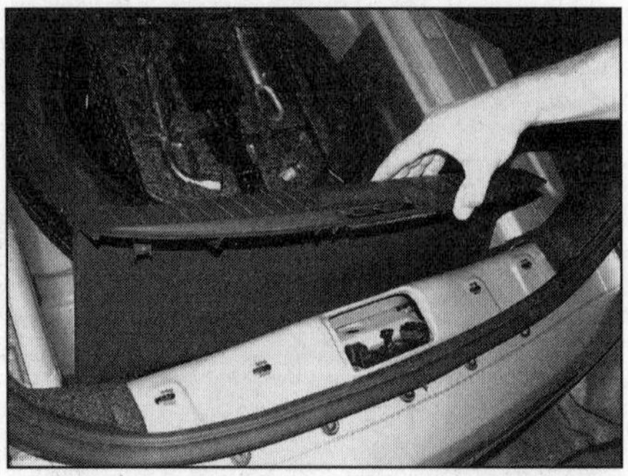

25.81 Unclip the boot rear trim panel at the top, and pull forwards

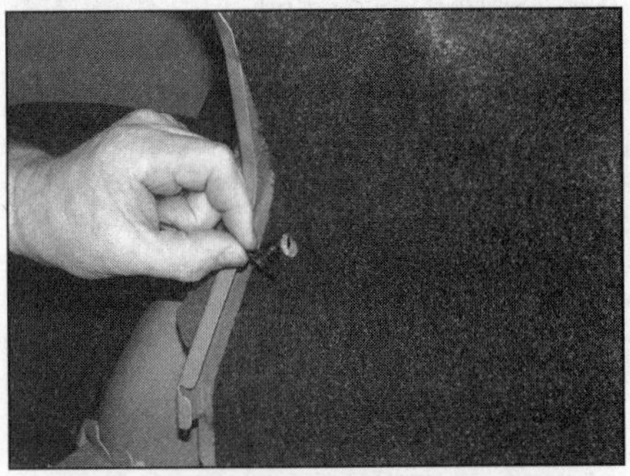

25.82a Prise out the clip at the front (behind the rear seat) . . .

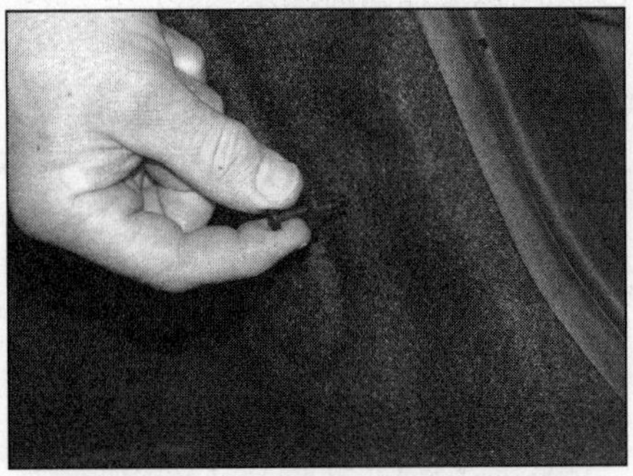

25.82b . . . one behind the rear light cluster . . .

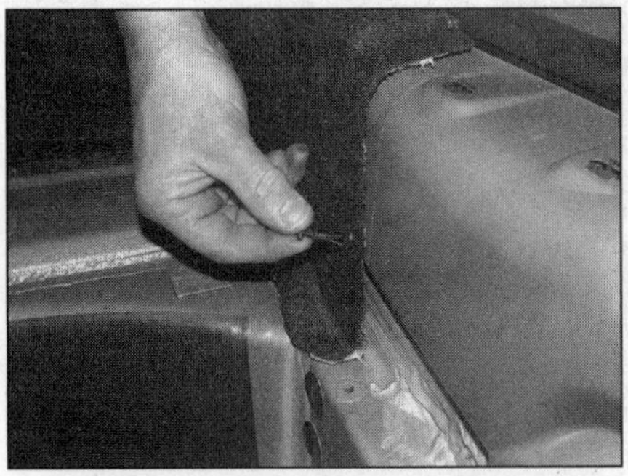

25.82c . . . and one at the rear . . .

25.82d . . . and remove the boot side trim panel

25.85a Remove the screw . . .

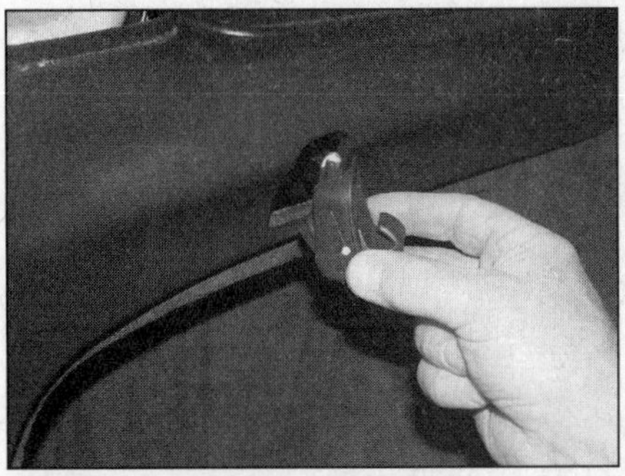

25.85b . . . and take off the side carry hook

82 Prise out the clips at the front and rear of the side trim panels, and remove them **(see illustrations)**.

83 Refitting is a reversal of removal.

Boot trim panels – Tourer

Side trim panels

84 Remove the D-pillar trim panel as described later in this Section.

85 Remove the carry hook from the rearmost trim panel, which is secured by a single screw **(see illustrations)**.

86 Starting at one end, work around the panel, and release a total of seven clips. Remove the rear trim panel **(see illustration)**.

87 Fold the rear seat forwards, then unclip and remove the side bolster, starting at the top, and pulling forwards. The bolsters have a hooked-over plastic clip at the top, and a wire clip at the base **(see illustration)**.

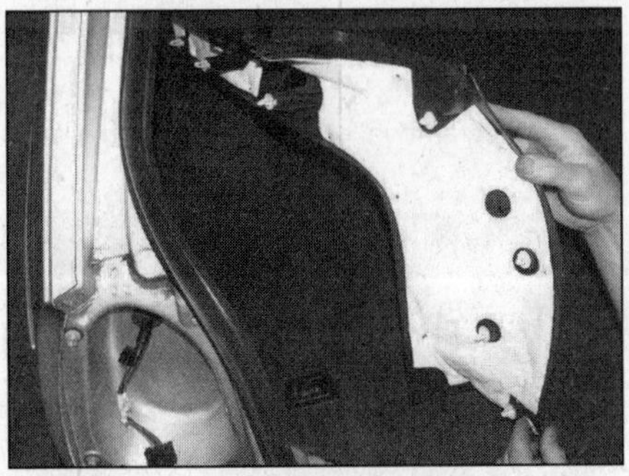

25.86 Unclip and remove the rear trim panel

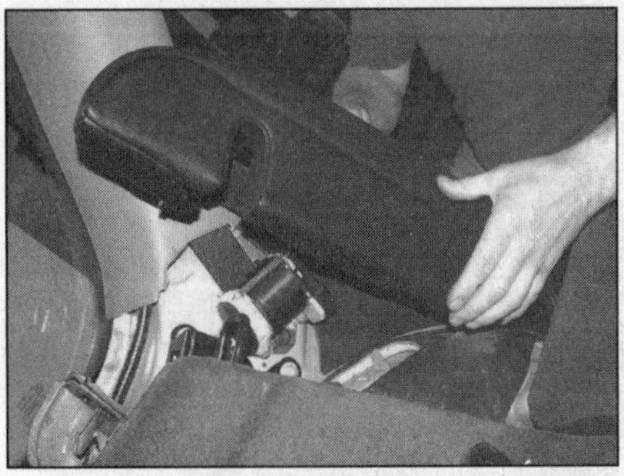

25.87 Pull off the rear seat side bolster

88 Remove the loadspace cover. Unclip and lift off the trim cover from the loadspace cover mounting bracket **(see illustration)**.

89 Remove the screw at the front of the trim panel, just next to the seat belt reel **(see illustration)**.

90 Moving to the rear of the car, remove the two upper screws and one rear screw from the trim panel **(see illustrations)**.

91 Prise out the screw covers, then remove the two Torx screws from the two anchorage

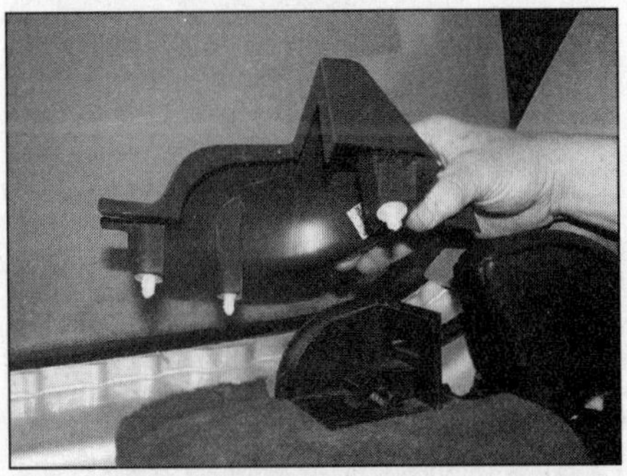

25.88 The loadspace cover bracket trim is secured by three clips

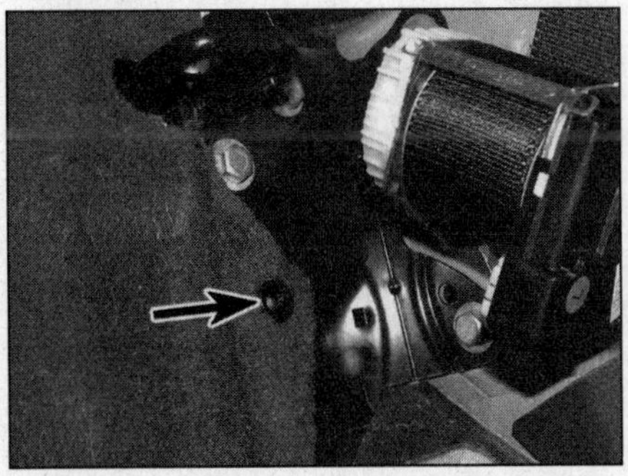

25.89 Remove the trim panel front screw

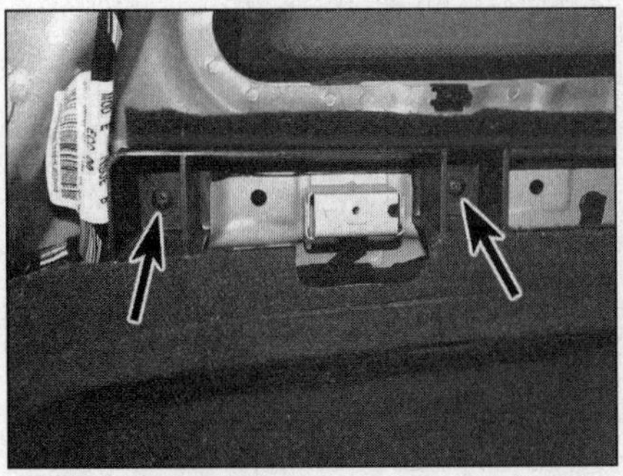

25.90a At the rear, remove the two screws at the top . . .

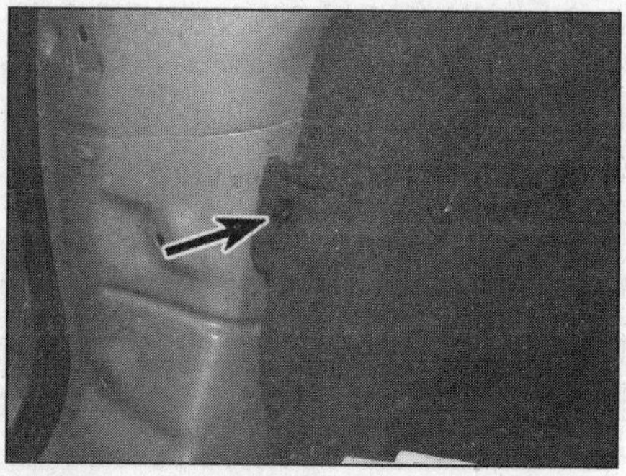

25.90b . . . and a further screw at the rear of the panel

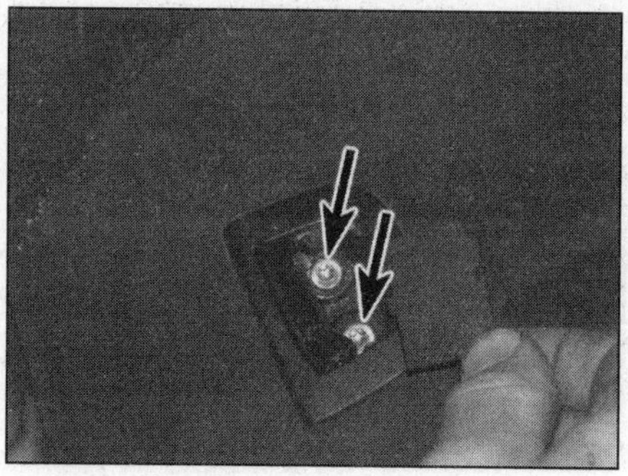

25.91a Prise out the screw cover . . .

25.91b . . . then remove the screws and the anchorage points

points, and remove them from the side panel **(see illustrations)**.

92 Raise the spare wheel cover, and prise out the two push-in clips securing the base of the panel to the floor **(see illustration)**.

93 Loosely close the spare wheel cover, and remove the trim panel from the car, tipping it on its side so that the lip on its base can be lifted clear of the spare wheel cover **(see illustration)**. On the right-hand panel, unclip the manual fuel filler flap release.

94 Refitting is a reversal of removal.

Spare wheel cover

95 Remove the rear seat as described in Section 23.

96 Lift and support the spare wheel cover, using a suitable temporary prop.

97 Disconnect the wiring plug from the cover light.

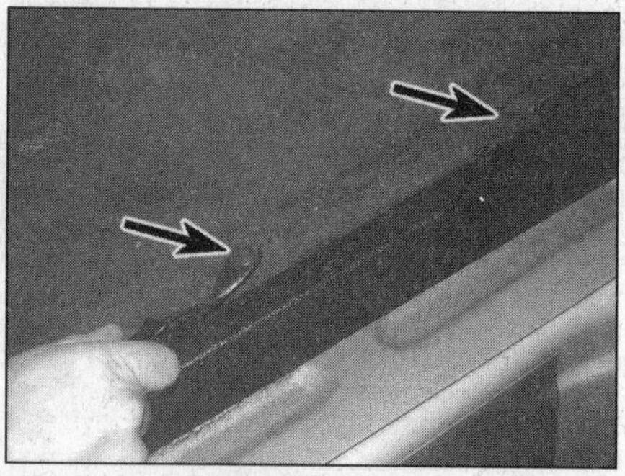

25.92 Prise out the two clips securing the panel to the floor

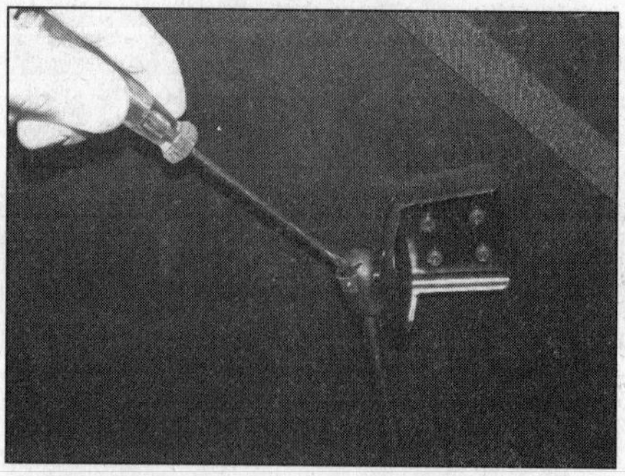

25.98 Prise out the spring clip from the spare wheel cover support strut

98 Pull out the spring clip at the top of the cover support strut, and disconnect it from the cover bracket **(see illustration)**.

99 Remove the two bolts from each cover hinge, and remove the cover from the car.

100 Refitting is a reversal of removal. Check the operation of the cover before refitting the rear seat as described in Section 23.

D-pillar trim panel - Tourer

101 The D-pillar trim panel is secured by four clips – carefully prise the panel away, and remove it **(see illustration)**.

102 Refitting is a reversal of removal.

Carpets

103 The carpet is held in position by the sill trim panels, and other surrounding panels and components.

104 Carpet removal and refitting is reasonably straightforward, but very time-consuming, due to the fact that many of the adjoining trim panels must be removed first. It will also be necessary to remove components such as the seats and their mountings, the centre console, etc.

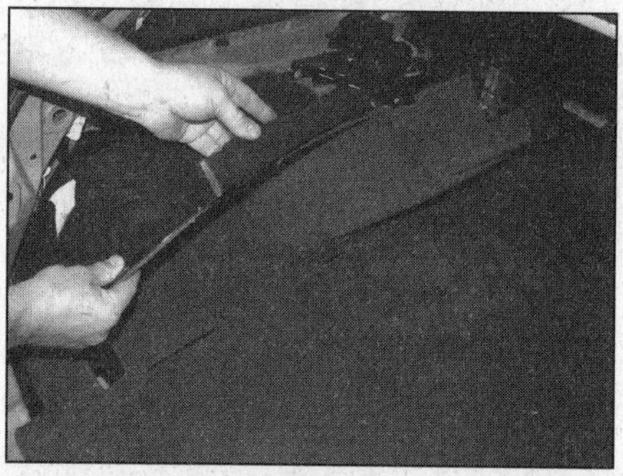

25.93 Tip the panel on its side, then lift up and remove

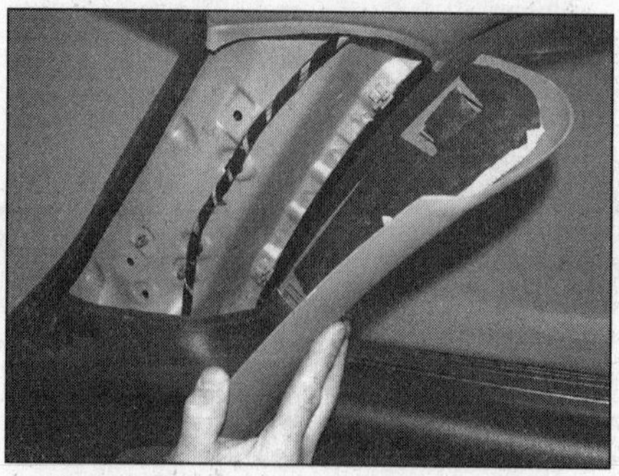

25.101 The D-pillar trim panel can be unclipped by hand

Headlining

Warning: Remove the ignition key, disconnect both battery leads, negative first (see 'Disconnecting the battery'), then wait for 10 minutes before proceeding. This is a precaution against accidentally disconnecting the side curtain airbags, which (where fitted) are located behind and above the A-pillar trim panels.

105 The headlining is held in place by the grab handles, sun visors, sunroof trim, door pillar trim panels, weatherseals, etc. On Tourer models, the rear of the headlining is also secured by the boot light, cargo net retainers, and two additional rear clips. When all the fittings have been removed or prised clear, it can then be withdrawn out through one of the doors, or the tailgate aperture. Disconnect the wiring plugs for the side curtain airbags as they become accessible.

106 Note that headlining removal requires considerable skill and patience if it is to be carried out without damage, and is therefore best entrusted to an expert.

26 Centre console - removal and refitting

Warning: Remove the ignition key, disconnect both battery leads, negative first (see 'Disconnecting the battery'), then wait for 10 minutes before proceeding. If this waiting period is not observed, there is danger of activating the airbags and seat belt tensioners. The airbag control unit wiring plug is disconnected as part of this procedure.

Removal

1 Removing the centre console is made easier if both front seats are removed as described in Section 23.

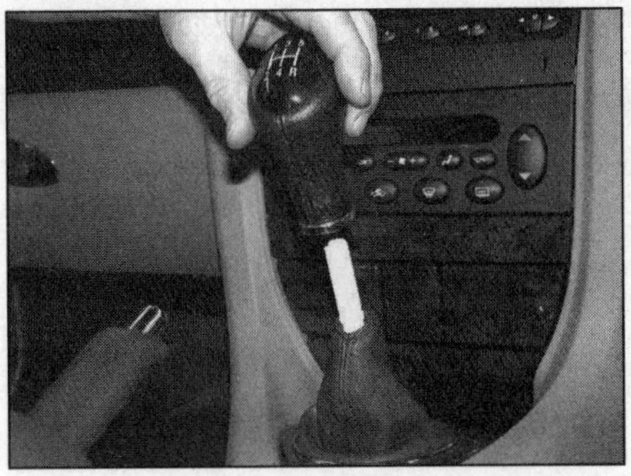
26.3 Pull off the gear/selector lever knob

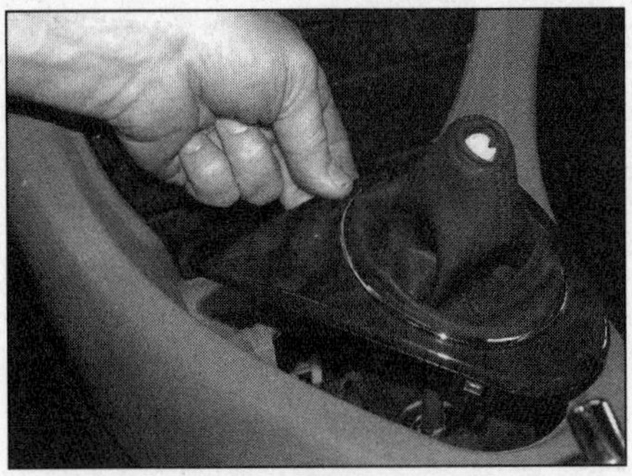
26.4 Unclip the gear/selector lever trim panel

26.5a Unclip the handbrake lever gaiter at the top initially . . .

2 Release the clip securing the ashtray at the rear of the console, and remove it.
3 Pull up sharply to disengage the gear/selector knob's securing tab, and remove the knob **(see illustration)**.
4 Unclip the gear/selector lever gaiter trim panel from the centre console, and lift it off the lever **(see illustration)**. On automatic transmission models, disconnect two wiring plugs from the trim panel/gaiter.
5 Unclip the handbrake lever gaiter from the centre console – start at the top, then unhook the gaiter at the front. Turn the gaiter inside-out, and carefully slide it off the lever **(see illustrations)**.
6 The hazard warning light switch panel does not have to be removed from the console, as the switch wiring is disconnected via the console harness plug later on.
7 Remove the audio unit (radio/CD/sat-nav) as described in Chapter 12.
8 Remove the heater control panel as described in Chapter 3.

High-specification models

9 On models with a row of switches below the heater control panel, the switches must now be removed. Working in the radio aperture, release the clip either side on top of the switch panel above the ashtray. Withdraw the switch assembly, and disconnect the wiring plugs from it.
10 Release the clips either side at the top, and withdraw the front ashtray assembly from the centre console. Disconnect the wiring plugs from behind the ashtray, and remove it.

All models

11 Remove a total of eight screws/bolts securing the console – four at the front, two in the rear ashtray aperture, and one on either side towards the rear **(see illustrations)**. Pull the console back slightly from the facia.
12 Disconnect the main harness wiring plug (which includes the airbag control unit wiring) at the front of the console. On our car, there were two plugs visible once the console was pulled back – only the grey one had to be disconnected **(see illustration)**.
13 Pull the console fully rearwards, and lift it over the handbrake lever. If this proves difficult, unscrew the handbrake adjuster nut (in front of

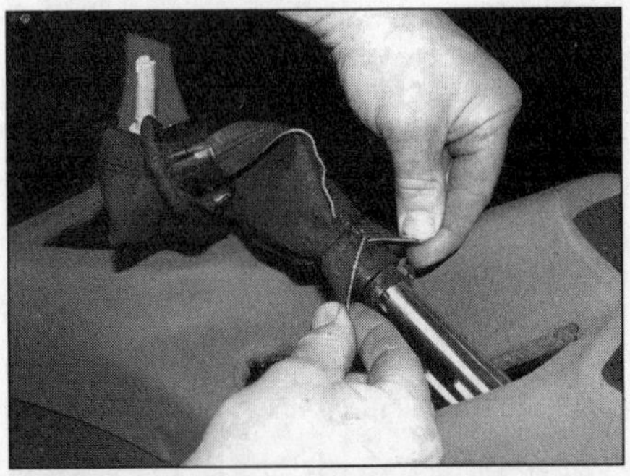
26.5b . . . then turn inside-out and remove from the lever

26.11a Remove the two (black) screws . . .

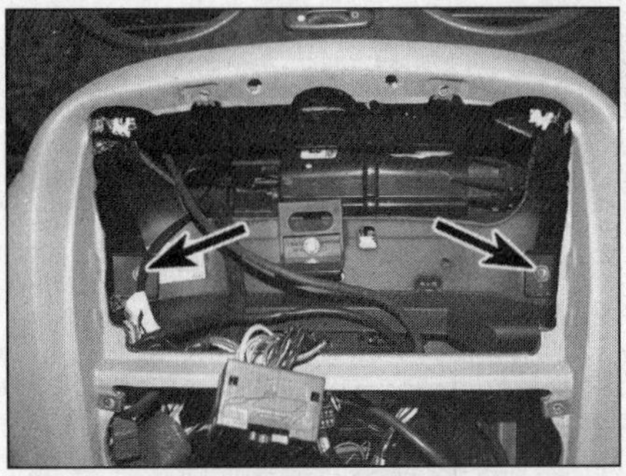
26.11b . . . and two (brass) screws inside the radio aperture . . .

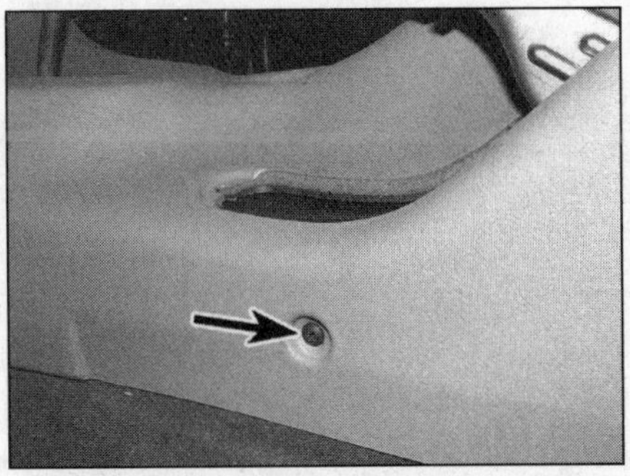
26.11c . . . one more screw on each side . . .

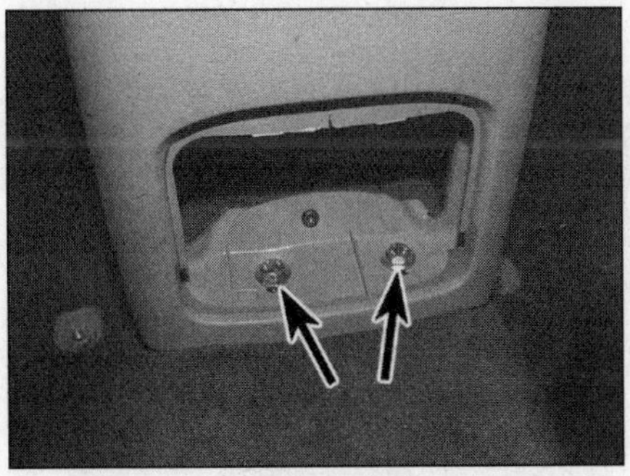
26.11d . . . and two bolts in the rear ashtray aperture

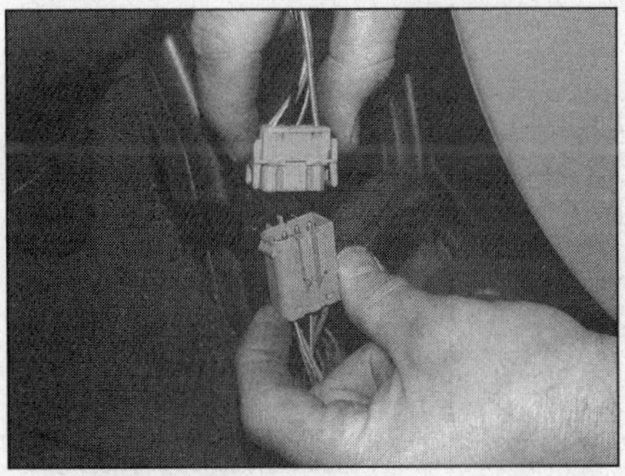
26.12 Disconnect the (grey) console harness connector at the front

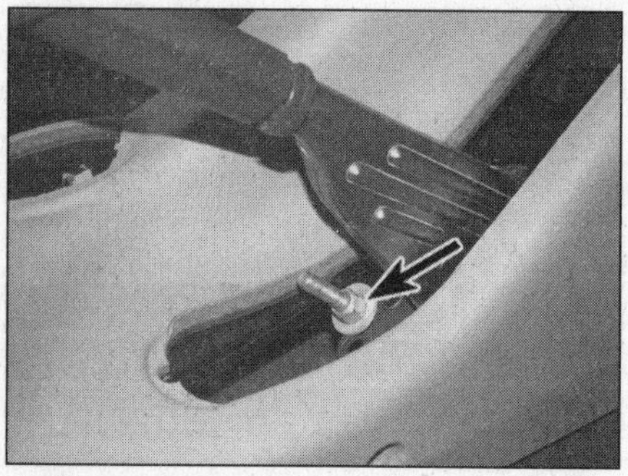

26.13a If the console won't lift over the handbrake, loosen the adjuster nut

26.13b Removing the centre console

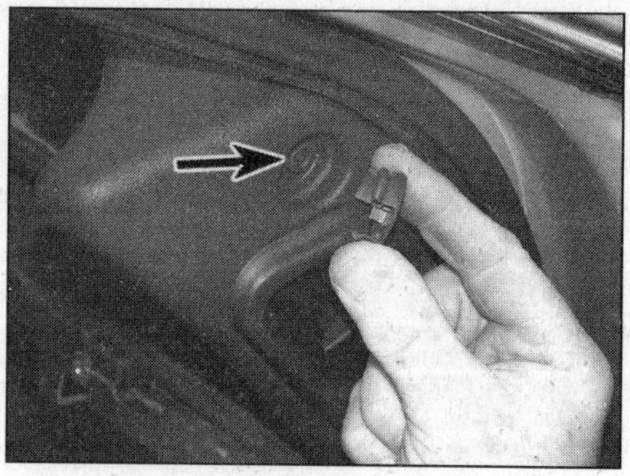

27.4 Prise out the facia end plug, and remove the bolt underneath

the lever) by a few turns, which will allow the lever to be pulled up higher **(see illustrations)**.

Refitting

14 Refitting is a reversal of removal. If necessary, adjust the handbrake as described in Chapter 9 on completion.

27 Facia panel and crossmember – removal and refitting

Note: *This is a difficult procedure, carried out in two stages – removing the plastic facia panel, and then the large metal crossmember underneath it. Both facia sections have to be removed, for example, to gain access to the heater assembly. It is strongly recommended that this Section is read through thoroughly before starting the procedure.*

Warning: Remove the ignition key, disconnect both battery leads, negative first (see 'Disconnecting the battery'), then wait for 10 minutes before proceeding. If this waiting period is not observed, there is danger of activating the airbags and seat belt tensioners.

Removal

Facia panel

1 Remove the centre console as described in Section 26.

2 Remove the A-pillar trim panels, facia veneer trim panels, facia closing panels, and glovebox, as described in Section 25.

3 Remove the headlight main switch, instrument panel and airbag rotary coupler (clockspring) as described in Chapter 12.

4 Open both front doors, and prise out the two plugs on the end of the facia. Unscrew and remove the bolt under each plug **(see illustration)**.

5 On models with the top-specification navigation system, disconnect the wiring plug from the remote control interface unit, located behind the radio unit. Release the interface unit from its mounting bracket, and remove it.

6 Remove the central facia mounting bolt, and recover the small mounting bracket **(see illustration)**.

7 Remove the mounting bolt at each end of the facia. On the passenger side, the bolt is hidden under a cover which is prised out **(see illustrations)**.

8 To the right of the glovebox aperture, there is a further cross-head screw which must be removed **(see illustration)**.

27.6 Remove the central mounting bolt, and take off the mounting bracket

9 On models with air conditioning, disconnect the wiring plug from behind the cabin temperature sensor, located to the left of the steering column **(see illustration)**.

10 Disconnect the facia wiring harness plug (black on our car) in front of the centre console location **(see illustration)**.

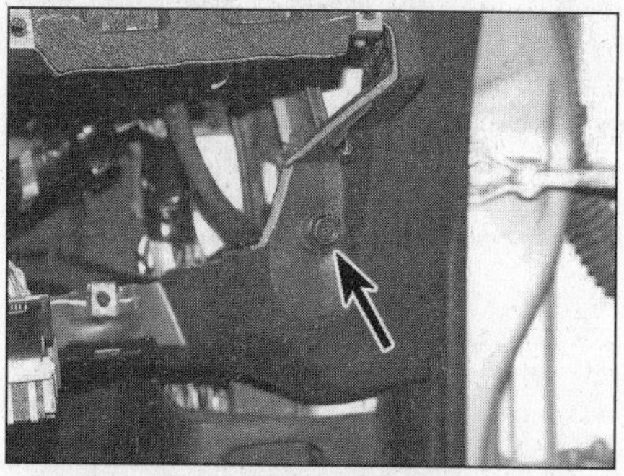

27.7a Facia mounting bolt on the driver's side . . .

27.7b . . . on the passenger side, the bolt is hidden under a cover

27.8 Remove the cross-head screw to the right of the glovebox

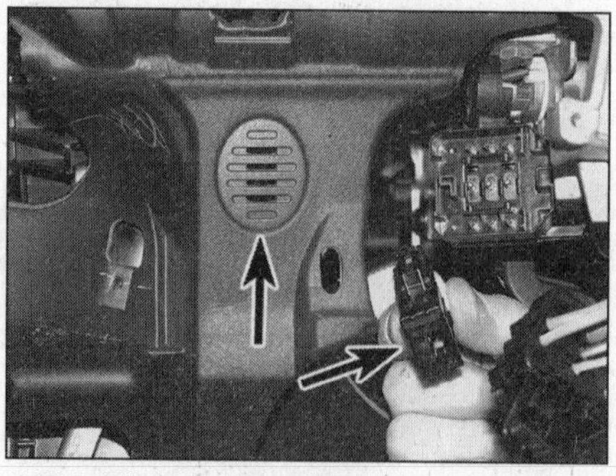

27.9 Disconnect the cabin temperature sensor wiring plug

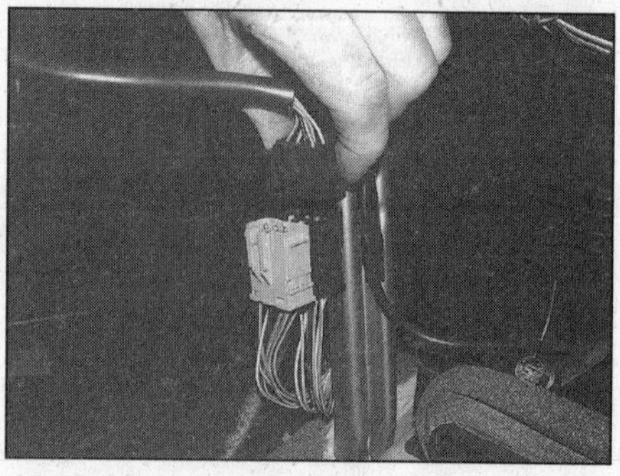

27.10 Disconnect the facia wiring harness connector

27.11 Ease the facia panel back, then lift it and remove from the car

27.14a Disconnect the passenger airbag wiring plug . . .

27.14b . . . then remove the two bolts each end . . .

27.14c . . . and remove the airbag unit

27.15a Disconnect the immobiliser reader coil plug . . .

27.15b . . . then unclip the wiring harness along the steering column

11 With the help of an assistant, ease the facia away, noting that it will 'hang up' on the driver's side brackets behind it. Remove the facia through one of the front doors **(see illustration)**.

12 Refitting is a reversal of removal, noting the following points:

a) *Before starting, ensure that the battery is still disconnected – do not reconnect it until all the work is complete.*
b) *When offering the facia back into place, ensure that the facia heating/ventilation ducts are correctly aligned and engaged with the heater unit.*
c) *Tighten all the facia mounting bolts securely.*

Crossmember

13 Removing the metal crossmember requires some studying of the wiring harness beforehand, to ensure its correct routing when refitting. If possible, take some photos before starting, to use as a guide later.

14 Disconnect the passenger airbag wiring plug, then unscrew the two Torx mounting bolts at each end, and remove the airbag **(see illustrations)**.

15 Disconnect the immobiliser reader coil wiring plug from the ignition switch. Release the ignition switch wiring harness clips along the steering column as necessary, and move the harness clear **(see illustrations)**.

16 Unscrew the four bolts securing the steering column to the facia crossmember – note the positions of the bolts, as they are of different types **(see illustrations)**.

17 Support the steering column, then remove two further screws underneath, then lower the column into the footwell. Recover the two washers on top of the column for the upper mounting bolts **(see illustrations)**.

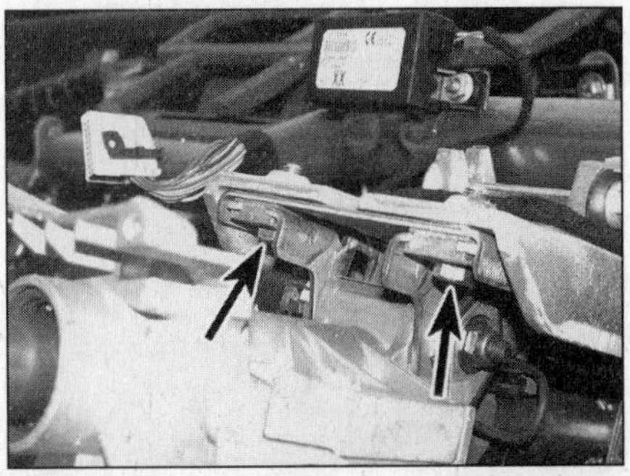

27.16a Unscrew the steering column upper . . .

27.16b . . . and lower main mounting bolts

27.17a Remove the two remaining screws underneath . . .

27.17b . . . then lower the column into the footwell – recover the top washers

18 Noting carefully how the wiring is routed, cut the cable-ties securing the harness to the crossmember, and to the floor of the car. Move the wiring clear. Unclip the facia wiring

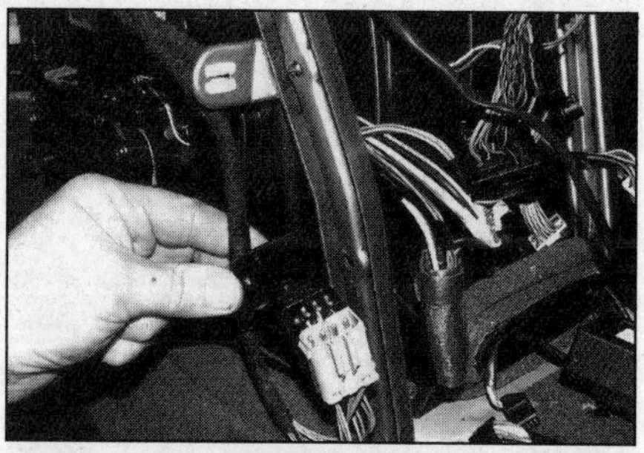

27.18 Unclip the wiring sockets from the central support

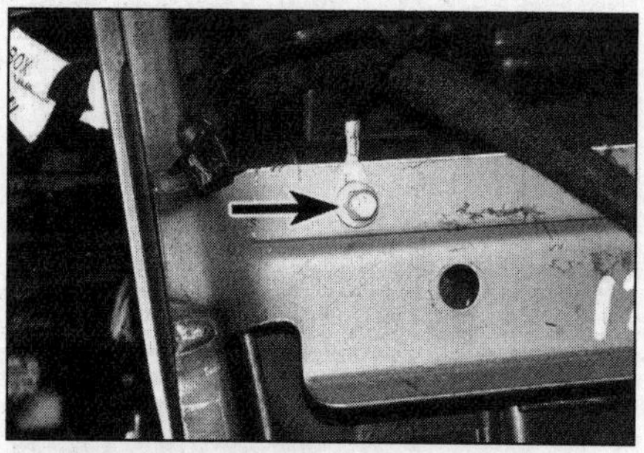

27.19 Unscrew the nut and bolt, and disconnect the earth lead

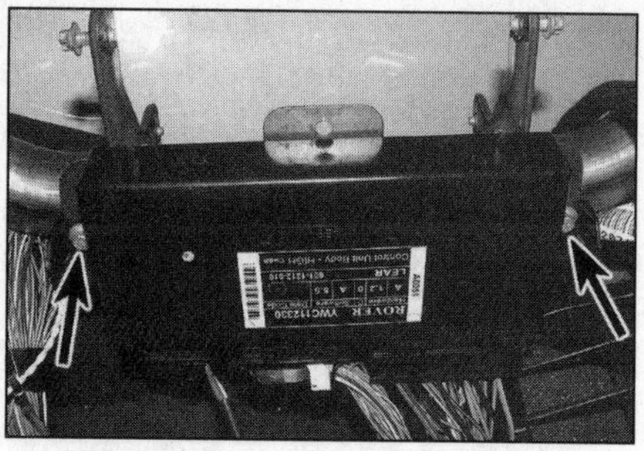

27.20a Loosen the two mounting bolts . . .

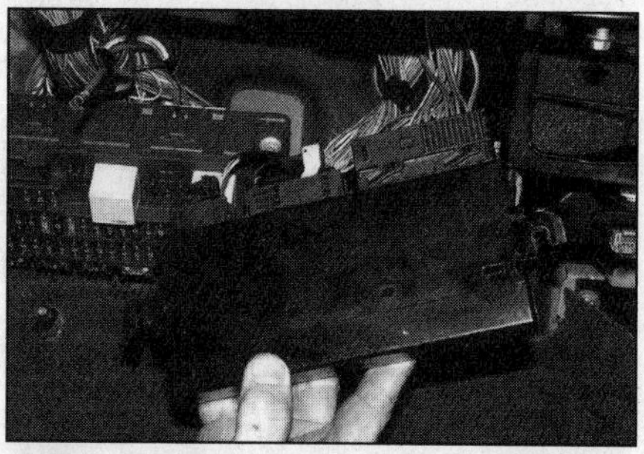

27.20b . . . and lower the body control unit away from the crossmember

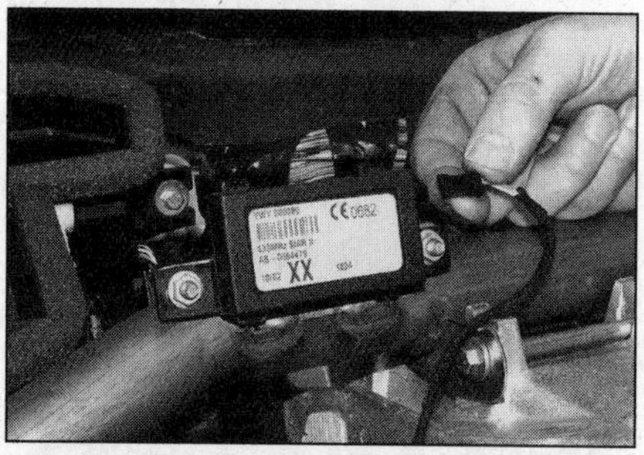

27.22 Where applicable, disconnect the remote locking receiver

harness sockets from the central support **(see illustration)**.

19 Remove the nut and bolt securing the earth lead to the crossmember **(see illustration)**.

20 Loosen the two mounting bolts securing the body control unit (BCU) to the centre of the crossmember. Lower the unit without disconnecting the wiring plugs **(see illustrations)**.

21 Similarly, on models with traction control, release the traction control ECU from the facia crossmember, and move it clear without disconnecting it.

22 On later models, disconnect the wiring plug from the central locking remote receiver, located in the instrument cluster aperture **(see illustration)**.

23 The crossmember cannot be withdrawn unless the steering column support bracket is also removed. The bracket is secured by two long horizontal bolts to the crossmember, and under the windscreen are three further bolts (the sound insulation should be pulled down for access). Remove the bolts, and withdraw the bracket **(see illustrations)**.

24 The crossmember is secured by a total of six bolts – two at either end, and one at the base of each central support leg (pull back the carpet for access). Unscrew the bolts then, with the help of an assistant, remove the crossmember from the car **(see illustrations)**.

Refitting

25 Refitting is a reversal of removal, bearing in mind the following points:

a) Ensure that the wiring harnesses, aerial lead, etc, are routed as noted before removal.

b) Tighten all bolts securely, or to the specified torque.

27.23a Remove the upper horizontal bolts (and nuts) . . .

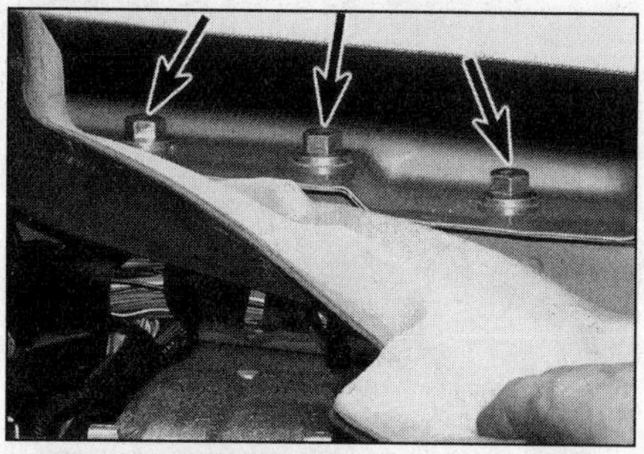

27.23b . . . followed by the three bolts at the front . . .

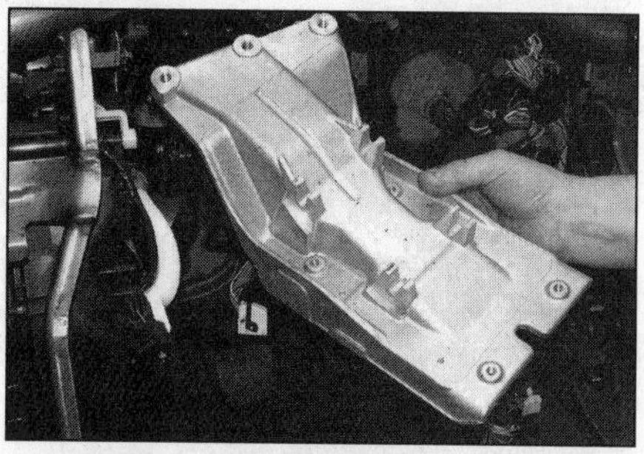

27.23c . . . then remove the steering column mounting bracket

27.24a Remove the two mounting bolts at each end . . .

27.24b . . . and the bolt at the base of each central support

27.24c Removing the facia crossmember

Chapter 12
Body electrical system

Contents

Degrees of difficulty

Easy, suitable for novice with little experience	**Fairly easy,** suitable for beginner with some experience	**Fairly difficult,** suitable for competent DIY mechanic	**Difficult,** suitable for experienced DIY mechanic	**Very difficult,** suitable for expert DIY or professional

Specifications

General

System type	12 volt, negative-earth

Bulbs

	Wattage
Exterior lights	
Direction indicator	21 (orange bulb)
Direction indicator side repeater	5 (wedge-base, orange bulb)
Front foglight	55 (H1 or H11 type)
Front sidelight	5 (wedge-base)
Headlight with halogen bulbs:	
Main beam	55 (H1 type)
Dip beam	55 (H7 type)
Headlight with xenon or projector (blue vision) bulbs:	
Main beam	65 (H9 type)
Dip beam	- (xenon) or 55 (H7 blue type)
High-level brake light	LEDs (no bulbs fitted)
Number plate light	5 (festoon)
Rear foglight	21
Reversing light	21
Stop-light	21
Tail light	5 (wedge-base)
Interior lights	
Boot light:	
Saloon	10
Tourer	5
Glovebox light	5 (festoon)
Interior lights	3 (wedge-base)

Torque wrench settings

	Nm	lbf ft
Airbag control unit mounting bolts	9	7
Crash sensor mounting bolts	10	7
Driver's airbag mounting screws	9	7
Passenger airbag mounting bolts	9	7

1 General information and precautions

Warning: Before carrying out any work on the electrical system, read through the precautions given in 'Safety first!' at the beginning of this manual, and in Chapter 5A.

The electrical system is of 12 volt negative-earth type. Power for the lights and all electrical accessories is supplied by a lead-acid type battery, which is charged by the alternator.

This Chapter covers repair and service procedures for the various electrical components not associated with the engine. Information on the battery, alternator and starter motor can be found in Chapter 5A.

It should be noted that, prior to working on any component in the electrical system, the battery negative terminal should first be disconnected, to prevent the possibility of electrical short-circuits and/or fires.

Caution: Before disconnecting the battery, refer to the information given in 'Disconnecting the battery' in the Reference Section of this manual.

2 Electrical fault finding – general information

Note: *Refer to the precautions given in Safety first!' and at the beginning of Chapter 5A before starting work.*

Warning: Since this is a multiplex wiring system, many circuits in the car pass through at least one 'ECU'. For this reason, it is inadvisable to use any kind of self-powered test equipment, as this may cause damage to the electronic modules fitted.

General

1 A typical electrical circuit consists of an electrical component, any switches, relays, motors, fuses, fusible links or circuit breakers related to that component, and the wiring and connectors which link the component to both the battery and the chassis. To help to pinpoint a problem in an electrical circuit, wiring diagrams are included at the end of this Chapter.

2 Before attempting to diagnose an electrical fault, first study the appropriate wiring diagram, to obtain a more complete understanding of the components included in the particular circuit concerned. The possible sources of a fault can be narrowed down by noting whether other components related to the circuit are operating properly. If several components or circuits fail at one time, the problem is likely to be related to a shared fuse or earth connection.

3 Multiplex wiring makes traditional electrical fault-finding more difficult, as inter-related circuits are connected together as required by the multiplex modules. This factor makes tracing faults from one end of the car to the other almost impossible, with the added factor that the multiplex modules may also be at fault, in not switching/connecting the circuits correctly. Once testing has passed beyond the basic stage, it may be more time-efficient to have the fault diagnosed by an MG Rover specialist.

4 Electrical problems usually stem from simple causes, such as loose or corroded connections, a faulty earth connection, a blown fuse, a melted fusible link, or a faulty relay (refer to Section 3 for details of testing relays). Visually inspect the condition of all fuses, wires and connections in a problem circuit before testing the components. Use the wiring diagrams to determine which terminal connections will need to be checked, in order to pinpoint the trouble-spot.

5 The basic tools required for electrical fault-finding include a voltmeter (a 12 volt bulb with a set of test leads can also be used for certain tests), an ohmmeter (to measure resistance), and a jumper wire, preferably with a circuit breaker or fuse incorporated, which can be used to bypass suspect wires or electrical components. Before attempting to locate a problem with test instruments, use the wiring diagram to determine where to make the connections.

6 To find the source of an intermittent wiring fault (usually due to a poor or dirty connection, or damaged wiring insulation), a 'wiggle' test can be performed on the wiring. This involves wiggling the wiring by hand, to see if the fault occurs as the wiring is moved. It should be possible to narrow down the source of the fault to a particular section of wiring. This method of testing can be used in conjunction with any of the tests described in the following sub-Sections.

7 Apart from problems due to poor connections, two basic types of fault can occur in an electrical circuit – open-circuit, or short-circuit.

8 Open-circuit faults are caused by a break somewhere in the circuit, which prevents current from flowing. An open-circuit fault will prevent a component from working, but will not cause the relevant circuit fuse to blow.

9 Short-circuit faults are caused by a 'short' somewhere in the circuit, which allows the current flowing in the circuit to 'escape' along an alternative route, usually to earth. Short-circuit faults are normally caused by a breakdown in wiring insulation, which allows a feed wire to touch either another wire, or an earthed component such as the bodyshell. A short-circuit fault will normally cause the relevant circuit fuse to blow.

Finding an open-circuit

10 To check for an open-circuit, connect one lead of a test light or voltmeter to either the negative battery terminal or a known good earth.

11 Connect the other lead to a connector in the circuit being tested, preferably nearest to the battery or fuse.

12 Switch on the circuit, bearing in mind that some circuits are live only when the ignition is on.

13 If voltage is present (indicated either by the tester bulb lighting or a voltmeter reading, as applicable), this means that the section of the circuit between the relevant connector and the battery is problem-free.

14 Continue to check the remainder of the circuit in the same fashion.

15 When a point is reached at which no voltage is present, the problem must lie between that point and the previous test point with voltage. Most problems can be traced to a broken, corroded or loose connection.

Finding a short-circuit

16 To check for a short-circuit, first disconnect the load(s) from the circuit (loads are the components which draw current from a circuit, such as bulbs, motors, heating elements, etc).

17 Remove the relevant fuse from the circuit, and connect a test light or voltmeter to the fuse connections.

18 Switch on the circuit, bearing in mind that some circuits are live only when the ignition is on.

19 If voltage is present (indicated either by the test bulb lighting or a voltmeter reading, as applicable), this means that there is a short-circuit.

20 If no voltage is present, but the fuse still blows with the load(s) connected, this indicates an internal fault in the load(s).

Finding an earth fault

21 The battery negative terminal is connected to 'earth' – the metal of the engine/transmission unit and the car body – and most systems are wired so that they only receive a positive feed, the current returning via the metal of the car body. This means that the component mounting and the body form part of that circuit. Loose or corroded mountings can therefore cause a range of electrical faults, ranging from total failure of a circuit, to a puzzling partial fault.

22 In particular, lights may shine dimly (especially when another circuit sharing the same earth point is in operation), motors (eg, wiper motors or the radiator cooling fan motor) may run slowly, and the operation of one circuit may have an apparently-unrelated effect on another.

23 Note that on many cars, earth straps are used between certain components, such as the engine/transmission and the body, usually where there is no metal-to-metal contact between components, due to flexible rubber mountings, etc.

24 To check whether a component is properly earthed, disconnect the battery, and connect one lead of an ohmmeter to a known good earth point. Connect the other lead to the wire or earth connection being tested. The resistance reading should be zero; if not, check the connection as follows.

25 If an earth connection is thought to be faulty, dismantle the connection, and clean back to bare metal both the bodyshell and the wire terminal or the component earth connection mating surface. Be careful to remove all traces of dirt and corrosion, then use a knife to trim away any paint, so that a clean metal-to-metal joint is made.

26 On reassembly, tighten the joint fasteners securely; if a wire terminal is being refitted, use serrated washers between the terminal and the bodyshell, to ensure a clean and secure connection.

27 When the connection is remade, prevent the onset of corrosion in the future by applying a coat of petroleum jelly or silicone-based grease, or by spraying on (at regular intervals) a proprietary ignition sealer.

3 Fuses, relays and multiplex modules – general information

Fuses

1 Fuses are designed to break a circuit when a predetermined current is reached, in order to protect the components and wiring which could be damaged by excessive current flow. Any excessive current flow will be due to a fault in the circuit, usually a short-circuit (see Section 2).

2 The main fuses are located in the passenger compartment fusebox, below the glovebox.

3 Release the two turn-buckle fasteners which secure the top edge of the facia closing panel, and lower the panel to access the fusebox **(see illustrations)**.

4 The fuse ratings and circuits protected are shown on a label inside the facia closing panel.

5 A blown fuse can be recognised from its melted or broken wire.

6 To remove a fuse, first ensure that the ignition and the relevant circuit are switched off – for maximum safety, disconnect the battery (see *Disconnecting the battery*).

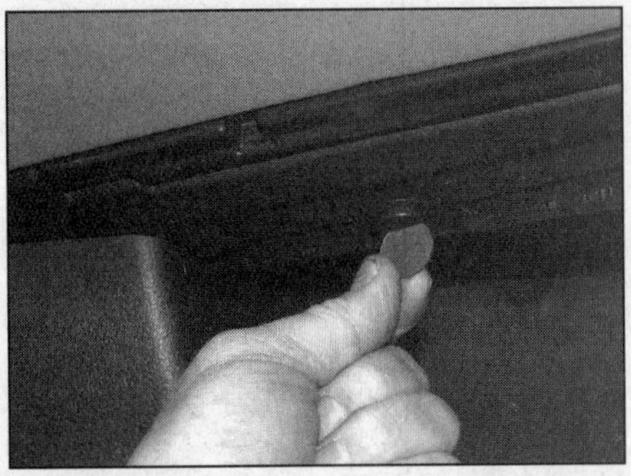

3.3a Release the turn-buckle fasteners at the front . . .

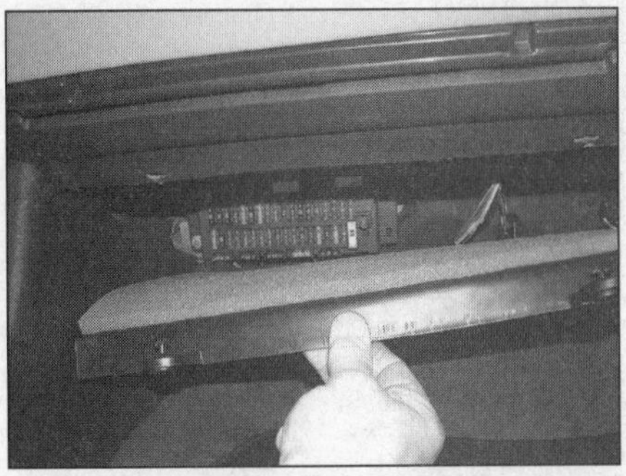

3.3b . . . and lower the facia closing panel to access the fusebox

7 Pull the fuse from its location, using the plastic tweezer tool provided **(see illustration)**. Spare fuses are provided in the cover panel, and below the fusebox.

8 Before renewing a blown fuse, trace and rectify the cause, and always use a fuse of the correct rating. Never substitute a fuse of a higher rating, or make temporary repairs using wire or metal foil; more serious damage, or even fire, could result.

9 Additional fuses are located in the engine compartment fusebox. Open the bonnet, then release the catch at the front of the fusebox, located behind the left-hand headlight **(see illustration)**.

10 Larger fuses, known as fusible links, are also included in the engine compartment fusebox; however, if one of these has blown, it indicates a serious wiring fault. Refer the car to an MG Rover specialist or automotive electrical specialist.

Relays

11 A relay is an electrically-operated switch, which is used for the following reasons:

a) *A relay can switch a heavy current remotely from the circuit in which the current is flowing, allowing the use of lighter-gauge wiring and switch contacts.*
b) *A relay can receive more than one control input, unlike a mechanical switch.*
c) *A relay can have a timer function – for example, the intermittent wiper relay.*

12 Some switching functions previously performed by relays are contained within the multiplex modules. Most of the relays are located in the engine compartment fusebox, but there are a couple in the interior fusebox **(see illustration)**. Refer to the wiring diagrams at the end of this Chapter for more information.

13 If a circuit or system controlled by a relay develops a fault, and the relay is suspect, operate the system. If the relay is functioning, it should be possible to hear it 'click' as it is energised. If this is the case, the fault lies with the components or wiring of the system. If the relay is not being energised, then either the relay is not receiving a main supply or a switching voltage, or the relay itself is faulty. Testing is by the substitution of a known good unit, but be careful – while some relays are identical in appearance and in operation, others look similar but perform different functions.

Multiplex modules

14 The body control unit (BCU) controls many of the car's ancillary systems (such as the central locking, wipers and electric windows), and is part of the multiplex vehicle wiring system (or K-bus network) fitted to the 75 and ZT, which enables communication between the other control units fitted to the car.

15 To gain access to the module, remove the glovebox as described in Chapter 11, Section 25.

16 Unscrew the two mounting bolts securing

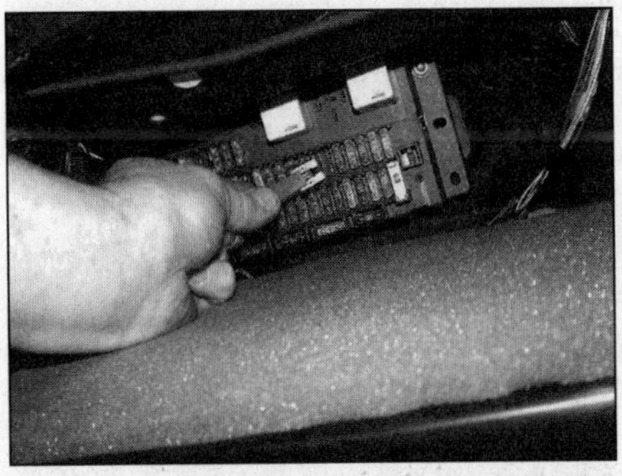

3.7 Pull the fuse out using the tweezer tool

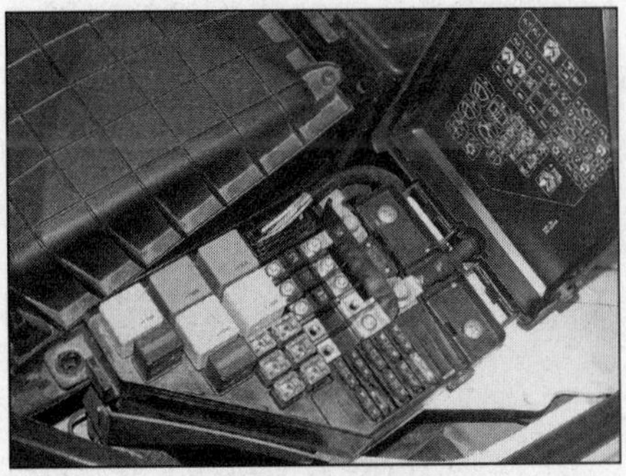

3.9 More fuses are located in the engine compartment fusebox

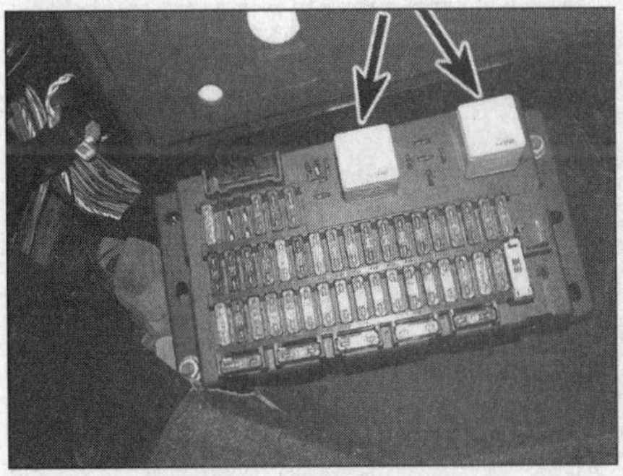

3.12 Two relays are located at the top of the interior fusebox

3.16a Remove the two BCU mounting bolts – seen from below . . .

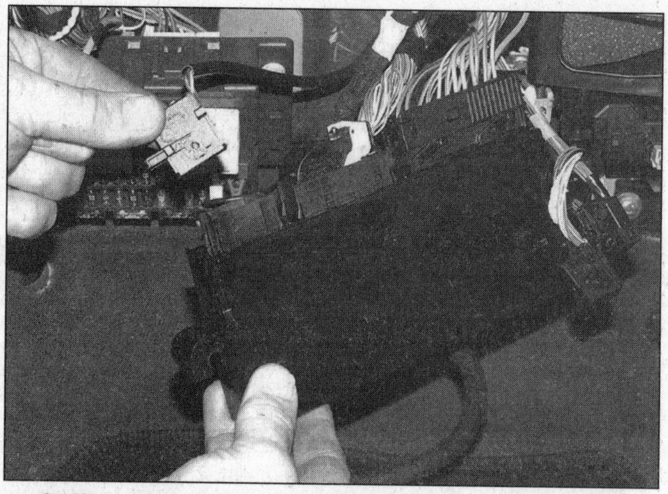

3.16b . . . then withdraw it and disconnect the wiring plugs

the body control unit to the centre of the facia crossmember. Lower the unit and disconnect the wiring plugs **(see illustrations)**.

17 Various other modules are used for controlling the rest of the car's functions – for example, the engine control module (see the relevant Part of Chapter 4) and the lighting module (removed with the headlight main switch, in Section 4 of this Chapter).

18 Any suspected problems with the modules are best referred to an MG Rover specialist, who will have the dedicated diagnostic equipment available to determine the problem. Fitting a module from another car will probably mean reprogramming the module to the car before it will work properly.

4 Switches – removal and refitting

Note: *Before removing any switch, at least make sure the ignition is off (take out the key). Ideally, disconnect the battery negative lead, and position the lead away from the battery (see 'Disconnecting the battery').*

Ignition switch

1 Refer to Chapter 10.

Heated seat switches

2 Using a small screwdriver, starting at one end, carefully unclip the switch surround panel, which is secured by two clips.

3 Unclip and remove the switch from the housing, then disconnect the wiring plug.

4 Refitting is a reversal of removal.

Traction control switch

5 Proceed as described in paragraphs 2 to 4.

Rear sunblind switch

6 Proceed as described in paragraphs 2 to 4.

Horn switches

7 Remove the driver's airbag from the steering wheel as described in Section 27.

8 Release the upper and lower clips, and detach the two horn buttons from the wheel **(see illustration)**. The horn wiring is combined with that for the radio remote and cruise control switches (as applicable), forming a single harness with one wiring plug at the top of the wheel. Therefore, the horn buttons must be removed with the other steering wheel switches, as follows.

9 The radio remote and cruise control switches (as applicable) are secured by two screws – remove the screws from each switch assembly, and release the switches from the wheel **(see illustration)**.

10 Release the wiring harness from the six securing clips, then disconnect the single wiring plug at the top of the wheel, and remove the switches as an assembly **(see illustration)**.

11 Check with your parts supplier as to what wiring will be provided with the new switch assembly. Particularly if a secondhand switch is being fitted, it may be necessary to cut the wires from the old one, and join in the new. Ensure any such joins in the wiring are made correctly and securely – we recommend soldering the bared ends of wire, and insulating with tape or heat-shrink sleeve.

12 Refitting is a reversal of removal. Ensure that the battery is still disconnected, then refit the driver's airbag as described in Section 27.

Radio remote controls

13 Proceed as described for the horn switches in paragraphs 7 to 12.

Cruise control switches

14 To renew the master switch in the centre console, proceed as described in paragraphs 2 to 4.

15 The steering wheel switches can be renewed by following the procedure for the horn switches, in paragraphs 7 to 12.

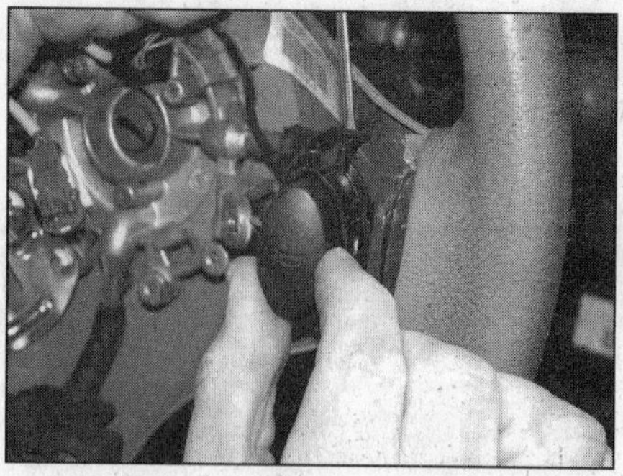

4.8 Release the clips above and below to remove the horn switch

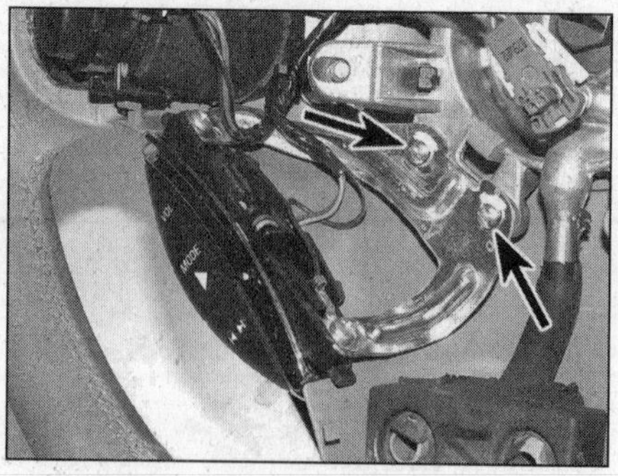

4.9 Radio remote control switches are secured by two screws

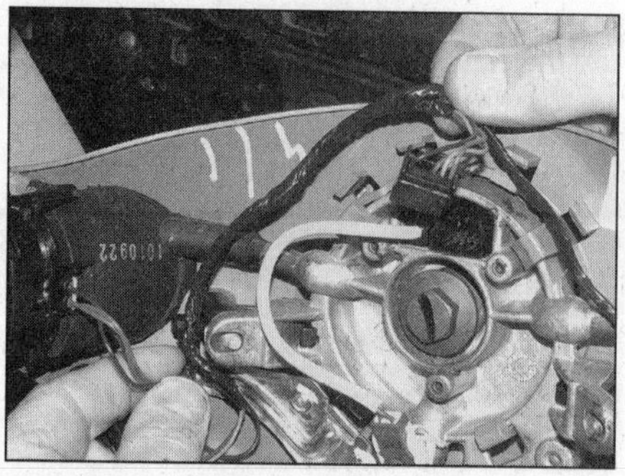

4.10 Disconnect the wiring plug at the top, and release the wiring

4.19a Remove the three screws . . .

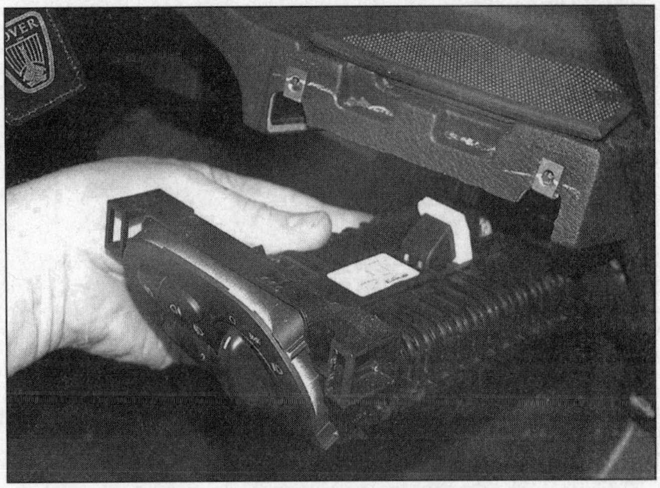

4.19b . . . and withdraw the switch module

Blower and air conditioning switches

16 These switches are built into the heater control panel – remove the panel as described in Chapter 3.

Heated rear window switch

17 This switch is built into the heater control panel – remove the panel as described in Chapter 3.

Headlight main switch

18 Remove the driver's side lower facia panel as described in Chapter 11, Section 25.

19 Remove the three switch module mounting screws (one either side, one underneath), and withdraw the module from the facia **(see illustrations)**.

20 Unlock the wiring multi-plug by swinging the locking lever forwards, then remove the module completely **(see illustration)**.

21 The switch part of the module is removed by releasing the two catches at the top, then disconnecting the wiring plug at the rear. The individual switches are not available separately – if necessary, the whole switch panel must be renewed.

22 Refitting is a reversal of removal.

4.20 Unlock the wiring plug using the lever

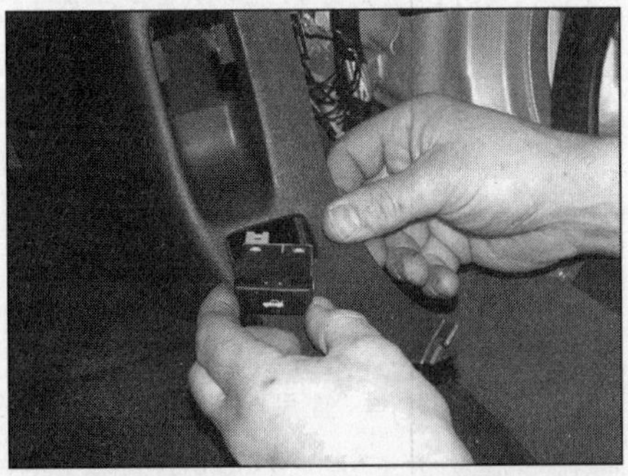

4.27 Removing the boot lid/tailgate remote release switch

Foglight switches

23 The foglight switches are integral with the headlight main switch – see paragraphs 18 to 22.

Headlight adjuster switch

24 The headlight adjuster switch is integral with the headlight main switch – see paragraphs 18 to 22.

Instrument dimmer switch

25 The instrument dimmer switch is integral with the headlight main switch – see paragraphs 18 to 22.

Boot lid/tailgate remote release switch

26 Remove the driver's footwell trim panel as described in Chapter 11, Section 25.

27 Using a small screwdriver, release the switch retaining tabs and withdraw it from the back of the panel **(see illustration)**.

28 Refitting is a reversal of removal.

Steering column switches

29 Remove the steering column shrouds as described in Chapter 11, Section 25.

30 Disconnect the wiring plug at the rear of the switch **(see illustration)**.

31 Remove the two switch mounting screws, and withdraw the switch from its location **(see illustrations)**.

32 Refitting is a reversal of removal.

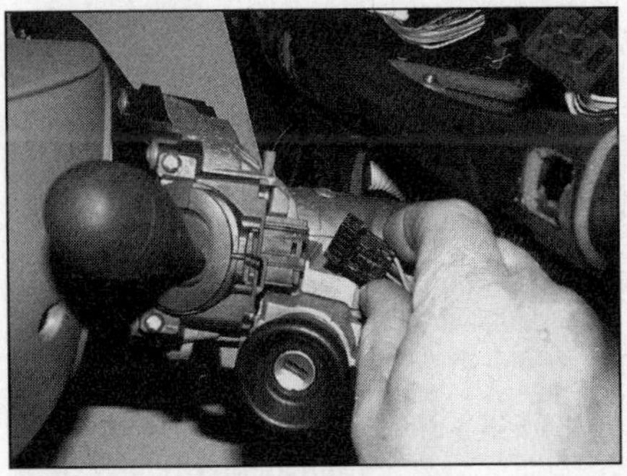

4.30 Disconnect the wiring plug from the back of the switch

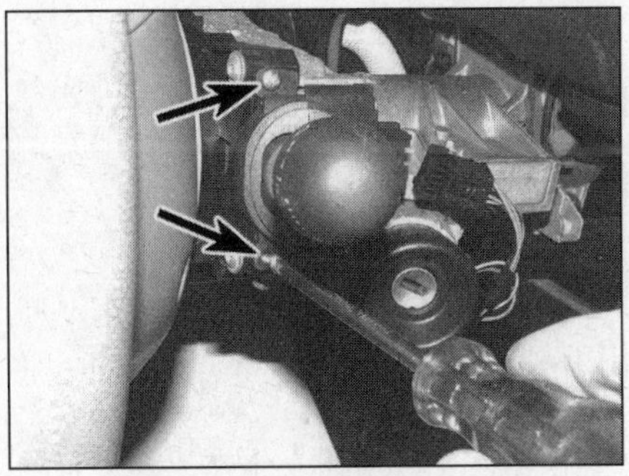

4.31a Remove the screw above and below the stalk . . .

4.31b . . . and remove the switch assembly

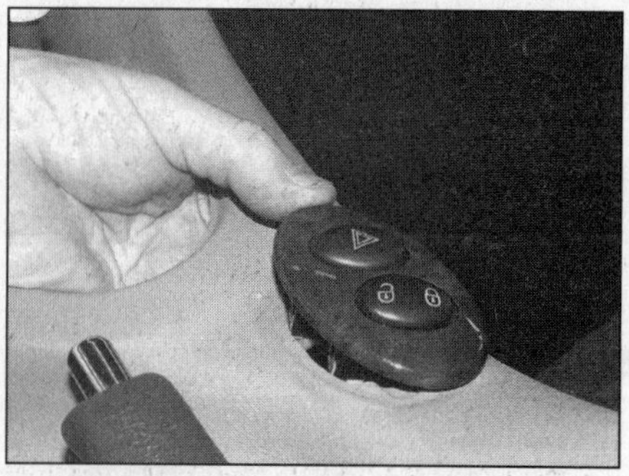

4.37a Push the switch panel out from behind if possible . . .

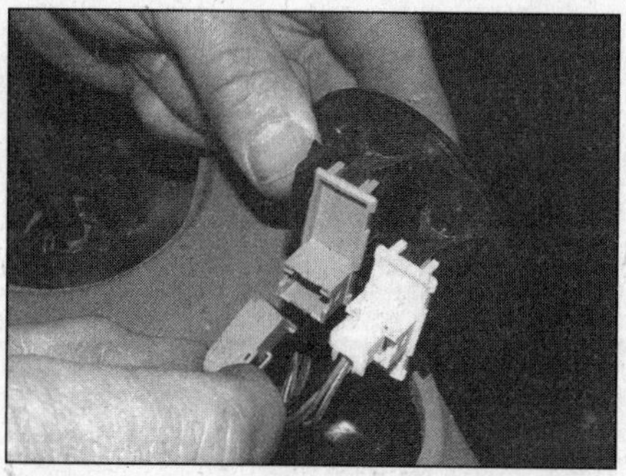

4.37b . . . and disconnect the two wiring plugs

4.41 Disconnect the wiring plug, then push out the switch

Electric seat switches

33 Remove the relevant front seat as described in Chapter 11.

34 Lay the seat down so that the underside is accessible. Remove the seat outer trim panel, which is secured by two screws, a nut and four clips. Disconnect the wiring plug(s) and remove the seat trim panel.

35 The switches are clipped to the seat trim panel, and can be released using a small screwdriver.

36 Refitting is a reversal of removal.

Hazard warning light switch

37 Carefully prise the switch panel out of the centre console, and disconnect the wiring plugs **(see illustrations)**. Removing the panel is most easily done from behind, after first prising out the gear/selector lever panel.

38 The individual switches can be removed from the switch panel by releasing their retaining tabs with a small screwdriver.

39 Refitting is a reversal of removal.

Central locking switch

40 Proceed as described for the hazard warning light switch, in paragraphs 37 to 39.

Automatic transmission mode switch

41 Carefully prise the switch panel out of the centre console, and disconnect the wiring plug **(see illustration)**. Squeeze the switch retaining tabs at either end, and push the switch out of the panel from behind.

42 Refitting is a reversal of removal.

Electric window switches

43 Carefully prise up the window switch assembly, and lift it out of the door pull handle **(see illustration)**.

4.43 Prise out the switch panel, taking care not to mark the trim

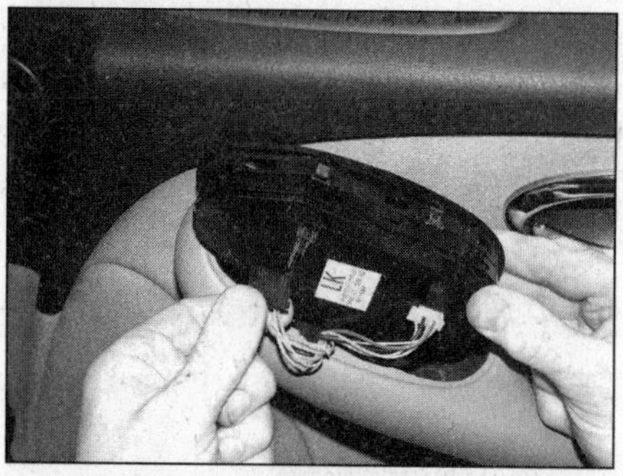

4.44 Disconnect the wiring plug(s) from the switch assembly

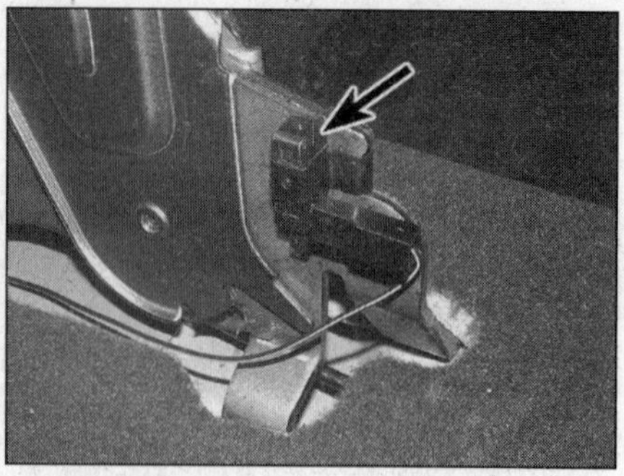

4.54 Handbrake warning light switch location

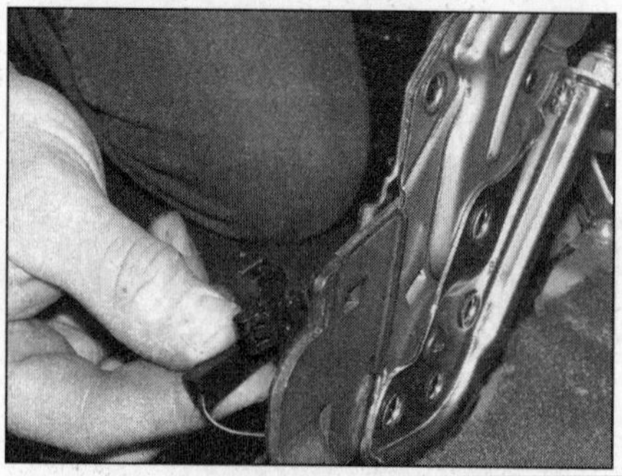

4.55 Unclip the switch, then disconnect the wiring plug

44 Disconnect the wiring plug(s) and remove the switch **(see illustration)**.

45 The window switches are not available separately – if faulty, the whole switch panel must be renewed.

46 Refitting is a reversal of removal.

Electric mirror switch

47 The mirror switches are integral with the driver's window switch panel – see paragraphs 43 to 46.

48 Refitting is a reversal of removal.

Interior light switches

49 The interior/courtesy lights are operated by the body control unit (see Section 3), using information from the central locking system to determine when a door is open. Conventional switches are therefore not used.

Sunroof switch

50 Prise the switch out of the interior light, and disconnect the wiring plug from it.

51 Refitting is a reversal of removal.

Brake light switch

52 The brake light switch is removed as described in Chapter 9.

Handbrake warning light switch

53 Remove the centre console as described in Chapter 11.

54 The handbrake warning light switch is clipped to the rear of the handbrake lever **(see illustration)**.

55 Release the clip securing the switch to the handbrake lever, then disconnect the wiring plug and remove the switch **(see illustration)**.

56 Refitting is a reversal of removal. Check the switch operation before refitting the centre console.

Inertia (fuel cut-off) switch

57 Refer to the relevant Part of Chapter 4.

Bonnet switch (anti-theft alarm)

58 Open the bonnet, then unclip the rubber boot from the base of the switch.

59 Reach in under the bonnet lock platform, and release the retaining tab on each side of the bonnet switch.

60 Lift the switch out of the bonnet lock platform, and disconnect its wiring plug.

61 Refitting is a reversal of removal.

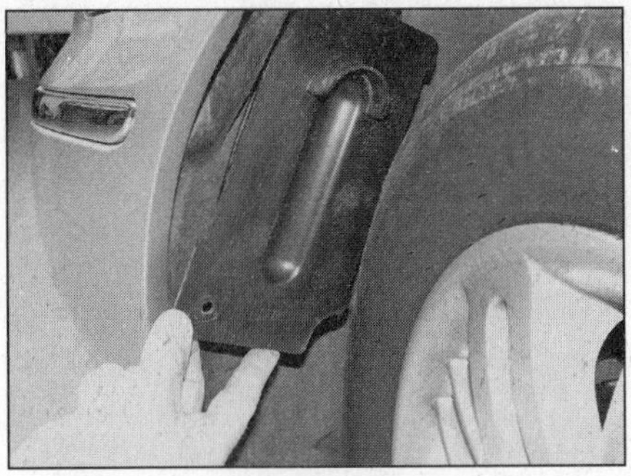
5.5 Removing the bulb access panel from the wheel arch liner

5 Bulbs (exterior lights) - renewal

General

1 Whenever a bulb is renewed, note the following points:

a) Disconnect the battery negative lead, or at least make sure that the lighting circuit is switched off, before starting work.
b) Remember that if the light has recently been in use, the bulb may be extremely hot.
c) Always check the bulb contacts and/or holder (as applicable). Ensure that there is clean metal-to-metal contact between the bulb contacts and the contacts in the holder, and/or the holder and the wiring plug. Clean off any corrosion or dirt before fitting a new bulb.
d) Ensure that the new bulb is of the correct rating and that it is completely clean before fitting; this applies particularly to headlight bulbs.

Headlight dipped beam - except xenon

2 If removing the right-hand bulb on V6 engine models, loosen the clamp nut and lift out the power steering fluid reservoir.

3 To remove the right-hand bulb on diesel engine models, disconnect the battery negative lead, and move the lead away from the battery (see *Disconnecting the battery*).

4 Turn the steering to full right lock (for the left-hand bulb) or to full left lock (for the right-hand bulb).

5 The bulb access panel is at the front of the wheel arch. Release the turn-buckle fastener with a screwdriver, and detach the panel, noting how it is fitted **(see illustration)**. To gain more room, try removing the wheel arch liner completely, as described in Chapter 11, Section 22. Opening the bonnet does not help bulb access, but does allow more light in.

Left-hand bulb

Note: *Access to the left-hand bulb on petrol models is poor. However, our mechanic has large hands, and had little difficulty changing the bulb using the following method.*

6 Working through the bulb access panel, lift the air inlet hose from its mounting, then push it down and to the left **(see illustration)**. Note, however, that this hose deteriorates with age, and may be damaged if roughly handled. Work your hand in past the wiring harness to the back of the headlight.

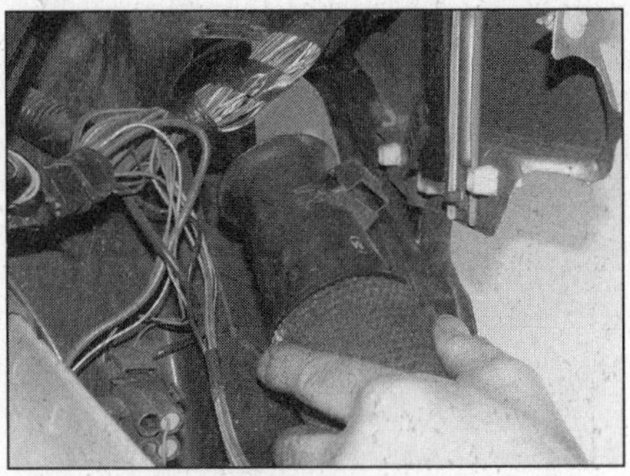
5.6 Unhooking the air inlet hose - seen from the front, with bumper removed

7 For better access from above, we tried removing the engine compartment fusebox, which is secured by a bolt at the front, and two screws inside the box. However, the fusebox can only be lifted so far, limited by the attached wiring **(see illustration)**.

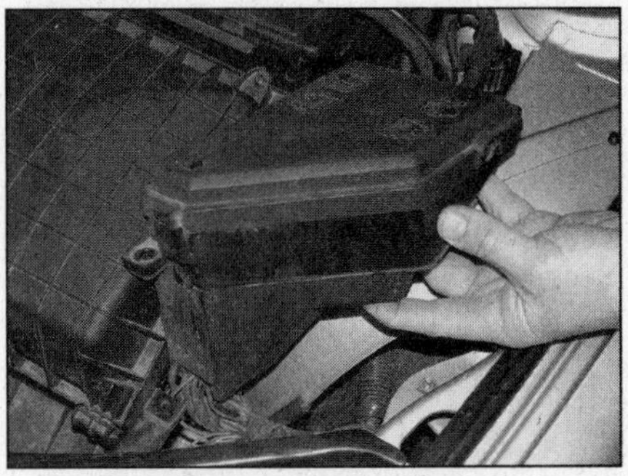
5.7 Lifting out the fusebox only improves access slightly from above

All bulbs

8 Pull off the dust cover from the back of the headlight **(see illustration)**.

9 Disconnect the wiring plug from the bulb. Press the wire retaining clip inwards and down, then swing it to the side, and withdraw the bulb **(see illustrations)**.

10 When handling the new bulb, use a tissue or clean cloth to avoid touching the glass with the fingers; moisture and grease from the skin can cause blackening and rapid failure of this type of bulb.

11 Refitting is a reversal of removal. Offer the new bulb into place, with the locating lug facing upwards.

Headlight dipped beam - xenon

Warning: Before carrying out any operations on xenon headlight units, it is recommended that protective gloves and safety glasses are worn. It is essential that the wiring connectors are disconnected from the rear of the headlight unit, then wait until the bulbs have completely cooled down before removal. DO NOT switch the headlights on with the bulb removed as it is harmful to the eyes.

5.8 Pull off the headlight rubber cover . . .

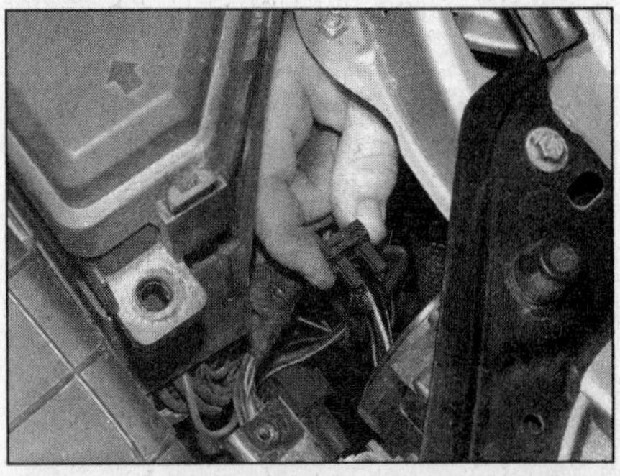
5.9a . . . then disconnect the bulb wiring plug . . .

5.9b . . . push the wire clip in, then down, to release . . .

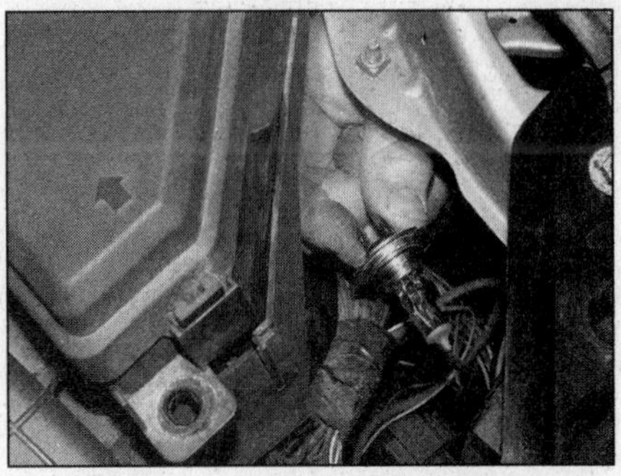
5.9c . . . and withdraw the bulb

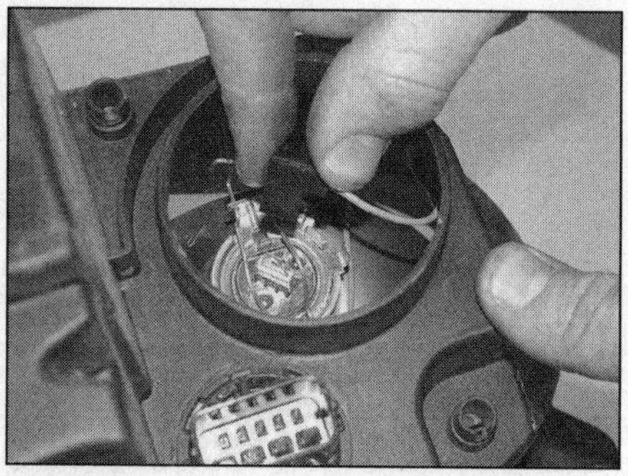
5.18a Disconnect the bulb wiring plug . . .

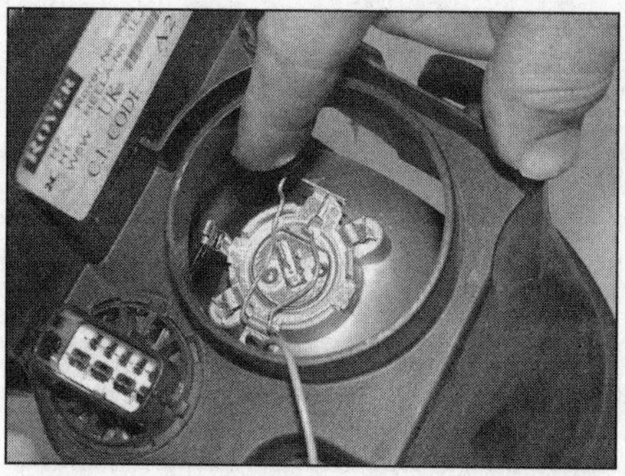
5.18b . . . unhook the wire clip sideways at the top . . .

5.19 . . . and withdraw the bulb

12 Remove the headlight unit as described in Section 7.

13 Unscrew the three Torx screws securing the rear cap, then disconnect the wiring multi-plug and remove the cap.

14 Hold the ribbed collar surrounding the 'bulb' to stop it turning, then twist the igniter unit anti-clockwise and remove it from the back of the 'bulb'. Disconnect the igniter wiring plug when it is accessible.

15 Release the centre catch on the back, then twist the 'bulb' anti-clockwise and withdraw it from the headlight.

16 Refitting is a reversal of removal. Refit the headlight as described in Section 7.

Headlight main beam – halogen

17 Open the bonnet, then reach in behind the headlight and pull off the dust cover from the inboard light.

18 Disconnect the wiring plug from the bulb, then release the bulb's retaining wire clip by unhooking the end, then fold the clip down **(see illustrations)**.

19 Withdraw the bulb from the light **(see illustration)**.

20 When handling the new bulb, use a tissue or clean cloth to avoid touching the glass with the fingers; moisture and grease from the skin can cause blackening and rapid failure of this type of bulb.

21 Refitting is a reversal of removal.

Headlight main beam – blue vision and xenon

22 Open the bonnet, then reach in behind the headlight and pull off the dust cover from the inboard light.

23 Twist the bulbholder anti-clockwise to release it, then withdraw the bulb from the light.

24 Disconnect the bulbholder wiring plug by releasing the catches on either side, and remove the bulb with its holder.

25 Refitting is a reversal of removal.

Front sidelight

26 On models with halogen headlight bulbs, the sidelight bulb is located below the dipped beam (outer) bulb, and is accessed as described in paragraphs 2 to 8.

27 On models with blue vision or xenon bulbs, the sidelight bulb is underneath the main beam (inner) bulb – gain access as described in paragraph 22.

28 Pull out the bulbholder from its location, then pull out the wedge-base bulb **(see illustrations)**.

29 Refitting is a reversal of removal. Press the bulb into place, then locate the bulbholder in the hole under the headlight bulb and press it home.

Front indicator

Note: *On pre-facelift Rover 75 models, MG Rover's suggested method of bulb renewal involves removing the indicator from the bumper. However, we found removing the light is near-impossible unless it was pushed out from behind (see Section 7). With access from behind, you can also change the bulb, so the light does not have to be removed.*

30 The light unit is accessed via a removable panel under the bumper, secured by five cross-head screws **(see illustration)**. To improve access, jack up the front of the car, and support it on axle stands (see *Jacking and vehicle support*).

31 Reach up under the bumper, twist the bulbholder anti-clockwise to release it from the light, then push and twist the bayonet bulb to remove it **(see illustrations)**.

32 Refitting is a reversal of removal.

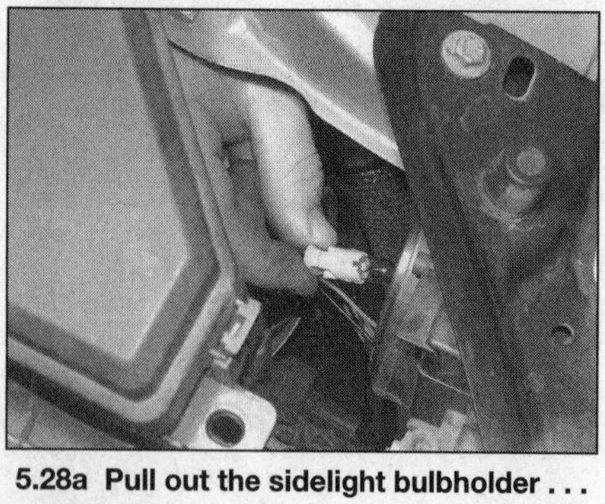
5.28a Pull out the sidelight bulbholder . . .

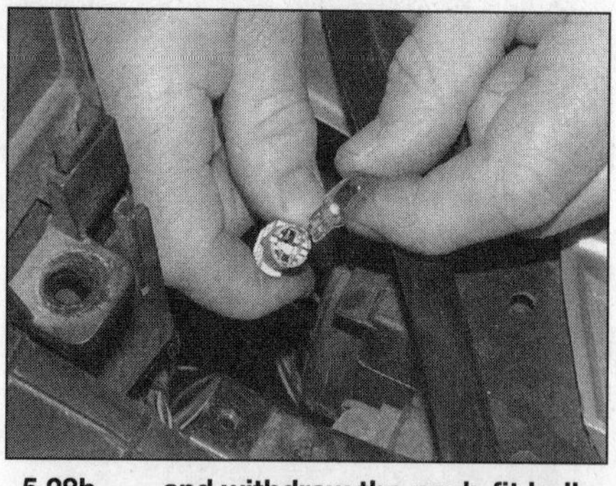
5.28b . . . and withdraw the push-fit bulb

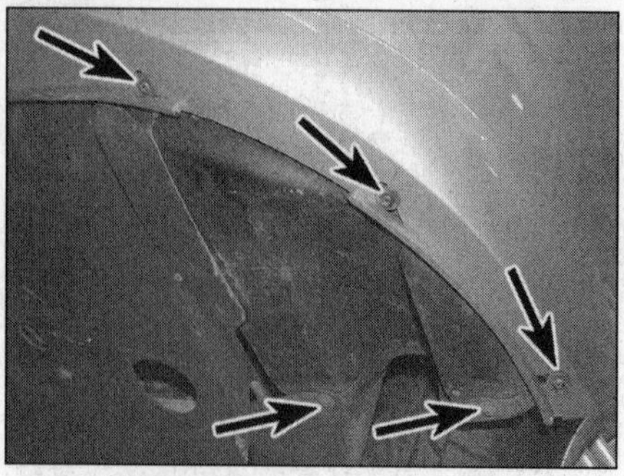
5.30 Remove the five screws and take off the bulb access panel

5.31a Twist the bulbholder from the back of the indicator . . .

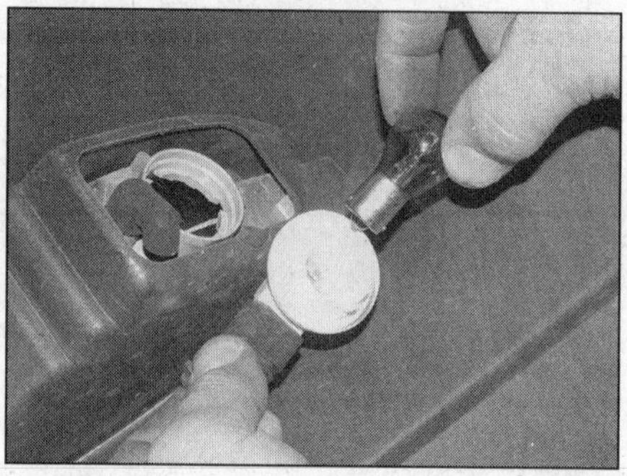
5.31b . . . and remove the bayonet-fit bulb

5.34a Twist the foglight bulbholder anti-clockwise . . .

5.34b . . . and disconnect the wiring plug

5.38 Push the side repeater forwards, and unhook at the rear . . .

Front foglight

33 The light unit is accessed via a removable panel under the bumper, secured by five cross-head screws **(see illustration 5.30)**. To improve access, jack up the front of the car, and support it on axle stands (see *Jacking and vehicle support*).

34 Reach up under the bumper, and twist the bulbholder anti-clockwise to release it from the light. Disconnect the wiring plug from the bulbholder **(see illustrations)**.

H1 type bulb

35 Release the bulb from the holder, helping it out by prising the base with a small screwdriver if necessary. Note how the bulb is fitted, with the flat on the bulb's base aligned with the one on the bulbholder.

H11 type bulb

36 This type of bulb cannot be removed from its holder, so the bulb and holder are renewed as one. The holder should be marked 'H11' on the back, to identify it, but the bulb on this type is visibly welded in place.

All bulbs

37 Refitting is a reversal of removal, noting the following points:

a) *When handling the new bulb, use a tissue or clean cloth to avoid touching the glass with the fingers; moisture and grease from the skin can cause blackening and rapid failure of this type of bulb. If the glass is accidentally touched, wipe it clean using methylated spirit.*

b) *On H1 bulbs, ensure the new bulb is secure in its holder.*

Front indicator side repeater

38 Push the light unit forwards, and pull the light outwards at the rear to unhook the spring clip **(see illustration)**.

39 Twist the bulbholder anti-clockwise to release it from the light, then pull out the wedge-base bulb **(see illustrations)**.

40 Refitting is a reversal of removal. Push the bulb firmly into its holder, and ensure the light is properly clipped back into the wing.

Rear light cluster

Saloon

41 Open the boot, and release the carpet trim panel by removing one of the 'scrivet' fixings as follows. Prise out the centre expander pin using a small screwdriver, then prise out the body of the clip **(see illustration)**. When refitting, insert the body of the clip, then fit the expander pin and tap it home to secure.

42 Fold back the carpet trim panel, then push the rear light cluster bulbholder's catch sideways to release it. Withdraw the bulbholder from the light, starting at the bottom edge **(see illustrations)**.

43 Push and twist to release the relevant bayonet bulb from the holder **(see illustration)**.

5.39a . . . then twist the bulbholder anti-clockwise . . .

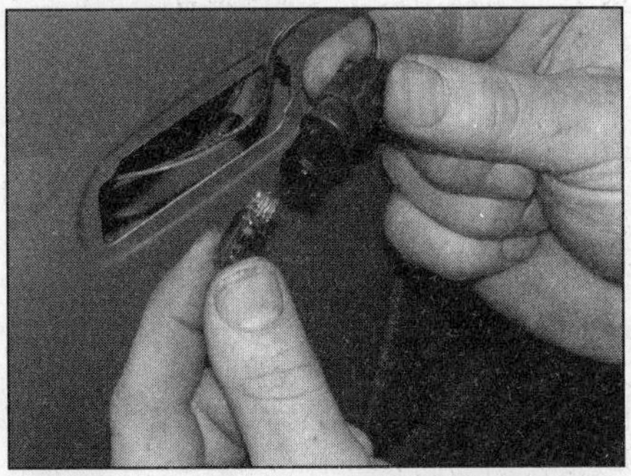

5.39b . . . and pull out the wedge-base bulb

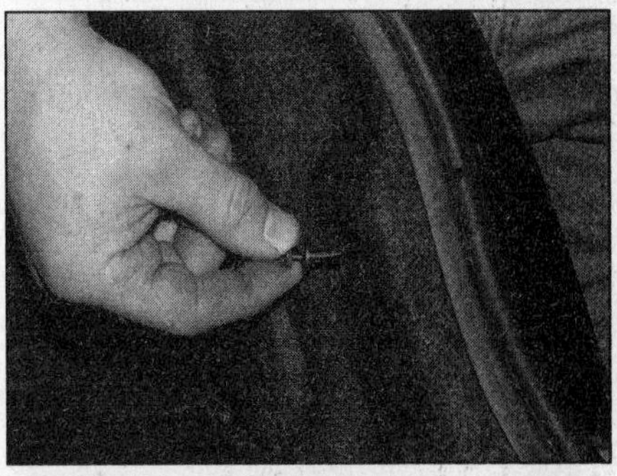

5.41 Pull out the expanding clip to release the boot carpet

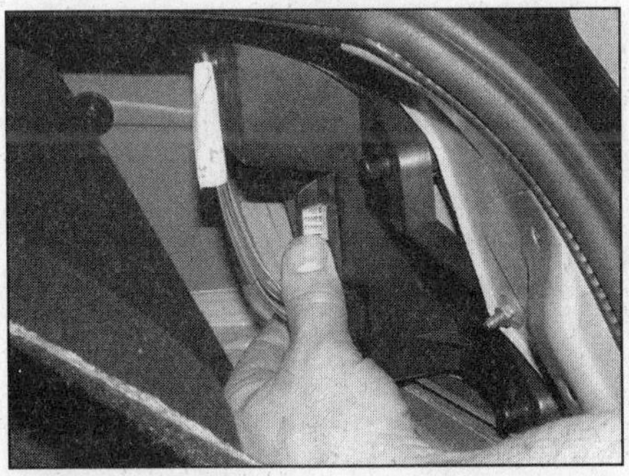

5.42a Press the bulbholder catch sideways to release . . .

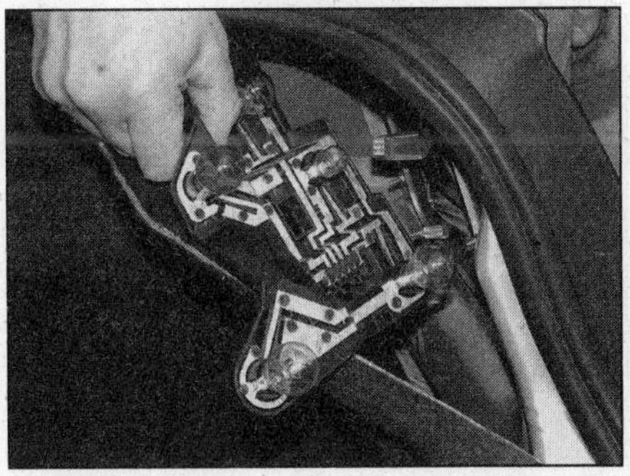

5.42b . . . then withdraw the bulbholder

5.43 Remove the relevant bulb from the holder

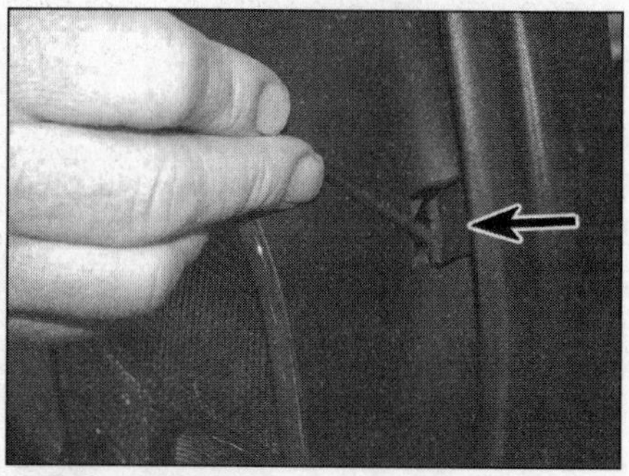

5.46a Prise up the two screw covers . . .

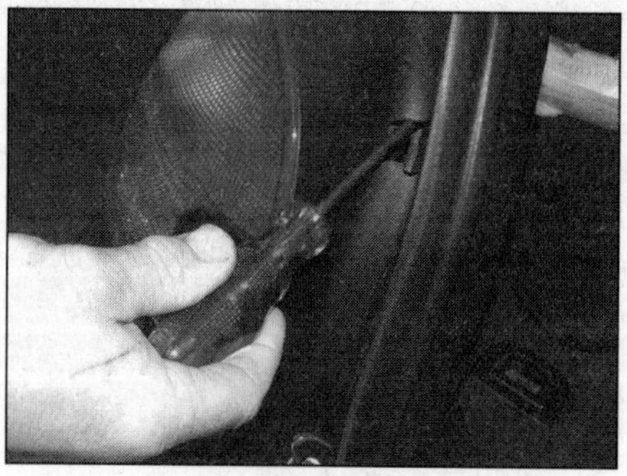

5.46b . . . then remove the rear cluster retaining screws

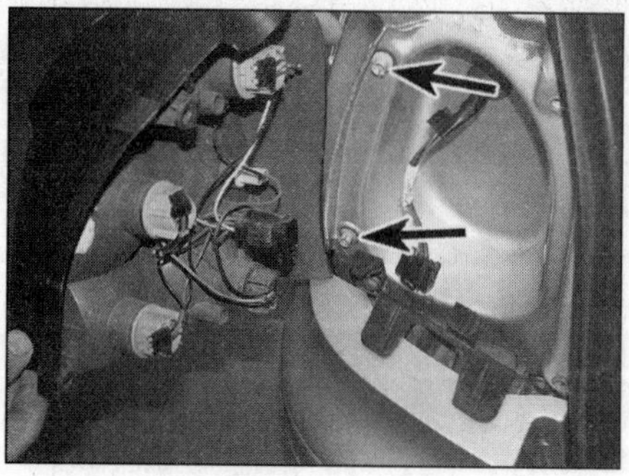

5.47a Pull the light unit pegs from the locating sockets . . .

44 If required, the bulbholder can be removed completely, after disconnecting its wiring plug. For bulb renewal, however, this isn't necessary.

45 Refitting is a reversal of removal. Hook the bulbholder in at the top edge first, and ensure it is securely clipped in place.

Tourer

46 Open the tailgate then, using a small screwdriver, prise up the two covers on the inner side of the light cluster, to reveal the mounting screws. Unscrew and remove the two screws **(see illustrations)**.

47 The light unit locates on two ball-and-socket pegs on the outer side, and there are two locating lugs at the base. Pull the light squarely backwards to release the two outer pegs – note that the sockets are brittle, and quite likely to break. To remove the light completely, disconnect the wiring plug from the back **(see illustrations)**.

48 Twist the bulbholder anti-clockwise to release it from the light. Push and twist to release the larger bayonet bulbs – in the case of the tail light, the smaller wedge-base bulb just pulls out **(see illustrations)**.

49 Refitting is a reversal of removal, noting the following points:

a) Apply a little grease to the cluster's outer pegs and sockets, to make future removal easier.

b) Ensure that the rear light is aligned correctly when refitting.

High-level stop-light

50 The 'bulbs' in the high-level stop-light are non-renewable LEDs. If the light has stopped working, this will probably be due to a blown fuse, loose connector or damaged wiring. The high-level stop-light unit can be removed as described in Section 7. If none of the brake lights work, check the stop-light switch with reference to Chapter 9.

Rear number plate lights

Saloon

51 Open the boot lid to improve access. Remove the two screws and withdraw the light unit lens **(see illustrations)**.

52 Withdraw the festoon-type bulb from the spring contacts **(see illustration)**.

53 Refitting is a reversal of removal. Check that the light unit's contacts are clean, and (if the bulb appears to be loose when fitted), bend the contacts together slightly.

Tourer

54 Open the tailgate to improve access. Prise down the outer end of the light unit lens with a

5.47b . . . and disconnect the wiring plug

5.48a Twist out the relevant bulbholder . . .

5.48b . . . then push and twist to remove the bayonet-fit bulbs

5.51a Remove the two screws . . .

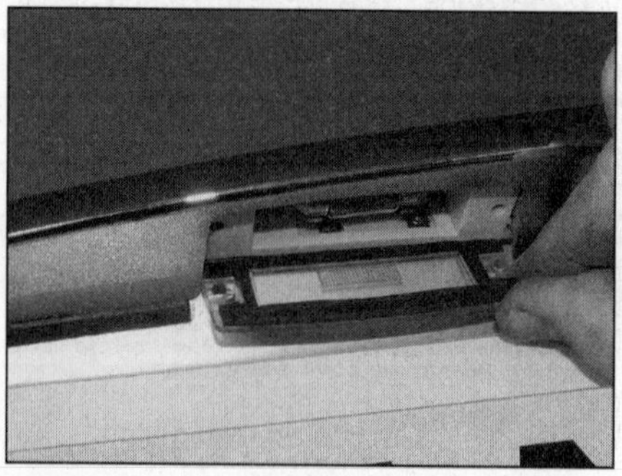

5.51b . . . and withdraw the number plate light lens

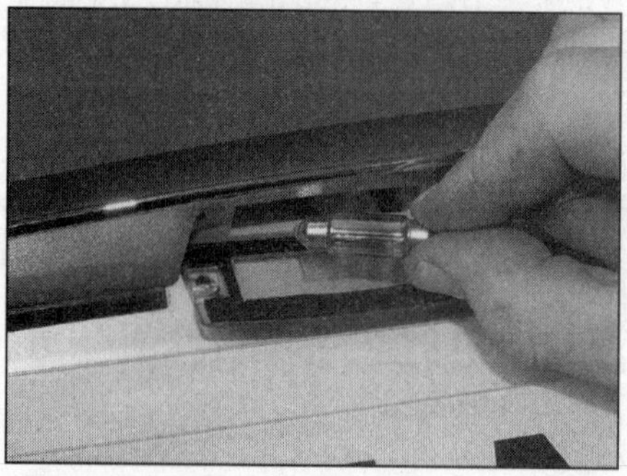

5.52 Withdraw the festoon bulb from the contacts

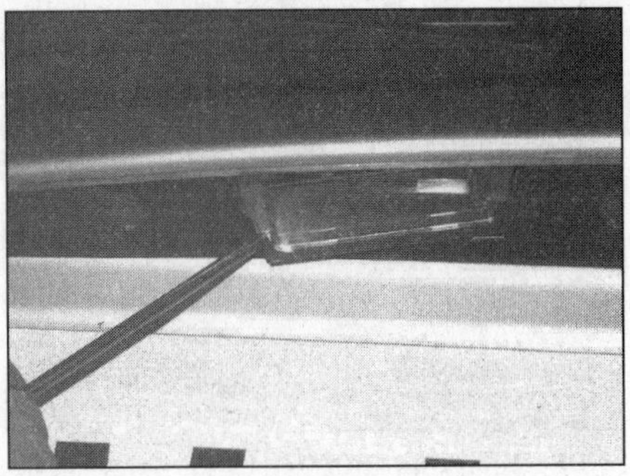

5.54a Prise down the outer end of the lens . . .

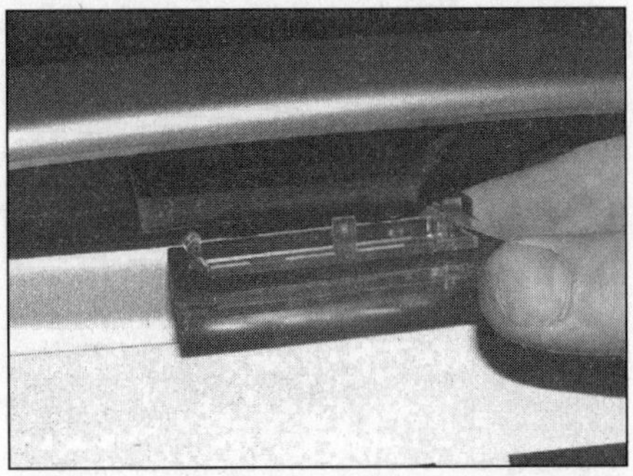

5.54b . . . and withdraw it from the handle

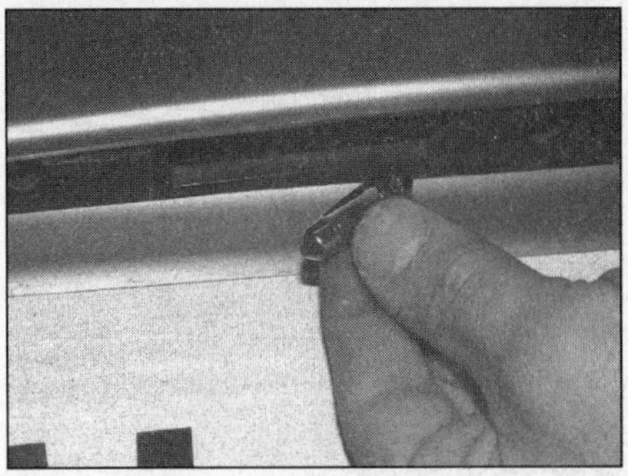

5.55 Pull the festoon-type bulb from the contacts

small screwdriver, and withdraw the lens **(see illustrations)**.

55 Withdraw the festoon-type bulb from the spring contacts **(see illustration)**.

56 Refitting is a reversal of removal. Check that the light unit's contacts are clean, and (if the bulb appears to be loose when fitted), bend the contacts together slightly.

6 Bulbs (interior lights) - renewal

General

1 Refer to Section 5, paragraph 1.

Interior lights

Front

2 Insert a small screwdriver blade into the indent at the back of the light lens, and prise the lens down. The lens also has retaining lugs at the front and sides.

3 Pull out the relevant wedge-base bulb, and press in the new one.

4 Refit the lens at the front first, then engage the side and rear clips to complete.

Rear

5 Release the unit from the headlining – this should be possible without using any tools **(see illustration)**.

6 Twist out the bulbholder, then pull out the relevant wedge-base bulb, and press in the new one **(see illustrations)**.

7 Refitting is a reversal of removal. Ensure the light unit is securely clipped back into the headlining.

Glovebox light

8 Open the glovebox, then prise down the light unit on the left-hand side.

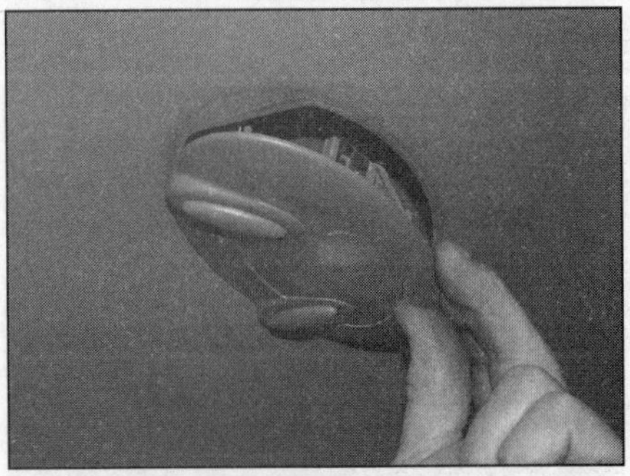

6.5 Unclip the interior light unit from the roof

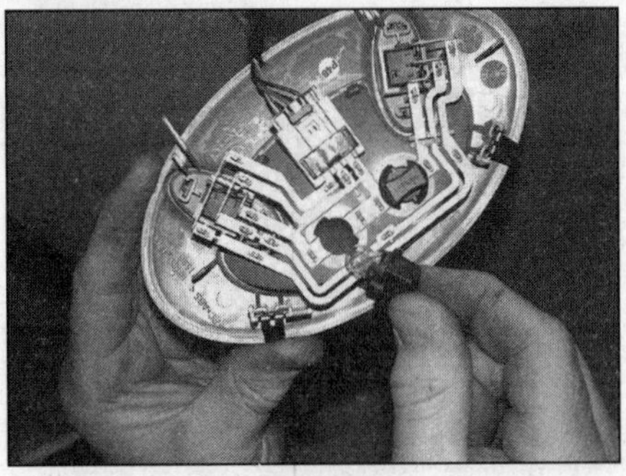

6.6a Twist out the bulbholder . . .

9 Withdraw the festoon-type bulb from the spring contacts.

10 Refitting is a reversal of removal. Check that the light unit's contacts are clean, and (if the bulb appears to be loose when fitted), bend the contacts together slightly.

Instrument panel and warning lights

11 The instrument panel is a 'solid-state' type, which means the 'bulbs' are non-renewable LEDs. The instrument panel is removed as described in Section 10.

Cigar lighter illumination

12 Remove the cigar lighter as described in Section 14.

13 The bulb may have to be renewed as part of the holder, check with your MG Rover specialist for availability. Reassemble and refit the cigar lighter using a reversal of the removal procedure.

Heater control illumination

14 The heater control panel is a 'solid-state' type, which means the 'bulbs' are non-renewable LEDs. The heater control panel is removed as described in Chapter 3.

Luggage compartment light

Saloon

15 Insert a small screwdriver blade into the indent at the end of the light lens, and prise the lens out **(see illustration)**.

16 Twist and remove the bayonet bulb **(see illustration)**. The light can be removed if required, after disconnecting the two wiring plugs

17 Refitting is a reversal of removal.

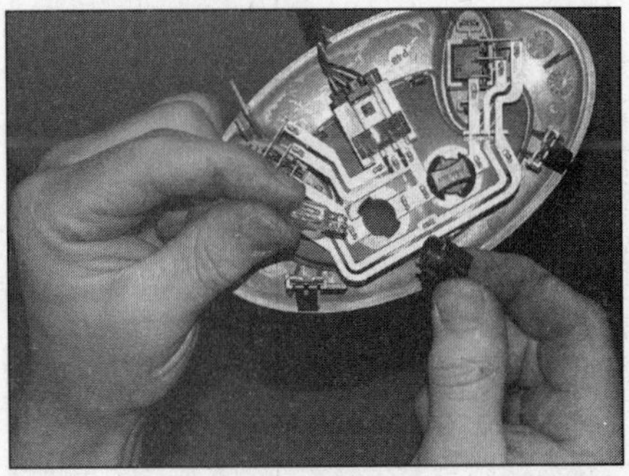

6.6b . . . and pull out the wedge-base bulb

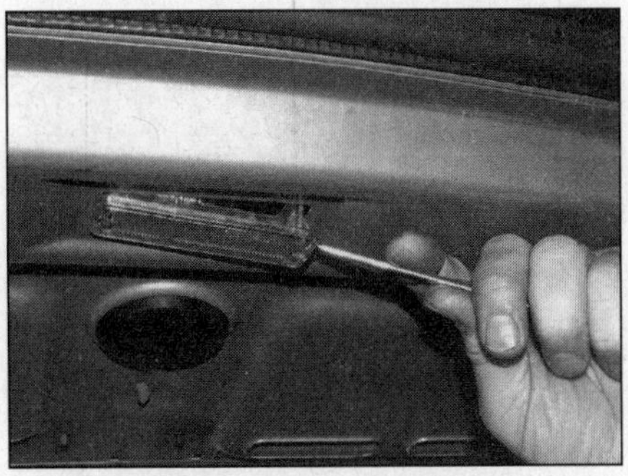

6.15 Prise down the boot light . . .

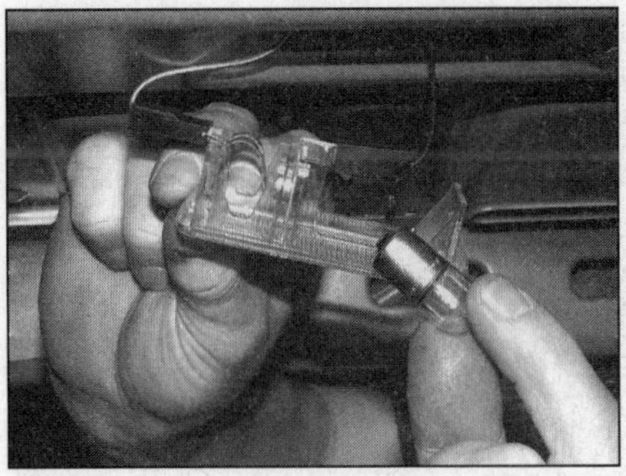

6.16 . . . and twist out the bayonet bulb

Tourer

18 Prise out the light unit lens using a small screwdriver **(see illustration)**.

19 Withdraw the festoon-type bulb from the spring contacts **(see illustration)**.

20 Refitting is a reversal of removal. Check that the light unit's contacts are clean, and (if the bulb appears to be loose when fitted) bend the contacts together slightly.

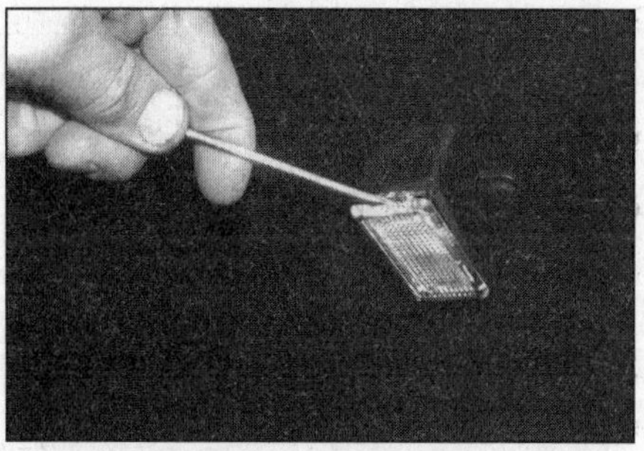

6.18 Prise out the light unit lens (spare wheel cover light shown) . . .

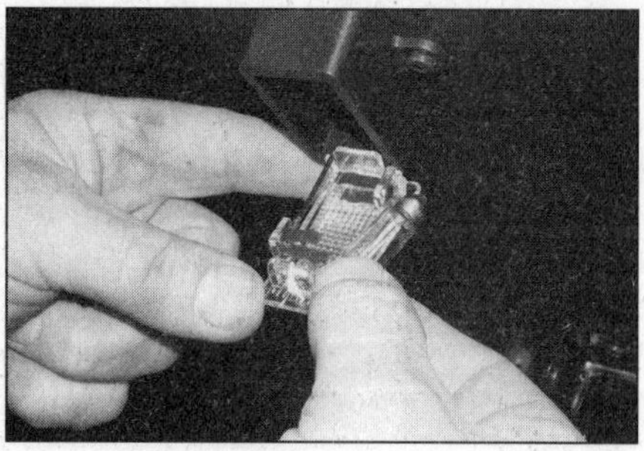

6.19 . . . and pull out the festoon-type bulb

7 Exterior light units – removal and refitting

Note: *Before removing any light, at least make sure the light concerned is switched off, and that the ignition is also off (take out the key). Ideally, disconnect the battery negative lead, and position the lead away from the battery (see 'Disconnecting the battery').*

Headlight

Warning: Before carrying out any operations on xenon headlight units, it is recommended that protective gloves and safety glasses are worn. It is essential that the wiring connectors are disconnected from the rear of the headlight unit, then wait until the bulbs have cooled down before removal. DO NOT switch the headlights on with the bulb removed, as it is harmful to the eyes.

1 Remove the front bumper as described in Chapter 11.

2 Mark the position of the headlight mounting bolts against the headlight lugs, using white paint – this is advisable due to the large amount of lateral movement possible once the bolts are loosened. Remove the four headlight mounting bolts, and withdraw the light unit from its location **(see illustrations)**.

3 Disconnect the wiring plug from the back of the light, and remove it **(see illustration)**.

4 Refitting is a reversal of removal. Align the mounting bolts with the marks made prior to removal – if this is not possible, assume that the correct fitted position is when the bolt heads are central on the lugs.

5 On completion, the headlight beam alignment should be checked, ideally using optical setting equipment. This check should be carried out by a MG Rover specialist or a suitably-equipped garage (see Section 9).

Front indicator

Pre-facelift Rover 75 models

6 Disconnect the bulbholder from the light as described in Section 5.

7 When viewed from behind, the light is held in place by a spring clip on the right, and is hooked into a clip on the left. Depress the spring clip on the right, and push the light out on the right-hand side – this may take a few tries, as the clip catches several times on its way out **(see illustration)**.

8 Unhook the light on the left-hand side, and remove it completely **(see illustration)**.

9 Refitting is a reversal of removal.

Round unit and post-facelift models

10 Disconnect the bulbholder from the light as described in Section 5.

11 Remove the two indicator mounting screws at the rear, and remove the light from the bumper.

12 Refitting is a reversal of removal.

Front foglight

Oval unit (pre-facelift models)

13 Pull the inner edge of the foglight front surround panel outwards, and unclip the panel from the light **(see illustration)**. If necessary,

7.2a Remove the two mounting bolts on top . . .

7.2b . . . and two more underneath

7.3 Withdraw the headlight and disconnect the wiring plug

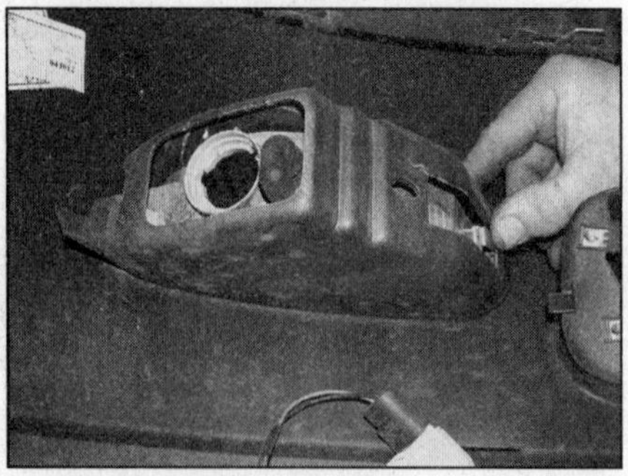

7.7 From behind, depress the clip and push out the light . . .

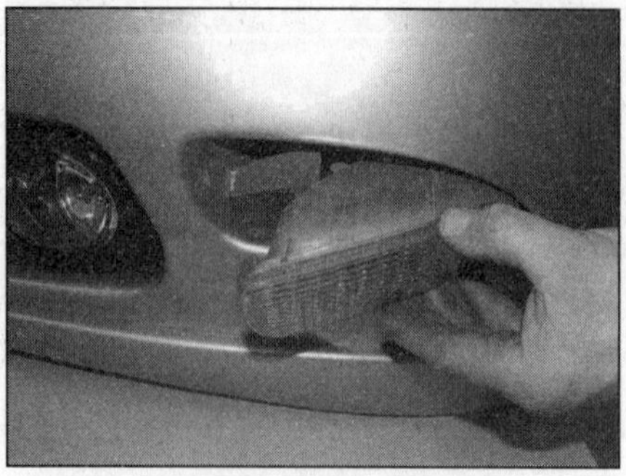

7.8 . . . then unhook it on the left, and remove it

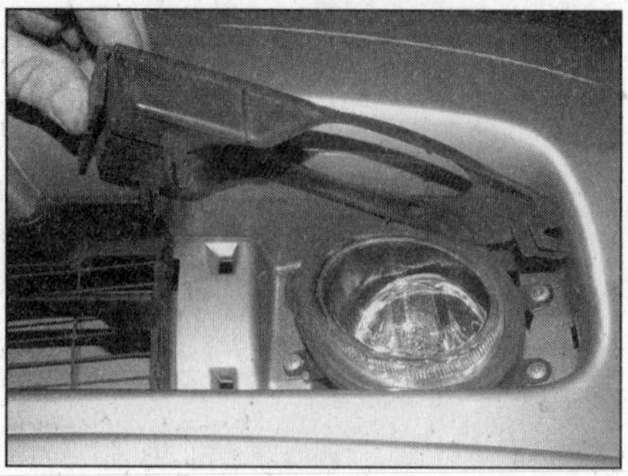

7.13 Unclip the foglight surround panel

7.14 Remove the three mounting screws

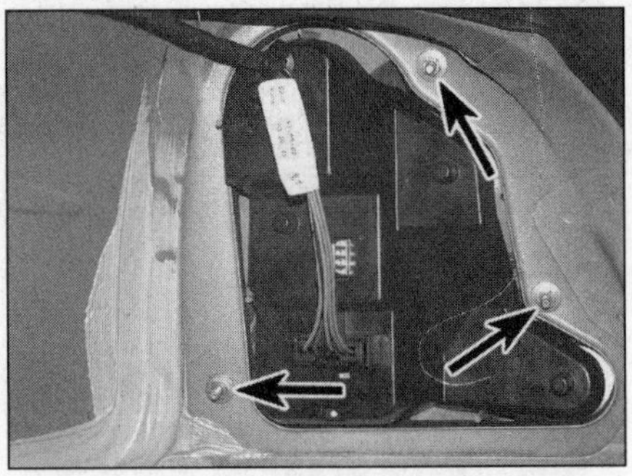

7.22a Remove the three mounting nuts . . .

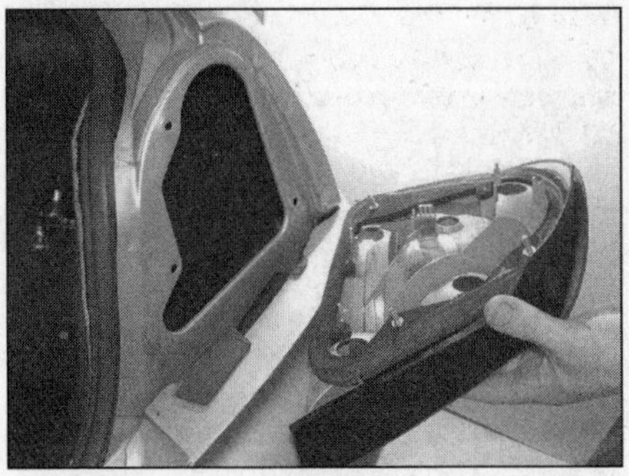

7.22b . . . and withdraw the rear light cluster

prise the surround with a screwdriver, taking care not to damage the paintwork.

14 Remove the three foglight mounting screws, and withdraw the light from the bumper **(see illustration)**.

15 Twist the bulbholder anti-clockwise to release it from the light.

16 Refitting is a reversal of removal.

Round unit

17 Remove the bulb as described in Section 5.

18 Remove the two foglight mounting screws from the rear of the unit, and remove the light from the bumper.

19 Refitting is a reversal of removal. It is advisable to have the foglight beam alignment checked on completion.

Front indicator side repeater

20 The procedure is described in the bulb renewal sequence, in Section 5.

Rear light cluster

Saloon

21 Remove the bulbholder as described in Section 5.

22 The light unit is secured by three nuts on the inside. Remove the nuts and withdraw the light from the car **(see illustrations)**.

23 Refitting is a reversal of removal. Check the condition of the light unit seal – if in poor condition, this may lead to water leaks into the boot.

Tourer

24 The procedure is described in the bulb renewal sequence, in Section 5.

High-level stop-light

Saloon

25 Working in the back seat, remove the two screws securing the light unit cover **(see illustrations)**.

26 Disconnect the wiring plug, then unscrew the two mounting nuts and withdraw the light from the rear window **(see illustrations)**.

27 Refitting is a reversal of removal.

Tourer

28 Open the tailgate window.

29 The high-level stop-light is clipped at each end to the glass – carefully prise the unit free, then disconnect its wiring plug **(see illustrations)**.

30 If required, the light unit can be dismantled by removing the two Torx cover screws (not that there is much to be gained by doing so).

31 Refitting is a reversal of removal.

Rear number plate light

32 The bulb renewal sequence in Section 5 only covers removal of the light unit lens.

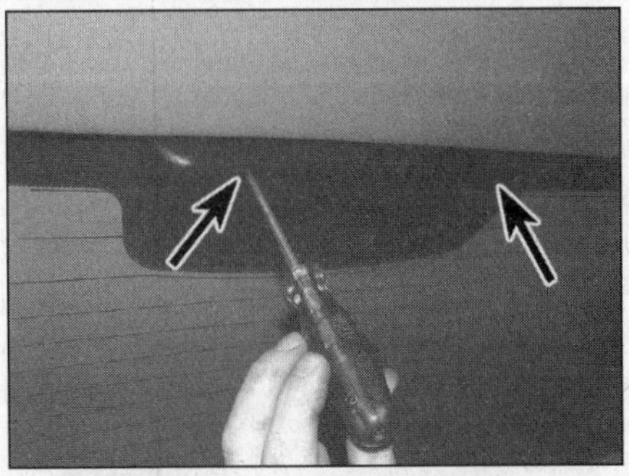

7.25a Remove the two screws . . .

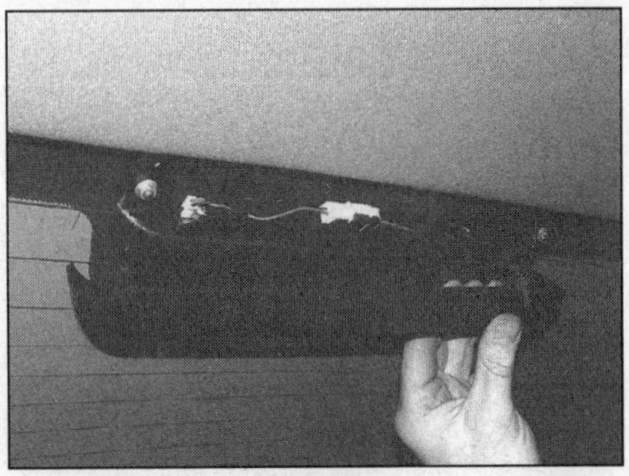

7.25b . . . and withdraw the stop-light cover

7.26a Disconnect the wiring plug, then undo the mounting nuts . . .

7.26b . . . and lower out the high-level stop-light

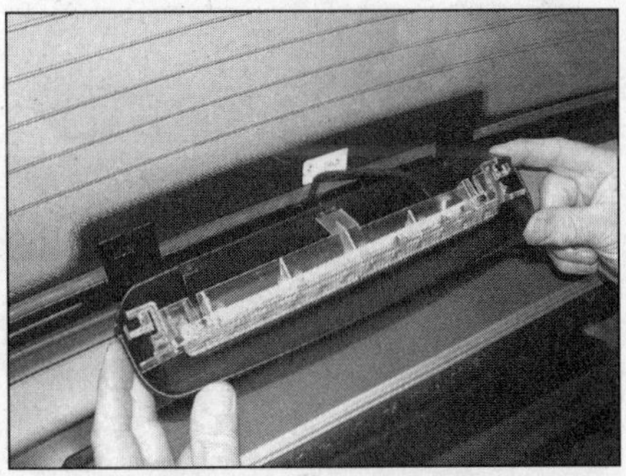

7.29a Release the clips and either end, and remove the light . . .

7.29b . . . then disconnect the wiring plug

8.4 Prise out the light unit, and disconnect the wiring plug

9.2a Headlight beam vertical adjuster

9.2b Headlight beam horizontal adjuster

Saloon

33 To remove the light unit itself, first remove the boot lid trim/handle – refer to Chapter 11, Section 16.

34 Trace the wiring to the number plate light, and disconnect it.

35 The light unit is attached to the boot lid using strong double-sided tape, so care is needed in removing it. Protect the surrounding paintwork with several strips of masking tape, and warm the area to soften the adhesive before carefully prising at one end with a wide-bladed tool.

36 Refitting is a reversal of removal, noting the following points:

a) Before sticking the light unit in place, it may be advisable to connect it up and check its operation.

b) Clean the mating surfaces and use new double-sided tape – take care over aligning the unit before pressing into place.

c) Refit the trim/handle over the light unit, referring to Chapter 11 as necessary.

Tourer

37 On Tourer models, the lights are integral with the tailgate release handle. Handle removal and refitting details are given in Chapter 11, Section 17.

8 Interior light units – removal and refitting

Interior lights

Front

1 Insert a small screwdriver blade into the indent at the back of the light lens, and prise the lens down. The lens also has retaining lugs at the front and sides.

2 Remove the two light unit mounting screws at the front, then carefully prise down the light at the rear to release the two clips. Disconnect the multi-plugs and remove the light.

3 Refitting is a reversal of removal.

Rear

4 Carefully prise the light unit from the headlining, then disconnect the wiring plug **(see illustration)**.

5 Refitting is a reversal of removal.

Glovebox light

6 The procedure is described in the bulb renewal sequence, in Section 6.

Luggage compartment light

Saloon

7 The procedure is described in the bulb renewal sequence, in Section 6.

Tourer

8 Prise out the light unit lens using a small screwdriver.

9 Remove the two light unit mounting screws and withdraw the light. Disconnect the wiring plug and remove the light completely.

10 Refitting is a reversal of removal.

9 Headlight beam alignment – general information

1 Accurate adjustment of the headlight beam is only possible using optical beam-setting equipment, and this work should therefore be carried out by a MG Rover specialist or suitably-equipped garage.

2 To make a temporary adjustment of the headlights, position the car on a level surface 10 metres from a wall. The tyres must all be at the correct pressure, and the manual adjustment switch inside the car set at 0. Use the adjuster screws at the rear of the headlight to reset the beams accordingly **(see illustrations)**.

3 Most models have a headlight beam manual adjustment control, which allows the aim of the headlights to be adjusted to compensate for variation in the car's payload. The aim is altered by means of facia-mounted switch, which controls electric adjuster motors located in the rear of the headlight assemblies.

4 Models with xenon headlights have an automatic levelling system. If a fault occurs in the system, a warning light will show up on the instrument panel, and the headlights will be angled down to avoid dazzling oncoming traffic. If this happens, the driving speed must be adjusted accordingly to allow for decreased visibility.

10 Instrument panel – removal and refitting

Removal

1 Remove the two screws under the top edge of the instrument panel shroud, then lower and withdraw the shroud **(see illustrations)**.

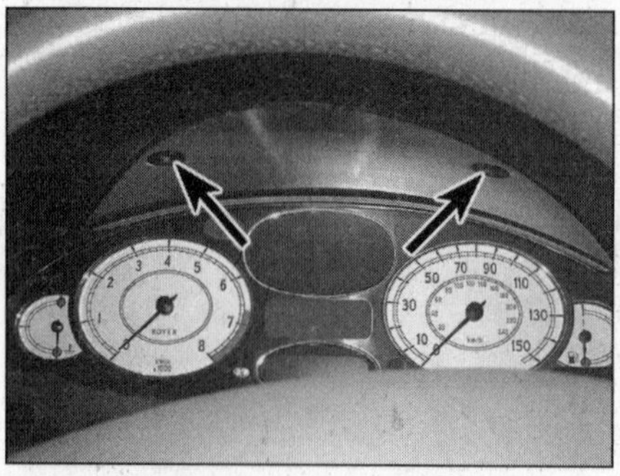

10.1a Remove the two upper screws . . .

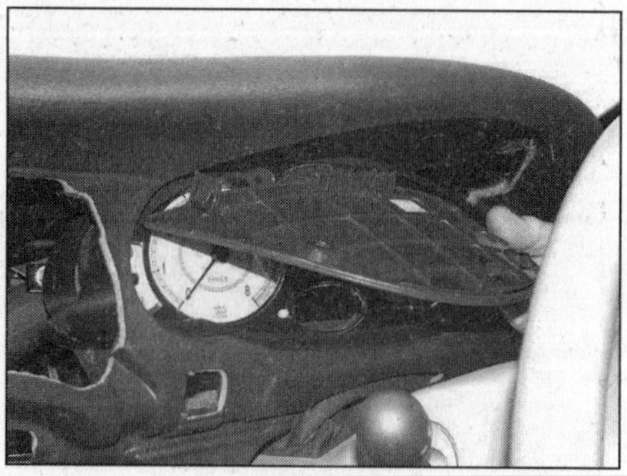

10.1b . . . and lower out the panel's top shroud

2 Unscrew the mounting screw at the top, and the instrument panel can be removed **(see illustrations)**. However, it is a tight fit, and there is a plastic clip on each lower corner which can easily break if care is not taken – try to withdraw the panel squarely to prevent this, and lift the lower edge if at all possible.
3 Disconnect the two multi-plugs on the back, and the panel can be removed completely **(see illustration)**.

Refitting

4 Refitting is a reversal of removal.

11 Clock – removal and refitting

Removal

1 Referring to Chapter 11, Section 25, remove the driver's side facia veneer trim panel.
2 Remove the facia vents from the back of the panel – each is secured by four Torx screws. However, note carefully the fitted positions of the panel's metal securing clips and brackets, which are also retained by the vent screws **(see illustrations)**. If possible, take some photos of the panel clips and brackets, to use as a guide for refitting.
3 Lift off the vent operating wheel and cable **(see illustration)**.
4 Remove the clock from the panel, noting how it is fitted **(see illustration)**.

10.2a Unscrew the top mounting screw . . .

Refitting

5 Refitting is a reversal of removal. Ensure that the panel clips are refitted as noted before removal, and remember to reconnect the clock wiring plug as the panel is refitted.

12 Exterior temperature sensor – removal and refitting

Refer to Chapter 4B, Section 11.

13 Rain sensor – removal and refitting

General information

1 The sensor used to automatically switch on the wipers (on models so equipped) consists

10.2b . . . and withdraw the instrument panel

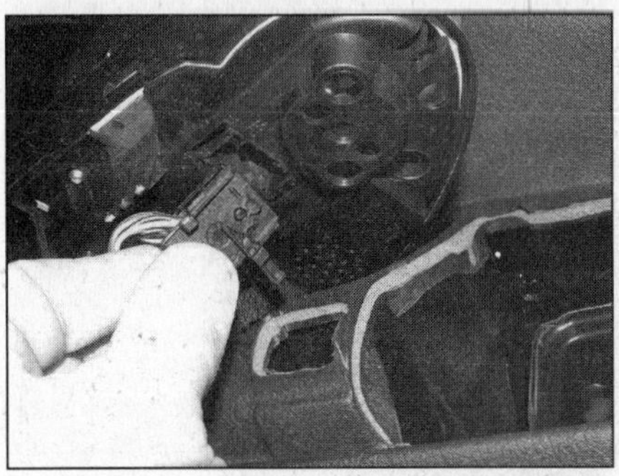

10.3 Disconnect the panel wiring plugs

of several photo-electric cells fitted at the top of the windscreen, detecting the amount of light coming through. If the light is refracted by raindrops on the glass, the sensor signals the body control unit to operate the wipers, independently of the driver.

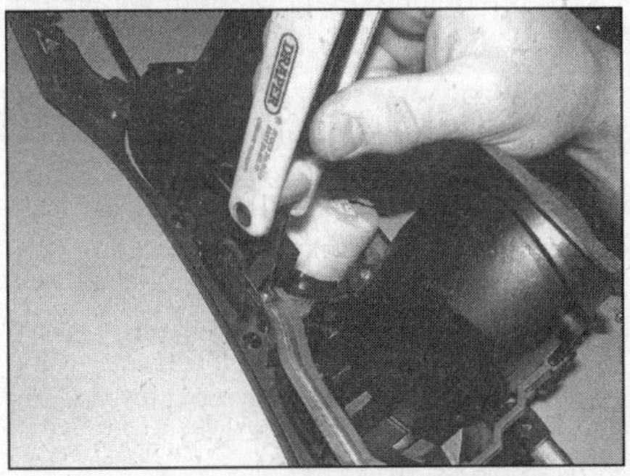

11.2a Remove the Torx screws . . .

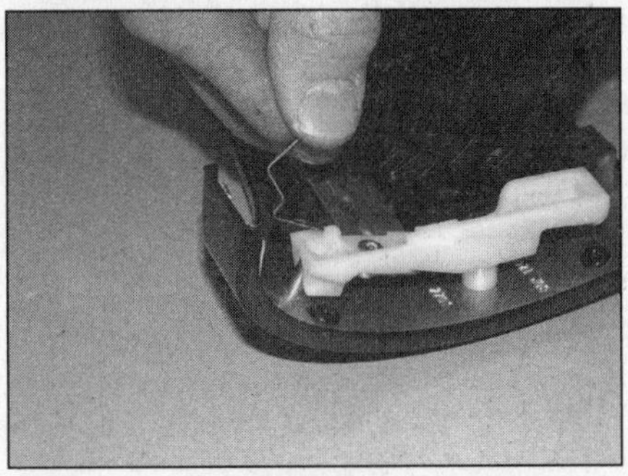

11.2b . . . noting the fitted positions of the panel clips . . .

11.2c . . . and mounting brackets . . .

11.2d . . . then lift off the two centre vents

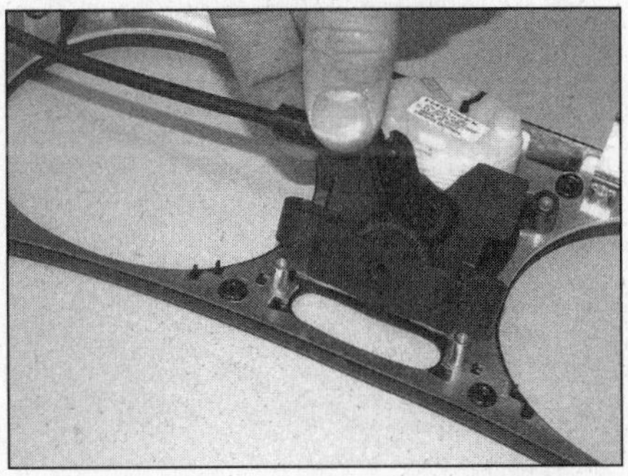

11.3 Lift off the vent operating wheel and cable

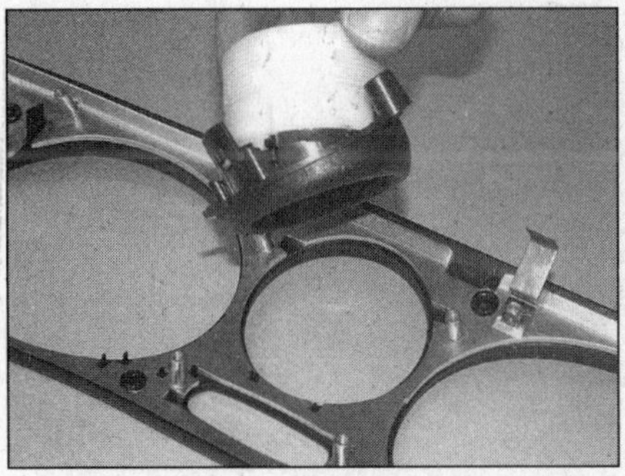

11.4 Remove the clock from the panel

2 Since the sensor is highly sensitive, it is vital for its correct operation that the windscreen be as clean as possible. Also, any damage to the glass, such as a stone chip in the vicinity of the sensor, will seriously affect it.

Removal

3 This sensor is not really intended for DIY removal and refitting. It works through a clear gel coating on the inside of the windscreen, which if damaged or contaminated in any way will result in faulty operation of the sensor. Though the procedure is given below, it is recommended that the advice of an MG Rover specialist is sought before disturbing the sensor.
4 Release the four clips and remove the two sensor half-trims above the interior mirror.
5 Disconnect the wiring plug from the side of the sensor.
6 Support the sensor, then prise out the thin two-legged clips at the front and rear which secure it in position. Carefully lower the sensor from the windscreen, and remove it.
7 If the same sensor is to be refitted, keep its upper surface clean while it is removed – any dirt particles will cause faulty operation on refitting, and could result in wipers which are on all the time.

Refitting

8 Refitting is a reversal of removal. Take care that nothing contaminates the sensor's upper surface during refitting.

14 Cigar lighter – removal and refitting

Removal

1 Remove the heater control panel as described in Chapter 3. For extra working room, also remove the audio unit (radio/CD/sat-nav) – this should not be necessary, but it helps.
2 Working through the heater panel/radio aperture, press to release the clip either side on top of the panel above the ashtray. Withdraw the assembly as far as permitted by the attached wiring, and disconnect the wiring plugs from it – the cigar lighter plugs are recessed, and will need long-nosed pliers to pull them off.
3 Release the clips either side at the top, and withdraw the ashtray assembly from the centre console. Disconnect the wiring plugs from behind the ashtray, and remove it.
4 Release the clips securing the cigar lighter to the console panel from behind, and withdraw it through the front. If not already done, disconnect the wiring plug as the lighter is removed.

Refitting

5 Refitting is a reversal of removal.

15 Horn – removal and refitting

Removal

1 The two horn units are located at the front of the car, behind the grille.
2 On Rover 75 models, remove the radiator grille as described in Chapter 11. Where applicable, release a total of sixteen clips from the two grille cowls, and remove them.
3 On MG ZT models, remove the front bumper as described in Chapter 11.
4 Unscrew the mounting bolt, and withdraw the horn from the front of the car **(see illustration)**.

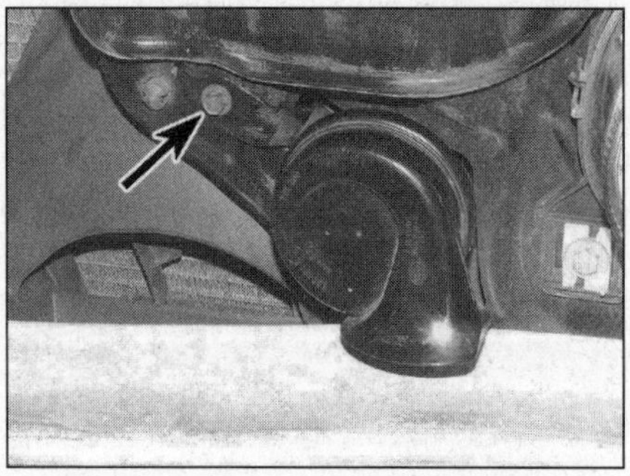

15.4 Horn mounting bolt (arrowed)

15.5 Withdraw the horn, and disconnect the wiring plug

5 Disconnect the wiring plug from the horn, and remove it completely **(see illustration)**.

Refitting

6 Refitting is a reversal of removal.

16 Wiper arms – removal and refitting

Removal

1 The wiper motor should be in the parked position before removing the wiper arm (switch the wipers on, then immediately off, and let them come to rest). Mark the position of the blade on the glass with adhesive tape, as a guide to refitting **(see illustration)**.
2 If both windscreen wiper arms are to be removed, identify them so that they can be refitted in their original positions.

Windscreen wipers

3 Prise out the plastic cap, and remove the nut underneath securing the arm to the spindle **(see illustration)**.
4 Pull or prise the arm from the spindle, using a puller or screwdriver if necessary. Take care not to damage the trim or paintwork. Recover the spacer collar which is fitted under the wiper arm nut, and keep it for refitting **(see illustration)**.

Tailgate wiper

5 Lift up and unclip the hinged cover over the

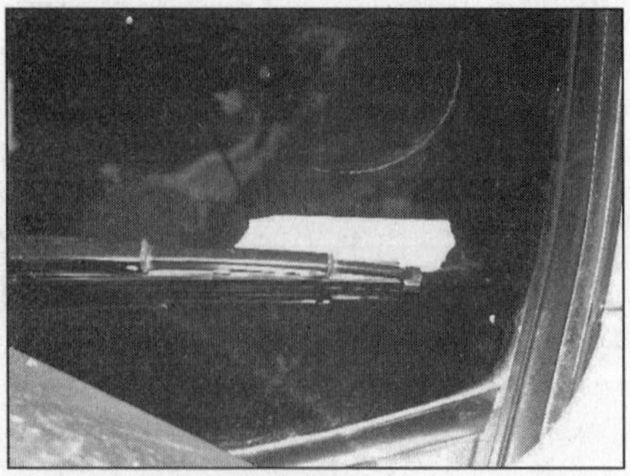

16.1 Mark the position of the wiper blade with tape

16.3 Prise off the cap to access the wiper arm nut

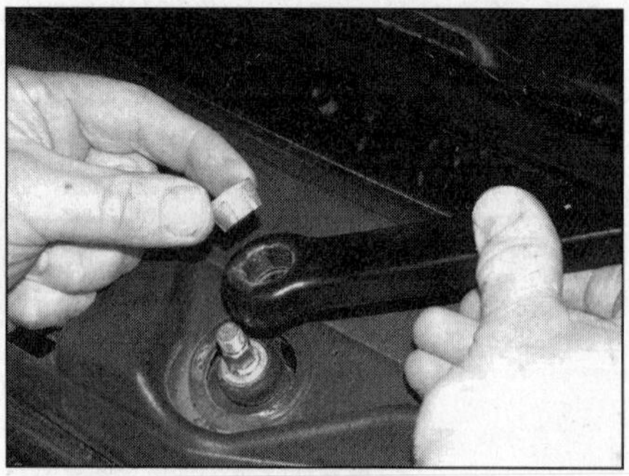

16.4 Pull off the arm, and recover the spacer collar

16.5 Unclip the wiper arm nut cover . . .

16.6 . . . then unscrew the nut and pull off the wiper arm

arm mounting nut, then unscrew the nut **(see illustration)**.

6 Pull or prise the arm from the spindle, using a puller or screwdriver if necessary **(see illustration)**.

Refitting

7 Refitting is a reversal of removal. Position the arms so that the blades align with the tape applied to the glass before removal.

17 Windscreen wiper motor and linkage – removal and refitting

Removal

1 Remove the windscreen wiper arms as described in Section 16.

2 Remove the windscreen cowl panels, as described in Chapter 11.

3 Disconnect the wiring plug from the wiper motor **(see illustration)**.

4 Remove the three wiper linkage mounting bolts, then lift the linkage/motor assembly out **(see illustrations)**.

5 To remove the motor, mark the relative positions of the motor shaft and crank, then unscrew the retaining nut and washer and free the wiper linkage from the motor spindle. Unscrew the three motor retaining bolts and separate the motor from the linkage.

Refitting

6 Refitting is a reversal of removal.

18 Tailgate wiper motor components – removal and refitting

Wiper motor

1 Remove the tailgate inner trim panel as described in Chapter 11, Section 17.

2 Disconnect the wiring plugs from the wiper motor and tailgate window lock module. Remove the three large-headed Torx bolts securing the wiper motor **(see illustrations)**.

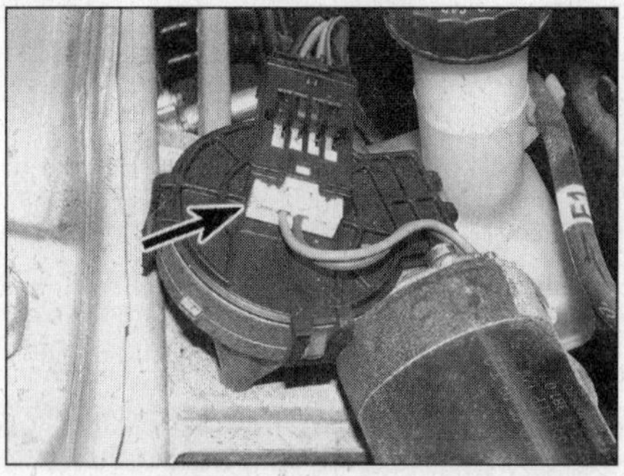

17.3 Disconnect the wiper motor wiring plug

17.4a Two of the wiper linkage mounting bolts . . .

17.4b . . . and the third, near the centre of the car

18.2a Disconnect the wiring plugs from the wiper motor . . .

18.2b . . . and from the tailgate window lock module . . .

18.2c . . . then remove the three Torx bolts on the inside

3 Close the tailgate, and open the tailgate window.

4 Remove the remaining large-headed wiper motor Torx bolt, and withdraw the motor from the tailgate **(see illustrations)**.

5 Refitting is a reversal of removal.

Wiper motor spindle

6 Remove the tailgate wiper arm as described in Section 16.

7 Prise off the C-clip at the top of the spindle, then take off the plain washer, nut and O-ring from outside.

8 Open the tailgate window, then remove the spindle and two washers.

9 Refitting is a reversal of removal.

18.4a Remove the remaining bolt . . .

18.4b . . . and withdraw the motor assembly

19 Windscreen/tailgate/headlight washer system components – removal and refitting

Washer jets

Windscreen

1 Open the bonnet.

2 Prise out the ten clips used to retain the soundproofing panel to the underside of the bonnet, and remove the panel **(see illustration)**.

3 On models with heated washer jets, peel off the tape securing the wiring multi-plugs to the underside of the bonnet, then disconnect the plugs.

4 Disconnect the windscreen washer hose at the T-piece, or from the jet itself **(see illustration)**.

5 The washer jets are secured by a single clip at the front – it may be possible to simply lift the jet at the rear and unhook it **(see illustrations)**.

6 Refitting is a reversal of removal. Ensure the washer hose is pushed fully onto the jet, to avoid leaks.

Tailgate

7 Carefully prise the washer jet from the glass – it is a tight fit inside the supply tube.

8 Refitting is a reversal of removal.

Headlight

9 Remove the front bumper as described in Chapter 11.

10 Release the clips securing the washer hoses to the jet under each headlight. The original factory clips are of the crimped type, and should be carefully cut off. Small Jubilee clips or even some small cable-ties could be used as substitutes when refitting.

11 The jets are clipped to the inside of the bumper – release the clips and remove them.

12 Refitting is a reversal of removal. Ensure the jet is clipped in and the hose reconnected securely.

Screen washer pump

13 Remove the right-hand front wheel arch liner as described in Chapter 11, Section 22.

14 Position a suitable container under the reservoir – most of the contents will be lost when the pump is removed.

15 Disconnect the wiring plug and washer tube(s) from the washer pump, which is situated low down on the reservoir **(see illustrations)** – the headlight washer pump, where fitted, is higher up.

16 Carefully release the pump from its

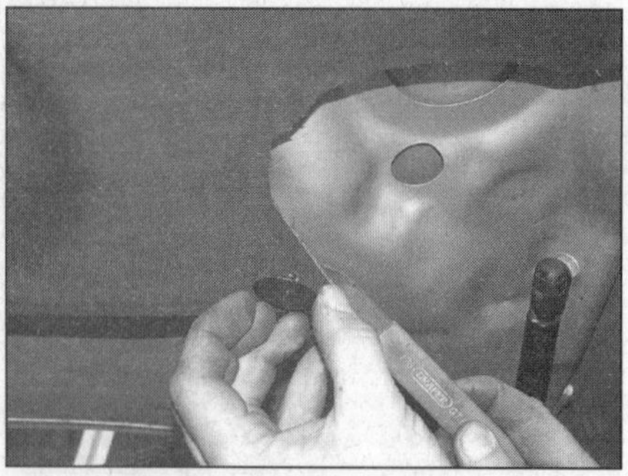

19.2 Prise out the clips and remove the bonnet soundproofing

19.4 Disconnect the washer hose from the jet

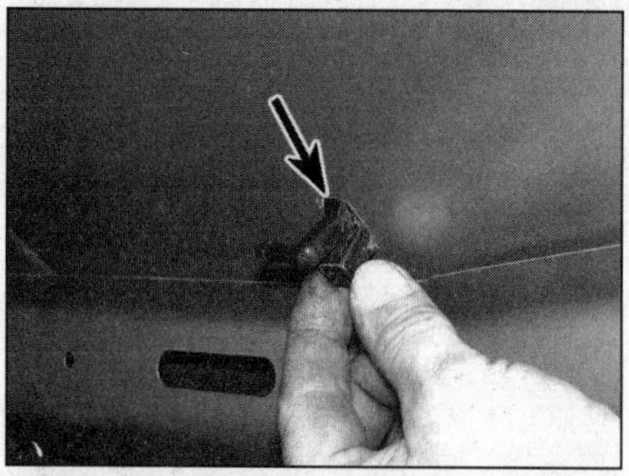

19.5a Press the clip at the front to release the jet . . .

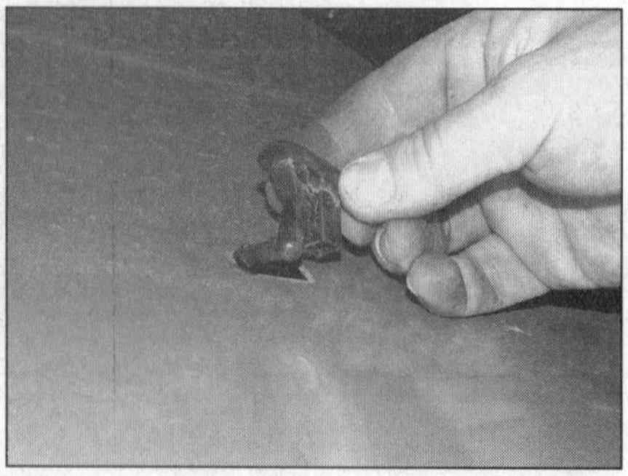

19.5b . . . and withdraw it from the bonnet

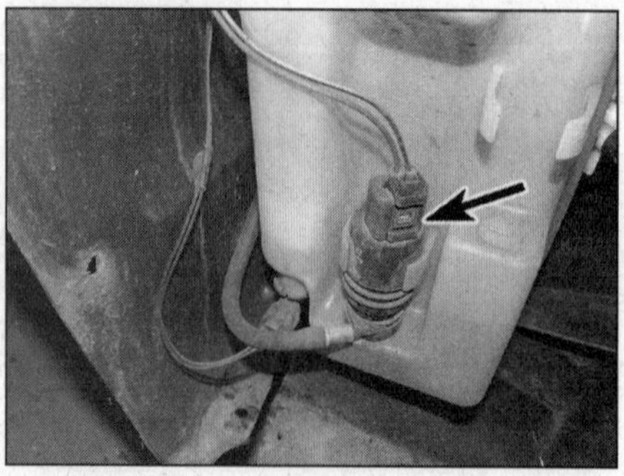

19.15a Screen washer pump location

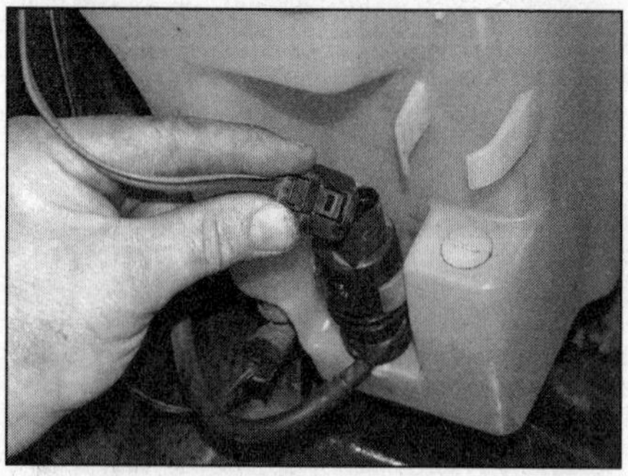

19.15b Disconnect the wiring plug from the pump

retaining clip. Pull the washer pump upwards out of the reservoir – it's likely that the rubber grommet will come with it, in which case this should be refitted to the reservoir before the pump goes back in.

17 Refitting is a reversal of removal. Refill the reservoir and check for leaks before refitting the wheel arch liner.

Headlight washer pump

18 Remove the right-hand front wheel arch liner as described in Chapter 11, Section 22.

19 Position a suitable container under the reservoir – roughly half of the contents will be lost when the pump is removed.

20 Disconnect the wiring plug and washer tube from the washer pump, which is situated halfway up the reservoir.

21 Carefully release the pump from its retaining clip. Pull the washer pump upwards out of the reservoir – it's likely that the rubber grommet will come with it, in which case this should be refitted to the reservoir before the pump goes back in.

22 Refitting is a reversal of removal. Refill the reservoir and check for leaks before refitting the wheel arch liner.

Fluid level sensor

23 Remove the right-hand front wheel arch liner as described in Chapter 11, Section 22.

24 Disconnect the sensor wiring plug, which is at the base of the reservoir – do not confuse this with the plug for the washer pump, which is higher up.

25 Position a suitable container under the reservoir, then twist and pull the sensor down from the reservoir **(see illustration)**. Recover the O-ring seal.

26 Refitting is a reversal of removal. Partially fill the reservoir and check for leaks before refitting the wheel arch liner.

Washer reservoir

27 Remove the right-hand front wheel arch liner as described in Chapter 11, Section 22.

28 Remove the four screws securing the brake air duct to the base of the bumper, and remove it.

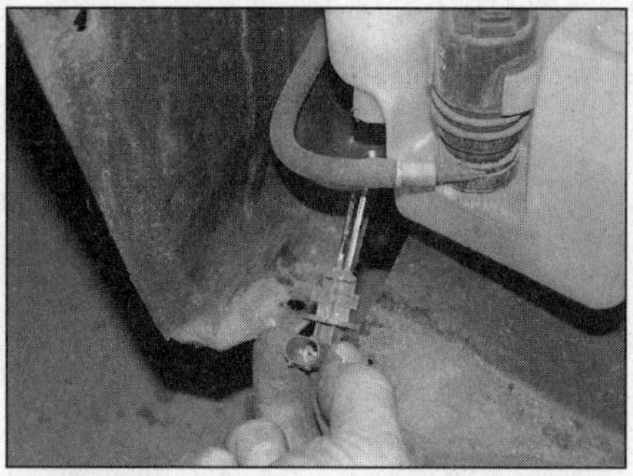

19.25 Removing the fluid level sensor

19.32 One of the washer reservoir mounting screws (arrowed)

29 Position a suitable container under the reservoir.

30 Disconnect the wiring plugs and washer tubes from the reservoir, noting their locations for refitting.

31 Working in the engine compartment, twist and pull out the reservoir filler tube.

32 Remove the two mounting screws/clips, then release the two clips and withdraw the reservoir from under the wheel arch **(see illustration)**.

33 If a new reservoir is being fitted, transfer the washer pump(s) and level sensor as described previously in this Section.

34 Refitting is a reversal of removal. Partially fill the reservoir and check for leaks before refitting the wheel arch liner.

20 Radio/cassette and CD player – removal and refitting

Note: *Do not remove the radio unit unless the security code is known, otherwise the unit will not work when refitted. Instructions for re-entering the radio code should be found in the handbook or audio booklet which came with the car – if not, a car audio dealer may be able to help.*

Standard units (entry-level)

1 A standard unit can be identified by its rectangular shape. Several different units have been fitted during the production life of the 75/ZT, but in all cases, removal is similar.

2 Using the removal tools provided, release the locking catches at the sides of the mounting cage, and slide the unit out forwards.

3 Disconnect the main wiring multi-plug, aerial lead, and (where applicable) the CD changer lead from the back of the set.

4 If required, the mounting cage can be released from the panel – typically, this will be secured by a few bent-over tabs or spring clips. Try not to bend or distort the cage as it is removed, or the radio unit will be difficult to refit.

5 Refitting is a reversal of removal. Reconnect the unit, then press it firmly into the mounting cage until the locking catches are heard to engage.

'Harmony' and 'Symphony' units

6 Higher-specification models have a larger radio/cassette which is shaped to match the centre console. The 'Harmony' set has a narrow control panel, while that on the 'Symphony' set is fuller, with a larger display panel (and possibly, satellite navigation controls).

7 First, the curved trim panel fitted above the top of the unit must be removed. Release the two clips underneath the front edge of the panel, and unclip the panel's inner cover. Remove the two screws now revealed, and take off the trim panel, noting its two locating pegs **(see illustrations)**.

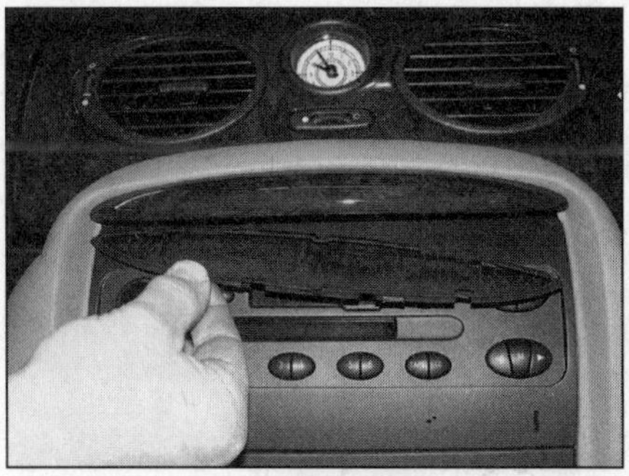

20.7a Unclip and remove the inner cover . . .

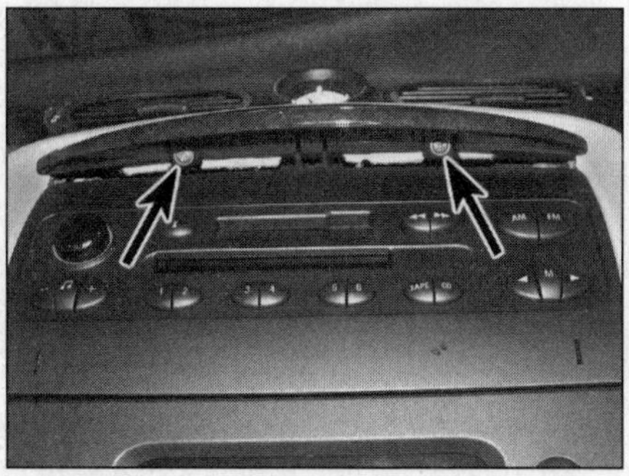

20.7b . . . to reveal the two screws inside . . .

20.7c . . . remove the screws and take off the trim panel

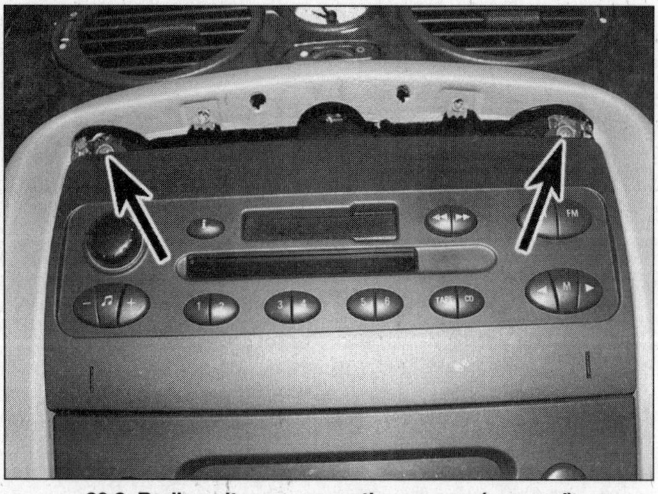

20.8 Radio unit upper mounting screws (arrowed)

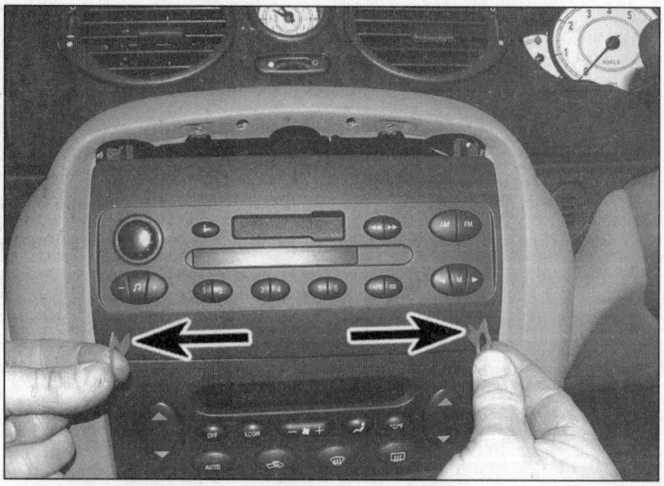

20.9a Insert the removal tools into the slots at the base . . .

8 Remove the two screws which secure the top of the unit to the centre console **(see illustration)**.

9 Using the removal tools provided, release the two locking catches at the base of the unit, and slide the unit out **(see illustrations)**.

10 Disconnect the main wiring multi-plug, aerial lead, and (where applicable) the CD changer lead from the back of the set **(see illustrations)**. On a Symphony set which has low-end navigation, disconnect the switch panel wiring plug.

11 Refitting is a reversal of removal. Reconnect the unit, then press it firmly into place until the lower locking catches are heard to engage.

High-end navigation unit

12 The high-end navigation unit has a display panel which is almost the full height of the unit, as opposed to the smaller screen of the low-end system ('Symphony' unit). For more information on the satellite navigation system, see Section 23.

13 First, the curved trim panel fitted above the top of the unit must be removed. Release the two clips underneath the front edge of the panel, and unclip the panel's outer cover. Remove the two screws now revealed, and take off the trim panel.

14 Remove the two screws which secure the top of the unit to the centre console.

15 Carefully pull off the left-hand rotary knob from the unit. Turn the screw behind this knob anti-clockwise by a quarter-turn – this retracts and locks the unit's lower locking catches.

16 Slide the unit out forwards, disconnect the two multi-plugs and remove it.

17 Refitting is a reversal of removal, noting the following points:

a) Before refitting, depress the raised screw spindle on the back of the unit, to release the lower locking catches.

b) Reconnect the unit, then press it firmly into place until the lower locking catches are heard to engage.

Radio receiver

18 On models with the high-end navigation unit, the radio controls operate a radio receiver which is actually mounted behind the spare wheel.

19 Lift up the spare wheel cover, then unclip the central trim panel at the base of the boot lid/tailgate aperture to reveal the radio receiver.

20 The receiver unit lifts out of its mounting bracket. Slide the wiring plug's locking cage upwards to release it, then disconnect the two aerial leads and remove the unit completely.

21 Refitting is a reversal of removal.

CD changer

22 The CD changer fitted to some models may be located inside the glovebox, or on the right-hand side of the luggage compartment.

Glovebox

23 Working in the passenger footwell, release the two turn-buckle fasteners at the top, and lower down the carpet panel underneath the glovebox.

24 Unscrew the four nuts now visible which secure the CD changer inside the glovebox.

25 Open the glovebox. Lift and turn the changer as necessary until the lead can be disconnected, then remove the changer from the glovebox.

26 If the changer lead is to be removed completely, the radio unit will have to be removed as described previously in this Section (otherwise, the lead can be left in place until the changer is refitted). Note the routing of the lead as it is removed, so it can be refitted the same way.

27 Refitting is a reversal of removal.

Luggage compartment

28 With the boot lid or tailgate open, the CD changer is mounted on the right-hand side.

29 Remove the two mounting bolts, and withdraw the changer from its support bracket.

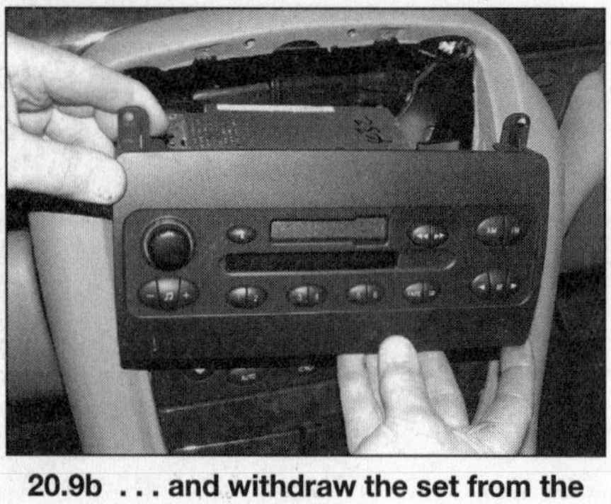

20.9b . . . and withdraw the set from the facia

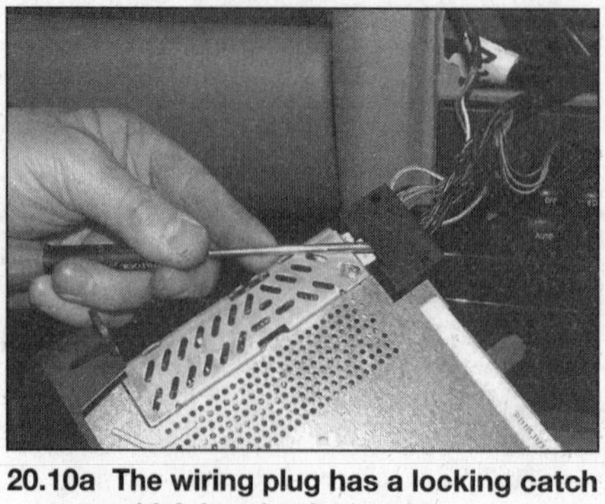

20.10a The wiring plug has a locking catch which is prised upwards . . .

20.10b . . . before it can be disconnected

21.2 Unclip the window frame trim, and disconnect the tweeter wiring plug

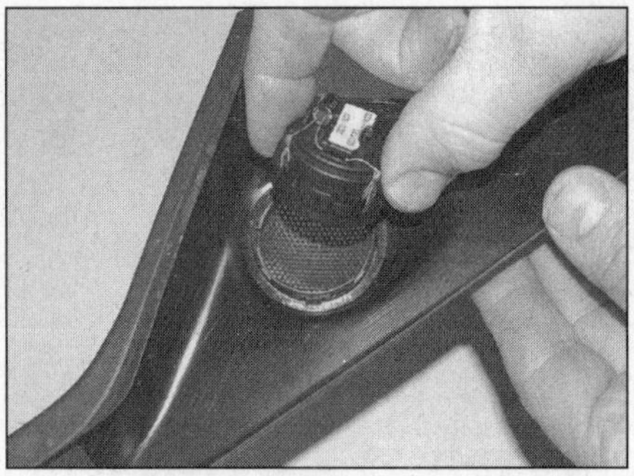

21.3 Release the clips and withdraw the tweeter

21.5a Remove the four mounting screws . . .

Disconnect the wiring plug, and remove the unit.

30 Removing the CD lead will mean the removal of several trim panels, and tracing the lead to the front of the car, where the radio unit will also have to be removed.

31 Refitting is a reversal of removal.

21 Speakers – removal and refitting

Front door speakers

1 Remove the door trim panel as described in Chapter 11.

Tweeter

2 Work around the inside edge of the window frame, and unclip the trim strip. At the front of the window trim, disconnect the wiring plugs for the electric window anti-trap sensor (where applicable) and for the tweeter **(see illustration)**.

3 Unclip and remove the tweeter from the window trim panel **(see illustration)**.

4 Refitting is a reversal of removal.

Main speaker

5 Remove the four screws securing the speaker and its mounting bracket to the door. Withdraw the assembly, and disconnect the speaker wiring plug **(see illustrations)**.

6 If required, the speaker can be separated from the bracket after removing the three screw/clips.

7 Refitting is a reversal of removal.

Rear door speakers

8 Remove the door trim panel as described in Chapter 11.

Tweeter

9 Release the three clips securing the tweeter to the inside of the door trim panel, and remove it.

10 Refitting is a reversal of removal.

Main speaker

11 Remove the three screws securing the speaker and its mounting bracket to the door. Withdraw the assembly, and disconnect the speaker wiring plug **(see illustrations)**.

12 If required, the speaker can be separated from the bracket after removing the three screw/clips.

13 Refitting is a reversal of removal.

Subwoofers (Saloon)

14 Fold the rear seats forwards to gain access to the underside of the rear shelf.

Speakers

15 Disconnect the two speaker wiring connectors from the subwoofer.

16 Support the speaker, then unscrew the four mounting screws and withdraw the subwoofer.

17 Refitting is a reversal of removal.

Speaker/baffle assembly

18 Disconnect the wiring multi-plug on the right-hand side of the assembly.

19 Support the assembly, then remove the four mounting bolts securing it to the underside of the shelf. Lower the assembly into the boot, and withdraw it from the car.

20 Refitting is a reversal of removal.

22 Radio aerial components – removal and refitting

Aerial

1 On the 75/ZT, the radio aerial is actually the heated rear window element. A filter is used to remove any interference which may occur while the heated rear window is in use, and an aerial amplifier is used to boost the signal.

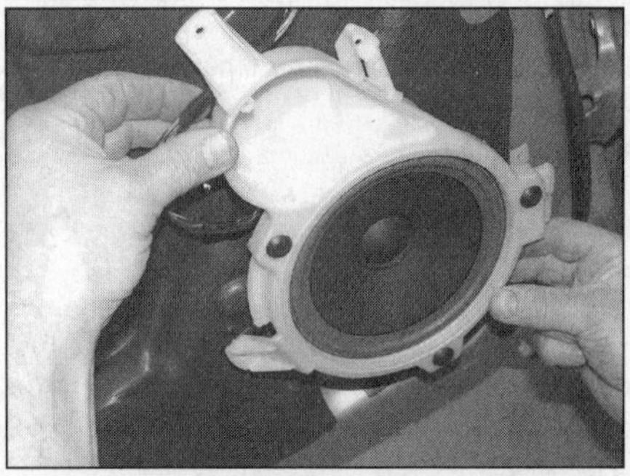

21.5b . . . then withdraw the speaker and bracket . . .

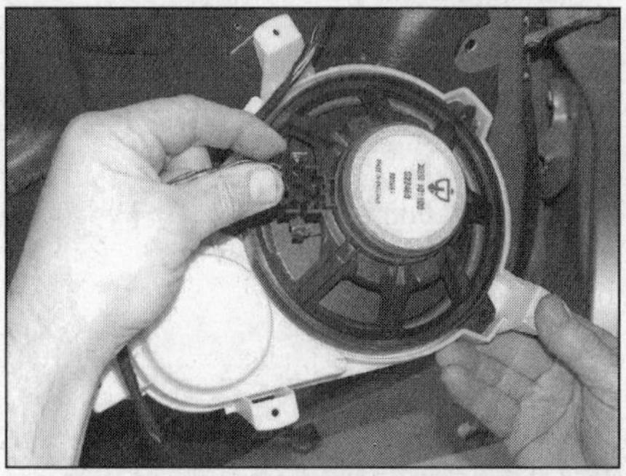

21.5c . . . and disconnect the wiring plug behind

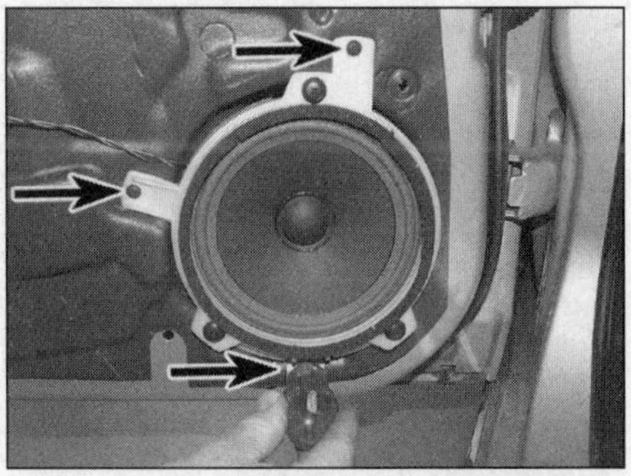

21.11a Remove the three mounting screws . . .

21.11b . . . then disconnect the speaker wiring plug

22.3 Aerial amplifier location – Saloon models

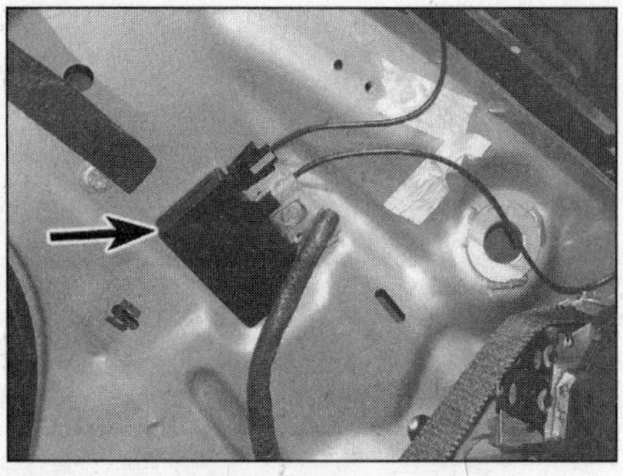

22.11 Aerial filter location – Saloon models

Aerial amplifier

Saloon

2 Remove the left-hand C-pillar trim panel as described in Chapter 11, Section 25.
3 Disconnect the various wiring connectors from the amplifier, noting how each one is fitted **(see illustration)**.
4 Unscrew the mounting bolt, and withdraw the amplifier from the car.
5 Refitting is a reversal of removal. Ensure that all the connections are clean, and securely remade, to reduce interference.

Tourer

6 On Tourer models, the amplifier is mounted at the rear of the roof, and the headlining has to be lowered for access. Removing the headlining is not a simple operation, but can be achieved if care is taken, using the information in Chapter 11, Section 25.
7 Disconnect the various wiring connectors from the amplifier, noting how each one is fitted.
8 Unscrew the two Torx mounting bolts, and withdraw the amplifier from the car.
9 Refitting is a reversal of removal. Ensure that all the connections are clean, and securely remade, to reduce interference.

Amplifier filter

Saloon

10 Remove the right-hand C-pillar trim panel as described in Chapter 11, Section 25.
11 Disconnect the three wiring connectors from the amplifier filter **(see illustration)**.
12 Unscrew the mounting bolt, and withdraw the amplifier filter from the car.
13 Refitting is a reversal of removal. Ensure that all the connections are clean, and securely remade, to reduce interference.

Tourer

14 On Tourer models, the amplifier filter is mounted at the rear of the roof, and the headlining has to be lowered for access. Removing the headlining is not a simple operation, but can be achieved if care is taken, using the information in Chapter 11, Section 25.
15 Disconnect the various wiring connectors from the amplifier filter, noting how each one is fitted.
16 Unscrew the Torx mounting bolt, and withdraw the unit from the car.
17 Refitting is a reversal of removal. Ensure that all the connections are clean, and securely remade, to reduce interference.

23 Satellite navigation system components – removal and refitting

Main display unit

1 The facia-mounted navigation unit is removed as described in Section 20.

GPS aerial

Saloon

2 Remove the parcel shelf as described in Chapter 11, Section 25.
3 Disconnect the aerial lead fitting, then remove the two mounting screws and withdraw the aerial unit from the car.
4 Refitting is a reversal of removal.

Tourer

5 On Tourer models, the GPS aerial is mounted at the rear of the roof, and the headlining has to be lowered for access. Removing the headlining is not a simple operation, but can be achieved if care is taken, using the information in Chapter 11, Section 25.
6 Disconnect the multi-plug from the aerial unit.
7 Loosen the nut which secures the unit to the roof, and recover the multi-plug support bracket.
8 Unclip the aerial unit from the roof, and collect the plastic bush.
9 Refitting is a reversal of removal.

GPS receiver

10 Remove the access panel on the right-hand side of the boot.
11 Remove the three mounting bolts, then withdraw the receiver. Disconnect the aerial lead and the wiring multi-plug (which is secured with a locking lever), and remove the receiver from the car.
12 Refitting is a reversal of removal.

Navigation computer

13 Remove the access panel on the right-hand side of the boot.
14 Using removal tools similar to those typically used to remove radio units, inserted into the two holes at either end of the unit, release the computer from its mounting bracket.
15 Pull out the computer, then disconnect the aerial lead and the wiring multi-plugs (which are secured with locking levers) and remove it.
16 Refitting is a reversal of removal. Reconnect the wiring, then push the unit firmly into place until the locking catches engage.

Speaker

17 Remove the trim panel fitted above the pedals on the driver's side – two screws are used at the top corners, with two push clips at the base.
18 Disconnect the wiring plug from the speaker, which is fitted above the pedals in its own support bracket.
19 Release the speaker from its bracket, and remove it.
20 Refitting is a reversal of removal.

24 Parking sensor system – information and component renewal

General information

1 The parking distance control (PDC) system is a driver aid which warns of objects located behind the car while reversing. The system comprises four ultrasonic sensors fitted to the rear bumper, an ECU and a boot-mounted speaker. The system is only operational when reverse gear is selected, as signalled by the reversing light switch (manual transmission) or reversing light relay (automatic transmission).
2 The system ECU uses the four sensors to monitor the area behind the car. If an obstacle of sufficient size and height is detected by the sensors when reversing, this is signalled to the ECU, which then outputs a warning signal through the speaker. The system is disabled when a trailer or caravan is being used, as the lighting module can detect the extra connections to the rear lighting circuit. The system is also disabled if reversing at more than 10 mph, as signalled by the ABS sensors. If a towbar is fitted, the system will detect it, and extend the range of the two central sensors to compensate.
3 The ultrasonic detection area extends to 1.5 metres behind the car. When reversing towards an object, the tone emitted by the system will be intermittent until the distance reduces to 35 cm or less, at which point the tone will become continuous.
4 Any faults detected with the system are signalled by a high-pitched tone, 5 seconds in duration, when the system becomes active.

Parking sensors

5 Remove the rear bumper as described in Chapter 11.

6 Disconnect the multi-plug from each sensor.
7 Release the retaining clip on either side of the sensor, and withdraw the sensor from the bumper.
8 Refitting is a reversal of removal. Though the four sensors are identical, it is important for the correct operation of the system that the sensors are aligned correctly – the retaining clips are offset to ensure this.

Parking sensor ECU

9 The parking sensor ECU is located on the right-hand side of the boot.

Saloon models

10 On models with satellite navigation, use the removal tools (similar to audio unit removal tools) to release the unit, then pull it out of the side trim panel and disconnect the wiring plugs.
11 Release the clips at the front and rear of the boot side trim panel, and remove it.
12 The parking sensor ECU is the one nearest the rear light cluster. Disconnect the two wiring plugs, then unscrew the two mounting bolts and remove the ECU.
13 Refitting is a reversal of removal.

Tourer models

14 Release the turnbuckle fastener and remove the trim panel from the right-hand side of the boot.
15 On models with satellite navigation, remove the four bolts securing the navigation computer mounting bracket, and withdraw the bracket and computer into the boot.
16 Disconnect the two wiring plugs, then unscrew the two mounting bolts and remove the parking sensor ECU.
17 Refitting is a reversal of removal.

Parking sensor speaker

Saloon models

18 Remove the parcel shelf as described in Chapter 11, Section 25.
19 Disconnect the wiring plug from the back of the speaker.
20 Remove the bolt at the front securing the speaker bracket to the car, then unscrew the nut and washer holding the speaker to the bracket.
21 Refitting is a reversal of removal.

Tourer models

22 Release the turnbuckle fastener and remove the trim panel from the right-hand side of the boot.
23 On models with satellite navigation, the speaker is in front of the navigation computer, secured to its mounting bracket by a single nut. Unscrew the nut, and withdraw the speaker around the front of the computer. Disconnect the wiring plug and remove the speaker.
24 Refitting is a reversal of removal.

25 Anti-theft alarm and immobiliser systems – general information

All models are fitted with an anti-theft alarm system, which uses various sensing systems and warning sirens, depending on model. Any faults should be referred to an MG Rover specialist for diagnosis.

An engine immobiliser system is fitted as standard to all models, and the system is operated automatically every time the ignition key is inserted/removed.

The immobiliser system ensures that the car can only be started using the original MG Rover keys supplied with the car when new. Each key contains an electronic chip (transponder) which is programmed with a code. When the key is inserted into the ignition switch, it uses the current present in the reader coil (which is fitted to the switch housing) to send a signal to the immobiliser electronic control unit (ECU). The ECU checks this code every time the ignition is switched on. If the key code does not match the ECU code, the ECU will disable the starter circuits to prevent the engine being started.

The car's central locking and alarm systems are controlled by the body control unit (BCU) – see Section 3 for more information. The immobiliser system has its own ECU, located in the driver's footwell.

26 Airbag system – general information and precautions

General information

All models are equipped with a comprehensive airbag system. In addition to front airbags for the driver and front passenger, there are side airbags fitted to the front seats, and side curtain airbags which are deployed from modules in the headlining.

The airbag system is triggered in the event of a heavy frontal or side impact above a predetermined force; depending on the point of impact, not all the airbags will necessarily be fired. The airbags inflate within milliseconds to form a safety cushion which prevents contact with the internal surfaces of the car, greatly reducing the risk of injury. The airbags then deflate almost immediately.

The system is armed only when the ignition is on. However, a reserve power source maintains power to the system in the event of a break in the main electrical supply for a short period – for this reason, it is essential to wait before disconnecting any of the system wiring.

The system is activated by a 'g' sensor (deceleration sensor), incorporated in the electronic control unit, fitted under the rear of the centre console. Note that the airbag control unit also controls the seat belt tensioners. Impact sensors at the base of the B-pillars detect side impacts which, if severe enough, will cause the side and curtain airbags to be fired on the side concerned.

The airbags are inflated by gas generators, which force the bags out from their locations. Although these are safety items, their deployment is violently rapid, and this may cause injury if they are triggered unintentionally.

Linked to the airbag system are the seat belt tensioners fitted to each seat belt. The seat belt tensioners are fired with the airbags in the event of an accident, to take up the slack in the belts, and hold the occupants in their seats.

Precautions

Warning: The following precautions must be observed when working on vehicles equipped with an airbag system, to prevent the possibility of personal injury.

General precautions

The following precautions **must** be observed when carrying out work on a vehicle equipped with an airbag:

a) Do not disconnect the battery with the engine running.
b) Before carrying out any work in the vicinity of the airbag, removal of any of the airbag components, or any welding work on the car, de-activate the system as described in the following sub-Section.
c) Do not attempt to test any of the airbag system circuits using test meters or any other test equipment.
d) If the airbag warning light comes on, or any fault in the system is suspected, consult an MG Rover specialist without delay. Do not attempt to carry out fault diagnosis, or any dismantling of the components.

Precautions when handling an airbag

a) Transport the airbag by itself, bag upward.
b) Do not put your arms around the airbag.
c) Carry the airbag close to the body, bag outward.
d) Do not drop the airbag or expose it to impacts.
e) Do not attempt to dismantle the airbag unit.
f) Do not connect any form of electrical equipment to any part of the airbag circuit.

Precautions when storing an airbag

a) Store the unit in a cupboard with the airbag upward.
b) Do not expose the airbag to temperatures above 80°C.
c) Do not expose the airbag to flames.
d) Do not attempt to dispose of the airbag – consult a MG Rover specialist.
e) Never refit an airbag which is known to be faulty or damaged.

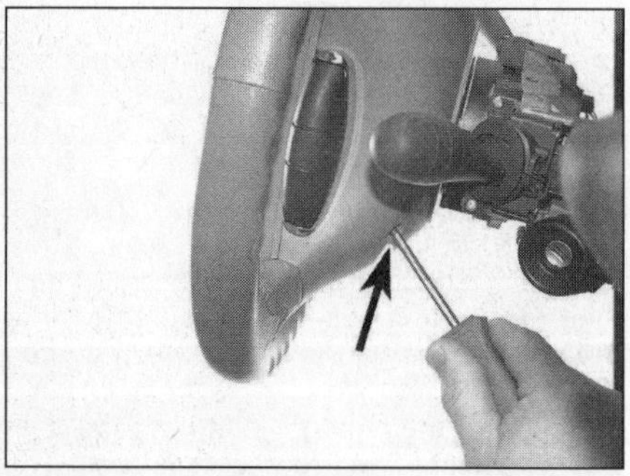

27.3 The driver's airbag Torx screws are accessed from the back of the wheel

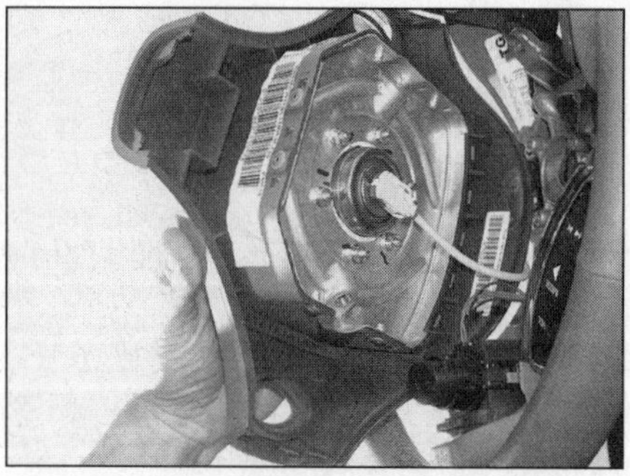

27.4a Release the airbag from the wheel . . .

27.4b . . . then prise up the locking catch with a slim screwdriver . . .

De-activation of airbag system

The system must be de-activated as follows, before carrying out any work on the airbag components or surrounding area.

a) Switch off the engine.
b) Remove the ignition key.
c) Switch off all electrical equipment.
d) Disconnect the battery negative lead (see 'Disconnecting the battery').
e) Insulate the battery negative terminal and the end of the battery negative lead with electrical tape, to prevent any possibility of contact.
f) ***Wait for at least 10 minutes*** *before carrying out any further work.*

27 Airbag system components – removal and refitting

Note: *Refer to the precautions in Section 26 before carrying out the following operations.*

1 Disconnect the battery negative lead and wait for at least 10 minutes. This will allow the reserve power capacitors in the control unit to discharge and disable the airbag system (see Section 26).

Driver's airbag

2 Remove the steering column shrouds as described in Chapter 11, Section 25.

3 The airbag's two Torx screws are fitted to the back of the steering wheel centre pad, and are recessed. It is likely the screws will be quite tight, especially if they have not been disturbed recently – use only the proper tools to remove them **(see illustration)**. The screws cannot be removed completely – when the screw head is flush with the back of the wheel pad, it has been released.

4 Release the unit from the wheel, and disconnect the yellow wiring plug on the back, after prising up the locking catch **(see illustrations)**.

5 Remove the airbag from the car, taking care not to knock or drop it, and keeping the front uppermost. Store it somewhere safe while it is removed.

6 When refitting, ensure that the wiring connectors are securely reconnected, and seat the airbag unit centrally in the steering wheel, making sure the wires do not become trapped. Tighten the airbag mounting screws securely, or to the specified torque if possible.

7 Ensuring no one is inside the car, reconnect the battery. Insert the ignition key through the driver's window, and check the operation of the airbag warning light – it should come on for approximately 4 seconds, then go out.

Airbag rotary connector (clockspring)

8 Remove the driver's airbag as described previously in this Section, and the steering wheel as described in Chapter 10.

9 Stick some adhesive tape across the face of the rotary connector, to prevent it from turning from Its reference position **(see illustration)**.

10 Unscrew the four Torx screws securing the rotary connector to the steering column **(see illustration)**.

11 Carefully withdraw the connector without turning it, then disconnect the wiring plugs from the back, and remove it completely **(see illustration)**. Store the connector carefully if it will be refitted – damage will result if the unit is dropped, for instance.

12 If required, the steering column switch assemblies can be removed, after unscrewing the two Torx screws from each.

13 If a new rotary connector is being fitted, check that its blue locking peg is intact. Don't fit any connector which has been dropped or roughly handled.

14 Check that the front wheels are still pointing straight-ahead, and that the connector is set to its centre position. Provided the connector has not been turned, or that the blue locking peg is in place, this should be the case. However, if the centre position has been lost, remove the tape or locking peg, and gently turn the connector until the white segment appears on the indicator wheel.

27.4c . . . and disconnect the yellow wiring plug

27.9 Secure the clockspring using a piece of tape

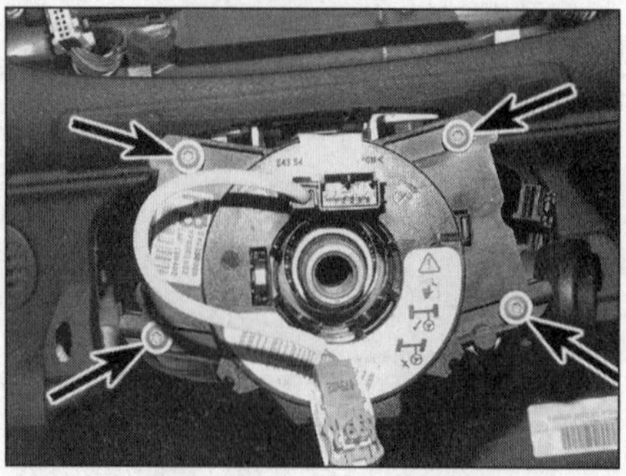

27.10 Airbag clockspring four Torx screws

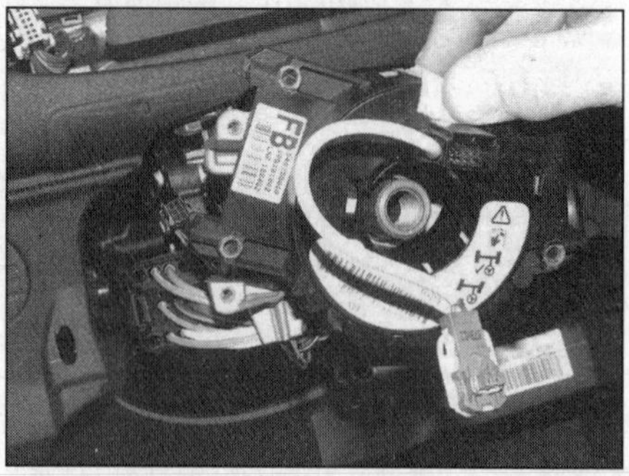

27.11 Withdraw the clockspring without turning it

27.18a Prise out the locking catch, and disconnect the yellow plug . . .

27.18b . . . then undo the two Torx bolts each end . . .

27.18c . . . and withdraw the passenger airbag from the crossmember

15 Offer the connector into place, reconnect the wiring plugs, and secure it with the four Torx screws. If not already done, remove the tape or locking peg.

16 Refit the column shrouds, then refit the steering wheel as described in Chapter 10, and the driver's airbag as described previously in this Section. On completion, reconnect the battery and check the operation of the airbag warning light.

Passenger's airbag

17 Remove the facia panel as described in Chapter 11 – the crossmember does not have to be removed.

18 Disconnect the airbag wiring plug, after prising out the locking catch. Remove the four airbag unit Torx mounting bolts (two each end), and withdraw the airbag from the crossmember **(see illustrations)**.

19 Refitting is a reversal of removal.

Front side airbags

20 The side airbags are located internally within the front seat backrest, and no attempt should be made to remove them. Any suspected problems with the side airbag system should be referred to an MG Rover specialist, but it may be worth checking the wiring and plugs under the seats for problems first (disconnect the battery before disturbing the wiring).

Side curtain airbags

21 The modules for the side curtain airbags are located at the sides of the headlining. It is strongly recommended that any work which requires even just the removal of the headlining, never mind any work on the side curtain airbags, be referred to an MG Rover specialist or experienced garage.

Airbag control unit

22 Remove the centre console as described in Chapter 11, then lift off the protective rubber cover **(see illustration)**.

23 Release the locking lever, and disconnect the wiring plug from the side of the unit **(see illustration)**.

24 Unscrew and remove the three Torx mounting bolts, and lift out the unit.

25 Refitting is a reversal of removal, noting the following points:

a) *Ensure that the battery is still disconnected, then reconnect the unit wiring plug.*
b) *Ensure that the mating faces of the unit and the floor are clean, with nothing trapped in between. One of the crash sensors is located in the unit, and this will not operate correctly if the unit is badly fitted.*
c) *Tighten the mounting bolts to the specified torque.*
d) *Refit the centre console as described in Chapter 11.*

Side impact sensors

26 Remove the front seat on the side concerned, as described in Chapter 11.

27 Also as described in Chapter 11, Section 25, remove the B-pillar trim panels on the side concerned.

28 Release the carpet at the base of the B-pillar, and lift it for access to the side impact sensor.

29 Disconnect the sensor multi-plug, then unscrew the two Torx mounting bolts and remove the sensor.

30 Refitting is a reversal of removal, noting the following points:

a) *Ensure that the battery is still disconnected, then reconnect the sensor wiring plug.*
b) *Ensure that the mating faces of the sensor and B-pillar are clean, with nothing trapped in between. The sensor will not operate correctly if badly fitted.*
c) *Tighten the mounting bolts to the specified torque.*
d) *Refit the trim panels and front seat as described in Chapter 11.*

Seat belt tensioners

31 Refer to the seat belt procedures in Chapter 11, Section 24.

27.22 Lift off the cover for access to the airbag control unit

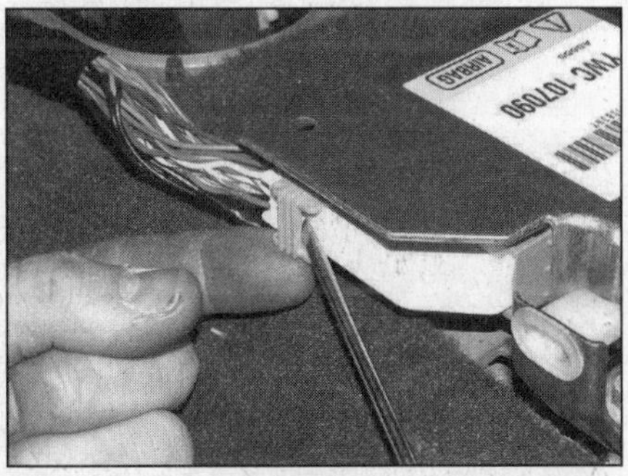

27.23a Use a screwdriver to release the locking lever . . .

27.23b . . . and disconnect the wiring plug from the side

ROVER 75 & MG ZT wiring diagrams

Diagram 1

Key to symbols

- Bulb
- Flashing bulb
- Switch
- Multiple contact switch (ganged)
- Fuse/fusible link with rating (F28 15A)
- Resistor
- Variable resistor
- Variable resistor
- Wire splice, unspecified connector or soldered joint
- Connecting wires
- Item no. (2)
- Single speed pump/motor
- Twin speed motor
- Gauge/meter
- Earth point location (E4)
- Diode
- Light emitting diode (LED)
- Solenoid actuator
- Heating element
- Plug and socket connection
- Wire colour (green with pink tracer) G/K

Dashed component outline denotes part of a larger item.

'2' denotes pin 2 of single connector.
'a2' denotes pin 2 of connector a.

Earth locations

E1	At base of LH 'A' pillar
E2	Behind LH headlight
E3	At base of RH 'A' pillar
E4	At base of LH 'A' pillar
E5	On top of engine
E6	At base of LH 'A' pillar
E7	LH inner wing
E8	At base of RH 'A' pillar
E9	Behind LH headlight
E9	Behind LH headlight
E10	Right hand side of boot
E11	Left hand side of boot
E12	At base of RH 'A' pillar
E13	At base of LH 'A' pillar
E14	Left hand side of boot
E15	At base of RH 'A' pillar
E16	Below centre console
E17	Behind centre console

Engine fusebox 6

Fuse	Rating	Circuit protected
F1	15A	Engine management
F2	30A	TCS control unit (KV6 with traction control)
F2	20A	Fuel injectors & ignition coils, engine management control unit (KV6 & K1.8))
F2	30A	Engine management control unit (Diesel)
F3	15A	Engine management
F4	15A	Engine cooling fan, compressor clutch, auto. transmission selector, reversing light switch
F5	10A	Engine management control unit (KV6 & K1.8))
F6	15A	Front foglight relay
F7	30A	ABS control unit
F8	15A	Fuel burning heater (Diesel)
F9	10A	Compressor clutch relay
F10	20A	Windscreen wiper relays 1 & 2

Passenger compartment fusebox 5

Fuse	Rating	Circuit protected
F1	20A	Body control unit
F2	30A	TCS control unit
F3	5A	Clock, diagnostic socket, memory seat control unit
F4	5A	RH front window switch, air temperature control unit, fresh/recirculated air motor, electric mirrors
F5	5A	Body control unit
F6	5A	Instrument cluster
F7	5A	Light switch control unit
F8	5A	Body control unit
F9	10A	Windscreen washer pump
F10	5A	Instrument cluster
F11	5A	RH front window switch, air temperature control unit & temperature sensor, cigar lighter relay, audio system
F12	10A	Torch socket, park distance control unit, sunblind switch, rain sensor, gearbox solenoid, interior mirror, folding mirrors
F13	10A	Body control unit
F14	20A	Body control unit
F15	15A	Cigar lighter relay
F16	20A	Accessory socket relay
F17	5A	Instrument cluster
F18	5A	Airbag control unit
F19	30A	Memory seat control unit
F20	20A	Inertia switch, fuel pump relay
F21	30A	Memory seat control unit
F22	15A	Audio system
F23	20A	Sunroof control unit
F24	30A	Body control unit
F25	20A	Ignition switch
F26	5A	Battery back-up sounder, engine immobiliser control unit
F27	5A	Instrument cluster
F28	15A	PETROL MODELS - cruise control switch, steering wheel clock springs, horn switch, light switch control unit, clock & diagnostic connector
F28	15A	DIESEL MODELS - steering wheel clock springs, horn relay, light switch control unit, clock & diagnostic connector
F29	-	Not used
F30	30A	Washer pump
F31	15A	Alarm sounder
F32	10A	K1.8 MODELS - ABS control unit
F32	10A	KV6 MODELS - ABS control unit, TCS control unit & switch
F32	10A	DIESEL MODELS - ABS control unit, TCS switch
F33	5A	Air temperature control control unit, driver's seat belt switch
F34	10A	Fuel pump relay, engine control unit, automatic transmission cooling fan relay
F35	5A	Heated washer jets, heated door mirrors, trailer socket relay
F36	5A	Alternator
F37	-	Not used
F38	-	Not used
F39	-	Not used
F40	5A	Switch lighting control unit
F41	10A	Cruise control, reversing light, interlock control unit
F42	-	Not used

Engine fusebox 6

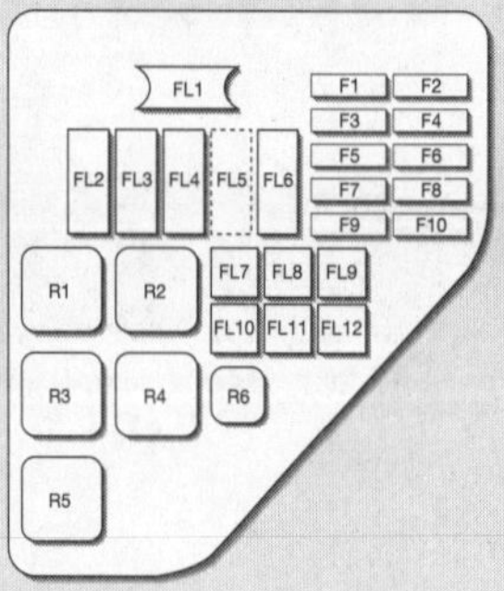

Passenger compartment fusebox 5

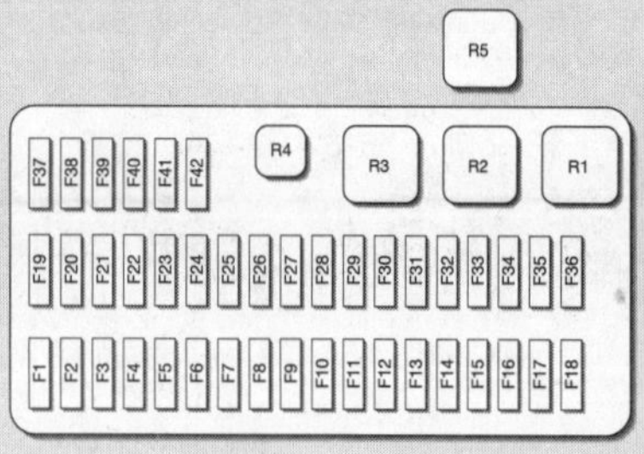

H33394

Diagram 2

Wire colours

B	Black	P	Purple
G	Green	R	Red
K	Pink	S	Grey
Lg	Light green	U	Blue
N	Brown	W	White
O	Orange	Y	Yellow

Key to items

1 Battery
2 Ignition switch
3 Starter motor
4 Alternator
5 Passenger compartment fusebox
 a = horn relay
 b = cigar lighter relay
6 Engine fusebox
 R4 = main relay
7 A/T selector switch
8 Immobiliser control unit
9 Immobiliser coil
10 Horn
11 Steering wheel clock springs
12 Horn switch
13 Accessory socket relay
14 Accessory socket
15 Torch socket
16 Cigar lighter

H33395

Typical starting & charging system

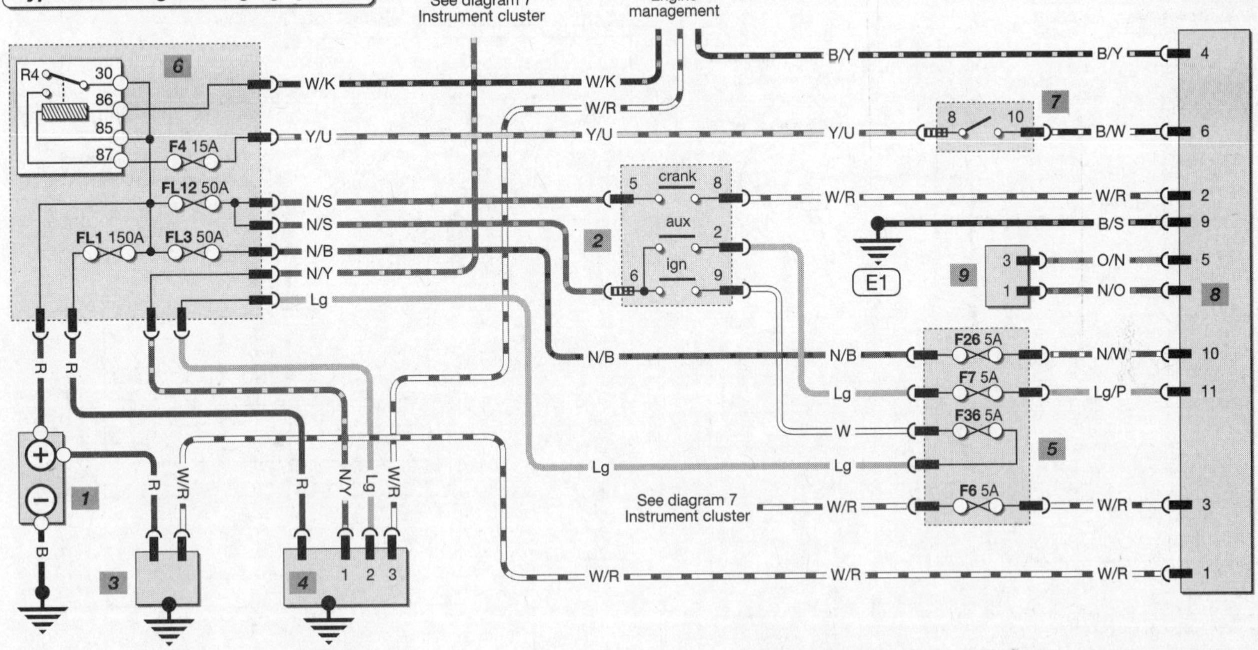

Horn

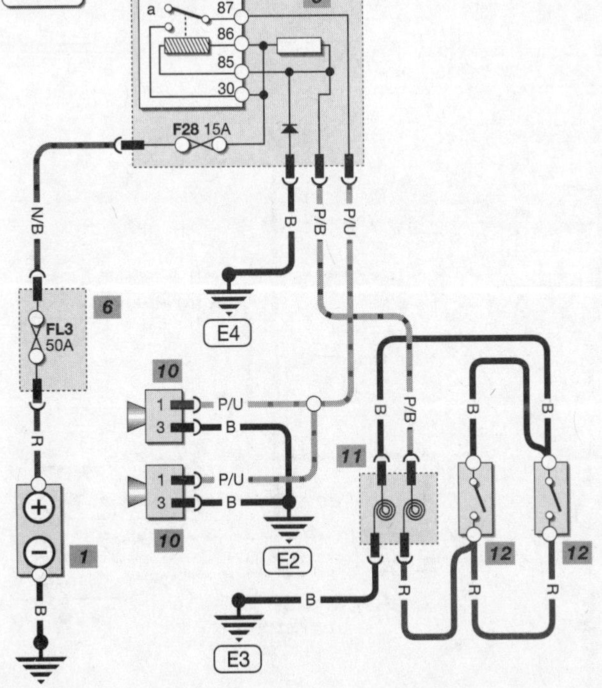

Cigar lighter & accessory socket

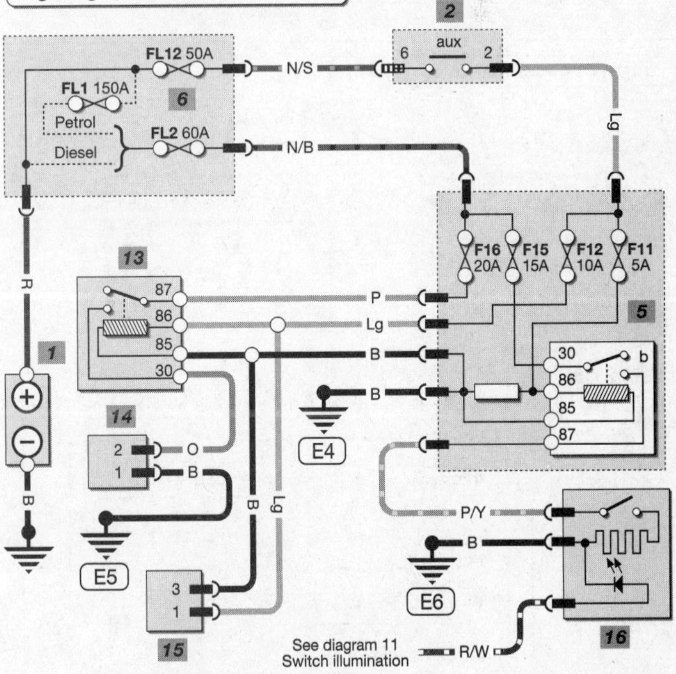

Wire colours

B	Black	**P**	Purple
G	Green	**R**	Red
K	Pink	**S**	Grey
Lg	Light green	**U**	Blue
N	Brown	**W**	White
O	Orange	**Y**	Yellow

Key to items

1 Battery
6 Engine fusebox
  R4 = main relay
  R5 = heater blower relay
18 Engine cooling fan unit
  a = low speed fan relay
  b = medium speed fan relay
  c = high speed relay
  d = medium pressure relay
  e = control unit
  f = engine cooling fan
19 Engine management control unit
20 Coolant temperature sensor
21 Heater blower motor
22 Heater blower resistors
23 Blower motor switch

Diagram 3

H33396

Engine cooling fan (Diesel)

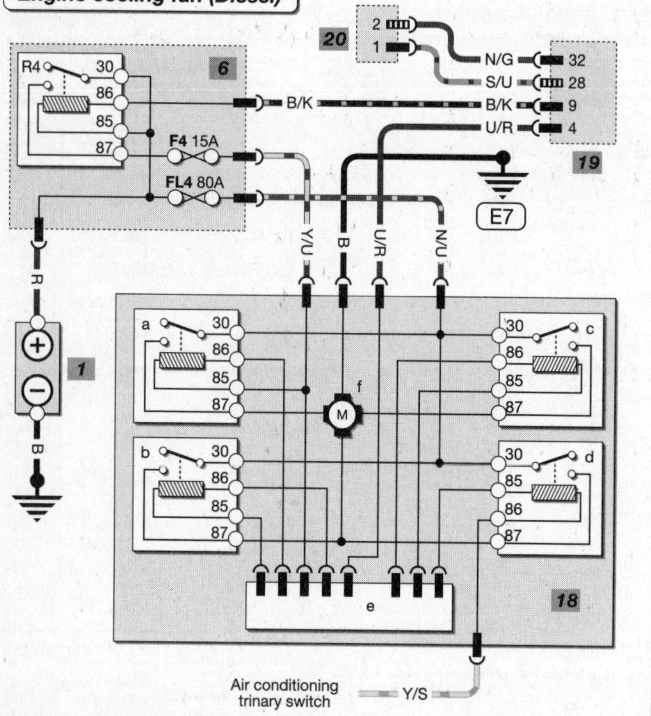

Engine cooling fan (K series 1.8)

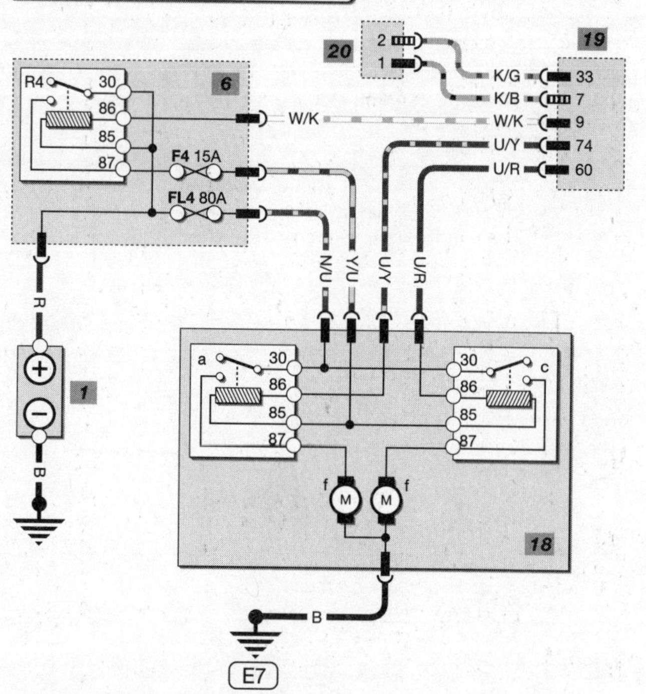

Engine cooling fan (K series V6)

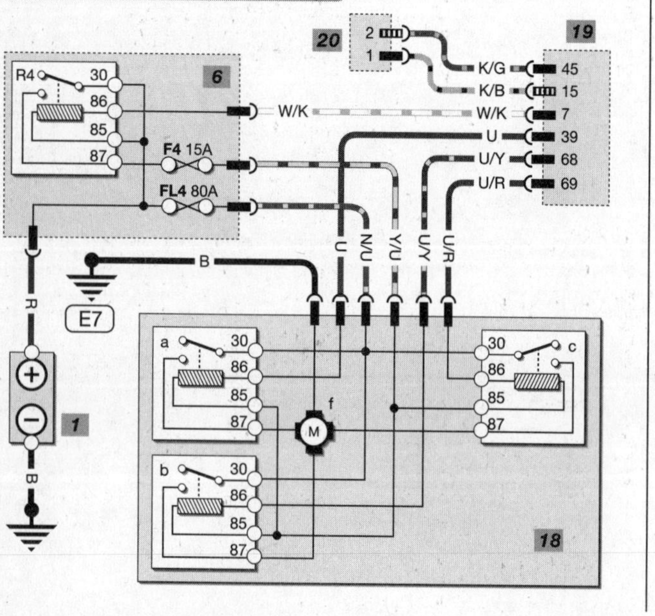

Heater blower (part of A/C)

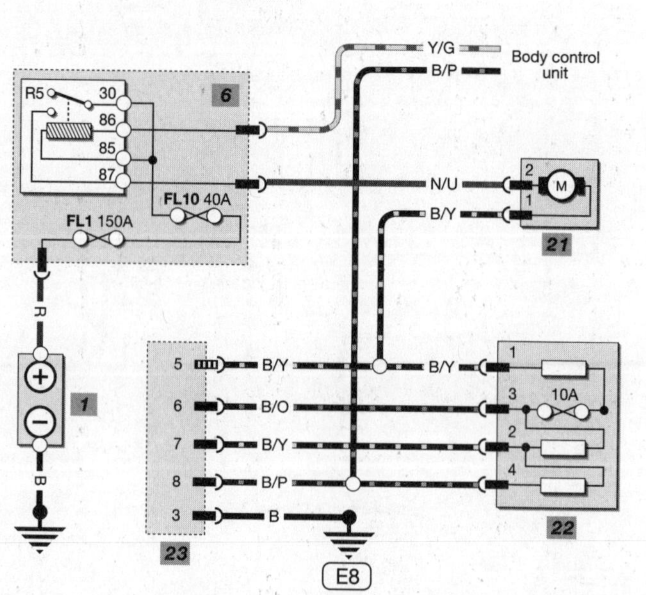

Diagram 4

Wire colours

B	Black	**P**	Purple
G	Green	**R**	Red
K	Pink	**S**	Grey
Lg	Light green	**U**	Blue
N	Brown	**W**	White
O	Orange	**Y**	Yellow

Key to items

1 Battery
2 Ignition switch
5 Passenger fusebox
  R4 = reversing light relay (auto)
6 Engine fusebox
  R4 = main relay
7 A/T selector switch (reversing light switch)
25 Light switch control unit
26 Steering column switch
  a = direction indicator
  b = main, dip, flash
27 LH headlight unit
  a = sidelight
  b = main beam
  c = dip beam
28 RH headlight unit (as above)
29 Number plate light
30 LH rear light cluster
  a = tail light
  b = stop light
  c = reversing light
31 RH rear light cluster (as above)
32 Reversing light switch
33 High level brake light
34 Stop light switch

H33397

Side, head & tail lights

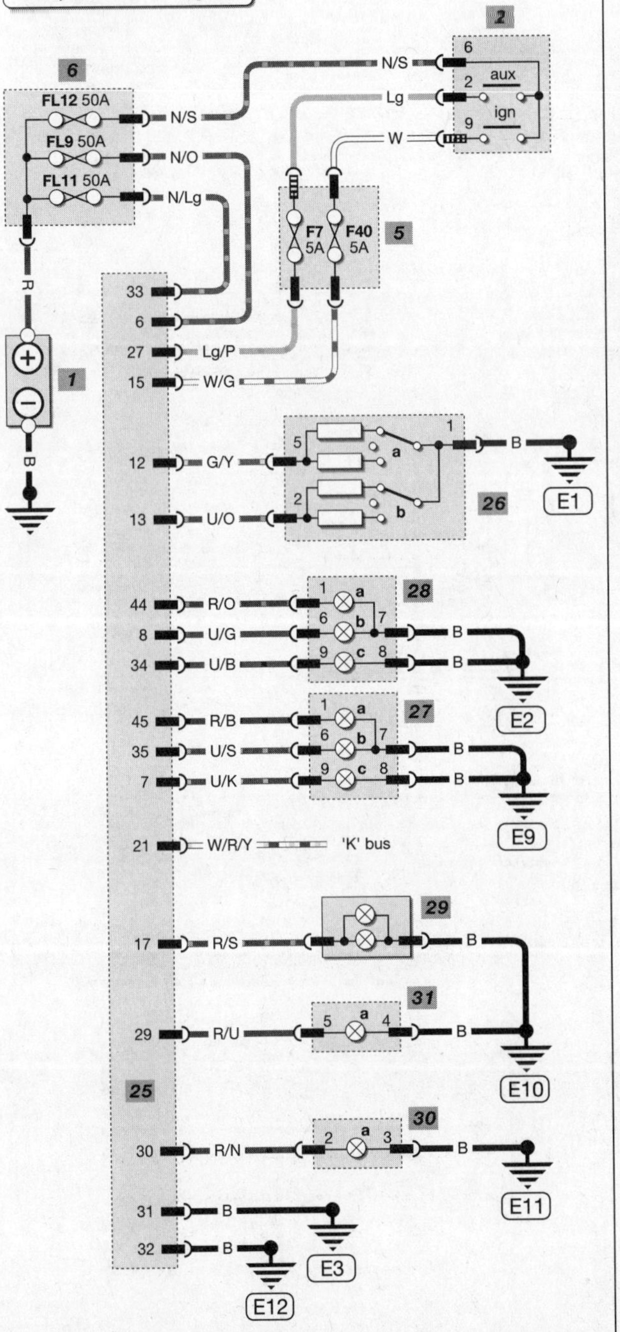

Stop & reversing lights

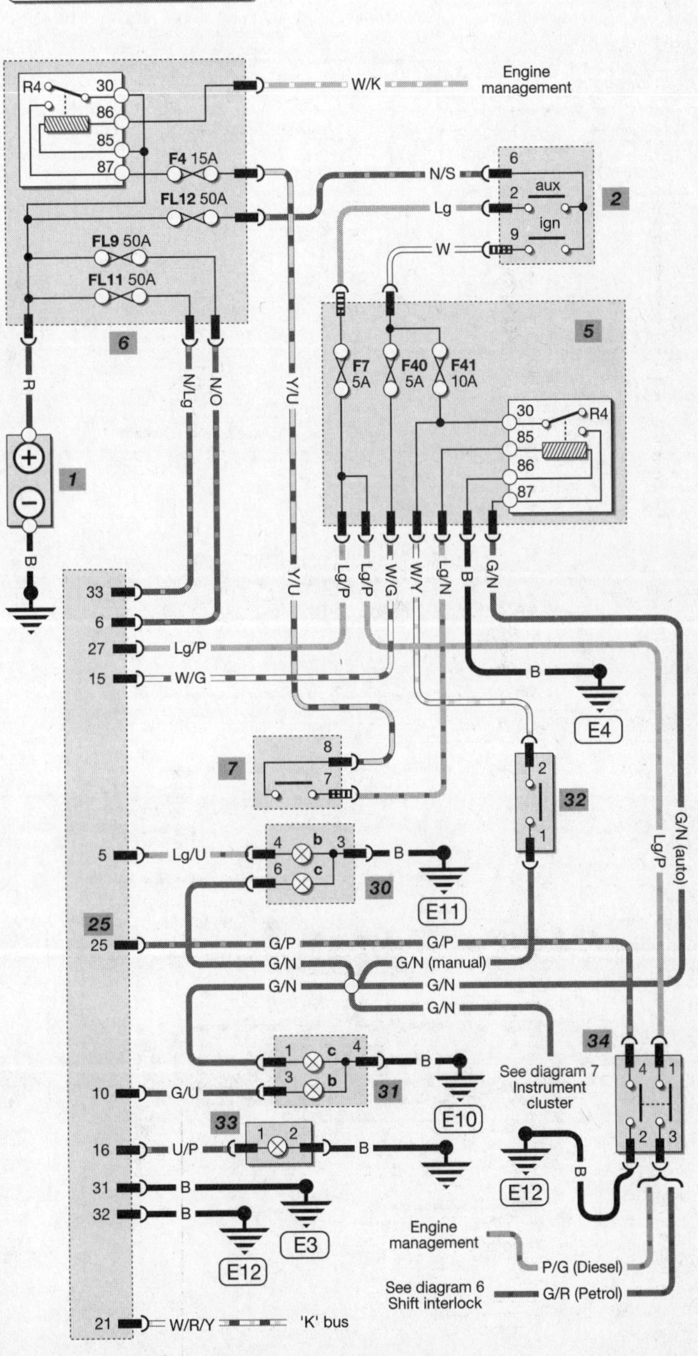

Diagram 5

Wire colours

B	Black	**P**	Purple
G	Green	**R**	Red
K	Pink	**S**	Grey
Lg	Light green	**U**	Blue
N	Brown	**W**	White
O	Orange	**Y**	Yellow

Key to items

1 Battery
2 Ignition switch
5 Passenger fusebox
6 Engine fusebox
  R6 = front foglight relay
25 Light switch control unit
26 Steering column switch
  a = direction indicator
  b = main, dip, flash
27 LH headlight unit
  d = headlight levelling
28 RH headlight unit
  d = headlight levelling
30 LH rear light cluster
  d = direction indicator
  e = rear foglight
31 RH rear light cluster
  d = direction indicator
  e = rear foglight
36 LH front direction indicator
37 RH front direction indicator
38 LH indicator side repeater
39 RH indicator side repeater
40 Hazard warning light switch
41 LH front foglight
42 RH front foglight

H33398

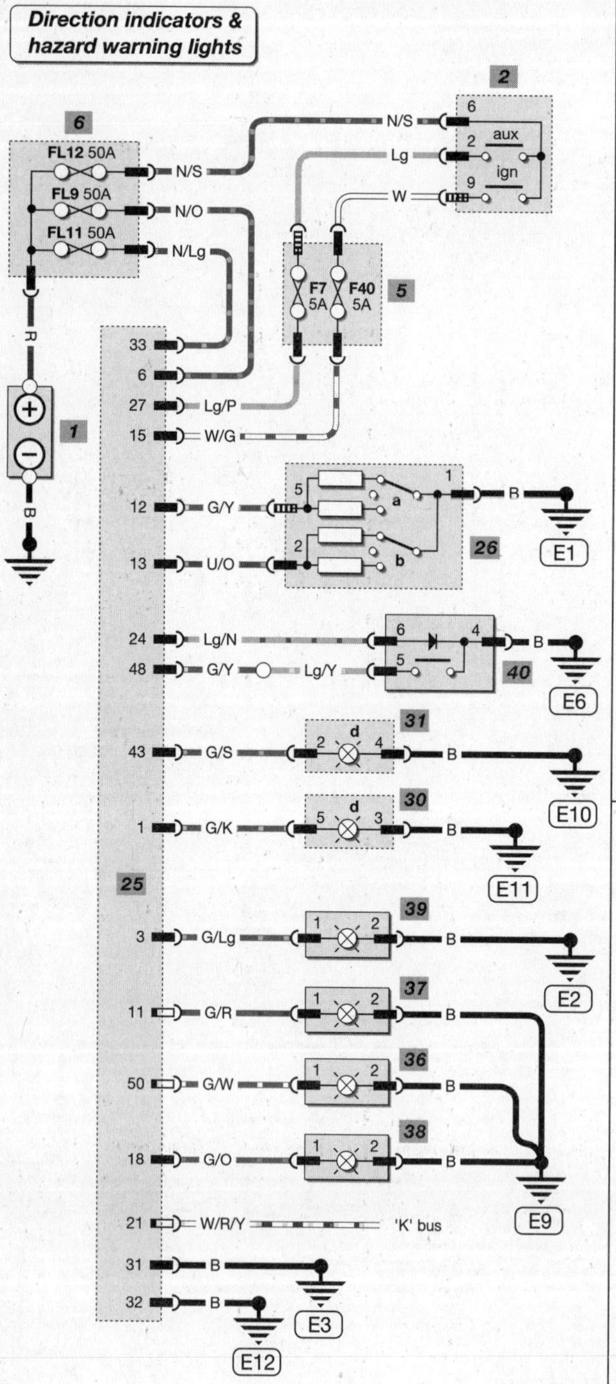

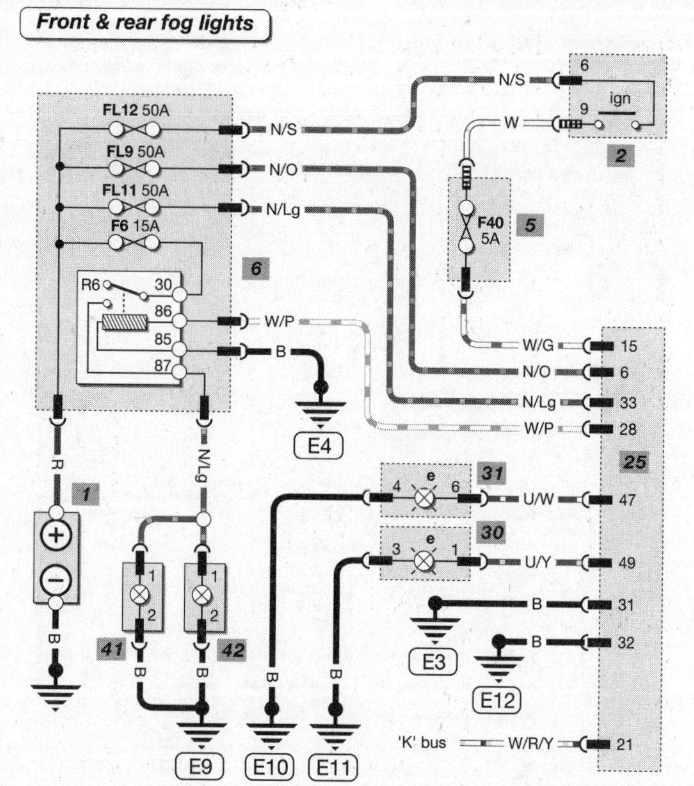

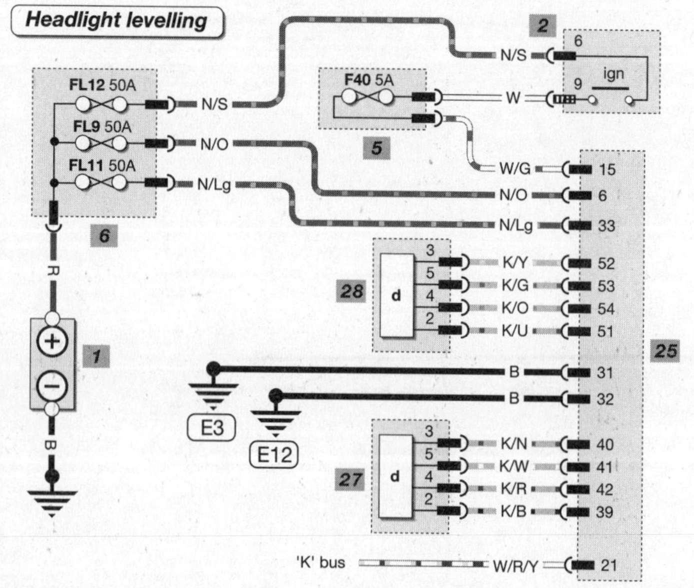

Diagram 6

Wire colours

B	Black	P	Purple
G	Green	R	Red
K	Pink	S	Grey
Lg	Light green	U	Blue
N	Brown	W	White
O	Orange	Y	Yellow

Key to items

1 Battery
2 Ignition switch
5 Passenger fusebox
6 Engine fusebox
25 Light switch control unit
30 LH rear light cluster
a = tail light
b = stop light
c = reversing light
d = direction indicator
31 RH rear light cluster (as above)
43 Trailer control unit
44 Trailer fuse
45 Single trailer socket
46 Twin trailer socket
47 Clock
48 Diagnostic connector
49 Interlock control unit
50 Shift interlock solenoid

H33399

Trailer socket

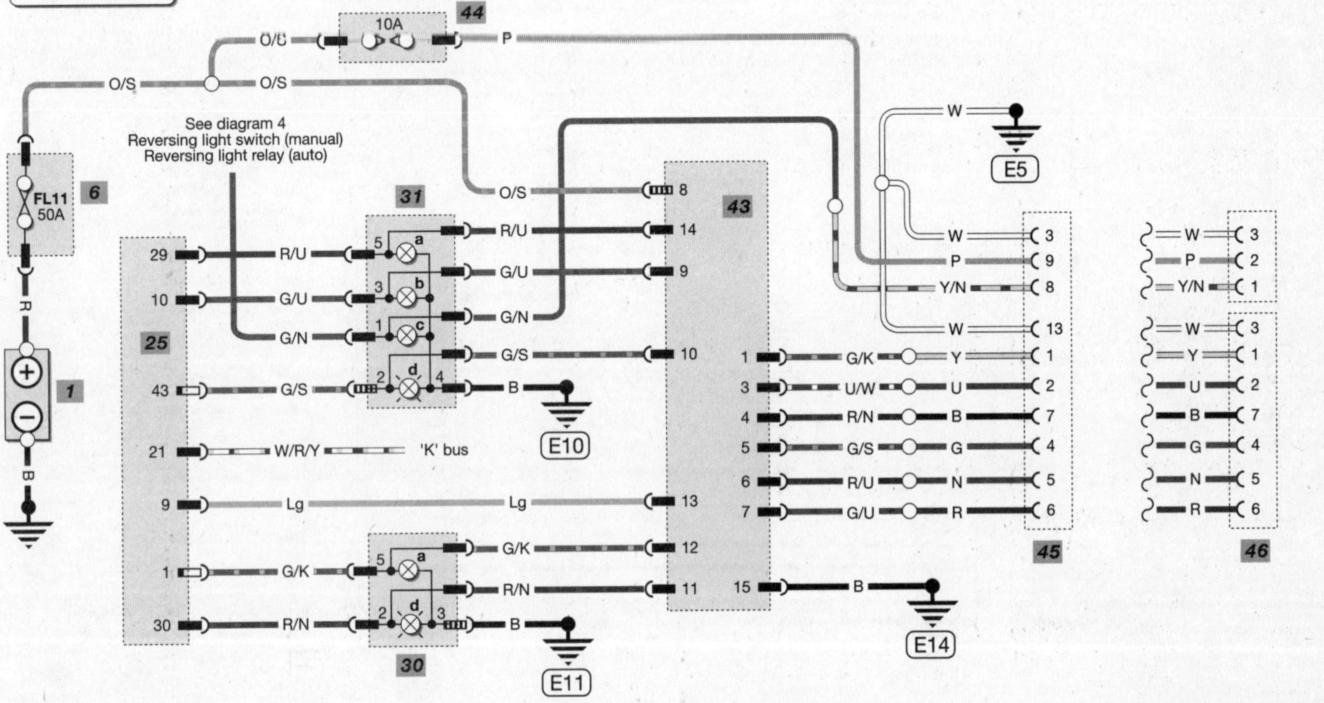

Clock & diagnostic connector

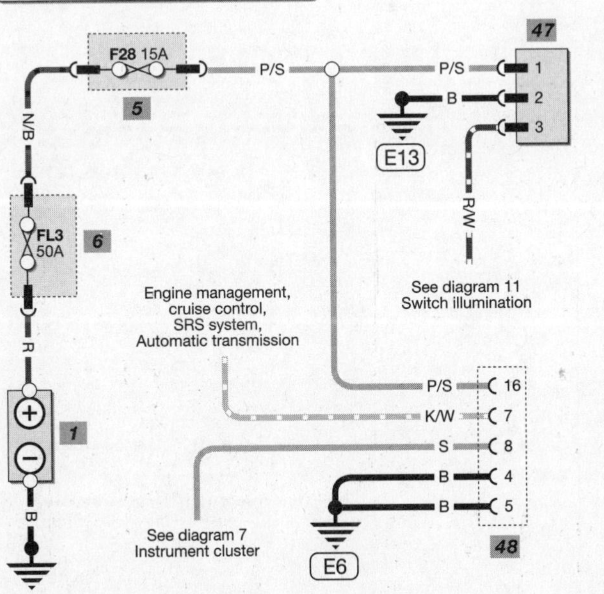

A/T shift interlock

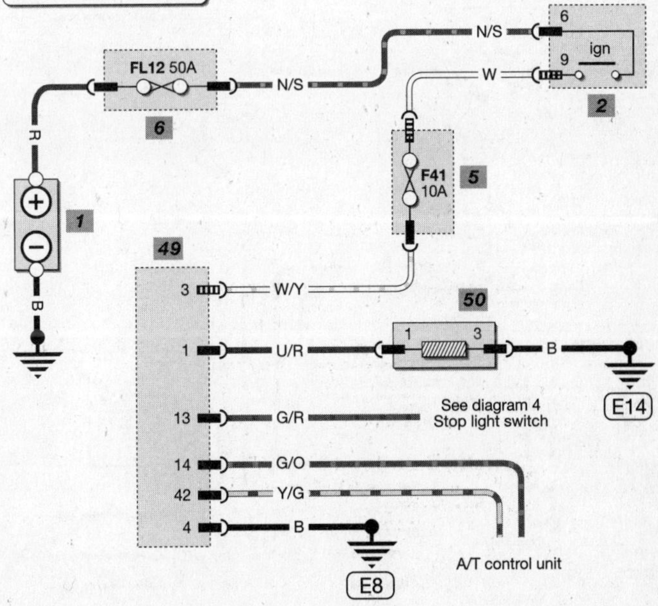

Diagram 7

Wire colours

B	Black	**P**	Purple
G	Green	**R**	Red
K	Pink	**S**	Grey
Lg	Light green	**U**	Blue
N	Brown	**W**	White
O	Orange	**Y**	Yellow

Key to items

1 Battery
2 Ignition switch
5 Passenger fusebox
6 Engine fusebox
R2 = heated rear window relay
26 Steering column switch
a = direction indicator
55 Instrument cluster
56 Oil pressure switch
57 Low washer fluid switch
58 Airbag control unit
59 Body control unit
60 Seatbelt switch
61 ABS control unit
62 Brake fluid switch
63 Handbrake switch
64 Fuel tank unit
65 Air temperature sensor
66 Pad wear sensor
67 Air temperature control unit
68 Filter
69 Heated rear window
70 Heated rear window switch
71 Heated washer jet

H33400

Instrument cluster

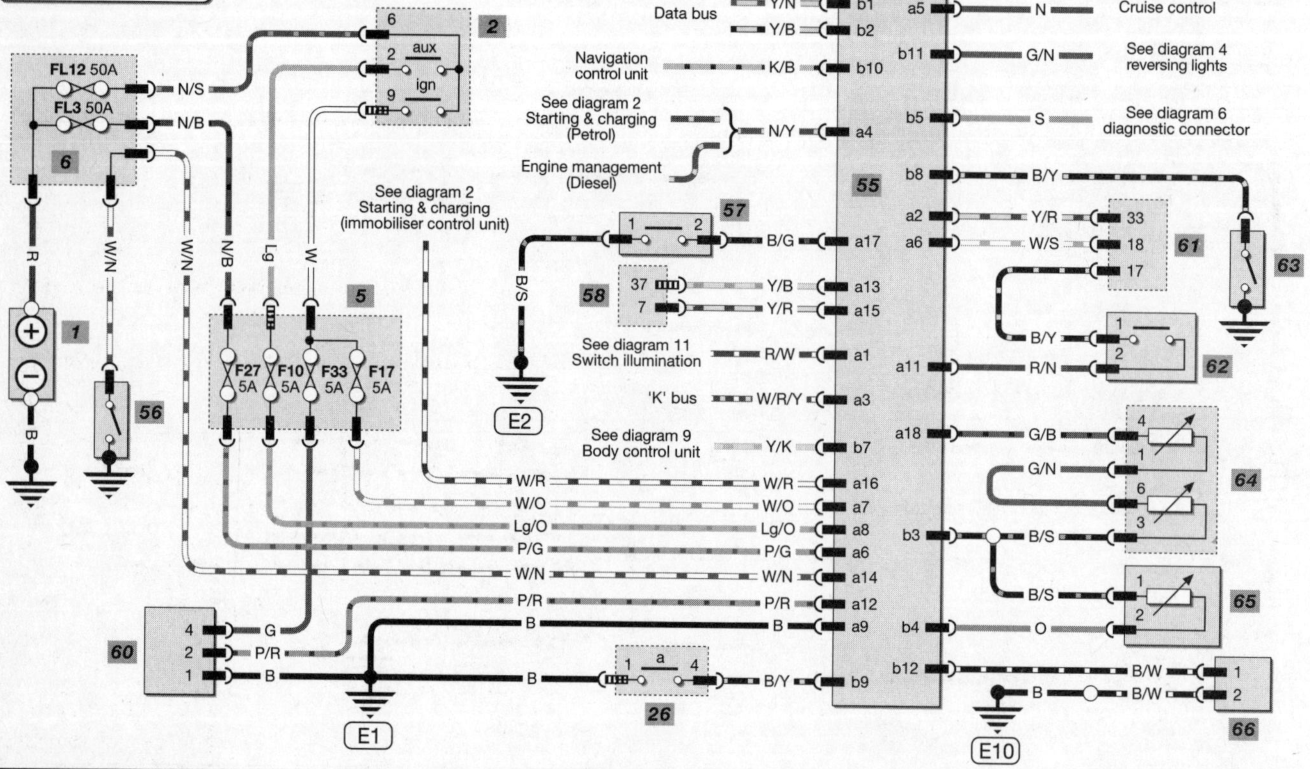

Heated rear window

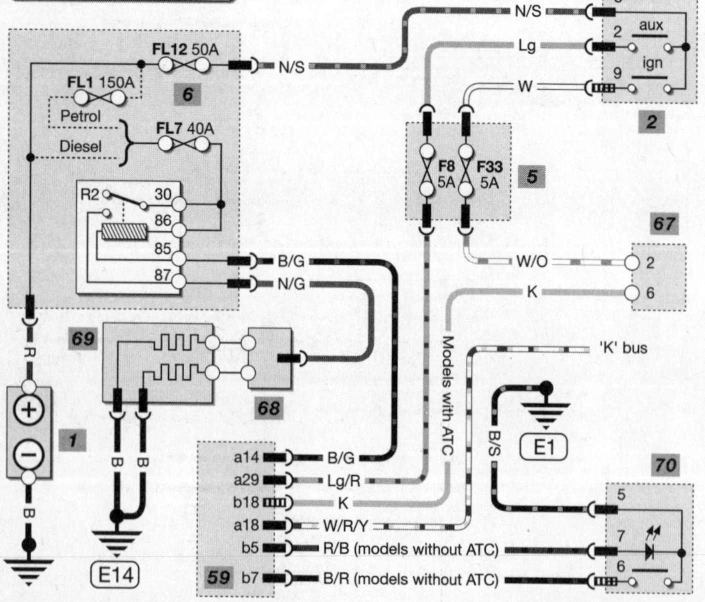

Heated washer jets

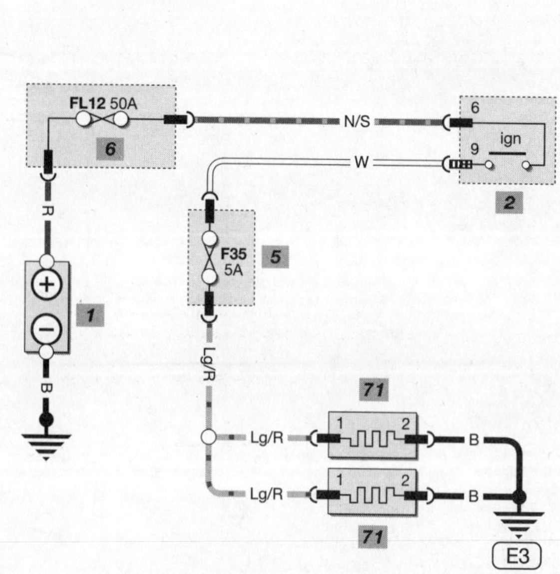

Wire colours

B	Black	P	Purple
G	Green	R	Red
K	Pink	S	Grey
Lg	Light green	U	Blue
N	Brown	W	White
O	Orange	Y	Yellow

Key to items

Diagram 8

1 Battery
2 Ignition switch
5 Passenger fusebox
R3 = power washer relay
6 Engine fusebox
R1 = wiper relay 1
R3 = wiper relay 2
25 Light switch control unit
59 Body control unit
75 Headlight washer pump
76 Wash/wipe switch
a = slow/fast
b = flick
c = intermittent
d = washer
77 Front wiper motor
78 Rain sensor
79 Windscreen washer pump
80 Sunroof control unit
81 Sunroof switch

H33401

Headlight washer

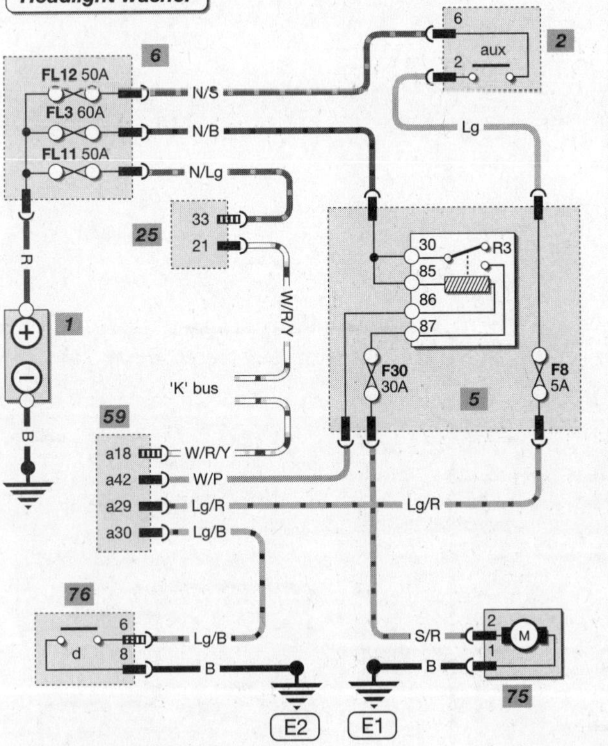

Wash/wipe

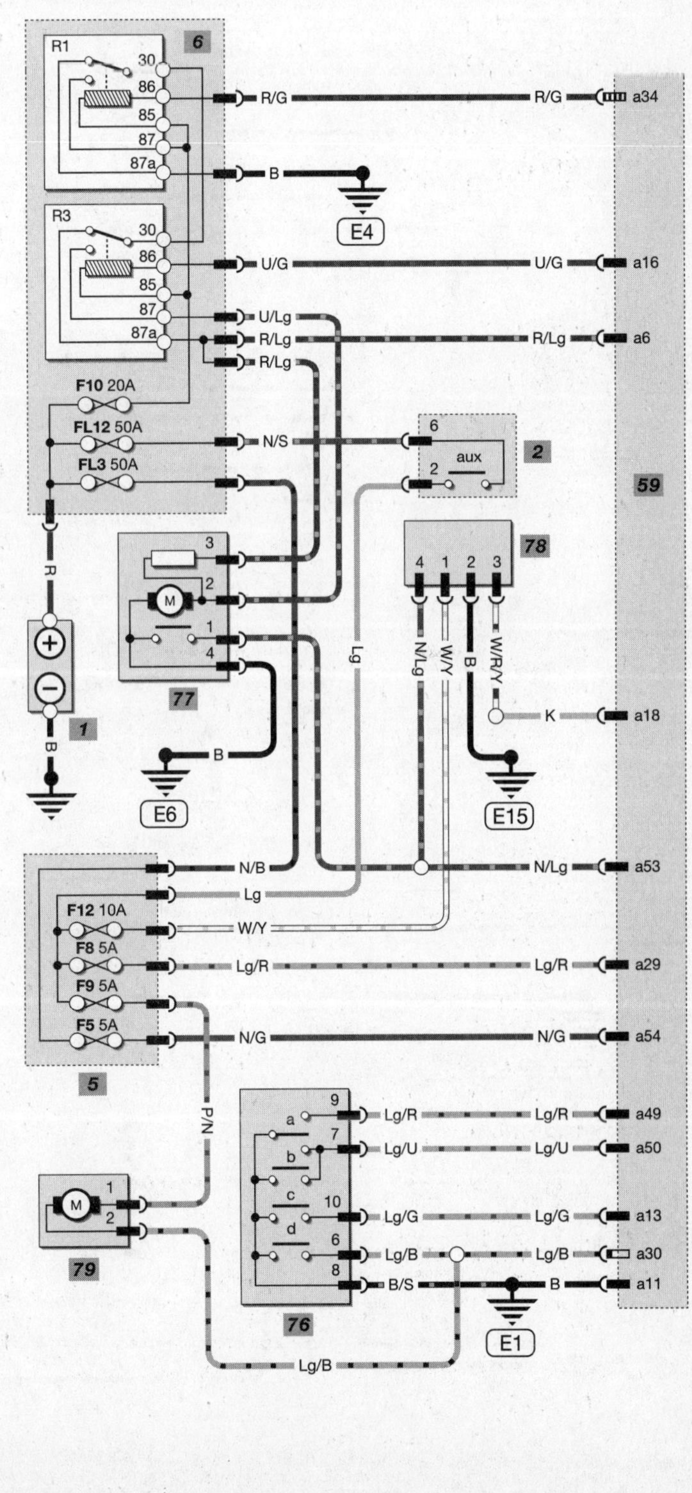

Sunroof

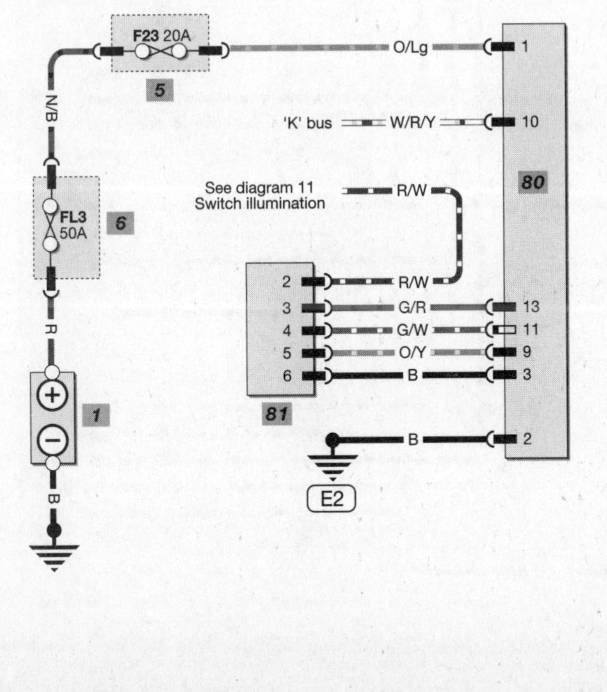

Wire colours

B	Black	**P**	Purple
G	Green	**R**	Red
K	Pink	**S**	Grey
Lg	Light green	**U**	Blue
N	Brown	**W**	White
O	Orange	**Y**	Yellow

Key to items

1 Battery
5 Passenger fusebox
6 Engine fusebox
59 Body control unit
85 Inertia switch
86 Ultra sonic module
87 Fuel filler flap motor
88 LH front door lock
89 LH rear door lock
90 RH front door lock
91 RH rear door lock
92 Boot release switch
93 RF receiver
94 Boot lock motor
95 Boot ajar switch
96 Bonnet ajar switch
97 Central locking switch

Diagram 9

H33402

Central locking

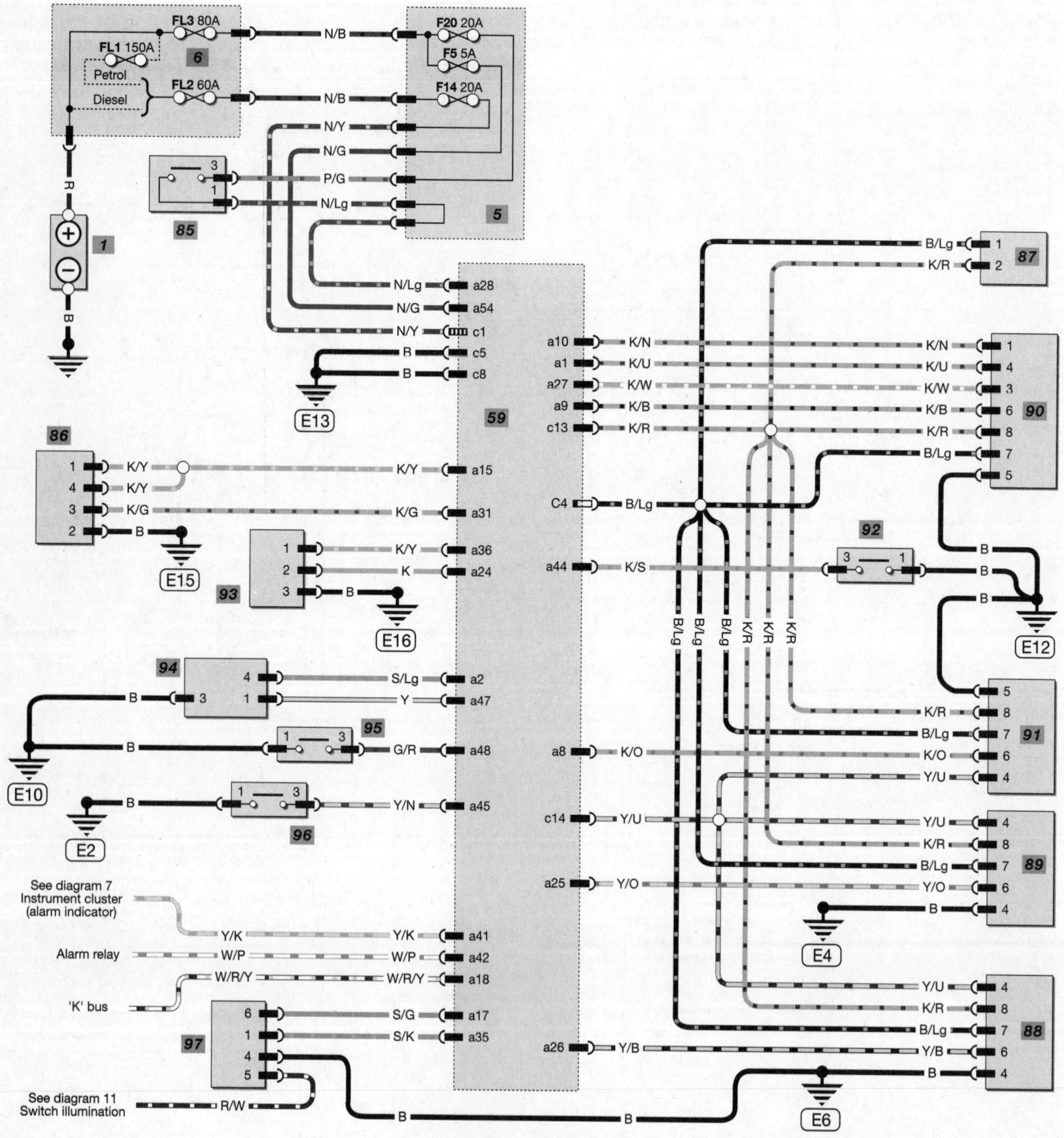

Diagram 10

Wire colours

B	Black	P	Purple
G	Green	R	Red
K	Pink	S	Grey
Lg	Light green	U	Blue
N	Brown	W	White
O	Orange	Y	Yellow

Key to items

1 Battery
2 Ignition switch
5 Passenger fusebox
6 Engine fusebox
59 Body control unit
100 LH front window switch
101 LH rear window switch
102 RH front window switch
103 RH rear window switch
104 LH front window motor
105 LH rear window motor
106 RH front window motor
107 RH rear window motor
108 Driver's anti-trap switch
109 Mirror control switch
110 LH door mirror assembly
a = fold motor
b = vertical adjustment
c = horizontal adjustment
d = heater
111 RH door mirror assembly
(items a to d as above)

H33403

Electric windows

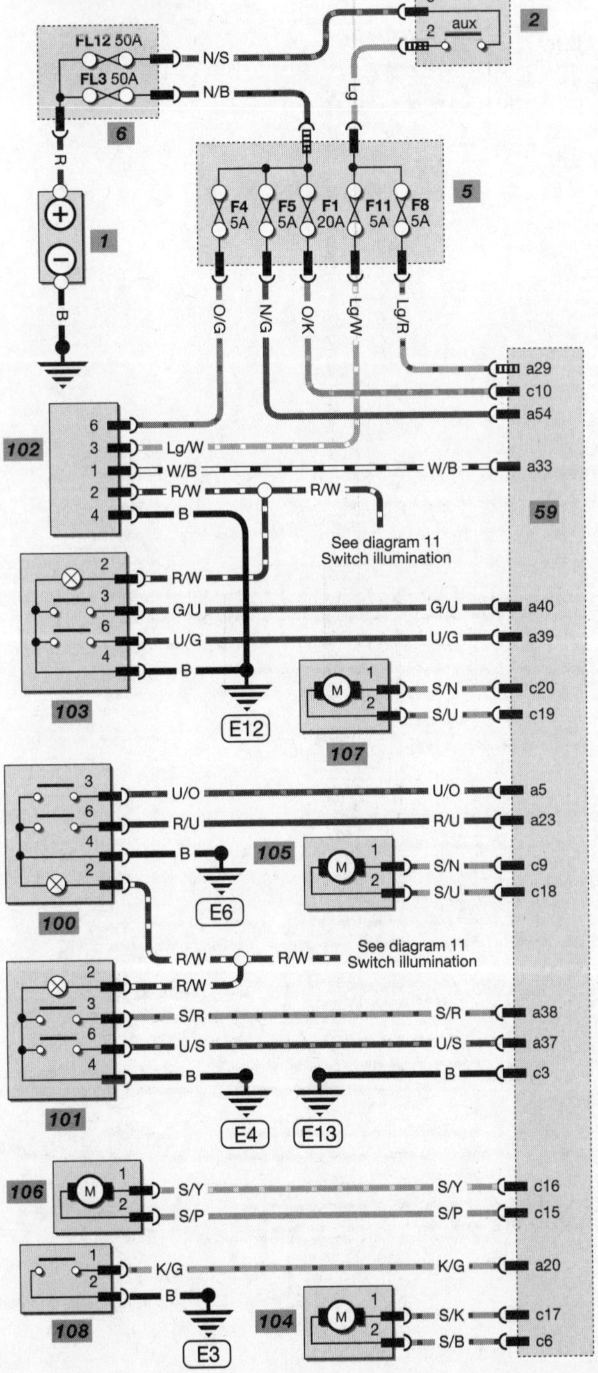

Electric mirrors

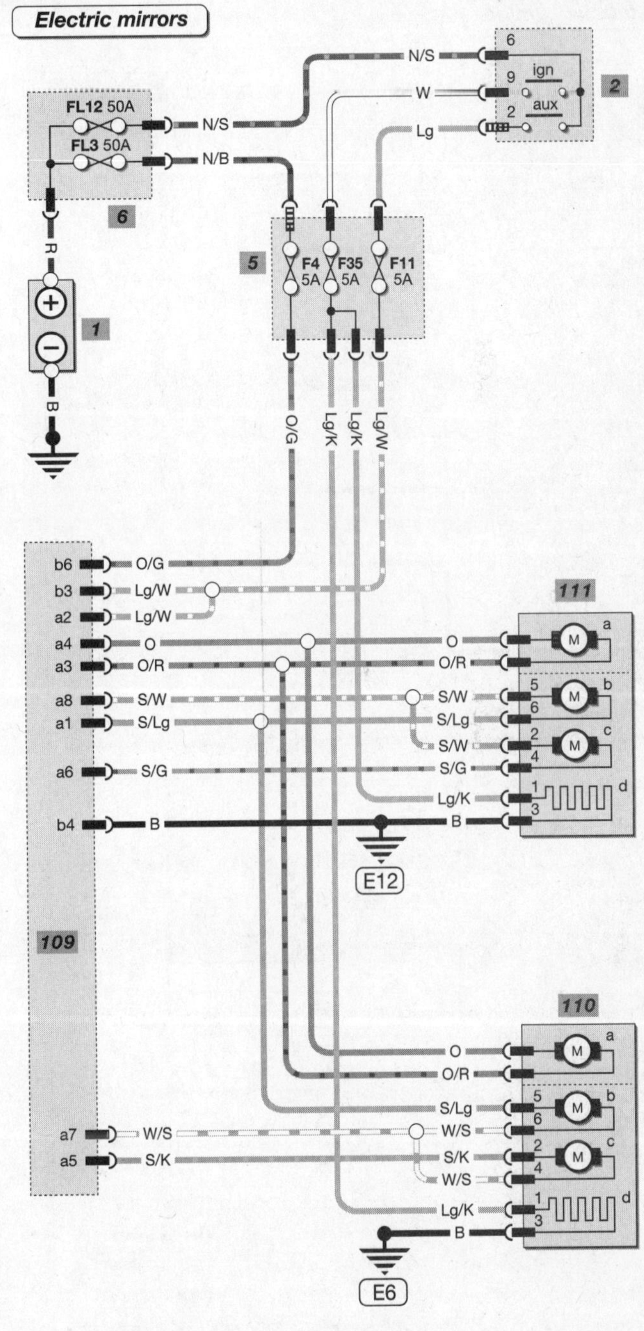

Diagram 11

Wire colours

B	Black	P	Purple
G	Green	R	Red
K	Pink	S	Grey
Lg	Light green	U	Blue
N	Brown	W	White
O	Orange	Y	Yellow

Key to items

1 Battery
2 Ignition switch
5 Passenger fusebox
6 Engine fusebox
11 Steering wheel clock springs
25 Light switch control unit
59 Body control unit
115 Boot light
116 Front interior/map reading light
117 Rear map reading light
118 LH vanity mirror illumination
119 RH vanity mirror illumination
120 Glovebox light
121 Radio/cassette player
122 CD player
123 Remote control switches
124 Aerial
125 LH front speaker
126 LH front tweeter
127 LH rear speaker
128 RH front speaker
129 RH front tweeter
130 RH rear speaker

H33404

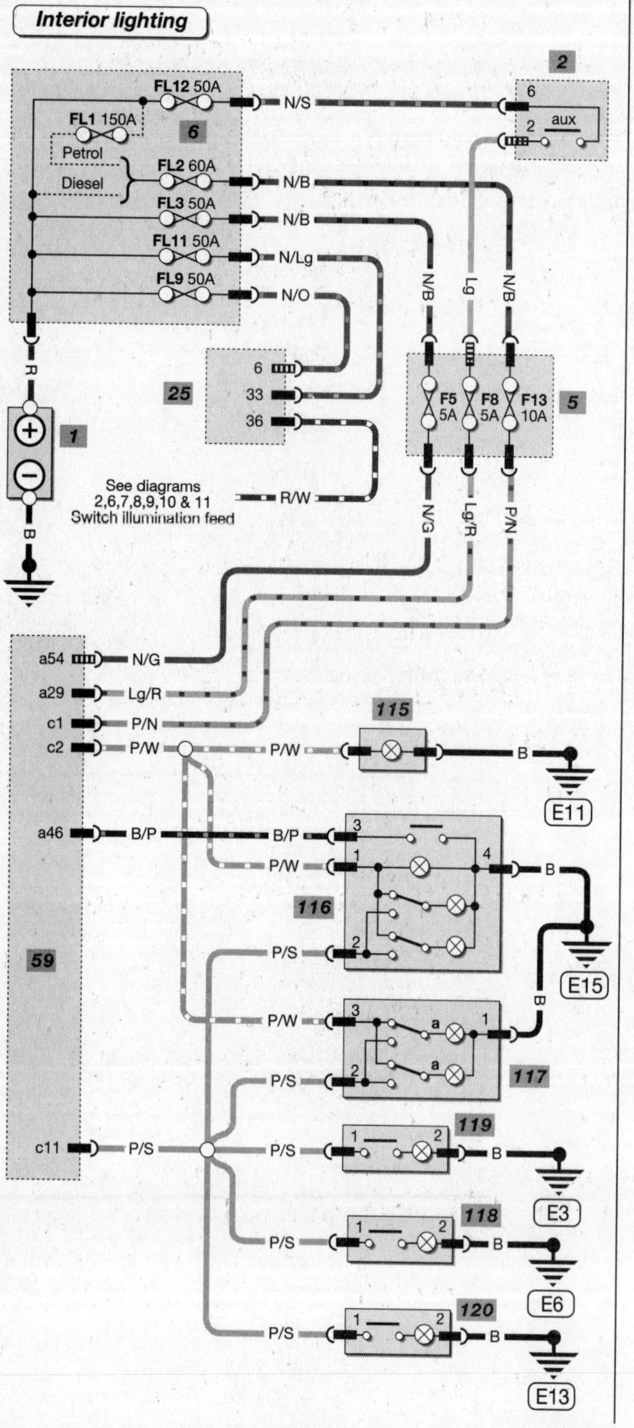

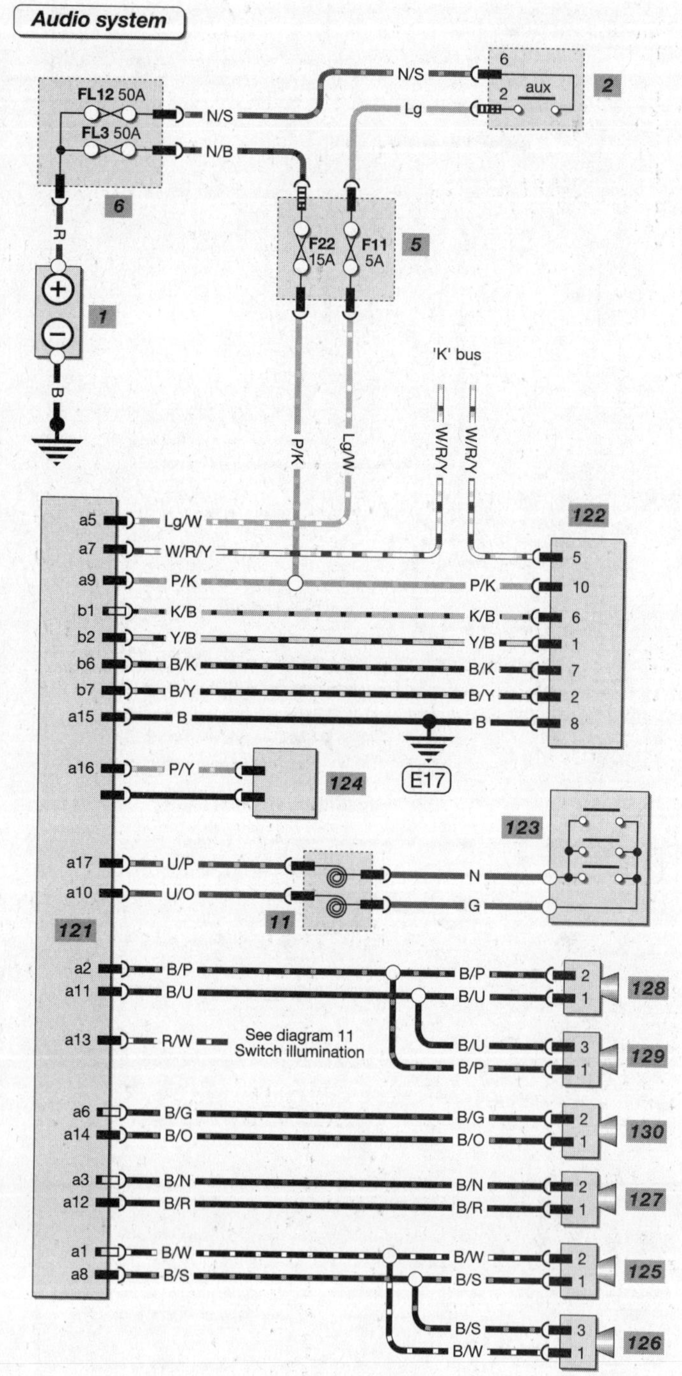

Dimensions and weights

Note: *All figures are approximate, and may vary according to model. Refer to manufacturer's data for exact figures.*

Dimensions

Overall length:	
Saloon	4747 mm
Tourer	4791 mm
Overall width – excluding mirrors	1778 mm
Overall height (unladen):	
Saloon	1424 mm
Estate	477 mm
Wheelbase	2746 mm

Kerb weights

Saloon:	
Petrol models (typical):	
1.8 litre engines	1400 to 1530 kg
V6 engines	1470 to 1625 kg
Diesel models (typical)	1510 to 1635 kg
Maximum gross vehicle weight	1940 to 2030 kg
Tourer:	
Petrol models (typical):	
1.8 litre engines	1460 to 1580 kg
V6 engines	1535 to 1680 kg
Diesel models (typical)	1560 to 1670 kg
Maximum gross vehicle weight	1980 to 2120 kg

Conversion factors

Length (distance)

Inches (in)	x 25.4	= Millimetres (mm)	x 0.0394	= Inches (in)
Feet (ft)	x 0.305	= Metres (m)	x 3.281	= Feet (ft)
Miles	x 1.609	= Kilometres (km)	x 0.621	= Miles

Volume (capacity)

Cubic inches (cu in; in³)	x 16.387	= Cubic centimetres (cc; cm³)	x 0.061	= Cubic inches (cu in; in³)
Imperial pints (Imp pt)	x 0.568	= Litres (l)	x 1.76	= Imperial pints (Imp pt)
Imperial quarts (Imp qt)	x 1.137	= Litres (l)	x 0.88	= Imperial quarts (Imp qt)
Imperial quarts (Imp qt)	x 1.201	= US quarts (US qt)	x 0.833	= Imperial quarts (Imp qt)
US quarts (US qt)	x 0.946	= Litres (l)	x 1.057	= US quarts (US qt)
Imperial gallons (Imp gal)	x 4.546	= Litres (l)	x 0.22	= Imperial gallons (Imp gal)
Imperial gallons (Imp gal)	x 1.201	= US gallons (US gal)	x 0.833	= Imperial gallons (Imp gal)
US gallons (US gal)	x 3.785	= Litres (l)	x 0.264	= US gallons (US gal)

Mass (weight)

Ounces (oz)	x 28.35	= Grams (g)	x 0.035	= Ounces (oz)
Pounds (lb)	x 0.454	= Kilograms (kg)	x 2.205	= Pounds (lb)

Force

Ounces-force (ozf; oz)	x 0.278	= Newtons (N)	x 3.6	= Ounces-force (ozf; oz)
Pounds-force (lbf; lb)	x 4.448	= Newtons (N)	x 0.225	= Pounds-force (lbf; lb)
Newtons (N)	x 0.1	= Kilograms-force (kgf; kg)	x 9.81	= Newtons (N)

Pressure

Pounds-force per square inch (psi; lbf/in²; lb/in²)	x 0.070	= Kilograms-force per square centimetre (kgf/cm²; kg/cm²)	x 14.223	= Pounds-force per square inch (psi; lbf/in²; lb/in²)
Pounds-force per square inch (psi; lbf/in²; lb/in²)	x 0.068	= Atmospheres (atm)	x 14.696	= Pounds-force per square inch (psi; lbf/in²; lb/in²)
Pounds-force per square inch (psi; lbf/in²; lb/in²)	x 0.069	= Bars	x 14.5	= Pounds-force per square inch (psi; lbf/in²; lb/in²)
Pounds-force per square inch (psi; lbf/in²; lb/in²)	x 6.895	= Kilopascals (kPa)	x 0.145	= Pounds-force per square inch (psi; lbf/in²; lb/in²)
Kilopascals (kPa)	x 0.01	= Kilograms-force per square centimetre (kgf/cm²; kg/cm²)	x 98.1	= Kilopascals (kPa)
Millibar (mbar)	x 100	= Pascals (Pa)	x 0.01	= Millibar (mbar)
Millibar (mbar)	x 0.0145	= Pounds-force per square inch (psi; lbf/in²; lb/in²)	x 68.947	= Millibar (mbar)
Millibar (mbar)	x 0.75	= Millimetres of mercury (mmHg)	x 1.333	= Millibar (mbar)
Millibar (mbar)	x 0.401	= Inches of water (inH$_2$O)	x 2.491	= Millibar (mbar)
Millimetres of mercury (mmHg)	x 0.535	= Inches of water (inH$_2$O)	x 1.868	= Millimetres of mercury (mmHg)
Inches of water (inH$_2$O)	x 0.036	= Pounds-force per square inch (psi; lbf/in²; lb/in²)	x 27.68	= Inches of water (inH$_2$O)

Torque (moment of force)

Pounds-force inches (lbf in; lb in)	x 1.152	= Kilograms-force centimetre (kgf cm; kg cm)	x 0.868	= Pounds-force inches (lbf in; lb in)
Pounds-force inches (lbf in; lb in)	x 0.113	= Newton metres (Nm)	x 8.85	= Pounds-force inches (lbf in; lb in)
Pounds-force inches (lbf in; lb in)	x 0.083	= Pounds-force feet (lbf ft; lb ft)	x 12	= Pounds-force inches (lbf in; lb in)
Pounds-force feet (lbf ft; lb ft)	x 0.138	= Kilograms-force metres (kgf m; kg m)	x 7.233	= Pounds-force feet (lbf ft; lb ft)
Pounds-force feet (lbf ft; lb ft)	x 1.356	= Newton metres (Nm)	x 0.738	= Pounds-force feet (lbf ft; lb ft)
Newton metres (Nm)	x 0.102	= Kilograms-force metres (kgf m; kg m)	x 9.804	= Newton metres (Nm)

Power

Horsepower (hp)	x 745.7	= Watts (W)	x 0.0013	= Horsepower (hp)

Velocity (speed)

Miles per hour (miles/hr; mph)	x 1.609	= Kilometres per hour (km/hr; kph)	x 0.621	= Miles per hour (miles/hr; mph)

Fuel consumption*

Miles per gallon, Imperial (mpg)	x 0.354	= Kilometres per litre (km/l)	x 2.825	= Miles per gallon, Imperial (mpg)
Miles per gallon, US (mpg)	x 0.425	= Kilometres per litre (km/l)	x 2.352	= Miles per gallon, US (mpg)

Temperature

Degrees Fahrenheit = (°C x 1.8) + 32

Degrees Celsius (Degrees Centigrade; °C) = (°F - 32) x 0.56

* *It is common practice to convert from miles per gallon (mpg) to litres/100 kilometres (l/100km), where mpg x l/100 km = 282*

Spare parts are available from many sources, including maker's appointed garages, accessory shops, and motor factors. To be sure of obtaining the correct parts, it will sometimes be necessary to quote the vehicle identification number (see *Vehicle identification*). If possible, it can also be useful to take the old parts along for positive identification. Items such as starter motors and alternators may be available under a service exchange scheme – any parts returned should always be clean.

Our advice regarding spare part sources is as follows.

Officially-appointed garages

Following the collapse of MG Rover in 2005, there is no longer any such thing as an official MG Rover dealer. In the UK, a company called XPart (main suppliers of MG Rover genuine spare parts) have set up a network of AutoService centres – most of these are former dealers, now reborn as MG Rover specialists, offering servicing and spare parts support. At the time of writing, we also understand that Unipart spares continue to be available from motor factors, and that Lincoln-based Rimmer Brothers can supply MG Rover spares by mail order.

Accessory shops

These are very good places to buy materials and components needed for the maintenance of your car (oil, air and fuel filters, spark plugs, light bulbs, drivebelts, oils and greases, brake pads, touch-up paint, etc). Components of this nature sold by a reputable shop are of the same standard as those used by the car manufacturer.

Besides components, these shops also sell tools and general accessories, usually have convenient opening hours, charge lower prices, and can often be found not far from home. Some accessory shops have parts counters where the components needed for almost any repair job can be purchased or ordered.

Motor factors

Good factors will stock all the more important components which wear out comparatively quickly, and can sometimes supply individual components needed for the overhaul of a larger assembly (eg brake seals and hydraulic parts, bearing shells, pistons, valves, alternator brushes). They may also handle work such as cylinder block reboring, crankshaft regrinding and balancing, etc.

Tyre and exhaust specialists

These outlets may be independent, or members of a local or national chain. They frequently offer competitive prices when compared with a main dealer or local garage, but it will pay to obtain several quotes before making a decision. When researching prices, also ask what 'extras' may be added – for instance, fitting a new valve and balancing the wheel are both commonly charged on top of the price of a new tyre.

Other sources

Beware of parts or materials obtained from market stalls, car boot sales or similar outlets. Such items are not invariably sub-standard, but there is little chance of compensation if they do prove unsatisfactory. In the case of safety-critical components such as brake pads, there is the risk not only of financial loss but also of an accident causing injury or death.

Second-hand components or assemblies obtained from a car breaker can be a good buy in some circumstances, but this sort of purchase is best made by the experienced DIY mechanic.

Vehicle identification

Modifications are a continuing and unpublicised process in car manufacture, quite apart from major model changes. Spare parts manuals and lists are compiled upon a numerical basis, the individual vehicle identification numbers being essential to correct identification of the component concerned.

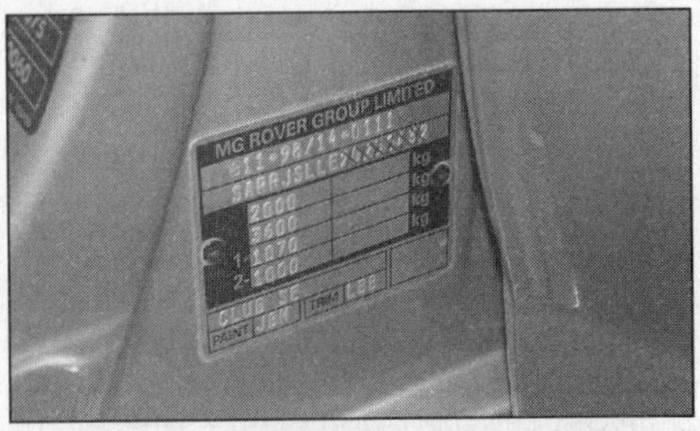

Vehicle identification plate location

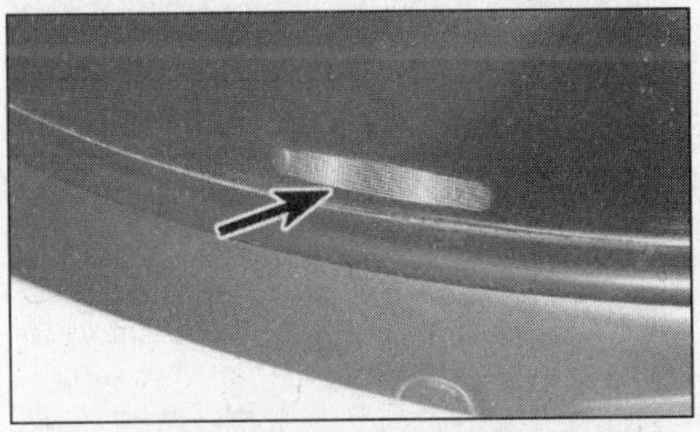

The VIN can also be viewed through the windscreen

When ordering spare parts, always give as much information as possible. Quote the car model, year of manufacture, body and engine numbers as appropriate.

The *vehicle identification plate* is located at the base of the passenger's door B-pillar, and can be viewed with the door open. In addition to many other details, it carries the Vehicle Identification Number (VIN), maximum vehicle weight information, and codes for interior trim and body colours **(see illustration)**.

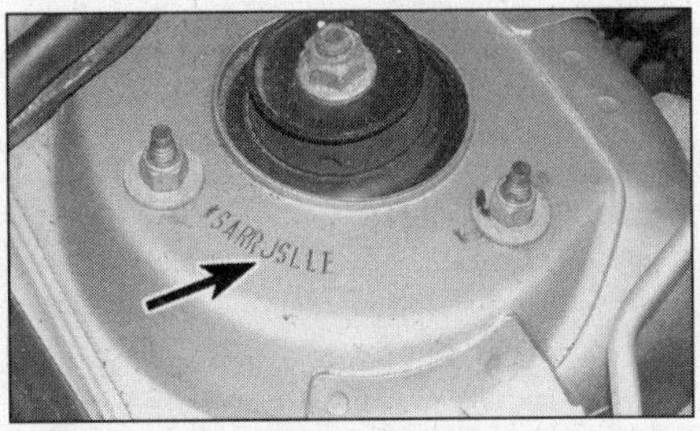

The VIN is stamped into the suspension strut mounting

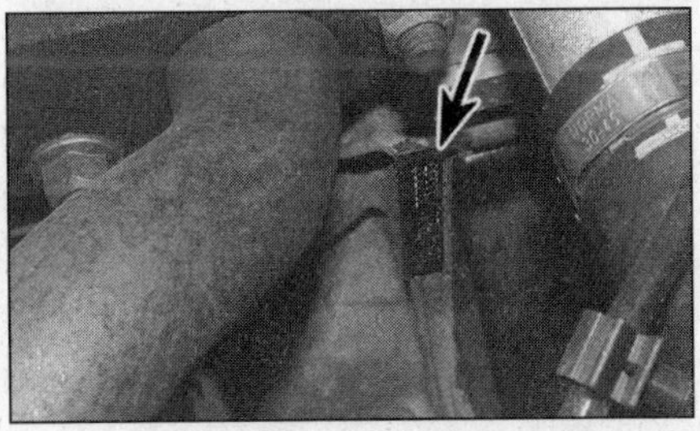

1.8 litre engine number location

The *Vehicle Identification Number (VIN)* is given on the vehicle identification plate. It is also stamped on the right-hand front suspension strut mounting in the engine compartment, and may also be viewed through the base of the windscreen on the passenger's side **(see illustrations)**.

The *body number and paint code numbers* are located on the vehicle identification plate.

The *engine number* is stamped on the front of the petrol engine block, at the transmission end – on V6 engines, the front cylinder head may make viewing difficult, and this may be easier from below **(see illustrations)**. On diesel engines, the number appears on a raised boss just above the sump, halfway along the front.

V6 engine number location (transmission removed)

Whenever servicing, repair or overhaul work is carried out on the car or its components, observe the following procedures and instructions. This will assist in carrying out the operation efficiently and to a professional standard of workmanship.

Joint mating faces and gaskets

When separating components at their mating faces, never insert screwdrivers or similar implements into the joint between the faces in order to prise them apart. This can cause severe damage which results in oil leaks, coolant leaks, etc upon reassembly. Separation is usually achieved by tapping along the joint with a soft-faced hammer in order to break the seal. However, note that this method may not be suitable where dowels are used for component location.

Where a gasket is used between the mating faces of two components, a new one must be fitted on reassembly; fit it dry unless otherwise stated in the repair procedure. Make sure that the mating faces are clean and dry, with all traces of old gasket removed. When cleaning a joint face, use a tool which is unlikely to score or damage the face, and remove any burrs or nicks with an oilstone or fine file.

Make sure that tapped holes are cleaned with a pipe cleaner, and keep them free of jointing compound, if this is being used, unless specifically instructed otherwise.

Ensure that all orifices, channels or pipes are clear, and blow through them, preferably using compressed air.

Oil seals

Oil seals can be removed by levering them out with a wide flat-bladed screwdriver or similar implement. Alternatively, a number of self-tapping screws may be screwed into the seal, and these used as a purchase for pliers or some similar device in order to pull the seal free.

Whenever an oil seal is removed from its working location, either individually or as part of an assembly, it should be renewed.

The very fine sealing lip of the seal is easily damaged, and will not seal if the surface it contacts is not completely clean and free from scratches, nicks or grooves. If the original sealing surface of the component cannot be restored, and the manufacturer has not made provision for slight relocation of the seal relative to the sealing surface, the component should be renewed.

Protect the lips of the seal from any surface which may damage them in the course of fitting. Use tape or a conical sleeve where possible. Lubricate the seal lips with oil before fitting and, on dual-lipped seals, fill the space between the lips with grease.

Unless otherwise stated, oil seals must be fitted with their sealing lips toward the lubricant to be sealed.

Use a tubular drift or block of wood of the appropriate size to install the seal and, if the seal housing is shouldered, drive the seal down to the shoulder. If the seal housing is unshouldered, the seal should be fitted with its face flush with the housing top face (unless otherwise instructed).

Screw threads and fastenings

Seized nuts, bolts and screws are quite a common occurrence where corrosion has set in, and the use of penetrating oil or releasing fluid will often overcome this problem if the offending item is soaked for a while before attempting to release it. The use of an impact driver may also provide a means of releasing such stubborn fastening devices, when used in conjunction with the appropriate screwdriver bit or socket. If none of these methods works, it may be necessary to resort to the careful application of heat, or the use of a hacksaw or nut splitter device.

Studs are usually removed by locking two nuts together on the threaded part, and then using a spanner on the lower nut to unscrew the stud. Studs or bolts which have broken off below the surface of the component in which they are mounted can sometimes be removed using a stud extractor. Always ensure that a blind tapped hole is completely free from oil, grease, water or other fluid before installing the bolt or stud. Failure to do this could cause the housing to crack due to the hydraulic action of the bolt or stud as it is screwed in.

When tightening a castellated nut to accept a split pin, tighten the nut to the specified torque, where applicable, and then tighten further to the next split pin hole. Never slacken the nut to align the split pin hole, unless stated in the repair procedure.

When checking or retightening a nut or bolt to a specified torque setting, slacken the nut or bolt by a quarter of a turn, and then retighten to the specified setting. However, this should not be attempted where angular tightening has been used.

For some screw fastenings, notably cylinder head bolts or nuts, torque wrench settings are no longer specified for the latter stages of tightening, "angle-tightening" being called up instead. Typically, a fairly low torque wrench setting will be applied to the bolts/nuts in the correct sequence, followed by one or more stages of tightening through specified angles.

Locknuts, locktabs and washers

Any fastening which will rotate against a component or housing during tightening should always have a washer between it and the relevant component or housing.

Spring or split washers should always be renewed when they are used to lock a critical component such as a big-end bearing retaining bolt or nut. Locktabs which are folded over to retain a nut or bolt should always be renewed.

Self-locking nuts can be re-used in non-critical areas, providing resistance can be felt when the locking portion passes over the bolt or stud thread. However, it should be noted that self-locking stiffnuts tend to lose their effectiveness after long periods of use, and should then be renewed as a matter of course.

Split pins must always be replaced with new ones of the correct size for the hole.

When thread-locking compound is found on the threads of a fastener which is to be re-used, it should be cleaned off with a wire brush and solvent, and fresh compound applied on reassembly.

Special tools

Some repair procedures in this manual entail the use of special tools such as a press, two or three-legged pullers, spring compressors, etc. Wherever possible, suitable readily-available alternatives to the manufacturer's special tools are described, and are shown in use. In some instances, where no alternative is possible, it has been necessary to resort to the use of a manufacturer's tool, and this has been done for reasons of safety as well as the efficient completion of the repair operation. Unless you are highly-skilled and have a thorough understanding of the procedures described, never attempt to bypass the use of any special tool when the procedure described specifies its use. Not only is there a very great risk of personal injury, but expensive damage could be caused to the components involved.

Environmental considerations

When disposing of used engine oil, brake fluid, antifreeze, etc, give due consideration to any detrimental environmental effects. Do not, for instance, pour any of the above liquids down drains into the general sewage system, or onto the ground to soak away. Many local council refuse tips provide a facility for waste oil disposal, as do some garages. If none of these facilities are available, consult your local Environmental Health Department, or the National Rivers Authority, for further advice.

With the universal tightening-up of legislation regarding the emission of environmentally-harmful substances from motor vehicles, most vehicles have tamperproof devices fitted to the main adjustment points of the fuel system. These devices are primarily designed to prevent unqualified persons from adjusting the fuel/air mixture, with the chance of a consequent increase in toxic emissions. If such devices are found during servicing or overhaul, they should, wherever possible, be renewed or refitted in accordance with the manufacturer's requirements or current legislation.

OIL BANK LINE
0800 66 33 66
www.oilbankline.org.uk

Note: It is antisocial and illegal to dump oil down the drain. To find the location of your local oil recycling bank, call this number free.

The jack supplied with the car's tool kit should only be used for changing the roadwheels - see *Wheel changing* at the front of this book. When carrying out any other kind of work, raise the car using a hydraulic (or 'trolley') jack, and always supplement the jack with axle stands positioned under the jacking/support points. If the roadwheels do not have to be removed, consider using wheel ramps - if wished, these can be placed under the wheels once the car has been raised using a hydraulic jack, and then lowered onto the ramps so that it is resting on its wheels.

Only ever jack the car up on a solid, level surface. If there is even a slight slope, take great care that the car cannot move as the wheels are lifted off the ground. Jacking up on an uneven or gravelled surface is not recommended, as the weight of the car will not be evenly distributed, and the jack may slip as the car is raised.

As far as possible, do not leave the car unattended once it has been raised, particularly if children are playing nearby.

Before jacking up the front of the car, ensure that the handbrake is firmly applied. When jacking up the rear of the car, place wooden chocks in front of the front wheels, and engage first gear (or P).

To raise the front of the car, position the jack head underneath the front subframe, on or near one of the mounting bolts, and use a flat piece of wood to spread the load. A front jacking point is provided in the centre of the subframe, at the front – this should be used where possible. Always supplement the jack with axle stands under the sill jacking points **(see illustrations)**.

At the rear, a central lifting point is again provided, under the central towing eye **(see illustration)**. Otherwise, place a wide, flat piece of wood centrally under the rear jacking points to spread the load, and position the jack head and axle stand as close together either side of the jacking point as possible.

Do not jack the car under any other part of the sill, sump, floor pan, or directly under any of the steering or suspension components.

Never work under, around, or near a raised vehicle, unless it is adequately supported on stands. Do not rely on a jack alone, as even a hydraulic jack could fail under load.

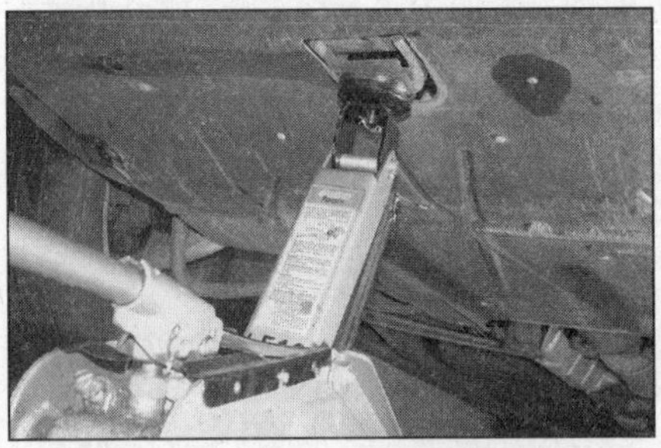

Trolley jack positioned under the jacking point on the front subframe

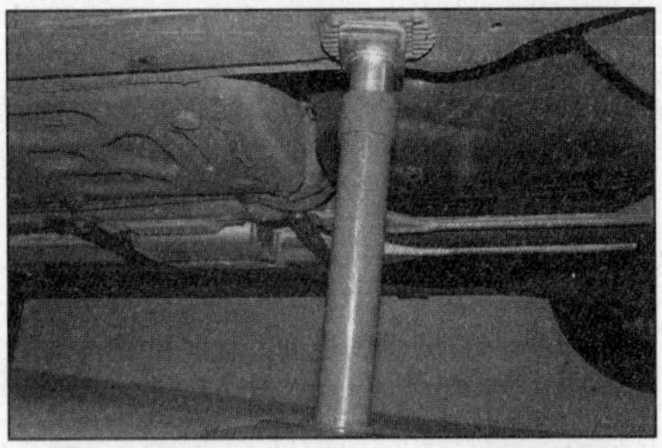

Place axle stands under the sill jacking points

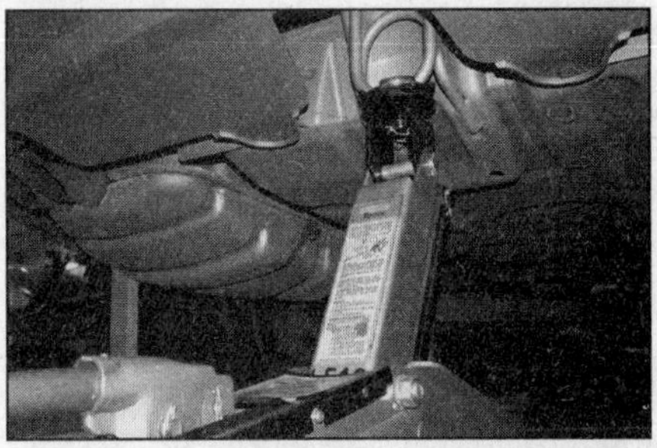

Trolley jack under the rear towing eye

Disconnecting the battery

Several systems fitted to the car require battery power to be available at all times, either to ensure that their continued operation (such as the clock) or to maintain control unit memories (such as that in the engine management system's control module) which would be wiped if the battery were to be disconnected. Whenever the battery is to be disconnected therefore, first note the following, to ensure that there are no unforeseen consequences of this action:

a) *First, on any vehicle with central locking, it is a wise precaution to remove the ignition key, and to keep it with you, so that it does not get locked in, if the central locking should engage accidentally when the battery is reconnected.*

b) *The car's engine control module (ECM) will lose the information stored in its memory when the battery is disconnected. This includes idling and operating values, and any fault codes detected – in the case of the fault codes, if it is thought likely that the system has developed a fault for which the corresponding code has been logged, the car must be taken to a suitably-equipped garage for the codes to be read, using the special diagnostic equipment necessary for this. Whenever the battery is disconnected, the information relating to idle speed control and other operating values will have to be re-programmed into the unit's memory. The ECM does this by itself, but until then, there may be surging, hesitation, erratic idle and a generally inferior level of performance. To allow the ECM to relearn these values, start the engine and let it run as close to idle speed as possible until it reaches its normal operating temperature, then run it for approximately two minutes at 1200 rpm. Next, drive the car as far as necessary – approximately 5 miles of varied driving conditions is usually sufficient – to complete the relearning process.*

c) *If the battery is disconnected while the alarm system is armed or activated, the alarm will remain in the same state when the battery is reconnected. The same applies to the engine immobiliser system.*

d) *If a standard audio unit is fitted, and the unit and/or the battery is disconnected, the unit will not function again on reconnection until the correct security code is entered. Details of this procedure, which varies according to the unit and model year, are given in the audio operating guide supplied with the car when new. Ensure you have the correct code before you disconnect the battery. For obvious security reasons, the procedure is not given in this manual. If you do not have the code or details of the correct procedure, but can supply proof of ownership and a legitimate reason for wanting this information, an MG Rover specialist or car audio dealer may be able to help.*

e) *Where electric windows with 'one-touch' operation are fitted, this function may not work correctly until each window has been reset. This is done by fully opening the window with the button pressed, then keeping the button pressed for a few seconds after opening, so the system can 'learn' the fully-open position. Close the window, and again keep the button pressed for a few seconds after closing.*

Devices known as 'memory-savers' (or 'code-savers') can be used to avoid some of the above problems. Precise details vary according to the device used. Typically, it is plugged into the cigarette lighter, and is connected by its own wires to a spare battery; the car's own battery is then disconnected from the electrical system, leaving the 'memory-saver' to pass sufficient current to maintain audio unit security codes and ECU memory values, and also to run permanently-live circuits such as the clock, all the while isolating the battery in the event of a short-circuit occurring while work is carried out.

Warning: Some of these devices allow a considerable amount of current to pass, which can mean that many of the car's systems are still operational when the main battery is disconnected. If a 'memory-saver' is used, ensure that the circuit concerned is actually 'dead' before carrying out any work on it!

Introduction

A selection of good tools is a fundamental requirement for anyone contemplating the maintenance and repair of a motor vehicle. For the owner who does not possess any, their purchase will prove a considerable expense, offsetting some of the savings made by doing-it-yourself. However, provided that the tools purchased meet the relevant national safety standards and are of good quality, they will last for many years and prove an extremely worthwhile investment.

To help the average owner to decide which tools are needed to carry out the various tasks detailed in this manual, we have compiled three lists of tools under the following headings: *Maintenance and minor repair*, *Repair and overhaul*, and *Special*. Newcomers to practical mechanics should start off with the *Maintenance and minor repair* tool kit, and confine themselves to the simpler jobs around the vehicle. Then, as confidence and experience grow, more difficult tasks can be undertaken, with extra tools being purchased as, and when, they are needed. In this way, a *Maintenance and minor repair* tool kit can be built up into a *Repair and overhaul* tool kit over a considerable period of time, without any major cash outlays. The experienced do-it-yourselfer will have a tool kit good enough for most repair and overhaul procedures, and will add tools from the *Special* category when it is felt that the expense is justified by the amount of use to which these tools will be put.

Maintenance and minor repair tool kit

The tools given in this list should be considered as a minimum requirement if routine maintenance, servicing and minor repair operations are to be undertaken. We recommend the purchase of combination spanners (ring one end, open-ended the other); although more expensive than open-ended ones, they do give the advantages of both types of spanner.

☐ *Combination spanners:*
Metric - 8 to 19 mm inclusive
☐ *Adjustable spanner - 35 mm jaw (approx.)*
☐ *Spark plug spanner (with rubber insert) - petrol models*
☐ *Spark plug gap adjustment tool - petrol models*
☐ *Set of feeler gauges*
☐ *Brake bleed nipple spanner*
☐ *Screwdrivers:*
Flat blade - 100 mm long x 6 mm dia
Cross blade - 100 mm long x 6 mm dia
Torx - various sizes (not all vehicles)
☐ *Combination pliers*
☐ *Hacksaw (junior)*
☐ *Tyre pump*
☐ *Tyre pressure gauge*
☐ *Oil can*
☐ *Oil filter removal tool*
☐ *Fine emery cloth*
☐ *Wire brush (small)*
☐ *Funnel (medium size)*
☐ *Sump drain plug key (not all vehicles)*

Repair and overhaul tool kit

These tools are virtually essential for anyone undertaking any major repairs to a motor vehicle, and are additional to those given in the *Maintenance and minor repair* list. Included in this list is a comprehensive set of sockets. Although these are expensive, they will be found invaluable as they are so versatile - particularly if various drives are included in the set. We recommend the half-inch square-drive type, as this can be used with most proprietary torque wrenches.

The tools in this list will sometimes need to be supplemented by tools from the *Special* list:

☐ *Sockets (or box spanners) to cover range in previous list (including Torx sockets)*
☐ *Reversible ratchet drive (for use with sockets)*
☐ *Extension piece, 250 mm (for use with sockets)*
☐ *Universal joint (for use with sockets)*
☐ *Flexible handle or sliding T "breaker bar" (for use with sockets)*
☐ *Torque wrench (for use with sockets)*
☐ *Self-locking grips*
☐ *Ball pein hammer*
☐ *Soft-faced mallet (plastic or rubber)*
☐ *Screwdrivers:*
Flat blade - long & sturdy, short (chubby), and narrow (electrician's) types
Cross blade – long & sturdy, and short (chubby) types
☐ *Pliers:*
Long-nosed
Side cutters (electrician's)
Circlip (internal and external)
☐ *Cold chisel - 25 mm*
☐ *Scriber*
☐ *Scraper*
☐ *Centre-punch*
☐ *Pin punch*
☐ *Hacksaw*
☐ *Brake hose clamp*
☐ *Brake/clutch bleeding kit*
☐ *Selection of twist drills*
☐ *Steel rule/straight-edge*
☐ *Allen keys (inc. splined/Torx type)*
☐ *Selection of files*
☐ *Wire brush*
☐ *Axle stands*
☐ *Jack (strong trolley or hydraulic type)*
☐ *Light with extension lead*
☐ *Universal electrical multi-meter*

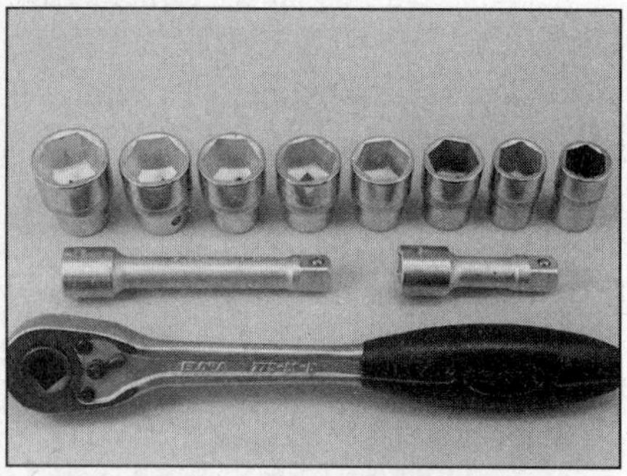

Sockets and reversible ratchet drive

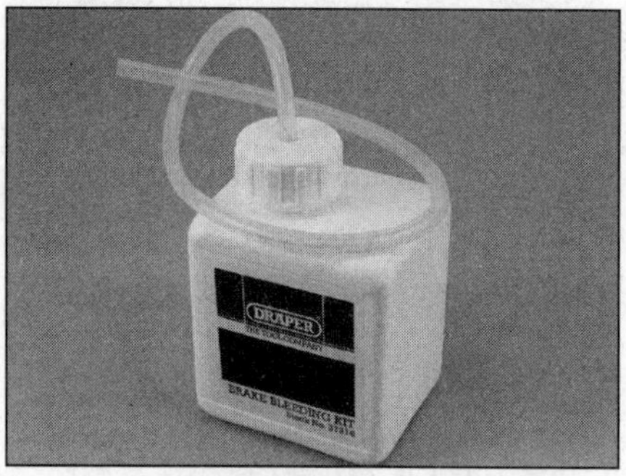

Brake bleeding kit

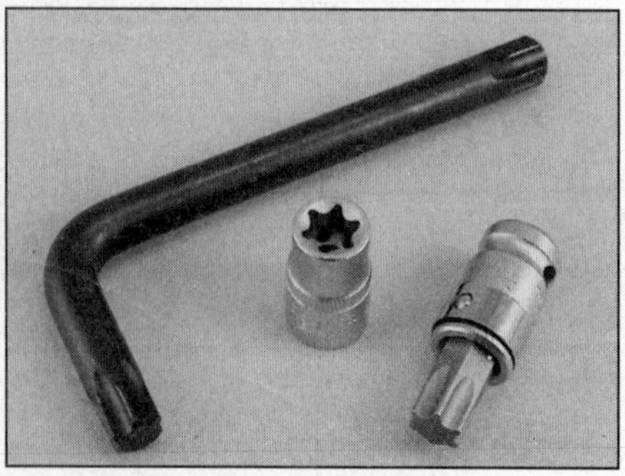

Torx key, socket and bit

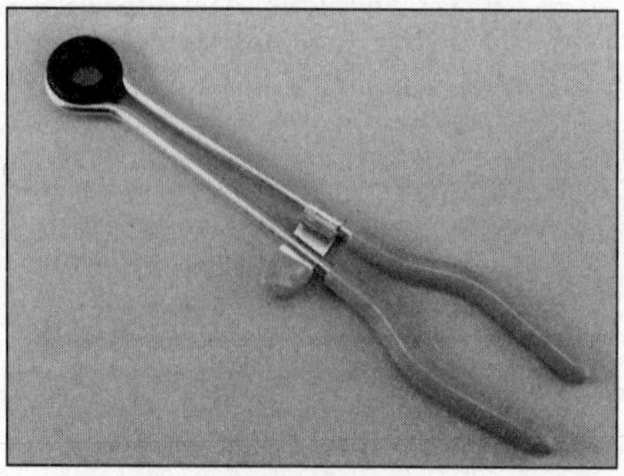

Hose clamp

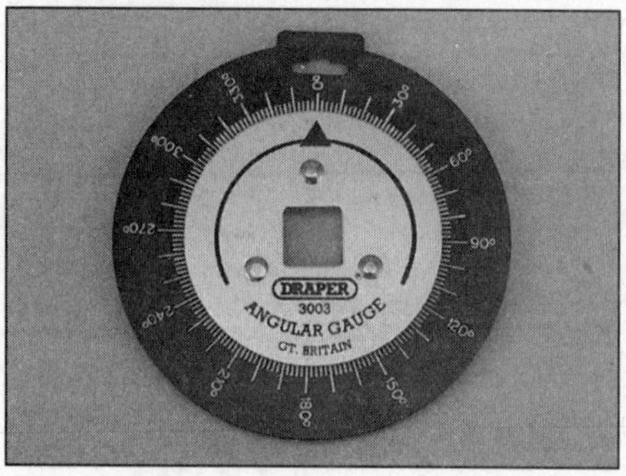

Angular-tightening gauge

Special tools

The tools in this list are those which are not used regularly, are expensive to buy, or which need to be used in accordance with their manufacturers' instructions. Unless relatively difficult mechanical jobs are undertaken frequently, it will not be economic to buy many of these tools. Where this is the case, you could consider clubbing together with friends (or joining a motorists' club) to make a joint purchase, or borrowing the tools against a deposit from a local garage or tool hire specialist. It is worth noting that many of the larger DIY superstores now carry a large range of special tools for hire at modest rates.

The following list contains only those tools and instruments freely available to the public, and not those special tools produced by the vehicle manufacturer specifically for its dealer network. You will find occasional references to these manufacturers' special tools in the text of this manual. Generally, an alternative method of doing the job without the vehicle manufacturers' special tool is given. However, sometimes there is no alternative to using them. Where this is the case and the relevant tool cannot be bought or borrowed, you will have to entrust the work to a dealer.

- ☐ *Angular-tightening gauge*
- ☐ *Valve spring compressor*
- ☐ *Valve grinding tool*
- ☐ *Piston ring compressor*
- ☐ *Piston ring removal/installation tool*
- ☐ *Cylinder bore hone*
- ☐ *Balljoint separator*
- ☐ *Coil spring compressors (where applicable)*
- ☐ *Two/three-legged hub and bearing puller*
- ☐ *Impact screwdriver*
- ☐ *Micrometer and/or vernier calipers*
- ☐ *Dial gauge*
- ☐ *Stroboscopic timing light*
- ☐ *Dwell angle meter/tachometer*
- ☐ *Fault code reader*
- ☐ *Cylinder compression gauge*
- ☐ *Hand-operated vacuum pump and gauge*
- ☐ *Clutch plate alignment set*
- ☐ *Brake shoe steady spring cup removal tool*
- ☐ *Bush and bearing removal/installation set*
- ☐ *Stud extractors*
- ☐ *Tap and die set*
- ☐ *Lifting tackle*
- ☐ *Trolley jack*

Buying tools

Reputable motor accessory shops and superstores often offer excellent quality tools at discount prices, so it pays to shop around.

Remember, you don't have to buy the most expensive items on the shelf, but it is always advisable to steer clear of the very cheap tools. Beware of 'bargains' offered on market stalls or at car boot sales. There are plenty of good tools around at reasonable prices, but always aim to purchase items which meet the relevant national safety standards. If in doubt, ask the proprietor or manager of the shop for advice before making a purchase.

Care and maintenance of tools

Having purchased a reasonable tool kit, it is necessary to keep the tools in a clean and serviceable condition. After use, always wipe off any dirt, grease and metal particles using a clean, dry cloth, before putting the tools away. Never leave them lying around after they have been used. A simple tool rack on the garage or workshop wall for items such as screwdrivers and pliers is a good idea. Store all normal spanners and sockets in a metal box. Any measuring instruments, gauges, meters, etc, must be carefully stored where they cannot be damaged or become rusty.

Take a little care when tools are used. Hammer heads inevitably become marked, and screwdrivers lose the keen edge on their blades from time to time. A little timely attention with emery cloth or a file will soon restore items like this to a good finish.

Working facilities

Not to be forgotten when discussing tools is the workshop itself. If anything more than routine maintenance is to be carried out, a suitable working area becomes essential.

It is appreciated that many an owner-mechanic is forced by circumstances to remove an engine or similar item without the benefit of a garage or workshop. Having done this, any repairs should always be done under the cover of a roof.

Wherever possible, any dismantling should be done on a clean, flat workbench or table at a suitable working height.

Any workbench needs a vice; one with a jaw opening of 100 mm is suitable for most jobs. As mentioned previously, some clean dry storage space is also required for tools, as well as for any lubricants, cleaning fluids, touch-up paints etc, which become necessary.

Another item which may be required, and which has a much more general usage, is an electric drill with a chuck capacity of at least 8 mm. This, together with a good range of twist drills, is virtually essential for fitting accessories.

Last, but not least, always keep a supply of old newspapers and clean, lint-free rags available, and try to keep any working area as clean as possible.

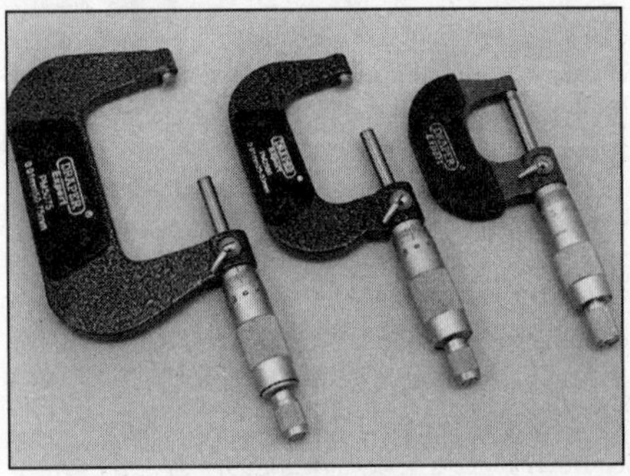

Micrometers

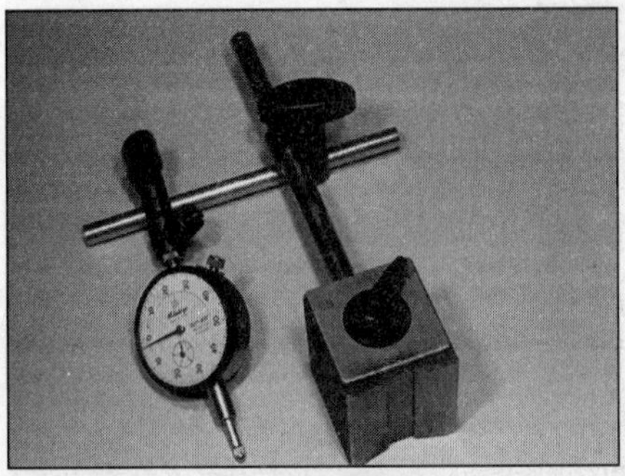

Dial test indicator ("dial gauge")

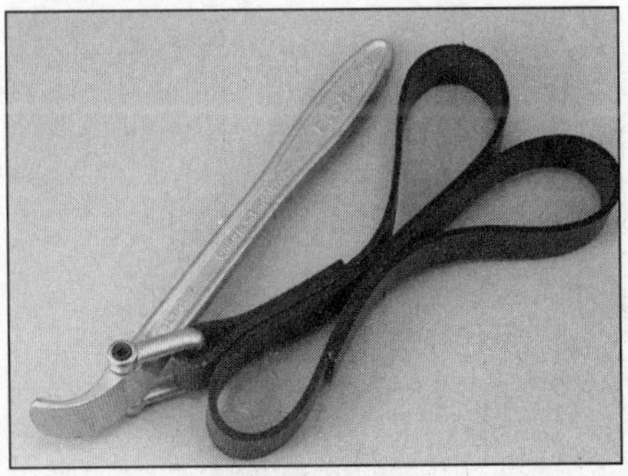

Strap wrench

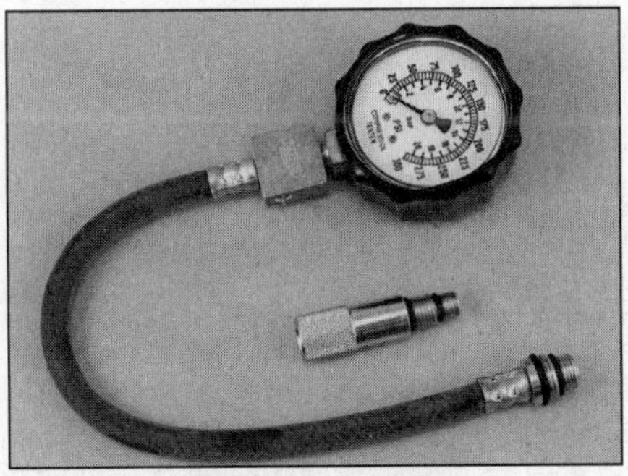

Compression tester

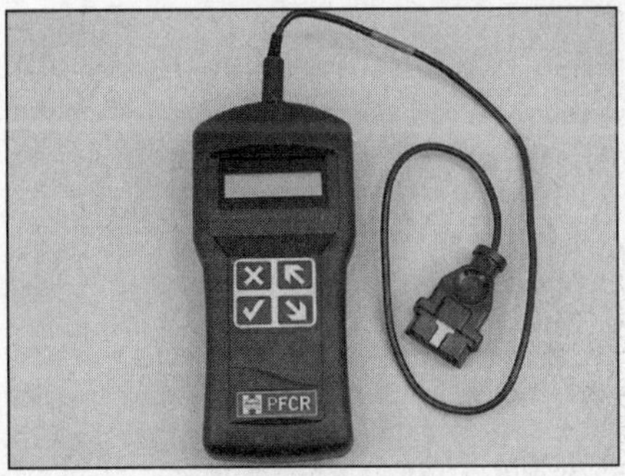

Fault code reader

MOT test checks

This is a guide to getting your vehicle through the MOT test. Obviously it will not be possible to examine the vehicle to the same standard as the professional MOT tester. However, working through the following checks will enable you to identify any problem areas before submitting the vehicle for the test.

Where a testable component is in borderline condition, the tester has discretion in deciding whether to pass or fail it. The basis of such discretion is whether the tester would be happy for a close relative or friend to use the vehicle with the component in that condition. If the vehicle presented is clean and evidently well cared for, the tester may be more inclined to pass a borderline component than if the vehicle is scruffy and apparently neglected.

It has only been possible to summarise the test requirements here, based on the regulations in force at the time of printing. Test standards are becoming increasingly stringent, although there are some exemptions for older vehicles.

An assistant will be needed to help carry out some of these checks.

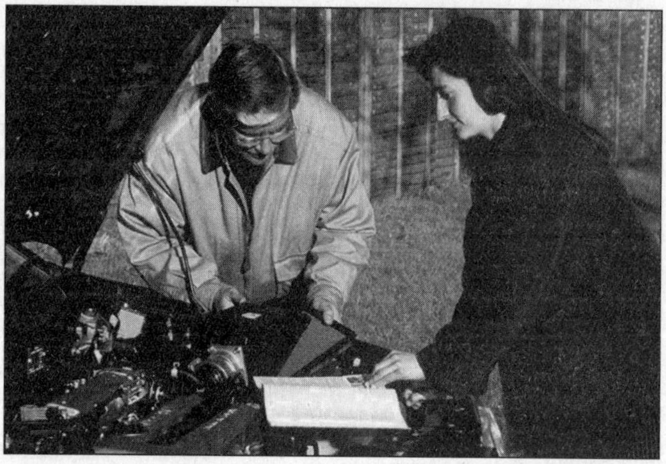

The checks have been sub-divided into four categories, as follows:

1 Checks carried out **FROM THE DRIVER'S SEAT**

2 Checks carried out **WITH THE VEHICLE ON THE GROUND**

3 Checks carried out **WITH THE VEHICLE RAISED AND THE WHEELS FREE TO TURN**

4 Checks carried out on **YOUR VEHICLE'S EXHAUST EMISSION SYSTEM**

1 Checks carried out FROM THE DRIVER'S SEAT

Handbrake

☐ Test the operation of the handbrake. Excessive travel (too many clicks) indicates incorrect brake or cable adjustment.

☐ Check that the handbrake cannot be released by tapping the lever sideways. Check the security of the lever mountings.

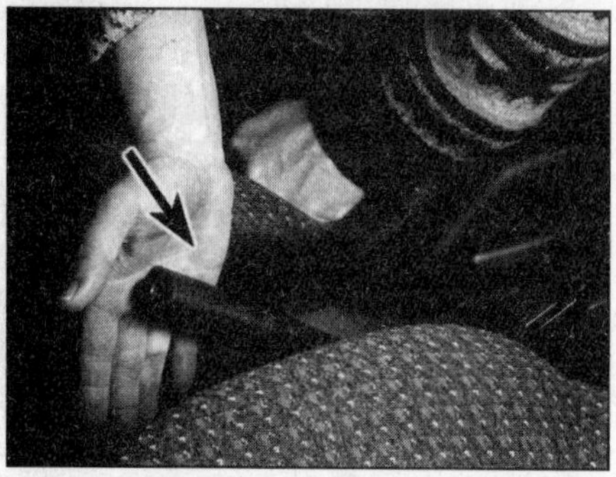

Footbrake

☐ Depress the brake pedal and check that it does not creep down to the floor, indicating a master cylinder fault. Release the pedal, wait a few seconds, then depress it again. If the pedal travels nearly to the floor before firm resistance is felt, brake adjustment or repair is necessary. If the pedal feels spongy, there is air in the hydraulic system which must be removed by bleeding.

☐ Check that the brake pedal is secure and in good condition. Check also for signs of fluid leaks on the pedal, floor or carpets, which would indicate failed seals in the brake master cylinder.

☐ Check the servo unit (when applicable) by operating the brake pedal several times, then keeping the pedal depressed and starting the engine. As the engine starts, the pedal will move down slightly. If not, the vacuum hose or the servo itself may be faulty.

Steering wheel and column

☐ Examine the steering wheel for fractures or looseness of the hub, spokes or rim.

☐ Move the steering wheel from side to side and then up and down. Check that the steering wheel is not loose on the column, indicating wear or a loose retaining nut. Continue moving the steering wheel as before, but also turn it slightly from left to right.

☐ Check that the steering wheel is not loose on the column, and that there is no abnormal

movement of the steering wheel, indicating wear in the column support bearings or couplings.

Windscreen, mirrors and sunvisor

☐ The windscreen must be free of cracks or other significant damage within the driver's field of view. (Small stone chips are acceptable.) Rear view mirrors must be secure, intact, and capable of being adjusted.

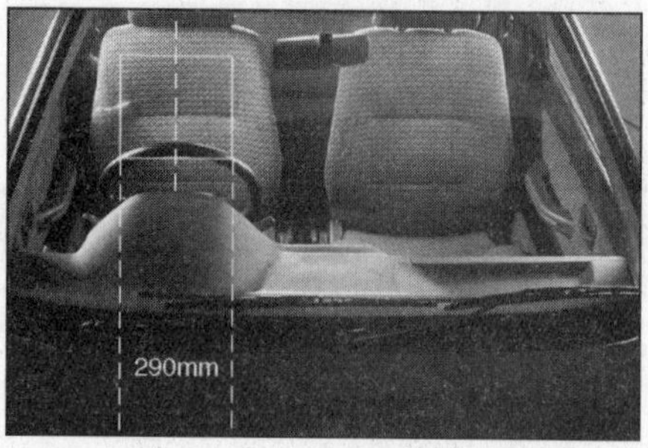

☐ The driver's sunvisor must be capable of being stored in the "up" position.

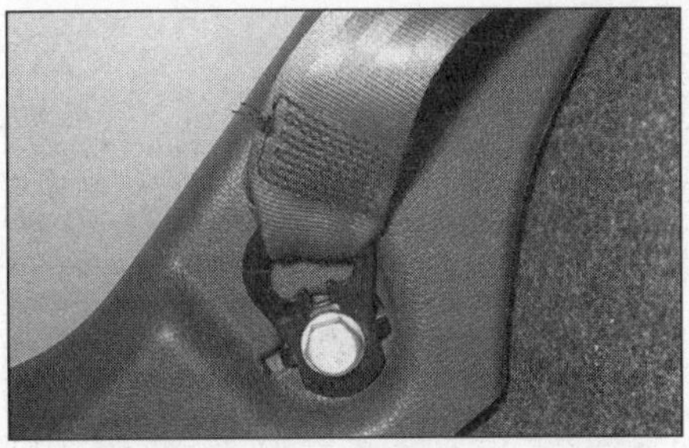

Seat belts and seats

Note: *The following checks are applicable to all seat belts, front and rear.*

☐ Examine the webbing of all the belts (including rear belts if fitted) for cuts, serious fraying or deterioration. Fasten and unfasten each belt to check the buckles. If applicable, check the retracting mechanism. Check the security of all seat belt mountings accessible from inside the vehicle.

☐ Seat belts with pre-tensioners, once activated, have a "flag" or similar showing on the seat belt stalk. This, in itself, is not a reason for test failure.

☐ The front seats themselves must be securely attached and the backrests must lock in the upright position.

Doors

☐ Both front doors must be able to be opened and closed from outside and inside, and must latch securely when closed.

2 Checks carried out WITH THE VEHICLE ON THE GROUND

Vehicle identification

☐ Number plates must be in good condition, secure and legible, with letters and numbers correctly spaced – spacing at (A) should be at least twice that at (B).

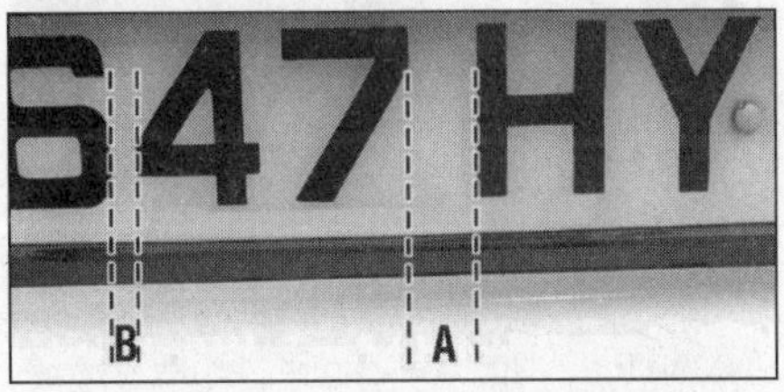

☐ The VIN plate and/or homologation plate must be legible.

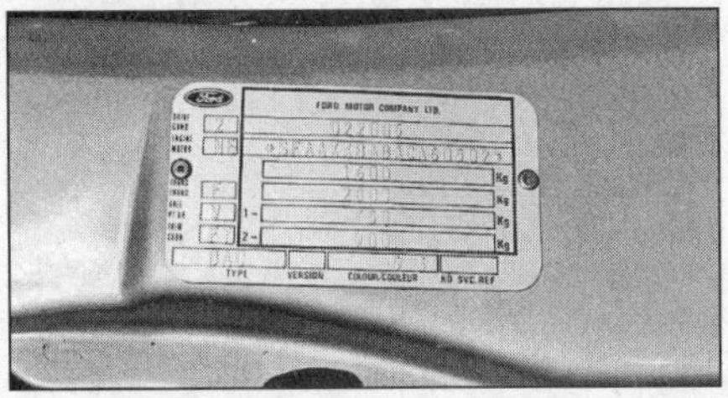

Electrical equipment

☐ Switch on the ignition and check the operation of the horn.

☐ Check the windscreen washers and wipers, examining the wiper blades; renew damaged or perished blades. Also check the operation of the stop-lights.

☐ Check the operation of the sidelights and number plate lights. The lenses and reflectors must be secure, clean and undamaged.

☐ Check the operation and alignment of the headlights. The headlight reflectors must not be tarnished and the lenses must be undamaged.

☐ Switch on the ignition and check the operation of the direction indicators (including the instrument panel tell-tale) and the hazard warning lights. Operation of the sidelights and stop-lights must not affect the indicators - if it does, the cause is usually a bad earth at the rear light cluster.

☐ Check the operation of the rear foglight(s), including the warning light on the instrument panel or in the switch.

☐ The ABS warning light must illuminate in accordance with the manufacturers' design. For most vehicles, the ABS warning light should illuminate when the ignition is switched on, and (if the system is operating properly) extinguish after a few seconds. Refer to the owner's handbook.

Footbrake

☐ Examine the master cylinder, brake pipes and servo unit for leaks, loose mountings, corrosion or other damage.

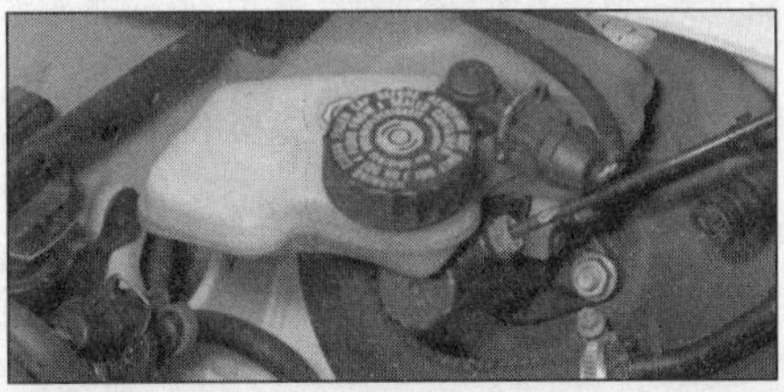

☐ The fluid reservoir must be secure and the fluid level must be between the upper (**A**) and lower (**B**) markings.

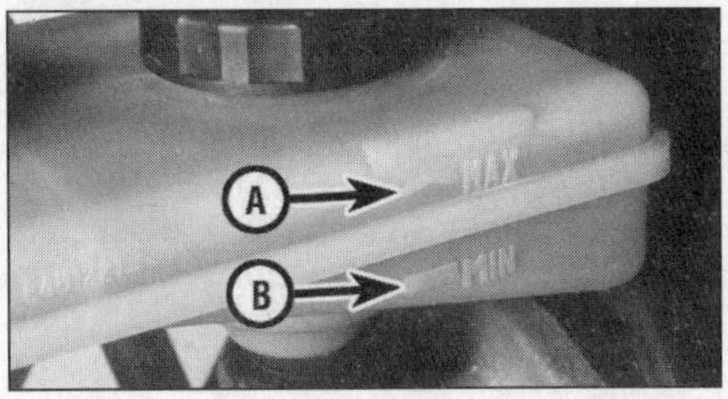

☐ Inspect both front brake flexible hoses for cracks or deterioration of the rubber. Turn the steering from lock to lock, and ensure that the hoses do not contact the wheel, tyre, or any part of the steering or suspension mechanism. With the brake pedal firmly depressed, check the hoses for bulges or leaks under pressure.

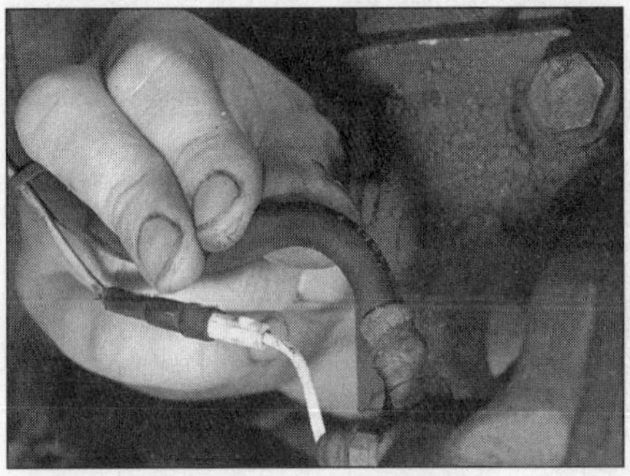

Steering and suspension

☐ Have your assistant turn the steering wheel from side to side slightly, up to the point where the steering gear just begins to transmit this movement to the roadwheels. Check for excessive free play between the steering wheel and the steering gear, indicating wear or insecurity of the steering column joints, the column-to-steering gear coupling, or the steering gear itself.

☐ Have your assistant turn the steering wheel more vigorously in each direction, so that the roadwheels just begin to turn. As this is done, examine all the steering joints, linkages, fittings and attachments. Renew any component that shows signs of wear or damage. On vehicles with power steering, check the security and condition of the steering pump, drivebelt and hoses.

☐ Check that the vehicle is standing level, and at approximately the correct ride height.

Shock absorbers

☐ Depress each corner of the vehicle in turn, then release it. The vehicle should rise and then settle in its normal position. If the vehicle continues to rise and fall, the shock absorber is defective. A shock absorber which has seized will also cause the vehicle to fail.

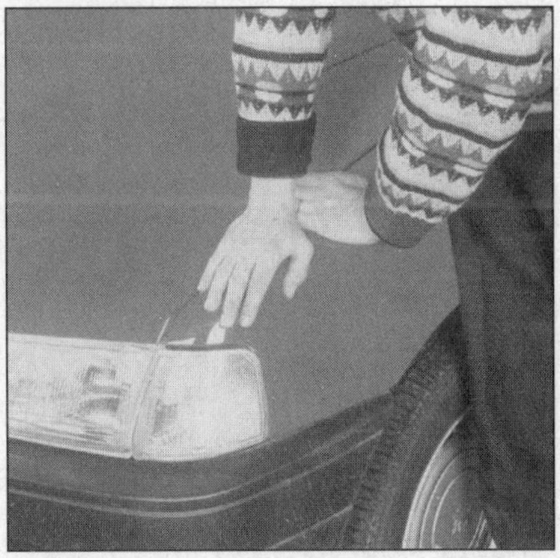

Exhaust system

☐ Start the engine. With your assistant holding a rag over the tailpipe, check the entire system for leaks. Repair or renew leaking sections.

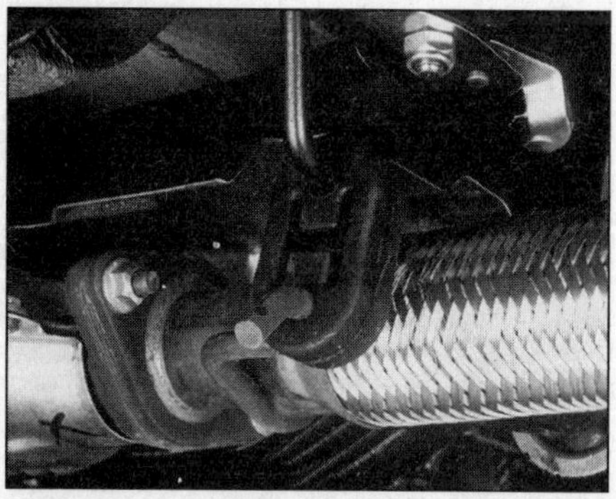

3 Checks carried out WITH THE VEHICLE RAISED AND THE WHEELS FREE TO TURN

Jack up the front and rear of the vehicle, and securely support it on axle stands. Position the stands clear of the suspension assemblies. Ensure that the wheels are clear of the ground and that the steering can be turned from lock to lock.

Steering mechanism

☐ Have your assistant turn the steering from lock to lock. Check that the steering turns smoothly, and that no part of the steering mechanism, including a wheel or tyre, fouls any brake hose or pipe or any part of the body structure.

☐ Examine the steering rack rubber gaiters for damage or insecurity of the retaining clips. If power steering is fitted, check for signs of damage or leakage of the fluid hoses, pipes or connections. Also check for excessive stiffness or binding of the steering, a missing split pin or locking device, or severe corrosion of the body structure within 30 cm of any steering component attachment point.

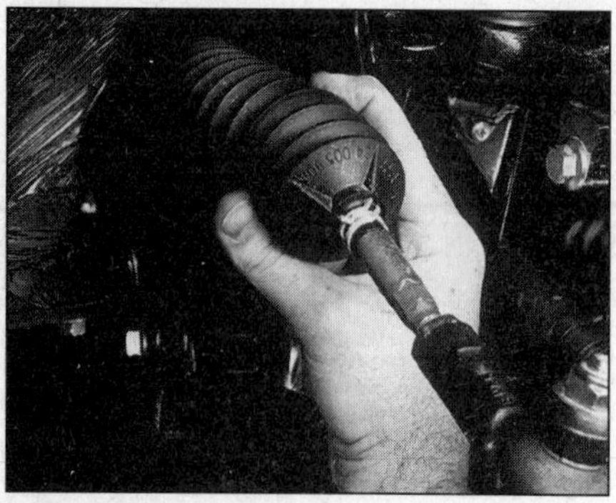

Front and rear suspension and wheel bearings

☐ Starting at the front right-hand side, grasp the roadwheel at the 3 o'clock and 9 o'clock positions and rock gently but firmly. Check for free play or insecurity at the wheel bearings, suspension balljoints, or suspension mountings, pivots and attachments.

☐ Now grasp the wheel at the 12 o'clock and 6 o'clock positions and repeat the previous inspection. Spin the wheel, and check for roughness or tightness of the front wheel bearing.

☐ If excess free play is suspected at a component pivot point, this can be confirmed by using a large screwdriver or similar tool and levering between the mounting and the component attachment. This will confirm whether the wear is in the pivot bush, its retaining bolt, or in the mounting itself (the bolt holes can often become elongated).

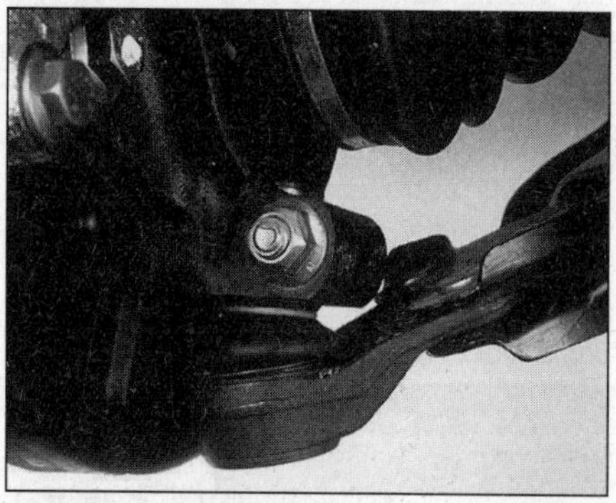

☐ Carry out all the above checks at the other front wheel, and then at both rear wheels.

Springs and shock absorbers

☐ Examine the suspension struts (when applicable) for serious fluid leakage, corrosion, or damage to the casing. Also check the security of the mounting points.

☐ If coil springs are fitted, check that the spring ends locate in their seats, and that the spring is not corroded, cracked or broken.

☐ If leaf springs are fitted, check that all leaves are intact, that the axle is securely attached to each spring, and that there is no deterioration of the spring eye mountings, bushes, and shackles.

☐ The same general checks apply to vehicles fitted with other suspension types, such as torsion bars, hydraulic displacer units, etc. Ensure that all mountings and attachments are secure, that there are no signs of excessive wear, corrosion or damage, and (on hydraulic types) that there are no fluid leaks or damaged pipes.

☐ Inspect the shock absorbers for signs of serious fluid leakage. Check for wear of the mounting bushes or attachments, or damage to the body of the unit.

Driveshafts (fwd vehicles only)

☐ Rotate each front wheel in turn and inspect the constant velocity joint gaiters for splits or damage. Also check that each driveshaft is straight and undamaged.

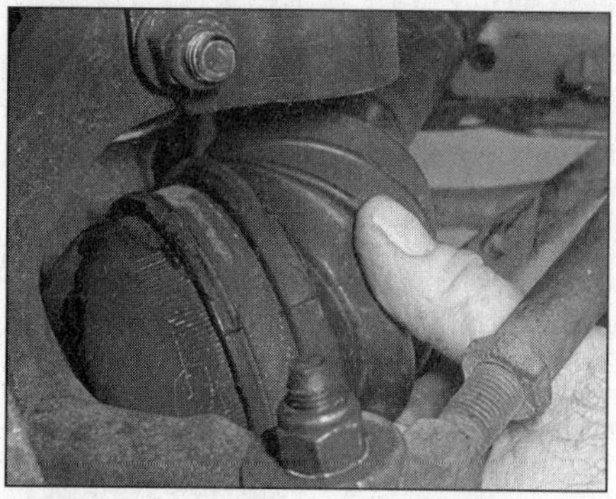

Braking system

☐ If possible without dismantling, check brake pad wear and disc condition. Ensure that the friction lining material has not worn excessively, (A) and that the discs are not fractured, pitted, scored or badly worn (B).

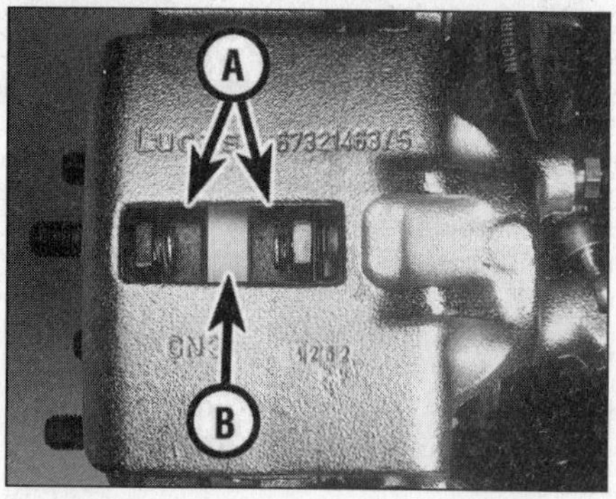

☐ Examine all the rigid brake pipes underneath the vehicle, and the flexible hose(s) at the rear. Look for corrosion, chafing or insecurity of the pipes, and for signs of bulging under pressure, chafing, splits or deterioration of the flexible hoses.

☐ Look for signs of fluid leaks at the brake calipers or on the brake backplates. Repair or renew leaking components.

☐ Slowly spin each wheel, while your assistant depresses and releases the footbrake. Ensure that each brake is operating and does not bind when the pedal is released.

☐ Examine the handbrake mechanism, checking for frayed or broken cables, excessive corrosion, or wear or insecurity of the linkage. Check that the mechanism works on each relevant wheel, and releases fully, without binding.

☐ It is not possible to test brake efficiency without special equipment, but a road test can be carried out later to check that the vehicle pulls up in a straight line.

Fuel and exhaust systems

☐ Inspect the fuel tank (including the filler cap), fuel pipes, hoses and unions. All components must be secure and free from leaks.

☐ Examine the exhaust system over its entire length, checking for any damaged, broken or missing mountings, security of the retaining clamps and rust or corrosion.

Wheels and tyres

☐ Examine the sidewalls and tread area of each tyre in turn. Check for cuts, tears, lumps, bulges, separation of the tread, and exposure of the ply or cord due to wear or damage. Check that the tyre bead is correctly seated on the wheel rim, that the valve is sound and properly seated, and that the wheel is not distorted or damaged.

☐ Check that the tyres are of the correct size for the vehicle, that they are of the same size

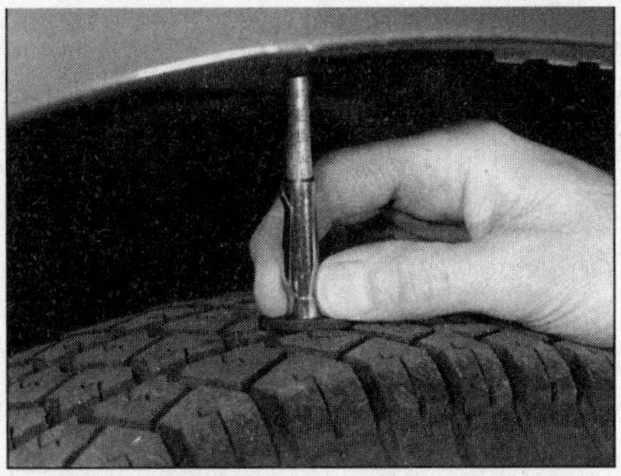

and type on each axle, and that the pressures are correct.

☐ Check the tyre tread depth. The legal minimum at the time of writing is 1.6 mm over at least three-quarters of the tread width. Abnormal tread wear may indicate incorrect front wheel alignment.

Body corrosion

☐ Check the condition of the entire vehicle structure for signs of corrosion in load-bearing areas. (These include chassis box sections, side sills, cross-members, pillars, and all suspension, steering, braking system and seat belt mountings and anchorages.) Any corrosion which has seriously reduced the thickness of a load-bearing area is likely to cause the vehicle to fail. In this case professional repairs are likely to be needed.

☐ Damage or corrosion which causes sharp or otherwise dangerous edges to be exposed will also cause the vehicle to fail.

4 Checks carried out on **YOUR VEHICLE'S EXHAUST EMISSION SYSTEM**

Petrol models

☐ The engine should be warmed up, and running well (ignition system in good order, air filter element clean, etc).

☐ Before testing, run the engine at around 2500 rpm for 20 seconds. Let the engine drop to idle, and watch for smoke from the exhaust. If the idle speed is too high, or if dense blue or black smoke emerges for more than 5 seconds, the vehicle will fail. Typically, blue smoke signifies oil burning (engine wear); black smoke means unburnt fuel (dirty air cleaner element, or other fuel system fault).

☐ An exhaust gas analyser for measuring carbon monoxide (CO) and hydrocarbons (HC) is now needed. If one cannot be hired or borrowed, have a local garage perform the check.

CO emissions (mixture)

☐ The MOT tester has access to the CO limits for all vehicles. The CO level is measured at idle speed, and at 'fast idle' (2500 to 3000 rpm). The following limits are given as a general guide:

At idle speed – Less than 0.5% CO
At 'fast idle' – Less than 0.3% CO
Lambda reading – 0.97 to 1.03

☐ If the CO level is too high, this may point to poor maintenance, a fuel injection system problem, faulty lambda (oxygen) sensor or catalytic converter. Try an injector cleaning treatment, and check the vehicle's ECU for fault codes.

HC emissions

☐ The MOT tester has access to HC limits for all vehicles. The HC level is measured at 'fast idle' (2500 to 3000 rpm). The following limits are given as a general guide:

At 'fast idle' – Less then 200 ppm

☐ Excessive HC emissions are typically caused by oil being burnt (worn engine), or by a blocked crankcase ventilation system ('breather'). If the engine oil is old and thin, an oil change may help. If the engine is running badly, check the vehicle's ECU for fault codes.

Diesel models

☐ The only emission test for diesel engines is measuring exhaust smoke density, using a calibrated smoke meter. The test involves accelerating the engine at least 3 times to its maximum unloaded speed.

Note: *On engines with a timing belt, it is VITAL that the belt is in good condition before the test is carried out.*

☐ With the engine warmed up, it is first purged by running at around 2500 rpm for 20 seconds. A governor check is then carried out, by slowly accelerating the engine to its maximum speed. After this, the smoke meter is connected, and the engine is accelerated quickly to maximum speed three times. If the smoke density is less than the limits given below, the vehicle will pass:

Non-turbo vehicles: 2.5m-1
Turbocharged vehicles: 3.0m-1

☐ If excess smoke is produced, try fitting a new air cleaner element, or using an injector cleaning treatment. If the engine is running badly, where applicable, check the vehicle's ECU for fault codes. Also check the vehicle's EGR system, where applicable. At high mileages, the injectors may require professional attention.

Engine
- ☐ Engine fails to rotate when attempting to start
- ☐ Engine rotates, but will not start
- ☐ Engine difficult to start when cold
- ☐ Engine difficult to start when hot
- ☐ Starter motor noisy or excessively-rough in engagement
- ☐ Engine starts, but stops immediately
- ☐ Engine misfires, or idles unevenly
- ☐ Engine stalls, or lacks power
- ☐ Engine backfires
- ☐ Engine noises
- ☐ Oil consumption excessive
- ☐ Oil pressure warning light illuminated with engine running

Cooling system
- ☐ Overheating
- ☐ Overcooling
- ☐ External coolant leakage
- ☐ Internal coolant leakage
- ☐ Corrosion

Fuel and exhaust systems
- ☐ Fuel consumption excessive
- ☐ Fuel leakage and/or fuel odour
- ☐ Black smoke in exhaust
- ☐ Blue or white smoke in exhaust
- ☐ Excessive noise or fumes from exhaust system

Clutch
- ☐ Pedal travels to floor – no pressure or very little resistance
- ☐ Clutch fails to disengage (unable to select gears)
- ☐ Clutch slips (engine speed increases, with no increase in vehicle speed)
- ☐ Judder as clutch is engaged
- ☐ Noise when depressing or releasing clutch pedal

Manual transmission
- ☐ Noisy in neutral with engine running
- ☐ Noisy in one particular gear
- ☐ Difficulty engaging gears
- ☐ Jumps out of gear
- ☐ Vibration
- ☐ Lubricant leaks

Automatic transmission
- ☐ Fluid leakage
- ☐ Transmission fluid brown, or has burned smell
- ☐ General gear selection problems
- ☐ Transmission will not downshift (kickdown) with accelerator fully depressed
- ☐ Engine will not start in any gear, or starts in gears other than Park or Neutral
- ☐ Transmission slips, shifts roughly, is noisy, or has no drive in forward or reverse gears

Driveshafts
- ☐ Vibration when accelerating or decelerating
- ☐ Clicking or knocking noise on turns (at slow speed on full-lock)

Braking system
- ☐ Car pulls to one side under braking
- ☐ Noise (grinding or high-pitched squeal) when brakes applied
- ☐ Excessive brake pedal travel
- ☐ Brake pedal feels spongy when depressed
- ☐ Excessive brake pedal effort required to stop vehicle
- ☐ Judder felt through brake pedal or steering wheel when braking
- ☐ Brakes binding
- ☐ Rear wheels locking under normal braking

Suspension and steering
- ☐ Car pulls to one side
- ☐ Wheel wobble and vibration
- ☐ Excessive pitching and/or rolling around corners, or during braking
- ☐ Wandering or general instability
- ☐ Excessively-stiff steering
- ☐ Excessive play in steering
- ☐ Lack of power assistance
- ☐ Tyre wear excessive

Electrical system
- ☐ Battery will only hold a charge for a few days
- ☐ Ignition (no-charge) warning light remains illuminated with engine running
- ☐ Ignition (no-charge) warning light fails to come on
- ☐ Lights inoperative
- ☐ Instrument readings inaccurate or erratic
- ☐ Horn faults
- ☐ Windscreen/tailgate wiper faults
- ☐ Windscreen/tailgate washer faults
- ☐ Electric window faults
- ☐ Central locking system faults

Introduction

The car owner who does his or her own maintenance according to the recommended service schedules should not have to use this section of the manual very often. Modern component reliability is such that, provided those items subject to wear or deterioration are inspected or renewed at the specified intervals, sudden failure is comparatively rare. Faults do not usually just happen as a result of sudden failure, but develop over a period of time. Major mechanical failures in particular are usually preceded by characteristic symptoms over hundreds or even thousands of miles. Those components which do occasionally fail without warning are often small and easily carried in the car.

With any fault-finding, the first step is to decide where to begin investigations. Sometimes this is obvious, but on other occasions, a little detective work will be necessary. The owner who makes half a dozen haphazard adjustments or replacements may be successful in curing a fault (or its symptoms), but will be none the wiser if the fault recurs, and ultimately may have spent more time and money than was necessary. A calm and logical approach will be found to be more satisfactory in the long run. Always take into account any warning signs or abnormalities that may have been noticed in the period preceding the fault – power loss, high or low gauge readings, unusual smells, etc – and remember that failure of components such as fuses may only be pointers to some underlying fault.

The pages which follow provide an easy-reference guide to the more common problems which may occur during the operation of the vehicle. These problems and their possible causes are grouped under headings denoting various components or systems, such as Engine, Cooling system, etc. The general

Chapter which deals with the problem is also shown in brackets; refer to the relevant part of that Chapter for system-specific information. Whatever the fault, certain basic principles apply. These are as follows:

Verify the fault. This is simply a matter of being sure that you know what the symptoms are before starting work. This is particularly important if you are investigating a fault for someone else, who may not have described it very accurately.

Don't overlook the obvious. For example, if the car won't start, is there fuel in the tank? (Don't take anyone else's word on this particular point, and don't trust the fuel gauge either!) If an electrical fault is indicated, look for loose or broken wires before using the test gear.

Cure the disease, not the symptom. Substituting a flat battery with a fully-charged one will get you off the hard shoulder, but if the underlying cause is not attended to, the new battery will go the same way.

Don't take anything for granted. Particularly, don't forget that a 'new' component may itself be defective (especially if it's been rattling around in the boot for months), and don't leave components out of a fault diagnosis sequence just because they are new or recently fitted. When you do finally diagnose a difficult fault, you'll probably realise that all the evidence was there from the start.

Consider what work, if any, has recently been carried out. Many faults arise through careless or hurried work. For instance, if any work has been performed under the bonnet, could some of the wiring have been dislodged or incorrectly routed, or a hose trapped? Have all the fasteners been properly tightened? Were new, genuine parts and new gaskets used? There is often a certain amount of detective work to be done in this case, as an apparently-unrelated task can have far-reaching consequences.

Diesel fault diagnosis

The majority of starting problems on small diesel engines are electrical in origin. The mechanic who is familiar with petrol engines but less so with diesel may be inclined to view the diesel's injectors and pump in the same light as the spark plugs and distributor, but this is generally a mistake.

When investigating complaints of difficult starting for someone else, make sure that the correct starting procedure is understood and is being followed. Some drivers are unaware of the significance of the preheating warning light – many modern engines are sufficiently forgiving for this not to matter in mild weather, but with the onset of winter problems begin.

As a rule of thumb, if the engine is difficult to start but runs well when it has finally got going, the problem is electrical (battery, starter motor or preheating system). If poor performance is combined with difficult starting, the problem is likely to be in the fuel system. The low pressure (supply) side of the fuel system should be checked before suspecting the injectors and injection pump. The most common fuel supply problem is air getting into the system, and any pipe from the fuel tank forwards must be scrutinised if air leakage is suspected. Normally the pump is the last item to suspect, since unless it has been tampered with, there is no reason for it to be at fault.

Engine

Engine fails to rotate when attempting to start

- ☐ Battery terminal connections loose or corroded (*Weekly checks*).
- ☐ Battery discharged or faulty (Chapter 5A).
- ☐ Broken, loose or disconnected wiring in the starting circuit (Chapter 5A).
- ☐ Defective starter solenoid or ignition switch (Chapter 5A or 12).
- ☐ Defective starter motor (Chapter 5A).
- ☐ Flywheel ring gear or starter pinion teeth loose or broken (Chapter 2A, 2B, 2C or 5A).
- ☐ Engine earth strap broken or disconnected.
- ☐ Engine suffering 'hydraulic lock' (eg from water ingested after traversing flooded roads, or from a serious internal coolant leak) – remove the spark / glow plugs and retry. Engine may be damaged – perform compression test.
- ☐ Immobiliser or anti-theft alarm faulty or incorrectly used, or 'uncoded' ignition key being used (Chapter 12).
- ☐ Automatic transmission not in position N or P (Chapter 7B).

Engine rotates, but will not start

- ☐ Fuel tank empty, or fuel pump faulty (Chapter 4A, 4B, or 4C).
- ☐ Battery discharged or inadequate capacity (engine rotates slowly) (Chapter 5A).
- ☐ Battery terminal connections loose or corroded (*Weekly checks*).
- ☐ Ignition components damp or damaged – petrol engines (Chapter 1A or 5B)
- ☐ Worn, faulty or incorrectly-gapped spark plugs – petrol engines (Chapter 1A)
- ☐ Incorrect use of diesel preheating system, or preheating system fault (Chapter 5B).
- ☐ Diesel fuel waxing (in very cold weather).
- ☐ Crankshaft sensor, or other engine management system sensor, fault (Chapter 4A, 4B, or 4C)
- ☐ Air filter element dirty or clogged (Chapter 1A or 1B).
- ☐ Blockage in exhaust system (Chapter 4A, 4B, or 4C).
- ☐ Poor compressions (Chapter 2A, 2B or 2C).
- ☐ Air in diesel fuel system (Chapter 4C).
- ☐ Valve timing incorrect, possibly through a poorly-fitted timing belt or chain (Chapter 2A, 2B or 2C).
- ☐ Major mechanical failure (eg camshaft drive) (Chapter 2A, 2B, or 2C).

Engine difficult to start when cold

- ☐ Battery discharged (Chapter 5A).
- ☐ Battery terminal connections loose or corroded (see *Weekly checks*).
- ☐ Worn, faulty or incorrectly-gapped spark plugs – petrol models (Chapter 1A).
- ☐ Other ignition system fault – petrol models (Chapter 5B).
- ☐ Fuel system fault (Chapter 4).
- ☐ Diesel glow plug(s) defective (Chapter 5C).
- ☐ Wrong grade of engine oil used (*Weekly checks* or Chapter 1A or 1B).
- ☐ Low cylinder compressions (Chapter 2A, 2B, or 2C)

Engine difficult to start when hot

- ☐ Air filter element dirty or clogged (Chapter 1A or 1B).
- ☐ Fuel system fault (Chapter 4).
- ☐ Low cylinder compressions (Chapter 2A, 2B, or 2C).
- ☐ Diesel – crankshaft sensor fault (Chapter 4C).

Starter motor noisy or excessively-rough

- ☐ Starter pinion or flywheel ring gear teeth loose or broken (Chapter 2A, 2B, 2C or 5A).
- ☐ Starter motor mounting bolts loose or missing (Chapter 5A).
- ☐ Starter motor internal components worn or damaged (Chapter 5A).

Engine starts, but stops immediately

- ☐ Loose or faulty electrical connections in the ignition circuit – petrol models (Chapter 1A or 5B).
- ☐ Vacuum leak at the throttle body, inlet manifold or associated hoses – petrol models (Chapter 4A or 4B).
- ☐ Blocked injectors/fuel system fault (Chapter 4).
- ☐ Fuel very low in tank.
- ☐ Restriction in fuel feed or return.
- ☐ Air in diesel fuel system (Chapter 4C).
- ☐ Air cleaner dirty or blockage in air intake system (Chapter 1A, 1B, 4A, 4B or 4C).
- ☐ Blockage in exhaust system (Chapter 4A, 4B, or 4C).

Engine (continued)

Engine misfires, or idles unevenly

- ☐ Air cleaner dirty or blockage in air intake system (Chapter 1A, 1B, 4A, 4B or 4C).
- ☐ Vacuum leak at the throttle body, inlet manifold or associated hoses – petrol models (Chapter 4A or 4B).
- ☐ Worn, faulty or incorrectly-gapped spark plugs – petrol models (Chapter 1A).
- ☐ Uneven or low cylinder compressions (Chapter 2A, 2B, or 2C)
- ☐ Camshaft lobes worn (Chapter 2A, 2B, or 2C).
- ☐ Timing belt/chain incorrectly fitted (Chapter 2A, 2B, or 2C).
- ☐ Blocked injectors/fuel injection system fault (Chapter 4).
- ☐ Valve(s) sticking, valve spring(s) weak or broken, or poor compressions (Chapter 2A, 2B, or 2C).
- ☐ Overheating (Chapter 3).
- ☐ Cylinder head gasket blown (Chapter 2A, 2B, or 2C).

Engine stalls, or lacks power

- ☐ Diesel fuel filter choked (Chapter 1B).
- ☐ In-tank fuel pump faulty, or delivery pressure low (Chapter 4A, 4B, or 4C).
- ☐ Diesel lift pump faulty, or delivery pressure low (Chapter 4C).
- ☐ Air in diesel fuel system (Chapter 4C).
- ☐ Vacuum leak at the throttle body, inlet manifold or associated hoses – petrol models (Chapter 4A or 4B).
- ☐ Worn, faulty or incorrectly-gapped spark plugs – petrol models (Chapter 1A).
- ☐ Faulty ignition coils – petrol models (Chapter 5B).
- ☐ Uneven or low cylinder compressions (Chapter 2A, 2B, or 2C).
- ☐ Blocked injector/fuel system fault (Chapter 4).
- ☐ Blocked catalytic converter (Chapter 4A, 4B, or 4C).
- ☐ Engine overheating (Chapter 3).
- ☐ Air filter element blocked (Chapter 1A or 1B).
- ☐ Throttle position sensor fault (Chapter 4A, 4B, or 4C).
- ☐ Engine warning light on (fault code in system) (Chapter 4A, 4B, or 4C).
- ☐ Timing belt/chain worn, or incorrectly fitted (Chapter 2A, 2B, or 2C).
- ☐ Turbo boost pressure inadequate – 1.8 litre turbo and diesel models (Chapter 4A or 4C).
- ☐ V6 engine VIS motor failure (Chapter 4B).
- ☐ Diesel airflow meter failure (Chapter 4C).
- ☐ Brakes binding (Chapter 1 or 9).
- ☐ Clutch slipping (Chapter 6).

Engine backfires

- ☐ Timing belt or chain incorrectly fitted (Chapter 2A, 2B, or 2C).
- ☐ Vacuum leak at the throttle body, inlet manifold or associated hoses – petrol models (Chapter 4A or 4B).
- ☐ Blocked catalytic converter (Chapter 4A, 4B, or 4C).
- ☐ Ignition coil faulty – petrol models (Chapter 5B).

Engine noises

Pre-ignition (pinking) or knocking during acceleration or under load

- ☐ Ignition system fault – petrol models (Chapter 1A or 5B).
- ☐ Incorrect grade of spark plug – petrol models (Chapter 1A).
- ☐ Incorrect grade (or type) of fuel used (Chapter 4A, 4B, or 4C).
- ☐ Vacuum leak at the throttle body, inlet manifold or associated hoses – petrol models (Chapter 4A or 4B).
- ☐ Excessive carbon build-up in cylinder head/pistons (Chapter 2A, 2B, or 2C).
- ☐ Blocked injector/fuel injection system fault (Chapter 4A or 4B).

Whistling or wheezing noises

- ☐ Leaking inlet manifold or throttle body gasket – petrol models (Chapter 4A or 4B).
- ☐ Leaking exhaust manifold gasket, or pipe-to-manifold joint (Chapter 4A, 4B, or 4C).
- ☐ Leaking vacuum hose (Chapter 4 or 9).
- ☐ Blowing cylinder head gasket (Chapter 2A, 2B, or 2C).
- ☐ Partially blocked or leaking crankcase ventilation system (Chapter 4D).

Tapping or rattling noises

- ☐ Worn camshaft (Chapter 2A, 2B, or 2C)
- ☐ Ancillary component fault (coolant pump, alternator, etc) (Chapter 3, 5A, etc).
- ☐ Air in diesel fuel system (Chapter 4C).

Knocking or thumping noises

- ☐ Worn big-end bearings (regular heavy knocking, perhaps less under load) (Chapter 2D).
- ☐ Worn main bearings (rumbling and knocking, perhaps worsening under load) (Chapter 2D).
- ☐ Piston slap - most noticeable when cold, caused by piston/bore wear (Chapter 2D).
- ☐ Ancillary component fault (coolant pump, alternator, etc) (Chapter 3, 5A, etc).
- ☐ Engine mountings worn or defective (Chapter 2A, 2B, or 2C).
- ☐ Front suspension or steering components worn (Chapter 10).

Oil consumption excessive

- ☐ External leakage (standing or running) – eg sump gasket, crankshaft oil seals (Chapter 2A, 2B or 2C).
- ☐ New engine not yet run-in.
- ☐ Engine oil incorrect grade/poor quality, or oil level too high (*Weekly checks*).
- ☐ Crankcase ventilation system obstructed (Chapter 4D).
- ☐ Engine oil cooler failed – V6 engines (Chapter 2B).
- ☐ Burning oil due to general engine wear – pistons and/or bores, valve stem oil seals, etc (Chapter 2D).

Oil pressure warning light illuminated with engine running

- ☐ Low oil level or incorrect oil grade (*Weekly checks*).
- ☐ Faulty oil pressure warning light switch (Chapter 2A, 2B, or 2C).
- ☐ Worn engine bearings and/or oil pump (Chapter 2).
- ☐ High engine operating temperature (Chapter 3).
- ☐ Oil pick-up strainer clogged – remove sump to check (Chapter 2A, 2B, or 2C).

Cooling system

Overheating

- ☐ Insufficient coolant in system (*Weekly checks*).
- ☐ Thermostat faulty (Chapter 3).
- ☐ Radiator core blocked or grille restricted (Chapter 3).
- ☐ Radiator electric cooling fan(s) or coolant temperature sensor faulty (Chapter 3).
- ☐ Pressure cap faulty (Chapter 3).
- ☐ Inaccurate coolant temperature gauge sender (Chapter 3).
- ☐ Airlock in cooling system (Chapter 1A or 1B).
- ☐ Engine management system fault (Chapter 4A, 4B, or 4C).
- ☐ Blockage in exhaust system (Chapter 4A, 4B, or 4C).
- ☐ Engine oil cooler failed – V6 engines (Chapter 2B).
- ☐ Cylinder head gasket blown (Chapter 2A, 2B, or 2C).

Overcooling

- ☐ Thermostat faulty (Chapter 3).
- ☐ Inaccurate coolant temperature gauge sender (Chapter 3).

External coolant leakage

- ☐ Deteriorated or damaged hoses or hose clips (Chapter 1A or 1B).
- ☐ Radiator core or heater matrix leaking (Chapter 3).
- ☐ Pressure cap faulty (Chapter 1A or 1B).
- ☐ Water pump or thermostat housing leaking (Chapter 3).
- ☐ Boiling due to overheating (Chapter 3).
- ☐ Engine oil cooler failed – V6 engines (Chapter 2B).
- ☐ Core plug leaking (Chapter 2D).

Internal coolant leakage

- ☐ Engine oil cooler failed – V6 engines (Chapter 2B).
- ☐ Leaking cylinder head gasket (Chapter 2A, 2B, or 2C).
- ☐ Cracked cylinder head or cylinder bore (Chapter 2D).

Corrosion

- ☐ Infrequent draining and flushing (Chapter 1A or 1B).
- ☐ Incorrect antifreeze mixture, or inappropriate antifreeze type (*Weekly checks* and Chapter 1A or 1B).

Fuel and exhaust systems

Fuel consumption excessive

- ☐ New engine not yet run-in.
- ☐ Air cleaner element dirty, or blockage in air intake system (Chapter 1A, 1B, 4A, 4B, or 4C).
- ☐ Fuel system fault (Chapter 4A, 4B or 4C).
- ☐ Crankcase ventilation system blocked (Chapter 4D).
- ☐ Unsympathetic driving style, or adverse conditions.
- ☐ Tyres under-inflated (see *Weekly checks*).
- ☐ Brakes binding (Chapter 1 or 9).
- ☐ Fuel leak, causing apparent high consumption (Chapter 1A, 1B, 4A, 4B, or 4C).
- ☐ Valve timing incorrect, possibly through a poorly-fitted timing belt/chain (Chapter 2A, 2B, or 2C).

Fuel leakage and/or fuel odour

- ☐ Damaged or corroded fuel tank, pipes or connections (Chapter 1A or 1B).
- ☐ Evaporative emissions system fault – petrol models (Chapter 4D).

Black smoke in exhaust

- ☐ Air cleaner element dirty, or blockage in air intake system (Chapter 1A, 1B, 4A, 4B, or 4C).
- ☐ Turbo boost pressure inadequate – 1.8 litre turbo and diesel models (Chapter 4A or 4C).
- ☐ Exhaust gas recirculation system fault – diesel models (Chapter 4D).
- ☐ Fuel system fault (Chapter 4A, 4B or 4C).

Blue or white smoke in exhaust

- ☐ Engine oil incorrect grade or poor quality, or fuel passing into sump (worn piston rings/bores).
- ☐ Diesel glow plug(s) defective (white smoke at start-up only) (Chapter 5C).
- ☐ Air cleaner element dirty, or blockage in air intake system (Chapter 1A, 1B, 4A, 4B, or 4C).
- ☐ Injector(s) faulty (Chapter 4A, 4B or 4C).
- ☐ Blocked or damaged emissions system hoses or components (Chapter 4D).
- ☐ General engine wear - pistons and/or bores, valve stem oil seals, etc (Chapter 2D).

Excessive noise or fumes from exhaust system

- ☐ Leaking exhaust system or manifold joints (Chapter 1A, 1B, 4A, 4B or 4C).
- ☐ Leaking, corroded or damaged silencers or pipe (Chapter 1A, 1B, 4A, 4B or 4C).
- ☐ Exhaust gas recirculation system fault – diesel models (Chapter 4D).
- ☐ Oxygen sensors loose or damaged – petrol models (Chapter 4D).
- ☐ Broken mountings, causing body or suspension contact (Chapter 1A, 1B, 4A, 4B or 4C).

Clutch

Pedal travels to floor – no pressure or very little resistance

- ☐ Air in hydraulic system/faulty master or slave cylinder (Chapter 6).
- ☐ Faulty hydraulic release system (Chapter 6).
- ☐ Clutch pedal return spring detached or broken (Chapter 6).
- ☐ Broken clutch release bearing or fork (Chapter 6).
- ☐ Broken diaphragm spring in clutch pressure plate (Chapter 6).

Clutch fails to disengage (unable to select gears)

- ☐ Air in hydraulic system/faulty master or slave cylinder (Chapter 6).
- ☐ Faulty hydraulic release system (Chapter 6).
- ☐ Clutch disc sticking on transmission input shaft splines (Chapter 6).
- ☐ Clutch disc sticking to flywheel or pressure plate (Chapter 6).
- ☐ Faulty pressure plate assembly (Chapter 6).
- ☐ Clutch release mechanism worn or incorrectly assembled (Chapter 6).

Clutch slips (engine speed increases, with no increase in vehicle speed)

- ☐ Faulty hydraulic release system (Chapter 6).
- ☐ Clutch disc linings excessively worn (Chapter 6).
- ☐ Clutch disc linings contaminated with oil or grease (Chapter 6).
- ☐ Faulty pressure plate or weak diaphragm spring (Chapter 6).

Judder as clutch is engaged

- ☐ Clutch disc linings contaminated with oil or grease (Chapter 6).
- ☐ Clutch disc linings excessively worn (Chapter 6).
- ☐ Faulty or distorted pressure plate or diaphragm spring (Chapter 6).
- ☐ Worn or loose engine/transmission mountings (Chapter 2A, 2B, or 2C).
- ☐ Clutch disc hub or transmission input shaft splines worn (Chapter 6 or 7A).

Noise when depressing or releasing clutch pedal

- ☐ Worn clutch release bearing (Chapter 6).
- ☐ Worn or dry clutch pedal bushes (Chapter 6).
- ☐ Worn or dry clutch master cylinder piston (Chapter 6).
- ☐ Faulty pressure plate assembly (Chapter 6).
- ☐ Pressure plate diaphragm spring broken (Chapter 6).
- ☐ Broken clutch disc cushioning springs (Chapter 6).

Manual transmission

Noisy in neutral with engine running

- ☐ Lack of oil (Chapter 1A or 1B).
- ☐ Input shaft bearings worn (noise apparent with clutch pedal released, but not when depressed) (Chapter 7A).*
- ☐ Clutch release bearing worn (noise apparent with clutch pedal depressed, possibly less when released) (Chapter 6).

Noisy in one particular gear

- ☐ Worn, damaged or chipped gear teeth (Chapter 7A).*

Difficulty engaging gears

- ☐ Clutch fault (Chapter 6).
- ☐ Worn or damaged gear cables (Chapter 7A).
- ☐ Incorrectly-fitted gear cables (Chapter 7A).
- ☐ Worn synchroniser assemblies (Chapter 7A).*

Jumps out of gear

- ☐ Worn or damaged gear cables (Chapter 7A).
- ☐ Incorrectly-fitted gear cables (Chapter 7A).
- ☐ Worn synchroniser assemblies (Chapter 7A).*
- ☐ Worn selector forks (Chapter 7A).*

Vibration

- ☐ Lack of oil (Chapter 1).
- ☐ Worn bearings (Chapter 7A).*

Lubricant leaks

- ☐ Leaking differential side gear oil seal (Chapter 7A).
- ☐ Leaking housing joint (Chapter 7A).*
- ☐ Leaking input shaft oil seal (Chapter 7A).*
- ☐ Leaking selector shaft oil seal (Chapter 7A).

** Although the corrective action necessary to remedy the symptoms described is beyond the scope of the home mechanic, the above information should be helpful in isolating the cause of the condition, so that the owner can communicate clearly with a professional mechanic.*

Driveshafts

Vibration when accelerating or decelerating

- ☐ Worn inner constant velocity joint (Chapter 1A, 1B, or 8).
- ☐ Bent or distorted driveshaft (Chapter 8).
- ☐ Worn intermediate bearing (Chapter 8).
- ☐ Loose or damaged driveshaft nut (Chapter 1A, 1B, or 8).

Clicking or knocking noise on turns (at slow speed on full-lock)

- ☐ Lack of constant velocity joint lubricant (Chapter 8).
- ☐ Worn outer constant velocity joint (Chapter 1A, 1B, or 8).
- ☐ Worn intermediate bearing (Chapter 8).
- ☐ Loose or damaged driveshaft nut (Chapter 1A, 1B, or 8).

Automatic transmission

Note: *Due to the complexity of the automatic transmission, it is difficult for the home mechanic to properly diagnose and service this unit. For problems other than the following, the car should be taken to a dealer service department or automatic transmission specialist. Do not be too hasty in removing the transmission if a fault is suspected, as most of the testing is carried out with the unit still fitted.*

Fluid leakage

- ☐ Automatic transmission fluid is usually dark in colour. Fluid leaks should not be confused with engine oil, which can easily be blown onto the transmission by airflow.
- ☐ To determine the source of a leak, first remove all built-up dirt and grime from the transmission housing and surrounding areas using a degreasing agent, or by steam-cleaning. Drive the car at low speed, so airflow will not blow the leak far from its source. Raise and support the car, and determine where the leak is coming from.

General gear selection problems

- ☐ Chapter 7B deals with checking and adjusting the selector cable on automatic transmissions. The following are common problems which may be caused by a poorly-adjusted cable:
  - *a) Engine starting in gears other than Park or Neutral.*
  - *b) Indicator panel indicating a gear other than the one actually being used.*
  - *c) Car moves when in Park or Neutral.*
  - *d) Poor gear shift quality or erratic gear changes.*
- ☐ Refer to Chapter 7B for the selector cable adjustment procedure.

Transmission will not downshift (kickdown) with accelerator pedal fully depressed

- ☐ Low transmission fluid level (Chapter 1).
- ☐ Incorrect selector cable adjustment (Chapter 7B).

Engine will not start in any gear, or starts in gears other than Park or Neutral

- ☐ Incorrect selector cable adjustment (Chapter 7B).

Transmission slips, shifts roughly, is noisy, or has no drive in forward or reverse gears

- ☐ There are many probable causes for the above problems, but unless there is a very obvious reason (such as a loose or corroded wiring plug connection on or near the transmission), the car should be taken to an MG Rover specialist, or automatic transmission expert, for the fault to be diagnosed. The transmission control unit incorporates a self-diagnosis facility, and any fault codes can quickly be read and interpreted by someone with the proper diagnostic equipment.

Braking system

Note: *Before assuming that a brake problem exists, make sure that the tyres are in good condition and correctly inflated, that the front wheel alignment is correct, and that the car is not loaded with weight in an unequal manner. Apart from checking the condition of all pipe and hose connections, any faults occurring on the Anti-lock Braking System (ABS) should be referred to an MG Rover specialist, experienced garage, or Bosch agent, for diagnosis.*

Car pulls to one side under braking

- ☐ Worn, defective, damaged or contaminated front or rear brake pads on one side (Chapter 1A or 1B).
- ☐ Seized or partially-seized caliper piston (Chapter 9).
- ☐ A mixture of brake pad lining materials fitted between sides (Chapter 1A or 1B).
- ☐ Brake caliper mounting bolts loose (Chapter 9).
- ☐ Worn or damaged steering or suspension components (Chapter 10).

Noise (grinding or high-pitched squeal) when brakes applied

- ☐ Brake pad friction lining material worn down to metal backing Chapter 1A or 1B).
- ☐ Excessive corrosion of brake disc (may be apparent after the car has been standing for some time) (Chapter 1A or 1B).

Excessive brake pedal travel

- ☐ Faulty master cylinder (Chapter 9).
- ☐ Air in hydraulic system (Chapter 9).

Brake pedal feels spongy when depressed

- ☐ Air in hydraulic system (Chapter 9).
- ☐ Deteriorated flexible rubber brake hoses (Chapter 9).
- ☐ Master cylinder mounting nuts loose (Chapter 9).
- ☐ Faulty master cylinder (Chapter 9).

Excessive brake pedal effort required to stop car

- ☐ Faulty vacuum servo unit (Chapter 9).
- ☐ Disconnected, damaged or insecure brake servo vacuum hoses (Chapter 9).
- ☐ Brake vacuum pump leaking or faulty – diesel models (Chapter 9).
- ☐ Primary or secondary hydraulic circuit failure (Chapter 9).
- ☐ Seized brake caliper piston (Chapter 9).
- ☐ Brake pads incorrectly fitted (Chapter 9).
- ☐ Incorrect grade of brake pads fitted (Chapter 1A or 1B).
- ☐ Brake pads contaminated (Chapter 1A or 1B).

Judder felt through brake pedal or steering wheel when braking

- ☐ Excessive run-out or distortion of front or rear discs (Chapter 9).
- ☐ Brake pads worn (Chapter 1A or 1B).
- ☐ Brake caliper mounting bolts loose (Chapter 9).
- ☐ Wear in suspension or steering components or mountings (Chapter 10).

Brakes binding

- ☐ Seized brake caliper piston (Chapter 9).
- ☐ Faulty handbrake mechanism (Chapter 9).
- ☐ Faulty master cylinder (Chapter 9).

Rear wheels locking under normal braking

- ☐ Rear brake pads contaminated (Chapter 1A or 1B).
- ☐ Faulty ABS unit (Chapter 9).

Suspension and steering

Note: *Before diagnosing suspension or steering faults, be sure that the trouble is not due to incorrect tyre pressures, mixtures of tyre types, or binding brakes.*

Car pulls to one side

- ☐ Defective tyre (Chapter 1A or 1B).
- ☐ Excessive wear in suspension or steering components (Chapter 10).
- ☐ Incorrect front wheel alignment (Chapter 10).
- ☐ Accident damage to steering or suspension components (Chapter 10).

Wheel wobble and vibration

- ☐ Front roadwheels out of balance (vibration felt mainly through the steering wheel) (Chapter 1A or 1B).
- ☐ Rear roadwheels out of balance (vibration felt throughout the car) (Chapter 1A or 1B).
- ☐ Roadwheels damaged or distorted (Chapter 1A or 1B).
- ☐ Faulty or damaged tyre (*Weekly checks*).
- ☐ Worn steering or suspension joints, bushes or components (Chapter 10).
- ☐ Roadwheel bolts loose (Chapter 1A or 1B).
- ☐ Wear in driveshaft joint, or loose driveshaft nut (vibration worst when under load) (Chapter 1A, 1B, or 8).

Excessive pitching and/or rolling around corners, or during braking

- ☐ Defective shock absorbers (Chapter 10).
- ☐ Broken or weak coil spring and/or suspension components (Chapter 10).
- ☐ Worn or damaged anti-roll bar or mountings (Chapter 10).

Wandering or general instability

- ☐ Incorrect front wheel alignment (Chapter 10).
- ☐ Worn steering or suspension joints, bushes or components (Chapter 10).
- ☐ Tyres out of balance (*Weekly checks*).
- ☐ Faulty or damaged tyre (*Weekly checks*).
- ☐ Roadwheel bolts loose (Chapter 1A or 1B).
- ☐ Defective shock absorbers (Chapter 10).

Excessively-stiff steering

- ☐ Lack of steering gear lubricant (Chapter 10).
- ☐ Seized track-rod end balljoint or suspension balljoint (Chapter 10).
- ☐ Broken or slipping auxiliary drivebelt (Chapter 1A or 1B).
- ☐ Incorrect front wheel alignment (Chapter 10).
- ☐ Steering rack or column bent or damaged (Chapter 10).

Excessive play in steering

- ☐ Worn steering column universal joint (Chapter 10).
- ☐ Worn steering track-rod end balljoints (Chapter 10).
- ☐ Worn rack-and-pinion steering gear (Chapter 10).
- ☐ Worn steering or suspension joints, bushes or components (Chapter 10).

Lack of power assistance

- ☐ Broken or slipping auxiliary drivebelt (Chapter 1A or 1B).
- ☐ Incorrect power steering fluid level (*Weekly checks*).
- ☐ Restriction in power steering fluid hoses (Chapter 10).
- ☐ Faulty power steering pump (Chapter 10).
- ☐ Faulty rack-and-pinion steering gear (Chapter 10).

Tyre wear excessive

Tyres worn on inside or outside edges

- ☐ Tyres under-inflated (wear on both edges) (*Weekly checks*).
- ☐ Incorrect camber or castor angles (wear on one edge only) (Chapter 10).
- ☐ Worn steering or suspension joints, bushes or components (Chapter 10).
- ☐ Excessively-hard cornering.
- ☐ Accident damage.

Tyre treads exhibit feathered edges

- ☐ Incorrect toe setting (Chapter 10).

Tyres worn in centre of tread

- ☐ Tyres over-inflated (*Weekly checks*).

Tyres worn on inside and outside edges

- ☐ Tyres under-inflated (*Weekly checks*).

Tyres worn unevenly

- ☐ Tyres out of balance (*Weekly checks*).
- ☐ Excessive wheel or tyre run-out (Chapter 1A or 1B).
- ☐ Worn shock absorbers (Chapter 10).
- ☐ Faulty tyre (*Weekly checks*).

Electrical system

Note: *For problems associated with the starting system, refer to the faults listed under Engine earlier in this Section.*

Battery will only hold a charge for a few days

- ☐ Battery defective internally (Chapter 5A).
- ☐ Battery electrolyte level low (Chapter 5A).
- ☐ Battery terminal connections loose or corroded (*Weekly checks*).
- ☐ Auxiliary drivebelt worn or slipping (Chapter 1A or 1B).
- ☐ Alternator not charging at correct output (Chapter 5A).
- ☐ Alternator or voltage regulator faulty (Chapter 5A).
- ☐ Short-circuit causing continual battery drain (Chapters 5A and 12).

Ignition (no-charge) warning light remains illuminated with engine running

- ☐ Auxiliary drivebelt broken, worn, or slipping (Chapter 1A or 1B).
- ☐ Alternator brushes worn, sticking, or dirty (Chapter 5A).
- ☐ Alternator brush springs weak or broken (Chapter 5A).
- ☐ Internal fault in alternator or voltage regulator (Chapter 5A).
- ☐ Disconnected or loose wiring in charging circuit (Chapter 5A).

Ignition (no-charge) warning light fails to come on

- ☐ Warning light bulb blown (Chapter 12).
- ☐ Broken, disconnected, or loose wiring in warning light circuit (Chapters 5A and 12).
- ☐ Alternator faulty (Chapter 5A).

Lights inoperative

- ☐ Bulb blown (Chapter 12).
- ☐ Corrosion of bulb or bulbholder contacts (Chapter 12).
- ☐ Blown fuse (Chapter 12).
- ☐ Faulty relay (Chapter 12).
- ☐ Broken, loose, or disconnected wiring (Chapter 12).
- ☐ Body control unit (BCU) fault (Chapter 12).
- ☐ Faulty switch (Chapter 12).

Instrument readings inaccurate or erratic

Gauges give no reading

- ☐ Faulty gauge sender unit (Chapter 3 or 4A).
- ☐ Wiring open-circuit (Chapter 12).
- ☐ Faulty gauge (Chapter 12).
- ☐ Body control unit (BCU) fault (Chapter 12).

Gauges give continuous maximum reading

- ☐ Faulty gauge sender unit (Chapter 3 or 4A).
- ☐ Wiring short-circuit (Chapter 12).
- ☐ Faulty gauge (Chapter 12).
- ☐ Body control unit (BCU) fault (Chapter 12).

Horn faults

Horn fails to operate

- ☐ Blown fuse (Chapter 12).
- ☐ Cable or cable connections loose or disconnected (Chapter 12).
- ☐ Faulty horn (Chapter 12).

Horn emits intermittent or unsatisfactory sound

- ☐ Cable connections loose (Chapter 12).
- ☐ Horn mountings loose (Chapter 12).
- ☐ Faulty horn (Chapter 12).

Horn operates all the time

- ☐ Horn push either earthed or stuck down (Chapter 12).
- ☐ Horn cable to horn push earthed (Chapter 12).

Windscreen/tailgate wiper faults

Wipers fail to operate, or operate very slowly

- ☐ Wiper blades stuck to screen, or linkage seized (Chapter 12).
- ☐ Blown fuse (Chapter 12).
- ☐ Cable or cable connections loose or disconnected (Chapter 12).
- ☐ Faulty relay (Chapter 12).
- ☐ Faulty wiper motor (Chapter 12).
- ☐ Body control unit (BCU) fault (Chapter 12).

Wiper blades sweep over the wrong area of glass

- ☐ Wiper arms incorrectly-positioned on spindles (Chapter 12).
- ☐ Excessive wear of wiper linkage (Chapter 12).
- ☐ Wiper motor or linkage mountings loose or insecure (Chapter 12).

Wiper blades fail to clean the glass effectively

- ☐ Wiper blade rubbers worn or perished (*Weekly checks*).
- ☐ Wiper arm tension springs broken, or arm pivots seized (Chapter 12).
- ☐ Insufficient windscreen washer additive to adequately remove road film (*Weekly checks*).

Windscreen/tailgate washer faults

One or more washer jets inoperative

- ☐ Blocked washer jet (*Weekly checks* or Chapter 12).
- ☐ Disconnected, kinked or restricted fluid hose (Chapter 12).
- ☐ Insufficient fluid in washer reservoir (*Weekly checks*).

Washer pump fails to operate

- ☐ Broken or disconnected wiring or connections (Chapter 12).
- ☐ Blown fuse (Chapter 12).
- ☐ Faulty washer switch (Chapter 12).
- ☐ Faulty washer pump (Chapter 12).

Washer pump runs for some time before fluid is emitted from jets

- ☐ Faulty one-way valve in fluid supply hose (Chapter 12).

Electric window faults

Window glass will only move in one direction

- ☐ Faulty switch (Chapter 12).

Window glass slow to move

- ☐ Regulator seized or damaged, or lack of lubrication (Chapter 11).
- ☐ Door internal components or trim fouling regulator (Chapter 11).
- ☐ Faulty motor (Chapter 12).

Window glass fails to move

- ☐ Blown fuse (Chapter 12).
- ☐ Faulty relay (Chapter 12).
- ☐ Broken or disconnected wiring or connections (Chapter 12).
- ☐ Faulty motor (Chapter 12).

Central locking system faults

Complete system failure

- ☐ Blown fuse (Chapter 12).
- ☐ Faulty relay (Chapter 12).
- ☐ Broken or disconnected wiring or connections (Chapter 12).
- ☐ Body control unit (BCU) fault (Chapter 12).

Latch locks but will not unlock, or unlocks but will not lock

- ☐ Faulty lock (Chapter 11).

One lock motor fails to operate

- ☐ Broken or disconnected wiring or connections (Chapter 12).
- ☐ Faulty lock motor (Chapter 11).
- ☐ Fault in door latch (Chapter 11).

A

ABS (Anti-lock brake system) A system, usually electronically controlled, that senses incipient wheel lockup during braking and relieves hydraulic pressure at wheels that are about to skid.
Air bag An inflatable bag hidden in the steering wheel (driver's side) or the dash or glovebox (passenger side). In a head-on collision, the bags inflate, preventing the driver and front passenger from being thrown forward into the steering wheel or windscreen.
Air cleaner A metal or plastic housing, containing a filter element, which removes dust and dirt from the air being drawn into the engine.
Air filter element The actual filter in an air cleaner system, usually manufactured from pleated paper and requiring renewal at regular intervals.

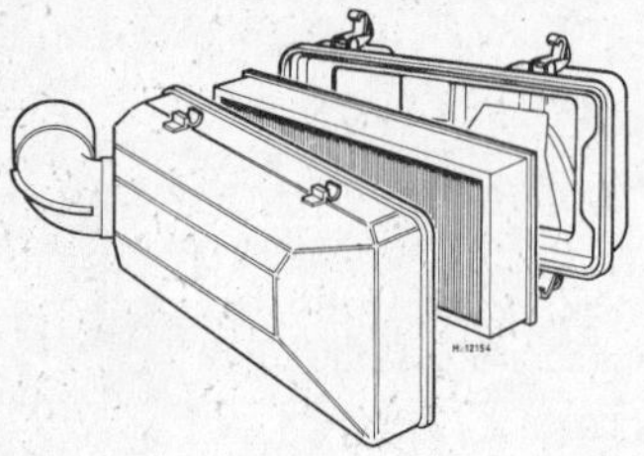

Air filter

Allen key A hexagonal wrench which fits into a recessed hexagonal hole.
Alligator clip A long-nosed spring-loaded metal clip with meshing teeth. Used to make temporary electrical connections.
Alternator A component in the electrical system which converts mechanical energy from a drivebelt into electrical energy to charge the battery and to operate the starting system, ignition system and electrical accessories.
Ampere (amp) A unit of measurement for the flow of electric current. One amp is the amount of current produced by one volt acting through a resistance of one ohm.
Anaerobic sealer A substance used to prevent bolts and screws from loosening. Anaerobic means that it does not require oxygen for activation. The Loctite brand is widely used.
Antifreeze A substance (usually ethylene glycol) mixed with water, and added to a vehicle's cooling system, to prevent freezing of the coolant in winter. Antifreeze also contains chemicals to inhibit corrosion and the formation of rust and other deposits that would tend to clog the radiator and coolant passages and reduce cooling efficiency.
Anti-seize compound A coating that reduces the risk of seizing on fasteners that are subjected to high temperatures, such as exhaust manifold bolts and nuts.
Asbestos A natural fibrous mineral with great heat resistance, commonly used in the composition of brake friction materials. Asbestos is a health hazard and the dust created by brake systems should never be inhaled or ingested.
Axle A shaft on which a wheel revolves, or which revolves with a wheel. Also, a solid beam that connects the two wheels at one end of the vehicle. An axle which also transmits power to the wheels is known as a live axle.
Axleshaft A single rotating shaft, on either side of the differential, which delivers power from the final drive assembly to the drive wheels. Also called a driveshaft or a halfshaft.

B

Ball bearing An anti-friction bearing consisting of a hardened inner and outer race with hardened steel balls between two races.
Bearing The curved surface on a shaft or in a bore, or the part assembled into either, that permits relative motion between them with minimum wear and friction.

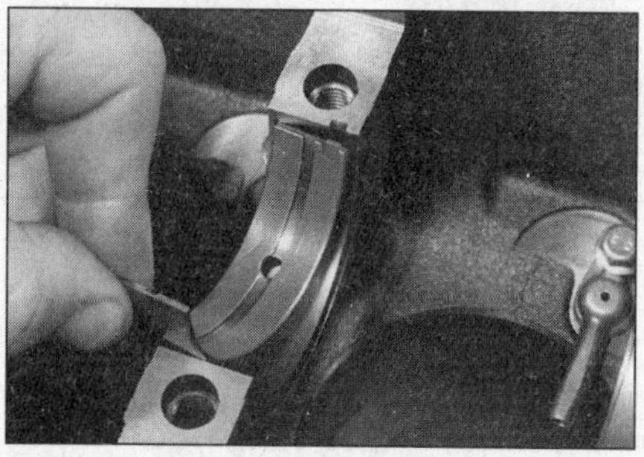

Bearing

Big-end bearing The bearing in the end of the connecting rod that's attached to the crankshaft.
Bleed nipple A valve on a brake wheel cylinder, caliper or other hydraulic component that is opened to purge the hydraulic system of air. Also called a bleed screw.
Brake bleeding Procedure for removing air from lines of a hydraulic brake system.

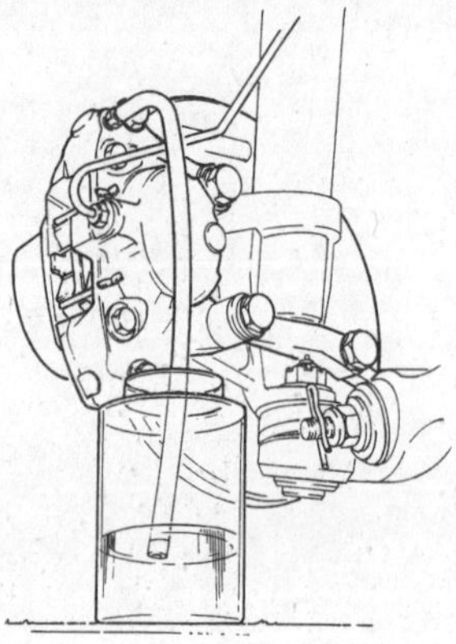

Brake bleeding

Brake disc The component of a disc brake that rotates with the wheels.
Brake drum The component of a drum brake that rotates with the wheels.
Brake linings The friction material which contacts the brake disc or drum to retard the vehicle's speed. The linings are bonded or riveted to the brake pads or shoes.
Brake pads The replaceable friction pads that pinch the brake disc when the brakes are applied. Brake pads consist of a friction material bonded or riveted to a rigid backing plate.
Brake shoe The crescent-shaped carrier to which the brake linings are mounted and which forces the lining against the rotating drum during braking.
Braking systems For more information on braking systems, consult the *Haynes Automotive Brake Manual*.
Breaker bar A long socket wrench handle providing greater leverage.
Bulkhead The insulated partition between the engine and the passenger compartment.

C

Caliper The non-rotating part of a disc-brake assembly that straddles the disc and carries the brake pads. The caliper also contains the hydraulic components that cause the pads to pinch the disc when the brakes are applied. A caliper is also a measuring tool that can be set to measure inside or outside dimensions of an object.
Camshaft A rotating shaft on which a series of cam lobes operate the valve mechanisms. The camshaft may be driven by gears, by sprockets and chain or by sprockets and a belt.
Canister A container in an evaporative emission control system; contains activated charcoal granules to trap vapours from the fuel system.

Canister

Carburettor A device which mixes fuel with air in the proper proportions to provide a desired power output from a spark ignition internal combustion engine.
Castellated Resembling the parapets along the top of a castle wall. For example, a castellated balljoint stud nut.
Castor In wheel alignment, the backward or forward tilt of the steering axis. Castor is positive when the steering axis is inclined rearward at the top.

Catalytic converter A silencer-like device in the exhaust system which converts certain pollutants in the exhaust gases into less harmful substances.

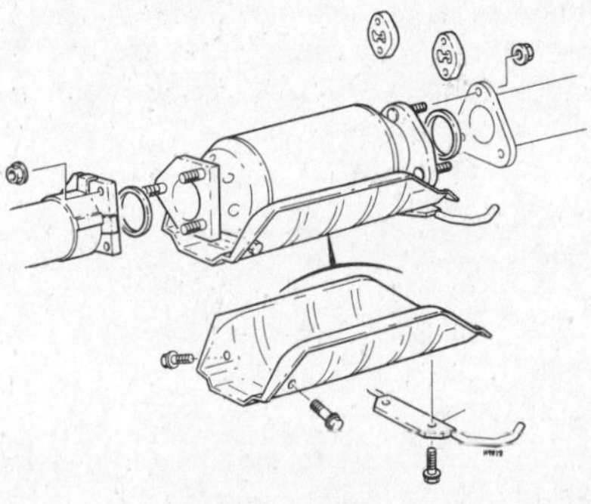

Catalytic converter

Circlip A ring-shaped clip used to prevent endwise movement of cylindrical parts and shafts. An internal circlip is installed in a groove in a housing; an external circlip fits into a groove on the outside of a cylindrical piece such as a shaft.

Clearance The amount of space between two parts. For example, between a piston and a cylinder, between a bearing and a journal, etc.

Coil spring A spiral of elastic steel found in various sizes throughout a vehicle, for example as a springing medium in the suspension and in the valve train.

Compression Reduction in volume, and increase in pressure and temperature, of a gas, caused by squeezing it into a smaller space.

Compression ratio The relationship between cylinder volume when the piston is at top dead centre and cylinder volume when the piston is at bottom dead centre.

Constant velocity (CV) joint A type of universal joint that cancels out vibrations caused by driving power being transmitted through an angle.

Core plug A disc or cup-shaped metal device inserted in a hole in a casting through which core was removed when the casting was formed. Also known as a freeze plug or expansion plug.

Crankcase The lower part of the engine block in which the crankshaft rotates.

Crankshaft The main rotating member, or shaft, running the length of the crankcase, with offset "throws" to which the connecting rods are attached.

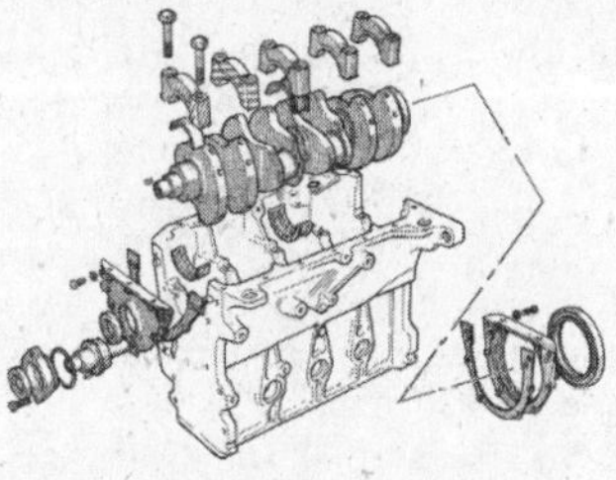

Crankshaft assembly

Crocodile clip See Alligator clip

D

Diagnostic code Code numbers obtained by accessing the diagnostic mode of an engine management computer. This code can be used to determine the area in the system where a malfunction may be located.

Disc brake A brake design incorporating a rotating disc onto which brake pads are squeezed. The resulting friction converts the energy of a moving vehicle into heat.

Double-overhead cam (DOHC) An engine that uses two overhead camshafts, usually one for the intake valves and one for the exhaust valves.

Drivebelt(s) The belt(s) used to drive accessories such as the alternator, water pump, power steering pump, air conditioning compressor, etc. off the crankshaft pulley.

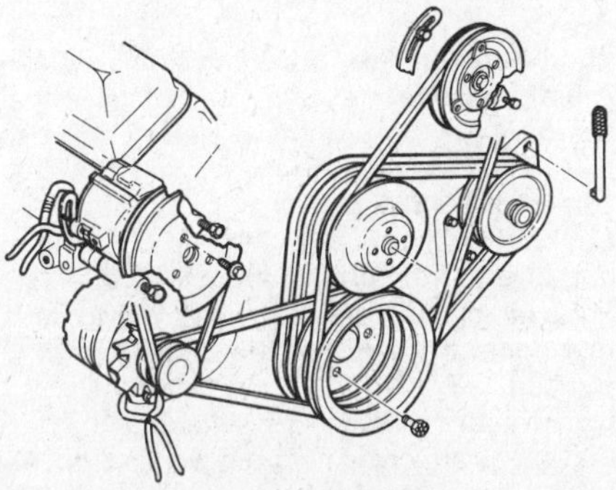

Accessory drivebelts

Driveshaft Any shaft used to transmit motion. Commonly used when referring to the axleshafts on a front wheel drive vehicle.

Drum brake A type of brake using a drum-shaped metal cylinder attached to the inner surface of the wheel. When the brake pedal is pressed, curved brake shoes with friction linings press against the inside of the drum to slow or stop the vehicle.

E

EGR valve A valve used to introduce exhaust gases into the intake air stream.

Electronic control unit (ECU) A computer which controls (for instance) ignition and fuel injection systems, or an anti-lock braking system. For more information refer to the *Haynes Automotive Electrical and Electronic Systems Manual.*

Electronic Fuel Injection (EFI) A computer controlled fuel system that distributes fuel through an injector located in each intake port of the engine.

Emergency brake A braking system, independent of the main hydraulic system, that can be used to slow or stop the vehicle if the primary brakes fail, or to hold the vehicle stationary even though the brake pedal isn't depressed. It usually consists of a hand lever that actuates either front or rear brakes mechanically through a series of cables and linkages. Also known as a handbrake or parking brake.

Endfloat The amount of lengthwise movement between two parts. As applied to a crankshaft, the distance that the crankshaft can move forward and back in the cylinder block.

Engine management system (EMS) A computer controlled system which manages the fuel injection and the ignition systems in an integrated fashion.

Exhaust manifold A part with several passages through which exhaust gases leave the engine combustion chambers and enter the exhaust pipe.

F

Fan clutch A viscous (fluid) drive coupling device which permits variable engine fan speeds in relation to engine speeds.

Feeler blade A thin strip or blade of hardened steel, ground to an exact thickness, used to check or measure clearances between parts.

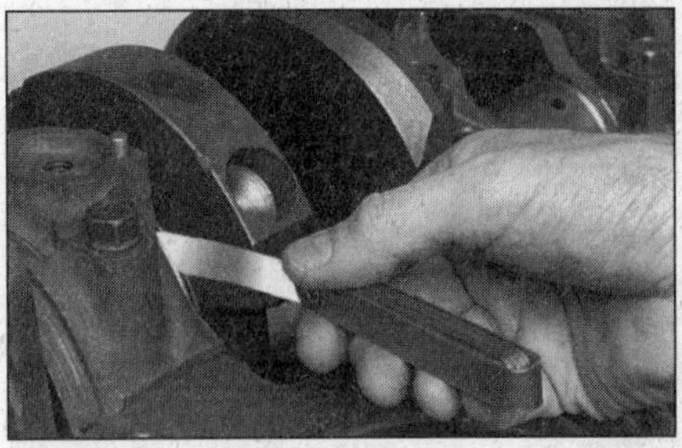

Feeler blade

Firing order The order in which the engine cylinders fire, or deliver their power strokes, beginning with the number one cylinder.

Flywheel A heavy spinning wheel in which energy is absorbed and stored by means of momentum. On cars, the flywheel is attached to the crankshaft to smooth out firing impulses.

Free play The amount of travel before any action takes place. The "looseness" in a linkage, or an assembly of parts, between the initial application of force and actual movement. For example, the distance the brake pedal moves before the pistons in the master cylinder are actuated.

Fuse An electrical device which protects a circuit against accidental overload. The typical fuse contains a soft piece of metal which is calibrated to melt at a predetermined current flow (expressed as amps) and break the circuit.

Fusible link A circuit protection device consisting of a conductor surrounded by heat-resistant insulation. The conductor is smaller than the wire it protects, so it acts as the weakest link in the circuit. Unlike a blown fuse, a failed fusible link must frequently be cut from the wire for replacement.

G

Gap The distance the spark must travel in jumping from the centre electrode to the side electrode in a spark plug. Also refers to the spacing between the points in a contact breaker assembly in a conventional points-type ignition, or to the distance between the reluctor or rotor and the pickup coil in an electronic ignition.

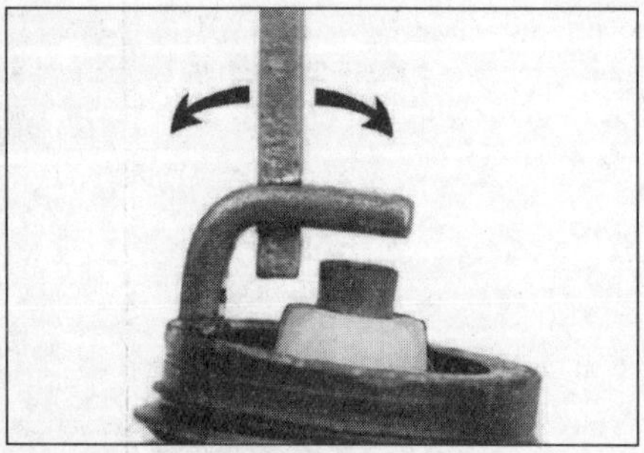

Adjusting spark plug gap

Gasket Any thin, soft material - usually cork, cardboard, asbestos or soft metal - installed between two metal surfaces to ensure a good seal. For instance, the cylinder head gasket seals the joint between the block and the cylinder head.

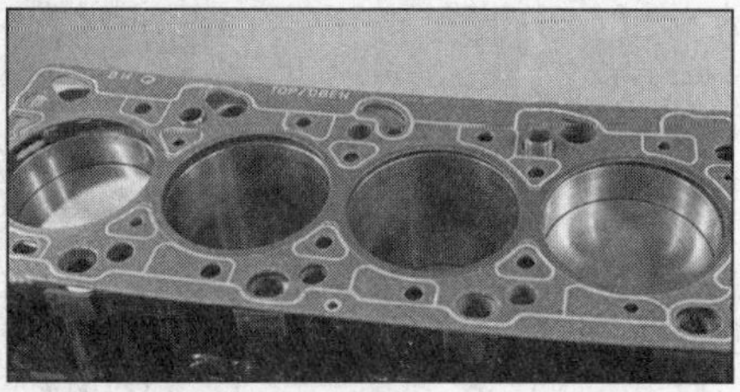

Gasket

Gauge An instrument panel display used to monitor engine conditions. A gauge with a movable pointer on a dial or a fixed scale is an analogue gauge. A gauge with a numerical readout is called a digital gauge.

H

Halfshaft A rotating shaft that transmits power from the final drive unit to a drive wheel, usually when referring to a live rear axle.

Harmonic balancer A device designed to reduce torsion or twisting vibration in the crankshaft. May be incorporated in the crankshaft pulley. Also known as a vibration damper.

Hone An abrasive tool for correcting small irregularities or differences in diameter in an engine cylinder, brake cylinder, etc.

Hydraulic tappet A tappet that utilises hydraulic pressure from the engine's lubrication system to maintain zero clearance (constant contact with both camshaft and valve stem). Automatically adjusts to variation in valve stem length. Hydraulic tappets also reduce valve noise.

I

Ignition timing The moment at which the spark plug fires, usually expressed in the number of crankshaft degrees before the piston reaches the top of its stroke.

Inlet manifold A tube or housing with passages through which flows the air-fuel mixture (carburettor vehicles and vehicles with throttle body injection) or air only (port fuel-injected vehicles) to the port openings in the cylinder head.

J

Jump start Starting the engine of a vehicle with a discharged or weak battery by attaching jump leads from the weak battery to a charged or helper battery.

L

Load Sensing Proportioning Valve (LSPV) A brake hydraulic system control valve that works like a proportioning valve, but also takes into consideration the amount of weight carried by the rear axle.

Locknut A nut used to lock an adjustment nut, or other threaded component, in place. For example, a locknut is employed to keep the adjusting nut on the rocker arm in position.

Lockwasher A form of washer designed to prevent an attaching nut from working loose.

M

MacPherson strut A type of front suspension system devised by Earle MacPherson at Ford of England. In its original form, a simple lateral link with the anti-roll bar creates the lower control arm. A long strut - an integral coil spring and shock absorber - is mounted between the body and the steering knuckle. Many modern so-called MacPherson strut systems use a conventional lower A-arm and don't rely on the anti-roll bar for location.

Multimeter An electrical test instrument with the capability to measure voltage, current and resistance.

N

NOx Oxides of Nitrogen. A common toxic pollutant emitted by petrol and diesel engines at higher temperatures.

O

Ohm The unit of electrical resistance. One volt applied to a resistance of one ohm will produce a current of one amp.

Ohmmeter An instrument for measuring electrical resistance.

O-ring A type of sealing ring made of a special rubber-like material; in use, the O-ring is compressed into a groove to provide the sealing action.

Overhead cam (ohc) engine An engine with the camshaft(s) located on top of the cylinder head(s).

Overhead valve (ohv) engine An engine with the valves located in the cylinder head, but with the camshaft located in the engine block.

Oxygen sensor A device installed in the engine exhaust manifold, which senses the oxygen content in the exhaust and converts this information into an electric current. Also called a Lambda sensor.

P

Phillips screw A type of screw head having a cross instead of a slot for a corresponding type of screwdriver.

Plastigage A thin strip of plastic thread, available in different sizes, used for measuring clearances. For example, a strip of Plastigage is laid across a bearing journal. The parts are assembled and dismantled; the width of the crushed strip indicates the clearance between journal and bearing.

Plastigage

Propeller shaft The long hollow tube with universal joints at both ends that carries power from the transmission to the differential on front-engined rear wheel drive vehicles.

Proportioning valve A hydraulic control valve which limits the amount of pressure to the rear brakes during panic stops to prevent wheel lock-up.

R

Rack-and-pinion steering A steering system with a pinion gear on the end of the steering shaft that mates with a rack (think of a geared wheel opened up and laid flat). When the steering wheel is turned, the pinion turns, moving the rack to the left or right. This movement is transmitted through the track rods to the steering arms at the wheels.

Radiator A liquid-to-air heat transfer device designed to reduce the temperature of the coolant in an internal combustion engine cooling system.

Refrigerant Any substance used as a heat transfer agent in an air-conditioning system. R-12 has been the principle refrigerant for many years; recently, however, manufacturers have begun using R-134a, a non-CFC substance that is considered less harmful to the ozone in the upper atmosphere.

Rocker arm A lever arm that rocks on a shaft or pivots on a stud. In an overhead valve engine, the rocker arm converts the upward movement of the pushrod into a downward movement to open a valve.

Rotor In a distributor, the rotating device inside the cap that connects the centre electrode and the outer terminals as it turns, distributing the high voltage from the coil secondary winding to the proper spark plug. Also, that part of an alternator which rotates inside the stator. Also, the rotating assembly of a turbocharger, including the compressor wheel, shaft and turbine wheel.
Runout The amount of wobble (in-and-out movement) of a gear or wheel as it's rotated. The amount a shaft rotates "out-of-true." The out-of-round condition of a rotating part.

S

Sealant A liquid or paste used to prevent leakage at a joint. Sometimes used in conjunction with a gasket.
Sealed beam lamp An older headlight design which integrates the reflector, lens and filaments into a hermetically-sealed one-piece unit. When a filament burns out or the lens cracks, the entire unit is simply replaced.
Serpentine drivebelt A single, long, wide accessory drivebelt that's used on some newer vehicles to drive all the accessories, instead of a series of smaller, shorter belts. Serpentine drivebelts are usually tensioned by an automatic tensioner.

Serpentine drivebelt

Shim Thin spacer, commonly used to adjust the clearance or relative positions between two parts. For example, shims inserted into or under bucket tappets control valve clearances. Clearance is adjusted by changing the thickness of the shim.
Slide hammer A special puller that screws into or hooks onto a component such as a shaft or bearing; a heavy sliding handle on the shaft bottoms against the end of the shaft to knock the component free.
Sprocket A tooth or projection on the periphery of a wheel, shaped to engage with a chain or drivebelt. Commonly used to refer to the sprocket wheel itself.
Starter inhibitor switch On vehicles with an automatic transmission, a switch that prevents starting if the vehicle is not in Neutral or Park.
Strut See MacPherson strut.

T

Tappet A cylindrical component which transmits motion from the cam to the valve stem, either directly or via a pushrod and rocker arm. Also called a cam follower.
Thermostat A heat-controlled valve that regulates the flow of coolant between the cylinder block and the radiator, so maintaining optimum engine operating temperature. A thermostat is also used in some air cleaners in which the temperature is regulated.
Thrust bearing The bearing in the clutch assembly that is moved in to the release levers by clutch pedal action to disengage the clutch. Also referred to as a release bearing.
Timing belt A toothed belt which drives the camshaft. Serious engine damage may result if it breaks in service.
Timing chain A chain which drives the camshaft.
Toe-in The amount the front wheels are closer together at the front than at the rear. On rear wheel drive vehicles, a slight amount of toe-in is usually specified to keep the front wheels running parallel on the road by offsetting other forces that tend to spread the wheels apart.
Toe-out The amount the front wheels are closer together at the rear than at the front. On front wheel drive vehicles, a slight amount of toe-out is usually specified.
Tools For full information on choosing and using tools, refer to the *Haynes Automotive Tools Manual.*
Tracer A stripe of a second colour applied to a wire insulator to distinguish that wire from another one with the same colour insulator.
Tune-up A process of accurate and careful adjustments and parts replacement to obtain the best possible engine performance.
Turbocharger A centrifugal device, driven by exhaust gases, that pressurises the intake air. Normally used to increase the power output from a given engine displacement, but can also be used primarily to reduce exhaust emissions (as on VW's "Umwelt" Diesel engine).

U

Universal joint or U-joint A double-pivoted connection for transmitting power from a driving to a driven shaft through an angle. A U-joint consists of two Y-shaped yokes and a cross-shaped member called the spider.

V

Valve A device through which the flow of liquid, gas, vacuum, or loose material in bulk may be started, stopped, or regulated by a movable part that opens, shuts, or partially obstructs one or more ports or passageways. A valve is also the movable part of such a device.
Valve clearance The clearance between the valve tip (the end of the valve stem) and the rocker arm or tappet. The valve clearance is measured when the valve is closed.
Vernier caliper A precision measuring instrument that measures inside and outside dimensions. Not quite as accurate as a micrometer, but more convenient.
Viscosity The thickness of a liquid or its resistance to flow.
Volt A unit for expressing electrical "pressure" in a circuit. One volt that will produce a current of one ampere through a resistance of one ohm.

W

Welding Various processes used to join metal items by heating the areas to be joined to a molten state and fusing them together. For more information refer to the *Haynes Automotive Welding Manual.*
Wiring diagram A drawing portraying the components and wires in a vehicle's electrical system, using standardised symbols. For more information refer to the *Haynes Automotive Electrical and Electronic Systems Manual.*

Note: *References throughout this index are in the form* **"Chapter number" • "Page number"**. *So, for example, 2C•15 refers to page 15 of Chapter 2C.*

Note: *References throughout this index are in the form* "**Chapter number**" • "**Page number**". *So, for example, 2C•15 refers to page 15 of Chapter 2C.*

Note: *References throughout this index are in the form* **"Chapter number" • "Page number"**. *So, for example, 2C•15 refers to page 15 of Chapter 2C.*

Note: *References throughout this index are in the form* **"Chapter number" • "Page number"**. *So, for example, 2C•15 refers to page 15 of Chapter 2C.*

Haynes Manuals – The Complete **UK Car** List

Title	Book No.
ALFA ROMEO Alfasud/Sprint (74 - 88) up to F *	0292
Alfa Romeo Alfetta (73 - 87) up to E *	0531
AUDI 80, 90 & Coupe Petrol (79 - Nov 88) up to F	0605
Audi 80, 90 & Coupe Petrol (Oct 86 - 90) D to H	1491
Audi 100 & 200 Petrol (Oct 82 - 90) up to H	0907
Audi 100 & A6 Petrol & Diesel (May 91 - May 97) H to P	3504
Audi A3 Petrol & Diesel (96 - May 03) P to 03	4253
Audi A4 Petrol & Diesel (95 - 00) M to X	3575
Audi A4 Petrol & Diesel (01 - 04) X to 54	4609
AUSTIN A35 & A40 (56 - 67) up to F *	0118
Austin/MG/Rover Maestro 1.3 & 1.6 Petrol (83 - 95) up to M	0922
Austin/MG Metro (80 - May 90) up to G	0718
Austin/Rover Montego 1.3 & 1.6 Petrol (84 - 94) A to L	1066
Austin/MG/Rover Montego 2.0 Petrol (84 - 95) A to M	1067
Mini (59 - 69) up to H *	0527
Mini (69 - 01) up to X	0646
Austin/Rover 2.0 litre Diesel Engine (86 - 93) C to L	1857
Austin Healey 100/6 & 3000 (56 - 68) up to G *	0049
BEDFORD CF Petrol (69 - 87) up to E	0163
Bedford/Vauxhall Rascal & Suzuki Supercarry (86 - Oct 94) C to M	3015
BMW 316, 320 & 320i (4-cyl) (75 - Feb 83) up to Y *	0276
BMW 320, 320i, 323i & 325i (6-cyl) (Oct 77 - Sept 87) up to E	0815
BMW 3- & 5-Series Petrol (81 - 91) up to J	1948
BMW 3-Series Petrol (Apr 91 - 99) H to V	3210
BMW 3-Series Petrol (Sept 98 - 03) S to 53	4067
BMW 520i & 525e (Oct 81 - June 88) up to E	1560
BMW 525, 528 & 528i (73 - Sept 81) up to X *	0632
BMW 5-Series 6-cyl Petrol (April 96 - Aug 03) N to 03	4151
BMW 1500, 1502, 1600, 1602, 2000 & 2002 (59 - 77) up to S *	0240
CHRYSLER PT Cruiser Petrol (00 - 03) W to 53	4058
CITROËN 2CV, Ami & Dyane (67 - 90) up to H	0196
Citroën AX Petrol & Diesel (87 - 97) D to P	3014
Citroën Berlingo & Peugeot Partner Petrol & Diesel (96 - 05) P to 55	4281
Citroën BX Petrol (83 - 94) A to L	0908
Citroën C15 Van Petrol & Diesel (89 - Oct 98) F to S	3509
Citroën C3 Petrol & Diesel (02 - 05) 51 to 05	4197
Citroën CX Petrol (75 - 88) up to F	0528
Citroën Saxo Petrol & Diesel (96 - 04) N to 54	3506
Citroën Visa Petrol (79 - 88) up to F	0620
Citroën Xantia Petrol & Diesel (93 - 01) K to Y	3082
Citroën XM Petrol & Diesel (89 - 00) G to X	3451
Citroën Xsara Petrol & Diesel (97 - Sept 00) R to W	3751
Citroën Xsara Picasso Petrol & Diesel (00 - 02) W to 52	3944
Citroën ZX Diesel (91 - 98) J to S	1922
Citroën ZX Petrol (91 - 98) H to S	1881
Citroën 1.7 & 1.9 litre Diesel Engine (84 - 96) A to N	1379
FIAT 126 (73 - 87) up to E *	0305
Fiat 500 (57 - 73) up to M *	0090
Fiat Bravo & Brava Petrol (95 - 00) N to W	3572
Fiat Cinquecento (93 - 98) K to R	3501
Fiat Panda (81 - 95) up to M	0793
Fiat Punto Petrol & Diesel (94 - Oct 99) L to V	3251
Fiat Punto Petrol (Oct 99 - July 03) V to 03	4066
Fiat Regata Petrol (84 - 88) A to F	1167
Fiat Tipo Petrol (88 - 91) E to J	1625
Fiat Uno Petrol (83 - 95) up to M	0923
Fiat X1/9 (74 - 89) up to G *	0273
FORD Anglia (59 - 68) up to G *	0001
Ford Capri II (& III) 1.6 & 2.0 (74 - 87) up to E *	0283
Ford Capri II (& III) 2.8 & 3.0 V6 (74 - 87) up to E	1309

Title	Book No.
Ford Cortina Mk I & Corsair 1500 ('62 - '66) up to D*	0214
Ford Cortina Mk III 1300 & 1600 (70 - 76) up to P *	0070
Ford Escort Mk I 1100 & 1300 (68 - 74) up to N *	0171
Ford Escort Mk I Mexico, RS 1600 & RS 2000 (70 - 74) up to N *	0139
Ford Escort Mk II Mexico, RS 1800 & RS 2000 (75 - 80) up to W *	0735
Ford Escort (75 - Aug 80) up to V *	0280
Ford Escort Petrol (Sept 80 - Sept 90) up to H	0686
Ford Escort & Orion Petrol (Sept 90 - 00) H to X	1737
Ford Escort & Orion Diesel (Sept 90 - 00) H to X	4081
Ford Fiesta (76 - Aug 83) up to Y	0334
Ford Fiesta Petrol (Aug 83 - Feb 89) A to F	1030
Ford Fiesta Petrol (Feb 89 - Oct 95) F to N	1595
Ford Fiesta Petrol & Diesel (Oct 95 - Mar 02) N to 02	3397
Ford Fiesta Petrol & Diesel (Apr 02 - 05) 02 to 54	4170
Ford Focus Petrol & Diesel (98 - 01) S to Y	3759
Ford Focus Petrol & Diesel (Oct 01 - 05) 51 to 05	4167
Ford Galaxy Petrol & Diesel (95 - Aug 00) M to W	3984
Ford Granada Petrol (Sept 77 - Feb 85) up to B *	0481
Ford Granada & Scorpio Petrol (Mar 85 - 94) B to M	1245
Ford Ka (96 - 02) P to 52	3570
Ford Mondeo Petrol (93 - Sept 00) K to X	1923
Ford Mondeo Petrol & Diesel (Oct 00 - Jul 03) X to 03	3990
Ford Mondeo Petrol & Diesel (July 03 - 07) 03 to 56	4619
Ford Mondeo Diesel (93 - 96) L to N	3465
Ford Orion Petrol (83 - Sept 90) up to H	1009
Ford Sierra 4-cyl Petrol (82 - 93) up to K	0903
Ford Sierra V6 Petrol (82 - 91) up to J	0904
Ford Transit Petrol (Mk 2) (78 - Jan 86) up to C	0719
Ford Transit Petrol (Mk 3) (Feb 86 - 89) C to G	1468
Ford Transit Diesel (Feb 86 - 99) C to T	3019
Ford 1.6 & 1.8 litre Diesel Engine (84 - 96) A to N	1172
Ford 2.1, 2.3 & 2.5 litre Diesel Engine (77 - 90) up to H	1606
FREIGHT ROVER Sherpa Petrol (74 - 87) up to E	0463
HILLMAN Avenger (70 - 82) up to Y	0037
Hillman Imp (63 - 76) up to R *	0022
HONDA Civic (Feb 84 - Oct 87) A to E	1226
Honda Civic (Nov 91 - 96) J to N	3199
Honda Civic Petrol (Mar 95 - 00) M to X	4050
Honda Civic Petrol & Diesel (01 - 05) X to 55	4611
Honda Jazz (01 - Feb 08) 51 - 57	4735
HYUNDAI Pony (85 - 94) C to M	3398
JAGUAR E Type (61 - 72) up to L *	0140
Jaguar MkI & II, 240 & 340 (55 - 69) up to H *	0098
Jaguar XJ6, XJ & Sovereign; Daimler Sovereign (68 - Oct 86) up to D	0242
Jaguar XJ6 & Sovereign (Oct 86 - Sept 94) D to M	3261
Jaguar XJ12, XJS & Sovereign; Daimler Double Six (72 - 88) up to F	0478
JEEP Cherokee Petrol (93 - 96) K to N	1943
LADA 1200, 1300, 1500 & 1600 (74 - 91) up to J	0413
Lada Samara (87 - 91) D to J	1610
LAND ROVER 90, 110 & Defender Diesel (83 - 07) up to 56	3017
Land Rover Discovery Petrol & Diesel (89 - 98) G to S	3016
Land Rover Discovery Diesel (Nov 98 - Jul 04) S to 04	4606
Land Rover Freelander Petrol & Diesel (97 - Sept 03) R to 53	3929
Land Rover Freelander Petrol & Diesel (Oct 03 - Oct 06) 53 to 56	4623
Land Rover Series IIA & III Diesel (58 - 85) up to C	0529
Land Rover Series II, IIA & III 4-cyl Petrol (58 - 85) up to C	0314

Title	Book No.
MAZDA 323 (Mar 81 - Oct 89) up to G	1608
Mazda 323 (Oct 89 - 98) G to R	3455
Mazda 626 (May 83 - Sept 87) up to E	0929
Mazda B1600, B1800 & B2000 Pick-up Petrol (72 - 88) up to F	0267
Mazda RX-7 (79 - 85) up to C *	0460
MERCEDES-BENZ 190, 190E & 190D Petrol & Diesel (83 - 93) A to L	3450
Mercedes-Benz 200D, 240D, 240TD, 300D & 300TD 123 Series Diesel (Oct 76 - 85)	1114
Mercedes-Benz 250 & 280 (68 - 72) up to L *	0346
Mercedes-Benz 250 & 280 123 Series Petrol (Oct 76 - 84) up to B *	0677
Mercedes-Benz 124 Series Petrol & Diesel (85 - Aug 93) C to K	3253
Mercedes-Benz C-Class Petrol & Diesel (93 - Aug 00) L to W	3511
MGA (55 - 62) *	0475
MGB (62 - 80) up to W	0111
MG Midget & Austin-Healey Sprite (58 - 80) up to W *	0265
MINI Petrol (July 01 - 05) Y to 05	4273
MITSUBISHI Shogun & L200 Pick-Ups Petrol (83 - 94) up to M	1944
MORRIS Ital 1.3 (80 - 84) up to B	0705
Morris Minor 1000 (56 - 71) up to K	0024
NISSAN Almera Petrol (95 - Feb 00) N to V	4053
Nissan Almera & Tino Petrol (Feb 00 - 07) V to 56	4612
Nissan Bluebird (May 84 - Mar 86) A to C	1223
Nissan Bluebird Petrol (Mar 86 - 90) C to H	1473
Nissan Cherry (Sept 82 - 86) up to D	1031
Nissan Micra (83 - Jan 93) up to K	0931
Nissan Micra (93 - 02) K to 52	3254
Nissan Primera Petrol (90 - Aug 99) H to T	1851
Nissan Stanza (82 - 86) up to D	0824
Nissan Sunny Petrol (May 82 - Oct 86) up to D	0895
Nissan Sunny Petrol (Oct 86 - Mar 91) D to H	1378
Nissan Sunny Petrol (Apr 91 - 95) H to N	3219
OPEL Ascona & Manta (B Series) (Sept 75 - 88) up to F *	0316
Opel Ascona Petrol (81 - 88)	3215
Opel Astra Petrol (Oct 91 - Feb 98)	3156
Opel Corsa Petrol (83 - Mar 93)	3160
Opel Corsa Petrol (Mar 93 - 97)	3159
Opel Kadett Petrol (Nov 79 - Oct 84) up to B	0634
Opel Kadett Petrol (Oct 84 - Oct 91)	3196
Opel Omega & Senator Petrol (Nov 86 - 94)	3157
Opel Rekord Petrol (Feb 78 - Oct 86) up to D	0543
Opel Vectra Petrol (Oct 88 - Oct 95)	3158
PEUGEOT 106 Petrol & Diesel (91 - 04) J to 53	1882
Peugeot 205 Petrol (83 - 97) A to P	0932
Peugeot 206 Petrol & Diesel (98 - 01) S to X	3757
Peugeot 206 Petrol & Diesel (02 - 06) 51 to 06	4613
Peugeot 306 Petrol & Diesel (93 - 02) K to 02	3073
Peugeot 307 Petrol & Diesel (01 - 04) Y to 54	4147
Peugeot 309 Petrol (86 - 93) C to K	1266
Peugeot 405 Petrol (88 - 97) E to P	1559
Peugeot 405 Diesel (88 - 97) E to P	3198
Peugeot 406 Petrol & Diesel (96 - Mar 99) N to T	3394
Peugeot 406 Petrol & Diesel (Mar 99 - 02) T to 52	3982
Peugeot 505 Petrol (79 - 89) up to G	0762
Peugeot 1.7/1.8 & 1.9 litre Diesel Engine (82 - 96) up to N	0950
Peugeot 2.0, 2.1, 2.3 & 2.5 litre Diesel Engines (74 - 90) up to H	1607
PORSCHE 911 (65 - 85) up to C	0264

* Classic reprint

Title	Book No.
Porsche 924 & 924 Turbo (76 - 85) up to C	0397
PROTON (89 - 97) F to P	3255
RANGE ROVER V8 Petrol (70 - Oct 92) up to K	0606
RELIANT Robin & Kitten (73 - 83) up to A *	0436
RENAULT 4 (61 - 86) up to D *	0072
Renault 5 Petrol (Feb 85 - 96) B to N	1219
Renault 9 & 11 Petrol (82 - 89) up to F	0822
Renault 18 Petrol (79 - 86) up to D	0598
Renault 19 Petrol (89 - 96) F to N	1646
Renault 19 Diesel (89 - 96) F to N	1946
Renault 21 Petrol (86 - 94) C to M	1397
Renault 25 Petrol & Diesel (84 - 92) B to K	1228
Renault Clio Petrol (91 - May 98) H to R	1853
Renault Clio Diesel (91 - June 96) H to N	3031
Renault Clio Petrol & Diesel (May 98 - May 01) R to Y	3906
Renault Clio Petrol & Diesel (June '01 - '05) Y to 55	4168
Renault Espace Petrol & Diesel (85 - 96) C to N	3197
Renault Laguna Petrol & Diesel (94 - 00) L to W	3252
Renault Laguna Petrol & Diesel (Feb 01 - Feb 05) X to 54	4283
Renault Mégane & Scénic Petrol & Diesel (96 - 99) N to T	3395
Renault Mégane & Scénic Petrol & Diesel (Apr 99 - 02) T to 52	3916
Renault Megane Petrol & Diesel (Oct 02 - 05) 52 to 55	4284
Renault Scenic Petrol & Diesel (Sept 03 - 06) 53 to 06	4297
ROVER 213 & 216 (84 - 89) A to G	1116
Rover 214 & 414 Petrol (89 - 96) G to N	1689
Rover 216 & 416 Petrol (89 - 96) G to N	1830
Rover 211, 214, 216, 218 & 220 Petrol & Diesel (Dec 95 - 99) N to V	3399
Rover 25 & MG ZR Petrol & Diesel (Oct 99 - 04) V to 54	4145
Rover 414, 416 & 420 Petrol & Diesel (May 95 - 98) M to R	3453
Rover 45 / MG ZS Petrol & Diesel (99 - 05) V to 55	4384
Rover 618, 620 & 623 Petrol (93 - 97) K to P	3257
Rover 75 / MG ZT Petrol & Diesel (99 - 06) S to 06	4292
Rover 820, 825 & 827 Petrol (86 - 95) D to N	1380
Rover 3500 (76 - 87) up to E *	0365
Rover Metro, 111 & 114 Petrol (May 90 - 98) G to S	1711
SAAB 95 & 96 (66 - 76) up to R *	0198
Saab 90, 99 & 900 (79 - Oct 93) up to L	0765
Saab 900 (Oct 93 - 98) L to R	3512
Saab 9000 (4-cyl) (85 - 98) C to S	1686
Saab 9-3 Petrol & Diesel (98 - Aug 02) R to 02	4614
Saab 9-5 4-cyl Petrol (97 - 04) R to 54	4156
SEAT Ibiza & Cordoba Petrol & Diesel (Oct 93 - Oct 99) L to V	3571
Seat Ibiza & Malaga Petrol (85 - 92) B to K	1609
SKODA Estelle (77 - 89) up to G	0604
Skoda Fabia Petrol & Diesel (00 - 06) W to 06	4376
Skoda Favorit (89 - 96) F to N	1801
Skoda Felicia Petrol & Diesel (95 - 01) M to X	3505
Skoda Octavia Petrol & Diesel (98 - Apr 04) R to 04	4285
SUBARU 1600 & 1800 (Nov 79 - 90) up to H *	0995
SUNBEAM Alpine, Rapier & H120 (67 - 74) up to N *	0051
SUZUKI SJ Series, Samurai & Vitara (4-cyl) Petrol (82 - 97) up to P	1942
Suzuki Supercarry & Bedford/Vauxhall Rascal (86 - Oct 94) C to M	3015
TALBOT Alpine, Solara, Minx & Rapier (75 - 86) up to D	0337

Title	Book No.
Talbot Horizon Petrol (78 - 86) up to D	0473
Talbot Samba (82 - 86) up to D	0823
TOYOTA Avensis Petrol (98 - Jan 03) R to 52	4264
Toyota Carina E Petrol (May 92 - 97) J to P	3256
Toyota Corolla (80 - 85) up to C	0683
Toyota Corolla (Sept 83 - Sept 87) A to E	1024
Toyota Corolla (Sept 87 - Aug 92) E to K	1683
Toyota Corolla Petrol (Aug 92 - 97) K to P	3259
Toyota Corolla Petrol (July 97 - Feb 02) P to 51	4286
Toyota Hi-Ace & Hi-Lux Petrol (69 - Oct 83) up to A	0304
Toyota Yaris Petrol (99 - 05) T to 05	4265
TRIUMPH GT6 & Vitesse (62 - 74) up to N *	0112
Triumph Herald (59 - 71) up to K *	0010
Triumph Spitfire (62 - 81) up to X	0113
Triumph Stag (70 - 78) up to T *	0441
Triumph TR2, TR3, TR3A, TR4 & TR4A (52 - 67) up to F *	0028
Triumph TR5 & 6 (67 - 75) up to P *	0031
Triumph TR7 (75 - 82) up to Y *	0322
VAUXHALL Astra Petrol (80 - Oct 84) up to B	0635
Vauxhall Astra & Belmont Petrol (Oct 84 - Oct 91) B to J	1136
Vauxhall Astra Petrol (Oct 91 - Feb 98) J to R	1832
Vauxhall/Opel Astra & Zafira Petrol (Feb 98 - Apr 04) R to 04	3758
Vauxhall/Opel Astra & Zafira Diesel (Feb 98 - Apr 04) R to 04	3797
Vauxhall/Opel Astra Petrol (04 - 07) 04 - 07	4732
Vauxhall/Opel Astra Diesel (04 - 07) 04 - 07	4733
Vauxhall/Opel Calibra (90 - 98) G to S	3502
Vauxhall Carlton Petrol (Oct 78 - Oct 86) up to D	0480
Vauxhall Carlton & Senator Petrol (Nov 86 - 94) D to L	1469
Vauxhall Cavalier Petrol (81 - Oct 88) up to F	0812
Vauxhall Cavalier Petrol (Oct 88 - 95) F to N	1570
Vauxhall Chevette (75 - 84) up to B	0285
Vauxhall/Opel Corsa Diesel (Mar 93 - Oct 00) K to X	4087
Vauxhall Corsa Petrol (Mar 93 - 97) K to R	1985
Vauxhall/Opel Corsa Petrol (Apr 97 - Oct 00) P to X	3921
Vauxhall/Opel Corsa Petrol & Diesel (Oct 00 - Sept 03) X to 53	4079
Vauxhall/Opel Corsa Petrol & Diesel (Oct 03 - Aug 06) 53 to 06	4617
Vauxhall/Opel Frontera Petrol & Diesel (91 - Sept 98) J to S	3454
Vauxhall Nova Petrol (83 - 93) up to K	0909
Vauxhall/Opel Omega Petrol (94 - 99) L to T	3510
Vauxhall/Opel Vectra Petrol & Diesel (95 - Feb 99) N to S	3396
Vauxhall/Opel Vectra Petrol & Diesel (Mar 99 - May 02) T to 02	3930
Vauxhall/Opel Vectra Petrol & Diesel (June 02 - Sept 05) 02 to 55	4618
Vauxhall/Opel 1.5, 1.6 & 1.7 litre Diesel Engine (82 - 96) up to N	1222
VW 411 & 412 (68 - 75) up to P *	0091
VW Beetle 1200 (54 - 77) up to S	0036
VW Beetle 1300 & 1500 (65 - 75) up to P	0039
VW 1302 & 1302S (70 - 72) up to L *	0110
VW Beetle 1303, 1303S & GT (72 - 75) up to P	0159
VW Beetle Petrol & Diesel (Apr 99 - 01) T to 51	3798
VW Golf & Jetta Mk 1 Petrol 1.1 & 1.3 (74 - 84) up to A	0716
VW Golf, Jetta & Scirocco Mk 1 Petrol 1.5, 1.6 & 1.8 (74 - 84) up to A	0726

Title	Book No.
VW Golf & Jetta Mk 1 Diesel (78 - 84) up to A	0451
VW Golf & Jetta Mk 2 Petrol (Mar 84 - Feb 92) A to J	1081
VW Golf & Vento Petrol & Diesel (Feb 92 - Mar 98) J to R	3097
VW Golf & Bora Petrol & Diesel (April 98 - 00) R to X	3727
VW Golf & Bora 4-cyl Petrol & Diesel (01 - 03) X to 53	4169
VW Golf & Jetta Petrol & Diesel (04 - 07) 53 to 07	4610
VW LT Petrol Vans & Light Trucks (76 - 87) up to E	0637
VW Passat & Santana Petrol (Sept 81 - May 88) up to E	0814
VW Passat 4-cyl Petrol & Diesel (May 88 - 96) E to P	3498
VW Passat 4-cyl Petrol & Diesel (Dec 96 - Nov 00) P to X	3917
VW Passat Petrol & Diesel (Dec 00 - May 05) X to 05	4279
VW Polo & Derby (76 - Jan 82) up to X	0335
VW Polo (82 - Oct 90) up to H	0813
VW Polo Petrol (Nov 90 - Aug 94) H to L	3245
VW Polo Hatchback Petrol & Diesel (94 - 99) M to S	3500
VW Polo Hatchback Petrol (00 - Jan 02) V to 51	4150
VW Polo Petrol & Diesel (02 - May 05) 51 to 05	4608
VW Scirocco (82 - 90) up to H *	1224
VW Transporter 1600 (68 - 79) up to V	0082
VW Transporter 1700, 1800 & 2000 (72 - 79) up to V *	0226
VW Transporter (air-cooled) Petrol (79 - 82) up to Y *	0638
VW Transporter (water-cooled) Petrol (82 - 90) up to H	3452
VW Type 3 (63 - 73) up to M *	0084
VOLVO 120 & 130 Series (& P1800) (61 - 73) up to M *	0203
Volvo 142, 144 & 145 (66 - 74) up to N *	0129
Volvo 240 Series Petrol (74 - 93) up to K	0270
Volvo 262, 264 & 260/265 (75 - 85) up to C *	0400
Volvo 340, 343, 345 & 360 (76 - 91) up to J	0715
Volvo 440, 460 & 480 Petrol (87 - 97) D to P	1691
Volvo 740 & 760 Petrol (82 - 91) up to J	1258
Volvo 850 Petrol (92 - 96) J to P	3260
Volvo 940 petrol (90 - 98) H to R	3249
Volvo S40 & V40 Petrol (96 - Mar 04) N to 04	3569
Volvo S40 & V50 Petrol & Diesel (Mar 04 - Jun 07) 04 to 07	4731
Volvo S70, V70 & C70 Petrol (96 - 99) P to V	3573
Volvo V70 / S80 Petrol & Diesel (98 - 05) S to 55	4263
AUTOMOTIVE TECHBOOKS	
Automotive Electrical and Electronic Systems Manual	3049
Automotive Gearbox Overhaul Manual	3473
Automotive Service Summaries Manual	3475
Automotive Timing Belts Manual – Austin/Rover	3549
Automotive Timing Belts Manual – Ford	3474
Automotive Timing Belts Manual – Peugeot/Citroën	3568
Automotive Timing Belts Manual – Vauxhall/Opel	3577
DIY MANUAL SERIES	
The Haynes Air Conditioning Manual	4192
The Haynes Car Electrical Systems Manual	4251
The Haynes Manual on Bodywork	4198
The Haynes Manual on Brakes	4178
The Haynes Manual on Carburettors	4177
The Haynes Manual on Diesel Engines	4174
The Haynes Manual on Engine Management	4199
The Haynes Manual on Fault Codes	4175
The Haynes Manual on Practical Electrical Systems	4267
The Haynes Manual on Small Engines	4250
The Haynes Manual on Welding	4176

* Classic reprint

CL23.12/07